Missing something? Instructors may assign the online materials that accompany this text. For access to them, visit **macmillanhighered.com /frominquiry3e**.

Inside LaunchPad Solo for *From Inquiry to Academic Writing: A Text and Reader*, Third Edition

Multimodal readings, such as video, audio, images, and Web texts

Laura Hartigan, "Understanding the Unique Affordances of Multimodal, Creative Writing, and Academic Writing" [annotated multimedia research paper and poster presentation]

Dylan Garity, "Rigged Game" [video]

Trailers for *Miss Representation* and *The Mask You Live In* [videos]

From *Cracking the Codes: The System of Racial Inequality* [video]

"Linda Loma University Medical Center's Orthotics and Prosthetics Team Gives Brazilian Athlete Ability to Walk" [online article with video]

Terri Oda, "The Clearest Graphs You Will Ever See Refuting the Idea that Women Are Bad at Math" [click-through presentation]

Trailer for *Food Patriots* [video]

"The Sins of Greenwashing: Home and Family Edition" [interactive quiz]

Paul Mulhauser and Kelly Bradbury, "How Genders Work: Putting Together the J. Crew Catalogue" [interactive flip-book]

Interactive exercises and tutorials for reading, writing, and research

Active Reading Strategies

Reading Visuals: Purpose

Reading Visuals: Audience

Do I Need to Cite That?

How to Cite an Article in MLA Style

How to Cite a Book in MLA Style

How to Cite a Database in MLA Style

How to Cite a Database in APA Style

How to Cite a Web Site in MLA Style

How to Cite a Website in APA Style

LearningCurve

Working with Sources [MLA]

Working with Sources [APA]

FROM INQUIRY TO ACADEMIC WRITING

A Text and Reader

THIRD EDITION

Stuart Greene
University of Notre Dame

April Lidinsky
Indiana University South Bend

Bedford/St. Martin's   BOSTON ■ NEW YORK

For Bedford/St. Martin's

Vice President, Editorial, Macmillan Higher Education Humanities: Edwin Hill
Executive Director for English and Music: Karen S. Henry
Publisher for Composition and Business and Technical Writing: Leasa Burton
Senior Executive Editor: Stephen A. Scipione
Senior Production Editor: Gregory Erb
Publishing Services Manager: Katie Watterson, MPS North America LLC
Senior Production Supervisor: Jennifer Wetzel
Marketing Manager: Jane Helms
Copyeditor: Dawn Adams
Indexer: MPS North America LLC
Photo Researcher: Christine End
Director of Rights and Permissions: Hilary Newman
Senior Art Director: Anna Palchik
Text Design: Jean Hammond and MPS North America LLC
Cover Design: Donna Lee Dennison
Cover Art: Charles Biederman, *#8 Untitled,* painted aluminum, 1977–1979.
   Reproduced with permission of private collection, Minneapolis, and the
   Weisman Art Museum, Minneapolis. Photo courtesy of B & W Arts.
Composition: MPS North America LLC
Printing and Binding: RR Donnelley and Sons

Manufactured in the United States of America.

9 8 7 6 5 4
f   e   d   c   b   a

For information, write: Bedford/St. Martin's, 75 Arlington Street, Boston, MA
02116   (617-399-4000)

ISBN 978-1-4576-5344-5

Preface for Instructors

A cademic writing can be a challenging hurdle for students entering college. They must learn new habits of writing, reading, and even thinking. That's where *From Inquiry to Academic Writing* comes in. It addresses the challenges of academic writing, offering a clear, methodical approach to meeting those challenges. Our students, and many others, have told us that our approach demystifies academic writing, while helping them to see that its skills carry over to civic participation and life issues beyond their college years.

Specifically, *From Inquiry to Academic Writing: A Text and Reader* is a composition rhetoric and thematic anthology that introduces students to college-level inquiry, analysis, and argument. It is based on a first-year composition course in which we guide students to produce essays that use evidence and sources in increasingly complex ways. In this book, as in our classes, we present academic writing as a collaborative conversation, undertaken to pursue new knowledge. We teach students to see that academic writing is a social act that involves working responsibly with the ideas of others. At the same time, we encourage students to see themselves as makers of knowledge who use sources to advance arguments about important academic and cultural issues.

This third edition encompasses a greater range of academic habits and skills than the second, particularly strategies and genres of research. The anthology features two new multidisciplinary themes. Overall, more than half the readings are new and explore issues that have become more prominent in academia and public life over the past few years. And for the first time, *From Inquiry to Academic Writing* is available with LaunchPad Solo, book-specific multimodal materials in a customizable course space. Read on for details about what's new to the text and to the reader.

▪ A Closer Look at the Rhetoric Text

The chapters in the rhetoric begin with academic thinking and proceed through academic reading and research, integrating academic writing throughout. Yet Chapters 1 through 11 are freestanding enough to be taught in any order that suits your course. What unites them is our constant emphasis on the recursive nature of these skills and the centrality of the writing process. We punctuate every chapter with short readings and activities that prompt students to practice what we teach.

Chapter 1 is an overview of academic writing as a process motivated by inquiry and introduces academic habits of mind. Chapter 2 encourages students to practice writerly reading — the rhetorical analysis of other writers' decisions — to learn appropriate strategies for their own writing. While Chapters 2 through 5 address essentials of getting started on writing, from how to mark a text to forming questions and developing a working thesis, we recognize that this process is rarely linear, and that it benefits from conversation with invested readers. Chapters 6 and 7 help students develop and support their theses by providing strategies for finding and working with sources, for example, showing students how they can use summary, paraphrase, and synthesis to serve their purposes as writers. Chapters 8 and 9 again link writerly reading with readerly writing — this time with writing that reflects rhetorical appeals (including visual appeals) and strategies of structure and development.

Chapter 10 presents revision in the context of peer groups. The responses of classmates can help students determine when they might need to read additional material to shape more effective research questions, or when they might need more evidence to support an argument. Our supporting materials for peer workshops foster productive group interaction at every stage of the peer review process. Finally, in Chapter 11, we provide students with strategies for conducting original research that build upon earlier chapters about using personal experience or writing a researched argument.

Although the process of developing an academic argument can be unruly, the structured step-by-step pedagogy in the rhetoric text should support students during each stage of the process. Most readings are followed by "Reading as a Writer" questions that send students back into the reading to respond to the rhetorical moves writers make. "Steps to" boxes summarize the major points about each stage of thinking, reading, and writing, offering quick references that bring key information into focus for review. "Practice Sequences" ask students to try out and build on the strategies we have explained or demonstrated. We also provide templates, formulas, and worksheets that students may use to organize information as they read and write.

Your students should feel further supported and encouraged by the abundance of student writing (annotated to highlight the rhetorical moves students make) that we use as examples in the rhetoric text, side by side with the examples of professional writing we include.

■ What's New in the Rhetoric Chapters?

Among many smaller revisions, we made the following additions in response to numerous comments by instructors:

- **New treatment of composing a rhetorical analysis**, with advice on writing one's way into academic conversations, appears in Chapter 2.
- **An alternative variety of thesis statement**, the hypothesis-testing model, is introduced in Chapter 5.
- **The annotated bibliography**, a crucial genre, is presented in Chapter 6.
- **New treatment of other genres of research**, including the literature review, a model idea sheet, and a research proposal, appear in Chapter 11.
- **Throughout, ten of the readings are new**, including six annotated student papers.

Additionally, **LaunchPad Solo** features an annotated multimedia student research paper and a poster presentation that take students beyond the confines of the printed page. **LearningCurve** adaptive quizzing focuses students on writing and common grammar topics they need the most help with.

■ A Closer Look at the Thematic Reader

The thematic reader chapters (12 through 17) are organized into interdisciplinary issues and include many lengthy, documented selections. They approximate the kinds of reading and writing that college students are expected to do in other college classes. Although the selections may be longer and more complex than those found in most other first-year composition readers, students who have had some practice with the reading and writing strategies in the first part of the book and who use the guidelines in the headnotes and questions after the readings are generally more than up to the task of working with these selections. Moreover, our students are usually exhilarated by what they discover in the readings—the kind of "big thinking" they came to college to experience.

As you would expect in a book that emphasizes cross-curricular writing, many of the readings come from journals and publications intended for scholarly audiences and thus model what would traditionally be considered academic writing. Among these are selections from the work of Agustín Fuentes, Noël Sturgeon, and Beverly Daniel Tatum, scholars whose texts are especially influential among their peers in academe. Other selections are drawn from thought-provoking and engaging books on recent "best-seller" lists, the kind of books that become popular and sometimes required reading on college campuses. The authors of these books—Sherry Turkle, Diane Ravitch, Steven D. Levitt, Stephen J. Dubner, and Michael Pollan, to name a few—are intellectuals who use the same kinds of strategies of research and analysis as academic writers, and like academic writers they use those skills to take on big ideas, frame them in interesting new ways, and offer striking examples that present them provocatively to readers. Still other readings—by Barbara Ehrenreich and Gary Steiner, for instance—are brief and accessible, chosen to draw students into the conversation of ideas that longer selections unpack and extend in greater detail.

While all these readings are at some level researched essays—texts that build on ideas others have written—they also provide students with a wide range of rhetorical styles to use as models. Some readings take a journalistic approach and some occasionally dip into autobiographical details, with authors using personal anecdotes to explain their interest in an issue or illustrate an example, while other readings take a more formal tone, relying on research and expertise to build their arguments. We chose these selections in part because of the many different strategies they use to make many different kinds of connections—from the personal to the scholarly, from individual experiences to larger social patterns. This multileveled inquiry is at the heart of the thinking and writing we invite students to learn in this book.

We have divided the selections in the reader into six chapters, each focused on an issue broadly associated with a particular discipline:

Chapter 12 on Education contains readings that ask, "What does it mean to be educated, and who decides?" The authors in this chapter ask us to question our common assumptions about how classrooms operate, from the dynamics between teacher and student to the very material that has been designated "important knowledge." These readings help students to see their past and present educational experiences through fresh eyes, prompting them to consider the relationship between education and social power, and to envision alternatives to standard educational practices and goals.

Chapter 13 on Media Studies explores the question of "What can we learn from what entertains us?" with probing readings on popular culture, from Jean Kilbourne's classic analysis of fashion advertisements to contemporary examinations of Disney Pixar films and the social networking phenomenon. Too often students are reluctant to think critically about popular entertainment, but these readings provide the provocations and tools to do so.

Chapter 14 on Sociology plunges into questions of how shifting cultural understandings of race, class, and gender influence us. The authors in this chapter suggest models for making sense of those three interrelated concerns that shape our daily lives, whether we are conscious of them or not. Concepts such as "the myth of race," "white privilege," and "fag discourse" offer arresting perspectives on this complex arena of ideas.

Chapter 15 delves into the disciplines of Biology and Psychology, taking a broad view in response to the question of how our physical and cultural selves intersect. Many of the selections reveal how cultural assumptions occlude our vision of where nature ends and nurture begins, from performance on math tests, to the number of genders we are willing to accept, to the effects of negative body image on physical health.

Chapter 16 on Environmental Studies raises topics of environmental damage and sustainability as it explores the issue of how our decisions affect our environment. For example, Anna Lappé connects our eating habits to global climate problems, and Michael Pollan makes the case that small personal efforts can have a cumulative positive effect on the environment—an argument challenged by Derrick Jensen and Stephanie McMillan in an excerpt from their graphic text *As the World Burns: 50 Simple Things You Can Do to Stay in Denial*.

Chapter 17 looks at the world of Business and Marketing through the dual lenses of these questions: "What is the present and future of marketing? Are we what we buy?" The readings range widely, encouraging critical thinking about such topics as brand logic, green businesses, neuromarketing, global capitalism, and the implications of marketing multicultural ideas to children.

Every selection in the thematic reader is introduced by a headnote that provides biographical and contextual information, as well as some tactics for students (and instructors) to engage the text actively on first and subsequent readings. Further, every reading is followed by two types of questions, "Reading as a Writer: Analyzing Rhetorical Choices," which ask students to consider the stylistic decisions a writer makes in crafting the piece, and "Writing as a Reader: Entering the Conversation of Ideas," which use each essay as a launching point for further inquiry, research, and discovery about an issue raised in the text. The questions and assignments in the reader support students by reinforcing the skills and strategies presented in the rhetoric.

More ways to work with the readings appear in the Assignment Sequences (p. 874) for instructors to implement or adapt to their specific needs. They define a subject for inquiry and offer a sequential path through readings and several writing assignments that build on one another. Assignment sequences give students the opportunity to engage in intellectual inquiry that lasts longer than one assignment. Rather than writing an essay and then moving on to a completely new topic, then, each essay students write in a sequence will help them develop the ideas in their next essay, as they consider an issue from many perspectives, and with a range of sources. In other words, these assignment sequences invite students to read, research, and write with the habits of mind and practices of academic writers who are in conversation with other thinkers, and who also bring scholarly analysis to experiences beyond the classroom. The book concludes with an Appendix that introduces the basics of documentation in MLA and APA styles.

■ What's New in the Thematic Reader?

- **Many, many new readings on arresting topics**. While we retained the most popular readings from our second edition, well over half of the selections are new, and many of them encourage and model interdisciplinary cultural analysis, often on popular topics that students will find eye-opening and personally engaging. For example, Joni Adamson traces the worldwide impact of the movie *Avatar* in raising awareness of the plight of indigenous cultures—often inspiring activism in those very cultures. And Matthew Immergut offers surprising and entertaining insights on "manscaping" in his semiotic take on patterns of contemporary male grooming behavior.

- **Two new interdisciplinary themes.** At the suggestion of many adopters of the second edition, a new Sociology chapter addresses some of the latest academic thinking on the continually morphing issues of race, class, and gender. The intersections of nature and nurture are probed in a chapter that combines readings oriented to Biology and Psychology.

- **LaunchPad Solo** integrates multimodal selections, showcasing video and interactive examples that illustrate arguments beyond the page, with guiding questions and assignments to shape in-class activities and writing projects. For example, Dylan Garity inveighs against the "Rigged Game" of bilingual education in a mesmerizing poetic performance, and an interactive "flip book" helps students critique fashion advertising.

▪ Available as an e-Book to Go

From Inquiry to Academic Writing is available as an e-Book to Go and in a variety of other electronic formats. Online, interactive, and at a value price, our e-books can be purchased standalone or packaged with a print book. Get an exam copy, adopt for your course, or have students purchase a copy at **macmillanhighered.com**. Please contact your Bedford/ St. Martin's representative for more details.

▪ The Text Is Available Separately

If you are interested in assigning only the rhetoric chapters, they are available without the thematic chapters as *From Inquiry to Academic Writing: A Practical Guide*, Third Edition, in print and as an e-Book to Go.

▪ An Instructor's Manual Is Available for Download

We have prepared an instructor's manual, *Resources for Teaching From Inquiry to Academic Writing: A Text and Reader*, Third Edition. The first part of the manual addresses every step of the process of academic writing we set forth in the rhetoric text, with additional comments on the readings integrated in the text chapters. Not only do we discuss many of the issues involved in taking our rhetorical approach to academic argument—problems and questions students and instructors may have—but we also suggest background readings on the research informing our approach. The second part of the manual provides concrete strategies for teaching the selections in the thematic reader, and is based on our own experiences working with these readings. We also suggest possible responses to the questions that follow the readings in Part Two. The instructor's manual can be downloaded via the catalog page, **macmillanhighered.com/catalog/frominquiry**.

▪ Acknowledgments

We would first like to thank the many reviewers who commented on the proposal, the manuscript, and the first edition, as well as the reviewers of the second edition in both its full and compact iterations. Invariably their comments were useful, and frequently helpful and cheering as well. The list of reviewers includes Andrea Acker, Seton Hill University; Angela Adams, Loyola University–Chicago; Steve Adkison, Idaho State University; Teresa Fernandez Arab, University of Kansas; Yesho Atil, Asheville-Buncombe Technical Community College; Anthony Atkins, University of North Carolina, Wilmington; Paula Bacon, Pace University–Pleasantville; Susan Bailor, Front Range Community College; Mary Ellen Bertolini, Middlebury College; Laurel Bollinger, University of Alabama–Huntsville; Margaret Bonesteel, Syracuse University; James Brill, University of California, Chico; Laurie Britt-Smith, St. Louis University; Christina Riley Brown, Mercyhurst University; Siobhan Brownson, Winthrop University; William Brugger, Brigham Young University Idaho; Lise Buranen, California State University–Los Angeles; Robin Caine, Montclair State University; Bettina Caluori, Mercer County Community College; Jeffrey Cebulski, Kennesaw State University; Kathleen Chriest, Mercyhurst University; Marie Coffey, San Antonio College; Carolyn Cole, Oklahoma Baptist University; Tami Comstock-Peavy, Arapahoe Community College; Emily Cosper, Delgado Community College; Karen Cox, City College of San Francisco; Donna Craine, Front Range Community College; Ryan Crider, Missouri State University; Calum Cunningham, Fanshawe College–London; Sarah Dangelantonio, Franklin Pierce University; Alexis Davis, University of Mount Olive; J. Madison Davis, University of Oklahoma–Norman; Anne DeMarzio, University of Scranton; Erin Denney, Community College of San Francisco; Jason DePolo, North Carolina A&T State University; Brock Dethier, Utah State University; Clark Draney, College of Southern Idaho; Eugenia C. Eberhart, Garden City Community College; Lisa Egan, Brown University; Ed Eleazer, Francis Marion University; Brant Ellsworth, Penn State Harrisburg; Larry Eson, Front Range Community College; Elaine Fredericksen, University of Texas–El Paso; Hannah Furrow, University of Michigan–Flint; Christine A. Geyer, Cazenovia University; Rhoda Greenstone, Long Beach City College; Rima Gulshan, George Mason University; Sinceree Gunn, University of Alabama–Huntsville; Clinton Hale, Blinn College; Juli E. Hale, King College; Jane Hammons, University of California, Berkeley; Amy Hankins, Blue River Community College; Ann Hartney, Fort

Lewis College; Beth Hedengren, Brigham Young University; Tara Hembrough, Southern Illinois University, Carbondale; Virginia Scott Hendrickson, Missouri State University; Zachery Hickman, University of Miami; Wilbur Higgins, University of Massachusetts Dartmouth; Monica Hogan, Johnson County Community College; Jean Incampo, Gateway Community College; T. Christine Jesperson, Western State College of Colorado; Margaret Johnson, Idaho State University; Laura Katsaros, Monmouth University; Karen Keaton Jackson, North Carolina Central University; Dennis Jerz, Seton Hill University; Christine Jespersen, Western State Colorado University; Therese Jones, Lewis University; Michael Kaufmann, Indiana University–Purdue and University Fort Wayne; Trevor Kearns, Greenfield Community College; Howard Kerner, Polk Community College; Lynn Kilpatrick, Salt Lake Community College; Jeff Klausman, Whatcom Community College; Tamara Kuzmenkov, Tacoma Community College; Michelle LaFrance, UMass Dartmouth; Erin Lebacqz, University of New Mexico; Lindsay Lewan, Arapahoe Community College; April Lewandowski, Front Range Community College–Westminster; Meredith Love-Steinmetz, Francis Marion University; Renee Major, Louisiana State University; Mark McBeth, John Jay College; Diane L. Maldonado, Point Park University; Gina Maranto, University of Miami; Loren Loving Marquez, Salisury University; Carola Mattord, Kennesaw State University; Timothy McGinn, Northwest Arkansas Community College; Erica Messenger, Bowling Green State University–Main; Alyce Miller, Indiana University; Deborah Miller, University of Georgia; Whitney Myers, University of New Mexico; Lamata Mitchell, Rock Valley College; Robert Mohrenne, University of Central Florida; Erin Nelson, Blinn College; Teddy Norris, St. Charles Community College; Lolly J. Ockerstrom, Park University; Judy Olson, California State University, Los Angeles; Jill Onega, University of Alabama–Huntsville; Robert Peltier, Trinity College; Valeries L. Perry, Lewis University; Jeanette Pierce, San Antonio College; Mary Jo Reiff, University of Tennessee; Tonya Ritola, Georgia Gwinnett College; Mary Roma, New York University; Claudia Rubner, Mercer County Community College; David Ryan, University of San Francisco; Daniel Schenker, University of Alabama–Huntsville; Amanda McGuire Rzicznek, Bowling Green State University; Roy Stamper, North Carolina State University; Scott Stevens, Western Washington University; Sarah Stone, University of California–Berkeley; Joseph Sullivan, Marietta College; Mark Todd, Western State Colorado University; Gretchen Treadwell, Fort Lewis College; Tisha Turk, University of Minnesota, Morris; Raymond M. Vince, University of Tampa; Charles Warren, Salem State College; Patricia Webb, Arizona State University; Susan Garrett Weiss, Goucher College; Worth Weller, Indiana University–Purdue University–Fort Wayne; Jackie White, Lewis University; and Audrey Wick, Blinn College.

We are also grateful to the many people at Bedford/St. Martin's, starting with vice president and editorial director of humanities Edwin Hill, composition publisher Leasa Burton, and executive director for English Karen Henry.

Molly Parke, now an executive editor, did a remarkable job marketing the second edition, and we appreciate the shrewd insights she continues to offer in her new position. As he has since the first edition, senior executive editor Steve Scipione has been a terrific collaborator who read our work carefully and who offered sage advice every step of the way. Senior editor Adam Whitehurst and associate editor Sherry Mooney were invaluable advisors who helped us incorporate the new LaunchPad readings and activities. Steve could not have helped us complete this project without the tireless assistance of Laura Horton, Rachel Greenhaus, Arrin Kaplan, and Amanda Legee. We are grateful to Jane Helms for her wise and imaginative marketing efforts, assisted by Allie Rottman. The talented production department steered the manuscript through a demanding schedule to create the book you hold. We thank Susan Brown, Elise Kaiser, Michael Granger, and especially Greg Erb, the book's accommodating and masterly production editor. Dawn Adams provided exceptionally alert and constructive copyediting. Kalina Ingham, James Toftness, and Christine End negotiated the complicated process of permissions acquisition. Donna Dennison designed the cover.

Stuart Greene writes: I wish to thank the many students and faculty with whom I have worked over the years. Specifically, I would like to thank Kelly Kinney, Stephen Fox, Rebecca Nowacek, and Katherine Weese, who served as my assistant directors in the past and who taught me a great deal about the teaching of writing. I would also like to thank Robert Kachur who contributed a great deal to our early iterations of this book. And I will always appreciate the many discussions I have had with John Duffy during these many years and to Connie Mick, a tireless and innovative teacher of writing. Susan Ohmer provided much insight into my understanding of media and student culture. A special thanks to Mike Palmquist, with whom I taught writing as "conversation" over twenty years ago and who gave this book direction. Finally, to Denise Della Rossa, who has listened to me rehearse these ideas for years. I dedicate this book to her.

April Lidinsky writes: I am grateful for the superb pedagogical mentorship I received from Lou Kelly at the University of Iowa. I thank Kurt Spellmeyer, Hugh English, and Ron Christ at Rutgers, the State University of New Jersey, for my training in both hermeneutical and rhetorical approaches to teaching writing. My colleagues and graduate student instructors at the University of Notre Dame, especially Julie Bruneau, Connie Mick, Marion C. Rohrleitner, Misty Schieberle, and Scott T. Smith, inspired early versions of this text. Thanks to Christy Jespersen, Joel Langston, Grace Lidinsky-Smith, and Rachel Stein for their excellent suggestions for readings for this third edition. My students continue to challenge and sharpen my teaching and especially my own learning. Finally, I am indebted to my parents, JoElla Hunter and Tom Lidinsky, for their model of lifelong reading and learning, and to Ken Smith, Grace Lidinsky-Smith, and Miriam Lidinsky-Smith for ensuring every day is filled with wit and wisdom.

GET THE MOST OUT OF YOUR COURSE WITH *FROM INQUIRY TO ACADEMIC WRITING: A TEXT AND READER,* THIRD EDITION

Bedford/St. Martin's offers resources and format choices that help you and your students get even more out of your book and course. To learn more about or to order any of the following products, contact your Bedford/ St. Martin's sales representative, e-mail sales support (**sales_support @bfwpub.com**), or visit the Web site at **macmillanhighered.com /catalog/frominquiry**.

■ LaunchPad Solo for *From Inquiry to Academic Writing:* Where Students Learn

LaunchPad Solo provides engaging content and new ways to get the most out of your course. Get **unique, book-specific materials** in a fully customizable course space; then assign and mix our resources with yours.

- **Curated Content**—including readings, videos, tutorials, and more—is **easy to adapt and assign** by adding your own materials and mixing them with our high-quality multimedia content and ready-made assessment options, such as **LearningCurve** adaptive quizzing. For instance, students will enjoy clicking though a presentation refuting the idea that women are bad at math, and watching a slam poetry champion mount a critique against bad teaching. LaunchPad Solo also provides access to a **gradebook** that provides a clear window on the performance of your whole class, individual students, and even individual assignments.

- A **streamlined interface** helps students focus on what's due, and social commenting tools let them **engage**, make connections, and learn from each other. Use LaunchPad Solo on its own or integrate it with your school's learning management system so that your class is always on the same page.

To get the most out of your course, order LaunchPad Solo for *From Inquiry to Academic Writing* packaged with the print book **at no additional charge**. (LaunchPad Solo for *From Inquiry to Academic Writing* can also be purchased on its own.) An activation code is required. To order Launch-Pad Solo for *From Inquiry to Academic Writing* with the print book, use ISBN 978-1-319-01310-3.

■ Choose from Alternative Formats of *From Inquiry to Academic Writing*

Bedford/St. Martin's offers a range of affordable formats, allowing students to choose the one that works best for them. For details, visit

macmillanhighered.com/frominquiry/formats. A *Bedford e-Book to Go*, a portable, downloadable e-book, is available at about half the price of the print book. To order the *Bedford e-Book to Go* for *From Inquiry to Academic Writing*, use ISBN 978-1-4576-6380-2. For details about other popular e-book formats, visit **macmillanhighered.com/ebooks**.

▪ Package with Another Bedford/St. Martin's Title at a Significant Discount

Get the most value for your students by packaging *From Inquiry to Academic Writing* with a Bedford/St. Martin's handbook or any other Bedford/St. Martin's title for a significant discount. To order, please request a package ISBN from your sales representative or e-mail sales support (**sales_support@bfwpub.com**).

▪ Select Value Packages

Add value to your text by packaging one of the following resources with *From Inquiry to Academic Writing*. To learn more about package options for any of the following products, contact your Bedford/St. Martin's sales representative or visit **macmillanhighcred.com/catalog/frominquiry**.

LearningCurve for Readers and Writers, Bedford/St. Martin's adaptive quizzing program, quickly learns what students already know and helps them practice what they don't yet understand. Game-like quizzing motivates students to engage with their course, and reporting tools help teachers discern their students' needs. *LearningCurve for Readers and Writers* can be packaged with *From Inquiry to Academic Writing* at a significant discount. An activation code is required. To order *LearningCurve* packaged with the print book, use ISBN 978-1-319-01513-8. For details, visit **learningcurveworks.com**.

i-series This popular series presents multimedia tutorials in a flexible format—because there are things you can't do in a book.

- *ix visualizing composition 2.0* helps students put into practice key rhetorical and visual concepts.
- *i-claim: visualizing argument* offers a new way to see argument—with six multimedia tutorials, an illustrated glossary, and a wide array of multimedia arguments.

Portfolio Keeping, **Third Edition, by Nedra Reynolds and Elizabeth Davis,** provides all the information students need to use the portfolio method successfully in a writing course. *Portfolio Teaching*, a companion guide for instructors, provides the practical information instructors and writing program administrators need to use the portfolio method successfully in a writing course.

■ Make Learning Fun with *Re:Writing 3*

bedfordstmartins.com/rewriting
New open online resources with videos and interactive elements engage students in new ways of writing. You'll find tutorials about using common digital writing tools, an interactive peer review game, Extreme Paragraph Makeover, and more—all for free and for fun. Visit **bedfordstmartins.com /rewriting**.

INSTRUCTOR RESOURCES

macmillanhighered.com/catalog/frominquiry
You have a lot to do in your course. Bedford/St. Martin's wants to make it easy for you to find the support you need—and to get it quickly.

Resources for Teaching From Inquiry to Academic Writing: A Text and Reader, **Third Edition** is available as a PDF that can be downloaded from the Bedford/St. Martin's online catalog at the URL above. In addition to chapter overviews and teaching tips, the instructor's manual includes sample syllabi, correlations to the Council of Writing Program Administrators' Outcomes Statement, commentaries on all the readings, and classroom activities.

Teaching Central offers the entire list of Bedford/St. Martin's print and online professional resources in one place. You'll find landmark reference works, sourcebooks on pedagogical issues, award-winning collections, and practical advice for the classroom—all free for instructors. Visit **macmillanhighered.com/teachingcentral**.

Bits collects creative ideas for teaching a range of composition topics in an easily searchable blog format. A community of teachers—leading scholars, authors, and editors—discuss revision, research, grammar and style, technology, peer review, and much more. Take, use, adapt, and pass the ideas around. Then, come back to the site to comment or share your own suggestion. Visit **bedfordbits.com**.

Brief Contents

Contents

 To access **Tutorials, LearningCurve** activities, and **E-readings,** visit **macmillanhighered.com/frominquiry3e**.

2 From Reading as a Writer to Writing as a Reader   29

To access **Tutorials, LearningCurve** activities, and **E-readings,** visit **macmillanhighered.com/frominquiry3e**.

5   From Formulating to Developing a Thesis   106

To access **Tutorials, LearningCurve** activities, and **E-readings,** visit
macmillanhighered.com/frominquiry3e.

6 From Finding to Evaluating Sources 129

7 From Summary to Synthesis

Using Sources to Build an Argument   151

To access **Tutorials, LearningCurve** activities, and **E-readings,** visit **macmillanhighered.com/frominquiry3e.**

9 From Introductions to Conclusions

Drafting an Essay   257

To access **Tutorials, LearningCurve** activities, and **E-readings,** visit **macmillanhighered.com/frominquiry3e.**

11 Other Methods of Inquiry

Interviews and Focus Groups 313

To access **Tutorials, LearningCurve** activities, and **E-readings,** visit
macmillanhighered.com/frominquiry3e.

Entering the Conversation of Ideas   343

12   Education

What does it mean to be educated, and who decides?   345

13 Media Studies

What can we learn from what entertains us?   427

14 Sociology

How do race, class, and gender influence us? 513

15 Biology and Psychology

16 Environmental Studies
How do our decisions affect our environment?   692

To access **Tutorials, LearningCurve** activities, and **E-readings,** visit **macmillanhighered.com/frominquiry3e.**

17 Business and Marketing

What are the present and future of marketing? Are we what we buy?   *774*

How This Book Supports WPA Outcomes for First-Year Composition

Note: This chart aligns with the latest WPA Outcomes Statement, ratified in July 2014.

WPA Outcomes	RELEVANT FEATURES OF *FROM INQUIRY TO ACADEMIC WRITING: A TEXT AND READER,* THIRD EDITION
Rhetorical Knowledge	
Learn and use key rhetorical concepts through analyzing & composing a variety of texts.	A full range of rhetorical concepts is presented throughout the text. For example, see: • the treatment of rhetorical analysis in Chapter 2, From Reading as a Writer to Writing as a Reader (pp. 29–54); • the treatment of argument in Chapter 3, From Identifying Claims to Analyzing Arguments (pp. 55–79); • the treatment of rhetorical appeals in Chapter 8, From Ethos to Logos (pp. 211–256)
Gain experience reading and composing in several genres to understand how genre conventions shape and are shaped by readers' and writers' practices and purposes.	A wide range of genres is represented in the text and the reader for analysis and composition. For example, see: • The literacy narratives that conclude Chapter 1 and the Practice Sequence that follows (pp. 16–27). • Chapter 2 presents rhetorical context as a tool for analysis (pp. 29–54). • Throughout the text chapters, all student essays are annotated to indicate particular practices for particular purposes. • The reader chapters feature a range of texts from many academic and popular sources, each introduced by headnotes and "Reading as a Writer" questions that prompt students to consider context and conventions.

WPA Outcomes	RELEVANT FEATURES OF *FROM INQUIRY TO ACADEMIC WRITING: A TEXT AND READER*, THIRD EDITION
Develop facility in responding to a variety of situations and contexts, calling for purposeful shifts in voice, tone, level of formality, design, medium, and/or structure.	Throughout the text chapters students are instructed to attend to situations and contexts and given strategies for recognizing and responding to them in their composing. For example: • Chapter 4 concludes with an activity for considering genre and audience shifts (p. 105). • Chapter 5 shows how to establish a context for a thesis (pp. 106–128). • Chapter 8 shows analysis and modulation of appeals, including examples of visual appeals. • Numerous texts in Chapters 12 through 17 model the uses of charts, diagrams, and graphs for evidence in different disciplines.
Understand and use a variety of technologies to address a range of audiences.	The range of texts and technologies in the print text and available through LaunchPad Solo help students understand and analyze different technologies they can use in their own composing. • A poster presentation in LaunchPad Solo is affiliated with the student research paper in Chapter 11. • Multimodal e-readings affiliated with Chapters 12 through 17 deploy a range of strategies via different technologies, for example video, PowerPoint, performance, documentaries.
Match the capacities of different environments (e.g., print & electronic) to varying rhetorical situations.	• The rhetorical and analytical instruction in the text chapters (1–11) help students match the capacities of different composing technologies to different rhetorical situations in the reader chapters (12–17) including both print and multimodal examples.
Critical Thinking, Reading, and Composing	
Use composing and reading for inquiry, learning, thinking, and communicating in various rhetorical contexts.	• Chapter 1 sets the stage for academic writing as a form of inquiry (pp. 1–28). • Chapters 2, 3, and 4 show critical reading in action. • Chapters 5, 8, and 9 show how to generate texts and compositions from reading in various rhetorical contexts.
Read a diverse range of texts, attending especially to relationships between assertion and evidence, to patterns of organization, to interplay between verbal and nonverbal elements, and how these features function for different audiences and situations.	• Chapter 3 offers instruction in identifying claims and assertions and relating them to evidence (pp. 55–79). • Chapter 5 presents the thesis statements as ways of developing claims and using evidence depending on the situation (pp. 106–128). • Chapter 9 shows how to shape a composition via different patterns of organization (pp. 257–285). • Chapters 12 through 17 present a wide range of diverse texts that demonstrate relationships between assertion and evidence, patterns of organization, the interplay between verbal and nonverbal elements, and how these features function for different audiences and situations.
Locate and evaluate primary and secondary research materials, including journal articles, essays, books, databases, & informal Internet sources.	• Chapter 6, From Finding to Evaluating Sources, presents instruction in locating and evaluating primary and secondary research materials, including journal articles, essays, books, databases, and informal internet sources. • Chapter 11, Other Methods of Inquiry, helps students do primary research via interviews and focus groups.

WPA Outcomes	Relevant Features of *From Inquiry to Academic Writing: A Text and Reader*, Third Edition
Use strategies—such as interpretation, synthesis, response, critique, and design/redesign—to compose texts that integrate the writer's ideas with those from appropriate sources.	• Chapter 7, From Summary to Synthesis, helps students compose texts that integrate the writer's ideas with those from appropriate sources. • Writing as a Reader assignments after every selection in Chapters 12 through 17 ask students to put various texts in conversation and join those conversation. • Assignment Sequences (pp. 874–882) provide practice in developing a writing project by using the ideas of a sequence of several readings.
Processes	
Develop a writing project through multiple drafts.	• Chapters 1 through 11 provide instruction in the various stages of developing writing projects. • Within chapters, the Practice Sequences often present compound activities for chapter-specific writing projects, such as comparing arguments in Chapter 3 (pp. 78–79) and developing a synthesis in Chapter 7 (p. 182). • Assignment Sequences (pp. 874–882) provide practice in developing a writing project by using the ideas of a sequence of several readings
Develop flexible strategies for reading, drafting, reviewing, collaboration, revising, rewriting, rereading, and editing.	• Chapters 2 and 4 offer flexible strategies for rhetorical reading and inventive reading, such as reading to extend the ideas of others. • Chapters 9 and 10 feature concrete strategies on drafting, collaborating, revising, and editing.
Use composing processes and tools as a means to discover and reconsider ideas.	• Throughout, the text chapters, the importance of rereading and rewriting to discover and reconsider ideas is emphasized • Chapter 5 teaches the importance of revising a thesis in light of new evidence. • The Assignment Sequences (pp. 874–882) are predicated on the importance of rereading and rewriting to discover and rediscover ideas.
Experience the collaborative and social aspects of writing processes.	• The habits of mind of academic writing set forth in Chapter 1 (pp. 1–28) emphasize the importance of collaboration and the idea of academic writing as conversation. • Chapter 10, From Revising to Editing: Working with Peer Groups (pp. 286–312), presents collaboration and revision as essential to academic writing.
Learn to give and act on productive feedback to works in progress.	• Chapter 10 includes sample documents and worksheets for the various stages of productive feedback readers can give writings
Adapt composing processes for a variety of technologies and modalities.	• Chapter 8's section on visual analysis fosters an awareness of how rhetorical concepts function across various technologies and modalities • Responding to various multimodal texts and assignments available through LaunchPad Solo prompts reflection composing processes.
Reflect on the development of composing practices and how those practices influence their work.	• Practice Sequences and Writing as a Reader assignments often encourage students to reflect on their composing practices and how those practices influence their work.

WPA Outcomes	RELEVANT FEATURES OF *FROM INQUIRY TO ACADEMIC WRITING: A TEXT AND READER*, THIRD EDITION
Knowledge of Conventions	
Develop knowledge of linguistic structures, including grammar, punctuation, and spelling, through practice in composing and revising.	• Chapters 9 and 10 on drafting, revising, and editing help students develop knowledge of linguistic structures, including grammar, punctuation, and spelling.
Understand why genre conventions for structure, paragraphing, tone, and mechanics vary.	• The overarching emphasis on rhetorical context and situation in the text chapters fosters critical thinking about genre conventions. • The headnotes and Reading as a Writer questions that surround the selections in the reader chapters (12–17) make students aware of genre conventions, encouraging meta-aware thinking.
Gain experience negotiating variations in genre conventions.	• Critical reading of the variety of formats and genres represented by the multidisciplinary selections in the text and reader chapters and multimodal texts available through LaunchPad Solo impart experience negotiating variations in genre conventions.
Learn common formats and/or design features for different kinds of texts.	• Annotated texts such as the student essays in the text chapters impart awareness of common formats and/or design features for difference kinds of texts. • Appendix on documentation styles gives specific instruction in formats and design. • The range of multidisciplinary readings in Chapters 12 through 17 foregrounds a variety of formats used in the humanities, social sciences, and sciences.
Explore the concepts of intellectual property (such as fair use and copyright) that motivate documentation conventions.	• A Practice Sequence in Chapter 7 concerns critical thinking about copyright and intellectual property. • The Appendix on documenting sources (specifically MLA and APA formats) raises issues of different documentation conventions. • Practice Sequence in the Appendix encourages research into concepts of intellectual property that motivate documentations conventions.
Practice applying citation conventions systematically in their own work.	• The Appendix enables students to apply citation conventions of MLA and APA styles systematically in their own work.

FROM INQUIRY TO ACADEMIC WRITING

A Text and Reader

Starting with Inquiry
Habits of Mind of Academic Writers

WHAT IS ACADEMIC WRITING?

In the strictest sense, *academic writing* is what scholars do to communicate with other scholars in their fields of study, their *disciplines*. It's the research report a biologist writes, the interpretive essay a literary scholar composes, the media analysis a film scholar produces. At the same time, *academic writing* is what you have to learn so that you can participate in the different disciplinary conversations that take place in your courses. You have to learn to *think* like an academic, *read* like an academic, *do research* like an academic, and *write* like an academic—even if you have no plans to continue your education and become a scholar yourself. Learning these skills is what this book is about.

Fair warning: It isn't easy. Initially you may be perplexed by the vocabulary and sentence structure of many of the academic essays you read. Scholars use specialized language to capture the complexity of an issue or to introduce specific ideas from their discipline. Every discipline has its own vocabulary. You probably can think of words and phrases that are not used every day but that are necessary, nevertheless, to express certain ideas precisely. For example, consider the terms *centrifugal force*, *Oedipus complex*, and *onomatopoeia*. These terms carry with them a history of study; when you learn to use them, you also are learning to use the ideas they represent. Such terms help us describe the world specifically rather than generally; they help us better understand how things work and how to make better decisions about what matters to us.

Sentence structure presents another challenge. The sentences in academic writing are often longer and more intricate than the sentences in popular magazines. Academics strive to go beyond what is quick, obvious, and general. They ask questions based on studying a subject from multiple points of view, to make surprising connections that would not occur to someone who has not studied the subject carefully. It follows that academic writers are accustomed to extensive reading that prepares them to examine an issue, knowledgeably, from many different perspectives, and to make interesting intellectual use of what they discover in their research. To become an adept academic writer, you have to learn these practices as well.

Academic writing will challenge you, no doubt. But hang in there. Any initial difficulty you have with academic writing will pay off when you discover new ways of looking at the world and of making sense of it. Moreover, the habits of mind and core skills of academic writing are highly valued in the world outside the academy.

Basically, academic writing entails making an **argument**—text crafted to persuade an audience—often in the service of changing people's minds and behaviors. When you write an academic essay, you have to

- define a situation that calls for some response in writing;

- demonstrate the timeliness of your argument;

- establish a personal investment;

- appeal to readers whose minds you want to change by understanding what they think, believe, and value;

- support your argument with good reasons; and

- anticipate and address readers' reasons for disagreeing with you, while encouraging them to adopt your position.

Academic argument is not about shouting down an opponent. Instead, it is the careful expression of an idea or perspective based on reasoning and the insights garnered from a close examination of the arguments others have made on the issue.

Making academic arguments is also a social act, like joining a conversation. When we sit down to write an argument intended to persuade someone to do or to believe something, we are never really the first to broach the topic about which we are writing. Thus, learning how to write a researched argument is a process of learning how to enter conversations that are already going on in written form. This idea of writing as dialogue—not only between author and reader but between the text and everything that has been said or written about its subject beforehand—is important. Writing is a process of balancing our goals with the history of similar kinds of communication, particularly others' arguments that have been made on the same subject. The conversations that have already been going on about a subject are the subject's historical context.

WHAT ARE THE HABITS OF MIND OF ACADEMIC WRITERS?

The chapters in the first part of this book introduce you to the habits of mind and core skills of academic writing. By **habits of mind**, we mean the patterns of thought that lead you to question assumptions and opinions, explore alternative opinions, anticipate opposing arguments, compare one type of experience to another, and identify the causes and consequences of ideas and events. These forms of **critical thinking** demand an inquiring mind that welcomes complexities and seeks out and weighs many different points of view, a mind willing to enter complex conversations both in and out of the academy. We discuss academic habits of mind in the rest of Chapter 1 and refer to them throughout this book.

Such habits of mind are especially important today, when we are bombarded with appeals to buy this or that product and with information that may or may not be true. For example, in "106 Science Claims and a Truckful of Baloney" (*The Best American Science and Nature Writing*, 2005), William Speed Weed illustrates the extent to which the claims of science vie for our attention alongside the claims of advertising. He notes that advertisers often package their claims as science, but wonders whether a box of Cheerios really can reduce cholesterol.

As readers we have a responsibility to test the claims of both science and advertising in order to decide what to believe and act upon. Weed found that "very few of the 100 claims" he evaluated "proved completely true" and that "a good number were patently false." Testing the truth of claims—learning to consider information carefully and critically and to weigh competing points of view before making our own judgments—gives us power over our own lives.

The habits of mind and practices valued by academic writers are probably ones you already share. You are behaving "academically" when you comparison-shop, a process that entails learning about the product in the media and on the Internet and then looking at the choices firsthand before you decide which one you will purchase. You employ these same habits of mind when you deliberate over casting a vote in an election. You inform yourself about the issues that are most pressing; you learn about the candidates' positions on these issues; you consider other arguments for and against both issues and candidates; and you weigh those arguments and your own understanding to determine which candidate you will support.

Fundamentally, academic habits of mind are *analytical*. When you consider a variety of factors—the quality and functionality of the item you plan to buy, how it meets your needs, how it compares to similar items before making a shopping choice—you are conducting an **analysis**. That is, you are pausing to examine the reasons why you should buy something, instead of simply handing over your cash and saying, "I want one of those."

To a certain extent, analysis involves breaking something down into its various parts and reflecting on how the parts do or don't work together. For example, when you deliberate over your vote, you may consult one of those charts that newspapers often run around election time: A list of candidates appears across the top of the chart, and a list of issues appears on the side. You can scan the columns to see where each candidate stands on the issues, and you can scan the rows to see how the candidates compare on a particular issue. The newspaper editors have performed a preliminary analysis for you. They've asked, "Who are the candidates?" "What are the issues?" and "Where does each candidate stand on the issues?"; and they have presented the answers to you in a format that can help you make your decision.

But you still have to perform your own analysis of the information before you cast your ballot. Suppose no candidate holds your position on every issue. Whom do you vote for? Which issues are most important to you? Or suppose two candidates hold your position on every issue. Which one do you vote for? What characteristics or experience are you looking for in an elected official? And you may want to investigate further by visiting the candidates' Web sites or by talking with your friends to gather their thoughts on the election.

As you can see, analysis involves more than simply disassembling or dissecting something. It is a process of continually asking questions and looking for answers. Analysis reflects, in the best sense of the word, a *skeptical* habit of mind, an unwillingness to settle for obvious answers in the quest to understand why things are the way they are and how they might be different.

This book will help you develop the questioning, evaluating, and conversational skills you already have into strategies that will improve your ability to make careful, informed judgments about the often conflicting and confusing information you are confronted with every day. With these strategies, you will be in a position to use your writing skills to create change where you feel it is most needed.

The first steps in developing these skills are to recognize the key academic habits of mind and then to refine your practice of them. We explore four key habits of mind in the rest of this chapter:

1. inquiring,
2. seeking and valuing complexity,
3. understanding that academic writing is a conversation, and
4. understanding that writing is a process.

ACADEMIC WRITERS MAKE INQUIRIES

Academic writers usually study a body of information so closely and from so many different perspectives that they can ask questions that may not occur to people who are just scanning the information. That is, academic writers learn to make **inquiries**. Every piece of academic writing begins with a question about the way the world works, and the best questions lead to rich, complex insights that others can learn from and build on.

You will find that the ability to ask good questions is equally valuable in your daily life. Asking thoughtful questions about politics, popular culture, work, or anything else—questions like, What exactly did that candidate mean by "Family values are values for all of us," anyway? What is lost and gained by bringing Tolkien's *Lord of the Rings* trilogy to the screen? What does it take to move ahead in this company?—is the first step in understanding how the world works and how it can be changed.

Inquiry typically begins with **observation**, a careful noting of phenomena or behaviors that puzzle you or challenge your beliefs and values (in a text or in the real world). Observing phenomena prompts an attempt to understand them by **asking questions** (Why does this exist? Why is this happening? Do things have to be this way?) and **examining alternatives** (Maybe this doesn't need to exist. Maybe this could happen another way instead.).

For example, Mark Edmundson, a professor of English at the University of Virginia, *observes* that his students seem to prefer classes they consider "fun" over those that push them to work hard. This prompts him to *ask* how the consumer culture—especially the entertainment culture—has altered the college experience. In his essay "On the Uses of a Liberal Education," he wonders what it means that colleges increasingly see students as customers they need to please with Club Med–style exercise facilities that look "like a retirement spread for the young" more than as minds to be educated. He further *asks* what will happen if we don't change course—if entertaining students and making them feel good about themselves continue to be higher priorities than challenging students to stretch themselves with difficult ideas. Finally, he looks at alternatives to entertainment-style education and *examines those alternatives* to see what they would offer students.

In her reading on the American civil rights movement of the 1950s and 1960s, one of our students *observed* that the difficulties many immigrant groups experienced when they first arrived in the United States are not acknowledged as struggles for civil rights. This student of Asian descent *wondered why* the difficulties Asians faced in assimilating into American culture are not seen as analogous to the efforts of African Americans to gain civil rights (Why are things this way?). In doing so, she *asked* a number of relevant questions: What do we leave out when we tell stories about ourselves? Why reduce the struggle for civil rights to black-and-white terms? How can we represent the multiple struggles of people who have contributed to building our nation? Then she *examined alternatives*—different ways of presenting the history of a nation that prides itself on justice and the protection of its people's civil rights (Maybe this doesn't need to exist. Maybe this could happen another way.). The academic writing you will read—and write yourself—starts with questions and seeks to find rich answers.

Steps to Inquiry

1 **Observe.** Note phenomena or behaviors that puzzle you or challenge your beliefs and values.

2 **Ask questions.** Consider why things are the way they are.

3 **Examine alternatives.** Explore how things could be different.

A Practice Sequence: Inquiry Activities

The activities below will help you practice the strategies of observing, asking questions, and examining alternatives.

1   Find an advertisement for a political campaign (you can find many political ads on the Internet), and write down anything about what you observe in the ad that puzzles you or that challenges your beliefs and values. Next, write down questions you might have (Do things have to be this way?). Finally, write down other ways you think the ad could persuade you to vote for this particular candidate (Maybe this could happen another way instead.).

2   Locate and analyze data about the students at your school. For example, you might research the available majors and determine which departments have the highest and lowest enrollments. (Some schools have fact books that can be accessed online; and typically the registrar maintains a database with this information.) Is there anything that puzzles you? Write down any questions you have (Why are things the way they are?). What alternative explanations can you provide to account for differences in the popularity of the subjects students major in?

ACADEMIC WRITERS SEEK AND VALUE COMPLEXITY

Seeking and valuing complexity are what inquiry is all about. As you read academic arguments (for example, about school choice), observe how the media work to influence your opinions (for example, in political ads), or analyze data (for example, about candidates in an election), you will explore reasons why things are the way they are and how they might be different. When you do so, we encourage you not to settle for simple either/ or reasons. Instead, look for multiple explanations.

When we rely on **binary thinking**—imagining there are only two sides to an issue—we tend to ignore information that does not fall tidily into one side or the other. Think of the sound-bite assertions you hear bandied about on talk shows on the pretext of "discussing" a hot-button issue like stem-cell research or abortion: "It's just wrong/right because it is!" Real-world questions (How has the Internet changed our sense of what it means to be a writer? What are the global repercussions of fast food? How do we make sense of terrorism?) don't have easy for-or-against answers. Remember that an **issue** is open to dispute and can be explored and debated. Issue-based questions, then, need to be approached with a mind open to complex possibilities. (We say more about identifying issues and formulating issue-based questions in Chapter 4.)

If we take as an example the issue of terrorism, we would discover that scholars of religion, economics, ethics, and politics tend to ask very different questions about terrorism and to propose very different approaches for addressing this worldwide problem. This doesn't mean that one approach is right and the others are wrong; it means that complex issues are likely to have multiple explanations, rather than a simple choice between A and B.

In her attempt to explain the popularity of hip-hop culture, Bronwen Low, a professor of education, provides a window on the steps we can take to examine the complexity of a topic. In the introductory chapters of her book, *Slam School: Learning Through Conflict in the Hip Hop and Spoken Word Classroom*, she begins with the observation that hip-hop "is the single-most influential cultural force shaping contemporary urban youth culture in the United States, and its international reach is growing." She then defines what she means by hip-hop culture, distinguishing it from "rapping," and helps readers understand hip-hop culture as encompassing graffiti art and "a whole culture of style," including "fashion" and "sensibility." Motivated by a sense of curiosity, if not puzzlement, Low asks questions that guide her inquiry: What is it that makes hip-hop culture so compelling to young people across such a wide spectrum of race, culture, and gender? Further, how can social, cultural, and literary critics better understand the evolution of new forms of language and performance, such as spoken-word poetry, in "youth-driven popular culture"? Notice that she indicates that she will frame her inquiry using the multiple perspectives of social, cultural, and literary critics. In turn, Low explains that she began to answer these questions by giving herself a "hip-hop education." She attended spoken-word poetry festivals ("slams") across the United States, listened to the music, and read both "academic theory and journalism" to see what others had to say about "poetry's relevance and coolness to youth."

One of our students was curious about why a well-known musician, Eminem, was at once so widely popular and so bitterly reviled, a phenomenon he observed in discussions with friends and in reviews of Eminem's music. He set out to understand these conflicting responses by examining the differing perspectives of music critics, politicians, religious evangelists, and his peers; and then he formulated an issue-based question: "How can we explain Eminem's popularity given the ways people criticize Eminem personally and his music?" In looking at this issue, the student opened himself to complexity by resisting simple answers to his question about why Eminem and his music evoked such different and conflicting responses.

Steps to Seeking and Valuing Complexity

1 **Reflect on what you observe.** Clarify your initial interest in a phenomenon or behavior by focusing on its particular details. Then reflect on what is most interesting and least interesting to you about these details, and why.

2 **Examine issues from multiple points of view.** Imagine more than two sides to the issue, and recognize that there may well be other points of view too.

3 **Ask issue-based questions.** Try to put into words questions that will help you explore why things are the way they are.

A Practice Sequence: Seeking and Valuing Complexity

These activities build on the previous exercises we asked you to complete.

1   Look again at the political ad. Think about other perspectives that would complicate your understanding of how the ad might persuade voters.

2   Imagine other perspectives on the data you found on the students in your school. Let's say, for example, that you've looked at data on student majors. How did you explain the popularity of certain majors and the unpopularity of others? How do you think other students would explain these discrepancies? What explanations would faculty members offer?

ACADEMIC WRITERS SEE WRITING AS A CONVERSATION

Another habit of mind at the heart of academic writing is the understanding that ideas always build on and respond to other ideas, just as they do in the best kind of conversations. Of course, conversations in academic writing happen on the page; they are not spoken. Still, these conversations are quite similar to the conversations you have through e-mail and instant messaging: You are responding to something someone else has written (or said) and are writing back in anticipation of future responses.

Academic writing also places a high value on the belief that good, thoughtful ideas come from conversations with others, *many* others. As your exposure to other viewpoints increases, as you take more and different points of view into consideration and build on them, your own ideas will develop more fully and fairly. You already know that to get a full picture of something, often you have to ask for multiple perspectives. When you want to find out what "really" happened at an event when your friends are telling you different stories, you listen to all of them and then evaluate the evidence to draw conclusions you can stand behind—just as academic writers do.

Theologian Martin Marty starts a conversation about hospitality in his book *When Faiths Collide* (2004). *Hospitality* is a word he uses to describe a human behavior that has the potential to bring about real understanding among people who do not share a common faith or culture. As Marty points out, finding common ground is an especially important and timely concern "in a world where strangers meet strangers with gunfire, barrier walls, spiritually land-mined paths, and the spirit of revenge." He believes that people need opportunities to share their stories, their values, and their beliefs; in doing so, they feel less threatened by ideas they do not understand or identify with.

Yet Marty anticipates the possibility that the notion of hospitality will be met with skepticism or incomprehension by those who find the term "dainty." Current usage of the term—as in "hospitality suites" and "hospitality industries"—differs from historical usage, particularly biblical usage. To counter the incredulity or incomprehension of those who do not immediately understand his use of the term *hospitality*, Marty gives his readers entrée to a conversation with other scholars who understand the complexity and power of the kind of hospitality shown by people who welcome a stranger into their world. The stranger he has in mind may simply be the person who moves in next door; but that person could also be an immigrant, an exile, or a refugee.

Marty brings another scholar, Darrell Fasching, into the conversation to explain that hospitality entails welcoming "the stranger . . . [which] inevitably involves us in a sympathetic passing over into the other's life and stories" (cited in Marty, p. 132). And John Koenig, another scholar Marty cites, traces the biblical sources of the term in an effort to show the value of understanding those we fear. That understanding, Marty argues, might lead to peace among warring factions. The conversation Marty begins on the page helps us see that his views on bringing about peace have their source in other people's ideas. In turn, the fact that he draws on multiple sources gives strength to Marty's argument.

The characteristics that make for effective oral conversation are also in play in effective academic conversation: empathy, respect, and a willingness to exchange and revise ideas. **Empathy** is the ability to understand the perspectives that shape what people think, believe, and value. To express both empathy and respect for the positions of all people involved in the conversation, academic writers try to understand the conditions under which each opinion might be true and then to represent the strengths of that position accurately.

For example, imagine that your firm commitment to protecting the environment is challenged by those who see the value of developing land rich with oil and other resources. In challenging their position, it would serve you well to understand their motives, both economic (lower gas prices, new jobs that will create a demand for new houses) and political (less dependence on foreign oil). If you can demonstrate your knowledge of these factors, those committed to developing resources in protected areas will listen to you. To convey empathy and respect while presenting your own point of view, you might introduce your argument by saying:

> Although it is important to develop untapped resources in remote areas of the United States both to lower gas prices and create new jobs and to eliminate our dependence on other countries' resources, it is in everyone's interest to use alternative sources of power and protect our natural resources.

As you demonstrate your knowledge and a sense of shared values, you could also describe the conditions under which you might change your own position.

People engaging in productive conversation try to create change by listening and responding to one another rather than dominating one another. Instead of trying to win an argument, they focus on reaching a mutual understanding. This does not mean that effective communicators do not take strong positions; more often than not they do. However, they are more likely to achieve their goals by persuading others instead of ignoring them and their points of view. Similarly, writers come to every issue with an agenda. But they realize that they may have to compromise on certain points to carry those that mean the most to them. More important, they understand that their perceptions and opinions may be flawed or limited, and they are willing to revise them when valid new perspectives are introduced.

In an academic community, ideas develop through give-and-take, through a conversation that builds on what has come before and grows stronger from multiple perspectives. You will find this dynamic at work in your classes, when you discuss your ideas: You will build on other people's insights, and they will build on yours. As a habit of mind, paying attention to academic conversations can improve the thinking and writing you do in every class you take.

Steps to Joining an Academic Conversation

1 **Be receptive to the ideas of others.** Listen carefully and empathetically to what others have to say.

2 **Be respectful of the ideas of others.** When you refer to the opinions of others, represent them fairly and use an evenhanded tone. Avoid sounding scornful or dismissive.

3 **Engage with the ideas of others.** Try to understand how people have arrived at their feelings and beliefs.

4 **Be flexible in your thinking about the ideas of others.** Be willing to exchange ideas and to revise your own opinions.

A Practice Sequence: Joining an Academic Conversation

The following excerpt is taken from Thomas Patterson's *The Vanishing Voter* (2002), an examination of voter apathy. Read the excerpt and then complete the exercises that follow.

> Does a diminished appetite for voting affect the health of American politics? Is society harmed when the voting rate is low or in decline? As the *Chicago Tribune* said in an editorial, it may be "humiliating" that the United States, the oldest continuous democracy, has nearly the lowest voting rate in the world. But does it have any practical significance? . . .
>
> The increasing number of nonvoters could be a danger to democracy. Although high participation by itself does not trigger radical change, a flood of new voters into the electorate could possibly do it. It's difficult to imagine a crisis big and divisive enough to prompt millions of new voters to suddenly flock to the polls, especially in light of Americans' aversion to political extremism. Nevertheless, citizens who are outside the electorate are less attached to the existing system. As the sociologist Seymour Martin Lipset observed, a society of nonvoters "is potentially more explosive than one in which most citizens are regularly involved in activities which give them some sense of participation in decisions which affect their lives."
>
> Voting can strengthen citizenship in other ways, too. When people vote, they are more attentive to politics and are better informed about issues affecting them. Voting also deepens community involvement, as the philosopher John Stuart Mill theorized a century ago. Studies indicate that voters are more active in community affairs than nonvoters are. Of course, this association says more about the type of person who votes as opposed to the effect of voting. But recent evidence, as Harvard University's Robert Putnam notes, "suggests that the act of voting itself encourages volunteering and other forms of government citizenship."

1   In this excerpt, Patterson presents two arguments: that increasing voter apathy is a danger to democracy and that voting strengthens citizenship. With which of these arguments do you sympathize more? Why? Can you imagine reasons that another person might not agree with you? Write them down. Now do the same exercise with the argument you find less compelling.

2   Your instructor will divide the class into four groups and assign each group a position—pro or con—on one of Patterson's arguments. Brainstorm with the members of your group to come up with examples or reasons why your group's position is valid. Make a list of those examples or reasons, and be prepared to present them to the class.

3   Your instructor will now break up the groups into new groups, each with at least one representative of the original groups. In turn with the other members of your new group, take a few moments

to articulate your position and the reasons for it. Remember to be civil and as persuasive as possible.

4   Finally, with the other members of your new group, talk about the merits of the various points of view. Try to find common ground ("I understand what you are saying; in fact, it's not unlike the point I was making about . . ."). The point of this discussion is not to pronounce a winner (who made the best case for his or her perspective) but to explore common ground, exchange and revise ideas, and imagine compromises.

ACADEMIC WRITERS UNDERSTAND THAT WRITING IS A PROCESS

Academic writing is a process of defining issues, formulating questions, and developing sound arguments. This view of writing counters a number of popular myths: that writing depends on inspiration, that writing should happen quickly, that learning to write in one context prepares you to write in other contexts, and that revision is the same as editing. The writing process addresses these myths. First, choosing an idea that matters to you is one way to make your writing matter. And there's a better chance that writing you care about will contribute in a meaningful way to the conversation going on about a given issue in the academic community. Second, writers who invest time in developing and revising their ideas will improve the quality of both their ideas and their language—their ability to be specific and express complexity.

There are three main stages to the writing process: collecting information, drafting, and revising. We introduce them here and expand on them throughout this book.

■ Collect Information and Material

Always begin the process of writing an essay by collecting *in writing* the material—the information, ideas, and evidence—from which you will shape your own argument. Once you have read and marked the pages of a text, you have begun the process of building your own argument. The important point here is that you start to put your ideas on paper. Good writing comes from returning to your ideas on your own and with your classmates, reconsidering them, and revising them as your thinking develops. This is not something you can do with any specificity unless you have written down your ideas. The following box shows the steps for gathering information from your reading, the first stage in the process of writing an academic essay. (In Chapter 2, these steps are illustrated and discussed in more detail.)

Steps to Collecting Information and Material

1 **Mark your texts as you read.** Note key terms; ask questions in the margins; indicate connections to other texts.

2 **List quotations you find interesting and provocative.** You might even write short notes to yourself about what you find significant about the quotes.

3 **List your own ideas in response to the reading or readings.** Include what you've observed about the way the author or authors make their arguments.

4 **Sketch out the similarities and differences among the authors whose work you plan to use in your essay.** Where would they agree or disagree? How would each respond to the others' arguments and evidence?

▪ Draft, and Draft Again

The next stage in the writing process begins when you are ready to think about your focus and how to arrange the ideas you have gathered in the collecting stage. Writers often find that writing a first draft is an act of discovery, that their ultimate focus emerges during this initial drafting process. Sometimes it is only at the end of a four-page draft that a writer says, "Aha! This is what I really want to talk about in this essay!" Later revisions of an essay, then, are not simply editing or cleaning up the grammar of a first draft. Instead, they truly involve *re*vision, seeing the first draft again to establish the clearest possible argument and the most persuasive evidence. This means that you do not have to stick with the way a draft turns out the first time. You can—and must!—be willing to rewrite a substantial amount of a first draft if the focus of the argument changes, or if in the process of writing new ideas emerge that enrich the essay. This is why it's important not to agonize over wording in a first draft: It's difficult to toss out a paragraph you've sweated over for hours. Use the first draft to get your ideas down on paper so that you and your peers can discuss what you see there, with the knowledge that you (like your peers) will need to stay open to the possibility of changing an aspect of your focus or argument.

Steps to Drafting

1 **Look through the materials** you have collected to see what interests you most and what you have the most to say about.

2 **Identify what is at issue** what is open to dispute.

3 Formulate a question that your essay will respond to.

4 Select the material you will include, and decide what is outside your focus.

5 Consider the types of readers who might be most interested in what you have to say.

6 Gather more material once you've decided on your purpose—what you want to teach your readers.

7 Formulate a working thesis that conveys the point you want to make.

8 Consider possible arguments against your position and your response to them.

■ Revise Significantly

The final stage, revising, might involve several different drafts as you continue to sharpen your insights and the organization of what you have written. As we discuss in Chapter 10, you and your peers will be reading one another's drafts, offering feedback as you move from the larger issues to the smaller ones. It should be clear by now that academic writing is done in a community of thinkers: That is, people read other people's drafts and make suggestions for further clarification, further development of ideas, and sometimes further research. This is quite different from simply editing someone's writing for grammatical errors and typos. Instead, drafting and revising with real readers, as we discuss in Chapter 10, allow you to participate in the collaborative spirit of the academy, in which knowledge making is a group activity that comes out of the conversation of ideas. Importantly, this process approach to writing in the company of real readers mirrors the conversation of ideas carried on in the pages of academic books and journals.

Steps to Revising

1 Draft and revise the introduction and conclusion.

2 Clarify any obscure or confusing passages your peers have pointed out.

3 Provide details and textual evidence where your peers have asked for new or more information.

4 Check to be sure you have included opposing points of view and have addressed them fairly.

5 Consider reorganization.

> **6** Check to be sure that every paragraph contributes clearly to your thesis or main claim and that you have included signposts along the way, phrases that help a reader understand your purpose ("Here I turn to an example from current movies to show how this issue is alive and well in pop culture.")
>
> **7** Consider using strategies you have found effective in other reading you have done for class (repeating words or phrases for effect, asking rhetorical questions, varying your sentence length).

The four academic habits of mind we have discussed throughout this chapter—making inquiries, seeking and valuing complexity, understanding writing as a conversation, and understanding writing as a process—are fundamental patterns of thought you will need to cultivate as an academic writer. The core skills we discuss through the rest of the book build on these habits of mind.

Moreover, the kind of writing we describe in this chapter may challenge some models of writing that you learned in high school, particularly the five-paragraph theme. The five-paragraph essay is a **genre,** or kind, of writing that offers writers a conventional formula for transmitting information to readers. While there is nothing wrong with such a formula, it does not effectively represent the conversations of ideas that transpire in the academy. By contrast, academic writing is a genre responsive to the role that readers play in guiding writing and the writing process. That is, academic writing is about shaping and adapting information for the purpose of influencing how readers think about a given issue, not simply placing information in a conventional organizational pattern. We expect academic readers to critically analyze what we have written and anticipate writers' efforts to address their concerns. Therefore, as writers, we need to acknowledge different points of view, make concessions, recognize the limitations of what we argue, and provide counterarguments. Reading necessarily plays a prominent role in the many forms of writing that you do, but not necessarily as a process of simply gathering information. Instead, as James Crosswhite suggests in his book *The Rhetoric of Reason,* reading "means making judgments about which of the many voices and encounters can be brought together into productive conversation."

BECOMING ACADEMIC: TWO NARRATIVES

In the following passages, two writers describe their early experiences as readers. Trained as academic writers, Richard Rodriguez and Gerald Graff are well known outside the academy. In this excerpt from *Hunger of Memory,* Rodriguez describes what it was like growing up as a bookish bilingual "scholarship boy" in a Spanish-speaking household. In the other excerpt, from *Beyond the Culture Wars,* Graff narrates how he disliked reading books, especially literature and history books, well into his under-graduate years as an English major. Both of their narratives turn around moments of recognition triggered by exposure to the ideas of others. As you read the selections, consider these questions:

- Where are the turning points in each narrative? What are the most important things the writers seem to learn?
- What incidents or insights did you find most interesting in the narratives? Why?
- What seem to be the key ideas in each narrative? Do these ideas strike you as being potentially useful in your own work as a thinker and writer?
- Do you find that the writers exhibit academic habits of mind (making inquiries, seeking and valuing complexity, seeing writing as a kind of conversation)? If so, where?

RICHARD RODRIGUEZ

Scholarship Boy

Richard Rodriguez was born into a Mexican immigrant family in San Francisco, California, and spoke only Spanish until age six. He had a formi-dable education, receiving a BA from Stanford University and an MA from Columbia University; studying for a PhD at the University of California, Berkeley; and attending the Warburg Institute in London on a Fulbright fellowship. Instead of pursuing a career in academia, he became a journalist. He is perhaps best known for his contributions to PBS's *The NewsHour with Jim Lehrer* and for his controversial opposition to affirmative action and bilingual education. His books include *Hunger of Memory: The Education of Richard Rodriguez* (1981), *Mexico's Children* (1990), *Days of Obligation: An Argument with My Mexican Father* (1992), and *Brown: The Last Discovery of America* (2002).

■ ■ ■

I stand in the ghetto classroom—"the guest speaker"—attempting to lecture on the mystery of the sounds of our words to rows of diffident students. "Don't you hear it? Listen! The music of our words. '*Sumer is i-cumen in. . . .*' And songs on the car radio. We need Aretha Franklin's voice to fill plain words with music—her life." In the face of their empty stares, I try to create an enthusiasm. But the girls in the back row turn to watch some boy passing outside. There are flutters of smiles, waves. And someone's mouth elongates heavy, silent words through the barrier of glass. Silent words—the lips straining to shape each voiceless syllable: "*Meet meee late errr.*" By the door, the instructor smiles at me,

1

apparently hoping that I will be able to spark some enthusiasm in the class. But only one student seems to be listening. A girl, maybe fourteen. In this gray room her eyes shine with ambition. She keeps nodding and nodding at all that I say; she even takes notes. And each time I ask a question, she jerks up and down in her desk like a marionette, while her hand waves over the bowed heads of her classmates. It is myself (as a boy) I see as she faces me now (a man in my thirties).

The boy who first entered a classroom barely able to speak English, twenty years later concluded his studies in the stately quiet of the reading room in the British Museum. Thus with one sentence I can summarize my academic career. It will be harder to summarize what sort of life connects the boy to the man.

2

With every award, each graduation from one level of education to the next, people I'd meet would congratulate me. Their refrain always the same: "Your parents must be very proud." Sometimes then they'd ask me how I managed it—my "success." (How?) After a while, I had several quick answers to give in reply. I'd admit, for one thing, that I went to an excellent grammar school. (My earliest teachers, the nuns, made my success their ambition.) And my brother and both my sisters were very good students. (They often brought home the shiny school trophies I came to want.) And my mother and father always encouraged me. (At every graduation they were behind the stunning flash of the camera when I turned to look at the crowd.)

3

As important as these factors were, however, they account inadequately for my academic advance. Nor do they suggest what an odd success I managed. For although I was a very good student, I was also a very bad student. I was a "scholarship boy," a certain kind of scholarship boy. Always successful, I was always unconfident. Exhilarated by my progress. Sad. I became the prized student—anxious and eager to learn. Too eager, too anxious—an imitative and unoriginal pupil. My brother and two sisters enjoyed the advantages I did, and they grew to be as successful as I, but none of them ever seemed so anxious about their schooling. A second-grade student, I was the one who came home and corrected the "simple" grammatical mistakes of our parents. ("Two negatives make a positive.") Proudly I announced—to my family's startled silence—that a teacher had said I was losing all trace of a Spanish accent. I was oddly annoyed when I was unable to get parental help with a homework assignment. The night my father tried to help me with an arithmetic exercise, he kept reading the instructions, each time more deliberately, until I pried the textbook out of his hands, saying, "I'll try to figure it out some more by myself."

4

When I reached the third grade, I outgrew such behavior. I became more tactful, careful to keep separate the two very different worlds of my day. But then, with ever-increasing intensity, I devoted myself to my

5

studies. I became bookish, puzzling to all my family. Ambition set me apart. When my brother saw me struggling home with stacks of library books, he would laugh, shouting: "Hey, Four Eyes!" My father opened a closet one day and was startled to find me inside, reading a novel. My mother would find me reading when I was supposed to be asleep or helping around the house or playing outside. In a voice angry or worried or just curious, she'd ask: "What do you see in your books?" It became the family's joke. When I was called and wouldn't reply, someone would say I must be hiding under my bed with a book.

(How did I manage my success?) 6

What I am about to say to you has taken me more than twenty years 7 to admit: *A primary reason for my success in the classroom was that I couldn't forget that schooling was changing me and separating me from the life I enjoyed before becoming a student.* That simple realization! For years I never spoke to anyone about it. Never mentioned a thing to my family or my teachers or classmates. From a very early age, I understood enough, just enough about my classroom experiences to keep what I knew repressed, hidden beneath layers of embarrassment. Not until my last months as a graduate student, nearly thirty years old, was it possible for me to think much about the reasons for my academic success. Only then. At the end of my schooling, I needed to determine how far I had moved from my past. The adult finally confronted, and now must publicly say, what the child shuddered from knowing and could never admit to himself or to those many faces that smiled at his every success. ("Your parents must be very proud. . . .")

At the end, in the British Museum (too distracted to finish my disser- 8 tation) for weeks I read, speed-read, books by modern educational theorists, only to find infrequent and slight mention of students like me. (Much more is written about the more typical case, the lower-class student who barely is helped by his schooling.) Then one day, leafing through Richard Hoggart's *The Uses of Literacy*, I found, in his description of the scholarship boy, myself. For the first time I realized that there were other students like me, and so I was able to frame the meaning of my academic success, its consequent price—the loss.

Hoggart's description is distinguished, at least initially, by deep 9 understanding. What he grasps very well is that the scholarship boy must move between environments, his home and the classroom, which are at cultural extremes, opposed. With his family, the boy has the intense pleasure of intimacy, the family's consolation in feeling public alienation. Lavish emotions texture home life. *Then*, at school, the instruction bids him to trust lonely reason primarily. Immediate needs set the pace of his parents' lives. From his mother and father the boy learns to trust spontaneity and nonrational ways of knowing. *Then*, at school, there is mental calm. Teachers emphasize the value of a reflectiveness that opens a space between thinking and immediate action.

Years of schooling must pass before the boy will be able to sketch   *10*
the cultural differences in his day as abstractly as this. But he senses those differences early. Perhaps as early as the night he brings home an assignment from school and finds the house too noisy for study.

> He has to be more and more alone, if he is going to "get on." He will have, probably unconsciously, to oppose the ethos of the hearth, the intense gregariousness of the working-class family group. Since everything centers upon the living-room, there is unlikely to be a room of his own; the bedrooms are cold and inhospitable, and to warm them or the front room, if there is one, would not only be expensive, but would require an imaginative leap—out of the tradition—which most families are not capable of making. There is a corner of the living-room table. On the other side Mother is ironing, the wireless is on, someone is singing a snatch of song or Father says intermittently whatever comes into his head. The boy has to cut himself off mentally, so as to do his homework, as well as he can.[1]

The next day, the lesson is as apparent at school. There are even rows of desks. Discussion is ordered. The boy must rehearse his thoughts and raise his hand before speaking out in a loud voice to an audience of classmates. And there is time enough, and silence, to think about ideas (big ideas) never considered at home by his parents.

Not for the working-class child alone is adjustment to the classroom   *11*
difficult. Good schooling requires that any student alter early childhood habits. But the working-class child is usually least prepared for the change. And, unlike many middle-class children, he goes home and sees in his parents a way of life not only different but starkly opposed to that of the classroom. (He enters the house and hears his parents talking in ways his teachers discourage.)

Without extraordinary determination and the great assistance of   *12*
others—at home and at school—there is little chance for success. Typically most working-class children are barely changed by the classroom. The exception succeeds. The relative few become scholarship students. Of these, Richard Hoggart estimates, most manage a fairly graceful transition. Somehow they learn to live in the two very different worlds of their day. There are some others, however, those Hoggart pejoratively terms "scholarship boys," for whom success comes with special anxiety. Scholarship boy: good student, troubled son. The child is "moderately endowed," intellectually mediocre, Hoggart supposes—though it may be more pertinent to note the special qualities of temperament in the child. High-strung child. Brooding. Sensitive. Haunted by the knowledge that one *chooses* to become a

---

[1] All quotations in this selection are from Richard Hoggart, *The Uses of Literacy* (London: Chatto and Windus, 1957), chapter 10.

student. (Education is not an inevitable or natural step in growing up.) Here is a child who cannot forget that his academic success distances him from a life he loved, even from his own memory of himself.

Initially, he wavers, balances allegiance. ("The boy is himself [until he reaches, say, the upper forms] very much of *both* the worlds of home and school. He is enormously obedient to the dictates of the world of school, but emotionally still strongly wants to continue as part of the family circle.") Gradually, necessarily, the balance is lost. The boy needs to spend more and more time studying, each night enclosing himself in the silence permitted and required by intense concentration. He takes his first step toward academic success, away from his family. 13

From the very first days, through the years following, it will be with his parents—the figures of lost authority, the persons toward whom he feels deepest love—that the change will be most powerfully measured. A separation will unravel between them. Advancing in his studies, the boy notices that his mother and father have not changed as much as he. Rather, when he sees them, they often remind him of the person he once was and the life he earlier shared with them. He realizes what some Romantics also know when they praise the working class for the capacity for human closeness, qualities of passion and spontaneity, that the rest of us experience in like measure only in the earliest part of our youth. For the Romantic, this doesn't make working-class life childish. Working-class life challenges precisely because it is an *adult* way of life. 14

The scholarship boy reaches a different conclusion. He cannot afford to admire his parents. (How could he and still pursue such a contrary life?) He permits himself embarrassment at their lack of education. And to evade nostalgia for the life he has lost, he concentrates on the benefits education will bestow upon him. He becomes especially ambitious. Without the support of old certainties and consolations, almost mechanically, he assumes the procedures and doctrines of the classroom. The kind of allegiance the young student might have given his mother and father only days earlier, he transfers to the teacher, the new figure of authority. "[The scholarship boy] tends to make a father-figure of his form-master," Hoggart observes. 15

But Hoggart's calm prose only makes me recall the urgency with which I came to idolize my grammar school teachers. I began by imitating their accents, using their diction, trusting their every direction. The very first facts they dispensed, I grasped with awe. Any book they told me to read, I read—then waited for them to tell me which books I enjoyed. Their every casual opinion I came to adopt and to trumpet when I returned home. I stayed after school "to help"—to get my teacher's undivided attention. It was the nun's encouragement that mattered most to me. (She understood exactly what—my parents never seemed to appraise so well—all my achievements entailed.) Memory gently 16 caressed each word of praise bestowed in the classroom so that compliments teachers paid me years ago come quickly to mind even today.

The enthusiasm I felt in second-grade classes I flaunted before both my parents. The docile, obedient student came home a shrill and precocious son who insisted on correcting and teaching his parents with the remark: "My teacher told us. . . ."

I intended to hurt my mother and father. I was still angry at them for having encouraged me toward classroom English. But gradually this anger was exhausted, replaced by guilt as school grew more and more attractive to me. I grew increasingly successful, a talkative student. My hand was raised in the classroom; I yearned to answer any question. At home, life was less noisy than it had been. (I spoke to classmates and teachers more often each day than to family members.) Quiet at home, I sat with my papers for hours each night. I never forgot that schooling had irretrievably changed my family's life. That knowledge, however, did not weaken ambition. Instead, it strengthened resolve. Those times I remembered the loss of my past with regret, I quickly reminded myself of all the things my teachers could give me. (They could make me an educated man.) I tightened my grip on pencil and books. I evaded nostalgia. Tried hard to forget. But one does not forget by trying to forget. One only remembers. I remembered too well that education had changed my family's life. I would not have become a scholarship boy had I not so often remembered.

Once she was sure that her children knew English, my mother would tell us, "You should keep up your Spanish." Voices playfully groaned in response. "¡*Pochos*!" my mother would tease. I listened silently.

After a while, I grew more calm at home. I developed tact. A fourth-grade student, I was no longer the show-off in front of my parents. I became a conventionally dutiful son, politely affectionate, cheerful enough, even—for reasons beyond choosing—my father's favorite. And much about my family life was easy then, comfortable, happy in the rhythm of our living together: hearing my father getting ready for work; eating the breakfast my mother had made me; looking up from a novel to hear my brother or one of my sisters playing with friends in the backyard; in winter, coming upon the house all lighted up after dark.

But withheld from my mother and father was any mention of what most mattered to me: the extraordinary experience of first-learning. Late afternoon: In the midst of preparing dinner, my mother would come up behind me while I was trying to read. Her head just over mine, her breath warmly scented with food. "What are you reading?" Or, "Tell me all about your new courses." I would barely respond, "Just the usual things, nothing special." (A half smile, then silence. Her head moving back in the silence. Silence! Instead of the flood of intimate sounds that had once flowed smoothly between us, there was this silence.) After dinner, I would rush to a bedroom with papers and books. As often as possible, I resisted parental pleas to "save lights" by coming to the kitchen to work. I kept so

17

18

19

20

21

much, so often, to myself. Sad. Enthusiastic. Troubled by the excitement of coming upon new ideas. Eager. Fascinated by the promising texture of a brand-new book. I hoarded the pleasures of learning. Alone for hours. Enthralled. Nervous. I rarely looked away from my books—or back on my memories. Nights when relatives visited and the front rooms were warmed by Spanish sounds, I slipped quietly out of the house.

It mattered that education was changing me. It never ceased to matter. My brother and sisters would giggle at our mother's mispronounced words. They'd correct her gently. My mother laughed girlishly one night, trying not to pronounce *sheep* as *ship*. From a distance I listened sullenly. From that distance, pretending not to notice on another occasion, I saw my father looking at the title pages of my library books. That was the scene on my mind when I walked home with a fourth-grade companion and heard him say that his parents read to him every night. (A strange-sounding book—*Winnie the Pooh*.) Immediately, I wanted to know, "What is it like?" My companion, however, thought I wanted to know about the plot of the book. Another day, my mother surprised me by asking for a "nice" book to read. "Something not too hard you think I might like." Carefully I chose one, Willa Cather's *My Ántonia*. But when, several weeks later, I happened to see it next to her bed unread except for the first few pages, I was furious and suddenly wanted to cry. I grabbed up the book and took it back to my room and placed it in its place, alphabetically on my shelf.

"Your parents must be very proud of you." People began to say that to me about the time I was in sixth grade. To answer affirmatively, I'd smile. Shyly I'd smile, never betraying my sense of the irony: I was not proud of my mother and father. I was embarrassed by their lack of education. It was not that I ever thought they were stupid, though stupidly I took for granted their enormous native intelligence. Simply, what mattered to me was that they were not like my teachers.

But, "Why didn't you tell us about the award?" my mother demanded, her frown weakened by pride. At the grammar school ceremony several weeks after, her eyes were brighter than the trophy I'd won. Pushing back the hair from my forehead, she whispered that I had "shown" the *gringos*. A few minutes later, I heard my father speak to my teacher and felt ashamed of his labored, accented words. Then guilty for the shame. I felt such contrary feelings. (There is no simple roadmap through the heart of the scholarship boy.) My teacher was so soft-spoken and her words were edged sharp and clean. I admired her until it seemed to me that she spoke too carefully. Sensing that she was condescending to them, I became nervous. Resentful. Protective. I tried to move my parents away. "You both must be very proud of Richard," the nun said. They responded quickly. (They were proud.) "We are proud of all our children." Then this afterthought: "They sure didn't get their brains from us." They all laughed. I smiled.

GERALD GRAFF

Disliking Books

Gerald Graff received his BA in English from the University of Chicago and his PhD in English and American literature from Stanford University. In his distinguished academic career, he has taught at numerous universities and is currently a professor of English and education at the University of Illinois at Chicago. He is probably best known for his pedagogical theories, especially "teaching the controversies," an approach he argues for most famously in his book *Beyond the Culture Wars: How Teaching the Conflicts Can Revitalize American Education* (1993), from which this excerpt is taken. His other well-known books include *Literature Against Itself: Literary Ideas in Modern Society* (1979), *Professing Literature: An Institutional History* (1987), and *Clueless in Academe: How Schooling Obscures the Life of the Mind* (2003).

I like to think I have a certain advantage as a teacher of literature because when I was growing up I disliked and feared books. My youthful aversion to books showed a fine impartiality, extending across the whole spectrum of literature, history, philosophy, science, and what by then (the late 1940s) had come to be called social studies. But had I been forced to choose, I would have singled out literature and history as the reading I disliked most. Science at least had some discernible practical use, and you could have fun solving the problems in the textbooks with their clear-cut answers. Literature and history had no apparent application to my experience, and any boy in my school who had cultivated them — I can't recall one who did — would have marked himself as a sissy.

As a middle-class Jew growing up in an ethnically mixed Chicago neighborhood, I was already in danger of being beaten up daily by rougher working-class boys. Becoming a bookworm would have only given them a decisive reason for beating me up. Reading and studying were more permissible for girls, but they, too, had to be careful not to get too intellectual, lest they acquire the stigma of being "stuck up."

In *Lives on the Boundary*, a remarkable autobiography of the making of an English teacher, Mike Rose describes how the "pain and confusion" of his working-class youth made "school and knowledge" seem a saving alternative. Rose writes of feeling "freed, as if I were untying fetters," by his encounters with certain college teachers, who helped him recognize that "an engagement with ideas could foster competence and lead me out into the world."[1] Coming at things from my middle-class

---

[1] Mike Rose, *Lives on the Boundary* (New York: Free Press, 1989), pp. 46–47.

perspective, however, I took for granted a freedom that school, knowledge, and engagement with ideas seemed only to threaten.

My father, a literate man, was frustrated by my refusal to read anything besides comic books, sports magazines, and the John R. Tunis and Clair Bee sports novels. I recall his once confining me to my room until I finished a book on the voyages of Magellan, but try as I might, I could do no better than stare bleakly at the pages. I could not, as we would later say, "relate to" Magellan or to any of the other books my father brought home—detective stories, tales of war and heroism, adventure stories with adolescent heroes (the *Hardy Boys*, *Hans Brinker*, or *The Silver Skates*), stories of scientific discovery (Paul de Kruif's *Microbe Hunters*), books on current events. Nothing worked.

It was understood, however, that boys of my background would go to college and that once there we would get serious and buckle down. For some, "getting serious" meant prelaw, premed, or a major in business to prepare for taking over the family business. My family did not own a business, and law and medicine did not interest me, so I drifted by default into the nebulous but conveniently noncommittal territory of the liberal arts. I majored in English.

At this point the fear of being beaten up if I were caught having anything to do with books was replaced by the fear of flunking out of college if I did not learn to deal with them. But though I dutifully did my homework and made good grades (first at the University of Illinois, Chicago branch, then at the University of Chicago, from which I graduated in 1959), I continued to find "serious" reading painfully difficult and alien. My most vivid recollections of college reading are of assigned classics I failed to finish: *The Iliad* (in the Richmond Lattimore translation); *The Autobiography of Benvenuto Cellini*, a major disappointment after the paperback jacket's promise of "a lusty classic of Renaissance ribaldry"; E. M. Forster's *Passage to India*, sixty agonizing pages of which I managed to slog through before giving up. Even Hemingway, Steinbeck, and Fitzgerald, whose contemporary world was said to be "close to my own experience," left me cold. I saw little there that did resemble my experience.

Even when I had done the assigned reading, I was often tongue-tied and embarrassed when called on. What was unclear to me was what I was supposed to *say* about literary works, and why. Had I been born a decade or two earlier, I might have come to college with the rudiments of a literate vocabulary for talking about culture that some people older than I acquired through family, high school, or church. As it was, "cultured" phrases seemed effete and sterile to me. When I was able to produce the kind of talk that was required in class, the intellectualism of it came out sounding stilted and hollow in my mouth. If *Cliffs Notes* and other such crib sheets for the distressed had yet come into existence, with their ready-to-copy summaries of widely taught literary works,

I would have been an excellent customer. (As it was, I did avail myself of the primitive version then in existence called *Masterplots*.)

What first made literature, history, and other intellectual pursuits seem attractive to me was exposure to critical debates. There was no single conversion experience, but a gradual transformation over several years, extending into my first teaching positions, at the University of New Mexico and then Northwestern University. But one of the first sparks I remember was a controversy over *Adventures of Huckleberry Finn* that arose in a course during my junior year in college. On first attempt, Twain's novel was just another assigned classic that I was too bored to finish. I could see little connection between my Chicago upbringing and Huck's pre–Civil War adventures with a runaway slave on a raft up the Mississippi.

My interest was aroused, however, when our instructor mentioned that the critics had disagreed over the merits of the last part of the novel. He quoted Ernest Hemingway's remark that "if you read [the novel] you must stop where the nigger Jim is stolen by the boys. This is the real end. The rest is cheating." According to this school of thought, the remainder of the book trivializes the quest for Jim's freedom that has motivated the story up to that point. This happens first when Jim becomes an object of Tom Sawyer's slapstick humor, then when it is revealed that unbeknownst to Huck, the reader, and himself, Jim has already been freed by his benevolent owner, so that the risk we have assumed Jim and Huck to be under all along has been really no risk at all.

Like the critics, our class divided over the question: Did Twain's ending vitiate the book's profound critique of racism, as Hemingway's charge of cheating implied? Cheating in my experience up to then was something students did, an unthinkable act for a famous author. It was a revelation to me that famous authors were capable not only of mistakes but of ones that even lowly undergraduates might be able to point out. When I chose to write my term paper on the dispute over the ending, my instructor suggested I look at several critics on the opposing sides, T. S. Eliot and Lionel Trilling, who defended the ending, and Leo Marx, who sided with Hemingway.

Reading the critics was like picking up where the class discussion had left off, and I gained confidence from recognizing that my classmates and I had had thoughts that, however stumbling our expression of them, were not too far from the thoughts of famous published critics. I went back to the novel again and to my surprise found myself rereading it with an excitement I had never felt before with a serious book. Having the controversy over the ending in mind, I now had some issues *to watch out for* as I read, issues that reshaped the way I read the earlier chapters as well as the later ones and focused my attention. And having issues to watch out for made it possible not only to concentrate, as I had not been able to do earlier, but to put myself in the text—to read with a sense of

8

9

10

11

personal engagement that I had not felt before. Reading the novel with the voices of the critics running through my mind, I found myself thinking of things that I might say about what I was reading, things that may have belonged partly to the critics but also now belonged to me. It was as if having a stock of things to look for and to say about a literary work had somehow made it possible for me to read one.

One of the critics had argued that what was at issue in the debate   *12* over *Huckleberry Finn* was not just the novel's value but its cultural significance: If *Huckleberry Finn* was contradictory or confused in its attitude toward race, then what did that say about the culture that had received the novel as one of its representative cultural documents and had made Twain a folk hero? This critic had also made the intriguing observation—I found out only later it was a critical commonplace at that time—that judgments about the novel's aesthetic value could not be separated from judgments about its moral substance. I recall taking in both this critic's arguments and the cadence of the phrases in which they were couched; perhaps it would not be so bad after all to become the sort of person who talked about "cultural contradictions" and the "inseparability of form and content." Perhaps even mere literary-critical talk could give you a certain power in the real world. As the possibility dawned on me that reading and intellectual discussion might actually have something to do with my real life, I became less embarrassed about using the intellectual formulas.

The Standard Story

It was through exposure to such critical reading and discussion over a   *13* period of time that I came to catch the literary bug, eventually choosing the vocation of teaching. This was not the way it is supposed to happen. In the standard story of academic vocation that we like to tell ourselves, the germ is first planted by an early experience of literature itself. The future teacher is initially inspired by some primary experience of a great book and only subsequently acquires the secondary, derivative skills of critical discussion. A teacher may be involved in instilling this inspiration, but a teacher who seemingly effaces himself or herself before the text. Any premature or excessive acquaintance with secondary critical discourse, and certainly with its sectarian debates, is thought to be a corrupting danger, causing one to lose touch with the primary passion for literature. . . .

The standard story ascribes innocence to the primary experience of   *14* literature and sees the secondary experience of professional criticism as corrupting. In my case, however, things had evidently worked the other way around: I had to be corrupted first in order to experience innocence. It was only when I was introduced to a critical debate about

Huckleberry Finn that my helplessness in the face of the novel abated and I could experience a personal reaction to it. Getting into immediate contact with the text was for me a curiously triangular business; I could not do it directly but needed a conversation of other readers to give me the issues and terms that made it possible to respond.

As I think back on it now, it was as if the critical conversation I needed   15
had up to then been withheld from me, on the ground that it could only interfere with my direct access to literature itself. The assumption was that leaving me alone with literary texts themselves, uncontaminated by the interpretations and theories of professional critics, would enable me to get on the closest possible terms with those texts. But being alone with the texts only left me feeling bored and helpless, since I had no language with which to make them mine. On the one hand, I was being asked to speak a foreign language — literary criticism — while on the other hand, I was being protected from that language, presumably for my own safety.

The moral I draw from this experience is that our ability to read well   16
depends more than we think on our ability to *talk well* about what we read. Our assumptions about what is "primary" and "secondary" in the reading process blind us to what actually goes on. Many literate people learned certain ways of talking about books so long ago that they have forgotten they ever had to learn them. These people therefore fail to understand the reading problems of the struggling students who have still not acquired a critical vocabulary.

How typical my case was is hard to say, but many of the students I   17
teach seem to have grown up as the same sort of nonintellectual, non-bookish person I was, and they seem to view literature with some of the same aversions, fears, and anxieties. That is why I like to think it is an advantage for a teacher to know what it feels like to grow up being indifferent to literature and intimidated by criticism and what it feels like to overcome a resistance to talking like an intellectual.

A Practice Sequence: Composing a Literacy Narrative

A *literacy narrative* — a firsthand, personal account about reading or composing — is a well-established genre that is popular both inside and outside the academy. Rodriguez's and Graff's autobiographical stories dealing with aspects of how they became literate and their relationship with reading and writing are literacy narratives. Rodriguez's narrative is part of *Hunger of Memory: The Education of Richard Rodriguez*, a memoir that also explores the politics of language in American culture. Graff's narrative is embedded in his *Beyond the Culture Wars: How Teaching the Conflicts Can Revitalize American Education*, which, as the subtitle suggests, presents arguments and proposals for altering educational practices.

We would like you to write your own literacy narrative. The following practice sequence suggests some strategies for doing so.

1   Reflect on your experiences as a reader. Spend some time jotting down answers to these questions (not necessarily in this order) or to other related questions that occur to you as you write.

- Can you recall the time when you first began to read?
- What are the main types of reading you do? Why?
- How would you describe or characterize yourself as a reader?
- Is there one moment or event that encapsulates who you are as a reader?
- What are your favorite books, authors, and types of books? Why are they favorites?
- In what ways has reading changed you for the better? For the worse?
- What is the most important thing you've learned from reading?
- Have you ever learned something important from reading, only to discover later that it wasn't true, or sufficient? Explain.

2   Write your literacy narrative, focusing on at least one turning point, at least one moment of recognition or lesson learned. Write no fewer than two pages but no more than five pages. See where your story arc takes you. What do you conclude about your own "growing into literacy"?

3   Then start a conversation about literacy. Talk with some other people about their experiences. You might talk with some classmates—and not necessarily those in your writing class—about their memories of becoming literate. You might interview some people you grew up with—a parent, a sibling, a best friend—about their memories of you as a reader and writer and about their own memories of becoming literate. Compare their memories to your own. Did you all have similar experiences? How were they different? Do you see things the same way? Then write down your impressions and what you think you may have learned.

4   Recast your literacy narrative, incorporating some of the insights you gathered from other people. How does your original narrative change? What new things now have to be accounted for?

5   Like Graff, who takes his own experience as a starting point for proposing new educational policies, can you imagine your insights having larger implications? Explain. Do you think what you've learned from reading Graff's and Rodriguez's literacy narratives has implications for the ways reading is taught in school?

From Reading as a Writer to Writing as a Reader

Reading for class and then writing an essay might seem to be separate tasks, but reading is the first step in the writing process. In this chapter we present methods that will help you read more effectively and move from reading to writing your own college essays. These methods will lead you to understand a writer's purpose in responding to a situation, the motivation for asserting a claim in an essay and entering a particular conversation with a particular audience.

Much if not all of the writing you do in college will be based on what you have read. This is the case, for example, when you summarize a philosopher's theory, analyze the significance of an experiment in psychology, or, perhaps, synthesize different and conflicting points of view in making an argument about race and academic achievement in sociology.

As we maintain throughout this book, writing and reading are inextricably linked to each other. Good academic writers are also good critical readers: They leave their mark on what they read, identifying issues, making judgments about the truth of what writers tell them, and evaluating the adequacy of the evidence in support of an argument. This is where writing and inquiry begin: understanding our own position relative to the scholarly conversations that we want to enter. Moreover, critical readers try to understand the strategies that writers use to persuade readers to agree with them. At times, these are strategies that we can adapt in advancing our arguments.

READING AS AN ACT OF COMPOSING: ANNOTATING

Leaving your mark on the page—**annotating**—is your first act of composing. When you mark the pages of a text, you are reading critically, engaging with the ideas of others, questioning and testing those ideas, and inquiring into their significance. **Critical reading** is sometimes called *active reading* to distinguish it from memorization, when you just read for the main idea so that you can "spit it back out on a test." When you read actively and critically, you bring your knowledge, experiences, and interests to a text, so that you can respond to the writer, continuing the conversation the writer has begun.

Experienced college readers don't try to memorize a text or assume they must understand it completely before they respond to it. Instead they read strategically, looking for the writer's claims, for the writer's key ideas and terms, and for connections with key ideas and terms in other texts. They also read to discern what conversation the writer has entered, and how the writer's argument is connected to those he or she makes reference to.

When you annotate a text, your notes in the margins might address the following questions:

- What arguments is this author responding to?
- Is the issue relevant or significant?
- How do I know that what the author says is true?
- Is the author's evidence legitimate? Sufficient?
- Can I think of an exception to the author's argument?
- What would the counterarguments be?

Good readers ask the same kinds of questions of every text they read, considering not just *what* a writer says (the content), but *how* he or she says it given the writer's purpose and audience.

The marks you leave on a page might indicate your own ideas and questions, patterns you see emerging, links to other texts, even your gut response to the writer's argument—agreement, dismay, enthusiasm, confusion. They reveal your own thought processes as you read and signal that you are entering the conversation. In effect, they are traces of your own responding voice.

Developing your own system of marking or annotating pages can help you feel confident when you sit down with a new reading for your classes. Based on our students' experiences, we offer this practical tip: Although wide-tipped highlighters have their place in some classes, it is more useful to read with a pen or pencil in your hand, so that you can do more than draw a bar of color through words or sentences you find important. Experienced readers write their responses to a text in the margins, using personal codes (boxing key words, for example), writing out definitions of words they have looked up, drawing lines to connect ideas on facing pages, or writing notes to themselves ("Connect this to Edmundson on consumer culture"; "Hirsch would disagree big time—see his ideas on memorization in primary grades"; "You call THIS evidence?!"). These notes help you get started on your own writing assignments, and you cannot make them with a highlighter.

Annotating your readings benefits you twice. First, it is easier to participate in class discussions if you have already marked passages that are important, confusing, or linked to specific passages in other texts you have read. It's a sure way to avoid that sinking feeling you get when you return to pages you read the night before but now can't remember at all. Second, by marking key ideas in a text, noting your ideas about them, and making connections to key ideas in other texts, you have begun the process of writing an essay. When you start writing the first draft of your essay, you can quote the passages you have already marked and explain what you find significant about them based on the notes you have already made to yourself. You can make the connections to other texts in the paragraphs of your own essay that you have already begun to make on the pages of your textbook. If you mark your texts effectively, you'll never be at a loss when you sit down to write the first draft of an essay.

Let's take a look at how one of our students marked several paragraphs of Douglas Massey and Nancy Denton's *American Apartheid: Segregation and the Making of the Underclass* (1993). In the excerpt below, the student underlines what she believes is important information and begins to create an outline of the authors' main points.

1. racist attitudes

2. private behaviors

3. & institutional practices lead to ghettos (authors' claim?)

Ghetto = multistory, high-density housing projects. Post-1950

I remember this happening where I grew up, but I didn't know the government was responsible. Is this what happened in There Are No Children Here?

The spatial isolation of black Americans was achieved by a conjunction of racist attitudes, private behaviors, and institutional practices that disenfranchised blacks from urban housing markets and led to the creation of the ghetto. Discrimination in employment exacerbated black poverty and limited the economic potential for integration, and black residential mobility was systematically blocked by pervasive discrimination and white avoidance of neighborhoods containing blacks. The walls of the ghetto were buttressed after 1950 by government programs that promoted slum clearance and relocated displaced ghetto residents into multi-story, high-density housing projects.   *1*

Authors say situation of "spatial isolation" remains despite court decisions. Does it?

In theory, this self-reinforcing cycle of prejudice, discrimination, and segregation was broken during the 1960s by a growing rejection of racist sentiments by whites and a series of court decisions and federal laws that banned discrimination in public life. (1) The Civil Rights Act of 1964 outlawed racial discrimination in employment, (2) the Fair Housing Act of 1968 banned discrimination in housing, and (3) the *Gautreaux* and *Shannon* court decisions prohibited public authorities from placing housing projects exclusively in black neighborhoods. Despite these changes, however, the nation's largest black communities remained as segregated as ever in 1980. Indeed, many urban areas displayed a pattern of intense racial isolation that could only be described as hypersegregation.   *2*

Subtler racism, not on public record.

Lack of enforcement of Civil Rights Act? Fair Housing Act? Gautreaux and Shannon? Why? Why not?

Although the racial climate of the United States improved outwardly during the 1970s, racism still restricted the residential freedom of black Americans; it just did so in less blatant ways. In the aftermath of the civil rights revolution, few whites voiced openly racist sentiments; realtors no longer refused outright to rent or sell to blacks; and few local governments went on record to oppose public housing projects because they would contain blacks. This lack of overt racism, however, did not mean that prejudice and discrimination had ended.   *3*

Notice how the student underlines information that helps her understand the argument the authors make.

1. She numbers the three key factors (racist attitudes, private behaviors, and institutional practices) that influenced the formation of ghettos in the United States.

2. She identifies the situation that motivates the authors' analysis: the extent to which "the spatial isolation of black Americans" still exists despite laws and court decisions designed to end residential segregation.

3. She makes connections to her own experience and to another book she has read.

By understanding the authors' arguments and making these connections, the student begins the writing process. She also sets the stage for her own research, for examining the authors' claim that residential segregation still exists.

READING AS A WRITER: ANALYZING A TEXT RHETORICALLY

When you study how writers influence readers through language, you are analyzing the **rhetoric** (available means of persuasion) of what you read. When you identify a writer's purpose for responding to a situation by composing an essay that puts forth claims meant to sway a particular audience, you are performing a rhetorical analysis. Such an analysis entails identifying the features of an argument to better understand how the argument works to persuade a reader. We discuss each of these elements

- how the writer sees the situation that calls for a response in writing,
- the writer's purpose for writing,
- intended audience,
- kinds of claims, and
- types of evidence,

as we analyze the following preface from E. D. Hirsch's book *Cultural Literacy: What Every American Needs to Know* (1987). Formerly a professor of English, Hirsch has long been interested in educational reform. That interest developed from his (and others') perception that today's students do not know as much as students did in the past. Although Hirsch wrote the book more than twenty years ago, many observers still believe that the contemporary problems of illiteracy and poverty can be traced to a lack of cultural literacy.

Read the preface. You may want to mark it with your own questions and responses, and then consider them in light of our analysis (following the preface) of Hirsch's rhetorical situation, purpose, claims, and audience.

E. D. HIRSCH JR.

Preface to *Cultural Literacy*

E. D. Hirsch Jr., a retired English professor, is the author of many acclaimed books, including *The Schools We Need and Why We Don't Have Them* (1996) and *The Knowledge Deficit* (2006). His book *Cultural Literacy* was a best seller in 1987 and had a profound effect on the focus of education in the late 1980s and 1990s.

■ ■ ■

> Rousseau points out the facility with which children lend themselves to our false methods: . . ."The apparent ease with which children learn is their ruin."
>
> —JOHN DEWEY

> There is no matter what children should learn first, any more than what leg you should put into your breeches first. Sir, you may stand disputing which is best to put in first, but in the meantime your backside is bare. Sir, while you stand considering which of two things you should teach your child first, another boy has learn't 'em both.
>
> —SAMUEL JOHNSON

To be culturally literate is to possess the basic information needed to thrive in the modern world. The breadth of that information is great, extending over the major domains of human activity from sports to science. It is by no means confined to "culture" narrowly understood as an acquaintance with the arts. Nor is it confined to one social class. Quite the contrary. Cultural literacy constitutes the only sure avenue of opportunity for disadvantaged children, the only reliable way of combating the social determinism that now condemns them to remain in the same social and educational condition as their parents. That children from poor and illiterate homes tend to remain poor and illiterate is an unacceptable failure of our schools, one which has occurred not because our teachers are inept but chiefly because they are compelled to teach a fragmented curriculum based on faulty educational theories. Some say that our schools by themselves are powerless to change the cycle of poverty and illiteracy. I do not agree. They *can* break the cycle, but only if they themselves break fundamentally with some of the theories and practices that education professors and school administrators have followed over the past fifty years. 1

Although the chief beneficiaries of the educational reforms advocated in this book will be disadvantaged children, these same reforms will also enhance the literacy of children from middle-class homes. The educational goal advocated is that of mature literacy for *all* our citizens. 2

The connection between mature literacy and cultural literacy may already be familiar to those who have closely followed recent 3 discussions of education. Shortly after the publication of my essay "Cultural Literacy," Dr. William Bennett, then chairman of the National Endowment for the Humanities and subsequently secretary of education in President Ronald Reagan's second administration, championed its ideas. This endorsement from an influential person of conservative views gave my ideas some currency, but such an endorsement was not likely to recommend the concept to liberal thinkers, and in fact the idea of cultural literacy has been attacked by some liberals on the assumption that I must be advocating a list of great books that every child in the land should be forced to read.

But those who examine the Appendix to this book will be able to   4
judge for themselves how thoroughly mistaken such an assumption is. Very few specific titles appear on the list, and they usually appear as words, not works, because they represent writings that culturally literate people have read about but haven't read. *Das Kapital* is a good example. Cultural literacy is represented not by a *prescriptive* list of books but rather by a *descriptive* list of the information actually possessed by literate Americans. My aim in this book is to contribute to making that information the possession of all Americans.

The importance of such widely shared information can best be under-   5
stood if I explain briefly how the idea of cultural literacy relates to currently prevailing theories of education. The theories that have dominated American education for the past fifty years stem ultimately from Jean Jacques Rousseau, who believed that we should encourage the natural development of young children and not impose adult ideas upon them before they can truly understand them. Rousseau's conception of education as a process of natural development was an abstract generalization meant to apply to all children in any time or place: to French children of the eighteenth century or to Japanese or American children of the twentieth century. He thought that a child's intellectual and social skills would develop naturally without regard to the specific content of education. His content-neutral conception of educational development has long been triumphant in American schools of education and has long dominated the "developmental," content-neutral curricula of our elementary schools.

In the first decades of this century, Rousseau's ideas powerfully influ-   6
enced the educational conceptions of John Dewey, the writer who has the most deeply affected modern American educational theory and practice. Dewey's clearest and, in his time, most widely read book on education, *Schools of Tomorrow*, acknowledges Rousseau as the chief source of his educational principles. The first chapter of Dewey's book carries the telling title "Education as Natural Development" and is sprinkled with quotations from Rousseau. In it Dewey strongly seconds Rousseau's opposition to the mere accumulation of information.

Development emphasizes the need of intimate and extensive personal acquaintance with a small number of typical situations with a view to mastering the way of dealing with the problems of experience, not the piling up of information.

Believing that a few direct experiences would suffice to develop the skills that children require, Dewey assumed that early education need not be tied to specific content. He mistook a half-truth for the whole. He placed too much faith in children's ability to learn general skills from a few typical experiences and too hastily rejected "the piling up of information." Only by piling up specific, communally shared information can children learn to participate in complex cooperative activities with other members of their community.   7

This old truth, recently rediscovered, requires a countervailing theory of education that once again stresses the importance of specific information in early and late schooling. The corrective theory might be described as an anthropological theory of education, because it is based on the anthropological observation that all human communities are founded upon specific shared information. Americans are different from Germans, who in turn are different from Japanese, because each group possesses specifically different cultural knowledge. In an anthropological perspective, the basic goal of education in a human community is acculturation, the transmission to children of the specific information shared by the adults of the group or polis.   8

Plato, that other great educational theorist, believed that the specific contents transmitted to children are by far the most important elements of education. In *The Republic* he makes Socrates ask rhetorically, "Shall we carelessly allow children to hear any casual tales which may be devised by casual persons, and to receive into their minds ideas for the most part the very opposite of those which we shall wish them to have when they are grown up?" Plato offered good reasons for being concerned with the specific contents of schooling, one of them ethical: "For great is the issue at stake, greater than appears—whether a person is to be good or bad."   9

Time has shown that there is much truth in the durable educational theories of both Rousseau and Plato. But even the greatest thinkers, being human, see mainly in one direction at a time, and no thinkers, however profound, can foresee the future implications of their ideas when they are translated into social policy. The great test of social ideas is the crucible of history, which, after a time, usually discloses a one-sidedness in the best of human generalizations. History, not superior wisdom, shows us that neither the content-neutral curriculum of Rousseau and Dewey nor the narrowly specified curriculum of Plato is adequate to the needs of a modern nation.   10

Plato rightly believed that it is natural for children to learn an adult culture, but too confidently assumed that philosophy could devise the one best culture. (Nonetheless, we should concede to Plato that within our culture we have an obligation to choose and promote our best traditions.) On the other side, Rousseau and Dewey wrongly believed that   11 adult culture is "unnatural" to young children. Rousseau, Dewey, and their present-day disciples have not shown an adequate appreciation of the need for transmission of specific cultural information.

In contrast to the theories of Plato and Rousseau, an anthropological theory of education accepts the naturalness as well as the relativity of human cultures. It deems it neither wrong nor unnatural to teach young children adult information before they fully understand it. The anthropological view stresses the universal fact that a human group must have effective communications to function effectively, that effective communications require shared culture, and that shared culture requires transmission of specific information to children. Literacy, an essential aim of education in the modern world, is no autonomous, empty skill but depends upon literate culture. Like any other aspect of acculturation, literacy requires the early and continued transmission of specific information. Dewey was deeply mistaken to disdain "accumulating information in the form of symbols." Only by accumulating shared symbols, and the shared information that the symbols represent, can we learn to communicate effectively with one another in our national community.

12

Now let's take a look at the steps for doing a rhetorical analysis.

■ Identify the Situation

The **situation** is what moves a writer to write. To understand what motivated Hirsch to write, we need look no further than the situation he identifies in the first paragraph of the preface: "the social determinism that now condemns [disadvantaged children] to remain in the same social and educational condition as their parents." Hirsch wants to make sure his readers are aware of the problem so that they will be motivated to read his argument (and take action). He presents as an urgent problem the situation of disadvantaged children, an indication of what is at stake for the writer and for the readers of the argument. For Hirsch, this situation needs to change.

The urgency of a writer's argument is not always triggered by a single situation; often it is multifaceted. Again in the first paragraph, Hirsch identifies a second concern when he states that poverty and illiteracy reflect "an unacceptable failure of our schools, one which has occurred not because our teachers are inept but chiefly because they are compelled to teach a fragmented curriculum based on faulty educational theories." When he introduces a second problem, Hirsch helps us see the interconnected and complex nature of the situations authors confront in academic writing.

■ Identify the Writer's Purpose

The **purpose** for writing an essay may be to respond to a particular situation; it also can be what a writer is trying to accomplish. Specifically, what does the writer want readers to do? Does the writer want us to think about an issue, to change our opinions? Does the writer want to make us aware of a problem that we may not have recognized? Does the writer advocate for some type of change? Or is some combination of all three at work?

Hirsch's main purpose is to promote educational reforms that will produce a higher degree of literacy for all citizens. He begins his argument with a broad statement about the importance of cultural literacy: "Cultural literacy constitutes the only sure avenue of opportunity for disadvantaged children, the only reliable way of combating the social determinism that now condemns them to remain in the same social and educational condition as their parents" (para. 1). As his argument unfolds, his purpose continues to unfold as well. He identifies the schools as a source of the problem and suggests how they must change to promote literacy:

> Some say that our schools by themselves are powerless to change the cycle of poverty and illiteracy. I do not agree. They can break the cycle, but only if they themselves break fundamentally with some of the theories and practices that education professors and school administrators have followed over the past fifty years. (para. 1)

The "educational goal," Hirsch declares at the end of paragraph 2, is "mature literacy for *all* our citizens." To reach that goal, he insists, education must break with the past. In paragraphs 5 through 11, he cites the influence of Jean-Jacques Rousseau, John Dewey, and Plato, tracing what he sees as the educational legacies of the past. Finally, in the last paragraph of the excerpt, Hirsch describes an "anthropological view, . . . the universal fact that a human group must have effective communications to function effectively, that effective communications require shared culture, and that shared culture requires transmission of specific information to children." It is here, Hirsch argues, in the "transmission of specific information to children," that schools must do a better job.

■ Identify the Writer's Claims

Claims are assertions that authors must justify and support with evidence and good reasons. The **thesis**, or **main claim**, is the controlling idea that crystallizes a writer's main point, helping readers track the idea as it develops throughout the essay. A writer's purpose clearly influences the way he or she crafts the main claim of an argument, the way he or she presents all assertions and evidence.

Hirsch's main claim is that "cultural literacy constitutes the only sure avenue of opportunity for disadvantaged children, the only reliable way of combating the social determinism that now condemns them to remain in the same social and educational condition as their parents" (para. 1). Notice that his thesis also points to a solution: making cultural literacy the core of public school curricula. Here we distinguish the main claim, or thesis, from the other claims or assertions that Hirsch makes. For example, at the very outset, Hirsch states that "to be culturally literate is to possess the basic information needed to thrive in the modern world." Although this is an assertion that requires support, it is a **minor claim**; it does not shape what Hirsch writes in the remainder of his essay. His main claim, or thesis, is really his call for reform.

■ Identify the Writer's Audience

A writer's language can help us identify his or her **audience**, the readers whose opinions and actions the writer hopes to influence or change. In Hirsch's text, words and phrases like *social determinism*, *cycle of poverty and illiteracy*, *educational reforms*, *prescriptive*, and *anthropological* indicate that Hirsch believes his audience is well educated. References to Plato, Socrates, Rousseau, and Dewey also indicate the level of knowledge Hirsch expects of his readers.

Finally, the way the preface unfolds suggests that Hirsch is writing for an audience that is familiar with a certain **genre**, or type, of writing: the formal argument. Notice how the author begins with a statement of the situation and then asserts his position. The very fact that he includes a preface speaks to the formality of his argument. Hirsch's language, his references, and the structure of the document all suggest that he is very much in conversation with people who are experienced and well-educated readers.

More specifically, the audience Hirsch invokes is made up of people who are concerned about illiteracy in the United States and the kind of social determinism that appears to condemn the educationally disadvantaged to poverty. Hirsch also acknowledges directly "those who have closely followed recent discussions of education," including the conservative William Bennett and liberal thinkers who might be provoked by Bennett's advocacy of Hirsch's ideas (para. 3). Moreover, Hirsch appears to assume that his readers have achieved "mature literacy," even if they are not actually "culturally literate." He is writing for an audience that not only is well educated but also is deeply interested in issues of education as they relate to social policy.

Steps to Analyzing a Text Rhetorically

1 **Identify the situation.** What motivates the writer to write?

2 **Identify the writer's purpose.** What does the writer want readers to do or think about?

3 **Identify the writer's claims.** What is the writer's main claim? What minor claims does he or she make?

4 **Identify the writer's audience.** What do you know about the writer's audience? What does the writer's language imply about the readers? What about the writer's references? The structure of the essay?

Hirsch's writings on cultural literacy have inspired and provoked many responses to the conversation he initiated more than twenty years ago. Eugene F. Provenzo's book *Critical Literacy: What Every American Needs to Know*, published in 2005, is a fairly recent one. Provenzo examines the source of Hirsch's ideas, his critiques of scholars like John Dewey, the extent to which Hirsch's argument is based on sound research, and the implications of Hirsch's notion of cultural literacy for teaching and learning. Despite the passage of time, Hirsch's book remains relevant in discussions about the purpose of education, demonstrating how certain works become touchstones and the ways academic and cultural conversations can be sustained over time.

A Practice Sequence: Analyzing a Text Rhetorically

To practice the strategies of rhetorical analysis, read "Hirsch's Desire for a National Curriculum," an excerpt from Eugene F. Provenzo's book, using these questions as a guide:

- What motivates Provenzo as a writer?
- What does he want readers to think about?
- What is Provenzo's main point?
- Given the language Provenzo uses, who do you think his main audience is?

EUGENE F. PROVENZO JR.

Hirsch's Desire for a National Curriculum

Eugene F. Provenzo Jr. is a professor in the Department of Teaching and Learning in the School of Education at the University of Miami in Coral Gables, Florida. His career as a researcher has been interdisciplinary in nature. Throughout his work, his primary focus has been on education as a social and cultural phenomenon. One of his prime concerns has been the role of the teacher in American society. He is also interested in the impact of computers on contemporary children, education, and culture. He is author or co-author of numerous books, including *Teaching, Learning, and Schooling: A Twenty-first Century Perspective* (2001); *Internet and Online Research for Teachers* (Third Edition, 2004); and *Observing in Schools: A Guide for Students in Teacher Education* (2005).

■ ■ ■

To a large extent, Hirsch, in his efforts as an educational reformer, wants to establish a national curriculum.

Our elementary schools are not only dominated by the content-neutral ideas of Rousseau and Dewey, they are also governed by approximately sixteen thousand independent school districts. We have viewed this dispersion of educational authority as an insurmountable obstacle to altering the fragmentation of the school curriculum even when we have questioned that fragmentation. We have permitted school policies that have shrunk the body of information that Americans share and these policies have caused our national literacy to decline.

This is an interesting argument when interpreted in a conservative political context. While calling for greater local control, Hirsch and other conservatives call for a curriculum that is controlled not at the state and local level, but at the national level by the federal government.

Putting contradictions like this aside, the question arises as to whether or not Hirsch even has a viable curriculum. In an early review of Hirsch's *Cultural Literacy*, Hazel Whitman Hertzberg criticized the book and its list of 5,000 things every American needs to know for its fragmentation. As she explained:

> Hirsch's remedy for curricular fragmentation looks suspiciously like more fragmentation. Outside of the dubious claim that his list represents what literate people know, there is nothing that holds it together besides its arrangement in alphabetical order. Subject-matter organization is ignored. It is not hard to imagine how Hirsch's proposal would have been greeted by educational neoconservatives had it been made by one of those professors of education who he charges are responsible for the current state of cultural illiteracy.

Hertzberg wonders what Hirsch's "hodgepodge of miscellaneous, arbitrary, and often trivial information" would look like if it were put into a coherent curriculum.

In 1988 Hirsch did in fact establish the Core Knowledge Foundation, which had as its purpose the design of a national curriculum. Called the "Core Knowledge Sequence," the sequence offered a curriculum in six content areas: history, geography, mathematics, science, language arts, and fine arts. Hirsch's curriculum was intended to represent approximately half of the total curriculum for K–6 schools. Subsequent curriculum revisions include a curriculum for grades seven and eight as well as one at the preschool level.

Several hundred schools across the United States currently use Hirsch's model. A national conference is held each year, which draws several thousand people. In books like *What Your First Grader Needs to Know* (1991) as well as *A First Dictionary of Cultural Literacy: What Our Children Need to Know* (1989) and *The Dictionary of Cultural Literacy* (1993), along with the Core Knowledge Sequence, one finds a fairly conservative but generally useful curriculum that conforms to much of the content already found in local school systems around the country.

Hirsch seems not to recognize that there indeed is a national curriculum, one whose standards are set by local communities through their acceptance and rejection of textbooks and by national accreditation groups ranging from the National Council of Teachers of Mathematics to the National Council for Social Studies Teachers and the National

Council of Teachers of English. One need only look at standards in different subject areas in school districts across the country to realize the extent to which there is indeed a national curriculum.

Whether the current curriculum in use in the schools across the country is adequate is of course open to debate. Creating any curriculum is by definition a deeply political act, and is, or should be, subject to considerable negotiation and discussion at any level. But to act as though there is not a de facto national curriculum is simply inaccurate. First graders in most school districts across the country learn about the weather and the seasons, along with more basic skills like adding and subtracting. Students do not learn to divide before they learn how to add or multiply. Local and state history is almost universally introduced for the first time in either third or fourth grade. It is reintroduced in most states at the seventh or eighth grade levels. Algebra is typically taught in the ninth grade. Traditions, developmental patterns of students, textbook content, and national subject standards combine to create a fairly uniform national curriculum.

Hirsch's complaint that there is no national curriculum is not motivated by a desire to establish one but rather a desire to establish a curriculum that reflects his cultural and ideological orientation. It is a sophisticated assault on more inclusive and diverse models of curriculum and culture—one that represents a major battle in the culture wars of the last twenty years in the United States.

WRITING AS A READER: COMPOSING A RHETORICAL ANALYSIS

One of our favorite exercises is to ask students to choose a single paragraph or a brief section from a text they have read and to write a rhetorical analysis. We first ask our students to identify the writer's key claims and ideas to orient them to the main points they want to make in their analysis. We then ask our students to consider such features as the situation that calls for a response in writing and the writer's purpose, intended audience, kinds of claims, and types of evidence. In their rhetorical analyses, we encourage our students to analyze the ways writers develop their ideas and the extent to which these strategies succeed. That is, we ask our students to consider how writers express their ideas, develop their points of view, respond to a given situation, and use evidence to persuade readers. Once you are able to identify *how* writers make arguments, look critically at what works and what doesn't in making a persuasive argument; then you will be able to make use of their strategies in your own writing.

For example, one of our students wrote a rhetorical analysis of an excerpt from David Tyack's book on education, *Seeking Common Ground: Public Schools in a Diverse Society* (2004). In his book, Tyack examines the extent to which the purpose of education in American schools has developed out of and reflected the political, economic, and moral concerns of the nation. His analysis begins with the emergence of public schools in the nineteenth century and demonstrates a sense of continuity in twenty-first-century education, particularly in light of contemporary debates around national standards, teacher evaluation, social justice, equity, civic engagement, and the common good. This continuity is best represented in the quest for a common denominator of political and moral truths, often evidenced in textbooks that point to the progress of history and American democracy, the focus on great men who understood the grandeur of America's destiny, and the importance of individual character in building a strong nation founded on shared values. For Tyack, history textbooks have served as a significant source of civic education—that is, "what adults thought children should learn about the past"—and assimilation. However, the search for common values in official histories (what he calls "stone monuments") has not been without dissent, given their focus on white, male, Protestant ideology. Tyack also writes about the ways in which educators have dealt with questions of social and educational diversity, particularly race, immigration and ethnicity, and gender; efforts to establish models of educational governance to meet the needs of a pluralistic society; and the implications of opening public education to a free market.

Note that in the following passage, Tyack assesses the state of American history textbooks by citing a number of writers, sometimes generally and at other times more specifically, to address ways to solve the problems he identifies (for example, Patricia Nelson Limerick's proposal for a "pluralistic model of history").

As you read the Tyack's passage, take notes on the rhetorical situation, purpose, main claim, audience, and language. You may want to underline passages or circle words and phrases where the writer makes the following points explicit:

- the situation that motivates his writing,
- the purpose of his analysis and argument,
- his main claim or thesis, and
- who he believes his audience is.

DAVID TYACK

Whither History Textbooks?

David Tyack is the Vida Jacks Professor of Education and Professor of History, Emeritus, at Stanford University. In addition to writing *Seeking Common Ground*, he is the author of *The One Best System: A History of American Urban Education* (1974) and coauthor of *Tinkering Toward Utopia: A Century of Public School Reform* (1997), *Law and the Shaping of Public Education, 1785–1954* (1991), *Learning Together: A History of Coeducation in American Public Schools* (1992), and *Public Schools in Hard Times: The Great Depression and Recent Years* (1984).

■ ■ ■

A history textbook today is hardly the republican catechism that Noah Webster appended to his famous speller. It is more like pieces of a sprawling novel with diverse characters and fascinating subplots waiting for an author to weave them into a broader narrative. Now a noisy confusion reigns about what stories the textbooks should tell. Special-interest groups of the right and left pressure publishers to include or drop topics, especially in big states such as California or Texas. Worries abound about old truths betrayed and new truths ignored. Many groups want to vet or veto what children learn, and it is unclear what roles teachers, parents, ethnic groups, religious activists, historians, and others should play. Tempers rise. In New York debates over a multicultural curriculum, Catherine Cornbleth and Dexter Waugh observed, "both sides engaged in a rhetoric of crisis, doom, and salvation." *1*

In the United States, unlike most other nations, private agencies—publishing companies—create and sell textbooks. Thus commerce plays an important part in deciding which historical truths shall be official. To be sure, public agencies usually decide which textbooks to adopt (about half of the states delegate text adoption to local districts, and the rest use some form of state adoption). For all the conventionality of the product, the actual production and sale of textbooks is still a risky business. It's very expensive to create and print textbooks, and the market (the various agencies that actually decide which to adopt) is somewhat unpredictable. In addition, at any time some citizens are likely to protest whatever messages the texts send. Textbook adoption can be a free-for-all. *2*

Thus it is not surprising that textbooks still beget textbooks. To control risk, companies find it wise to copy successes. Old icons (Washington) remain, but publishers respond to new demands by multiplying new state-approved truths. It has been easier to add those ubiquitous sidebars to the master narrative than to rethink it, easier to incorporate new content into a safe and profitable formula than to create new accounts. American history textbooks are enormous—888 pages, on average—in part because publishers seek to neutralize or anticipate criticisms by adding topics. The result is often not comprehensive coverage but a bloated book devoid of style or coherence. *3*

The traditional American fear of centralized power, salient today in debates over national standards and tests, has resulted in a strange patchwork of agencies and associations—textbook companies, state and local governments, lobby groups of many persuasions, individuals who want to play Grand Inquisitor—to choose and monitor the public truths taught in the texts. One of the most rapid ways of changing what students learn in American schools is to transform the textbooks, but the present Rube Goldberg system of creating and selecting textbooks makes such a change very difficult (though fine history textbooks have on occasion appeared). *4*

What are some strategies to cope with the cross-cutting demands on history textbooks? Three possible ones are these: muddling through with modest improvements; turning over the task of writing textbooks to experts; or devising texts that depart from the model of state-approved truths and embrace instead the taking of multiple perspectives. Each of these has some advantages and faults that are worth contemplating. 5

Muddling through may seem sensible to people who believe that there is a vast gap between superheated policy talk about the defects of textbooks and the everyday reality teachers face in classrooms. Is all the debate over bad textbooks a dust-devil masquerading as a tornado? For many teachers, the big challenge is to prepare students for high-stakes tests they must take for graduation, and textbooks are a key resource in that task. 6

Teachers tend to find the status quo in textbooks more bearable than do the critics. When a sample of classroom teachers was asked their opinion of the textbooks they used, they generally said that the books are good and getting better. Teachers rely heavily on textbooks in their instruction, employing them for about 70 percent of class time. 7

A commonsense argument for muddling through, with gradual improvement of textbooks, is that pedagogical reforms rarely work well if they are imposed on teachers. Study after study has shown that teachers tend to avoid controversy in teaching American history (indeed, being "nonpartisan" is still judged a virtue, as it was in the past). And parents and school board members, like teachers, have their own ideas about what is "real history." Too sharp a turn in the historical highway might topple reform. So some teachers argue that the best way to improve education is to keep the old icons and welcome the newcomers in the textbooks. And hope that the students in fact *do read* the textbooks! Common sense—that's the way to cope amid all the confusion. 8

An alternate approach to reform of textbooks is to set good state or local standards for history courses and turn the writing of textbooks over to experts—an approach used in many nations and sometimes advocated in the United States today. Muddling through just maintains the status quo and guarantees incoherence in textbooks and hence in learning. In the current politics and commerce of text publishing, "truth" becomes whatever the special interests (left or right) pressure textbook companies to say. Current textbooks are often victims of commercial timidity, veto groups, and elephantiasis (888 pages!). 9

What is missing, proponents of this view argue, is a clear set of national standards about what students should know and a vivid and cogent text 10 that engages students in learning. Those who call for expertise suggest that history is too important *not* to be left to the historians.

But this response to the faults of history texts presents its own prob-   *11*
lems. Calling in the experts doesn't eliminate disputes; PhDs love to differ among themselves. Teachers are adept at sabotaging reforms dropped on them from above. And amid all the commercialism and special interests now rife in the process of selecting textbooks, the public still deserves some say in deciding what American students learn about the past, expert or not.

Patricia Nelson Limerick, professor of history at the University of   *12*
Colorado, suggests a pluralistic model of history that contrasts with both muddling through and textbooks by experts. She recently suggested that the Little Bighorn Battlefield, where Sioux and Cheyenne fought George Armstrong Custer, needed not two monuments, one in honor of the Indians and one to recognize Custer and his soldiers, but "a different kind of memorial—one in which no point of view dominates." She imagines visitors walking among memorials to the warriors and Custer, but also to the enlisted men dragooned into the slaughter, to Custer's widow, to the families of the white soldiers, and to the children and wives of the Indian warriors.

Such perspective-taking lies at the core of historical understanding of a   *13*
socially diverse nation. Pluralistic history can enhance ethnic self-respect and empathy for other groups. Parallel to the monuments Limerick proposes, texts for a pluralistic civic education might have not one master narrative but several, capturing separate identities and experiences.

But the history of Americans in their separate groups would be par-   *14*
tial without looking as well at their lives in interaction. Our society is pluralistic in character, and so should be the history we teach to young citizens. But alongside that *pluribus* citizens have also sought an *unum*, a set of shared political aspirations and institutions. One reason there have been so many textbook wars is that group after group has, in turn, sought to become part of a common story told about our past. The *unum* and the *pluribus* have been in inescapable tension, constantly evolving as Americans struggled to find common ground and to respect their differences.

AN ANNOTATED STUDENT RHETORICAL ANALYSIS

Now read our student's rhetorical analysis about David Tyack's discussion of history textbooks in "Whither History Textbooks?" We have annotated the student's analysis to point out how he identifies the author's situation, purpose, argument, and audience.

Quentin Collie   Collie 1

A Rhetorical Analysis of
"Whither History Textbooks?"

The student pro-
vides an overview
of the author's
argument.

In my analysis, I will focus on "Whither History Textbooks?"
which serves as a conclusion to David Tyack's chapter on American
history textbooks in his book *Seeking Common Ground*. In this section,
Tyack explains the state of history textbooks in American schools
today, the causes and influences that result in what he sees as a
problem with trying to cover too many topics without much depth,
and possible ways in which history textbooks can be changed and
improved. In advocating for a pluralistic account of history, Tyack use
specific words and phrases that convey his impatience with American
history textbooks and presents a number of options to make his
discussion appear fair.

The student
summarizes the
author's argument
in more detail and,
specifically, the
source of what
the author sees
as a problem in
teaching history.
This is the situa-
tion that calls for
some response
in writing: that
textbooks have
become "heavy"
and "boring."
The student
then describes
three possible
approaches that
the author takes
to address the
problem he identi-
fies in teaching
history in school.

Tyack points out that in this section that today's textbooks
are, for the most part, bulky and disjointed. Many storylines and
historic figures are pieced together without any all-encompassing
narrative flow or style. Textbooks have come to take this form
because of two significant influences. On one hand, nearly every
interest group argues for certain events, figures, or issues to be
included in the history curriculum. On the other hand, in a more
economical sense, textbooks that present the traditional and generic
American narrative have been the most successful. As a result,
textbook authors and producers attempt to intersperse the variety
of new pieces into the original American narrative. This results in
the heavy and boring textbooks that students use in the classroom
today. Tyack offers three possibilities for how to navigate through
the demands and difficulties involved in history textbook production:
continuing the use of current textbooks with moderate additions and
improvements, delegating the writing of textbooks to experts, and
embracing a new style of textbook which emphasizes the multiple
perspectives of Americans.

In this particular section of the book, Tyack's purpose seems
to be a call for change. In describing the current types of textbooks,
he implies his personal stance through his word choice. Tyack's use
of vivid imagery throughout this part of his book allows him to

1

2

3

Collie 2

The student underscores the author's purpose. He then shows how language reflects the author's point of view. In addition, the student helps us see that the situation the author responds to is not only about how textbooks are written, but how educators choose to adopt textbooks.

delve into the textbook problem by appealing to the emotions of the reader. For instance, Tyack explains that the average American history textbook is 888 pages long and laments this length as the reason that most of today's history books are "bloated" and "devoid of style or coherence" (para. 3). He also alludes to anarchy when he claims that "textbook adoption can be a free-for-all" (para. 2), establishing his skeptical perspective on the decision processes of textbook writers as well as of those who buy them. Another way Tyack explains his views on the methodology behind buying and selling textbooks is through an allusion to a "Rube Goldberg system" (para. 4) in his description of how textbooks are created and sold. This reference implies that our current method has become unnecessarily complex and has rendered making changes in history textbooks difficult or impossible.

He points out the author's strategy for developing the argument, one that forces knowledgeable readers to draw their own conclusions.

Tyack does not advocate for just any change, but, rather, a particular change and ideal type of textbook. He does not make an outright statement of support for a particular plan. Instead, he presents an examination of possibilities that leads the audience to decide which one option is superior. The possibilities include using the same format with slight changes, having experts write the textbooks, and departing from the regular model of textbooks to include new truths and multiple perspectives. He makes a point to state that each option has both pros and cons to be considered.

4

The student points to the author's concession that not everyone agrees that the quality of textbook writing is a problem. The student again demonstrates how word choice conveys an author's point of view and that the author does not find this first solution very tenable.

Tyack writes that teachers, in general, do not have a large problem with the current types of textbooks, and pedagogical reforms rarely work if imposed on teachers. This evidence argues in favor of using the same types of textbooks. The discussion of this particular option, however, ends with its success resting on a "hope that the students in fact *do read* the textbooks!" (para. 8). This statement carries a tone of sarcasm, leaving the reader with a feeling that Tyack believes that students will not read this type of textbook, so this particular plan of action is not likely to improve the schools. In addition, Tyack's exact phrasing for this possibility is "muddling through with modest improvements" (para. 5). From word choice alone, the reader can see that Tyack discredits this idea. The verb *muddle* is associated with things being confused, messed up, and unclear, so his choice of this word implies that he thinks using

5

Collie 3

the current format for textbooks results in teachers and students having a confused and incorrect view of American history. Eventually, he concludes that "muddling through just maintains the status quo and guarantees incoherence in textbooks and hence learning" (para. 9).

He summarizes the author's second possible solution to the problem but explains why the author is not sympathetic to that position.

His next suggested approach is using textbooks written by experts. This option could set clear national standards about what students should be learning about history by those most informed. This option, however, also has its faults as Tyack argues that the experts differ in their opinions. Furthermore, the public does deserve some input about material to be taught to its children, which this option would take away.

6

Although it would seem that the author lets readers draw their own conclusions, the student explains how Tyack uses research to give credence to this last solution to the problem. This is the one solution that the author is not critical of.

Tyack's final option is "a pluralistic model of history that contrasts with both muddling through and textbooks by experts" (para. 12). Tyack argues that "such perspective-taking lies at the core of historical understanding of a socially diverse nation. Pluralistic history can enhance ethnic self-respect and empathy for other groups" (para. 13). Tyack supports this point of view with quotations from a professor of history, which gives credibility to this option. In addition, Tyack does not discuss any possible difficulties in pursuing this type of textbook, even though he stated earlier that each option has both benefits and faults. In this, Tyack appears to be considering multiple possibilities for textbook reform, but, at the same time, he dismisses two of the options and advocates for a particular course of action through his writing strategy.

7

WRITING A RHETORICAL ANALYSIS

By now you should have a strong sense of what is involved in rhetorical analysis. You should be ready to take the next steps: performing a rhetorical analysis of your own and then sharing your analysis and the strategies you've learned with your classmates.

Read the next text, "The Flight from Conversation" by Sherry Turkle, annotating it to help you identify her situation, purpose, thesis, and audience. As you read, also make a separate set of annotations — possibly with a different color pen or pencil, circled, or keyed with asterisks — in which you comment on or evaluate the effectiveness of her essay. What do you like or dislike about it? Why? Does Turkle persuade you to accept her point of view? What impressions do you have of her as a person? Would you like to be in a conversation with her?

SHERRY TURKLE

The Flight from Conversation

Sherry Turkle—the Abby Rockefeller Mauzé Professor of the Social Studies of Science and Technology in the Program in Science, Technology, and Society at the Massachusetts Institute of Technology—is a licensed clinical psychologist with a joint doctorate in sociology and personality psychology from Harvard University. Director of the MIT Initiative on Technology and Self, she is the author or editor of many books, including The *Second Self: Computers and the Human Spirit* (1984), *Life on the Screen: Identity in the Age of the Internet* (1995), *Simulation and Its Discontents* (2009), and *Alone Together: Why We Expect More from Technology and Less from Each Other* (2011). "The Flight from Conversation" appeared in the April 12, 2012, issue of *The New York Times Magazine*.

■ ■ ■

W e live in a technological universe in which we are always communicating. And yet we have sacrificed conversation for mere connection. 1

At home, families sit together, texting and reading e-mail. At work executives text during board meetings. We text (and shop and go on Facebook) during classes and when we're on dates. My students tell me about an important new skill: It involves maintaining eye contact with someone while you text someone else; it's hard, but it can be done. 2

Over the past fifteen years, I've studied technologies of mobile connection and talked to hundreds of people of all ages and circumstances about their plugged-in lives. I've learned that the little devices most of us carry around are so powerful that they change not only what we do, but also who we are. 3

We've become accustomed to a new way of being "alone together." Technology-enabled, we are able to be with one another, and also elsewhere, connected to wherever we want to be. We want to customize our lives. We want to move in and out of where we are because the thing we value most is control over where we focus our attention. We have gotten used to the idea of being in a tribe of one, loyal to our own party. 4

Our colleagues want to go to that board meeting but pay attention only to what interests them. To some this seems like a good idea, but we can end up hiding from one another, even as we are constantly connected to one another. 5

A businessman laments that he no longer has colleagues at work. He doesn't stop by to talk; he doesn't call. He says that he doesn't want to interrupt them. He says they're "too busy on their e-mail." But then he pauses and corrects himself. "I'm not telling the truth. I'm the one who doesn't want to be interrupted. I think I should. But I'd rather just do things on my BlackBerry." 6

A 16-year-old boy who relies on texting for almost everything says   7
almost wistfully, "Someday, someday, but certainly not now, I'd like to
learn how to have a conversation."

In today's workplace, young people who have grown up fearing con-   8
versation show up on the job wearing earphones. Walking through a college library or the campus of a high-tech start-up, one sees the same
thing: We are together, but each of us is in our own bubble, furiously
connected to keyboards and tiny touch screens. A senior partner at a
Boston law firm describes a scene in his office. Young associates lay out
their suite of technologies: laptops, iPods, and multiple phones. And
then they put their earphones on. "Big ones. Like pilots. They turn their
desks into cockpits." With the young lawyers in their cockpits, the office
is quiet, a quiet that does not ask to be broken.

In the silence of connection, people are comforted by being in touch   9
with a lot of people—carefully kept at bay. We can't get enough of one
another if we can use technology to keep one another at distances we
can control: not too close, not too far, just right. I think of it as a Goldi-
locks effect.

Texting and e-mail and posting let us present the self we want   10
to be. This means we can edit. And if we wish to, we can delete. Or
retouch: the voice, the flesh, the face, the body. Not too much, not too
little—just right.

Human relationships are rich; they're messy and demanding. We   11
have learned the habit of cleaning them up with technology. And the
move from conversation to connection is part of this. But it's a process
in which we shortchange ourselves. Worse, it seems that over time we
stop caring, we forget that there is a difference.

We are tempted to think that our little "sips" of online connection   12
add up to a big gulp of real conversation. But they don't. E-mail, Twitter, Facebook, all of these have their places—in politics, commerce,
romance, and friendship. But no matter how valuable, they do not substitute for conversation.

Connecting in sips may work for gathering discrete bits of infor-   13
mation or for saying, "I am thinking about you." Or even for saying, "I
love you." But connecting in sips doesn't work as well when it comes to
understanding and knowing one another. In conversation we tend to one
another. (The word itself is kinetic; it's derived from words that mean to
move, together.) We can attend to tone and nuance. In conversation, we
are called upon to see things from another's point of view.

Face-to-face conversation unfolds slowly. It teaches patience. When   14
we communicate on our digital devices, we learn different habits. As
we ramp up the volume and velocity of online connections, we start to
expect faster answers. To get these, we ask one another simpler questions; we dumb down our communications, even on the most important
matters. It is as though we have all put ourselves on cable news. Shakespeare might have said, "We are consum'd with that which we were
nourish'd by."

And we use conversation with others to learn to converse with our-   *15*
selves. So our flight from conversation can mean diminished chances to
learn skills of self-reflection. These days, social media continually asks
us what's "on our mind," but we have little motivation to say something
truly self-reflective. Self-reflection in conversation requires trust. It's
hard to do anything with 3,000 Facebook friends except connect.

As we get used to being shortchanged on conversation and to getting   *16*
by with less, we seem almost willing to dispense with people altogether.
Serious people muse about the future of computer programs as psychia-
trists. A high school sophomore confides to me that he wishes he could
talk to an artificial intelligence program instead of his dad about dating;
he says the AI would have so much more in its database. Indeed, many
people tell me they hope that as Siri, the digital assistant on Apple's
iPhone, becomes more advanced, "she" will be more and more like a
best friend—one who will listen when others won't.

During the years I have spent researching people and their rela-   *17*
tionships with technology, I have often heard the sentiment "No one is
listening to me." I believe this feeling helps explain why it is so appealing to have a Facebook page or a Twitter feed—each provides so many
automatic listeners. And it helps explain why—against all reason— so
many of us are willing to talk to machines that seem to care about
us. Researchers around the world are busy inventing sociable robots,
designed to be companions to the elderly, to children, to all of us.

One of the most haunting experiences during my research came   *18*
when I brought one of these robots, designed in the shape of a baby seal,
to an elder-care facility, and an older woman began to talk to it about the
loss of her child. The robot seemed to be looking into her eyes. It seemed
to be following the conversation. The woman was comforted.

And so many people found this amazing. Like the sophomore who   *19*
wants advice about dating from artificial intelligence and those who look
forward to computer psychiatry, this enthusiasm speaks to how much we
have confused conversation with connection and collectively seem to have
embraced a new kind of delusion that accepts the simulation of compassion as sufficient unto the day. And why would we want to talk about love
and loss with a machine that has no experience of the arc of human life?
Have we so lost confidence that we will be there for one another?

We expect more from technology and less from one another and seem   *20*
increasingly drawn to technologies that provide the illusion of companionship
without the demands of relationship. Always-on/always-on-you devices provide three powerful fantasies: that we will always be heard; that we can put our
attention wherever we want it to be; and that we never have to be alone. Indeed
our new devices have turned being alone into a problem that can be solved.

When people are alone, even for a few moments, they fidget and reach   *21*
for a device. Here connection works like a symptom, not a cure, and our
constant, reflexive impulse to connect shapes a new way of being.

Think of it as "I share, therefore I am." We use technology to define   *22*
ourselves by sharing our thoughts and feelings as we're having them. We

used to think, "I have a feeling; I want to make a call." Now our impulse is, "I want to have a feeling; I need to send a text."

So, in order to feel more, and to feel more like ourselves, we connect. But in our rush to connect, we flee from solitude, our ability to be separate and gather ourselves. Lacking the capacity for solitude, we turn to other people but don't experience them as they are. It is as though we use them, need them as spare parts to support our increasingly fragile selves.   23

We think constant connection will make us feel less lonely. The opposite is true. If we are unable to be alone, we are far more likely to be lonely. If we don't teach our children to be alone, they will know only how to be lonely.   24

I am a partisan for conversation. To make room for it, I see some first, deliberate steps. At home, we can create sacred spaces: the kitchen, the dining room. We can make our cars "device-free zones." We can demonstrate the value of conversation to our children. And we can do the same thing at work. There we are so busy communicating that we often don't have time to talk to one another about what really matters. Employees asked for casual Fridays; perhaps managers should introduce conversational Thursdays. Most of all, we need to remember—in between texts and e-mails and Facebook posts—to listen to one another, even to the boring bits, because it is often in unedited moments, moments in which we hesitate and stutter and go silent, that we reveal ourselves to one another.   25

I spend the summers at a cottage on Cape Cod, and for decades I walked the same dunes that Thoreau once walked. Not too long ago, people walked with their heads up, looking at the water, the sky, the sand and at one another, talking. Now they often walk with their heads down, typing. Even when they are with friends, partners, children, everyone is on their own devices.   26

So I say, look up, look at one another, and let's start the conversation.   27

A Practice Sequence: Writing a Rhetorical Analysis

1   Write a brief rhetorical analysis of Sherry Turkle's essay, referring to your notes and citing passages where she indicates her situation, purpose, main claim, and audience.

2   An option for group work: As a class, divide into three or more groups. Each group should answer the following questions in response to their reading of Turkle's essay:

Group 1: Identify the situation(s) motivating Turkle to write. Then evaluate: How well does her argument function as a conversation with other authors who have written on the same topic?

Group 2: Analyze the audience's identity, perspectives, and conventional expectations. Then evaluate: How well does the argument function as a conversation with the audience?

Group 3: Analyze the writer's purpose. Then evaluate: Do you believe Turkle achieves her purpose in this essay? Why or why not?

Then, as a class, share your observations:

- To what extent does the author's ability as a conversationalist— that is, her ability to enter into a conversation with other authors and her audience—affect your evaluation of whether she achieves her purpose in this essay?

- If you were to meet this writer, what suggestions or advice would you give her for making her argument more persuasive?

WRITING YOURSELF INTO ACADEMIC CONVERSATIONS

Sherry Turkle laments the erosion of conversation in our culture, blaming technology that encourages broad and shallow connection without real face-to-face engagement. But much academic conversation occurs on the page or screen, involving the exchange of ideas through writing. The philosopher Kenneth Burke uses his metaphor of an ongoing parlor conversation to capture the spirit of academic writing:

> Imagine that you enter a parlor. You come late. When you arrive, others have long preceded you, and they are engaged in a heated discussion, a discussion too heated for them to pause and tell you exactly what it is about. In fact, the discussion had already begun long before any of them got there, so that no one present is qualified to retrace for you all the steps that had gone before. You listen for a while, until you decide that you have caught the tenor of the argument; then you put in your oar. Someone answers; you answer him; another comes to your defense; another aligns himself against you, to either the embarrassment or gratification of your opponent, depending upon the quality of your ally's assistance. However, the discussion is interminable. The hour grows late, you must depart. And you do depart, with the discussion still vigorously in progress.*

As this passage describes, every argument you make is connected to other arguments. Think of how Eugene F. Provenzo Jr. responds to aspects of E. D. Hirsh's arguments about education earlier in this chapter, and the position he takes.

Now that you have learned how to use the tools of rhetorical analysis, we present a series of steps using those tools to write yourself into academic conversations of ideas. Every time you write an argument, the way you position yourself will depend on three things:

- which previously stated arguments you share;
- which previously stated argument you want to refute; and
- what new opinions and supporting information you are going to bring to the conversation.

*Kenneth Burke, *The Philosophy of Literary Form* (Berkeley: University of California Press, 1941), pp. 110–111.

You may, for example, affirm others for raising important issues, but assert that they have not given those issues the thought or emphasis that they deserve. Or you may raise a related issue that has been ignored entirely.

Steps to Writing Yourself into an Academic Conversation

- **Retrace the conversation**, including the relevance of the topic and situation, for readers by briefly discussing an author's key claims and ideas. This discussion can be as brief as a sentence or two and include a quotation for each author you cite.

- **Respond to the ideas of others** by helping readers understand the context in which another's claims make sense. "I get this if I see it this way."

- **Discuss possible implications** by putting problems aside and asking, "Do their claims make sense?"

- **Introduce conflicting points of view** and raise possible criticisms to indicate something the authors whose ideas you discuss may have overlooked.

- **Formulate your own claim** to assert what you think.

- **Ensure that your own purpose as a writer is clear to readers.**

A Practice Sequence: Writing Yourself into an Academic Conversation

1   Now that you have done a rhetorical analysis of Sherry Turkle's "The Flight from Conversation," follow the steps to writing yourself into the conversation and write a short one-page argument. You should retrace the conversation, explain Turkle's argument in ways that demonstrate you understand her argument and underlying assumptions, and formulate your own position with a clear sense of purpose.

2   An option for group work:

- As a group, discuss Turkle's argument, listing reasons why it makes sense and reasons that members of the group take issue with it.

- In turn, formulate your own point of view on the argument.

- Each individual in the class should write an argument that follows the steps above in "Writing Yourself into an Academic Conversation."

3   As an alternative, work individually or in groups to develop an argument in which you enter the conversation with E. D. Hirsch and Eugene Provenzo. Retrace the conversation, discuss the claims they make, explain why their ideas are worth taking seriously, identify what they may have ignored, and formulate your own claim.

From Identifying Claims to Analyzing Arguments

A **claim** is an assertion of fact or belief that needs to be supported with **evidence** — the information that backs up a claim. A main claim, or **thesis**, summarizes the writer's position on a situation and answers the question(s) the writer addresses. It also encompasses all of the minor claims, along with their supporting evidence, that the writer makes throughout the argument.

As readers, we need to identify a writer's main claim, or thesis, because it helps us organize our own understanding of the writer's argument. It acts as a signpost that tells us, "This is what the essay is about," "This is what I want you to pay attention to," and "This is how I want you to think, change, or act."

When you evaluate a claim, whether it is an argument's main claim or a minor claim, it is helpful to identify the type of claim it is: a claim of fact, a claim of value, or a claim of policy. You also need to evaluate the reasons for and the evidence that supports the claim. Because academic argument should acknowledge multiple points of view, you also should be prepared to identify what, if any, concessions a writer offers his or her readers, and what counterarguments he or she anticipates from others in the conversation.

IDENTIFYING TYPES OF CLAIMS

To illustrate how to identify a writer's claims, let's take a look at a text by educators Myra and David Sadker that examines gender bias in schools. The text is followed by our analyses of the types of claims (fact, value, and policy) and then, in the next section, of the nature of the arguments (use of evidence, concessions, and counterarguments) the authors present.

MYRA SADKER AND DAVID SADKER

Hidden Lessons

Myra Sadker was a professor of education at American University until 1995, the year she died. Dr. Sadker coauthored *Sexism in School and Society*, the first book on gender bias in America's schools, in 1973 and became a leading advocate for equal educational opportunities.

David Sadker is a professor at American University and has taught at the elementary, middle school, and high school levels. David Sadker and his late wife earned a national reputation for their groundbreaking work in confronting gender bias and sexual harassment. "Hidden Lessons" is an excerpt from their book *Failing at Fairness: How Our Schools Cheat Girls* (1994).

■ ■ ■

Sitting in the same classroom, reading the same textbook, listening to the same teacher, boys and girls receive very different educations. From grade school through graduate school female students are more likely to be invisible members of classrooms. Teachers interact with males more frequently, ask them better questions, and give them more precise and helpful feedback. Over the course of years the uneven distribution of teacher time, energy, attention, and talent, with boys getting the lion's share, takes its toll on girls. Since gender bias is not a noisy problem, most people are unaware of the secret sexist lessons and the quiet losses they engender.   1

Girls are the majority of our nation's schoolchildren, yet they are second-class educational citizens. The problems they face—loss of self-esteem, decline in achievement, and elimination of career options—are at the heart of the educational process. Until educational sexism is eradicated, more than half our children will be shortchanged and their gifts lost to society.   2

Award-winning author Susan Faludi discovered that backlash "is most powerful when it goes private, when it lodges inside a woman's mind and turns her vision inward, until she imagines the pressure is all in her head, until she begins to enforce the backlash too—on herself."[1] Psychological backlash internalized by adult women is a frightening concept, but what is even more terrifying is a curriculum of sexist school   3

[1] Editor's note: Journalist Susan Faludi's book *Backlash: The Undeclared War Against American Women* (1991) was a response to the antifeminist backlash against the women's movement.

lessons becoming secret mind games played against female children, our daughters, and tomorrow's women.

After almost two decades of research grants and thousands of hours of classroom observation, we remain amazed at the stubborn persistence of these hidden sexist lessons. When we began our investigation of gender bias, we looked first in the classrooms of one of Washington, D.C.'s elite and expensive private schools. Uncertain of exactly what to look for, we wrote nothing down; we just observed. The classroom was a whirlwind of activity so fast paced we could easily miss the quick but vital phrase or gesture, the insidious incident, the tiny inequity that held a world of meaning. As we watched, we had to push ourselves beyond the blind spots of socialization and gradually focus on the nature of the interaction between teacher and student. On the second day we saw our first example of sexism, a quick, jarring flash within the hectic pace of the school day:

> Two second-graders are kneeling beside a large box. They whisper excitedly to each other as they pull out wooden blocks, colored balls, counting sticks. So absorbed are these two small children in examining and sorting the materials, they are visibly startled by the teacher's impatient voice as she hovers over them. "Ann! Julia! Get your cottonpickin' hands out of the math box. Move over so the boys can get in there and do their work."

Isolated here on the page of a book, this incident is not difficult to interpret. It becomes even more disturbing if you think of it with the teacher making a racial distinction. Picture Ann and Julia as African American children moved away so white children can gain access to the math materials. If Ann and Julia's parents had observed this exchange, they might justifiably wonder whether their tuition dollars were well spent. But few parents actually watch teachers in action, and fewer still have learned to interpret the meaning behind fast-paced classroom events.

The incident unsettles, but it must be considered within the context of numerous interactions this harried teacher had that day. While she talked to the two girls, she was also keeping a wary eye on fourteen other active children. Unless you actually shadowed the teacher, stood right next to her as we did, you might not have seen or heard the event. After all, it lasted only a few seconds.

It took us almost a year to develop an observation system that would register the hundreds of daily classroom interactions, teasing out the gender bias embedded in them. Trained raters coded classrooms in math, reading, English, and social studies. They observed students from different racial and ethnic backgrounds. They saw lessons taught by women and by men, by teachers of different races. In short, they analyzed America's classrooms. By the end of the year we had thousands of observation sheets, and after another year of statistical analysis, we discovered a syntax of sexism so elusive that most teachers and students were completely unaware of its influence.

Recently a producer of NBC's *Dateline* contacted us to learn more about our discovery that girls don't receive their fair share of education. Jane Pauley, the show's anchorwoman, wanted to visit classrooms, capture these covert sexist lessons on videotape, and expose them before a television audience. The task was to extricate sound bites of sexism from a fifth-grade classroom where the teacher, chosen to be the subject of the exposé, was aware she was being scrutinized for sex bias. *8*

Dateline had been taping in her class for two days when we received a concerned phone call. "This is a fair teacher," the producer said. "How can we show sexism on our show when there's no gender bias in this teacher's class?" We drove to the NBC studio in Washington, D.C., and found two *Dateline* staffers, intelligent women concerned about fair treatment in school, sitting on the floor in a darkened room staring at the videotape of a fifth-grade class. "We've been playing this over and over. The teacher is terrific. There's no bias in her teaching. Come watch." *9*

After about twenty minutes of viewing, we realized it was a case of déjà vu: The episodal sexist themes and recurring incidents were all too familiar. The teacher was terrific, but she was more effective for half of the students than she was for the other. She was, in fact, a classic example of the hundreds of skillful well-intentioned professionals we have seen who inadvertently teach boys better than girls. *10*

We had forgotten how difficult it was to recognize subtle sexism before you learn how to look. It was as if the *Dateline* staff members were wearing blinders. We halted the tape, pointed out the sexist behaviors, related them to incidents in our research, and played the tape again. There is a classic "aha!" effect in education when people finally "get it." Once the hidden lessons of unconscious bias are understood, classrooms never look the same again to the trained observer. *11*

Much of the unintentional gender bias in that fifth-grade class could not be shown in the short time allowed by television, but the sound bites of sexism were also there. *Dateline* chose to show a segregated math group: boys sitting on the teacher's right side and girls on her left. After giving the math book to a girl to hold open at the page of examples, the teacher turned her back to the girls and focused on the boys, teaching them actively and directly. Occasionally she turned to the girls' side, but only to read the examples in the book. This teacher, although aware that she was being observed for sexism, had unwittingly transformed the girls into passive spectators, an audience for the boys. All but one, that is: The girl holding the math book had become a prop. *12*

Dateline also showed a lively discussion in the school library. With both girls' hands and boys' hands waving for attention, the librarian *13* chose boy after boy to speak. In one interaction she peered through the forest of girls' hands waving directly in front of her to acknowledge the raised hand of a boy in the back of the room. Startled by the teacher's attention, the boy muttered, "I was just stretching."

The next day we discussed the show with future teachers, our students at The American University. They were bewildered. "Those teachers really were sexist. They didn't mean to be, but they were. How could that happen—with the cameras and everyone watching?" When we took those students into classrooms to discover the hidden lessons for themselves, they began to understand. It is difficult to detect sexism unless you know precisely how to observe. And if a lifetime of socialization makes it difficult to spot gender bias even when you're looking for it, how much harder it is to avoid the traps when you are the one doing the teaching.

14

Now let's consider the types of claims in the Sadkers' argument.

▪ Identify Claims of Fact

Claims of fact are assertions (or arguments) that seek to define or classify something or establish *that a problem or condition has existed, exists, or will exist*. Claims of fact are made by individuals who believe that something is true; but claims are never simply facts, and some claims are more objective, and so easier to verify, than others.

For example, "It's raining in Portland today" is a "factual" claim of fact; it's easily verified. But consider the argument some make that the steel and automotive industries in the United States have depleted our natural resources and left us at a crisis point. This is an assertion that a condition exists. A careful reader must examine the basis for this kind of claim: Are we truly facing a crisis? And if so, are the steel and automotive industries truly responsible? A number of politicians counter this claim of fact by insisting that if the government were to harness the vast natural resources in Alaska, there would be no "crisis." This is also a claim of fact, in this case an assertion that a condition will exist in the future. Again, it is based on evidence, evidence gathered from various sources that indicates sufficient resources in Alaska to keep up with our increasing demands for resources and to allay a potential crisis.

Our point is that most claims of fact are debatable and challenge us to provide evidence to verify our arguments. They may be based on factual information, but they are not necessarily true. Most claims of fact present **interpretations** of evidence derived from **inferences**. That is, a writer will examine evidence (for example, about the quantity of natural resources in Alaska and the rate that industries harness those resources and process them into goods), draw a conclusion based on reasoning (an inference), and offer an explanation based on that conclusion (an interpretation).

So, for example, an academic writer will study the evidence on the quantity of natural resources in Alaska and the rate that industries harness those resources and process them into goods; only after the writer makes an informed decision on whether Alaska's resources are sufficient to keep pace with the demand for them will he or she take a position on the issue.

Another claim of fact is one that seeks to define or classify. For example, researchers have sought to define a range of behaviors such as autism that actually resist simple definition. After all, autism exists along a behavioral spectrum attributed variably to genetics and environment. Psychologists have indeed tried to define autism using a diagnostic tool to characterize behaviors associated with communication and social interaction. However, definitions of autism have changed over time, reflecting changing criteria for assessing human behavior and the perspective one takes. So do we in fact have a "crisis" in the over diagnosis of autistic behaviors as some have claimed? For that matter, who gets to decide what counts as a crisis?

Let's now come to the Sadkers' claim of fact that female students are "more likely to be invisible members of classrooms" and that teachers interact differently with female students than they do with male students. The careful reader will want to see how the Sadkers support these claims of fact throughout the essay. Can they convincingly present their argument about "the secret sexist lessons and the quiet losses they engender" in the paragraphs that follow?

▪ Identify Claims of Value

A claim of fact is different from a **claim of value**, which *expresses an evaluation of a problem or condition that has existed, exists, or will exist.* Is a condition good or bad? Is it important or inconsequential?

For example, an argument that developing the wilderness in Alaska would irreversibly mar the beauty of the land indicates that the writer values the beauty of the land over the possible benefits of development. A claim of value presents a judgment, which is sometimes signaled by a value-laden word like *ugly, beautiful*, or *immoral*, but may also be conveyed more subtly by the writer's tone and attitude.

Sadker and Sadker make a claim of value when they suggest that a "majority of our nation's schoolchildren" have become "second-class educational citizens" and point out that the consequences of treating girls differently from boys in school has resulted in a "loss of self-esteem, decline in achievement, and elimination of career options" for girls (para. 2). Of course, the critical reader's task is to question these evaluations: Does gender bias in the classroom affect self-esteem, achievement, and career options? Both of these statements are minor claims, but they make assertions that require support. After all, how do the Sadkers know these things? Whether or not readers are persuaded by these claims depends on the evidence or reasons that the authors use to support them. We discuss the nature of evidence and what constitutes "good reasons" later in this chapter.

■ Identify Claims of Policy

A **claim of policy** is an argument for what should be the case, *that a condition should exist*. It is a call for change or a solution to a problem.

Two recent controversies on college campuses center on claims of policy. One has activists arguing that universities and colleges should have a policy that all workers on campus earn a living wage. The other has activists arguing that universities and colleges should have a policy that prevents them from investing in countries where the government ignores human rights.

Claims of policy are often signaled by words like *should* and *must*: "For public universities to live up to their democratic mission, they *must* provide all their workers with a living wage." Myra and David Sadker make a claim of policy when they assert that "educational sexism" must be eradicated; otherwise, they point out, "more than half our children will be shortchanged and their gifts lost to society" (para. 2).

Not all writers make their claims as explicitly as the Sadkers do, and it is possible that claims of fact may seem like interpretive claims as they are based on the inferences we draw from evidence. Thus, it is the writer's task to make a distinction between a claim of fact and interpretation with sufficient evidence. But you should be able to identify the three different types of claims. Moreover, you should keep in mind what the situation is and what kind of argument can best address what you see as a problem. Ask yourself: Does the situation involve a question of fact? Does the situation involve a question of value? Does the situation require a change in policy? Or is some combination at work?

Steps to Identifying Claims

1 **Ask:** Does the argument assert that a problem or condition has existed, exists, or will exist? If so, it's a claim of fact.

2 **Ask:** Does the argument express an evaluation of a problem or condition that has existed, exists, or will exist? If so, it's a claim of value.

3 **Ask:** Does the argument call for change, and is it directed at some future action? If so, it's a claim of policy.

A Practice Sequence: Identifying Claims

What follows is a series of claims. Identify each one as a claim of fact, value, or policy. Be prepared to justify your categorizations.

1 Taxing the use of fossil fuels will end the energy crisis.

2 We should reform the welfare system to ensure that people who receive support from the government also work.

3 Images of violence in the media create a culture of violence in schools.

4 The increase in homelessness is a deplorable situation that contradicts the whole idea of democracy.

5 Distributing property taxes more equitably is the one sure way to end poverty and illiteracy.

6 Individual votes don't really count.

7 Despite the 20 percent increase in the number of females in the workforce over the past forty years, women are still not treated equitably.

8 Affirmative action is a policy that has outlived its usefulness.

9 There are a disproportionate number of black males in American prisons.

10 The media are biased, which means we cannot count on newspapers or television news for the truth.

ANALYZING ARGUMENTS

Analyzing an argument involves identifying the writer's main and minor claims and then examining (1) the reasons and evidence given in support of each claim, (2) the writer's concessions, and (3) the writer's attempts to handle counterarguments.

■ Analyze the Reasons Used to Support a Claim

Stating a claim is one thing; supporting that claim is another. As a critical reader, you need to evaluate whether a writer has provided *good reasons* to support his or her position. Specifically, you will need to decide whether the support for a claim is recent, relevant, reliable, and accurate. As a writer, you will need to use the same criteria when you support your claims.

Is the source recent?   Knowledgeable readers of your written arguments not only will be aware of classic studies that you should cite as "intellectual touchstones"; they will also expect you to cite recent evidence, evidence published within five years of when you are writing.

Of course, older research can be valuable. For example, in a paper about molecular biology, you might very well cite James Watson and Francis Crick's groundbreaking 1953 study in which they describe the structure of DNA. That study is an intellectual touchstone that changed the life sciences in a fundamental way.

Or if you were writing about educational reform, you might very well mention E. D. Hirsch's 1987 book *Cultural Literacy.* Hirsch's book did not change the way people think about curricular reform as profoundly as Watson and Crick's study changed the way scientists think about biology, but his term *cultural literacy* continues to serve as useful shorthand for a particular way of thinking about curricular reform that remains influential to this day.

Although citing Hirsch is an effective way to suggest you have studied the history of an educational problem, it will not convince your readers that there is a crisis in education today. To establish that, you would need to use as evidence studies published over the past few years to show, for example, that there has been a steady decline in test scores since Hirsch wrote his book. And you would need to support your claim that curricular reform is the one sure way to bring an end to illiteracy and poverty with data that are much more current than those available to Hirsch in the 1980s. No one would accept the judgment that our schools are in crisis if your most recent citation is more than twenty years old.

Is the source relevant?   Evidence that is relevant must have real bearing on your issue. It also depends greatly on what your readers expect. For example, suppose two of your friends complain that they were unable to sell their condominiums for the price they asked. You can claim there is a crisis in the housing market, but your argument won't convince most readers if your only evidence is personal anecdote.

Such *anecdotal evidence* may alert you to a possible topic and help you connect with your readers, but you will need to test the **relevance** of your friends' experience—Is it pertinent? Is it typical of a larger situation or condition?—if you want your readers to take your argument seriously. For example, you might scan real estate listings to see what the asking prices are for properties comparable to your friends' properties. By comparing listings, you are defining the grounds for your argument. If your friends are disappointed that their one-bedroom condominiums sold for less than a three-bedroom condominium with deeded parking in the same neighborhood, it may well be that their expectations were too high.

In other words, if you aren't comparing like things, your argument is going to be seriously flawed. If your friends' definition of what constitutes a "reasonable price" differs dramatically from everyone else's, their experience is probably irrelevant to the larger question of whether the local housing market is depressed.

Is the source reliable?   You also need to evaluate whether the data you use to support your argument are reliable. After all, some researchers present findings based on a very small sample of people that can also be rather selective.

For example, a researcher might argue that 67 percent of the people he cited believe that school and residential integration are important concerns. But how many people did this person interview? More important, who responded to the researcher's questions? A reliable claim cannot be based on a few of the researcher's friends.

Let's return to the real estate example. You have confirmed that your friends listed their condominiums at prices that were not out of line with the market. Now what? You need to seek out reliable sources to continue testing your argument. For example, you might search the real estate or business section of your local newspaper to see if there are any recent stories about a softening of the market; and you might talk with several local real estate agents to get their opinions on the subject.

In consulting local newspapers and local agents, you are looking for **authoritative sources** against which to test your anecdotal evidence—the confirmation of experts who report on, study, evaluate, and have an informed opinion on local real estate. Local real estate agents are a source of **expert testimony**, firsthand confirmation of the information you have discovered. You would probably not want to rely on the testimony of a single real estate agent, who may have a bias; instead, talk with several agents to see if a consensus emerges.

Is the source accurate?   To determine the accuracy of a study that you want to use to support your argument, you have to do a little digging to find out who else has made a similar claim. For instance, if you want to cite authoritative research that compares the dropout rate for white students with the rate for students of color, you could look at research conducted by the Civil Rights Project. Of course, you don't need to stop your search there. You could also check the resources available through the National Center for Education Statistics. You want to show your readers that you have done a relatively thorough search to make your argument as persuasive as possible.

The accuracy of **statistics**—factual information presented numerically or graphically (for example, in a pie or bar chart)—is difficult to verify. To a certain extent, then, their veracity has to be taken on faith. Often the best you can do is assure yourself that the source of your statistical information is authoritative and reliable—government and major research universities generally are "safe" sources—and that whoever is interpreting the statistical information is not distorting it.

Returning again to our real estate example, let's say you've read a newspaper article that cites statistical information about the condition of the local real estate market (for example, the average price of property and volume of sales this year in comparison to last year). Presumably the author of the article is an expert, but he or she may be interpreting rather than simply reporting on the statistics.

To reassure yourself one way or the other, you may want to check the sources of the author's statistics—go right to your source's sources—which a responsible author will cite. That will allow you to look over the raw data and come to your own conclusions. A further step you could take would be to discuss the article with other experts—local real estate agents—to find out what they think of the article and the information it presents.

Now, let's go back to Myra and David Sadker's essay. How do they develop their assertion that girls are treated differently from boys in classrooms from "grade school through graduate school"? First, they tell us (in para. 4) that they have been conducting research continuously for "almost two decades" and that they have accumulated "thousands of hours of classroom observation." This information suggests that their research is both recent and relevant.

But are their studies reliable and accurate? That their research meets the reliability criterion is confirmed by the grants they received over the years: Granting institutions (experts) have assessed their work and determined that it deserved to be funded. Grants confer authority on research. In addition, the Sadkers explain that they observed and refined their analyses over time to achieve accuracy: "As we watched, we had to push ourselves beyond the blind spots of socialization and gradually focus on the nature of the interaction between teacher and student."

In paragraph 7, the authors provide more evidence that the observations that support their claim are accurate. Not only have they observed many instances of gender bias in classrooms; so have trained "raters." The raters add objectivity to the findings because they did not share the Sadkers' interest in drawing a specific conclusion about whether gender bias exists in classrooms. Also the raters observed a wide cross section of students and teachers from "different racial and ethnic backgrounds." At the end of their study, the Sadkers had collected thousands of pieces of data and could feel quite confident about their conclusion—that they had "discovered a syntax of sexism so elusive that most teachers and students were completely unaware of its influence."

Steps to Evaluating Support for a Claim

Ask yourself:

1 **Is the source recent?** Has it been published in the past few years? How have things changed since then? If the source was not published recently, is it still an important part of the conversation worth acknowledging?

2 **Is the source relevant?** Does the evidence have real bearing on the claim? Is it pertinent? Is it typical of a larger situation or condition?

3 **Is the source reliable?** Does the evidence come from recognized experts and authoritative institutions?

4 **Is the source accurate?** Are the data presented in the source sufficient? Have they been gathered, interpreted, and reported responsibly? How do they compare with other data you have found?

▪ Identify Concessions

Part of the strategy of developing a main claim supported with good reasons is to offer a **concession**, an acknowledgment that readers may not agree with every point the writer is making. A concession is a writer's way of saying, "Okay, I can see that there may be another way of looking at the issue or another way to interpret the evidence used to support the argument I am making."

For instance, you may not want your energy costs to go up, but after examining the reasons why it may be necessary to increase taxes on gasoline—to lower usage and conserve fossil fuels—you might concede that a tax increase on gasoline could be useful. The willingness to make concessions is valued in academic writing because it acknowledges both complexity and the importance of multiple perspectives. It also acknowledges the fact that information can always be interpreted in different ways.

The Sadkers make a concession when they acknowledge in the last paragraph of the excerpt that "it is difficult to detect sexism unless you know precisely how to observe." And, they explain, "if a lifetime of socialization makes it difficult to spot gender bias even when you're looking for it, how much harder it is to avoid the traps when you are the one doing the teaching."

Notice that these concessions do not weaken their argument. The authors' evidence appears overwhelmingly to support their thesis. The lesson here is that conceding a point in your argument shows that you have acknowledged there are other ways of seeing things, other interpretations. This is an important part of what it means to enter a conversation of ideas.

Often a writer will signal a concession with phrases like the following:

- "It is true that . . ."
- "I agree with X that Y is an important factor to consider."
- "Some studies have convincingly shown that . . ."

Generally, the writer will then go on to address the concession, explaining how it needs to be modified or abandoned in the light of new evidence or the writer's perspective on the issue.

▪ Identify Counterarguments

As the term suggests, a **counterargument** is an argument raised in response to another argument. You want to be aware of and acknowledge what your readers may object to in your argument. Anticipating readers' objections is an important part of developing a conversational argument.

For example, if you were arguing in support of universal health care, you would have to acknowledge that the approach departs dramatically from the traditional role the federal government has played in providing health insurance. That is, most people's access to health insurance has depended on their individual ability to afford and purchase this kind of insurance. You would have to anticipate how readers would respond to your proposal, especially readers who do not feel that the federal government should ever play a role in what has heretofore been an individual responsibility.

Anticipating readers' objections demonstrates that you understand the complexity of the issue and are willing at least to entertain different and conflicting opinions.

In the excerpt from "Hidden Lessons," the Sadkers describe the initial response of *Dateline* staffers to what they observed in the classroom they were videotaping: "This is a fair teacher. . . . [T]here's no gender bias in this teacher's class." Two women whom the Sadkers describe as "intelligent" and "concerned about fair treatment in school" agreed: "We've been playing this over and over. The teacher is terrific. There's no bias in her teaching. Come watch" (para. 9).

Notice the Sadkers' acknowledgment that even intelligent, concerned people may not see the problems that the Sadkers spent more than twenty years studying. In addressing the counterargument—that sexism does not exist—the authors are both empathetic to and respectful of what any reasonable person might or might not see. This is in keeping with what we would call a conversational argument: that writers listen to different points of view, that they respect arguments that diverge from their own, and that they be willing to exchange ideas and revise their own points of view.

In an argument that is more conversational than confrontational, writers establish areas of common ground, both to convey different views that are understood and to acknowledge the conditions under which those different views are valid. Writers do this by making concessions and anticipating and responding to counterarguments.

This conversational approach is what many people call a **Rogerian approach to argument**, based on psychologist Carl Rogers's approach to psychotherapy. The objective of a Rogerian strategy is to reduce listeners' sense of threat so that they are open to alternatives. For academic writers, it involves four steps:

1. Conveying to readers that their different views are understood.
2. Acknowledging conditions under which readers' views are valid.
3. Helping readers see that the writer shares common ground with them.
4. Creating mutually acceptable solutions to agreed-on problems.

The structure of an argument, according to the Rogerian approach, grows out of the give-and-take of conversation between two people and the topic under discussion. In a written conversation, the give-and-take of face-to-face conversation takes the form of anticipating readers' counterarguments and uses language that is both empathetic and respectful, to put the readers at ease.

AN ANNOTATED STUDENT ARGUMENT

We have annotated the following essay to show the variety of claims the student writer uses, as well as some of the other argumentative moves he performs. The assignment was to write an argument out of personal experience and observation about the cultural impact of a recent innovation. Marques Camp chose to write about the Kindle, an electronic reading device developed by the online retailer Amazon that allows users to download books for a fee. However, the user cannot share the download electronically with other users. Camp touches on a number of issues reflected in his claims.

As you read the essay, imagine how you would respond to his various claims. Which do you agree with, which do you disagree with, and why? What evidence would you present to support or counter his claims? Do you detect a main claim? Do you think his overall essay develops and supports it?

Camp 1

Marques Camp
Professor Fells
English 1020
January 28, 20—
   The End of the World May Be Nigh, and It's the Kindle's Fault

"Libraries will in the end become cities."
   — Gottfried Wilhelm Leibniz, German polymath

The student presents a claim of fact that others have made.

The future of written human history will come, as they will have us believe, in the form of the Amazon Kindle, all 10.2 ounces of it, all 2 GB and 532 MHz of it, all 240,000+ titles of it, ready to change the way people read, ready to revolutionize the way people see the world.

1

He lays the basis for a counterargument by questioning whether this is a real threat at all, citing some technological precedents.

The Kindle is a signpost for our times, the final checkpoint in our long and adventurous journey from the world of printed paper to the twenty-first-century world of digitalization. We first saw this paradigm shift with newspapers, where weekly columns were taken over by daily blog posts, where 48-point sans-serif headlines transformed into 12-point Web links. We then moved on into television, where Must-See TV was replaced with On-Demand TV, where consumers no longer sat around in the living room with their families during prime time but rather watched the latest episode of their favorite show commercial-free from the comfortable and convenient confines of their

2

Camp 2

laptop, able to fast-forward, rewind, and pause with a delightful and devilish sense of programming omnipotence. We are now seeing it, slowly but surely, slay the giant that we never thought could be slain: the world of books.

In this paragraph, he makes a claim of fact about unequal access to technological innovation and offers a concession to what many see as the value of the Kindle.

Contrary to popular belief, easier access to a wider quantity of literature is not a universal revolution. The Kindle speaks to the world that measures quantity by the number of cable television channels it has, speed by the connectivity of its wireless networks, and distance by the number of miles a family travels for vacation. Yes, the Kindle is the new paradigm for universal access and literary connectivity. But it is much like a college degree in the sense that it is merely a gateway to a wealth of opportunity. The problem, however, is gaining access to this gateway in the first place.

3

He supports his claim of fact with evidence based on experience: that sharing books provides something technology cannot offer.

Books often pass from hand to hand, from friend to friend, from generation to generation, many times with the mutual understanding that remuneration is not necessary — merely the promise of hope that the new reader is as touched and enlightened by the book as the previous one. This transfer serves more than a utilitarian function; symbolically, it represents the passage of hope, of knowledge, of responsibility.

4

Evidence from observation: not everyone has access to new technologies, but people will always have access to books.

The book, in many cases, represents the only sort of hope for the poorest among us, the great equalizer in a world full of financial and intellectual capital and highly concentrated access to this capital. The wonderful quality of the book is that its intellectual value is very rarely proportional to its financial value; people often consider their most valuable book to be one they happened to pick up one day for free.

5

An evaluative claim — that the widening gap between rich and poor is dangerous — adds another layer to the argument.

The proliferation of the Kindle technology, however, will result in a wider disconnect between the elite and the non-elite — as the old saying goes, the rich will get richer and the poor will get poorer. Unfortunately for the poor, this is no financial disconnect — this is a widening of the gap in the world of ideas. And this is, perhaps, the most dangerous gap of all.

6

A further evaluative claim — that new technological devices offer little hope to "victims" of illiteracy — is followed by a claim of fact that

The Kindle Revolution, ironically, may end up contributing to the very disease that is antithetical to its implied function: illiteracy. Make no mistake, the Kindle was not designed with the poor in mind. For those in most need of the printed

7

Camp 3

books inspire people to create change in the world.

word, for those who are the most vulnerable victims of the illiteracy threat, the $359 Kindle offers little in the way of hope. One book for a poor person is all he or she needs to be inspired and change the world; with the Kindle, that one book is consolidated and digitized, transformed from a tangible piece of hope and the future into a mere collection of words in the theoretically infinite dimension of cyberspace. A "book" on the Kindle is a book wedged among many other books, separated by nothing more than title, devoid of essence, devoid of uniqueness, devoid of personality, devoid of its unique position in space — precisely what makes a book a "book," as opposed to a mere collection of words. It is no longer singular, no longer serendipitous, no longer distinguishable.

An evaluative claim in which the author observes that technology can make reading passive. Then a claim of fact: that the experience of reading can be transformative.

The e-book cannot, like a bound book, pass through multiple hands and eventually settle itself on the right person, ready to be unleashed as a tool to change the world. Due to the restrictions on sharing and reselling e-books with the Kindle, the very nature of reading books transforms from highly communal to individualistic, from highly active to somewhat passive. The Kindle will lead to the mystification of books, wherein they become less unique capsules of thoughts and ideas and experiences and more utility-oriented modes of information-giving. What many Kindle advocates fail to realize is that oftentimes, the transformative quality of books resides less in the actual words comprising the book and more in the actual experience of reading.

8

The student offers a final evaluative claim, observing that the Kindle threatens to mask the relationship between ideas and the world.

There is also something to be said for the utter corporeality of books that lies at the heart of Leibniz's metaphor. Libraries are physical testaments to all that we have learned and recorded during human history. The sheer size of libraries, the sheer number of volumes residing in them, tell us, in a spatial sense, of all the theoretical knowledge we have accumulated in the course of our existence, and all the power we have to further shape and define the world we live in. The Kindle and other digital literary technologies are threatening the very connection between the world of ideas and the material world, threatening to take our literal measures of progress and hide them away in the vast database of words and ideas,

9

Camp 4

His concluding claim falls just short of making a proposal — but he does suggest that those in positions of power must ensure the proliferation of books.

available only to those with $359 to spare and a credit card for further purchases.

If libraries will indeed become cities, then we need to carefully begin to lay the foundations, book on top of book on top of book, and we are going to have to ensure that we have enough manpower to do it.

10

Steps to Analyzing an Argument

1 **Identify the type of claim.** Is it a claim of fact? Value? Policy?

2 **Analyze the reasons used to support the claim.** Are they recent? Relevant? Reliable? Accurate?

3 **Identify concessions.** Is there another argument that even the author acknowledges is legitimate?

4 **Identify counterarguments.** What arguments contradict or challenge the author's position?

A Practice Sequence: Analyzing an Argument

Use the criteria in the "Steps to Analyzing an Argument" box to analyze the following blog post by Susan D. Blum. What types of claim does she advance? What seems to be her main claim? Do you find her reasons recent, relevant, reliable, and accurate? What sort of concessions does she make? What counterarguments would you raise?

SUSAN D. BLUM

The United States of (Non)Reading: The End of Civilization or a New Era?

Susan D. Blum is a Professor of Anthropology at the University of Notre Dame, whose wide areas of professional interest and expertise include Asian Studies and education. She has written or edited many publications, including *Portraits of "Primitives": Ordering Human Kinds in the Chinese Nation (2001), My Word! Plagiarism and College Culture* (2009), and *Making Sense of Language: Readings in Culture and Communication* (2009; 2013). She also writes the Learning versus Schooling blog for the *Huffington Post,* where this essay was posted on October 8, 2013.

■ ■ ■

Just the other day one of my undergraduate assistants reported a *1*
friend's boast that he had not read anything for school since fifth
grade. A student at an excellent university, successful, "clever," "smart,"
he can write papers, take exams, participate in class or online discussions. Why would he have to read?

Students sometimes don't buy the class books. Professors are shocked. *2*

Several years ago a student told me that she regarded all assigned *3*
reading as "recommended," even if the professors labeled it "required."
Were professors so dumb that they didn't know that?

The idea of assigned reading, as the core activity of college students, *4*
is old. Students don't see it as central; faculty do.

And though I used to, and sometimes still do, spend a lot of energy *5*
lamenting this, by taking a broader view of the nature of reading and
writing, I have come to understand it and even to some extent accept it.

Student avoidance of reading is not an entirely new problem. When *6*
I was in graduate school, in the 1980s, one of my most indelible memories was of a new classmate, straight out of a first-rate college, complaining in our anthropology theory class that we had to keep finding
out what other people thought. When was it time for us to convey our
viewpoints? Why all that reading?

Some college course evaluations ask students what percentage of the *7*
reading they did. Some report they did as much as 90 percent. Some as
little as 25 percent.

In a systematic study of college students' reading, Kylie Baier and *8*
four colleagues reported that students mostly (40 percent) read for
exams. Almost 19 percent don't read for class. In terms of time, 94 percent of students spend less than two hours on any given reading for
class; 62 percent spend less than an hour. Thirty-two percent believe
they could get an A without reading; 89 percent believe they could get
at least a C.

Among many other educational crises, there is a perceived crisis *9*
given that "students are increasingly reading less and less."

When faculty enter new institutions, they often ask colleagues: *10*
How much reading should I assign? Some departments offer guidelines about the number of pages: Assign twenty-five pages for each
meeting of first-year classes, but no more than one hundred pages a
week for any course. This has always struck me as strange, given that
a page of a novel and a page of a double-column textbook have completely different amounts of text, and take different kinds of attention
and time. In response to this faculty challenge, Steve Volk—named the
Carnegie Professor of the Year in 2011, so he knows something about
teaching—wrote on the Web site of Oberlin College's Center for Teaching Innovation and Excellence that there is no magic formula for numbers of pages. He suggests instead that faculty consider "What do you
want the reading to do?"

But it is not only college teachers who worry about how much people *11* are reading. There is a widespread belief that Americans in general read less and less. This perception builds on public conversations about the lack of reading. In 2007 a National Endowment for the Arts study concluded that adults' reading habits were in severe decline. Only 57 percent of adults read a book voluntarily in 2002, down from 61 percent in 1992.

This was supposed to have all sorts of terrible consequences: educa- *12* tional, of course, but also economic, social, moral, you name it.

Reversing the cup-half-empty conclusion, a 2013 study showed that *13* more than half read books for pleasure—just not what the NEA defines (or would if the Government were functioning) as "literature."

And the Pew interpretation was that if reading for work and school *14* is added to "voluntary reading," then almost all people read "books" at some point during the year: 79 percent of 18 to 24 year-olds, and 90 percent of 16 to 17 year-olds.

It is undeniable that people are reading (looking at) writing all the *15* time. It may not be in physical books, however. And just this week, *USA Today* argued that digital devices increase book reading (on the devices).

David Carr wrote in 2008 about the decline in attention—not only *16* in our students. Attention spans, focus, mindfulness . . . all these are shrinking. Technology plays a role in this, as many of us spend much of our lives looking at short items. The Onion, the humor website, puts most of its efforts into its headlines. Blogs should be at most one thousand words, but three hundred is better. (This one is too long.)

So if students are sipping text constantly on their devices, and sud- *17* denly they are asked to consume what sounds like an insurmountable mountain of pages in some other form—and for what!?—they are likely to avoid it entirely.

"Flipping the classroom" has attempted to seek some kind of account- *18* ability from students for their reading, so that they have to engage in one way or another with their material prior to assembling for the precious moment of face-to-face interaction. This requires reading—but reading with a goal. Students often like to do that, as a kind of scavenger hunt for what is useful and important. Just having them read for background ideas seems to be fading.

Actually, I have stopped worrying constantly about this. Students *19* are reading. The public is reading. They may not sit for hours, still and attentive, and focus on one item. They may confuse their facts. They may miss a complex argument.

Don't misunderstand. I worship reading. When I travel for three *20* days, in addition to all my devices I bring six books and five (print) magazines. Yet I cannot concentrate the way I used to. So those less devoted. . . . Should we cut them off from the world, isolate them in soundproof rooms with no WiFi, and force them to read a book?

Writing has evolved, and will evolve. And with it reading changes.   *21*
From clay tablets designed to record debts to bronze proclamations of
kings and emperors, from bamboo strips recording rituals to complex
philosophical arguments on paper, from paintings for the royal afterlife
to paperback novels, from stone tablets proclaiming a new moral code
to infinitesimal elements on a shiny handheld device—from its origins,
writing has transformed, and will continue to change. It is not entirely
that the medium is the message, but the medium affects the message.
Since humans are the ones doing the writing, we get the writing that
suits our purposes.

We are all getting a front-row seat to a sudden change in medium, and   *22*
therefore in writing and reading. What a quick and shocking ride this is!

Read all about it!   *23*

ANALYZING AND COMPARING ARGUMENTS

As an academic writer, you will often need to compare disparate claims
and evidence from multiple arguments addressing the same topic. Rarely,
however, will those arguments be simplistic pro/con pairs meant to represent two opposing sides to an issue. Certainly the news media thrive on
such black-and-white conflict, but academic writers seek greater complexity and do not expect to find simple answers. Analyzing and comparing essays on the same topic or issue will often reveal the ways writers
work with similar evidence to come up with different, and not necessarily
opposed, arguments.

The next two selections are arguments about grade inflation. Both are
brief, and we recommend you read through them quickly as a prelude to
the activity in analyzing and comparing arguments that follows them. As
you read, try to note their claims, the reasons used to support them, concessions, and counterarguments.

STUART ROJSTACZER

Grade Inflation Gone Wild

A former professor of geophysics at Duke University with a PhD in applied
earth sciences, Stuart Rojstaczer has written or coauthored many geo-
logical studies in his career as a scientist. He has also published a book,
Gone for Good: Tales of University Life After the Golden Age (1999), and
numerous articles on higher education and grading. He is the creator of
gradeinflation.com, where he posts a variety of charts and graphs chronicling his data about grade inflation. This op-ed piece appeared in the
Christian Science Monitor on March 24, 2009.

■ ■ ■

A bout six years ago, I was sitting in the student union of a small lib-eral arts college when I saw a graph on the cover of the student newspaper that showed the history of grades given at that institution in the past 30 years.

Grades were up. Way up.

I'm a scientist by training and I love numbers. So when I looked at that graph, I wondered, "How many colleges and universities have data like this that I can find?" The answer is that a lot of schools have data like this hidden somewhere. Back then, I found more than 80 col-leges and universities with data on grades, mostly by poking around the Web. Then I created a website (gradeinflation.com) so that others could find this data. I learned that grades started to shoot up nationwide in the 1960s, leveled off in the 1970s, and then started rising again in the 1980s. Private schools had much higher grades than public schools, but virtually everyone was experiencing grade inflation.

What about today?

Grades continue to go up regardless of the quality of education. At a time when many are raising questions about the quality of U.S. higher education, the average GPA at public schools is 3.0, with many flagship state schools having average GPAs higher than 3.2. At a private college, the average is now 3.3. At some schools, it tops 3.5 and even 3.6. "A" is average at those schools! At elite Brown University, two-thirds of all letter grades given are now A's.

These changes in grading have had a profound influence on college life and learning. When students walk into a classroom knowing that they can go through the motions and get a B+ or better, that's what they tend to do, give minimal effort. Our college classrooms are filled with students who do not prepare for class. Many study less than 10 hours a week—that's less than half the hours they spent studying 40 years ago. Paradoxically, students are spending more and more money for an edu-cation that seems to deliver less and less content.

With so few hours filled with learning, boredom sets in and students have to find something to pass the time. Instead of learning, they drink. A recent survey of more than 30,000 first-year students across the coun-try showed that nearly half were spending more hours drinking than they were studying. If we continue along this path, we'll end up with a generation of poorly educated college graduates who have used their four years principally to develop an addiction to alcohol.

There are many who say that grade inflation is a complicated issue with no easy fix. But there are solutions. At about the same time that I started to collect data on rising grades, Princeton University began to actually do something about its grade-inflation problem. Its guidelines have the effect of now limiting A's on average to 35 percent of students in a class. Those guidelines have worked. Grades are going back down at Princeton and academic rigor is making a comeback. A similar successful effort has taken place at Wellesley College in Massachusetts. And through a concerted effort on the part of faculty and leadership, grades at Reed College in Oregon have stayed essentially constant for 20 years.

Princeton, Wellesley, and Reed provide evidence that the effort to keep grade inflation in check is not impossible. This effort takes two major steps. First, school officials must admit that there is a problem. Then they must implement policies or guidelines that truly restore excellence.   9

I asked Dean Nancy Malkiel at Princeton why so few schools seem to be following Princeton's lead. "Because it's hard work," she answered. "Because you have to persuade the faculty that it's important to do the work."   10

Making a switch will take hard work, but the effort is worthwhile. The alternative is a student body that barely studies and drinks out of boredom. That's not acceptable. Colleges and universities must roll up their sleeves, bring down inflated grades, and encourage real learning. It's not an impossible task. There are successful examples that can be followed. I'm looking forward to the day when we can return to being proud of the education that our nation's colleges and universities provide.   11

PHIL PRIMACK

Doesn't Anybody Get a C Anymore?

Phil Primack is a journalist, editor, and policy analyst who teaches journalism at Tufts University, where he is a senior fellow at the Jonathan M. Tisch College of Citizenship and Public Service. His articles have appeared in many regional and national publications, including the *New York Times*, the *Boston Globe*, and *Columbia Journalism Review*. The following piece appeared in the *Boston Globe* on October 5, 2008.

■ ■ ■

The student deserved a B-minus. Maybe even a C-plus, I had decided. One paper was especially weak; another was late. But then I began to rationalize. The student had been generally prepared and contributed to class discussion, so I relented and gave what I thought was a very generous B. At least I wouldn't get a complaint about this grade, I figured. Then came the e-mail.   1

Why such a "low grade," the indignant student wrote.   *2*

"Low grade"? Back when I attended Tufts in the late 1960s, a B in   *3*
certain courses was something I could only dream about. But grade
inflation, the steady rise in grade point averages that began in the
1960s, now leaves many students regarding even the once-acceptable
B—which has always stood for "good"—as a transcript wrecker, and
a C—that is, "average"—as unmitigated disaster. More and more academic leaders may lament grade inflation, but precious few have been
willing to act against it, leaving their professors all alone in the mine-
field between giving marks that reflect true merit and facing the wrath
of students for whom entitlement begins with the letter A.

Grade inflation "is a huge problem," says former U.S. senator Hank   *4*
Brown, who tried to make it a priority issue as president of the University of Colorado in 2006. "Under the current system at a lot of schools,
there is no way to recognize the difference between an outstanding job
and a good job. Grade inflation hides laziness on the part of the students, and as long as it exists, even faculty who want to do a good job [in
grading] don't feel they can."

That's because many professors fear that "tough grading" will trig-   *5*
ger poor student evaluations or worse, which in turn can jeopardize the
academic career track. "In my early years, students would say they liked
my class, but the grades were low and the work level high," says retired
Duke University professor Stuart Rojstaczer. "I had to get with the program and reduce my own expectations of workload and increase grades
in order to have students leave my class with a positive impression to
give to other students so they would attend [next year]. I was teaching
worse, but the student response was much more positive."

Harvard University is the poster campus for academic prestige—and   *6*
for grade inflation, even though some of its top officials have warned
about grade creep. About 15 percent of Harvard students got a B-plus
or better in 1950, according to one study. In 2007, more than half of all
Harvard grades were in the A range. Harvard declined to release more
current data or officially comment for this article. At the University of
Massachusetts at Amherst, the average GPA in 2007 was 3.19 (on a four-
point scale), up from 3.02 a decade earlier. That "modest increase" simply reflects better students, UMass spokesman Ed Blaguszewski says in
an e-mail. "Since our students have been increasingly well-prepared . . .
it makes sense that their UMass grades have crept up. Essentially, the
profile of the population has changed over time, so we don't consider
this to be grade inflation."

That's certainly the most common argument to explain away grade   *7*
inflation—smarter students naturally get higher grades. But is it that
simple? Privately, many faculty members and administrators say colleges are unwilling to challenge and possibly offend students and their
hovering, tuition-paying parents with some tough grade love. And

without institutional backing, individual faculty members simply yield to whining students.

But not everywhere. The most cited—and extreme—case of taking on grade inflation is at Princeton University, which in 2004 directed that A's account for less than 35 percent of undergraduate course grades. From 2004 to 2007, A's (A-plus, A, A-minus) accounted for 40.6 percent of undergraduate course grades, down from 47 percent in the period 2001 to 2004.

Closer to home, Wellesley College calls for the average grade in basic undergraduate courses to be no higher than a B-plus (3.33 GPA). "It's not that we're trying to get grades down, but we're trying to get grades to mean something," says associate dean of the college Adele Wolfson, who teaches chemistry. Wellesley's GPA, which stood at 3.47 in 2002 and was 3.4 when the policy was implemented two years later, fell to 3.3 this year, mainly because of more B grades and fewer A's. "The A has really become the mark of excellence," she says, "which is what it should be."

The problem, says Rojstaczer, is that such policies are the exceptions, and that grade inflation will be reduced only through consistent prodding and action by top officials. "In truth, some university leaders are embarrassed that grading is so lax, but they are loath to make any changes," he says in an e-mail. "Grade inflation in academia is like the alcoholic brother you pretend is doing just fine. When someone calls your brother a drunk, you get angry and defend him, although privately you worry. That's where we are with grade inflation: public denial and private concern."

A Practice Sequence: Analyzing and Comparing Arguments

1 To practice these strategies, first break up into small groups to discuss four different concerns surrounding grade inflation:

Group 1: Define what you think grade inflation is.

Group 2: Discuss whether you think grade inflation is a problem at the university or college you attend. What evidence can you provide to suggest that it is or is not a problem?

Group 3: Why should students or faculty be concerned with grade inflation? What's at stake?

Group 4: How would you respond if the administration at your university or college decided to limit the number of A's that faculty could give students?

Reassemble as a class and briefly report on the discussions.

2 Analyze Stuart Rojstaczer's argument in "Grade Inflation Gone Wild," addressing the following questions:

- What evidence does Rojstaczer use to indicate that there is a problem?

- How would you characterize this evidence (for example, scientific, anecdotal), and to what extent are you persuaded by the evidence he provides to suggest that grade inflation has a profound effect on "life and learning"?

- To what extent does he persuade you that a change in policy is necessary or that such a change would make a difference?

3 Now compare Phil Primack's and Stuart Rojstaczer's strategies for developing an argument.

- How does Primack establish that there is a problem? To what extent is his approach as persuasive as Rojstaczer's?

- What strategies would you identify in either argument as strategies that you might employ to develop your own argument?

- To what extent are you persuaded by the counterargument that Primack introduces?

- What do you think Primack wants you to do or think about in his analysis?

- In the end, does Primack add anything to your understanding of the problem of whether your college or university should introduce a policy to limit grade inflation?

4 As an alternative assignment, write a three-page essay in which you compare the arguments student Marques Camp and Professor Susan D. Blum make about the state of reading today. Consider their main claims and how they support them. Explain which argument you find more persuasive, and why. Feel free to draw on your own experience and make use of personal anecdotes to make your case.

4

From Identifying Issues
to Forming Questions

Remember that inquiry is central to the process of composing. As you move from reading texts to writing them, you will discover that writing grows out of answering these questions:

- What are the concerns of the authors I've been reading?
- What situations motivate them to write?
- What frames or contexts do they use to construct their arguments?
- What is my argument in response to their writing?
- What is at stake in my argument?
- Who will be interested in reading what I have to say?
- How can I connect with both sympathetic and antagonistic readers?
- What kinds of evidence will persuade my readers?
- What objections are they likely to raise?

To answer these questions, you must read in the role of writer, with an eye toward

- *identifying an issue* (an idea or a statement that is open to dispute) that compels you to respond in writing,
- *understanding the situation* (the factors that give rise to the issue and shape your response), and
- *formulating a question* (what you intend to answer in response to the issue).

In Table 4.1, we identify a series of situations and one of the issues and questions that derive from each of them. Notice that the question

TABLE 4.1   A Series of Situations with Related Issues and Questions

Situation	Issue	Question
Different state legislatures are passing legislation to prevent Spanish-speaking students from using their own language in schools.	Most research on learning contradicts the idea that students should be prevented from using their own language in the process of learning a new language.	Under what conditions should students be allowed to use their own language while they learn English?
A manufacturing company has plans to move to your city with the promise of creating new jobs in a period of high unemployment.	You feel that this company will compromise the quality of life for the surrounding community because the manufacturing process will pollute the air.	What would persuade the city to prevent this company from moving in, even though the company will provide much-needed jobs?
Your school has made an agreement with a local company to supply vending machines that sell drinks and food. The school plans to use its share of the profits to improve the library and purchase a new scoreboard for the football field.	You see that the school has much to gain from this arrangement, but you also know that obesity is a growing problem at the school.	Is there another way for the school to generate needed revenue without putting students' health at risk?
An increasing number of homeless people are seeking shelter on your college campus.	Campus security has stepped up its efforts to remove the homeless, even though the shelters off campus are overcrowded.	How can you persuade the school to shelter the homeless and to provide funds to support the needs of the homeless in your city?

you ask defines the area of inquiry as you read; it also can help you formulate your working thesis, the statement that answers your question. (We say more about developing a thesis in Chapter 5.) In this chapter, in addition to further discussing the importance of situation, we look at how you can identify issues and formulate questions to guide your reading and writing.

IDENTIFYING ISSUES

In this section we present several steps to identifying an issue. You don't have to follow them in this particular order, and you may find yourself going back and forth among them as you try to bring an issue into focus.

Keep in mind that issues do not simply exist in the world well formed. Instead, writers construct what they see as issues from the situations they observe. For example, consider legislation to limit downloads from the Internet. If such legislation conflicts with your own practices and sense of freedom, you may have begun to identify an issue: the clash of values over what constitutes fair use and what does not. Be aware that others may not understand your issue and that in your writing you will have to explain carefully what is at stake.

■ Draw on Your Personal Experience

You may have been taught that formal writing is objective, that you must keep a dispassionate distance from your subject, and that you should not use *I* in a college-level paper. The fact is, however, that our personal experiences influence how we read, what we pay attention to, and what inferences we draw. It makes sense, then, to begin with you—where you are and what you think and believe.

We all use personal experience to make arguments in our everyday lives. In an academic context, the challenge is to use personal experience to argue a point, to illustrate something, or to illuminate a connection between theories and the sense we make of our daily experience. You don't want simply to tell your story. You want your story to strengthen your argument.

For example, in *Cultural Literacy*, E. D. Hirsch personalizes his interest in reversing the cycle of illiteracy in America's cities. To establish the nature of the problem in the situation he describes, he cites research showing that student performance on standardized tests in the United States is falling. But he also reflects on his own teaching in the 1970s, when he first perceived "the widening knowledge gap [that] caused me to recognize the connection between specific background knowledge and mature literacy." And he injects anecdotal evidence from conversations with his son, a teacher. Those stories heighten readers' awareness that school-aged children do not know much about literature, history, or government. (For example, his son mentions a student who challenged his claim that Latin is a "dead language" by demanding, "What do they speak in Latin America?")

Hirsch's use of his son's testimony makes him vulnerable to criticism, as readers might question whether Hirsch can legitimately use his son's experience to make generalizations about education. But in fact, Hirsch is using personal testimony—his own and his son's—to augment and put a human face on the research he cites. He presents his issue, that schools must teach cultural literacy, both as something personal and as something with which we should all be concerned. The personal note helps readers see Hirsch as someone who has long been concerned with education and who has even raised a son who is an educator.

■ Identify What Is Open to Dispute

An issue is something that is open to dispute. Sometimes the way to clarify an issue is to think of it as a *fundamental tension* between two or more conflicting points of view. If you can identify conflicting points of view, an issue may become clear.

Consider E. D. Hirsch, who believes that the best approach to educational reform (the subject he writes about) is to change the curriculum in schools. His position: A curriculum based on cultural literacy is the one sure way to reverse the cycle of poverty and illiteracy in urban areas.

What is the issue? Hirsch's issue emerges in the presence of an alternative position. Jonathan Kozol, a social activist who has written extensively about educational reform, believes that policymakers need to address reform by providing the necessary resources that all students need to learn. Kozol points out that students in many inner-city schools are reading outdated textbooks and that the dilapidated conditions in these schools—windows that won't close, for example—make it impossible for students to learn.

In tension are two different views of the reform that can reverse illiteracy: Hirsch's view that educational reform should occur through curricular changes, and Kozol's view that educational reform demands socioeconomic resources.

■ Resist Binary Thinking

As you begin to define what is at issue, try to tease out complexities that may not be immediately apparent. That is, try to resist the either/or mindset that signals binary thinking.

If you considered only what Hirsch and Kozol have to say, it would be easy to characterize the problems facing our schools as either curricular or socioeconomic. But it may be that the real issue combines these arguments with a third or even a fourth, that neither curricular nor socioeconomic changes by themselves can resolve the problems with American schools.

After reading essays by both Hirsch and Kozol, one of our students pointed out that both Hirsch's focus on curriculum and Kozol's socioeconomic focus ignore another concern. She went on to describe her school experience in racial terms. In the excerpt below, notice how this writer uses personal experience (in a new school, she is not treated as she had expected to be treated) to formulate an issue.

> Moving from Colorado Springs to Tallahassee, I was immediately struck by the differences apparent in local home life, school life, and community unity, or lack thereof. Ripped from my sheltered world at a small Catholic school characterized by racial harmony, I was thrown into a large public school where outward prejudice from classmates and teachers and "race wars" were common and tolerated. . . .
>
> In a school where students and teachers had free rein to abuse anyone different from them, I was constantly abused. As the only black student in English honors, I was commonly belittled in front of my "peers" by my teacher. If I developed courage enough to ask a question, I was always answered with the use of improper grammar and such words as "ain't" as my teacher attempted to simplify

the material to "my level" and to give me what he called "a little learning." After discussing several subjects, he often turned to me, singling me out of a sea of white faces, and asked, "Do *you* understand, Mila?" When asking my opinion of a subject, he frequently questioned, "What do *your* people think about this?" Although he insisted on including such readings as Martin Luther King's "I Have a Dream" speech in the curriculum, the speech's themes of tolerance and equity did not accompany his lesson.

Through her reading, this student discovered that few prominent scholars have confronted the issue of racism in schools directly. Although she grants that curricular reform and increased funding may be necessary to improve education, she argues that scholars also need to address race in their studies of teaching and learning.

Our point is that issues may be more complex than you first think they are. For this student, the issue wasn't one of two positions—reform the curriculum or provide more funding. Instead, it combined a number of different positions, including race ("prejudice" and "race wars") and the relationship between student and teacher ("Do *you* understand, Mila?") in a classroom.

In this passage, the writer uses her experience to challenge binary thinking. Like the student writer, you should examine issues from different perspectives, avoiding either/or propositions that oversimplify the world.

■ Build on and Extend the Ideas of Others

Academic writing builds on and extends the ideas of others. As an academic writer, you will find that by extending other people's ideas, you will extend your own. You may begin in a familiar place, but as you read more and pursue connections to other readings, you may well end up at an unexpected destination.

For example, one of our students was troubled when he read Melissa Stormont-Spurgin's description of homeless children. The student uses details from her work (giving credit, of course) in his own:

> The children . . . went to school after less than three hours of sleep. They wore the same wrinkled clothes that they had worn the day before. What will their teachers think when they fall asleep in class? How will they get food for lunch? What will their peers think? What could these homeless children talk about with their peers? They have had to grow up too fast. Their worries are not the same as other children's worries. They are worried about their next meal and where they will seek shelter. Their needs, however, are the same. They need a home and all of the securities that come with it. They also need an education (Stormont-Spurgin 156).

Initially the student was troubled by his own access to quality schools, and the contrast between his life and the lives of the children Stormont-Spurgin describes. Initially, then, his issue was the fundamental tension between his own privileged status, something he had taken for granted, and the struggle that homeless children face every day.

However, as he read further and grew to understand homelessness as a concern in a number of studies, he connected his personal response to a larger conversation about democracy, fairness, and education:

> Melissa Stormont-Spurgin, an author of several articles on educational studies, addresses a very real and important, yet avoided issue in education today. Statistics show that a very high percentage of children who are born into homeless families will remain homeless, or in poverty, for the rest of their lives. How can this be, if everyone actually does have the same educational opportunities? There must be significant educational disadvantages for children without homes. In a democratic society, I feel that we must pay close attention to these disadvantages and do everything in our power to replace them with equality.

Ultimately, the student refined his sense of what was at issue: *Although all people should have access to public education in a democratic society, not everyone has the opportunity to attend quality schools in order to achieve personal success.* In turn, his definition of the issue began to shape his argument:

> Parents, teachers, homeless shelters, and the citizens of the United States who fund [homeless] shelters must address the educational needs of homeless children, while steering them away from any more financial or psychological struggles. Without this emphasis on education, the current trend upward in the number of homeless families will inevitably continue in the future of American society.

The student shifted away from a personal issue—the difference between his status and that of homeless children—to an issue of clashing values: the principle of egalitarian democracy on the one hand and the reality of citizens in a democracy living in abject poverty on the other. When he started to read about homeless children, he could not have made the claim he ends up making, that policymakers must make education a basic human right.

This student offers us an important lesson about the role of inquiry and the value of resisting easy answers. He has built on and extended his own ideas—and the ideas of others—after repeating the process of reading, raising questions, writing, and seeing problems a number of times.

■ Read to Discover a Writer's Frame

A more specialized strategy of building on and extending the ideas of others involves reading to discover a writer's **frame**, the perspective through which a writer presents his or her arguments. Writers want us to see the world a certain way, so they frame their arguments much the same way photographers and artists frame their pictures.

For example, if you were to take a picture of friends in front of the football stadium on campus, you would focus on what you would most like to remember—your friends' faces—blurring the images of the people walking behind your friends. Setting up the picture, or framing it, might require using light and shade to make some details stand out more than others. Writers do the same with language.

E. D. Hirsch uses the concept of *cultural literacy* to frame his argument for curricular reform. For Hirsch, the term is a benchmark, a standard: People who are culturally literate are familiar with the body of information that every educated citizen should know. Hirsch's implication, of course, is that people who are not culturally literate are not well educated. But that is not necessarily true. In fact, a number of educators insist that literacy is simply a means to an end—reading to complete an assignment, for example, or to understand the ramifications of a decision—not an end in itself. By defining and using *cultural literacy* as the goal of education, Hirsch is framing his argument; he is bringing his ideas into focus.

When writers use framing strategies, they also call attention to the specific conversations that set up the situation for their arguments. Framing often entails quoting specific theories and ideas from other authors and then using those quotations as a perspective, or lens, through which to examine other material. In his memoir *Hunger of Memory: The Education of Richard Rodriguez* (1982), Richard Rodriguez uses this method to examine his situation as a nonnative speaker of English desperate to enter the mainstream culture, even if it means sacrificing his identity as the son of Mexican immigrants. Reflecting on his life as a student, Rodriguez comes across Richard Hoggart's book *The Uses of Literacy* (1957). Hoggart's description of "the scholarship boy" presents a lens through which Rodriguez can see his own experience. Hoggart writes:

> With his family, the boy has the intense pleasure of intimacy, the family's consolation in feeling public alienation. Lavish emotions texture home life. *Then*, at school, the instruction bids him to trust lonely reason primarily. Immediate needs set the pace of his parents' lives. From his mother and father the boy learns to trust spontaneity and nonrational ways of knowing. *Then*, at school, there is mental calm. Teachers emphasize the value of a reflectiveness that opens a space between thinking and immediate action.
>
> Years of schooling must pass before the boy will be able to sketch the cultural differences in his day as abstractly as this. But he senses those differences early. Perhaps as early as the night he brings home an assignment from school and finds the house too noisy for study. He has to be more and more alone, if he is going to "get on." He will have, probably unconsciously, to oppose the ethos of the hearth, the intense gregariousness of the working-class family group. . . . The boy has to cut himself off mentally, so as to do his homework, as well as he can.

Here is Rodriguez's response to Hoggart's description of the scholarship boy:

For weeks I read, speed-read, books by modern educational theorists, only
to find infrequent and slight mention of students like me. . . . Then one day,
leafing through Richard Hoggart's *The Uses of Literacy*, I found, in his description of the scholarship boy, myself. For the first time I realized that there were
other students like me, and so I was able to frame the meaning of my academic success, its consequent price—the loss.

Notice how Rodriguez introduces ideas from Hoggart "to frame" his
own ideas: "I found, in his description of the scholarship boy, myself. For
the first time I realized that there were other students like me, and so I
was able to frame the meaning of my academic success, its consequent
price—the loss." Hoggart's scholarship boy enables Rodriguez to revisit
his own experience with a new perspective. Hoggart's words and idea advance Rodriguez's understanding of the problem he identifies in his life:
his inability to find solace at home and within his working-class roots.
Hoggart's description of the scholarship boy's moving between cultural
extremes—spontaneity at home and reflection at school—helps Rodriguez bring his own youthful discontent into focus.

Rodriguez's response to Hoggart's text shows how another writer's
lens can help frame an issue. If you were using Hoggart's term *scholarship
boy* as a lens through which to clarify an issue in education, you might
ask how the term illuminates new aspects of another writer's examples
or your own. And then you might ask, "To what extent does Hirsch's cultural literacy throw a more positive light on what Rodriguez and Hoggart
describe?" or "How do my experiences challenge, extend, or complicate
the scholarship-boy concept?"

■ Consider the Constraints of the Situation

In identifying an issue, you have to understand the situation that gives rise
to the issue, including the contexts in which it is raised and debated. One of
the contexts is the *audience*. In thinking about your issue, you must consider
the extent to which your potential readers are involved in the dialogue you
want to enter, and what they know and need to know. In a sense, audience
functions as both context and **constraint**, a factor that narrows the choices
you can make in responding to an issue. An understanding of your potential
readers will help you choose the depth of your discussion; it will also determine the kind of evidence you can present and the language you can use.

Another constraint on your response to an issue is the form that
response takes. For example, if you decide to make an issue of govern-
ment- imposed limits on what you can download from the Internet, your
response in writing might take the form of an editorial or a letter to a leg-
islator. In this situation, length is an obvious constraint: Newspapers limit
the word count of editorials, and the best letters to legislators tend to be
brief and very selective about the evidence they cite. A few personal examples and a few statistics may be all you can include to support your claim
about the issue. By contrast, if you were making your case in an academic

journal, a very different set of constraints would apply. You would have more space for illustrations and support, for example.

Finally, the situation itself can function as a major constraint. For instance, suppose your topic is the decline of educational standards. It's difficult to imagine any writer making the case for accelerating that decline, or any audience being receptive to the idea that a decline in standards is a good thing.

Steps to Identifying Issues

1 **Draw on your personal experience.** Start with your own sense of what's important, what puzzles you, or what you are curious about. Then build your argument by moving on to other sources to support your point of view.

2 **Identify what is open to dispute.** Identify a phenomenon or some idea in a written argument that challenges what you think or believe.

3 **Resist binary thinking.** Think about the issue from multiple perspectives.

4 **Build on and extend the ideas of others.** As you read, be open to new ways of looking at the issue. The issue you finally write about may be very different from what you set out to write about.

5 **Read to discover a writer's frame.** What theories or ideas shape the writer's focus? How can these theories or ideas help you frame your argument?

6 **Consider the constraints of the situation.** Craft your argument to meet the needs of and constraints imposed by your audience and form.

IDENTIFYING ISSUES IN AN ESSAY

In the following editorial, published in 2002 in *Newsweek*, writer Anna Quindlen addresses her concern that middle-class parents overschedule their children's lives. She calls attention to the ways leisure time helped her develop as a writer and urges parents to consider the extent to which children's creativity depends on having some downtime. They don't always have to have their time scheduled. As you read Quindlen's "Doing Nothing Is Something," note what words and phrases Quindlen uses to identify the situation and to indicate who her audience is. Identify her main claim as one of fact, value, or policy. Finally, answer the questions that follow the selection to see if you can discern how she locates, defines, and advances her issue.

ANNA QUINDLEN

Doing Nothing Is Something

Anna Quindlen is a best-selling author of novels and children's books, but she is perhaps most widely known for her nonfiction and commentary on current events and contemporary life. She won a Pulitzer Prize in 1992 for her "Public and Private" column in the *New York Times*, and for ten years wrote a biweekly column for *Newsweek*. Some of her novels are *Object Lessons* (1991), *Blessings* (2002), and *Every Last One* (2010). Her nonfiction works and collections include *Living Out Loud* (1988), *Thinking Out Loud* (1994), *Loud and Clear* (2004), and *Good Dog. Stay.* (2007).

＊ ＊ ＊

Summer is coming soon. I can feel it in the softening of the air, but I can see it, too, in the textbooks on my children's desks. The number of uncut pages at the back grows smaller and smaller. The loose-leaf is ragged at the edges, the binder plastic ripped at the corners. An old remembered glee rises inside me. Summer is coming. Uniform skirts in mothballs. Pencils with their points left broken. Open windows. Day trips to the beach. Pickup games. Hanging out.   1

How boring it was.   2

Of course, it was the making of me, as a human being and a writer. Downtime is where we become ourselves, looking into the middle distance, kicking at the curb, lying on the grass, or sitting on the stoop and staring at the tedious blue of the summer sky. I don't believe you can write poetry, or compose music, or become an actor without downtime, and plenty of it, a hiatus that passes for boredom but is really the quiet moving of the wheels inside that fuel creativity.   3

And that, to me, is one of the saddest things about the lives of American children today. Soccer leagues, acting classes, tutors—the calendar of the average middle-class kid is so over the top that soon Palm handhelds will be sold in Toys "R" Us. Our children are as overscheduled as we are, and that is saying something.   4

This has become so bad that parents have arranged to schedule times for unscheduled time. Earlier this year the privileged suburb of Ridgewood, New Jersey, announced a Family Night, when there would be no homework, no athletic practices, and no after-school events. This was terribly exciting until I realized that this was not one night a week, but one single night. There is even a free-time movement, and Web site: familylife1st.org. Among the frequently asked questions provided online: "What would families do with family time if they took it back?"   5

Let me make a suggestion for the kids involved: How about nothing? It is not simply that it is pathetic to consider the lives of children who don't have a moment between piano and dance and homework to talk   6 about their day or just search for split ends, an enormously satisfying leisure-time activity of my youth. There is also ample psychological research suggesting that what we might call "doing nothing" is when human beings actually do their best thinking, and when creativity comes to call. Perhaps we are creating an entire generation of people whose ability to think outside the box, as the current parlance of business has it, is being systematically stunted by scheduling.

A study by the University of Michigan quantified the downtime   7
deficit; in the last twenty years American kids have lost about four unstructured hours a week. There has even arisen a global Right to Play movement: in the Third World it is often about child labor, but in the United States it is about the sheer labor of being a perpetually busy child. In Omaha, Nebraska, a group of parents recently lobbied for additional recess. Hooray, and yikes.

How did this happen? Adults did it. There is a culture of adult distrust   8
that suggests that a kid who is not playing softball or attending science-enrichment programs—or both—is huffing or boosting cars: If kids are left alone, they will not stare into the middle distance and consider the meaning of life and how come your nose in pictures never looks the way you think it should, but instead will get into trouble. There is also the culture of cutthroat and unquestioning competition that leads even the parents of preschoolers to gab about prestigious colleges without a trace of irony: This suggests that any class in which you do not enroll your first grader will put him at a disadvantage in, say, law school.

Finally, there is a culture of workplace presence (as opposed to pro-   9
ductivity). Try as we might to suggest that all these enrichment activities are for the good of the kid, there is ample evidence that they are really for the convenience of parents with way too little leisure time of their own. Stories about the resignation of presidential aide Karen Hughes unfailingly reported her dedication to family time by noting that she arranged to get home at 5:30 one night a week to have dinner with her son. If one weekday dinner out of five is considered laudable, what does that say about what's become commonplace?

Summer is coming. It used to be a time apart for kids, a respite from   10
the clock and the copybook, the organized day. Every once in a while, either guilty or overwhelmed or tired of listening to me keen about my monumental boredom, my mother would send me to some rinky-dink park program that consisted almost entirely of three-legged races and making things out of Popsicle sticks. Now, instead, there are music camps, sports camps, fat camps, probably thin camps. I mourn hanging out in the backyard. I mourn playing Wiffle ball in the street without a sponsor and matching shirts. I mourn drawing in the dirt with a stick.

Maybe that kind of summer is gone for good. Maybe this is the lead-   11
ing edge of a new way of living that not only has no room for contemplation but is contemptuous of it. But if downtime cannot be squeezed

during the school year into the life of frantic and often joyless activity with which our children are saddled while their parents pursue frantic and often joyless activity of their own, what about summer? Do most adults really want to stand in line for Space Mountain or sit in traffic to get to a shore house that doesn't have enough saucepans? Might it be even more enriching for their children to stay at home and do nothing? For those who say they will only watch TV or play on the computer, a piece of technical advice: The cable box can be unhooked, the modem removed. Perhaps it is not too late for American kids to be given the gift of enforced boredom for at least a week or two, staring into space, bored out of their gourds, exploring the inside of their own heads. "To contemplate is to toil, to think is to do," said Victor Hugo. "Go outside and play," said Prudence Quindlen. Both of them were right.

Reading as a Writer

1. What evidence of Quindlen's personal responses and experiences can you identify?

2. What phenomenon has prompted her to reflect on what she thinks and believes? How has she made it into an issue?

3. Where does she indicate that she has considered the issue from multiple perspectives and is placing her ideas in conversation with those of others?

4. What sort of lens does she seem to be using to frame her argument?

5. What constraints (such as the format of an editorial) seem to be in play in the essay?

A Practice Sequence: Identifying Issues

This sequence of activities will give you practice in identifying and clarifying issues based on your own choice of reading and collaboration with your classmates.

1　Draw on your personal experience. Reflect on your own responses to what you have been reading in this class or in other classes, or issues that writers have posed in the media. What concerns you most? Choose a story that supports or challenges the claims people are making in what you have read or listened to. What questions do you have? Make some notes in response to these questions, explaining your personal stake in the issues and questions you formulate.

2　Identify what is open to dispute. Take what you have written and formulate your ideas as an issue, using the structure we used in our example of Hirsch's and Kozol's competing arguments:

- Part 1: Your view of a given topic
- Part 2: At least one view that is in tension with your own

If you need to, read further to understand what others have to say about this issue.

3   Resist binary thinking. Share your statement of the issue with one or more peers and ask them if they see other ways to formulate the issue that you may not have thought about. What objections, if any, do they make to your statement in part 1? Write these objections down in part 2 so that you begin to look at the issue from multiple perspectives.

4   Build on and extend the ideas of others. Now that you have formulated an issue from different perspectives, explaining your personal stake in the issue, connect what you think to a broader conversation in what you are reading. Then try making a claim using this structure: "Although some people would argue _____, I think that _____."

5   Read to discover a writer's frame. As an experiment in trying out multiple perspectives, revise the claim you make in exercise 4 by introducing the frame, or lens, through which you want readers to understand your argument. You can employ the same sentence structure. For example, here is a claim framed in terms of race: "Although people should have access to public education, recent policies have worsened racial inequalities in public schools." In contrast, here is a claim that focuses on economics: "Although people should have access to public education, the unequal distribution of tax money has created what some would call an 'economy of education.'" The lens may come from reading you have done in other courses or from conversations with your classmates, and you may want to attribute the lens to a particular author or classmate: "Although some people would argue_____, I use E. D. Hirsch's notion of cultural literacy to show_____."

6   Consider the constraints of the situation. Building on these exercises, develop an argument in the form of an editorial for your local newspaper. This means that you will need to limit your argument to about 250 words. You also will need to consider the extent to which your potential readers are involved in the conversation. What do they know? What do they need to know? What kind of evidence do you need to use to persuade readers?

FORMULATING ISSUE-BASED QUESTIONS

As we have said, when you identify an issue, you need to understand it in the context of its situation. Ideally, the situation and the issue will be both relevant and recent, making the task of connecting to your audience that much easier when you write about the issue. For example, the student writer who was concerned about long-standing issues of homelessness and lack of educational opportunity connected to his readers by citing recent statistics and giving the problem of homelessness a face: "The children . . . went to school after less than three hours of sleep. They wore the same wrinkled clothes that they had worn the day before." If your issue does not immediately fulfill the criteria of relevance and timeliness, you need to take that into consideration as you continue your reading and research on the issue. Ask yourself, "What is on people's minds these days?" "What do they need to know about?" Think about why the issue matters to you, and imagine why it might matter to others. By the time you write, you should be prepared to make the issue relevant for your readers.

In addition to understanding the situation and defining the issue that you feel is most relevant and timely, you can formulate an issue-based question that can help you think through what you might be interested in writing about. This question should be specific enough to guide inquiry into what others have written. An issue-based question can also help you accomplish the following:

- clarify what you know about the issue and what you still need to know;
- guide your inquiry with a clear focus;
- organize your inquiry around a specific issue;
- develop an argument, rather than simply collecting information by asking "how," "why," "should," or "the extent to which something is or is not true";
- consider who your audience is;
- determine what resources you have, so that you can ask a question that you will be able to answer with the resources available to you.

A good question develops out of an issue, some fundamental tension that you identify within a conversation. In "Doing Nothing Is Something," Anna Quindlen identifies a problem that middle-class parents need to know about: that overscheduling their children's lives may limit their children's potential for developing their creativity. As she explores the reasons why children do not have sufficient downtime, she raises a question that encourages parents to consider what would happen if they gave their children time to do nothing: "Might it be even more enriching for their children to stay at home and do nothing?" (para. 11). Through identifying what is at issue, you should begin to understand for whom it is an issue— for whom you are answering the question. In turn, the answer to your question will help you craft your thesis.

In the following section, we trace the steps one of our students took to formulate an issue-based question on the broad topic of language diversity. Although we present the steps in sequence, be aware that they are guidelines only: The steps often overlap, and there is a good deal of room for rethinking and refining along the way.

■ Refine Your Topic

Generally speaking, a **topic** is the subject you want to write about. For example, homelessness, tests, and violence are all topics. So are urban homelessness, standardized tests, and video game violence. And so are homelessness in New York City, aptitude tests versus achievement tests, and mayhem in the video game *Grand Theft Auto*. As our list suggests, even a specific topic needs refining into an issue before it can be explored effectively in writing.

The topic our student wanted to focus on was language diversity, a subject her linguistics class had been discussing. She was fascinated by the extraordinary range of languages spoken in the United States, not just by immigrant groups but by native speakers whose dialects and varieties of English are considered nonstandard. She herself had relatives for whom English was not a first language. She began refining her topic by putting her thoughts into words:

> I want to describe the experience of being raised in a home where non–Standard English is spoken.

> I'd like to know the benefits and liabilities of growing up bilingual.

> I am curious to know what it's like to live in a community of nonnative speakers of English while trying to make a living in a country where the dominant language is English.

Although she had yet to identify an issue, her attempts to articulate what interested her about the topic were moving her toward the situation of people in the United States who don't speak Standard English or don't have English as their first language.

■ Explain Your Interest in the Topic

At this point, the student encountered E. D. Hirsch's *Cultural Literacy* in her reading, which had both a provocative and a clarifying effect on her thinking. She began to build on and extend Hirsch's ideas. Reacting to Hirsch's assumption that students should acquire the same base of knowledge and write in Standard Written English, her first, somewhat mischievous thought was, "I wonder what Hirsch would think about cultural literacy being taught in a bilingual classroom?" But then her thinking took another turn, and she began to contemplate the effect of Hirsch's cultural-literacy agenda on speakers whose English is not standard or for whom English is not a first language. She used a demographic fact that she had learned in her linguistics class in her explanation of her interest in the topic: "I'm curious about the consequences of limiting language diversity when the presence of ethnic minorities in our educational system is growing."

▪ Identify an Issue

The more she thought about Hirsch's ideas, and the more she read about language diversity, the more concerned our student grew. It seemed to her that Hirsch's interest in producing students who all share the same base of knowledge and all write in Standard Written English was in tension with her sense that this kind of approach places a burden on people whose first language is not English. That tension clarified the issue for her. In identifying the issue, she wrote:

> Hirsch's book actually sets some priorities, most notably through his list of words and phrases that form the foundations of what it means to be "American." However, this list certainly overlooks several crucial influences in American culture. Most oversights generally come at the expense of the minority populations.

These two concerns—with inclusion and with exclusion—helped focus the student's inquiry.

▪ Formulate Your Topic as a Question

To further define her inquiry, the student formulated her topic as a question that pointed toward an argument: "To what extent can E. D. Hirsch's notion of 'cultural literacy' coexist with our country's principles of democracy and inclusion?" Notice that her choice of the phrase *To what extent* implies that both goals do not go hand in hand. If she had asked, "Can common culture coexist with pluralism?" her phrasing would imply that a yes or no answer would suffice, possibly foreclosing avenues of inquiry and certainly ignoring the complexity of the issue.

Instead, despite her misgivings about the implications of Hirsch's agenda, the student suspended judgment, opening the way to genuine inquiry. She acknowledged the usefulness and value of sharing a common language and conceded that Hirsch's points were well taken. She wrote:

> Some sort of unification is necessary. Language, . . . on the most fundamental level of human interaction, demands some compromise and chosen guidelines. . . . How can we learn from one another if we cannot even say hello to each other?

Suspending judgment led her to recognize the complexity of the issue, and her willingness to examine the issue from different perspectives indicated the empathy that is a central component of developing a conversational argument.

▪ Acknowledge Your Audience

This student's question ("To what extent can E. D. Hirsch's notion of 'cultural literacy' coexist with our country's principles of democracy and inclusion?") also acknowledged an audience. By invoking cultural literacy, she assumed an audience of readers who are familiar with Hirsch's ideas, probably including policymakers and educational administrators. In gesturing toward democracy, she cast her net very wide: Most Americans probably admire the "principles of democracy." But in specifying inclusion as a democratic principle, she wisely linked all Americans who believe in democratic principles, including the parents of schoolchildren, with all people who have reason to feel excluded by Hirsch's ideas, especially nonnative speakers of English, among them immigrants from Mexico and speakers of African American Vernacular English. Thus, this student was acknowledging an audience of policymakers, administrators, parents (both mainstream and marginalized), and those who knew about and perhaps supported cultural literacy.

Steps to Formulating an Issue-Based Question

1 **Refine your topic.** Examine your topic from different perspectives. For example, what are the causes of homelessness? What are its consequences?

2 **Explain your interest in the topic.** Explore the source of your interest in this topic and what you want to learn.

3 **Identify an issue.** Determine what is open to dispute.

4 **Formulate your topic as a question.** Use your question to focus your inquiry.

5 **Acknowledge your audience.** Reflect on what readers may know about the issue, why they may be interested, and what you would like to teach them.

A Practice Sequence: Formulating an Issue-Based Question

As you start developing your own issue-based question, it might be useful to practice a five-step process that begins with a topic, a word or phrase that describes the focus of your interests. Here, apply the process to the one-word topic *homelessness*.

1   Expand your topic into a phrase. "I am interested in the *consequences* of homelessness," "I want to *describe* what it means to be homeless," or "I am interested in discussing the *cause* of homelessness."

2   Explain your interest in this topic. "I am interested in the consequences of homelessness because it challenges democratic principles of fairness."

3   Identify an issue. "The persistence of homelessness contradicts my belief in social justice."

4   Formulate your topic as a question. "To what extent can we allow homelessness to persist in a democratic nation that prides itself on providing equal opportunity to all?"

5   Acknowledge your audience. "I am interested in the consequences of homelessness because I want people who believe in democracy to understand that we need to work harder to make sure that everyone has access to food, shelter, and employment."

The answer to the question you formulate in step 4 should lead to an assertion, your main claim, or *thesis*. For example, you could state your main claim this way: "Although homelessness persists as a widespread problem in our nation, we must develop policies that eliminate homelessness, ensuring that everyone has access to food, shelter, and employment. This is especially important in a democracy that embraces social justice and equality."

The thesis introduces a problem and makes an assertion that you will need to support: "We must develop policies that eliminate homelessness, ensuring that everyone has access to food, shelter, and employment." What is at issue? Not everyone would agree that policies must be implemented to solve the problem. In fact, many would argue that homelessness is an individual problem, that individuals must take responsibility for lifting themselves out of poverty, homelessness, and unemployment. Of course, you would need to read quite a bit to reach this final stage of formulating your thesis.

Try using the five-step process we describe above to formulate your own topic as a question, or try formulating the following topics as questions:

- violence in video games
- recycling
- the popularity of a cultural phenomenon (a book, a film, a performer, an icon)
- standardized tests
- professional sports injuries
- town-gown relationships
- media representation and gender
- government and religion
- vegetarianism

AN ACADEMIC ESSAY FOR ANALYSIS

The following essay by William Deresiewicz provides an intriguing academic extension of the homely topic that Anna Quindlen writes about (p. 89): the need for the young to have solitary, unscheduled time. His essay illustrates many of the strategies we have discussed thus far: raising questions, stating a thesis by placing an argument in the stream of a broader conversation, using evidence to support his claims. As you read Deresiewicz's essay, you might use the following questions as a guide:

- What is Deresiewicz's thesis? Would you characterize his claim as one of fact? Value?
- What types of evidence does he use to support his claim?
- What do Deresiewicz's vocabulary and citations indicate about his target audience?
- What does Deresiewicz want his readers to do or think about?

WILLIAM DERESIEWICZ

The End of Solitude

William Deresiewicz taught English at Yale University from 1998 to 2008. He is now a contributing writer at *The Nation* and was nominated for a 2009 National Magazine Award for his reviews and criticism. His essay "The End of Solitude" appeared in *The Chronicle of Higher Education* in January 2009 and represents one of many debates about literacy that scholars have waged concerning the benefits and limits of new technologies. Deresiewicz observes that technology fulfills a human impulse to be known, to be connected with others. Posting on MySpace, Twitter, and Facebook enables us to be visible and helps validate who we are as individuals. However, he worries that this instinct to be connected also has an adverse effect: We lose a sense of solitude and the space he believes we all need to have in order to understand who we are, what we believe, and what we value. He worries, too, that a new generation does not see the point of solitude because so many young people equate solitude with loneliness.

◾ ◾ ◾

W hat does the contemporary self want? The camera has created a culture of celebrity; the computer is creating a culture of connectivity. As the two technologies converge—broadband tipping the Web from text to image, social-networking sites spreading the mesh of interconnection ever wider—the two cultures betray a common impulse. Celebrity and connectivity are both ways of becoming known. This is what the contemporary self wants. It wants to be recognized, wants to be connected: It wants to be visible. If not to the millions, on *Survivor* or *Oprah*, then to the hundreds, on Twitter or Facebook. This is the quality that validates us, this is how we become real to ourselves—by being seen by others. The great contemporary terror is anonymity. If Lionel Trilling was right, if the property that grounded the self, in Romanticism, was sincerity, and in modernism it was authenticity, then in postmodernism it is visibility.

So we live exclusively in relation to others, and what disappears from our lives is solitude. Technology is taking away our privacy and our concentration, but it is also taking away our ability to be alone. Though I shouldn't say taking away. We are doing this to ourselves; we are discarding these riches as fast as we can. I was told by one of her older relatives that a teenager I know had sent 3,000 text messages one recent month. That's 100 a day, or about one every 10 waking minutes, morning, noon, and night, weekdays and weekends, class time, lunch time, homework time, and toothbrushing time. So on average, she's never alone for more than 10 minutes at once. Which means, she's never alone.

I once asked my students about the place that solitude has in their lives. One of them admitted that she finds the prospect of being alone so unsettling that she'll sit with a friend even when she has a paper to write. Another said, why would anyone want to be alone?

To that remarkable question, history offers a number of answers. Man may be a social animal, but solitude has traditionally been a societal value. In particular, the act of being alone has been understood as an essential dimension of religious experience, albeit one restricted to a self-selected few. Through the solitude of rare spirits, the collective renews its relationship with divinity. The prophet and the hermit, the sadhu and the yogi, pursue their vision quests, invite their trances, in desert or forest or cave. For the still, small voice speaks only in silence. Social life is a bustle of petty concerns, a jostle of quotidian interests, and religious institutions are no exception. You cannot hear God when people are chattering at you, and the divine word, their pretensions notwithstanding, demurs at descending on the monarch and the priest. Communal experience is the human norm, but the solitary encounter with God is the egregious act that refreshes that norm. (Egregious, for no man is a prophet in his own land. Tiresias was reviled before he was vindicated, Teresa interrogated before she was canonized.) Religious solitude is a kind of self-correcting social mechanism, a way of burning out the underbrush of moral habit and spiritual custom. The seer returns with new tablets or new dances, his face bright with the old truth.

Like other religious values, solitude was democratized by the Reformation and secularized by Romanticism. In Marilynne Robinson's interpretation, Calvinism created the modern self by focusing the soul inward, leaving it to encounter God, like a prophet of old, in "profound isolation." To her enumeration of Calvin, Marguerite de Navarre, and

Milton as pioneering early-modern selves we can add Montaigne, Hamlet, and even Don Quixote. The last figure alerts us to reading's essential role in this transformation, the printing press serving an analogous function in the sixteenth and subsequent centuries to that of television and the Internet in our own. Reading, as Robinson puts it, "is an act of great inwardness and subjectivity." "The soul encountered itself in response to a text, first Genesis or Matthew and then *Paradise Lost* or *Leaves of Grass*." With Protestantism and printing, the quest for the divine voice became available to, even incumbent upon, everyone.

But it is with Romanticism that solitude achieved its greatest cultural salience, becoming both literal and literary. Protestant solitude is still only figurative. Rousseau and Wordsworth made it physical. The self was now encountered not in God but in Nature, and to encounter Nature one had to go to it. And go to it with a special sensibility: The poet displaced the saint as social seer and cultural model. But because Romanticism also inherited the eighteenth-century idea of social sympathy, Romantic solitude existed in a dialectical relationship with sociability—if less for Rousseau and still less for Thoreau, the most famous solitary of all, then certainly for Wordsworth, Melville, Whitman, and many others. For Emerson, "the soul environs itself with friends, that it may enter into a grander self-acquaintance or solitude; and it goes alone, for a season, that it may exalt its conversation or society." The Romantic practice of solitude is neatly captured by Trilling's "sincerity": the belief that the self is validated by a congruity of public appearance and private essence, one that stabilizes its relationship with both itself and others. Especially, as Emerson suggests, one beloved other. Hence the famous Romantic friendship pairs: Goethe and Schiller, Wordsworth and Coleridge, Hawthorne and Melville.

Modernism decoupled this dialectic. Its notion of solitude was harsher, more adversarial, more isolating. As a model of the self and its interactions, Hume's social sympathy gave way to Pater's thick wall of personality and Freud's narcissism—the sense that the soul, self-enclosed and inaccessible to others, can't choose but be alone. With exceptions, like Woolf, the modernists fought shy of friendship. Joyce and Proust disparaged it; D. H. Lawrence was wary of it; the modernist friendship pairs—Conrad and Ford, Eliot and Pound, Hemingway and Fitzgerald—were altogether cooler than their Romantic counterparts. The world was now understood as an assault on the self, and with good reason.

The Romantic ideal of solitude developed in part as a reaction to the emergence of the modern city. In modernism, the city is not only more menacing than ever, it has become inescapable, a labyrinth: Eliot's London, Joyce's Dublin. The mob, the human mass, presses in. Hell is other people. The soul is forced back into itself—hence the development of a more austere, more embattled form of self-validation, Trilling's "authenticity," where the essential relationship is only with oneself. (Just as there are few good friendships in modernism, so are there few good marriages.) Solitude becomes, more than ever, the arena of heroic self-discovery, a voyage through interior realms made vast and terrifying by Nietzschean and Freudian insights. To achieve authenticity is to look upon these visions without flinching; Trilling's exemplar here is Kurtz. Protestant self-examination becomes Freudian analysis, and the culture hero, once a prophet of God and then a poet of Nature, is now a novelist of self—a Dostoyevsky, a Joyce, a Proust.

But we no longer live in the modernist city, and our great fear is not submersion by the mass but isolation from the herd. Urbanization gave way to suburbanization, and with it the universal threat of loneliness. What technologies of transportation exacerbated—we could live farther and farther apart—technologies of communication redressed—we could bring ourselves closer and closer together. Or at least, so we have imagined. The first of these technologies, the first simulacrum of proximity, was the telephone. "Reach out and touch someone." But through the 1970s and 1980s, our isolation grew. Suburbs, sprawling ever farther, became exurbs. Families grew smaller or splintered apart, mothers left the home to work. The electronic hearth became the television in every room. Even in childhood, certainly in adolescence, we were each trapped inside our own cocoon. Soaring crime rates, and even more sharply escalating rates of moral panic, pulled children off the streets. The idea that you could go outside and run around the neighborhood with your friends, once unquestionable, has now become unthinkable. The child who grew up between the world wars as part of an extended family within a tight-knit urban community became the grandparent of a kid who sat alone in front of a big television, in a big house, on a big lot. We were lost in space.

Under those circumstances, the Internet arrived as an incalculable blessing. We should never forget that. It has allowed isolated people to communicate with one another and marginalized people to find one another. The busy parent can stay in touch with far-flung friends. The gay teenager no longer has to feel like a freak. But as the Internet's dimensionality has grown, it has quickly become too much of a good thing. Ten years ago we were writing e-mail messages on desktop computers and transmitting them over dial-up connections. Now we are sending text messages on our cell phones, posting pictures on our Facebook pages, and following complete strangers on Twitter. A constant stream of mediated contact, virtual, notional, or simulated, keeps us wired in to the electronic hive—though contact, or at least two-way contact, seems increasingly beside the point. The goal now, it seems, is simply to become known, to turn oneself into a sort of miniature celebrity. How many friends do I have on Facebook? How many people are reading my blog? How many Google hits does my name generate? Visibility secures our self-esteem, becoming a substitute, twice removed, for genuine connection. Not long ago, it was easy to feel lonely. Now, it is impossible to be alone.

As a result, we are losing both sides of the Romantic dialectic. *11* What does friendship mean when you have 532 "friends"? How does it enhance my sense of closeness when my Facebook News Feed tells me that Sally Smith (whom I haven't seen since high school, and wasn't all that friendly with even then) "is making coffee and staring off into space"? My students told me they have little time for intimacy. And of course, they have no time at all for solitude.

But at least friendship, if not intimacy, is still something they want. *12* As jarring as the new dispensation may be for people in their 30s and 40s, the real problem is that it has become completely natural for people in their teens and 20s. Young people today seem to have no desire for solitude, have never heard of it, can't imagine why it would be worth having. In fact, their use of technology—or to be fair, our use of technology—seems to involve a constant effort to stave off the possibility of solitude, a continuous attempt, as we sit alone at our computers, to maintain the imaginative presence of others. As long ago as 1952, Trilling wrote about "the modern fear of being cut off from the social group even for a moment." Now we have equipped ourselves with the means to prevent that fear from ever being realized. Which does not mean that we have put it to rest. Quite the contrary. Remember my student, who couldn't even write a paper by herself. The more we keep aloneness at bay, the less are we able to deal with it and the more terrifying it gets.

There is an analogy, it seems to me, with the previous generation's *13* experience of boredom. The two emotions, loneliness and boredom, are closely allied. They are also both characteristically modern. The *Oxford English Dictionary*'s earliest citations of either word, at least in the contemporary sense, date from the nineteenth century. Suburbanization, by eliminating the stimulation as well as the sociability of urban or traditional village life, exacerbated the tendency to both. But the great age of boredom, I believe, came in with television, precisely because television was designed to palliate that feeling. Boredom is not a necessary consequence of having nothing to do, it is only the negative experience of that state. Television, by obviating the need to learn how to make use of one's lack of occupation, precludes one from ever discovering how to enjoy it. In fact, it renders that condition fearsome, its prospect intolerable. You are terrified of being bored—so you turn on the television.

I speak from experience. I grew up in the 1960s and 1970s, the age *14* of television. I was trained to be bored; boredom was cultivated within me like a precious crop. (It has been said that consumer society wants to condition us to feel bored, since boredom creates a market for stimulation.) It took me years to discover—and my nervous system will never fully adjust to this idea; I still have to fight against boredom, am permanently damaged in this respect—that having nothing to do doesn't have to be a bad thing. The alternative to boredom is what Whitman called idleness: a passive receptivity to the world.

So it is with the current generation's experience of being alone. That is precisely the recognition implicit in the idea of solitude, which is to loneliness what idleness is to boredom. Loneliness is not the absence of company, it is grief over that absence. The lost sheep is lonely; the shepherd is not lonely. But the Internet is as powerful a machine for the production of loneliness as television is for the manufacture of boredom. If six hours of television a day creates the aptitude for boredom, the inability to sit still, a hundred text messages a day creates the aptitude for loneliness, the inability to be by yourself. Some degree of boredom and loneliness is to be expected, especially among young people, given the way our human environment has been attenuated. But technology amplifies those tendencies. You could call your schoolmates when I was a teenager, but you couldn't call them 100 times a day. You could get together with your friends when I was in college, but you couldn't always get together with them when you wanted to, for the simple reason that you couldn't always find them. If boredom is the great emotion of the TV generation, loneliness is the great emotion of the Web generation. We lost the ability to be still, our capacity for idleness. They have lost the ability to be alone, their capacity for solitude. 15

And losing solitude, what have they lost? First, the propensity for introspection, that examination of the self that the Puritans, and the Romantics, and the modernists (and Socrates, for that matter) placed at the center of spiritual life—of wisdom, of conduct. Thoreau called it fishing "in the Walden Pond of [our] own natures," "bait[ing our] hooks with darkness." Lost, too, is the related propensity for sustained reading. The Internet brought text back into a televisual world, but it brought it back on terms dictated by that world—that is, by its remapping of our attention spans. Reading now means skipping and skimming; five minutes on the same Web page is considered an eternity. This is not reading as Marilynne Robinson described it: the encounter with a second self in the silence of mental solitude. 16

But we no longer believe in the solitary mind. If the Romantics had Hume and the modernists had Freud, the current psychological model— and this should come as no surprise—is that of the networked or social mind. Evolutionary psychology tells us that our brains developed to interpret complex social signals. According to David Brooks, that reliable index of the social-scientific zeitgeist, cognitive scientists tell us that "our decision-making is powerfully influenced by social context"; neuroscientists, that we have "permeable minds" that function in part through a process of "deep imitation"; psychologists, that "we are organized by our attachments"; sociologists, that our behavior is affected by "the power of social networks." The ultimate implication is that there is 17 no mental space that is not social (contemporary social science dove-tailing here with postmodern critical theory). One of the most striking things about the way young people relate to one another today is that they no longer seem to believe in the existence of Thoreau's "darkness."

The MySpace page, with its shrieking typography and clamorous im-agery, has replaced the journal and the letter as a way of creating and communicating one's sense of self. The suggestion is not only that such communication is to be made to the world at large rather than to one-self or one's intimates, or graphically rather than verbally, or performa-tively rather than narratively or analytically, but also that it can be made completely. Today's young people seem to feel that they can make them-selves fully known to one another. They seem to lack a sense of their own depths, and of the value of keeping them hidden.   *18*

If they didn't, they would understand that solitude enables us to   *19* secure the integrity of the self as well as to explore it. Few have shown this more beautifully than Woolf. In the middle of *Mrs. Dalloway*, between her navigation of the streets and her orchestration of the party, between the urban jostle and the social bustle, Clarissa goes up, "like a nun withdrawing," to her attic room. Like a nun: She returns to a state that she herself thinks of as a kind of virginity. This does not mean she's a prude. Virginity is classically the outward sign of spiritual inviolability, of a self untouched by the world, a soul that has preserved its integrity by refusing to descend into the chaos and self-division of sexual and social relations. It is the mark of the saint and the monk, of Hippolytus and Antigone and Joan of Arc. Solitude is both the social image of that state and the means by which we can approximate it. And the supreme image in *Mrs. Dalloway* of the dignity of solitude itself is the old woman whom Clarissa catches sight of through her window. "Here was one room," she thinks, "there another." We are not merely social beings. We are each also separate, each solitary, each alone in our own room, each miracu-lously our unique selves and mysteriously enclosed in that selfhood.

To remember this, to hold oneself apart from society, is to begin to   *20* think one's way beyond it. Solitude, Emerson said, "is to genius the stern friend." "He who should inspire and lead his race must be defended from traveling with the souls of other men, from living, breathing, read-ing, and writing in the daily, time-worn yoke of their opinions." One must protect oneself from the momentum of intellectual and moral consensus—especially, Emerson added, during youth. "God is alone," Thoreau said, "but the Devil, he is far from being alone; he sees a great deal of company; he is legion." The university was to be praised, Emerson believed, if only because it provided its charges with "a separate cham-ber and fire"—the physical space of solitude. Today, of course, universi-ties do everything they can to keep their students from being alone, lest they perpetrate self-destructive acts, and also, perhaps, unfashionable thoughts. But no real excellence, personal or social, artistic, philosophi-cal, scientific, or moral, can arise without solitude. "The saint and poet seek privacy," Emerson said, "to ends the most public and universal." We are back to the seer, seeking signposts for the future in splendid isolation.

Solitude isn't easy, and isn't for everyone. It has undoubtedly never been the province of more than a few. "I believe," Thoreau said, "that men are generally still a little afraid of the dark." Teresa and Tiresias will always be the exceptions, or to speak in more relevant terms, the young people—and they still exist—who prefer to loaf and invite their soul, who step to the beat of a different drummer. But if solitude disappears as a social value and social idea, will even the exceptions remain possible? Still, one is powerless to reverse the drift of the culture. One can only save oneself—and whatever else happens, one can still always do that. But it takes a willingness to be unpopular.

21

The last thing to say about solitude is that it isn't very polite. Thoreau knew that the "doubleness" that solitude cultivates, the ability to stand back and observe life dispassionately, is apt to make us a little unpleasant to our fellows, to say nothing of the offense implicit in avoiding their company. But then, he didn't worry overmuch about being genial. He didn't even like having to talk to people three times a day, at meals; one can only imagine what he would have made of text-messaging. We, however, have made of geniality —the weak smile, the polite interest, the fake invitation—a cardinal virtue. Friendship may be slipping from our grasp, but our friendliness is universal. Not for nothing does "gregarious" mean "part of the herd." But Thoreau understood that securing one's self-possession was worth a few wounded feelings. He may have put his neighbors off, but at least he was sure of himself. Those who would find solitude must not be afraid to stand alone.

22

Writing as a Reader

1. Recast Deresiewicz's essay as Anna Quindlen might in her *Newsweek* column. Obviously, her *Newsweek* column is much shorter (an important constraint). She also writes for a more general audience than Deresiewicz, and her tone is quite different. To strengthen your sense of her approach, you may want to browse some of Quindlen's other essays in editions of *Newsweek* or in some of her essay collections listed in the headnote on page 89.

2. Recast Deresiewicz's essay in terms of a writer you read regularly—for example, a columnist in your local newspaper or a blogger in some online venue. Use your imagination. What is the audience, and how will you have to present the issue to engage and persuade them?

5

From Formulating to Developing a Thesis

Academic writing explores complex issues that grow out of relevant, timely conversations in which something is at stake. An academic writer reads as a writer to understand the issues, situations, and questions that lead other writers to make claims. Readers expect academic writers to take a clear, specific, logical stand on an issue, and they evaluate how writers support their claims and anticipate counterarguments. The logical stand is the **thesis**, an assertion that academic writers make at the beginning of what they write and then support with evidence throughout their essay. The illustrations and examples that a writer includes must relate to and support the thesis. Thus, a thesis encompasses all of the information writers use to further their arguments; it is not simply a single assertion at the beginning of an essay.

One of our students aptly described the thesis using the metaphor of a shish kebab: The thesis penetrates every paragraph, holding the paragraphs together, just as a skewer penetrates and holds the ingredients of a shish kebab together. Moreover, the thesis serves as a signpost throughout an essay, reminding readers what the argument is and why the writer has included evidence—examples, illustrations, quotations—relevant to that argument.

An academic thesis

- makes an assertion that is clearly defined, focused, and supported.
- reflects an awareness of the conversation from which the writer has taken up the issue.
- is placed at the beginning of the essay.

- penetrates every paragraph like the skewer in a shish kebab.
- acknowledges points of view that differ from the writer's own, reflecting the complexity of the issue.
- demonstrates an awareness of the readers' assumptions and anticipates possible counterarguments.
- conveys a significant fresh perspective.

It is a myth that writers first come up with a thesis and then write their essays. The reality is that writers use issue-based questions to read, learn, and develop a thesis throughout the process of writing. Through revising and discussing their ideas, writers hone their thesis, making sure that it threads through every paragraph of the final draft. The position writers ultimately take in writing—their thesis—comes at the end of the writing process, after not one draft but many.

WORKING VERSUS DEFINITIVE THESES

Writers are continually challenged by the need to establish their purpose and to make a clear and specific assertion of it. To reach that assertion, you must first engage in a prolonged process of inquiry, aided by a well-formulated question. The question serves as a tool for inquiry that will help you formulate your **working thesis**, your first attempt at an assertion of your position. A working thesis is valuable in the early stages of writing because it helps you read selectively, in the same way that your issue-based question guides your inquiry. Reading raises questions, helping you see what you know and need to know, and challenging you to read on.

Never accept your working thesis as your final position. Instead, continue testing your assertion as you read and write, and modify your working thesis as necessary. A more definitive thesis will come once you are satisfied that you have examined the issue from multiple perspectives.

For example, one of our students wanted to study representations of femininity in the media. In particular, she focused on why the Barbie doll has become an icon of femininity despite what many cultural critics consider Barbie's "outrageous and ultimately unattainable physical characteristics." Our student's working thesis suggested she would develop an argument about the need for change:

> The harmful implications of ongoing exposure to these unattainable ideals, such as low self-esteem, eating disorders, unhealthy body image, and acceptance of violence, make urgent the need for change.

The student assumed that her research would lead her to argue that Barbie's unattainable proportions have a damaging effect on women's self-image and that something needs to be done about it. However, as she read scholarly research to support her tentative thesis, she realized that a more compelling project would be less Barbie-centric. Instead, she chose to examine the broader phenomenon of how the idea of femininity is created and reinforced by society. That is, her personal interest in Barbie was supplanted by her discoveries about cultural norms of beauty and the power they have to influence self-perception and behavior. In her final draft, this was her definitive thesis:

> Although evidence may be provided to argue that gender is an innate characteristic, I will show that it is actually the result of one's actions, which are then labeled *masculine* or *feminine* according to society's definitions of ideal gender. Furthermore, I will discuss the communication of such definitions through the media, specifically in music videos, on TV, and in magazines, and the harmful implications of being exposed to these ideals.

Instead of arguing for change, the student chose to show her readers how they were being manipulated, leaving it to them to decide what actions they might want to take.

DEVELOPING A WORKING THESIS: FOUR MODELS

What are some ways to develop a working thesis? We suggest four models that may help you organize the information you gather in response to the question guiding your inquiry.

▪ The Correcting-Misinterpretations Model

This model is used to correct writers whose arguments you believe have misconstrued one or more important aspects of an issue. The thesis typically takes the form of a factual claim. Consider this example and the words we have underlined:

> <u>Although scholars have addressed curriculum</u> to explain low achievement in schools, <u>they have failed to fully appreciate the impact of limited resources</u> to fund up-to-date textbooks, quality teachers, and computers. Therefore, reform in schools must focus on economic need as well as curriculum.

The clause beginning with "Although" lays out the assumption that many scholars make, that curriculum explains low educational achievement; the clause beginning with "they have failed" identifies the error those scholars have made by ignoring the economic reasons for low achievement in schools. Notice that the structure of the sentence reinforces the author's position. He explains what he sees as the faulty assumption in a subordinate clause and reserves the main clause for his own position. The two clauses indicate that different authors hold conflicting opinions. Note that the writer could have used a phrase such as "they [scholars] have *understated* the impact of limited resources" as a way to reframe the problem in his thesis. In crafting your thesis, choose words that signal to readers that you are correcting others' ideas, or even misinterpretations, without being dismissive. One more thing: Although it is a common myth that a thesis can be phrased in a single sentence (a legacy of the five-paragraph theme, we suspect), this example shows that a thesis can be written in two (or more) sentences.

■ The Filling-the-Gap Model

The gap model points to what other writers may have overlooked or ignored in discussing a given issue. The gap model typically makes a claim of value. Consider this student's argument that discussions of cultural diversity in the United States are often framed in terms of black and white. Our underlining indicates the gap the writer has identified:

> If America is truly a "melting pot" of cultures, as it is often called, then why is it that stories and events seem only to be in black and white? Why is it that when history courses are taught about the period of the civil rights movement, only the memoirs of African Americans are read, like those of Melba Pattillo Beals and Ida Mae Holland? Where are the works of Maxine Hong Kingston, who tells the story of alienation and segregation in schools through the eyes of a Chinese child? African Americans were denied the right to vote, and many other citizenship rights; but Chinese Americans were denied even the opportunity to become citizens. I am not diminishing the issue of discrimination against African Americans, or belittling the struggles they went through. I simply want to call attention to discrimination against other minority groups and their often-overlooked struggles to achieve equality.

In the student's thesis, the gap in people's knowledge stems from their limited understanding of history. They need to understand that many minority groups were denied their rights.

A variation on the gap model also occurs when a writer suggests that although something might appear to be the case, a closer look reveals something different. For example: "Although it would *appear* that women have achieved equality in the workplace, their paychecks suggest that this is not true."

One of our students examined two poems by the same author that appeared to contradict each other. She noticed a gap others had not seen:

> In both "The Albatross" and "Beauty," Charles Baudelaire chooses to explore the plight of the poet. Interestingly, despite their common author, the two poems' portrayals of the poet's struggles appear contradictory. "The Albatross" seems to give a somewhat sympathetic glimpse into the exile of the poet — the "winged voyager" so awkward in the ordinary world. "Beauty" takes what appears to be a less

> forgiving stance: The poet here is docile, simply a mirror. Although both pieces depict the poet's struggles, a closer examination demonstrates how the portrayals differ.

In stating her thesis, the student indicates that although readers might expect Baudelaire's images of poets to be similar, a closer examination of his words would prove them wrong.

■ The Modifying-What-Others-Have-Said Model

The modification model of thesis writing assumes that mutual understanding is possible. For example, in proposing a change in policy, one student asserts:

> Although scholars have claimed that the only sure way to reverse the cycle of homelessness in America is to provide an adequate education, we need to build on this work, providing school-to-work programs that ensure graduates have access to employment.

Here the writer seeks to modify other writers' claims, suggesting that education alone does not solve the problem of homelessness. The challenge he sets for himself is to understand the complexity of the problem by building on and extending the ideas of others. In effect, he is in a constructive conversation with those whose work he wants to build on, helping readers see that he shares common ground with the other writers and that he hopes to find a mutually acceptable solution to the agreed-on problem.

■ The Hypothesis-Testing Model

The hypothesis-testing model begins with the assumption that writers may have good reasons for supporting their arguments, but that there are also a number of legitimate reasons that explain why something is, or is not, the case. The questions motivating your research will often lead you to a number of possible answers, but none are necessarily more correct than others. That is, the evidence is based on a hypothesis that researchers will continue to test by examining individual cases through an inductive method until the evidence refutes that hypothesis.

For example, researchers have generated a number of hypotheses to explain the causes of climate change. Some argue that climate change, or global warming, can be explained by natural causes, that change is a cyclical process. Those who adopt such a view might use evidence to demonstrate that oceans produce heat and that change can be attributed to a steady increase in heat production over time. Others have persuasively shown that humans have caused global warming by burning fossil fuels that increase the amount of carbon in the air, which creates what scientists call the "greenhouse effect." Each assertion is based on a set of inferences from observation and the data available to test each hypothesis. Moreover, the truth value of any assertion is based on the probability that global warming can be attributed to any one cause or explanation. At this point, we don't have definitive evidence that an array of natural phenomena or human behavior cause global warming.

The hypothesis-testing model assumes that the questions you raise will likely lead you to multiple answers that compete for your attention. The following is one way to formulate such an argument in which you examine rival hypotheses before coming to a conclusion.

> Some people explain *this* by suggesting *that*, but a close analysis of the problem reveals several compelling, but competing explanations.

You may not find a definitive explanation, so you will need to sort through the evidence you find, develop an argument, and acknowledge the reasonable counterarguments that critical readers will raise. In the end, you are not really proving that something is the case, such as the causes of global warming, but you are helping readers understand what you see as the best case given the available evidence.

Steps to Formulating a Working Thesis: Four Models

1 **Misinterpretations model:** "Although many scholars have argued about A and B, a careful examination suggests C."

2 **Gap model:** "Although scholars have noted A and B, they have missed the importance of C."

3 **Modification model:** "Although I agree with the A and B ideas of other writers, it is important to extend/refine/limit their ideas with C."

4 **Hypothesis-testing model:** "Some people explain A by suggesting B, but a close analysis of the problem reveals the possibility of several competing/complementary explanations such as C, D, and E."

A Practice Sequence: Identifying Types of Theses

Below is a series of working theses. Read each one and then identify the model—misinterpretations, gap, modification, or hypothesis-testing—that it represents.

1 A number of studies indicate that violence on television has a detrimental effect on adolescent behavior. However, few researchers have examined key environmental factors like peer pressure, music, and home life. In fact, I would argue that many researchers have oversimplified the problem.

2 Although research indicates that an increasing number of African American and Hispanic students are dropping out of high school, researchers have failed to fully grasp the reasons why this has occurred.

3 I want to argue that studies supporting single-sex education are relatively sound. However, we don't really know the long-term effects of single-sex education, particularly on young women's career paths.

4 Although recent studies of voting patterns in the United States indicate that young people between the ages of 18 and 24 are apathetic, I want to suggest that not all of the reasons these studies provide are valid.

5 Indeed, it's not surprising that students are majoring in fields that will enable them to get a job after graduation. But students may not be as pragmatic as we think. Many students choose majors because they feel that learning is an important end in itself.

6 Some reformers have assumed that increasing competition will force public schools to improve the quality of education, but it seems that a number of recent initiatives can be used to explain why students have begun to flourish in math and reading, particularly in the primary grades.

7 It is clear that cities need to clean up the dilapidated housing projects that were built over half a century ago; but few, if any, studies have examined the effects of doing so on the life chances of those people who are being displaced.

8 In addition to its efforts to advance the cause of social justice in the new global economy, the university must make a commitment to ending poverty on the edge of campus.

9 Although the writer offers evidence to explain the sources of illiteracy in America, he overstates his case when he ignores other factors, among them history, culture, and economic well-being. Therefore, I will argue that we place the discussion in a broader context.

10 More and more policymakers argue that English should be the national language in the United States. Although I agree that English is important, we should not limit people's right to maintain their own linguistic and cultural identity.

ESTABLISHING A CONTEXT FOR A THESIS

In addition to defining the purpose and focus of an essay, a thesis must set up a **context** for the writer's claim. The process of establishing a background for understanding an issue typically involves four steps:

1. Establish that the topic of conversation, the issue, is current and relevant—that it is on people's minds or should be.

2. Briefly summarize what others have said to show that you are familiar with the topic or issue.

3. Explain what you see as the problem—a misinterpretation, a gap, or a modification that needs to be made in how others have addressed the topic or issue—perhaps by raising the questions you believe need to be answered.

4. State your thesis, suggesting that your view on the issue may present readers with something new to think about as it builds on and extends what others have argued.

You need not follow these steps in this order as long as your readers come away from the first part of your essay knowing why you are discussing a given issue and what your argument is.

AN ANNOTATED STUDENT INTRODUCTION: PROVIDING A CONTEXT FOR A THESIS

We trace these four steps below in our analysis of the opening paragraphs of a student's essay. Motivating his argument is his sense that contemporary writers and educators may not fully grasp the issues that limit the opportunities for low-income youth to attend college. His own family struggled financially, and he argues that a fuller appreciation of the problem can help educators partner with families to advise youth in more informed ways.

Colin O'Neill   O'Neill 1

Money Matters:
Framing the College Access Debate

The student establishes the timeliness and relevance of an issue that challenges widely held assumptions about the value of attending college.

College is expensive. And with prices continuing to rise each year, there are those who are beginning to question whether or not college is a worthy investment. In a recent *Newsweek* article, journalist Megan McArdle (2012) asserts that the process of obtaining a college degree has morphed into a "national neurosis" and calls upon Americans to question whether college is necessary for lifelong success. McArdle joins a chorus of voices calling upon

He begins to summarize what others have said to demonstrate his familiarity with the conversation in popular media and scholarship.

a reevaluation of the current educational pipeline at a time when the number of American students who are ill-prepared to face the rigors of a college curriculum has increased. Some writers suggest that a renaissance of vocational education may, in fact, begin to compensate for the disparate nature of American education. Based on research conducted by Bozick and DeLuca (2011), it is clear that these opinions are grounded in reality.

Of nearly 3,000 surveyed "college non-enrollees," roughly 50 percent attributed their withdrawal from the education system

1

2

O'Neill 2

The student identifies what he sees as a problem signaled by words like "however," "overlooked," and "instead" and begins to formulate his own argument.

to either the high cost of college education or the desire to look for work and embark along their chosen career path. However, for those like me, who believe strongly that higher education is a right that ought to be available to all students, McArdle's and others' assertions add to the list of physical and social barriers that keep students of poorer backgrounds from pursuing their educational aspirations. The ability to pay for college may not be the only consideration keeping students from exploring higher education. Instead, researchers have overlooked the extent to which knowledge (or the lack of it) of college costs and awareness of different financing options (such as grants, scholarships, and loans) may preemptively alter the way in which children envision themselves within the college experience.

He points out a misconception that he wants to correct.

The student cites research to further define the problem and show that he is aware of the very real barriers that affect college access for low-income youth.

In many cities where the median household income often hovers slightly above $30,000, college is, according to some educators, a pipedream to which nearly every family aspires, but most are not convinced this goal will ever become a reality (United States Census Bureau). Indeed, with the average cost of a college education rising to upwards of $20,000, it is unclear whether this dream will, in fact, come true. Although parents have a strong desire to send their kids to college, the financial numbers do not seem to add up. While educators have tended to leave parents responsible for educating their children on the financial realities of higher education, researchers such as Elliot, Sherraden, Johnson, and Guo (2010) make the case that awareness of college costs makes its way into the worldview of students as young as second grade. In light of this work, it becomes important to note that the large price tag of a college degree may have implications that spread far beyond a particular family's capacity to fund their children's education. As the recent research of Bozick and DeLuca (2011) suggests, the cost of college is changing and challenging the way students begin to examine the purpose and necessity of college education. College costs are diminishing one's access to college in more ways than restricting their ability to foot the bill. For low-income students and their families, for whom every day is filled with financial burdens of all sorts, high college costs are changing the way they perceive college as an institution.

He uses research to understand further a problem that others may have overlooked or ignored.

3

The correlation between the college choice process and students' perceptions of the cost of higher education is not an

4

O'Neill 3

unexamined phenomenon. Many researchers have looked at the ways in which the cost of a college education affects the ways low-income students begin to foster a relationship with the college system. The existing body of research, however, has tended to focus solely on high school students, students who are mere months away from beginning the college search process. According to Cabrera and La Nasa (2000), the college choice process actually begins much earlier, commencing between the time a child enters middle school and embarks upon his or her high school journey. It is this process that ultimately dictates the level of college access a particular student does or does not have. Therefore, my study will focus primarily on what Cabrera and La Nasa (2000) termed the "predisposition" stage. Between grades seven and nine, predisposition draws upon parental encouragement, socioeconomic status, and "information about college." Along the trajectory set in place by Cabrera and La Nasa (2000), these factors have a profound influence on the search and choice stages of the college-access process. Recognizing the interrelational nature of these different stages, that is, both how they are different and how each one builds upon the other, is key to navigating the ill-defined nature of the pre-collegiate experience.

Given the findings of prior research, it is important to push back the discussion about college affordability and college access to examine how the notion of cost impacts the fragile, emerging relationship that middle school students are just beginning to develop. To recognize how students begin to understand college and develop college aspirations, then, I conducted interviews with middle school children to assess how early awareness of college costs plays a role in shaping families' decisions about the need, desire for, and accessibility of higher education. By doing so, I have tried to fill gap left behind by previous research and add to the wider discussion of college affordability and its overall impact on college access amongst students of all ages. Although educators may argue that American education ought to revert to an old, draconian system of vocational education, preparing low-income students to enter technical fields, I argue that it is important to create programs that encourage parents, teachers, and students to think early about the costs of college and the possibilities that exist to help children pursue a college degree.

Citing a key study, the student under-scores a gap in the research, again sig-naled by "however."

He adopts a frame through which to think about the issue and narrow his focus.

He begins to offer a solution to a problem research-ers have not fully appreciated.

The student explains that the purpose of his research is to fill the gap he identifies above and correct a misunderstanding.

Here he makes a policy-related claim that chal-lenges a conflicting point of view.

5

■ Establish That the Issue Is Current and Relevant

Ideally, you should convey to readers that the issue you are discussing is both current (what's on people's minds) and relevant (of sufficient importance to have generated some discussion and written conversation). In the first two sentences of the first paragraph, O'Neill explains that the increase in college costs has not only become a focus of national attention, evidenced in a recent issue of *Newsweek*, but has motivated writers to question whether the cost to low-income families is a worthwhile investment. In the next sentence, he explains that the author of this recent piece, Megan McArdle, is not alone in challenging some widely held assumptions about the value of attending college. In fact, O'Neill indicates that McArdle "joins a chorus of voices calling upon a reevaluation of the current educational pipeline at a time when the number of American students who are ill-prepared to face the rigors of a college curriculum has increased." Thus, O'Neill demonstrates that the issue he focuses on is part of a lively conversation and debate that has captured the imagination of many writers at the time he was writing about college access.

■ Briefly Present What Others Have Said

It is important to introduce who has said what in the conversation you are entering. After all, you are interrupting that conversation to make your contribution, and those who are in that conversation expect you to have done your homework and acknowledge those who have already made important contributions.

In the first few sentences of his introduction, O'Neill sets the stage for his review of research by citing McArdle's *Newsweek* article. Although he takes issue with McArdle, he is careful to explain her argument. In addition, he refers to research in the final sentence of the first paragraph to suggest the extent to which her argument may be "grounded in reality." Indeed, in the second paragraph, he cites a study that reports on the significant number of students surveyed who dropped out of college, nearly half attributing their decision to the high costs of pursuing a college degree. However, O'Neill, who makes clear that he believes everyone has a "right" to an education, uses his review to reframe the issue, in particular the extent to which McArdle and others have "overlooked the extent to which knowledge (or the lack of it) of college costs and awareness of different financing options (such as grants, scholarships, and loans) may preemptively alter the way in which children envision themselves within the college experience." In turn, O'Neill calls attention to research that focuses on parents' and children's perceptions of college access as a way to challenge those writers who call for a "reevaluation of the current educational pipeline."

By pointing out what journalists and researchers may have overlooked in discussing the college-going prospects of low-income youth, O'Neill is doing more than listing the sources he has read. He is establishing that a problem, or issue, exists. Moreover, his review gives readers intellectual touchstones, the scholars (e.g., Cabrera and La Nasa [2000]) who need to be cited in any academic conversation about college access. A review is not a catchall for anyone writing on a topic. Instead it should represent a writer's choice of the most relevant participants in the conversation. O'Neill's choice of sources, and how he presents them, convey that he is knowledgeable about his subject. (Of course, it is his readers' responsibility to read further to determine whether he has reviewed the most relevant work and has presented the ideas of others accurately. If he has, readers will trust him, whether or not they end up agreeing with him on the issue.)

▪ Explain What You See as the Problem

If a review indicates a problem, as O'Neill's review does, the problem can often be couched in terms of the models we discussed earlier: misinterpretations, gaps, modification, or hypothesis testing. In paragraph 5, O'Neill identifies what he sees as a gap in how journalists and researchers approach the cost of attending college and who question "whether college is necessary to lifelong success." He suggests that such a view is the consequence of a gap in knowledge (notice our underlining):

> The existing body of research, however, has tended to focus solely on high school students, students who are mere months away from beginning the college search process. According to Cabrera and La Nasa (2000), the college choice process actually begins much earlier, commencing between the time a child enters middle school and embarks upon his or her high school journey.

While O'Neill acknowledges the value of others' writing, his review of research culminates with his assertion that it is important to understand the problem of college costs with greater depth and precision. After all, researchers and print media have overlooked or ignore important sources of information. At stake for O'Neill is that limiting low-income youth's access to higher education challenges a more equitable view that all children deserve a chance to have a successful life. Moreover, at the end of paragraph 4, he shifts the burden from parents, alone, to educators who clearly influence the "way students begin to examine the purpose and necessity of college education."

▪ State Your Thesis

An effective thesis statement helps readers see the reasoning behind a writer's claim; it also signals what readers should look for in the remainder of the essay. O'Neill closes paragraph 5 with a statement that speaks to both the purpose and the substance of what he writes:

> Although educators have argued that American education ought to revert to an old, draconian system of vocational education, preparing low-income students to enter technical fields, I argue that it is important to create programs that encourage

parents, teachers, and students to think early about the costs of college and the possibilities that exist to help children pursue a college degree.

In your own writing, you can make use of the strategies that O'Neill uses in his essay. Words like *although*, *however*, *but*, *instead*, and *yet* can set up the problem you identify. Here is a variation on what O'Neill writes: "One might argue that vocational programs may provide a reasonable alternative to meeting the needs of low-income students for whom college seems unaffordable and out of reach; however [but, yet], such an approach ignores the range of possibilities that exist for changing policies to ensure that all children have access to a college education."

Steps to Establishing a Context for a Thesis

1 **Establish that the issue is current and relevant.** Point out the extent to which others have recognized the problem, issue, or question that you are writing about.

2 **Briefly present what others have said.** Explain how others have addressed the problem, issue, or question you are focusing on.

3 **Explain what you see as the problem.** Identify what is open to dispute.

4 **State your thesis.** Help readers see your purpose and how you intend to achieve it—by correcting a misconception, filling a gap, modifying a claim others have accepted, or stating an hypothesis.

▪ Analyze the Context of a Thesis

In "Teaching Toward Possibility," educator Kris Gutiérrez argues that teaching should focus on student learning and provide students with multiple tools from different disciplines to ensure that students engage in what she describes as "deep learning." She also explains that culture plays a key role in learning, particularly for students from nondominant groups. However, she reframes the notion of culture as a set of practices, as a verb, which she distinguishes from inert conceptions of culture based on individuals' membership in a particular ethnic community. Her essay, published in 2011, is addressed to educators, teachers, and policy makers. As you read the following excerpt, you may be puzzled by some of Gutiérrez's vocabulary and perhaps even excluded from the conversation at times. Our purpose in reprinting this excerpt is to show through our annotations how Gutiérrez has applied the strategies we have been discussing in this chapter. As you read, make your own annotations, and then try to answer the questions—which may involve careful rereading—that we pose after the selection. In particular, watch for signpost words or phrases that signal the ideas the writer is challenging.

KRIS GUTIÉRREZ

From "Teaching Toward Possibility: Building Cultural Supports for Robust Learning"

The author establishes the relevance and timeliness of the issue.

This is particularly relevant for an audience of teachers who want to know how to motivate students whose backgrounds they may unfamiliar with.

Gutiérrez further establishes the relevance of teaching non-dominant students and seeks to correct a misconception about the nature of teaching, learning, and culture.

Consider the potential learning power of a unit on environmental inequities or environment racism for middle or high school students in which students are provided the opportunity to examine the issue deeply and broadly. We did just this over a number of years in rigorous summer programs for high school students from migrant farm worker backgrounds. Students learned environmental science, learned traditional information about the environment, learned about the history of the area of study, as well as the history of environmental issues in their local and immediate communities. This way of learning required interdisciplinary reading, including reading across genres, points of view, and across historical time and space. These learning practices enticed students to want to learn more, to research, and to make connections across relevant ideas and their varied meanings within and across academic and home communities. In short, instruction was coherent, historicized, textured, layered, and deeply supported in ways that allowed students to access and engage with rigorous texts and high status knowledge, as well as work in and through the contradictions and tensions inherent in knowledge production and authentic science/learning issues.

In the following section, I draw on the case of teaching science to migrant students mentioned above to elaborate a challenge to reductive approaches to teaching and learning that offer the "quick-fix" and provide "off the shelf" solutions to education; that is, those relying on silver bullet solutions to solve complex educational problems or using theory and research uncritically or without sufficient understanding because it is fashionable to do so. One such quick-fix approach is found in learning styles approaches to learning, particularly cultural learning styles conceptions in which regularities in cultural

1

2

communities are characterized as static and unchanging and general traits of individuals are attributable categorically to ethnic group membership.

She cites her own work to support her argument and then reviews relevant studies to challenge approaches to teaching and learning that fail to conceptualize the notion of culture adequately.

In my work (Gutiérrez, 2002; Gutiérrez & Rogoff, 2003), I have argued the importance of moving beyond such narrow assumptions of cultural communities by focusing both on regularity and variance in a community's practices (as well as those of individuals). Employing a cultural-historical-activity theoretical approach to learning and development (Cole & Engeström, 2003; Engeström, 1987; Leontiev, 1981) is one productive means toward challenging static and a historical understandings of cultural communities and their practices, as this view focuses attention on variations in individual and group histories of engagement in cultural practices. Variations, then, are best understood as proclivities of people who have particular histories of engagement with specific cultural activities, not as traits of individuals or collections of individuals. In other words, individual and group experience in activities-not their traits-become the focus.

Gutiérrez reframes the way educators should view culture and this new frame is the lens through which she develops her argument.

Through this new conception of culture, Gutiérrez defines what she sees is a gap in what educators know and need to know. She attributes this gap to what educators have ignored and cites additional research to make her point.

Within this view, it becomes easier to understand the limitations of learning styles approaches in which individuals from one group might be characterized as "holistic learners"—where individuals from another group may be characterized as learning analytically or individuals may be divided into cooperative versus individualist learners on the basis of membership in a particular cultural group. Such methods ignore or minimize variation and focus on perceived or overgeneralized regularities. Further, learning styles pedagogical practices have been used to distinguish the learning styles of "minority" group members and to explain "minority" student failure (see Foley, 1997; Kavale & Forness, 1987; Irvine & York, 1995 for reviews). Of consequence, addressing learning styles as traits linked to membership in cultural communities also seems to be a common way to prepare teachers about diversity (Guild, 1994; Matthews, 1991). Understandably, teaching to a difference that can be labeled (e.g., learning modalities) may be appealing to teachers who have limited resources, support, or training to meet the challenges of new student

3

4

populations. However, attribution of learning style or difference based on group membership can serve to buttress persistent deficit model orientations to teaching students from nondominant communities; without acknowledging both the regularity and variance makes it harder to understand the relation of individual learning and the practices of cultural communities, which in turn can hinder effective assistance to student learning (Gutiérrez & Rogoff, 2003).

The key issue here is that learning styles approaches are grounded in reductive notions of culture that conflate race/ethnicity with culture—a practice that often leads to one-size-fits-all approaches and understandings of the learning process of students from nondominant communities. Consider familiar statements such as "My Latino students learn this way" or "I need to teach to the cultural background of my African American students" and even, "Asian students are good at math." Such generalizations are based on the assumption that people hold uniform cultural practices based on their membership in a particular community. Culture from this perspective is something

you can observe from people's phenotype, physical characteristics, national origin, or language. Culture, then, is best considered a verb or said differently, culture is better understood as people's practices or how people live culturally (Moll, 1998). This more dynamic and instrumental role of culture should help us avoid the tendency to conflate culture with race and ethnicity and assumptions about people's cultural practices.

To avoid conflating race/ethnicity with culture, I often remind researchers and educators to invoke the "100-percent Piñata rule"—that is, 100-percent of Mexicans do not hit piñatas 100-percent of the time. While piñatas may in fact be a prevalent cultural artifact in many Mexican and Mexican-descent communities (and now across many household and communities in the Southwest), we would not make generalizations about their use and would expect variation in piñata practices,

their meaning, value, and use. Thus, while cultural artifacts mediate human activity, they have varying functions in use and in practice, just as there is regularity and variance in any cultural community and its practices.

Reading as a Writer

1. What specific places can you point to in the selection that illustrate what is at issue for Gutiérrez?

2. How does she use her review to set up her argument?

3. What specific words and phrases does she use to establish what she sees as the problem? Is she correcting misinterpretations, filling a gap, or modifying what others have said?

4. What would you say is Gutiérrez's thesis? What specifics can you point to in the text to support your answer?

5. What would you say are the arguments Gutiérrez wants you to avoid? Again, what specific details can you point to in the text to support your answer?

A Practice Sequence: Building a Thesis

We would like you to practice some of the strategies we have covered in this chapter. If you have already started working on an essay, exercises 1 through 4 present an opportunity to take stock of your progress, a chance to sort through what you've discovered, identify what you still need to discover, and move toward refining your thesis. Jot down your answer to each of the questions below and make lists of what you know and what you need to learn.

1   Have you established that your issue is current and relevant, that it is or should be on people's minds? What information would you need to do so?

2   Can you summarize briefly what others have said in the past to show that you are familiar with how others have addressed the issue? List some of the key texts you have read and the key points they make.

3   Have you identified any misunderstandings or gaps in how others have addressed the issue? Describe them. Do you have any ideas or information that would address these misunderstandings or help fill these gaps? Where might you find the information you need? Can you think of any sources you should reread to learn more? (For example, have you looked at the works cited or bibliographies in the texts you've already read?)

4   At this point, what is your take on the issue? Try drafting a working thesis statement that will present readers with something new to think about, building on and extending what others have argued. In drafting your thesis statement, try out the

models discussed in this chapter and see if one is an especially good fit:

- *Misinterpretations model*: "Although many scholars have argued about A and B, a careful examination suggests C."

- *Gap model*: "Although scholars have noted A and B, they have missed the importance of C."

- *Modification model*: "Although I agree with A and B ideas of other writers, it is important to extend/refine/limit their ideas with C."

- *Hypothesis-testing model:* "Some people explain A by suggesting B, but a close analysis of the problem reveals the possibility of several competing/complementary explanations such as C, D, and E."

5   If you haven't chosen a topic yet, try a group exercise. Sit down with a few of your classmates and choose one of the following topics to brainstorm about as a group. Choose a topic that everyone in the group finds interesting, and work through exercises 1 through 4 in this practice sequence. Here are some suggestions:

- the moral obligation to vote
- the causes or consequences of poverty
- the limits of academic freedom
- equity in education
- the popularity of _____
- gender stereotypes in the media
- linguistic diversity
- the uses of a liberal education
- journalism and truth
- government access to personal information

AN ANNOTATED STUDENT ESSAY: STATING AND SUPPORTING A THESIS

We have annotated the following student essay to illustrate the strategies we have discussed in this chapter for stating a thesis that responds to a relevant, timely problem in a given context. The assignment was to write an argument focusing on literacy based on research. Veronica Stafford chose to write about her peers' habit of texting and the ways in which this type of social interaction affects their intellectual development. Stafford develops a thesis that provides a corrective to a misconception that she sees in the ongoing conversations about texting. Her approach is a variation on the strategy in which writers correct a misinterpretation. In turn, you will see that she makes claims of fact and evaluation in making an argument for changing her peers' penchant for texting.

As you read the essay, reflect on your own experiences: Do you think the issue she raises is both timely and relevant? How well do you think she places her ideas in conversation with others? How would you respond to her various claims? Which do you agree with and disagree with, and why? What evidence would you present to support or counter her claims? Do you think she offers a reasonable corrective to what she believes is a misconception about texting?

Stafford 1

Veronica Stafford
Professor Wilson
English 1102
April 20 —

Texting and Literacy

As students walk to class each day, most do not notice the other people around them. Rather than talking with others, they are texting their friends in the next building, in their dorm, or back home. Although social networking is the most common use for text messages, they are not used solely for socializing. While texting is a quick and easy way to keep up with friends, it threatens other aspects of our lives. When students spend time texting rather than focusing on those other important aspects, texting becomes detrimental. Students' enjoyment of reading, their schoolwork, and their relationships with others are all negatively affected by text messaging.

The student identifies an issue, or problem, and states her thesis as an evaluative claim that attempts to correct a misconception.

Due to the mass appeal of text messaging, students pass their free time chatting through their cell phones rather than enjoying a great book. Texting is so widespread because 25 percent of students under age eight, 89 percent of students ages eleven to thirteen, and over 95 percent of students over age fifteen have a cell phone ("Mobile Phones"). On average, 75.6 million text messages are sent in a day, with 54 percent of the population texting more than five times per day ("Mobile Phones"). In contrast to the time they spend texting, fifteen- to

She summarizes research, placing the conversation in a larger context. Her citations also indicate that the problem she identifies is relevant and timely.

1

2

Stafford 2

twenty-four-year-olds read a mere seven minutes per day for fun and only 1.25 hours a week (NEA 10), which is less than half the time that seventh-grade students spend texting: 2.82 hours a week (Bryant, Sanders-Jackson and Smallwood). While more than half of the population texts every day, almost as many (43 percent) have not read a single book in the past year (NEA 7). It seems there is a direct correlation between reading and texting because, as text messaging increases in popularity, reading decreases. The National Endowment for the Arts surveyed eighteen- to twenty-four-year-olds and discovered that the enjoyment of reading in this age group is declining the fastest. Inversely, it is the group that sends the most text messages: 142 billion a year (NEA 10). From 1992 to 2002, 2.1 million potential readers, aged eighteen to twenty-four years old, were lost (NEA 27). As proved by the direct correlation, reading does not have the same appeal because of texting. Students prefer to spend time in the technological world rather than sitting with a book.

However, reading well is essential to being successful academically. Although some argue that text messages force students to think quickly and allow them to formulate brief responses to questions, their habit is actually stifling creativity. When a group of twenty students was given a chance to write responses to open-ended questions, the students who owned cell phones with text messaging wrote much less. They also had more grammatical errors, such as leaving apostrophes out of contractions and substituting the letter "r" for the word "are" (Ward). Because of text messages, students perceive writing as a fun way to communicate with friends and not as a way to strongly voice an opinion. Students no longer think of writing as academic, but rather they consider it social. For instance, in Scotland, a thirteen-year-old student wrote this in a school essay about her summer vacation: "My smmr hols wr CWOT. B4 we used 2 go to NY 2C my bro, & 3 kids FTF ILNY, its gr8 . . ." (Ward). She used writing that would appear in a text message for a friend rather than in a report for school. Furthermore,

She uses evidence to support her thesis — that we take for granted a mode of communication that actually threatens the development of literacy.

She refines her thesis, first stating what people assume is true and then offering a corrective in the second part of her thesis.

She also makes a secondary claim related to her thesis.

Stafford 3

And she elaborates on this claim to point out one of the detrimental effects of texting.

students who text become so accustomed to reading this type of shorthand lingo that they often overlook it in their own writing (O'Connor). This means that teachers have to spend even longer correcting these bad habits. Regardless, Lily Huang, a writer for *Newsweek*, believes that text messages increase literacy because a student must first know how to spell a word to abbreviate it in texting. However, texting affects not only the way that students

The student presents a possible counter-argument from a published writer and then restates her thesis in an effort to correct a misconception.

write, but also the way in which they think about language. As a critic of Huang's article writes, "Habitual use of shorthand isn't just about choppy English, but choppy thinking" (Muffie). Writers who text will have trouble thinking creatively, and will especially have trouble composing intricate works like poetry because of the abridged way of thinking to which they are accustomed.

Outside of school, students' interactions with one another are similarly altered. Three in five teens would argue with a friend and one in three would break up with someone through a text message ("Technology Has Tremendous Impact"). Text messaging is now the most popular way for students to arrange to meet with friends, have a quick conversation, contact a friend when bored, or invite friends to a party ("Technology Has Tremendous Impact"). Eight out of ten teens would rather text than call ("Mobile Phones"). Although it is true that text

She restates an evaluative claim that runs through the essay like the skewer we discussed earlier.

messaging has made conversations much simpler and faster, it has not improved communication. Texting may make it more convenient to stay in contact with friends, but it does not ensure that the contact is as beneficial as talking in person. Text messages do not incorporate all of the body language and vocal inflections that a face-to-face conversation does. These nonverbal cues are essential to fully comprehending what is

She provides current research to support her thesis.

being communicated. Only 7 percent of a message is verbal. When the message is not communicated face-to-face, 93 percent of that message is lost ("Importance of Nonverbal"), and this nonverbal message is crucial to maintaining close relationships. According to Don McKay, a contributor to healthinfosource.com, the most important aspect of lasting friendships is effective

4

Stafford 4

communication. Friends must be able to convey emotions and empathize with others (McKay). However, friends who communicate solely through text messages will miss out on any truly personal interaction because they can never see the other person's posture, body language, or gestures.

5

All of the negative effects of text messaging additionally deteriorate literacy. The enjoyment of reading leads to avid readers who eagerly absorb written words. A devotion to schoolwork encourages students to read so that they may be informed about important topics. Through book clubs and conversations about great literature, even relationships can foster a love for reading. However, text messaging is detracting from all three. In today's society, literacy is important. Schools focus on teaching English at an early age because of the active role that it forces students to take (Le Guin). While students can passively text message their friends, they need to focus on reading to enjoy it. In order to really immerse themselves in the story, they need to use a higher level of thinking than that of texting. This learning is what causes avid readers to become so successful. Those who read for fun when they are young score better on standardized tests, are admitted to more selective universities, and are able to secure the most competitive jobs (NEA 69). The decline in literacy caused by text messaging could inevitably cost a student a selective job. If students spent less time texting and more time reading, it could give them an advantage over their peers. Imagine a scenario between classes without any students' eyes to the ground. Imagine that Notre Dame students are not texting acquaintances hours away. Perhaps instead they are all carrying a pen and notebook and writing a letter to their friends. Maybe they are conversing with those around them. Instead of spending time every week text messaging, they are reading. When those other students text "lol," it no longer is an abbreviation for "laugh out loud," but for "loss of literacy."

She concludes by restating her premise about the value of reading and her evaluation of texting as a form of communication that erodes what she considers the very definition of literacy.

She also concludes with a claim in which she proposes that students need to elevate the way they read and write.

Works Cited

Bryant, J. Alison, Ashley Sanders-Jackson, and Amber M. K. Smallwood. "IMing, Text Messaging, and Adolescent Social Networks." *Journal of Computer-Mediated Communication* 11.2 (2006): n. pag. Web. 28 Mar. 20--.

Huang, Lily. "The Death of English (LOL)." *Newsweek.* Newsweek, 2 Aug. 2008. Web. 28 Mar. 20--.

"The Importance of Nonverbal Communication." *EruptingMind Self Improvement Tips.* N.p., 2008. Web. 1 Apr. 20--.

Le Guin, Ursula K. "Staying Awake: Notes on the Alleged Decline of Reading." *Harper's Magazine.* The Harper's Magazine Foundation, Feb. 2008. Web. 30 Mar. 20--.

McKay, Don. "Communication and Friendship." *EzineArticles.* EzineArticles.com, 22 Feb. 2006. Web. 27 Mar. 20--.

"Mobile Phones, Texting, and Literacy." *National Literacy Trust.* NLT, 2008. Web. 1 Apr. 20--.

Muffie. Member comment. "The Death of English (LOL)." *Newsweek.* Newsweek, 18 Aug. 2008. Web. 28 Mar. 20--.

National Endowment for the Arts. *To Read or Not To Read: A Question of National Consequence.* Washington, NEA, Nov. 2007. PDF file.

O'Connor, Amanda. "Instant Messaging: Friend or Foe of Student Writing." *New Horizons for Learning.* New Horizons for Learning, Mar. 2005. Web. 27 Mar. 20--.

"Technology Has Tremendous Impact on How Teens Communicate." *Cellular-news.* Cellular-news, 20 Feb. 2007. Web. 27 Mar. 20--.

Ward, Lucy. "Texting 'Is No Bar to Literacy.'" *Guardian.co.uk.* Guardian News and Media Limited, 23 Dec. 2004. Web. 2 Apr. 20--.

6

From Finding to Evaluating Sources

In this chapter, we look at strategies for expanding the base of sources you work with to support your argument. The habits and skills of close reading and analysis that we have discussed and that you have practiced are essential for evaluating the sources you find. Once you find sources, you will need to assess the claims the writers make, the extent to which they provide evidence in support of those claims, and the recency, relevance, accuracy, and reliability of the evidence. The specific strategies we discuss here are those you will use to find and evaluate the sources you locate in your library's electronic catalog or on the Internet. These strategies are core skills for developing a researched academic argument. They are also essential to avoid being overwhelmed by the torrent of information unleashed at the click of a computer mouse.

Finding sources is not difficult; finding and identifying good sources is challenging. You know how simple it is to look up a subject in an encyclopedia or to use a search engine like Google or Yahoo! to discover basic information on a subject or topic. Unfortunately, this kind of research will only take you so far. What if the information you find doesn't really address your question? True, we have emphasized the importance of thinking about an issue from multiple perspectives — and finding multiple perspectives is easy when you search the Internet. But how do you know whether a perspective is authoritative or trustworthy or even legitimate? Without knowing how to find and identify good sources, you can waste a lot of time reading material that will not contribute to your essay. Our goal is to help you use your time wisely to collect the sources you need to support your argument.

IDENTIFYING SOURCES

We assume that by the time you visit the library or log on to the Internet to find sources, you are not flying blind. At the very least you will have chosen a topic you want to explore (something in general you want to write about), possibly will have identified an issue (a question or problem about the topic that is arguable), and perhaps will even have a working thesis (a main claim that you want to test against other sources).

Let's say, for example, that you are interested in the topic of nutrition and obesity. Perhaps you have begun to formulate an issue: Trends show that obesity is increasing at a time when published reports are also showing that the food industry may have been complicit by engineering processed foods with high fat, sugar, and salt content. In fact, these reports point to the lack of nutritional value of processed foods. The issue might be between what you see as an unfortunate trend that affects the health of a growing population of children and adults in the United States and the extent to which food manufacturers contribute to the problem. You may have begun to formulate a question about who is responsible for addressing this problem. Should individuals be more responsible for making good choices? Should food manufacturers monitor themselves and be more responsible to consumers? Should the government intervene to ensure that processed foods provide adequate nutrients and less fat, sugar, and salt? The closer you are to identifying an issue or question, the more purposeful your research will be and the more you will be able to home in on the materials that will be most useful. As you read, your research will help you refine, formulate a question, and develop a working thesis.

However, a working thesis is just a place to begin. As you digest all of the perspectives that your research yields, your interest in the topic or issue may shift significantly. Maybe you'll end up writing about the extent to which the government should have a role, any role, in regulating the food industry rather than about obesity. Perhaps you become interested in trends in food distribution and end up writing about what some call the "locavore" movement. Be open to revising your ideas and confronting the complexities inherent in any topic. Pursue what interests you and what is timely and relevant to your readers. The question, then, is what are you trying to learn and demonstrate?

If you are unsure about where to start, we provide a list of standard types of sources for doing research in Table 6.1. For example, you could begin by looking up abstracts, a tool researchers use to get a brief snapshot of the field and summaries of potentially relevant articles. You can simply do a Google search, type in "abstracts," and add the topic that interests you ("Abstracts in Health Sciences"). You can also look up book reviews to see how others might have responded to a book where you first learned about the problems of obesity, nutrition, food production, and the like. More specialized searches will take you to databases available on a given library's website.

TABLE 6.1   Standard Types of Sources for Doing Research

Source	Type of Information	Purpose	Limitations	Examples
Abstract	Brief summary of a text and the bibliographic information needed to locate the complete text	To help researchers decide whether they want to read the entire source	May be too brief to fully assess the value of a source	*Biological Abstracts* *Historical Abstracts* *New Testament Abstracts* *Reference Sources in History: An Introductory Guide*
Bibliography	List of works, usually by subject and author, with full publication information	For an overview of what has been published in a field and who the principal researchers in the field are	Difficult to distinguish the best sources and the most prominent researchers	Bibliography of the History of Art *MLA International Bibliography*
Biography	Story of an individual's life and the historical, cultural, or social context in which he or she lived	For background on a person of importance	Lengthy and reflects the author's bias	Biography and Genealogy Master Index Biography Resource Center Biography.com Literature Resource Center *Oxford Dictionary of National Biography*
Book review	Description and usually an evaluation of a recently published book	To help readers stay current with research and thought in their field and to evaluate scholarship	Reflects the reviewer's bias	ALA *Booklist* *Book Review Digest* *Book Review Index* *Bowker Books in Print*
Database	Large collection of citations and abstracts from books, journals, and digests, often updated daily	To give researchers access to a wide range of current sources	Lacks evaluative information	EBSCOhost Education Resources Information Center (ERIC) Humanities International Index Index to Scientific & Technical Proceedings United Nations Bibliographic Information System
Data, statistics	Measurements derived from studies or surveys	To help researchers identify important trends (e.g., in voting, housing, residential segregation)	Requires a great deal of scrutiny and interpretation	American FactFinder American National Election Studies Current Index to Statistics Current Population Survey *U.S. Census Bureau National Data Book*

(*continued on next page*)

TABLE 6.1   *(continued)*

SOURCE	TYPE OF INFORMATION	PURPOSE	LIMITATIONS	EXAMPLES
Dictionary	Alphabetical list of words and their definitions	To explain key terms and how they are used		*Merriam-Webster's Collegiate Dictionary* *Oxford English Dictionary* *The Oxford Dictionary of Current English*
Encyclopedia	Concise articles about people, places, concepts, and things	A starting point for very basic information	Lack of in-depth information	*The CQ Researcher* Encyclopedia Brittanica Online *McGraw-Hill Encyclopedia of Science & Technology*
Internet search engine	Web site that locates online information by keyword or search term	For quickly locating a broad array of current resources	Reliability of information open to question	Google Yahoo! Google Scholar
Newspaper, other news sources	Up-to-date information	To locate timely information	May reflect reporter's or medium's bias	America's Historical Newspapers LexisNexis Academic Newspaper Source ProQuest Historical Newspapers World News Connection
Thesaurus	Alphabetical list of words and their synonyms	For alternative search terms		*Roget's II: The New Thesaurus* *Pro Quest Thesaurus*

■ Consult Experts Who Can Guide Your Research

Before you embark on a systematic hunt for sources, you may want to consult with experts who can help guide your research. The following experts are nearer to hand and more approachable than you may think.

Your writing instructor.   Your first and best expert is likely to be your writing instructor, who can help you define the limits of your research and the kinds of sources that would prove most helpful. Your writing instructor can probably advise you on whether your topic is too broad or too narrow, help you identify your issue, and perhaps even point you to specific reference works or readings you should consult. He or she can also help you figure out whether you should concentrate mainly on popular or scholarly sources (for more about popular and scholarly sources, see pages 134–37).

Librarians at your campus or local library.   In all likelihood, there is no bet-ter repository of research material than your campus or local library, and no better guide to those resources than the librarians who work there. Their job is to help you find what you need (although it's up to you to make the most of what you find). Librarians can give you a map or tour of the library and provide you with booklets or other handouts that instruct you in the specific resources available and their uses. They can explain the catalog system and reference system. And, time allowing, most librarians are willing to give you personal help in finding and using specific sources, from books and journals to indexes and databases.

Experts in other fields.   Perhaps the idea for your paper originated outside your writing course, in response to a reading assigned in, say, your psy-chology or economics course. If so, you may want to discuss your topic or issue with the instructor in that course, who can probably point you to other readings or journals you should consult. If your topic originated outside the classroom, you can still seek out an expert in the appropriate field. If so, you may want to read the advice on interviewing we present in Chapter 11.

Manuals, handbooks, and dedicated web sites.   These exist in abundance, for general research as well as for discipline-specific research. They are especially helpful in identifying a wide range of authoritative search tools and resources, although they also offer practical advice on how to use and cite them. Indeed, your writing instructor may assign one of these manuals or handbooks, or recommend a Web site, at the beginning of the course. If not, he or she can probably point you to the one that is best suited to your research.

▪ Develop a Working Knowledge of Standard Sources

As you start your hunt for sources, it helps to know broadly what kinds of sources are available and what they can help you accomplish. Table 6.1 lists a number of the resources you are likely to rely on when you are looking for material, the purpose and limitations of each type of resource, and some well-known examples. Although it may not help you pinpoint specific resources that are most appropriate for your research, the table does provide a basis for finding sources in any discipline. And familiariz-ing yourself with the types of resources here should make your conversa-tions with the experts more productive.

▪ Distinguish Between Primary and Secondary Sources

As you define the research task before you, you will need to understand the difference between primary and secondary sources and figure out which you will need to answer your question. Your instructor may specify which he or she prefers, but chances are you will have to make the decision yourself. A **primary source** is a firsthand, or eyewitness, account, the kind of account you find in letters or newspapers or research reports in which the researcher explains his or her impressions of a particular phenomenon. For example, "Hidden Lessons," the Sadkers' study of gender bias in schools, is a primary source. The authors report their own experiences of the phenomenon in the classroom. A **secondary source** is an analysis of information reported in a primary source. For example, even though it may cite the Sadkers' primary research, an essay that analyzes the Sadkers' findings along with other studies of gender dynamics in the classroom would be considered a secondary source.

If you were exploring issues of language diversity and the English-only movement, you would draw on both primary and secondary sources. You would be interested in researchers' firsthand (primary) accounts of language learning and use by diverse learners for examples of the challenges nonnative speakers face in learning a standard language. And you would also want to know from secondary sources what others think about whether national unity and individuality can and should coexist in communities and homes as well as in schools. You will find that you are often expected to use both primary and secondary sources in your research.

▪ Distinguish Between Popular and Scholarly Sources

To determine the type of information to use, you also need to decide whether you should look for popular or scholarly books and articles. **Popular sources** of information—newspapers like *USA Today* and *The Chronicle of Higher Education*, and large-circulation magazines like *Time Magazine* and *Field & Stream*—are written for a general audience. This is not to say that popular sources cannot be specialized: *The Chronicle of Higher Education* is read mostly by academics; *Field & Stream*, by people who love the outdoors. But they are written so that any educated reader can understand them. **Scholarly sources,** by contrast, are written for experts in a particular field. *The New England Journal of Medicine* may be read by people who are not physicians, but they are not the journal's primary audience. In a manner of speaking, these readers are eavesdropping on the journal's conversation of ideas; they are not expected to contribute to it (and in fact would be hard pressed to do so). The articles in scholarly journals undergo **peer review.** That is, they do not get published until they have been carefully evaluated by the author's peers, other experts in the academic conversation being conducted in the journal. Reviewers may comment at length about an article's level of research and writing, and an author may have to revise an article several times before it sees print. And if the reviewers cannot reach a consensus that the research makes an important contribution to the academic conversation, the article will not be published.

When you begin your research, you may find that popular sources provide helpful information about a topic or an issue—the results of a national poll, for example. Later, however, you will want to use scholarly sources to advance your argument. You can see from Table 6.2 that popular magazines and scholarly journals can be distinguished by a number of characteristics. Does the source contain advertisements? If so, what kinds of advertisements? For commercial products? Or for academic events and resources? How do the advertisements appear? If you find ads and glossy pictures and illustrations, you are probably looking at a popular magazine. This is in contrast to the tables, charts, and diagrams you are likely to find in an education, psychology, or microbiology journal. Given your experience with rhetorical analyses, you should also be able to determine the makeup of your audience—specialists or nonspecialists—and the level of language you need to use in your writing.

TABLE 6.2 Popular Magazines Versus Scholarly Journals

CRITERIA	POPULAR MAGAZINES	SCHOLARLY JOURNALS
Advertisements	Numerous full-page color ads	Few if any ads
Appearance	Eye-catching; glossy; pictures and illustrations	Plain; black-and-white graphics, tables, charts, and diagrams
Audience	General	Professors, researchers, and college students
Author	Journalists	Professionals in an academic field or discipline
Bibliography	Rarely give full citations	Extensive bibliography at the end of each article; footnotes and other documentation
Content	General articles to inform, update, or introduce a contemporary issue	Research projects, methodology, and theory
Examples	*Newsweek, National Review, PC World, Psychology Today*	*International Journal of Applied Engineering Research, New England Journal of Medicine*
Language	Nontechnical, simple vocabulary	Specialized vocabulary
Publisher	Commercial publisher	Professional organization, university, research institute, or scholarly press

SOURCE: Adapted from materials at the Hesburgh Library, University of Notre Dame.

Again, as you define your task for yourself, it is important to consider why you would use one source or another. Do you want facts? Opinions? News reports? Research studies? Analyses? Personal reflections? The extent to which the information can help you make your argument will serve as your basis for determining whether a source of information is of value.

Steps to Identifying Sources

1 **Consult experts who can guide your research.** Talk to people who can help you formulate issues and questions.

2 **Develop a working knowledge of standard sources.** Identify the different kinds of information that different types of sources provide.

3 **Distinguish between primary and secondary sources.** Decide what type of information can best help you answer your research question.

4 **Distinguish between popular and scholarly sources.** Determine what kind of information will persuade your readers.

A Practice Sequence: Identifying Sources

We would now like you to practice using some of the strategies we have discussed so far: talking with experts, deciding what sources of information you should use, and determining what types of information can best help you develop your paper and persuade your readers. We assume you have chosen a topic for your paper, identified an issue, and perhaps formulated a working thesis. If not, think back to some of the topics mentioned in earlier chapters. Have any of them piqued your interest? If not, here are five very broad topics you might work with:

- higher education student loans
- science and religion
- the media and gender
- immigration
- global health

Once you've decided on a topic, talk to experts and decide which types of sources you should use: primary or secondary, popular or scholarly. Consult with your classmates to evaluate the strengths and weaknesses of different sources of information and the appropriateness of using different types of information. Here are the steps to follow:

1   Talk to a librarian about the sources you might use to get information about your topic (for example, databases, abstracts, or bibliographies). Be sure to take notes.

2 Talk to an expert who can provide you with some ideas about current issues in the field of interest. Be sure to take detailed notes.

3 Decide whether you should use primary or secondary sources. What type of information would help you develop your argument?

4 Decide whether you should use popular or scholarly sources. What type of information would your readers find compelling?

SEARCHING FOR SOURCES

Once you've decided on the types of sources you want to use—primary or secondary, popular or scholarly—you can take steps to locate the information you need. You might begin with a tour of your university or local library, so that you know where the library keeps newspapers, government documents, books, journals, and other sources of information. Notice where the reference desk is: This is where you should head to ask a librarian for help if you get stuck. You also want to find a computer where you can log on to your library's catalog to start your search. Once you have located your sources in the library, you can begin to look through them for the information you need.

You may be tempted to rely on the Internet and a search engine like Google or Yahoo! But keep in mind that the information you retrieve from the Internet may not be trustworthy: Anyone can post his or her thoughts on a Web site. Of course, you can also find excellent scholarly sources on the Internet. (For example, Johns Hopkins University Press manages Project MUSE, a collection of 300-plus academic journals that can be accessed online through institutional subscription.) School libraries also offer efficient access to government records and other sources essential to scholarly writing.

Let's say you are about to start researching a paper on language diversity and the English-only movement. When you log on to the library's site, you find a menu of choices: Catalog, Electronic Resources, Virtual Reference Desk, and Services & Collections. (The wording may vary slightly from library to library, but the means of locating information will be the same.) When you click on Catalog, another menu of search choices appears: Keyword, Title, Author, and Subject (Figure 6.1). The hunt is on.

FIGURE 6.1   Menu of Basic Search Strategies

■ Perform a Keyword Search

A **keyword** is essentially your topic: It defines the topic of your search. To run a keyword search, you can look up information by author, title, or subject. You would search by author to locate all the works a particular author has written on a subject. So, for example, if you know that Paul Lang is an expert on the consequences of the English-only movement, you might begin with an author search. You can use the title search to locate all works with a key word or phrase in the title. The search results are likely to include a number of irrelevant titles, but you should end up with a list of authors, titles, and subject headings to guide another search.

A search by subject is particularly helpful as you begin your research, while you are still formulating your thesis. You want to start by thinking of as many words as possible that relate to your topic. (A thesaurus can help you come up with different words you can use in a keyword search.) Suppose you type in the phrase "English only." A number of different sources appear on the screen, but the most promising is Paul Lang's book *The English Language Debate: One Nation, One Language?* You click on this record, and another screen appears with some valuable pieces of information, including the call number (which tells you where in the library you can find the book) and an indication that the book has a bibliography, something you can make use of once you find the book (Figure 6.2). Notice that the subject listings—*Language policy*,

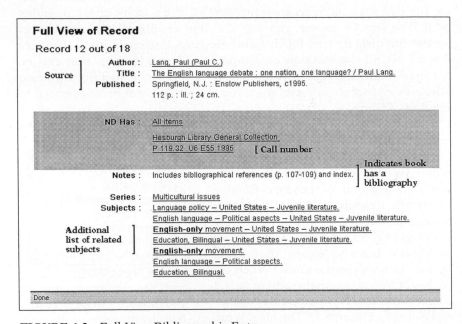

FIGURE 6.2   Full-View Bibliographic Entry

English language–Political aspects, English-only movement, Bilingual education — also give you additional keywords to use in finding relevant information. The lesson here is that it is important to generate keywords to get initial information and then to look at that information carefully for more keywords and to determine if the source has a bibliography. Even if this particular source isn't relevant, it may lead you to other sources that are.

▪ Try Browsing

Browse is a headings search; it appears in the menu of choices in Figure 6.1 as "Subject begins with . . ." This type of search allows you to scroll through an alphabetical index. Some of the indexes available are the Author Index, the Title Index, and the Library of Congress Subject Headings, a subject index. Browse

- displays an alphabetical list of entries;
- shows the number of records for each entry;
- indicates whether there are cross-references for each entry.

What appears in the window is "Browse List: Choose a field, enter a phrase and click the 'go' button." Figure 6.3 shows the results of a preliminary browse when the words "English-only" are entered. Notice that a list of headings or titles appears on the screen. This is not a list of books, and not all of the entries are relevant. But you can use the list to determine which headings are relevant to your topic, issue, or question.

For your paper on the English-only movement, the first two headings seem relevant: *English-only debate* and *English-only movement*. A further

No. of Recs	Entry
	Browse List: Subjects
	English one-act plays - [LC Authority Record]
	See: One-act plays, English
	English-only debate - [LC Authority Record]
	See: English-only movement
4	English-only movement - [LC Authority Record]
1	English-only movement – California – Case studies
1	English-only movement – Colorado
4	English-only movement – United States
1	English-only movement – United States – Juvenile literature
	English-only question - [LC Authority Record]
	See: English-only movement
1	English – Ontario – Correspondence
1	English oration

FIGURE 6.3   Preliminary Browse of "English-only" Subject Heading

#	Year	Author	Title
1	☐ 2006	United States.	**English as the official language : hearing before the Subcommittee on Education Reform of the Co <Book>** Click for ONLINE ACCESS (Text version:) Documents Center Owned: 1 Checked Out: 0 Display full record
2	☐ 1996	United States.	**S. 356—Language of Government Act of 1995 : hearings before the Committee on Governmental Affai <Book>** Documents Center Display full record
3	☐ 1996	United States.	**Hearing on English as the common language : hearing before the Subcommittee on Early Childhood, <Book>** Documents Center Display full record
4	☐ 1995	United States.	**Hearing on English as a common language : hearing before the Subcommittee on Early Childhood, Yo <Book>** Documents Center Display full record

Done

FIGURE 6.4   Results of Browsing Deeper: A New List of Sources

click would reveal the title of a relevant book and a new list of subject headings (Figure 6.4) that differs from those of your initial search. This list gives you a new bibliography from which you can gather new leads and a list of subject headings to investigate.

We suggest that you do a keyword search first and then a browse search to home in on a subject. Especially when you don't know the exact subject, you can do a quick keyword search, retrieve many sets of results, and then begin looking at the subjects that correspond to each title. Once you find a subject that fits your needs, you can click on the direct subject (found in each bibliographic record) and execute a new search that will yield more-relevant results.

■ Perform a Journal or Newspaper Title Search

Finally, you can search by journal or newspaper title. For this kind of search, you will need exact information. You can take the name of a journal, magazine, or newspaper cited in your keyword or browse search. The journal or newspaper title search will tell you if your library subscribes to the publication and in what format—print, microform or microfilm, or electronic.

Suppose you want to continue your search in the *New York Times* for information on the English-only movement by searching for articles in the *New York Times*. You would run a basic search under the category "Periodicals": "Periodical Title begins with . . ." That would give you access to a limited number of articles that focused on the debate surrounding the English-only movement. To find more recent articles, you could go to the *New York Times* Web site (nytimes.com), where you could find many potentially useful listings. Recent newspaper articles will lack the depth and complexity of more scholarly studies, but they are undeniably useful in helping you establish the timeliness and relevance of your research. To see the full text of the articles, you must subscribe or pay a nominal fee, although you can usually preview the articles because the Web site will include a few sentences describing the content of each article.

Steps to Searching for Sources

1 **Perform a keyword search.** Choose a word or phrase that best describes your topic.

2 **Try browsing.** Search an alphabetical list by subject.

3 **Perform a journal or newspaper title search.** Find relevant citations by identifying the exact title of a journal or newspaper, or by subject.

A Practice Sequence: Searching for Sources

If you tried the practice sequence on identifying sources (p. 136), explore your topic further by practicing the types of searches discussed in this section: a keyword search; a browse; and a journal or newspaper title search (or a subject search).

EVALUATING LIBRARY SOURCES

The information you collect can and will vary in terms of its relevance and overall quality. You will want to evaluate this information as systematically as possible to be sure that you are using the most appropriate sources to develop your argument. Once you have obtained at least some of the sources you located by searching your library's catalog, you should evaluate the material as you read it. In particular, you want to evaluate the following information for each article or book:

- the author's background and credentials (What is the author's educational background? What has he or she written about in the past? Is this person an expert in the field?)
- the writer's purpose
- the topic of discussion
- the audience the writer invokes and whether you are a member of that audience

- the nature of the conversation (How have others addressed the problem?)
- what the author identifies as a misinterpretation or a gap in knowledge, an argument that needs modifying, or a hypothesis.
- what the author's own view is
- how the author supports his or her argument (that is, with primary or secondary sources, with popular or scholarly articles, with facts or opinions)
- the accuracy of the author's evidence (Can you find similar information elsewhere?)

If your topic is current and relevant, chances are your searches are going to turn up a large number of possible sources. How do you go about choosing which sources to rely on in your writing? Of course, if time were not an issue, you would read them all from start to finish. But in the real world, assignments come with due dates. To decide whether a library source merits a close reading and evaluation, begin by skimming each book or article. **Skimming**—briefly examining the material to get a sense of the information it offers—involves four steps:

1. Read the introductory sections.
2. Examine the table of contents and index.
3. Check the notes and bibliographic references.
4. Skim for the argument.

■ Read the Introductory Sections

Turn to the introductory sections of the text first. Many authors use a preface or an introduction to explain the themes they focus on in a book. An **abstract** serves a similar purpose, but article abstracts are usually only 250 words long. In the introductory sections, writers typically describe the issue that motivated them to write and indicate whether they believe the work corrects a misconception, fills a gap, or builds on and extends the research of others. For example, in the preface to her book *Learning and Not Learning English: Latino Students in American Schools* (2001), Guadalupe Valdés explains that even after two years of language instruction, many students remain at a low level of language competence. In this passage, Valdés makes clear the purpose of her work:

> This book examines the learning of English in American schools by immigrant children. It focuses on the realities that such youngsters face in trying to acquire English in settings in which they interact exclusively with other non-English-speaking youngsters the entire school day. It is designed to fill a gap in the existing literature on non-English-background youngsters by offering a glimpse of the challenges and difficulties faced by four middle-school students

enrolled in the United States for the first time when they were 12 or 13 years old. It is my purpose here to use these youngsters' lives and experiences as a lens through which to examine the policy and instructional dilemmas that now surround the education of immigrant children in this country. (p. 2)

If you were looking for sources for a paper on the English-only movement, in particular the consequences of that movement for young students, you might very well find Valdés's words compelling and decide the book is worth a closer reading.

■ Examine the Table of Contents and Index

After reading the introductory sections, you will find it useful to analyze the **table of contents** to see how much emphasis the writer gives to topics that are relevant to your own research. For example, the table of contents to *Learning and Not Learning English* includes several headings that may relate to your interest: "Educating English-Language Learners," "Challenges and Realities," "Implications for Policy and Practice," and the "Politics of Teaching English." You also should turn to the back of the book to examine the **index,** an alphabetical list of the important and recurring concepts in a book, and the page numbers on which they appear. An index also would include the names of authors cited in the book. In the index to Valdés's book, you would find references to "English-language abilities and instruction" with specific page numbers where you can read what the author has to say on this subject. You would also find references to "English-only instruction," "equal educational opportunities," and "sheltered instruction."

■ Check the Notes and Bibliographic References

Especially in the initial stages of writing, you should look closely at writers' notes and bibliographies to discern who they feel are the important voices in the field. Frequent citation of a particular researcher's work may indicate that the individual is considered to be an expert in the field you are studying. Notes usually provide brief references to people, concepts, or context; the bibliography includes a long list of related works. Mining Valdés's bibliography, you would find such titles as "Perspectives on Official English," "Language Policy in Schools," "Not Only English," "Language and Power," and "The Cultural Politics of English."

■ Skim for the Argument

Skimming a book or an article entails briefly looking over the elements we have discussed so far: the preface or abstract, the table of contents and the index, and the notes and bibliography. Skimming also can mean reading chapter titles, headings, and the first sentence of each paragraph to determine the relevance of a book or an article.

Skimming the first chapter of *Learning and Not Learning English*, you would find several topic sentences that reveal the writer's purpose:

> "In this book, then, I examine and describe different expressions that both learning and not-learning English took among four youngsters."

> "In the chapters that follow . . ."

> "What I hope to suggest . . ."

These are the types of phrases you should look for to get a sense of what the writer is trying to accomplish and whether the writer's work will be of use to you.

If, after you've taken these steps, a source still seems promising, you should reflect on whether it might help you answer your research question. Keep in mind the critical reading skills you've learned and see if you can discern the author's overall situation, purpose, claims, and audience. Assess the evidence used to support the claims—is it recent, relevant, accurate, reliable? What kinds of evidence does the author use? Primary or secondary? Popular or scholarly? What kind of data, facts, or statistical evidence? Note whether facts or opinions seem to predominate. Ultimately you have to determine whether to set the source aside or commit yourself to a thorough understanding of its argument and all the note taking and critical thinking that will entail.

Steps to Evaluating Library Sources

1 **Read the introductory sections.** Get an overview of the researcher's argument.

2 **Examine the table of contents and index.** Consider the most relevant chapters to your topic and the list of relevant subjects.

3 **Check the notes and bibliographic references.** Identify the authors a researcher refers to (do the names come up in many different books?) and the titles of both books and articles.

4 **Skim for the argument.** Read chapter titles, headings, and topic sentences to determine the source's relevance to your research. Go deeper to assess the type and quality of evidence the author uses. Note whether the researcher uses credible evidence to support the argument.

A Practice Sequence: Evaluating Library Sources

For this exercise, we would like you to choose a specific book or article to examine in order to practice these strategies. If you are far along on your own research, use a book or an article you have identified as potentially useful.

1   Read the introductory sections. What issue is the author responding to? What is the writer's purpose? To correct a misconception? To fill a gap? To build on or extend the work of others? To address a hypothesis?

2   Examine the table of contents and index. What key words or phrases are related to your own research? Which topics does the author focus on? Are you intending to give these topics similar emphasis? (Will you give more or less emphasis?)

3   Check the notes and bibliographic references. Make a list of the sources you think you want to look up for your own research. Do certain sources seem more important than others?

4   Skim for the argument. What is the author's focus? Is it relevant to your own topic, issue, question, working thesis? What kinds of evidence does the author use? Does the author use primary or secondary sources? Popular or scholarly articles? Statistics? Facts or opinions? Do you want to commit yourself to grappling with the author's argument?

EVALUATING INTERNET SOURCES

Without question, the World Wide Web has revolutionized how research is conducted. It has been a particular boon to experienced researchers who have a clear sense of what they are looking for, giving them access to more information more quickly than ever before. But the Internet is rife with pitfalls for inexperienced researchers. That is, sites that appear accurate and reliable may prove not to be. The sources you find on the Internet outside your school library's catalog pose problems because anyone can post anything he or she wants. Unfortunately, there is no way to monitor the accuracy of what is published on the Internet. Although Internet sources can be useful, particularly because they are current, you must take steps to evaluate them before using information from them.

■ Evaluate the Author of the Site

If an author's name appears on a Web site, ask the following: Who is this person? What credentials and professional affiliations qualify this person to make a legitimate argument in the field being investigated?

One of our students googled "English only" and clicked on the first result, "Language Policy—English Only Movement," which eventually led her to James Crawford's Language Policy Web Site & Emporium. On the site, Crawford explains that he is "a writer and lecturer—formerly the Washington editor of *Education Week*—who specializes in the politics of language."* He notes that "since 1985, I have been reporting on the English Only movement, English Plus, bilingual education, Native American language revitalization, and language rights in the U.S.A." Between 2004 and 2006, he served as executive director of the National Association for Bilingual Education. Perhaps most important, Crawford has authored four books and a number of articles and has testified before Congress on "Official English Legislation." From this biographical sketch, the student inferred that Crawford is credentialed to write about the English-only movement.

Less certain, however, are the credentials of the writer who penned an article titled "Should the National Anthem Be Sung in English Only?" which appeared on another Web site our student visited. Why? Because the writer's name never appears on the site. An anonymous posting is the first clue that you want to move on to a more legitimate source of information.

■ Evaluate the Organization That Supports the Site

You have probably noticed that Internet addresses usually end with a suffix: .edu, .gov, .org, or .com. The .edu suffix means the site is associated with a university or college, which gives it credibility. The same holds true for .gov, which indicates a government agency. Both types of sites have a regulatory body that oversees their content. The suffix .org indicates a nonprofit organization; .com, a commercial organization. You will need to approach these Web sites with a degree of skepticism because you cannot be sure that they are as carefully monitored by a credentialed regulatory body. (In fact, even .edu sites may turn out to be postings by a student at a college or university.)

Our student was intrigued by James Crawford's site because he appears to be a credible source on the English-only movement. She was less sure about the reference to the Institute for Language and Education Policy. Is the institute a regulatory body that oversees what appears on the site? How long has the institute existed? Who belongs to the institute? Who sits on its board of directors? As a critical thinker, the student had to ask these questions.

Education Week has been published since 1981 by Editorial Projects in Education, a nonprofit organization that was founded with the help of a Carnegie grant. The publication covers issues related to primary and secondary education. If you are not familiar with a publication and are uncertain about its legitimacy, you can always ask your instructor, a librarian, or another expert to vouch for its reliability.

■ Evaluate the Purpose of the Site

Information is never objective, so whenever you evaluate a book, an article, or a Web site, you should consider the point of view the writer or sponsor is taking. It's especially important to ask if there is a particular bias among members of the group that sponsors the site. Can you tell what the sponsors of the site advocate? Are they hoping to sell or promote a product, or to influence opinion?

Not all Web sites provide easy answers to these questions. However, James Crawford's Language Policy Web Site & Emporium is quite explicit. In fact, Crawford writes that "the site is designed to encourage discussion of language policy issues, expose misguided school 'reforms,'" and, among other goals, "promote [his] own publications." (Notice "Emporium" in the name of the site.) He is candid about his self-interest, which does raise a question about his degree of objectivity.

What about a site like Wikipedia ("The Free Encyclopedia")? The site appears to exist to convey basic information. Although the popularity of Wikipedia recommends it as a basic resource, you should approach the site with caution because it is not clear whether and how the information posted on the site is regulated. It is prudent to confirm information from Wikipedia by checking on sites that are regulated more transparently rather than take Wikipedia as an authoritative source.

■ Evaluate the Information on the Site

In addition to assessing the purpose of a Web site like Wikipedia, you need to evaluate the extent to which the information is recent, accurate, and consistent with information you find in print sources and clearly regulated sites. For example, clicking on "The modern English-only movement" on Wikipedia takes you to a timeline of sorts with a number of links to other sites. But again, what is the source of this information? What is included? What is left out? You should check further into some of these links, reading the sources cited and keeping in mind the four criteria for evaluating a claim—recency, relevance, reliability, and accuracy. Because you cannot be certain that Internet sources are reviewed or monitored, you need to be scrupulous about examining the claims they make: How much and what kind of evidence supports the writer's (or site's) argument? Can you offer counterarguments?

In the last analysis, it comes down to whether the information you find stands up to the criteria you've learned to apply as a critical reader and writer. If not, move on to other sources. In a Web-based world of information, there is no shortage of material, but you have to train yourself not to settle for the information that is most readily available if it is clearly not credible.

Steps to Evaluating Internet Sources

1 **Evaluate the author of the site.** Determine whether the author is an expert.

2 **Evaluate the organization that supports the site.** Find out what the organization stands for and the extent of its credibility.

3 **Evaluate the purpose of the site.** What interests are represented on the site? What is the site trying to do? Provide access to legitimate statistics and information? Advance an argument? Spread propaganda?

4 **Evaluate the information on the site.** Identify the type of information on the site and the extent to which the information is recent, relevant, reliable, and accurate.

A Practice Sequence: Evaluating Internet Sources

For this exercise, we would like you to work in groups on a common topic. The class can choose its own topic or use one of the topics we suggest on pages 145–47. Then google the topic and agree on a Web site to analyze:

Group 1: Evaluate the author of the site.

Group 2: Evaluate the organization that supports the site.

Group 3: Evaluate the purpose of the site.

Group 4: Evaluate the information on the site.

Next, each group should share its evaluation. The goal is to determine the extent to which you believe you could use the information on this site in writing an academic essay.

WRITING AN ANNOTATED BIBLIOGRAPHY

In this chapter, we have suggested some strategies that you can use to locate information to help you learn more about a topic, issue, or question and to assess the extent to which this information can help you develop a legitimate, credible, and well-supported argument. As you read, it is important to write down the citation, or bibliographic information, of each source, including the author's name, date of publication, the title of an article or book, the journal title where an article appears, page numbers, and publishing information for a book.

Collecting the basic information about each source is useful, but we also suggest that you write an annotated bibliography to give some shape to the information you find. In writing an annotation, you should include the key ideas and claims from each source. You can also identify where you see gaps, misconceptions, and areas that you can build upon in developing your own argument. That is, in addition to stating what a given source is about, you can address the following questions: What is the issue the author responds to? What is the writer's purpose? To what extent is the argument persuasive? Does it overlook any issues that are important? Finally, you can explain the relevance of this work to your own research, given your own purpose for writing and what you want to demonstrate.

You can limit each annotation to a few sentences in which you present another writer's key claims and ideas, briefly analyze the writer's argument, and then explain how you will use that information in your own researched argument. The annotation below provides one such example, using APA format for the citation.

> Loftstrom, M., & Tyler, J. H. (2009). Finishing high school: Alternative pathways and dropout recovery. *The Future of Children, 19* (1), 77–103. Retrieved August 28, 2012 from JSTOR at http://www.jstor.org/stable/27795036
>
> This article provides a good history and analysis of the present dropout problem facing our nation. Researchers examine the discrepancy in statewide high school completion requirements that have led to debates about reality of dropout rates. The authors also examine social and economic consequences of failure to complete high school and the inadequacy of a GED certificate as a replacement for a high school diploma. The researchers conclude by examining some dropout prevention programs and by calling for more research in this area. In doing so, they identify a gap that my research at an alternative high school can help to fill, especially my interviews with students currently enrolled in the program and those who have dropped out.

Steps to Writing an Annotated Bibliography

1 Present key ideas. Describe in just a few sentences what this research is about and what you have learned.

2 Analyze. Explain the situation the author responds to, the purpose of the research, possible gaps in reasoning or misconceptions, and adequacy of evidence.

3 Determine relevance. Discuss how you might use this research in developing your own argument. As background for your own work? To explain how you fill a gap or correct a misconception? Will you build upon and extend this work?

A Practice Sequence: Writing an Annotated Bibliography

Write an annotation of a book, book chapter, or article that you have read for your research. Follow the steps in the previous box by first discussing the content of what you have read and analyzing the author's argument. Then determine the relevance of this research to your own work. If you have not chosen a topic yet, we invite you to write an annotation of a book, book chapter, or article related to any of the following broad topics:

- higher education student loans
- the media and gender
- global health
- science and religion
- immigration

From Summary to Synthesis
Using Sources to Build an Argument

When you start to use sources to build your argument, there are certain strategies for working with the words and ideas of others that you will need to learn. Often you can quote the words of an author directly; but just as often you will restate and condense the arguments of others (paraphrasing and summarizing) or make comparisons to the ideas of others in the process of developing your own argument (synthesizing). We walk you through these more challenging strategies in this chapter. We also briefly discuss plagiarism and ways to avoid it and how to integrate quotations into your writing.

SUMMARIES, PARAPHRASES, AND QUOTATIONS

In contrast to quotations, which involve using another writer's exact words, paraphrases and summaries are both restatements of another writer's ideas in your own words, but they differ in length:

- A paraphrase is usually about the same length as the original passage.
- A summary generally condenses a significantly longer text, conveying the argument not only of a few sentences but also of entire paragraphs, essays, or books.

In your own writing, you might paraphrase a few sentences or even a few paragraphs, but you certainly would not paraphrase a whole essay (much less a whole book). In constructing your arguments, however, you will often have to summarize the main points of the lengthy texts with which you are in conversation.

Both paraphrasing and summarizing are means to inquiry. That is, the act of recasting someone else's words or ideas into your own language, to suit your argument and reach your readers, forces you to think critically: What does this passage really mean? What is most important about it for my argument? How can I best present it to my readers? It requires making choices, not least of which is the best way to present the information—through paraphrase, summary, or direct quotation. In general, the following rules apply:

- *Paraphrase* when all the information in the passage is important, but the language may be difficult for your readers to understand.
- *Summarize* when you need to present only the key ideas of a passage (or an essay or a book) to advance your argument.
- *Quote* when the passage is so effective—so clear, so concise, so authoritative, so memorable—that you would be hard-pressed to improve on it.

WRITING A PARAPHRASE

A **paraphrase** is a restatement of all the information in a passage in your own words, using your own sentence structure and composed with your own audience in mind to advance your argument.

- When you paraphrase a passage, start by identifying key words and phrases and substituting synonyms for them. A dictionary or thesaurus can help, but you may also have to reread what led up to the passage to remind yourself of the context. For example, did the writer define terms earlier that he or she uses in the passage and now expects you to know?
- Continue by experimenting with word order and sentence structure, combining and recombining phrases to convey what the writer says without replicating his or her style, in the best sequence for your readers. As you shuffle words and phrases, you should begin arriving at a much better understanding of what the writer is saying. By thinking critically, then, you are clarifying the passage for yourself as much as for your readers.

Let's look at a paraphrase of a passage from science fiction writer and scholar James Gunn's essay "Harry Potter as Schooldays Novel"*:

ORIGINAL PASSAGE

The situation and portrayal of Harry as an ordinary child with an extraordinary talent make him interesting. He elicits our sympathy at every turn. He plays a Cinderella-like role as the abused child of mean-spirited foster parents

*Gunn's essay appears in *Mapping the World of Harry Potter: An Unauthorized Exploration of the Bestselling Fantasy Series of All Time*, edited by Mercedes Lackey (Dallas: BenBella, 2006).

who favor other, less-worthy children, and also fits another fantasy role, that of changeling. Millions of children have nursed the notion that they cannot be the offspring of such unremarkable parents; in the Harry Potter books, the metaphor is often literal truth.

PARAPHRASE

According to James Gunn, the circumstances and depiction of Harry Potter as a normal boy with special abilities captivate us by playing on our empathy. Gunn observes that, like Cinderella, Harry is scorned by his guardians, who treat him far worse than they treat his less-admirable peers. And like another fairy-tale figure, the changeling, Harry embodies the fantasies of children who refuse to believe that they were born of their undistinguished parents (146).

In this paraphrase, synonyms have replaced main words (*circumstances and depiction* for "situation and portrayal," *guardians* for "foster parents"), and the structure of the original sentences has been rearranged. But the paraphrase is about the same length as the original and says essentially the same things as Gunn's original.

Now, compare the paraphrase with this summary:

SUMMARY

James Gunn observes that Harry Potter's character is compelling because readers empathize with Harry's fairy-tale-like plight as an orphan whose gifts are ignored by his foster parents (146).

The summary condenses the passage, conveying Gunn's main point without restating the details. Notice how both the paraphrase and the summary indicate that the ideas are James Gunn's, not the writer's — "According to James Gunn," "James Gunn observes" — and signal, with page references, where Gunn's ideas end. *It is essential that you acknowledge your sources*, a subject we come back to in our discussion of plagiarism on page 192. The point we want to make here is that borrowing from the work of others is not always intentional. Many students stumble into plagiarism, especially when they are attempting to paraphrase. Remember that it's not enough to change the words in a paraphrase; you must also change the structure of the sentences. The only sure way to protect yourself is to cite your source.

You may be wondering: "If paraphrasing is so tricky, why bother? What does it add? I can see how the summary of Gunn's paragraph presents information more concisely and efficiently than the original, but the paraphrase doesn't seem to be all that different from the source and doesn't seem to add anything to it. Why not simply quote the original or summarize it?"

Good questions. The answer is that you paraphrase when the ideas in a passage are important but are conveyed in language your readers may have difficulty understanding. When academics write for their peers, they draw on the specialized vocabulary of their disciplines to make their arguments. By paraphrasing, you may be helping your readers, providing a translation of sorts for those who do not speak the language.

Consider this paragraph by George Lipsitz from his academic book *Time Passages: Collective Memory and American Popular Culture*, 1990), and compare the paraphrase that follows it:

ORIGINAL PASSAGE

The transformations in behavior and collective memory fueled by the contradictions of the nineteenth century have passed through three major stages in the United States. The first involved the establishment and cod-ification of commercialized leisure from the invention of the telegraph to the 1890s. The second involved the transition from Victorian to consumer-hedonist values between 1890 and 1945. The third and most important stage, from World War II to the present, involved extraordinary expansion in both the dis-tribution of consumer purchasing power and in both the reach and scope of electronic mass media. The dislocations of urban renewal, suburbanization, and deindustrialization accelerated the demise of tradition in America, while the worldwide pace of change undermined stability elsewhere. The period from World War II to the present marks the final triumph of commercialized leisure, and with it an augmented crisis over the loss of connection to the past.

PARAPHRASE

Historian George Lipsitz argues that Americans' sense of the past is rooted in cultural changes dating from the 1800s and has evolved through three stages. In the first stage, technological innovations of the nineteenth century gave rise to widespread commercial entertainment. In the second stage, dating from the 1890s to about 1945, attitudes toward the consumption of goods and ser-vices changed. Since 1945, in the third stage, increased consumer spending and the growth of the mass media have led to a crisis in which Americans find themselves cut off from their traditions and the memories that give meaning to them (12).

Notice that the paraphrase is not a word-for-word translation of the origi-nal. Instead, the writer has made choices that resulted in a slightly briefer and more accessible restatement of Lipsitz's thinking. (Although this para-phrase is shorter than the original passage, a paraphrase can also be a little longer than the original if extra words are needed to help readers understand the original.)

Notice too that several specialized terms and phrases from the original passage—the "codification of commercialized leisure," "the transition from Victorian to consumer-hedonist values," "the dislocations of urban renewal, suburbanization, and deindustrialization"—have disappeared. The writer not only looked up these terms and phrases in the dictionary but also reread the several pages that preceded the original passage to understand what Lip-sitz meant by them.

The paraphrase is not an improvement on the original passage—in fact, historians would probably prefer what Lipsitz wrote—but it may help readers who do not share Lipsitz's expertise understand his point without distorting his argument.

Now compare this summary to the paraphrase:

SUMMARY

Historian George Lipsitz argues that technological, social, and economic changes dating from the nineteenth century have culminated in what he calls a "crisis over the loss of connection to the past," in which Americans find themselves cut off from the memories of their traditions (12).

Which is better, the paraphrase or the summary? Neither is better or worse in and of itself. Their correctness and appropriateness depend on how the restatements are used in a given argument. That is, the decision to paraphrase or summarize depends entirely on the information you need to convey. Would the details in the paraphrase strengthen your argument? Or is a summary sufficient? In this case, if you plan to focus your argument on the causes of America's loss of cultural memory (the rise of commercial entertainment, changes in spending habits, globalization), then a paraphrase might be more helpful. But if you plan to define *loss of cultural memory*, then a summary may provide enough context for the next stage of your argument.

Steps to Writing a Paraphrase

1 **Decide whether to paraphrase.** If your readers don't need all the information in the passage, consider summarizing it or presenting the key points as part of a summary of a longer passage. If a passage is clear, concise, and memorable as originally written, consider quoting instead of paraphrasing. Otherwise, and especially if the original was written for an academic audience, you may want to paraphrase the original to make its substance more accessible to your readers.

2 **Understand the passage.** Start by identifying key words, phrases, and ideas. If necessary, reread the pages leading up to the passage, to place it in context.

3 **Draft your paraphrase.** Replace key words and phrases with synonyms and alternative phrases (possibly gleaned from the context provided by the surrounding text). Experiment with word order and sentence structure until the paraphrase captures your understanding of the passage, in your own language, for your readers.

4 **Acknowledge your source.** That's the only sure way to protect yourself from a charge of plagiarism.

A Practice Sequence: Paraphrasing

1 In one of the sources you've located in your research, find a sentence of some length and complexity, and paraphrase it. Share the original and your paraphrase of it with a classmate, and discuss the effectiveness of your restatement. Is the meaning clear to your reader? Is the paraphrase written in your own language, using your own sentence structure?

2 Repeat the activity using a short paragraph from the same source. You and your classmate may want to attempt to paraphrase the same paragraph and then compare results. What differences do you detect?

WRITING A SUMMARY

As you have seen, a **summary** condenses a body of information, presenting the key ideas and acknowledging the source. A common activity or assignment in a composition class is to *summarize* a text. You may be asked to read a text, reduce it to its main points, and convey them, without any details or examples, in a written summary. The goal of this assignment is to sharpen your reading and thinking skills as you learn to distinguish between main ideas and supporting details. Being able to distill information in this manner is crucial to critical thinking.

However, summarizing is not an active way to make an argument. While summaries do provide a common ground of information for your readers, you must shape that information to support the purposes of your researched argument with details that clarify, illustrate, or support their main ideas for your readers.

We suggest a method of summarizing that involves

1. describing the author's key claims,
2. selecting examples to illustrate the author's argument,
3. presenting the gist of the author's argument, and
4. contextualizing what you summarize.

We demonstrate these steps for writing a summary following Clive Thompson's article "On the New Literacy."

CLIVE THOMPSON

On the New Literacy

A print journalist at *New York Magazine*, Clive Thompson started his blog, Collision Detection, in September 2002, when he was beginning his year as a Knight Fellow in Science Journalism at MIT. Collision Detection has become one of the most well-regarded blogs on technology and culture. The blog receives approximately 3,000 to 4,000 hits a day. His piece on literacy appeared in *Wired* magazine in 2009.

■ ■ ■

As the school year begins, be ready to hear pundits fretting once again about how kids today can't write—and technology is to blame. Facebook encourages narcissistic blabbering, video and PowerPoint have replaced carefully crafted essays, and texting has dehydrated language into "bleak, bald, sad shorthand" (as University College of London English professor John Sutherland has moaned). An age of illiteracy is at hand, right? *1*

Andrea Lunsford isn't so sure. Lunsford is a professor of writing and rhetoric at Stanford University, where she has organized a mammoth project called the Stanford Study of Writing to scrutinize college students' prose. From 2001 to 2006, she collected 14,672 student writing samples—everything from in-class assignments, formal essays, and journal entries to e-mails, blog posts, and chat sessions. Her conclusions are stirring. *2*

"I think we're in the midst of a literacy revolution the likes of which we haven't seen since Greek civilization," she says. For Lunsford, technology isn't killing our ability to write. It's reviving it—and pushing our literacy in bold new directions. *3*

The first thing she found is that young people today write far more than any generation before them. That's because so much socializing takes place online, and it almost always involves text. Of all the writing that the Stanford students did, a stunning 38 percent of it took place out of the classroom—life writing, as Lunsford calls it. Those Twitter updates and lists of 25 things about yourself add up. *4*

It's almost hard to remember how big a paradigm shift this is. Before the Internet came along, most Americans never wrote anything, ever, that wasn't a school assignment. Unless they got a job that required producing text (like in law, advertising, or media), they'd leave school and virtually never construct a paragraph again. *5*

But is this explosion of prose good, on a technical level? Yes. Lunsford's team found that the students were remarkably adept at what rhetoricians call *kairos*—assessing their audience and adapting their tone and technique to best get their point across. The modern world of online writing, particularly in chat and on discussion threads, is conversational and public, which makes it closer to the Greek tradition of argument than the asynchronous letter and essay writing of 50 years ago. *6*

The fact that students today almost always write for an audience (something virtually no one in my generation did) gives them a different sense of what constitutes good writing. In interviews, they defined good *7* prose as something that had an effect on the world. For them, writing is about persuading and organizing and debating, even if it's over something as quotidian as what movie to go see. The Stanford students were almost always less enthusiastic about their in-class writing because it had no audience but the professor: It didn't serve any purpose other than to get them a grade. As for those texting short-forms and smileys defiling *serious* academic writing? Another myth. When Lunsford examined the work of first-year students, she didn't find a single example of texting speak in an academic paper.

Of course, good teaching is always going to be crucial, as is the mastering of formal academic prose. But it's also becoming clear that online media are pushing literacy into cool directions. The brevity of texting and status updating teaches young people to deploy haiku-like concision. At the same time, the proliferation of new forms of online pop-cultural exegesis—from sprawling TV-show recaps to 15,000-word videogame walkthroughs—has given them a chance to write enormously long and complex pieces of prose, often while working collaboratively with others.   8

We think of writing as either good or bad. What today's young people know is that knowing who you're writing for and why you're writing might be the most crucial factor of all.   9

■ Describe the Key Claims of the Text

As you read through a text with the purpose of summarizing it, you want to identify how the writer develops his or her argument. You can do this by what we call "chunking," grouping related material together into the argument's key claims. Here are two strategies to try.

Notice how paragraphs begin and end.   Often, focusing on the first and last sentences of paragraphs will alert you to the shape and direction of an author's argument. It is especially helpful if the paragraphs are lengthy and full of supporting information, as much academic writing is.

Because of his particular journalistic forum, *Wired* magazine, Thompson's paragraphs are generally rather short, but it's still worth taking a closer look at the first and last sentences of his opening paragraphs:

> *Paragraph 1:* As the school year begins, be ready to hear pundits fretting once again about how kids today can't write—and technology is to blame. Facebook encourages narcissistic blabbering, video and PowerPoint have replaced carefully crafted essays, and texting has dehydrated language into "bleak, bald, sad shorthand" (as University College of London English professor John Sutherland has moaned). An age of illiteracy is at hand, right?

> *Paragraph 2:* Andrea Lunsford isn't so sure. Lunsford is a professor of writing and rhetoric at Stanford University, where she has organized a mammoth project called the Stanford Study of Writing to scrutinize college students' prose. From 2001 to 2006, she collected 14,672 student writing

samples—everything from in-class assignments, formal essays, and journal entries to e-mails, blog posts, and chat sessions. Her conclusions are stirring.

Right away you can see that Thompson has introduced a topic in each paragraph—pundits' criticism of students' use of electronic media in the first, and a national study designed to examine students' literacy in the second—and has indicated a connection between them. In fact, Thompson is explicit in doing so. He asks a question at the end of the first paragraph and then raises doubts as to the legitimacy of critics' denunciation of young people's reliance on blogs and posts to communicate. How will Thompson elaborate on this connection? What major points does he develop?

Notice the author's point of view and use of transitions. Another strategy for identifying major points is to pay attention to descriptive words and transitions. For example, Thompson uses a rhetorical question ("An age of illiteracy is at hand, right?") and then offers a tentative answer ("Andrea Lunsford isn't so sure") that places some doubt in readers' minds.

Notice, too, the words that Thompson uses to characterize the argument in the first paragraph, which he appears to challenge in the second paragraph. Specifically, he describes these critics as "pundits," a word that traditionally refers to an expert or knowledgeable individual. However, the notion of a pundit, someone who often appears on popular talk shows, has also been used negatively. Thompson's description of pundits "fretting," wringing their hands in worry that literacy levels are declining, underscores this negative association of what it means to be a pundit. Finally, Thompson indicates that he does not identify with those who describe students as engaging in "narcissistic blabbering." This is clear when he characterizes the professor as having "moaned."

Once you identify an author's point of view, you will start noticing contrasts and oppositions in the argument—instances where the words are less positive, or neutral, or even negative—which are often signaled by how the writer uses transitions.

For example, Thompson begins with his own concession to critics' arguments when he acknowledges in paragraph 8 that educators should expect students to "[master] formal academic prose." However, he follows this concession with the transition word "but" to signal his own stance in the debate he frames in the first two paragraphs: "online media are pushing literacy into cool directions." Thompson also recognizes that students who write on blogs tend to write short, abbreviated texts. Still, he qualifies his concern with another transition, "at the same time." This transition serves to introduce Thompson's strongest claim: New media have given students "a chance to write enormously long and complex pieces of prose, often while working collaboratively with others."

These strategies can help you recognize the main points of an essay and explain them in a few sentences. For example, you could describe Thompson's key claims in this way:

1. Electronic media give students opportunities to write more than in previous generations, and students have learned to adapt what they

are writing in order to have some tangible effect on what people think and how they act.

2. Arguably, reliance on blogging and posting on Twitter and Facebook can foster some bad habits in writing.

3. But at least one major study demonstrates that the benefits of using the new media outweigh the disadvantages. This study indicates that students write lengthy, complex pieces that contribute to creating significant social networks and collaborations.

■ Select Examples to Illustrate the Author's Argument

A summary should be succinct, which means you should limit the number of examples or illustrations you use. As you distill the major points of the argument, try to choose one or two examples to illustrate each major point. Here are the examples (in italics) you might use to support Thompson's main points:

1. Electronic media give students opportunities to write more than in previous generations, and students have learned to adapt what they are writing in order to have some tangible effect on what people think and how they act. *Examples from the Stanford study: Students "defined good prose as something that had an effect on the world. For them, writing is about persuading and organizing and debating"* (para. 7).

2. Arguably, reliance on blogging and posting on Twitter and Facebook can foster some bad habits in writing. *Examples of these bad habits include critics' charges of "narcissistic blabbering," "bleak, bald, sad shorthand," and "dehydrated language"* (para. 1). *Thompson's description of texting's "haiku-like concision"* (para. 8) *seems to combine praise (haiku can be wonderful poetry) with criticism (it can be obscure and unintelligible).*

3. But at least one major study demonstrates that the benefits of using the new media outweigh the disadvantages. *Examples include Thompson's point that the writing in the new media constitutes a "paradigm shift"* (para. 5). *Andrea Lunsford observes that students are "remarkably adept at what rhetoricians call* kairos—*assessing their audience and adapting their tone and technique to best get their point across"* (para. 6).

A single concrete example may be sufficient to clarify the point you want to make about an author's argument. Throughout the essay, Thompson derives examples from the Stanford study to support his argument in the final two paragraphs. The most concrete, specific example of how the new media benefit students as writers appears in paragraph 6, where the primary research of the Stanford study describes students' acquisition of important rhetorical skills of developing writing that is opportune (*kairos*) and purposeful. This one example may be sufficient for the purposes of summarizing Thompson's essay.

■ Present the Gist of the Author's Argument

When you present the **gist** of an argument, you are expressing the author's central idea in a sentence or two. The gist is not quite the same thing as the author's thesis statement. Instead, it is your formulation of the author's main idea, composed for the needs of your own argument.

Thompson's observations in paragraph 8 represent his thesis: "But it's also becoming clear that online media are pushing literacy into cool directions. . . . [T]he proliferation of new forms of online pop-cultural exegesis—from sprawling TV-show recaps to 15,000-word videogame walkthroughs—has given [students] a chance to write enormously long and complex pieces of prose, often while working collaboratively with others." In this paragraph, Thompson clearly expresses his central ideas in two sentences, while also conceding some of the critics' concerns. However, in formulating the gist of his argument, you want to do more than paraphrase Thompson. You want to use his position to support your own. For example, suppose you want to qualify the disapproval that some educators have expressed in drawing their conclusions about the new media. You would want to mention Thompson's own concessions when you describe the gist of his argument:

GIST

In his essay "On the New Literacy," Clive Thompson, while acknowledging some academic criticism of new media, argues that these media give students opportunities to write more than in previous generations and that students have learned to adapt what they are writing in order to have some tangible effect on what people think and how they act.

Notice that this gist could not have been written based only on Thompson's thesis statement. It reflects knowledge of Thompson's major points, his examples, and his concessions.

■ Contextualize What You Summarize

Your summary should help readers understand the context of the conversation:

- Who is the author?
- What is the author's expertise?
- What is the title of the work?
- Where did the work appear?
- What was the occasion of the work's publication? What prompted the author to write the work?
- What are the issues?
- Who else is taking part in the conversation, and what are their perspectives on the issues?

Key Claim(s)	Examples	Gist	Context
1. Electronic media prompt more student writing than ever before, and students use their writing to make a difference.	The Stanford study: Students "defined good prose as something that had an effect on the world" (para. 7).	In his essay "On the New Literacy," Clive Thompson, while acknowledging some academic criticism of new media, argues that these media give students opportunities to write more than in previous generations and that students have learned to adapt what they are writing in order to have some tangible effect on what people think and how they act.	Thompson is a journalist who has written widely on issues in higher education. His essay "On the New Literacy" appeared in *Wired* in August 2009 (http://www.wired .com/techbiz/people /magazine/17-09 /st_thompson). Under consideration is the debate that he frames in his opening paragraphs.
2. Arguably, reliance on blogging and posting can foster some bad writing habits.	Complaints of "bleak, bald, sad shorthand" and "narcissistic blabbering" (para. 1); texting can be obscure.		
3. But one major study shows the benefits of new media on student writing.	A "paradigm shift" (para. 5) to fluency in multiple formats and skill in assessing and persuading audiences.		

FIGURE 7.1   Worksheet for Writing a Summary

Again, because a summary must be concise, you must make decisions about how much of the conversation your readers need to know. If your assignment is to practice summarizing, it may be sufficient to include only information about the author and the source. However, if you are using the summary to build your own argument, you may need to provide more context. Your practice summary of Thompson's essay should mention that he is a journalist and should cite the title of and page references to his essay. You also may want to include information about Thompson's audience, publication information, and what led to the work's publication. Was it published in response to another essay or book, or to commemorate an important event?

We compiled our notes on Thompson's essay (key claims, examples, gist, context) in a worksheet (Figure 7.1). All of our notes in the worksheet constitute a type of prewriting, our preparation for writing the summary. Creating a worksheet like this can help you track your thoughts as you plan to write a summary. (You can download a template of this worksheet at macmillanhighered.com/frominquiry3e.)

Here is our summary of Thompson's essay:

The gist of Thompson's argument.

In his essay "On the New Literacy," Clive Thompson, while acknowledging some academic criticism of new media, argues that these media give students opportunities to write more than in previous generations and that students have learned to adapt what they are writing in order to have some tangible effect on what people think and how they act.

This concession helps to balance enthusiasm based on a single study.

Thompson's main point with example.

Arguably, reliance on blogging and posting on Twitter and Facebook can foster some bad habits in writing. But at least one major study demonstrates that the benefits of using the new media outweigh the disadvantages. Students write lengthy, complex pieces that contribute to creating significant social networks and collaborations.

Steps to Writing a Summary

1 **Describe the key claims of the text.** To understand the shape and direction of the argument, study how paragraphs begin and end, and pay attention to the author's point of view and use of transitions. Then combine what you have learned into a few sentences describing the key claims.

2 **Select examples to illustrate the author's argument.** Find one or two examples to support each key claim. You may need only one example when you write your summary.

3 **Present the gist of the author's argument.** Describe the author's central idea in your own language with an eye to where you expect your argument to go.

4 **Contextualize what you summarize.** Cue your readers into the conversation. Who is the author? Where and when did the text appear? Why did the author write? Who else is in the conversation?

A Practice Sequence: Writing a Summary

1   Summarize a text that you have been studying for research or for one of your other classes. You may want to limit yourself to an excerpt of just a few paragraphs or a few pages. Follow the four steps we've described, using a summary worksheet for notes, and write a summary of the text. Then share the excerpt and your summary of it with two of your peers. Be prepared to justify your choices in composing the summary. Do your peers agree that your summary captures what is important in the original?

2   With a classmate, choose a brief text of about three pages. Each of you should use the method we describe above to write a summary of the text. Exchange your summaries and worksheets, and discuss the effectiveness of your summaries. Each of you should be prepared to discuss your choice of key claims and examples and your wording of the gist. Did you set forth the context effectively?

SYNTHESIS VERSUS SUMMARY

A **synthesis** is a discussion that forges connections between the arguments of two or more authors. Like a summary, a synthesis requires you to understand the key claims of each author's argument, including his or her use of supporting examples and evidence. Also like a summary, a synthesis requires you to present a central idea, a *gist*, to your readers. But in contrast to a summary, which explains the context of a source, a synthesis creates a context for your own argument. That is, when you write a synthesis comparing two or more sources, you demonstrate that you are aware of the larger conversation about the issue and begin to claim your own place in that conversation.

Most academic arguments begin with a synthesis that sets the stage for the argument that follows. By comparing what others have written on a given issue, writers position themselves in relation to what has come before them, acknowledging the contributions of their predecessors as they advance their own points of view.

Like a summary, a synthesis requires analysis: You have to break down arguments and categorize their parts to see how they work together. In our summary of Thompson's essay (pp. 162–63), the parts we looked at were the key claims, the examples and evidence that supported them, the central idea (conveyed in the gist), and the context. But in a synthesis, your main purpose is not simply to report what another author has said. Rather, you must think critically about how multiple points of view intersect on your issue, and decide what those intersections mean.

Comparing different points of view prompts you to ask why they differ. It also makes you more aware of *counterarguments*—passages where claims conflict ("writer X says this, but writer Y asserts just the opposite") or at least differ ("writer X interprets this information this way, while writer Y sees it differently"). And it starts you formulating your own counterarguments: "Neither X nor Y has taken this into account. What if they had?"

Keep in mind that the purpose of a synthesis is not merely to list the similarities and differences you find in different sources or to assert your agreement with one source as opposed to others. Instead, it sets up your argument. Once you discover connections among texts, you have to decide what those connections mean to you and your readers. What bearing do they have on your own thinking? How can you make use of them in your argument?

WRITING A SYNTHESIS

To compose an effective synthesis, you must (1) make connections among ideas in different texts, (2) decide what those connections mean, and (3) formulate the gist of what you've read, much like you did when you wrote a summary. The difference is that in a synthesis, your gist should be a succinct statement that brings into focus not the central idea of one text but the relationship among different ideas in multiple texts.

To help you grasp strategies of writing a synthesis, read the following essays by journalists Cynthia Haven and Josh Keller, which, like Clive Thompson's essay, deal with the effects of new media on the quality of students' writing. We have annotated the Haven and Keller readings not only to comment on their ideas but also to connect their ideas with those of Thompson. Annotating your texts in this manner is a useful first step in writing a synthesis.

Following the Haven and Keller selections, we explain how annotating contributes to writing a synthesis. Then we show how you can use a worksheet to organize your thinking when you are formulating a gist of your synthesis. Finally, we present our own synthesis based on the texts of Thompson, Haven, and Keller.

CYNTHIA HAVEN

The New Literacy: Stanford Study Finds Richness and Complexity in Students' Writing

Cynthia Haven has written for *The Times Literary Supplement, The Virginia Quarterly Review, The Washington Post, The Los Angeles Times, The San Francisco Chronicle, World Literature Today,* and other publications. Her work has also appeared in *Le Monde, La Repubblica, The Kenyon Review, Quarterly Conversation, The Georgia Review, Civilization,* and others. She has been a Milena Jesenská Journalism Fellow with the Institut für die Wissenschaften vom Menschen in Vienna. *Peter Dale in Conversation with Cynthia Haven* was published in London, 2005. Her *Czeslaw Milosz: Conversations* was published in 2006; *Joseph Brodsky: Conversations* in 2003; and *An Invisible Rope: Portraits of Czeslaw Milosz* was published in 2011 with Ohio University Press/Swallow Press. She is currently a visiting scholar at Stanford, working on a book about René Girard.

■ ■ ■

Begins with claims in the first two paragraphs for our consideration.

Today's kids don't just write for grades anymore. They write to shake the world. *1*

Moreover, they are writing more than any previous generation, ever, in history. They navigate in a bewildering new arena where writers and their audiences have merged. *2*

Cites a study that supports these claims and sets up the terms of a debate: that new media may not be eroding literacy as "conventional wisdom" might suggest.

These are among the startling findings in the Stanford Study of Writing, spearheaded by Professor Andrea Lunsford, director of Stanford's Program in Writing and Rhetoric. The study refutes conventional wisdom and provides a wholly new context for those who wonder "whether Google is making us stupid and whether Facebook is frying our brains," said Lunsford. *3*

The five-year study investigated the writing of Stanford students during their undergraduate careers and their first year afterward, whether at a job or in graduate school. *4*

Observing the way the study employed a random sample helps give legitimacy to the study and support for the study's claims.

The study began in September 2001, when Lunsford invited a random sample of the freshman class to participate in the study. Of the 243 invited, 189 accepted the invitation—about 12 percent of that year's class. *5*

Students agreed to submit the writing they did for all their classes, including multimedia presentations, problem sets, lab reports, and honors theses. They also submitted as much as they wanted of what Lunsford calls "life writing," that is, the writing they did for themselves, their families, their friends, and the world at large. *6*

The volume and range of writing reinforces the initial claim: Today's students are writing more than previous generations.

Lunsford was unprepared for the avalanche of material that ensued: about 15,000 pieces of writing, including e-mails in 11 languages, blog postings, private journal entries, and poetry. The last, in particular, surprised her: "If there's any closeted group at Stanford, it's poets." *7*

Only 62 percent of the writing was for their classwork. *8*

While data analysis is ongoing, Lunsford said the study's first goal was "to paint a picture of the writing that these young writers do" and to portray "its richness and complexity." *9*

Her conclusion: Although today's kids are "writing more than ever before in history," it may not look like the writing of yesterday. The focus of today's writing is "more about instantaneous communication." It's also about audience. *10*

Writing as Vehicle of Change

Implied comparison between the current generation, which communicates to create change, and previous generations, who wrote to fulfill classroom assignments.

For these students, "Good writing changes something. It doesn't just sit on the page. It gets up, walks off the page, and changes something," whether it's a web site or a poster for a walkathon.

11

More than earlier generations, said Lunsford, "Young people today are aware of the precarious nature of our lives. They understand the dangers that await us." Hence, "Writing is a way to get a sense of power."

12

Haven provides a representative case example from the study to illustrate one of the conclusions drawn from the research: that students are writing more outside of class to "get something done."

Twenty-six-year-old Mark Otuteye, one of thirty-six students in the study group who agreed to be interviewed once a year, is in many ways representative. While at Stanford, he started a performance poetry group in response to 2003 student protests against growing involvement in Iraq.

13

"Academic writing seemed to be divorced from a public audience. I was used to communicating not only privately, with e-mails, but publicly, with web sites, blogs, and social networks," said Otuteye, CEO of AES Connect, a social media design company (he's also worked at Google).

14

"I was used to writing transactionally—not just for private reflection, but writing to actually get something done in the world." For Otutcye, a half-Ghanaian student in the Program in African and African American Studies who went on to get a Stanford master's degree in modern thought and literature (2005) and, with a Marshall Scholarship, a master's degree from the University of Sussex in artificial intelligence (2008), academic writing was often "less important" than his writing for the "real world"—for example, the fliers he put up all over Stanford to promote his poetry group.

15

Lunsford cautioned that "audiences are very slippery," and that, in the Internet age, "in a way the whole world can be your audience. It's inspirational, really, but it's hard to know who they are or what they'll do."

16

Anyone anywhere can be an overnight pundit with an audience of millions—or can ramble on in

17

Haven raises a question that many critics have about students being trapped in a limited view of the world.

an unregarded cyberspace tirade. A lively blog "conversation" may consist largely of one writer assuming different masks. Does much of this writing, moreover, trap them in a world of other 19-year-olds, their peers?

Audiences Change over Time

Otuteye noted that the students in the study were already writing for professors, friends, and parents. Moreover, as they transition into the work world after graduation, they begin to see "those audiences begin to mix and overlap. All the communication that they do online, with the exception of e-mail, can become public."   18

The case example helps support the claim that new media enable students to learn to value rhetorical skills.

"The skill of being able to manage multiple, overlapping audiences is a principle of rhetoric, a skill I was able to hone and perfect not only in academic writing, but in the performance writing I did and all the rhetorical activity I was engaged in at Stanford."   19

He said that even the computer code he writes now follows "the same principles of rhetoric, specifically around audience, that is used in poetry and academic writing." A line of code, he said, could have four or more audiences, including other engineers and computers.   20

Is it higher education — not students — that needs to change to meet the demands of new media?

Lunsford underscored the need for higher education to adapt; for example, students could post their essays online, accommodating their preference for an audience and online discussion. But Lunsford said adaptation must go even further: What does an English professor say when a student approaches her and says, "I know you'd like me to write an essay, but I'd like to make a documentary"?   21

This is Haven's own stand. It's clear that these prognosticators were wrong, and they may be wrong again.

In light of this brave new world, it can be hard to remember that only a few decades ago doomsday prophets were predicting the death of the written word, as telephones and television increased their domination over a culture, and business CEOs dictated their letters into Dictaphones.   22

In those days, graduation from college largely meant goodbye to writing. An office memo, letters, or   23 "annotated cookbooks" were about the only written expressions of the adult world, said Lunsford, unless they were headed for jobs in the media or in academia. Writing was "instrumental"—designed for a purpose, such as a purchasing agreement, or advertising to sell a product.

Redefining "Writing"

Today's landscape alters fundamental notions of what writing is. According to Lunsford, "The everyday understanding of writing is usually operational as opposed to epistemic." 24

Defines a specialized term, "epistemic."

Epistemic writing creates knowledge. (Think of all those times when you don't know what to think till you begin writing.) Such epistemic writing is an exploration, rather than declaration. It's the writing that dominates journals, letters, and many blogs. Clearly, the students' sense of agency extends to self-knowledge as well as changing the world. 25

But is the writing "three times" as effective? Is it good writing?

Comparing the Stanford students' writing with their peers from the mid-1980s, Lunsford found that the writing of today's students is about three times as long —they have "the ability to generate more prose." 26

They are also likely to make different kinds of errors. The number one error twenty years ago was spelling—a problem easily circumvented today by a spellchecker. Today's number one error is using the wrong word—"constraint" instead of "constrained," for example, or using the wrong preposition. 27

Lunsford recalls one student writing "I feel necrotic" rather than "neurotic." 28

Counterargument to Lunsford's position: Students have not mastered the technical aspects of writing. However, the quotation does not really answer the question.

Some nevertheless insist that writing today is substandard, littered with too many LOLs and OMGs. However, Lunsford noted that Stanford students were adept at different writing for different audiences. Moreover, they are changing the game: For a graphic novel such as Chris Ware's *Jimmy Corrigan: The Smartest Kid on Earth*, "traditional reading strategies do not work. Every single word is important." And web sites, though they can be skimmed with a click, can be very labor- and thought-intensive. 29

"College writers need to be able to retain the best 30
of print literacy, and know how to deploy it for their
own purposes," said Lunsford. "They also need and
deserve to be exposed to new forms of expression."

With the more playful, inventive and spontaneous 31
forms of writing available to them, are today's students losing the taste for more complex English?

*Concludes with a
quotation about how
the use of new media
does not devalue tra-
ditional conceptions
of literacy, writing,
and classic literature.*

"Every time I pick up Henry James, I have to 32
relearn how to read Henry James. We don't want to
lose the ability to do that kind of reading and writing," said Lunsford.

"Thinking about hard things requires hard prose. 33
We can boil things down, prepare for different audiences, but when it comes to hard things, I don't think
it can be worked out in 140 characters."

JOSH KELLER

Studies Explore Whether the Internet Makes Students Better Writers

Josh Keller was a reporter for *The Chronicle of Higher Education* in Washington, D.C. The weekly publication focuses on issues in higher education and on news and serves as a job-information source for college and
university faculty members, administrators, and students. His piece
appeared in 2009.

■ ■ ■

As a student at Stanford University, Mark Otuteye 1
wrote in any medium he could find. He wrote blog
posts, slam poetry, to-do lists, teaching guides, e-mail
and Facebook messages, diary entries, short stories. He
wrote a poem in computer code, and he wrote a computer program that helped him catalog all the things he
had written.

*Keller uses the same
student example as
Haven to make the
same point about
college writing
assignments.*

But Mr. Otuteye hated writing academic papers. 2
Although he had vague dreams of becoming an English professor, he saw academic writing as a "soul-
less exercise" that felt like "jumping through hoops."
When given a writing assignment in class, he says, he

would usually adopt a personal tone and more or less ignore the prompt. "I got away with it," says Mr. Otuteye, who graduated from Stanford in 2006. "Most of the time."

The rise of online media has helped raise a new generation of college students who write far more, and in more diverse forms, than their predecessors did. But the implications of the shift are hotly debated, both for the future of students' writing and for the college curriculum.

Sums up two opposed points of view on the debate.

Some scholars say that this new writing is more engaged and more connected to an audience, and that colleges should encourage students to bring lessons from that writing into the classroom. Others argue that tweets and blog posts enforce bad writing habits and have little relevance to the kind of sustained, focused argument that academic work demands.

A new generation of longitudinal studies, which track large numbers of students over several years, is attempting to settle this argument. The "Stanford Study of Writing," a five-year study of the writing lives of Stanford students—including Mr. Otuteye—is probably the most extensive to date.

Goes beyond Haven to cite an additional study at Michigan State that reached similar conclusions as the Stanford study.

In a shorter project, undergraduates in a first-year writing class at Michigan State University were asked to keep a diary of the writing they did in any environment, whether blogging, text messaging, or gaming. For each act of writing over a two-week period, they recorded the time, genre, audience, location, and purpose of their writing.

"What was interesting to us was how small a percentage of the total writing the school writing was," says Jeffrey T. Grabill, the study's lead author, who is director of the Writing in Digital Environments Research Center at Michigan State. In the diaries and in follow-up interviews, he says, students often described their social, out-of-class writing as more persistent and meaningful to them than their in-class work was.

Additional evidence that supports the Stanford study.

"Digital technologies, computer networks, the Web—all of those things have led to an explosion in

3

4

5

6

7

8

writing," Mr. Grabill says. "People write more now than ever. In order to interact on the Web, you have to write."

Keller adds the voices of scholars of writing to comment on the value of new media.

Kathleen Blake Yancey, a professor of English at Florida State University and a former president of the National Council of Teachers of English, calls the current period "the age of composition" because, she says, new technologies are driving a greater number of people to compose with words and other media than ever before.

9

"This is a new kind of composing because it's so variegated and because it's so intentionally social," Ms. Yancey says. Although universities may not consider social communication as proper writing, it still has a strong influence on how students learn to write, she says. "We ignore it at our own peril."

10

Unlike Thompson and Haven, Keller provides the counterarguments of scholars who dispute the findings of the Stanford study.

But some scholars argue that students should adapt their writing habits to their college course work, not the other way around. Mark Bauerlein, a professor of English at Emory University, cites the reading and writing scores in the National Assessment of Educational Progress, which have remained fairly flat for decades. It is a paradox, he says: "Why is it that with young people reading and writing more words than ever before in human history, we find no gains in reading and writing scores?"

11

The Right Writing

Determining how students develop as writers, and why they improve or not, is difficult. Analyzing a large enough sample of students to reach general conclusions about how the spread of new technologies affects the writing process, scholars say, is a monumental challenge.

12

The sheer amount of information that is relevant to a student's writing development is daunting and difficult to collect: formal and informal writing, scraps of notes and diagrams, personal histories, and fleeting conversations and thoughts that never make it onto the printed page.

13

Underscores the
difficulty of drawing
conclusions either
way. This summary
of the Stanford
study suggests that
researchers there
have responded to
the complexity of
measuring outcomes
of writing in any
medium.

The Stanford study is trying to collect as much of   *14*
that material as possible. Starting in 2001, researchers at the university began collecting extensive writing samples from 189 students, roughly 12 percent
of the freshman class. Students were given access to
a database where they could upload copies of their
work, and some were interviewed annually about
their writing experiences. By 2006 researchers had
amassed nearly 14,000 pieces of writing.

Students in the study "almost always" had more   *15*
enthusiasm for the writing they were doing outside
of class than for their academic work, says Andrea A.
Lunsford, the study's director. Mr. Otuteye submitted
about 700 pieces of writing and became the study's
most prolific contributor.

The report's authors say they included nonaca-   *16*
demic work to better investigate the links between
academic and nonacademic writing in students' writing development. One of the largest existing longitudinal studies of student writing, which started at
Harvard University in the late 1990s, limited its sample to academic writing, which prevented researchers
from drawing direct conclusions about that done outside of class.

In looking at students' out-of-class writing, the   *17*
Stanford researchers say they found several traits that
were distinct from in-class work. Not surprisingly, the
writing was self-directed; it was often used to connect
with peers, as in social networks; and it usually had a
broader audience.

Cites the study at
George Mason.
Writing on blogs is
more engaging than
writing in school, and
it represents the
ways students sus-
tain social networks
(paras 17-20).

The writing was also often associated with accom-   *18*
plishing an immediate, concrete goal, such as organizing a group of people or accomplishing a political
end, says Paul M. Rogers, one of the study's authors.
The immediacy might help explain why students
stayed so engaged, he says. "When you talked to
them about their out-of-class writing, they would
talk about writing to coordinate out-of-class activity,"
says Mr. Rogers, an assistant professor of English at
George Mason University. "A lot of them were a lot

more conscious of the effect their writing was having on other people."

Mr. Rogers believes from interviews with students *19* that the data in the study will help show that students routinely learn the basics of writing concepts wherever they write the most. For instance, he says, students who compose messages for an audience of their peers on a social-networking Web site were forced to be acutely aware of issues like audience, tone, and voice.

"The out-of-class writing actually made them more *20* conscious of the things writing teachers want them to think about," the professor says.

Mr. Otuteye, who recently started a company that *21* develops Web applications, says he paid close attention to the writing skills of his peers at Stanford as the co-founder of a poetry slam. It was the students who took their out-of-class writing seriously who made the most progress, he says. "Everybody was writing in class, but the people who were writing out of and inside of class, that was sort of critical to accelerating their growth as writers."

Although analysis of the Stanford study is still at an *22* early stage, other scholars say they would like to start similar studies. At the University of California, several writing researchers say they are trying to get financial support for a longitudinal study of 300 students on the campuses in Irvine, Santa Barbara, and Davis.

Curricular Implications

Why does it have to be "either/or"? Isn't it possible that there's a middle ground?

The implications of the change in students' writing habits for writing and literature curricula are up for debate. Much of the argument turns on whether online writing should be seen as a welcome new direction or a harmful distraction. *23*

Grabill criticizes the critics, pointing out that they have lost sight of an important goal: Students should be able to

Mr. Grabill, from Michigan State, says college writing instruction should have two goals: to help students become better academic writers, and to help them become better writers in the outside world. The second, broader goal is often lost, he says, either *24 write to general, public audience, not just academic readers (paras. 24–30).*

because it is seen as not the college's responsibility, or because it seems unnecessary.

"The unstated assumption there is that if you can write a good essay for your literature professor, you can write anything," Mr. Grabill says. "That's utter nonsense."   25

The writing done outside of class is, in some ways, the opposite of a traditional academic paper, he says. Much out-of-class writing, he says, is for a broad audience instead of a single professor, tries to solve real-world problems rather than accomplish academic goals, and resembles a conversation more than an argument.   26

Rather than being seen as an impoverished, secondary form, online writing should be seen as "the new normal," he says, and treated in the curriculum as such: "The writing that students do in their lives is a tremendous resource."   27

This seems rather anecdotal.

Ms. Yancey, at Florida State, says out-of-class writing can be used in a classroom setting to help students draw connections among disparate types of writing. In one exercise she uses, students are asked to trace the spread of a claim from an academic journal to less prestigious forms of media, like magazines and newspapers, in order to see how arguments are diluted. In another, students are asked to pursue the answer to a research question using only blogs, and to create a map showing how they know if certain information is trustworthy or not.   28

But does this occur — avoiding a "fire wall"?

The idea, she says, is to avoid creating a "fire wall" between in-class and out-of-class writing.   29

"If we don't invite students to figure out the lessons they've learned from that writing outside of school and bring those inside of school, what will happen is only the very bright students" will do it themselves, Ms. Yancey says. "It's the rest of the population that we're worried about."   30

One critic concedes that writing in electronic media can help struggling writers, but he also

Writing in electronic media probably does benefit struggling students in a rudimentary way, says Emory's Mr. Bauerlein, because they are at least forced to string sentences together: "For those kids who   31

*warns that educa-
tors should temper
their enthusiasm for
blogging and other
online writing (paras.
32–35).*

wouldn't be writing any words anyway, that's going to improve their very low-level skills."

But he spends more of his time correcting, not inte- 32
grating, the writing habits that students pick up out-side of class. The students in his English courses often turn in papers that are "stylistically impoverished," and the Internet is partly to blame, he says. Writing for one's peers online, he says, encourages the kind of quick, unfocused thought that results in a scarcity of coherent sentences and a limited vocabulary.

Has he studied this?

"When you are writing so much to your peers, 33
you're writing to other 17-year-olds, so your vocabu-lary is going to be the conventional vocabulary of the 17-year-old idiom," Mr. Bauerlein says.

Students must be taught to home in on the words 34
they write and to resist the tendency to move quickly from sentence to sentence, he says. Writing scholars, too, should temper their enthusiasm for new tech-nologies before they have fully understood the impli-cations, he says. Claims that new forms of writing should take a greater prominence in the curriculum, he says, are premature.

"The sweeping nature of their pronouncements 35
to me is either grandiose or flatulent, or you could say that this is a little irresponsible to be pushing for practices so hard that are so new," Mr. Bauerlein says. "We don't know what the implications of these things will be. Slow down!?"

*Another scholar
reaffirms a finding in
the Stanford study:
that electronic media
represent a cultural
shift that educators
must learn to accept
and adapt to.*

Deborah Brandt, a professor of English at the 36
University of Wisconsin at Madison who studies the recent history of reading and writing, says the growth of writing online should be seen as part of a broader cultural shift toward mass authorship. Some of the resistance to a more writing-centered curriculum, she says, is based on the view that writing without reading can be dangerous because students will be untethered to previous thought, and reading levels will decline.

*Really, people are not
shaped by what they
read?*

But that view, she says, is "being challenged by the 37
literacy of young people, which is being developed primarily by their writing. They're going to be read-ing, but they're going to be reading to write, and not to be shaped by what they read."

■ Make Connections Among Different Texts

The texts by Thompson, Haven, and Keller all deal with the emergence of new electronic media and their effects on students' development as writers. These texts are very much in conversation with one another, as each author focuses on what research tells us are the benefits of the new media and the potential ways that electronic media can limit young writers' growth:

- Thompson uses the Stanford study to emphasize the ways that students' participation on blogs and the like helps students learn to adapt their writing for specific audiences and to write fairly complex texts to affect the ways readers think and act.

- Haven provides a more elaborate analysis of the Stanford study to argue that we are witnessing a revolution in literacy, the likes of which we have not experienced since the development of classical rhetoric.

- Keller offers converging pieces of evidence to support the findings from the Stanford study that Thompson and Haven discuss, but additionally he provides a more detailed counterargument that is also based on research.

All three authors seem to agree that the introduction of new electronic media has contributed to a paradigm shift in the uses of writing—to create agency and community—but they seem to vary in the concessions they make to counterarguments.

Notice how our annotations call out connections. "Keller uses the same student example as Haven to make the same point about college writing assignments." "Keller adds the voices of scholars of writing to comment on the value of new media." "Unlike Thompson and Haven, Keller provides the counterarguments of scholars who dispute the findings of the Stanford study."

With these annotations, we are starting to think critically about the ideas in the essays. Notice, however, that not all of the annotations make connections. Some note examples that support the argument that electronic media benefit writers, while others point to examples that provide compelling evidence for the counterargument. Still other annotations raise questions about the basis on which researchers and teachers reached their conclusions. In the end, you should not expect that every annotation will contribute to your synthesis. Instead, use them to record your responses and also to spur your thinking.

■ Decide What Those Connections Mean

Having annotated the selections, we filled out the worksheet in Figure 7.2, making notes in the grid to help us see the three texts in relation to one another. Our worksheet included columns for

- author and source information,
- the gist of each author's arguments,

- supporting examples and illustrations,
- counterarguments, and
- our own thoughts.

A worksheet like this one can help you concentrate on similarities and differences in the texts to determine what the connections among texts mean. (You can download a template for this worksheet at macmillanhighered .com/frominquiry3e.) Of course, you can design your own worksheet as well, tailoring it to your needs and preferences. If you want to take very detailed notes about your authors and sources, for example, you may want to have separate columns for each.

Once you start making connections, including points of agreement and disagreement, you can start identifying counterarguments in the reading—for example, Keller quotes a scholar who cites a national study, the National Assessment of Education Progress, to dampen enthusiasm for the claims that Thompson and Haven give so much attention to. Identifying counterarguments gives you a sense of what is at issue for each author. And determining what authors think in relation to one another can help you realize what is at issue for you. Suppose you are struck by Haven's implicit argument that a revolution in literacy is occurring and that institutions of higher education, not students, need to respond to changes in the nature of literacy and communication. But you also recognize in Keller's analysis that questions persist about studies conducted to assess the development of students' growth and development as writers. How persuasive are the studies conducted at Stanford, Michigan State, and George Mason? What do we really know? And how can we further test the claims experts make about electronic media and paradigm shifts? Turning these ideas and questions over in your mind, you may be able to decide on a topic you want to explore and develop.

■ Formulate the Gist of What You've Read

Remember that your gist should bring into focus the relationship among different ideas in multiple texts. Looking at the information juxtaposed on the worksheet, you can begin to construct the gist of your synthesis:

- Clive Thompson cites research conducted at Stanford to challenge prevailing arguments about electronic media's effects on students' literacy. Indeed, despite pundits' complaints, students may be more literate than in the past.
- Cynthia Haven also analyzes the Stanford study, which indicates that we may very well be experiencing a revolution in literacy. Students use electronic media to sustain social networks and create change. As Thompson also points out, students are writing more than ever before and are more adept at applying principles of rhetoric than were students in previous generations. Those in higher education may have to change in order to respond to students' uses of electronic media, not the other way around.

Author and Source	Gist of Argument	Examples/ Illustrations	Counterarguments	What I Think
Clive Thompson, "On the New Literacy," *Wired* (2009)	Research challenges prevailing arguments about electronic media's effects on students' literacy, suggesting they may be more literate than in the past.	The Stanford study, with its sample of more than 14,000 pieces of writing and randomized sample of student participants. One case example.	Student writing is full of "texting-speak."	The Stanford study is persuasive, especially given the size of the study. Not much counter-evidence.
Cynthia Haven, "The New Literacy: Stanford Study Finds Richness and Complexity in Students' Writing," *Stanford Report* (2009)	A study indicates a possible revolution in literacy. Using online social networks to create change, students now write more, more persuasively, and more adaptively than ever before.	Stanford study and case example of one student.	Students who spend most of their time writing on electronic networks do not attend to the technical aspects of communication and have a limited sense of their audience.	This is a more thorough review of the Stanford study. It emphasizes how much more meaningful writing is outside of the classroom.
Josh Keller, "Studies Explore Whether the Internet Makes Students Better Writers," *Chronicle of Higher Education* (2009)	Two studies suggest that electronic media, in giving students more opportunities to write and honing their sense of audience, have made them better writers than previous generations. But an emerging body of evidence challenges these recent claims, which force educators to consider what they consider good writing.	Studies at Stanford, Michigan State, and George Mason. Expert opinion from faculty at Florida State and the University of Wisconsin.	Critics like Professor Bauerlein at Emory University argue that literacy is not progressing steadily, as some have observed, at least not based on standardized tests. He suggests that writing solely to one's peers online encourages spontaneous but unfocused thought and a limited vocabulary.	The three studies together are quite powerful. I am not sure that standardized tests developed a generation ago are the best way to measure increases in literacy. And Bauerlein relies on anecdotal evidence to make his argument: that writing in electronic media limits thinking or writing quality. I should check if any studies exist to support Baeurlein.

FIGURE 7.2   Worksheet for Writing a Synthesis

- Josh Keller points to two additional studies of writing to suggest that students are developing literate practices that are more impressive than those of previous generations. This can be attributed to the fact that current students have more opportunities to write and they know what it means to write for an audience. But he also observes that an emerging body of evidence challenges these recent claims, forcing educators to consider what constitutes good writing.

How do you formulate this information into a gist? You can use a transition word such as *although* or *however* to connect ideas that different authors bring together while conveying their differences. Thus, a gist of these essays might read:

GIST OF A SYNTHESIS

Although Clive Thompson and Cynthia Haven suggest that new electronic media have created a paradigm shift in the ways educators think about writing, journalists such as Josh Keller have also cited evidence that dampens enthusiasm for the benefits of writing on blogs without students' having instruction in formal, academic writing.

Having drafted the gist, we returned to our notes on the worksheet to complete the synthesis, presenting examples and using transitions to signal the relationships among the texts and their ideas. Here is our brief synthesis of the three texts:

The gist of our synthesis. "Although" signals that Thompson's and Haven's arguments are qualified.

Although Clive Thompson and Cynthia Haven suggest that new electronic media have created a paradigm shift in the ways educators think about writing, journalists such as Josh Keller have also cited evidence that dampens enthusiasm for the benefits of writing on blogs without students' hav-

Specific example of a key piece of evidence that has sparked debate.

ing instruction in formal, academic writing. In particular, Thompson cites research conducted at Stanford University to challenge prevailing arguments about electronic media's effects on students' literacy. The Stanford study, with its sample of more than 14,000 pieces of writing and randomized sample of student participants, seems very persuasive. Indeed, despite pundits' complaints, students may be more literate than in the past.

Cynthia Haven also analyzes the Stanford study, indicating that we may very well be experiencing a revolution in literacy. Students use electronic media to sustain social networks and create change. As Thompson also points out, students are writing more than ever before and are more adept at applying principles of rhetoric than were students in previous generations. Those in higher education may have to change in order to respond to students' uses of electronic media, not the other way around.

Finally, Josh Keller points to two additional studies of writing to suggest that students are developing literate practices that are more impressive than those of previous generations. This can be attributed to the fact that current students have more opportunities to write and they know what it means to write for an audience. However, Keller, more than Thompson and Haven, observes that an emerging body of evidence challenges these recent claims, forcing educators to consider what constitutes good writing. Keller's analysis reveals that questions persist about studies conducted to assess the development of students' growth and development as writers. How persuasive are the studies conducted at Stanford, Michigan State, and George Mason? What do we really know, and what do we need to know? Further, how can we test the claims experts make about electronic media and paradigm shifts?

Transition: Both Thompson and Haven give less attention to the counterargument than they should.

Questions set up direction of what is to follow.

Writing a synthesis, like writing a summary, is principally a strategy for framing your own argument. In writing a synthesis, you are conveying to your readers how various points of view in a conversation intersect and diverge. The larger point of this exercise is to find your own issue—your own position in the conversation—and make your argument for it.

Steps to Writing a Synthesis

1 **Make connections between and among different texts.** Annotate the texts you are working with, with an eye to comparing them. As you would for a summary, note major points in the texts, choose relevant examples, and formulate the gist of each text.

2 **Decide what those connections mean.** Fill out a worksheet to compare your notes on the different texts, track counterarguments, and record your thoughts. Decide what the similarities and differences mean to you and what they might mean to your readers.

3 **Formulate the gist of what you've read.** Identify an overarching idea that brings together the ideas you've noted, and write a synthesis that forges connections and makes use of the examples you've noted. Use transitions to signal the direction of your synthesis.

A Practice Sequence: Writing a Synthesis

1 To practice the strategies for synthesizing that we describe in this chapter, read the following three essays, which focus on the role that electronic media play in conveying information to diverse groups of readers or viewers. As you discuss the strategies the authors use to develop their arguments, consider these questions:

- How would you explain the popularity of blogs, Twitter, and YouTube?

- What themes have the writers focused on as they have sought to enter the conversation surrounding the use of electronic media?

- To what extent do you think the criticisms of new media presented by the authors are legitimate?

- Do blogs, Twitter, and YouTube pose a threat to traditional journalism?

- Do you think that blogs, Twitter, and YouTube add anything to print journalism? If so, what?

2 To stimulate a conversation, or a debate, we suggest that you break up into four different groups:

Group 1: Print journalism

Group 2: Blogs

Group 3: Twitter

Group 4: YouTube

Students in each group should prepare an argument indicating the strengths and limitations of the particular mode of communication that they represent. In preparing the argument, be sure to acknowledge what other modes of communication might add to the ways we learn about news and opinions. One student from each group will present this argument to the other groups.

3 Based on the discussion you have had in exercise 1 and/or exercise 2, write a synthesis of the three essays using the steps we have outlined in this chapter.

- Summarize each essay.

- Explain the ways in which the authors' arguments are similar or different, using examples and illustrations to demonstrate the similarities and differences.

- Formulate an overall gist that synthesizes the points each author makes.

DAN KENNEDY

Political Blogs: Teaching Us Lessons About Community

Dan Kennedy, an assistant professor of journalism at Northeastern University, writes on media issues for *The Guardian* and for *CommonWealth* magazine. His blog, Media Nation, is online at dankennedy.net.

■ ■ ■

The rise of blogging as both a supplement and a challenge to traditional journalism has coincided with an explosion of opinion mongering. Blogs—and the role they play in how Americans consume and respond to information—are increasingly visible during our political season, when our ideological divide is most apparent. From nakedly partisan sites such as Daily Kos on the left and Little Green Footballs on the right, to more nuanced but nevertheless ideological enterprises such as Talking Points Memo, it sometimes seems there is no room in blogworld for straight, neutral journalism.   1

The usual reasons given for this are that reporting is difficult and expensive and that few bloggers know how to research a story, develop and interview sources, and assemble the pieces into a coherent, factual narrative. Far easier, so this line of thinking goes, for bloggers to sit in their pajamas and blast their semi-informed opinions out to the world.   2

There is some truth to this, although embracing this view wholeheartedly requires us to overlook the many journalists who are now writing blogs, as well as the many bloggers who are producing journalism to a greater or lesser degree. But we make a mistake when we look at the opinion-oriented nature of blogs and ask whether bloggers are capable of being "objective," to use a hoary and now all but meaningless word. The better question to ask is why opinion-oriented blogs are so popular—and what lessons the traditional media can learn from them without giving up their journalistic souls.   3

Perhaps what's happening is that the best and more popular blogs provide a sense of community that used to be the lifeblood of traditional news organizations and, especially, of newspapers. Recently I reread part of Jay Rosen's book, *What Are Journalists For?*, his 1999 postmortem on the public journalism movement. What struck me was Rosen's description of public journalism's origins, which were grounded in an attempt to recreate a sense of community so that people might discover a reason to read newspapers. "Eventually I came to the conclusion . . . that journalism's purpose was to see the public into fuller existence," Rosen writes. "Informing people followed that."   4

Rosen's thesis—that journalism could only be revived by reawak-   5
ening the civic impulse—is paralleled by Robert Putnam's 2000 book,
Bowling Alone, in which he found that people who sign petitions,
attend public meetings, and participate in religious and social organizations are more likely to be newspaper readers than those who do
not. "Newspaper readers are older, more educated, and more rooted in
their communities than is the average American," Putnam writes.

Unfortunately for the newspaper business, the traditional idea   6
of community, based mainly on geography, remains as moribund today
as it was when Rosen and Putnam were analyzing its pathologies. But
if old-fashioned communities are on the decline, the human impulse to
form communities is not. And the Internet, as it turns out, is an ideal
medium for fostering a new type of community in which people have
never met, and may not even know each other's real names, but share
certain views and opinions about the way the world works. It's interesting that Rosen has become a leading exponent of journalism tied
to these communities, both through his PressThink blog and through
NewAssignment.net, which fosters collaborations between professional
and citizen journalists.

Attitude First, Facts Second

This trend toward online community-building has given us a mediascape   7
in which many people—especially those most interested in politics
and public affairs—want the news delivered to them in the context of
their attitudes and beliefs. That doesn't mean they want to be fed a diet
of self-reinforcing agit-prop (although some do). It does mean they see
their news consumption as something that takes place within their community, to be fit into a preexisting framework of ideas that may be challenged but that must be acknowledged.

Earlier this year John Lloyd, a contributing editor for the *Financial*   8
Times, talked about the decline of just-the-facts journalism on *Open*
Source, a Web-based radio program hosted by the veteran journalist
Christopher Lydon. It has become increasingly difficult, Lloyd said, to
report facts that are not tied to an ideological point of view. The emerging paradigm, he explained, may be "that you can only get facts through
by attaching them to a very strong left-wing, right-wing, Christian, athe-
ist position. Only then, only if you establish your bona fides within this
particular community, will they be open to facts."

No less a blogging enthusiast than Markos Moulitsas, founder of Daily   9
Kos, has observed that political blogs are a nonentity in Britain, where

the newspapers themselves cater to a wide range of different opinions. "You look at the media in Britain, it's vibrant and it's exciting and it's fun, because they're all ideologically tinged," Moulitsas said at an appearance in Boston last fall. "And that's a good thing, because people buy them and understand that their viewpoints are going to be represented."

The notion that journalism must be tied to an ideological community   *10* may seem disheartening to traditionalists. In practice, though, journalism based on communities of shared interests and beliefs can be every bit as valuable as the old model of objectivity, if approached with rigor and respect for the truth.

Last year, for instance, Talking Points Memo (TPM) and its related   *11* blogs helped break the story of how the U.S. Department of Justice had fired eight U.S. attorneys for what appeared to be politically motivated reasons, a scandal that led to the resignation of Attorney General Alberto Gonzales. TPM's reporting was based in part on information dug up and passed along by its liberal readership. The founder and editor, Joshua Micah Marshall, received a George Polk Award, but it belonged as much to the community he had assembled as it did to him personally.

Of course, we still need neutral, non-opinionated journalism to help   *12* us make sense of the world around us. TPM's coverage of the U.S. attorneys scandal was outstanding, but it was also dismissive of arguments that it was much ado about nothing, or that previous administrations had done the same or worse. Liberals or conservatives who get all of their news from ideologically friendly sources don't have much incentive to change their minds.

Connecting to Communities of Shared Interests

Even news outlets that excel at traditional, "objective" journalism do so   *13* within the context of a community. Some might not find liberal bias in the news pages of the *New York Times,* as the paper's conservative critics would contend, but there's little doubt that the *Times* serves a community of well-educated, affluent, culturally liberal readers whose preferences and tastes must be taken into account. Not to be a journalistic relativist, but all news needs to be evaluated within the context in which it was produced, even an old-fashioned, inverted-pyramid-style dispatch from the wires. Who was interviewed? Who wasn't? Why? These are questions that must be asked regardless of the source.

We might now be coming full circle as placeblogs—chatty, conver-   *14* sational blogs that serve a particular geographic community—become more prevalent. Lisa Williams, founder of H2Otown, a blog that serves her community of Watertown, Massachusetts, believes that such forums could help foster the sense of community that is a necessary precondition to newspaper readership. Williams also runs a project called Placeblogger.com, which tracks local blogs around the world.

"The news creates a shared pool of stories that gives us a way to talk *15* to people who aren't family or close friends or people who we will never meet—in short, our fellow citizens," Williams says by e-mail. "The truth is, people still want those neighbor-to-neighbor contacts, but the traditional ways of doing it don't fit into the lives that people are actually living today. Your core audience is tired, sitting on the couch with their laptop, and watching *Lost* with one eye. Give them someone to sit with."

Critics of blogs have been looking at the wrong thing. While tradition- *16* alists disparage bloggers for their indulgence of opinion and hyperbole, they overlook the sense of community and conversation that blogs have fostered around the news. What bloggers do well, and what news organizations do poorly or not at all, is give their readers someone to sit with. News consumers—the public, citizens, us—still want the truth. But we also want to share it and talk about it with our like-minded neighbors and friends. The challenge for journalism is not that we'll lose our objectivity; it's that we won't find a way to rebuild a sense of community.

JOHN DICKERSON

Don't Fear Twitter

John Dickerson is *Slate* magazine's chief political correspondent and political director of CBS News. Before joining *Slate*, Dickerson covered politics for *Time* magazine, including four years as the magazine's White House correspondent. Dickerson has also written for the *New York Times* and *Washington Post* and is a regular panelist on *Washington Week in Review*. This essay first appeared in the Summer 2008 issue of *Nieman Reports*.

∎ ∎ ∎

If I were cleverer, this piece on Twitter and journalism would fit in *1* Twitter's 140-character limitation. The beauty of Twitter when properly used—by both the reader and the writer—is that everyone knows what it is. No reader expects more from Twitter than it offers, and no one writing tries to shove more than necessary into a Twitter entry, which is sometimes called a Tweet, but not by me, thank you.

Not many people know what Twitter is, though, so I'm going to go on *2* for a few hundred words. Twitter is a Web site that allows you to share your thoughts instantly and on any topic with other people in the Twitter network as long as you do so in tight little entries of 140 characters or less. If you're wondering how much you can write with that space limitation, this sentence that you're reading right now hits that mark perfectly.

For some, journalism is already getting smaller. Newspapers are 3 shrinking. Serious news is being pushed aside in favor of entertainment and fluff stories. To many journalists and guardians of the trade, the idea that any journalist would willingly embrace a smaller space is horrifying and dumb. One journalism professor drew himself up to his full height and denounced Twitter journalism—or microjournalism, as someone unfortunately called it—as the ultimate absurd reduction of journalism. (I think he may have dislodged his monocle, he was waving his quill pen so violently.) Venerable CBS newsman Roger Mudd had a far lighter touch when he joked to me that he could barely say the word "texting" when he and I were talking about the idea of delivering a couple of sentences and calling it journalism.

We can all agree that journalism shouldn't get any smaller, but Twit- 4 ter doesn't threaten the traditions of our craft. It adds, rather than subtracts, from what we do.

As I spend nearly all of my time on the road these days reporting on 5 the presidential campaigns, Twitter is the perfect place for all of those asides I've scribbled in the hundreds of notebooks I have in my garage from the campaigns and stories I've covered over the years. Inside each of those notebooks are little pieces of color I've picked up along the way. Sometimes these snippets are too off-topic or too inconsequential to work into a story. Sometimes they are the little notions or sideways thoughts that become the lead of a piece or the kicker. All of them now have found a home on Twitter.

As journalists we take people places they can't go. Twitter offers a 6 little snapshot way to do this. It's informal and approachable and great for conveying a little moment from an event. Here's an entry from a McCain rally during the Republican primaries: "Weare, NH: Audience man to McCain: 'I heard that Hershey is moving plants to Mexico and I'll be damned if I'm going to eat Mexican chocolate.'" In Scranton covering Barack Obama I sent this: "Obama: 'What's John McCain's problem?' Audience member: 'He's too old.' Obama: 'No, no that's not the problem. There are a lot of wise people. . . .'" With so many Democrats making an issue of McCain's age, here was the candidate in the moment seeming to suggest that critique was unfair.

Occasionally, just occasionally, reporters can convey a piece of news 7 that fits into 140 characters without context. If Twitter had been around when the planes hit the World Trade Center, it would have been a perfect way for anyone who witnessed it to convey at that moment what they'd seen or heard. With Twitter, we can also pull back the curtain on our lives a little and show readers what it's like to cover a campaign. ("Wanna be a reporter? On long bus rides learn to sleep in your own hand.")

The risk for journalism, of course, is that people spend all day Twit-   8
tering and reading other people's Twitter entries and don't engage with
the news in any other way. This seems a pretty small worry. If written
the right way, Twitter entries build a community of readers who find
their way to longer articles because they are lured by these moment-
by-moment observations. As a reader, I've found that I'm exposed to
a wider variety of news because I read articles suggested to me by the
wide variety of people I follow on Twitter. I'm also exposed to some
keen political observers and sharp writers who have never practiced
journalism.

Twitter is not the next great thing in journalism. No one should try   9
to make Twitter do more than it can and no reader should expect too
much from a 140-character entry. As for the critics, their worries about
Twitter and journalism seem like the kind of obtuse behavior that would
make a perfect observational Twitter entry: "A man at the front of the
restaurant is screaming at a waiter and gesticulating wildly. The snacks
on the bar aren't a four-course meal!"

STEVE GROVE

YouTube: The Flattening of Politics

Steve Grove is Director of Community Partnerships at Google, and formerly directed all news, political programming, and citizen journalism for
YouTube. He has been quoted as saying that he regards himself less as an
editor than as a curator of the Web site's "chaotic sea of content." A native
of Northfield, Minnesota, he worked as a journalist at the *Boston Globe* and
ABC News before moving to YouTube.

■ ■ ■

For a little over a year, I've served as YouTube's news and political   1
director—perhaps a perplexing title in the eyes of many journalists.
Such wonderment might be expected since YouTube gained its early
notoriety as a place with videos of dogs on skateboards or kids falling
off of trampolines. But these days, in the ten hours of video uploaded to
YouTube every minute of every day (yes—every minute of every day),
an increasing amount of the content is news and political video. And
with YouTube's global reach and ease of use, it's changing the way that
politics—and its coverage—is happening.

Each of the sixteen one-time presidential candidates had YouTube   2
channels; seven announced their candidacies on YouTube. Their staffs
uploaded thousands of videos that were viewed tens of millions of times.
By early March of this year, the Obama campaign was uploading two to

three videos to YouTube every day. And thousands of advocacy groups and nonprofit organizations use YouTube to get their election messages into the conversation. For us, the most exciting aspect is that ordinary people continue to use YouTube to distribute their own political content; these range from "gotcha" videos they've taken at campaign rallies to questions for the candidates, from homemade political commercials to video mash-ups of mainstream media coverage.

What this means is that average citizens are able to fuel a new meritocracy for political coverage, one unburdened by the gatekeeping "middleman." Another way of putting it is that YouTube is now the world's largest town hall for political discussion, where voters connect with candidates — and the news media — in ways that were never before possible.   *3*

In this new media environment, politics is no longer bound by traditional barriers of time and space. It doesn't matter what time it is, or where someone is located — as long as they have the means to connect through the Web, they can engage in the discussion. This was highlighted in a pair of presidential debates we produced with CNN during this election cycle during which voters asked questions of the candidates via YouTube videos they'd submitted online. In many ways, those events simply brought to the attention of a wider audience the sort of exchanges that take place on YouTube all the time. . . .   *4*

News Organizations and YouTube

Just because candidates and voters find all sorts of ways to connect directly on YouTube does not mean there isn't room for the mainstream media, too. In fact, many news organizations have launched YouTube channels, including the Associated Press, the *New York Times*, the BBC, CBS, and the *Wall Street Journal*.   *5*

Why would a mainstream media company upload their news content to YouTube?   *6*

Simply put, it's where eyeballs are going. Research from the Pew Internet & American Life project found that 37 percent of adult Internet users have watched online video news, and well over half of online adults have used the Internet to watch video of any kind. Each day on YouTube hundreds of millions of videos are viewed at the same time that television viewership is decreasing in many markets. If a mainstream news organization wants its political reporting seen, YouTube offers visibility without a cost. The ones that have been doing this for a while rely on a strategy of building audiences on YouTube and then trying to drive viewers back to their Web sites for a deeper dive into the content. And these organizations can earn revenue as well by running ads against their video content on YouTube.   *7*

In many ways, YouTube's news ecosystem has the potential to offer   8
much more to a traditional media outlet. Here are some examples:

1. **Interactivity:** YouTube provides an automatic focus group for
   news content. How? YouTube wasn't built as merely a "series of
   tubes" to distribute online video. It is also an interactive platform.
   Users comment on, reply to, rank, and share videos with one
   another and form communities around content that they like. If
   news organizations want to see how a particular piece of content
   will resonate with audiences, they have an automatic focus group
   waiting on YouTube. And that focus group isn't just young people:
   20 percent of YouTube users are over age 55—which is the same
   percentage that is under 18. This means the YouTube audience
   roughly mirrors the national population.

2. **Partner with Audiences:** YouTube provides news media organizations new ways to engage with audiences and involve them
   in the programming. Modeled on the presidential debates we
   cohosted last year, YouTube has created similar partnerships,
   such as one with the BBC around the mayoral election in London
   and with a large public broadcaster in Spain for their recent presidential election. Also on the campaign trail, we worked along with
   Hearst affiliate WMUR-TV in New Hampshire to solicit videos
   from voters during that primary. Hundreds of videos flooded in
   from across the state. The best were broadcast on that TV station,
   which highlighted this symbiotic relationship: On the Web, online
   video bubbles the more interesting content to the top and then
   TV amplifies it on a new scale. We did similar arrangements with
   news organizations in Iowa, Pennsylvania, and on Super Tues-
   day, as news organizations leveraged the power of voter-generated
   content. What the news organizations discover is that they gain
   audience share by offering a level of audience engagement—with
   opportunities for active as well as passive experiences.

For news media organizations, audience engagement is much eas-   9
ier to achieve by using platforms like YouTube than it is to do on their
own. And we just made it easier: Our open API (application programming interface), nicknamed "YouTube Everywhere"—just launched
a few months ago—allows other companies to integrate our upload
functionality into their online platforms. It's like having a mini YouTube on
your Web site and, once it's there, news organizations can encourage—and
publish—video responses and comments on the reporting they do.

Finally, reporters use YouTube as source material for their stories.   10
With hundreds of thousands of video cameras in use today, there is a
much greater chance than ever before that events will be captured—by

someone—as they unfold. No need for driving the satellite truck to the scene if someone is already there and sending in video of the event via their cell phone. It's at such intersections of new and old media that YouTube demonstrates its value. It could be argued, in fact, that the YouTube platform is the new frontier in newsgathering. On the election trail, virtually every appearance by every candidate is captured on video—by someone—and that means the issues being talked about are covered more robustly by more people who can steer the public discussion in new ways. The phenomenon is, of course, global, as we witnessed last fall in Burma (Myanmar) after the government shut down news media outlets during waves of civic protests. In time, YouTube was the only way to track the violence being exercised by the government on monks who'd taken to the streets. Videos of this were seen worldwide on YouTube, creating global awareness of this situation—even in the absence of journalists on the scene.

Citizen journalism on YouTube—and other Internet sources—is   *11*
often criticized because it is produced by amateurs and therefore lacks a degree of trustworthiness. Critics add that because platforms like YouTube are fragmenting today's media environment, traditional newsrooms are being depleted of journalists, and thus the denominator for quality news coverage is getting lower and lower. I share this concern about what is happening in the news media today, but I think there are a couple of things worth remembering when it comes to news content on YouTube.

Trusting What We See

When it comes to determining the trustworthiness of news content   *12*
on YouTube, it's important to have some context. People tend to know what they're getting on YouTube, since content is clearly labeled by username as to where it originated. A viewer knows if the video they're watching is coming from "jellybean109" or "thenewyorktimes." Users also know that YouTube is an open platform and that no one verifies the truth of content better than the consumer. The wisdom of the crowd on YouTube is far more likely to pick apart a shoddy piece of "journalism" than it is to elevate something that is simply untrue. In fact, because video is ubiquitous and so much more revealing and compelling than text, YouTube can provide a critical fact-checking platform in today's media environment. And in some ways, it offers a backstop for accuracy since a journalist can't afford to get the story wrong; if they do, it's likely that someone else who was there got it right—and posted it to YouTube.

Scrutiny cuts both ways. Journalists are needed today for the work   *13* they do as much as they ever have been. While the wisdom of crowds might provide a new form of fact checking, and the ubiquity of technology might provide a more robust view of the news, citizens desperately need the Fourth Estate to provide depth, context, and analysis that only comes with experience and the sharpening of the craft. Without the work of journalists, the citizens—the electorate—lose a critical voice in the process of civic decision-making.

This is the media ecosystem in which we live in this election cycle.   *14* Candidates and voters speak directly to one another, unfiltered. News organizations use the Internet to connect with and leverage audiences in new ways. Activists, issue groups, campaigns, and voters all advocate for, learn about, and discuss issues on the same level platform. YouTube has become a major force in this new media environment by offering new opportunities and new challenges. For those who have embraced them—and their numbers grow rapidly every day—the opportunity to influence the discussion is great. For those who haven't, they ignore the opportunity at their own peril.

AVOIDING PLAGIARISM

Whether you paraphrase, summarize, or synthesize, it is essential that you acknowledge your sources. Academic writing requires you to use and document sources appropriately, making clear to readers the boundaries between your words and ideas and those of other writers. Setting boundaries can be a challenge because so much of academic writing involves interweaving the ideas of others into your own argument. Still, no matter how difficult, you must acknowledge your sources. It's only fair. Imagine how you would feel if you were reading a text and discovered that the writer had incorporated a passage from one of your papers, something you slaved over, without giving you credit. You would see yourself as a victim of plagiarism, and you would be justified in feeling very angry indeed.

In fact, **plagiarism**—the unacknowledged use of another's work, passed off as one's own—is a most serious breach of academic integrity, and colleges and universities deal with it severely. If you are caught plagiarizing in your work for a class, you can expect to fail that class and may even be expelled from your college or university. Furthermore, although a failing grade on a paper or in a course, honestly come by, is unlikely to deter an employer from hiring you, the stigma of plagiarism can come back to haunt you when you apply for a job. Any violation of the principles set forth in Table 7.1 could have serious consequences for your academic and professional career.

TABLE 7.1   Principles Governing Plagiarism

1. All written work submitted for any purpose is accepted as your own work. This means it must not have been written even in part by another person.

2. The wording of any written work you submit is assumed to be your own. This means you must not submit work that has been copied, wholly or partially, from a book, an article, an essay, a newspaper, another student's paper or notebook, or any other source. Another writer's phrases, sentences, or paragraphs can be included only if they are presented as quotations and the source acknowledged.

3. The ideas expressed in a paper or report are assumed to originate with you, the writer. Written work that paraphrases a source without acknowledgment must not be submitted for credit. Ideas from the work of others can be incorporated in your work as starting points, governing issues, illustrations, and the like, but in every instance the source must be cited.

4. Remember that any online materials you use to gather information for a paper are also governed by the rules for avoiding plagiarism. You need to learn to cite electronic sources as well as printed and other sources.

5. You may correct and revise your writing with the aid of reference books. You also may discuss your writing with your peers in a writing group or with peer tutors at your campus writing center. However, you may not submit writing that has been revised substantially by another person.

Even if you know what plagiarism is and wouldn't think about doing it, you can still plagiarize unintentionally. Again, paraphrasing can be especially tricky: Attempting to restate a passage without using the original words and sentence structure is, to a certain extent, an invitation to plagiarism. If you remember that your paper is *your* argument, and understand that any paraphrasing, summarizing, or synthesizing should reflect *your* voice and style, you will be less likely to have problems with plagiarism. Your paper should sound like you. And, again, the surest way to protect yourself is to cite your sources.

Steps to Avoiding Plagiarism

1 **Always cite the source.** Signal that you are paraphrasing, summarizing, or synthesizing by identifying your source at the outset—"According to James Gunn," "Clive Thompson argues," "Cynthia Haven and Josh Keller . . . point out." And if possible, indicate the end of the paraphrase, summary, or synthesis with relevant page references to the source. If you cite a source several times in your paper, don't assume that your first citation has you covered; acknowledge the source as often as you use it.

2 **Provide a full citation in your bibliography.** It's not enough to cite a source in your paper; you must also provide a full citation for every source you use in the list of sources at the end of your paper.

INTEGRATING QUOTATIONS INTO YOUR WRITING

When you integrate quotations into your writing, bear in mind a piece of advice we've given you about writing the rest of your paper: Take your readers by the hand and lead them step by step. When you quote other authors to develop your argument—using their words to support your thinking or to address a counterargument—discuss and analyze the words you quote, showing readers how the specific language of each quotation contributes to the larger point you are making in your essay. When you integrate quotations, then, there are three basic things you want to do: (1) Take an active stance, (2) explain the quotations, and (3) attach short quotations to your own sentences.

■ Take an Active Stance

Critical reading requires that you adopt an active stance toward what you read—that you raise questions in response to a text. You should be no less active when you are using other authors' texts to develop your own argument.

Taking an active stance when you are quoting means knowing when to quote. Don't quote when a paraphrase or summary will convey the information from a source more effectively. More important, you have to make fair and wise decisions about what and how much you should quote to make your argument.

- You want to show that you understand the writer's argument, and you want to make evenhanded use of it in your own argument. It's not fair (or wise) to quote selectively—choosing only passages that support your argument—when you know you are distorting the argument of the writer you are quoting.

- Remember that your ideas and argument—your thesis—are what is most important to the readers and what justifies a quotation's being included at all. It's not wise (or fair to yourself) to flesh out your paper with an overwhelming number of quotations that could make readers think that you do not know your topic well or do not have your own ideas. Don't allow quotations to take over your paragraphs.

Above all, taking an active stance when you quote means taking control of your writing. You want to establish your own argument and guide your readers through it, allowing sources to contribute to but not dictate its direction. You are responsible for plotting and pacing your essay. Always keep in mind that your thesis is the skewer that runs through every paragraph, holding all of the ideas together. When you use quotations, then, you must organize them to enrich, substantiate, illustrate, and help support your central claim or thesis.

▪ Explain the Quotations

When you quote an author to support or advance your argument, make sure that readers know exactly what they should learn from the quotation.

Read the excerpt below from one student's early draft of an argument that focuses on the value of service learning in high schools. The student reviews several relevant studies—but then simply drops in a quotation, expecting readers to know what they should pay attention to in it.

> Other research emphasizes community service as an integral and integrated part of moral identity. In this understanding, community service activities are not isolated events but are woven into the context of students' everyday lives (Yates, 1995); the personal, the moral, and the civic become "inseparable" (Colby, Ehrlich, Beaumont, & Stephens, 2003, p. 15). In their study of minority high schoolers at an urban Catholic school who volunteered at a soup kitchen for the homeless as part of a class assignment, Youniss and Yates (1999) found that the students underwent significant identity changes, coming to perceive themselves as lifelong activists. The researchers' findings are worth quoting at length here because they depict the dramatic nature of the students' changed viewpoints. Youniss and Yates wrote:
>
>> Many students abandoned an initially negative view of homeless people and a disinterest in homelessness by gaining appreciation of the humanity of homeless people and by showing concern for homelessness in relation to poverty, job training, low-cost housing, prison reform, drug and alcohol rehabilitation, care for the mentally ill, quality urban education, and welfare policy. Several students also altered perceptions of themselves from politically impotent teenagers to involved citizens who now and in the future could use their talent and power to correct social problems. They projected articulated pictures of themselves as adult citizens who could affect housing policies, education for minorities, and government programs within a clear framework of social justice. (p. 362)

The student's introduction to the quoted passage provided a rationale for quoting Youniss and Yates at length, but it did not help her readers see how the research related to her argument. The student needed to frame the quotation for her readers. Instead of introducing the quotation by saying "Youniss and Yates wrote," she should have made clear that the study supports the argument that community service can create change. A more appropriate frame for the quotation might have been a summary like this one:

Frames the quotations, explaining it in the context of the student's argument.

One particular study underscores my argument that service can motivate change, particularly when that change begins within the students who are involved in service. Youniss and Yates (1999) wrote that over the course of their research, the students developed both

> an "appreciation of the humanity of homeless people" and a sense
> that they would someday be able to "use their talent and power to
> correct social problems" (p. 362).

In the following example, notice that the student writer uses Derrick
Bell's text to say something about how the effects of desegregation have
been muted by political manipulation.* The writer shapes what he wants
readers to focus on, leaving nothing to chance.

> The effectiveness with which the meaning of *Brown v. Board of Education* has been
> manipulated, Derrick Bell argued, is also evidenced by the way in which such thinking
> has actually been embraced by minority groups. Bell claimed that a black school board
> member's asking "But of what value is it to teach black children to read in all-black
> schools?" indicates this unthinking acceptance that whiteness is an essential ingredient
> to effective schooling for blacks. Bell continued:
>
>> The assumption that even the attaining of academic skills is worthless
>> unless those skills are acquired in the presence of white students illustrates
>> dramatically how a legal precedent, namely the Supreme Court's decision in
>> Brown v. Board of Education, has been so constricted even by advocates that
>> its goal — equal educational opportunity — is rendered inaccessible, even
>> unwanted, unless it can be obtained through racial balancing of the school
>> population. (p. 255)
>
> Bell's argument is extremely compelling, particularly when one considers the
> extent to which "racial balancing" has come to be defined in terms of large white
> majority populations and small nonwhite minority populations.

Notice that the student's last sentence helps readers understand what
the quoted material suggests and why it's important by embedding and
extending Bell's notion of racial balancing into his explanation.

In sum, you should always explain the information that you quote so
that your readers can see how the quotation relates to your own argument.
("Take your readers by the hand . . .") As you read other people's writing,
keep an eye open to the ways writers introduce and explain the sources
they use to build their arguments.

▪ Attach Short Quotations to Your Sentences

The quotations we discussed above are **block quotations**, lengthy quotations of more than five lines that are set off from the text of a paper with
indention. Make shorter quotations part of your own sentences so that
your readers can understand how the quotations connect to your argument and can follow along easily. How do you make a quotation part of
your own sentences? There are two main methods:

---

*This quotation is from Derrick Bell's *Silent Covenants: Brown v. Board of Education
and the Unfulfilled Hopes for Racial Reform* (New York: Oxford UP, 2005).

- Integrate quotations within the grammar of your writing.
- Attach quotations with punctuation.

If possible, use both to make your integration of quotations more interesting and varied.

Integrate quotations within the grammar of a sentence.   When you integrate a quotation into a sentence, the quotation must make grammatical sense and read as if it is part of the sentence:

> Fine, Weiss, and Powell (1998) expanded upon what others call "equal status contact theory" by using a "framework that draws on three traditionally independent literatures — those on community, difference, and democracy" (p. 37).

If you add words to the quotation, use square brackets around them to let readers know that the words are not original to the quotation:

> Smith and Wellner (2002) asserted that they "are not alone [in believing] that the facts have been incorrectly interpreted by Mancini" (p. 24).

If you omit any words in the middle of a quotation, use an **ellipsis**, three periods with spaces between them, to indicate the omission:

> Riquelme argues that "Eliot tries . . . to provide a definition by negations, which he also turns into positive terms that are meant to correct misconceptions" (p. 156).

If you omit a sentence or more, make sure to put a period before the ellipsis points:

> Eagleton writes, "What Eliot was in fact assaulting was the whole ideology of middle-class liberalism. . . . Eliot's own solution is an extreme right-wing authoritarianism: men and women must sacrifice their petty 'personalities' and opinions to an impersonal order" (p. 39).

Whatever you add (using square brackets) or omit (using ellipses), the sentence must read grammatically. And, of course, your additions and omissions must not distort the author's meaning.

> Leah is also that little girl who "stares at her old street and look[s] at the abandoned houses and cracked up sidewalks."

Attach quotations with punctuation.   You also can attach a quotation to a sentence by using punctuation. For example, this passage attaches the run-in quotation with a colon:

> For these researchers, there needs to be recognition of differences in a way that will include and accept all students. Specifically, they asked: "Within multiracial settings, when are young people invited to discuss, voice, critique, and re-view the very notions of race that feel so fixed, so hierarchical, so damaging, and so accepted in the broader culture?" (p. 132).

In conclusion, if you don't connect quotations to your argument, your readers may not understand why you've included them. You need to explain a significant point that each quotation reveals as you introduce or end it. This strategy helps readers know what to pay attention to in a quotation, particularly if the quotation is lengthy.

Steps to Integrating Quotations into Your Writing

1 **Take an active stance.** Your sources should contribute to your argument, not dictate its direction.

2 **Explain the quotations.** Explain what you quote so your readers understand how each quotation relates to your argument.

3 **Attach short quotations to your sentences.** Integrate short quotations within the grammar of your own sentences, or attach them with appropriate punctuation.

A Practice Sequence: Integrating Quotations

1 Using several of the sources you are working with in developing your paper, try integrating quotations into your essay. Be sure you are controlling your sources. Carefully read the paragraphs where you've used quotations. Will your readers clearly understand why the quotations are there — the points the quotations support? Do the sentences with quotations read smoothly? Are they grammatically correct?

2 Working in a small group, agree on a substantial paragraph or passage (from this book or some other source) to write about. Each member should read the passage and take a position on the ideas, and then draft a page that quotes the passage using both strategies for integrating these quotations. Compare what you've written, examining similarities and differences in the use of quotations.

AN ANNOTATED STUDENT RESEARCHED ARGUMENT: SYNTHESIZING SOURCES

The student who wrote the essay "A Greener Approach to Groceries: Community-Based Agriculture in LaSalle Square" did so in a first-year writing class that gave students the opportunity to do service in the local community. For this assignment, students were asked to explore debates about community and citizenship in contemporary America and to focus their research and writing on a social justice–related issue of their choice. The context of the course guided their inquiry as all the students in the course explored community service as a way to engage meaningfully and to develop relationships in the community.

We have annotated her essay to show the ways that she summarized and paraphrased research to show the urgency of the problem of food insecurity that exists around the world and to offer possible solutions. Notice how she synthesizes her sources, taking an active stance in using what she has read to advance her own argument.

Nancy Paul   Paul 1
Professor McLaughlin
English 2102
May 11, 20—

A Greener Approach to Groceries:
Community-Based Agriculture in LaSalle Square

In our post–9/11 society, there is incessant concern for   *1*
the security of our future. Billions of dollars are spent tightening borders, installing nuclear detectors, and adjudicating safety measures so that the citizens of the United States can grow and prosper without fear. Unfortunately, for some urban poor, the threat from terrorism is minuscule compared to the cruelty of their immediate environment. Far from the sands of the Afghan plains and encapsulated in the midst of inner-city deterioration, many find themselves in gray-lot deserts devoid of vegetation

The student's thesis — and reliable food sources. Abandoned by corporate supermarkets, millions of Americans are maimed by a "food insecurity" — the nutritional poverty that cripples them developmentally, physically, and psychologically.

The midwestern city that surrounds our university has   *2*
a food-desert sitting just west of the famously lush campus. Known as LaSalle Square, it was once home to the lucrative Bendix plant and has featured both a Target and a Kroger super-

She calls attention to both the immediacy and urgency of the problem — market in recent years. But previous economic development decisions have driven both stores to the outskirts of town, and without a local supplier, the only food available in the neighborhood is prepackaged and sold at the few small convenience stores. This available food is virtually devoid of nutrition and

Paul 2

inhibits the ability of the poor to prosper and thrive. Thus, an aging strip mall, industrial site, and approximately three acres of an empty grass lot between the buildings anchor — and unfortunately define — the neighborhood.

She proposes a possible solution.

While there are multiple ways of providing food to the destitute, I am proposing a co-op of community gardens built on the grassy space in LaSalle Square and on smaller sites within the neighborhood, supplemented by extra crops from Michiana farmers, which would supply fresh fruit and vegetables to be sold or distributed to the poor. Together the co-op could meet the nutritional needs of the people, provide plenty of nutritious food, not cost South Bend any additional money, and contribute to neighborhood revitalization, yielding concrete increases in property values. Far from being a pipe dream, LaSalle Square already hosted an Urban Garden Market this fall, so a co-op would simply build upon the already recognized need and desire for healthy food in the area. Similar coalitions around the world are harnessing the power of community to remedy food insecurity without the aid of corporate enterprise, and South Bend is perfectly situated to reproduce and possibly exceed their successes.

She places her solution in a larger context to indicate its viability.

3

Many, myself previously included, believe that the large-volume, cheap industrialization of food and the welfare system have obliterated hunger in the United States. Supermarkets like Wal-Mart and Kroger seem ubiquitous in our communities, and it is difficult to imagine anyone being beyond their influence. However, profit-driven corporate business plans do not mix well with low-income, high-crime populations, and the gap between the two is growing wider. This polarization, combined with the vitamin deficiency of our high-fructose corn syrup society, has created food deserts in already struggling communities where malnutrition is the enemy *inconnu* of the urban poor.

4

More context

LaSalle Square's food insecurity is typical of many urban areas. The grocery stores that used to serve the neighborhood have relocated to more attractive real estate on the outskirts of the city, and only local convenience stores, stocking basic necessary items and tobacco products, remain profitable. Linda Wolfson, a member of the steering committee for the LaSalle Square

5

Paul 3

Redevelopment Plan, notes that if the community was fiscally
healthy, it would be reasonable to expect the inhabitants to simply drive the six miles to the strip mall district, but unfortunately
many are marginally employed and do not have access to cars. For
them, it is economically irresponsible to spend the extra money
to get to the supermarket, and so they feed their families on the
cheap soda, chips, and processed food that are readily available
at the convenience store. Especially since high-calorie, low-nutri-
ent, packaged food tends to be denser, urban mothers find that it
helps their children feel full (Garnett). Sadly, a health investigation released in 2006 concluded that by the age of three, more
than one-third of urban children are obese, due in large part to
the consumption of low-quality food obtained from corner stores
(Smith). A recent analysis of urban stores in Detroit found that
only 19 percent offer the healthy food array suggested by the FDA
food pyramid (Brown and Carter 5). The food that is offered contains 25 percent less nutrient density, and consequently, under-
privileged socioeconomic populations consume significantly lower
levels of the micronutrients that form the foundation for proper
protein and brain development. In a recent study of poor house
holds, it was found that two-thirds of children were nutritionally
poor and that more than 25 percent of women were deficient in
iron, vitamin A, vitamin C, vitamin B6, thiamin, and riboflavin
(Garnett). Of course, some may challenge the relevance of these
vitamins and nutrients since they are not something the average
person consciously incorporates into his or her diet on a daily
basis. Yet modern research, examining the severely homogenous
diets of the poor, has found severe developmental consequences
associated with the lack of nutritional substance. For those
afflicted, these deficiencies are not simply inconvenient, but
actually exacerbate their plight and hinder their progress toward
a sustainable lifestyle.

The human body is a complex system that cannot be
sustained merely on the simple sugars and processed carbo-
hydrates that comprise most cheap and filling foodstuffs, and
research shows a relationship between nutritional deficiencies
and a host of cognitive and developmental impairments that are
prevalent in the undernourished families from urban America.

*Synthesizing helps
illustrate the extent
of the problem and
bolster her view that
the poor suffer the
most from the problem
she identifies (Garnett;
Smith; Brown and
Carter).*

*Here she paraphrases
findings.*

6

7

*Again she both sum-
marizes and cites
a relevant study to
advance her argument.*

Standardized tests of impoverished siblings, one of whom
received nutritional supplements and the other who did not,
showed cognitive gains in the well-nourished child as well as
increased motor skills and greater interest in social interactions
when compared to the other child. In the highly formative toddler years, undernutrition can inhibit the myelination of nerve
fibers, which is responsible for neurotransmitting and proper
brain function. Collaborators Emily Tanner from the University of
Oxford and Matia Finn-Stevenson from Yale University published
a comprehensive analysis of the link between nutrition and
brain development in 2002. Their analysis, which they linked
to social policy, indicated that a shortage of legumes and leafy
green vegetables, which are nearly impossible to find in corner
stores, is the leading cause of the iron-deficiency anemia afflicting 25 percent of urban children. This extreme form of anemia
is characterized by impaired neurotransmission, weaker memory,
and reduced attention span (Tanner and Finn-Stevenson 186).
For those who do not have access to the vitamins, minerals, and
micronutrients found in fruits and vegetables, these maladies
are not distant risks, but constant, inescapable threats.

     In light of these severe consequences of undernutrition,
the term "food insecurity" encapsulates the condition wherein
the economically disadvantaged are vulnerable simply because
their bodies are unable to receive adequate fuel for optimal
functioning. Just as one cannot expect a dry, parched plant to
bloom and pollinate a garden, by constraining the development
of individuals, food insecurity also constrains the development
of the neighborhoods in which the individuals contribute. For
the health of a city and its communities, all roadblocks to progress must be removed, and food insecurity must be cut out at its
roots so that individuals have the resources for advancement.

     As socially conscious citizens and local governments
have recognized the prevalence and danger of food insecurity in
inner cities, there have been attempts at a remedy. Obviously,
the easiest solution is simply to introduce a grocery store that
would provide a variety of quality, healthful foods. However, for
big-box supermarkets driven by the bottom line, urban areas are
less than desirable business locales from a standpoint of both

7

8

Paul 5

profitability and maintenance. It is simply irrational for a supermarket to invest in an urban area with less revenue potential,
size constraints, an unattractive locale, and an increased threat
of theft and defacement when it is so easy to turn a profit in
spacious and peaceful suburbia (Eisenhauer 131). Supermarkets
must have significant incentive, beyond humanitarian ends, if
they are to take the financial risk of entering a poor, urban
marketplace.

*She takes an active
stance in citing initia-
tives that could be
applied more effectively
to alleviate the problem
of food insecurity.*

Certain cities are using the power of Tax Increment
Financing (TIF) districts to encourage supermarkets to invest in
urban centers. Under these redevelopment laws, tax revenues
from retail development or other commercial enterprises are
devoted, for a specified number of years, to infrastructural
improvement of the district ("TIF Reform"). This approach has
been effective in enticing new businesses; in fact, the exterior
growth around South Bend is the result of a TIF district estab
lished in the late 1980s. LaSalle Square is currently part of a TIF
district, but there is discussion as to how the TIF monies should
best be applied (Wolfson). It may be possible to use the power
of the TIF to encourage another large retailer such as Kroger to
establish a presence in the square, but a smaller enterprise may
be a better option. Experts indicate that for the destitute and
food-insecure, reliance on a corporate entity is not optimal.
Elizabeth Eisenhauer, a researcher from the State University of
New York, investigated the interplay between supermarkets and

*She paraphrases a
researcher's findings.*

the urban poor; she concluded that large big-box stores lack a
commitment to the communities they serve and can be relied
on only when it is clear they will make a profit, which may or
may not happen when TIF benefits expire (131). Even when a
portion of proceeds is used in the community, the majority of
the cash flow from a supermarket is going to a corporate headquarters elsewhere, not directly supporting the surrounding
neighborhood. Likewise, while some employees may be local,
the highest-salary management positions are generally given
to outsiders, making the stores and their employees set apart,
rather than integrated into the neighborhood (Eisenhauer 130).
Certainly a supermarket in an urban area will greatly contribute
to the reduction of food insecurity, but it is not the only

9

Paul 6

available option, and the city of South Bend is ripe for alternative solutions. The city is primed for a cooperative effort that
could shift the paradigm for urban renewal from a quick, corporate solution, to a long-term enterprise built on community
contributions and under local control.

She cites a number of examples as evidence to demonstrate the viability of the solution she offers.

Around the globe, many destitute urban areas have
found the means to reverse nutritional poverty through a literal
and figurative grassroots effort. In an effort to avoid packaged,
convenience store food, neighbors in the Bronx, San Francisco,
Los Angeles, London, and most successfully in Philadelphia,
have been planting their own crops right in the heart of the city
(Brown and Carter 3-4). Truly farming the food desert, coalitions that link community gardens, local farmers, and urban
markets are providing healthy, sustainable food sources without
a supermarket. Interestingly, in the process, such coalitions are
generating jobs, increasing property value, and, in some cases,
actually reversing the effects of poverty. The city of South Bend,
uniquely situated in the breadbasket of the United States, is
in the perfect position to launch a "greening" effort, modeled
after the successes in other parts of the world, which would
both solve the problem of food insecurity of LaSalle Square and
invigorate the local economy.

10

While modern Americans have the tendency to think that
food production should be, and always has been, industrialized,
countries around the world, especially economically disadvantaged nations, are exemplifying the possibilities of local garden-

11

The use of multiple sources would make her case even stronger than using just one source of information, in this case Brown and Carter.

ing efforts. Far removed from industrial farms, Cubans grow half
their vegetables within the city; vacant land in Russian cities
produces 80 percent of the nation's vegetables, and specifically
in Moscow, 65 percent of families contribute to food production. Singapore has 10,000 urban farmers, and nearly half of
the residents of Vancouver grow food in their gardens (Brown
and Carter 10). These habits are not simply a novelty; rather,
populations that garden tend to be healthier, eating six out of
the fourteen vegetable categories more regularly than nongar-
deners and also consuming fewer sweet and sugary foods per
capita (Brown and Carter 13). These data, compiled by the North
American Urban Agriculture Committee, were synthesized from

Paul 7

the *Journal of Public Health Policy* and the *Journal of Nutrition Education* and show the interrelatedness of nutritional access and availability to healthy personal choices. While these trends toward healthful lifestyles and gardening have been gaining ground slowly in the United States, when food insecurity and poverty take their toll, cities are finding that urban agriculture is an increasingly attractive and profitable alternative.

American communities have shown that creativity and collaboration can be quite effective at reversing food inse curity. The Garden Project of the Greater Lansing Food Bank has successfully combined gardening and Midwest access to local farms to bring food security to urban residents and senior citizens. Their eighteen community gardens and volunteers provide fresh fruits and vegetables year-round to low-income families, food pantries, the elderly, and social service organizations. Completely bypassing the commercial market, the Garden Project has trained 500 families to grow their own food in backyard plots so that they can always have healthy food in the midst of the city (Brown and Carter 1). The gardens are supplemented by a process known as "gleaning," in which volunteers harvest extra crops from local farmers that would otherwise go to waste, and deliver it to residents of subsidized housing ("Gleaning"). In 2008 alone, the Garden Project actively involved 2,500 individual gardeners and was able to provide over 250,000 pounds of produce from gleaning alone, plus the yields of the community plots that were used directly by the gardeners ("GLFB Facts"). This Lansing coalition serves over 5,000 individuals per month, yet only 4,400 reside under the poverty line in the LaSalle Square area (*City-Data.com*). If half of the inhabitants of LaSalle Square became engaged in the gardening effort, a similar collaboration could meet the needs of the region, and greater participation could yield an excess.

Similar efforts have demonstrated not only that inner-city food production is achievable but also that it can be cost-effective and self-sufficient, unlike a food bank. Frustrated by the inner-city downturn she describes as "an overgrown dog toilet," industrious London entrepreneur Julie Brown created a community gardening company aimed at providing unmecha-

12

13

She synthesizes different sources to make her point.

Paul 8

In this paragraph, she
summarizes research
to address the possible
counter-argument.

nized, local, sustainable food. The company, Growing Communities, uses organic box gardens and small farms to supply
more than 400 homes with weekly deliveries of organic fruits
and vegetables. After a ten-year investment in local farmers
and mini-gardens within the city, Growing Communities is now
financially independent and generates over $400,000 per year
(Willis 53). Compelled by both capitalism and social concern,
Brown's efforts have shown that community-supported agriculture not only is possible but can be profitable as well! Our own
community agriculture program should not be an entrepreneurial
endeavor, but Brown's work in London indicates that it need not
be a financial burden to the city either. Rather, the co-op would
be financially self-sufficient, with the potential to generate revenues and fiscal growth in the city.

There are environmental factors that make South Bend
an even better place to launch a profitable community agriculture program than London. Chiefly, South Bend has many more
farms in the immediate vicinity than Ms. Brown could ever have
dreamed of in the U.K. While Brown was limited to twenty-five
local farms within 100 miles of the city, South Bend has over fifty
farms within 25 miles of LaSalle Square (*Local Harvest*). Offering
a broader production base creates more potential for profits by
decreasing transportation time and increasing product, thereby
making it easier for a coalition to become financially self-
sufficient in a shorter time frame than Ms. Brown's ten-year plan.

14

Urban Philadelphia has led the way in demonstrating
the profitability of community solutions to food insecurity
through an offshoot of the Pennsylvania Horticultural Society
(PHS) known as Philadelphia Greens. Since the 1970s, this
coalition has reclaimed parks, planted trees, and created community gardens, both to revitalize the neighborhood and to
serve the nutritionally and economically poor. Through a process
that plants trees, builds wooden fences, and gardens the more
than 1,000 vacant lots of Philadelphia, PHS combines housing
projects and reclaimed space to "green" and reinvigorate the
neighborhood ("The Effects"). Since LaSalle Square is essentially a large empty grassy area at the moment, a community
agricultural co-op should turn this vacant lot and others in

15

She again cites
research to address
the counterargument.

Paul 9

the neighborhood into community gardens, which would work
in tandem with the gleaning from local farms. Similar to the
Philadelphia project, these gardens would simultaneously yield
produce and improve the appearance of the neighborhood.

One PHS project, in the New Kensington neighborhood of
north Philadelphia, was the subject of a recent socioeconomic
study conducted by the University of Pennsylvania's renowned
Wharton School of Business. In the New Kensington area,
PHS recently planted 480 new trees, cleaned 145 side yards,
developed 217 vacant lots, and established 15 new community
gardens. The effort was a model of the collaborative strategy
between PHS and the local community development corporation,
making it the ideal subject of the Wharton study. The findings,
published in 2004, showed significant increases in property values around the PHS greening projects and were the first step in
quantifying the fiscal returns of neighborhood greening beyond
the qualitative benefits of remedying food insecurity. After analyzing the sales records of thousands of New Kensington homes
between 1980 and 2003, the study reported that PHS greening
had led to a $4 million gain in property value from tree plant-
ings alone and a $12 million gain from vacant lot improvements.
Simply greening a vacant lot increased nearby property values
by as much as 30 percent ("Seeing Green"). While a supermarket
might modestly improve property values for those immediately
near the store, community greening involves multiple plots
across an area, benefiting many more people and properties. The
Wharton study showed that community greening would provide
increases in the value of any property near a green space, up
to multiple millions of dollars. The New Kensington neighborhood covers 1.4 square miles, which is approximately the size
of LaSalle Square, so while the overall property values are lower
simply because South Bend is a smaller city, the gains might be
proportional (*City-Data.com*). It is reasonable to believe that
cleaning up LaSalle Square and planting gardens would quantitatively benefit the fiscal situation of the city and increase
assets of the homeowners while subsequently improving the
quality of life over many acres.

16

*She summarizes a
study and then para-
phrases.*

Paul 10

Certainly there are challenges to the sort of dynami-
cal, community-based solution that I am proposing. Such an
agricultural co-op hinges on the participation of the people it
serves and cannot be successful without the dedicated support
of the neighborhood. It could be noted that lower-income economic groups are less socially involved than their higher-income
counterparts, and some might believe that they are unlikely to
contribute to, or care about, a greening effort. Yet I believe
that there is a distinction between political involvement and
neighborhood interaction. Middle-class Americans are conscious
of gas prices and the fluctuations of the stock market that affect
their job security and ability to provide for their families; yet
the unemployed poor without cars must rely on their neighborhoods to eke out a living. Their sustenance comes not from a
salary, but from odd jobs, welfare, and the munificence of fate.
The battle to put food on the table is more familiar to the poor
than foreign conflict and is one that they fight every day. Therefore, while the poor are less inclined to vote or worry about governmental affairs because of the difficulties associated simply
with daily living, they are acutely aware of their immediate surroundings and how those surroundings challenge or contribute
to their success. This position makes them uniquely inclined to
invest in the betterment of their surroundings since it can have
a dramatic effect on their personal lives. The real success of
the sustainable food movement may come from harnessing the
power of urban communities that can derive great, immediate,
and lasting benefit from neighborhood revitalization.

In this paragraph, she takes an active stance in using research to alleviate fears that the local community would have to start from scratch with limited expertise.

It has been argued that urban growers, especially from
lower socioeconomic classes, do not have the expertise or knowledge base to generate successful yields that will ensure food security. Fortunately, agriculture is Indiana's fourth-largest industry,
and the state boasts over 63,000 farms ("A Look"). In addition to
the many inhabitants of LaSalle Square who have a background in
agriculture, there is a wealth of knowledge about proper planting
methods available from the farmers around the local area. Many of
these farmers have already shown a willingness to help by selling
or donating their produce to the local Urban Market. Additionally,
national urban agriculture nonprofit groups, such as Master

17

18

Paul 11

Gardening and Cooperative Extension, offer free public education to cities beginning community agriculture programs, and
some will even perform on-site training (Brown and Carter 16).
By harnessing the assets of local, gratuitous knowledge and
supplementing that knowledge with national support groups,
South Bend has multiple resources available to train and encourage its burgeoning urban farmers.

  The economic and nutritional gains of the people would *19*
only be heightened by the personal well-being that is born of interpersonal collaboration that crosses racial and social boundaries.
Such an effort is ambitious; it will indeed require the time and talents of many people who care about the health of their community.
But the local community is rich with the necessary seeds for such a
project, which may, in time, blossom and grow to feed its people.

Paul 12

Works Cited

Brown, Katherine H., and Anne Carter. *Urban Agriculture and
  Community Food Security in the United States: Farming from
  the City Center to the Urban Fringe*. Venice, CA: Community
  Food Security Coalition, Oct. 2003. PDF file.

City-Data.com. Advameg, 2008. Web. 16 Apr. 20—.

"The Effects of Neighborhood Greening." *PHS*. Pennsylvania
  Horticultural Society, Jan. 2001. Web. 8 Apr. 20—.

Eisenhauer, Elizabeth. "In Poor Health: Supermarket Redlining
  and Urban Nutrition." *GeoJournal* 53.2 (2001): 125–33.
  Print.

Garnett, Tara. "Farming the City." *Ecologist* 26.6 (1996): 299.
  Academic Search Premier. Web. 8 Apr. 20—.

"Gleaning." *Greater Lansing Food Bank*. Greater Lansing Food
  Bank, n.d. Web. 15 Apr. 20—.

"GLFB Facts." *Greater Lansing Food Bank*. Greater Lansing Food
  Bank, 2005. Web. 15 Apr. 20—.

Paul 13

Local Harvest. LocalHarvest, 2008. Web. 15 Apr. 20—.

"A Look at Indiana Agriculture." *Agriculture in the Classroom*.
      USDA-CSREES, n.d. PDF file.

"Seeing Green: Study Finds Greening Is a Good Investment."
      PHS. Pennsylvania Horticultural Society, 2005. Web. 8 Apr.
      20—.

Smith, Stephen. "Obesity Battle Starts Young for Urban Poor."
      Boston Globe. NY Times, 29 Dec. 2006. Web. 18 Apr. 20—.

Tanner, Emily M., and Matia Finn-Stevenson. "Nutrition and
      Brain Development: Social Policy Implications." *American
      Journal of Orthopsychiatry* 72.2 (2002): 182–93. *Academic
      Search Premier*. Web. 8 Apr. 20—.

"TIF Reform." *New Rules Project*. Institute for Local Self-Reliance,
      2008. Web. 15 Apr. 20—.

Willis, Ben. "Julie Brown of Growing Communities." *The Ecologist*
      June 2008: 52–55. Print.

Wolfson, Linda. Personal interview. 20 Apr. 20—.

A Practice Sequence: Thinking about Copyright

1   Now that you have read about steps to avoiding plagiarism
    (pp. 192–93) and Nancy Paul's essay on community gardens
    (p. 199) we would like you to examine the idea of copyright. That
    is, who owns the rights to images that the organizers of a commu-
    nity garden use to market their idea? What if you wanted to use
    that image in a paper? Or what if you wanted to use a published
    ad in your own paper? Under what circumstances would you be
    able to use that ad for your own purposes?

2   After conducting your own inquiry into copyright, what would
    you conclude about the need to document the use of images,
    ideas, and text? Are the guidelines clear or are there some ambig-
    uous areas for what to cite and how? What advice would you give
    your peers?

8

From Ethos to Logos
Appealing to Your Readers

Your understanding of your readers influences how you see a particular situation, define an issue, explain the ongoing conversation surrounding that issue, and formulate a question. You may need to read widely to understand how different writers have dealt with the issue you address. And you will need to anticipate how others might respond to your argument—whether they will be sympathetic or antagonistic—and to compose your essay so that readers will "listen" whether or not they agree with you.

To achieve these goals, you will no doubt use reason in the form of evidence to sway readers. But you can also use other means of persuasion: That is, you can use your own character, by presenting yourself as someone who is knowledgeable, fair, and just; and you can appeal to your readers' emotions. Although you may believe that reason alone should provide the means for changing people's minds, people's emotions also color the way they see the world.

Your audience is more than your immediate reader, your instructor, or a peer. Your audience encompasses those you cite in writing about an issue and those you anticipate responding to your argument. This is true no matter what you write about, whether it be an interpretation of the novels of a particular author, an analysis of the cultural work of horror films, the ethics of treating boys and girls differently in schools, or the moral issues surrounding homelessness in America.

In this chapter we discuss different ways of engaging your readers, centering on three kinds of appeals: **ethos**, appeals from character; **pathos,** appeals to emotion; and **logos**, appeals to reason. *Ethos, pathos,* and *logos* are terms derived from ancient Greek writers, but they are still of great value today when considering how to persuade your audience. Readers will judge your argument on whether or not you present an argument that is fair and just, one that creates a sense of goodwill. All three appeals rely on these qualities.

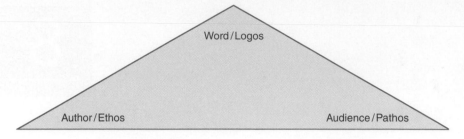

FIGURE 8.1   The Rhetorical Triangle

Figure 8.1, the **rhetorical triangle**, visually represents the interrelationship among ethos, pathos, and logos. Who we think our readers are (pathos: which of their emotions do we appeal to?) influences decisions about the ways we should represent ourselves to them (ethos: how can we come across as fair, credible, and just?). In turn, we use certain patterns of argument (logos: how do we arrange our words to make our case?) that reflect our interpretation of the situation to which we respond and that we believe will persuade readers to accept our point of view. Effective communication touches on each of the three points of the triangle. Your task as a writer is to determine the proper balance of these different appeals in your argument, based on your thesis, the circumstances, and your audience.

CONNECTING WITH READERS: A SAMPLE ARGUMENT

To see how an author connects with his audience, read the following excerpt from James W. Loewen's book *Lies My Teacher Told Me: Everything Your American History Textbook Got Wrong.* As you read the excerpt, note Loewen's main points and select key examples that illustrate his argument. As a class, test the claims he makes: To what extent do you believe that what Loewen argues is true? This may entail recalling your own experiences in high school history classes or locating one or more of the books that Loewen mentions.

JAMES W. LOEWEN

The Land of Opportunity

In addition to *Lies My Teacher Told Me* (1995), James Loewen, who holds a PhD in sociology, has written several other books, including *Lies Across America: What Our Historic Sites Get Wrong* (1999) and *Sundown Towns: A Hidden Dimension of American Racism* (2005). As the titles of these books suggest, Loewen is a writer who questions the assumptions about history that many people take for granted. This is especially true of the following excerpt, from a chapter in which Loewen challenges a common American belief—that everyone has an equal chance in what he calls the "land of opportunity"—by arguing that we live in a class system that privileges some people and raises barriers for others. History textbook writers, he points out, are guilty of complicity in this class system because they leave a great deal of history out of their textbooks.

■ ■ ■

High school students have eyes, ears, and television sets (all too many have their own TV sets), so they know a lot about relative privilege in America. They measure their family's social position against that of other families, and their community's position against other communities. Middle-class students, especially, know little about how the American class structure works, however, and nothing at all about how it has changed over time. These students do not leave high school merely ignorant of the workings of the class structure; they come out as terrible sociologists. "Why are people poor?" I have asked first-year college students. Or, if their own class position is one of relative privilege, "Why is your family well off?" The answers I've received, to characterize them charitably, are half-formed and naïve. The students blame the poor for not being successful. They have no understanding of the ways that opportunity is not equal in America and no notion that social structure pushes people around, influencing the ideas they hold and the lives they fashion.

High school history textbooks can take some of the credit for this state of affairs. Some textbooks cover certain high points of labor history, such as the 1894 Pullman strike near Chicago that President Cleveland broke with federal troops, or the 1911 Triangle Shirtwaist fire that killed 146 women in New York City, but the most recent event mentioned in most books is the Taft-Hartley Act of fifty years ago. No book mentions the Hormel meat-packers' strike in the mid-1980s or the air traffic controllers' strike broken by President Reagan. Nor do textbooks describe any continuing issues facing labor, such as the growth of multinational corporations and their exporting of jobs overseas. With such omissions, textbook authors can construe labor history as something that happened long ago, like slavery, and that, like slavery, was corrected long ago. It logically follows that unions appear anachronistic. The idea that they might be necessary in order for workers to have a voice in the workplace goes unstated.

Textbooks' treatments of events in labor history are never anchored in any analysis of social class. This amounts to delivering the footnotes instead of the lecture! Six of the dozen high school American history textbooks I examined contain no index listing at all for "social class," "social stratification," "class structure," "income distribution," "inequality," or any conceivably related topic. Not one book lists "upper class," "working class," or "lower class." Two of the textbooks list "middle class," but only to assure students that America is a middle-class country. "Except for slaves, most of the colonists were members of the 'middling ranks,'" says *Land of Promise,* and nails home the point that we are a middle-class country by asking students to "Describe three 'middle-class' values that united free Americans of all classes." Several of the textbooks note the explosion of middle-class suburbs after World War II. Talking about the middle class is hardly equivalent to discussing social stratification, however; in fact, as Gregory Mantsios has pointed out, "such references appear to be acceptable precisely because they mute class differences."

Stressing how middle-class we all are is particularly problematic today, because the proportion of households earning between 75 percent and 125 percent of the median income has fallen steadily since 1967. The Reagan-Bush administrations accelerated this shrinkage of the middle class, and most families who left its ranks fell rather than rose. This is the kind of historical trend one would think history books would take as appropriate subject matter, but only four of the twelve books in my sample provide any analysis of social stratification in the United States. Even these fragmentary analyses are set mostly in colonial America. *Land of Promise* lives up to its reassuring title by heading its discussion of social class "Social Mobility." "One great difference between colonial and European society was that the colonists had more social mobility," echoes *The American Tradition.* "In contrast with contemporary Europe, eighteenth-century America was a shining land of equality and opportunity—with the notorious exception of slavery," chimes in *The American Pageant.* Although *The Challenge of Freedom* identifies three social classes—upper, middle, and lower—among whites in colonial society, compared to Europe "there was greater *social mobility.*"

Never mind that the most violent class conflicts in American history— Bacon's Rebellion and Shays's Rebellion—took place in and just after colonial times. Textbooks still say that colonial society was relatively classless and marked by upward mobility. And things have gotten rosier since. "By 1815," *The Challenge of Freedom* assures us, two classes had withered away and "America was a country of middle class people and of middle class goals." This book returns repeatedly, at intervals of every fifty years or so, to the theme of how open opportunity is in America. "In the years after 1945, *social mobility*—movement from one social class to another—became more widespread in America," *Challenge* concludes. "This meant that people had a better chance to move upward in society." The stress on upward mobility is striking. There is almost nothing in any of these textbooks about class inequalities or barriers of any kind to social mobility. "What conditions made it possible for poor white immigrants to become richer in the colonies?" *Land of Promise* asks. "What conditions made/make it difficult?" goes unasked.

4

5

Textbook authors thus present an America in which, as preachers were fond of saying in the nineteenth century, men start from "humble origins" and attain "the most elevated positions."

Social class is probably the single most important variable in society. From womb to tomb, it correlates with almost all other social characteristics of people that we can measure. Affluent expectant mothers are more likely to get prenatal care, receive current medical advice, and enjoy general health, fitness, and nutrition. Many poor and working-class mothers-to-be first contact the medical profession in the last month, sometimes the last hours, of their pregnancies. Rich babies come out healthier and weighing more than poor babies. The infants go home to very different situations. Poor babies are more likely to have high levels of poisonous lead in their environments and their bodies. Rich babies get more time and verbal interaction with their parents and higher quality day care when not with their parents. When they enter kindergarten, and through the twelve years that follow, rich children benefit from suburban schools that spend two to three times as much money per student as schools in inner cities or impoverished rural areas. Poor children are taught in classes that are often 50 percent larger than the classes of affluent children. Differences such as these help account for the higher school-dropout rate among poor children.

Even when poor children are fortunate enough to attend the same school as rich children, they encounter teachers who expect only children of affluent families to know the right answers. Social science research shows that teachers are often surprised and even distressed when poor children excel. Teachers and counselors believe they can predict who is "college material." Since many working-class children give off the wrong signals, even in first grade, they end up in the "general education" track in high school. "If you are the child of low-income parents, the chances are good that you will receive limited and often careless attention from adults in your high school," in the words of Theodore Sizer's best-selling study of American high schools, *Horace's Compromise.* "If you are the child of upper-middle-income parents, the chances are good that you will receive substantial and careful attention." Researcher Reba Page has provided vivid accounts of how high school American history courses use rote learning to turn off lower-class students. Thus schools have put into practice Woodrow Wilson's recommendation: "We want one class of persons to have a liberal education, and we want another class of persons, a very much larger class of necessity in every society, to forgo the privilege of a liberal education and fit themselves to perform specific difficult manual tasks."

As if this unequal home and school life were not enough, rich teenagers then enroll in the Princeton Review or other coaching sessions for the Scholastic Aptitude Test. Even without coaching, affluent children are advantaged because their background is similar to that of the

6

7

8

test-makers, so they are comfortable with the vocabulary and subtle subcultural assumptions of the test. To no one's surprise, social class correlates strongly with SAT scores.

All these are among the reasons why social class predicts the rate   9
of college attendance and the type of college chosen more effectively than does any other factor, including intellectual ability, however measured. After college, most affluent children get white-collar jobs, most working-class children get blue-collar jobs, and the class differences continue. As adults, rich people are more likely to have hired an attorney and to be a member of formal organizations that increase their civic power. Poor people are more likely to watch TV. Because affluent families can save some money while poor families must spend what they make, wealth differences are ten times larger than income differences. Therefore most poor and working-class families cannot accumulate the down payment required to buy a house, which in turn shuts them out from our most important tax shelter, the write-off of home mortgage interest. Working-class parents cannot afford to live in elite subdivisions or hire high-quality day care, so the process of educational inequality replicates itself in the next generation. Finally, affluent Americans also have longer life expectancies than lower- and working-class people, the largest single cause of which is better access to health care. Echoing the results of Helen Keller's study of blindness, research has determined that poor health is not distributed randomly about the social structure but is concentrated in the lower class. Social Security then becomes a huge transfer system, using monies contributed by all Americans to pay benefits disproportionately to longer-lived affluent Americans.

Ultimately, social class determines how people think about social   10
class. When asked if poverty in America is the fault of the poor or the fault of the system, 57 percent of business leaders blamed the poor; just 9 percent blamed the system. Labor leaders showed sharply reversed choices: only 15 percent said the poor were at fault while 56 percent blamed the system. (Some replied "don't know" or chose a middle position.) The largest single difference between our two main political parties lies in how their members think about social class: 55 percent of Republicans blamed the poor for their poverty, while only 13 percent blamed the system for it; 68 percent of Democrats, on the other hand, blamed the system, while only 5 percent blamed the poor.

Few of these statements are news, I know, which is why I have not   11
documented most of them, but the majority of high school students do not know or understand these ideas. Moreover, the processes have changed over time, for the class structure in America today is not the same as it was in 1890, let alone in colonial America. Yet in *Land of Promise*, for example, social class goes unmentioned after 1670.

Reading as a Writer

1. List what you think are Loewen's main points. What appeals does he seem to draw on most when he makes those points: appeals based on his own character (ethos), on the emotions of his reader (pathos), or on the reasonableness of his evidence (logos)? Are the appeals obvious or difficult to tease out? Does he combine them? Discuss your answers with your classmates.

2. Identify what you think is the main claim of Loewen's argument, and choose key examples to support your answer. Compare your chosen claim and examples to those chosen by your classmates. Do they differ significantly? Can you agree on Loewen's gist and his key examples?

3. As a class, test the claims Loewen makes by thinking about your own experiences in high school history classes. Do you remember finding out that something you were taught from an American history textbook was not true? Did you discover on your own what you considered to be misrepresentations in or important omissions from your textbook? If so, did these misrepresentations or omissions tend to support or contradict the claims about history textbooks that Loewen makes?

APPEALING TO ETHOS

Although we like to believe that our decisions and beliefs are based on reason and logic, in fact they are often based on what amounts to character judgments. That is, if a person you trust makes a reasonable argument for one choice, and a person you distrust makes a reasonable argument for another choice, you are more likely to be swayed by the argument of the person you trust. Similarly, the audience for your argument will be more disposed to agree with you if its members believe you are a fair, just person who is knowledgeable and has good judgment. Even the most well-developed argument will fall short if you do not leave this kind of impression on your readers. Thus, it is not surprising that ethos may be the most important component of your argument.

There are three strategies for evoking a sense of ethos:

1. Establish that you have good judgment.
2. Convey to readers that you are knowledgeable.
3. Show that you understand the complexity of the issue.

These strategies are interrelated: A writer who demonstrates good judgment is more often than not someone who is both knowledgeable about an issue and who acknowledges the complexity of it by weighing the strengths *and* weaknesses of different arguments. However, keep in mind that these characteristics do not exist apart from what readers think and believe.

▪ Establish That You Have Good Judgment

Most readers of academic writing expect writers to demonstrate good judgment by identifying a problem that readers agree is worth addressing. In turn, good judgment gives writers credibility.

Loewen crafts his introduction to capture the attention of educators as well as concerned citizens when he claims that students leave high school unaware of class structure and as a consequence "have no understanding of the ways that opportunity is not equal in America and no notion that social structure pushes people around, influencing the ideas they hold and the lives they may fashion" (para. 1). Loewen does not blame students, or even instructors, for this lack of awareness. Instead, he writes, "textbooks can take some of the credit for this state of affairs" (para. 2) because, among other shortcomings, they leave out important events in "labor history" and relegate issues facing labor to the past.

Whether an educator—or a general reader for that matter—will ultimately agree with Loewen's case is, at this point, up for grabs, but certainly the possibility that high schools in general, and history textbooks in particular, are failing students by leaving them vulnerable to class-based manipulation would be recognized as a problem by readers who believe America should be a society that offers equal opportunity for all. At this point, Loewen's readers are likely to agree that the problem of omission he identifies may be significant if its consequences are as serious as he believes them to be.

Writers also establish good judgment by conveying to readers that they are fair-minded and just and have the best interests of readers in mind. Loewen is particularly concerned that students understand the persistence of poverty and inequality in the United States and the historical circumstances of the poor, which they cannot do unless textbook writers take a more inclusive approach to addressing labor history, especially "the growth of multinational corporations and their exporting of jobs overseas" (para. 2). It's not fair to deny this important information to students, and it's not fair to the poor to leave them out of official histories of the United States. Loewen further demonstrates that he is fair and just when he calls attention in paragraph 6 to the inequality between rich and poor children in schools, a problem that persists despite our forebears' belief that class would not determine the fate of citizens of the United States.

▪ Convey to Readers That You Are Knowledgeable

Being thoughtful about a subject goes hand in hand with being knowledgeable about the subject. Loewen demonstrates his knowledge of class issues and their absence from textbooks in a number of ways (not the least of which is his awareness that a problem exists—many people, including educators, may not be aware of this problem).

In paragraph 3, Loewen makes a bold claim: "Textbooks' treatments of events in labor history are never anchored in any analysis of social class." As readers, we cannot help wondering: How does the author know this? How will he support this claim? Loewen anticipates these questions by demonstrating that he has studied the subject through a systematic examination of American history textbooks. He observes that six of the twelve textbooks he examined "contain no index listing at all for 'social class,' 'social stratification,' 'class structure,' 'income distribution,' 'inequality,' or any conceivably related topic" and that "not one book lists 'upper class,' 'working class,' or 'lower class.'" Loewen also demonstrates his grasp of class issues in American history, from the "violent class conflicts" that "took place in and just after colonial times" (para. 5), which contradict textbook writers' assertions that class conflicts did not exist during this period, to the more recent conflicts in the 1980s and early 1990s (paras. 2 and 4).

Moreover, Loewen backs up his own study of textbooks with references to a number of studies from the social sciences to illustrate that "social class is probably the single most important variable in society" (para. 6). Witness the statistics and findings he cites in paragraphs 6 through 10. The breadth of Loewen's historical knowledge and the range of his reading should convince readers that he is knowledgeable, and his trenchant analysis contributes to the authority he brings to the issue and to his credibility.

■ Show That You Understand the Complexity of a Given Issue

Recognizing the complexity of an issue helps readers see the extent to which authors know that any issue can be understood in a number of different ways. Loewen acknowledges that most of the history he recounts is not "news" (para. 11) to his educated readers, who by implication "know" and "understand" his references to historical events and trends. What may be news to his readers, he explains, is the extent to which class structure in the United States has changed over time. With the steady erosion of middle-class households since 1967, "class inequalities" and "barriers . . . to social mobility" (para. 5) are limiting more and more Americans' access to even the most fundamental of opportunities in a democratic society—health care and education.

Still, even though Loewen has introduced new thinking about the nature of class in the United States and has demonstrated a provocative play of mind by examining an overlooked body of data (high school history textbooks) that may influence the way class is perceived in America, there are still levels of complexity he hasn't addressed explicitly. Most important, perhaps, is the question of why history textbooks continue to ignore issues of class when there is so much research that indicates its importance in shaping the events history textbooks purport to explain.

Steps to Appealing to Ethos

1 **Establish that you have good judgment.** Identify an issue your readers will agree is worth addressing, and demonstrate that you are fair-minded and have the best interests of your readers in mind when you address it.

2 **Convey to readers that you are knowledgeable.** Support your claims with credible evidence that shows you have read widely on, thought about, and understand the issue.

3 **Show that you understand the complexity of the issue.** Demonstrate that you understand the variety of viewpoints your readers may bring—or may not be able to bring—to the issue.

APPEALING TO PATHOS

An appeal to pathos recognizes that people are moved to action by their emotions as well as by reasonable arguments. In fact, pathos is a vital part of argument that can predispose readers one way or another. Do you want to arouse readers' sympathy? Anger? Passion? You can do that by knowing what readers value.

Appeals to pathos are typically indirect. You can appeal to pathos by using examples or illustrations that you believe will arouse the appropriate emotions and by presenting them using an appropriate tone.

To acknowledge that writers play on readers' emotions is not to endorse manipulative writing. Rather, it is to acknowledge that effective writers use all available means of persuasion to move readers to agree with them. After all, if your thoughtful reading and careful research have led you to believe that you must weigh in with a useful insight on an important issue, it stands to reason that you would want your argument to convince your readers to believe as strongly in what you assert as you do.

For example, if you genuinely believe that the conditions some families are living in are abysmal and unfair, you want your readers to believe it too. And an effective way to persuade them to believe as you do, in addition to convincing them of the reasonableness of your argument and of your own good character and judgment, is to establish a kind of emotional common ground in your writing—the common ground of pathos.

■ Show That You Know What Your Readers Value

Let's consider some of the ways James Loewen signals that he knows what his readers value.

In the first place, Loewen assumes that readers feel the same way he does: Educated people should know that the United States has a class structure despite the democratic principles that the nation was founded on. He also expects readers to identify with his unwillingness to accept the injustice that results from that class structure. He believes that women living in poverty should have access to appropriate health care, that children living in poverty should have a chance to attend college, and that certain classes of people should not be written off to "perform specific difficult manual tasks" (para. 7).

Time and again, Loewen cites examples that reveal that the poor are discriminated against by the class structure in the United States not for lack of ability, lack of desire, lack of ambition, or lack of morality, but for no better reason than lack of money—and that such discrimination has been going on for a long time. He expects that his readers also will find such discrimination an unacceptable affront to their values of fair play and democracy and that they will experience the same sense of outrage that he does.

■ Use Illustrations and Examples That Appeal to Readers' Emotions

You can appeal to readers' emotions indirectly through the illustrations and examples you use to support your argument.

For instance, in paragraph 2, Loewen contends that textbook writers share responsibility for high school students' not knowing about the continued relevance of class issues in American life. Loewen's readers—parents, educators, historians—may very well be angered by the omissions he points out. Certainly he would expect them to be angry when they read about the effects of economic class on the health care expectant mothers and then their children receive (para. 6) and on their children's access to quality education (paras. 6–8). In citing the fact that social class "correlates strongly with SAT scores" (para. 8) and so "predicts the rate of college attendance and the type of college chosen" (para. 9), Loewen forces his readers to acknowledge that the educational playing field is far from level.

Finally, he calls attention to the fact that accumulated wealth accounts for deep class divisions in our society—that their inability to save prevents the poor from hiring legal counsel, purchasing a home, or taking advantage of tax shelters. The result, Loewen observes, is that "educational inequality replicates itself in the next generation" (para. 9).

Together, these examples strengthen both Loewen's argument and what he hopes will be readers' outrage that history textbooks do not address class issues. Without that information, Americans cannot fully understand or act to change the existing class structure.

■ Consider How Your Tone May Affect Your Audience

The **tone** of your writing is your use of language that communicates your attitude toward yourself, your material, and your readers. Of course, your tone is important in everything you write, but it is particularly crucial when you are appealing to pathos.

When you are appealing to your readers' emotions, it is tempting to use loaded, exaggerated, and even intemperate language to convey how you feel (and hope your readers will feel) about an issue. Consider these sentences: "The Republican Party has devised the most ignominious means of filling the pockets of corporations." "These wretched children suffer heartrending agonies that can barely be imagined, much less described." "The ethereal beauty of the Brandenburg concertos thrill one to the deepest core of one's being." All of these sentences express strong and probably sincere beliefs and emotions, but some readers might find them overwrought and coercive and question the writer's reasonableness.

Similarly, some writers rely on irony or sarcasm to set the tone of their work. **Irony** is the use of language to say one thing while meaning quite another. **Sarcasm** is the use of heavy-handed irony to ridicule or attack someone or something. Although irony and sarcasm can make for vivid and entertaining writing, they also can backfire and end up alienating readers. The sentence "Liberals will be pleased to hear that the new budget will be making liberal use of their hard-earned dollars" may entertain some readers with its irony and wordplay, but others may assume that the writer's attitude toward liberals is likely to result in an unfairly slanted argument. And the sentence "In my opinion, there's no reason why Christians and Muslims shouldn't rejoice together over the common ground of their both being deluded about the existence of a God" may please some readers, but it risks alienating those who are uncomfortable with breezy comments about religious beliefs. Again, think of your readers and what they value, and weigh the benefits of a clever sentence against its potential to detract from your argument or offend your audience.

You often find colorful wording and irony in op-ed and opinion pieces, where a writer may not have the space to build a compelling argument using evidence and has to resort to shortcuts to readers' emotions. However, in academic writing, where the careful accumulation and presentation of evidence and telling examples are highly valued, the frequent use of loaded language, exaggeration, and sarcasm is looked on with distrust.

Consider Loewen's excerpt. Although his outrage comes through clearly, he never resorts to hectoring. For example, in paragraph 1, he writes that students are "ignorant of the workings of the class structure" and that their opinions are "half-formed and naïve." But he does not imply that students are ignoramuses or that their opinions are foolish. What they lack, he contends, is understanding. They need to be taught something about class structure that they are not now being taught. And paragraph 1 is about as close to name-calling as Loewen comes. Even textbook writers, who are the target of his anger, are not vilified.

Loewen does occasionally make use of irony, for example in paragraph 5, where he points out inconsistencies and omissions in textbooks: "Never mind that the most violent class conflicts in American history— Bacon's Rebellion and Shays's Rebellion—took place in and just after colonial times. Textbooks still say that colonial society was relatively classless and marked by upward mobility. And things have gotten rosier since." But he doesn't resort to ridicule. Instead, he relies on examples and illustrations to connect with his readers' sense of values and appeal to their emotions.

Steps to Appealing to Pathos

1 **Show that you know what your readers value.** Start from your own values and imagine what assumptions and principles would appeal to your readers. What common ground can you imagine between your values and theirs? How will it need to be adjusted for different kinds of readers?

2 **Use illustrations and examples that appeal to readers' emotions.** Again, start from your own emotional position. What examples and illustrations resonate most with you? How can you present them to have the most emotional impact on your readers? How would you adjust them for different kinds of readers?

3 **Consider how your tone may affect your audience.** Be wary of using loaded, exaggerated, and intemperate language that may put off your readers; and be careful in your use of irony and sarcasm

---

A Practice Sequence: Appealing to Ethos and Pathos

Discuss the language and strategies the writers use in the following passages to connect with their audience, in particular their appeals to both ethos and pathos. After reading each excerpt, discuss who you think the implied audience is and whether you think the strategies the writers use to connect with their readers are effective or not.

1 Almost a half century after the U.S. Supreme Court concluded that Southern school segregation was unconstitutional and "inherently unequal," new statistics from the 1998–99 school year show that segregation continued to intensify throughout the 1990s, a period in which there were three major Supreme Court decisions authorizing a return to segregated neighborhood schools and limiting the reach and duration of desegregation orders. For African American students, this trend is particularly apparent in the South, where most blacks live and where the 2000 Census shows a continuing return from the North. From 1988 to 1998, most of the progress of the previous two decades in increasing integration in the region was lost. The South is still much more integrated than it was before the civil rights revolution, but it is moving backward at an accelerating rate.

—GARY ORFIELD, "Schools More Separate:
Consequences of a Decade of Resegregation"

2   No issue has been more saturated with dishonesty than the issue of racial quotas and preferences, which is now being examined by the Supreme Court of the United States. Many defenders of affirmative action are not even honest enough to admit that they are talking about quotas and preferences, even though everyone knows that that is what affirmative action amounts to in practice.

Despite all the gushing about the mystical benefits of "diversity" in higher education, a recent study by respected academic scholars found that "college diversity programs fail to raise standards" and that "a majority of faculty members and administrators recognize this when speaking anonymously."

This study by Stanley Rothman, Seymour Martin Lipset, and Neil Nevitte found that "of those who think that preferences have some impact on academic standards those believing it negative exceed those believing it positive by 15 to 1."

Poll after poll over the years has shown that most faculty members and most students are opposed to double standards in college admissions. Yet professors who will come out publicly and say what they say privately in these polls are as rare as hens' teeth.

Such two-faced talk is pervasive in academia and elsewhere. A few years ago, in Berkeley, there was a big fight over whether a faculty vote on affirmative action would be by secret ballot or open vote. Both sides knew that the result of a secret ballot would be the direct opposite of the result in a public vote at a faculty meeting.

—Thomas Sowell, "The Grand Fraud:
Affirmative Action for Blacks"

3   When the judgment day comes for every high school student—that day when a final transcript is issued and sent to the finest institutions, with every sin of class selection written as with a burning chisel on stone—on that day a great cry will go up throughout the land, and there will be weeping, wailing, gnashing of teeth, and considerable grumbling against guidance counselors, and the cry of a certain senior might be, "WHY did no one tell me that Introduction to Social Poker wasn't a solid academic class?" At another, perhaps less wealthy school, a frustrated and under-nurtured sculptress will wonder, "Why can't I read, and why don't I care?" The reason for both of these oversights, as they may eventually discover, is that the idea of the elective course has been seriously mauled, mistreated, and abused under the current middle-class high school system. A significant amount of the blame for producing students who are stunted, both cognitively and morally, can be traced back to this pervasive fact. Elective courses, as shoddily planned and poorly funded as they may be, constitute the only formation that many students get in their own special types of intelligences. Following the model of

Howard Gardner, these may be spatial, musical, or something else. A lack of stimulation to a student's own intelligence directly causes a lack of identification with the intelligence of others. Instead of becoming moderately interested in a subject by noticing the pleasure other people receive from it, the student will be bitter, jealous, and without empathy. These are the common ingredients in many types of tragedy, violent or benign. Schools must take responsibility for speaking in some way to each of the general types of intelligences. Failure to do so will result in students who lack skills, and also the inspiration to comfort, admire, emulate, and aid their fellow humans.

"All tasks that really call upon the power of attention are interesting for the same reason and to an almost equal degree," wrote Simone Weil in her *Reflections on Love and Faith*, her editor having defined attention as "a suspension of one's own self as a center of the world and making oneself available to the reality of another being." In Parker Palmer's *The Courage to Teach*, modern scientific theorist David Bohm describes "a holistic underlying implicate order whose information unfolds into the explicate order of particular fields." Rilke's euphemism for this "holistic . . . implicate order," which Palmer borrows, is "the grace of great things." Weil's term would be "God." However, both agree that eventual perception of this singular grace, or God, is accessible through education of a specific sort, and for both it is doubtless the most necessary experience of a lifetime. Realizing that this contention is raining down from different theorists, and keeping in mind that the most necessary experience of a lifetime should not be wholly irrelevant to the school system, educators should therefore reach the conclusion that this is a matter worth looking into. I assert that the most fruitful and practical results of their attention will be a wider range of electives coupled with a new acknowledgment and handling of them, one that treats each one seriously.

—ERIN MEYERS,
"The Educational Smorgasbord as Saving Grace"

APPEALING TO LOGOS: USING REASON AND EVIDENCE TO FIT THE SITUATION

To make an argument persuasive, you need to be in dialogue with your readers, using your own character (ethos) to demonstrate that you are a reasonable, credible, fair person and appealing to your readers' emotions (pathos), particularly their sense of right and wrong. Both types of appeal go hand in hand with appeals to logos, using converging pieces of evidence—statistics, facts, observations—to advance your claim. Remember that the type of evidence you use is determined by the issue, problem, situation, and readers' expectations. As an author, you should try to anticipate and address readers' beliefs and values. Ethos and pathos are concerned with the content of your argument; logos addresses both form and content.

An argument begins with one or more premises and ends with a conclusion. A **premise** is an assumption that you expect your readers to agree with, a statement that is either true or false—for example, "Alaska is cold in the winter"—that is offered in support of a claim. That claim is the **conclusion** you want your readers to draw from your premises. The conclusion is also a sentence that is either true or false.

For instance, Loewen's major premise is that class is a key factor in Americans' access to health care, education, and wealth. Loewen also offers a second, more specific premise: that textbook writers provide little discussion of the ways class matters. Loewen crafts his argument to help readers draw the following conclusion: "We live in a class system that runs counter to the democratic principles that underlie the founding of the United States, and history textbooks must tell this story. Without this knowledge, citizens will be uninformed."

Whether readers accept this as true depends on how Loewen moves from his initial premises to reach his conclusion—that is, whether we draw the same kinds of inferences, or reasoned judgments, that he does. He must do so in a way that meets readers' expectations of what constitutes relevant and persuasive evidence and guides them one step at a time toward his conclusion.

There are two main forms of argument: deductive and inductive. A **deductive argument** is an argument in which the premises support (or appear to support) the conclusion. If you join two premises to produce a conclusion that is taken to be true, you are stating a **syllogism**. This is the classic example of deductive reasoning through a syllogism:

1. All men are mortal. (First premise)
2. Socrates is a man. (Second premise)
3. Therefore, Socrates is mortal. (Conclusion)

In a deductive argument, it is impossible for both premises to be true and the conclusion to be false. That is, the truth of the premises means that the conclusion must also be true.

By contrast, an **inductive argument** relies on evidence and observation to reach a conclusion. Although readers may accept a writer's premises as true, it is possible for them to reject the writer's conclusion.

Let's consider this for a moment in the context of Loewen's argument. Loewen introduces the premise that class matters, then offers the more specific premise that textbook writers leave class issues out of their narratives of American history, and finally draws the conclusion that citizens need to be informed of this body of knowledge in order to create change:

1. Although class is a key factor in Americans' access to health care, education, and wealth, students know very little about the social structure in the United States.

2. In their textbooks, textbook writers do not address the issue of class, an issue that people need to know about.

3. Therefore, if people had this knowledge, they would understand that poverty cannot be blamed on the poor.

Notice that Loewen's premises are not necessarily true. For example, readers could challenge the premise that "textbook writers do not address issues of class." After all, Loewen examined just twelve textbooks. What if he had examined a different set of textbooks? Would he have drawn the same conclusion? And even if Loewen's evidence convinces us that the two premises are true, we do not have to accept that the conclusion is true.

The conclusion in an inductive argument is never definitive. That is the nature of any argument that deals with human emotions and actions. Moreover, we have seen throughout history that people tend to disagree much more on the terms of an argument than on its form. Do we agree that Israel's leaders practice apartheid? (What do we mean by *apartheid* in this case?) Do we agree with the need to grant women reproductive rights? (When does life begin?) Do we agree that all people should be treated equally? (Would equality mean equal access to resources or to outcomes?)

Deductive arguments are conclusive. In a deductive argument, the premises are universal truths—laws of nature, if you will—and the conclusion must follow from those premises. That is, a^2 plus b^2 always equals c^2, and humans are always mortal.

By contrast, an inductive argument is never conclusive. The premises may or may not be true; and even if they are true, the conclusion may be false. We might accept that class matters and that high school history textbooks don't address the issue of class structure in the United States; but we still would not know that students who have studied social stratification in America will necessarily understand the nature of poverty. It may be that social class is only one reason for poverty; or it may be that textbooks are only one source of information about social stratification in the United States, that textbook omissions are simply not as serious as Loewen claims. That the premises of an argument are true only establishes that the conclusion is probably true and, perhaps, true only for some readers.

Inductive argument is the basis of academic writing; it is also the basis of any appeal to logos. The process of constructing an inductive argument involves three steps:

1. State the premises of your argument.

2. Use credible evidence to show readers that your argument has merit.

3. Demonstrate that the conclusion follows from the premises.

In following these three steps, you will want to determine the truth of your premises, help readers understand whether or not the inferences you draw are justified, and use word signals to help readers fully grasp the connections between your premises and your conclusion.

■ State the Premises of Your Argument

Stating a premise establishes what you have found to be true and what you want to persuade readers to accept as truth as well. Let's return to Loewen, who asserts his premise at the very outset of the excerpt: "Middle-class students . . . know little about how the American class structure works . . . and nothing at all about how it has changed over time." Loewen elaborates on this initial premise a few sentences later, arguing that students "have no understanding of the ways that opportunity is not equal in America and no notion that the social structure pushes people around, influencing the ideas they hold and the lives they fashion."

Implicit here is the point that class matters. Loewen makes this point explicit several paragraphs later, where he states that "social class is probably the single most important variable in society" (para. 6). He states his second, more specific premise in paragraph 2: "High school history textbooks can take some of the credit for this state of affairs." The burden of demonstrating that these premises are true is on Loewen. If readers find that either of the premises is not true, it will be difficult, if not impossible, for them to accept his conclusion that with more knowledge, people will understand that poverty is not the fault of the poor (para. 10).

■ Use Credible Evidence

The validity of your argument depends on whether the inferences you draw are justified, and whether you can expect a reasonable person to draw the same conclusion from those premises. Loewen has to demonstrate throughout (1) that students do not have much, if any, knowledge about the class structure that exists in the United States and (2) that textbook writers are in large part to blame for this lack of knowledge. He also must help readers understand how this lack of knowledge contributes to (3) his conclusion that greater knowledge would lead Americans to understand that poor people are not responsible for poverty. He can help readers with the order in which he states his premises and by choosing the type and amount of evidence that will enable readers to draw the inferences that he does.

Interestingly, Loewen seems to assume that one group of readers— educators—will accept his first premise as true. He does not elaborate on what students know or do not know. Instead, he moves right to his second premise, which involves first acknowledging what high school history textbooks typically cover, then identifying what he believes are the important events that textbook writers exclude, and ultimately asserting that "treatments of events in labor history are never anchored in any analysis of social class" (para. 3). He supports this point with his own study of twelve textbooks (paras. 3–5) before returning to his premise that "social class is probably the single most important variable in society" (para. 6). What follows is a series of observations about the rich and references to researchers' findings on inequality (paras. 7–9). Finally, he asserts that "social class determines how people think about social class" (para. 10), implying that fuller knowledge would lead business leaders and conservative voters to think differently about the source of poverty. The question to explore is whether or not Loewen supports this conclusion.

■ Demonstrate That the Conclusion Follows from the Premises

Authors signal their conclusion with words like *consequently*, *finally*, *in sum*, *in the end*, *subsequently*, *therefore*, *thus*, *ultimately*, and *as a result*. Here is how this looks in the structure of Loewen's argument:

1. Although class is a key factor in Americans' access to health care, education, and wealth, students know very little about the social structure in the United States.

2. In their textbooks, textbook writers do not address the issue of class, an issue that people need to know about.

3. Ultimately, if people had this knowledge, they would understand that poverty cannot be blamed on the poor.

We've reprinted much of paragraph 9 of Loewen's excerpt below. Notice how Loewen pulls together what he has been discussing. He again underscores the importance of class and achievement ("All these are among the reasons"). And he points out that access to certain types of colleges puts people in a position to accumulate and sustain wealth. Of course, this is not true of the poor "because affluent families can save some money while poor families must spend what they make." This causal relationship ("Because") heightens readers' awareness of the class structure that exists in the United States.

> All these are among the reasons why social class predicts the rate of college attendance and the type of college chosen more effectively than does any other factor, including intellectual ability, however measured. After college, most affluent children get white-collar jobs, most working-class children get blue-collar jobs, and the class differences continue. As adults, rich people are more likely to have hired an attorney and to be a member of formal organizations that increase their civic power. Poor people are more likely to watch TV. Because affluent families can save some money while poor families must spend what they make, wealth differences are ten times larger than income differences. Therefore most poor and working-class families cannot accumulate the down payment required to buy a house, which in turn shuts them out from our most important tax shelter, the write-off of home mortgage interest.

Working-class parents cannot afford to live in elite subdivisions or hire high-quality day care, so the process of educational inequality replicates itself in the next generation. Finally, affluent Americans also have longer life expectancies than lower- and working-class people, the largest single cause of which is better access to health care. . . .

Once Loewen establishes this causal relationship, he concludes ("Therefore," "Finally") with the argument that poverty persists from one generation to the next.

In paragraph 10, Loewen uses the transition word *ultimately* to make the point that social class matters, so much so that it limits the ways in which people see the world, that it even "determines how people think about social class." (We discuss how to write conclusions in Chapter 9.)

Steps to Appealing to Logos

1 **State the premises of your argument.** Establish what you have found to be true and what you want readers to accept as well.

2 **Use credible evidence.** Lead your readers from one premise to the next, making sure your evidence is sufficient and convincing and your inferences are logical and correct.

3 **Demonstrate that the conclusion follows from the premises.** In particular, use the right words to signal to your readers how the evidence and inferences lead to your conclusion.

RECOGNIZING LOGICAL FALLACIES

We turn now to **logical fallacies,** flaws in the chain of reasoning that lead to a conclusion that does not necessarily follow from the premises, or evidence. Logical fallacies are common in inductive arguments for two reasons: Inductive arguments rely on reasoning about probability, not certainty; and they derive from human beliefs and values, not facts or laws of nature.

Here we list fifteen logical fallacies. In examining them, think about how to guard against the sometimes-faulty logic behind statements you might hear from politicians, advertisers, and the like. That should help you examine the premises on which you base your own assumptions and the logic you use to help readers reach the same conclusions you do.

1. *Erroneous Appeal to Authority.* An authority is someone with expertise in a given subject. An *erroneous authority* is an author who claims to be an authority but is not, or someone an author cites as an authority who is not. In this type of fallacy, the claim might be true, but the fact that an unqualified person is making the claim means there is no reason for readers to accept the claim as true.

Because the issue here is the legitimacy of authority, your concern should be to prove to yourself and your readers that you or the people you are citing have expertise in the subject. An awareness of this type of fallacy has become increasingly important as celebrities offer support for candidates running for office or act as spokespeople for curbing global warming or some other cause. The candidate may be the best person for the office, and there may be very good reasons to control global warming; but we need to question the legitimacy of a nonexpert endorsement.

2. *Ad Hominem.* An ad hominem argument focuses on the person making a claim instead of on the claim itself. (*Ad hominem* is Latin for "to the person.") In most cases, an ad hominem argument does not have a bearing on the truth or the quality of a claim.

Keep in mind that it is always important to address the claim or the reasoning behind it, rather than the person making the claim. "Of course Senator Wiley supports oil drilling in Alaska—he's in the pocket of the oil companies!" is an example of an ad hominem argument. Senator Wiley may have good reasons for supporting oil drilling in Alaska that have nothing to do with his alleged attachment to the oil industry. However, if an individual's character is relevant to the argument, then an ad hominem argument can be valid. If Senator Wiley has been found guilty of accepting bribes from an oil company, it makes sense to question both his credibility and his claims.

3. *Shifting the Issue.* This type of fallacy occurs when an author draws attention away from the issue instead of offering evidence that will enable people to draw their own conclusions about the soundness of an argument. For example:

> Affirmative action proponents accuse me of opposing equal opportunity in the workforce. I think my positions on military expenditures, education, and public health speak for themselves.

The author of this statement does not provide a chain of reasoning that would enable readers to judge his or her stance on the issue of affirmative action.

4. *Either/Or Fallacy.* At times, an author will take two extreme positions to force readers to make a choice between two seemingly contradictory positions. For example:

> Either you support the war in Iraq, or you are against it.

Although the author has set up an either/or condition, in reality one position does not exclude the other. Many people support the troops in Iraq even though they do not support the reasons for starting the war.

5. *Sweeping Generalizations.* When an author attempts to draw a conclusion without providing sufficient evidence to support the conclusion or examining possible counterarguments, he or she may be making sweeping generalizations. For example:

> Despite the women's movement in the 1960s and 1970s, women still do not receive equal pay for equal work. Obviously, any attempt to change the status quo for women is doomed to failure.

As is the case with many fallacies, the author's position may be reasonable, but we cannot accept the argument at face value. Reading critically entails testing assumptions like this one—that any attempt to create change is doomed to failure because women do not receive equal pay for equal work. We could ask, for example, whether inequities persist in the public sector. And we could point to other areas where the women's movement has had measurable success. Title IX, for example, has reduced the dropout rate among teenage girls; it has also increased the rate at which women earn college and graduate degrees.

6. *Bandwagon.* When an author urges readers to accept an idea because a significant number of people support it, he or she is making a bandwagon argument. This is a fairly common mode of argument in advertising; for example, a commercial might attempt to persuade us to buy a certain product because it's popular.

> Because Harvard, Stanford, and Berkeley have all added a multicultural component to their graduation requirements, other institutions should do so as well.

The growing popularity of an idea is not sufficient reason to accept that it is true.

7. *Begging the Question.* This fallacy entails advancing a circular argument that asks readers to accept a premise that is also the conclusion readers are expected to draw:

> We could improve the undergraduate experience with coed dorms because both men and women benefit from living with members of the opposite gender.

Here readers are being asked to accept that the conclusion is true despite the fact that the premises—men benefit from living with women, and women benefit from living with men—are essentially the same as the conclusion. Without evidence that a shift in dorm policy could improve on the undergraduate experience, we cannot accept the conclusion as true. Indeed, the conclusion does not necessarily follow from the premise.

8. *False Analogy.* Authors (and others) often try to persuade us that something is true by using a comparison. This approach is not in and of itself a problem, as long as the comparison is reasonable. For example:

> It is ridiculous to have a Gay and Lesbian Program and a Department of African American Culture. We don't have a Straight Studies Program or a Department of Caucasian Culture.

Here the author is urging readers to rethink the need for two academic departments by saying that the school doesn't have two other departments. That, of course, is not a reason for or against the new departments. What's needed is an analysis that compares the costs (economic and otherwise) of starting up and operating the new departments versus the contributions (economic and otherwise) of the new departments.

9. *Technical Jargon.* If you've ever had a salesperson try to persuade you to purchase a television or an entertainment system with capabilities you absolutely *must* have—even if you didn't understand a word the salesperson was saying about alternating currents and circuit splicers—then you're familiar with this type of fallacy. We found this passage in one of our student's papers:

> You should use this drug because it has been clinically proven that it inhibits the reuptake of serotonin and enhances the dopamine levels of the body's neurotransmitters.

The student's argument may very well be true, but he hasn't presented any substantive evidence to demonstrate that the premises are true and that the conclusion follows from the premises.

10. *Confusing Cause and Effect.* It is challenging to establish that one factor causes another. For example, how can we know for certain that economic class predicts, or is a factor in, academic achievement? How do we know that a new president's policies are the cause of a country's economic well-being? Authors often assume cause and effect when two factors are simply associated with each other:

> The current recession came right after the president was elected.

This fallacy states a fact, but it does not prove that the president's election caused the recession.

11. *Appeal to Fear.* One type of logical fallacy makes an appeal to readers' irrational fears and prejudices, preventing them from dealing squarely with a given issue and often confusing cause and effect:

> We should use whatever means possible to avoid further attack.

The reasoning here is something like this: "If we are soft on defense, we will never end the threat of terrorism." But we need to consider whether there is indeed a threat, and, if so, whether the presence of a threat should lead to action, and, if so, whether that action should include "whatever means possible." (Think of companies that sell alarm systems by pointing to people's vulnerability to harm and property damage.)

12. *Fallacy of Division.* A fallacy of division suggests that what is true of the whole must also be true of its parts:

> Conservatives have always voted against raising the minimum wage, against stem cell research, and for defense spending. Therefore, we can assume that conservative Senator Harrison will vote this way.

The author is urging readers to accept the premise without providing evidence of how the senator has actually voted on the three issues.

13. *Hasty Generalization.* This fallacy is committed when a person draws a conclusion about a group based on a sample that is too small to be representative. Consider this statement:

> Seventy-five percent of the seniors surveyed at the university study just
> 10 hours a week. We can conclude, then, that students at the university are
> not studying enough.

What you need to know is how many students were actually surveyed. Seventy-five percent may seem high, but not if the researcher surveyed just 400 of the 2,400 graduating seniors. This sample of students from a total population of 9,600 students at the university is too small to draw the conclusion that students in general are not studying enough.

14. *The Straw Man Argument.* A straw man fallacy makes a generalization about what a group believes without actually citing a specific writer or work:

> Democrats are more interested in running away than in trying to win the war on terrorism.

Here the fallacy is that the author simply ignores a person's actual position and substitutes a distorted, exaggerated, or misrepresented version of that position. This kind of fallacy often goes hand in hand with assuming that what is true of the group is true of the individual, what we call the fallacy of division.

15. *Fallacy of the Middle Ground.* The fallacy of the middle ground assumes that the middle position between two extreme positions must be correct. Although the middle ground may be true, the author must justify this position with evidence.

> E. D. Hirsch argues that cultural literacy is the only sure way to increase test scores, and Jonathan Kozol believes schools will improve only if state legislators increase funding; but I would argue that school reform will occur if we change the curriculum and provide more funding.

This fallacy draws its power from the fact that a moderate or middle position is often the correct one. Again, however, the claim that the moderate or middle position is correct must be supported by legitimate reasoning.

ANALYZING THE APPEALS IN A RESEARCHED ARGUMENT

Now that you have studied the variety of appeals you can make to connect with your audience, we would like you to read a paper on urban health problems by Meredith Minkler and analyze her strategies for appealing to her readers. The paper is long and carefully argued, so we suggest you take detailed notes about her use of appeals to ethos, pathos, and logos as you read. You may want to refer to the Practice Sequence questions on page 248 to help focus your reading. Ideally, you should work through the text with your classmates, in groups of three or four, appointing one student to record and share each group's analysis of Minkler's argument.

MEREDITH MINKLER

Community-Based Research Partnerships: Challenges and Opportunities

Meredith Minkler is a professor of health and social behavior at the School of Public Health, University of California, Berkeley. She is an activist and researcher whose work explores community partnerships, community organizing, and community-based participatory research. With more than one hundred books and articles to her credit, she is coeditor of the influential *Community Based Participatory Research for Health* (2003). The following article appeared in *The Journal of Urban Health* in 2005.

Abstract
The complexity of many urban health problems often makes them ill suited to traditional research approaches and interventions. The resultant frustration, together with community calls for genuine partnership in the research process, has highlighted the importance of an alternative paradigm. Community-based participatory research (CBPR) is presented as a promising collaborative approach that combines systematic inquiry, participation, and action to address urban health problems. Following a brief review of its basic tenets and historical roots, key ways in which CBPR adds value to urban health research are introduced and illustrated. Case study examples from diverse international settings are used to illustrate some of the difficult ethical challenges that may arise in the course of CBPR partnership approaches. The concepts of partnership synergy and cultural humility, together with protocols such as Green et al.'s guidelines for appraising CBPR projects, are highlighted as useful tools for urban health researchers seeking to apply this collaborative approach and to deal effectively with the difficult ethical challenges it can present.

Keywords
Community-based participatory research, Ethical issues in research, Participatory action research, Partnership, Urban health.

Introduction

The complexity of urban health problems has often made them poorly suited to traditional "outside expert"–driven research and intervention approaches.[1] Together with community demands for authentic partnerships in research that are locally relevant and "community based" rather than merely "community placed," this frustration has led to a burgeoning of interest in an alternative research paradigm.[1,2] Community-based participatory research (CBPR) is an overarching term that increasingly is used to encompass a variety of approaches to research that have as their centerpiece three interrelated elements: participation, research, and action.[3] As defined by Green et al.[4] for the Royal Society of Canada, CBPR may concisely be described as "systematic investigation with the participation of those affected by an issue for purposes of education and action or affecting social change." The approach further has been characterized as

> [A] collaborative process that equitably involves all partners in the research process and recognizes the unique strengths that each brings. CBPR begins with a research topic of importance to the community with the aim of combining knowledge and action for social change to improve community health and eliminate health disparities.[5,6]

This article briefly describes CBPR's roots and core principles and summarizes the value added by this approach to urban health research. Drawing on examples from a variety of urban health settings nationally and internationally, it discusses and illustrates several of the key challenges faced in applying this partnership approach to inquiry and

action. The article concludes by suggesting that despite such challenges and the labor-intensive nature of this approach, CBPR offers an
exceptional opportunity for partnering with communities in ways that
can enhance both the quality of research and its potential for helping
address some of our most intractable urban health problems.

Historical Roots and Core Principles

The roots of CBPR may be traced in part to the action research school
developed by the social psychologist Kurt Lewin[7] in the 1940s, with its
emphasis on the active involvement in the research of those affected
by the problem being studied through a cyclical process of fact finding, action, and reflection. But CBPR is most deeply grounded in the
more revolutionary approaches to research that emerged, often independently from one another, from work with oppressed communities in
South America, Asia, and Africa in the 1970s.[3,8,9] Brazilian adult educator Paulo Freire[9] provided critical grounding for CBPR in his development of a dialogical method accenting co-learning and action based on
critical reflection. Freire,[9] Fals-Borda,[10] and other developing countries'
scholars developed their alternative approaches to inquiry as a direct
counter to the often "colonizing" nature of research to which oppressed
communities were subjected, with feminist and postcolonialist scholars
adding further conceptual richness.[11,12]

Among the tenets of participatory action approaches to research outlined by McTaggart[13] are that it is a political process, involves lay people
in theory-making, is committed to improving social practice by changing it, and establishes "self-critical communities." As Israel et al.[6] adds,
other core principles are that CBPR "involves systems development and
local community capacity development," is "a co-learning process" to
which community members and outside researchers contribute equally,
and "achieves a balance between research and action." CBPR reflects a
profound belief in "partnership synergy." As described by Lasker et al.[14]:

> [T]he synergy that partners seek to achieve through collaboration is more
> than a mere exchange of resources. By combining the individual perspec-
> tives, resources, and skills of the partners, the group creates something new
> and valuable together — something that is greater than the sum of its parts.

Moreover, CBPR embodies a deep commitment to what Tervalon
and Murray-Garcia[15] have called cultural humility. As they point out,
although we can never become truly competent in another's culture,
we can demonstrate a "lifelong commitment to self evaluation and
self-critique," to redress power imbalances and "develop and maintain
mutually respectful and dynamic partnerships with communities."[15]
Although the term *cultural humility* was coined primarily in reference

3

4

5

to race and ethnicity, it also is of value in helping us understand and address the impacts of professional cultures (which tend to be highly influenced by white, western, patriarchal belief systems), as these help shape interactions between outside researchers and their community partners.[15]

CBPR is not a method per se but an orientation to research that may employ any of a number of qualitative and quantitative methodologies. As Cornwall and Jewkes[16] note, what is distinctive about CBPR is "the attitudes of researchers, which in turn determine how, by and for whom research is conceptualized and conducted [and] the corresponding location of power at every stage of the research process." The accent placed by CBPR on individual, organizational, and community empowerment also is a hallmark of this approach to research.

With the increasing emphasis on partnership approaches to improving urban health, CBPR is experiencing a rebirth of interest and unprecedented new opportunities for both scholarly recognition and financial support. In the United States, for example, the Institute of Medicine[17] recently named "community-based participatory research" as one of eight new areas in which all schools of public health should be offering training.

Although the renewed interest in CBPR provides a welcome contrast to more traditional top-down research approaches, it also increases the dangers of co-optation as this label is loosely applied to include research and intervention efforts in search of funding that do not truly meet the criteria for this approach. The sections below illustrate some of the value added to urban research when authentic partnership approaches are taken seriously and then briefly highlight some of the ethical challenges such work may entail.

The Value Added to Urban Health Research by a CBPR Approach

CBPR can enrich and improve the quality and outcomes of urban health research in a variety of ways. On the basis of the work of many scholars and institutions,[4,6,8,18] and as summarized by the National Institutes of Health (http://grants.nih.gov/grants/guide/pa-files/PAR-05-026.html), some of its primary contributions may be characterized and illustrated as follows.

CBPR Can Support the Development of Research Questions That Reflect Health Issues of Real Concern to Community Members

Ideally, CBPR begins with a research topic or question that comes from the local community, as when the nongovernmental organization

(NGO) Alternatives for Community and Environment (ACE) in the low-income Roxbury section of Boston, reached out to Harvard University's School of Public Health and other potential partners to study and address the high rates of asthma in their neighborhood. Collaborative studies using air-monitoring and other approaches yielded data supporting the hypothesis that Roxbury was indeed a hot spot for pollution contributing to asthma. This in turn paved the way for a variety of policy and community education actions and outcomes.[19]

Although having a community partner such as ACE identify an issue   *11* and catalyze a research partnership may be the ideal, it is often the privileged outside researcher who initiates a CBPR project. In these instances too, however, a genuine commitment to high-level community involvement in issue selection, with NGOs and formal and informal community leaders engaged as equal partners, can help ensure that the research topic decided upon really is of major concern to the local population.

CBPR Can Improve Our Ability to Achieve Informed Consent, and to Address Issues of "Costs and Benefits" on the Community, and Not Simply the Individual Level[20]

With its accent on equitable community involvement in all stages of   *12* the research process,[6] CBPR often finds creative means of ensuring informed consent. The "One Hand, One Heart" study in urban and rural Tibet, which included a randomized controlled clinical trial of an indigenous medicine to prevent maternal hemorrhaging, actively involved local midwives and other community partners on the research team who played a key role in helping find locally translatable concepts to improve informed consent. Their help in early ethnographic work thus revealed that the concept of disclosing risk was highly problematic, because such disclosure was believed to disturb the wind element responsible for emotions, potentially leading to emotional upset and other adverse outcomes. By reframing risk disclosure as "safety issues," needed information could be conveyed in a far more culturally acceptable manner.[21]

CBPR also offers an important potential opening for extending the   *13* gaze of our ethical review processes such that we examine and address risks and benefits for the community. In Toronto, Travers and Flicker[20] have pioneered in developing such guidelines, pointing out the importance of having us ask such questions as "Will the methods used be sensitive and appropriate to various communities?" "What training or capacity building opportunities will you build in?" and "How will you balance scientific rigor and accessibility?" The strong philosophical fit between questions such as these and CBPR's commitments to equitable partnership and community capacity building reflect another source of value added to urban health research through this approach.

CBPR Can Improve Cultural Sensitivity and the Reliability and Validity of Measurement Tools Through High-Quality Community Participation in Designing and Testing Study Instruments

Particularly in survey research, community advisory boards (CABs) and other partnership structures can improve measurement instruments by making sure that questions are worded in ways that will elicit valid and reliable responses. In a study of urban grandparents raising grandchildren due to the crack cocaine epidemic, the author and her colleagues used validated instruments, such as those for depressive symptomatology. However, they also learned from CAB members how to word other questions about sensitive topics. Rather than asking a standard (and disliked) question about income, for example, the CAB encouraged us to rephrase the question as "How much money is available to help you in raising this child?" When this alternate wording was used, a wealth of detailed income data was obtained, which improved our understanding of the challenges faced by this population.[22]

CBPR Can Uncover Lay Knowledge Critical to Enhancing Understanding of Sensitive Urban Health Problems

Through the cultural humility and partnership synergy involved in deeply valuing lay knowledge and working in partnership with community residents, CBPR can uncover hidden contributors to health and social problems. The high rates of HIV/AIDS in India and the often sensitive nature of this subject among young men led the Deepak Charitable Trust to develop a research committee for a study in the industrial area of Nandesari, in Gujarat, comprised of several male village health workers and other young men from the area. Working closely with a medical anthropologist, the research committee planned the research, including developing a sampling plan and the phrasing of culturally sensitive questions. Their insider knowledge helped reveal that AIDS itself was not perceived as a major problem by the young men in this area. Instead, men who were engaging in high-risk behaviors wanted to find sex partners at least partly to avoid "thinning of the semen" and sexual dysfunction and fatigue, which were believed to be long-term consequences of masturbation and nocturnal emissions. These fears appeared to be contributing to high rates of unprotected intercourse with sex workers at the area's many truck stops and with other sex partners.[23] This insider knowledge both strengthened the research and led to subsequent interventions to help dispel such misinformation.

By Increasing Community Trust and Ownership, CBPR Can Improve Recruitment and Retention Efforts

In a participatory epidemiology project on diabetes in an urban Aboriginal community in Melbourne, Australia, a marked increase in recruitment was experienced following the hiring of a community codirector and the changing of the project's name to one chosen by the local community.[24] Similarly, a 69 percent response rate achieved in a CBPR study of the health and working conditions of the largely immigrant hotel room cleaner population (many of them undocumented) in several of San Francisco's major tourist hotels was heavily attributed to the hiring and training of a core group of twenty-five room cleaners as key project staff. That high response rate, together with the high quality of data collected, made a substantial contribution when results later were presented and used to help negotiate a new contract.[25]

CBPR Can Help Increase Accuracy and Cultural Sensitivity in the Interpretation of Findings

Even highly engaged community members of the research team may not wish to be involved in the labor-intensive data analysis phase of a research project,[26] nor do all methodological approaches lend themselves to such involvement. Yet when applicable and desired, community involvement in data analysis can make real contributions to our understanding of the themes and findings that emerge. In a U.S. study of and with people with disabilities on the contentious topic of death with dignity legislation in their community, the author and an "insider/outsider" member of the research team met on alternate Saturdays with a subcommittee of the CAB to engage in joint data analysis. Using redacted transcripts, and applying lessons learned in qualitative data interpretation, the diverse CAB members came up with far richer codes and themes than outside researchers could have achieved alone.[27]

CBPR Can Increase the Relevance of Intervention Approaches and Thus the Likelihood of Success

One of the strengths of CBPR is its commitment to action as part of the research process. But without strong community input, researchers not infrequently design interventions that are ill suited to the local context in which they are applied. In the Gujarat case study mentioned above, partnership with local community members helped in the design of culturally relevant interventions, such as street theater performed by locally recruited youth at *melas* (or fairs), and the dissemination of study findings through the fifteen local credit and savings groups that often provided platforms for discussing reproductive health and related issues. Both these approaches provided critical means of information dissemination on this culturally and emotionally charged topic.[23]

Ethical and Other Challenges in Community-Based Participatory Research

Engaging in urban health research with diverse community partners can indeed enrich both the quality and the outcomes of such studies. At the same time, CBPR is fraught with ethical and related challenges, several of which are now highlighted.

"Community Driven" Issue Selection

A key feature of CBPR involves its commitment to ensuring that the research topic comes from the community. Yet many such projects "paradoxically . . . would not occur without the initiative of someone outside the community who has the time, skill, and commitment, and who almost inevitably is a member of a privileged and educated group."[28] In such instances, outside researchers must pay serious attention to community understandings of what the real issue or topic of concern is.

In South Africa, for example, high rates of cervical cancer in the Black and Colored populations led Mosavel et al.[29] to propose an investigation of this problem. In response to community feedback, however, they quickly broadened their initial topic to "cervical health," a concept which "acknowledged the fact that women's health in South Africa extends well beyond the risk of developing cervical cancer, and includes HIV-AIDS and STDs, sexual violence, and multiple other social problems." In other instances, the outside researcher as an initiator of a potential CBPR project needs to determine whether the topic he or she has identified really is of concern to the local community—and whether outsider involvement is welcome. The Oakland, California–based Grandmother Caregiver Study mentioned above grew out of the interests of my colleague and me in studying the strengths of as well as the health and social problems faced by the growing number of urban African American grandmothers who were raising grandchildren in the context of a major drug epidemic. As privileged white women, however, we had to determine first whether this was a topic of local concern and, if so, whether there might be a role for us in working with the community to help study and address it. We began by enlisting the support of an older African American colleague with deep ties in the community, who engaged with us in a frank discussion with two prominent African American NGOs. It was only after getting their strong support for proceeding that we wrote a grant, with funds for these organizations, which in turn helped us pull together an outstanding CAB that was actively involved in many stages of the project.[21,26]

We were lucky in this case that a topic we as outsiders identified turned out to represent a deep concern in the local community. Yet not infrequently "the community" is in fact deeply divided over an issue.

Indeed, as Yoshihama and Carr[30] have argued, "communities are not places that researchers enter but are instead a set of negotiations that inherently entail multiple and often conflicting interests." In such situations, outside researchers can play a useful role in helping community partners think through who "the community" in fact is in relation to a proposed project and the pros and cons of undertaking the project to begin with. The holding of town hall meetings and other forums may then be useful in helping achieve consensus on an issue that is truly of, by, and for the community, however it is defined.[26]

Insider–Outsider Tensions

Urban health researchers in many parts of the world have written poignantly about the power dynamics and other sources of insider–outsider tensions and misunderstandings in CBPR and related partnership efforts. Ugalde[31] points out how in Latin America participants may be exploited as cheap sources of labor or may become alienated from their communities because of their participation. In her work with Native American and other marginalized groups in New Mexico, Wallerstein[32] further illustrates how even outsiders who pride ourselves on being trusted community friends and allies often fail to appreciate the extent of the power that is embedded in our own, often multiple sources of privilege, and how it can affect both process and outcomes in such research.   *23*

One major source of insider–outsider tensions involves the differential reward structures for partners in CBPR. For although a major aim of such research is to benefit the local community, the outside researchers typically stand to gain the most from such collaborations, bringing in grants, getting new publications, and so forth. The common expectation that community partners will work for little or no pay and the fact that receipt of compensation may take months if the funds are coming through a ministry of health or a university are also sources of understandable resentment.[6,26]   *24*

To address these and other sources of insider–outsider tensions in work with indigenous communities in both urban and rural areas, researchers in New Zealand,[33] Australia,[34] the United States,[35] and Canada[36] have worked with their community partners to develop ethical guidelines for their collaborative work, including protocols that address   *25*

1. negotiating with political and spiritual leaders in the community to obtain their input and their approval for the proposed research,

2. ensuring equitable benefits to participants (e.g., appropriate training and hiring of community members) in return for their contributions and resources,

3. developing agreements about the ownership and publication of findings, and the early review of findings by key community leaders.

Although such protocols cannot begin to address all of the conflicts   26
that may arise in CBPR, they can play a critical role in helping pave the
way for the continued dialogue and negotiation that must be an integral
part of the process.

Constraints on Community Involvement

Outside researchers committed to a CBPR approach not infrequently   27
express frustration at the difficulty moving from the goal of heavy community partner involvement in the research process to the reality. As
Diaz and Simmons[37] found in their Reproductive Health Project in Brazil, despite a strong commitment to involving the most marginalized
and vulnerable classes (in this case, women who were users of the public sector services being studied), such individuals often "are least likely
to be in a position to donate their time and energy." Further, and even
when outside researchers are careful to provide child care and transportation, there are differential costs of participation by gender.[30]

Still another set of challenges may arise when community desires   28
with respect to research design and methods clash with what outsider
researchers consider to be "good science." In an oft-cited CBPR study
with a local Mohawk community in Québec, Chataway[38] describes
how community members at first strongly objected to the idea of using
a questionnaire approach which they saw as "putting their thoughts in
boxes." Through respectful listening on both sides, the value of such an
approach was realized and a more qualitative methodology developed,
through which community members would then be actively involved in
helping analyze and interpret the quantitative findings that emerged. As
such case studies illustrate, CBPR does not condone an abandonment of
one's own scientific standards and knowledge base. But it does advocate
a genuine co-learning process through which lay and professional ways
of knowing both are valued and examined for what they can contribute.[26]

Dilemmas in the Sharing and Release of Findings

A crucial step in CBPR involves returning data to the community and   29
enabling community leaders and participants to have an authentic role
in deciding how that data will be used. As Travers and Flicker[20] suggest,
ethical research review processes that ask questions such as "Are there
built-in mechanisms for how unflattering results will be dealt with?"
should be employed at the front end of our CBPR projects. In addition
to the formal IRB process they propose, which offers a critical next step
for the field, CBPR partners can look to a variety of formal or informal
research protocols and particularly to the detailed guidelines for health
promotion research developed by Green et al.,[4,39] which help partnerships decide in advance how potentially difficult issues concerning the
sharing and release of findings and other matters will be handled.

Challenges in the Action Dimensions of CBPR

Numerous ethical challenges lastly may arise in relation to the critical   30
action component of CBPR. In some instances, community partners
may wish to move quickly into action, whereas academic and other
outside research partners may want to "put the breaks on" until findings have been published or other steps brought to fruition. In other
cases, the nature of funding (e.g., from a government body) may constrain action on the policy level that is prohibited or discouraged by the
funder. And in still other instances, including the Brazilian Reproductive Health Project[37] cited above, community members may not wish to
be associated with a CBPR project that appears connected to a broader
political agenda.

Participation in the action phase of CBPR projects may sometimes   31
present risks to community participants, as when immigrant hotel
room cleaners in the San Francisco study took part in a Labor Day sit-
in and in some cases faced arrest.[25] And for both professionally trained
researchers and their community partners, actions that involve challenging powerful corporate or other entrenched interests may have
negative consequences for those involved. At the same time, CBPR's
fundamental commitment to action and to redressing power imbalances makes this aspect of the work a particularly important contributor to urban health improvement through research.

Conclusion

Difficult ethical challenges may confront urban health researchers who   32
engage in CBPR. Yet this approach can greatly enrich the quality of our
research, helping ensure that we address issues of genuine community
concern and use methods and approaches that are culturally sensitive
and that improve the validity and reliability of our findings. Moreover,
through its commitment to action as an integral part of the research
process, CBPR can help in translating findings as we work with community partners to help address some of our most intractable urban
health problems.

Acknowledgement

Many current and former community and academic partners have con-   33
tributed to my understanding of the advantages and pitfalls of collaborative urban health research and I am deeply grateful. Particular thanks
are extended to Nina Wallerstein, Kathleen M. Roe, Barbara Israel,
Lawrence W. Green, and Ronald Labonte, who have greatly stimulated
my own thinking and scholarship in this area. I am grateful to former

students, Rima Shaw and Caroline Bell, as well as other individuals who have shared some of the cases drawn upon in this paper. My gratitude is extended to Claire Murphy for assistance with manuscript preparation.

References

1. Minkler M, Wallerstein N. Community Based Participatory Research for Health. San Francisco, CA: Jossey-Bass; 2003.

2. Green LW, Mercer SL. Can public health researchers and agencies reconcile the push from funding bodies and the pull from communities? *Am J Public Health.* 2001;91:1926–1929.

3. Hall BL. From margins to center: the development and purpose of participatory action research. *Am Sociol.* 1992;23:15–28.

4. Green LW, George A, Daniel M, et al. *Study of Participatory Research in Health Promotion.* Ottawa, Ontario: Royal Society of Canada; 1995.

5. Community Health Scholars Program. *The Community Health Scholars Program: Stories of Impact.* Ann Arbor, MI; 2002.

6. Israel BA, Schulz AJ, Parker EA, Becker AB. Review of community-based research: assessing partnership approaches to improve public health. *Annu Rev Public Health.* 1998;19:173–202.

7. Lewin K. Action research and minority problems. *J Soc Issues.* 1946;2:34–46.

8. Brown LD, Tandon R. Ideology and political economy in inquiry: action research and participatory research. *J Appl Behav Sci.* 1983; 19:277–294.

9. Freire P. *Pedagogy of the Oppressed.* New York, NY: Seabury Press; 1970.

10. Fals-Borda O. The application of participatory action-research in Latin America. *Int Sociol.* 1987;2:329–347.

11. Maguire P. *Doing Participatory Research: A Feminist Approach.* Amherst, MA: Center for International Education; 1987.

12. Duran E, Duran B. *Native American Postcolonial Psychology.* Albany, NY: State University of New York Press; 1995.

13. McTaggart R. Sixteen tenets of participatory action research. In: Wadsworth Y, ed. *Everyday Evaluation on the Run.* Sydney, Australia: Allen & Unwin; 1997:79.

14. Lasker RD, Weiss ES, Miller R. Partnership synergy: a practical framework for studying and strengthening the collaborative advantage. *Milbank Q.* 2001;79:179–205, III–IV.

15. Tervalon M, Murray-Garcia J. Cultural humility vs. cultural competence: a critical distinction in defining physician training outcomes in medical education. *J Health Care Poor Underserved.* 1998; 9:117–125.

16. Cornwall A, Jewkes R. What is participatory research? *Soc Sci Med.* 1995;41:1667–1676.

17. Gebbie K, Rosenstock L, Hernandez LM. *Who Will Keep the Public Healthy? Educating Public Health Professionals for the 21st Century.* Washington, DC: Institute of Medicine; 2002.

18. O'Fallon LR, Dearry A. Community-based participatory research as a tool to advance environmental health sciences. *Environ Health Perspect.* 2002;110:155–159.

19. Loh P, Sugerman-Brozan J. Environmental justice organizing for environmental health: case study on asthma and diesel exhaust in Roxbury, Massachusetts. *Environ Health Perspect.* 2002;584: 110–124.

20. Travers R, Flicker S. Ethical issues in community based research. In: *Urban Health Community-Based Research Series Workshop.* Wellesley, MA; 2004.

21. Bell C. *One HEART (Health Education and Research in Tibet) Community Based Participatory Research on Top of the World.* Unpublished manuscript, University of California, Berkeley, School of Public Health; 2004.

22. Roe KM, Minkler M, Saunders FF. Combining research, advocacy and education: the methods of the Grandparent Caregiving Study. *Health Educ Q.* 1995;22:458–475.

23. Shah R. *A Retrospective Analysis of an HIV Prevention Program for Men in Gujarat, India.* Unpublished manuscript, University of California, Berkeley, School of Public Health; 2004.

24. Thompson SJ. Participatory epidemiology: methods of the Living With Diabetes Project. *Intl Q Community Health Educ.* 2000; 19:3–18.

25. Lee P, Krause N, Goetchius C. Participatory action research with hotel room cleaners: from collaborative study to the bargaining table. In: Minkler M, Wallerstein N, eds. *Community Based Participatory Research for Health.* San Francisco, CA: Jossey-Bass; 2003: 390–404.

26. Minkler M. Ethical challenges for the "outside" researcher in community based participatory research. *Health Educ Behav.* 2004;31: 684–701.

27. Fadem P, Minkler M, Perry M, et al. Ethical challenges in community based participatory research: a case study from the San Francisco Bay Area disability community. In: Minkler M,

Wallerstein N, eds. *Community Based Participatory Research for Health*. San Francisco, CA: Jossey-Bass; 2003.

28. Reason P. *Participation in Human Inquiry*. London, UK: Sage; 1994.

29. Mosavel M, Simon C, van Stade D, Buchbinder M. *Community Based Participatory Research (CBPR) in South Africa: Engaging Multiple Constituents to Shape the Research Question*. Unpublished manuscript; 2004.

30. Yoshihama M, Carr ES. Community participation reconsidered: feminist participatory action research with Hmong women. *J Community Pract*. 2002;10:85–103.

31. Ugalde A. Ideological dimensions of community participation in Latin American health programs. *Soc Sci Med*. 1985;21:41–53.

32. Wallerstein N. Power between evaluator and community: research relationships within New Mexico's healthier communities. *Soc Sci Med*. 1999;49:39–53.

33. Cram F. Rangahau Maori: Tona tika, tona pono: The validity and integrity of Maori research. In: Tolich M, ed. *Research Ethics in Aotearoa New Zealand*. Longman, Auckland: Pearson Education; 2001:35–52.

34. Anderson I. Ethics and health research in Aboriginal communities. In: Daly J, ed. *Ethical Intersections: Health Research, Methods and Researcher Responsibility*. St. Leonards, New South Wales: Allen & Unwin; 1996:153–165.

35. Turning Point, National Association of County and City Health Officials. Thirteen policy principles for advancing collaborative activity among and between tribal communities and surrounding jurisdictions. In: Minkler M, Wallerstein N, eds. *Community Based Participatory Research for Health*. San Francisco, CA: Jossey-Bass; 2003:436, Appendix E.

36. Stuart CA. Care and concern: an ethical journey in participatory action research. *Can J Couns*. 1998;32:298–314.

37. Diaz M, Simmons R. When is research participatory? Reflections on a Reproductive Health Project in Brazil. *J Women's Health*. 1999;8:175–184.

38. Chataway CJ. Examination of the constraints of mutual inquiry in a participatory action research project. *J Soc Issues*. 1997;53: 747–765.

39. Green LW, George MA, Daniel M, et al. Guidelines for participatory research in health promotion. In: Minkler M, Wallerstein N, eds. *Community Based Participatory Research for Health*. San Francisco, CA: Jossey-Bass; 2003:419, Appendix C.

A Practice Sequence: Analyzing the Appeals in a Researched Argument

1   Make a list of the major premises that inform Minkler's argu-
    ment, and examine the evidence she uses to support them. To
    what extent do you find her evidence credible? Do you generally
    agree or disagree with the conclusions she draws? Be prepared to
    explain your responses to your class or peer group.

2   Note instances where Minkler appeals to ethos, pathos, and
    logos. How would you describe the ways she makes these three
    types of appeals? How does she present herself? What does she
    seem to assume? How does she help you understand the chain of
    reasoning by which she moves from premises to conclusion?

3   Working in groups of three or four, compose a letter to Minkler
    in which you take issue with her argument. This does not mean
    your group has to disagree with her entire argument, although of
    course you may. Rather, present your group's own contribution
    to the conversation in which she is participating. You may want
    to ask her to further explain one or more of her points, or suggest
    what she might be leaving out, or add your own take or evidence
    to her argument. As a group, you will have to agree on your focus.
    In the letter, include a summary of Minkler's argument or the part
    of it on which your group is focusing. Pay close attention to your
    own strategies for appealing to her—how you present yourselves,
    how you appeal to her values and emotions, and how you present
    your reasons for your own premises and conclusion.

ANALYZING VISUAL RHETORIC: ADVERTISEMENTS

This section focuses on visual rhetoric; that is, how visual images communicate and create an argument designed to move a specific audience to
think or act in a specific way. Every day we view films and television, read
magazines, browse the Internet, and walk the aisles of stores where sign-
age and packaging encourage us to buy products we may not need. Everywhere we are confronted by visual images that aim to persuade us.

To examine the strategies you can use to understand how images
and texts convey meaning, we would like you to analyze a public service
announcement (PSA) for Feeding America, distributed by the Ad Council,
a nonprofit institution founded in 1942 for the purpose of bringing attention to social issues. The long horizontal advertisement shows a blurry
group of children in the background playing street hockey. In the foreground to the right is a bright red alarm bell attached to a wooden telephone pole. The text reads, "School may be out for summer but lunch is
always in session." A sentence in smaller text below it reads, "If your kids

FIGURE 8.2   Feeding America Advertisement

rely on free school meals, call your Feeding America member food bank or visit FeedingAmerica.org/SummerMeals." Examine the advertisement (Figure 8.2) and try to answer the questions below.

1. Record what you think is the ad's overall message. What does the Ad Council want you to do or think about? What appeals does the ad seem to draw on most: appeals based on our cultural relationship to children (ethos), on the emotional reaction of potential viewers/readers (pathos), or on the ways text and image work together to convey an argument (logos)? Do you find that the appeals overlap and are difficult to tease out? Discuss with your classmates.

2. Formulate what you think is the ad's argument, and point out specific details that seem to support it. Compare your ideas with those of your classmates. Do they differ significantly? Can you agree on what the argument is?

3. As a class, test the assumption that the ad makes: When school is in session, policies are in place to insure federally funded schools feed children in need. Less certain is the extent to which children in need receive sufficient nutrition during the summer when school is out.

Let's begin with the assumption that everything in an advertisement appears for a specific reason in a particular place to direct your attention in an exact sequence. The "economy of the genre," its constraints, dictate that the message come across quickly in a limited space.

■ Notice Where the Ad Appears

Analyzing an ad begins with noting where the ad appears. In this case, the Ad Council posted the Feeding America ad on billboards in a wide range of cities across the United States. An ad on a billboard will reach many people whose assumptions about hunger in America will vary, as will their levels of education, race, gender, and ethnicity. Therefore, it's worthwhile to consider how an ad about hunger will connect with such a wide range of possible viewers who will clearly interpret the ad in different ways and act upon its message differently. It is also worth considering the Ad Council's choice to post the ad in urban areas, as opposed to rural towns in the United States. Does the Ad Council assume there are greater hunger issues in urban areas? Is this a fair assumption? And equally important, can we assume that the people who should have access to the information on the ad will actually see it and get the support they require?

Imagine for a moment that the ad had appeared in an issue of *Time* magazine, which has the largest circulation of any news weekly in the United States. As a news magazine, not an entertainment magazine such as *People*, *Time* aims to reach a broad, educated, even affluent, readership interested in keeping up with current events. Knowing your readers' demographics is important because producers of ads always have a target audience in mind when they design and place an ad. They assume that the audience shares certain beliefs and values, and that the ad will move the audience to think and act in particular ways.

As you compare the effects of posting an ad on a billboard versus placing an ad in a widely read magazine, you will inevitably discuss how a particular advertisement will travel from one medium to another. Certainly this Feeding America ad could appear in other weekly news magazines such as *Newsweek*. How effective would it be in a weekly tabloid? A fashion magazine? Or some place more public, such as in a bus terminal or waiting area in a public service office?

■ Identify What Draws Your Attention

The second step is to examine the main image or text that captures your attention. In the Feeding America ad, our attention is drawn to the central image of four children playing street hockey on a summer day. Their appearance suggests that they are healthy, happy, and well-cared for. The seemingly carefree scene of children playing with friends is familiar to most viewers.

■ Reflect on What Draws Your Attention

Then reflect on what draws your attention to this image or text. Is there something startling or shocking about the image or text, about the situation depicted? Something puzzling that holds your attention? Something about the use of color, the size of the image or text, or the font that catches your eye?

The Feeding America ad draws our attention to the center of the page where images of children, though blurred and in the background, catch our gaze. Evidently the ad was composed to emphasize the children's presence in our imagination. Who are these children? Where are they from? What are they like? Are they like us?

We are puzzled by the alarm bell in the foreground to the right. (In the original full-color ad, the alarm bell is bright red and demands our attention.) What does the designer want us to understand by juxtaposing children playing during the summer with an image that for many of us represents school? It's difficult to grasp the significance of these juxtapositions without further inquiry, in this case without looking at the text in the foreground of the ad. We assume that the designer expects readers to look there next, because of its size and the distinct way the letters are drawn— like children's chalk writing on the sidewalk. Finally, our eyes are drawn to the Feeding America logo. What is Feeding America and what values does it espouse?

■ Consider the Ethos of the Ad

The fourth step is to evaluate the ethos of the creator or sponsor of the ad. Ethos works in visual rhetoric just as it does in written rhetoric. Like writing, images are meant to convey how their composers or sponsors wish to be perceived. Thus, especially if you don't recognize a sponsor's logo or brand, it's important to ask: What is the sponsor's mission? What values does the sponsor embrace? What is the sponsor's track record? You need to know such things to determine how willing you are to believe what the ad promotes. In this case, you might find it helpful to go to the Feeding America Web site (listed in the ad) or to do a simple search on the Internet to see whether the organization has been discussed in blogs about hunger. Has Feeding America done significant work in the area of hunger? Is it a charity? If so, is it a reputable charity?

■ Analyze the Pathos in the Ad

The fifth step is to analyze the pathos in the ad—how images and text appeal to your emotions. An appeal to pathos is meant to evoke emotions such as empathy (which might prompt us to identify with an image) or outrage (which might spur us to act in a certain way). In this case, the image of children playing outdoors with friends on a neighborhood street is likely to appeal to many of us, evoking as it does idyllic childhood memories. Its nostalgic appeal invites us into an apparently calm, innocent world of peaceful play.

■ Understand the Logos of the Ad

The sixth and final step requires that we understand the entire composition of the ad—what the cluster of images and text convey. What is the logic of the ad? How do the images and text work together to persuade us? What is the takeaway message?

The text in the Feeding America ad helps clarify the meaning of the central images of the children and the alarm bell. The alarm bell ties the image in the background to the foregrounded text—"School may be out for summer, but lunch is always in session." Food insecurity is a problem everyday for children in need. But where do these children get their food when school is not in session?

Hunger is not readily visible to most of us. Images of playfulness, even childlike innocence, can mask the deprivation that any of the people surrounding us may experience in their own lives. The text makes the appeal in the ad explicit. Those living in hunger are all around us.

The smaller text answers the question of where children in need can receive the nutrition they require. Children who are eligible for free lunch during the school year are also eligible to receive free meals during the summer.

Translating the discrete images and text into a coherent argument requires inductive reasoning, moving from specific pieces of evidence to a major premise. We would conclude that the argument in the ad goes something like this:

1. Hunger in America is a reality in the lives of many children and families.

2. Food insecurity exists for children year round—whether school is in session or not.

3. Feeding America can help children and families gain access to the nutrition they require.

There are other ways to formulate the argument, and we invite you to discuss these alternatives as a class. Our main point, though, is that visual images make claims on us as viewers in much the same ways as any written text does. Having the tools of visual rhetoric can help you discern how images and text work together to produce an argument.

Steps to Visual Analysis

1 **Notice where the ad appears.** What is its target audience? To what extent does the placement of the ad in a magazine or newspaper or on a billboard determine the potential viewers of the ad?

2 **Identify what draws your attention.** Where does your eye go? To an image, some text, some odd juxtaposition?

3 **Reflect on what draws your attention.** Is there something startling or shocking about the image or text, about the situation depicted? Something puzzling that holds your attention? Something about the use of color, the size of the image or text, or the font that catches your eye?

4 **Consider the ethos of the ad.** Evaluate the legitimacy, or ethos, of the ad's sponsor. For example, what do you know about the corporation or institution sponsoring the ad? To what extent do you share its values?

5 **Analyze the pathos in the ad.** How do the images and text appeal to your emotions? What does the image or text make you feel or think about?

6 **Understand the logos of the ad.** What is the logic of the ad? Taken together, what do the cluster of images and text convey? How are the different images and text related to the claim that the ad is making?

A Practice Sequence: Analyzing the Rhetoric of an Advertisement

To practice these strategies, we would like you to choose and analyze the following ad for Microsoft (Figure 8.3). The photograph is of a girl in a robe and slippers sitting on her bed looking at a laptop. The text above the image reads, "You have your best ideas in the shower. Now you can work in the next room." Below the image the text reads, "Office and an online workspace from Microsoft let you work from almost anywhere inspiration finds you. It's easier than ever to store, view, and share all your important documents from pretty much anywhere you happen to be. That's because Microsoft Office works so easily with a free online workspace from Microsoft. So work no longer requires clothes, just Internet access. Buy it for your PC this holiday season." Text at the bottom of the ad reads, "Office2007.com Microsoft Office Real life tools." (Other advertisements for analysis appear on pages 254–256.)

First, evaluate the ethos that the ad tries to project. Do some research on the Internet to find out what Microsoft, which designs and manufactures computer software, represents as a company. In doing this research, write a brief summary of the company's values. Do you share those values? Are you confident in the company's ability to produce a good product that you want to use?

Second, reflect on and write about what the images and text make you feel about your own experiences working from home. In what ways do you identify with the message that the workplace extends into personal space?

Third, work in small groups to identify the logic of the narrative that the images and text convey. What do you see as the main premise of the ad? How did you arrive at your conclusion? Report your group's findings to the class. Be sure to present the evidence to support your claim.

FIGURE 8.3   Microsoft Advertisement

▪ Further Ads for Analysis: Figures 8.4–8.5

FIGURE 8.4   Drinking and Driving PSA   The image is of a full beer glass representing a mixture of light and dark beers. The main text heading reads: The "It's Only Another Beer" Black and Tan. A list of "ingredients" follows: 8 oz. pilsner lager. 8 oz. stout lager. 1 frosty mug. 1 icy road. 1 pick-up truck. 1 10-hour day. 1 tired worker. A few rounds with the guys. Mix ingredients. Add 1 totalled vehicle. Never underestimate 'just a few.' Buzzed driving is drunk driving. Sponsors appear at the bottom of the page: AdCouncil.org and U.S. Department of Transportation.

FIGURE 8.5   Health Care PSA   A tongue depressor appears against a plain white background next to a headline that reads: open up and say anything. The text underneath it reads: want better health care? start asking more questions. to your doctor. to your pharmacist. to your nurse. what are the test results? what about side effects? don't fully understand your prescriptions? don't leave confused. because the most important question is the one you should have asked. go to *www.ahrq.gov/questionsaretheanswer* or call *1-800-931-AHRQ (2477)* for the 10 questions every patient should ask. questions are the answer. The sponsors appear at the bottom of the ad: Ad Council, the U.S. Department of Health & Human Services, and AHRQ Agency for Healthcare Research and Quality.

9

From Introductions to Conclusions
Drafting an Essay

In this chapter, we describe strategies for crafting introductions that set up your argument. We then describe the characteristics of well-formulated paragraphs that will help you build your argument. Finally, we provide you with some strategies for writing conclusions that reinforce what is new about your argument, what is at stake, and what readers should do with the knowledge you convey.

DRAFTING INTRODUCTIONS

The introduction is where you set up your argument. It's where you identify a widely held assumption, challenge that assumption, and state your thesis. Writers use a number of strategies to set up their arguments. In this section we look at five of them:

- Moving from a general topic to a specific thesis (inverted-triangle introduction)
- Introducing the topic with a story (narrative introduction)
- Beginning with a question (interrogative introduction)
- Capturing readers' attention with something unexpected (paradoxical introduction)
- Identifying a gap in knowledge (minding-the-gap introduction)

Remember that an introduction need not be limited to a single paragraph. It may take several paragraphs to effectively set up your argument.

Keep in mind that you have to make these strategies your own. That is, we can suggest models, but you must make them work for your own argument. You must imagine your readers and what will engage them. What tone do you want to take? Playful? Serious? Formal? Urgent? The attitude you want to convey will depend on your purpose, your argument, and the needs of your audience.

■ The Inverted-Triangle Introduction

An **inverted-triangle introduction**, like an upside-down triangle, is broad at the top and pointed at the base. It begins with a general statement of the topic and then narrows its focus, ending with the point of the paragraph (and the triangle), the writer's thesis. We can see this strategy at work in the following introduction from a student's essay. The student writer (1) begins with a broad description of the problem she will address, (2) then focuses on a set of widely held but troublesome assumptions, and (3) finally, responding to what she sees as a pervasive problem, presents her thesis.

The student begins with a general set of assumptions about education that she believes people readily accept.

In today's world, many believe that education's sole purpose is to communicate information for students to store and draw on as necessary. By storing this information, students hope to perform well on tests. Good test scores assure good grades. Good grades eventually lead to acceptances into good colleges, which ultimately guarantee good jobs. Many teachers and students, convinced that education exists as a tool to secure good jobs, rely

She then cites author bell hooks, to identify an approach that makes use of these assumptions — the "banking system" of education, a term hooks borrows from educator Paulo Freire.

on the *banking system*. In her essay "Teaching to Transgress," bell hooks defines the *banking system* as an "approach to learning that is rooted in the notion that all students need to do is consume information fed to them by a professor and be able to memorize and store it" (185). Through the banking system, students focus solely on facts, missing the important themes and life lessons

The student then points to the banking system as the problem. This sets up her thesis about the "true purpose" of education.

available in classes and school materials. The banking system misdirects the fundamental goals of education. Education's true purpose is to prepare students for the real world by allowing them access to pertinent life knowledge available in their studies. Education should then entice students to apply this pertinent life knowledge to daily life struggles through praxis. In addition to her definition of the banking system, hooks offers the idea of praxis from the work of Paulo Freire. When incorporated into education, *praxis*, or "action and reflection upon the world in order to change it" (185), offers an advantageous educational tool that enhances the true purpose of education and overcomes the banking system.

The strategy of writing an introduction as an inverted triangle entails first identifying an idea, an argument, or a concept that people appear to accept as true; next, pointing out the problems with that idea, argument, or concept; and then, in a few sentences, setting out a thesis—how those problems can be resolved.

■ The Narrative Introduction

Opening with a short **narrative**, or story, is a strategy many writers use successfully to draw readers into a topic. A narrative introduction relates a sequence of events and can be especially effective if you think you need to coax indifferent or reluctant readers into taking an interest in the topic. Of course, a narrative introduction delays the declaration of your argument, so it's wise to choose a short story that clearly connects to your argument, and get to the thesis as quickly as possible (within a few paragraphs) before your readers start wondering "What's the point of this story?"

Notice how the student writer uses a narrative introduction to her argument in her essay titled "Throwing a Punch at Gender Roles: How Women's Boxing Empowers Women."

The student's entire first paragraph is a narrative that takes us into the world of women's boxing and foreshadows her thesis.

Glancing at my watch, I ran into the gym, noting to myself that being late to the first day of boxing practice was not the right way to make a good first impression. I flew down the stairs into the basement, to the room the boxers have lovingly dubbed "The Pit." What greeted me when I got there was more than I could ever have imagined. Picture a room filled with boxing gloves of all sizes covering an entire wall, a mirror covering another, a boxing ring in a corner, and an awesome collection of framed newspaper and magazine articles chronicling the boxers whose pictures were hanging on every wall. Now picture that room with seventy-plus girls on the floor doing push-ups, sweat dripping down their faces. I was immediately struck by the discipline this sport would take from me, but I had no idea I would take so much more from it.

With her narrative as a backdrop, the student identifies a problem, using the transition word yet to mark her challenge to the conditions she observes in the university's women's boxing program.

The university offers the only nonmilitary-based college-level women's boxing program in America, and it also offers women the chance to push their physical limits in a regulated environment. Yet the program is plagued with disappointments. I have experienced for myself the stereotypes female boxers face and have dealt with the harsh reality that boxing is still widely recognized as only a men's sport. This paper will show that the women's boxing program at Notre Dame serves as a much-needed outlet for females to come face-to-face with aspects of themselves they would not typically get a chance to explore. It will also examine how

The writer then states her thesis (what her paper "will show"): Despite the problems of stereotyping, women's boxing offers women significant opportunities for growth.

viewing this sport as a positive opportunity for women at ND indicates that there is growing hope that very soon more activities similar to women's boxing may be better received by society in general. I will accomplish these goals by analyzing scholarly journals, old *Observer* [the school newspaper] articles, and survey questions answered by the captains of the 20-- women's boxing team of ND.

The student writer uses a visually descriptive narrative to introduce us to the world of women's college boxing; then, in the second paragraph, she steers us toward the purpose of the paper and the methods she will use to develop her argument about what women's boxing offers to young women and to the changing world of sports.

■ The Interrogative Introduction

An **interrogative introduction** invites readers into the conversation of your essay by asking one or more questions, which the essay goes on to answer. You want to think of a question that will pique your readers' interest, enticing them to read on to discover how your insights shed light on the issue. Notice the question Daphne Spain, a professor of urban and environmental planning, uses to open her essay "Spatial Segregation and Gender Stratification in the Workplace."

Spain sets up her argument by asking a question and then tentatively answering it with a reference to a published study.

In the third sentence, she states her thesis — that men and women have very little contact in the workplace.

Finally, she outlines the effects that this lack of contact has on women.

To what extent do women and men who work in different occupations also work in different space? Baran and Teegarden propose that occupational segregation in the insurance industry is "tantamount to spatial segregation by gender" since managers are overwhelmingly male and clerical staff are predominantly female. This essay examines the spatial conditions of women's work and men's work and proposes that working women and men come into daily contact with one another very infrequently. Further, women's jobs can be classified as "open floor," but men's jobs are more likely to be "closed door." That is, women work in a more public environment with less control of their space than men. This lack of spatial control both reflects and contributes to women's lower occupational status by limiting opportunities for the transfer of knowledge from men to women.

By the end of this introductory paragraph, Spain has explained some of the terms she will use in her essay (*open floor* and *closed door*) and has offered in her final sentence a clear statement of her thesis.

In "Harry Potter and the Technology of Magic," literature scholar Elizabeth Teare begins by contextualizing the Harry Potter publishing phenomenon. Then she raises a question about what is fueling this success story.

In her first four sentences, Teare describes something she is curious about and she hopes readers will be curious about — the growing popularity of the Harry Potter books.

The July/August 2001 issue of *Book* lists J. K. Rowling as one of the ten most influential people in publishing. She shares space on this list with John Grisham and Oprah Winfrey, along with less famous but equally powerful insiders in the book industry. What these industry leaders have in common is an almost magical power to make books succeed in the marketplace, and this magic, in addition to that performed with wands, Rowling's novels appear to practice. Opening weekend sales charted like those of a blockbuster movie (not to mention the blockbuster movie itself), the reconstruction of the venerable *New York Times* bestseller lists, the creation of a new nation's worth of web sites in the territory of cyberspace, and of course the legendary inspiration of tens of millions of child readers — the Harry Potter books have

In the fifth sentence, Teare asks the question she will try to answer in the rest of the essay.

transformed both the technologies of reading and the way we understand those technologies. What is it that makes these books — about a lonely boy whose first act on learning he is a wizard is to go shopping for a wand — not only an international phenomenon among children and parents and teachers but also a topic of compelling interest to literary,

Finally, in the last sentence, Teare offers a partial answer to her question — her thesis.

social, and cultural critics? I will argue that the stories the books tell, as well as the stories we're telling about them, enact both our fantasies and our fears of children's literature and publishing in the context of twenty-first-century commercial and technological culture.

In the final two sentences of the introduction, Teare raises her question about the root of this "international phenomenon" and then offers her thesis. By the end of the opening paragraph, then, the reader knows exactly what question is driving Teare's essay and the answer she proposes to explain throughout the essay.

■ The Paradoxical Introduction

A **paradoxical introduction** appeals to readers' curiosity by pointing out an aspect of the topic that runs counter to their expectations. Just as an interrogative introduction draws readers in by asking a question, a paradoxical introduction draws readers in by saying, in effect, "Here's something completely surprising and unlikely about this issue, but my essay will go on to show you how it is true." In this passage from "'Holding Back': Negotiating a Glass Ceiling on Women's Muscular Strength," sociologist Shari L. Dworkin points to a paradox in our commonsense understanding of bodies as the product of biology, not culture.

In the first sentence, Dworkin quotes from a study to identify the thinking that she is going to challenge.

Notice how Dworkin signals her own position "However" relative to commonly held assumptions.

Dworkin ends by stating her thesis, noting a paradox that will surprise readers.

Current work in gender studies points to how "when examined closely, much of what we take for granted about gender and its causes and effects either does not hold up, or can be explained differently." These arguments become especially contentious when confronting nature/culture debates on gendered *bodies*. After all, "common sense" frequently tells us that flesh and blood bodies are about biology. However, bodies are also shaped and constrained through cumulative social practices, structures of opportunity, wider cultural meanings, and more. Paradoxically, then, when we think that we are "really seeing" naturally sexed bodies, perhaps we are seeing the effect of internalizing gender ideologies — carrying out social practices — and this constructs our vision of "sexed" bodies.

Dworkin's strategy in the first three sentences is to describe common practice, the understanding that bodies are biological. Then, in the sentences beginning "However" and "Paradoxically," she advances the surprising idea that our bodies — not just the clothes we wear, for example — carry cultural gender markers. Her essay then goes on to examine women's weight lifting and the complex motives driving many women to create a body that is perceived as muscular but not masculine.

▪ The Minding-the-Gap Introduction

This type of introduction takes its name from the British train system, the voice on the loudspeaker that intones "Mind the gap!" at every stop, to call riders' attention to the gap between the train car and the platform. In a **minding-the-gap introduction**, a writer calls readers' attention to a gap in the research on an issue and then uses the rest of the essay to fill in the "gap." A minding-the-gap introduction says, in effect, "Wait a minute. There's something missing from this conversation, and my research and ideas will fill in this gap."

For example, in the introductory paragraphs to their book *Men's Lives*, Michael S. Kimmel and Michael A. Messner explain how the book is different from other books that discuss men's lives, and how it serves a different purpose.

The authors begin with an assumption and then challenge it. A transition word "but" signals the challenge.

This is a book about men. But, unlike other books about men, which line countless library shelves, this is a book about men as men. It is a book in which men's experiences are not taken for granted as we explore the "real" and significant accomplishments of men, but a book in which those experiences are treated as significant and important in themselves.

But what does it mean to examine men "as men"? Most courses in a college curriculum are about men, aren't they?

The authors follow with a question that provokes readers' interest and points to the gap they summarize in the last sentence.

But these courses routinely deal with men only in their public roles, so we come to know and understand men as scientists, politicians, military figures, writers, and philosophers. Rarely, if ever, are men understood through the prism of gender.

Kimmel and Messner use these opening paragraphs to highlight both what they find problematic about the existing literature on men and to introduce readers to their own approach.

Steps to Drafting Introductions: Five Strategies

1 **Use an inverted triangle.** Begin with a broad situation, concept, or idea, and narrow the focus to your thesis.

2 **Begin with a narrative.** Capture readers' imagination and interest with a story that sets the stage for your argument.

3 **Ask a question that you will answer.** Provoke readers' interest with a question, and then use your thesis to answer the question.

4 **Present a paradox.** Begin with an assumption that readers accept as true, and formulate a thesis that not only challenges that assumption but may very well seem paradoxical.

5 **Mind the gap.** Identify what readers know and then what they don't know (or what you believe they need to know).

A Practice Sequence: Drafting an Introduction

1 Write or rewrite your introduction (which, as you've seen, may involve more than one paragraph), using one of the strategies described above. Then share your introduction with one of your peers and ask the following questions:

- To what extent did the strategy compel you to want to read further?

- To what extent is my thesis clear?

- How effectively do I draw a distinction between what I believe others assume to be true and my own approach?

- Is there another way that I might have made my introduction more compelling?

After listening to the responses, try a second strategy and then ask your peer which introduction is more effective.

2   If you do not have your own introduction to work on, revise the introduction below from one of our students' essays, combining two of the strategies we describe above.

> News correspondent Pauline Frederick once commented, "When a man gets up to speak people listen then look. When a woman gets up, people look; then, if they like what they see, they listen." Ironically, the harsh reality of this statement is given life by the ongoing controversy over America's most recognizable and sometimes notorious toy, Barbie. Celebrating her fortieth birthday this year, Barbie has become this nation's most beleaguered soldier (a woman no less) of idolatry who has been to the front lines and back more times than the average "Joe." This doll, a piece of plastic, a toy, incurs both criticism and praise spanning both ends of the ideological spectrum. Barbie's curvaceous and basically unrealistic body piques the ire of both liberals and conservatives, each contending that Barbie stands for the distinct view of the other. One hundred and eighty degrees south, others praise Barbie's (curves and all) ability to unlock youthful imagination and potential. M. G. Lord explains Barbie best: "To study Barbie, one sometimes has to hold seemingly contradictory ideas in one's head at the same time. . . . The doll functions like a Rorschach test: people project wildly dissimilar and often opposing meanings on it. . . . And her meaning, like her face, has not been static over time." In spite of the extreme polarity, a sole unconscious consensus manifests itself about Barbie. Barbie is "the icon" of womanhood and the twentieth century. She is the American dream. Barbie is "us." The question is always the same: What message does Barbie send? Barbie is a toy. She is the image of what we see.

DEVELOPING PARAGRAPHS

In your introduction, you set forth your thesis. Then, in subsequent paragraphs, you have to develop your argument. Remember our metaphor: If your thesis, or main claim, is the skewer that runs through each paragraph in your essay, then these paragraphs are the "meat" of your argument. The paragraphs that follow your introduction carry the burden of evidence in your argument. After all, a claim cannot stand on its own without supporting evidence. Generally speaking, each paragraph should include a topic sentence that brings the main idea of the paragraph into focus, be unified around the main idea of the topic sentence, and adequately develop the idea. At the same time, a paragraph does not stand on its own; as part of your overall argument, it can refer to what you've said earlier, gesture toward where you are heading, and connect to the larger conversation to which you are contributing.

We now ask you to read an excerpt from "Reinventing 'America': Call for a New National Identity," by Elizabeth Martínez, and answer some questions about how you think the author develops her argument, paragraph by paragraph. Then we discuss her work in the context of the three key elements of paragraphs: *topic sentences*, *unity*, and *adequate development*. As you read, pay attention to how, sentence by sentence, Martínez develops her paragraphs. We also ask that you consider how she makes her argument provocative, impassioned, and urgent for her audience.

ELIZABETH MARTÍNEZ

From Reinventing "America": Call for a New National Identity

Elizabeth Martínez is a Chicana activist who since 1960 has worked in and documented different movements for change, including the civil rights, women's, and Chicano movements. She is the author of six books and numerous articles. Her best-known work is *500 Years of Chicano History in Pictures* (1991), which became the basis of a two-part video she scripted and codirected. Her latest book is *De Colores Means All of Us: Latina Views for a Multi-Colored Century* (1998). In "Reinventing 'America,'" Martínez argues that Americans' willingness to accept a "myth" as "the basis for [the] nation's self-defined identity" has brought the country to a crisis.

■ ▨ ▪

For some fifteen years, starting in 1940, 85 percent of all U.S. elementary schools used the Dick and Jane series to teach children how to read. The series starred Dick, Jane, their white middle-class parents, their dog Spot, and their life together in a home with a white picket fence.   1

"Look, Jane, look! See Spot run!" chirped the two kids. It was a house full of glorious family values, where Mom cooked while Daddy went to work in a suit and mowed the lawn on weekends. The Dick and Jane books also taught that you should do your job and help others. All this affirmed an equation of middle-class whiteness with virtue.   2

In the mid-1990s, museums, libraries, and eighty Public Broadcasting Service (PBS) stations across the country had exhibits and programs commemorating the series. At one museum, an attendant commented, "When you hear someone crying, you know they are looking at the Dick and Jane books." It seems nostalgia runs rampant among many Euro-Americans: a nostalgia for the days of unchallenged White Supremacy—both moral and material—when life was "simple."   3

We've seen that nostalgia before in the nation's history. But today it signifies a problem reaching a new intensity. It suggests a national identity crisis that promises to bring in its wake an unprecedented nervous breakdown for the dominant society's psyche.   4

Nowhere is this more apparent than in California, which has long been on the cutting edge of the nation's present and future reality.   5

Warning sirens have sounded repeatedly in the 1990s, such as the fierce battle over new history textbooks for public schools, Proposition 187's ugly denial of human rights to immigrants, the 1996 assault on affirmative action that culminated in Proposition 209, and the 1997 move to abolish bilingual education. Attempts to copycat these reactionary measures have been seen in other states.

The attack on affirmative action isn't really about affirmative action. Essentially it is another tactic in today's war on the gains of the 1960s, a tactic rooted in Anglo resentment and fear. A major source of that fear: the fact that California will almost surely have a majority of people of color in twenty to thirty years at most, with the nation as a whole not far behind.   6

Check out the February 3, 1992, issue of *Sports Illustrated* with its double-spread ad for *Time* magazine. The ad showed hundreds of newborn babies in their hospital cribs, all of them Black or brown except for a rare white face here and there. The headline says, "Hey, whitey! It's your turn at the back of the bus!" The ad then tells you, read *Time* magazine to keep up with today's hot issues. That manipulative image could have been published today; its implication of shifting power appears to be the recurrent nightmare of too many potential Anglo allies.   7

Euro-American anxiety often focuses on the sense of a vanishing national identity. Behind the attacks on immigrants, affirmative action, and multiculturalism, behind the demand for "English Only" laws and the rejection of bilingual education, lies the question: with all these new people, languages, and cultures, what will it mean to be an American? If that question once seemed, to many people, to have an obvious, universally applicable answer, today new definitions must be found. But too often Americans, with supposed scholars in the lead, refuse to face that need and instead nurse a nostalgia for some bygone clarity. They remain trapped in denial.   8

An array of such ostriches, heads in the sand, began flapping their feathers noisily with the publication of Allan Bloom's 1987 best-selling book, *The Closing of the American Mind*. Bloom bemoaned the decline of our "common values" as a society, meaning the decline of Euro-American cultural centricity (shall we just call it cultural imperialism?). Since then we have seen constant sniping at "diversity" goals across the land. The assault has often focused on how U.S. history is taught. And with reason, for this country's identity rests on a particular narrative about the historical origins of the United States as a nation.   9

The Great White Origin Myth

Every society has an origin narrative that explains that society to itself and the world with a set of stories and symbols. The origin myth, as scholar-activist Roxanne Dunbar Ortiz has termed it, defines how a   10 society understands its place in the world and its history. The myth provides the basis for a nation's self-defined identity. Most origin narratives can be called myths because they usually present only the most flattering view of a nation's history; they are not distinguished by honesty.

Ours begins with Columbus "discovering" a hemisphere where some   *11*
80 million people already lived but didn't really count (in what became the United States, they were just buffalo-chasing "savages" with no grasp of real estate values and therefore doomed to perish). It continues with the brave Pilgrims, a revolution by independence-loving colonists against a decadent English aristocracy, and the birth of an energetic young republic that promised democracy and equality (that is, to white male landowners). In the 1840s, the new nation expanded its size by almost one-third, thanks to a victory over that backward land of little brown people called Mexico. Such has been the basic account of how the nation called the United States of America came into being as presently configured.

The myth's omissions are grotesque. It ignores three major pillars   *12*
of our nationhood: genocide, enslavement, and imperialist expansion (such nasty words, who wants to hear them?—but that's the problem). The massive extermination of indigenous peoples provided our land base; the enslavement of African labor made our economic growth possible; and the seizure of half of Mexico by war (or threat of renewed war) extended this nation's boundaries north to the Pacific and south to the Rio Grande. Such are the foundation stones of the United States, within an economic system that made this country the first in world history to be born capitalist. . . .

Racism as Linchpin of the U.S. National Identity

A crucial embellishment of the origin myth and key element of the na-   *13*
tional identity has been the myth of the frontier, analyzed in Richard Slotkin's *Gunfighter Nation*, the last volume of a fascinating trilogy. He describes Theodore Roosevelt's belief that the West was won thanks to American arms, "the means by which progress and nationality will be achieved." That success, Roosevelt continued, "depends on the heroism of men who impose on the course of events the latent virtues of their 'race.'" Roosevelt saw conflict on the frontier producing a series of virile "fighters and breeders" who would eventually generate a new leadership class. Militarism thus went hand in hand with the racialization of history's protagonists. . . .

The frontier myth embodied the nineteenth-century concept of Man-   *14*
ifest Destiny, a doctrine that served to justify expansionist violence by means of intrinsic racial superiority. Manifest Destiny was Yankee conquest as the inevitable result of a confrontation between enterprise and progress (white) versus passivity and backwardness (Indian, Mexican).

"Manifest" meant "God-given," and the whole doctrine is profoundly rooted in religious conviction going back to the earliest colonial times. In his short, powerful book *Manifest Destiny: American Expansion and the Empire of Right*, Professor Anders Stephanson tells how the Puritans reinvented the Jewish notion of chosenness and applied it to this hemisphere so that territorial expansion became God's will. . . .

Manifest Destiny Dies Hard

The concept of Manifest Destiny, with its assertion of racial superiority sustained by military power, has defined U.S. identity for 150 years. . . .   *15*

Today's origin myth and the resulting concept of national identity make for an intellectual prison where it is dangerous to ask big questions about this society's superiority. When otherwise decent people are trapped in such a powerful desire not to feel guilty, self-deception becomes unavoidable. To cease our present falsification of collective memory should, and could, open the doors of that prison. When together we cease equating whiteness with Americanness, a new day can dawn. As David Roediger, the social historian, has said, "[Whiteness] is the empty and therefore terrifying attempt to build an identity on what one isn't, and on whom one can hold back."   *16*

Redefining the U.S. origin narrative, and with it this country's national identity, could prove liberating for our collective psyche. It does not mean Euro-Americans should wallow individually in guilt. It does mean accepting collective responsibility to deal with the implications of our real origin. A few apologies, for example, might be a step in the right direction. In 1997, the idea was floated in Congress to apologize for slavery; it encountered opposition from all sides. But to reject the notion because corrective action, not an apology, is needed misses the point. Having defined itself as the all-time best country in the world, the United States fiercely denies the need to make a serious official apology for anything. . . . To press for any serious, official apology does imply a new origin narrative, a new self-image, an ideological sea-change.   *17*

Accepting the implications of a different narrative could also shed light on today's struggles. In the affirmative-action struggle, for example, opponents have said that that policy is no longer needed because racism ended with the Civil Rights Movement. But if we look at slavery as a fundamental pillar of this nation, going back centuries, it becomes obvious that racism could not have been ended by thirty years of mild reforms. If we see how the myth of the frontier idealized the white male adventurer as the central hero of national history, with the woman as sunbonneted helpmate, then we might better understand the dehumanized ways in which women have continued to be treated. A more truthful origin narrative could also help break down divisions among peoples of color by revealing common experiences and histories of cooperation.   *18*

Reading as a Writer

1. To what extent does the narrative Martínez begins with make you want to read further?

2. How does she connect this narrative to the rest of her argument?

3. How does she use repetition to create unity in her essay?

4. What assumptions does Martínez challenge?

5. How does she use questions to engage her readers?

■ Use Topic Sentences to Focus Your Paragraphs

The **topic sentence** states the main point of a paragraph. It should

- provide a partial answer to the question motivating the writer.
- act as an extension of the writer's thesis and the question motivating the writer's argument.
- serve as a guidepost, telling readers what the paragraph is about.
- help create unity and coherence both within the paragraph and within the essay.

Elizabeth Martínez begins by describing how elementary schools in the 1940s and 1950s used the Dick and Jane series not only to teach reading but also to foster a particular set of values—values that she believes do not serve all children enrolled in America's schools. In paragraph 4, she states her thesis, explaining that nostalgia in the United States has created "a national identity crisis that promises to bring in its wake an unprecedented nervous breakdown for the dominant society's psyche." This is a point that builds on an observation she makes in paragraph 3: "It seems nostalgia runs rampant among many Euro-Americans: a nostalgia for the days of unchallenged White Supremacy—both moral and material—when life was 'simple.'" Martínez often returns to this notion of nostalgia for a past that seems "simple" to explain what she sees as an impending crisis.

Consider the first sentence of paragraph 5 as a topic sentence. With Martínez's key points in mind, notice how she uses the sentence to make her thesis more specific. Notice too, how she ties in the crisis and breakdown she alludes to in paragraph 4. Essentially, Martínez tells her readers that they can see these problems at play in California, an indicator of "the nation's present and future reality."

> *Nowhere is this more apparent than in California, which has long been on the cutting edge of the nation's present and future reality.* Warning sirens have sounded repeatedly in the 1990s, such as the fierce battle over new history textbooks for public schools, Proposition 187's ugly denial of human rights to immigrants, the 1996 assault on affirmative action that culminated in Proposition 209, and the 1997 move to abolish bilingual education. *Attempts to copycat these reactionary measures have been seen in other states.*

The final sentence of paragraph 5 sets up the remainder of the essay.

As readers, we expect each subsequent paragraph to respond in some way to the issue Martínez has raised. She meets that expectation by formulating a topic sentence that appears at the beginning of the paragraph. The topic sentence is what helps create unity and coherence in the essay.

▪ Create Unity in Your Paragraphs

Each paragraph in an essay should focus on the subject suggested by the topic sentence. If a paragraph begins with one focus or major point of discussion, it should not end with another. Several strategies can contribute to the unity of each paragraph.

Use details that follow logically from your topic sentence and maintain a single focus — a focus that is clearly an extension of your thesis.   For example, in paragraph 5, Martínez's topic sentence ("Nowhere is this more apparent than in California, which has long been on the cutting edge of the nation's present and future reality") helps to create unity because it refers back to her thesis (*this* refers to the "national identity crisis" mentioned in paragraph 4) and limits the focus of what she includes in the paragraph to "the fierce battle over new history textbooks" and recent pieces of legislation in California that follow directly from and support the claim of the topic sentence.

Repeat key words to guide your readers.   A second strategy for creating unity is to repeat (or use synonyms for) key words within a given paragraph. You can see this at work in paragraph 12 (notice the words we've underscored), where Martínez explains that America's origin narrative omits significant details:

> The myth's omissions are grotesque. It ignores three major pillars of our nationhood: genocide, enslavement, and imperialist expansion (such nasty words, who wants to hear them? — but that's the problem). The massive extermination of indigenous peoples provided our land base; the enslavement of African labor made our economic growth possible; and the seizure of half of Mexico by war (or threat of renewed war) extended this nation's boundaries north to the Pacific and south to the Rio Grande. Such are the foundation stones of the United States, within an economic system that made this country the first in world history to be born capitalist. . . .

Specifically, Martínez tells us that the origin narrative ignores "three major pillars of our nationhood: genocide, enslavement, and imperialist expansion." She then substitutes *extermination* for "genocide," repeats *enslavement*, and substitutes *seizure* for "imperialist expansion." By connecting words in a paragraph, as Martínez does here, you help readers understand that the details you provide are all relevant to the point you want to make.

Use transition words to link ideas from different sentences.   A third strategy for creating unity within paragraphs is to establish a clear relationship among different ideas by using **transition words** or phrases. Transition words or phrases signal to your readers the direction your ideas are taking. Table 9.1 lists common transition words and phrases grouped by function—that is, for adding a new idea, presenting a contrasting idea, or drawing a conclusion about an idea.

Martínez uses transition words and phrases throughout the excerpt here. In several places, she uses the word *but* to make a contrast—to draw a distinction between an idea that many people accept as true and an alternative idea that she wants to pursue. Notice in paragraph 17 how she signals the importance of an official apology for slavery—and by implication genocide and the seizure of land from Mexico:

> . . . A few apologies, for example, might be a step in the right direction. In 1997, the idea was floated in Congress to apologize for slavery; it encountered opposition from all sides. But to reject the notion because corrective action, not an apology, is needed misses the point. Having defined itself as the all-time best country in the world, the United States fiercely denies the need to make a serious official apology for anything. . . . To press for any serious, official apology does imply a new origin narrative, a new self-image, an ideological sea-change.

Similarly, in the last paragraph, Martínez counters the argument that affirmative action is not necessary because racism no longer exists:

> . . . In the affirmative-action struggle, for example, opponents have said that that policy is no longer needed because racism ended with the Civil Rights Movement. But if we look at slavery as a fundamental pillar of this nation, going back centuries, it becomes obvious that racism could not have been ended by thirty years of mild reforms.

There are a number of ways to rephrase what Martínez is saying in paragraph 18. We could substitute *however* for "but." Or we could combine the two sentences into one to point to the relationship between the two competing ideas: *Although some people oppose affirmative action, believing that racism no longer exists, I would argue that racism remains a fundamental pillar of this nation.* Or we could pull together Martínez's different points to draw a logical conclusion using a transition word like *therefore.* Martínez observes that our country is in crisis as a result of increased immigration. *Therefore, we need to reassess our conceptions of national*

TABLE 9.1   Common Transition Words and Phrases

Adding an Idea	Presenting a Contrasting Idea	Drawing a Logical Conclusion
also, and, further, moreover, in addition to, in support of, similarly	although, alternatively, as an alternative, but, by way of contrast, despite, even though, however, in contrast to, nevertheless, nonetheless, rather than, yet	as a result, because of, consequently, finally, in sum, in the end, subsequently, therefore, thus

identity to account for the diversity that increased immigration has created. We can substitute any of the transition words in Table 9.1 for drawing a logical conclusion.

The list of transition words and phrases in Table 9.1 is hardly exhaustive, but it gives you a sense of the ways to connect ideas so that readers understand how your ideas are related. Are they similar ideas? Do they build on or support one another? Are you challenging accepted ideas? Or are you drawing a logical connection from a number of different ideas?

■ Use Critical Strategies to Develop Your Paragraphs

To develop a paragraph, you can use a range of strategies, depending on what you want to accomplish and what you believe your readers will need in order to be persuaded by what you argue. Among these strategies are using examples and illustrations; citing data (facts, statistics, evidence, details); analyzing texts; telling a story or an anecdote; defining terms; making comparisons; and examining causes and evaluating consequences.

Use examples and illustrations.   Examples make abstract ideas concrete through illustration. Using examples is probably the most common way to develop a piece of writing. Of course, Martínez's essay is full of examples. In fact, she begins with an example of a series of books—the Dick and Jane books—to show how a generation of schoolchildren were exposed to white middle-class values. She also uses examples in paragraph 5, where she lists several pieces of legislation (Propositions 187 and 209) to develop the claim in her topic sentence.

Cite data.   **Data** are factual pieces of information. They function in an essay as the bases of propositions. In the first few paragraphs of the excerpt, Martínez cites statistics ("85 percent of all U.S. elementary schools used the Dick and Jane series to teach children how to read") and facts ("In the mid-1990s, museums, libraries, and eighty Public Broadcasting Service . . . stations across the country had exhibits and programs commemorating the series") to back up her claim about the popularity of the Dick and Jane series and the nostalgia the books evoke.

Analyze texts.   Analysis is the process of breaking something down into its elements to understand how they work together. When you analyze a text, you point out parts of the text that have particular significance to your argument and explain what they mean. By *texts*, we mean both verbal and visual texts. In paragraph 7, Martínez analyzes a visual text, an advertisement that appeared in *Sports Illustrated*, to reveal "its implication of shifting power"—a demographic power shift from Anglos to people of color.

Provide narratives or anecdotes.   Put simply, a narrative is an account of something that happened. More technically, a narrative relates a sequence of events that are connected in time; and an **anecdote** is a short narrative that recounts a particular incident. An anecdote, like an example, can bring an abstraction into focus. Consider Martínez's third paragraph, where the anecdote about the museum attendant brings her point about racially charged nostalgia among white Americans into memorable focus: The tears of the museum-goers indicate just how profound their nostalgia is.

By contrast, a longer narrative, in setting out its sequence of events, often opens up possibilities for analysis. Why did these events occur? Why did they occur in this sequence? What might they lead to? What are the implications? What is missing?

In paragraph 11, for example, Martínez relates several key events in the origin myth of America. Then, in the next paragraph, she explains what is omitted from the myth, or narrative, and builds her argument about the implications and consequences of those omissions.

Define terms.   A definition is an explanation of what something is and, by implication, what it is not. The simplest kind of definition is a synonym, but for the purpose of developing your argument, a one-word definition is rarely enough.

When you define your terms, you are setting forth meanings that you want your readers to agree on, so that you can continue to build your argument on the foundation of that agreement. You may have to stipulate that your definition is part of a larger whole to develop your argument. For example: "Nostalgia is a bittersweet longing for things of the past; but for the purposes of my essay, I focus on white middle-class nostalgia, which combines a longing for a past that never existed with a hostile anxiety about the present."

In paragraph 10, Martínez defines the term *origin narrative* — a myth that explains "how a society understands its place in the world and its history . . . the basis for a nation's self-defined identity." The "Great White Origin Myth" is an important concept in her developing argument about a national crisis of identity.

Make comparisons.   Technically, a **comparison** shows the similarities between two or more things, and a **contrast** shows the differences. In practice, however, it is very difficult, if not impossible, to develop a comparison that does not make use of contrast. Therefore, we use the term *comparison* to describe the strategy of comparing *and* contrasting.

Doubtless you have written paragraphs or even whole essays that take as a starting point a version of this sentence: "X and Y are similar in some respects and different in others." This neutral formulation is seldom helpful when you are developing an argument. Usually, in making your comparison — in setting forth the points of similarity and difference — you have to take an evaluative or argumentative stance.

Note the comparison in this passage:

> Although there are similarities between the current nostalgias for Dick and Jane books and for rhythm and blues music of the same era — in both cases, the object of nostalgia can move people to tears — the nostalgias spring from emotional responses that are quite different and even contradictory. I will argue that the Dick and Jane books evoke a longing for a past that is colored by a fear of the present, a longing for a time when white middle-class values were dominant and unquestioned. By contrast, the nostalgia for R&B music may indicate a yearning for a past when multicultural musicians provided white folks with a sweaty release on the dance floor from those very same white-bread values of the time.

The writer does more than list similarities and differences; she offers an analysis of what they mean and is prepared to argue for her interpretation.

Certainly Elizabeth Martínez takes an evaluative stance when she compares versions of American history in paragraphs 11 and 12. In paragraph 11, she angrily relates the sanitized story of American history, setting up a contrast in paragraph 12 with the story that does not appear in history textbooks, a story of "genocide, enslavement, and imperialist expansion." Her evaluative stance comes through clearly: She finds the first version repugnant and harmful, its omissions "grotesque."

Examine causes and evaluate consequences.   In any academic discipline, questions of cause and consequence are central. Whether you are analyzing the latest election results in a political science course, reading about the causes of the Vietnam War in a history course, or speculating about the long-term consequences of global warming in a science course, questions of why things happened, happen, or will happen are inescapable.

Examining causes and consequences usually involves identifying a phenomenon and asking questions about it until you gather enough information to begin analyzing the relationships among its parts and deciding which are most significant. You can then begin to set forth your own analysis of what happened and why.

Of course, this kind of analysis is rarely straightforward, and any phenomenon worthy of academic study is bound to generate a variety of conversations about its causes and consequences. In your own thinking and research, avoid jumping to conclusions and continue to sift evidence until plausible connections present themselves. Be prepared to revise your thinking — perhaps several times — in light of new evidence.

In your writing, you also want to avoid oversimplifying. A claim like this — "The answer to curbing unemployment in the United States is to restrict immigration" — does not take into account corporate outsourcing of jobs overseas or the many other possible causes of unemployment. At the very least, you may need to explain the basis and specifics of your analysis and qualify your claim: "Recent studies of patterns of immigration and unemployment in the United States suggest that unrestricted immigration is a major factor in the loss of blue-collar job opportunities in the Southwest." Certainly this sentence is less forceful and provocative than the other one, but it does suggest that you have done significant and focused research and respect the complexity of the issue.

Throughout her essay, Martínez analyzes causes and consequences. In paragraph 8, for example, she speculates that the *cause* of "attacks on immigrants, affirmative action, and multiculturalism" is "Euro-American anxiety," "the sense of a vanishing national identity." In paragraph 13, she concludes that a *consequence* of Theodore Roosevelt's beliefs about race and war was a "militarism [that] went hand in hand with the racialization of history's protagonists." In paragraph 16, the topic sentence itself is a statement about causes and consequences: "Today's origin myth and the resulting concept of national identity make for an intellectual prison where it is dangerous to ask big questions about this society's superiority."

Having shown where and how Martínez uses critical strategies to develop her paragraphs, we must hasten to add that these critical strategies usually work in combination. Although you can easily develop an entire paragraph (or even an entire essay) using comparison, it is almost impossible to do so without relying on one or more of the other strategies. What if you need to tell an anecdote about the two authors you are comparing? What if you have to cite data about different rates of economic growth to clarify the main claim of your comparison? What if you are comparing different causes and consequences?

Our point is that the strategies described here are methods for exploring your issue in writing. How you make use of them, individually or in combination, depends on which can help you best communicate your argument to your readers.

Steps to Developing Paragraphs

1 **Use topic sentences to focus your paragraphs.** Remember that a topic sentence partially answers the question motivating you to write; acts as an extension of your thesis; indicates to your readers what the paragraph is about; and helps create unity both within the paragraph and within the essay.

2 **Create unity in your paragraphs.** The details in your paragraph should follow logically from your topic sentence and maintain a single focus, one tied clearly to your thesis. Repetition and transition words also help create unity in paragraphs.

3 **Use critical strategies to develop your paragraphs.** Use examples and illustrations; cite data; analyze texts; tell stories or anecdotes; define terms; make comparisons; and examine causes and evaluate consequences.

A Practice Sequence: Working with Paragraphs

We would like you to work in pairs on paragraphing. The objective of this exercise is to gauge the effectiveness of your topic sentences and the degree to which your paragraphs are unified and fully developed.

Make a copy of your essay and cut it up into paragraphs. Shuffle the paragraphs to be sure they are no longer in the original order, and then exchange cut-up drafts with your partner. The challenge is to put your partner's essay back together again. When you both have finished, compare your reorderings with the original drafts. Were you able to reproduce the original organization exactly? If not, do the variations make sense? If one or the other of you had trouble putting the essay back together, talk about the adequacy of your topic sentences, ways to revise topic sentences in keeping with the details in a given paragraph, and strategies for making paragraphs more unified and coherent.

DRAFTING CONCLUSIONS

In writing a conclusion to your essay, you are making a final appeal to your audience. You want to convince readers that what you have written is a relevant, meaningful interpretation of a shared issue. You also want to remind them that your argument is reasonable. Rather than summarize all of the points you've made in the essay—assume your readers have carefully read what you've written—pull together the key components of your argument in the service of answering the question "So what?" Establish why your argument is important: What will happen if things stay the same? What will happen if things change? How effective your conclusion is depends on whether or not readers feel that you have adequately addressed "So what?"—that you have made clear what is significant and of value.

In building on the specific details of your argument, you can also place what you have written in a broader context. (What are the sociological implications of your argument? How far-reaching are they? Are there political implications? Economic implications?) Finally, explain again how your ideas contribute something new to the conversation by building on, extending, or even challenging what others have argued.

In her concluding paragraph, Elizabeth Martínez brings together her main points, puts her essay in a broader context, indicates what's new in her argument, and answers the question "So what?":

> Accepting the implications of a different narrative could also shed light on today's struggles. In the affirmative-action struggle, for example, opponents have said that that policy is no longer needed because racism ended with the Civil Rights Movement. But if we look at slavery as a fundamental pillar of this nation, going back centuries, it becomes obvious that racism could not have

been ended by thirty years of mild reforms. If we see how the myth of the frontier idealized the white male adventurer as the central hero of national history, with the woman as sunbonneted helpmate, then we might better understand the dehumanized ways in which women have continued to be treated. A more truthful origin narrative could also help break down divisions among peoples of color by revealing common experiences and histories of cooperation.

Let's examine this concluding paragraph:

1. Although Martínez refers back to important events and ideas she has discussed, she does not merely summarize. Instead, she suggests the implications of those important events and ideas in her first sentence (the topic sentence), which crystallizes the main point of her essay: Americans need a different origin narrative.

2. Then she puts those implications in the broader context of contemporary racial and gender issues.

3. She signals what's new in her argument with the word *if* (if we look at slavery in a new way, if we look at the frontier myth in a new way).

4. Finally, her answers to why this issue matters culminate in the last sentence. This last sentence connects and extends the claim of her topic sentence, by asserting that a "more truthful origin narrative" could help heal divisions among peoples of color who have been misrepresented by the old origin myth. Clearly, she believes the implications of her argument matter: A new national identity has the potential to heal a country in crisis, a country on the verge of a "nervous breakdown" (para. 4).

Martínez also does something else in the last sentence of the concluding paragraph: She looks to the future, suggesting what the future implications of her argument could be. Looking to the future is one of five strategies for shaping a conclusion. The others we discuss are echoing the introduction, challenging the reader, posing questions, and concluding with a quotation. Each of these strategies appeals to readers in different ways; therefore, we suggest you try them all out in writing your own conclusions. Also, remember that some of these strategies can be combined. For example, you can write a conclusion that challenges readers, poses a question, looks to the future, and ends with a quotation.

■ Echo the Introduction

Echoing the introduction in your conclusion helps readers come full circle. It helps them see how you have developed your idea from beginning to end. In the following example, the student writer begins with a voice speaking from behind an Islamic veil, revealing the ways that Western culture misunderstands the symbolic value of wearing the veil. The writer repeats this visual image in her conclusion, quoting from the Koran: "Speak to them from behind a curtain."

Notice that the author begins with "a voice from behind the shrouds of an Islamic veil" and then echoes this quotation in her conclusion: "Speak to them from behind a curtain."

Introduction: A voice from behind the shrouds of an Islamic veil exclaims: "I often wonder whether people see me as a radical, fundamentalist Muslim terrorist packing an AK-47 assault rifle inside my jean jacket. Or maybe they see me as the poster girl for oppressed womanhood everywhere." In American culture where shameless public exposure, particularly of females, epitomizes ultimate freedom, the head-to-toe covering of a Muslim woman seems inherently oppressive. Driven by an autonomous national attitude, the inhabitants of the "land of the free" are quick to equate the veil with indisputable persecution. Yet Muslim women reveal the enslaving hijab as a symbolic display of the Islamic ideals — honor, modesty, and stability. Because of an unfair American assessment, the aura of hijab mystery cannot be removed until the customs and ethics of Muslim culture are genuinely explored. It is this form of enigmatic seclusion that forms the feminist controversy between Western liberals, who perceive the veil as an inhibiting factor against free will, and Islamic disciples, who conceptualize the veil as a sacred symbol of utmost morality.

Conclusion: By improperly judging an alien religion, the veil becomes a symbol of oppression and devastation, instead of a representation of pride and piety. Despite Western images, the hijab is a daily revitalization and reminder of the Islamic societal and religious ideals, thereby upholding the conduct and attitudes of the Muslim community. Americans share these ideals yet fail to recognize them in the context of a different culture. By sincerely exploring the custom of Islamic veiling, one will realize the vital role the hijab plays in shaping Muslim culture by sheltering women, and consequently society, from the perils that erupt from indecency. The principles implored in the Koran of modesty, honor, and stability construct a unifying and moral view of the Islamic Middle Eastern society when properly investigated. As it was transcribed from Allah, "Speak to them from behind a curtain. This is purer for your hearts and their hearts."

Notice how the conclusion echoes the introduction in its reference to a voice speaking from behind a curtain.

▪ Challenge the Reader

By issuing a challenge to your readers, you create a sense of urgency, provoking them to act to change the status quo. In this example, the student writer explains the unacceptable consequences of preventing young women from educating themselves about AIDS and the spread of a disease that has already reached epidemic proportions.

The changes in AIDS education that I am suggesting are necessary and relatively simple to make. Although the current curriculum in high school health classes is helpful and informative, it simply does not pertain to young women as much as it should. AIDS is killing women at an alarming rate, and many people do not realize this. According to Daniel DeNoon, AIDS is one of the six leading causes of death among women aged 18 to 45, and women "bear the brunt of the worldwide AIDS epidemic." For this reason, DeNoon argues, women are one of the most important new populations that are contracting HIV at a high rate. I challenge young women to be more well-informed about AIDS and their link to the disease; otherwise, many new cases may develop. As the epidemic continues to spread, women need to realize that they can stop the spread of the disease and protect themselves from infection and a number of related complications. It is the responsibility of health educators to present this to young women and inform them of the powerful choices that they can make.

Here the author cites a final piece of research to emphasize the extent of the problem.

Here she begins her explicit challenge to readers about what they have to do to protect themselves or their students from infection.

■ Look to the Future

Looking to the future is particularly relevant when you are asking readers to take action. To move readers to action, you must establish the persistence of a problem and the consequences of letting a situation continue unchanged. In the concluding paragraph below, the student author points out a number of things that teachers need to do to involve parents in their children's education. She identifies a range of options before identifying what she believes is perhaps the most important action teachers can take.

The second through fifth sentences present an array of options.

First and foremost, teachers must recognize the ways in which some parents are positively contributing to their children's academic endeavors. Teachers must recognize nontraditional methods of participation as legitimate and work toward supporting parents in these tasks. For instance, teachers might send home suggestions for local after-school tutoring programs. Teachers must also try to make urban parents feel welcome and respected in their school. Teachers might call parents to ask their opinion about a certain difficulty their child is having, or invite them to talk about something of interest to them. One parent, for instance, spoke highly of the previous superintendent who had let him use his work as a film producer to help with a show for students during homeroom. If teachers can develop innovative ways to utilize parents' talents and interests rather than just inviting them to be

In the last two sentences, the writer looks to the future with her recommendations.

passively involved in an already-in-place curriculum, more parents might respond. Perhaps, most importantly, if teachers want parents to be involved in their students' educations, they must make the parents feel as though their opinions and concerns have real weight. When parents such as those interviewed for this study voice concerns and questions over their child's progress, it is imperative that teachers acknowledge and answer them.

■ Pose Questions

Posing questions stimulates readers to think about the implications of your argument and to apply what you argue to other situations. This is the case in the following paragraph, in which the student writer focuses on immigration and then shifts readers' attention to racism and the possibility of hate crimes. It's useful to extrapolate from your argument, to raise questions that test whether what you write can be applied to different situations. These questions can help readers understand what is at issue.

The first question.

Other speculative questions follow from possible responses to the writer's first question.

Also, my research may apply to a broader spectrum of sociological topics. There has been recent discussion about the increasing trend of immigration. Much of this discussion has involved the distribution of resources to immigrants. Should immigrants have equal access to certain economic and educational resources in America? The decision is split. But it will be interesting to see how this debate will play out. If immigrants are granted more resources, will certain Americans mobilize against the distribution of these resources? Will we see another rise in racist groups such as the Ku Klux Klan in order to prevent immigrants from obtaining more resources? My research can also be used to understand global conflict or war. In general, groups mobilize when their established resources are threatened by an external force. Moreover, groups use framing processes to justify their collective action to others.

■ Conclude with a Quotation

A quotation can add authority to your argument, indicating that others in positions of power and prestige support your stance. A quotation also can add poignancy to your argument, as it does in the following excerpt, in which the quotation amplifies the idea that people use Barbie to advance their own interests.

The question still remains, what does Barbie mean? Is she the spokeswoman for the empowerment of women, or rather is she performing the dirty work of conservative patriarchy? I do not think we will ever know the answer. Rather, Barbie is the undeniable "American Icon." She is a toy, and she is what we want her to be. A test performed by Albert M. Magro at Fairmont State College titled "Why Barbie Is Perceived as Beautiful" shows that Barbie is the epitome of what we as humans find beautiful. The test sought to find human preferences on evolutionary changes in the human body. Subjects were shown a series of photos comparing different human body parts, such as the size and shape of the eyes, and asked to decide which feature they preferred: the primitive or derived (more evolved traits). The test revealed that the subjects preferred the derived body traits. Ironically, it is these preferred evolutionary features that are utilized on the body of Barbie. Barbie is truly an extension of what we are and what we perceive. Juel Best concludes his discourse on Barbie with these words: "Toys do not embody violence or sexism or occult meanings. People must assign toys their meanings." Barbie is whoever we make her out to be. Barbie grabs hold of our imaginations and lets us go wild.

The writer quotes an authority to amplify the idea that individually and collectively, we project significance on toys.

Steps to Drafting Conclusions: Five Strategies

1 **Pull together the main claims of your essay.** Don't simply repeat points you make in the paper. Instead, show readers how the points you make fit together.

2 **Answer the question "So what?"** Show your readers why your stand on the issue is significant.

3 **Place your argument in a larger context.** Discuss the specifics of your argument, but also indicate its broader implications.

4 **Show readers what is new.** As you synthesize the key points of your argument, explain how what you argue builds on, extends, or challenges the thinking of others.

5 **Decide on the best strategy for writing your conclusion.** Will you echo the introduction? Challenge the reader? Look to the future? Pose questions? Conclude with a quotation? Choose the best strategy or strategies to appeal to your readers.

A Practice Sequence: Drafting a Conclusion

1   Write your conclusion, using one of the strategies described in this section. Then share your conclusion with a classmate. Ask this person to address the following questions:

- Did I pull together the key points of the argument?
- Did I answer "So what?" adequately?

> • Are the implications I want readers to draw from the essay clear?
>
> After listening to the responses, try a second strategy, and then ask your classmate which conclusion is more effective.
>
> 2   If you do not have a conclusion of your own, analyze each example conclusion above to see how well each appears to (1) pull together the main claim of the essay, (2) answer "So what?" (3) place the argument in a larger context, and (4) show readers what is new.

ANALYZING STRATEGIES FOR WRITING: FROM INTRODUCTIONS TO CONCLUSIONS

Now that you have studied the various strategies for writing introductions, developing your ideas in subsequent paragraphs, and drafting conclusions, read Barbara Ehrenreich's essay, "Cultural Baggage," and analyze the strategies she uses for developing her argument about diversity. It may help to refer to the practice sequences for drafting introductions (p. 263) and conclusions (p. 281), as well as Steps to Developing Paragraphs (p. 275). Ideally, you should work with your classmates, in groups of three or four, assigning one person to record your ideas and share with the whole class.

Alternatively, you could put the essays by Ehrenreich and Elizabeth Martínez "in conversation" with one another. How do Martínez and Ehrenreich define the issues around diversity? What is at stake for them in the arguments they develop? What things need to change? How would you compare the way each uses stories and personal anecdote to develop her ideas? Would you say that either writer is a more effective "conversationalist" or more successful in fulfilling her purpose?

BARBARA EHRENREICH

Cultural Baggage

Barbara Ehrenreich is a social critic, activist, and political essayist. Her book *Nickel and Dimed: On (Not) Getting By in America* (2001) describes her attempt to live on low-wage jobs; it became a national best seller in the United States. Her book, *Bait and Switch: The (Futile) Pursuit of the American Dream* (2005), explores the shadowy world of the white-collar unemployed. Recent books of cultural analysis by Ehrenreich include *Bright-Sided: How the Relentless Promotion of Positive Thinking Has Undermined America* and *This Land Is Their Land: Reports from a Divided Nation* (both published in 2009). Ehrenreich has also written for *Mother Jones, The Atlantic, Ms., The New Republic, In These Times,* Salon.com, and other publications. "Cultural Baggage" was originally published in the *New York Times Magazine* in 1992. Her most recent book is *Living with a Wild God,* a memoir that she published in 2014.

■ ■ ■

An acquaintance was telling me about the joys of rediscovering her ethnic and religious heritage. "I know exactly what my ancestors were doing 2,000 years ago," she said, eyes gleaming with enthusiasm, "and *I can do the same things now.*" Then she leaned forward and inquired politely, "And what is your ethnic background, if I may ask?"

"None," I said, that being the first word in line to get out of my mouth. Well, not "none," I backtracked. Scottish, English, Irish—that was something, I supposed. Too much Irish to qualify as a WASP; too much of the hated English to warrant a "Kiss Me, I'm Irish" button; plus there are a number of dead ends in the family tree due to adoptions, missing records, failing memories, and the like. I was blushing by this time. Did "none" mean I was rejecting my heritage out of Anglo-Celtic self-hate? Or was I revealing a hidden ethnic chauvinism in which the Britannically derived serve as a kind of neutral standard compared with the ethnic "others"?

Throughout the 1960s and 70s, I watched one group after another—African Americans, Latinos, Native Americans—stand up and proudly reclaim their roots while I just sank back ever deeper into my seat. All this excitement over ethnicity stemmed, I uneasily sensed, from a past in which *their* ancestors had been trampled upon by *my* ancestors, or at least by people who looked very much like them. In addition, it had begun to seem almost un-American not to have some sort of hyphen at hand, linking one to more venerable times and locales.

But the truth is, I was raised with none. We'd eaten ethnic foods in my childhood home, but these were all borrowed, like the pasties, or Cornish meat pies, my father had picked up from his fellow miners in Butte, Montana. If my mother had one rule, it was militant ecumenism in all manners of food and experience. "Try new things," she would say, meaning anything from sweetbreads to clams, with an emphasis on the "new."

As a child, I briefly nourished a craving for tradition and roots. I immersed myself in the works of Sir Walter Scott. I pretended to believe that the bagpipe was a musical instrument. I was fascinated to learn from a grandmother that we were descended from certain Highland clans and longed for a pleated skirt in one of their distinctive tartans.

But in *Ivanhoe*, it was the dark-eyed "Jewess" Rebecca I identified with, not the flaxen-haired bimbo Rowena. As for clans: Why not call them "tribes," those bands of half-clad peasants and warriors whose idea of cuisine was stuffed sheep gut washed down with whiskey? And then there was the sting of Disraeli's remark—which I came across in my early teens—to the effect that his ancestors had been leading orderly, literate lives when my ancestors were still rampaging through the Highlands daubing themselves with blue paint.

Motherhood put the screws on me, ethnicity-wise. I had hoped that by marrying a man of Eastern European Jewish ancestry I would acquire for my descendants the ethnic genes that my own forebears so sadly lacked. At one point, I even subjected the children to a seder of my own design, including a little talk about the flight from Egypt and its relevance to modern social issues. But the kids insisted on buttering their matzos and snickering through my talk. "Give me a break, Mom," the older one said. "You don't even believe in God."   7

After the tiny pagans had been put to bed, I sat down to brood over Elijah's wine. What had I been thinking? The kids knew that their Jewish grandparents were secular folks who didn't hold seders themselves. And if ethnicity eluded me, how could I expect it to take root in my children, who are not only Scottish English Irish, but Hungarian Polish Russian to boot?   8

But, then, on the fumes of Manischewitz, a great insight took form in my mind. It was true, as the kids said, that I didn't "believe in God." But this could be taken as something very different from an accusation—a reminder of a genuine heritage. My parents had not believed in God either, nor had my grandparents or any other progenitors going back to the great-great level. They had become disillusioned with Christianity generations ago—just as, on the in-law side, my children's other ancestors had shaken their Orthodox Judaism. This insight did not exactly furnish me with an "identity," but it was at least something to work with: We are the kind of people, I realized—whatever our distant ancestors' religions—who do *not* believe, who do not carry on traditions, who do not do things just because someone has done them before.   9

The epiphany went on: I recalled that my mother never introduced a procedure for cooking or cleaning by telling me, "Grandma did it this way." What did Grandma know, living in the days before vacuum cleaners and disposable toilet mops? In my parents' general view, new things were better than old, and the very fact that some ritual had been performed in the past was a good reason for abandoning it now. Because what was the past, as our forebears knew it? Nothing but poverty, superstition, and grief. "Think for yourself," Dad used to say. "Always ask why."   10

In fact, this may have been the ideal cultural heritage for my particular ethnic strain—bounced as it was from the Highlands of Scotland across the sea, out to the Rockies, down into the mines, and finally spewed out into high-tech, suburban America. What better philosophy,   11 for a race of migrants, than "Think for yourself"? What better maxim, for a people whose whole world was rudely inverted every thirty years or so, than "Try new things"?

The more tradition-minded, the newly enthusiastic celebrants of Purim and Kwanzaa and Solstice, may see little point to survival if the survivors cany no cultural freight—religion, for example, or ethnic tradition. To which I would say that skepticism, curiosity, and wide-eyed ecumenical tolerance are also worthy elements of the human tradition and are at least as old as such notions as "Serbian" or "Croatian," "Scottish" or "Jewish." I make no claims for my personal line of progenitors except that they remained loyal to the values that may have induced all of our ancestors, long, long ago, to climb down from the trees and make their way into the open plains.

A few weeks ago, I cleared my throat and asked the children, now mostly grown and fearsomely smart, whether they felt any stirrings of ethnic or religious identity, etc., which might have been, ahem, insufficiently nourished at home. "None," they said, adding firmly, "and the world would be a better place if nobody else did, either." My chest swelled with pride, as would my mother's, to know that the race of "none" marches on.

10

From Revising to Editing
Working with Peer Groups

Academic writing is a collaborative enterprise. By reading and commenting on your drafts, your peers can support your work as a writer. And you can support the work of your peers by reading their drafts with a critical but constructive eye.

In this chapter, we set out the differences between revising and editing, discuss the peer editing process in terms of the composition pyramid, present a model peer editing session, and then explain the writer's and reader's responsibilities through early drafts, later drafts, and final drafts, providing opportunities for you to practice peer response on three drafts of a student paper.

REVISING VERSUS EDITING

We make a distinction between revising and editing. By **revising**, we mean making changes to a paper to reflect new thinking or conceptualizing. If a reader finds that the real focus of your essay comes at the end of your draft, you need to revise the paper with this new focus in mind. Revising differs from **editing**, which involves minor changes to what will be the final draft of a paper—replacing a word here and there, correcting misspellings, or substituting dashes for commas to create emphasis, for example.

When you're reading a first or second draft, the niceties of style, spelling, and punctuation are not priorities. After all, if the writer had to change the focus of his or her argument, significant changes to words, phrases, and punctuation would be inevitable. Concentrating on editing errors early on, when the writer is still trying to develop an argument with evidence, organize information logically, and anticipate counterarguments, is inefficient and even counterproductive.

Here are some characteristics of revising and editing that can guide how you read your own writing and the comments you offer to other writers:

REVISING	EDITING
Treats writing as a work in progress	Treats writing as an almost-finished product
Focuses on new possibilities both within and beyond the text	Addresses obvious errors and deficiencies
Focuses on new questions or goals	Focuses on the text alone
Considers both purpose and readers' needs	Considers grammar, punctuation, spelling, and style
Encourages further discovery	Polishes up the essay

Again, writing is a process, and revising is an integral part of that process. Your best writing will happen in the context of real readers' responding to your drafts. Look at the acknowledgments in any academic book, and you will see many people credited with having improved the book through their comments on drafts and ideas. All academic writers rely on conversations with others to strengthen their work.

THE PEER EDITING PROCESS

We emphasize that the different stages of writing—early, later, and final—call for different work from both readers and writers because writers' needs vary with each successive draft. These stages correspond to what has been called the composition pyramid (Figure 10.1).* The composition

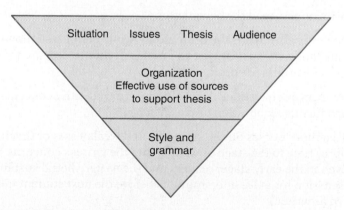

FIGURE 10.1 The Composition Pyramid

*We thank Susannah Brietz-Monta and Anthony Monta for this idea.

pyramid represents elements of writing that can help you decide what to pay attention to at different stages of writing.

1. The top of this inverted pyramid corresponds to the early stages of writing. At this point, members of the writing group should identify the situation the writer is responding to (for example, homelessness, inequality, or air pollution), the issue the writer has defined (for example, the economic versus the social costs of homelessness), the thesis or argument the writer advances, and the extent to which the writer addresses a given audience appropriately.

2. The middle portion of the pyramid corresponds to a later stage of the writing process, the point at which members of the group should move on to discuss the extent to which the writer has organized the argument logically and used sources effectively to support the thesis. Has the writer integrated quotations smoothly into the paper? Is the evidence relevant, recent, and credible?

3. Finally, the bottom of the pyramid corresponds to the final stages of drafting. As the writer's focus shifts to grammar and style, so should the group's. Questions to ask: Is this specific language appropriate to the intended audience? Has the writer presented the argument in ways that will compel readers—even those who disagree—to listen?

Steps in the Peer Editing Process

1 The writer distributes copies of the draft to each member of the writing group. (Ideally, the group should not exceed four students.)

2 The writer distributes a cover letter, setting an agenda for each member of the group.

3 The members read the cover letter.

4 The writer then reads the draft aloud, while members follow along, underlining passages and making notes to prepare themselves to discuss the draft.

5 Members ask questions that help the writer identify concepts that need further elaboration or clarification.

6 Discussion focuses on the strengths and weaknesses of the draft appropriate to the stage of writing and the writer's concerns. (Even in the early stage, readers and the writer should sustain discussion for at least ten minutes before the next student takes a turn as writer.)

PEER GROUPS IN ACTION: A SAMPLE SESSION

Let's take a look at one writing group in action to see the potential of this approach to writing. One student, Rebecca Jegier, worked collaboratively with three other students—Jasmine, Michaela, and Kevin—on a paper about the purpose of education and the extent to which school reforms reflect what she refers to as "a growing culture of impatience." She explained to her group that she struggled to draw a parallel between what she sees as a worn-out factory model of education (students sitting in rows) and the story of Blockbuster, a once-successful business that failed to respond to customers' changing needs. She also felt that she still needed to sharpen her argument.

> Rebecca: I think we are expected to argue what we think the purpose of education should be and to place our argument in the larger context of how others have defined the purpose historically.
>
> Jasmine: I am still trying to decide what I think the purpose of education should be. I sort of think that education should prepare people for a job, but we also read that article, you know, the one that said we may not even know what jobs will be available in ten years. He wrote that schools should prepare people to be creative, innovative, critical thinkers. That other essay explained that school should help people flourish. I haven't decided what that means.
>
> Michaela: I think the important thing we need to decide is the issue. I agree that schools don't really prepare us to be very creative or innovative. I guess that's the issue.

Rebecca restated her understanding of the assignment before giving Jasmine, Michaela, and Kevin a copy of her draft. This is a valuable starting point because a writer's interpretation of the writing assignment—the task, the purpose, and the audience—helps readers understand why she is taking a particular approach. If readers disagree with the writer's interpretation, they should discuss their differences before the writer shares the draft and determine an appropriate response to the assignment. Rebecca then read her paper aloud while her group members listened and wrote notes to indicate specific words, phrases, and ideas that they wanted to discuss.

AN ANNOTATED STUDENT DRAFT

Here we reprint the main part of Rebecca's draft, with annotations on passages that elicited comments from her peers. Following the draft, we present their discussion in more detail.

Jegier 1

Rebecca Jegier

Student-Centered Learning: Catering to Students' Impatience

In today's world of high-speed Internet and fast food, Americans have gotten used to receiving instant gratification and immediate results. If a Web site takes four seconds or longer to load, an average of one in four Internet users will get fed up with waiting and abandon the page ("Loading time," 2013). In a survey conducted by the Associated Press, the majority of Americans report losing patience after being kept waiting on the telephone for more than five minutes, and half of those surveyed reported that they have refused to return to a business because of long waits (AP, 2006). This paper is about two hundred times as long as the average tweet—how many teenage students would be willing to read it until the end? With the growing culture of impatience, it comes as no surprise that Americans today are frustrated with recent reforms in education and their lack of immediate results. It is also not a surprising issue that American children have trouble staying focused and engaged in today's standardized and "factory-based" education system driven by worksheets and mandated testing. This outdated system has created an environment that is completely contradictory to the interactive, personalized, and relevant world in which students spend most of their lives.

According to Dr. Martin Luther King Jr. (1947), "Intelligence plus character—that is the goal of true education. The complete education gives one not only power of concentration, but worthy objectives upon which to concentrate." In order for education in America to be "complete" and to reach its full potential of empowering students to concentrate and reach their goals, educators and school reformers might very well explore the issue of impatience. In some cases, such as investing in stocks, the unwillingness to be patient can cause people to make a poor trade-off between immediate, although mediocre, results or receiving something much better after a wait; in the example of the stock market, a larger return on investment usually comes with time. In other circumstances, however, impatience can be largely beneficial if it is handled correctly; successful businesses will improve as they make efforts to become

Rebecca's group member, Kevin, says he likes the introduction and agrees with the point that we are all becoming impatient. But he worries that the introduction should state the purpose of education more directly since this is the assignment. Jasmine agrees.

Kevin and Michaela both tell Rebecca that they like this phrase, "the culture of impatience."

They all discuss whether or not this is the argument and if Rebecca could restate her key claim.

Rebecca provides one important way that Americans can think about the purpose of education and tries to connect this perspective to her own ideas about impatience.

She also anticipates readers' different interpretations of impatience and whether it can be seen in positive terms.

1

2

more efficient and provide better customer service to those who
do not want to wait.

*She goes on to
explain that school
reformers have
been impatient, but
their approach has
been detrimental to
learning.*

School reformers' impatience belongs in the first
category: detrimental and unproductive. Making quality
reforms that will be both effective and enduring is a long-term
investment that must be carefully planned instead of hastily
implemented. The expectation that coming out with new legislation will immediately change schools for the better is, to
put it gently, ludicrous. And it is almost as ridiculous to think
that small reforms will be effective when they don't change the
underlying problem and allow the system to become relevant
to current society.

3

*Rebecca's peer group
is intrigued by this
analogy and even its
relevance. However,
Jasmine thinks
Rebecca is beginning
to lose the focus of
her argument.*

Take movies, for example. The first Blockbuster store
opened in the 1980s, boasting convenience and the ability to
customize movie selection to location. By September 2012,
however, Blockbuster had filed for bankruptcy and had closed
hundreds of stores in a sad attempt to get back on its feet.
How did such a successful idea turn into a disaster? The problem with Blockbuster was that it made small improvements to
its traditional, formerly successful model and disregarded consumers' changing desires and demands. Netflix had no problem
stepping in to fill the gaps with new and innovative methods.
In fact, Netflix had been patiently operating and steadily
gaining market share for six years before Blockbuster finally
came out with its own movie-by-mail service. Albert Einstein
once defined insanity as "doing the same thing over and over
again and expecting different results." Although schools
monopolize the education business, it is still vital for them
to adapt and conform to that which is relevant in today's
world. Instead of continuing to take a "Blockbuster" attitude
towards education — an arguably "insane" route — the U.S.
education system needs to examine reforms that have happened in the past as well as reevaluate what its goals are for
the children of tomorrow.

4

*In the following three
paragraphs, Rebecca
shifts the focus from
the present to the
past, which is part of*

Ever since education began in America with one-room
schoolhouses in the nineteenth century, schools have constantly
been adapting to meet the needs of the students and those
of the country depending on the time period (Tyack, 2007).

5

Jegier 3

the assignment, to
offer some historical
context for contem-
porary efforts to
define the purpose of
education.

As the goals of the country have changed, so have the schools. Initially, Thomas Jefferson and Noah Webster wanted children to emerge from school as functioning, self-governing citizens who could contribute to the democracy in a new fragile republic. Later, goals were revised due to changes or events in the world such as immigration, the space race, and the *Brown v. Board of Education* decision. When immigrants began to come to America in the late 1800s, the school system had to adapt to find a way to assimilate immigrants into the established education system. In the 1950s when the Supreme Court delivered its *Brown v. Board of Education* decision, schools had to adapt to desegregation and address the effects of opening their doors to those who formerly had no access to education. In 1957, when the Soviets launched the first satellite and effectively "won" the space race, the United States immediately shifted its focus to math and science classes. These reforms were specific to the time, as well as necessary to the relevant situations of that society, and were eventually effective even though they were not seen in this way at first.

In 1983, the National Commission on Excellence in Education published "A Nation at Risk," a report that pointed out flaws in the U.S. education system — flaws that the nation is still addressing today. It recommended that we should raise the standards of high school graduation requirements and college admissions requirements, as well as increase teacher salaries and raise standards for those who wish to teach, in addition to many other suggestions for reform (National Commission on Excellence in Education, 1983). Since this landmark report was produced, school reformers have repeatedly tried to confront the system head-on. 6

President George W. Bush's No Child Left Behind Act of 2001 (NCLB) is a commonly cited and criticized reform that requires states to assess all students at select grade levels in order for schools to receive federal funding. Intended to increase the quality of education for everyone by requiring schools to improve their performance, NCLB is limited in that it does not address the root of the problem and places the focus 7 on achievement instead of the teaching and learning process. Although some improvement in test scores has been reported since its implementation (Dee & Jacob, 2011), frustration with this act has been growing because the tests and the standards sometimes contradict each other and are very often not aligned. NCLB represents an attempt to provide a simple solution for a complex problem. Modern America's "get-rich-quick" attitude toward changes in general and school reforms in particular is a fallacy that must be remedied in order to promote effective reforms in the education system. Although Americans today tend to get frustrated after fifteen minutes of standing in line (AP, 2006), patience is necessary to develop quality reforms that will last in the long term.

Rebecca's group wonders about the point Rebecca makes here, one that implicitly connects to her idea that impatience can be a detriment. This is something Michaela wants Rebecca to say more about.

In contrast to the detrimental effects of citizens' and reformers' impatience with the current state of education, the "impatience" of our children in schools can actually be beneficial to the American education system, if responded to in the correct way. I place the word "impatience" in quotation marks because the pejorative quality of this word does not fully express what is going on in students' minds when they are categorized in this way by teachers, parents, or doctors. The underlying principle lies in their upbringing; kids are used to alleviating their natural curiosity through googling their questions or by texting a more knowledgeable friend who can respond within the hour (if not within the minute!). There is nothing inherently wrong with wanting to receive instant answers and quick results, especially when today's search engines and mobile apps can easily oblige. Similar to the way businesses constantly strive for better customer service, it is the responsibility of the school system to tailor education to its "impatient" (read: curious) students in relevant and timely ways.

Rebecca helps readers think of impatience as a positive trait that she believes educators overlook. Michaela and Kevin also think Rebecca needs to connect this point to what she says about the "culture of impatience."

Every child has unique talents and skills that are apparent at very early ages. In the 1980s, Harvard psychologist Howard Gardner proposed the theory of multiple intelligences (MI), which argues that intelligence should not be limited to the traditional "school smarts" that can be measured by Binet's IQ test or by the SAT (Gardner, 1987). In addition to the linguistic and logical-mathematical intelligences that

Although they agree with this point, Rebecca's group is not sure how this connects with her argument about impatience.

8

9

Jegier 5

are targeted in most school settings, Gardner proposes that people can be intelligent in other distinct ways. He came up with eight intelligences, including spatial, bodily-kinesthetic, musical, interpersonal, intrapersonal, and naturalist. Besides having different intelligences, students are unique because of their different learning styles (for example, one student might be a visual learner while another learns better from listening to a lecture) and the varying paces which they learn and retain material (Christensen, Horn & Johnson, 2008). This leads us to the question: if all students have different intelligences and learn in different ways, what reasoning do we have to support that standardizing their education would be an effective teaching method for all of them? Is providing the exact same instruction to all students fair, even if such a cookie-cutter method of teaching only caters to those who are "intelligent" in the linguistic and logical-mathematical sense? If the goal is to educate every student, standardization is not an effective way to do it.

Rebecca's group begins with a brief discussion of her introduction and then turn to Rebecca's argument. They ask questions and offer some reflections that they hoped would guide Rebecca toward making a more explicit claim about school reform.

Kevin:	I really like your introduction and agree with the idea that we live in a world where we expect instant gratification. I know I get pretty impatient when I have to wait for anything.
Michaela:	And you use a great phrase, "a culture of impatience," to describe the problem.
Jasmine:	Yes. But isn't the paper supposed to be about the purpose of education? You eventually connect the idea of impatience to the purpose of education, you know, to respond to a generation of students like us who have been brought up on technology. School isn't very responsive to the way we learn. Isn't that what you are arguing?
Rebecca:	Okay, I see what you are saying. But I wanted to write an introduction that would capture your attention with something relevant. I'll have to think about that.

Michaela:	She does make her argument at the end of the first paragraph. Like Jasmine said, you are arguing that schools need to be more responsive to kids' needs, who they are, and how they learn. I know you are not saying it that way, but is that what you are saying?
Rebecca:	I think so, yes.
Kevin:	Could you say that?

Kevin begins with a supportive comment that initiates a more specific conversation about the way Rebecca frames her ideas with the phrase, "a culture of impatience." However, Jasmine asks a pointed question that challenges Rebecca and the others in the group to think about the assignment and the role that an introduction should play. In particular, everyone seems to agree that Rebecca's key claim centers on school's lack of responsiveness to a new generation of students who tend to be impatient. The way that Rebecca states this is different from the way Jasmine and Michaela phrase the argument, and Kevin urges her to restate her claim in keeping with their interpretation. In the course of this conversation, then, peer group members provide support, but also question, even challenge, the way that Rebecca frames her argument. Importantly, the questions and advice are specific enough for Rebecca to use what they suggest to change her approach to writing about the purpose of education. Can or should she lead up to her claim with a story that does not directly address the purpose of education? And should she rephrase her claim? If Rebecca took their advice, this would mean revising an evaluative claim that schools are based on a worn-out factory model of education to a policy-driven claim about what school reform should require.

Group members also extended the conversation to helping Rebecca connect the different ideas that she introduces in her paper: school reforms as a negative example of impatience, the comparison she makes to corporations that fail to recognize "a culture of impatience," and recent research on individual learning styles.

Jasmine:	So now I get what you are saying about impatience and the purpose of school, but now you want to compare this to what happened to Blockbuster. The last sentence of your paragraph is good, but it takes you a while to make this point. In the paragraph above it, you say (*reads*) "Take movies, for example. The first Blockbuster store opened in the 1980s, boasting convenience and the ability to customize movie selection to location." But I think you need to connect your two points earlier. Otherwise, I think you are losing focus by introducing the example of Blockbuster.
Michaela:	I think the same thing happens when you start to talk about No Child Left Behind. Your last sentence talks about "patience." But you start by summarizing, not making clear that there is a connection here.

Kevin (*interrupting*): Yeah, I think you keep summarizing different ideas and I get lost in how you are connecting everything.

Michaela: One way to handle this problem is to say something that connects all the dots and not leave your main points until the end of each paragraph. The same thing happens again when you introduce the idea of learning styles.

Rebecca: Wow, okay. That's a lot. I am going to have to think about all of this.

Rebecca's draft reflects her first attempt to get her ideas down. It's fine for a first draft to explore ideas. When writers formulate a working thesis (or when they fail to do so), readers in a peer group can offer support, noting strengths or pointing to places of greatest interest to sustain the writer's energy for writing. The more specific the advice, the better the writer will be able to translate that advice into action. Rebecca's group helped her generate a plan for taking some next steps by pointing out how she could define the issue and connect different parts of her paper: " . . . say something that connects all the dots and not leave your main points until the end of each paragraph."

A peer group can also ask questions to help a writer set new goals, so that revision is really a process of reenvisioning or reseeing the key concepts in the writer's draft. As a reader, it is useful to paraphrase particular parts of the draft, so that the writer can hear how you have understood what he or she is trying to say. This is what Michaela did when she explained in a questioning sort of way: "You are arguing that schools need to be more responsive to kids' needs, who they are, and how they learn. I know you are not saying it that way, but is that what you are saying?"

WORKING WITH EARLY DRAFTS

▪ Understand the Writer's Responsibilities

When you present an early draft of your essay to your writing group, you want the group to focus on top-level pyramid concerns—situation, issue, thesis, and audience. You should explain this and any other concerns you have in a cover letter. Use the template in Figure 10.2 as a model for what needs explaining in the letter to your readers.

During the session, it's important to be open to suggestions. Although you don't have to incorporate every suggestion your group makes when you revise your draft, be sure you at least understand the members' comments and concerns. If you don't understand what the members are saying about your draft, ask them to clarify or give you an example.

Finally, if you decide not to take someone's suggestion, have a good reason for doing so. If a suggested change means you won't be addressing the terms of the assignment or that you would no longer be interested in the issue, it's fine to say no.

1. What is your question (or assignment)?

2. What is the issue motivating you to write?

3. How have published writers addressed the issue about which you are writing?

4. What is your working thesis?

5. Who is your audience, and what kind of response do you want form your readers?

6. What do you think is working best?

7. What specific aspect of the essay are you least satisfied with at this time?

8. What kind of feedback do you especially want today?

FIGURE 10.2   The Writer's Cover Letter: Early Drafts

■ Understand the Reader's Responsibilities

Your task as a reader is to follow along as the early draft is read, paying special attention to the concerns the writer has explained in the cover letter and focusing on the top of the pyramid: situation, issue, thesis, and audience. Take notes directly on the draft copy, circling or underlining sections you find confusing or have questions about, so that you can refer to them specifically in the discussion.

When it's your turn to talk, have a conversation about your reactions to the draft—where the draft amused, confused, or persuaded you, for example. Don't just jump in and start telling the writer what he or she should be doing in the paper. Your role as a reader is to give the writer a live audience: Your responses can help the writer decide what parts of the paper are working and what parts need serious revision. There are times, however, when you should play the role of *deferring reader*, putting off certain comments. You don't want to overwhelm the writer with problems no matter how many questions the essay raises.

Offer both positive and negative remarks. Start by pointing out what is working well in the paper, so the writer knows where he or she is on the right track. This also leaves the writer more open to constructive criticism. But don't shy away from telling the writer what should be working better. It's your job as a reader to offer honest and specific responses to the draft, so the writer can develop it into an effective piece of writing. Figure 10.3 lists key questions you should ask as a reader of an early draft.

■ Analyze an Early Draft

Keep these questions in mind as you read the following excerpt from a student's early draft. After reading a number of scholarly articles on the Civil Rights Movement, Tasha Taylor decided to address what she sees as

1. Are the questions and issues that motivate the writer clear?
2. Has the writer effectively realted the conversation that published writers are engaged in?
3. What is at issue?
4. What is the writer's thesis?
5. Is the writer addressing the audience's concerns effectively?
6. What passages of the draft are most effective?
7. What passages of the draft are least effective?

FIGURE 10.3   A Reader's Questions: Early Drafts

the difference between scholars' understanding of the movement and more popular treatments in textbooks and photographs. She also tries to tie in the larger question of historical memory to her analysis of southern blacks' struggle for equality—what people remember about the past and what they forget. In fact, she begins her essay with a quotation she believes summarizes what she wants to argue ("The struggle of man against power is the struggle of memory against forgetting").

As you read Taylor's essay, take detailed notes, and underline passages that concern you. Then write a paragraph or two explaining what she could do to strengthen the draft. Keep in mind that this is an early draft, so focus on the top level of the pyramid: the situation or assignment, the issue, the thesis, and the audience.

Taylor 1

Tasha Taylor
Professor Winters
English 111
October 23, 20—

Memory through Photography

The struggle of man against power is the struggle of memory against forgetting.

—Milan Kundera

Ask the average American what the key components of the civil rights movement are, and most people will probably recall Martin Luther King Jr. speaking of a dream in front of the Lincoln Memorial,

Taylor 2

Rosa Parks riding a bus, a few court decisions, and perhaps a photograph of Elizabeth Eckford cowering before an angry mob in front of Central High School in Little Rock. Few people are aware A. Philip Randolph planned the march on Washington. Few could describe Rosa Parks's connection to the civil rights movement (for example, the fact that she had been a member of the NAACP since 1943) before her legendary refusal to give up her seat in December 1955, which led to the Montgomery Bus Boycott. Few recognize the years of struggle that existed between the *Brown v. Board of Education* decision and the actual desegregation of schools. Few consider the fate of Elizabeth Eckford after federal troops were sent to protect her and the other members of the Little Rock Nine had left Central High or the months of abuse (physical and emotional) that they endured in the name of integration. What most people know is limited to textbooks they read in school or the captions under photographs that describe where a particular event occurred.

Why is it that textbooks exclusively feature the stories of larger than life figures like Martin Luther King? Why is it that we remember things the way we do? Historical events "have little meaning without human interpretation, without our speaking about them within the contexts of our lives and our culture, without giving them names and meanings" (Kolker xix). Each person experiencing the exact same event will carry a different memory from that event. Trying to decipher what memories reveal about each person is a fascinating yet difficult endeavor, because each retelling of a memory and each additional memory alters existing ones.

The story that photographs and textbooks tell us does not even begin to describe the depth of the movement or the thousands who risked their lives and the lives of their families to make equality a reality. Embracing this selective memory as a nation prevents understanding and acknowledgment of the harsh reality of other images from the civil rights movement (demonstrators being plowed down by fire hoses, beatings, and the charred bodies of bombing victims) which are key aspects of understanding who we are as a society. The question therefore is why. Why is it that textbook writers and publishers have allowed so much of this history to be skewed and forgotten? How can it be that barely 50 years after these events so many have been forgotten or diluted?

Reading as a Writer

1. What is working well in Taylor's draft?
2. What is Taylor's thesis or argument?
3. To what extent does she connect her analysis of the civil rights movement and historical memory?
4. What parts of her analysis could Taylor explain further? (What do you still need to know?)
5. What would you suggest Taylor do next?

WORKING WITH LATER DRAFTS

■ Understand the Writer's Responsibilities

At a later stage, after you've had the opportunity to take readers' suggestions and do further research, you should be able to state your thesis more definitively than you did in your earlier draft. You also should be able to support your thesis with evidence, anticipating possible counter-arguments. Ideally, your readers will still provide constructive criticism, offering their support, as in the first draft, but they will also question and challenge more than before.

Here, too, you want to help readers focus on your main concerns, which you should explain in a cover letter. You may still need to work on one or two top-level pyramid concerns, but your focus will likely be mid-level concerns—organization and the effective use of sources. Use the list of questions in Figure 10.4 to help you write your cover letter.

---

1. What is your research question?
2. What is the issue motivating you to write?
3. What is your thesis?
4. How do you go about identifying a gap in readers' knowledge, modifying other's ideas, or trying to correct readers' misunderstandings?
5. To what extent do you distinguish your argument from the information you quote, summarize, or paraphrase from the sources you have read?
6. To what extent have you organized your ideas in ways that will help readers follow the logic of your argument?
7. To what extent have you anticipated potential counterarguments to your thesis?
8. What do you think is working best?
9. What specific aspect of the essay are you least satisfied with at this time?

FIGURE 10.4   The Writer's Cover Letter: Later Drafts

■ Understand the Reader's Responsibilities

In a later draft, your focus as a reader should be on midlevel concerns in the composition pyramid: places in the writer's text that are confusing, that require better transitions, or that could use sources more effectively. You can challenge writers at this stage of the composing process, perhaps playing the role of *naive reader*, suggesting places in the draft where the writer has left something out or isn't clear. The naive reader's comments tend to take the form of questions: "Do you mean to suggest that everyone who learns to write well succeeds in life? What kind of success are you talking about?" Closely related to the naive reader is the *devil's advocate reader*. This reader's comments also challenge the writer, often taking the form of a question like this: "But why couldn't this be attributed to the effects of socialization rather than heredity?" Figure 10.5 offers questions for reading later drafts.

■ Analyze a Later Draft

Now read the following excerpt from Taylor's second draft. You will see that she begins with her discussion of historical memory. She also has included an analysis of a book of photographs that Nobel Prize–winning author Toni Morrison compiled. Take notes as you read the draft and write a paragraph in which you describe what you see as some of the strengths of what Taylor has written and what she can do to make other elements stronger. In particular, focus on the middle level of the composition pyramid—on organization and the effective use of sources and evidence to support her thesis.

---

1. To what extent is it clear what questions and issues motivate the writer?

2. What is the writers' thesis?

3. How effectively does the writer establish the conversation—identify a gap in people's knowledge, attempt to modify an existing argument, or try to correct some misunderstanding?

4. How effectively does the writer distinguish between his or ideas and the ideas he or she summarizes, paraphrases, or quotes?

5. How well does the writer help you follow the logic of his or her argument?

6. To what extent are you persuaded by the writer's argument?

7. To what extent does the writer anticipate possible counterarguments?

8. To what extent does the writer make clear how he or she wants readers to respond?

9. What do you think is working best? Explain by pointing to specific passages in the writer's draft.

10. What specific aspect of the draft is least effective? Explain by pointing to a specific passage in the writer's draft.

FIGURE 10.5 A Reader's Questions: Later Drafts

Taylor 1

Tasha Taylor
Professor Winters
English 111
November 14, 20—

Memory through Photography

> The struggle of man against power is the struggle of
> memory against forgetting.
>
> —Milan Kundera

Memory is such an integral part of what it is to be human, yet is something so often taken for granted: People assume that their memories are accurate to protect themselves from the harsh realities of the atrocities committed by ordinary people. Even the pictures used to represent the much-celebrated civil rights movement give us a false sense of security and innocence. For example, the Ku Klux Klan is most often depicted by covered faces and burning crosses; the masks allow us to remove ourselves from responsibility. Few could describe Rosa Parks's connection to the civil rights movement (for example, the fact that she had been a member of the NAACP since 1943) before her legendary refusal to give up her seat in December 1955, which led to the Montgomery Bus Boycott. Few recognize the years of struggle that existed between the *Brown v. Board of Education* decision and the actual desegregation of schools. Few consider the fate of Elizabeth Eckford after federal troops were sent to protect her and the other members of the Little Rock Nine had left Central High or the months of abuse (physical and emotional) that they endured in the name of integration. What most people know is limited to textbooks they read in school or the captions under photographs that describe where a particular event occurred.

1

It is important, therefore, to analyze what is remembered and even more importantly to recognize what is forgotten: to question why it is that it is forgotten, what that says about society today, how far it has come and how much it has unwittingly fallen back into old patterns such as prejudice and ignorance. The discrepancies in cultural memory are due more to a society's desire to remember itself in the best light and protect itself from the reality of its brutality and responsibility. Such selective memory only temporarily heals the wounds of society; lack of awareness does not cause healing.

2

Taylor 2

Although there have been many recent moves to increase awareness, they are tainted by unavoidable biases and therefore continue to perpetuate a distorted memory.

Images play a central role in the formation of cultural memory because people can point to photographs and claim them as concrete evidence: "Images entrance us because they provide a powerful illusion of owning reality. If we can photograph reality or paint or copy it, we have exercised an important kind of power" (Kolker 3). A picture of black and white children sitting at a table together is used to reinforce the cultural perception that the problems of racism are over, that it has all been fixed.

In her book *Remember*, Toni Morrison strives to revitalize the memory of school integration through photographs. The book is dedicated to Denise McNair, Carole Robertson, Addie Mae Collins, and Cynthia Wesley, the four girls killed in the 16th Street Baptist Church bombing in 1963. Morrison writes, "Things are better now. Much, much better. But remember why and please remember us" (Morrison 72). The pictures are of black and white children happily eating together, solemnly saluting the flag together, and holding hands. The photographs of the four murdered girls show them peacefully and innocently smiling as if everything really is better now. In reality, according to the United States Bureau of Alcohol, Tobacco and Firearms, between 1995 and 1997 there were 162 incidents of arson or bombing in African American houses of worship. There are a few images of people protesting integration, but they are also consistent with the cultural memory (protesters are shown simply holding signs and yelling, not beating and killing innocent children). Finally, the captions are written in a child's voice. Yet it is not a child's voice at all it is merely a top down view of children that serves to perpetuate a distorted cultural memory.

The photographs used to suggest how things are much, much better now are misleading. For example, the last photograph is of a black girl and a white girl holding hands through a bus window, which was transporting them to an integrated school. The caption reads: "Anything can happen. Anything at all. See?" (71). It is a very powerful image of how the evil of Jim Crow and segregation exists in a distant past and the nation has come together and healed.

Taylor 3

However, Morrison neglects to point out that the picture was taken in Boston, Massachusetts, not the deep south, the heart of racism. Children holding hands in Boston is much less significant than if they were in Birmingham where that action would be concrete evidence of how far we as a nation have come.

Morrison also glorifies Martin Luther King Jr. and Rosa Parks, pointing to them as epitomizing the movement. Unfortunately, she perpetuates the story that one needs to be special or somehow larger than life to affect change. Paul Rogat Loeb writes in *Soul of a Citizen*: 6

> Once we enshrine our heroes, it becomes hard for mere mortals to measure up in our eyes . . . in our collective amnesia we lose the mechanisms through which grassroots social movements of the past successfully shifted public sentiment and challenged entrenched institutional power. Equally lost are the means by which their participants managed to keep on, sustaining their hope and eventually prevailing in circumstances at least as difficult as those we face today. (Loeb 36, 38)

Placing a select few on pedestals and claiming them as next to divine heroes of the movement does society a disservice; people fail to realize that ordinary people can serve as agents of change. 7

Morrison's book ignores the thousands of ordinary people who risked their lives for the cause to bring about equality. The caption besides the picture of Rosa Parks in *Remember* reads "because if I ever feel helpless or lonely I just have to remember that all it takes is one person" (Morrison 62). Ironically, Morrison gives credit for the Montgomery Bus Boycott to one person, ignoring the months of planning and dozens of planners involved. Even the photograph presents Rosa Parks in a position of power. It is a low-angle shot up at Parks that makes her appear larger than life and authoritative. The photographs of Martin Luther King Jr. also further the impression of power with a close up shot of his face as he stands above thousands of participants in the March on Washington. Although these photographs were selected to perpetuate the hero illusion, it is more inspiring to remember the ordinary people who took a stand and were able to accomplish extraordinary feats because of their dedication and persistence rather than glorify extraordinary people who were destined for greatness. 8

Reading as a Writer

1. What is Taylor's thesis or argument?
2. How well does she help you follow the logic of her argument with transitions?
3. How effectively does she distinguish between her ideas and the ideas she summarizes, paraphrases, or quotes?
4. To what extent are you persuaded by her argument?
5. What should Taylor do next?

WORKING WITH FINAL DRAFTS

■ Understand the Writer's Responsibilities

Your final draft should require editing, not revising. At this stage, readers should focus on errors in style and grammar in the text, not on the substance of your work. Here, too, indicate your main concerns in a cover letter (Figure 10.6).

■ Understand the Reader's Responsibilities

Once a writer's ideas are developed and in place, readers should turn their attention to the bottom level of the composition pyramid, to matters of style and grammar. At this stage, details are important: Is this the best word to use? Would this sentence be easier to follow if it was broken into two sentences? Which spelling is correct—*Freedman* or *Friedman*? Are citations handled consistently? Should this question mark precede or follow the quotation mark? The *grammatically correct reader* evaluates and makes judgments about the writer's work. This reader may simply indicate with a mark of some sort that there's a problem in a sentence or paragraph, or may even correct the writer's work. Figure 10.7 is a list of questions a reader should ask of a final draft.

---

1. What is your unique perspective on your issue?
2. To what extent do the words and phrases you use reflect who you believe your readers are?
3. Does your style of citation reflect accepted conventions for academic writing?
4. What do you think is working best?
5. What specific aspect of the essay are you least satisfied with at this time?

FIGURE 10.6 The Writer's Cover Letter: Final Drafts

1. How does the writer go about contributing a unique perspective on the issue?

2. To what extent does the writer use words and phrases that are appropriate for the intended audience?

3. To what extent does the style of citation reflect accepted conventions for academic writing?

4. What do you think is working best?

5. What specific aspect of the essay are you least satisfied with at this time?

FIGURE 10.7 A Reader's Questions: Final Drafts

■ Analyze a Near-Final Draft

Now read Taylor's near-final draft and write a paragraph detailing what she can do to strengthen it. Again, you will see that Taylor has made substantial changes. She compares Morrison's book of photographs to a Spike Lee documentary that she watched with her class. As you read the essay, focus on the bottom level of the composition pyramid: Does the writer use appropriate language? Does she adhere to appropriate conventions for using and citing sources? (See the Appendix for information on MLA and APA formats.)

Tasha Taylor   Taylor 1
Professor Winters
English 111
December 5, 20—
                    Memory through Photography
          Memory is such an integral part of what it is to be human,   *1*
yet it is something so often taken for granted: people assume that
their memories are accurate to protect themselves from the harsh
realities of the atrocities committed by ordinary people. Even the
pictures used to represent the much-celebrated civil rights movement give us a false sense of security and innocence. For example,
the Ku Klux Klan is most often depicted by covered faces and burning crosses; the masks allow us to remove ourselves from responsibility. Few could describe Rosa Parks's connection to the civil

rights movement before her legendary refusal to give up her seat in December 1955, which led to the Montgomery Bus Boycott (for example, the fact that she had been a member of the NAACP since 1943). Few recognize the years of struggle that existed between the 1954 *Brown v. Board of Education* decision and the actual desegregation of schools. Few consider the fate of Elizabeth Eckford after the federal troops sent to protect her and the other members of the Little Rock Nine had left Central High or the months of abuse (physical and emotional) that they endured in the name of integration. What most people know is limited to the textbooks they read in school or the captions under photographs that describe where a particular event occurred.

It is important, then, to analyze what is remembered, and even more important to recognize what is forgotten: to question why it is that it is forgotten, what that says about society today, how far it has come and how much it has unwittingly fallen back into old patterns of prejudice and ignorance. The discrepancies in cultural memory are due more to society's desire to remember itself in the best light and protect itself from the reality of its brutality and responsibility. Such selective memory only temporarily heals the wounds of society; lack of awareness does not cause healing. Although there have been many recent moves to increase awareness, they are tainted by unavoidable biases and therefore continue to perpetuate a distorted memory.

Images play a central role in the formation of cultural memory because people can point to photographs and claim them as concrete evidence: "Images entrance us because they provide a powerful illusion of owning reality. If we can photograph reality or paint or copy it, we have exercised an important kind of power" (Kolker 3). A picture of black and white children sitting at a table together is used to reinforce the cultural perception that the problems of racism are over, that they have all been fixed.

In her book *Remember*, Toni Morrison strives to revitalize the memory of school integration through photographs. The book is dedicated to Denise McNair, Carole Robertson, Addie Mae Collins, and Cynthia Wesley, the four girls killed in the 16th Street Baptist Church bombing in 1963. Morrison writes: "Things are better now. Much, much better. But remember why and please remember us" (72). The pictures are of black and white children happily eating together, solemnly saluting the flag together, and holding hands. The photographs of the four murdered girls show them peacefully and innocently smiling as if everything really is better now. In reality, according to the United States Bureau of Alcohol, Tobacco and Firearms, between 1995 and 1997 there were 162 incidents of arson or bombing in African American houses of worship. There are a few images of people protesting integration, but they are also consistent with the cultural memory (protesters are shown simply holding signs and yelling, not beating and killing innocent children). Finally, the captions are written in a child's voice. Yet it is not a child's voice at all; it is merely a top-down view of children that serves to perpetuate a distorted cultural memory.

The photographs used to suggest how things are much, much better now are misleading. For example, the last photograph, taken through a bus window, is of a black girl and a white girl holding hands; the bus was transporting them to an integrated school. The caption reads: "Anything can happen. Anything at all. See?" (Morrison 71). It is a very powerful image of how the evil of Jim Crow and segregation exists in a distant past and the nation has come together and healed. However, Morrison neglects to point out that the picture was taken in Boston, not in the Deep South, the heart of racism. Children holding hands in Boston is much less significant than if they were in Birmingham, where that action would be concrete evidence of how far we as a nation have come.

Morrison also glorifies Martin Luther King Jr. and Rosa Parks, pointing to them as epitomizing the movement. Unfortunately, she perpetuates the story that one needs to be special or somehow larger than life to effect change. Paul Rogat Loeb writes in *Soul of a Citizen*:

> Once we enshrine our heroes, it becomes hard for mere mortals to measure up in our eyes. . . . In our collective amnesia we lose the mechanisms through which grassroots social movements of

Taylor 4

the past successfully shifted public sentiment and challenged
entrenched institutional power. Equally lost are the means by
which their participants managed to keep on, sustaining their
hope and eventually prevailing in circumstances at least as
difficult as those we face today. (36, 38)

Placing a select few on pedestals and claiming them as next-
to-divine heroes of the movement does society a disservice; people
fail to realize that ordinary people can serve as agents of change.

Morrison's book ignores the thousands of ordinary people who
risked their lives for the cause to bring about equality. The caption
beside the picture of Rosa Parks in *Remember* reads "Because if I
ever feel helpless or lonely I just have to remember that all it takes
is one person" (Morrison 62). Ironically, Morrison gives credit for
the Montgomery Bus Boycott to one person, ignoring the months
of planning that involved dozens of planners. Even the photograph
presents Rosa Parks in a position of power. It is a low-angle shot up
at Parks that makes her appear larger than life and authoritative. The
photographs of Martin Luther King Jr. also further the impression
of power with a close-up shot of his face as he stands above thousands of participants in the March on Washington. Although these
photographs were selected to perpetuate the hero illusion, it is more
inspiring to remember the ordinary people who took a stand and were
able to accomplish extraordinary feats because of their dedication
and persistence rather than to glorify extraordinary people who were
destined for greatness.

In contrast, Spike Lee's 1998 documentary titled *4 Little Girls*
is a stirring depiction of the lives and deaths of the girls who died in
the 1963 16th Street Baptist Church bombing. In his film, Spike Lee
looks behind what some would call "societal amnesia" to disclose
the harsh realities of the civil rights movement. Lee interviews family
members and friends of the murdered girls, revealing the pain and
anger that they grapple with more than forty years after the tragedy.
Lee includes not only images of the bombed church but also the
charred and nearly unrecognizable bodies of the murdered girls.

Taylor 5

These disturbing images underscore the reality of their deaths without appearing sensationalist. The film does an exceptional job of reminding the viewer of the suffering and mindless hate that were prevalent during the civil rights movement.

However, the documentary is also biased. For instance, the girls were not little; they were fourteen, not really little girls. Lee chose to describe them as little to elicit emotion and sympathy for their tragic deaths. They were victims. They had not marched through the streets demanding equality; instead, Denise McNair, Carole Robertson, Addie Mae Collins, and Cynthia Wesley were simply attending Sunday school and were ruthlessly murdered. Victimizing Denise, Carole, Addie Mae, and Cynthia is not detrimental to the cultural memory in and of itself. The problem is that the victimization of the four girls is expanded to encompass the entire black community, undermining the power and achievement of the average black citizen. We need to remember the people who struggled to gain employment for blacks in the labor movement of the 1940s and 1950s that initiated the civil rights movement.

One can argue that despite the presence of misleading images in Spike Lee's film and Toni Morrison's book, at least some of the story is preserved. Still, it is easy to fall victim to the cliché: Those who do not remember history are doomed to repeat it. Just because a portion of the story is remembered, it does not mean that society is immune to falling back into its old habits. This cultural amnesia not only perpetuates the injustices of the time but leaves open the possibility that these atrocities can occur again. If people believe the government can simply grant black equality, then they may believe that it can also take it away. In essence memory is about power: "The struggle of man against power is the struggle of memory against forgetting" (Kundera). Those who are remembered hold power over the forgotten. Their legacy is lost and so is their ability to inspire future generations through their memory.

9

10

Taylor 6

Works Cited

4 Little Girls. Dir. Spike Lee. 40 Acres & A Mule Filmworks, 1997. Film.

Kolker, Robert. *Film, Form, and Culture*. New York: McGraw Hill, 1998. Print.

Kundera, Milan. *QuotationsBook*. QuotationsBook, 2007. Web. 22 Nov. 20—.

Loeb, Paul Rogat. *Soul of a Citizen: Living with Conviction in a Cynical Time*. New York: St. Martin's/Griffin, 1999. Print.

Morrison, Toni. *Remember*. Boston: Houghton Mifflin, 2004. Print.

United States. Dept. of the Treasury. Bureau of Alcohol, Tobacco and Firearms. "Arson and Explosives: Incidents Report 1994." *ATF. gov*. US Dept. of Justice, 1995. Web. 15 Nov. 20—.

Reading as a Writer

1   What would you say is Taylor's argument?

2. To what extent does she provide transitions to help you understand how her analysis supports her argument?

3. To what extent does she integrate quotations appropriately into the text of her argument?

4. To what extent does the style of citation reflect accepted conventions for academic writing?

5. If Taylor had more time to revise, what would you suggest she do?

FURTHER SUGGESTIONS FOR PEER EDITING GROUPS

Monitoring your own writing group can help ensure that the group is both providing and receiving the kinds of responses the members need. Here is a list of questions you might ask of one another after a session:

- What topics were discussed?

- Were most questions and comments directed at the level of ideas? Structure? Language?

- Were topics always brought up with a question or a comment?
- Who initiated talk more frequently—the writer or the readers?
- What roles did different group members play?
- Did each author open with specific questions or concerns?
- Did the readers begin by giving specific reactions?

After answering these questions, identify two things that are working well in your group. Then identify two things that you could improve. How would you go about making those improvements?

When we asked our students what they thought contributed to effective conversation in their writing groups, here is what they told us:

- honest and spontaneous expression
- free interaction among members
- high levels of personal involvement
- members' commitment to insight and change
- the sense that self-disclosure is safe and highly valued
- members' willingness to take responsibility for the group's effectiveness
- members' belief that the group is important
- members' belief that they are primary agents of help for one another
- members' focus on communication within the group over other discussions

Other Methods of Inquiry
Interviews and Focus Groups

Sometimes to advance your argument you may need to do original research. By **original research**, we mean using primary sources of evidence you gather yourself. (Another common term for this type of investigation is *field research*.) Remember that primary sources of evidence include firsthand or eyewitness accounts like those found in letters or newspapers, or in research reports in which the researcher explains his or her impressions of a particular phenomenon—for example, gender relations in classroom interactions. (In contrast, a secondary source is an analysis of information contained in primary sources.)

The type of original research we discuss in this chapter relies on people—interviewees and members of focus groups—as primary sources of information. To inquire into gender dynamics in college science classrooms, then, you might conduct interviews with young women to understand their perceptions of how gender affects teaching. Or you might convene a focus group to put a variety of perspectives into play on questions about gendered teaching practices. The pages that follow present strategies for conducting interviews and setting up focus groups that can generate multiple responses to your research questions.

When you conduct research, keep in mind that you are not setting out to prove anything; instead, the process of inquiry will enable you to answer the questions *you* ask, address problems, and move readers to rethink their positions. Good critical readers know that the arguments they produce as writers are influenced by what they choose to discuss and how they construe the evidence they provide.

Although there is really no way to avoid the limitations of writing from one point of view, writers can provide readers with multiple sources of information so that they can make their own judgments about what to believe or not believe. In fact, this is the argument we make above in studying inequities in education. Relying on a single source of data will inevitably limit your field of vision. Multiple sources of information add complexity and texture to your analysis, conveying to readers the thoroughness of your approach.

WHY DO ORIGINAL RESEARCH?

We can think of four reasons (all of which overlap to some extent) why you might do original research for a writing class.

To increase your ability to read critically.   When you do original research, you learn, at a basic and pragmatic level, how the studies you consult in a researched argument come into being. You're on the ground floor of knowledge making.

As a critical reader, you know it's important to ask questions like these: What is the source of the author's claim? Why should I believe the author? What is the source of the author's authority? What are the possible counterarguments? When you are doing original research, you are in the position of that author, with a real stake in establishing your own authority. By coming to understand what it takes to establish your own authority, you are in a better position to evaluate how effectively other researchers establish theirs.

Let's say your research question concerns gender differences in math education. You might read a study that asserts that girls and young women are being shortchanged in math classes, impeding their ability to go into math-related fields. You would want to ask about the nature of the data used to support this claim. If the author of the study states that 56 percent of the female students interviewed said they were discouraged from going into math-related fields, you might wonder where the figure of 56 percent came from. How many girls and young women were interviewed? How was this sample selected? What were the students asked? Questions like these inform your own use of interviews and focus groups.

To increase your own research skills.   Doing original research broadens your own range of research methods. By developing a repertoire of research methods, you will be better able to explore questions that may be too complex to answer by examining texts alone. One scholar put it this way: "I couldn't see what a text was doing without looking at the worlds in which these texts served as significant activities."* After all, it is one thing to read a research report and understand its purpose, its intended

---

*C. Bazerman, *Shaping Written Knowledge: The Genre and Activity of the Scientific Article in Science* (Madison: University of Wisconsin Press, 1988), p. 4.

audience, the nature of its claims, and the like. But it is quite another to watch scientists at work and begin to understand how they have come to know what they know. The discovery of DNA, for example, was the result of an arduous process that involved much risk, collaboration, chance, error, and competition. The neat structure of a scientific report could mislead you into thinking that science is a linear process that begins with a question, moves on to an experiment, and ends with an answer. Real research is messier than that. Original research takes us behind the words we read, introducing levels of complexity.

To broaden your scope of inquiry.   Doing original research may also broaden the scope of your inquiry. First, it is useful to use different research methods than the ones you are accustomed to using. Learning to interview and run focus groups, at the very least, can give you insight and practice for nonacademic applications—market research, for example. Second, it can make you aware of how people outside your field address the questions you raise. Consider, for example, the different perspectives an educator, a sociologist, and an economist would bring to the question of educational inequities. An educator might study educational inequities as a curricular problem and therefore analyze the content of different curricula within and across schools. A sociologist might visit students' homes, noting the presence or absence of books or asking parents how they go about preparing their children for school. An economist might examine income levels in both wealthy and impoverished neighborhoods. The point is that each field brings its own perspective to a problem, adding complexity and richness to your own discussion of that problem.

To make a unique contribution to a conversation of ideas.   Finally, doing original research affords you the opportunity to make a unique contribution to a conversation of ideas. Instead of relying exclusively on texts others have written as evidence for your claims, you can offer your own data to address a question or problem, data that others do not have available. For instance, if you wanted to examine claims that primary school teachers pay more attention to boys in class than to girls, you could review the relevant literature and then add to that literature a study that systematically analyzes the ways in which teachers in different classrooms treat boys and girls.

GETTING STARTED: WRITING AN IDEA SHEET

The purpose of writing an **idea sheet** is to help you explore not just what you might want to learn by conducting research but why you are interested in a particular topic, issue, or problem. An idea sheet is a form of exploratory writing that can serve as the basis for a more formal research proposal.

We encourage our students to jot down some ideas about the topic they are interested in, why they find the topic of interest, and why it might be compelling to others. Moreover, we want them to answer the kinds of questions we have addressed throughout this book: What's at stake in conducting this research? What other related ideas compete for our attention and limit our ability to see what you think is important, and why?

To compose an idea sheet, you should follow these steps:

Step One: Explain your topic so that others can understand what you want to study.

Step Two: Detail the personal reasons why you are interested in the topic.

Step Three: Identify what is at issue—what is open to dispute for you.

Step Four: Describe for whom this issue might be significant or important.

Step Five: Formulate an issue-based question.

It is important to discuss an issue in the context of a current situation, so that readers will understand why you are raising a particular issue. As a writer, you will need to familiarize yourself with what people are talking and writing about. What is on people's minds? What is at issue for people? What about for you? What do your readers need to know about? In turn, you will need to help readers understand why they are reading your essay and fulfill their expectations that what you are writing about is both relevant and timely.

Formulating an issue-based question can help you think through what you might be interested in writing about and guide your research. As we suggest in Chapter 4, a good question develops out of an issue, some fundamental tension that you identify within a conversation. Your issue-based question should be specific enough to guide inquiry into what others have written and help you accomplish the following:

- Clarify what you know about the issue and what you still need to know.
- Guide your inquiry with a clear focus.
- Organize your inquiry around a specific issue.
- Develop an argument, rather than simply collecting information by asking "how," "why," "should," or the "extent to which something is true or not."
- Consider who your audience is.
- Determine what resources you have, so that you can ask a question that you will be able answer with the resources available to you.

A STUDENT'S ANNOTATED IDEA SHEET

Dan Grace   Grace 1
Professor Greene
English 320
March 10, 20—

Idea Sheet for Parent/Child Autism Study

The student explains the purpose of his research and begins to explain the method he would use to get the information he is interested in.

I would like to study the parent-child home interaction/ dynamic between an individual with autism and his or her parents in the student's home. I would like to research different intervention programs and interview the parents about their own programs with their child, both home- and school-implemented, as well as observe the parent-child interactions in both school work and natural daily activities such as conversations and meals. I would do this by spending at least fifty hours with the student with autism in his or her home, both individually with him or her and also observing his or her parental interactions. I would like to see how these interactions compare with the research performed in this field.

He explains why he is interested in this subject and this provides a rationale for what he will study.

The summer after my freshman year, I worked at a school for children with autism for six weeks. I also worked at a research facility that looked into the effects high vitamin and mineral diets had on individuals with autism. The next summer, and during several breaks in school, I worked at the school for a total of fifteen to twenty weeks. My experiences there have spurred an interest in autism and autism education. I've worked extensively in the classroom setting; however, I've never witnessed the home setting for anyone with autism. Also, I've heard many stories about parents and their different mindsets and levels of involvement with their children, but have never met any parents, except for one at the end of my first summer working at the school. I want to interact with a student outside of the classroom, as well as see the interactions between the student and his or her parents.

He casts his interest in a particular topic in terms of an issue that is perhaps more implicit than explicit. That is,

Children with autism lack the social, emotional, and cognitive (in many cases) skills that healthy individuals possess/have the potential to have. Early intervention is a very important thing in a child with autism's life, since it has been shown that early intervention can significantly help the child's social, emotional, and cognitive

1

2

3

Grace 2

he recognizes the importance of early intervention, but he is not altogether sure what that means in a child's everyday life.

The student provides a broad context for understanding autism and who else might be interested in this topic.

Finally, he formulates the topic as a series of questions that need to be answered.

development. Early intervention includes the parents as well. It is important for parents to interact with their children early and often, and to work with them to help them develop. Though the individual that I will be working with is already at the end of elementary school, it will still be useful to observe the parent-child interactions, as well as question the parents about what measures were taken early in the child's life.

This topic is important/significant for all those working with children with autism, as well as parents of children with autism. Autism is becoming ever more prevalent in this country, and the world, with more than one in every one hundred children being diagnosed with some form of autism spectrum disorder (ASD). The parents need to know how best to interact with, and better understand, their child.

4

How can parent-child interaction influence the development of a child with autism? This might be a vague question with many different directions in which to take it, but it is still a pertinent question. How might parental interaction in adolescence affect adolescent development? Why should parents work hard to interact with their children with autism? What are the benefits of early intervention? What are the long-term benefits of early intervention programs? What are the effects of good versus poor parental interaction? These questions need to be answered to fully understand the topic and research question.

5

WRITING A PROPOSAL

A **proposal** is a formal plan that outlines your objectives for conducting a research project, specifies the methods you intend to use, and describes the implications of your work. In its most basic form, a proposal is an argument that provides a rationale for conducting research and persuades readers that the research is worth pursuing. It is also a tool that helps guide you through various stages of the project. The most immediate benefit of writing a proposal is that through the act of writing—by setting forth an outline of your project—your thinking will become more focused and precise. And yet your thinking may change as you read more about your topic.

Typically, a research proposal should include four sections: introduction/purpose, review of relevant research, method, and implications. You may also want to include additional sections with materials that provide concrete support for your proposal—some of the tools that will help you get the job done. You should arrange your plan and use headings so that readers can find information quickly.

■ Describe Your Purpose

In the introduction, you should describe the purpose of your study and establish that the issue you want to study is relevant and timely. Then, briefly summarize how others have treated the issue you are focusing on in order to explain whether you are trying to fill a gap, correct a misconception, build upon and extend others' research, or test a hypothesis. As we point out throughout this book, it is important to help readers understand the context by retracing the conversation. After you provide some context to help readers understand the purpose of your study, you should then formulate the question that is motivating your research.

Finally, you should explain why you are interested in this issue area, why it is important, and what is at stake. Ask yourself why others should be interested in your effort to answer the question.

■ Review Relevant Research

Following the introduction, you should provide a review of the relevant research. For a proposal, you should demonstrate that you have a firm grasp of the issue as part of the argument you are making to justify your study. The more effectively you convince readers that you know the issue, the more persuasive your argument. Therefore, you will want to show that you have read widely, that you are aware of the most important studies conducted in your area of research, that you are also aware of current research within the past five years, and that you understand the strengths and limitations of your own approach.

More specifically, you can use your review to accomplish some of the following:

- Define a key term that is central to your study that others may not necessary agree upon.
- Discuss the history relevant to your research.
- Explain the strengths and limitations of different methodological approaches to answering similar research questions.
- Analyze the different theoretical approaches that authors have used to frame the issue (e.g., psychological, sociological, socioeconomic, racial).
- Identify trends in what researchers are finding or, perhaps, the lack of agreement.
- Point to more comprehensive reviews of research that others have written.

■ Define Your Method

In your method section, you should first explain how you will answer the research question motivating your study using the tools that are available. Some of the tools and strategies you might use include the following:

- conducting interviews or focus groups;
- taking notes;
- recording particular activities;
- doing background, historical, or archival work, and
- observing or coming to terms with your own impressions.

Since this is a proposal for research you will conduct, you should write this section in the future tense. "To answer the question(s) motivating this study, I will conduct interviews and focus groups and take detailed notes. . . ."

Second, describe how you plan to collect your data. You will need to tell readers whether or not you will audio-record interviews and/or focus groups, and, if so, that you will transcribe the data. If you are taking notes, you will want to explain whether or not you plan to take notes during or after the session. Be sure to explain where you are conducting the interview or focus group. If you are observing classes, meetings, or some event, you will need to explain how often you will observe, for how long, and whether you will be taking notes or transcribing data.

Third, justify why you are using some methods of collecting data and not others. Discuss the appropriateness of these methods given your research question. Given the objectives you have set for yourself and the constraints of doing the research, are some methods better than others? How will the methods you have chosen to use enable you to answer your question(s)?

Finally, you should have some sense of how you will analyze the data you collect. That is, readers will expect that you have done more than simply read your transcripts from interviews and focus groups to form impressions. Therefore, you will want to explain the principles you will use to analyze the data in light of the research question(s) you are asking.

■ Discuss Your Implications

It may seem a little premature to talk about what you hope to find in your study, but it is important to address "So what?" to explain what you believe is the significance of your study. Place your argument in the context of the conversation you want to join, and explain how your study can contribute to that conversation. Write about how your study will build upon, challenge, or extend the studies in your area of research. And finally, identify what you believe will be new about your findings.

▪ Include Additional Materials That Support Your Research

Depending on your instructor and the level of formality of your proposal, you may be asked to include additional materials that reveal other dimensions of your research. Those materials may include (1) an annotated bibliography, (2) scripts of the questions you plan to ask in interviews and focus groups, (3) the consent forms you will ask participants to sign, and (4) approval from your university's Institutional Review Board (IRB).

Annotated bibliography.   An **annotated bibliography** is a list of sources (arranged alphabetically by author) that you plan to consult and use in your research paper. Typically you provide a citation (author, date, title of source, and publication information) and a short summary of the source. You can present all your sources in one long list or organize them by type of source (books, journals, and so forth). See pages 148–150 in Chapter 6 for a more complete description of how to write an annotated bibliography and an example.

Questions you plan to ask.   Including a list (or lists) of the questions you expect to ask those you plan to interview or survey will help focus your thinking. What personal information do you need to know? What information do you need to know about your issue? What opinions and recommendations would be helpful? Each list should include at least five good questions but can include many more. A sample set of questions, focusing on parents of homeless children, appears in Figure 11.1.

Consent forms.   Whenever you plan to solicit information in an interview or focus group, you need to get permission from the interviewees or participants to use their comments and contributions in your research paper. The Institutional Review Board on your campus probably has a model for writing a consent form that you can use, but we have included a sample consent form for an interview in Figure 11.2.

IRB approval.   Your school's Institutional Review Board ensures that researchers hold high ethical standards in the research they conduct and protect the rights of "human subjects" who participate in a study. It is

---

Sample Interview Questions

Parent(s)

1. a. Describe your current living and family situation (parents, siblings, how long homeless, where living, where child attends school).

   b. Describe your child.

   c. Describe your relationship with your child.

2. a. Do you think homelessness is affecting your child's schooling?

   b. If so, tell me how (grades, friends, attendance, transportation).

3. Tell me about enrolling your child in school. What was the process like? Were there any problems? Conditions? Challenges?

4. a. Do you feel that your child's right to an education has been recognized?

   b. Why or why not? What experiences can you point to to support your answer?

5. Describe the relationship between your child and his or her teachers.

6. a. What types of support services is your child currently being offered in school and in the community?

   b. How effective are those services?

   c. How supportive of your child's educational and developmental growth do you feel your child's school has been?

   d. What about the Center for the Homeless?

   e. Do you have any recommendations for these sources of help or requests for other types of help or services for your child that are not currently offered?

7. How do you envision your child's future?

FIGURE 11.1 Sample Interview Questions

possible that research conducted for a class will not require IRB approval. You should contact the appropriate office (for example, the Office for Research) on your campus for details and exceptions.

■ Establish a Timeline

To write a proposal, you'll need to draw up a schedule for your research and identify when you expect to complete specific tasks. For example, when will you do the following?

- Submit proposal to Institutional Review Board (if necessary).
- Contact participants and get their commitments.
- Conduct interviews, focus groups, and the like.
- Compile an annotated bibliography.

Sample Interview Consent Form

You are invited to participate in a study of homelessness and education conducted by Mary Ronan, an undergraduate at the University of Notre Dame, during the next few months. If you decide to participate, you will

1. provide up to two interviews with the researcher,

2. allow the researcher to use excerpts from the interviews in publications about research with the understanding that your identity will not be revealed at any time.

Participation is completely voluntary. You may choose to stop participating at any time prior to completion of the project. Should you have any questions at any time, you are welcome to contact the researcher by phone or e-mail. Your decision to participate will have no effect on or prejudice your future relationship with the University of Notre Dame. One possible benefit of participating in the study is that you will have the opportunity to learn about the implications of homelessness on education.

If you are willing to participate in this research, please read and sign the consent form below. You will be given a copy of this form to keep.

CONSENT FORM

I agree to participate in all of the procedures above. I understand that my identity will be protected during the study and that others will not have access to the interviews I provide. I also understand that my name will not be revealed when data from the research are presented in publications. I have read the above and give the researcher, Mary Ronan, permission to use excerpts from transcripts of tapes without identifying me as the writer or speaker.

_____

Date   Signature

_____

Signature of Researcher
[Telephone number]/[E-mail address]

FIGURE 11.2   Sample Interview Consent Form

- Transcribe the data.
- Analyze the data.
- Draft an introduction, methods, and findings.

This timeline should include the dates when you expect to finish the proposal, when you will conduct interviews and focus groups, when you expect to have a draft, and when you will complete the project. Be realistic about how long it will actually take to complete the different stages of collecting data and writing. Anticipate that events will prevent everything from going exactly as planned. People cannot always meet with you when you would like them to, and you may have to change your own schedule. Therefore, be sure to contact participants well in advance of the time when you would like to speak with them in interviews or focus groups.

Steps to Writing a Proposal

1 **Describe your purpose in the introduction.** Summarize your issue, describing how it has led you to the question motivating your research.

2 **Review relevant research.** Show that you are aware of the most important studies conducted in your area of research, identify points of agreement and disagreement, and define key terms.

3 **Define your method.** What tools and strategies are you planning to use? Why are they appropriate and sufficient for your purposes?

4 **Discuss your implications.** What is the context of the conversation you are entering? What significant information do you expect your study to uncover?

5 **Include additional materials that support your research.** These may include an annotated bibliography, a series of interview questions, and blank consent forms.

AN ANNOTATED STUDENT PROPOSAL

Our student Laura Hartigan submitted a formal proposal for a study of different types of writing. Hartigan's proposal was exceptionally well prepared, thorough, and thoughtful, and she included a number of additional materials: a script of questions for focus groups with students; sample questions for the teacher and students she planned to interview; and consent forms. We reprint only the main part of her proposal—the part that includes a brief overview of the conversation about different modes of writing, her aims for conducting her study, methods, and implications sections—for you to consider as a model for proposal writing. A more complete example would include a separate review of relevant research. Notice how Hartigan summarizes her issue, explains how it motivated the study she proposes, formulates a set of guiding research questions, and helps readers understand why her research is important, particularly in the implications she draws.

 To view Laura Hartigan's completed paper, with guidelines for a presentation poster, visit **macmillanhighered.com/frominquiry3e**.

Laura Hartigan   Hartigan 1
Professor Greene
English 385
March 28, 20—

Proposal for Research: The Affordances of Multimodal,
Creative, and Academic Writing

The student
retraces the
recent, and
important,
conversation
about writing
and alternative
conceptions
that challenge
some widely held
assumptions.

Researchers (Hughes, 2009; Vasudevan, Schultz & Bateman, 2010) have called attention to the unique ways that writing can foster student learning and have for some time now argued that teachers in elementary and high schools should give students more opportunities to write fiction and poetry using image, music, and text to express themselves. Within the last decade, even more alternative modes of writing have gained prominence. Researchers (Hughes, 2009; Hull & Katz, 2006) argue that "multimodal digital storytelling" provides students with ways to help them engage more deeply with their written work. Digital storytelling in particular enables students to examine their experiences by writing personal narratives in which they confront key turning points in their lives and the challenges they face. In turn, they can use images, music, and voice-over to amplify and give meaning to their written stories. Allowing for what researchers call "new literate spaces" creates the opportunity for multiple modes of learning, understanding, and collaboration that challenge the limited ways that students use writing as a mode of learning in school (Hughes, 2009; Hull & Katz, 2006). Students may learn to write persuasive essays, but they also need opportunities to learn about themselves and use their writing as a way to create changes in their lives. Thus researchers urge educators to reform curricular and pedagogical practices to help students use writing to help them develop a sense of identity and ownership of their writing, to see the decision-making power they have as individuals.

She summarizes
recent studies and
evidence supporting
the value of
alternative modes
of writing. But she
also identifies a gap
in the argument
writing researchers
make.

When they argue that multimodal, digital literacy practices have a place in the standard curriculum, researchers (Hall, 2011; Hughes, 2009; Hull & Katz, 2006; Ranker, 2007; Vasudevan et al., 2010) provide evidence to show how youth grow and develop, become more confident learners, and use what they learn in and out of school. This is particularly true when youth have opportunities to reflect on their lives and use multiple literacies to give meaning to their

1

2

Hartigan 2

experience. They can use image, music, and text to confront how things in their lives look and feel, to examine the decisions they have made, and to consider the decisions they might make in confronting hardship, discrimination, and loss. However, most research fails to provide a satisfactory or compelling rationale for why new literacies *should* be used in the classroom (Alverman, Marshall, McLean, Huddleston, Joaquin, 2012; Binder & Kotsopoulos, 2011; Hull and Katz, 2006; Ranker, 2007) or how the seemingly unique gains could be positively integrated into the standard curriculum. The lack of assessment focusing on how academic and new literacies affect one another reveals a flaw in the conclusions drawn from studies that neglect the realities of teaching in K-12 schools. Increased emphasis on standards, testing, and accountability seem to preclude the kind of focus that new literacies seem to require. Thus, if educators are to allow for "new literate spaces," they need to know how to do so within the standard curriculum.

Recognizing this gap, she explores what she sees is a common problem in a number of studies.

Specifically, few researchers explore students' sense of their literate identity in academic and creative writing or how context matters in how students feel about themselves and their writing. While most researchers (Binder & Kostopoulos, 2011; Hughes, 2009; Hull & Katz, 2006; Vasudevan et al., 2010) refer to what they call "the mono-literacy landscape" of schools, the limits of literate experience to print, none really compare the opportunities that academic writing gives students versus, say, creative writing before, during, and after the study. That is, focusing only on the value of digital storytelling, for example, or creative writing is not sufficient to effect reform in school. Are there really significant differences between different kinds of writing? What are these differences? Such a gap in research seems to necessitate an inquiry into a student's emergent sense of authorship in different forms of composing, even academic writing in and out of school. Therefore, I propose a study that will provide an analysis of both academic and creative writing in an after-school program that helps children develop as learners through tutoring and enrichment. One implication of my research would be to show why educators might expand the types of literate experiences that students have in school.

In turn, this gap serves as a rationale for conducting her own study. She also points to the possible implications for doing the study she proposes.

3

Having defined the problem, she describes the aims of her study.

In order to investigate the possible differences between multimodal, creative, and standardized academic writing, this proposed study aims to explore (a) the unique opportunities afforded by the

4

multiple means of expression inherent in digital storytelling, (b) how
and if these opportunities create an alternative space for the growth of
empowered literate identities and a sense of agency, (c) the extent to
which writing supports a student's development of an authorial voice,
and (d) why schools should be concerned with the affordances given
to the development of a student's written voice and individual identity
by including multimodal digital storytelling in the curriculum. The
study focuses on analyzing the students' sense of authorship in both
their academic and creative assignments. To what extent can standard
academic and creative multimodal expression help students develop
an authorial identity and the skills they need to flourish in and out of
school? Considering the current atmosphere of accountability and federal
testing (Hull & Katz, 2006), it is important to ask what role multimodal
composing can play in the standard and narrow curriculum.

She reformulates the four aims of her study as questions to guide her inquiry.

Method

To address the aims of my study, I will conduct interviews and
focus groups to examine students' attitudes about writing in and out
of school at the Crusoe Community Learning Center (CCLC) in a small
midwestern city. Interviews and focus groups will enable me to discover
student attitudes and feelings about writing across the in-school and
out-of-school contexts in order to develop some insight into how
writing can enable or disengage students. I will also take field notes
taken by a participant-observer in the afterschool creative writing
workshop to develop a picture of the after-school classroom dynamics.

She describes the approach she will take to answer her questions.

5

Context

The CCLC is an off-campus educational initiative of a nearby
private university in partnership with the surrounding neighborhood
residents. Serving around 600 participants in the regular programming,
the CCLC also partners with the community schools in the surrounding
area with program outreach connecting to nearly 8,000 additional youths
throughout the year. Located in a high-traffic, low-income neighborhood,
the CCLC's mission centers around promoting hospitality, education,
partnership, civic engagement, and sustainability in the surrounding
area and all the participants. Organized around operating as a learning
center and gathering space, the CCLC fosters relationships with the
students, the surrounding residents, and the city's universities in a safe,

To help orient readers, she explains where her study will take place.

6

Hartigan 4

collaborative atmosphere. Classes and programming range from English as a New Language (ENL) to financial literacy, entrepreneurship, basic computing, and one-on-one tutoring for area children conducted by college volunteers.

She identifies the specific class that she will focus on in her research and why the context for conducting this study makes sense.

The creative writing class and the CCLC's curricular environment will provide an appropriate population and unique space to explore the possible affordances between creative and academic writing. With the after-school programming divided in weekly, day-by-day activities centered on enrichment, academic tutoring, and creative writing, the CCLC's after-school context is inherently connected to the student's school context. Thus the CCLC's efforts to help students with their day-to-day school work and also offer enrichment unique to an after-school program can enrich my understanding of the way students' contexts (in school and after school) influence how they see themselves as writers.

7

Participants

Importantly, she describes who will participate in the study and why she has chosen this particular teacher and class. Note that at this preliminary stage, she offers a brief sketch of the teacher and her credentials. However, she has not yet met the students.

At the CCLC, I will focus on Ms. Smith's class. Ms. Smith is a former fourth-grade teacher serving the center as a full-time AmeriCorps member. As an AmeriCorps member, Ms. Smith works in a federal program funded by the state of Indiana for a full-time forty-hour week at the CCLC. Taking place every Wednesday, the creative writing class centers around brainstorming, drafting, and publishing the student work for display inside the center and on a developing Web log. I have chosen this specific class and student population because it offered the opportunity to talk to students about their school and after-school writing experiences alongside the physical creative artifacts they created in Ms. Smith's class. Due to the participants' weekly experience of academic tutoring and creative class time, the choice was based on the wide range of writing activities that could be probed by the broad, experience-based focus of the question script.

8

Data Collection Procedure and Analysis

She explains the methods she will use to collect the information she needs to answer her research questions and, importantly, notes

I will conduct focus groups and interviews with the students in Ms. Smith's class over the course of three weeks. To obtain parental consent in order to conduct the focus groups and subsequent interviews, I will e-mail consent forms requesting each student's participation in my research. I will do so two weeks prior to the study's

9

Hartigan 5

start in order to provide the necessary time for the forms to be
sent home and signed by the parents. (For the complete list
of questions, see Appendix A.) Upon receiving confirmation
from Ms. Smith that the consent forms had been completed,
I can then conduct focus groups and interviews with the
participating students.

    I will audio-record the focus groups and interviews.
Following the end of each session, I will transcribe the
recordings. Though I will not take notes during the focus
groups and interviews in order to maintain total engagement
with the participants, I will type a series of reflections and
field notes after the completion of each audio-recorded
session. Following the completion of the transcriptions, I
will also take more notes to identify the themes that emerge
in both interviews with individual children and in the focus
groups.

    After analyzing student responses, I will construct
several categories to explore the CCLC participants' sense
of self and authorial identity across contexts: safe spaces,
expressing interest and meaningful message, and ownership.

Implications

    Though many unique and compelling findings support
a pedagogical shift toward new literacies, researchers
(Vasudevan et al., 2010) tend to ignore the impact of a
student's outside knowledge, experience, and contexts
for writing. Moreover, without clearly understanding the
differences and similarities between academic writing and
multimodal writing, educators may not see the importance
of including alternative modes of literacy in the standard
curriculum. Hughes (2009) notes that the multimodal
assignments and digital media in her research helped students
engage more deeply with language and their own personal
sense of command over their written work. The need to explore
the changing materiality of texts figures as Hughes's intriguing
concern due to its impact on the ways students construct
meaning in what they write. Hughes frames performance "as

10

11

12

a vehicle for exploration and learning, rather than as a fixed product to be rehearsed and delivered as a final event" (p. 262) that works in tandem with (not in isolation from) literacy practices. Digital media allowed for the students to become what Hughes termed "co-creators," which helped students move beyond simply observing and analyzing poetry as a generally traditional and boring academic topic. However, the shift from print culture to new, performative media has yet to be reflected in classroom culture.

She also reminds readers of a significant gap in current research.

Sharpening the ideas drawn from the conclusions of Hughes (2009) points to the necessity of documenting the development of a student's voice and presence in multimodal, digital, and academic writing. In essence, research must avoid implying that one form of literacy is somehow more advantageous to the other without also looking at how context influences the ways students feel about themselves and what they write. To address this gap, my study will analyze the differences, and perhaps similarities, in how students develop and perceive their authorial presence and power in both kinds of writing — multimodal and academic — and the influence of context. After all, the mode of writing may not be as significant as the extent to which children feel they have a safe space place to write, where they can take risks without being afraid that their peers and teacher will criticize them. They also need to know that they have ownership of their writing as a means of expression and performance of who they are, who they imagine themselves to be, and what they want for themselves in the future.

Moreover, after detailing how she will address her research questions above, she justifies the importance of her proposed study.

13

Working Bibliography

Alvermann, D., Marshall, J., McLean, C., Huddleston, A., Joaquin, J., et al. (2012). Adolescents' Web-based literacies, identity construction, and skill development. *Literacy Research and Instruction*, *51*(3), 179–195.

Binder, M., & Kotsopoulos, S. (2011). Multimodal literacy narratives: Weaving the threads of young children's identity through the arts. *Journal of Research in Childhood Education, 25*(4), 339–363.

Buckingham, D. (2007). Digital media literacies: Rethinking media education in the age of the Internet. *Research in Comparative and International Education, 2*(1), 43–55.

Hall, T. (2011). Designing from their own social worlds: The digital story of three African American young women. *English Teaching: Practice and Critique, 10*(1), 7–20.

Hughes, J. (2009). New media, new literacies and the adolescent learner. *E-Learning, 6*(3), 259–271.

Hull, G., & Katz, M. (2006). Crafting an agentive self: Case studies of digital storytelling. *Research in the Teaching of English, 41*(1), 43–81.

Ranker, J. (2007). Designing meaning with multiple media sources: A case study of an eight-year-old student's writing processes. *Research in the Teaching of English, 41*(4), 402–434.

Vasudevan, L., Schultz, K., & Bateman, J. (2010). Rethinking composing in a digital age: Authoring literate identities through multimodal storytelling. *Written Communication, 27*(4), 442–468.

INTERVIEWING

An **interview** helps to answer the research question(s) motivating your study by gathering concrete details and stories from various people. In her book *Critical Ethnography: Method, Ethics, and Performance,* D. Soyini Madison offers this advice: "When you first begin to formulate questions, a useful exercise is to reread your research question or problem over several times and then ask yourself, 'If this is what I am to understand, then what is it that I need to know about it to answer the questions or address the problem?' You will then list everything of interest that comes to mind" (p. 31). It's certainly possible to conduct an interview by phone, especially if the interviewee is not local, but a face-to-face conversation, in which you can note physical details and body language, is preferable.

The ways writers incorporate interviews into their writing appears almost seamless, but keep in mind that a finished text hides the process that went into a successful interview. You don't see the planning that occurs. Writers have to make appointments with the people they interview, develop a script or list of questions before the interview, and test the questions beforehand to see if they're likely to lead to the kind of information they're seeking. In other words, the key to a successful interview is preparation. The following information should help you plan your interview and prepare you for writing down your results.

■ Plan the Interview

You'll want to do some preliminary research to identify people who can help you understand more about your topic: What kind of expertise or experience do they have? Then you have to contact them to find out if they are willing to be interviewed. You can send a brief e-mail or letter to initiate a conversation and then follow up with a phone call.

Based on our own experience, it is important to explain the project for participants in plain terms. In fact, when you contact potential participants, we suggest you do so in writing and address the following: Who are you? What are you doing, and why?

What will you do with what you find? What are possible benefits and risks? How will you assure confidentiality? How often and how long would you like to meet for interviews? and the like.

If you are planning to record the interview—always a wise idea—make sure each individual consents to being recorded. Then make the necessary arrangements. For example, you may need to reserve a room where you can conduct your interview without being disturbed. Try to choose a location that is convenient for the individual(s) you want to interview and familiar, such as a room in a public library.

It's important to set up appointments with people early. To keep on schedule, list the names of people who have agreed to be interviewed:

Interviewee 1:_____ Contacted? __ yes/no __ date:_____

Interviewee 2:_____ Contacted? __ yes/no __ date:_____

Interviewee 3:_____ Contacted? __ yes/no __ date:_____

■ Prepare Your Script

As you prepare the script of questions for your interview, keep coming back to the question motivating your research. To what extent will the questions you want to ask in your interview enable you to answer the broader question motivating your research? That is, what is the story you want to tell in your research? The more specific the questions you ask, the more specific the answers or story that the person you interview will tell.

Build rapport.   In any conversation, you want to build rapport and perhaps establish some common ground. More than getting information from someone, an interview can serve as a means to produce knowledge collaboratively and in ways that are mutually satisfying to you and the people you want to talk to. To create this kind of conversation, you can help the interviewee feel at ease and then move on to the issues you want to learn more about.

Start with nonthreatening questions.   For example, "How long have you been teaching writing?" "When did you start teaching writing in a hybrid classroom?" "What digital tools do you use to teach writing in a hybrid classroom?"

Ask open-ended questions.   Your questions should encourage the person you are interviewing to tell stories that will help you learn about your subject. This means phrasing questions in ways that avoid simple yes/no answers. For instance, you might ask for an explanation of how children at a homeless center can overcome the obstacles they face as opposed to asking something like this: "Do you think children can overcome the obstacles they face?" Asking for an explanation invites someone to explain the process by which overcoming obstacles is possible. In turn, you can ask specific questions such as the following: "Can you tell me about a specific instance to illustrate the extent to which a child can overcome the obstacles they face?" "Can you help me understand what made this possible?"

Avoid leading questions.   It may be tempting to ask leading questions to keep the conversation going in an interview or to fill in something that an individual implies but does not actually say. For example, "Do you think that the food industry has contributed to the problem of obesity?" "So are you saying that the government should formulate policies to regulate the industry?" In each case, the question supplies a possible answer. This is not appropriate. The questions you ask should allow the person you are interviewing to come to his or her own conclusions. Alternatively, you can ask: "Tell me more about what you are saying about the government's role." Similarly, try not to reinforce the answers that an interviewee gives, such as "That's what I was thinking." "That's great." "You're right." Reinforcing answers may indicate to an interviewee that there is a correct answer to the questions you are asking. Instead, you want to this person to explore his or her thoughts in an open, honest way.

Only share experiences occasionally.   Although we have suggested that conducting interviews can be like conversations, you should resist providing your own experiences and stories. Listen to answers and follow up with questions that encourage the person you are interviewing to elaborate.

Rehearse and then revise the script.   After you develop a script of questions, rehearse it with your writing group or a friend who can play the role of the person you want to interview. In doing so, you want to get a sense of how an interviewee is going to respond to your questions. The following questions can serve as a guide for assessing the interview and what you might change:

- What would you point to as a good example of an effective exchange?
- What questions helped you get concrete details to tell the story you wanted to tell?
- What would you point to as an example of an exchange that didn't go as well as you had hoped? How would you explain what happened?
- What questions would you rephrase if you were to do the interview again?
- To what extent do you feel that you might have lost some opportunities to follow up?
- Are there follow-up questions you should have asked?

After you answer these questions, revise the script to improve the content, order, and pacing of your questions.

▪ Conduct the Interview

On the day before the interview, contact the individual you plan to interview to confirm that he or she remembers the time of the interview and knows how to find the location where the interview will take place. Also, as you prepare for your interview, look over your questions and check your recorder to make sure it is functioning and has sufficient recording capacity for the interview. Be on time. Have a brief conversation to put this individual at ease and then ask this person to read and sign the consent form (see Figure 11.2).

Explain use of technology.   Explain why recording the interview is necessary ("I know what you're saying is really important, and I want to listen to you during your interview, not take notes as you speak. As a result, I will record our conversation so I can remember the important things you tell me").

Describe the interview process.   Explain what types of questions you will ask in the interview ("Today, I'm going to ask you questions about school and your family"). In addition, explain why you're interested in knowing this information ("I want to learn more about you and your family so I can understand what techniques for school, family, etc. are helpful for you").

Keep the interview conversational.   Use your script as a guide, but be flexible, treating the interview as a conversation. This might mean following the direction that the person you interview takes in answering a question. Listen. Don't interrupt. That is, you might ask what you think is a pointed question and this person might begin to tell a story that may not seem relevant. Let the person finish and patiently return to the questions you would like this person to address. You can also try rephrasing your question(s) to be more specific about the information you need. If you think at some point that the interviewee is implying something of special interest to you, ask for clarification.

Respect silence.   If any interviewee is silent for a while after you ask a question, be patient and don't immediately repeat or ask another question. The interviewee may need time to gather his or her thoughts or understand the question. After some time has passed, you can ask this person the question again or ask another question.

Keep track of important questions.   Toward the end of the interview, check your script for important questions you may have forgotten to ask. If there are several, try to ask only the most important ones in the time remaining. You can also ask to have a follow-up meeting to ensure that you have gotten the information you need.

Follow up after the interview is over. Continue getting to know the interviewee. Even though the formal interview is done, you still want this person to feel as though he or she matters to you. Just because this person has completed the interview doesn't mean that his or her relationship with the research project is over.

■ Make Sense of the Interview

Conducting an interview is only part of the challenge; you then have to make sense of what was said. That process involves four steps:

1. *Familiarize yourself with the conversation.* If you recorded the interview, listen to it a couple of times to become really familiar with what was said. Read through your notes several times too.

2. *Transcribe the interview.* Transcribing entails listening carefully to and typing up the audio recording of your interview in order to analyze the conversation. A transcript provides a more manageable way to identify key points in the interview, details that you might miss if you only listened to the interview, and stories that you might recount in your research. Keep in mind that transcribing an interview is an important part of doing this kind of research, but it is time-consuming. Therefore, you need to plan accordingly. An hour-long interview usually takes about three hours to transcribe.

3. *Analyze the interview.* Read through the interview again. Look for answers to the questions motivating your research, and look for recurring patterns or themes. Make a list of those ideas relevant to the issues you intend to focus on, especially evidence that might support your argument.

4. *Find one good source.* Using the themes you identify in your analysis as a guide, find one good source that relates to your interview in some way. Maybe your subject's story fits into an educational debate (for example, public versus private education). Or maybe your subject's story counters a common conception about education (that inner-city schools are hopelessly inadequate). You're looking for a source you can link to your interview in an interesting and effective way.

■ Turn Your Interview into an Essay

Try to lay out in paper, in paragraphs, the material you've collected that addresses the question motivating your research and the focus of your paper. In a first draft, you might take these steps:

1. State your argument, or the purpose of your essay. What do you want to teach your readers?

2. Provide evidence to support your thesis. What examples from your reading, observations, or interviews do you want to offer your readers? How do those examples illuminate your claim?

3. Place quotations from more than one source in as many paragraphs as you can, so that you can play the quotations off against one another. What is significant about the ways you see specific quotations "in conversation" with one another? How do these conversations between quotations help you build your own argument?

4. Consider possible counterarguments to the point you want to make.

5. Help readers understand what is at stake in adopting your position.

Steps to Interviewing

1 Plan the interview. After you've identified the people you might like to talk to, contact them to explain your project and set up appointments if they are willing to participate.

2 Prepare your script. Draft your questions, rehearse them with your classmates or friends, and then make revisions based on their responses.

3 Conduct the interview. Be flexible with your script as you go, making sure to take good notes even if you are recording the interview.

4 Make sense of the interview. Review the recording and your notes of the interview, transcribe the interview, analyze the transcript, and connect the conversation to at least one good source.

5 Turn your interview into an essay. State your argument, organize your evidence, use quotes to make your point, consider counterarguments, and help your readers understand what's at stake.

USING FOCUS GROUPS

Like interviews, focus groups can provide you with an original source of evidence to complement (or complicate, contradict, or extend) the evidence you find in books and articles. According to Bruce L. Berg in *Qualitative Research Methods for the Social Sciences,* a **focus group** "may be defined as an interview style designed for small groups . . . addressing a particular topic of interest or relevance to the group and the researcher." College administrators often speak with groups of students to understand the nature of a problem—for instance, whether writing instruction is as effective as it should be beyond a first-year writing course, or whether technology is used to best effect in classes across the curriculum. One advantage of a focus group, as opposed to an interview, is that once one person starts talking, others join in. It is generally easier to get a conversation going in a focus group than to get an interview started with a single person.

As a method, focus groups provide a supportive environment for discussing an issue that people may feel less comfortable talking about in an interview. The conversations that emerge in focus groups may also prompt individuals to tell stories that they may not have considered relevant or interesting until they hear others telling their stories. Finally, listening to a focus group discussion can give you a pretty good idea of individuals you may want to interview.

A typical focus group session is guided by a facilitator, or moderator. The moderator's job is much like the interviewer's: to draw out information from the participants on topics of importance to a given investigation. The informal atmosphere of the focus group is intended to encourage participants to speak freely and completely about their behaviors, attitudes, and opinions. Interaction among group members often takes the form of brainstorming, generating a larger number of ideas, issues, topics, and even solutions to problems than could be produced through individual conversations.

The following are several basic tasks necessary to orchestrating a focus group.

■ Select Participants for the Focus Group

Focus groups should consist of five to seven participants, in addition to you, the moderator. Think carefully about the range of participants you'll need in order to gather the information you're hoping to find. Depending on your issue, you might choose participants based on gender, ethnicity, major, year in school, living situation, or some other factor. Do you want a wide range of participants? Or do you want to control the focus of the conversation by looking at just one particular group of people? For instance, if you wanted to find out if technology is serving students' needs, would you talk only to people in the sciences? Or would you want a cross section of disciplines represented? Or if your question is whether colleges and universities should take race and ethnicity into consideration when selecting students from the applicant pool, would you limit participation to the admissions staff? Where should you look for input on the purpose of giving preference to minority students or the advantages of a diverse campus?

■ Plan the Focus Group

Planning is as important for a focus group as it is for an interview. Make specific arrangements with participants about the time and place of the focus group session, and be clear about how much time it will take, usually thirty to forty-five minutes. You should audio-record the session and take notes. Jot down important information during the session, and allow yourself time to make more extensive notes as soon as it is over. You will need to get permission from respondents to use the information they give you and ensure their anonymity. (In your essay, you can refer to participants by letter, number, or some other designation.) Make a sheet with your signature that spells this out clearly, and make sure all your participants sign it before the session. You should include a statement pointing out that people have the right not to participate. We have included sample consent forms in Figures 11.3 and 11.4.

Focus Group Consent Form

You are invited to participate in a study of academic writing at the university over the next four years. You were selected from a random sample of all first-year students. If you decide to participate, you will

1. provide the researcher with copies of the writing you complete for every class and the assignment, when available.

2. attend up to four focus group sessions during a given academic year.

3. allow the researcher to use excerpts from the writing you complete and the focus group sessions in publications about research with the understanding that your identity will not be revealed at any time.

In all, out-of-class participation will take no more than four hours during an academic year.

Participation is completely voluntary; you may stop participating at any time prior to completion of the project. Should you have any questions at any time, you are welcome to contact the researcher at the address below or via e-mail. Your decision to participate or not will have no effect on your grade in any course or prejudice your future relationship with the university. One benefit of participating in the study is that you will have the opportunity to learn important information about writing.

If you are willing to participate in this research, please read and sign the consent form below. You will be given a copy of this form to keep.

CONSENT FORM

I agree to participate in all of the procedures above. I understand that my identity will be protected during the study and that instructors will not have access to the statements I make in focus group sessions. I also understand that my name will not be revealed when data from the research are presented in publications. (Digital files will be kept for five years and then removed from relevant databases.) I have read the above and give the researcher, Stuart Greene, and his coauthors permission to use excerpts from what I write or transcripts of tapes without identifying me as the writer or speaker.

Date   Signature

Signature of Researcher
[Telephone number]/[E-mail address]

FIGURE 11.3   Sample Consent Form for a Focus Group

■ Prepare Your Script

Many of the guidelines for designing interview questions (see pp. 332–34) apply equally well to focus group questions. So, for example, you might start by establishing common ground or with a couple of nonthreatening questions. For variety, and to keep the discussion moving, use open-ended questions. Consider asking participants for definitions, impressions, examples, their ideas of others' perceptions, and the like. Also, you might quote from key

---

Alternative Focus Group Consent Form

Should colleges and universities take race and ethnicity into consideration when selecting new freshmen from the applicant pool? What is the purpose of giving preference to minority status in admissions? What does a diverse campus offer its students? These are some of the issues I want to discuss in today's focus group. But before we start, let me tell you about the assignment and your involvement.

The focus group is an interview style designed for small groups of five to seven participants. Focus group interviews are guided discussions that address a particular topic of interest or relevance to the group and the researcher. The informality of the focus group structure is intended to encourage participants to speak freely about their behaviors, attitudes, and opinions. For the purposes of my research, focus groups are a way to include multiple perspectives in my paper.

This session will be recorded so that I can prove my research. No names will be used in any drafts or in my final paper; instead, I will use letters (A, B, C) to identify different speakers. Two focus groups — one for minority students at Notre Dame and another for nonminority students — are being held so that I can obtain opinions and viewpoints from both sides of the issue and discuss their similarities and differences in my report. Some things to keep in mind during the session:

- Because I need to transcribe the dialogue, try not to talk over another person.

- Feel free to agree or disagree with a question, statement, or another person's answer.

- Focus on the discussion, not the question.

- Avoid going off on tangents.

- Be open and honest in all your responses.

Thank you for taking the time to be involved in my research. By signing below you give me permission to use the comments you provide for my paper. You understand that in no way will your identity be revealed, except by your minority or nonminority status. If you would like a copy of the results of the focus groups, please include your e-mail address, and the documents will be sent to you.

Name _____

E-mail address _____

Ethnicity _____   Male / Female   Class of _____
                                             (circle one)

FIGURE 11.4 Alternative Sample Consent Form for a Focus Group

passages in the scholarly research you will be using and ask for the group's responses to these "expert" theories. Not only will this be interesting; it also will help you organize and integrate your focus group evidence with evidence from library sources in your essay. Ask a wider range of questions than you think you might need so that you can explore side issues if they arise.

■ Conduct the Focus Group

On the day before you conduct the focus group, contact those who have agreed to participate to remind them of when and where it will happen. Show up ahead of time to make sure that your recording device is in good working order and that the room has sufficient seating for the participants. And don't forget your script. Here are three other guidelines.

Ask questions that draw people out.   During the focus group, be ready to draw out participants with follow-up questions ("Can you offer an example?" "Where do you think this impression comes from?"). Encourage all participants to speak; don't allow one member to dominate the discussion. (You may need to ask a facilitating question like "Do the rest of you agree with X's statement?" or "How would you extend what X has said?" or "Has anyone had a different experience?")

Limit the time of a focus group session.   It's a good idea to limit the session to thirty to forty-five minutes. When deciding how long the session should last, remember that it will take approximately three times longer to transcribe it. You must transcribe the session so that you can read through the participants' comments and quote them accurately.

Notice nonverbal interactions.   The recording device you use will give you a record of what was said, but be sure to notice nonverbal interactions and responses in your session, taking notes of body language, reluctance or eagerness to speak, and dynamics among group members that either open up or shut down conversation. These responses should be part of the data you analyze.

■ Interpret the Data from the Focus Group

Once you transcribe your focus group session, decide how you will refer anonymously to your participants. You then need to interpret the significance of the way participants talk about issues, as well as the information they relate. Interpret the nonverbal communication in the group as well as the verbal communication.

In making claims based on focus group data, remember that data from focus group interviews are not the same as data from individual interviews. They reflect collective thinking, ideas shared and negotiated by the group. Also, although you might speculate that data from a focus group are indicative of larger trends, be careful about the kinds of claims you make. One first-year student's idea is not necessarily every first-year student's idea.

The principal aim of doing original research is to make a contribution to a conversation using primary material as evidence to support your argument. For instance, when you conduct interviews or focus group discussions, you are collecting information (or data) that can offer a unique perspective. And doing original research also can enable you to test others' claims or assumptions and broaden your scope of inquiry beyond secondary materials. An effective piece of original research still relies on secondary materials, particularly as you find ways to locate what you discover in the context of what other authors have observed and argued. Moreover, there is the value of using multiple sources of information to support your claims — using your observations and the findings of others to say something about your subject. Also important, the research methods you choose depend on the question you ask. A focus on the types of educational opportunities available to the homeless lends itself more to close observation, interviews, and perhaps focus groups.

■ Important Ethical Considerations

Finally, we want to end with an ethical reminder: *Be fair to your sources.* Throughout this chapter, we have included a number of forms on which you can base your own consent forms when you conduct interviews and focus groups. When people give you their consent to use their words, it is incumbent on you—really it is essential—that you represent as faithfully as possible what people have said. As a researcher, you are given a kind of power over the people you interview and write about, using what they tell you for your own purposes. You cannot abuse the trust they place in you when they consent to be part of your research. It is important that they understand why you're doing the research and how your theories and assumptions will likely figure into your interpretation of the information you gather. You must also be aware of how their words will be construed by those who read what you write.

Steps for Conducting a Focus Group

1 **Select participants for the focus group.** Identify the range of your five to seven participants. Are you looking for diverse perspectives or a more specialized group?

2 **Plan the focus group.** Make sure that you have a specified time and place and that your participants are willing to sign consent forms.

3 **Prepare your script.** Prepare a variety of open-ended questions; consider quoting research you are interested in using in your paper to get participants' responses; and try to rehearse and revise.

4 **Conduct the focus group.** Record the session; ask questions that draw people out; limit the time of the session; and notice nonverbal interactions. And don't forget the consent forms.

5 **Interpret the data from the focus group.** Transcribe and analyze the data, including nonverbal communications; draw conclusions, but be careful not to overgeneralize from your small sample.

Entering
the Conversation
of Ideas

Education

What does it mean to be educated, and who decides?

© Shutterstock/Dim Dimich

Students do not always get a chance to step back and reflect on the many elements that shape the educational system—elements that at this very moment affect what you are learning, how you are learning it, and the kind of educated person you will be when you graduate. The readings in this chapter take a range of inventive approaches to two central questions: What does it mean to be educated? Who decides?

Some of these authors invite you to reflect on your own educational experiences, both good and bad. For example, Jonathan Kozol and Diane Ravitch draw on specific examples of early education to demonstrate the ways school settings can empower or disempower their students. They also describe political and social debates around bilingualism, integration, poverty, and privatizing education that illuminate some classroom dynamics, helping us reflect on what Kozol provocatively calls the "educational apartheid" of the present. Although public education is widely thought to be the most crucial element of a democracy, clearly not all public education in the United States is equal. These writers use interviews with students and personal experiences to argue that many American schools fall far short of their democratic potential. Deborah Tannen, a professor of linguistics, examines classroom dynamics through another lens, noticing the way girls and boys are socialized into different speech patterns that can affect learning environments at all levels of education. Like Kozol and Ravitch, Tannen analyzes specific examples of instructors and students interacting in a classroom in order to help us see conversational patterns that limit both males and females, though in different ways. Keep your own experiences in mind as you consider the ways these authors explain these educational problems and possible solutions.

Beverly Daniel Tatum is also in conversation with Kozol and Ravitch about what Ravitch calls the "opportunity gap" in education, which often cuts along racial lines. These authors focus on the larger social dynamics — particularly social dynamics around racial differences — that shape the way others respond to us. Tatum's essay, pointedly titled "Why Are All the Black Kids Sitting Together in the Cafeteria?," provides tools for analyzing social dynamics of high schools that may be very familiar to you, and visible in your college setting, too. Tatum's interviews with students invite us to see with fresh eyes how school environments might more often than not reinforce racial stereotyping rather than providing tools for resisting these inequitable assumptions.

Mark Edmundson and coauthors Constance Steinkuehler and Sean Duncan take on another kind of conversation about education — how enjoyable should it be to learn? Edmudson attacks what he calls the "lite" college education experience, in which instructors and campuses cater mostly to the pleasure of the student consumer. He suggests something is wrong when college students "shop" for classes they will "enjoy" rather than aiming to be challenged by them. Edmundson argues for courses that stretch students beyond their comfort zones. Steinkeuhler and Duncan approach this issue from another angle, arguing for *more play* in education — in fact, they argue that video games may be just the right tools for teaching skills crucial to scientific literacy! As you read these pieces and evaluate the claims, examples, data, and conclusions, consider how your own experiences figure into these debates. What would you say to these authors?

All the writers in this chapter push us to ask what it means in contemporary culture to be educated, and who has access to which kinds of education. These readings invite you to question common assumptions about how classrooms operate, from teacher-student dynamics to the material that has been designated "important knowledge." These readings should help you see your past and present educational experiences through fresh eyes, to consider the relationship between education and social power, and to ask an important question: What do *you* think it should mean to be an educated person in the contemporary United States?

 Visit **macmillanhighered.com/frominquiry3e** to view College National Poetry Slam Champion Dylan Garity's energetic condemnation of current standardized methods for teaching non-native English speakers.

JONATHAN KOZOL

From Still Separate, Still Unequal: America's Educational Apartheid

Jonathan Kozol is an award-winning writer and public lecturer who focuses on social injustice in the United States, an interest that began in the 1960s, when he taught in the Boston public school system. This first experience of learning about the lives of the country's poor and under-educated led him to investigate and write extensively about Americans who suffer from what he calls social and educational "apartheid" in the United States, which keeps many people in a cycle of poverty that he believes is nearly impossible to break. An Internet search of Kozol's name will demonstrate how widely he is quoted and how often he appears in the media as an expert on social inequality.

This essay, published in *Harper's Magazine* in September 2005, was adapted from his book, *The Shame of the Nation: The Restoration of Apartheid Schooling in America* (Crown, 2005). You will see that while Kozol uses many different sources to support his argument, this is written in the style of magazine journalism, and so he does not use bibliographic footnotes. Try to track all of the different kinds of sources in this piece to see what connections you can make between Kozol's central argument and the voices he includes here. Kozol makes his case in part by juxtaposing the words of the powerless and the powerful and contexualizing these individual speakers with statistics and facts that demonstrate what he believes is a profoundly unjust system of keeping the haves and have-nots separated though a variety of policies and belief systems.

Before you read, you might consider what you know about the No Child Left Behind policy, which plays a role in Kozol's examination of urban school systems. You might even research the strong feelings held by supporters and opponents of this policy, so that you have a sense of this high-stakes conversation before you read Kozol's analysis. Also keep your own schooling experience in mind, and think about your childhood sense of what other kids had or didn't have. Kozol taps into a discussion about education that is linked to almost every other kind of social division in our country. What does he hope to illuminate, and what solutions does he propose? What do you have to say about who has access to a quality education in the U.S. and who does not?

Many Americans who live far from our major cities and who have 1
no firsthand knowledge of the realities to be found in urban public schools seem to have the rather vague and general impression that the
great extremes of racial isolation that were matters of grave national significance some thirty-five or forty years ago have gradually but steadily
diminished in more recent years. The truth, unhappily, is that the trend,
for well over a decade now, has been precisely the reverse. Schools that
were already deeply segregated twenty-five or thirty years ago are no less
segregated now, while thousands of other schools around the country that
had been integrated either voluntarily or by the force of law have since
been rapidly resegregating.

In Chicago, by the academic year 2002–2003, 87 percent of public- 2
school enrollment was black or Hispanic; less than 10 percent of children
in the schools were white. In Washington, D.C., 94 percent of children were
black or Hispanic; less than 5 percent were white. In St. Louis, 82 percent of the student population were black or Hispanic; in Philadelphia and
Cleveland, 79 percent; in Los Angeles, 84 percent; in Detroit, 96 percent; in
Baltimore, 89 percent. In New York City, nearly three quarters of the students were black or Hispanic.

Even these statistics, as stark as they are, cannot begin to convey 3
how deeply isolated children in the poorest and most segregated sections
of these cities have become. In the typically colossal high schools of the
Bronx, for instance, more than 90 percent of students (in most cases, more
than 95 percent) are black or Hispanic. At John F. Kennedy High School
in 2003, 93 percent of the enrollment of more than 4,000 students were
black and Hispanic; only 3.5 percent of students at the school were white.
At Harry S. Truman High School, black and Hispanic students represented
96 percent of the enrollment of 2,700 students; 2 percent were white. At
Adlai Stevenson High School, which enrolls 3,400 students, blacks and
Hispanics made up 97 percent of the student population; a mere eight-
tenths of 1 percent were white.

A teacher at P.S. 65 in the South Bronx once pointed out to me one of 4
the two white children I had ever seen there. His presence in her class was
something of a wonderment to the teacher and to the other pupils. I asked
how many white kids she had taught in the South Bronx in her career. "I've
been at this school for eighteen years," she said. "This is the first white student I have ever taught."

One of the most disheartening experiences for those who grew up in 5
the years when Martin Luther King Jr. and Thurgood Marshall were alive
is to visit public schools today that bear their names, or names of other
honored leaders of the integration struggles that produced the temporary progress that took place in the three decades after *Brown v. Board
of Education*, and to find out how many of these schools are bastions of
contemporary segregation. It is even more disheartening when schools
like these are not in deeply segregated inner-city neighborhoods but in
racially mixed areas where the integration of a public school would seem

to be most natural, and where, indeed, it takes a conscious effort on the part of parents or school officials in these districts to avoid the integration option that is often right at their front door.

In a Seattle neighborhood that I visited in 2002, for instance, where 6 approximately half the families were Caucasian, 95 percent of students at the Thurgood Marshall Elementary School were black, Hispanic, Native American, or of Asian origin. An African American teacher at the school told me—not with bitterness but wistfully—of seeing clusters of white parents and their children each morning on the corner of a street close to the school, waiting for a bus that took the children to a predominantly white school.

"At Thurgood Marshall," according to a big wall poster in the school's 7 lobby, "the dream is alive." But school-assignment practices and federal court decisions that have countermanded long-established policies that previously fostered integration in Seattle's schools make the realization of the dream identified with Justice Marshall all but unattainable today. In San Diego there is a school that bears the name of Rosa Parks in which 86 percent of students are black and Hispanic and only some 2 percent are white. In Los Angeles there is a school that bears the name of Dr. King that is 99 percent black and Hispanic, and another in Milwaukee in which black and Hispanic children also make up 99 percent of the enrollment. There is a high school in Cleveland that is named for Dr. King in which black students make up 97 percent of the student body, and the graduation rate is only 35 percent. In Philadelphia, 98 percent of children at a high school named for Dr. King are black. At a middle school named for Dr. King in Boston, black and Hispanic children make up 98 percent of the enrollment.

In New York City there is a primary school named for Langston 8 Hughes (99 percent black and Hispanic), a middle school named for Jackie Robinson (96 percent black and Hispanic), and a high school named for Fannie Lou Hamer, one of the great heroes of the integration movement in the South, in which 98 percent of students are black or Hispanic. In Harlem there is yet another segregated Thurgood Marshall School (also 98 percent black and Hispanic), and in the South Bronx dozens of children I have known went to a segregated middle school named in honor of Paul Robeson in which less than half of 1 percent of the enrollment was Caucasian.

There is a well-known high school named for Martin Luther King Jr. in 9 New York City too. This school, which I've visited repeatedly in recent years, is located in an upper-middle-class white neighborhood, where it was built in the belief—or hope—that it would draw large numbers of white students by permitting them to walk to school, while only their black and Hispanic classmates would be asked to ride the bus or come by train. When the school was opened in 1975, less than a block from Lincoln Center in Manhattan, "it was seen," according to the *New York Times*, "as a promising effort to integrate white, black and Hispanic students in a thriving neighborhood that held one of the city's cultural gems." Even from the start, however, parents in the neighborhood showed great reluctance to permit their children to enroll at Martin Luther King, and, despite "its prime location and its name, which itself creates the highest of expectations," notes the *Times*, the school before long came to be a destination for black and Hispanic students who could not obtain admission into more successful schools. It stands today as one of the nation's most visible and problematic symbols of an expectation rapidly receding and a legacy substantially betrayed.

Perhaps most damaging to any serious effort to address racial *10* segregation openly is the refusal of most of the major arbiters of culture in our northern cities to confront or even clearly name an obvious reality they would have castigated with a passionate determination in another section of the nation fifty years before—and which, moreover, they still castigate today in retrospective writings that assign it to a comfortably distant and allegedly concluded era of the past. There is, indeed, a seemingly agreed-upon convention in much of the media today not even to use an accurate descriptor like "racial segregation" in a narrative description of a segregated school. Linguistic sweeteners, semantic somersaults, and surrogate vocabularies are repeatedly employed. Schools in which as few as 3 or 4 percent of students may be white or Southeast Asian or of Middle Eastern origin, for instance—and where every other child in the building is black or Hispanic—are referred to as "diverse." Visitors to schools like these discover quickly the eviscerated meaning of the word, which is no longer a proper adjective but a euphemism for a plainer word that has apparently become unspeakable.

School systems themselves repeatedly employ this euphemism in de- *11* scribing the composition of their student populations. In a school I visited in the fall of 2004 in Kansas City, Missouri, for example, a document distributed to visitors reports that the school's curriculum "addresses the needs of children from diverse backgrounds." But as I went from class to class, I did not encounter any children who were white or Asian—or Hispanic, for that matter—and when I was later provided with precise statistics for the demographics of the school, I learned that 99.6 percent of students there were African American. In a similar document, the school board of another district, this one in New York State, referred to "the diversity" of its student population and "the rich variations of ethnic backgrounds." But when I looked at the racial numbers that the district had reported to the state, I learned that there were 2,800 black and Hispanic children in the system, 1 Asian child, and 3 whites. Words, in these cases, cease to have real meaning; or, rather, they mean the opposite of what they say.

High school students whom I talk with in deeply segregated neighbor- *12* hoods and public schools seem far less circumspect than their elders and far more open in their willingness to confront these issues. "It's more like being hidden," said a fifteen-year-old girl named Isabel[1] I met some years

---

[1] The names of children mentioned in this article have been changed to protect their privacy.

ago in Harlem, in attempting to explain to me the ways in which she and her classmates understood the racial segregation of their neighborhoods and schools. "It's as if you have been put in a garage where, if they don't have room for something but aren't sure if they should throw it out, they put it there where they don't need to think of it again."

I asked her if she thought America truly did not "have room" for her *13* or other children of her race. "Think of it this way," said a sixteen-year-old girl sitting beside her. "If people in New York woke up one day and learned that we were gone, that we had simply died or left for somewhere else, how would they feel?"

"How do you think they'd feel?" I asked. *14*

"I think they'd be relieved," this very solemn girl replied. *15*

Many educators make the argument today that given the demographics *16* of large cities like New York and their suburban areas, our only realistic goal should be the nurturing of strong, empowered, and well-funded schools in segregated neighborhoods. Black school officials in these situations have sometimes conveyed to me a bitter and clear-sighted recognition that they're being asked, essentially, to mediate and render functional an uncontested separation between children of their race and children of white people living sometimes in a distant section of their town and sometimes in almost their own immediate communities. Implicit in this mediation is a willingness to set aside the promises of *Brown* and—though never stating this or even thinking of it clearly in these terms—to settle for the promise made more than a century ago in *Plessy v. Ferguson,* the 1896 Supreme Court ruling in which "separate but equal" was accepted as a tolerable rationale for the perpetuation of a dual system in American society.

Equality itself—equality alone—is now, it seems, the article of faith *17* to which most of the principals of inner-city public schools subscribe. And some who are perhaps most realistic do not even dare to ask for, or expect, complete equality, which seems beyond the realm of probability for many years to come, but look instead for only a sufficiency of means—"adequacy" is the legal term most often used today—by which to win those practical and finite victories that appear to be within their reach. Higher standards, higher expectations, are repeatedly demanded of these urban principals, and of the teachers and students in their schools, but far lower standards—certainly in ethical respects—appear to be expected of the dominant society that isolates these children in unequal institutions.

"Dear Mr. Kozol," wrote the eight-year-old, "we do not have the things *18* you have. You have Clean things. We do not have. You have a clean bathroom. We do not have that. You have Parks and we do not have Parks. You have all the thing and we do not have all the thing. Can you help us?"

The letter, from a child named Alliyah, came in a fat envelope of *19* twenty-seven letters from a class of third-grade children in the Bronx. Other letters that the students in Alliyah's classroom sent me registered some of the same complaints. "We don't have no gardens," "no Music or Art," and "no fun places to play," one child said. "Is there a way to fix this

Problem?" Another noted a concern one hears from many children in such overcrowded schools: "We have a gym but it is for lining up. I think it is not fair." Yet another of Alliyah's classmates asked me, with a sweet misspelling, if I knew the way to make her school into a "good" school—"like the other kings have"—and ended with the hope that I would do my best to make it possible for "all the kings" to have good schools.

The letter that affected me the most, however, had been written by a [20] child named Elizabeth. "It is not fair that other kids have a garden and new things. But we don't have that," said Elizabeth. "I wish that this school was the most beautiful school in the whole why world."

"The whole why world" stayed in my thoughts for days. When I later [21] met Elizabeth, I brought her letter with me, thinking I might see whether, in reading it aloud, she'd change the "why" to "wide" or leave it as it was. My visit to her class, however, proved to be so pleasant, and the children seemed so eager to bombard me with their questions about where I lived, and why I lived there rather than in New York, and who I lived with, and how many dogs I had, and other interesting questions of that sort, that I decided not to interrupt the nice reception they had given me with questions about usages and spelling. I left "the whole why world" to float around unedited and unrevised in my mind. The letter itself soon found a resting place on the wall above my desk.

In the years before I met Elizabeth, I had visited many other schools [22] in the South Bronx and in one northern district of the Bronx as well. I had made repeated visits to a high school where a stream of water flowed down one of the main stairwells on a rainy afternoon and where green fungus molds were growing in the office where the students went for counseling. A large blue barrel was positioned to collect rainwater coming through the ceiling. In one makeshift elementary school housed in a former skating rink next to a funeral establishment in yet another nearly all-black-and- Hispanic section of the Bronx, class size rose to thirty-four and more; four kindergarten classes and a sixth-grade class were packed into a single room that had no windows. The air was stifling in many rooms, and the children had no place for recess because there was no outdoor playground and no indoor gym.

In another elementary school, which had been built to hold [23] 1,000 children but was packed to bursting with some 1,500, the principal poured out his feelings to me in a room in which a plastic garbage bag had been attached somehow to cover part of the collapsing ceiling. "This," he told me, pointing to the garbage bag, then gesturing around him at the other indications of decay and disrepair one sees in ghetto schools much like it elsewhere, "would not happen to white children."

Libraries, once one of the glories of the New York City school system, [24] were either nonexistent or, at best, vestigial in large numbers of the elementary schools. Art and music programs had also for the most part disappeared. "When I began to teach in 1969," the principal of an elementary school in the South Bronx reported to me, "every school had a full-time licensed art and music teacher and librarian." During the subsequent decades, he recalled, "I saw all of that destroyed."

School physicians also were removed from elementary schools during 25 these years. In 1970, when substantial numbers of white children still attended New York City's public schools, 400 doctors had been present to address the health needs of the children. By 1993 the number of doctors had been cut to 23, most of them part-time—a cutback that affected most severely children in the city's poorest neighborhoods, where medical facilities were most deficient and health problems faced by children most extreme. Teachers told me of asthmatic children who came into class with chronic wheezing and who at any moment of the day might undergo more serious attacks, but in the schools I visited there were no doctors to attend to them.

In explaining these steep declines in services, political leaders in 26 New York tended to point to shifting economic factors, like a serious budget crisis in the middle 1970s, rather than to the changing racial demographics of the student population. But the fact of economic ups and downs from year to year, or from one decade to the next, could not convincingly explain the permanent shortchanging of the city's students, which took place routinely in good economic times and bad. The bad times were seized upon politically to justify the cuts, and the money was never restored once the crisis years were past.

"If you close your eyes to the changing racial composition of the 27 schools and look only at budget actions and political events," says Noreen Connell, the director of the nonprofit Educational Priorities Panel in New York, "you're missing the assumptions that are underlying these decisions." When minority parents ask for something better for their kids, she says, "the assumption is that these are parents who can be discounted. These are kids who just don't count—children we don't value."

This, then, is the accusation that Alliyah and her classmates send our 28 way: "You have . . . We do not have." Are they right or are they wrong? Is this a case of naive and simplistic juvenile exaggeration? What does a third-grader know about these big-time questions of fairness and justice? Physical appearances apart, how in any case do you begin to measure something so diffuse and vast and seemingly abstract as having more, or having less, or not having at all?

Around the time I met Alliyah in the school year 1997–1998, 29 New York's Board of Education spent about $8,000 yearly on the education of a third-grade child in a New York City public school. If you could have scooped Alliyah up out of the neighborhood where she was born and plunked her down in a fairly typical white suburb of New York, she would have received a public education worth about $12,000 a year. If you were to lift her up once more and set her down in one of the wealthiest white suburbs of New York, she would have received as much as $18,000 worth of public education every year and would likely have had a third-grade teacher paid approximately $30,000 more than her teacher in the Bronx was paid.

The dollars on both sides of the equation have increased since then, 30 but the discrepancies between them have remained. The present per-pupil spending level in the New York City schools is $11,700, which may be compared with a per-pupil spending level in excess of $22,000 in the well-to-do suburban district of Manhasset, Long Island. The present New York City level is, indeed, almost exactly what Manhasset spent per pupil eighteen years ago, in 1987, when that sum of money bought a great deal more in services and salaries than it can buy today. In dollars adjusted for inflation, New York City has not yet caught up to where its wealthiest suburbs were a quarter-century ago.

Gross discrepancies in teacher salaries between the city and its afflu- 31 ent white suburbs have remained persistent as well. In 1997 the median salary for teachers in Alliyah's neighborhood was $43,000, as compared with $74,000 in suburban Rye, $77,000 in Manhasset, and $81,000 in the town of Scarsdale, which is only about eleven miles from Alliyah's school. Five years later, in 2002, salary scales for New York City's teachers rose to levels that approximated those within the lower-spending districts in the suburbs, but salary scales do not reflect the actual salaries that teachers typically receive, which are dependent upon years of service and advanced degrees. Salaries for first-year teachers in the city were higher than they'd been four years before, but the differences in median pay between the city and its upper-middle-income suburbs had remained extreme. The overall figure for New York City in 2002–2003 was $53,000, while it had climbed to $87,000 in Manhasset and exceeded $95,000 in Scarsdale.

"There are expensive children and there are cheap children," writes 32 Marina Warner, an essayist and novelist who has written many books for children, "just as there are expensive women and cheap women." The governmentally administered diminishment in value of the children of the poor begins even before the age of five or six, when they begin their years of formal education in the public schools. It starts during their infant and toddler years, when hundreds of thousands of children of the very poor in much of the United States are locked out of the opportunity for preschool education for no reason but the accident of birth and budgetary choices of the government, while children of the privileged are often given veritable feasts of rich developmental early education.

In New York City, for example, affluent parents pay surprisingly 33 large sums of money to enroll their youngsters, beginning at the age of two or three, in extraordinary early-education programs that give them social competence and rudimentary pedagogic skills unknown to children of the same age in the city's poorer neighborhoods. The most exclusive of the private preschools in New York, which are known to those who can afford them as "Baby Ivies," cost as much as $24,000 for a full-day program. Competition for admission to these pre-K schools is so extreme that private counselors are frequently retained, at fees as high as $300 an hour, to guide the parents through the application process.

At the opposite extreme along the economic spectrum in New York are *34* thousands of children who receive no preschool opportunity at all. Exactly how many thousands are denied this opportunity in New York City and in other major cities is almost impossible to know. Numbers that originate in governmental agencies in many states are incomplete and imprecise and do not always differentiate with clarity between authentic pre-K programs that have educative and developmental substance and those less expensive child-care arrangements that do not. But even where states do compile numbers that refer specifically to educative preschool programs, it is difficult to know how many of the children who are served are of low income, since admissions to some of the state-supported programs aren't determined by low income or they are determined by a complicated set of factors of which poverty is only one.

There are remarkable exceptions to this pattern in some sections of *35* the nation. In Milwaukee, for example, virtually every four-year-old is now enrolled in a preliminary kindergarten program, which amounts to a full year of preschool education, prior to a second kindergarten year for five-year-olds. More commonly in urban neighborhoods, large numbers of low-income children are denied these opportunities and come into their kindergarten year without the minimal social skills that children need in order to participate in class activities and without even such very modest early-learning skills as knowing how to hold a crayon or a pencil, identify perhaps a couple of shapes and colors, or recognize that printed pages go from left to right.

Three years later, in third grade, these children are introduced to what *36* are known as "high-stakes tests," which in many urban systems now determine whether students can or cannot be promoted. Children who have been in programs like those offered by the "Baby Ivies" since the age of two have, by now, received the benefits of six or seven years of education, nearly twice as many as the children who have been denied these opportunities; yet all are required to take, and will be measured by, the same examinations. Which of these children will receive the highest scores? The ones who spent the years from two to four in lovely little Montessori programs and in other pastel-painted settings in which tender and attentive and well-trained instructors read to them from beautiful storybooks and introduced them very gently for the first time to the world of numbers and the shapes of letters, and the sizes and varieties of solid objects, and perhaps taught them to sort things into groups or to arrange them in a sequence, or to do those many other interesting things that early childhood specialists refer to as pre-numeracy skills? Or the ones who spent those years at home in front of a TV or sitting by the window of a slum apartment gazing down into the street? There is something deeply hypocritical about a society that holds an eight-year-old inner-city child "accountable" for her performance on a high-stakes standardized exam but does not hold the high officials of our government accountable for robbing her of what they gave their own kids six or seven years earlier.

Perhaps in order to deflect these recognitions, or to soften them some- 37 what, many people, even while they do not doubt the benefit of making very large investments in the education of their own children, some- how—paradoxical as it may seem—appear to be attracted to the argument that money may not really matter that much at all. No matter with what regularity such doubts about the worth of spending money on a child's education are advanced, it is obvious that those who have the money, and who spend it lavishly to benefit their own kids, do not do it for no reason. Yet shockingly large numbers of well-educated and sophisticated people whom I talk with nowadays dismiss such challenges with a surprising ease. "Is the answer really to throw money into these dysfunctional and failing schools?" I'm often asked. "Don't we have some better ways to make them 'work'?" The question is posed in a variety of forms. "Yes, of course, it's not a perfectly fair system as it stands. But money alone is surely not the sole response. The values of the parents and the kids themselves must have a role in this as well—you know, housing, health conditions, social factors." "Other factors"—a term of overall reprieve one often hears—"have got to be considered, too." These latter points are obviously true but always seem to have the odd effect of substituting things we know we cannot change in the short run for obvious solutions like cutting class size and construct- ing new school buildings or providing universal preschool that we actually could put in place right now if we were so inclined.

Frequently these arguments are posed as questions that do not invite 38 an answer because the answer seems to be decided in advance. "Can you really buy your way to better education for these children?" "Do we know enough to be quite sure that we will see an actual return on the investment that we make?" "Is it even clear that this is the right starting point to get to where we'd like to go? It doesn't always seem to work, as I am sure that you already know," or similar questions that somehow assume I will agree with those who ask them.

Some people who ask these questions, although they live in wealthy 39 districts where the schools are funded at high levels, don't even send their children to these public schools but choose instead to send them to expen- sive private day schools. At some of the well-known private prep schools in the New York City area, tuition and associated costs are typically more than $20,000 a year. During their children's teenage years, they sometimes send them off to very fine New England schools like Andover or Exeter or Groton, where tuition, boarding, and additional expenses rise to more than $30,000. Often a family has two teenage children in these schools at the same time, so they may be spending more than $60,000 on their children's education every year. Yet here I am one night, a guest within their home, and dinner has been served and we are having coffee now; and this entirely likable, and generally sensible, and beautifully refined and thoughtful person looks me in the eyes and asks me whether you can really buy your way to better education for the children of the poor.

As racial isolation deepens and the inequalities of education finance *40* remain unabated and take on new and more innovative forms, the principals of many inner-city schools are making choices that few principals in public schools that serve white children in the mainstream of the nation ever need to contemplate. Many have been dedicating vast amounts of time and effort to create an architecture of adaptive strategies that promise incremental gains within the limits inequality allows....

Corporate leaders, when they speak of education, sometimes pay *41* lip-service to the notion of "good critical and analytic skills," but it is reasonable to ask whether they have in mind the critical analysis of *their* priorities. In principle, perhaps some do; but, if so, this is not a principle that seems to have been honored widely in the schools I have been visiting. In all the various business-driven inner-city classrooms I have observed in the past five years, plastered as they are with corporation brand names and managerial vocabularies, I have yet to see the two words "labor unions." Is this an oversight? How is that possible? Teachers and principals themselves, who are almost always members of a union, seem to be so beaten down that they rarely even question this omission.

It is not at all unusual these days to come into an urban school in *42* which the principal prefers to call himself or herself "building CEO" or "building manager." In some of the same schools teachers are described as "classroom managers."[2] I have never been in a suburban district in which principals were asked to view themselves or teachers in this way. These terminologies remind us of how wide the distance has become between two very separate worlds of education.

It has been more than a decade now since drill-based literacy methods *43* like Success for All began to proliferate in our urban schools. It has

[2]A school I visited three years ago in Columbus, Ohio, was littered with "Help Wanted" signs. Starting in kindergarten, children in the school were being asked to think about the jobs that they might choose when they grew up. In one classroom there was a poster that displayed the names of several retail stores: J. C. Penney, Wal-Mart, Kmart, Sears, and a few others. "It's like working in a store," a classroom aide explained. "The children are learning to pretend they're cashiers." At another school in the same district, children were encouraged to apply for jobs in their classrooms. Among the job positions open to the children in this school, there was an "Absence Manager" and a "Behavior Chart Manager," a "Form Collector Manager," a "Paper Passer Outer Manager," a "Paper Collecting Manager," a "Paper Returning Manager," an "Exit Ticket Manager," even a "Learning Manager," a "Reading Corner Manager," and a "Score Keeper Manager." I asked the principal if there was a special reason why those two words "management" and "manager" kept popping up throughout the school. "We want every child to be working as a manager while he or she is in this school," the principal explained. "We want to make them understand that, in this country, companies will give you opportunities to work, to prove yourself, no matter what you've done." I wasn't sure what she meant by "no matter what you've done," and asked her if she could explain it. "Even if you have a felony arrest," she said, "we want you to understand that you can be a manager someday."

been three and a half years since the systems of assessment that determine the effectiveness of these and similar practices were codified in the federal legislation, No Child Left Behind, that President Bush signed into law in 2002. Since the enactment of this bill, the number of standardized exams children must take has more than doubled. It will probably increase again after the year 2006, when standardized tests, which are now required in grades three through eight, may be required in Head Start programs and, as President Bush has now proposed, in ninth, tenth, and eleventh grades as well.

The elements of strict accountability, in short, are solidly in place; 44 and in many states where the present federal policies are simply reinforcements of accountability requirements that were established long before the passage of the federal law, the same regimen has been in place since 1995 or even earlier. The "tests-and-standards" partisans have had things very much their way for an extended period of time, and those who were convinced that they had ascertained "what works" in schools that serve minorities and children of the poor have had ample opportunity to prove that they were right.

What, then, it is reasonable to ask, are the results?   45

The achievement gap between black and white children, which nar- 46 rowed for three decades up until the late years of the 1980s—the period in which school segregation steadily decreased—started to widen once more in the early 1990s when the federal courts began the process of resegregation by dismantling the mandates of the *Brown* decision. From that point on, the gap continued to widen or remained essentially unchanged; and while recently there has been a modest narrowing of the gap in reading scores for fourth-grade children, the gap in secondary school remains as wide as ever.

The media inevitably celebrate the periodic upticks that a set of scores 47 may seem to indicate in one year or another in achievement levels of black and Hispanic children in their elementary schools. But if these upticks were not merely temporary "testing gains" achieved by test-prep regimens and were instead authentic education gains, they would carry over into middle school and high school. Children who know how to read—and read with comprehension—do not suddenly become nonreaders and hopelessly disabled writers when they enter secondary school. False gains evaporate; real gains endure. Yet hundreds of thousands of the inner-city children who have made what many districts claim to be dramatic gains in elementary school, and whose principals and teachers have adjusted almost every aspect of their school days and school calendars, forfeiting recess, canceling or cutting back on all the so-called frills (art, music, even social sciences) in order to comply with state demands—those students, now in secondary school, are sitting in subject-matter classes where they cannot comprehend the texts and cannot set down their ideas in the kind of sentences expected of most fourth-and fifth-grade students in the suburbs.

Students in this painful situation, not surprisingly, tend to be most likely to drop out of school.

In 48 percent of high schools in the nation's one hundred largest districts, which are those in which the highest concentrations of black and Hispanic students tend to be enrolled, less than half the entering ninth-graders graduate in four years. Nationwide, from 1993 to 2002, the number of high schools graduating less than half their ninth-grade class in four years has increased by 75 percent. In the 94 percent of districts in New York State where white children make up the majority, nearly 80 percent of students graduate from high school in four years. In the 6 percent of districts where black and Hispanic students make up the majority, only 40 percent do so. There are 120 high schools in New York, enrolling nearly 200,000 minority students, where less than 60 percent of entering ninth-graders even make it to twelfth grade.

The promulgation of new and expanded inventories of "what works," no matter the enthusiasm with which they're elaborated, is not going to change this. The use of hortatory slogans chanted by the students in our segregated schools is not going to change this. Desperate historical revisionism that romanticizes the segregation of an older order (this is a common theme of many separatists today) is not going to change this. Skinnerian instructional approaches, which decapitate a child's capability for critical reflection, are not going to change this. Posters about "global competition" will certainly not change this. Turning six-year-olds into examination soldiers and denying eight-year-olds their time for play at recess will not change this.

"I went to Washington to challenge the soft bigotry of low expectations," said President Bush in his campaign for reelection in September 2004. "It's working. It's making a difference." Here we have one of those deadly lies that by sheer repetition is at length accepted by surprisingly large numbers of Americans. But it is not the truth; and it is not an innocent misstatement of the facts. It is a devious appeasement of the heartache of the parents of the black and brown and poor, and if it is not forcefully resisted it will lead us further in a very dangerous direction.

Whether the issue is inequity alone or deepening resegregation or the labyrinthine intertwining of the two, it is well past the time for us to start the work that it will take to change this. If it takes people marching in the streets and other forms of adamant disruption of the governing civilities, if it takes more than litigation, more than legislation, and much more than resolutions introduced by members of Congress, these are prices we should be prepared to pay. "We do not have the things you have," Alliyah told me when she wrote to ask if I would come and visit her school in the South Bronx. "Can you help us?" America owes that little girl and millions like her a more honorable answer than they have received.

■ ■ ■

Reading as a Writer: Analyzing Rhetorical Choices

1. How would you describe Kozol's relationship to the people who are the subject of his essay? How does this relationship work to his advantage, or disadvantage, as he builds his argument? Be prepared to point to and explain several passages that support your responses to these questions.

2. Who is Kozol's audience (or audiences), and how can you tell? You might find it helpful to look for the counterarguments Kozol addresses, the kinds of sources he uses to make his argument, and the examples he uses to illustrate his points. Based on your findings, you could also consider who might be shut out of his audience, and why this matters.

Writing as a Reader: Entering the Conversation of Ideas

1. Kozol and Beverly Tatum both focus on conversational exchanges between those in power and those without power, within educational settings. Write an essay in which you analyze the similarities and differences in the points they raise and the conclusions they draw. What are the problems and potential each author sees in education in the United States when it comes to racial equity? Where do you stand on the issues they raise and the conclusions they draw? You may include a few of your own specific experiences and insights as you take a stance on this important topic.

2. In his essay, Kozol notes that certain school districts claim a diverse population, but he reveals what he calls the "eviscerated meaning of the word" (para. 10). Ann duCille is also interested in the ways that terms related to multiculturalism and diversity are often euphemisms for something else. Drawing on both Kozol's and duCille's points about how the language of diversity and multiculturalism is often used and misused, write an essay in which you consider the significance of this dynamic in the contemporary United States. Include your own analysis of Kozol's and duCille's examples and examples from your own experience that will help you make your point.

DIANE RAVITCH

The Facts about the Achievement Gap

Diane Ravitch is a research professor of education at New York University, served in the U.S. Department of Education from 1991 to 1993, and was a member of the National Assessment Governing Board, which oversees the federal educational testing, from 1997 to 2004. As a historian of education, Ravitch has written eleven books for the general public on the topic of education and the ethics of testing, has edited many others, and has written hundreds of articles for scholarly and popular journals. She is a frequent guest on television and a public lecturer on issues related to public education in the United States; she also writes a blog: dianeravitch.net. This piece is an excerpt from her 2013 book *Reign of Error: The Hoax of the Privatization Movement and the Danger to America's Public Schools*. What does the title of her book tell you about her perspective?

Ravitch opens her piece with an epigraph that establishes her corrective argument, designed to reveal that a common claim about U.S. public education—"The achievement gaps are large and getting worse"—is not actually supported by data. Ravitch traces the history of public education performance from 1990, citing statistics that support her claim that African American and Hispanic students have not been "left behind" by public schools, as supporters of privatization (or "reformers," as Ravitch calls them here) claim. Take time to discuss the data she cites in paragraphs 5 to 8; how effective do you find these numbers from the National Assessment of Educational Progress (NAEP) tests as you consider her perspective? What do you know about No Child Left Behind policies, which Ravitch brings up in paragraph 13?

Like other scholarly authors who seek to understand the complexity at the heart of social issues (rather than imitating the simplistic "for or against" debates that we often hear on talk-radio shows or bombastic opinion programs on television), Ravitch explores the many factors that contribute to student success (or failure), starting in paragraph 18. As you read these dense paragraphs, consider what she means when she describes these factors as "social and economic conditions that cause systemic disadvantages" (para. 20). What issues lie beyond the schools that help explain the persistence of achievement gaps, according to Ravitch?

In her penultimate paragraph, Ravitch claims that the phrase "achievement gap" does not accurately represent the problem: "What we call achievement gaps are in fact opportunity gaps," she says (para. 31). What is her point in this rephrasing? What solutions does she offer, given all the challenges she has described? In this brief piece, Ravitch covers a lot of ground on a topic that is in the news almost every day. Keep your own experiences with education in mind as you analyze this essay that begins with a critique of the charter and privatizing school movements and concludes with a critique of our cultural indifference to poverty. What key insights will you take away?

CLAIM   *The achievement gaps are large and getting worse.*

REALITY   *We have made genuine progress in narrowing the achievement gaps, but they will remain large if we do nothing about the causes of the gaps.*

One of the persistent claims of the corporate reform movement is that the reformers are leading the "civil rights issue of our time." Reformers point to the disparity between the test scores of white students and students of color as proof that the public schools are failing and that black and Hispanic students must be liberated from public schools to attend privately managed charter schools or to use vouchers to enroll in private and religious schools.

It defies reason to believe that Martin Luther King Jr. would march arm in arm with Wall Street hedge fund managers and members of ALEC to lead a struggle for the privatization of public education, the crippling of unions, and the establishment of for-profit schools. Privatization inevitably means deregulation, greater segregation, and less equity, with minimal oversight by public authorities. Privatization has typically not been a friend to powerless groups.

Reformers make the case for privatization by insisting that black and 3 Hispanic students are failing in the public schools and that they must be "saved."

Reformers often say that African American and Hispanic students 4 have made no progress for decades. But this is not true. The scores of black students in fourth-grade math increased dramatically in the two decades after 1990, when the federal tests were first offered; black student achievement was higher in 2009 than white student achievement in 1990. In addition, over this past generation there has been a remarkable decline in the proportion of African American and Hispanic students who register "below basic," the lowest possible academic rating on the NAEP tests.

If white achievement had stood still, the achievement gap would be 5 closed by now, but of course white achievement has also improved, so the gap remains large.

In mathematics, over the past two decades, all students made 6 dramatic progress. In 1990, 83 percent of black students in fourth grade scored "below basic," but that number fell to 34 percent in 2011. In eighth grade, 78 percent of black students were below basic in 1990, but by 2011 the proportion had dropped to 49 percent. Among Hispanic students, the proportion below basic in fourth grade fell from 67 percent to 28 percent; in eighth grade, that proportion declined from 66 percent to 39 percent. Among white students in fourth grade, the proportion below basic dropped in that time period from 41 percent to only 9 percent; in eighth grade, it declined from 40 percent to 16 percent. The proportion of fourth-grade Asian students below basic dropped from 38 percent in 1990 to 9 percent in 2011; in eighth grade, Asian students who were below basic declined from 36 percent to 14 percent.

This is truly remarkable progress.   7

The changes in reading scores were not as dramatic as in math, but 8 they nonetheless are impressive. In fourth-grade reading, the proportion of black students who were below basic in 1992 was 68 percent; by 2011, it was down to 51 percent. In eighth grade, the proportion of black students who were reading below basic was 55 percent; that had declined to 41 percent by 2011. Among fourth-grade white students, the proportion below basic declined from 29 percent to 22 percent in the same twenty-year period. Among fourth-grade Hispanic students, the proportion reading below basic dropped from 62 percent to 49 percent. Among eighth-grade Hispanic students, the proportion reading below basic declined from 51 percent to 36 percent. Among fourth-grade Asian students, the proportion below basic fell from 40 percent to 20 percent. In the eighth grade, it declined from 24 percent to 17 percent.

Clearly, performance on NAEP is not flat. The gains in reading have 9
been slow, steady, and significant. The gains in mathematics in both tested
grades have been remarkable for whites, blacks, Hispanics, and Asians.

Despite these increases, the achievement gaps remain between white 10
and black students and between white and Hispanic students because all
groups are improving their scores. Asian students perform as well as white
students in reading and better than white students in math. Reformers
ignore these gains and castigate the public schools for the persistence of
the gap.

Closing the racial achievement gap has been a major policy goal of 11
education policy makers for at least the past decade. There has been some
progress, but it has been slow and uneven. This is not surprising: It is hard
to narrow or close the gap if all groups are improving.

There is nothing new about achievement gaps between different racial 12
and ethnic groups and between children from families at different ends
of the income distribution. Such gaps exist wherever there is inequality,
not only in this country, but internationally. In every country, the students
from the most advantaged families have higher test scores on average than
students from the least advantaged families.[1]

One of the major reasons for the passage of the No Child Left Behind 13
law was the expectation that it would narrow, perhaps even close, the
black-white and also the Hispanic-white achievement gaps. Policy makers and legislators believed in 2001, when NCLB was debated, that testing
and accountability would suffice to close the gaps. Lawmakers believed
that the combination of test-based accountability and transparency would
produce the desired results.

The very act of publishing the disparate results, they expected, would 14
compel teachers to spend more time teaching the students who had low
scores, especially if there were punitive consequences for not raising those
scores. President George W. Bush staked his claim to being a "compassion-
ate conservative" because, as he put it, he opposed "the soft bigotry of low
expectations." If teachers were required by law to have high expectations
for all students, the theory went, then all students would learn and meet
high standards.

Now we know that, despite some gains, NCLB did not close the gaps. 15
Paul Barton and Richard Coley of the Educational Testing Service wrote an
overview of the black-white achievement gap over the course of the twentieth century and concluded that the period in which that gap narrowed most
was the 1970s and 1980s, in response to such things as desegregation, class
size reduction, early childhood education, the addition of federal resources
to schools enrolling poor children, and wider economic opportunities for
black families. From that time forward, the gap has wavered up and down
without resuming the sharp narrowing of the earlier period.[2]

What was impressive about the 1970s and 1980s was that black stu- 16
dents gained so much more ground than white students. In the years since

then, both white and black students improved their test scores, which made it hard to narrow the gap. So, for example, the black-white gap in fourth-grade reading was 30 points in 2002, but narrowed to 25 by 2011. White student scores increased by 2 points, while black scores increased by 6 points. The gap narrowed by a few points. It is still a sizable gap of 25 points, but there was improvement, not stasis or decline.[3]

In mathematics, where both white and black students made large test score gains, the gap in fourth grade narrowed from 31 points in 2000 to 25 points in 2011. That's a narrowing of 6 points. Two-thirds of that improvement occurred before the implementation of No Child Left Behind. The scores of black students rose from 203 on the NAEP scale to 224. At the same time, the scores of white students increased from 234 to 249, and two-thirds of that gain happened before the implementation of NCLB. Both groups recorded strong gains.[4]   *17*

The black-white achievement gap has existed as long as records have been kept. The source of the gap is no secret. African Americans have been subject to a long history of social and economic oppression and disadvantage; they have experienced higher levels of poverty and lower levels of education than white Americans. After the *Brown* decision of 1954, the federal government and many states adopted policies to redress past inequities, but those policies were insufficient to overcome generations of racism, which limited access to jobs and education. Despite significant progress in expanding educational access, educational attainment, and economic opportunities for black citizens in the past half century, blacks continue to be disproportionately poor, to attend racially segregated schools, to experience high rates of incarceration, and to live in racially isolated communities where children are likely to be exposed to violence, gangs, and drug use.   *18*

Today's reformers often imply that schools alone can close the achievement gaps among different groups. They like to point to exemplary charter schools with high test scores to prove their point. They say that teachers with high expectations can close the achievement gap. To date, no charter operator has taken responsibility for an entire school district and demonstrated that his or her pedagogical methods were powerful enough to overcome the disadvantages of poverty.   *19*

The impressive academic gains of the past two decades demonstrate that schools can significantly reduce the proportion of students who are poorly educated in reading and math. This is hugely important for students and for our society. But most people who study the achievement gap recognize that it cannot be sharply narrowed or closed without addressing the social and economic conditions that cause systemic disadvantages.   *20*

Achievement gaps begin long before children start kindergarten. On the first day of school, some children have had better medical care than others; are better nourished than others; are likelier to have a larger vocabulary because of having a parent who is college educated; are likelier to have books and computers in the home; and are likelier to live in sound   *21* housing in a safe neighborhood. The children at the wrong end of the gap are likelier to attend schools in overcrowded classrooms with inadequate resources and inexperienced teachers, as compared with the children at the advantaged end of the gap, whose schools are likelier to have small classes, experienced teachers, a full curriculum, laptops, libraries, playing fields, and a full staff. Schools that have large numbers of inexperienced teachers and inadequate resources are ill-prepared to reduce the achievement gap. If we were serious about narrowing the gap, the schools attended by African American and Hispanic children would have a stable, experienced staff, a rich curriculum, social services, after-school programs, and abundant resources to meet the needs of their students.

22 The black-white achievement gap is now smaller than the achievement gap between the poorest and the most affluent students, according to the sociologist Sean Reardon of Stanford University.

23 Strikingly, he found that "the achievement gap between children from high- and low-income families is roughly 30 to 40 percent larger among children born in 2001 than among those born twenty-five years earlier. In fact, it appears that the income achievement gap has been growing for at least fifty years, though the data are less certain for cohorts of children born before 1970." In contrast to the racial achievement gap, which has narrowed, the income achievement gap is growing. In fact, he found that the income achievement gap was nearly twice as large as the black-white achievement gap; the reverse was true fifty years earlier. The income achievement gap is already large when children start school, and according to the work of other researchers it "does not appear to grow (or narrow) appreciably as children progress through school." Reardon suggests that the income based gap is growing in part because affluent families invest in their children's cognitive development, with tutoring, summer camp, computers, and other enriching experiences. He concludes that "family income is now nearly as strong as parental education in predicting children's achievement."[5]

24 Thomas B. Timar of the University of California reviewed the efforts to close the black-white achievement gap and the Hispanic-white achievement gap and concluded that while there had been progress, the overall situation was discouraging. Why was there so little progress? He wrote: "One reason is that although schools can be held accountable for some of the disadvantage these students experience, *they have been given the entire responsibility for closing the achievement gap* [emphasis mine]. Yet the gap is the symptom of larger social, economic and political problems that go far beyond the reach of the school. . . . While schools are part of the solution, they alone cannot solve the problem of educational disparities."[6]

25 Another reason for the persistence of the gaps, Timar writes, is that policy makers have invested in strategies for thirty years that are "misdirected and ineffectual," managing to keep urban schools in a state of "policy spin," bouncing from one idea to another but never attaining the learning conditions or social capital that might make a difference.

Schools can't solve the problem alone, Timar acknowledges, as long 26
as society ignores the high levels of poverty and racial isolation in which
many of these youngsters live. He writes of children growing up in neighborhoods that experience high rates of crime and incarceration, violence,
and stress-related disorders. In the current version of reform, fixing schools
means more legislation, more mandates, and more regulations. What is
missing from reform, he says, is an appreciation for the value of local and
regional efforts, the small-scale programs that rely on local initiative for
implementation. Without local initiative, reforms cannot succeed.

Of great importance in creating lasting change is social capital, Timar 27
notes. This is the capital that grows because of relationships within the
school and between the school and the community. Social capital is a
necessary ingredient of reform, and it is built on a sense of community,
organizational stability, and trust. Successful schools in distressed communities have stable leadership and a shared vision for change. They have
"a sense of purpose, a coherent plan, and individuals with responsibility
to coordinate and implement the plan. Teachers worked collaboratively
to improve teaching and learning across the entire school curriculum. . . .
School improvement wasn't something done to them (like some sort of
medical procedure), but a collaborative undertaking. Students also realized that the school's engagement in school improvement activities was
meant for them, for their benefit."[7]

If we are serious about significantly narrowing the achievement gaps 28
between black and white students, Hispanic and white students, and
poor and affluent students, then we need to think in terms of long-term,
comprehensive strategies. Those strategies must address the problems of
poverty, unemployment, racial isolation, and mass incarceration. Income
inequality in the United States, he points out, cannot be ignored, since it
is greater now than at any time since the 1920s and more extreme than in
any other advanced nation. But American politics has grown so politically
conservative and unwilling to address structural issues that the chances of
this happening are slim.

So we are left with the short-term strategies. Timar says that the strat- 29
egies of "bureaucratizing the process of school improvement and turning
it into a chase for higher test scores" have not worked. They have not made
schools more stable, more coherent, and more professional. NCLB plus
the Obama administration's Race to the Top have made schools less stable, encouraged staff turnover, promoted policy churn, and undermined
professionalism.

Timar believes that the best hope for a school-based strategy for 30
reducing the gaps lies in a grassroots model of change. He points to
approaches like the Comer Process, developed by Dr. James Comer of Yale
University, which engages the school community in meeting the emotional,
psychological, social, and academic needs of students. What works best is
not regulation and mandates but professional collaboration, community

building, and cooperation. Such a scenario can happen only when those in the school have the authority to design their own improvement plans and act without waiting for instructions or permission from Washington or the state capital.

What we know from these scholars makes sense. The achievement 31 gaps are rooted in social, political, and economic structures. If we are unwilling to change the root causes, we are unlikely ever to close the gaps. What we call achievement gaps are in fact opportunity gaps.

Our corporate reformers insist that we must "fix" schools first, not 32 poverty. But the weight of evidence is against them. No serious social scientist believes that rearranging the organization or control or curriculum of schools will suffice to create income equality or to end poverty. The schools did not cause the achievement gaps, and the schools alone are not powerful enough to close them. So long as our society is indifferent to poverty, so long as we are willing to look the other way rather than act vigorously to improve the conditions of families and communities, there will always be achievement gaps.

NOTES

1. Martin Carnoy and Richard Rothstein, *What Do International Tests Really Show About U.S. Student Performance?* (Washington, D.C.: Economic Policy Institute, 2013).
2. Paul E. Barton and Richard J. Coley, *The Black-White Achievement Gap: When Progress Stopped* (Princeton, N.J.: Education Testing Service, 2010).
3. National Center for Education Statistics, *Nation's Report Card: Reading 2011*, 11.
4. National Center for Education Statistics, *Nation's Report Card: Mathematics 2011*, 12.
5. Sean F. Reardon, "The Widening Academic Achievement Gap Between the Rich and the Poor: New Evidence and Possible Explanations," in *Wither Opportunity? Rising Inequality, Schools, and Children's Life Chances,* ed. Greg J. Duncan and Richard J. Murnane (New York: Russell Sage Foundation, 2011).
6. Thomas B. Timar and Julie Maxwell-Jolly, eds., *Narrowing the Achievement Gap: Perspectives and Strategies for Challenging Times* (Cambridge, Mass.: Harvard Education Press, 2012), 230.
7. Ibid., 240–41.

■ ■ ■

Reading as a Writer: Analyzing Rhetorical Choices

1. One of the key words in the first sentence of Ravitch's piece is *corporate* in the phrase *corporate reform*. What does she mean, exactly? Divide into pairs or groups, and do some basic Internet research on corporate-financed school reform, and other education-related policies and practices that Ravitch mentions in passing: ALEC (para. 2), NAEP tests (para. 4), NCLB (para. 13), and any other acronyms or phrases that might be new to you. Share your findings.

2. After analyzing claims about "achievement gaps" in education throughout her piece, Ravitch makes an interesting move in her penultimate paragraph, arguing that this phrase is inaccurate: "What we call achievement gaps are in fact opportunity gaps" (para. 31). What does she mean by this? How do the examples and data she examines in this piece support her claim that "opportunity gap" is a more accurate term? Discuss how these two phrases reveal different perspectives on the problem of inequality in education.

Writing as a Reader: Entering the Conversation of Ideas

1. Ravitch notes in her second paragraph that privatization of schools often leads to greater segregation. What evidence does she offer in this essay? What might Beverly Tatum or Jonathan Kozol say about schools as spaces where we learn about difference and equality? Write an essay in which you draw on these scholars' examples and ideas to make a claim about the extent to which schools can be places that foster equality. What would need to change for improvements to be made?

2. Ravitch notes that race is a key element in conversations about educational inequalities. What might Agustín Fuentes say about the role of race in the education debate, as described by Ravitch? Compose an essay in which you build on these authors' insights to make an argument about the social impact of misunderstandings about racial categories

---

DEBORAH TANNEN

How Male and Female Students Use Language Differently

Deborah Tannen is a professor of linguistics at Georgetown University who is well known by both scholars and generalist readers with an interest in the ways people talk to one another. As a linguistic researcher, Tannen is curious about the relationship between the speech patterns we develop as a result of our socialization and the ways we are heard and misheard in the classroom, the workplace, our families, and our culture. This selection is from Tannen's book . . . *You Just Don't Understand: Women and Men in Conversation* (1990), which spent almost four years on the New York Times Best Seller list.

Tannen uses a writing style influenced by journalism. How does she express complex ideas within often short, punchy sentences? Pay attention to places where you see her moving smoothly between scholarly references to sociologists, anthropologists, and linguists, and personal anecdotes and observations about classroom behavior. Tannen argues that most classroom dynamics are "fundamentally male," and are characterized by an understanding that "the pursuit of knowledge is believed to be achieved by ritual opposition: public display followed by argument and challenge" (para. 5). How does this claim line up with your own experiences—good and bad—in the classroom?

Critics sometimes complain that Tannen's examples are too selective and that she makes generalizing claims from too little evidence, though she also has many admirers among academics, book award committees, and the millions of readers who purchase her books. It's difficult to be neutral about Tannen's work, because she asks us to question and analyze the ways we interact with others, and this feels very personal—as it should. This selection focuses on linguistic dynamics in the classroom, but you may find that her insights will make you reconsider conversations you have had in almost every part of your life.

■ ■ ■

When I researched and wrote . . . *You Just Don't Understand: Women and Men in Conversation*, the furthest thing from my mind was re-evaluating my teaching strategies. But that has been one of the direct benefits of having written the book. 1

The primary focus of my linguistic research always has been the language of everyday conversation. One facet of this is conversational style: how different regional, ethnic, and class backgrounds, as well as age and gender, result in different ways of using language to communicate. *You Just Don't Understand* is about the conversational styles of women and men. As I gained more insight into typically male and female ways of using language, I began to suspect some of the causes of the troubling facts that women who go to single-sex schools do better in later life, and that when young women sit next to young men in classrooms, the males talk more. This is not to say that all men talk in class, nor that no women do. It is simply that a greater percentage of discussion time is taken by men's voices. 2

The research of sociologists and anthropologists such as Janet Lever, Marjorie Harness Goodwin, and Donna Eder has shown that girls and boys learn to use language differently in their sex-separate peer groups. Typically, a girl has a best friend with whom she sits and talks, frequently telling secrets. It's the telling of secrets, the fact and the way that they talk to each other, that makes them best friends. For boys, activities are central: Their best friends are the ones they do things with. Boys also tend to play in larger groups that are hierarchical. High-status boys give orders and push low-status boys around. So boys are expected to use language to seize center stage: by exhibiting their skill, displaying their knowledge, and challenging and resisting challenges. 3

These patterns have stunning implications for classroom interaction. Most faculty members assume that participating in class discussion is a necessary part of successful performance. Yet speaking in a classroom is more congenial to boys' language experience than to girls', since it entails putting oneself forward in front of a large group of people, many of whom are strangers and at least one of whom is sure to judge speakers' knowledge and intelligence by their verbal display. 4

Another aspect of many classrooms that makes them more hospitable   5
to most men than to most women is the use of debatelike formats as a
learning tool. Our educational system, as Walter Ong argues persuasively
in his book *Fighting for Life* (Cornell University Press, 1981), is fundamentally male in that the pursuit of knowledge is believed to be achieved by ritual opposition: public display followed by argument and challenge. Father
Ong demonstrates that ritual opposition—what he calls "adversativeness"
or "agonism"—is fundamental to the way most males approach almost any
activity. (Consider, for example, the little boy who shows he likes a little girl
by pulling her braids and shoving her.) But ritual opposition is antithetical
to the way most females learn and like to interact. It is not that females
don't fight, but that they don't fight for fun. They don't *ritualize* opposition.

Anthropologists working in widely disparate parts of the world have found   6
contrasting verbal rituals for women and men. Women in completely
unrelated cultures (for example, Greece and Bali) engage in ritual laments:
spontaneously produced rhyming couplets that express their pain, for
example, over the loss of loved ones. Men do not take part in laments. They
have their own, very different verbal ritual: a contest, a war of words in
which they vie with each other to devise clever insults.

When discussing these phenomena with a colleague, I commented   7
that I see these two styles in American conversation: Many women bond
by talking about troubles, and many men bond by exchanging playful
insults and put-downs, and other sorts of verbal sparring. He exclaimed:
"I never thought of this, but that's the way I teach: I have students read an
article, and then I invite them to tear it apart. After we've torn it to shreds,
we talk about how to build a better model."

This contrasts sharply with the way I teach: I open the discussion of   8
readings by asking, "What did you find useful in this? What can we use
in our own theory building and our own methods?" I note what I see as
weaknesses in the author's approach, but I also point out that the writer's
discipline and purposes might be different from ours. Finally, I offer personal anecdotes illustrating the phenomena under discussion and praise
students' anecdotes as well as their critical acumen.

These different teaching styles must make our classrooms wildly dif-   9
ferent places and hospitable to different students. Male students are more
likely to be comfortable attacking the readings and might find the inclusion of personal anecdotes irrelevant and "soft." Women are more likely to
resist discussion they perceive as hostile, and, indeed, it is women in my
classes who are most likely to offer personal anecdotes.

A colleague who read my book commented that he had always taken for   10
granted that the best way to deal with students' comments is to challenge
them; this, he felt it was self-evident, sharpens their minds and helps them
develop debating skills. But he had noticed that women were relatively

silent in his classes, so he decided to try beginning discussion with relatively open-ended questions and letting comments go unchallenged. He found, to his amazement and satisfaction, that more women began to speak up.

Though some of the women in his class clearly liked this better, perhaps some of the men liked it less. One young man in my class wrote in a questionnaire about a history professor who gave students questions to think about and called on people to answer them: "He would then play devil's advocate . . . i.e., he debated us. . . . That class *really* sharpened me intellectually. . . . We as students do need to know how to defend ourselves." This young man valued the experience of being attacked and challenged publicly. Many, if not most, women would shrink from such "challenge," experiencing it as public humiliation. *11*

A professor at Hamilton College told me of a young man who was upset because he felt his class presentation had been a failure. The professor was puzzled because he had observed that class members had listened attentively and agreed with the student's observations. It turned out that it was this very agreement that the student interpreted as failure: Since no one had engaged his ideas by arguing with him, he felt they had found them unworthy of attention. *12*

So one reason men speak in class more than women is that many of them find the "public" classroom setting more conducive to speaking, whereas most women are more comfortable speaking in private to a small group of people they know well. A second reason is that men are more likely to be comfortable with the debatelike form that discussion may take. Yet another reason is the different attitudes toward speaking in class that typify women and men. *13*

Students who speak frequently in class, many of whom are men, assume that it is their job to think of contributions and try to get the floor to express them. But many women monitor their participation not only to get the floor but to avoid getting it. Women students in my class tell me that if they have spoken up once or twice, they hold back for the rest of the class because they don't want to dominate. If they have spoken a lot one week, they will remain silent the next. These different ethics of participation are, of course, unstated, so those who speak freely assume that those who remain silent have nothing to say, and those who are reining themselves in assume that the big talkers are selfish and hoggish. *14*

When I looked around my classes, I could see these differing ethics and habits at work. For example, my graduate class in analyzing conversation had twenty students, eleven women and nine men. Of the men, four were foreign students: two Japanese, one Chinese, and one Syrian. With the exception of the three Asian men, all the men spoke in class at least occasionally. The biggest talker in the class was a woman, but there were also five women who never spoke at all, only one of whom was Japanese. I decided to try something different. *15*

I broke the class into small groups to discuss the issues raised in the *16* readings and to analyze their own conversational transcripts. I devised three ways of dividing the students into groups: one by the degree program they were in, one by gender, and one by conversational style, as closely as I could guess it. This meant that when the class was grouped according to conversational style, I put Asian students together, fast talkers together, and quiet students together. The class split into groups six times during the semester, so they met in each grouping twice. I told students to regard the groups as examples of interactional data and to note the different ways they participated in the different groups. Toward the end of the term, I gave them a questionnaire asking about their class and group participation.

I could see plainly from my observation of the groups at work that *17* women who never opened their mouths in class were talking away in the small groups. In fact, the Japanese woman commented that she found it particularly hard to contribute to the all-woman group she was in because "I was overwhelmed by how talkative the female students were in the female-only group." This is particularly revealing because it highlights that the same person who can be "oppressed" into silence in one context can become the talkative "oppressor" in another. No one's conversational style is absolute; everyone's style changes in response to the context and others' styles.

Some of the students (seven) said they preferred the same-gender groups; *18* others preferred the same-style groups. In answer to the question "Would you have liked to speak in class more than you did?" six of the seven who said yes were women; the one man was Japanese. Most startlingly, this response did not come only from quiet women; it came from women who had indicated they had spoken in class never, rarely, sometimes, and often. Of the eleven students who said the amount they had spoken was fine, seven were men. Of the four women who checked "fine," two added qualifications indicating it wasn't completely fine: One wrote in "maybe more," and one wrote, "I have an urge to participate but often feel I should have something more interesting/relevant/wonderful/intelligent to say!!"

I counted my experiment a success. Everyone in the class found the *19* small groups interesting, and no one indicated he or she would have preferred that the class not break into groups. Perhaps most instructive, however, was the fact that the experience of breaking into groups, and of talking about participation in class, raised everyone's awareness about classroom participation. After we had talked about it, some of the quietest women in the class made a few voluntary contributions, though sometimes I had to ensure their participation by interrupting the students who were exuberantly speaking out.

Americans are often proud that they discount the significance of cul- *20* tural differences: "We are all individuals," many people boast. Ignoring such issues as gender and ethnicity becomes a source of pride: "I treat everyone the same." But treating people the same is not equal treatment if they are not the same.

The classroom is a different environment for those who feel comfort- 21
able putting themselves forward in a group than it is for those who find the prospect of doing so chastening, or even terrifying. When a professor asks, "Are there any questions?" students who can formulate statements the fastest have the greatest opportunity to respond. Those who need significant time to do so have not really been given a chance at all, since by the time they are ready to speak, someone else has the floor.

In a class where some students speak out without raising hands, those 22
who feel they must raise their hands and wait to be recognized do not have equal opportunity to speak. Telling them to feel free to jump in will not make them feel free; one's sense of timing, of one's rights and obligations in a classroom, are automatic, learned over years of interaction. They may be changed over time, with motivation and effort, but they cannot be changed on the spot. And everyone assumes his or her own way is best. When I asked my students how the class could be changed to make it easier for them to speak more, the most talkative woman said she would prefer it if no one had to raise hands, and a foreign student said he wished people would raise their hands and wait to be recognized.

My experience in this class has convinced me that small-group inter- 23
action should be part of any class that is not a small seminar. I also am convinced that having the students become observers of their own interaction is a crucial part of their education. Talking about ways of talking in class makes students aware that their ways of talking affect other students, that the motivations they impute to others may not truly reflect others' motives, and that the behaviors they assume to be self-evidently right are not universal norms.

The goal of complete equal opportunity in class may not be attainable, 24
but realizing that one monolithic classroom-participation structure is not equal opportunity is itself a powerful motivation to find more-diverse methods to serve diverse students—and every classroom is diverse.

■ ■ ■

Reading as a Writer: Analyzing Rhetorical Choices

1. Given that Tannen is concerned with classroom dynamics, why does she open her essay with a discussion of sociologists and anthropologists? How do the framing ideas of those experts contribute to her descriptions of classroom dynamics? In particular, how does she use the concept of "ritual opposition" to help build her argument?

2. How would you describe Tannen's own style of making an argument? Are there aspects of both "female" and "male" conversational styles, as she defines them? How successfully do you think she addresses readers who might disagree with her?

Writing as a Reader: Entering the Conversation of Ideas

1. Tannen's insights about gendered classroom conversational patterns may help bring aspects of Beverly Tatum's essay into clearer focus. Write an essay in which you use Tannen's insights about gender and conversational style to analyze some of the vocal exchanges you find most interesting in Tatum's essay. How might the sociological and anthropological ideas about gender dynamics that Tannen cites in her essay help you analyze both the problems and the solutions that Tatum describes in her essay?

2. Both Tannen and Jessie J. Prinz consider the way assumptions about gender can shape our educational experiences. Compose an essay in which you consider the ways Tannen's insights about gender dynamics in a classroom are in conversation with Prinz's ideas about "learned limitations" and other social forces that bear on learning. What solutions can you envision to the problems these authors raise?

BEVERLY DANIEL TATUM

"Why Are All the Black Kids Sitting Together in the Cafeteria?"

Dr. Beverly Daniel Tatum is a clinical psychologist and president of Spelman College in Atlanta. Her research often focuses on racial identity development and the role of race in education, including the very concrete experiences of race dynamics in the classroom. She is the author of several books, the most recent of which are *Can We Talk about Race? And Other Conversations in an Era of School Resegregation* (2007) and *"Why Are All the Black Kids Sitting Together in the Cafeteria?": A Psychologist Explains the Development of Racial Identity* (rev. 2003). Like many of the scholars in this book, she is an expert in her field, but she chooses language that is welcoming to any informed and interested reader.

This excerpt comes from her 2003 book and hinges on a very concrete example of the gathering patterns of kids in mixed high schools. Her title alone should get you thinking and talking with your peers. If you attended a high school with a diverse population, how would you answer her question? Tatum is aware that many Americans are uncomfortable talking about race and the effects of racial categorization, and so she offers her readers a set of tools for analyzing specific examples, like the cafeteria table example. She invites readers to see "racial identity formation" in a series of stages that we can analyze and reconsider. If cultural stereotypes are learned, as she argues, what will help us learn to think more open-mindedly about the potential of all people? Tatum's particular concern is the way schools—and high schools, in particular, in this excerpt—seem to be places where old patterns prevail more often than not.

As you read, evaluate the way Tatum frames both problems and solutions. Consider her claims and proposals in the context of your own experiences. How might your own racial identity, and even your gender, affect your insights and responses? This is a reading that might feel very close to home, which is not always comfortable. Tatum would argue, though, that facing discomfort head-on is better than never even asking obvious but difficult questions such as, "Why are all the black kids sitting together in the cafeteria?"

■ ■ ■

Walk into any racially mixed high school cafeteria at lunch time and *1* you will instantly notice that in the sea of adolescent faces, there is an identifiable group of Black students sitting together. Conversely, it could be pointed out that there are many groups of White students sitting together as well, though people rarely comment about that. The question on the tip of everyone's tongue is "Why are the Black kids sitting together?" Principals want to know, teachers want to know, White students want to know, the Black students who aren't sitting at the table want to know.

How does it happen that so many Black teenagers end up at the same *2* cafeteria table? They don't start out there. If you walk into racially mixed elementary schools, you will often see young children of diverse racial backgrounds playing with one another, sitting at the snack table together, crossing racial boundaries with an ease uncommon in adolescence. Moving from elementary school to middle school (often at sixth or seventh grade) means interacting with new children from different neighborhoods than before, and a certain degree of clustering by race might therefore be expected, presuming that children who are familiar with one another would form groups. But even in schools where the same children stay together from kindergarten through eighth grade, racial grouping begins by the sixth or seventh grade. What happens?

One thing that happens is puberty. As children enter adolescence, they *3* begin to explore the question of identity, asking "Who am I? Who can I be?" in ways they have not done before. For Black youth, asking "Who am I?" includes thinking about "Who am I ethnically and/or racially? What does it mean to be Black?"

As I write this, I can hear the voice of a White woman who asked me, *4* "Well, all adolescents struggle with questions of identity. They all become more self-conscious about their appearance and more concerned about what their peers think. So what is so different for Black kids?" Of course, she is right that all adolescents look at themselves in new ways, but not all adolescents think about themselves in racial terms.

The search for personal identity that intensifies in adolescence can *5* involve several dimensions of an adolescent's life: vocational plans, religious beliefs, values and preferences, political affiliations and beliefs, gender roles, and ethnic identities. The process of exploration may vary across these identity domains. James Marcia described four identity "statuses" to characterize the variation in the identity search process: (1) *diffuse*, a state in which there has been little exploration or active consideration of a particular domain, and no psychological commitment; (2) *foreclosed*, a state in which a commitment has been made to particular roles or belief systems, often those selected by parents, without actively considering alternatives; (3) *moratorium*, a state of active exploration of roles and beliefs in which no commitment has yet been made; and (4) *achieved*, a state of strong personal commitment to a particular dimension of identity following a period of high exploration.[1]

An individual is not likely to explore all identity domains at once; therefore it is not unusual for an adolescent to be actively exploring one dimension while another remains relatively unexamined. Given the impact of dominant and subordinate status, it is not surprising that researchers have found that adolescents of color are more likely to be actively engaged in an exploration of their racial or ethnic identity than are White adolescents.[2]   6

Why do Black youths, in particular, think about themselves in terms of race? Because that is how the rest of the world thinks of them. Our self-perceptions are shaped by the messages that we receive from those around us, and when young Black men and women enter adolescence, the racial content of those messages intensifies. A case in point: If you were to ask my ten-year-old son, David, to describe himself, he would tell you many things: that he is smart, that he likes to play computer games, that he has an older brother. Near the top of his list, he would likely mention that he is tall for his age. He would probably not mention that he is Black, though he certainly knows that he is. Why would he mention his height and not his racial group membership? When David meets new adults, one of the first questions they ask is "How old are you?" When David states his age, the inevitable reply is "Gee, you're tall for your age!" It happens so frequently that I once overheard David say to someone, "Don't say it, I know. I'm tall for my age." Height is salient for David because it is salient for others.   7

When David meets new adults, they don't say, "Gee, you're Black for your age!" If you are saying to yourself, of course they don't, think again. Imagine David at fifteen, six-foot-two, wearing the adolescent attire of the day, passing adults he doesn't know on the sidewalk. Do the women hold their purses a little tighter, maybe even cross the street to avoid him? Does he hear the sound of the automatic door locks on cars as he passes by? Is he being followed around by the security guards at the local mall? As he stops in town with his new bicycle, does a police officer hassle him, asking where he got it, implying that it might be stolen? Do strangers assume he plays basketball? Each of these experiences conveys a racial message. At ten, race is not yet salient for David, because it is not yet salient for society. But it will be.   8

Understanding Racial Identity Development

Psychologist William Cross, author of *Shades of Black: Diversity in African American Identity*, has offered a theory of racial identity development   9 that I have found to be a very useful framework for understanding what is happening not only with David, but with those Black students in the cafeteria.[3] According to Cross's model, referred to as the psychology of nigrescence, or the psychology of becoming Black, the five stages of racial identity development are *pre-encounter*, *encounter*, *immersion/emersion*, *internalization*, and *internalization-commitment*. For the moment, we will consider the first two stages as those are the most relevant for adolescents.

In the first stage, the Black child absorbs many of the beliefs and val- 10 ues of the dominant White culture, including the idea that it is better to be White. The stereotypes, omissions, and distortions that reinforce notions of White superiority are breathed in by Black children as well as White. Simply as a function of being socialized in a Eurocentric culture, some Black children may begin to value the role models, lifestyles, and images of beauty represented by the dominant group more highly than those of their own cultural group. On the other hand, if Black parents are what I call race-conscious—that is, actively seeking to encourage positive racial identity by providing their children with positive cultural images and messages about what it means to be Black—the impact of the dominant society's messages are reduced.[4] In either case, in the pre-encounter stage, the personal and social significance of one's racial group membership has not yet been realized, and racial identity is not yet under examination. At age ten, David and other children like him would seem to be in the pre-encounter stage. When the environmental cues change and the world begins to reflect his Blackness back to him more clearly, he will probably enter the encounter stage.

Transition to the encounter stage is typically precipitated by an event 11 or series of events that force the young person to acknowledge the personal impact of racism. As the result of a new and heightened awareness of the significance of race, the individual begins to grapple with what it means to be a member of a group targeted by racism. Though Cross describes this process as one that unfolds in late adolescence and early adulthood, research suggests that an examination of one's racial or ethnic identity may begin as early as junior high school.

In a study of Black and White eighth graders from an integrated urban 12 junior high school, Jean Phinney and Steve Tarver found clear evidence for the beginning of the search process in this dimension of identity. Among the forty-eight participants, more than a third had thought about the effects of ethnicity on their future, had discussed the issues with family and friends, and were attempting to learn more about their group. While White students in this integrated school were also beginning to think about ethnic identity, there was evidence to suggest a more active search among Black students, especially Black females.[5] Phinney and Tarver's research is consistent with my own study of Black youth in predominantly White communities, where the environmental cues that trigger an examination of racial identity often become evident in middle school or junior high school.[6]

Some of the environmental cues are institutionalized. Though many *13* elementary schools have self-contained classrooms where children of varying performance levels learn together, many middle and secondary schools use "ability grouping," or tracking. Though school administrators often defend their tracking practices as fair and objective, there usually is a recognizable racial pattern to how children are assigned, which often represents the system of advantage operating in the schools.[7] In racially mixed schools, Black children are much more likely to be in the lower track than in the honors track. Such apparent sorting along racial lines sends a message about what it means to be Black. One young honors student I interviewed described the irony of this resegregation in what was an otherwise integrated environment, and hinted at the identity issues it raised for him.

> It was really a very paradoxical existence, here I am in a school that's 35 percent Black, you know, and I'm the only Black in my classes. . . . That always struck me as odd. I guess I felt that I was different from the other Blacks because of that.

In addition to the changes taking place within school, there are *14* changes in the social dynamics outside school. For many parents, puberty raises anxiety about interracial dating. In racially mixed communities, you begin to see what I call the birthday party effect. Young children's birthday parties in multiracial communities are often a reflection of the community's diversity. The parties of elementary school children may be segregated by gender but not by race. At puberty, when the parties become sleepovers or boy-girl events, they become less and less racially diverse.

Black girls, especially in predominantly White communities, may *15* gradually become aware that something has changed. When their White friends start to date, they do not. The issues of emerging sexuality and the societal messages about who is sexually desirable leave young Black women in a very devalued position. One young woman from a Philadelphia suburb described herself as "pursuing White guys throughout high school" to no avail. Since there were no Black boys in her class, she had little choice. She would feel "really pissed off" that those same White boys would date her White friends. For her, "that prom thing was like out of the question."[8]

Though Black girls living in the context of a larger Black community *16* may have more social choices, they too have to contend with devaluing messages about who they are and who they will become, especially if they are poor or working-class. As social scientists Bonnie Ross Leadbeater and Niobe Way point out,

> The school drop-out, the teenage welfare mother, the drug addict, and the victim of domestic violence or of AIDS are among the most prevalent public images of poor and working-class urban adolescent girls. . . . Yet, despite the risks inherent in economic disadvantage, the majority of poor urban adolescent girls do not fit the stereotypes that are made about them.[9]

Resisting the stereotypes and affirming other definitions of themselves 17 is part of the task facing young Black women in both White and Black communities.

As was illustrated in the example of David, Black boys also face a 18 devalued status in the wider world. The all too familiar media image of a young Black man with his hands cuffed behind his back, arrested for a violent crime, has primed many to view young Black men with suspicion and fear. In the context of predominantly White schools, however, Black boys may enjoy a degree of social success, particularly if they are athletically talented. The culture has embraced the Black athlete, and the young man who can fulfill that role is often pursued by Black girls and White girls alike. But even these young men will encounter experiences that may trigger an examination of their racial identity.

Sometimes the experience is quite dramatic. *The Autobiography of* 19 *Malcolm X* is a classic tale of racial identity development, and I assign it to my psychology of racism students for just that reason. As a junior high school student, Malcolm was a star. Despite the fact that he was separated from his family and living in a foster home, he was an A student and was elected president of his class. One day he had a conversation with his English teacher, whom he liked and respected, about his future career goals. Malcolm said he wanted to be a lawyer. His teacher responded, "That's no realistic goal for a nigger," and advised him to consider carpentry instead.[10] The message was clear: You are a Black male, your racial group membership matters, plan accordingly. Malcolm's emotional response was typical—anger, confusion, and alienation. He withdrew from his White classmates, stopped participating in class, and eventually left his predominately white Michigan home to live with his sister in Roxbury, a Black community in Boston.

No teacher would say such a thing now, you may be thinking, but 20 don't be so sure. It is certainly less likely that a teacher would use the word *nigger*, but consider these contemporary examples shared by high school students. A young ninth-grade student was sitting in his homeroom. A substitute teacher was in charge of the class. Because the majority of students from this school go on to college, she used the free time to ask the students about their college plans. As a substitute she had very limited information about their academic performance, but she offered some suggestions. When she turned to this young man, one of few Black males in the class, she suggested that he consider a community college. She had recommended four-year colleges to the other students. Like Malcolm, this student got the message.

In another example, a young Black woman attending a desegregated 21 school to which she was bussed was encouraged by a teacher to attend the upcoming school dance. Most of the Black students did not live in the neighborhood and seldom attended the extracurricular activities. The young woman indicated that she wasn't planning to come. The well-intentioned teacher was persistent. Finally the teacher said, "Oh come on, I know you people love to dance." This young woman got the message, too.

Coping with Encounters: Developing an Oppositional Identity

What do these encounters have to do with the cafeteria? Do experiences   22
with racism inevitably result in so-called self-segregation? While certainly a desire to protect oneself from further offense is understandable, it is not the only factor at work. Imagine the young eighth-grade girl who experienced the teacher's use of "you people" and the dancing stereotype as a racial affront. Upset and struggling with adolescent embarrassment, she bumps into a White friend who can see that something is wrong. She explains. Her White friend responds, in an effort to make her feel better perhaps, and says, "Oh, Mr. Smith is such a nice guy, I'm sure he didn't mean it like that. Don't be so sensitive." Perhaps the White friend is right, and Mr. Smith didn't mean it, but imagine your own response when you are upset, perhaps with a spouse or partner. He or she asks what's wrong and you explain why you are offended. Your partner brushes off your complaint, attributing it to your being oversensitive. What happens to your emotional thermostat? It escalates. When feelings, rational or irrational, are invalidated, most people disengage. They not only choose to discontinue the conversation but are more likely to turn to someone who will understand their perspective.

In much the same way, the eighth-grade girl's White friend doesn't get   23
it. She doesn't see the significance of this racial message, but the girls at the "Black table" do. When she tells her story there, one of them is likely to say, "You know what, Mr. Smith said the same thing to me yesterday!" Not only are Black adolescents encountering racism and reflecting on their identity, but their White peers, even when they are not the perpetrators (and sometimes they are), are unprepared to respond in supportive ways. The Black students turn to each other for the much needed support they are not likely to find anywhere else.

In adolescence, as race becomes personally salient for Black youth,   24
finding the answer to questions such as, "What does it mean to be a young Black person? How should I act? What should I do?" is particularly important. And although Black fathers, mothers, aunts, and uncles may hold the answers by offering themselves as role models, they hold little appeal for most adolescents. The last thing many fourteen-year-olds want to do is to grow up to be like their parents. It is the peer group, the kids in the cafeteria, who hold the answers to these questions. They know how to be Black. They have absorbed the stereotypical images of Black youth in the popular culture and are reflecting those images in their self-presentation.

Based on their fieldwork in U.S. high schools, Signithia Fordham   25
and John Ogbu identified a common psychological pattern found among

African American high school students at this stage of identity development.[11] They observed that the anger and resentment that adolescents feel in response to their growing awareness of the systematic exclusion of Black people from full participation in U.S. society leads to the development of an oppositional social identity. This oppositional stance both protects one's identity from the psychological assault of racism and keeps the dominant group at a distance. Fordham and Ogbu write:

> Subordinate minorities regard certain forms of behavior and certain activities or events, symbols, and meanings as *not appropriate* for them because those behaviors, events, symbols, and meanings are characteristic of white Americans. At the same time they emphasize other forms of behavior as more appropriate for them because these are *not* a part of white Americans' way of life. To behave in the manner defined as falling within a white cultural frame of reference is to "act white" and is negatively sanctioned.[12]

Certain styles of speech, dress, and music, for example, may be embraced as "authentically Black" and become highly valued, while attitudes and behaviors associated with Whites are viewed with disdain. The peer group's evaluation of what is Black and what is not can have a powerful impact on adolescent behavior. 26

Reflecting on her high school years, one Black woman from a White neighborhood described both the pain of being rejected by her Black classmates and her attempts to conform to her peers' definition of Blackness: 27

> "Oh you sound White, you think you're White," they said. And the idea of sounding White was just so absurd to me. . . . So ninth grade was sort of traumatic in that I started listening to rap music, which I really just don't like. [I said] I'm gonna be Black, and it was just that stupid. But it's more than just how one acts, you know. [The other Black women there] were not into me for the longest time. My first year there was hell.

Sometimes the emergence of an oppositional identity can be quite dramatic, as the young person tries on a new persona almost overnight. At the end of one school year, race may not have appeared to be significant, but often some encounter takes place over the summer and the young person returns to school much more aware of his or her Blackness and ready to make sure that the rest of the world is aware of it, too. There is a certain "in your face" quality that these adolescents can take on, which their teachers often experience as threatening. When a group of Black teens are sitting together in the cafeteria, collectively embodying an oppositional stance, school administrators want to know not only why they are sitting together, but what can be done to prevent it. 28

We need to understand that in racially mixed settings, racial grouping is a developmental process in response to an environmental stressor, racism. Joining with one's peers for support in the face of stress is a positive coping strategy. What is problematic is that the young people are operating with a very limited definition of what it means to be Black, based largely on cultural stereotypes. 29

Oppositional Identity Development and Academic Achievement

Unfortunately for Black teenagers, those cultural stereotypes do not usu- *30*
ally include academic achievement. Academic success is more often associated with being White. During the encounter phase of racial identity
development, when the search for identity leads toward cultural stereotypes and away from anything that might be associated with Whiteness,
academic performance often declines. Doing well in school becomes
identified as trying to be White. Being smart becomes the opposite of
being cool.

While this frame of reference is not universally found among adoles- *31*
cents of African descent, it is commonly observed in Black peer groups.
Among the Black college students I have interviewed, many described
some conflict or alienation from other African American teens because
of their academic success in high school. For example, a twenty-year-old
female from a Washington, D.C., suburb explained:

> It was weird, even in high school a lot of the Black students were, like, "Well,
> you're not really Black." Whether it was because I became president of the
> sixth-grade class or whatever it was, it started pretty much back then. Junior
> high, it got worse. I was then labeled certain things, whether it was "the oreo"
> or I wasn't really Black.

Others described avoiding situations that would set them apart from *32*
their Black peers. For example, one young woman declined to participate
in a gifted program in her school because she knew it would separate her
from the other Black students in the school.

In a study of thirty-three eleventh-graders in a Washington, D.C., *33*
school, Fordham and Ogbu found that although some of the students had
once been academically successful, few of them remained so. These students also knew that to be identified as a "brainiac" would result in peer
rejection. The few students who had maintained strong academic records
found ways to play down their academic success enough to maintain some
level of acceptance among their Black peers.[13]

Academically successful Black students also need a strategy to find *34*
acceptance among their White classmates. Fordham describes one such
strategy as *racelessness*, wherein individuals assimilate into the dominant group by de-emphasizing characteristics that might identify them
as members of the subordinate group.[14] Jon, a young man I interviewed,
offered a classic example of this strategy as he described his approach to
dealing with his discomfort at being the only Black person in his advanced
classes. He said, "At no point did I ever think I was White or did I ever
want to be White.... I guess it was one of those things where I tried to
de-emphasize the fact that I was Black." This strategy led him to avoid
activities that were associated with Blackness. He recalled, "I didn't want
to do anything that was traditionally Black, like I never played basketball.

I ran cross-country. . . . I went for distance running instead of sprints." He felt he had to show his White classmates that there were "exceptions to all these stereotypes." However, this strategy was of limited usefulness. When he traveled outside his home community with his White teammates, he sometimes encountered overt racism. "I quickly realized that I'm Black, and that's the thing that they're going to see first, no matter how much I try to de-emphasize my Blackness."

A Black student can play down Black identity in order to succeed in 35 school and mainstream institutions without rejecting his Black identity and culture.[15] Instead of becoming raceless, an achieving Black student can become an *emissary*, someone who sees his or her own achievements as advancing the cause of the racial group. For example, social scientists Richard Zweigenhaft and G. William Domhoff describe how a successful Black student, in response to the accusation of acting White, connected his achievement to that of other Black men by saying, "Martin Luther King must not have been Black, then, since he had a doctoral degree, and Malcolm X must not have been Black since he educated himself while in prison." In addition, he demonstrated his loyalty to the Black community by taking an openly political stance against the racial discrimination he observed in his school.[16]

It is clear that an oppositional identity can interfere with academic 36 achievement, and it may be tempting for educators to blame the adolescents themselves for their academic decline. However, the questions that educators and other concerned adults must ask are, How did academic achievement become defined as exclusively White behavior? What is it about the curriculum and the wider culture that reinforces the notion that academic excellence is an exclusively White domain? What curricular interventions might we use to encourage the development of an empowered emissary identity?

An oppositional identity that disdains academic achievement has not 37 always been a characteristic of Black adolescent peer groups. It seems to be a post-desegregation phenomenon. Historically, the oppositional identity found among African Americans in the segregated South included a positive attitude toward education. While Black people may have publicly deferred to Whites, they actively encouraged their children to pursue education as a ticket to greater freedom.[17] While Black parents still see education as the key to upward mobility, in today's desegregated schools the models of success—the teachers, administrators, and curricular heroes— are almost always White.

Black Southern schools, though stigmatized by legally sanctioned seg- 38 regation, were often staffed by African American educators, themselves visible models of academic achievement. These Black educators may have presented a curriculum that included references to the intellectual legacy of other African Americans. As well, in the context of a segregated school, it was a given that the high achieving students would all be Black. Academic achievement did not have to mean separation from one's Black peers.

The Search for Alternative Images

This historical example reminds us that an oppositional identity discour- 39
aging academic achievement is not inevitable even in a racist society. If
young people are exposed to images of African American academic achievement in their early years, they won't have to define school achievement as
something for Whites only. They will know that there is a long history of
Black intellectual achievement.

This point was made quite eloquently by Jon, the young man I quoted 40
earlier. Though he made the choice to excel in school, he labored under
the false assumption that he was "inventing the wheel." It wasn't until he
reached college and had the opportunity to take African American studies courses that he learned about other African Americans besides Martin
Luther King, Malcolm X, and Frederick Douglass—the same three men he
had heard about year after year, from kindergarten to high school graduation. As he reflected on his identity struggle in high school, he said:

> It's like I went through three phases. . . . My first phase was being cool, doing
> whatever was particularly cool for Black people at the time, and that was
> like in junior high. Then in high school, you know, I thought being Black was
> basically all stereotypes, so I tried to avoid all of those things. Now in college,
> you know, I realize that being Black means a variety of things.

Learning his history in college was of great psychological importance 41
to Jon, providing him with role models he had been missing in high school.
He was particularly inspired by learning of the intellectual legacy of Black
men at his own college:

> When you look at those guys who were here in the Twenties, they couldn't live
> on campus. They couldn't eat on campus. They couldn't get their hair cut in
> town. And yet they were all Phi Beta Kappa. . . . That's what being Black really
> is, you know, knowing who you are, your history, your accomplishments. . . .
> When I was in junior high, I had White role models. And then when I got into
> high school, you know, I wasn't sure but I just didn't think having White role
> models was a good thing. So I got rid of those. And I basically just, you know,
> only had my parents for role models. I kind of grew up thinking that we were on
> the cutting edge. We were doing something radically different than everybody
> else. And not realizing that there are all kinds of Black people doing the very
> things that I thought we were the only ones doing. . . . You've got to do the very
> best you can so that you can continue the great traditions that have already
> been established.

This young man was not alone in his frustration over having learned 42
little about his own cultural history in grade school. Time and again in the
research interviews I conducted, Black students lamented the absence of
courses in African American history or literature at the high school level
and indicated how significant this new learning was to them in college,
how excited and affirmed they felt by this newfound knowledge. Sadly,

many Black students never get to college, alienated from the process of education long before high school graduation. They may never get access to the information that might have helped them expand their definition of what it means to be Black and, in the process, might have helped them stay in school. Young people are developmentally ready for this information in adolescence. We ought to provide it. . . .

An Alternative to the Cafeteria Table

The developmental need to explore the meaning of one's identity with others *43* who are engaged in a similar process manifests itself informally in school corridors and cafeterias across the country. Some educational institutions have sought to meet this need programmatically. Several colleagues and I recently evaluated one such effort, initiated at a Massachusetts middle school participating in a voluntary desegregation program known as the Metropolitan Council for Educational Opportunity (METCO) program.[18] Historically, the small number of African American students who are bussed from Boston to this suburban school have achieved disappointing levels of academic success. In an effort to improve academic achievement, the school introduced a program, known as Student Efficacy Training (SET), that allowed Boston students to meet each day as a group with two staff members. Instead of being in physical education or home economics or study hall, they were meeting, talking about homework difficulties, social issues, and encounters with racism. The meeting was mandatory and at first the students were resentful of missing some of their classes. But the impact was dramatic. Said one young woman,

> In the beginning of the year, I didn't want to do SET at all. It took away my
> study and it was only METCO students doing it. In the beginning all we did
> was argue over certain problems or it was more like a rap session and I didn't
> think it was helping anyone. But then when we looked at records . . .
> I know that last year out of all the students, sixth through eighth grade, there
> was, like, six who were actually good students. Everyone else, it was just
> pathetic, I mean, like, they were getting like Ds and Fs. . . . The eighth grade
> is doing much better this year. I mean, they went from Ds and Fs to Bs and Cs
> and occasional As. . . . And those seventh-graders are doing really good, they
> have a lot of honor roll students in seventh grade, both guys and girls. Yeah,
> it's been good. It's really good.

Her report is borne out by an examination of school records. The *44* opportunity to come together in the company of supportive adults allowed these young Black students to talk about the issues that hindered their performance—racial encounters, feelings of isolation, test anxiety, homework dilemmas—in the psychological safety of their own group. In the process, the peer culture changed to one that supported academic performance rather than undermined it, as revealed in these two students' comments:

Well, a lot of the Boston students, the boys and the girls, used to fight all the time. And now, they stopped yelling at each other so much and calling each other stupid.

It's like we've all become like one big family, we share things more with each other. We tease each other like brother and sister. We look out for each other with homework and stuff. We always stay on top of each other 'cause we know it's hard with African American students to go to a predominantly White school and try to succeed with everybody else.

The faculty, too, were very enthusiastic about the outcomes of the 45 intervention, as seen in the comments of these two classroom teachers:

This program has probably produced the most dramatic result of any single change that I've seen at this school. It has produced immediate results that affected behavior and academics and participation in school life.

My students are more engaged. They aren't battling out a lot of the issues of their anger about being in a White community, coming in from Boston, where do I fit, I don't belong here. I feel that those issues that often came out in class aren't coming out in class anymore. I think they are being discussed in the SET room, the kids feel more confidence. The kids' grades are higher, the home-work response is greater, they're not afraid to participate in class, and I don't see them isolating themselves within class. They are willing to sit with other students happily. . . . I think it's made a very positive impact on their place in the school and on their individual self-esteem. I see them enjoying themselves and able to enjoy all of us as individuals. I can't say enough, it's been the best thing that's happened to the METCO program as far as I'm concerned.[19]

Although this intervention is not a miracle cure for every school, it 46 does highlight what can happen when we think about the developmen-tal needs of Black adolescents coming to terms with their own sense of identity. It might seem counterintuitive that a school involved in a volun-tary desegregation program could improve both academic performance and social relationships among students by *separating* the Black students for one period every day. But if we understand the unique challenges fac-ing adolescents of color and the legitimate need they have to feel supported in their identity development, it makes perfect sense.

Though they may not use the language of racial identity development 47 theory to describe it, most Black parents want their children to achieve an internalized sense of personal security, to be able to acknowledge the reality of racism and to respond effectively to it. Our educational institu-tions should do what they can to encourage this development rather than impede it. When I talk to educators about the need to provide adolescents with identity-affirming experiences and information about their own cul-tural groups, they sometimes flounder because this information has not been part of their own education. Their understanding of adolescent development has been limited to the White middle-class norms included in most textbooks, their knowledge of Black history limited to Martin Luther King, Jr., and Rosa Parks. They sometimes say with frustration that parents should provide this kind of education for their children. Unfortunately Black parents often attended the same schools the teachers did and have the same informational gaps. We need to acknowledge that an important part of interrupting the cycle of oppression is constant re-education, and sharing what we learn with the next generation.

NOTES

1. J. Marcia, "Development and validation of ego identity status," *Journal of Personality and Social Psychology* 3 (1966): 551–58.
2. For a review of the research on ethnic identity in adolescents, see J. Phinney, "Ethnic identity in adolescents and adults: Review of research," *Psychological Bulletin* 108, no. 3 (1990): 499–514. See also "Part I: Identity development," in B. J. R. Leadbeater and N. Way (Eds.), *Urban girls: Resisting stereotypes, creating identities* (New York: New York University Press, 1996).
3. W. E. Cross, Jr., *Shades of Black: Diversity in African-American identity* (Philadelphia: Temple University Press, 1991).
4. For an expanded discussion of "race-conscious" parenting, see B. D. Tatum, *Assimilation blues*, ch. 6.
5. J. S. Phinney and S. Tarver, "Ethnic identity search and commitment in Black and White eighth graders," *Journal of Early Adolescence* 8, no. 3 (1988): 265–77.
6. See B. D. Tatum, "African-American identity, academic achievement, and missing history," *Social Education* 56, no. 6 (1992): 331–34; B. D. Tatum, "Racial identity and relational theory: The case of Black women in White communities," *in Work in progress, no. 63* (Wellesley MA: Stone Center Working Papers, 1992); B. D. Tatum, "Out there stranded? Black youth in White communities," pp. 214–33 in H. McAdoo (Ed.), *Black families*, 3d ed. (Thousand Oaks, CA: Sage, 1996).
7. For an in-depth discussion of the negative effects of tracking in schools, see J. Oakes, *Keeping track: How schools structure inequality* (New Haven: Yale University Press, 1985).
8 For further discussion of the social dynamics for Black youth in White communities, see Tatum, "Out there stranded?"
9. Leadbeater and Way, *Urban girls*, p. 5.
10. A. Haley and Malcolm X, *The autobiography of Malcolm X* (New York: Grove Press, 1965), p. 36.
11 S. Fordham and J. Ogbu, "Black students' school success: Coping with the burden of 'acting White,'" *Urban Review* 18 (1986): 176–206.
12. Ibid., p. 181.
13. For an expanded discussion of the "trying to be White" phenomenon, see Fordham and Ogbu, "Black students' school success," and S. Fordham, "Racelessness as a factor in Black students' school success: Pragmatic strategy or Pyrrhic victory?" *Harvard Educational Review* 58, no. 1 (1988): 54–84.
14. Fordham, "Racelessness as a factor in Black students' school success." See also S. Fordham, *Blacked out: Dilemmas of race, identity, and success at Capital High* (Chicago: University of Chicago Press, 1996).
15. For further discussion of this point, see R. Zweigenhaft and G. W Domhoff, *Blacks in the White establishment? A study of race and class in America* (New Haven: Yale University Press, 1991), p. 155.
16. Ibid.
17. Ibid., p. 156.
18. The Metropolitan Council for Educational Opportunity (METCO) program was established in 1966 under the state's Racial Imbalance Law passed by the Massachusetts General Court in 1965. METCO was established to provide (1) the opportunity for an integrated public school education for urban Black children and

other children of color from racially unbalanced schools in Boston by placing them in suburban schools, (2) a new learning experience for suburban children, and (3) a closer understanding and cooperation between urban and suburban parents and other citizens in the Boston metropolitan area. Thirty-four suburban communities participate in the METCO program.

19. For a more complete description of the program and its evaluation, see B. D. Tatum, P. C. Brown, P. Elliott, and T. Tatum, "Student efficacy training: An evaluation of one middle school's programmatic response to the Eastern Massachusetts Initiative" (presented at the American Educational Research Association Annual Meeting, April 9,1996, New York).

■ ■ ■

Reading as a Writer: Analyzing Rhetorical Choices

1. Tatum launches her essay with a pointed question in her title and in her first paragraph: "Why are the Black kids sitting together?" While the rest of her essay is a response to this big question, Tatum uses questions throughout her essay. Using an easy-to-see pen, mark all the questions in this essay. At what points in her argument do they appear, and what functions do they serve? What conclusions can you draw about the effect of question-asking strategies in persuasive writing?

2. Tatum moves between citing experts (particularly in psychology and education) and interviews with students. Locate the places where she shifts between experts and students, and discuss how exactly she makes these connections. How effectively does she explain and analyze the ideas in quotations from both experts and students? To what extent are the students she interviews experts, as well?

Writing as a Reader: Entering the Conversation of Ideas

1. Tatum and Diane Ravitch approach racial inequity and school curricula from different perspectives and with different kinds of examples, yet they share a commitment to making school a place where future citizens can develop fully the skills they will need to succeed in increasingly diverse environments. Write a paper in which you place these two scholars in conversation, considering how each envisions both the problems and solutions when they examine racial inequity in the school setting. Where do you stand in this conversation about the role schools can (and should?) play in fostering equity within the curriculum and school environment?

2. Both Tatum and Ann DuCille focus on adolescents and are concerned with the many ways cultural "norms" in the United States perpetuate very narrow ideas about what it means to be African American in the United States. Write an essay in which you draw on ideas and specific examples from both authors in order to consider how much of our "education" about race in American culture often happens in such small, seemingly innocuous exchanges. (You might find it interesting to develop and include in your essay a Peggy McIntosh–style list that helps you enumerate some of the concrete, daily ways we are "educated" into assumptions about racial identity.) Based on these writers' ideas, what conclusions can you draw about the most effective ways we might change this "education"?

MARK EDMUNDSON

On the Uses of a Liberal Education: As Lite Entertainment for Bored College Students

Mark Edmundson is a professor of English at the University of Virginia. He has published many scholarly articles on literary and cultural criticism, and has written books for academic specialists on the politics of reading and writing. Edmundson's popular press books on the business of teaching and learning include the acclaimed *Teacher: The One Who Made the Difference* (2003), about a quirky high school philosophy teacher who inspired Edmundson, a self-described "jock," to become a teacher himself.

In this piece, you will hear Edmundson's very distinctive voice, which can be funny as well as sharply critical. As you read, consider both his argument that higher education caters too much to consumerist tendencies of students, and the way he makes this argument, through specific examples of himself, his students, and his campus.

How on-target do you think he is about student culture? Consider, for example, how you and your friends talk about "good" versus "bad" professors, perhaps in terms of those who are "fun" or "boring."

Because this is an article for a general readership, Edmundson does not quote other scholars at length or cite them in a bibliography or Works Cited page. However, he does draw on a wide range of literary and historical references and assumes his readers know what he means when he refers to "Adorno and Horkheimer" in paragraph 48, or when he lists Lenin, Trotsky, Freud, and Blake in paragraph 52. As a reader, you might assess what it feels like to be put in the position of being expected to know these names. (Do you usually look up names and words you don't know, for example? How might your willingness—or unwillingness—to do this "extra" work be connected to Edmundson's argument?)

The bulk of Edmundson's evidence comes from his personal observations and exchanges with students, and as you read you should weigh the strengths and weaknesses of these kinds of examples. What kinds of examples draw you in and make you think about your own school experiences? In his conclusion, he challenges professors and students to embrace exuberance, despite the cultural tendency simply to shrug and mutter, "Whatever." This provocative essay aims to get under your skin so that such a response isn't likely.

■ ■ ■

Today is evaluation day in my Freud class, and everything has changed. The class meets twice a week, late in the afternoon, and the clientele, about fifty undergraduates, tends to drag in and slump, looking disconsolate and a little lost, waiting for a jump start. To get the discussion moving, they usually require a joke, an anecdote, an off-the-wall question—When you were a kid, were your Halloween getups ego costumes, id costumes, or superego costumes? That sort of thing. But today, as soon as I flourish the forms, a buzz rises in the room. Today they write their assessments of the course, their assessments of *me*, and they are without a doubt wide-awake. "What is your evaluation of the instructor?" asks question number eight, entreating them to circle a number between five (excellent) and one (poor). Whatever interpretive subtlety they've acquired during the term is now out the window. Edmundson: one to five, stand and shoot.

And they do. As I retreat through the door—I never stay around for 2 this phase of the ritual—I look over my shoulder and see them toiling away like the devil's auditors. They're pitched into high writing gear, even the ones who struggle to squeeze out their journal entries word by word, stoked on a procedure they have by now supremely mastered. They're playing the informed consumer, letting the provider know where he's come through and where he's not quite up to snuff.

But why am I so distressed, bolting like a refugee out of my own class- 3 room, where I usually hold easy sway? Chances are the evaluations will be much like what they've been in the past—they'll be just fine. It's likely that I'll be commended for being "interesting" (and I am commended, many times over), that I'll be cited for my relaxed and tolerant ways (that hap- pens, too), that my sense of humor and capacity to connect the arcana of the subject matter with current culture will come in for some praise (yup). I've been hassled this term, finishing a manuscript, and so haven't given their journals the attention I should have, and for that I'm called—quite civilly, though—to account. Overall, I get off pretty well.

Yet I have to admit that I do not much like the image of myself that 4 emerges from these forms, the image of knowledgeable, humorous detach- ment and bland tolerance. I do not like the forms themselves, with their number ratings, reminiscent of the sheets circulated after the TV pilot has just played to its sample audience in Burbank. Most of all I dislike the attitude of calm consumer expertise that pervades the responses. I'm disturbed by the serene belief that my function—and, more important, Freud's, or Shakespeare's, or Blake's—is to divert, entertain, and interest. Observes one respondent, not at all unrepresentative: "Edmundson has done a fantastic job of presenting this difficult, important, & controversial material in an enjoyable and approachable way."

Thanks but no thanks. I don't teach to amuse, to divert, or even, for that 5 matter, to be merely interesting. When someone says she "enjoyed" the course—and that word crops up again and again in my evaluations—some- where at the edge of my immediate complacency I feel encroaching self- dislike. That is not at all what I had in mind. The off-the-wall questions and the sidebar jokes are meant as lead-ins to stronger stuff—in the case of the Freud course, to a complexly tragic view of life. But the affability and the one-liners often seem to be all that land with the students; their journals and evaluations leave me little doubt.

I want some of them to say that they've been changed by the course. I 6 want them to measure themselves against what they've read. It's said that some time ago a Columbia University instructor used to issue a harsh two-part question. One: What book did you most dislike in the course? Two: What intellectual or characterological flaws in you does that dislike point to? The hand that framed that question was surely heavy. But at least it compels one to see intellectual work as a confrontation between two people, student and author, where the stakes matter. Those Columbia students were being asked to relate the quality of an *encounter*, not rate the action as though it had unfolded on the big screen.

Why are my students describing the Oedipus complex and the death   7
drive as being interesting and enjoyable to contemplate? And why am I coming across as an urbane, mildly ironic, endlessly affable guide to this intellectual territory, operating without intensity, generous, funny, and loose?

Because that's what works. On evaluation day, I reap the rewards of   8
my partial compliance with the culture of my students and, too, with the culture of the university as it now operates. It's a culture that's gotten little exploration. Current critics tend to think that liberal-arts education is in crisis because universities have been invaded by professors with peculiar ideas: deconstruction, Lacanianism, feminism, queer theory. They believe that genius and tradition are out and that P.C., multiculturalism, and identity politics are in because of an invasion by tribes of tenured radicals, the late millennial equivalents of the Visigoth hordes that cracked Rome's walls.

But mulling over my evaluations and then trying to take a hard,   9
extended look at campus life both here at the University of Virginia and around the country eventually led me to some different conclusions. To me, liberal-arts education is as ineffective as it is now not chiefly because there are a lot of strange theories in the air. (Used well, those theories *can* be illuminating.) Rather, it's that university culture, like American culture writ large, is, to put it crudely, ever more devoted to consumption and entertainment, to the using and using up of goods and images. For someone growing up in America now, there are few available alternatives to the cool consumer worldview. My students didn't ask for that view, much less create it, but they bring a consumer weltanschauung to school, where it exerts a powerful, and largely unacknowledged, influence. If we want to understand current universities, with their multiple woes, we might try leaving the realms of expert debate and fine ideas and turning to the classrooms and campuses, where a new kind of weather is gathering.

From time to time I bump into a colleague in the corridor and we have   10
what I've come to think of as a Joon Lee fest. Joon Lee is one of the best students I've taught. He's endlessly curious, has read a small library's worth, seen every movie, and knows all about showbiz and entertainment. For a class of mine he wrote an essay using Nietzsche's Apollo and Dionysus to analyze the pop group The Supremes. A trite, cultural-studies bonbon?

Not at all. He said striking things about conceptions of race in America and about how they shape our ideas of beauty. When I talk with one of his other teachers, we run on about the general splendors of his work and presence. But what inevitably follows a JL fest is a mournful reprise about the divide that separates him and a few other remarkable students from their contemporaries. It's not that some aren't nearly as bright—in terms of intellectual ability, my students are all that I could ask for. Instead, it's that Joon Lee has decided to follow his interests and let them make him into a singular and rather eccentric man; in his charming way, he doesn't mind being at odds with most anyone.

It's his capacity for enthusiasm that sets Joon apart from what I've *11* come to think of as the reigning generational style. Whether the students are sorority/fraternity types, grunge aficionados, piercer/tattooers, black or white, rich or middle class (alas, I teach almost no students from truly poor backgrounds), they are, nearly across the board, very, very self-contained. On good days they display a light, appealing glow; on bad days, shuffling disgruntlement. But there's little fire, little passion to be found.

This point came home to me a few weeks ago when I was wandering *12* across the university grounds. There, beneath a classically cast portico, were two students, male and female, having a rip-roaring argument. They were incensed, bellowing at each other, headstrong, confident, and wild. It struck me how rarely I see this kind of full-out feeling in students anymore. Strong emotional display is forbidden. When conflicts arise, it's generally understood that one of the parties will say something sarcastically propitiating ("whatever" often does it) and slouch away.

How did my students reach this peculiar state in which all passion *13* seems to be spent? I think that many of them have imbibed their sense of self from consumer culture in general and from the tube in particular. They're the progeny of one hundred cable channels and omnipresent Blockbuster outlets. TV, Marshall McLuhan famously said, is a cool medium. Those who play best on it are low-key and nonassertive; they blend in. Enthusiasm, à la Joon Lee, quickly looks absurd. The form of character that's most appealing on TV is calmly self-interested though never greedy, attuned to the conventions, and ironic. Judicious timing is preferred to sudden self-assertion. The TV medium is inhospitable to inspiration, improvisation, failures, slipups. All must run perfectly.

Naturally, a cool youth culture is a marketing bonanza for producers *14* of the right products, who do all they can to enlarge that culture and keep it grinding. The Internet, TV, and magazines now teem with what I call persona ads, ads for Nikes and Reeboks and Jeeps and Blazers that don't so much endorse the capacities of the product per se as show you what sort of person you will be once you've acquired it. The Jeep ad that features hip, outdoorsy kids whipping a Frisbee from mountaintop to mountaintop isn't so much about what Jeeps can do as it is about the kind of people who own them. Buy a Jeep and be one with them. The ad is of little consequence in itself, but expand its message exponentially and you have the central thrust of current consumer culture—buy in order to be.

Most of my students seem desperate to blend in, to look right, not to 15 make a spectacle of themselves. (Do I have to tell you that those two students having the argument under the portico turned out to be acting in a role-playing game?) The specter of the uncool creates a subtle tyranny. It's apparently an easy standard to subscribe to, this Letterman-like, Tarantino-like cool, but once committed to it, you discover that matters are rather different. You're inhibited, except on ordained occasions, from showing emotion, stifled from trying to achieve anything original. You're made to feel that even the slightest departure from the reigning code will get you genially ostracized. This is a culture tensely committed to a laid-back norm.

Am I coming off like something of a crank here? Maybe. Oscar Wilde, 16 who is almost never wrong, suggested that it is perilous to promiscuously contradict people who are much younger than yourself. Point taken. But one of the lessons that consumer hype tries to insinuate is that we must never rebel against the new, never even question it. If it's new—a new need, a new product, a new show, a new style, a new generation—it must be good. So maybe, even at the risk of winning the withered, brown laurels of crankdom, it pays to resist newness-worship and cast a colder eye.

Praise for my students? I have some of that too. What my students are, 17 at their best, is decent. They are potent believers in equality. They help out at the soup kitchen and volunteer to tutor poor kids to get a stripe on their résumés, sure. But they also want other people to have a fair shot. And in their commitment to fairness they are discerning; there you see them at their intellectual best. If I were on trial and innocent, I'd want them on the jury.

What they will not generally do, though, is indict the current system. 18 They won't talk about how the exigencies of capitalism lead to a reserve army of the unemployed and nearly inevitable misery. That would be getting too loud, too brash. For the pervading view is the cool consumer perspective, where passion and strong admiration are forbidden. "To stand in awe of nothing, Numicus, is perhaps the one and only thing that can make a man happy and keep him so," says Horace in the *Epistles,* and I fear that his lines ought to hang as a motto over the university in this era of high consumer capitalism.

It's easy to mount one's high horse and blame the students for this 19 state of affairs. But they didn't create the present culture of consumption. (It was largely my own generation, that of the Sixties, that let the counter-culture search for pleasure devolve into a quest for commodities.) And they weren't the ones responsible, when they were six and seven and eight years old, for unplugging the TV set from time to time or for hauling off and kicking a hole through it. It's my generation of parents who sheltered these students, kept them away from the hard knocks of everyday life, making them cautious and overfragile, who demanded that their teachers, from grade school on, flatter them endlessly so that the kids are shocked if their college profs don't reflexively suck up to them.

Of course, the current generational style isn't simply derived from cul- 20 ture and environment. It's also about dollars. Students worry that taking too many chances with their educations will sabotage their future prospects. They're aware of the fact that a drop that looks more and more like one wall of the Grand Canyon separates the top economic tenth from the rest of the population. There's a sentiment currently abroad that if you step aside for a moment, to write, to travel, to fall too hard in love, you might lose position permanently. We may be on a conveyor belt, but it's worse down there on the filth-strewn floor. So don't sound off, don't blow your chance.

But wait. I teach at the famously conservative University of Virginia. 21 Can I extend my view from Charlottesville to encompass the whole country, a whole generation of college students? I can only say that I hear comparable stories about classroom life from colleagues everywhere in America. When I visit other schools to lecture, I see a similar scene unfolding. There are, of course, terrific students everywhere. And they're all the better for the way they've had to strive against the existing conformity. At some of the small liberal-arts colleges, the tradition of strong engagement persists. But overall, the students strike me as being sweet and sad, hovering in a nearly suspended animation.

Too often now the pedagogical challenge is to make a lot from a little. 22 Teaching Wordsworth's "Tintern Abbey," you ask for comments. No one responds. So you call on Stephen. Stephen: "The sound, this poem really flows." You: "Stephen seems interested in the music of the poem. We might extend his comment to ask if the poem's music coheres with its argument. Are they consistent? Or is there an emotional pain submerged here that's contrary to the poem's appealing melody?" All right, it's not usually that bad. But close. One friend describes it as rebound teaching: They proffer a weightless comment, you hit it back for all you're worth, then it comes dribbling out again. Occasionally a professor will try to explain away this intellectual timidity by describing the students as perpetrators of postmodern irony, a highly sophisticated mode. Everything's a slick counterfeit, a simulacrum, so by no means should any phenomenon be taken seriously. But the students don't have the urbane, Oscar Wilde–type demeanor that should go with this view. Oscar was cheerful, funny, confident, strange. (Wilde, mortally ill, living in a Paris flophouse: "My wallpaper and I are fighting a duel to the death. One or the other of us has to go.") This generation's style is considerate, easy to please, and a touch depressed.

Granted, you might say, the kids come to school immersed in a con- 23 sumer mentality—they're good Americans, after all—but then the university and the professors do everything in their power to fight that dreary mind-set in the interest of higher ideals, right? So it should be. But let us look at what is actually coming to pass.

Over the past few years, the physical layout of my university has been *24*
changing. To put it a little indecorously, the place is looking more and
more like a retirement spread for the young. Our funds go to construction, into new dorms, into renovating the student union. We have a new
aquatics center and ever-improving gyms, stocked with StairMasters and
Nautilus machines. Engraved on the wall in the gleaming aquatics building is a line by our founder, Thomas Jefferson, declaring that everyone
ought to get about two hours' exercise a day. Clearly even the author of the
Declaration of Independence endorses the turning of his university into a
sports-and-fitness emporium.

But such improvements shouldn't be surprising. Universities need to *25*
attract the best (that is, the smartest *and* the richest) students in order to
survive in an ever more competitive market. Schools want kids whose parents can pay the full freight, not the ones who need scholarships or want
to bargain down the tuition costs. If the marketing surveys say that the
kids require sports centers, then, trustees willing, they shall have them. In
fact, as I began looking around, I came to see that more and more of what's
going on in the university is customer driven. The consumer pressures that
beset me on evaluation day are only a part of an overall trend.

From the start, the contemporary university's relationship with stu- *26*
dents has a solicitous, nearly servile tone. As soon as someone enters his
junior year in high school, and especially if he's living in a prosperous zip
code, the informational material—the advertising—comes flooding in.
Pictures, testimonials, videocassettes, and CD ROMs (some bidden, some
not) arrive at the door from colleges across the country, all trying to capture the student and his tuition cash. The freshman-to-be sees photos of
well-appointed dorm rooms, of elaborate phys-ed facilities; of fine dining
rooms; of expertly kept sports fields; of orchestras and drama troupes; of
students working alone (no overbearing grown-ups in range), peering with
high seriousness into computers and microscopes; or of students arrayed
outdoors in attractive conversational garlands.

Occasionally—but only occasionally, for we usually photograph rather *27*
badly; in appearance we tend at best to be styleless—there's a professor
teaching a class. (The college catalogues I received, by my request only,
in the late Sixties were austere affairs full of professors' credentials and
course descriptions; it was clear on whose terms the enterprise was going
to unfold.) A college financial officer recently put matters to me in concise,
if slightly melodramatic, terms: "Colleges don't have admissions offices
anymore, they have marketing departments." Is it surprising that someone
who has been approached with photos and tapes, bells and whistles, might
come in thinking that the Freud and Shakespeare she had signed up to
study were also going to be agreeable treats?

How did we reach this point? In part the answer is a matter of demo- *28*
graphics and (surprise) of money. Aided by the G.I. bill, the college-going
population in America dramatically increased after the Second World War.

Then came the baby boomers, and to accommodate them, schools continued to grow. Universities expand easily enough, but with tenure locking
faculty in for lifetime jobs, and with the general reluctance of administrators to eliminate their own slots, it's not easy for a university to contract.
So after the baby boomers had passed through—like a fat meal digested
by a boa constrictor—the colleges turned to energetic promotional strategies to fill the empty chairs. And suddenly college became a buyer's market. What students and their parents wanted had to be taken more and
more into account. That usually meant creating more comfortable, less
challenging environments, places where almost no one failed, everything
was enjoyable, and everyone was nice.

Just as universities must compete with one another for students, so 29
must the individual departments. At a time of rank economic anxiety, the
English and history majors have to contend for students against the more
success-insuring branches, such as the sciences and the commerce school.
In 1968, more than 21 percent of all the bachelor's degrees conferred in
America were in the humanities; by 1993, that number had fallen to about
13 percent. The humanities now must struggle to attract students, many of
whose parents devoutly wish they would study something else.

One of the ways we've tried to stay attractive is by loosening up. We 30
grade much more softly than our colleagues in science. In English, we
don't give many Ds, or Cs for that matter. (The rigors of Chem 101 create
almost as many English majors per year as do the splendors of Shakespeare.) A professor at Stanford recently explained grade inflation in the
humanities by observing that the undergraduates were getting smarter
every year; the higher grades simply recorded how much better they were
than their predecessors. Sure.

Along with softening the grades, many humanities departments have 31
relaxed major requirements. There are some good reasons for introducing more choice into curricula and requiring fewer standard courses. But
the move, like many others in the university now, jibes with a tendency
to serve—and not challenge—the students. Students can also float in
and out of classes during the first two weeks of each term without making any commitment. The common name for this time span—shopping
period—speaks volumes about the consumer mentality that's now in play.
Usually, too, the kids can drop courses up until the last month with only
an innocuous "W" on their transcripts. Does a course look too challenging? No problem. Take it pass-fail. A happy consumer is, by definition, one
with multiple options, one who can always have what he wants. And since
a course is something the students and their parents have bought and paid
for, why can't they do with it pretty much as they please?

A sure result of the university's widening elective leeway is to give students 32
more power over their teachers. Those who don't like you can simply avoid
you. If the clientele dislikes you en masse, you can be left without students,
period. My first term teaching I walked into my introduction to poetry

course and found it inhabited by one student, the gloriously named Bambi Lynn Dean. Bambi and I chatted amiably awhile, but for all that she and the pleasure of her name could offer, I was fast on the way to meltdown. It was all a mistake, luckily, a problem with the scheduling book. Everyone was waiting for me next door. But in a dozen years of teaching I haven't forgotten that feeling of being ignominiously marooned. For it happens to others, and not always because of scheduling glitches. I've seen older colleagues go through hot embarrassment at not having enough students sign up for their courses: They graded too hard, demanded too much, had beliefs too far out of keeping with the existing disposition. It takes only a few such instances to draw other members of the professoriat further into line.

And if what's called tenure reform — which generally just means the abolition of tenure — is broadly enacted, professors will be yet more vulnerable to the whims of their customer-students. Teach what pulls the kids in, or walk. What about entire departments that don't deliver? If the kids say no to Latin and Greek, is it time to dissolve classics? Such questions are being entertained more and more seriously by university administrators. 33

How does one prosper with the present clientele? Many of the most successful professors now are the ones who have "decentered" their classrooms. There's a new emphasis on group projects and on computer-generated exchanges among the students. What they seem to want most is to talk to one another. A classroom now is frequently an "environment," a place highly conducive to the exchange of existing ideas, the students' ideas. Listening to one another, students sometimes change their opinions. But what they generally can't do is acquire a new vocabulary, a new perspective, that will cast issues in a fresh light. 34

The Socratic method — the animated, sometimes impolite give-and-take between student and teacher — seems too jagged for current sensibilities. Students frequently come to my office to tell me how intimidated they feel in class; the thought of being embarrassed in front of the group fills them with dread. I remember a student telling me how humiliating it was to be corrected by the teacher, by me. So I asked the logical question: "Should I let a major factual error go by so as to save discomfort?" The student — a good student, smart and earnest — said that was a tough question. He'd need to think about it. 35

Disturbing? Sure. But I wonder, are we really getting students ready for Socratic exchange with professors when we push them off into vast lecture rooms, two and three hundred to a class, sometimes face them with only grad students until their third year, and signal in our myriad professorial ways that we often have much better things to do than sit in our offices and talk with them? How bad will the student-faculty ratios have to become, how teeming the lecture courses, before we hear students righteously complaining, as they did thirty years ago, about the impersonality of their schools, about their decline into knowledge factories? "This is a firm," said Mario Savio at Berkeley during the Free Speech protests of the 36

Sixties, "and if the Board of Regents are the board of directors . . . then . . .
the faculty are a bunch of employees and we're the raw material. But we're
a bunch of raw material that don't mean . . . to be made into any product."

Teachers who really do confront students, who provide significant   37
challenges to what they believe, *can* be very successful, granted. But sometimes such professors generate more than a little trouble for themselves.
A controversial teacher can send students hurrying to the deans and the
counselors, claiming to have been offended. ("Offensive" is the preferred
term of repugnance today, just as "enjoyable" is the summit of praise.) Colleges have brought in hordes of counselors and deans to make sure that
everything is smooth, serene, unflustered, that everyone has a good time.
To the counselor, to the dean, and to the university legal squad, that which
is normal, healthy, and prudent is best.

An air of caution and deference is everywhere. When my students   38
come to talk with me in my office, they often exhibit a Franciscan humility. "Do you have a moment?" "I know you're busy. I won't take up much of
your time." Their presences tend to be very light; they almost never change
the temperature of the room. The dress is nondescript: Clothes are in
earth tones; shoes are practical—cross-trainers, hiking boots, work shoes,
Dr. Martens, with now and then a stylish pair of raised-sole boots on one
of the young women. Many, male and female both, peep from beneath the
bills of monogrammed baseball caps. Quite a few wear sports, or even corporate, logos, sometimes on one piece of clothing but occasionally (and dis-
concertingly) on more. The walk is slow; speech is careful, sweet, a bit
weary, and without strong inflection. (After the first lively week of the term,
most seem far in debt to sleep.) They are almost unfailingly polite. They
don't want to offend me; I could hurt them, savage their grades.

Naturally, there are exceptions, kids I chat animatedly with, who offer   39
a joke, or go on about this or that new CD (almost never a book, no). But
most of the traffic is genially sleepwalking. I have to admit that I'm a touch
wary, too. I tend to hold back. An unguarded remark, a joke that's taken
to be off-color, or simply an uncomprehended comment can lead to difficulties. I keep it literal. They scare me a little, these kind and melancholy
students, who themselves seem rather frightened of their own lives.

Before they arrive, we ply the students with luscious ads, guarantee-   40
ing them a cross between summer camp and lotusland. When they get
here, flattery and nonstop entertainment are available, if that's what they
want. And when they leave? How do we send our students out into the
world? More and more, our administrators call the booking agents and
line up one or another celebrity to usher the graduates into the millennium. This past spring, Kermit the Frog won himself an honorary degree
at Southampton College on Long Island; Bruce Willis and Yogi Berra took
credentials away at Montclair State; Arnold Schwarzenegger scored at the
University of Wisconsin–Superior. At Wellesley, Oprah Winfrey gave the
commencement address. (*Wellesley*—one of the most rigorous academic
colleges in the nation.) At the University of Vermont, Whoopi Goldberg

laid down the word. But why should a worthy administrator contract the likes of Susan Sontag, Christopher Hitchens, or Robert Hughes—someone who might actually say something, something disturbing, something "offensive"—when he can get what the parents and kids apparently want and what the newspapers will softly commend—more lite entertainment, more TV?

Is it a surprise, then, that this generation of students—steeped in 41 consumer culture before going off to school, treated as potent customers by the university well before their date of arrival, then pandered to from day one until the morning of the final kiss-off from Kermit or one of his kin—are inclined to see the books they read as a string of entertainments to be placidly enjoyed or languidly cast down? Given the way universities are now administered (which is more and more to say, given the way that they are currently marketed), is it a shock that the kids don't come to school hot to learn, unable to bear their own ignorance? For some measure of self-dislike, or self-discontent—which is much different than simple depression—seems to me to be a prerequisite for getting an education that matters. My students, alas, usually lack the confidence to acknowledge what would be their most precious asset for learning: their ignorance.

Not long ago, I asked my Freud class a question that, however hoary, never 42 fails to solicit intriguing responses: Who are your heroes? Whom do you admire? After one remarkable answer, featuring T. S. Eliot as hero, a series of generic replies rolled in, one gray wave after the next: my father, my best friend, a doctor who lives in our town, my high school history teacher. Virtually all the heroes were people my students had known personally, people who had done something local, specific, and practical, and had done it for them. They were good people, unselfish people, these heroes, but most of all they were people who had delivered the goods.

My students' answers didn't exhibit any philosophical resistance to 43 the idea of greatness. It's not that they had been primed by their professors with complex arguments to combat genius. For the truth is that these students don't need debunking theories. Long before college, skepticism became their habitual mode. They are the progeny of Bart Simpson and David Letterman, and the hyper-cool ethos of the box. It's inane to say that theorizing professors have created them, as many conservative critics like to do. Rather, they have substantially created a university environment in which facile skepticism can thrive without being substantially contested.

Skeptical approaches have *potential* value. If you have no all- 44 encompassing religious faith, no faith in historical destiny, the future of the West, or anything comparably grand, you need to acquire your vision of the world somewhere. If it's from literature, then the various visions literature offers have to be inquired into skeptically. Surely it matters that women are denigrated in Milton and in Pope, that some novelistic voices assume an overbearing godlike authority, that the poor are, in this or that

writer, inevitably cast as clowns. You can't buy all of literature wholesale if
it's going to help draw your patterns of belief.

But demystifying theories are now overused, applied mechanically. *45*
It's all logocentrism, patriarchy, ideology. And in this the student
environment—laid-back, skeptical, knowing—is, I believe, central. Full-
out debunking is what plays with this clientele. Some have been doing it
nearly as long as, if more crudely than, their deconstructionist teachers. In
the context of the contemporary university, and cool consumer culture, a
useful intellectual skepticism has become exaggerated into a fundamentalist caricature of itself. The teachers have buckled to their students' views.

At its best, multiculturalism can be attractive as well-deployed theory. *46*
What could be more valuable than encountering the best work of far-flung
cultures and becoming a citizen of the world? But in the current consumer
environment, where flattery plays so well, the urge to encounter the other
can devolve into the urge to find others who embody and celebrate the
right ethnic origins. So we put aside the African novelist Chinua Achebe's
abrasive, troubling *Things Fall Apart* and gravitate toward hymns on
Africa, cradle of all civilizations.

What about the phenomenon called political correctness? Raising the *47*
standard of civility and tolerance in the university has been—who can
deny it?—a very good thing. Yet this admirable impulse has expanded to
the point where one is enjoined to speak well—and only well—of women,
blacks, gays, the disabled, in fact of virtually everyone. And we can owe
this expansion in many ways to the student culture. Students now do not
wish to be criticized, not in any form. (The culture of consumption never
criticizes them, at least not *overtly*.) In the current university, the movement for urbane tolerance has devolved into an imperative against critical
reaction, turning much of the intellectual life into a dreary Sargasso Sea.
At a certain point, professors stopped being usefully sensitive and became
more like careful retailers who have it as a cardinal point of doctrine never
to piss the customers off.

To some professors, the solution lies in the movement called cultural *48*
studies. What students need, they believe, is to form a critical perspective on pop culture. It's a fine idea, no doubt. Students should be able to
run a critical commentary against the stream of consumer stimulations
in which they're immersed. But cultural-studies programs rarely work,
because no matter what you propose by way of analysis, things tend to
bolt downhill toward an uncritical discussion of students' tastes, into what
they like and don't like. If you want to do a Frankfurt School–style analysis of *Braveheart*, you can be pretty sure that by mid-class Adorno and
Horkheimer will be consigned to the junk heap of history and you'll be
collectively weighing the charms of Mel Gibson. One sometimes wonders
if cultural studies hasn't prospered because, under the guise of serious
intellectual analysis, it gives the customers what they most want—easy
pleasure, more TV. Cultural studies becomes nothing better than what its
detractors claim it is—Madonna studies—when students kick loose from

the critical perspective and groove to the product, and that, in my experience teaching film and pop culture, happens plenty.

On the issue of genius, as on multiculturalism and political correct-   49
ness, we professors of the humanities have, I think, also failed to press
back against our students' consumer tastes. Here we tend to nurse a pair
of—to put it charitably—disparate views. In one mode, we're inclined to
a programmatic debunking criticism. We call the concept of genius into
question. But in our professional lives per se, we aren't usually disposed
against the idea of distinguished achievement. We argue animatedly about
the caliber of potential colleagues. We support a star system, in which
some professors are far better paid, teach less, and under better conditions than the rest. In our own profession, we are creating a system that
is the mirror image of the one we're dismantling in the curriculum. Ask
a professor what she thinks of the work of Stephen Greenblatt, a leading
critic of Shakespeare, and you'll hear it for an hour. Ask her what her views
are on Shakespeare's genius and she's likely to begin questioning the term
along with the whole "discourse of evaluation." This dual sensibility may
be intellectually incoherent. But in its awareness of what plays with students, it's conducive to good classroom evaluations and, in its awareness
of where and how the professional bread is buttered, to self-advancement
as well.

My overall point is this: It's not that a left-wing professorial coup has   50
taken over the university. It's that at American universities, left-liberal politics have collided with the ethos of consumerism. The consumer ethos is
winning.

Then how do those who at least occasionally promote genius and high lit-   51
erary ideals look to current students? How do we appear, those of us who
take teaching to be something of a performance art and who imagine that
if you give yourself over completely to your subject you'll be rewarded with
insight beyond what you individually command?

I'm reminded of an old piece of newsreel footage I saw once. The   52
speaker (perhaps it was Lenin, maybe Trotsky) was haranguing a large
crowd. He was expostulating, arm waving, carrying on. Whether it was
flawed technology or the man himself, I'm not sure, but the orator looked
like an intricate mechanical device that had sprung into fast-forward. To
my students, who mistrust enthusiasm in every form, that's me when I
start riffing about Freud or Blake. But more and more, as my evaluations
showed, I've been replacing enthusiasm and intellectual animation with
stand-up routines, keeping it all at arm's length, praising under the cover
of irony.

It's too bad that the idea of genius has been denigrated so far, because   53
it actually offers a live alternative to the demoralizing culture of hip
in which most of my students are mired. By embracing the works and
lives of extraordinary people, you can adapt new ideals to revise those
that came courtesy of your parents, your neighborhood, your clan—or

the tube. The aim of a good liberal-arts education was once, to adapt an observation by the scholar Walter Jackson Bate, to see that "we need not be the passive victims of what we deterministically call 'circumstances' (social, cultural, or reductively psychological-personal), but that by linking ourselves through what Keats calls an 'immortal free-masonry' with the great we can become freer—freer to be ourselves, to be what we most want and value."

But genius isn't just a personal standard; genius can also have politi- 54 cal effect. To me, one of the best things about democratic thinking is the conviction that genius can spring up anywhere. Walt Whitman is born into the working class and thirty-six years later we have a poetic image of America that gives a passionate dimension to the legalistic brilliance of the Constitution. A democracy needs to constantly develop, and to do so it requires the most powerful visionary minds to interpret the present and to propose possible shapes for the future. By continuing to notice and praise genius, we create a culture in which the kind of poetic gamble that Whitman made—a gamble in which failure would have entailed rank humiliation, depression, maybe suicide—still takes place. By rebelling against established ways of seeing and saying things, genius helps us to apprehend how malleable the present is and how promising and fraught with danger is the future. If we teachers do not endorse genius and self-overcoming, can we be surprised when our students find their ideal images in TV's latest persona ads?

A world uninterested in genius is a despondent place, whose sad deni- 55 zens drift from coffee bar to Prozac dispensary, unfired by ideals, by the glowing image of the self that one might become. As Northrop Frye says in a beautiful and now dramatically unfashionable sentence, "The artist who uses the same energy and genius that Homer and Isaiah had will find that he not only lives in the same palace of art as Homer and Isaiah, but lives in it at the same time." We ought not to deny the existence of such a place simply because we, or those we care for, find the demands it makes intimidating, the rent too high.

What happens if we keep trudging along this bleak course? What hap- 56 pens if our most intelligent students never learn to strive to overcome what they are? What if genius, and the imitation of genius, become silly, outmoded ideas? What you're likely to get are more and more one-dimensional men and women. These will be people who live for easy pleasures, for comfort and prosperity, who think of money first, then second, and third, who hug the status quo; people who believe in God as a sort of insurance policy (cover your bets); people who are never surprised. They will be people so pleased with themselves (when they're not in despair at the general pointlessness of their lives) that they cannot imagine humanity could do better. They'll think it their highest duty to clone themselves as frequently as possible. They'll claim to be happy, and they'll live a long time.

It is probably time now to offer a spate of inspiring solutions. Here 57 ought to come a list of reforms, with due notations about a core curriculum and various requirements. What the traditionalists who offer such solutions miss is that no matter what our current students are given to read, many of them will simply translate it into melodrama, with flat characters and predictable morals. (The unabated capitalist culture that conservative critics so often endorse has put students in a position to do little else.) One can't simply wave a curricular wand and reverse acculturation.

Perhaps it would be a good idea to try firing the counselors and sending 58 half the deans back into their classrooms, dismantling the football team and making the stadium into a playground for local kids, emptying the fraternities, and boarding up the student-activities office. Such measures would convey the message that American colleges are not northern outposts of Club Med. A willingness on the part of the faculty to defy student conviction and affront them occasionally—to be usefully offensive—also might not be a bad thing. We professors talk a lot about subversion, which generally means subverting the views of people who never hear us talk or read our work. But to subvert the views of our students, our customers, that would be something else again.

Ultimately, though, it is up to individuals—and individual students in 59 particular—to make their own way against the current sludgy tide. There's still the library, still the museum, there's still the occasional teacher who lives to find things greater than herself to admire. There are still fellow students who have not been cowed. Universities are inefficient, cluttered, archaic places, with many unguarded corners where one can open a book or gaze out onto the larger world and construe it freely. Those who do as much, trusting themselves against the weight of current opinion, will have contributed something to bringing this sad dispensation to an end. As for myself, I'm canning my low-key one-liners; when the kids' TV-based tastes come to the fore, I'll aim and shoot. And when it's time to praise genius, I'll try to do it in the right style, full-out, with faith that finer artistic spirits (maybe not Homer and Isaiah quite, but close, close), still alive somewhere in the ether, will help me out when my invention flags, the students doze, or the dean mutters into the phone. I'm getting back to a more exuberant style; I'll be expostulating and arm waving straight into the millennium, yes I will.

■ ■ ■

Reading as a Writer: Analyzing Rhetorical Choices

1. How would you describe Edmundson's ethos, or self-representation, in this essay? Pointing to specific words and phrases, how would you characterize his tone and attitude? Find three passages that you think best illustrate the author's self-representation and discuss how this contributes to, or detracts from, the argument he makes in this essay.

2. Edmundson writes at length about what he thinks is wrong with university culture, but he also makes recommendations for change. What does

he want students and professors to do differently? How practical do you find Edmundson's suggestions? Explain why you do—or do not—agree with his suggestions for change.

Writing as a Reader: Entering the Conversation of Ideas

1. Edmundson and Deborah Tannen both describe specific classroom dynamics in detail as they make their cases about some of the shortcomings of contemporary education. How do you think these very different authors would analyze each other's classroom examples and conclusions based on those examples? What do you think of these perspectives and insights? Write an essay in which you place yourself and these authors in conversation about the connection between classroom dynamics and the goals of education.

2. The college students Edmundson analyzes may seem at first to have little in common with the primary and secondary school children Jonathan Kozol describes in his essay. However, both authors address the goals of education and the methods that work best to meet those goals. Compose an essay in which you draw on the authors' arguments in order to take your own position on these issues. Draw on examples from your own education as you develop your argument.

CONSTANCE STEINKUEHLER AND SEAN DUNCAN
Scientific Habits of Mind in Virtual Worlds

Constance Steinkuehler is a professor at the University of Wisconsin–Madison, where she teaches courses on video games and education; she is also a senior policy analyst at the Office of Science and Technology Policy in the Executive Office of the President. She has written and edited many books and articles on gaming, technology, and literacy. Steinkuehler's Web site offers links to her blog and to news stories related to gaming and education: http://website.education.wisc.edu/steinkuehler/blog/. Steinkuehler's co-author, Sean Duncan, is a professor of at Indiana University–Bloomington, where he uses his research background in educational psychology to study game design and learning; he also directs the university's "Playful Culture Lab." He has written, cowritten, and edited research on many aspects of gaming culture, including pieces on *World of Warcraft*, *Minecraft*, and *Zelda*.

Steinkuehler and Duncan craft their essay in the IMRAD style (Introduction, Methods, Research, and Discussion), common to social science and science writing. They explain their argument in the "Leveraging Online Play" section, where they defend their idea that rather than being merely entertaining, video games can play a crucial role in "fostering scientific habits of mind" (para. 6). How, exactly? What skills do they claim are fostered through these games?

Read carefully through the "Data Collection and Research Methods" section, particularly paragraph 16, and be sure you understand their rationale for collecting data in these ways in order to evaluate "scientific discursive practices" (para. 16). How did they decide to code the behaviors they found, and what were some of the challenges of coding (see para. 32, for example)? As you read, think about your own experiences of playing video games, and weigh those experiences against the methods these authors use to collect and analyze data. What might make this data complicated to capture and evaluate?

In their final section, "Discussion and Implications," Steinkuehler and Duncan restate their argument and offer an overview of their data and findings. Underline the key sentences in which they evaluate their conclusions. For example, "Contrary to our initial hypotheses . . . " (para. 36), "This, however, was not at all the pattern we found . . . " (para. 38), "Such findings are useful . . . " (para. 40). In the final three paragraphs, they present what they see as the three major implications for their research. Take some time to discuss these ideas, in relation to your own experience with video games. To what extend to you agree that the future of education should contain more *play?*

■ ■ ■

In 1905, at a gathering of the world's greatest minds in the physical sciences, Henri Poincaré reflected on the rapid progress of scientific inquiry and the means through which the scientific community at the turn of the twentieth century and beyond would refine our understanding of the world. In his historical address, Poincaré warned against the seduction of reducing science to a domain of seeming facts, stating, "Science is built up of facts, as a house is built of stones; but an accumulation of facts is no more science than a heap of stones is a house" (1905/2001, p. 141). A century later, his admonition against the framing of science as a "rhetoric of conclusion" (Schwab 1962, p. 24) still holds, with science scholars and educators from Dewey on repeatedly warning us against the teaching of science as only content rather than process. In Dewey's own words, "the future of our civilization depends upon the widening spread and deepening hold of the *scientific habit of mind* [italics added] . . . the problem of problems in our education is therefore to discover how to mature and make effective this scientific habit" (1910, p. 127).

In today's world of massive globalization and technological interconnectivity, the need for a scientifically literate citizenry in the United States has only grown more urgent; yet, by some measures, it seems we have done a poor job at fostering the right habits of mind in our schools. Currently only one in five Americans is scientifically literate (Miller 2004), despite mandatory instruction in science. In a recent study of contemporary classroom practice, Chinn and Malhotra (2002) found that standard "inquiry" activities not only failed to engender scientific habits of mind, but in fact actually fostered epistemological beliefs directly *antithetical* to them. Recent assessment of high school laboratory activities by the National Research Council (Singer et al. 2005) reaches similar conclusions: science labs, long heralded as *the* site for engaging students in science practice, fail. Meanwhile, the public seems to grow increasingly hostile to the scientific enterprise (Elsner 2005).

Leveraging Online Play

But, if the inquiry activities used currently in education are unable to foster   3
the right attitudes toward science, what can? Games, potentially. Despite dismissals as "torpid" and inviting "inert reception" (Solomon 2004) in some mainstream press, videogame technologies may be one viable alternative—not to the role of teachers and classrooms in learning science, but rather to textbooks and science labs as educational experiences about the inquiry process. Recent studies indicate that the intellectual activities that constitute successful gameplay are nontrivial, including the construction of new identities (Gee 2003; Steinkuehler 2006b), collaborative problem solving (Squire 2005; Steinkuehler 2006a; cf. Nasir 2005), literacy practices that exceed our national standards (Steinkuehler 2007, 2008a), systemic thinking (Squire 2003), and, as one might expect, computer literacy (Hayes and Games in press; Steinkuehler and Johnson, 2007, unpublished manuscript).

Games, however, are more than just the sum of their intellectual prac-   4
tices (as important as those may be); they are, in fact, *simulated worlds:*

> The first step towards understanding how video games can (and we argue, will) transform education is changing the widely shared perspective that games are "mere entertainment." More than a multi-billion dollar industry, more than a compelling toy for both children and adults, more than a route to computer literacy, video games are important because they let people participate in new worlds. (Shaffer, Squire, Halverson, and Gee 2005, p. 106)

As simulations, games allow "just plain folk" (Lave 1988) to build sit-   5
uated understandings of important phenomena (physical laws, for example) that are instantiated in those worlds amid a culture of intellectual practice that render those phenomena culturally meaningful (Steinkuehler 2006c). Their affordances for learning have not gone unnoticed, and the last two years have witnessed a marked rise in interest across various academies in leveraging game technologies toward educational ends: the Woodrow Wilson Foundation's Serious Games Initiative; the Games, Learning and Society program at the University of Wisconsin-Madison; the Education Arcade project at MIT; the Games for Social Change Movement; and Stanford University's Media X "Gaming To Learn" Workshop, to name a few.

One genre of videogame in particular offers distinctive promise in terms 6 of fostering scientific habits of mind: *massively multiplayer online games.* Massively multiplayer online games (MMOs) are 2- or 3-D graphical, simulated worlds played online that allow individuals to interact, through their digital characters or "avatars," not only with the designed environment in which activities take place, but also with other individuals' avatars as well. For example, five friends or strangers could create an impromptu group and go hunting "boss" dragons in one of the virtual world's more difficult dungeons. Previous ethnography of such online worlds demonstrates their function as naturally occurring learning environments (Steinkuehler 2004, 2005), yet the forms of scientific argumentation, model-based reasoning, and theory-evidence coordination that arise in the context of MMO play warrant further investigation.

In MMOs, individuals collaborate to solve complex problems within 7 the virtual world, such as figuring out what combination of individual skills, proficiencies, and equipment are necessary to conquer an in-game boss dragon in the example above. As part of developing efficient and effective solutions, players are customarily expected to research various game strategies and tactics by consulting on- and offline manuals, databases, and discussions, as well as by using such knowledge as the basis for in-game action. Such research might include, to continue our example, consulting collective online databases about where the boss dragon lives, what its special skills are, and what previous strategies have been successful.

Members of the group then come to the activity well-versed in known 8 research on the problem and enter into collaborative work under the mutual expectation that each will apply known information to solving the problem. Should the solution not prove to be straightforward, the group learns from what fails, discounting some solution paths while raising others. In prior ethnographic work (2005), Steinkuehler found that it was not unusual for players to gather data about a specific monster or challenge in the virtual world in Excel spreadsheets, create models of the data in the form of simple mathematical equations, and then argue about whose model was "better" in terms of prediction and explanatory scope.

Thus, as part of standard gameplay (particularly beyond the beginning 9 levels), individuals share their own hypotheses about what strategies work by proposing models for solutions, justifying their "theories" with evidence (such as tabulated mathematical results aggregated across multiple trials), and debate the merits of conflicting hypotheses. This collaborative construction of knowledge, parallel to what takes place in the scientific community, is not aimless contentious discussion (although there is a bit of that as well), but rather part and parcel of the *collective intelligence* (Levy 1999) amassed through patterned participatory consumption (Jenkins 1992), which is a hallmark of interactive "entertainment" media such as games.

Innovative projects such as Harvard University's *River City* (e.g., Ketel- 10 hut 2007; Ketelhut et al. 2007; Nelson et al. 2007) and Indiana University-Bloomington's *Quest Atlantis* (e.g., Barab et al. 2005; Barab et al. 2007) have begun to tackle the complexities of designing MMOs for science learning, offering proof of concept of the argument presented above. Yet, as Lave and Wenger (1991) note, understanding informal contexts for learning is crucial if we are to advance educational theory and practice beyond the contexts we ourselves contrive. Therefore, in order to extend our understanding of the forms of scientific reasoning that emerge as a natural part of gameplay in informal MMOs and the design features that appear to foster them, this paper presents an examination of discussions on the official online forum for the commercial MMO *World of Warcraft*.

In this investigation, we analyzed a random sample of nearly 2,000 discussion posts in which participants discuss various game-related topics. Using codes based on national benchmarks for scientific literacy (American Association for the Advancement of Science 1993), Chinn and Malhotra's (2002) theoretical framework for evaluating inquiry tasks, and Kuhn's (1992) epistemological framework, we highlight the scientific habits of mind displayed within the forum discussions and the features of the game—both as designed object and emergent culture—that appear to foster them. This study moves beyond arguments about the *potential* of MMOs for learning by documenting and assessing which *specific* literacy practices emerge within such game-related online communities (and which do not). Based on those findings, we then take a first step toward identifying the characteristics of MMOs that may be enabling such practices to emerge.

Data Collection and Research Methods

Context of the Research and Data Corpus

The context for this investigation is *World of Warcraft* (*WoW*), a successful MMO released in November 2004 and currently boasting the single largest share of the global MMO market with well over ten million subscribers globally (Woodcock 2008). The game is set in a fantasy world in which players of various classes (nine total, at the time of this article's writing) wander the environment hunting, gathering, questing, battling, and crafting in order to strengthen or "level" their character in various ways.

The data analyzed for this particular study consist of threaded discussions that took place early November of 2006 (before the release of the expansion, *World of Warcraft: The Burning Crusade*) on the "priest forum" of the official *World of Warcraft* website (http://forums.worldofwarcraft .com). Although there are a number of relevant online forums to be found, the official website alone featured thirty-one separate forums totaling well over 270,000 separate, active threads. Therefore, we chose to limit our data corpus by selecting a single character class-related forum rather than, say, the guild recruitment or bug report forum. Class-related forums are just like any other discussion forum, except the content is ostensibly focused on class-related topics for discussion. Content is not restricted in any way (other than by the overarching rules of the forums, such as decency), but posters are expected to discuss something related to the respected character class in some way, whether that be anecdotes, strategies, complaints, preferences, or what have you. We pulled a random sample of 1,984 posts across eighty-five threads of 4,656 threads total ($\overline{X}$ = 23, σ = 38 posts per thread), resulting in a confidence level of approximately 91 percent. Data from the discussion forums were saved as text files, extraneous information and HTML markup tags were removed, and descriptive information (such as data on the "level" of each poster) was collected in a separate spreadsheet. The final corpus included discussion posts made by 1,087 unique *WoW* characters.

Method of Analysis

In order to assess the *scientific habits of mind* that characterize (or fail to _14_ characterize) the data corpus examined here, we developed a set of codes (following methods outlined in Chi 1997) based in combination on a subset of the AAAS benchmarks for scientific literacy (American Association for the Advancement of Science 1993), Chinn and Malhotra's (2002) theoretical framework for evaluating inquiry tasks, and Kuhn's (1992) framework for categorizing epistemological stances in argumentation. Both the AAAS benchmarks and the Chinn and Malhotra report have been quite influential in science education, with the former serving as the basis of the National Research Council's (1996) Science Standards and many state science standards for K–12 education in the United States. Kuhn's work has also proven quite influential in its own right in research on argumentation in informal scientific reasoning. The codes were selected from these sources based on a combination of a priori assumptions about the forms of scientific reasoning such spaces ought to generate (e.g., understanding systems and feedback among components of a system), previous games related literature (Gee 2003; Squire 2003, 2005; Steinkuehler 2004, 2005, 2006a, 2006b, 2006c), and a pilot study conducted in preparation for this investigation (Steinkuehler and Chmiel 2006).

Our goal was to focus on scientific reasoning as "the building of houses" _15_ rather than the "collection of stones," per the vision of science practice articulated by Poincaré (1905/2001) and science education forwarded by Dewey (1910) and Schwab (1962). Therefore, important aspects to scientific understanding that are specific to *content knowledge* rather than practice per se (e.g. an understanding of natural forces) are notably absent. However, given the focus of our interests (scientific practices rather than content) and the nature of the phenomenon under investigation (a simulated world that makes no claims of correspondence with the natural one), such omission was justified. Table 12.1 includes the full set of eighteen codes and their definitions.

Together, the coding set addresses aspects of scientific thinking as _16_ seen through three major groups of codes: scientific discursive practices (including social knowledge construction), systems- and model-based reasoning, and tacit epistemologies. The scientific discursive practices codes each addressed a different aspect of argumentation, discourse, and the use of evidence or other resources in the formulation of an argument. The systems- and model-based reasoning codes each addressed a different aspect

TABLE 12.1 The Full Set of Analytic Codes Used to Assess Scientific Habits of Mind

Scientific discursive practices

Social knowledge construction	Scientists construct knowledge in collaborative groups; students do not (AAAS.D.12.6 & 1.A. 12.2; Chinn and Malhotra 2002)
Build on others' ideas	Participate in group discussions on scientific topics by restating or summarizing accurately what others have said, asking for clarification or elaboration (AAAS)
Use of counter-arguments	Suggest alternative claims or arguments, criticize arguments in which data, explanations, or conclusions are represented as the only ones worth consideration with no mention of other possibilities, suggest alternative trade-offs in decisions and designs, criticize designs in which major trade-offs are not acknowledged (AAAS.I2.E)
Uses data/evidence	Use data or evidence in making arguments and claims (AAAS)
Alternative explanations of data	No matter how well one theory fits observations, a new theory might fit them just as well or better, or might fit a wider range of observations. In science, the testing, revising, and occasional discarding of theories, new and old, never ends. This ongoing process leads to an increasingly better understanding of how things work in the world but not to absolute truth (AAAS.1.A.12.3, AAAS.12.A.8.3)
References outside resources	References outside resources in making arguments and claims (e.g., other threads or stickies, online articles, databases) (AAAS12.D.8.3/Chinn and Malhotra 2002)

Systems- and model-based reasoning

Systems-based reasoning	Reasons about some phenomenon or problem in terms of a system—a collection of components and processes that interact in some way (ie. have relationships to one another of some form). Defined systems have boundaries, subsystems, relation to other systems, and inputs & outputs (AAAS.11.A)
Understanding feedback	Thinking about things as systems means looking for how its components relate to each other. Output from one part of a system can function as input to other parts of a system. A change in one component's state can result in changes in another component's state. This includes relationships among components within a system or between systems (AAAS. 11.A.8.2)
Model-based reasoning	Model-based reasoning involves the envision of a principle-based mechanism with interacting components that represents the operation of system within the natural (virtual) world. A model may concretize phenomena that are not directly observable (Mayer 1992; AAAS.11.B)
Model testing and prediction	The usefulness of a model can be tested by comparing its predictions to actual observations in the real world. But a close match docs not necessarily mean that the model is the only "true" model of the only one that would work (AAAS.11.B. 12.2)
Mathematical modeling	The basic idea of mathematical modeling is to find a mathematical relationship (e.g. algebraic equation, relationship between two quantities, etc) that behaves in the same ways as the objects or processes under investigation. A mathematical model may give insight about how something really works or may fit observations very well without any intuitive meaning (AAAS.11.B.12.1)
Mathematical computation	Explicitly gives some form of mathematical calculation in their argument or thesis that is not given by the game itself (e.g., not merely the DPS listed on a weapon). For example, demonstrates how an algebraic equation (a mathematical model) can be solved for (or predict) the relative trade off between two variables, or compares two groups using their mean, median, variance, standard deviation, etc. (AAAS.12.B)
Not relevant to sci reason	Social banter, non science related topics, etc.
Uncodable	Cannot tell if it is science related or not

Tacit epistemologies

Absolutist	Knowledge is objective, certain, and simply accumulates (Kuhn 1992)
Relativist	Knowledge is subjective, dictated only by personal tastes and wishes of the knower. Nothing is certain, all opinions arc of equal validity, and even experts disagree (Kuhn 1992)
Evaluative	Knowledge is an open-ended process of evaluation and argument (Kuhn 1992)
Uncodable	Cannot tell what epistemology the poster tacitly holds

of scientific thinking, cutting across specific scientific domains, including reasoning using systems and models; understanding feedback, prediction and testing; and the use of mathematics to investigate the problem under discussion. Finally, the tacit epistemology codes addressed the implicit conception of knowledge employed by an author in a given post—that knowledge is objective and absolute, or that it is subjective and nothing is certain, or that knowledge is shaped through evaluation and argument. Four raters, each of whom had at least 4 months of experience as participant observer within the game, coded the data; four-way interrater reliability, calculated on a subset of roughly 10% of the corpus, was 92%.

In addition, a second set of codes were developed in order to characterize the *WoW*-specific content discussed in each post. Two raters, both with over a year of participant-observer experience within the game, coded the data; two-way interrater reliability, calculated again on roughly 10% of the corpus, was 93%. Additionally, for each poster, we collected virtual "demographic" information—including character level, race, class, guild status, and player-vs.-player rank—in addition to the total number of occurrences of each scientific reasoning and content code their posts received and the total number of posts per individual made.

Findings

The results from this analysis are presented in Figure 12.1, which shows the percentage of posts that exhibit each code we focused on for analysis. Here, we see the saturation of key characteristics of scientific reasoning skills and dispositions across the sample. Several interesting patterns emerge from this analysis.

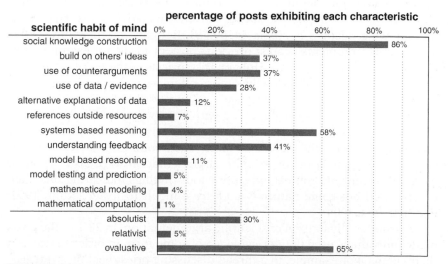

FIGURE 12.1 Proportion of posts within the data corpus that exhibit each scientific habit of mind and tacit epistemology under examination.

Social Knowledge Construction

The first and most obvious pattern is the large proportion of productive *19* discussion found on the boards: We found that 86% of the *WoW* discussion forums consisted of talk that could be considered "social knowledge construction"—meaning, the collective development of understanding, often through joint problems solving and argumentation. In other words, in the overwhelming majority of forum talk, participants were solving problems through discussion, knowledge sharing, and debate through threads that began with posts such as "I notice that high level priests carry around a great deal of potions . . . Which potions do you carry around constantly and why?" (post #3357.0) Only 8% of the discussion posts were mere social banter (the remaining 6% were uncodable with this coding scheme)—perhaps a surprising result for those who presume that discussions around videogames are a "torpid" waste of time.

One of our initial hypotheses was that only the more experienced *20* *WoW* players would engage in higher order intellectual work on the discussion forums. In fact, we found no relationship between a given poster's character level (which represents their experience with the game) and the quality or quantity of the attributes for which we coded, other than a very mild and negative correlation ($r = -0.08$) between author's character level and social banter. Thus, while we cannot disprove the notion that only the "hardcore" gamers engage in the forms of informal science literacy investigated here, we find no evidence that such is indeed the case.

Scientific Discursive Practices

Of the 86% of the forum posts that were not social banter or simply *21* uncodable, roughly one-third (37%) built on ideas that previous posters had raised; for example, by stating "Given your advice, I've spec'd out the following talents . . ." (post #4109.29). Roughly another third (37%) used counterarguments against previous posters' ideas; for example, stating "The real question is 'Are Holy or Disc priests going to kill as much?' And the answer is no. Shadow has more offensive utility, which is just as important as the increase in damage. . . ." (post #2143.5) That *WoW* players either elaborated on or disagreed with previous people's comments in the context of a forum should come as no surprise given the "collectively intelligent" (Levy 1999) nature of many such communities. However, it is interesting that forms of *scientific* argumentation were also prevalent within this informal context, given previous findings indicating that such practices do not come naturally and are difficult to foster (Kuhn 1992; Osborne et al. 2004).

As another illustration of scientific argumentation, in 28% of the posts *22* made individuals used data or evidence of some form in order to warrant their claims. For example, in a thread discussing priest healing strategies, one poster argues for his strategy by stating, "my +355 healing allows me to use Heal4 [spell] to hit around 1k+ every time, ignoring crits [critical hits]. That's good enough to spam [cast repeatedly] for most battles while throwing in a Fheal [flash heal] now and then" (post #3247.20). In another 12%, individuals challenge one another's hypotheses by providing alternative explanations of evidence used to support those suppositions with statements such as the following:

> The calculations correctly show that mind flay [spell] receives just as much +damage percentage as mind blast. However mind blast has a 1.5 second cast time, and mind flay has a 3 second cast time. And therefore mind flay receives half the dps [damage per second] boost it should. (post #2609.43)

And in 7% of the posts, participants cited a variety of information resources beyond the current discussion thread itself (see Table 12.2). For example, one poster: recommended a particular character configuration (i.e. "talent build," discussed below) over another with the statement "I would be more inclined to go with a build similar to: http://www.wowhead.com/?talent=bVMhzZZxOgtczR if you would like to go Shadow [one particular form of character specialization]" (post #3374.9). 23

What did the typical "social knowledge construction" discussion thread containing "scientific discursive practices" look like? As the example in Figure 12.2 illustrates, most such discussions began with an initial question about a given mechanic in the game or game-playing strategy, often coupled with the proposal of some theory. A second poster would typically then elaborate in answering the question or responding to the proposed theory, at times using data from the game to warrant the claims made. The response would then be discussed and debated by a larger group. Often a second, alternative hypothesis or explanation would eventually be offered (or, more rarely, the interpretation of the data used in the first explanation was reinterpreted), followed by an additional round of discussion and debate, and so on. Occasionally, confirming or disconfirming claims or evidence from other resources, such as collaborative online manuals to the game (e.g., WoWWiki, http://wowwiki.com) or other 24

TABLE 12.2   Types of Outside Resources Referenced by Forum Poster Within the Sample

	Outside Resources Referenced
Talent calculators/builds	Links to an official or unofficial tools for calculating talent point allocations
Personal talent builds	Links to a player's specific talent build
WoW databases and Wikis	Links to information on publicly accessible *WoW* databases and Wikis created by *WoW* players themselves
Official blizzard documents	Links to official information published by Blizzard
Other *WoW* forums	Links to other discussions in the *WoW* forums (beyond current forum)
Personal websites	Links to a player's personal website or other online material

post#	social knowledge construction	build on others' ideas	use of counterarguments	use of data / evidence	alternative explanations outside data	references outside resources	systems based reasoning	understanding of data	model based reasoning	model testing and prediction	understanding feedback	mathematical modeling	mathematical computation	absolutist	relativist	evaluative
0 Poses question: group healing strategy (A) or (B)?	●			●			●	●	●							●
1 Advocates (B) & gives strategy (C)	●				●		●	●								●
2 Compares (A) & (B) on use conditions, advocates (A)	●														●	
3 Critiques (A) & (B), advocates (C), raise issue (X)	●	●					●	●								●
4 Elaborates (X)	●	●		●			●	●								●
5 Elaborates (X)	●	●			●		●	●						●		
6 Argues (A) > (B)	●	●	●				●	●								●
7 Elaborates (X)	●						●	●								●
8 Elaborates (A) > (B) but dependent on conditions	●	●					●	●							●	
9 Argues (A) = (B) under the right conditions for each	●	●	●		●		●	●							●	
10 Counterargues (B) > (A)	●	●	●	●			●	●						●		
11 Elaborates counterargument (B) > (A)	●	●	●	●			●	●	●	●	●	●				
12 Details scenario with (B) strategy & issue (X)	●		●				●	●	●							●
13 Details scenario with both (A) & (B) strategies	●		●				●	●	●							●
14 Details scenario with (A) strategy & new issue (Y)	●		●													●
15 Challenges detail of scenario with (A)	●	●														
16 Argues (A) > (B)	●		●	●			●	●								●
17 Argues (B) > (A) & details issue (X)	●	●	●	●			●	●	●					●		
18 Elaborates (A) > (B)	●						●									
19 Counterargues (B) > (A)	●						●									●
20 Argues (B) > (A)	●		●				●	●								●
21 Compares (A) & (B) on use conditions, advocates (A)	●		●	●	●		●	●								●
22 Original poster acknowledges discussion	●															
23 Argues both (A) & (B) strategies	●						●	●								●
24 Argues (A) > (B)	●			●			●	●							●	
25 Counterargues (B) > (A)	●		●	●			●	●								●
26 Argues (A) = (B) under right conditions based on (X)	●	●	●	●	●		●	●	●							●
27 Details scenario w/ (A) & (B) & (C) strategies given (X)	●		●				●	●	●							●
28 Argues (A) > (B)	●		●	●												
29 Argues (A) = (B) under right conditions based on (X)	●			●			●	●	●							
30 Elaborates detail of scenario with (A) & (B) & (C)	●						●	●								
31 Counterargues (B) > (A)	●	●	●	●			●	●	●	●	●					●
32 Argues (B) > (A)	●			●			●	●								●
33 Challenges initial characterization of (B)	●													●		
34 Argues (A) > (B) & raises issue (X)	●		●	●			●	●	●					●		
35 Argues (A) > (B)	●		●	●						●	●			●		
36 Details scenario with both (A) & (B) strategies	●		●	●			●	●	●							●

scientific habit of mind

A = spam PoH   B = Holy Nova   C = renew   X = FR gear   Y = FR pots

FIGURE 12.2 An example "social knowledge" construction thread (#329) of thirty-six posts detailed in terms of both the augmentative moves made within each and the codes applied to them.

archived discussions on this or other forums, would be introduced into the discussion. In some threads, a comparison or synthesis of the two or more explanations would culminate the discussion; in others, the conversation simply petered out as though the participants had accepted the most recently posted theory or explanation as the preferred one or had perhaps tired of the topic and moved on.

System- and Model-Based Reasoning

Over half (58%) of the *WoW* forum posts evinced *systems-based reasoning*,   25 the majority of which also demonstrate an understanding of feedback among components of the system. For example, participants discussed the game in terms of components and processes that interact in ways such that changes in one impact cause changes in another, as in the following post:

> By choosing a slower spell [variable one] and the lowest rank [variable two] you can live comfortably with (or your tank can live with, in our case), you are still making the most of your mana [variable three], given your gear [variable four]. (post #3247.12)

Roughly one tenth of the forum posts illustrated *model-based reason-*   26 *ing*—essentially, using some form of model to understand a given system under consideration—with about half of those (5% of posts total) including some comparison between the model's predictions and actual observations of the phenomenon it is intended to capture or explain in some way. One example of such discussion focused on a phenomenon called "scaling." Imagine that, for a level 2 priest, a given spell does ten damage; when the priest reaches to level 20, that ten damage accomplishes much less because the level 20 priest is now fighting much harder monsters. In order to balance ability with challenge, *WoW* makes higher level, stronger spells available as one's character level increases. In place of a spell that does ten damage would be a spell that does one hundred damage, for example, so that the ability to do damage to monsters using a given spell "scales" as character level increases. Scaling is not the same for every spell or character class, and one way that designers "balance" their game mechanics is to monitor and tweak scaling. In the following excerpt, a participant proposes one particular model of how the in-game scaling mechanics work and considers that model's predictions given changes in input:

> If mind flay [priest spell] actually got the full scaling of a 3 second cast spell, then by combining mind flay with both dots [priest damage over time spells] and all available talents [point system for specializing character types] to improve those, you would actually see a shadow priest's scaling maxing out at a little under 80% of what a fire mage's scaling would max out at with 40 fire and nothing more. (post #2609.51)

Thus, posters orient toward the usefulness of a model in terms if its   27 ability (or inability) to make predictions that match actual observations. Slightly less than half of those models (4% of posts total) were explicitly mathematical, and only 1% of the total forum posts included actual computations as well. An example illustrating both is the following post excerpt raising issues about the balance of priest versus mage abilities:

> By intuition, you should notice a problem . . .
> but I'll give you the numbers anyways
> For Mindflay, SW:P, and presumably VT [3 priest spells]:
> Damage = (base_spell_damage + modifier * damage_
> gear) * darkness * weaving * shadowform * misery
> For Frostbolt [mage spell]
> Average Damage = (base_spell_damage + (modifier + empowered frost)
> * damage_gear) * (1 * (1 − critrate − winter's chill − empowered frost) +
> (1.5 + ice shards) * (critrate + winter's chill + empowered frost)) * piercing ice
> mindflay = (426 + 0.45 * dam) * 1.1 * 1.15 * 1.15 * 1.05
> 650.7 + 0.687 * dam
> frostbolt = (530 + (0.814 + 0.10)*dam) * ((1 − crit − 0.10 − 0.05) +
> (1.5 + 0.5) * (crit + 0.10 + 0.05)) * 1.06
> (530 + 0.914 * dam) * ((0.85 − crit) + 2 * (crit + 0.15)) * 1.06
> 0.968 * (dam + 579.7) * (crit + 1.15)
> Please notice the 0.687 versus the 0.968. That's the scaling factor. (post #2609.18)

In this example, the author makes an argument about the relative *28* scaling of priest skills compared to mage skills based on a thoroughly mathematical argument, using computation as a form of evidence for the points made. His conclusion—that the scaling factor of each class type (0.687 and 0.968 respectfully) is unequal—is his climactic justification for the initial claim that the two character classes are not balanced.

What did a typical "systems- and model-based reasoning" forum post *29* discussion thread look like? Figure 12.3 shows the analysis of one post-containing relevant codes.

Typically, such posts would occur in context of broader "social knowl- *30* edge construction" threads (described above). In order to make an argument for one particular hypothesis or solution for some in-game system, the poster would often present a model to explain the system as evidence for their claim. In some rare cases, that model would be mathematical in nature, and fidelity between the model's prediction and actual in-game observations would function as evidence of its explanatory power. More frequently, evidence would include direct observations taken in-game and references to outside resources such as collective data sets, heuristics in the form of online database backed websites, or fan-created user manuals and guides. Generally speaking, the proportion of model-based reasoning, model testing and prediction, use of mathematics, and explicit computation (11%, 5%, 4%, 1%, respectively) were rather low; however, the sophistication of arguments that leverage such models warrants consideration. For example, Figure 12.4 shows the model linked in the post detailed in Figure 12.3.

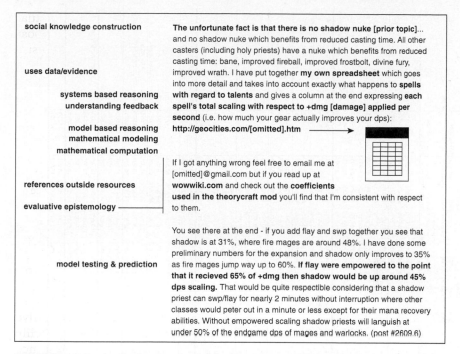

social knowledge construction	The unfortunate fact is that there is no shadow nuke [prior topic]... and no shadow nuke which benefits from reduced casting time. All other casters (including holy priests) have a nuke which benefits from reduced casting time: bane, improved fireball, improved frostbolt, divine fury,
uses data/evidence	improved wrath. I have put together **my own spreadsheet** which goes into more detail and takes into account exactly what happens to **spells**
systems based reasoning understanding feedback	**with regard to talents** and gives a column at the end expressing **each spell's total scaling with respect to +dmg [damage] applied per**
model based reasoning mathematical modeling mathematical computation	**second** (i.e. how much your gear actually improves your dps): http://geocities.com/[omitted].htm
references outside resources	If I got anything wrong feel free to email me at [omitted]@gmail.com but if you read up at **wowwiki.com** and check out the **coefficients**
evaluative epistemology	**used in the theorycraft mod** you'll find that I'm consistent with respect to them.
model testing & prediction	You see there at the end - if you add flay and swp together you see that shadow is at 31%, where fire mages are around 48%. I have done some preliminary numbers for the expansion and shadow only improves to 35% as fire mages jump way up to 60%. **If flay were empowered to the point that it recieved 65% of +dmg then shadow would be up around 45% dps scaling.** That would be quite respectible considering that a shadow priest can swp/flay for nearly 2 minutes without interruption where other classes would peter out in a minute or less except for their mana recovery abilities. Without empowered scaling shadow priests will languish at under 50% of the endgame dps of mages and warlocks. (post #2609.6)

FIGURE 12.3   Analysis of an individual post exemplifying system- and model-based reasoning.

Tacit Epistemologies

We chose to examine the dispositions toward knowledge exhibited in the data corpus because previous pilot work indicated that, while we may find informal science reasoning and argumentation in *WoW* forum discussions, it may also be the case that the stance authors in such contexts take toward their claims is appropriate for *reverse engineering*, but inappropriate for *scientific inquiry* (Steinkuehler and Chmiel 2006). An "absolutist" epistemology, for example, might serve someone well when operating in a virtual world where there really is a single algorithm (or set of algorithms) underlying a given phenomenon and success is only a matter of finding them. However, such an absolutist approach does not serve someone well for understanding science in the real world. Instead, in science, an evaluative disposition is most appropriate, one that treats knowledge as an open-ended process of evaluation and argument of hypotheses about whether and how "algorithms" govern natural phenomena.

The epistemology tacitly displayed in 27% of the data corpus was too ambiguous to code. Of the remaining data corpus that could be coded for epistemological disposition, we found that 65% of the forum posts displayed an evaluative epistemology through rhetorical moves that treat

FIGURE 12.4 An example model of an in-game phenomenon called scaling (Basic n.d.) that illustrates the complexity of the models sometimes discussed.

Constants: Crit Rate = 5%

Solo Caster Classes at Level 60

Class	Spec	Spell (+ talent conditions)	Spell Damage Scale (Cast Time / 3.5)	Damage Talents (per talents)	Target Debuffs (per abilities)	Damage Scale (talents * debuffs)	Spell Damage Total Scale (scale * talents * debuffs)	Crit Bonus (no benefit for dots)	Crit Rate Bonus (per talents)	Crit Scale (total scale * crit bonus)	Damage Interval (limited by dots)	Cast Interval	Cast Time	Casts Per Interval	DPS Scale (total scale / dmg interval)	Time Ratio Scale	Max Crit DPS Scale	Modified Crit Rate	TOTAL DPS SCALE	Notes
Priest	Shadow	Mind Flay	45.7%	125%	115%	144%	65.7%	100%	0%	65.7%	3	3	3	1	21.90%	100.00%	21.90%	5.00%	21.90%	Channeled
		SWP	133.3%	125%	115%	144%	191.7%	100%	0%	191.7%	18	18	18	1	10.65%	100.00%	10.65%	5.00%	10.65%	Dot
		Mind Blast	42.9%	125%	115%	144%	61.6%	150%	0%	92.4%	1.5	5.5	5.5	1.5	41.07%	27.27%	61.61%	5.00%	42.10%	
	Disc/Holy	Smite	71.4%	115%	100%	115%	82.1%	150%	15%	123.2%	2	2	2	1	41.07%	100.00%	61.61%	20.00%	45.18%	
		Holy Fire	75.0%	115%	100%	115%	86.3%	150%	15%	129.4%	3	3	3	1	28.75%	100.00%	43.13%	20.00%	31.63%	Dot
		Holy Fire Dot	25.0%	115%	100%	115%	28.8%	100%	0%	28.8%	10	10	10	1.5	2.88%	100.00%	2.88%	5.00%	2.88%	
		SWP	100.0%	105%	100%	105%	105.0%	100%	0%	105.0%	18	18	18	1.5	5.83%	100.00%	5.83%	5.00%	5.83%	
		PI + Smite	71.4%	135%	100%	135%	96.4%	150%	15%	144.6%	2	2	180	6	48.21%	6.67%	72.32%	20.00%	53.04%	Cooldown
		PI + Holy Fire	75.0%	135%	100%	135%	101.3%	150%	15%	151.9%	3	3	180	3	33.75%	8.33%	50.63%	20.00%	37.13%	Dot + Cooldown
		PI Holy Fire Dot	25.0%	135%	100%	135%	33.8%	100%	15%	33.8%	10	10	180	3	3.38%	11.11%	3.38%	20.00%	3.38%	
Warlock	SM/Ruin	Shadowbolt	85.7%	110%	110%	121%	103.7%	200%	0%	207.4%	2.5	2.5	2.5	1	41.49%	100.00%	82.97%	10.00%	45.63%	
		Corruption	100.0%	110%	110%	121%	121.0%	100%	0%	121.0%	18	18	18	1.5	6.72%	100.00%	6.72%	5.00%	6.72%	
		Curse of Agony	100.0%	110%	110%	121%	121.0%	100%	0%	121.0%	24	24	24	1.5	5.04%	100.00%	5.04%	5.00%	5.04%	improved CoA does not apply to gear
		Shadowburn	42.9%	110%	110%	121%	51.9%	200%	5%	103.7%	1.5	10	10	1.5	34.57%	15.00%	69.14%	10.00%	38.03%	Luck
		Improved Shadowbolt	85.7%	110%	132%	145%	124.5%	200%	5%	248.9%	2.5	2.5	2.5	1	49.78%	100.00%	99.57%	10.00%	54.76%	Luck
	SM/DS	Shadowbolt	100.0%	125%	110%	138%	137.5%	150%	0%	206.3%	3	3	3	1	45.83%	100.00%	68.75%	5.00%	46.98%	
		Corruption	100.0%	125%	110%	138%	137.5%	100%	0%	137.5%	18	18	18	1.5	7.64%	100.00%	7.64%	5.00%	7.64%	
		Curse of Agony	100.0%	131%	110%	144%	144.1%	100%	0%	144.1%	24	24	24	1.5	6.00%	100.00%	6.00%	5.00%	6.00%	
	Ember/DS	Soul Fire	100.0%	125%	110%	138%	137.5%	200%	5%	275.0%	6	6	6	2.5	22.92%	100.00%	45.83%	10.00%	25.21%	Reagent
		Searing Pain	42.9%	125%	110%	138%	58.9%	200%	15%	117.9%	1.5	1.5	1.5	1.5	39.29%	100.00%	78.57%	20.00%	47.14%	
		Immolate	19.8%	150%	110%	165%	32.7%	200%	5%	65.3%	1.5	1.5	1.5	3	21.78%	100.00%	43.56%	10.00%	23.96%	Dot
		Immolate Dot	65.3%	125%	110%	138%	89.8%	100%	5%	89.8%	15	15	15	3	5.99%	100.00%	5.99%	10.00%	5.99%	
	MD/Ruin	Shadowbolt	85.7%	115%	110%	127%	108.4%	200%	5%	216.9%	2.5	2.5	2.5	1	43.37%	100.00%	86.74%	10.00%	47.71%	
		Corruption	100.0%	115%	110%	127%	126.5%	100%	0%	126.5%	18	18	18	1.5	7.03%	100.00%	7.03%	5.00%	7.03%	
		Curse of Agony	100.0%	115%	110%	127%	126.5%	100%	5%	126.5%	24	24	24	1.5	5.27%	100.00%	5.27%	5.00%	5.27%	improved CoA does not apply to gear
		Shadowburn	42.9%	115%	110%	127%	54.2%	200%	5%	108.4%	1.5	10	10	1.5	36.14%	15.00%	72.29%	10.00%	39.76%	
		Improved Shadowbolt	85.7%	115%	132%	152%	130.1%	200%	5%	260.2%	2.5	2.5	2.5	1	52.05%	100.00%	104.09%	10.00%	57.25%	Luck
Mage	Frost	Frostbolt	81.4%	106%	100%	106%	86.3%	200%	10%	172.6%	2.5	2.5	2.5	1	34.53%	100.00%	69.05%	15.00%	39.70%	winter's chill for all ice
		Frozen + Frostbolt	81.4%	106%	100%	106%	86.3%	200%	60%	172.6%	2.5	2.5	2.5	1	34.53%	100.00%	69.05%	65.00%	56.97%	Frozen target
	AP/Frost	Frostbolt	81.4%	109%	100%	109%	88.8%	200%	3%	177.5%	2.5	2.5	2.5	1	35.50%	100.00%	71.01%	8.00%	38.34%	
		Frozen + Frostbolt	81.4%	109%	100%	109%	88.8%	200%	63%	177.5%	2.5	2.5	2.5	1	35.50%	100.00%	71.01%	68.00%	59.64%	Frozen target
		AP + Frostbolt	81.4%	139%	100%	139%	113.2%	200%	3%	226.4%	2.5	2.5	180	5	45.27%	6.94%	90.55%	8.00%	48.90%	Cooldown
		AP + Frozen Frostbolt	81.4%	139%	100%	139%	113.2%	200%	63%	226.4%	2.5	2.5	180	5	45.27%	6.94%	90.55%	68.00%	76.06%	Cooldown + Frozen target
	Fire	Fireball	100.0%	110%	115%	127%	126.5%	219%	10%	277.0%	3	3	3	1	42.17%	100.00%	92.35%	11.00%	47.69%	imp scorch for all fire mage
		Fire Blast	42.9%	110%	115%	127%	54.2%	219%	10%	118.7%	1.5	8	8	1.5	36.14%	18.75%	79.15%	15.00%	42.59%	ignite is 150% + 150% * 40% * debuffs
		Scorch	42.9%	110%	115%	127%	54.2%	219%	10%	118.7%	1.5	1.5	1.5	1.5	36.14%	100.00%	79.15%	15.00%	42.59%	
	AP/Fire	Fireball	100.0%	103%	115%	118%	118.5%	219%	6%	259.4%	3	3	3	1	39.48%	100.00%	86.47%	11.00%	44.65%	
		Scorch	42.9%	103%	115%	118%	50.8%	219%	6%	111.2%	1.5	1.5	1.5	1.5	33.84%	100.00%	74.12%	11.00%	38.27%	
		AP + Fireball	100.0%	133%	115%	153%	153.0%	219%	6%	335.0%	3	3	180	3	50.98%	6.67%	111.65%	11.00%	57.66%	Cooldown
Druid	Balance	Moonfire	20.0%	110%	100%	110%	22.0%	200%	13%	44.0%	1.5	1.5	1.5	1.5	14.67%	100.00%	29.33%	18.00%	17.31%	Dot, imp MF doesn't apply to gear
			57.1%	110%	100%	110%	62.9%	100%	13%	62.9%	12	12	12	1.5	5.24%	100.00%	5.24%	18.00%	5.24%	
		Wrath	57.1%	110%	100%	110%	62.9%	200%	3%	125.7%	1.5	1.5	1.5	1.5	41.90%	100.00%	83.81%	8.00%	45.26%	
		Starfire	100.0%	110%	100%	110%	110.0%	200%	3%	220.0%	3	3	3	3	36.67%	100.00%	73.33%	8.00%	39.60%	
Shaman		Elemental Lightning Bolt	85.7%	105%	100%	105%	90.0%	200%	10%	180.0%	2	2	2	1	45.00%	100.00%	90.00%	15.00%	51.75%	
		Chain Lightning	71.4%	105%	100%	105%	75.0%	200%	10%	150.0%	1.5	1.5	1.5	1	50.00%	25.00%	100.00%	15.00%	57.50%	Cooldown

knowledge as an open-ended process of evaluation and argument such as "Shadow Affinity [priest talent] and Silent Resolve [priest talent]: Do they stack? If so, why would a shadow priest need a 45% reduction in threat?" (post #1937.0). Thirty percent displayed an absolutist epistemology, treating knowledge as objective, certain, and simply accumulative through statements such as: "There is a basic strategy for any one class vs any other class and whoever carries out that strategy most successfully will win" (post #415.92) [even though no such basic strategy exists]. Another 5% displayed a relativist epistemology, treating claims about the world as subjective and "to each his own" (post #215.58). Thus, the majority of posts that could be coded in terms of the attitude toward knowledge held fell into the "evaluative" category, which is consistent with scientific inquiry and inconsistent with reverse engineering. We discuss these findings in greater depth below.

Game Specific Content

What specific content areas of the game elicit these forms of informal science _33_ literacy practice? Examining the relationships among our scientific habits of mind codes (see Table 12.1) and our _WoW_ content codes (Table 12.3), we found that the only moderately strong and non-obvious relationship between the two was between systems-based reasoning (and its concomitant "understanding feedback") and discussion of the priest "talent tree" ($r = 0.48$ and 0.42, respectively), shown in Figure 12.5, whereby players allocate "talent points" toward customizing the functions and abilities of their online character or "avatar."

  In working through this system, participants are faced with the chal- _34_ lenge of finding the best-fit solution to a problem of limited resources (talent points) for distribution across multiple variables, each with their own mathematical relationship to underlying avatar characteristics (e.g., hit points, mana points, regeneration speed). Because _WoW_ is a complex system with no single obvious solution, a significant amount of time on the priest discussion boards is spent assessing how choices in one area of the talent tree affect outcomes elsewhere and debating which point allocations

TABLE 12.3   A Second Set of Codes Used to Describe the Game-Related Content of the Post

World of Warcraft *Content Codes*		
Guilds	Items, equipment, supplies	PvP content, battlegrounds
Quests, instances, raids	Talent trees, spells, abilities	Collaborative play
Other classes (than priests)	Addons, macros	Patches, expansions
Factions (horde vs. alliance)	*WoW* forums, trolling	Class/profession guides, how-to's
Reputation/experience grinding, leveling	Null/social banter	Uncodable

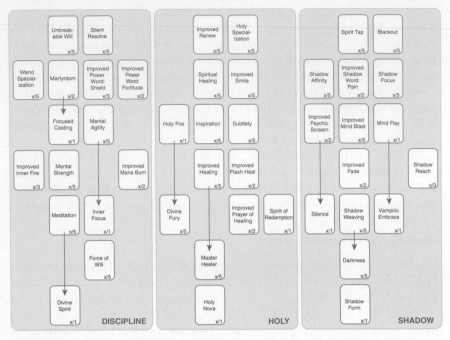

FIGURE 12.5   The *World of Warcraft* "talent tree" for the priest class (at the time of data collection), which enables players to customize their avatars.

are best given various play styles and goals. Many of the examples used throughout this paper are a testament to the intellectual labor spent on just this one game-related content area.

Discussion and Implications

Our goal has been to provide empirical evidence to substantiate claims of the potential of MMOs as sites fostering learning, especially informal science literacy. Given the overall representativeness of our sample (confidence level of 91%), we are in a good position to make reasonably strong claims. Overwhelmingly, game related forums like the one examined here are rich sites for social knowledge construction. That game communities engage in productive forms of discussion and problem solving is not surprising; that such an overwhelming majority of their conversation (86%) is dedicated to such labor *is* surprising. Discursive practices include argument, counterargument, and the use of evidence to warrant one's claims. In such contexts, much of the conversation focuses on puzzling through complex systems within the virtual world and the relationships among components within those systems. At times, that inquiry includes the

35

proposal of explanatory models of how the system under scrutiny functions. On rare occasions, posts debate the merits of their models in terms of their predictive power. On even rarer occasions still, those models take the form of mathematical equations whose computations are done explicitly and publicly.

The findings on tacit epistemology displayed throughout the discussions were also a surprise. Contrary to our initial hypotheses, the predominant epistemological disposition exhibited in the forum posts was "evaluative" and therefore appropriate to science. Such findings are quite encouraging. In an earlier study of argumentative reasoning in everyday contexts that examined Americans across gender, age, class, and educational level (Kuhn 1992), only 15% of those interviewed held an evaluative epistemology, 50% held an absolutist epistemology, and 35% held a relativist epistemology. In this earlier study, argumentative ability did not differ systematically as a function of gender or age but it did differ systematically in terms of level of education. Kuhn therefore concluded that classrooms are one promising context for the development of such skills. However, she also points out the limitations of teacher led dialogues, crediting the positive impact education has on such attributes to the "social environment of peers" that school, as a byproduct, enables rather than teacher led formal dialogues per se:

> . . . does school experience in fact offer the opportunity for the kinds of exchange of ideas and argumentative discourse that would enhance development of argumentative thinking? In one sense, the answer is yes; in another sense it is no. The answer is yes in the sense that from the earliest years, schooling provides a social environment of peers. In the informal social interaction that is a major part of school experience, ideas are tested and inevitably challenged; thus social experience serves as the natural challenge to individual thought. In a second deeper sense, however, the answer is no; schools do not provide this opportunity, or at least do not provide it optimally. Even in the best schools, what may appear to be genuine group debates about an issue are usually heavily controlled by the teacher . . . [who] already possesses the understanding of an issue that he or she wishes students to attain . . . Most often missing, even in the best of such "discovery-based" pedagogies, is genuine, open debate of complex, unanswered questions. (Kuhn 1992, pp. 175–176).

While Kuhn does not advocate the use of informal social dialogue necessarily either (in her own words, they "only occasionally leads students to think explicitly about their ideas—to reflect on their own thought" p. 175), these data suggest their efficacy, at least under certain conditions. In the context of game related forums, informal social dialogues are indeed "genuine, open debate of complex, unanswered questions" and therefore may very well lead participants toward a more reflective stance toward knowledge ultimately. Such a hypothesis is certainly worth future consideration in studies that follow. Of course, one could also argue that game forums (like the one studied here) tend to attract individuals with a more nuanced stance toward knowledge rather than fostering such a stance themselves. Regardless, we can at least say that the cultural norms that emerge in this part of *WoW* fandom preference an evaluative epistemology and that this preferencing of an evaluative disposition varies significantly from the disposition preferenced by other cultural norms, including but certainly not limited to the typical cultural norms of an American classroom.

In addition providing empirical evidence to substantiate the poten- 38 tial of such play contexts for informal science literacy learning, this study sheds some curious light on the nature of collective intelligence (Levy 1999). Discussion environments such as these are best characterized as *collective* rather than *collaborative*. It could have easily been the case that a handful of verbose posters engage in extended dialogue with each other, making it a highly collaborative (albeit small) community of exceptional minds who happen to make their cognition public. This, however, was not at all the pattern we found. Rather, as Figure 12.6 shows, the relationship between length of discussion thread and number of players contributing to it strongly linear.

In such contexts, solutions developed by one person are referenced, 39 debated, and built upon by masses of other participants, not merely a handful of designated experts. Thus, a large number of posters each make one or two contributions to the discussion, with the solution to the problem or answer to the inquiry emerging as a result of swarms of thinkers, not a lonely few.

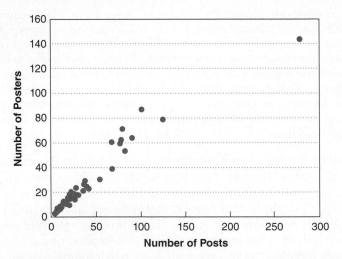

FIGURE 12.6 Scatter plot of number of posts by number of unique posters for each thread in the data corpus.

Such findings are useful in that they enable us to more accurately char- *40* acterize virtual worlds as learning contexts that stretch across both intra-game and extra-game spaces. As our study shows, forms of inquiry within play contexts such as these are *authentic* although *synthetic:* even though the worlds themselves are fantasy, the knowledge building communities around them are quite real. And, it is their designed nature that makes these communities so lively. For they were designed such that particular user-controlled configurations (e.g., how one builds her talent tree) has powerful and important implications for the success of one's game play. In fact, in these synthetic worlds designers can manipulate these dynamics so that they are most likely to breed rich conversations as users struggle with the most appropriate configurations.

What, then, are the implications for science education and future *41* research? There are several. First, the veritable firewall against games and gaming culture within schools might erode. While virtual worlds may seem "torpid" (Solomon 2004) to a non-gaming older generation, empirical analysis of what game communities do and value indicates that this interactive medium might well be a worthy vehicle of learning for those who value intellectual and academic play. In a school system sometimes sidetracked by testing regimes that pressure teachers and students to focus on only a narrow range of topics, popular culture contexts such as these might be a nice complement to classrooms, augmenting classroom instruction by situating informal science literacy in popular culture context.

Second, we should ask ourselves how these practices are distributed *42* across various groups by demographic variables known to be important, such as age, education level, and income. Demonstrating that game communities such as those in *WoW* engage in important forms of science literacy again raises the specter of a new form of digital divide—one not between the have and have-nots, but between the do and do-nots. We need to think deeply about what people are doing with the technologies that are becoming so ubiquitous and engaging. As educators, we have a responsibility to better understand what these different forms of technology afford and communicate this to the public more broadly.

Third and finally, we should actively seek out ways to build *bridging* *43* *third spaces* (Steinkuehler 2008b) between school and home that incubate forms of academic play such as those studied here. In so doing, we might address both growing digital divides at once. We can ameliorate the generational divide by educating the keepers of the canon as to the genuine merit of games and gaming cultures, and we can close the access gap by providing rich intellectual play spaces in technically and cognitively sophisticated environments to kids and young adults who might not otherwise happen upon them. As Dewey himself once argued, good education, effective and life-enhancing education, represents life "as real and vital to the child as that which he carries on in the home, in the neighborhood, or on the play-ground" (1897).

REFERENCES

American Association for the Advancement of Science (1993) Benchmarks for science literacy. Oxford University Press, New York

Barab S, Arcici A, Jackson C (2005) Eat your vegetables and do your homework: a design-based investigation of enjoyment and meaning in learning. Educ Technol 45(1):15–21

Barab SA, Sadler T, Heiselt C, Hickey D, Zuiker S (2007) Relating narrative, inquiry, and inscriptions: a framework for socio-scientific inquiry. J Sci Educ Technol 16(1):59–82. doi: 10.1007/s10956-006-9033-3

Basic (n.d.) Scaling model. Retrieved November 1, 2007 from http://geocities.com/karlthepagan/wow/damage_scale.htm

Chi MTH (1997) Quantifying qualitative analyses of verbal data: a practical guide. J Learn Sci 6(3):271–315. doi:10.1207/s15327809jls0603_1

Chinn CA, Malhotra B (2002) Epistemologically authentic inquiry in schools: a theoretical framework for evaluating inquiry tasks. Sci Educ 86(2):175–218. doi:10.1002/sce.10001

Dewey J (1897) My pedagogic creed. Sch J 14(3):77–80

Dewey J (1910) Science as subject matter and as method. Science 31(787):121–127. doi:10.1126/science.31.787.121

Elsner A (2005) Is US becoming hostile to science? CNN.com. Retrieved October 31, 2005 from http://www.cnn.com/2005/TECH/science/10/28/science.debate.reut

Friedman TL (2005) The world is flat. Farrar, Straus, and Giroux, New York

Gee JP (2003) What video games have to teach us about learning and literacy. Palgrave, New York

Hayes E Games I Learning through game design: a review of current software & research. Games Cult (in press)

Jenkins H III (1992) Textual poachers: television fans & participatory culture. Routledge, New York

Ketelhut DJ (2007) The impact of student self-efficacy on scientific inquiry skills: an exploratory investigation in River City, a multiuser virtual environment. J Sci Educ Technol 16(1):99–111. doi: 10.1007/s10956-006-9038-y

Ketelhut DJ, Dede C, Clarke J, Nelson B, Bowman C (2007) Studying situated learning in a multi-user virtual environment. In: Baker E, Dickieson J, Wulfeck W, O'Neil H (eds), Assessment of problem solving using simulations. Lawrence Erlbaum Associates, Mahwah, NJ

Kuhn D (1992) Thinking as argument. Harv Educ Rev 62(2):155–178

Lave J (1988) Cognition in practice. Cambridge University Press, Cambridge UK

Lave J, Wenger E (1991) Situated learning. Cambridge University Press, Cambridge

Levy P (1999) Collective intelligence. (Robert Bononno, trans.). Perseus Books, Cambridge MA

Mayer RE (1992) Thinking, problem solving, cognition, 2nd edn. WH Freeman, New York

Miller JD (2004) Public understanding of, and attitudes toward, scientific research: what we know and what we need to know. Public Underst Sci 13(3):273–294. doi:10.1177/0963662504044908

Nasir NS (2005) Individual cognitive structuring and the sociocultural context: strategy shifts in the game of dominoes. J Learn Sci 14(1):5–34. doi:10.1207/s15327809jls1401_2

National Research Council (1996) National science education standards. National Academy Press, Washington DC

Nelson B, Ketelhut DJ, Clarke J, Dieterle E, Dede C, Erlandson B (2007) Robust design strategies for scaling educational innovations: The River City MUVE case study.

In: Shelton BE, Wiley DA (eds) The design and use of simulation computer games in education. Sense Press, Rotterdam, The Netherlands

Osborne J, Erduren S, Simon S (2004) Enhancing the quality of argumentation in school science. J Res Sci Teach 41(10):994–1020. doi:10.1002/tea.20035

Poincaré H (2001) Science and hypothesis. In: Gould SJ (ed) The value of science: essential writings of Henri Poincaré. The Modern Library, New York, pp 7–180 (Original work published 1905)

Schwab JJ (1962) The teaching of science as enquiry. Harvard University Press, Cambridge MA

Shaffer DW, Squire KD, Halverson R, Gee JP (2005) Video games and the future of learning. Phi Delta Kappan 87(2):105–111

Singer SR, Hilton M, Schweingruber HA (2005) America's lab report: investigations in high school science. The National Academy Press, Washington DC

Solomon A (2004, July 10) The closing of the American book. The New York Times p. A17

Squire K (2003) Replaying history: learning world history through playing Civilization III. Unpublished dissertation. Indiana University, Bloomington IN

Squire KD (2005) Educating the fighter. Horizon 13(2):75–88. doi: 10.1108/10748120510608106

Steinkuehler CA (2004) Learning in massively multiplayer online games. In: Kafai YB, Sandoval WA, Enyedy N, Nixon AS, Herrera F (eds) Proceedings of the sixth ICLS. Erlbaum, Mahwah, NJ, pp 521–528

Steinkuehler CA (2005) Cognition and learning in massively multiplayer online games: a critical approach. Unpublished dissertation. University of Wisconsin, Madison WI

Steinkuehler C (2006a) The mangle of play. Games Cult 1(3):1–14

Steinkuehler CA (2006b) Massively multiplayer online videogaming as participation in a Discourse. Mind Cult Act 13(1):38–52. doi: 10.1207/s15327884mca1301_4

Steinkuehler CA (2006c) Why game (culture) studies now? Games Cult 1(1):1–6

Steinkuehler C, Chmiel M (2006) Fostering scientific habits of mind in the context of online play. In: Barab SA, Hay KE, Songer NB, Hickey DT (eds) Proceedings of the international conference of the learning sciences. Erlbuam, Mahwah NJ, pp 723–729

Steinkuehler C (2007) Massively multiplayer online gaming as a constellation of literacy practices. eLearning 4(3):297–318

Steinkuehler CA (2008a) Cognition and literacy in massively multiplayer online games. In: Coiro J, Knobel M, Lankshear C, Leu D (eds) Handbook of research on new literacies. Erlbaum, Mahwah NJ, pp 611–634

Steinkuehler C (2008b) Massively multiplayer online games as an educational technology: an outline for research. Educ Technol 48(1):10–21

Woodcock BS (2008) An analysis of MMOG subscription growth 23.0. Retrieved April 21, 2008 from http://www.mmogchart.com

■ ■ ■

Reading as a Writer: Analyzing Rhetorical Choices

1. In paragraphs 7, 8 and 9, Steinkuehler and Duncan list the skills they believe are crucial to scientific literacy and that are also fostered by video games. Divide into small groups and give each group one of the "scientific discursive practices" listed in paragraph 16. Each group should be sure they can define their practice, and then offer examples from this essay that demonstrate this skill in action, according to the authors.

2. The authors present some of their evidence in charts, many of which contain a lot of information. On your own, or in pairs, analyze the material presented in this visual medium. What are the strengths and weaknesses of this kind of presentation? Which charts are most helpful for explaining their argument, and why?

Writing as a Reader: Entering the Conversation of Ideas

1. Steinkuehler and Duncan's theories about valuing "play spaces" in education seems to run counter to Mark Edmundson's ideas that universities, at least, are catering too much to student pleasure. Compose an essay in which you draw on the authors' ideas to consider the strengths and weaknesses of fun in education, keeping in mind that a thoughtful response will do more than weigh "for" or "against" the role of pleasure in education. When is fun useful? What are its limits for learning?

2. Diane Ravitch's perspective on the "achievement gap" (which she redefines as the "opportunity gap") is interesting to consider in light of Steinkuehler and Duncan's claims in their essay's conclusion that the "growing digital divide" (as well as the generational divide) might be narrowed by expanding our uses and access to video game "play spaces." Conduct some additional research to discover what scholars are saying about this issue as you write an essay that makes a point about technology, inequality, and justice in education.

Media Studies

What can we learn from what entertains us?

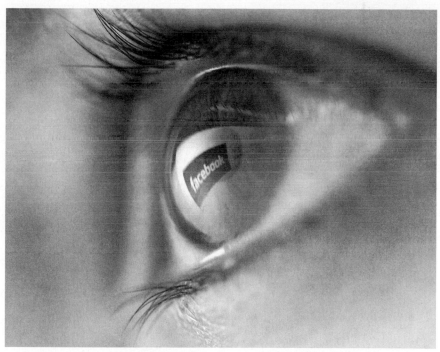

© Getty Images/Chris Jackson

People love to debate the virtues and vices of media culture. Is our obsession with video gaming dumbing us down, or making us smarter? Do mainstream advertising and the movie industry reinforce damaging stereotypes, or offer more equitable alternatives? Is popular culture worth taking seriously at all? The authors of this chapter's readings believe that far from being too "lite" to take seriously, media culture is the very ground we should be exploring carefully if we wish to make sense of our lives today. These writers discover meanings that may surprise you in the many pastimes, entertainments, and guilty pleasures that tempt us every day. When scholars study what we do for fun—enjoying online avatars, movies, and glossy advertising, to name just a few of the pleasures analyzed in these texts—we learn how every cultural artifact, no matter how seemingly insignificant, carries meaning that shapes our lives in often quite significant ways.

In this chapter, you will be invited to consider very different perspectives about the effects of online culture on our identities. Sherry Turkle suggests that there are clear downsides to our "tethered" or "collaborative" selves, particularly on social media. Jane McGonigal offers a different perspective on the problem-solving potential of collective game playing, which might offer inspiration for solving real-life challenges, too. Where would you chime into this complex conversation?

Some of the authors in this chapter focus specifically on television and films, such as Joni Adamson, who reveals the surprising popularity of the film *Avatar* among some indigenous environmental activists. Ken Gillam and Shannon R. Wooden examine unexpected role models for a new kind of masculinity in Pixar films, while bell hooks notes that films and television shows may not be so forward-thinking when it comes to depictions of poverty. Jean Kilbourne also examines the ways media can reinforce damaging stereotypes that limit the ways we see both women and men. What solutions do these writers offer?

The readings in this chapter acknowledge the positive potential of media culture, but they also help us understand that the past is always with us in our concerns for the present and hopes for the future. Whether you see media today as the end of culture as we knew it, the same old stuff, or something entirely new—or perhaps all three—these readings raise provocative questions about the significance of our "just-for-fun" pastimes.

 Visit **macmillanhighered.com/frominquiry3e** to view documentary videos from The Representation Project that explore how the media shapes our expectations of femininity and masculinity.

SHERRY TURKLE

Growing Up Tethered

Sherry Turkle is a professor in the Program in Science, Technology, and Society at MIT (Massachusetts Institute of Technology), where she also directs the MIT Initiative on Technology and Self. In her research and writing, Turkle focuses on people's subjective experiences with technology, and she has published many books and articles on this rich topic, both for scholarly and popular audiences. She is a frequent media commentator on the intersections of technology, media, psychology, and sociology, on programs that include NPR, *Nightline*, and *The Colbert Report*. Turkle gave a TED talk in 2012 titled, "Connected, but Alone?", which indicates one of her concerns about the effects of screen culture.

This piece comes from Turkle's 2011 book *Alone Together: Why We Expect More from Technology and Less from Each Other*, from a chapter titled, "Growing Up Tethered." What do her book and chapter titles suggest about her perspective on our use of technology? You might pause after reading the first five paragraphs to reflect on the conversations she reports having with teenagers, and her evaluation. Is it fair to call this generation a "tethered" one? What problems does Turkle find in not being able to separate from one's parents, and from one's friends?

As you read, weigh Turkle's description of this new way of being (what she calls the "tethered" or "collaborative self") against her analysis of this media-moderated behavior as either a "pathology" or as just a new norm — or perhaps both. (See paras. 22 to 26 in particular.) Turkle raises some different theories of the self in paragraphs 29 and 30. Slow down and be sure you understand the ideas she attributes to Erik Erikson, Jay Lifton, and her own theory of the narcissistic self. To what extent do her examples and explanations support this claim?

In her sections titled "The Avatar of Me" and "Presentation Anxiety," Turkle offers some extended examples of the ways we self-consciously craft our public personas on social media, whether through games like the Sims or in profiles on Facebook. Evaluate your own earliest — and then later — experiences with Facebook or other social media sites that require a kind of crafting of online identity. We suspect you could have some lively discussions with your classmates (or friends and family outside of your class) about the good and bad and stress-producing aspects of this form of media. How would you respond to Turkle's claims about the benefits versus the deficits of being a "tethered" or "collaborative" self? (And would you respond differently if you were speaking to her *in person* versus via text, tweet, or on another social media platform?)

■   ■   ■

Roman, eighteen, admits that he texts while driving and he is not going to stop. "I know I should, but it's not going to happen. If I get a Facebook message or something posted on my wall . . . I have to see it. I have to." I am speaking with him and ten of his senior classmates at the Cranston School, a private urban coeducational high school in Connecticut. His friends admonish him, but then several admit to the same behavior. Why do they text while driving? Their reasons are not reasons; they simply express a need to connect. "I interrupt a call even if the new call says 'unknown' as an identifier — I just have to know who it is. So I'll cut off a friend for an 'unknown,'" says Maury. "I need to know who wanted to connect. . . . And if I hear my phone, I have to answer it. I don't have a choice. I have to know who it is, what they are calling for." Marilyn adds, "I keep the sound on when I drive. When a text comes in, I have to look. No matter what. Fortunately, my phone shows me the text as a pop up right up front . . . so I don't have to do too much looking while I'm driving."

These young people live in a state of waiting for connection. And they are willing to take risks, to put themselves on the line. Several admit that tethered to their phones, they get into accidents when walking. One chipped a front tooth. Another shows a recent bruise on his arm. "I went right into the handle of the refrigerator."

I ask the group a question: "When was the last time you felt that you *2* didn't want to be interrupted?" I expect to hear many stories. There are none. Silence. "I'm waiting to be interrupted right now," one says. For him, what I would term "interruption" is the beginning of a connection.

Today's young people have grown up with robot pets and on the net- *3* work in a fully tethered life. In their views of robots, they are pioneers, the first generation that does not necessarily take simulation to be second best. As for online life, they see its power—they are, after all risking their lives to check their messages—but they also view it as one might the weather: to be taken for granted, enjoyed, and sometimes endured. They've gotten used to this weather but there are signs of weather fatigue. There are so many performances; it takes energy to keep things up; and it takes time, a lot of time. "Sometimes you don't have time for your friends except if they're online," is a common complaint. And then there are the compulsions of the networked life—the ones that lead to dangerous driving and chipped teeth.

Today's adolescents have no less need than those of previous genera- *4* tions to learn empathic skills, to think about their values and identity, and to manage and express feelings. They need time to discover themselves, time to think. But technology, put in the service of always-on communication and telegraphic speed and brevity, has changed the rules of engagement with all of this. When is downtime, when is stillness? The text-driven world of rapid response does not make self-reflection impossible but does little to cultivate it. When interchanges are reformatted for the small screen and reduced to the emotional shorthand of emoticons, there are necessary simplifications. And what of adolescents' need for secrets, for marking out what is theirs alone?

I wonder about this as I watch cell phones passed around high school *5* cafeterias. Photos and messages are being shared and compared. I cannot help but identify with the people who sent the messages to these wandering phones. Do they all assume that their words and photographs are on public display? Perhaps. Traditionally, the development of intimacy required privacy. Intimacy without privacy reinvents what intimacy means. Separation, too, is being reinvented. Tethered children know they have a parent on tap—a text or a call away.

Degrees of Separation

Mark Twain mythologized the adolescent's search for identity in the Huck *6* Finn story, the on-the-Mississippi moment, a time of escape from an adult world. Of course, the time on the river is emblematic not of a moment but of an ongoing process through which children separate from their parents. That rite of passage is now transformed by technology. In the traditional variant, the child internalizes the adults in his or her world before crossing the threshold of independence. In the modern, technologically tethered variant, parents can be brought along in an intermediate space, such as that created by the cell phone, where everyone important is on speed dial. In this sense, the generations sail down the river together, and adolescents don't face the same pressure to develop the independence we have associated with moving forward into young adulthood.

When parents give children cell phones—most of the teenagers I 7 spoke with were given a phone between the ages of nine and thirteen—the gift typically comes with a contract: Children are expected to answer their parents' calls. This arrangement makes it possible for the child to engage in activities—see friends, attend movies, go shopping, spend time at the beach—that would not be permitted without the phone. Yet, the tethered child does not have the experience of being alone with only him- or herself to count on. For example, there used to be a point for an urban child, an important moment, when there was a first time to navigate the city alone. It was a rite of passage that communicated to children that they were on their own and responsible. If they were frightened, they had to experience those feelings. The cell phone buffers this moment.

Parents want their children to answer their phones, but adolescents 8 need to separate. With a group of seniors at Fillmore, a boys' preparatory school in New York City, the topic of parents and cell phones elicits strong emotions. The young men consider, "If it is always possible to be in touch, when does one have the right to be alone?"

Some of the boys are defiant. For one, "It should be my decision about 9 whether I pick up the phone. People can call me, but I don't have to talk to them." For another, "To stay free from parents, I don't take my cell. Then they can't reach me. My mother tells me to take my cell, but I just don't." Some appeal to history to justify ignoring parents' calls. Harlan, a distinguished student and athlete, thinks he has earned the right to greater independence. He talks about older siblings who grew up before cell phones and enjoyed greater freedom: "My mother makes me take my phone, but I never answer it when my parents call, and they get mad at me. I don't feel I should have to. Cell phones are recent. In the last ten years, everyone started getting them. Before, you couldn't just call someone whenever. I don't see why I have to answer when my mom calls me. My older sisters didn't have to do that." Harlan's mother, unmoved by this argument from precedent, checks that he has his phone when he leaves for school in the morning; Harlan does not answer her calls. Things are at an unhappy stalemate.

Several boys refer to the "mistake" of having taught their parents 10 how to text and send instant messages (IMs), which they now equate with letting the genie out of the bottle. For one, "I made the mistake of teaching my parents how to text-message recently, so now if I don't call them when they ask me to call, I get an urgent text message." For another, "I taught my parents to IM. They didn't know how. It was the stupidest thing I could do. Now my parents IM me all the time. It is really annoying. My parents are upsetting me. I feel trapped and less independent."

Teenagers argue that they should be allowed time when they are not *11* "on call." Parents say that they, too, feel trapped. For if you know your child is carrying a cell phone, it is frightening to call or text and get no response. "I didn't ask for this new worry," says the mother of two high school girls. Another, a mother of three teenagers, "tries not to call them if it's not important." But if she calls and gets no response, she panics:

> I've sent a text. Nothing back. And I know they have their phones. Intellectually, I know there is little reason to worry. But there is something about this unanswered text. Sometimes, it made me a bit nutty. One time, I kept sending texts, over and over. I envy my mother. We left for school in the morning. We came home. She worked. She came back, say at six. She didn't worry. I end up imploring my children to answer my every message. Not because I feel I have a right to their instant response. Just out of compassion.

Adolescent autonomy is not just about separation from parents. Ado- *12* lescents also need to separate from each other. They experience their friendships as both sustaining and constraining. Connectivity brings complications. Online life provides plenty of room for individual experimentation, but it can be hard to escape from new group demands. It is common for friends to expect that their friends will stay available—a technology-enabled social contract demands continual peer presence. And the tethered self becomes accustomed to its support.

Traditional views of adolescent development take autonomy and *13* strong personal boundaries as reliable signs of a successfully maturing self. In this view of development, we work toward an independent self capable of having a feeling, considering it, and deciding whether to share it. Sharing a feeling is a deliberate act, a movement toward intimacy. This description was always a fiction in several ways. For one thing, the "gold standard" of autonomy validated a style that was culturally "male." Women (and indeed, many men) have an emotional style that defines itself not by boundaries but through relationships.[1] Furthermore, adolescent conversations are by nature exploratory, and this in healthy ways. Just as some writers learn what they think by looking at what they write, the years of identity formation can be a time of learning what you think by hearing what you say to others. But given these caveats, when we think about maturation, the notion of a bounded self has its virtues, if only as a metaphor. It suggests, sensibly, that before we forge successful life partnerships, it is helpful to have a sense of who we are.[2]

But the gold standard tarnishes if a phone is always in hand. You *14* touch a screen and reach someone presumed ready to respond, someone who also has a phone in hand. Now, technology makes it easy to express emotions while they are being formed. It supports an emotional style in which feelings are not fully experienced until they are communicated. Put otherwise, there is every opportunity to form a thought by sending out for comments.

The Collaborative Self

Julia, sixteen, a sophomore at Branscomb, an urban public high school in   *15* New Jersey, turns texting into a kind of polling. Julia has an outgoing and warm presence, with smiling, always-alert eyes. When a feeling bubbles up, Julia texts it. Where things go next is guided by what she hears next. Julia says,

> If I'm upset, right as I feel upset, I text a couple of my friends . . . just because I know that they'll be there and they can comfort me. If something exciting happens, I know that they'll be there to be excited with me, and stuff like that. So I definitely feel emotions when I'm texting, as I'm texting. . . . Even before I get upset and I know that I have that feeling that I'm gonna start crying, yeah, I'll pull up my friend . . . uh, my phone . . . and say like . . . I'll tell them what I'm feeling, and, like, I need to talk to them, or see them.

"I'll pull up my friend . . . uh, my phone." Julia's language slips tell-   *16* ingly. When Julia thinks about strong feelings, her thoughts go both to her phone and her friends. She mixes together "pulling up" a friend's name on her phone and "pulling out" her phone, but she does not really correct her-self so much as imply that the phone is her friend and that friends take on identities through her phone.

After Julia sends out a text, she is uncomfortable until she gets one   *17* back: "I am always looking for a text that says, 'Oh, I'm sorry,' or 'Oh, that's great.'" Without this feedback, she says, "It's hard to calm down." Julia describes how painful it is to text about "feelings" and get no response: "I get mad. Even if I e-mail someone, I want the response, like, right away.[3] I want them to be, like, right there answering me. And sometimes I'm like, 'Uh! Why can't you just answer me?' . . . I wait, like, depending on what it is, I wait like an hour if they don't answer me, and I'll text them again. 'Are you mad? Are you there? Is everything okay?'" Her anxiety is palpable. Julia must have a response. She says of those she texts, "You want them there, because you need them." When they are not there, she moves on with her nascent feelings, but she does not move on alone: "I go to another friend and tell them."

Claudia, seventeen, a junior at Cranston, describes a similar progres-   *18* sion. "I start to have some happy feelings as soon as I start to text." As with Julia, things move from "I have a feeling, I want to make a call" to "I want to have a feeling, I need to make a call," or in her case, send a text. What is not being cultivated here is the ability to be alone and reflect on one's emotions in private. On the contrary, teenagers report discomfort when they are without their cell phones.[4] They need to be connected in order to feel like themselves. Put in a more positive way, both Claudia and Julia share feelings as part of discovering them. They cultivate a collaborative self.

Estranged from her father, Julia has lost her close attachments to his 19 relatives and was traumatized by being unable to reach her mother during the day of the September 11 attacks on the Twin Towers. Her story illustrates how digital connectivity—particularly texting—can be used to manage specific anxieties about loss and separation. But what Julia does—her continual texting, her way of feeling her feelings only as she shares them—is not unusual. The particularities of every individual case express personal history, but Julia's individual "symptom" comes close to being a generational style.[5]

Sociologist David Riesman, writing in the mid-1950s, remarked on the 20 American turn from an inner- to an other-directed sense of self.[6] Without a firm inner sense of purpose, people looked to their neighbors for validation. Today, cell phone in hand, other-directedness is raised to a higher power. At the moment of beginning to have a thought or feeling, we can have it validated, almost prevalidated. Exchanges may be brief, but more is not necessarily desired. The necessity is to have someone be there.

Ricki, fifteen, a freshman at Richelieu, a private high school for girls 21 in New York City, describes that necessity: "I have a lot of people on my contact list. If one friend doesn't 'get it,' I call another." This marks a turn to a hyper-other-directedness. This young woman's contact or buddy list has become something like a list of "spare parts" for her fragile adolescent self. When she uses the expression "get it," I think she means "pick up the phone." I check with her if I have gotten this right. She says, "'Get it,' yeah, 'pick up,' but also 'get it,' 'get *me*.'" Ricki counts on her friends to finish her thoughts. Technology does not cause but encourages a sensibility in which the validation of a feeling becomes part of establishing it, even part of the feeling itself.

I have said that in the psychoanalytic tradition, one speaks about 22 narcissism not to indicate people who love themselves, but a personality so fragile that it needs constant support.[7] It cannot tolerate the complex demands of other people but tries to relate to them by distorting who they are and splitting off what it needs, what it can use. So, the narcissistic self gets on with others by dealing only with their made-to-measure representations. These representations (some analytic traditions refer to them as "part objects," others as "self-objects") are all that the fragile self can handle. We can easily imagine the utility of inanimate companions to such a self because a robot or a computational agent can be sculpted to meet one's needs. But a fragile person can also be supported by selected and limited contact with people (say, the people on a cell phone "favorites" list). In a life of texting and messaging, those on that contact list can be made to appear almost on demand. You can take what you need and move on. And, if not gratified, you can try someone else.

Again, technology, on its own, does not cause this new way of relating 23 to our emotions and other people. But it does make it easy. Over time, a new style of being with each other becomes socially sanctioned. In every era, certain ways of relating come to feel natural. In our time, if we can be continually in touch, needing to be continually in touch does not seem a problem or a pathology but an accommodation to what technology affords. It becomes the norm.

The history of what we think of as psychopathology is dynamic. If in 24 a particular time and place, certain behaviors seem disruptive, they are labeled pathological. In the nineteenth century, for example, sexual repression was considered a good and moral thing, but when women lost sensation or the ability to speak, these troubling symptoms were considered a disease, hysteria. With more outlets for women's sexuality, hysterical symptoms declined, and others took their place. So, the much-prescribed tranquilizers of the 1950s spoke to women's new anxieties when marginalized in the home after a fuller civic participation during World War II.

Now, we have symptoms born of fears of isolation and abandonment. 25 In my study of growing up in the networked culture, I meet many children and teenagers who feel cast off. Some have parents with good intentions who simply work several jobs and have little time for their children. Some have endured divorce—sometimes multiple divorces—and float from one parent to another, not confident of their true home. Those lucky children who have intact families with stable incomes can experience other forms of abandonment. Busy parents are preoccupied, often by what is on their cell phones. When children come home, it is often to a house that is empty until a parent returns from work.

For young people in all of these circumstances, computers and 26 mobile devices offer communities when families are absent. In this context, it is not surprising to find troubling patterns of connection and disconnection: teenagers who will only "speak" online, who rigorously avoid face-to-face encounters, who are in text contact with their parents fifteen or twenty times a day, who deem even a telephone call "too much" exposure and say that they will "text, not talk." But are we to think of these as pathologies? For as social mores change, what once seemed "ill" can come to seem normal. Twenty years ago, as a practicing clinical psychologist, if I had met a college junior who called her mother fifteen times a day, checking in about what shoes to buy and what dress to wear, extolling a new kind of decaffeinated tea, and complaining about the difficulty of a physics problem set, I would have thought her behavior problematic. I would have encouraged her to explore difficulties with separation. I would have assumed that these had to be addressed for her to proceed to successful adulthood. But these days, a college student who texts home fifteen times a day is not unusual.

High school and college students are always texting—while waiting 27
in line at the cafeteria, while eating, while waiting for the campus shuttle.
Not surprisingly, many of these texts are to parents. What once we might
have seen as a problem becomes how we do things. But a behavior that has
become typical may still express the problems that once caused us to see
it as pathological. Even a typical behavior may not be in an adolescent's
developmental interest.

Consider Leo, a college sophomore far from home, who feels crippling 28
loneliness. He tells me that he "handles" this problem by texting and calling his mother up to twenty times a day. He remarks that this behavior
does not make him stand out; everyone he knows is on a phone all day. But
even if invisible, he considers his behavior a symptom all the same.

These days, our relationship to the idea of psychological autonomy 29
is evolving. I have said that central to Erik Erikson's thinking about adolescents is the idea that they need a moratorium, a "time out," a relatively
consequence-free space for experimentation. But in Erikson's thinking, the
self, once mature, is relatively stable. Though embedded in relationships,
in the end it is bounded and autonomous.[8] One of Erikson's students, psychiatrist Robert Jay Lifton, has an alternative vision of the mature self. He
calls it *protean* and emphasizes its multiple aspects.[9] Thinking of the self
as protean accents connection and reinvention. This self, as Lifton puts it,
"fluid and many-sided," can embrace and modify ideas and ideologies. It
flourishes when provided with things diverse, disconnected, and global.

Publicly, Erikson expressed approval for Lifton's work, but after 30
Erikson's death in 1994, Lifton asked the Erikson family if he might have
the books he had personally inscribed and presented to his teacher. The
family agreed; the books were returned. In his personal copy of Lifton's
The Protean Self, Erikson had written extensive marginal notes. When he
came to the phrase "protean man," Erikson had scrawled "protean boy?"[10]
Erikson could not accept that successful maturation would not result in
something solid. By Erikson's standards, the selves formed in the cacophony of online spaces are not protean but juvenile. Now I suggest that the
culture in which they develop tempts them into narcissistic ways of relating to the world.

The Avatar of Me

Erikson said that identity play is the work of adolescence. And these days 31
adolescents use the rich materials of online life to do that work. For example, in a game such as The Sims Online (think of this as a very junior version of Second Life), you can create an avatar that expresses aspects of
yourself, build a house, and furnish it to your taste. Thus provisioned, you
can set about reworking in the virtual aspects of life that may not have
gone so well in the real.

Trish, a timid and anxious thirteen-year-old, has been harshly beaten 32
by her alcoholic father. She creates an abusive family on The Sims Online,
but in the game her character, also thirteen, is physically and emotionally
strong. In simulation, she plays and replays the experience of fighting off
her aggressor. A sexually experienced girl of sixteen, Katherine, creates an
online innocent. "I want to have a rest," she says. Beyond rest, Katherine
tells me she can get "practice at being a different kind of person. That's
what Sims is for me. Practice."

Katherine "practices" on the game at breakfast, during school recess, 33
and after dinner. She says she feels comforted by her virtual life. I ask her if
her activities in the game have led her to do anything differently in her life
away from it. She replies, "Not really," but then goes on to describe how her
life is in fact beginning to change: "I'm thinking about breaking up with my
boyfriend. I don't want to have sex anymore, but I would like to have a boyfriend. My character on Sims has boyfriends but doesn't have sex. They [the
boyfriends of her Sims avatar] help her with her job. I think to start fresh I
would have to break up with my boyfriend." Katherine does not completely
identify with her online character and refers to her avatar in the third person. Yet, The Sims Online is a place where she can see her life anew.

This kind of identity work can take place wherever you create an 34
avatar. And it can take place on social-networking sites as well, where one's
profile becomes an avatar of sorts, a statement not only about who you
are but who you want to be. Teenagers make it clear that games, worlds,
and social networking (on the surface, rather different) have much in common. They all ask you to compose and project an identity. Audrey, sixteen,
a junior at Roosevelt, a suburban public high school near New York City,
is explicit about the connection between avatars and profiles. She calls her
Facebook profile "my Internet twin" and "the avatar of me."

Mona, a freshman at Roosevelt, has recently joined Facebook. Her 35
parents made her wait until her fourteenth birthday, and I meet her shortly
after this long-awaited day. Mona tells me that as soon as she got on the
site, "Immediately, I felt power." I ask her what she means. She says, "The
first thing I thought was, 'I am going to broadcast the real me.'" But when
Mona sat down to write her profile, things were not so straightforward.
Whenever one has time to write, edit, and delete, there is room for performance. The "real me" turns out to be elusive. Mona wrote and rewrote her
profile. She put it away for two days and tweaked it again. Which pictures
to add? Which facts to include? How much of her personal life to reveal?
Should she give any sign that things at home were troubled? Or was this a
place to look good?

Mona worries that she does not have enough of a social life to make 36
herself sound interesting: "What kind of personal life should I *say* I have?"
Similar questions plague other young women in her class. They are starting to have boyfriends. Should they list themselves as single if they are
just starting to date someone new? What if they consider themselves in a

relationship, but their boyfriends do not? Mona tells me that "it's common sense" to check with a boy before listing yourself as connected to him, but "that could be a very awkward conversation." So there are misunderstandings and recriminations. Facebook at fourteen can be a tearful place. For many, it remains tearful well through college and graduate school. Much that might seem straightforward is fraught. For example, when asked by Facebook to confirm someone as a friend or ignore the request, Helen, a Roosevelt senior, says, "I always feel a bit of panic. . . . Who should I friend? . . . I really want to only have my cool friends listed, but I'm nice to a lot of other kids at school. So I include the more unpopular ones, but then I'm unhappy." It is not how she wants to be seen.

In the Victorian era, one controlled whom one saw and to whom one   37
was connected through the ritual of calling cards. Visitors came to call and, not necessarily expecting to be received, left a card. A card left at your home in return meant that the relationship might grow. In its own way, friending on Facebook is reminiscent of this tradition. On Facebook, you send a request to be a friend. The recipient of the request has the option to ignore or friend you. As was the case in the Victorian era, there is an intent to screen. But the Victorians followed socially accepted rules. For example, it was understood that one was most open to people of similar social standing. Facebook is more democratic—which leaves members to make up their own rules, not necessarily understood by those who contact them. Some people make a request to be a Facebook friend in the spirit of "I'm a fan" and are accepted on that basis. Other people friend only people they know. Others friend any friend of a friend, using Facebook as a tool to expand their acquaintanceships. All of this can be exciting or stressful—often both at the same time, because friending has consequences. It means that someone can see what you say about yourself on your profile, the pictures you post, and your friends' postings on your "wall," the shared communication space for you and your friends. Friending someone gives that person implicit permission to try to friend your friends. In fact, the system constantly proposes that they do so.

Early in this project, I was at a conference dinner, sitting next to an   38
author whose publisher insisted that she use Facebook as a way to promote her new book. The idea was to use the site to tell people where she would be speaking and to share the themes of her book with an ever-expanding potential readership. Her publisher hoped this strategy would make her book "go viral." She had expected the Facebook project to feel like business, but instead she described complicated anxieties about not having enough friends, and about envy of her husband, also a writer, who had more friends than she. It also felt wrong to use the word "friends" for all of those she had "friended," since so many of the friended were there for professional reasons alone. She left me with this thought: "This thing took me right back to high school."

I promised her that when I joined Facebook I would record my first   39
feelings, while the site was still new to me. My very first feelings now seem

banal: I had to decide between "friending" plan A (this will be a place for people I actually know) and plan B (I will include people who contact me because they say they appreciate my work). I tried several weeks on plan A and then switched to the more inclusive plan B, flattered by the attention of strangers, justifying my decision in professional terms.

But now that I had invited strangers into my life, would I invite myself *40* into the lives of strangers? I would have anticipated not, until I did that very thing. I saw that one of my favorite authors was a Facebook friend of a friend. Seized by the idea that I might be this writer's friend, I made my request, and he accepted me. The image of a cafeteria came to mind, and I had a seat at his virtual table. But I felt like a gatecrasher. I decided realistically that I was taking this way too seriously. Facebook is a world in which fans are "friends." But of course, they are not friends. They have been "friended." That makes all the difference in the world, and I couldn't get high school out of my mind.

Presentation Anxiety

What are the truth claims in a Facebook profile? How much can you *41* lie? And what is at stake if you do? Nancy, an eighteen-year-old senior at Roosevelt, answers this question. "On the one hand, low stakes, because no one is really checking." Then, with a grimace, she says, "No, high stakes. Everyone is checking." A few minutes later, Nancy comes back to the question: "Only my best friends will know if I lie a little bit, and they will totally understand." Then she laughs. "All of this, it is, I guess, a bit of stress."[11]

At Cranston, a group of seniors describe that stress. One says, *42* "Thirteen to eighteen are the years of profile writing." The years of identity construction are recast in terms of profile production. These private school students had to write one profile for their applications to middle school, another to get into high school, and then another for Facebook. Now they are beginning to construct personae for college applications. And here, says Tom, "You have to have a slightly different persona for the different colleges to which you are applying: one for Dartmouth, a different one, say, for Wesleyan." For this aficionado of profile writing, every application needs a different approach. "By the time you get to the questions for the college application, you are a professional profile writer," he says. His classmate Stan describes his online profiles in great detail. Each serves a different purpose, but they must overlap, or questions of authenticity will arise. Creating the illusion of authenticity demands virtuosity. Presenting a self in these circumstances, with multiple media and multiple goals, is not easy work. The trick, says Stan, is in "weaving profiles together . . . so that people can see you are not too crazy. . . . What I learned in high school was profiles, profiles, profiles, how to make a me."

Early in my study, a college senior warned me not to be fooled by "any- *43* one you interview who tells you that his Facebook page is 'the real me.' It's like being in a play. You make a character." Eric, a college-bound senior at Hadley, a boys' preparatory school in rural New Jersey, describes himself as savvy about how you can "mold a Facebook page." Yet, even he is shocked when he finds evidence of girls using "shrinking" software to appear thinner on their profile photographs. "You can't see that they do it when you look at the little version of the picture, but when you look at a big picture, you can see how the background is distorted." By eighteen, he has become an identity detective. The Facebook profile is a particular source of stress because it is so important to high school social life. Some students feel so in its thrall that they drop out of Facebook, if only for a while, to collect themselves.

Brad, eighteen, a senior at Hadley, is about to take a gap year to do community service before attending a small liberal arts college in the Midwest. His parents are architects; his passion is biology and swimming. Brad wants to be part of the social scene at Hadley, but he doesn't like texting or instant messaging. He is careful to make sure I know he is "no Luddite." He has plenty of good things to say about the Net. He is sure that it makes it easier for insecure people to function. Sometimes the ability to compose his thoughts online "can be reassuring," he says, because there is a chance to "think through, calculate, edit, and make sure you're as clear and concise as possible." But as our conversation continues, Brad switches gears. Even as some are able to better function because they feel in control, online communication also offers an opportunity to ignore other people's feelings. You can avoid eye contact. You can elect not to hear how "hurt or angry they sound in their voice." He says, "Online, people miss your body language, tone of voice. You are not really you." And worst of all, online life has led him to mistrust his friends. He has had his instant messages "recorded" without his knowledge and forwarded on "in a cut-and-paste world." 44

In fact, when I meet Brad in the spring of his senior year, he tells me he has "dropped out" of online life. "I'm off the Net," he says, "at least for the summer, maybe for my year off until I go to college." He explains that it is hard to drop out because all his friends are on Facebook. A few weeks before our conversation, he had made a step toward rejoining but immediately he felt that he was not doing enough to satisfy its demands. He says that within a day he felt "rude" and couldn't keep up. He felt guilty because he didn't have the time to answer all the people who wrote to him. He says that he couldn't find a way to be "a little bit" on Facebook—it does not easily tolerate a partial buy-in. Just doing the minimum was "pure exhaustion." 45

In the world of Facebook, Brad says, "your minute movie preferences matter. And what groups you join. Are they the right ones?" Everything is a token, a marker for who you are: 46

> When you have to represent yourself on Facebook to convey to anyone who
> doesn't know you what and who you are, it leads to a kind of obsession
> about minute details about yourself. Like, "Oh, if I like the band State Radio
> and the band Spoon, what does it mean if I put State Radio first or Spoon

first on my list of favorite musical artists? What will people think about me?" I know for girls, trying to figure out, "Oh, is this picture too revealing to put? Is it prudish if I don't put it?" You have to think carefully for good reason, given how much people will look at your profile and obsess over it. You have to know that everything you put up will be perused very carefully. And that makes it necessary for you to obsess over what you do put up and how you portray yourself. . . . And when you have to think that much about what you come across as, that's just another way that . . . you're thinking of yourself in a bad way.

For Brad, "thinking of yourself in a bad way" means thinking of your- 47 self in reduced terms, in "short smoke signals" that are easy to read. To me, the smoke signals suggest a kind of reduction and betrayal. Social media ask us to represent ourselves in simplified ways. And then, faced with an audience, we feel pressure to conform to these simplifications. On Facebook, Brad represents himself as cool and in the know—both qualities are certainly part of who he is. But he hesitates to show people online other parts of himself (like how much he likes Harry Potter). He spends more and more time perfecting his online Mr. Cool. And he feels pressure to perform him all the time because that is who he is on Facebook.

At first Brad thought that both his Facebook profile and his college 48 essays had gotten him into this "bad way" of thinking, in which he reduces himself to fit a stereotype. Writing his Facebook profile felt to him like assembling cultural references to shape how others would see him. The college essay demanded a victory narrative and seemed equally unhelpful: He had to brag, and he wasn't happy. But Brad had a change of heart about the value of writing his college essays. "In the end I learned a lot about how I write and think—what I know how to think about and some things, you know, I really can't think about them well at all." I ask him if Facebook might offer these kinds of opportunities. He is adamant that it does not: "You get reduced to a list of favorite things. 'List your favorite music'—that gives you no liberty at all about how to say it." Brad says that "in a conversation, it might be interesting that on a trip to Europe with my parents, I got interested in the political mural art in Belfast. But on a Facebook page, this is too much information. It would be the kiss of death. Too much, too soon, too weird. And yet . . . it is part of who I am, isn't it? . . . You are asked to make a lot of lists. You have to worry that you put down the 'right' band or that you *don't* put down some Polish novel that nobody's read." And in the end, for Brad, it is too easy to lose track of what is important:

> What does it matter to anyone that I prefer the band Spoon over State Radio? Or State Radio over Cake? But things like Facebook . . . make you think that it really does matter. . . . I look at someone's profile and I say, "Oh, they like these bands." I'm like, "Oh, they're a poser," or "they're really deep, and they're into good music." We all do that, I think. And then I think it doesn't matter, but . . .

the thing is, in the world of Facebook it *does* matter. Those minute details *do* matter.

Brad, like many of his peers, worries that if he is modest and doesn't 49 put down all of his interests and accomplishments, he will be passed over. But he also fears that to talk about his strengths will be unseemly. None of these conflicts about self presentation are new to adolescence or to Facebook. What is new is living them out in public, sharing every mistake and false step. Brad, attractive and accomplished, sums it up with the same word Nancy uses: "Stress. That's what it comes down to for me. It's just worry and stressing out about it." Now Brad only wants to see friends in person or talk to them on the telephone. "I can just act how I want to act, and it's a much freer way." But who will answer the phone?

NOTES

1. Carol Gilligan, *In a Different Voice: Psychological Theory and Women's Development* (1982; Cambridge, MA: Harvard University Press, 1993).
2. Erik Erikson, *Identity and the Life Cycle* (1952; New York: W. W. Norton, 1980) and *Childhood and Society* (New York: Norton, 1950).
3. In Julia's world, e-mail is considered "slow" and rarely used because texting has greater immediacy.
4. It is so common to see teenagers (and others) attending to their mobiles rather than what is around them, that it was possible for a fake news story to gain traction in Britain. Taken up by the media, the story went out that there was a trial program to pad lampposts in major cities. Although it was a hoax, I fell for it when it was presented online as news. In fact, in the year prior to the hoax, one in five Britons did walk into a lamppost or other obstruction while attending to a mobile device. This is not surprising because research reported that "62 per cent of Britons concentrate so hard on their mobile phone when texting they lose peripheral vision." See Charlie Sorrel, "Padded Lampposts Cause Fuss in London," *Wired*, March 10, 2008, www.wired.com/gadgetlab/2008/03/padded-lampposts (accessed October 5, 2009).
5. New communications technology makes it easier to serve up people as slivers of self, providing a sense that to get what you need from others you have multiple and inexhaustible options. On the psychology that needs these "slivers," see Paul H. Ornstein, ed., *The Search for Self: Selected Writings of Heinz Kohut (1950–1978)*, vol. 2 (New York: International Universities Press, 1978).
6. David Riesman, Nathan Glazer, and Reuel Denney, *The Lonely Crowd: A Study of the Changing American Character* (1950; New Haven, CT: Yale University Press, 2001).
7. Orenstein, *The Search for Self.* For an earlier work, of a very different time, that linked cultural change and narcissistic personality style, see Christopher Lasch, *The Culture of Narcissism* (New York: Norton, 1979). Lasch said that "pathology represents a heightened version of normality." This formulation is helpful in thinking about the "normal" self in a tethered society and those who suffer more acutely from its discontents. From a psychodynamic perspective, we all suffer from the same things, some of us more acutely than others.
8. See Erik Erikson, *Identity and the Life Cycle and Childhood and Society, Young Man Luther: A Study in Psychoanalysis and History* (New York: W. W. Norton and Company, 1958).

9. Robert Jay Lifton, *The Protean Self. Human Resilience in an Age of Fragmentation* (New York: Basic Books, 1993).

10. Lifton shared this story at a meeting of the Wellfleet Seminar in October 2009, an annual gathering that began as a forum for Erikson and his students as they turned their attention to psychohistory.

11. The performances of everyday life—playing the roles of father, mother, child, wife, husband, life partner, worker—also provide "a bit of stress." There is room for considerable debate about how much online life really shares with our performances of self in "real life." Some look to the sociology of "self-presentation" to argue that online and off, we are always onstage. Erving Goffman, *The Presentation of Self in Everyday Life* (Garden City, NY: Doubleday Anchor, 1959).

■ ■ ■

Reading as a Writer: Analyzing Rhetorical Choices

1. In her opening two sections, Turkle demonstrates that comparison between the past and present is part of her argumentative strategy. As you read through her examples, consider the extent to which she is analyzing or judging (or both) these new strategies and habits of using technology. You might begin, for example, with her claims in paragraph 5: "Intimacy without privacy reinvents what intimacy means. Separation, too, is being reinvented." Try marking places in her opening two sections where she offers examples, and places where she evaluates or makes claims about the examples. Where do they overlap?

2. Turkle opens with an example from an interview with an 18-year-old, and she uses interviews with teenagers and parents throughout her piece to help make her point. Discuss the effectiveness of this as a way of offering evidence. What are the strengths and limitations of these kinds of examples?

Writing as a Reader: Entering the Conversation of Ideas

1. Turkle's term "the tethered self" contrasts with Jane McGonigal's optimism about the power of collective play. Compose an essay in which you apply these authors' ideas to a specific video game, considering the strategies and goals of the game, and the significance you see in the intersection of technology, emotion, and social values. What conclusions can you draw?

2. How do Turkle's concerns and insights about technology intersect with Constance Steinkuehler and Sean Duncan's interest in technology and education (Chapter 12)? Write an essay that takes into consideration the multiple perspectives on technology in these readings in order to build your own argument about the extent to which technology improves our lives. Anchor your claims with specific examples, both from these readings and your own experiences.

JANE McGONIGAL

Becoming Part of Something Bigger Than Ourselves

Jane McGonigal is a designer of alternate reality video games created to help players confront real-life challenges. Her game SuperBetter is a good example, designed for players to take on health challenges such as depression, anxiety, and brain injury. McGonigal's PhD is in performance studies, and she has taught game theory and design at the San Francisco Art Institute and the University of California, Berkeley. She is a frequent public speaker on the potential value of games; you can view many of her talks and interviews from her website: janemcgonigal.com. This reading is from her 2011 book *Reality Is Broken: Why Games Make Us Better and How They Can Change the World*, a New York Times Best Seller.

Here, McGonigal writes in a journalistic style, with very short paragraphs and frequent use of sentence fragments for stylistic effect (see paras. 8 and 9, for example). However, she still uses scholarly strategies to build her argument, drawing on other scholars' theories to situate her ideas in an academic "conversation." As you read, mark the references to other writers, and take note of the ways she uses these ideas to frame her own examples from *Halo 3*. Use a pen of another color, perhaps, to mark the sentences where you see her clearly articulating her argument. How does her argument build throughout this piece?

McGonigal opens this chapter from her book, titled "Becoming a Part of Something Bigger Than Ourselves," with a long list of statistics that are meant to spur our thinking about the relationship between virtual worlds (in particular, the virtual world of *Halo 3*) and reality. How does the "epic" scale of those numbers support her argument that she develops in the section titled "Epic Context for Heroic Action" about the difference between "value" and "meaning" (paras. 9–12)? As she moves between examples from the video game and her argument about "epic scale" and the power of "awe," pay attention to the places where you find her evidence most persuasive. To what extent does your experience with video game play (or playing other games that have a collective goal) confirm or complicate her claims?

In paragraph 67, McGonigal begins to develop her conclusion by quoting Johan Huizinga's concept that "All play *means* something." How does she build from this insight about collective play to the significance of these virtual-world experiences in the real world? If "reality is broken," as she claims, how exactly might video games offer a fix? Her optimism about the power of gaming isn't shared by everyone; how effectively does she address her critics? What will you take away from this "epic" argument about the power of play?

■ ■ ■

In April 2009, *Halo 3* players celebrated a collective spine-tingling milestone: 10 billion kills against their virtual enemy, the Covenant. That's roughly one and a half times the total number of every man, woman, and child on earth.

To reach this monumental milestone, *Halo 3* players spent 565 days [2] fighting the third and final campaign in the fictional Great War, protecting earth from an alliance of malevolent aliens seeking to destroy the human race. Together, they averaged 17.5 million Covenant kills a day, 730,000 kills per hour, 12,000 kills a minute.

Along the way, they'd assembled the largest army on earth, virtual or [3] otherwise. More than 15 million people had fought on behalf of the science fiction game's United Nations Space Command. That's roughly the total number of active personnel of all twenty-five of the largest armed forces in the real world, combined.[1]

Ten billion kills wasn't an incidental achievement, stumbled onto blindly [4] by the gaming masses. *Halo* players made a concerted effort to get there. They embraced 10 billion kills as a symbol of just how much the *Halo* community could accomplish—and they wanted it to be something bigger than anything any other game community had achieved before. So they worked hard to make every single player as good at *Halo 3* as possible. Players shared tips and strategies with each other and organized round-the-clock "co-op," or cooperative, campaign shifts. They called on every registered member of *Halo* online to pitch in: "This could be something big, but we will need YOU to get it done."[2] They treated their mission like an urgent duty. "We know we'll be doing our part," one game blog declared. "Will you?"[3]

It's no wonder London *Telegraph* reporter Sam Leith observed in his [5] coverage of the *Halo 3* community that "a big shift has taken place, in recent years, in the way video games are played. What was once generally a solitary activity is now . . . overwhelmingly a communal one."[4] More and more, gamers aren't just in it for themselves. They're in it for each other—and for the thrill of being a part of something bigger.

When *Halo* players finally reached their goal, they flooded online [6] forums to congratulate each other and claim their contributions. "I just did some math and with my 32,388 kills I have .00032% of the 10 billion kills," one player wrote. "I feel like I could have contributed more . . . well, on to 100 billion then!"[5] This reaction was typical, and the new 100 billion goal was repeated widely on *Halo* forums. Fresh off one collective achievement, *Halo* players were ready to tackle an even more monumental goal. And they were fully prepared to recruit an even bigger community to do it. As one gamer proposed: "We did that with just a few million gamers. Imagine what we could do with the full force of six billion humans!!"[6]

Halo's creators, a Seattle, Washington–based game studio called Bun- [7] gie, joined in the celebration. They issued a major press release and an open letter to the *Halo* community, emphasizing the teamwork it had taken to get to 10 billion kills: "We've hit the Covenant where it hurts. Made them pay a price for setting foot on our soil. We're glad we've got you by our side, soldier. Mighty fine work. Here's to ten billion more."[7]

Perhaps you're thinking to yourself right now: *So?* What's the point? [8] The Covenant isn't real. It's just a game. What have the players actually *done* that's worth celebrating?

On one hand, nothing. There's no *value* to a Covenant kill, whether 9
you score one, 10 billion, or even 100 billion of them. Value is a measure of
importance and consequence. And even the most die-hard *Halo* fan knows
that there's no real importance or consequence to saving the human race
from a fictional alien invasion. There's no actual danger being averted.
There are no real lives being saved.

But on the other hand, just because the kills don't have value doesn't 10
mean they don't have *meaning*.

Meaning is the feeling that we're a part of something bigger than our- 11
selves. It's the belief that our actions matter beyond our own individual
lives. When something is meaningful, it has significance and worth not
just to ourselves, or even to our closest friends and family, but to a much
larger group: to a community, an organization, or even the entire human
species.

Meaning is something we're all looking for more of: more ways to 12
make a difference in the bigger picture, more chances to leave a lasting
mark on the world, more moments of awe and wonder at the scale of the
projects and communities we're a part of.

How do we get more meaning in our lives? It's actually quite simple. 13
Philosophers, psychologists, and spiritual leaders agree: The single best
way to add meaning to our lives is to *connect our daily actions to something bigger than ourselves* — and the bigger, the better. As Martin Seligman
says, "The self is a very poor site for meaning." We can't *matter* outside of
a large-scale social context. "The larger the entity you can attach yourself
to," Seligman advises, "the more meaning you can derive."[8]

And that's exactly the point of working together in a game like *Halo 3*. 14
It's not that the Covenant kills have value. It's that pursuing a massive
goal alongside millions of other people feels good. It feels meaningful.
When players dedicate themselves to a goal like 10 billion Covenant kills,
they're attaching themselves to a cause, and they're making a significant
contribution to it. As the popular gamer site Joystiq reported on the day
Halo players celebrated their 10 billionth kill: "Now we know for sure. . . .
Every kill you get in *Halo 3*'s campaign actually *means* something."[9]

To experience *real* meaning, we don't have to contribute something of 15
real value. We just have to be given the opportunity to contribute at all.
We need a way to connect with others who care about the same massively
scaled goal we do, no matter how arbitrary the goal. And we need a chance
to reflect on the truly epic scale of what we're doing together.

Which gives us one fix for our broken reality: 16

Epic Scale

Compared with games, reality is trivial. Games make us a part of something
bigger and give epic meaning to our actions.

"Epic" is the key word here. Blockbuster video games like *Halo*—the kind *17* of games that have a production budget of thirty, forty, or even fifty million dollars—aren't just "something bigger." They're big enough to be *epic.*

Epic is one of the most important concepts in gamer culture today. *18* It's how players describe their most memorable, gratifying game experiences. As one game critic writes, *"Halo 3 is epic. It empowers you the way no other game can. It doesn't have moments, but events. Experiences that tickle the soul, sending shivers down the spine."*[10]

A good working definition for "epic" is something that far surpasses *19* the ordinary, especially in size, scale, and intensity. Something epic is of *heroic proportions.* Blockbuster video games do epic scale better than any other medium of our time, and they're epic in three key ways:

> They create *epic contexts for action*: collective stories that help us connect our individual gameplay to a much bigger mission.

> They immerse us in *epic environments*: vast, interactive spaces that provoke feelings of curiosity and wonder.

> And they engage us in *epic projects*: cooperative efforts carried out by players on massive scales, over months or even years.

There's a reason why gamers love epic games. It's not just that bigger is *20* better. It's that bigger is more awe-inspiring.

Awe is a unique emotion. According to many positive psychologists, *21* it's the single most overwhelming and gratifying positive emotion we can feel. In fact, neuropsychologist Paul Pearsall calls awe "the orgasm of positive emotions."[11]

Awe is what we feel when we recognize that we're in the presence of *22* something bigger than ourselves. It's closely linked with feelings of spirituality, love, and gratitude—and more importantly, a desire to serve.

In *Born to Be Good,* Dacher Keltner explains, "The experience of awe *23* is about finding your place in the larger scheme of things. It is about quieting the press of self-interest. It is about folding into social collectives. It is about feeling reverential toward participating in some expansive process that unites us all and that ennobles our life's endeavors."[12]

In other words, awe doesn't just *feel* good; it inspires us to *do* good. *24*

Without a doubt, it's awe that a *Halo 3* player is feeling when he says *25* that the game sends "shivers down the spine." Spine tingling is one of the classic physiological symptoms of awe—along with chills, goose bumps, and that choked-up feeling in the throat.

Our ability to feel awe in the form of chills, goose bumps, or choking *26* up serves as a kind of emotional radar for detecting meaningful activity. Whenever we feel awe, we know we've found a potential source of meaning. We've discovered a real opportunity to be of service, to band together, to contribute to a larger cause.

In short, awe is a call to collective action. *27*

So it's no accident that *Halo* players are so inclined toward collective 28
efforts. It's the direct result of the game's epic, and awe-inspiring, aesthetic. Today's best game designers are experts at giving individuals the
chance to be a part of something bigger—and no one is better at it than
the creators *of Halo*. Everything about the *Halo* games—from the plot and
the sound track to the marketing and the way the community is organized
online—is intentionally crafted to make players feel that their gameplay
really means something. And the one simple trick used over and over again
is this: always connect the individual to something bigger.

Let's take a closer look at exactly how *Halo* does it. 29

Epic Context for Heroic Action

> It's five hundred years in the future. The Covenant, a hostile alliance of alien
> species, is hell-bent on destroying humanity. You are Master Chief Petty
> Officer John 117—once an ordinary person, now a supersoldier, augmented
> with biological technologies that give you superhuman speed, strength,
> intelligence, vision, and reflexes. Your job is to stop the Covenant and save
> the world.

That's the basic *Halo* story. It's not that different from many other 30
blockbuster video games. As veteran game developer Trent Polack puts
it, "To look at the majority of games today, one might think that gamers
care only about saving the world." He would know: Some of Polack's previous games have asked players to save the galaxy from malevolent aliens
(*Galactic Civilizations II*), save the universe from evil deities (*Demigod*),
and save the world from marauding Titans (*Elemental: War of Magic*).

Why *are* so many games about saving the world? In an industry 31
article about the rise of "epic scale" narratives in video games, Polack
suggests, "When games give players the epic scope of saving the galaxy,
destroying some reawakened ancient evil, or any other classical portrayal
of good versus evil on a grand scale, they're fulfilling gamers' power
fantasies."[13]

I agree with Polack, but it's important that we be clear on exactly what 32
kind of power fantasy is being fulfilled by these save-the-world stories.

Any video game that features a slew of high-powered weapons and 33
gameplay that consists largely of shooting and blowing things up is, at one
level, about the aesthetic pleasures of destruction and the positive feelings we get from exerting control over a situation.[14] This is true of any
shooter game on the market today. But we don't need an epic story about
saving the world to get those pleasures. We can get them quite effectively,
and more efficiently, from a simple, plotless game like Atari's *Breakout*.
Games that come with epic, save-the-world narratives are using them to
help players get a taste of a different kind of power. It's the power to act
with meaning: to do something that matters in a bigger picture. The story
is the bigger picture; the player's actions are what matters.

As Polack explains, "Story sets the stage for meaning. It frames the *34* player's actions. We, as designers, are not telling, we're not showing, we're informing the *doing*—the actions that players engage in and the feats they undergo." These feats make up the player's story, and the story is ultimately what has meaning.

Not every game feels like a larger cause. For a game to feel like a *cause*, *35* two things need to happen. First, the game's story needs to become a collective context for action—shared by other players, not just an individual experience. That's why truly epic games are always attached to large, online player communities—hundreds of thousands or millions of players acting in the same context together, and talking to each other on forums and wikis about the actions they're taking. And second, the actions that players take inside the collective context need to feel like service: Every effort by one player must ultimately benefit all the other players. In other words, every individual act of gameplay has to eventually add up to something bigger.

Halo is probably the best game in the world at turning a story into a *36* collective context and making personal achievement feel like service.

Like many other blockbuster video games, *Halo* has extensive online *37* community features: discussion forums, wikis, and file sharing (so that players can upload and share videos of their finest gameplay moments). But Bungie and Xbox have taken it much further than these traditional context-building tools. They've given players groundbreaking tools for tracking the magnitude of their collective effort and unprecedented opportunities to reflect on the epic scale of their collective service.

Every *Halo* player has their own story of making a difference, and it's *38* documented online in their "personal service record." It's an exhaustive record and analysis of their individual contributions to the *Halo* community and to the Great War effort—or as Bungie calls it, "Your entire *Halo* career."

The service record is stored on the official Bungie website, and it's *39* fully viewable by other players. It lists all the campaign levels you've completed, the medals you've earned, and the achievements you've unlocked. It also includes a minute-by-minute, play-by-play breakdown of *every single* Halo *level or match you've ever played online.* For many *Halo* players, that means thousands of games over the past six years—ever since the *Halo* series first went online in 2004—all laid out and perfectly documented in one place.

And it's more than just statistics. There are data visualizations of every *40* possible kind: interactive charts, graphs, heat maps. They help you learn about your own strengths and weaknesses: where you make the most mistakes, and where you consistently score your biggest victories; which weapons you're most proficient with, and which you're weakest with; even which teammates help you play better, and which don't.

Thanks to Bungie's exhaustive data collection and sharing, everything 41
you do in *Halo* adds up to something bigger: a multiyear history of your
own personal service to the Great War.

But it's not just your history—it's much bigger than that You're con- 42
tributing to the Great War effort alongside millions of other players, who
also have service records online. And *service* really is a crucial concept
here. A personal service record isn't just a profile. It's a history of a player's
contributions to a larger organization. The fact that your profile is called
a "service record" is a constant reminder. When you play *Halo* online, rack
up kills, and accomplish your missions, you're *contributing*. You're actively
creating new moments in the history of the Great War.[15]

The moments all add up. The millions of individual personal service 43
records taken together tell the real story of *Halo*, a collective history of
the Great War. They connect all the individual gamers into a community,
a network of people fighting for the same cause. And the unprecedented
scale of data collected and shared in these service records underscores
just how epic the players' collective story is. Bungie recently announced
to players that its personal-service-record servers handled more than
1.4 *quadrillion* bytes of data requests from players in the past nine months.
That's 1.4 petabytes in computer science terms.

To put that number in perspective, experts have estimated that the 44
entire written works of humankind, from the beginning of recorded history, in all languages, adds up to about 50 petabytes of data.[16] *Halo* players aren't quite there yet—but it's not a bad start, considering that they've
been playing together online for only six short years, compared to all of
recorded human history.

One of the best examples of innovative collective context building is 45
the *Halo* Museum of Humanity, an online museum that purports to be
from the twenty-seventh century, dedicated to "all who fought bravely
in the Great War." Of course, it's not a real museum; it was developed
by the Xbox marketing group to build a more meaningful context for
Halo 3.

The museum features a series of videos done in the classic style of 46
Ken Burns' *Civil War* series: interviews with Great War veterans and
historians, images from Covenant battles, all set to a hymnal score.
As one blogger wrote, "The videos in the *Halo* Museum of Humanity seem like they could have been pulled straight from The History
Channel. . . . It's nice to see video game lore treated with this kind of
reverence."[17]

Reverence—the expression of profound awe, respect and love, or ven- 47
eration is usually an emotion we reserve for very big, very serious things.
But that was precisely the point of the *Halo* Museum of Humanity: to
acknowledge how seriously *Halo* players take their favorite game, and to
inspire the kind of epic emotions that have always been the best part of
playing it.

It's worked. The video series packs a real emotional wallop, despite the *48*
fact that, in the words of one player, "it's meant to honor heroes that never
existed."[18] Brian Crecente, a leading games journalist, wrote, "It left me
with chills."[19] And online forums and blogs were full of comments expressing heartfelt emotion. One player put it best when he wrote, "Really poignant. They've made something real out of fiction."[20]

It's not that the museum is such a believable artifact from the future. *49*
It's that the *emotions* it provokes are believable. The online Museum of
Humanity is a place to reflect on the extreme scale of the *Halo* experience:
the years of service, the millions of players involved. The Great War isn't
real, but you really do feel awe when you think about the scale of the effort
so many different people have made to fight it.

In the end, as one player sums it up, *"Halo* proves that you can have *50*
a shooter game with a story that really means something. It draws you in
and makes you feel like you're part of something bigger."[21]

But *Halo* isn't just a bigger story. It's also a bigger environment—and *51*
this brings us to our next strategy for connecting players to something bigger: built epic environments, or highly immersive spaces that are intentionally designed to bring out the best in us.

Epic Environments—Or How to Build a Better Place

An epic environment is a space that, by virtue of its extreme scale, pro- *52*
vokes a profound sense of awe and wonder.

There are plenty of natural epic environments in the world: Mount *53*
Everest, the Grand Canyon, Victoria Falls, the Great Barrier Reef, for
example. These spaces humble us; they remind us of the power and grandeur of nature, and make us feel small by comparison.

A *built* epic environment is different: It's not the work of nature, but *54*
rather a feat of design and engineering. It's a *human* accomplishment. And
that makes it both humbling and empowering at the same time. It makes
us feel smaller as individuals, but it also makes us feel capable of much
bigger things, together. That's because a built epic environment—like the
Great Wall of China, the Taj Mahal, or Machu Picchu—is the result of
extreme-scale collaboration. It's proof of the extraordinary scale of things
humans can accomplish together.

Halo 3 is, without a doubt, such an environment. *55*

The game consists of thirty-four different playing environments span- *56*
ning more than two hundred thousand light-years of virtual space. From
one level to the next, you might find yourself traveling from the crowded
market city of Voi, Kenya, to the Ark, a desert far, far beyond the limits of
our own Milky Way galaxy.

It's not just how big the *Halo* playing field is; it's also how diverse *57*
and carefully rendered the environments are. As Sam Leith observes,
"The building of a game like *Halo 3* is a work of electronic engineering

comparable in scale to the building of a medieval cathedral." It took Bungie three years to craft this gaming cathedral, with a team of more than 250 artists, designers, writers, programmers, and engineers collaborating together. "You get a sense of the scale and intricacy of the task," Leith continues, "by considering the sound effects alone: The game contains 54,000 pieces of audio and 40,000 lines of dialogue. There are 2,700 different noises for footsteps alone, depending on whose foot is stepping on what."[22]

And that's what players are appreciating when they get goose bumps *58* from *Halo*: the unprecedented achievement it represents as a work of computer design and engineering. Gamers aren't so much in awe of the environment itself as they are in awe of the work and dedication and vision required to create it. In this regard, *Halo* players join a long tradition in human culture of feeling awe, wonder, and gratitude toward the builders of epic environments.

The very first epic environments were constructed more than eleven thou- *59* sand years ago, during the Neolithic period, or the New Stone Age. In other words, six thousand years before humans first used the written word, they were already building physical spaces to inspire awe and cooperation.

The world's oldest known example of an epic built environment is *60* the Gobekli Tepe. Discovered less than two decades ago in southeastern Turkey, it's believed to predate Stonehenge by a staggering six thousand years. It's a twenty-five-acre arrangement of at least twenty stone circles, between ten and thirty meters in diameter each, made from monolithic pillars three meters high.

In comparison with other stone houses, tombs, and temples from the *61* same period and location, this building was constructed on an extreme scale: It was much, *much* bigger, taller, and more formidable in its design than anything archaeologists had seen before at the time of its discovery. One archaeologist on the scene described it as "a place of worship on an unprecedented scale—humanity's first 'cathedral on a hill.'"[23]

And it wasn't just the scale of the building—it was its particular wind- *62* ing design. The Gobekli Tepe features an intricate series of passageways that would lead visitors through the dark to a cross-shaped inner sanctum, almost like a labyrinth. This particular architecture seems designed intentionally to trigger interest and curiosity, alongside a kind of trembling wonder. What would be around the next corner? Where would the path take them? They would need to hold on to other visitors for support, feeling their way through the darkness.

Crucially, the Gobekli Tepe wasn't an isolated example. As research- *63* ers have discovered since, epic stone cathedrals were common across the Neolithic landscape. Most recently, in August 2009, archaeologists working in northern Scotland unearthed the ruins of a 5,330-square-foot stone structure with twenty-foot ceilings and sixteen-foot-thick walls, also of a labyrinthine design, and also dating back to the New Stone Age.[24]

"A building of this scale and complexity was here to amaze, to create a sense of awe in the people who saw this place," Nick Card, director of the archaeological dig, said to reporters when the ancient cathedral was first unearthed.

In the wake of unearthing these types of structures all over the planet, 64 archaeologists have recently proposed a startling theory: that these stone cathedrals served an important purpose in the evolution of human civilization. They actually inspired and enabled human society to become dramatically more cooperative, completely reinventing civilization as it once existed. In an in-depth report in *Smithsonian* magazine on these Neolithic cathedrals, Andrew Curry wrote:

> Scholars have long believed that only after people learned to farm and live in settled communities did they have the time, organization and resources to construct temples and support complicated social structures. But. . . [perhaps] it was the other way around: the extensive, coordinated effort to build the monoliths literally laid the groundwork for the development of complex societies.[25]

In fact, as Curry quotes one scientist in his article, "You can make 65 a good case these constructs are the real origin of complex Neolithic societies."[26]

No wonder epic environments inspire gamers today to collective 66 efforts. They have been inspiring humans to work together to do amazing things for eleven thousand years and counting. . . .

Johan Huizinga, the great twentieth-century Dutch philosopher of 67 human play, once said, "All play *means* something."[27] Today, thanks to the increased scale of game worlds and advances in collective game design, gameplay often means something *more*. Game developers today are honing their ability to create awe-inspiring contexts for collective effort and heroic service. As a result, game communities are more committed than ever to setting extreme-scale goals and generating epic meaning.

When our everyday work feels trivial, or when we can't easily be of 68 direct service to a larger cause, games can fulfill an important need for us. As we play games at an epic scale, we're increasing our ability to rise to the occasion, to inspire awe, and to take part in something bigger than ourselves.

Earlier in this chapter I quoted a *Halo* player who wondered, "Imagine 69 what we could do with the full force of six billion humans!!"

Of course, there aren't enough Xboxes in the world to do it. Nor 70 could everyone afford them, of course. But it does make for an interesting thought experiment: What *could* you do in a game like *Halo 3* if you had the full force of humanity playing together?

On one hand, this is an absurd idea to even consider. What would be 71 the point of assembling 6 billion people to wage a fictional war?

But on the other: Can you imagine what it would feel like to have   72
6 billion people fighting *on the same side* of a fictional war?

I think it's pretty clear that such an effort would have real meaning,   73
even if it failed to generate any real-world value. If you were able to focus
the attention of the entire planet on a single goal, even if just for one day,
and even if it just involved dispatching aliens in a video game, it would
be a truly awe-inspiring occasion. It would be the single biggest collective
experience ever undertaken in the whole of human history. It would give
the whole earth goose bumps.

That's the epic scale that gamers are capable of thinking on. That's the   74
scale gamers are ready to work at.

Gamers can imagine 6 billion people coming together to fight a fic-   75
tional enemy, for the sheer awe and wonder of it. They are ready to work
together on extreme scales, toward epic goals, just for the spine-tingling
joy of it. And the more we seek out that kind of happiness as a planet, the
more likely we are to save it—not from fictional aliens, but from apathy
and wasted potential.

Jean M. Twenge, a professor of psychology and the author of *Gen-*   76
eration Me, has persuasively argued that the youngest generations
today—particularly anyone born after 1980—are, in her words, "more
miserable than ever before." Why? Because of our increased cultural
emphasis on "self-esteem" and "self-fulfillment." But real fulfillment, as
countless psychologists, philosophers, and spiritual leaders have shown,
comes from fulfilling commitments to others. We want to be esteemed in
the eyes of others, not for "who we are," but rather for what we've done
that really matters.

The more we focus on ourselves and avoid a commitment to others,   77
Twenge's research shows, the more we suffer from anxiety and depression.
But that doesn't stop us from trying to make ourselves happy alone. We
mistakenly think that by putting ourselves first, we'll finally get what we
want. In fact, true happiness comes not from thinking *more* of ourselves,
but rather from thinking *less* of ourselves—from seeing the truly small
role we play in something much bigger, much more important than our
individual needs.

Joining any collective effort and embracing feelings of awe can help   78
us unlock our potential to lead a meaningful life and to leave a meaningful
mark on the world.

Even if it's a virtual world we're leaving our mark on, we're still learn-   79
ing what it feels like to be of service to a larger cause. We're priming our
brains and bodies to value and to seek out epic meaning as an emotional
reward. And as recent research suggests, the more we enjoy these rewards
in game worlds, the more likely we may be to seek them out in real life.

Three scientific studies published in 2009 by a consortium of research-   80
ers from eight universities in the United States, Japan, Singapore, and

Malaysia studied the relationship between time spent playing games that require "helpful behavior" and the gamers' willingness to help others in everyday life. One study focused on children age thirteen and younger, another on teenagers, and the third on college students. The researchers worked with more than three thousand young gamers in total, and in all three studies they reached the same conclusion: Young people who spend more time playing games in which they're required to help each other are significantly more likely to help friends, family, neighbors, and even strangers in their real lives.[28]

Although these studies weren't specifically looking at epic-scale games,   *81*
the core findings seem likely to remain consistent, or even increase, at larger scales. As Brad Bushman, one coauthor of the studies and a professor of communications and psychology at the University of Michigan's Institute for Social Research, puts it, "These findings suggest there is an upward spiral of prosocial gaming and helpful behavior."[29] In other words, the more we help in games, the more we help in life. And so there's good reason to believe that the more we learn to enjoy serving epic causes in game worlds, the more we may find ourselves contributing to epic efforts in the real world.

The psychologist Abraham Maslow famously said, "It isn't normal to know   *82*
what we want. It is a rare and difficult psychological achievement."[30] But today's best games give us a powerful tool for achieving exactly that rare kind of self-knowledge.

Games are showing us exactly what we want out of life: more satis-   *83*
fying work, better hope of success, stronger social connectivity, and the chance to be a part of something bigger than ourselves. With games that help us generate these four rewards every day, we have unlimited potential to raise our own quality of life. And when we play these games with friends, family, and neighbors, we can enrich the lives of people we care about.

So games are teaching us to see what really makes us happy—and how   *84*
to become the best versions of ourselves. But can we apply that knowledge to the real world?

By supporting our four essential human cravings, and by providing a   *85*
reliable source of flow and fiero, the gaming industry has gone a long way toward making us happier and more emotionally, resilient—but only up to a point. We haven't learned how to enjoy our *real lives* more thoroughly. Instead, we've spent the last thirty-five years learning to enjoy our *game lives* more thoroughly.

Instead of fixing reality, we've simply created more and more attrac-   *86*
tive alternatives to the boredom, anxiety, alienation, and meaninglessness we run up against so often in everyday life. It's high time we start applying the lessons of games to the design of our everyday lives. We need to

engineer *alternate* realities: new, more gameful ways of interacting with the real world and living our real lives.

Fortunately, the project of making alternate realities is already under way. 87

NOTES

1. "13 Billion Kills: Join the Mission." *Halo 3* forum, Bungie.net, February 20, 2009. http://www.bungie.net/News/content.aspx?type=topnews&link=TenBillionKills.
2. Ibid.
3. "Players Attempt to Hit 7 Billion Kills While *Halo 3* Killcount Exceeds Global Population." Joystiq, June 27, 2008. http://xbox.joystiq.com/2008/06/27/players-attempt-to-hit-7-billion-kills-while-halo-3-killcount-ex/.
4. Leith, Sam. "*Halo 3*: Blown Away." *Telegraph*, September 22, 2007. http://www.telegraph.co.uk/culture/3668103/Halo-3-blown-away.hbnl.
5. "Campaign Kill Count: 10,000,000,000." *Halo 3* forum, Bungie.net, April 13, 2009. http://www.bungie.net/Forums/posts.aspx?postID=32064021&postRepeater]-p=3.
6. Ibid.
7. Ibid.
8. Seligman, *Learned Optimism*, 287.
9. "Bungie: 10 Billion Covenant Killed in *Halo 3* . . . and *Growing*." Joystiq, April 13, 2009. http.//xbox.joystiq.corn/2009/04/13/bungie-10-billion-covenaut-killed-in-halo-3-and-growing/.
10. "*Halo 3* Review." NZGamer, September 24, 2007. http://nzgamer.com/x360/reviews/538/halo-3.html.
11. Paul Pearsall. *Awe: The Delights and Dangers of Our Eleventh Emotion* (Deerfield Beach, Florida: HCl, 2007), 193.
12. Keltner, *Born to Be Good*, 268.
13. Polack, Trent. "Epic Scale." Gamasutra, July 16, 2009. http://www.gamasutra.com/blogs/IYerit Polack/20090716/7.412/Epic_Scale.php.
14. Kuhrcke, Tim, Christoph Klimmt, and Peter Vorderer. "Why Is Virtual Fighting Fun? Motivational Predictors of Exposure to Violent Video Games." Paper presented at the annual meeting of the International Communication Association, Dresden, Germany, May 25, 2009. http://www.allacademic.com/meta/p91358_indcx.html.
15. "Return of the New Hotness." Bungie.net, August 27, 2009. http://www.bungie.net/news/content.as px?type=topnews&Link=NewHotness.
16. Kelly, Kevin. "Scan This Book!" *New York Times*, March 14, 2006. http://www.nytimes.com/2006/ 05/14/magazine/14publishing.html.
17. "Watch New *Halo 3* Ad: 'Two Soldiers Reminisce.'" Joystiq, September 22, 2007. http://www.joystiq.com/2007/09/22/watch-new-halo-3-ad-two-soldiers-reminisce/.
18. "*Halo 3* Ad Brings Battle to Reality." *Escapist*, September 12, 2007. http://www.escapistmagazinc.com/forums/read/7.48542.
19. Crecente, Brian. "*Halo* Diorama May Tour Country." Kotaku, September 13, 2007. http://kotaku.com/gaming/gallery/halo-diorama-may-tour-country-299470.php.
20. "Watch New *Halo 3* Ad," Joystiq.
21. "Hindsight: *Halo 3*." Ascendant Justice, March 1, 2008. http://blog.ascendant justice.com/halo-3/hindsight-halo-3/.
22. Leith, "*Halo 3*: Blown Away."
23. Curry, Andrew. "Gobekli Tepe: The World's First Temple?" *Smithsonian*, November 2008. http.//www.smithsonianmag.com/history-archaeology/gobekli-tepe.html #ixzz0T0oKIRQ6.

24. McIntosh, Lindsay. "'Neolithic Cathedral Built to Amaze' Unearthed in Orkney Dig." *The Times* (UK), August 14, 2009. http://www.timesonline.co.uk/tol/news/uk/scotland/article6795316.ece.

25. Curry, "Gobekli Tepe."

26. Ibid.

27. Huizinga, Johan. *Homo Ludens* (Boston: Beacon Press, 1971), 446.

28. Gentile, Douglas A., Craig A. Anderson, Shintaro Yukawa, et al. "The Effects of Pro-social Video Games on Prosocial Behaviors: International Evidence From Correlational, Longitudinal, and Experimental Studies." *Personality and Social Psychology Bulletin*, 2009, 35:752–63.

29. "Some Video Games Can Make Children Kinder and More Likely to Help." Science Daily, June 18, 2009. http://www.sciencedaily.com/releases/2009/06/090617171819.htm.

30. Maslow, Abraham. *Motivation and Personality* (New York: Harper Collins, 1987), 113.

■ ■ ■

Reading as a Writer: Analyzing Rhetorical Choices

1. In paragraph 9, McGonigal begins to distinguish between "value" and "meaning" in video games. How does she define each of these terms, and how do her examples from *Halo 3* demonstrate this difference? What other examples can you generate from your own experience of playing games of one kind or another?

2. While McGonigal writes in a magazine style, she uses a scholarly strategy of drawing on other writers to build the context of her argument. Mark all the places in her piece where she quotes another author, and then examine the patterns you see in when and how she uses ideas from others. How, specifically, do these ideas contribute to the larger argument she makes in this piece?

Writing as a Reader: Entering the Conversation of Ideas

1. McGonigal argues that video game play can improve our emotional lives, while Turkle may seem to have quite a different perspective. There may be more similarities between these texts than are obvious, however. Where do these authors' ideas intersect, overlap, and diverge? Compose an essay that places these authors in conversation as you make an argument about technology and emotions. You might draw on your own specific experiences as you make your point.

2. McGonigal, like Ann duCille (Chapter 17), writes about play as a significant activity, worthy of careful analysis. Compose an essay in which you consider these authors' ideas in relation to one another and pull out some larger principles about the function and importance of play in our culture.

JONI ADAMSON

Indigenous Literatures, Multinaturalism, and *Avatar*: The Emergence of Indigenous Cosmopolitics

Joni Adamson is a professor of English and Environmental Humanities at Arizona State University and teaches courses in their Global Institute of Sustainability, one of the leading programs of its kind. While her original training is in literary studies, her current work is interdisciplinary, drawing together analysis of literature and film, environmental justice, global indigenous environmentalisms, and food studies, among other topics. She has published widely in journals and has written and edited many books, and she speaks on interdisciplinary environmental issues all over the world. This is a version of a longer article, published in a journal titled *American Literary History*; we have edited it here for space considerations, and because the literary texts that Adamson analyzes in the trimmed portions will not be familiar to many readers. In contrast, we expect that many readers are familiar with James Cameron's 2009 film *Avatar*, which is the focus of her analysis here.

You might want to watch the online trailer for *Avatar* before you read this piece, so that the images and tone of the film are fresh in your mind as you read the plot summary in paragraph 1, which sets up Adamson's piece. Adamson moves quickly from this summary to a flurry of examples of the surprisingly positive responses from Latin American, South American, and African thinkers who found that the film's perspective resonates with indigenous attitudes toward the environment. This sets up her claim that "blockbuster films and documentaries are playing an increasingly important role in global environmental justice struggles" (para. 6). Given the heavy dose of fantasy imagery in *Avatar*, this may be a somewhat unexpected argument.

You may find that some of the environmental disasters she mentions are unfamiliar to you; if so, take the time to look up events such as the "chemical spill at Bhopal" and the "nuclear disaster at Chernobyl" (para. 8) so that you understand what is at stake for those who are forming coalitions to combat these toxic disasters. As you read, pay attention to the way Adamson moves between her analysis of "the interrelations of cosmopolitanism, nationalism, localism, and environmentalism" (para. 7) and her analysis of the film. How exactly does she connect these big ideas to the film? How does she explain the ways the film is being used by different groups? What do you find most surprising, or striking, in these connections?

It is easy to find negative reviews of this film (and you might find it interesting to read some online critiques). Adamson reveals another perspective on this film, though, considering the way it speaks to ecological movements of diverse people who seek to teach others to see the interconnections of the planet and human life. In her conclusion, Adamson considers the relationship between these movements—what writer Marisol de la Cadena calls "multinaturalism"—and economic growth and development. How do we balance our desires for economic development and the health of our planet? This pressing question is at the heart of this rich exploration of *Avatar* and ecological issues. What do you think?

Light and color are often the only signs of these lives invisible to the
unaided eye.

STEFAN HELMREICH, ALIEN OCEAN

James Cameron's *Avatar* (2009) premiered to some predictably scath-   *1*
ing reviews comparing the film to Kevin Costner's *Dances with Wolves*
(1990) and Disney's *Pocahontas* (1995). Set 145 years in the future, the film
tells the story of the Na'vi, 10-foot-tall blue-skinned humanoids living on
an Earth-like moon called Pandora in a monolithic "Hometree." Humans
have come from Earth intent on mining "unobtainium," a rare mineral
located beneath Hometree and considered the solution to Earth's energy
crisis. Hero Jake Sully, a parapalegic ex-marine, is hired to gather intelligence and given a genetically engineered Na'vi body, or avatar, to pilot
in the alien Pandoran atmosphere. When he is attacked by wild animals,
he is saved by Neytiri, the daughter of the Na'vi chief, and they later fall
in love. Neytiri teaches Jake that Hometree and all living beings are alive
with the spirit of "Eywa," described as a "network of energy" represented
as bioluminescent, brightly colored seeds, trees, and animals. Given this
romantic plot and luminous setting, it is not surprising that most reviews
referenced the commonplace figure of the "ecological Indian" in movies
that seek absolution for the sins of industrialization and evoke desire for
the re-enchantment of nature (Newitz n.p.).

What *was* surprising about some of the first responses to the film were   *2*
the number of cautiously positive responses from indigenous groups,
political figures, community leaders and scholars. For example, Evo
Morales, the Aymara President of Bolivia, praised *Avatar* for its imaginative portrayal of an indigenous group fighting a greedy corporation ("Head
of State" n.p.). Morales's comments resonate with the language of the 2010
Universal Declaration on the Rights of Mother Earth written at the World
Peoples' Conference on Climate Change in Cochabamba, Bolivia. Organized by Morales after the failure of the United Nations climate talks in
Copenhagen, delegates declared that they would no longer be silent and
would make themselves visible in international spaces of political negotiation (Eshelman n.p.). Their authority as politicians was based on a
"cosmic spirituality linked to nature" thousands of years in the making
and they would no longer support the economic models promoted by
industrialized countries that had radically transformed their relationship
to Mother Earth or "Pachamama."[1]

Throughout Latin America, Pachamama is understood *not* as a female-   *3*
gendered planet but as "Source of Light" or "Source of Life" (de la Cadena
335, 350). Indigenous peoples and nations are mobilizing around the concept of earth-beings that "concentrate energy and life"; "being" is defined
as "ecosystems, natural communities, species and all other natural entities
which exist as part of Mother Earth" (UDRME Art. 4.1 n.p.). The resonance

---

[1] See the "Universal Declaration on the Rights of Mother Earth," hereafter cited as
UDRME.

between notions of sentient earth-beings and Cameron's representation of Na'vi relationship to Pandora's networked energy may be one reason for Morales's positive response to *Avatar*. Another might be explained using Rob Nixon's work on the concepts of "slow violence" (6) and "spectacle" (16). Nixon, who is noted for bridging postcolonial and ecocritical studies, analyzes the work of writer-activists in the Global South, including Ogoni organizer Ken Saro-Wiwa, a prolific creative writer, novelist, screenwriter, and politician. Saro-Wiwa's work helped to illuminate an inattention to the attritional lethality of environmental disasters which exacerbate the vulnerability of ecosystems and people who are poor, disempowered, and often involuntarily displaced. In an increasingly globalizing world, this is a pattern that is often repeated, with transnational corporations based in the Global North promising to contribute to the progress of modern society, then managing to evade resolution of "matters of environmental injury, remediation, and redress" for decades (Nixon 6). Since there is a deficit of spectacle or of "recognizable special effects that fill movie seats" in these communities, there is nothing to draw the global media's attention to their plight; consequently, slow violence often remains hidden (6).

Nixon has illustrated how a deficit of spectacle in Nigeria led to the *4* 1995 execution of Ken Saro-Wiwa on trumped-up charges. The Ogoni are an indigenous and ethnic minority group that has been subjected both to racism by Royal Dutch/Shell Oil and discrimination by an elite faction of dominant ethnic groups profiting from oil extraction. For their resistance to the degradation of their lands and water, the Ogoni were being murdered, raped, and tortured. Saro-Wiwa had been attempting to call the world's attention to this violence and to oil spills the size of the Exxon Valdez spill that had been occurring in the Niger Delta every year since 1958. But lacking the sudden spectacle of oiled Alaskan wildlife, no one seemed to care. By 1993, when he began traveling his country to give speeches for the United Nations International Year for the World's Indigenous People, Saro-Wiwa was only just beginning to imagine how he might capitalize on new forms of international organizing and attention. In his speeches, he outlined Ogoni territorial boundaries and settlement in terms of "six kingdoms" formed in a time in the past (Saro-Wiwa 11). His purpose was not to suggest that his people were "closer to nature," but to extend the world's gaze across time, to articulate the long-term perils lurking in 50 years of spills. Shortly before his execution, Saro-Wiwa learned that indigenous peoples in Ecuador had sued Texaco-Chevron for decades of oil and chemical spills. He thought this might be the kind of "spectacle" that could draw the world's gaze to the slow violence in Ogoniland. Soon after, Ogoni villagers sued Shell for spillages that had "robbed them of their livelihoods" as subsistence farmers and fishers (Nixon 119).[2]

---

[2] Today, these two groups are formally organized and linked; see *Justice in Nigeria Now!*, 25 May 2011 http://justiceinnigeria.wordpress.com/ and *Amazon Defense Coalition*, 25 May 2011 http://www.texacotoxico.org/eng/node/.

On the other side of the Atlantic, 10 years after Saro-Wiwa's execution 5 and several decades after the lawsuit in Ecuador had been filed against Texaco-Chevron, the case was still pending. The plaintiffs had learned that simply entering a courtroom was not "spectacular" enough to draw the world's gaze. So, in 2005, the legal team representing the plaintiffs persuaded famed documentarian Joe Berlinger to try to fill movie seats with a dramatic account of their David and Goliath battle. The result was *Crude: The Real Cost of Oil* (2009), an award-winning documentary which tells the story of substandard oil drilling practices, gas flaring, and untreated toxic wastes in the territory of the indigenous Cofán. Berlinger follows Pablo Fajardo, a young Cofán lawyer taking his first case, and his associate, Cofán environmental activist Luis Yanza, as they gather evidence of cancers, rashes, and death. They form an alliance with US human rights and criminal lawyer, Steven Donziger, himself just out of Harvard Law School, and his backers who include powerful US class action law firms. Berlinger also records the statements of Chevron and Ecuadoran politicians who deny causal links between contamination and ill health. Rock star Sting's wife, Trudie Styler, brings a missing element of celebrity to the jungle as she flies in to be the eyes of the Global North. The buzz created around the film undoubtedly drew the world's gaze to the Andes. In February 2011, an Ecuadoran court awarded the plaintiffs over $18.1 billion in compensation. However, Chevron has appealed the ruling and sued Berlinger, Donziger, and Farjardo for fraud. The Cofán, and the multiple species with which they coexist, must continue waiting for remediation and redress.

The notion, as Nixon has phrased it, that there is an ongoing, 6 crude" battle over spectacle taking place in the world points to the reasons why blockbuster films and documentaries are playing an increasingly important role in global environmental justice struggles and why Evo Morales, as I will discuss below, is not the only indigenous leader to link a political struggle to *Avatar*. . . . This analysis will allow me to explore further why indigenous groups are linking their movements to a blockbuster film that features a coalition of humans and bioluminescent nonhuman species fighting to shift audience focus from the spectacle of war and corporate greed to the ontology and agency of the material world.

Cosmopolitism and Ecocriticism

Questions of citizenship have long been at the heart of the field imagi- 7 nary in American studies and central to recent ecocritical debates about the interrelations of cosmopolitanism, nationalism, localism, and environmentalism. In a special issue of the *Journal of Transnational American Studies*, Günter Lenz surveys key texts and scholars that have been at the center of a rich discussion of the meaning and promises of new versions of cosmopolitanism.[3] He observes that this work is energizing the potential for "newly defined conceptions and practices of governance, justice, [and] citizenship . . . in a multi-polar world of unequal distribution of power and resources" (9). In the same issue, Alfred Hornung praises *Ursula Heise's Sense of Place and Sense of Planet* (2008) as a key example of this new work. Heise urges literary critics and environmentalists to consider how studies of globalization suggest new possibilities for "ecocosmopolitanism," a term she coins as a kind of shorthand for ecologically inflected notions of "world citizenship" (10). Heise surveys the tensions and contradictions that theories of globalization and cosmopolitanism present for ecocriticism, which she defines as environmentally oriented literary and cultural studies. She urges ecocritics to recognize the limitations of an "excessive investment in the local" (10) while cautioning that academic theories of globalization and cosmopolitanism must always be enriched by "environmental justice fieldwork" (Heise 159). Both Hornung and Lenz suggest that new work exploring cosmopolitanism and environmentalisms is revealing "new options for forging more complex, multifaceted" and "localized visions of communal politics and cultural practices in a globalizing world" (Lenz 7).

Lenz notes that new versions of cosmopolitanism are leading to a recognition of multiple new dimensions of "cultural citizenship, minority rights, [and] the right of ecological citizenship" (6). Rob Nixon's work on slow violence (which brilliantly answers Heise's call for environmental justice field work that forges more complex, multifaceted visions of localized communal politics) offers excellent examples of how some of these new concepts of ecological citizenship are developing. For example, in the after-math of the chemical spill at Bhopal, nuclear disaster at Chernobyl, and oil spills in the Niger Delta, new "varieties of biological citizenship" are produced when some of the survivors gain "official recognition as sufferers" while others are "dismissed as nonsufferers because their narratives of injury are deemed to fail the prevailing politico-scientific logic of causation" (Nixon 47). Stacy Alaimo and Susan Hekman's coedited work in *Material Feminisms* (2008) also addresses the ways in which mobilization around environmental justice issues is forging new possibilities for coalition and communal politics. Alaimo and Hekman analyze the "traffic in toxins," showing how toxic substances released into a community can bring together interest groups heretofore imagined separately (9). An oil spill, for example, studied from a cultural–natural perspective that does not separate the two realms, reveals how a toxin may affect the workers who produce it, the community in which it is produced, and the humans and animals (domesticated and wild) that ingest it. Saro-Wiwa's connection of Ogoni resistance to Ecuadoran indigenous groups through his work with the United Nations and

[3] See especially page 5, note 5.

Berlinger's *Crude* provide innovative examples of how coalitional groups can form around the siting and practices of extractive industries or environmental accidents.

Marisol de la Cadena's ethnographic study of indigenous organiz- 9 ing in Latin America also illustrates how coalitions are forming around the notion that multiple species and "things" that have heretofore not been considered deserving of the same rights and protections as humans should be granted the "right to regenerate . . . biocapacity and continue . . . vital cycles" (UDRME n.p.). De la Cadena draws from Isabelle Stengers's work to explicate an emerging "indigenous cosmopolitics" focused on recognition of the rights of "Pachamama." Stengers extracts from the word "cosmopolitan" its two constituents: cosmos and politics. Cosmos "refers to the unknown" constituted by multiple, divergent worlds and politics "to the articulation of which they would eventually be capable" (Stengers 995). Stengers argues that a cosmos detached from politics is irrelevant, then dives deep into the philosophies of politics and science to explore how "our modern world," to use Latour's phrase, separated humans from nature (27). The Declaration on the Rights of Mother Earth counters this separation by urging all the world's citizens to become more aware of multiple, divergent worlds and to build a politics that would support the "recovery, revalidation, and strengthening" of "cosmovisions based on ancient and ancestral indigenous knowledge" (UDRME Art. 1 n.p.).

Political rallies and events across Latin America are illustrating 10 what an "indigenous cosmovision" might look like in practice. At a protest in 2006 organized to oppose a proposed mining concession in Peru, for example, a coalition of indigenous peoples, environmentalists, and academics enlisted Ausangate, a mountain considered a "powerful earth-being, the source of life and death, of wealth and misery," as an ally (de la Cadena 338). They argued that Ausangate should have the right to exist in proper relationship with its surrounding mountains. A mine sited at Ausangate would prevent the maintenance and continuance of this relationship. But in the modern world, writes de la Cadena, the notion that a mountain can be sentient is dismissed as "anti-capitalist nonsense" (340). The President of Peru, Alan García, denied that Ausangate was sacred and described it as *tierra ociosas*, or "idle land" that could be developed for the "common good" of the "nation" (340). In dismissing the legitimacy of the protest, García calls upon ideas accepted by modern societies that agree that unscientific indigenous or "ethnic beliefs" block "progress." Despite García's views, protestors at the rally included indigenous people, many educated and already elected to political office, who believed in sentient entities. They were working to prevent unfortunate accidents that might be caused by the ire that would be triggered by a sentient mountain subject to desecration. Other protestors, some academics and some environmentalists, did not believe in sentient entities and were at the rally to protect local rivers and agriculture from the harm that erosion and pollution might cause. What was notable, observes de la Cadena, is that despite many differing views and opinions, indigenous politicians and nonindigenous academics and activists were able to commit to a politics of nature that included "disagreement on the definition of nature itself" (de la Cadena 346). This kind of commitment is emerging throughout Latin America. . . .

Multidimensional Relationship and Multinaturalism

"[W]hat forces—imaginative, scientific, and activist," asks Rob Nixon, *11* "can help us extend the temporal horizons of our gaze not just retrospectively" to past environmental injustices but prospectively to worlds we might see if we knew what to look for (62)? Many indigenous groups, scholars, and politicians around the world have raised *Avatar* like a red flag to begin suggesting answers. In eastern India, the Dongria Kondh tribe posted a YouTube video titled "The Real Avatar" that narrates their (successful) battle to stop mining giant Vedanta Resources from siting a bauxite mine on their sacred mountain, Niyam Raja. At an Ecuadoran fundraising event posted on YouTube, Shuar, Achuar, and Waorani tribal members enter a movie theater decked out in their plumes, feathered crowns, and jewelry, then watch *Avatar* wearing 3-D glasses. Achuar leader Luis Vargas objects to the main character being a "white guy [who] sweeps in to the rescue" but allows that such plot devices are to be expected from Hollywood (Spitzer n.p.). Vargas is more interested in the film's potential for calling attention to the plans of multinationals to drill for oil in Yasuni National Park, home to some of the world's still uncontacted tribes (Spitzer n.p.). At a fundraiser attended by James Cameron, near the site of a proposed dam which will dry up a 60-mile stretch of the Xingu River in Brazil and displace the Arara people, the media asks the chief for a response to the film and he says simply, "*Avatar* is happening here" (Barrionuevo A1).

In a review subtitled "An Indigenous Woman Considers *Avatar*," Julia *12* Good Fox analyzes the connections that indigenous communities are making to the film and argues that it is a willful oversimplification to reduce the film to "white savior" or "going native" metaphors. She is more interested in whether or not the imaginative, scientific, and activist forces portrayed in the film can move audience members toward better understanding of issues that indigenous groups face in a globalizing world. Jake Sully, she wryly observes, is no "savior" since he would be powerless, and literally unable to move, without the alliance formed between the Na'vi's ceremonial elder, Mo'at and her daughter, Neytiri, and without the scientist in charge of the Avatar program, Dr. Grace Augustine. This kind of alliance is typical in the context of Cameron's *oeuvre:* from *The Terminator* (1984), to *Aliens* (1986), to *Titanic* (1997), this director has spent his career exploring the "ways that representative individuals and cultures misconnect . . . . abuse connection, and, of course, connect" (Good Fox n.p.). He *wants* viewers to think of cowboys and Indians, militarization, and genocide and colonization. The film is a "deliberately pieced together metatext" whose embedded history encourages the audience to explore the possibilities of individuals "to connect to each other's humanity despite overwhelming hurdles" (Good Fox n.p.).

Good Fox explains that diverse tribes have various characteristics that *13* differentiate them from other tribes, but indigenous peoples share a general recognition of "multidimentional relationships," often referred to as "all my relations," or the notion that all life is connected.[4] Cameron represents this notion when Neytiri's mother, Mo'at, charges her daughter with leading Jake Sully from "insanity to sanity." In a scene in which Neytiri upbraids Sully for not fully understanding that hunting is not just a sport and animals are not just food, she emphatically teaches him the phrase "Oel ngati kameie" or "I see you," which implies, argues Good Fox, not just a glance, but an accurate and encompassing recognition, an insightful and respectful acknowledgment of connectedness or "relatedness" to elements of the world that cannot be seen by humans. Neytiri's extensive knowledge of the brightly colored, iridescent species of Pandora points to emerging fields of study that focus on multispecies relationship. Led by scholars such as Donna Haraway, Stacy Alaimo, and Stefan Helmreich, this field has gone well beyond the work of famed anthropologists such as Claude Lévi-Strauss to show that other-than-human species are not just "good to think" or "good to eat" but are also, in Haraway's formulation, "entities, and agents, 'to live with'" (qtd. in Kirksey and Helmreich 552). As Helmreich has observed in his "anthropological voyages in microbial seas," at the smallest of scales, light and color "are often the only signs of these lives invisible to the unaided eye" (187). Neytiri commandingly teaches Jake that interpreting light and color takes committed apprenticeship. Jake, whose last name, "Sully," means "to mar the luster of something," is secretly working to gather intelligence on the Na'vi for use by the mining corporation. This deceit is clouding his gaze and blinding him to the lustrous networked energy of Eywa that connects all the species and "things" on Pandora.

The relationships between Mo'at, Neytiri, and Grace illustrate that "all *14* our relations" also encompass relations between various human groups (Good Fox n.p.). This is the element of the film, writes Daniel Heath Justice, another indigenous scholar and reviewer, that prevented the Indigenous Studies community from dismissing the film (Justice n.p.). Grace's research on the Na'vi offers what Justice calls a "muted critique

---

[4] For a book-length consideration of this concept, see Winona LaDuke's *All Our Relations* (1999).

of academic colonialism" which focuses a spotlight on the danger—and potential—of historical "legacies of interface"—between indigenous peoples, colonizers, armies, teachers, preachers, and scholars (Justice n.p.). Grace's corporate funding has produced a bestselling ethnography that is offering humans insight into the Na'vi, but the information is also being used by the corporation to plan the forced removal of the indigenous population from Hometree. This aspect of the film highlights historically problematic relationships between indigenous peoples and other human groups, including today's academics, NGOs (non-governmental organization), and others, who may have good intentions, but whose activities lead to harmful consequences.

Grace's research on the bioluminescent botany of Pandora is also meant 15 to show how alliances between academics and local populations might extend human vision to different scales of time and space. Cameron became interested in bioluminescence while filming *Abyss* (1989), a deep-sea sci-fi thriller, and several documentaries on deep-ocean volcanoes, animals, and plankton. Because bioluminescence occurs only in marine life on earth (with a few exceptions, like fireflies), Cameron hired botanist Jodie Holt to ensure that the representation of Pandora's "networked energy" would be scientifically credible and adhere to "known laws of physics and biology" (Kozlowski n.p.) Plants do not have a nervous system, Holt told Cameron, so they cannot literally "communicate" with each other; however, communication among plants could credibly be explained with the language of the emerging field of biosemiotics, and, more specifically, with reference to the process of "signal transduction" (Kozlowski n.p.). Biosemiotics and signal transduction are areas of research, writes Stefan Helmreich, that deal with how living things "perceive and interpret their environments" through chemical gradients or intensities of light (187).

Before the corporation begins forcibly removing the Na'vi, Grace 16 tries to convince the head executive that the real wealth of Pandora is not "under the ground" but in understanding how signal transduction works. Her words fall on deaf ears and the corporation sends in bomb-dropping planes and missile-launching robots. As the sentient Hometree is violently blown apart and the Na'vi are scattered and killed, Cameron shows how blindness to scales of time and space prevents a precautionary approach that might have averted socionatural disaster or mitigated its effects. While humans see only a "thing," Hometree is actually a grove of mangrove-like trees that have grown and intertwined from just a few bioluminescent seeds over the course of 10,000 years. Each increases the strength of the whole and expands Hometree's ability to shelter a host of species. The Na'vi's relationship to Hometree and knowledge of the other species that live there offers insight into the meaning of "deep time" and phrases like "a cosmic spirituality in the making for thousands of years" (UDRME n.p.).

What is astonishing about indigenous groups linking their own 17 regionally specific movements to *Avatar* is not that a block buster film is playing in India or the Andes or the Amazon; it is that the "things" that *Avatar* is helping to "make public," to use the language of Bruno Latour, are living systems (mountains, rivers, forests, deserts) that may help inaugurate a politics that is more plural not because the people enacting it are bodies marked by race or ethnicity demanding rights, or by environmentalists representing nature, but because they force into visibility the culture–nature divide that has prevented multiple worlds and species from being recognized as deserving the right to maintain and continue their vital cycles (de la Cadena 346). The alliance between Mo'at, Neytiri, and Grace, observes Good Fox, calls upon the audience to consider how "independent thinkers and questioners" possess traits that allow them to move away from a "monolithic mindset" of profit and enter into coalitions seeking solutions to seemingly insurmountable cultural, territorial, and environmental conflicts (Good Fox n.p.). The plurality being called for, then, does not stop at multiculturalism, but is a project that de la Cadena suggests might more accurately be called "multinaturalism" (347). . . .

Allowing earth-beings to count in politics, writes de la Cadena, does 18 not remove other proposals for economic growth and development from the table (de la Cadena 362). People, citizens—indigenous or not—can still side with a mine or dam, and choose jobs or money, depending on local needs. Opening a space for the contemplation of earth-beings would allow for recognition of nature's multiple and heterogeneous ontologies (including its possibility as repository of mineral wealth). Multiple possibilities might weigh into discussions of differing, even competing political proposals without any of these proposals being dismissed as "right," "left," "superstitious" or "unscientific." Cameron imagines this kind of increasingly plural politics, or cosmovisions, that would allow for more innovative interpretations of "citizenship" for the culture–nature entity known to many as "Source of Light."

Works Cited

Alaimo, Stacy. "Trans-Corporeal Feminisms and the Ethnical Space of Nature." *Material Feminisms*. Eds. Stacy Alaimo and Susan J. Hekman. Bloomington: Indiana UP, 2008. 237–64.

Avatar. Dir. James Cameron. Perf. Sam Worthington, Zoe Saldana, Sigourney Weaver. Twentieth Century Fox Film Corporation, 2009.

Barrionuevo, Alexei. "Tribes of Amazon Find an Ally Out of *Avatar*." *New York Times* 11 Apr. 2010: A1.

Crude: The Real Price of Oil. Dir. Joe Berlinger. Entendre Films. 2009.

De la Cadena, Marisol. "Indigenous Cosmopolitics in the Andes: Conceptual Reflections beyond 'Politics.'" *Cultural Anthropology* 25.2 (2010): 334–70.

Eshelman, Robert S. "World Peoples Conference on Climate Change and the Rights of Mother Earth Kicks Off in Bolivia." *Huffington Post* 19 Apr. 2010 17 Sept. 2010.

<http://www.huffingtonpost.com/robert-s-eshelman/worldpeoples-conference_b_543211.html>.

Good Fox, Julia. *"Avatars* to the Left of Me, Pandora to the Right: An Indigenous Woman Considers James Cameron's *Avatar."* 21 Jan. 2010. 2 Mar 2010 <http://lastwoman.wordpress.com/2010/01/21/48_Avatar/>

"Head of State Fights for Environment: Evo Morales 'Identifies' with *Avatar* Film." *Buenos Aires Herald* 12 Jan. 2010. <http://www.buenosairesherald.com/article/22287/evo-morales-identifies-with-*Avatar*-film> 9 Aug. 2010.

Heise, Ursula. *Sense of Place and Sense of Planet: The Environmental Imagination of the Global.* New York: Oxford UP, 2008.

Helmreich, Stefan. *Alien Ocean: Anthropological Voyages in Microbial Seas.* Berkeley: U of California P, 2009.

Hornung, Alfred. "Planetary Citizenship." *Journal of Transnational American Studies* 3, 1 (2011): 37–46.

Justice, Daniel Heath. "James Cameron's *Avatar*: Missed Opportunities." *First People: New Directions in Indigenous Studies.* 20 Jan. 2010. 2 Mar 2010 <http://firstpeoplesnewdirections.org/blog/?p=169/>.

Kirksey, S. Eben and Stefen Helmreich. "The Emergence of Multispecies Ethnography." *Cultural Anthropology* 25.4 (2010): 545–76.

Kozlowski, Lori, *"Avatar* Team Brings in UC Riverside Professor to Dig in the Dirt of Pandora." *Los Angeles Times* 2 Jan. 2010. 25 Jan. 2010. <http://latimesblogs.latimes.com/herocomplex/2010/01/avatar-team-brought-in-uc-riverside-professor-to-dig-in-the-dirt-of-pandora.html>.

Lenz, Günter H. "Symposium: Redefinitions of Citizenship and Revisions of Cosmopolitanism— Transnational Perspectives." *Journal of Transnational American Studies* 3.1 (2011): 1–17.

Latour, Bruno. *We Have Never Been Modern.* Cambridge: Harvard UP, 1993.

Nixon, Rob. *Slow Violence and the Environmentalism of the Poor.* Cambridge: Harvard UP, 2011.

"The Real Avatar: Mine—Story of a Sacred Mountain." *Survival International* 31 Mar. 2009. 10 May 2011. <http://www.youtube.com/ watch?v=R4tuTFZ3wXQ>.

Saro-Wiwa, Ken. *Genocide in Nigeria: The Ogoni Tragedy.* Lagos: Saros International, 1991.

Spitzer, Melaina. "Avatar in the Amazon." *Public Radio International* 29 Jan. 2010. 8 Aug 2010. <http://www.youtube.com/watch?v=Qh_dFfoE6wo>.

Stengers, Isabelle. "The Cosmopolitical Proposal." *Making Things Public: Atmospheres of Democracy.* Eds. Latour Bruno and Weibel Peter. Cambridge: MIT P, 2005. 994–1004.

United Nations Declaration on the Rights of Indigenous Peoples. *The United Nations Permanent Forum on Indigenous Issues* 13 Sept. 2007. 11 Aug 2009. <http://www.un.org/esa/socdev/unpfii/en/declaration.html>.

Universal Declaration on the Rights of Mother Earth. *World People's Conference on Climate Change and the Rights of Mother Earth* 22 Apr. 2010. 17 Sept 2010. <http://www.globalresearch.ca/index. php?context=va&aid=18931>.

■ ■ ■

Reading as a Writer: Analyzing Rhetorical Choices

1. How and where does Adamson move between descriptions of the film and argument? Locate and discuss some specific passages. Is it possible to describe something without infusing the description with a perspective or argument? Provide evidence for your answer.

2. Adamson's first sentence in paragraph 7 contains a long list of key words
    that are important to her argument: "Questions of citizenship have long
    been at the heart of the field imaginary in American studies and central
    to recent ecocritical debates about the interrelations of cosmopolitanism,
    nationalism, localism, and environmentalism." Perhaps dividing into pairs
    or groups, look up the words "ecocritical," "cosmopolitanism," "national-
    ism," "localism," and "environmentalism." Discuss how these terms are
    connected to the analysis of *Avatar* in this essay.

Writing as a Reader: Entering the Conversation of Ideas

1. Adamson, Ken Gillam and Shannon R. Wooden, and bell hooks examine
    the ways film representations engage in social issues. Draw on ideas from
    these authors to craft an essay about the power of films to invite or repress
    (or both) critiques of social problems. What skills should viewers bring to
    the movie theater, according to these authors? You might select a film to
    analyze in your essay, as a means of applying these authors' ideas and pro-
    viding examples for your claims.

2. Adamson argues, as do Mark R. Tercek and Jonathan S. Adams in the
    excerpt from *Nature's Fortune* (Chapter 17), that environmental awareness
    need not be opposed to mainstream culture and values. Using the ideas
    from these authors, compose an essay that draws out some principles
    about effective ways for popular culture to engage fruitfully with environ-
    mental issues.

KEN GILLAM AND SHANNON R. WOODEN

Post-Princess Models of Gender: The New Man in Disney/Pixar

Ken Gillam directs the composition program at Missouri State University,
where he teaches courses on composition theory and pedagogy. Shannon
R. Wooden is a professor of English at the same university, where her specialty is British literature, creative writing, literature and science, and
adaptations of novels for the screen. This piece is part of the research for
their 2014 book, *Pixar's Boy Stories: Masculinity in a Postmodern Age*. You
may be familiar with the many critiques of Disney princesses, but less
has been written about the leading male characters. Gillam and Wooden's
work begins to fill this gap in the research.

　　While every scholarly article is in some way driven by inquiry, Gillam
and Wooden make their question explicit in their second paragraph: "Does
this nominal feminizing of male also-rans [in *Cars*] (and the simultaneous
gendering of success) constitute a meaningful pattern?" The rest of their

essay is an answer to this question, elaborating on their thesis that "Pixar consistently promotes a new model of masculinity, one that matures into acceptance of its more traditionally 'feminine' aspects" (para. 2). They argue that the male leads in Pixar films beginning with *Toy Story* in 1995 share a similar storyline of initially striving for an "alpha-male identity," but then, "finally, they achieve (and teach) a kinder, gentler understanding of what it means to be a man" (para. 4). How and where do they define this new kind of masculinity throughout their essay?

As you read, test their argument against the examples and interpretations the authors offer of films you may know well. You might try to remember your first responses to these Pixar classics, as well as what you see as you reflect on them now. Consider their claim that these films share a similar plot, which revolves around a male character: "As these characters begin the film in (or seeking) the tenuous alpha position among fellow characters, each of them is also stripped of this identity—dramatically emasculated—so that he may learn, reform, and emerge again with a different, and arguably more feminine, self-concept" (para. 11). How effectively do their examples from *Toy Story*, *The Incredibles*, and *Cars* support their claim?

In their conclusion, Gillam and Wooden turn their argument a new direction, looking critically at the Walt Disney Company's enormous audience and calling on the readers to retain "a critical consciousness of the main lessons taught by the cultural monolith of Disney" (para. 24). Slow down and be sure you understand the points the authors make in these densely packed final two paragraphs. What do they claim is at stake in becoming "conscientious cultural critics"? Can childhood movies really make that big of an impact? If you think back on your own childhood favorites and how much they meant to you (and perhaps still do), you may have at least the beginning of your own answer.

■ ■ ■

Lisping over the Steve McQueen allusion in Pixar's *Cars* (2006), our two- *1* year-old son, Oscar, inadvertently directed us to the definition(s) of masculinity that might be embedded in a children's animated film about NASCAR. The film overtly praises the "good woman" proverbially behind every successful man: The champion car, voiced by Richard Petty, tells his wife, "I wouldn't be nothin' without you, honey." But gender in this twenty-first-century bildungsroman is rather more complex, and Oscar's mispronunciation held the first clue. To him, a member of the film's target audience, the character closing in on the title long held by "The King" is not "Lightning McQueen" but "Lightning the queen"; his chief rival, the always-a-bridesmaid runner-up "Chick" Hicks.

Does this nominal feminizing of male also-rans (and the simultaneous *2* gendering of success) constitute a meaningful pattern? Piqued, we began examining the construction of masculinity in major feature films released by Disney's Pixar studios over the past thirteen years. Indeed, as we argue here, Pixar consistently promotes a new model of masculinity, one that matures into acceptance of its more traditionally "feminine" aspects.

Cultural critics have long been interested in Disney's cinematic prod- 3
ucts, but the gender critics examining the texts most enthusiastically gobbled up by the under-six set have so far generally focused on their retrograde representations of women. As Elizabeth Bell argues, the animated Disney features through *Beauty and the Beast* feature a "teenaged heroine at the idealized height of puberty's graceful promenade . . . [f]emale wickedness . . . rendered as middle-aged beauty at its peak of sexuality and authority . . . and [f]eminine sacrifice and nurturing . . . drawn in pear-shaped, old women past menopause" (108). Some have noted the models of masculinity in the classic animated films, primarily the contrast between the ubermacho Gaston and the sensitive, misunderstood Beast in *Beauty and the Beast*,[1] but the male protagonist of the animated classics, at least through *The Little Mermaid*, remains largely uninterrogated.[2] For most of the early films, this critical omission seems generally appropriate, the various versions of Prince Charming being often too two-dimensional to do more than inadvertently shape the definition of the protagonists' femininity. But if the feminist thought that has shaped our cultural texts for three decades now has been somewhat disappointing in its ability to actually rewrite the princess trope (the spunkiest of the "princesses," Ariel, Belle, Jasmine, and, arguably, even Mulan, remain thin, beautiful, kind, obedient or punished for disobedience, and headed for the altar), it has been surprisingly effective in rewriting the type of masculine power promoted by Disney's products.[3]

Disney's new face, Pixar studios, has released nine films—*Toy Story* 4 (1995) and *Toy Story 2* (1999); *A Bug's Life* (1998), *Finding Nemo* (2003); *Monsters, Inc.* (2001); *The Incredibles* (2004); *Cars* (2006); *Ratatouille* (2007); and now *WALL•E* (2008)—all of which feature interesting male

---

[1] See Susan Jeffords, "The Curse of Masculinity: Disney's *Beauty and the Beast*" for an excellent analysis of that plot's developing the cruel Beast into a man who can love and be loved in return: "Will he be able to overcome his beastly temper and terrorizing attitude in order to learn to love?" (168). But even in this film, she argues, the Beast's development is dependent on "other people, especially women," whose job it is to tutor him into the new model of masculinity, the "New Man" (169, 170).

[2] Two articles demand that we qualify this claim. Indirectly, they support the point of this essay by demonstrating a midcentury Disney model of what we call "alpha" masculinity. David Payne's "Bambi" parallels that film's coming-of-age plot, ostensibly representing a "natural" world, with the military mindset of the 1940s against which the film was drawn. Similarly, Claudia Card, in "Pinocchio," claims that the Disneyfied version of the nineteenth-century Carlo Collodi tale replaces the original's model of bravery and honesty with "a macho exercise in heroism [. . . and] avoid[ing] humiliation" (66–67).

[3] Outside the animated classics, critics have noted a trend toward a postfeminist masculinity—one characterized by emotional wellness, sensitivity to family, and a conscious rejection of the most alpha male values—in Disney-produced films of the 1980s and 1990s. Jeffords gives a sensible account of the changing male lead in films ranging from *Kindergarten Cop* to *Terminator 2*.

figures in leading positions. Unlike many of the princesses, who remain relatively static even through their own adventures, these male leads are actual protagonists; their characters develop and change over the course of the film, rendering the plot. Ultimately these various developing characters—particularly Buzz and Woody from *Toy Story*, Mr. Incredible from *The Incredibles*, and Lightning McQueen from *Cars*—experience a common narrative trajectory, culminating in a common "New Man" model:[4] they all strive for an alpha-male identity; they face emasculating failures; they find themselves, in large part, through what Eve Sedgwick refers to as "homosocial desire" and a triangulation of this desire with a feminized object (and/or a set of "feminine" values); and, finally, they achieve (and teach) a kinder, gentler understanding of what it means to be a man.

Emasculation of the Alpha Male

A working definition of *alpha male* may be unnecessary; although more tra- 5
ditionally associated with the animal kingdom than the Magic Kingdom, it familiarly evokes ideas of dominance, leadership, and power in human social organizations as well. The phrase "alpha male" may stand for all things stereotypically patriarchal: unquestioned authority, physical power and social dominance, competitiveness for positions of status and leadership, lack of visible or shared emotion, social isolation. An alpha male, like Vann in *Cars*, does not ask for directions; like Doc Hudson in the same film, he does not talk about his feelings. The alpha male's stresses, like Buzz Lightyear's, come from his need to save the galaxy; his strength comes from faith in his ability to do so. These models have worked in Disney for decades. The worst storm at sea is no match for *The Little Mermaid*'s uncomplicated Prince Eric—indeed, any charming prince need only ride in on his steed to save his respective princess. But the postfeminist world is a different place for men, and the post-princess Pixar is a different place for male protagonists.

Newsweek recently described the alpha male's new cinematic and 6
television rival, the "beta male": "The testosterone-pumped, muscle-bound Hollywood hero is rapidly deflating. . . . Taking his place is a new kind of leading man, the kind who's just as happy following as leading, or never getting off the sofa" (Yabroff 64). Indeed, as Susan Jeffords points out, at least since *Beauty and the Beast*, Disney has resisted (even ridiculed) the machismo once de rigueur for leading men (170). Disney cinema, one of

---

[4] In Disney criticism, the phrase "New Man" seems to belong to Susan Jeffords's 1995 essay on *Beauty and the Beast*, but it is slowly coming into vogue for describing other postfeminist trends in masculine identity. In popular culture, see Richard Collier's "The New Man: Fact or Fad?" online in *Achilles Heel: The Radical Men's Magazine* 14 (Winter 1992/1993). http://www.achillesheel.freeuk.com/article14_9.html. For a literary-historical account, see *Writing Men: Literary Masculinities from Frankenstein to the New Man* by Berthold Schoene-Harwood (Columbia UP, 2000).

the most effective teaching tools America offers its children, is not yet converting its model male protagonist all the way into a slacker, but the New Man model is quite clearly emerging.

Cars, *Toy Story,* and *The Incredibles* present their protagonists as unambiguously alpha in the opening moments of the films. Although Lightning McQueen may be an as-yet incompletely realized alpha when *Cars* begins, not having yet achieved the "King" status of his most successful rival, his ambition and fierce competitiveness still clearly valorize the alpha-male model: "Speed. I am speed . . . I eat losers for breakfast," he chants as a prerace mantra. He heroically comes from behind to tie the championship race, distinguishing himself by his physical power and ability, characteristics that catapult him toward the exclusively male culture of sports superstars. The fantasies of his life he indulges after winning the coveted Piston Cup even include flocks of female cars forming a worshipful harem around him. But the film soon diminishes the appeal of this alpha model. Within a few moments of the race's conclusion, we see some of Lightning's less positive macho traits; his inability to name any friends, for example, reveals both his isolation and attempts at emotional stoicism. Lightning McQueen is hardly an unemotional character, as can be seen when he prematurely jumps onto the stage to accept what he assumes to be his victory. For this happy emotional outburst, however, he is immediately disciplined by a snide comment from Chick. From this point until much later in the film, the only emotions he displays are those of frustration and anger.

Toy Story's Buzz Lightyear and Sheriff Woody similarly base their worth on a masculine model of competition and power, desiring not only to be the "favorite toy" of their owner, Andy, but to possess the admiration of and authority over the other toys in the playroom. Woody is a natural leader, and his position represents both paternalistic care and patriarchal dominance. In an opening scene, he calls and conducts a "staff meeting" that highlights his unambiguously dominant position in the toy community. Encouraging the toys to pair up so that no one will be lost in the family's impending move, he commands: "A moving buddy. If you don't have one, GET ONE." Buzz's alpha identity comes from a more exalted source than social governance—namely, his belief that he is the one "space ranger" with the power and knowledge needed to save the galaxy; it seems merely natural, then, that the other toys would look up to him, admire his strength, and follow his orders. But as with Lightning McQueen, these depictions of masculine power are soon undercut. Buzz's mere presence exposes Woody's strength as fragile, artificial, even arbitrary, and his "friends," apparently having been drawn to his authority rather than his character, are fair-weather at best. Buzz's authority rings hollow from the very beginning, and his refusal to believe in his own "toyness" is at best silly and at worst dangerous. Like Lightning, Buzz's and Woody's most commonly expressed emotions are anger and frustration, not sadness (Woody's, at having been "replaced") or fear (Buzz's, at having "crash-landed on a strange planet") or even wistful fondness (Woody's, at the loss of Slink's, Bo Peep's, and Rex's loyalty). Once again, the alpha-male position is depicted as fraudulent, precarious, lonely, and devoid of emotional depth.

An old-school superhero, Mr. Incredible opens *The Incredibles* by   9 displaying the tremendous physical strength that enables him to stop speeding trains, crash through buildings, and keep the city safe from criminals. But he too suffers from the emotional isolation of the alpha male. Stopping on the way to his own wedding to interrupt a crime in progress, he is very nearly late to the service, showing up only to say the "I dos." Like his car and toy counterparts, he communicates primarily through verbal assertions of power — angrily dismissing Buddy, his meddlesome aspiring sidekick; bantering with Elastigirl over who gets the pickpocket — and limits to anger and frustration the emotions apparently available to men.

Fraught as it may seem, the alpha position is even more fleeting: 10 In none of these Pixar films does the male protagonist's dominance last long. After Lightning ties, rather than wins, the race and ignores the King's friendly advice to find and trust a good team with which to work, he browbeats his faithful semi, Mack, and ends up lost in "hillbilly hell," a small town off the beaten path of the interstate. His uncontrolled physical might destroys the road, and the resultant legal responsibility — community service — keeps him far from his Piston Cup goals. When Buzz appears as a gift for Andy's birthday, he easily unseats Woody both as Andy's favorite and as the toy community's leader. When Buzz becomes broken, failing to save himself from the clutches of the evil neighbor, Sid, he too must learn a hard lesson about his limited power, his diminished status, and his own relative insignificance in the universe. Mr. Incredible is perhaps most obviously disempowered: Despite his superheroic feats, Mr. Incredible has been unable to keep the city safe from his own clumsy brute force. After a series of lawsuits against "the Supers," who accidentally leave various types of small-time mayhem in their wake, they are all driven underground, into a sort of witness protection program. To add insult to injury, Mr. Incredible's diminutive boss fires him from his job handling insurance claims, and his wife, the former Elastigirl, assumes the "pants" of the family.

Most of these events occur within the first few minutes of the characters' respective films. Only Buzz's downfall happens in the second half.   11 The alpha-male model is thus not only present and challenged in the films but also is, in fact, the very structure on which the plots unfold. Each of these films is about being a man, and they begin with an outdated, two-dimensional alpha prototype to expose its failings and to ridicule its logical extensions: the devastation and humiliation of being defeated in competition, the wrath generated by power unchecked, the paralyzing alienation and fear inherent in being lonely at the top. As these characters begin the film in (or seeking) the tenuous alpha position among fellow characters, each of them is also stripped of this identity—dramatically emasculated—so that he may learn, reform, and emerge again with a different, and arguably more feminine, self-concept.

"Emasculated" is not too strong a term for what happens to these male *12* protagonists; the decline of the alpha-male model is gender coded in all the films. For his community service punishment, Lightning is chained to the giant, snorting, tar-spitting "Bessie" and ordered to repair the damage he has wrought. His own "horsepower" (as Sally cheerfully points out) is used against him when literally put in the service of a nominally feminized figure valued for the more "feminine" orientation of service to the community. If being under the thumb of this humongous "woman" is not emasculating enough, Mater, who sees such subordination to Bessie as a potentially pleasurable thing, names the price, saying, "I'd give my left two lug nuts for something like that!"

Mr. Incredible's downfall is most clearly marked as gendered by *13* his responses to it. As his wife's domestic power and enthusiasm grow increasingly unbearable, and his children's behavior more and more out of his control, he surreptitiously turns to the mysterious, gorgeous "Mirage," who gives him what he needs to feel like a man: superhero work. Overtly depicting her as the "other woman," the film requires Elastigirl to intercept a suggestive-sounding phone call, and to trap her husband in a lie, to be able to work toward healing his decimated masculinity.

In *Toy Story*, the emasculation of the alpha male is the most overt, *14* and arguably the most comic. From the beginning, power is constructed in terms conspicuously gender coded, at least for adult viewers: As they watch the incoming birthday presents, the toys agonize at their sheer size, the longest and most phallic-shaped one striking true fear (and admiration?) into the hearts of the spectators. When Buzz threatens Woody, one toy explains to another that he has "laser envy." Buzz's moment of truth, after seeing himself on Sid's father's television, is the most clearly gendered of all. Realizing for the first time that Woody is right, he is a "toy," he defiantly attempts to fly anyway, landing sprawled on the floor with a broken arm. Sid's little sister promptly finds him, dresses him in a pink apron and hat, and installs him as "Mrs. Nesbit" at her tea party. When Woody tries to wrest him from his despair, Buzz wails, "Don't you get it? I AM MRS. NESBIT. But does the hat look good? Oh, tell me the hat looks good!" Woody's "rock bottom" moment finds him trapped under an overturned milk crate, forcing him to ask Buzz for help and to admit that he "doesn't stand a chance" against Buzz in the contest for Andy's affection, which constitutes "everything that is important to me." He is not figured into a woman, like Buzz is, or subordinated to a woman, like Lightning is, or forced to seek a woman's affirmation of his macho self, like Mr. Incredible is, but he does have to acknowledge his own feminine values, from his need for communal support to his deep, abiding (and, later, maternal) love of a boy. This "feminine" stamp is characteristic of the New Man model toward which these characters narratively journey.

Homosociality, Intimacy, and Emotion

Regarding the "love of a boy," the "mistress" tempting Mr. Incredible away *15* from his wife and family is not Mirage at all but Buddy, the boy he jilted in the opening scenes of the film (whose last name, Pine, further conveys the unrequited nature of their relationship). Privileging his alpha-male emotional isolation, but adored by his wannabe sidekick, Mr. Incredible vehemently protects his desire to "work alone." After spending the next years nursing his rejection and refining his arsenal, Buddy eventually retaliates against Mr. Incredible for rebuffing his advances. Such a model of homosocial tutelage as Buddy proposes at the beginning of the film certainly evokes an ancient (and homosexual) model of masculine identity; Mr. Incredible's rejection quickly and decisively replaces it with a heteronormative one, further supported by Elastigirl's marrying and Mirage's attracting the macho superhero.[5] But it is equally true that the recovery of Mr. Incredible's masculine identity happens primarily through his (albeit antagonistic) relationship with Buddy, suggesting that Eve Sedgwick's notion of a homosocial continuum is more appropriate to an analysis of the film's gender attitudes than speculations about its reactionary heteronormativity, even homophobia.

Same-sex (male) bonds—to temporarily avoid the more loaded term *16* *desire*—are obviously important to each of these films. In fact, in all three, male/male relationships emerge that move the fallen alphas forward in their journeys toward a new masculinity. In each case, the male lead's first and/or primary intimacy—his most immediate transformative relationship—is with one or more male characters. Even before discovering Buddy as his nemesis, Mr. Incredible secretly pairs up with his old pal Frozone, and the two step out on their wives to continue superheroing on the sly; Buddy and Frozone are each, in their ways, more influential on Mr. Incredible's sense of self than his wife or children are. Although Lightning falls in love with Sally and her future vision of Radiator Springs, his almost accidentally having befriended the hapless, warm Mater catalyzes more foundational lessons about the responsibilities of friendship—demanding honesty, sensitivity, and care—than the smell-the-roses lesson Sally represents. He also ends up being mentored and taught a comparable lesson about caring for

---

[5] Critics have described the superhero within some framework of queer theory since the 1950s, when Dr. Fredric Wertham's *Seduction of the Innocent* claimed that Batman and Robin were gay (Ameron Ltd, 1954). See Rob Lendrum's "Queering Super-Manhood: Superhero Masculinity, Camp, and Public Relations as a Textual Framework" (*International Journal of Comic Art* 7.1 [2005]: 287–303) and Valerie Palmer-Mehtan and Kellie Hay's "A Superhero for Gays? Gay Masculinity and Green Lantern" (*Journal of American Culture* 28.4 [2005]: 390–404), among myriad nonscholarly pop-cultural sources.

others by Doc Hudson, who even more explicitly encourages him to resist the alpha path of the Piston Cup world by relating his experiences of being used and then rejected. Woody and Buzz, as rivals-cum-allies, discover the necessary truths about their masculine strength only as they discover how much they need one another. Sedgwick further describes the ways in which the homosocial bond is negotiated through a triangulation of desire; that is, the intimacy emerging "between men" is constructed through an overt and shared desire for a feminized object. Unlike homosocial relationships between women—that is, "the continuum between 'women loving women' and 'women promoting the interests of women'"—male homosocial identity is necessarily homophobic in patriarchal systems, which are structurally homophobic (3). This means the same-sex relationship demands social opportunities for a man to insist on, or prove, his heterosexuality. Citing Rene Girard's *Deceit, Desire, and the Novel,* Sedgwick argues that "in any erotic rivalry, the bond that links the two rivals is as intense and potent as the bond that links either of the rivals to the beloved" (21); women are ultimately symbolically exchangeable "for the primary purpose of cementing the bonds of men with men" (26).

This triangulation of male desire can be seen in *Cars* and *Toy Story* [17] particularly, where the homosocial relationship rather obviously shares a desire for a feminized third. Buzz and Woody compete first, momentarily, for the affection of Bo Peep, who is surprisingly sexualized for a children's movie (purring to Woody an offer to "get someone else to watch the sheep tonight," then rapidly choosing Buzz as her "moving buddy" after his "flying" display). More importantly, they battle for the affection of Andy—a male child alternately depicted as maternal (it is his responsibility to get his baby sister out of her crib) and in need of male protection (Woody exhorts Buzz to "take care of Andy for me!").[6] *Cars* also features a sexualized romantic heroine; less coquettish than Bo Peep, Sally still fumbles over an invitation to spend the night "not with me, but . . ." in the motel she owns. One of Lightning and Mater's moments of "bonding" happens when Mater confronts Lightning, stating his affection for Sally and sharing a parallel story of heterosexual desire. The more principal objects of desire in *Cars,* however, are the (arguably) feminized "Piston Cup" and the Dinoco sponsorship. The sponsor itself is established in romantic terms: With Lightning stuck in Radiator Springs, his agent says Dinoco has had to "woo" Chick instead. Tia and Mia, Lightning's "biggest fans," who transfer their affection to Chick during his absence, offer viewers an even less subtly gendered goal, and Chick uses this to taunt Lightning. It is in the

---

[6] Interestingly, Andy and *Toy Story* in general are apparently without (human) male role models. The only father present in the film at all is Sid's, sleeping in front of the television in the middle of the day. Andy's is absent at a dinner out, during a move, and on the following Christmas morning. Andy himself, at play, imagines splintering a nuclear family: when he makes Sheriff Woody catch One-Eyed Black Bart in a criminal act, he says, "Say goodbye to the wife and tater tots . . . you're going to jail."

pursuit of these objects, and in competition with Chick and the King, that Lightning first defines himself as a man; the Piston Cup also becomes the object around which he and Doc discover their relationship to one another.

The New Man

With the strength afforded by these homosocial intimacies, the male characters triumph over their respective plots, demonstrating the desirable modifications that Pixar makes to the alpha-male model. To emerge victorious (and in one piece) over the tyrannical neighbor boy, Sid, Buzz and Woody have to cooperate not only with each other but also with the cannibalized toys lurking in the dark places of Sid's bedroom. Incidentally learning a valuable lesson about discrimination based on physical difference (the toys are not monsters at all, despite their frightening appearance), they begin to show sympathy, rather than violence born of their fear, to the victims of Sid's experimentation. They learn how to humble themselves to ask for help from the community. Until Woody's grand plan to escape Sid unfolds, Sid could be an object lesson in the unredeemed alpha-male type: Cruelly almighty over the toy community, he wins at arcade games, bullies his sister, and, with strategically placed fireworks, exerts militaristic might over any toys he can find. Woody's newfound ability to give and receive care empowers him to teach Sid a lesson of caring and sharing that might be microcosmic to the movie as a whole. Sid, of course, screams (like a girl) when confronted with the evidence of his past cruelties, and when viewers last see him, his younger sister is chasing him up the stairs with her doll. [18]

Even with the unceremonious exit of Sid, the adventure is not quite over for Buzz and Woody. Unable to catch up to the moving van as Sid's dog chases him, Woody achieves the pinnacle of the New Man narrative: Armed with a new masculine identity, one that expresses feelings and acknowledges community as a site of power, Woody is able to sacrifice the competition with Buzz for his object of desire. Letting go of the van strap, sacrificing himself (he thinks) to Sid's dog, he plainly expresses a caretaking, nurturing love, and a surrender to the good of the beloved: "Take care of Andy for me," he pleads. Buzz's own moment of truth comes from seizing his power as a toy: holding Woody, he glides into the family's car and back into Andy's care, correcting Woody by proudly repeating his earlier, critical words back to him: "This isn't flying; it's falling with style." Buzz has found the value of being a "toy," the self-fulfillment that comes from being owned and loved. "Being a toy is a lot better than being a space ranger," Woody explains. "You're *his toy*" (emphasis in original). [19]

Mr. Incredible likewise must embrace his own dependence, both physical and emotional. Trapped on the island of Chronos, at the mercy of [20]

Syndrome (Buddy's new super-persona), Mr. Incredible needs women —
his wife's superpowers and Mirage's guilty intervention—to escape. To
overpower the monster Syndrome has unleashed on the city, and to
achieve the pinnacle of the New Man model, he must also admit to his
emotional dependence on his wife and children. Initially confining them to
the safety of a bus, he confesses to Elastigirl that his need to fight the monster alone is not a typically alpha ("I work alone") sort of need but a loving
one: "I can't lose you again," he tells her. The robot/monster is defeated,
along with any vestiges of the alpha model, as the combined forces of the
Incredible family locate a new model of postfeminist strength in the family as a whole. This communal strength is not simply physical but marked
by cooperation, selflessness, and intelligence. The children learn that their
best contributions protect the others; Mr. Incredible figures out the robot/
monster's vulnerability and cleverly uses this against it.

In a parallel motif to Mr. Incredible's inability to control his strength,   21
Buddy/Syndrome finally cannot control his robot/monster; in the defeat,
he becomes the newly emasculated alpha male. But like his robot, he
learns quickly. His last attempt to injure Mr. Incredible, kidnapping his
baby Jack-Jack, strikes at Mr. Incredible's new source of strength and
value, his family. The strength of the cooperative family unit is even more
clearly displayed in this final rescue: For the shared, parental goal of saving Jack-Jack, Mr. Incredible uses his physical strength and, with her consent, the shape-shifting body of his super-wife. He throws Elastigirl into
the air, where she catches their baby and, flattening her body into a para-
chute, sails gently back to her husband and older children.

Through Lightning McQueen's many relationships with men, as well   22
as his burgeoning romance with Sally, he also learns how to care about
others, to focus on the well-being of the community, and to privilege nurture and kindness. It is Doc, not Sally, who explicitly challenges the race
car with his selfishness ("When was the last time you cared about something except yourself, hot rod?"). His reformed behavior begins with his
generous contributions to the Radiator Springs community. Not only does
he provide much-needed cash for the local economy, but he also listens
to, praises, and values the residents for their unique offerings to Radiator
Springs. He is the chosen auditor for Lizzy's reminiscing about her late
husband, contrasting the comic relief typically offered by the senile and
deaf Model T with poignancy, if not quite sadness. Repairing the town's
neon, he creates a romantic dreamscape from the past, a setting for both
courting Sally ("cruising") and, more importantly, winning her respect
with his ability to share in her value system. For this role, he is even physically transformed: He hires the body shop proprietor, Ramone, to paint
over his sponsors' stickers and his large race number, as if to remove himself almost completely from the Piston Cup world, even as he anticipates
being released from his community service and thus being able to return
to racing.

Perhaps even more than Buzz, Woody, and Mr. Incredible do, the New   23
Man McQueen shuns the remaining trappings of the alpha role, actually refusing the Piston Cup. If the first three protagonists are ultimately
qualified heroes—that is, they still retain their authority and accomplish
their various tasks, but with new values and perspectives acquired along
the way—Lightning completely and publicly refuses his former object of
desire. Early in the final race, he seems to somewhat devalue racing; his
daydreams of Sally distract him, tempting him to give up rather than to
compete. The plot, however, needs him to dominate the race so his decision
at the end will be entirely his own. His friends show up and encourage him
to succeed. This is where the other films end: The values of caring, sharing,
nurturing, and community being clearly present, the hero is at last able to
achieve, improved by having embraced those values. But Lightning, seeing
the wrecked King and remembering the words of Doc Hudson, screeches
to a stop inches before the finish line. Reversing, he approaches the King,
pushes him back on the track, and acknowledges the relative insignificance of the Piston Cup in comparison to his new and improved self. He
then declines the Dinoco corporate offer in favor of remaining faithful to
his loyal Rust-eze sponsors. Chick Hicks, the only unredeemed alpha male
at the end, celebrates his ill-gotten victory and is publicly rejected at the
end by both his fans, "the twins," and, in a sense, by the Piston Cup itself,
which slides onto the stage and hits him rudely in the side.

Conclusion

The trend of the New Man seems neither insidious nor nefarious, nor is it   24
out of step with the larger cultural movement. It is good, we believe, for
our son to be aware of the many sides of human existence, regardless of
traditional gender stereotypes. However, maintaining a critical consciousness of the many lessons taught by the cultural monolith of Disney remains
imperative. These lessons—their pedagogical aims or results—become
most immediately obvious to us as parents when we watch our son ingest
and express them, when he misunderstands and makes his own sense
of them, and when we can see ways in which his perception of reality is
shaped by them, before our eyes. Without assuming that the values of the
films are inherently evil or representative of an evil "conspiracy to undermine American youth" (Giroux 4), we are still compelled to critically
examine the texts on which our son bases many of his attitudes, behaviors,
and preferences.

Moreover, the impact of Disney, as Henry Giroux has effectively   25
argued, is tremendously more widespread than our household. Citing
Michael Eisner's 1995 "Planetized Entertainment," Giroux claims that 200
million people a year watch Disney videos or films, and in a week, 395 million watch a Disney TV show, 3.8 million subscribe to the Disney Channel,

and 810,000 make a purchase at a Disney store (19). As Benjamin Barber argued in 1995, "[T]he true tutors of our children are not schoolteachers or university professors but filmmakers, advertising executives and pop culture purveyors" (qtd. in Giroux 63). Thus we perform our "pedagogical intervention[s]" of examining Disney's power to "shap[e] national identity, gender roles, and childhood values" (Giroux 10). It remains a necessary and ongoing task, not just for concerned parents, but for all conscientious cultural critics.

WORKS CITED

Bell, Elizabeth. "Somatexts at the Disney Shop: Constructing the Pentimentos of Women's Animated Bodies." Bell, *From Mouse to Mermaid* 107–24.

Bell, Elizabeth, Lynda Haas, and Laura Sells, eds. *From Mouse to Mermaid: the Politics of Film, Gender, and Culture.* Bloomington: Indiana UP, 1995.

Card, Claudia. "Pinocchio." Bell, *From Mouse to Mermaid* 62–71.

Cars. Dir. John Lasseter. Walt Disney Pictures/Pixar Animation Studios, 2006.

Collier, Richard. "The New Man: Fact or Fad?" *Achilles Heel: The Radical Men's Magazine* 14 (1992–93). <http://www.achillesheel.freeuk.com/article14_9.html>.

Eisner, Michael. "Planetized Entertainment." *New Perspectives Quarterly* 12.4 (1995): 8.

Giroux, Henry. *The Mouse that Roared: Disney and the End of Innocence.* Oxford, Eng.: Rowman, 1999.

The Incredibles. Dir. Brad Bird. Walt Disney Pictures/Pixar Animation Studios, 2004.

Jeffords, Susan. "The Curse of Masculinity: Disney's *Beauty and the Beast*" Bell, *From Mouse to Mermaid* 161–72.

Lendrum, Rob. "Queering Super-Manhood: Superhero Masculinity, Camp, and Public Relations as a Textual Framework." *International Journal of Comic Art* 7.1 (2005): 287–303.

Palmer-Mehtan, Valerie, and Kellie Hay. "A Superhero for Gays? Gay Masculinity and Green Lantern." *Journal of American Culture* 28.4 (2005): 390–404.

Payne, David. "Bambi." Bell, *From Mouse to Mermaid* 137–47.

Schoene-Harwood, Berthold. *Writing Men: Literary Masculinities from Frankenstein to the New Man.* Columbia: Columbia UP, 2000.

Sedgwick, Eve Kosofsky. *Between Men: English Literature and Male Homosocial Desire.* New York: Columbia UP, 1985.

Toy Story. Dir. John Lasseter. Walt Disney Pictures/Pixar Animation Studios, 1995.

Wertham, Fredric. *Seduction of the Innocent.* New York: Reinhart, 1954.

Yabroff, Jennie. "Betas Rule." *Newsweek* 4 June 2007: 64–65.

■ ■ ■

Reading as a Writer: Analyzing Rhetorical Choices

1. While the topic of this essay comes from popular culture, the language is quite scholarly. Circle any words that might be new to you, and see what you can discern about their meaning from the context, and then look them up. For example, you might want to be sure you know the meaning of "bildungsroman" (para. 1), "patriarchal" (para. 5), "homosocial" (para. 16), and "pedagogical" (para. 24), among others. How are these terms important to the authors' argument?

2. You might have some fun applying the authors' argument to Pixar films produced after 2008 or to other films made for children. In pairs or groups, choose a film to use as a test case, and apply the authors' method of using specific examples from the film to analyze whether the lead character's gender role changes over the course of the film in the way they claim is standard, at least for Pixar films. What happens to the roles of leading female characters? What conclusions do you draw?

Writing as a Reader: Entering the Conversation of Ideas

1. Building on insights from Gillam and Wooden and also Allan G. Johnson (Chapter 14), compose an analysis of a film not mentioned in this reading that you believe raises interesting issues about gender roles. Be sure to use description and analysis of specific examples in the film as you make an argument about the significance of gender representations in the film.

2. How do Gillam and Wooden's ideas about changing attitudes toward masculinity intersect with Matthew Immergut's insights about "manscaping" (Chapter 14)? Write an essay in which you bring together ideas from these readings in order to make a point about changing—or unchanging— concepts of masculinity in the United States.

BELL HOOKS

Seeing and Making Culture: Representing the Poor

bell hooks is the pen name of Gloria Watkins, a cultural critic, scholar, and prolific writer. She has a wide range of intellectual interests, and her many books on race, gender, politics, and popular culture are taught frequently in both undergraduate and graduate courses. She is well-known for her collaborations with prominent scholars such as Cornel West on projects related to activism and spirituality. hooks also co-edited a collection of essays on the aftermath of Hurricane Katrina, *What Lies Beneath: Katrina, Race, and the State of the Nation* (2007). This selection was taken from *Outlaw Culture: Resisting Representations* (1994) and focuses on images of poverty in popular culture and what they tell us about "our" assumptions about "the poor."

Despite bell hooks's publishing success, some scholars have criticized her for refusing to follow the "rules" of academic publishing. For example, although she quotes and engages with numerous scholars in her writing, she does not use footnotes in her work because she believes many readers find them off-putting, and she is interested in making her ideas accessible to readers who are not necessarily academics. As you read, you might pay attention to the many different strategies she uses as a writer to invite readers to think about some challenging ideas—what Americans really think about poverty. Where does she use personal experiences to illustrate her arguments? How does she introduce other scholars into the conversation of her essay? You might mark some of the challenging phrases in this piece, such as some of the quotations by Cornel West in paragraph 1 or anthropologist Carol Stack's ideas about the "ethic of liberal individual-ism" (para. 11), and work with your peers to make sure you understand these terms, looking up information, if necessary. Noticing how exactly hooks moves between personal examples and these scholarly ones in her sentences can help you decide how to make these moves in your own writing.

hooks also cites specific popular culture representations of poverty in this essay, such as *Pretty Woman* and *Menace II Society*. While hooks's essay is as pertinent now as when she published it in 1994, these references are now a bit dated. As you read this piece, consider more recent represen-tations of poverty in television, film, or even news coverage (such as the coverage of Hurricane Katrina), and be ready to discuss the ways hooks's ideas help you make sense of those images and the stories that accom-pany them. What do the examples you come up with tell us about what we believe about poverty and those who are poor?

In this essay, hooks is interested in both illuminating what she consid-ers to be problematic in attitudes toward poverty in the United States, and in proposing solutions. Pay close attention to her closing paragraphs and assess what you think the solutions she suggests for developing less punishing attitudes toward poverty among people who are poor and those who are not. What values can poverty teach us all?

Cultural critics rarely talk about the poor. Most of us use words such as "underclass" or "economically disenfranchised" when we speak about being poor. Poverty has not become one of the new hot topics of radical discourse. When contemporary Left intellectuals talk about capitalism, few if any attempts are made to relate that discourse to the reality of being poor in America. In his collection of essays *Prophetic Thought in Post-mod-ern Times*, black philosopher Cornel West includes a piece entitled "The Black Underclass and Black Philosophers" wherein he suggests that black intellectuals within the "professional-managerial class in U.S. advanced capitalist society" must "engage in a kind of critical self-inventory, a his-torical situating and positioning of ourselves as persons who reflect on the situation of those more disadvantaged than us even though we may have relatives and friends in the black underclass." West does not speak of pov-erty or being poor in his essay. And I can remember once in conversation with him referring to my having come from a "poor" background; he cor-rected me and stated that my family was "working class." I told him that technically we *were* working class, because my father worked as a janitor at the post office, however the fact that there were seven children in our family meant that we often faced economic hardship in ways that made us children at least think of ourselves as poor. Indeed, in the segregated world of our small Kentucky town, we were all raised to think in terms of the haves and the have-nots, rather than in terms of class. We acknowledged the existence of four groups: the poor, who were destitute; the working folks, who were poor because they made just enough to make ends meet;

those who worked and had extra money; and the rich. Even though our family was among the working folks, the economic struggle to make ends meet for such a large family always gave us a sense that there was not enough money to take care of the basics. In our house, water was a luxury and using too much could be a cause for punishment. We never talked about being poor. As children we knew we were not supposed to see ourselves as poor but we felt poor.

I began to *see* myself as poor when I went away to college. I never had 2 any money. When I told my parents that I had scholarships and loans to attend Stanford University, they wanted to know how I would pay for getting there, for buying books, for emergencies. We were not poor, but there was no money for what was perceived to be an individualistic indulgent desire; there were cheaper colleges closer to family. When I went to college and could not afford to come home during breaks, I frequently spent my holidays with the black women who cleaned in the dormitories. Their world was my world. They, more than other folks at Stanford, knew where I was coming from. They supported and affirmed my efforts to be educated, to move past and beyond the world they lived in, the world I was coming from.

To this day, even though I am a well-paid member of what West calls 3 the academic "professional-managerial class," in everyday life, outside the classroom, I rarely think of myself in relation to class. I mainly think about the world in terms of who has money to spend and who does not. Like many technically middle-class folks who are connected in economic responsibility to kinship structures where they provide varying material support for others, the issue is always one of money. Many middle-class black folks have no money because they regularly distribute their earnings among a larger kinship group where folks are poor and destitute, where elder parents and relatives who once were working class have retired and fallen into poverty.

Poverty was no disgrace in our household. We were socialized early 4 on, by grandparents and parents, to assume that nobody's value could be measured by material standards. Value was connected to integrity, to being honest and hardworking. One could be hardworking and still be poor. My mother's mother Baba, who did not read or write, taught us—against the wishes of our parents—that it was better to be poor than to compromise one's dignity, that it was better to be poor than to allow another person to assert power over you in ways that were dehumanizing or cruel.

I went to college believing there was no connection between poverty 5 and personal integrity. Entering a world of class privilege which compelled me to think critically about my economic background, I was shocked by representations of the poor learned in classrooms, as well as by the comments of professors and peers that painted an entirely different picture. They almost always portrayed the poor as shiftless, mindless, lazy, dishonest, and unworthy. Students in the dormitory were quick to assume that anything missing had been taken by the black and Filipina women who worked there. Although I went through many periods of shame about my economic background (even before I educated myself for critical consciousness about class by reading and studying Marx, Gramsci, Memmi, and the like), I contested stereotypical negative representations of poverty. I was especially disturbed by the assumption that the poor were without values. Indeed one crucial value that I had learned from Baba, my grandmother, and other family members was not to believe that "schooling made you smart." One could have degrees and still not be intelligent or honest. I had been taught in a culture of poverty to be intelligent, honest, to work hard, and always to be a person of my word. I had been taught to stand up for what I believed was right, to be brave and courageous. These lessons were the foundation that made it possible for me to succeed, to become the writer I always wanted to be, and to make a living in my job as an academic. They were taught to me by the poor, the disenfranchised, the underclass.

Those lessons were reinforced by liberatory religious traditions 6 that affirmed identification with the poor. Taught to believe that poverty could be the breeding ground of moral integrity, of a recognition of the significance of communion, of sharing resources with others in the black church, I was prepared to embrace the teachings of liberatory theology, which emphasized solidarity with the poor. That solidarity was meant to be expressed not simply through charity, the sharing of privilege, but in the assertion of one's power to change the world so that the poor would have their needs met, would have access to resources, would have justice and beauty in their lives.

Contemporary popular culture in the United States rarely represents 7 the poor in ways that display integrity and dignity. Instead, the poor are portrayed through negative stereotypes. When they are lazy and dishonest, they are consumed with longing to be rich, a longing so intense that it renders them dysfunctional. Willing to commit all manner of dehumanizing and brutal acts in the name of material gain, the poor are portrayed as seeing themselves as always and only worthless. Worth is gained only by means of material success.

Television shows and films bring the message home that no one can 8 truly feel good about themselves if they are poor. In television sitcoms the working poor are shown to have a healthy measure of self-contempt; they dish it out to one another with a wit and humor that we can all enjoy, irrespective of our class. Yet it is clear that humor masks the longing to change their lot, the desire to "move on up" expressed in the theme song of the sitcom *The Jeffersons*. Films which portray the rags-to-riches tale continue to have major box-office appeal. Most contemporary films portraying black folks—*Harlem Nights, Boomerang, Menace II Society*, to name only a few—have as their primary theme the lust of the poor for material plenty and their willingness to do anything to satisfy that lust. *Pretty*

Woman is a perfect example of a film that made huge sums of money portraying the poor in this light. Consumed and enjoyed by audiences of all
races and classes, it highlights the drama of the benevolent, ruling-class
person (in this case a white man, played by Richard Gere) willingly sharing his resources with a poor white prostitute (played by Julia Roberts).
Indeed, many films and television shows portray the ruling class as generous, eager to share, as unattached to their wealth in their interactions with
folks who are not materially privileged. These images contrast with the
opportunistic avaricious longings of the poor.

Socialized by film and television to identify with the attitudes and val-   9
ues of privileged classes in this society, many people who are poor, or a few
paychecks away from poverty, internalize fear and contempt for those who
are poor. When materially deprived teenagers kill for tennis shoes or jackets they are not doing so just because they like these items so much. They
also hope to escape the stigma of their class by appearing to have the trappings of more privileged classes. Poverty, in their minds and in our society
as a whole, is seen as synonymous with depravity, lack, and worthlessness.
No one wants to be identified as poor. Teaching literature by African American women writers at a major urban state university to predominantly
black students from poor and working-class families, I was bombarded
by their questioning as to why the poor black women who were abused in
families in the novels we read did not "just leave." It was amazing to me
that these students, many of whom were from materially disadvantaged
backgrounds, had no realistic sense about the economics of housing or
jobs in this society. When I asked that we identify our class backgrounds,
only one student—a young single parent—was willing to identify herself
as poor. We talked later about the reality that although she was not the
only poor person in the class, no one else wanted to identify with being
poor for fear this stigma would mark them, shame them in ways that
would go beyond our class. Fear of shame-based humiliation is a primary
factor leading no one to want to identify themselves as poor. I talked with
young black women receiving state aid, who have not worked in years,
about the issue of representation. They all agree that they do not want to
be identified as poor. In their apartments they have the material posses-
sions that indicate success (a VCR, a color television), even if it means that
they do without necessities and plunge into debt to buy these items. Their
self-esteem is linked to not being seen as poor.

If to be poor in this society is everywhere represented in the language   10
we use to talk about the poor, in the mass media, as synonymous with
being nothing, then it is understandable that the poor learn to be nihilistic.
Society is telling them that poverty and nihilism are one and the same. If
they cannot escape poverty, then they have no choice but to drown in the
image of a life that is valueless. When intellectuals, journalists, or politicians speak about nihilism and the despair of the underclass, they do
not link those states to representations of poverty in the mass media. And
rarely do they suggest by their rhetoric that one can lead a meaningful,

contented, and fulfilled life if one *is* poor. No one talks about our individual and collective accountability to the poor, a responsibility that begins with the politics of representation.

When white female anthropologist Carol Stack looked critically at the *11* lives of black poor people more than twenty years ago and wrote her book *The Culture of Poverty,* she found a value system among them which emphasized the sharing of resources. That value system has long been eroded in most communities by an ethic of liberal individualism, which affirms that it is morally acceptable not to share. The mass media has been the primary teacher bringing into our lives and our homes the logic of liberal individualism, the idea that you make it by the privatized hoarding of resources, not by sharing them. Of course, liberal individualism works best for the privileged classes. But it has worsened the lot of the poor who once depended on an ethic of communalism to provide affirmation, aid, and support.

To change the devastating impact of poverty on the lives of masses of *12* folks in our society we must change the way resources and wealth are distributed. But we must also change the way the poor are represented. Since many folks will be poor for a long time before those changes are put in place that address their economic needs, it is crucial to construct habits of seeing and being that restore an oppositional value system affirming that one can live a life of dignity and integrity in the midst of poverty. It is precisely this dignity Jonathan Freedman seeks to convey in his book *From Cradle to Grave: The Human Face of Poverty in America,* even though he does not critique capitalism or call for major changes in the distribution of wealth and resources. Yet any efforts to change the face of poverty in the United States must link a shift in representation to a demand for the redistribution of wealth and resources.

Progressive intellectuals from privileged classes who are themselves *13* obsessed with gaining material wealth are uncomfortable with the insistence that one can be poor, yet lead a rich and meaningful life. They fear that any suggestion that poverty is acceptable may lead those who have to feel no accountability toward those who have not, even though it is unclear how they reconcile their pursuit with concern for and accountability towards the poor. Their conservative counterparts, who did much to put in place a system of representation that dehumanized the poor, fear that if poverty is seen as having no relation to value, the poor will not passively assume their role as exploited workers. That fear is masked by their insistence that the poor will not seek to work if poverty is deemed acceptable, and that the rest of us will have to support them. (Note the embedded assumption that to be poor means that one is not hardworking.) Of course, there are many more poor women and men refusing menial labor in low-paid jobs than ever before. This refusal is not rooted in laziness but in the assumption that it is not worth it to work a job where one is systematically dehumanized or exploited only to remain poor. Despite these individuals, the vast majority of poor people in our society want to work, even when jobs do not mean that they leave the ranks of the poor.

Witnessing that individuals can be poor and lead meaningful lives, I *14*
understand intimately the damage that has been done to the poor by a dehumanizing system of representation. I see the difference in self-esteem
between my grandparents' and parents' generations and that of my siblings, relatives, friends, and acquaintances who are poor, who suffer from
a deep-seated, crippling lack of self-esteem. Ironically, despite the presence
of more opportunity than that available to an older generation, low self-
esteem makes it impossible for this younger generation to move forward
even as it also makes their lives psychically unbearable. That psychic pain
is most often relieved by some form of substance abuse. But to change the
face of poverty so that it becomes, once again, a site for the formation of
values, of dignity and integrity, as any other class positionality in this society, we would need to intervene in existing systems of representation.

Linking this progressive change to radical/revolutionary political *15*
movements (such as eco-feminism, for example) that urge all of us to live
simply could also establish a point of connection and constructive interaction. The poor have many resources and skills for living. Those folks who
are interested in sharing individual plenty as well as working politically
for redistribution of wealth can work in conjunction with individuals who
are materially disadvantaged to achieve this end. Material plenty is only
one resource. Literacy skills are another. It would be exciting to see unemployed folks who lack reading and writing skills have available to them
community-based literacy programs. Progressive literacy programs connected to education for critical consciousness could use popular movies
as a base to begin learning and discussion. Theaters all across the United
States that are not used in the day could be sites for this kind of program
where college students and professors could share skills. Since many
individuals who are poor, disadvantaged, or destitute are *already* literate, reading groups could be formed to educate for critical consciousness,
to help folks rethink how they can organize life both to live well in poverty and to move out of such circumstances. Many of the young women I
encounter—black and white—who are poor and receiving state aid (and
some of whom are students or would-be students) are intelligent, critical
thinkers struggling to transform their circumstances. They are eager to
work with folks who can offer guidance, know-how, concrete strategies.
Freedman concludes his book with the reminder that

> It takes money, organization, and laws to maintain a social structure but
> none of it works if there are not opportunities for people to meet and help
> each other along the way. Social responsibility comes down to something
> simple—the ability to respond.

Constructively changing ways the poor are represented in every aspect of *16*
life is one progressive intervention that can challenge everyone to look at
the face of poverty and not turn away.

■ ■ ■

Reading as a Writer: Analyzing Rhetorical Choices

1. bell hooks includes personal anecdotes in this selection. Use a pen or high-lighter to mark all the places where she makes use of personal experiences, and discuss with your classmates the relationship you see between these personal experiences and the larger point she is making about perceptions of poverty in the United States. What do you notice about the structure of this essay? What conclusions can you draw about effective strategies for using personal experiences in scholarly writing?

2. In paragraphs 6, 7, and 8, hooks lays out varying cultural attitudes about the relationship between poverty and personal integrity. What do you notice about the order of the ideas in these paragraphs, and the examples she offers? Discuss the way she structures her argument here, and consider how some more recent examples from popular culture would fit with the claims she makes in this section. How do these ideas relate to the solutions she proposes in her final paragraphs?

Writing as a Reader: Entering the Conversation of Ideas

1. hooks, like Jonathan Kozol (Chapter 12), is committed to understanding the many subtle ways we learn who "counts" in our society and who doesn't. Both writers draw on examples of school dynamics that teach students far more than what is in their textbooks. Compose an essay that places these authors in conversation about the ways school settings can teach students, perhaps inadvertently, about who "counts," by analyzing some specific school examples in each text. What connections do you see, and what can you conclude? If you like, describe and analyze some specific examples from your own classroom or campus experiences to help establish your point.

2. Both hooks and Noël Sturgeon (Chapter 16) are concerned with the ways popular culture often reinforces stereotypes, whether those stereotypes are about poverty or attitudes toward "nature." Using specific examples from current popular culture (books, television, movies, etc.), write an essay in which you draw on insights from both authors in order to analyze the way your examples reinforce common stereotypes, counteract them, or (as is often the case), do both. What do you conclude?

JEAN KILBOURNE

"Two Ways a Woman Can Get Hurt": Advertising and Violence

Jean Kilbourne, EdD, is an award-winning author and educator who is best known for her lively campus lectures on the effects of media images on young people. Her academic interests stem from personal experience. Although Kilbourne was a superb student when she came of age in the 1960s, she found she was rewarded more for her looks than her intelligence. Later, after she began working in journalism and education, she noticed the absurd arguments that advertisements often make, many of them insulting to women's intelligence and self-esteem. Once she found her personal and professional interests intersecting, Kilbourne began collecting and analyzing advertisements, eventually shaping them into a lecture series and then a film titled *Killing Us Softly: Advertising's Image of Women* (1979). This film, its three subsequent versions, and other films Kilbourne has produced on anorexia and on tobacco and alcohol addiction, are taught frequently in college classes today. Kilbourne has also published many articles and several books on these topics, including the book from which this essay is excerpted, *Deadly Persuasion: Why Women and Girls Must Fight the Addictive Power of Advertising* (1999).

The first thing you may notice about Kilbourne's essay is that it is filled with advertising images. Before you read, flip through the essay to see if you can get a sense of Kilbourne's argument simply from the advertisements she includes. As you read, keep returning to these images, testing them against Kilbourne's argument and the information she includes from other scholars about violence in our culture (particularly sexualized violence) and the power of the media. Kilbourne's is an important voice among the many media critics who have discussed the ways advertising images normalize—and even make appealing—sexual and violent situations that most often threaten women and children. As you read, pay close attention to the connections Kilbourne makes between the media and social problems. Note the passages you find most and least convincing, and ask yourself why. Getting in the habit of evaluating evidence this way will help you immeasurably when you decide on the kinds of evidence you want to include in your own writing.

Kilbourne is sometimes criticized for being too selective in her choice of images and evidence and too narrow in her analysis. Throughout the essay, you will hear her addressing her critics, anticipating claims that she is simply reading too much into these images or taking advertising too seriously. Often she provides more than one interpretation of an image, for example, saying about the subject of one advertisement, "I suppose this could be a woman awaiting her lover, but it could as easily be a girl being preyed upon" (para. 33). Note the way she builds her claims about images on the research of experts in the fields of anthropology, addiction, gendered violence, and media criticism, and also the way she sites newspaper reports of crimes and trends she finds so dangerous.

Given our visually rich media culture, you are likely to find many familiar ideas and images in Kilbourne's essay, and you also are likely to find yourself strongly agreeing or disagreeing—or perhaps both—with her as she builds her case about the "deadly" power of the advertising industry. Even if you do not agree with her on every point, Kilbourne's strategy of analyzing the ways advertising makes dangerous behaviors seem "normal" and even appealing is one all consumers can use to make sense of marketing claims and popular culture.

■ ■ ■

Two Ways A Woman Can Get Hurt.

(Heartbreaker)

(Soap and water shave)

Skintimate® Shave Gel Ultra Protection formula contains 75% moisturizers, including vitamin E, to protect your legs from nicks, cuts and razor burn. So while guys may continue to be a pain, shaving most definitely won't.

SKINTIMATE® SHAVE GEL.
LOVE YOUR LEGS

© 1997 S.C. Johnson & Son, Inc. All rights reserved. www.skintimate.com

S ex in advertising is more about 1 disconnection and distance than connection and closeness. It is also more often about power than passion, about violence than violins. The main goal, as in pornography, is usually power over another, either by the physical dominance or preferred status of men or what is seen as the exploitative power of female beauty and female sexuality. Men conquer and women ensnare, always with the essential aid of a product. The woman is rewarded for her sexuality by the man's wealth, as in an ad for Cigarette boats in which the woman says, while lying in a man's embrace clearly after sex, "Does this mean I get a ride in your Cigarette?"

Sex in advertising is pornographic because it dehumanizes and objec- 2 tifies people, especially women, and because it fetishizes products, imbues them with an erotic charge—which dooms us to disappointment since products never can fulfill our sexual desires or meet our emotional needs. The poses and postures of advertising are often borrowed from pornography, as are many of the themes, such as bondage, sadomasochism, and

The right tie can make even the most casual evening more memorable

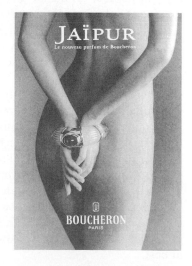

JAÏPUR
Le nouveau parfum de Boucheron

BOUCHERON
PARIS

the sexual exploitation of children. When a beer ad uses the image of a man licking the high-heeled boot of a woman clad in leather, when bondage is used to sell neckties in *The New York Times,* perfume in *The New Yorker,* and watches on city buses, and when a college magazine promotes an S&M Ball, pornography can be considered mainstream.

Most of us know all this by now and I suppose some consider it kinky   3 good fun. Pornography is more dangerously mainstream when its glorification of rape and violence shows up in mass media, in films and television shows, in comedy and music videos, and in advertising. Male violence is subtly encouraged by ads that encourage men to be forceful and dominant, and to value sexual intimacy more than emotional intimacy. "Do you want to be the one she tells her deep, dark secrets to?" asks a three-page ad for men's cologne. "Or do you want to be her deep, dark secret?" The last page advises

men, "Don't be such a good boy." There are two identical women looking adoringly at the man in the ad, but he isn't looking at either one of them. Just what is the deep, dark secret? That he's sleeping with both of them? Clearly the way to get beautiful women is to ignore them, perhaps mistreat them.

"Two ways a woman can get hurt,"   4 says an ad for shaving gel, featuring a razor and a photo of a handsome man. My first thought is that the man is a batterer or date rapist, but the ad informs us that he is merely a "heartbreaker." The gel will protect the woman so that "while guys may continue to be a pain, shaving most definitely won't." Desirable men are painful—heartbreakers at best.

Wouldn't it be wonderful if, realizing the importance of relationships 5 in all of our lives, we could seek to learn relational skills from women and to help men develop these strengths in themselves? In fact, we so often do the opposite. The popular culture usually trivializes these abilities in women, mocks men who have real intimacy with women (it is almost always married men in ads and cartoons who are jerks), and idealizes a

template for relationships between men and women that is a recipe for disaster: a template that views sex as more important than anything else, that ridicules men who are not in control of their women (who are "pussy-whipped"), and that disparages fidelity and commitment (except, of course, to brand names).

Indeed the very worst kind of 6 man for a woman to be in an intimate relationship with, often a truly dangerous man, is the one considered most sexy and desirable in the popular culture. And the men capable of real intimacy (the ones we tell our deep, dark secrets to) constantly have their very masculinity impugned. Advertising often

encourages women to be attracted to hostile and indifferent men while encouraging boys to become these men. This is especially dangerous for those of us who have suffered from "condemned isolation" in childhood: Like heat-seeking missiles, we rush inevitably to mutual destruction.

Men are also encouraged to never take no for an answer. Ad after ad 7 implies that girls and women don't really mean "no" when they say it, that women are only teasing when they resist men's advances. "NO" says an ad showing a man leaning over a woman against a wall. Is she screaming or laughing? Oh, it's an ad for deodorant and the second word, in very small print, is "sweat." Sometimes it's "all in good fun," as in the ad for Possession shirts and shorts featuring a man ripping the clothes off a woman who seems to be having a good time.

And sometimes it is more sinister. A perfume ad running in several 8 teen magazines features a very young woman, with eyes blackened by makeup or perhaps something else, and the copy, "Apply generously to your neck so he can smell the scent as you shake your head 'no.'" In other words, he'll understand that you don't really mean it and he can respond to the scent like any other animal.

Sometimes there seems to be no question but that a man should force a 9 woman to have sex. A chilling newspaper ad for a bar in Georgetown features a closeup of a cocktail and the headline, "If your date won't listen to reason, try a Velvet Hammer." A vodka ad pictures a wolf hiding in a flock of sheep, a hideous grin on its face. We all know what wolves do to sheep. A campaign for Bacardi Black rum features shadowy figures almost obliterated by darkness and captions such as "Some people embrace the night because the rules of the day do not apply." What it doesn't say is that people who are above the rules do enormous harm to other people, as well as to themselves.

Sip exotic cocktails. dine and dance to Swing Era music at Georgetown's top nightspot. 1232 36th St., NW. Reservations, call 342-0009. Free valet parking. Jackets required.

These ads are particu- *10* larly troublesome, given that between one-third and three-quarters of all cases of sexual assault involve alcohol consumption by the perpetrator, the victim, or both.[1] "Make strangers your friends, and your friends a lot stranger," says one of the ads in a Cuervo campaign that uses colorful cartoon beasts and emphasizes heavy drinking. This ad is especially disturbing when we consider the role of alcohol in date rape, as is another ad in the series that says, "The night began with a bottle of Cuervo and ended with a vow of silence." Over half of all reported rapes on college campuses occur when either the victim or the assailant has been drinking.[2] Alcohol's role has different meaning for men and women, however. If a man is drunk when he commits a rape, he is considered less responsible. If a woman is drunk (or has had a drink or two or simply met the man in a bar), she is considered more responsible.

In general, females are still held responsible and hold each other *11* responsible when sex goes wrong—when they become pregnant or are the victims of rape and sexual assault or cause a scandal. Constantly exhorted to be sexy and attractive, they discover when assaulted that that very sexiness is evidence of their guilt, their lack of "innocence." Sometimes the ads play on this by "warning" women of what might happen if they use the product. "Wear it but beware it," says a perfume ad. Beware what exactly? Victoria's Secret tempts young women with blatantly sexual ads promising that their lingerie will make them irresistible. Yet when a young woman accused William Kennedy Smith of raping her, the fact that she wore Victoria's Secret panties was used against her as an indication of her immorality. A jury acquitted Smith, whose alleged history of violence against women was not permitted to be introduced at trial.

It is sadly not surprising that the jury was composed mostly of women. *12* Women are especially cruel judges of other women's sexual behavior, mostly because we are so desperate to believe we are in control of what happens to us. It is too frightening to face the fact that male violence against women is irrational and commonplace. It is reassuring to believe that we can avoid it by being good girls, avoiding dark places, staying out of bars, dressing "innocently." An ad featuring two young women talking intimately at a coffee shop says, "Carla and Rachel considered themselves

---

[1] Wilsnack, Plaud, Wilsnack, and Klassen, 1997, 262.
[2] Abbey, Ross, and McDuffie, 1991. Also Martin, 1992, 230–37.

open-minded and non-judgmental people. Although they did agree Brenda was a tramp." These terrible judgments from other women are an important part of what keeps all women in line.

If indifference in a man is sexy, then violence is sometimes downright   13
erotic. Not surprisingly, this attitude too shows up in advertising. "Push my buttons," says a young woman, "I'm looking for a man who can totally floor me." Her vulnerability is underscored by the fact that she is in an elevator, often a dangerous place for women. She is young, she is submissive (her eyes are downcast), she is in a dangerous place, and she is dressed provocatively. And she is literally asking for it.

"Wear it out and make it scream,"   14
says a jeans ad portraying a man sliding his hands under a woman's transparent blouse. This could be a seduction, but it could as easily be an attack. Although the ad that ran in the Czech version of *Elle* portraying three men attacking a woman seems unambiguous, the terrifying image is being used to sell jeans *to women*. So someone must think that women would find this image compelling or attractive. Why would we? Perhaps it is simply designed to get our attention, by shocking us and by arousing unconscious anxiety. Or perhaps the intent is more subtle and it is designed to play into the

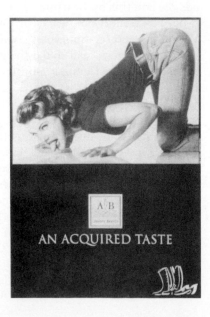

fantasies of domination and even rape that some women use in order to maintain an illusion of being in control (we are the ones having the fantasies, after all, we are the directors).

A camera ad features a woman's torso *15* wrapped in plastic, her hands tied behind her back. A smiling woman in a lipstick ad has a padlocked chain around her neck. An ad for MTV shows a vulnerable young woman, her breasts exposed, and the simple copy "Bitch." A perfume ad features a man shadowboxing with what seems to be a woman.

Sometimes women are shown dead or in *16* the process of being killed. "Great hair never dies," says an ad featuring a female corpse lying on a bed, her breasts exposed. An ad in the Italian version of *Vogue* shows a man aiming a gun at a nude woman wrapped in plastic, a leather briefcase covering her face. And an ad for Bitch skateboards, for God's sake, shows a cartoon version of a similar scene, this time clearly targeting young people. We believe we are not affected by these images, but most of us experience visceral shock when we pay conscious attention to them. Could they be any less shocking to us on an unconscious level?

Most of us become numb to these images, just as we become numb *17* to the daily litany in the news of women being raped, battered, and

ÉGOÏSTE
"PLATINUM"

CHANEL

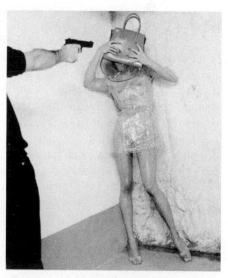

La Borsa è la Vita

killed. According to former surgeon general Antonia Novello, battery is the single greatest cause of injury to women in America, more common than automobile accidents, muggings, and stranger rapes combined, and more than one-third of women slain in this country die at the hands of husbands or boyfriends.[3] Throughout the world, the biggest problem for most women is simply surviving at home. The Global Report on Women's Human Rights concluded that "domestic violence is a leading cause of female

bitch skateboards

injury in almost every country in the world and is typically ignored by the state or only erratically punished."[4] Although usually numb to these facts on a conscious level, most women live in a state of subliminal terror, a state that, according to Mary Daly, keeps us divided both from each other and from our most passionate, powerful, and creative selves.[5]

Ads don't directly cause violence, of course. But the violent images *18* contribute to the state of terror. And objectification and disconnection create a climate in which there is widespread and increasing violence. Turning a human being into a thing, an object, is almost always the first step toward justifying violence against that person. It is very difficult, perhaps impossible, to be violent to someone we think of as an equal, someone we have empathy with, but it is very easy to abuse a thing. We see this with racism, with homophobia. The person becomes an object and violence is inevitable. This step is already taken with women. The violence, the abuse, is partly the chilling but logical result of the objectification.

An editorial in *Advertising Age* suggests that even some advertisers are *19* concerned about this: "Clearly it's time to wipe out sexism in beer ads; for the brewers and their agencies to wake up and join the rest of America in realizing that sexism, sexual harassment, and the cultural portrayal of women in advertising are inextricably linked."[6] Alas, this editorial was written in 1991 and nothing has changed.

It is this link with violence that makes the objectification of women *20* a more serious issue than the objectification of men. Our economic system constantly requires the development of new markets. Not surprisingly, men's bodies are the latest territory to be exploited. Although we are growing more used to it, in the beginning the male sex object came as a surprise. In 1994 a "gender bender" television commercial in which a bevy of

[3]Novello, 1991. Also Blumenthal, 1995.
[4]Wright, 1995, A2.
[5]Weil, 1999, 21.
[6]Brewers can help fight sexism, 1991, 28.

women office workers gather to watch a construction worker doff his shirt to quaff a Diet Coke led to so much hoopla that you'd have thought women were mugging men on Madison Avenue.[7]

There is no question that men are used as sex objects in ads now as *21* never before. We often see nude women with fully clothed men in ads (as in art), but the reverse was unheard of, until recently. These days some ads do feature clothed and often aggressive women with nude men. And women sometimes blatantly objectify men, as in the Metroliner ad that says, " 'She's reading Nietzsche,' Harris noted to himself as he walked towards the café car for a glass of cabernet. And as he passed her seat, Maureen looked up from her book and thought, 'Nice buns.' "

Although these ads are often funny, it is never a good thing for human *22* beings to be objectified. However, there is a world of difference between

the objectification of men and that of women. The most important difference is that there is no danger for most men, whereas objectified women are always at risk. In the Diet Coke ad, for instance, the women are physically separated from the shirtless man. He is the one in control. His body is powerful, not passive. Imagine a true role reversal of this ad: A group of businessmen gather to leer at a beautiful woman worker on her break, who removes her shirt before drinking her Diet Coke. This scene would be frightening, not funny, as the Diet Coke ad is. And why is the Diet Coke ad funny? Because we know it doesn't describe any truth. However, the

ads featuring images of male violence against women do describe a truth, a truth we are all aware of, on one level or another.

When power is unequal, when one group is oppressed and discrimi- *23* nated against *as a group*, when there is a context of systemic and historical oppression, stereotypes and prejudice have different weight and meaning. As Anna Quindlen said, writing about "reverse racism": "Hatred by the powerful, the majority, has a different weight—and often very different effects—than hatred by the powerless, the minority."[8] When men objectify women, they do so in a cultural context in which women are constantly objectified and in which there are consequences—from economic discrimination to violence—to that objectification.

For men, though, there are no such consequences. Men's bodies *24* are not routinely judged and invaded. Men are not likely to be raped, harassed, or beaten (that is to say, men presumed to be heterosexual

[7]Kilbourne, 1994, F13.
[8]Quindlen, 1992, E17.

are not, and very few men are abused in these ways by women). How many men are frightened to be alone with a woman in an elevator? How many men cross the street when a group of women approach? Jackson Katz, who writes and lectures on male violence, often begins his workshops by asking men to describe the things they do every day to protect themselves from sexual assault. The men are surprised, puzzled, sometimes amused by the question. The women understand the question easily and have no trouble at all coming up with a list of responses. We don't list our full names in the phone directory or on our mailboxes, we try not to be alone after dark, we carry our keys in our hands when we approach our cars, we always look in the back seat before we get in, we are wary of elevators and doorways and bushes, we carry pepper sprays, whistles, Mace.

Nonetheless, the rate of sexual assault in the United States is the high- 25 est of any industrialized nation in the world.[9] According to a 1998 study by the federal government, one in five of us has been the victim of rape or attempted rape, most often before our seventeenth birthday.[10] And more than half of us have been physically assaulted, most often by the men we live with. In fact, three of four women in the study who responded that they had been raped or assaulted as adults said the perpetrator was a current or former husband, a cohabiting partner, or a date. The article reporting the results of this study was buried on page twenty-three of my local newspaper, while the front page dealt with a long story about the New England Patriots football team.

A few summers ago, a Diet Pepsi commercial featured Cindy Craw- 26 ford being ogled by two boys (they seemed to be about twelve years old) as she got out of her car and bought a Pepsi from a machine. The boys made very suggestive comments, which in the end turned out to be about the Pepsi's can rather than Ms. Crawford's. There was no outcry: The boys' behavior was acceptable and ordinary enough for a soft-drink commercial.

Again, let us imagine the reverse: a sexy man gets out of a car in the 27 countryside and two preteen girls make suggestive comments, seemingly about his body, especially his buns. We would fear for them and rightly so. But the boys already have the right to ogle, to view women's bodies as property to be looked at, commented on, touched, perhaps eventually hit and raped. The boys have also learned that men ogle primarily to impress other men (and to affirm their heterosexuality). If anyone is in potential danger in this ad, it is the woman (regardless of the age of the boys). Men are not seen as *property* in this way by women. Indeed if a woman does whistle at a man or touches his body or even makes direct eye contact, it is still *she* who is at risk and the man who has the power.

[9]Blumenthal, 1995, 2.
[10]Tjaden and Thoennes, 1998.

"I always lower my eyes to see if a man is worth following," says the 28 woman in an ad for men's pants. Although the ad is offensive to everyone, the woman is endangering only herself.

"Where women are women and men are roadkill," says an ad for motor- 29 cycle clothing featuring an angry-looking African-American woman. Women

are sometimes hostile and angry in ads these days, especially women of color who are often seen as angrier and more threatening than white women. But, regardless of color, we all know that women are far more likely than men to end up as roadkill—and, when it happens, they are blamed for being on the road in the first place.

Even little girls are sometimes 30 held responsible for the violence against them. In 1990 a male Canadian judge accused a three-year-old girl of being "sexually aggressive" and suspended the sentence of her molester, who was then free to return to his job of babysitter.[11] The deeply held belief that all women, regardless of age, are really temptresses in disguise, nymphets, sexually insatiable and seductive, conveniently transfers all blame and responsibility onto women.

All women are vulnerable in a culture in which there is such wide- 31 spread objectification of women's bodies, such glorification of disconnection, so much violence against women, and such blaming of the victim.

When everything and everyone is sexualized, it is the powerless who are most at risk. Young girls, of course, are especially vulnerable. In the past twenty years or so, there have been several trends in fashion and advertising that could be seen as cultural reactions to the women's movement, as perhaps unconscious fear of female power. One has been the obsession with thinness. Another has been an increase in images of violence against women. Most disturbing has been the increasing sexualization of children, especially girls. Sometimes the little girl is made up and seductively posed. Sometimes the language is suggestive. "Very cherry," says

[11]Two men and a baby, 1990, 10.

the ad featuring a sexy little African-American girl who is wearing a dress with cherries all over it. A shocking ad in a gun magazine features a smiling little girl, a toddler, in a bathing suit that is tugged up suggestively in the rear.[12] The copy beneath the photo says, "short BUTTS from FLEMING FIRE-ARMS." Other times girls are juxtaposed with grown women, as in the ad for underpants that says "You already know the feeling."

This is not only an American phenomenon. A growing national obses- 32 sion in Japan with schoolgirls dressed in uniforms is called "Loli-con," after Lolita.[13] In Tokyo hundreds of "image clubs" allow Japanese men to act out their fantasies with make-believe schoolgirls. A magazine called *V-Club* featuring pictures of naked elementary-school girls competes with another called *Anatomical Illustrations of Junior High School Girls*. Masao Miyamoto, a male psychiatrist, suggests that Japanese men are turning to girls because they feel threatened by the growing sophistication of older women.[14]

In recent years, this sexualization of little girls has become even more 33 disturbing as hints of violence enter the picture. A three-page ad for Prada clothing features a girl or very young woman with a barely pubescent body, clothed in what seem to be cotton panties and perhaps a training bra, viewed through a partially opened door. She seems surprised, startled, worried, as if she's heard a strange sound or glimpsed someone watching her. I suppose this could be a woman awaiting her lover, but it could as

[12]Herbert, 1999, WK 17.
[13]Schoolgirls as sex toys, 1997, 2E.
[14]*Ibid.*

easily be a girl being preyed upon.

The 1996 mur- *34* der of six-year-old JonBenet Ramsey was a gold mine for the media, combining as it did child pornography and violence. In November of 1997 *Advertising Age* reported in an article entitled "JonBenet keeps hold on magazines" that the child had been on five magazine covers in October, "enough to capture the Cover Story lead for the month. The pre-adolescent beauty queen, found slain in her home last Christmas, garnered 6.5 points. The case earned a *triple play* [italics mine] on the *National Enquirer,* and one-time appearances on *People* and *Star.*"[15] Imagine describing a six-year-old child as "pre-adolescent."

Sometimes the models in ads are children, other times they just look *35* like children. Kate Moss was twenty when she said of herself, "I look twelve."[16] She epitomized the vacant, hollow-cheeked look known as "heroin chic" that was popular in the mid-nineties. She also often looked vulnerable, abused, and exploited. In one ad she is nude in the corner of a huge sofa, cringing as it braced for an impending sexual assault. In

---

[15] Johnson, 1997, 42.
[16] Leo, 1994, 27.

another, she is lying nude on her stomach, pliant, available, androgynous enough to appeal to all kinds of pedophiles. In a music video she is dead and bound to a chair while Johnny Cash sings "Delia's Gone."

It is not surprising that Kate Moss 36 models for Calvin Klein, the fashion designer who specializes in breaking taboos and thereby getting himself public outrage, media coverage, and more bang for his buck. In 1995 he brought the federal government down on himself by running a campaign that may have crossed the line into child pornography.[17] Very young models (and others who just seemed young) were featured in lascivious print ads and in television commercials designed to mimic child porn. The models were awkward, self-conscious. In one commercial, a boy stands in what seems to be a finished basement. A male voiceover tells him he has a great body and asks him to take off his shirt. The boy seems embarrassed but he complies. There was a great deal of protest, which brought the issue into national consciousness but which also gave Klein the publicity and free media coverage he was looking for. He pulled the ads but, at the same time, projected that his jeans sales would almost double from $115 million to $220 million that year, partly because of the free publicity but also because the controversy made his critics seem like prudes and thus positioned Klein as the daring rebel, a very appealing image to the majority of his customers.

[17] Sloan, 1996, 27.

Having learned from this, in 1999 Klein launched a very brief adver- 37
tising campaign featuring very little children frolicking in their under-

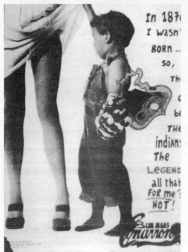

pants, which included a controversial billboard in Times Square.[18] Although in some ways this campaign was less offensive than the earlier one and might have gone unnoticed had the ads come from a department store catalog rather than from Calvin Klein, there was the expected protest and Klein quickly with- drew the ads, again getting a windfall of media coverage. In my opinion, the real obscenity of this campaign is the whole idea of people buying designer under- wear for their little ones, especially in a country in which at least one in five chil- dren doesn't have enough to eat.

Although boys are sometimes sexual- 38
ized in an overt way, they are more often portrayed as sexually precocious, as in the Pepsi commercial featuring the young boys ogling Cindy Crawford or the jeans ad portraying a very little boy looking up a woman's skirt. It may seem that I am reading too much into this ad, but imagine if the genders were reversed. We would fear for a little girl who was unzipping a man's fly in an ad (and we would be shocked, I would hope). Boys are vulnerable to sexual abuse too, but cul- tural attitudes make it difficult to take this seriously. As a result, boys are less likely to report abuse and to get treatment.

Many boys grow up feeling that they are unmanly if they are not 39
always "ready for action," capable of and interested in sex with any woman who is available. Advertising doesn't cause this attitude, of course, but it contributes to it. A Levi Strauss commercial that ran in Asia features the shock of a schoolboy who discovers that the seductive young woman who has slipped a note into the jeans of an older student is his teacher. And an ad for BIC pens pictures a young boy wearing X-ray glasses while ogling the derriere of an older woman. Again, these ads would be unthinkable if the genders were reversed. It is increas- ingly difficult in such a toxic environment to see children, boys or girls, as *children*.

In the past few years there has been a proliferation of sexually gro- 40
tesque toys for boys, such as a Spider Man female action figure whose exaggerated breasts have antennae coming out of them and a female Spawn figure with carved skulls for breasts. Meantime even children have easy access to pornography in video games and on the World Wide Web, which includes explicit photographs of women having intercourse with

[18] Associated Press, 1999, February 18.

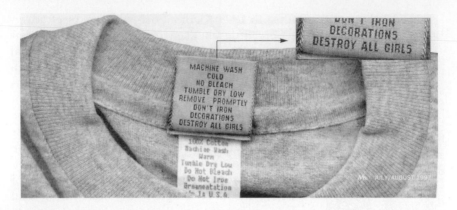

groups of men, with dogs, donkeys, horses, and snakes; photographs of women being raped and tortured; some of these women made up to look like little girls.

It is hard for girls not to learn self-hatred in an environment in which   41 there is such widespread and open contempt for women and girls. In 1997 a company called Senate distributed clothing with inside labels that included, in addition to the usual cleaning instructions, the line "Destroy all girls."[19] A Senate staffer explained that he thought it was "kind of cool." Given all this, it's not surprising that when boys and girls were asked in a recent study to write an essay on what it would be like to be the other gender, many boys wrote they would rather be dead. Girls had no trouble writing essays about activities, power, freedom, but boys were often stuck, could think of nothing.

It is also not surprising that, in such an environment, sexual harass-   42 ment is considered normal and ordinary. According to an article in the journal *Eating Disorders*:

> In our work with young women, we have heard countless accounts of this contempt being expressed by their male peers: the girls who do not want to walk down a certain hallway in their high school because they are afraid of being publicly rated on a scale of one to ten; the girls who are subjected to barking, grunting, and mooing calls and labels of "dogs, cows, or pigs" when they pass by groups of male students; those who are teased about not mea-suring up to buxom, bikini-clad [models]; and the girls who are grabbed, pinched, groped, and fondled as they try to make their way through the school corridors.
>
> Harassing words do not slide harmlessly away as the taunting sounds dis-sipate. . . . They are slowly absorbed into the child's identity and develop-ing sense of self, becoming an essential part of whom she sees herself to be. Harassment involves the use of words as weapons to inflict pain and assert

---

[19] Wire and *Times* staff reports, 1997, D1.

power. Harassing words are meant to instill fear, heighten bodily discomfort, and diminish the sense of self.[20]

It is probably difficult for those of us who are older to understand 43 how devastating and cruel and pervasive this harassment is, how different from the "teasing" some of us might remember from our own childhoods (not that that didn't hurt and do damage as well). A 1993 report by the American Association of University Women found that 76 percent of female students in grades eight to eleven and 56 percent of male students said they had been sexually harassed in school.[21] One high-school junior described a year of torment at her vocational school: "The boys call me slut, bitch. They call me a 10-timer, because they say I go with 10 guys at the same time. I put up with it because I have no choice. The teachers say it's because the boys think I'm pretty."[22]

High school and junior high school have always been hell for those 44 who were different in any way (gay teens have no doubt suffered the most, although "overweight" girls are a close second), but the harassment is more extreme and more physical these days. Many young men feel they have the right to judge and touch young women and the women often feel they have no choice but to submit. One young woman recalled that "the guys at school routinely swiped their hands across girls' legs to patrol their shaving prowess and then taunt them if they were slacking off. If I were running late, I'd protect myself by faux shaving—just doing the strip between the bottom of my jeans and the top of my cotton socks."[23]

Sexual battery, as well as inappropriate sexual gesturing, touching, 45 and fondling, is increasing not only in high schools but in elementary and middle schools as well.[24] There are reports of sexual assaults by students on other students as young as eight. A fifth-grade boy in Georgia repeatedly touched the breasts and genitals of one of his fellow students while saying, "I want to get in bed with you" and "I want to feel your boobs."[25] Authorities did nothing, although the girl complained and her grades fell. When her parents found a suicide note she had written, they took the board of education to court.

A high-school senior in an affluent suburban school in the Boston area 46 said she has been dragged by her arms so boys could look up her skirt and that boys have rested their heads on her chest while making lewd comments.[26] Another student in the same school was pinned down on a lunch table while a boy simulated sex on top of her. Neither student reported any of the incidents, for fear of being ostracized by their peers. In another

---

[20] Larkin, Rice, and Russell, 1996, 5–26.
[21] Daley and Vigue, 1999, A12.
[22] Hart, 1998, A12.
[23] Mackler, 1998, 56.
[24] Daley and Vigue, 1999, A1, A12.
[25] Shin, 1999, 32.
[26] Daley and Vigue, 1999, A12.

school in the Boston area, a sixteen-year-old girl, who had been digitally raped by a classmate, committed suicide.[27]

According to Nan Stein, a researcher at Wellesley College: 47

> Schools may in fact be training grounds for the insidious cycle of domestic violence. . . . The school's hidden curriculum teaches young women to suffer abuse privately, that resistance is futile. When they witness harassment of others and fail to respond, they absorb a different kind of powerlessness—that they are incapable of standing up to injustice or acting in solidarity with their peers. Similarly, in schools boys receive permission, even training, to become batterers through the practice of sexual harassment.[28]

This pervasive harassment of and contempt for girls and women constitute a kind of abuse. We know that addictions for women are rooted in trauma, that girls who are sexually abused are far more likely to become addicted to one substance or another. I contend that all girls growing up in this culture are sexually abused—abused by the pornographic images of female sexuality that surround them from birth, abused by all the violence against women and girls, and abused by the constant harassment and threat of violence. Abuse is a continuum, of course, and I am by no means implying that cultural abuse is as terrible as literally being raped and assaulted. However, it hurts, it does damage, and it sets girls up for addictions and self-destructive behavior. Many girls turn to food, alcohol, cigarettes, and other drugs in a misguided attempt to cope. 48

As Marian Sandmaier said in *The Invisible Alcoholics: Women and Alcohol Abuse in America*, "In a culture that cuts off women from many of their own possibilities before they barely have had a chance to sense them, that pain belongs to all women. Outlets for coping may vary widely, and may be more or less addictive, more or less self-destructive. But at some level, all women know what it is to lack access to their own power, to live with a piece of themselves unclaimed."[29] 49

Today, every girl is endangered, not just those who have been physically and sexually abused. If girls from supportive homes with positive role models are at risk, imagine then how vulnerable are the girls who have been violated. No wonder they so often go under for good—ending up in abusive marriages, in prison, on the streets. And those who do are almost always in the grip of one addiction or another. More than half of women in prison are addicts and most are there for crimes directly related to their addiction.[30] Many who are there for murder killed men who had been battering them for years. Almost all of the women who are homeless or in prisons and mental institutions are the victims of male violence. 50

Male violence exists within the same cultural and sociopolitical context that contributes to addiction. Both can be fully understood only within 51

---

[27] Vigue and Abraham, 1999, B6.
[28] Stein, 1993, 316–17.
[29] Sandmaier, 1980, xviii.
[30] Snell, 1991.

this context, way beyond individual psychology and family dynamics. It is a context of systemic violence and oppression, including racism, classism, heterosexism, weightism, and ageism, as well as sexism, all of which are traumatizing in and of themselves. Advertising is only one part of this cultural context, but it is an important part and thus is a part of what traumatizes.

All right, you might think, these ads are shocking. They are probably not good for us. But just what is the relationship of all these sexist and violent ads to addiction? Am I blaming advertisers for everything now? No. But I do contend that ads that contribute to a climate of disconnection also contribute to addiction. Ads that objectify women and sexualize children also play a role in the victimization of women and girls that often leads to addiction. When women are shown in positions of powerlessness, submission, and subjugation, the message to men is clear: Women are always available as the targets of aggression and violence, women are inferior to men and thus deserve to be dominated, and women exist to fulfill the needs of men.

There is a further connection between images that legitimize male domination of females and addiction. In his classic essay "The Cybernetics of Self" Gregory Bateson describes the fundamental belief of Western culture that we can dominate, control, and have power over almost every aspect of our experience.[31] We can get rid of pain, we can dominate people who threaten us, we can win in any interaction, we can be invulnerable. Bateson theorizes that this belief is fundamentally erroneous and leads to addiction, which he sees as a disordered attempt to get to a more "correct" state of mind, one in which we permit dependency, vulnerability, and mutuality. Bateson argues that we have no culturally sanctioned, nonaddictive way to achieve this state.

Claudia Bepko takes Bateson's theory further by arguing that the stage is set for addiction by the overriding belief system maintaining that men have power and women are the objects of that power.[32] This assumption is as erroneous as is the assumption that we can control our emotions. But our entire culture is predicated on this illusion of male dominance, and our institutions are set up in ways that perpetuate it. According to Bepko, being socialized in an erroneous belief system leads to addiction because incongruity may arise between what one believes and how one actually feels. A man who feels he must be dominant but who actually feels vulnerable might use an addictive substance to lessen his feeling of vulnerability or to enhance his sense of dominance. A woman forced to show dependence who really feels powerful might use a drug or other substance either to enhance or disqualify the impulse to be powerful (as the old Jefferson Airplane song says, "One pill makes you larger and one pill makes you small"). Thus gender-role socialization both shapes and is continually challenged by addictive behavior.

Bepko describes what she calls "the yin and yang of addiction." Both men and women become addicted and suffer, but their individual addictions arise from their different positions in the world and have different

[31] Bateson, 1972.
[32] Bepko, 1989.

effects. Men operate within a context in which both autonomy and entitlement to be taken care of are assumed; women within a context in which both dependency on a man and emotional and physical nurturing and caretaking are assumed. The contradictions in these prescriptions obviously create a bind: The male is independent but taken care of and the woman is dependent but the caretaker. Addiction is one response to the pain created by these contradictions.

Although the critical issues are dependency and control, these have radically different meanings and outcomes for women and men. Since money, sexuality, size, strength, and competitive work convey power and status for men, gambling, sexual addictions, and work addiction tend to be predominantly male forms of compulsive behavior (although women are catching up as gender roles change). Women are still socialized to be physically and emotionally nurturing, so eating disorders, obsessive shopping or cleaning, self-mutilation, and compulsive behavior in relationships are common female forms of addictive behavior, as is prescription drug abuse, which reflects the cultural belief that women's emotions need to be subdued and controlled. A man is more likely to engage in addictive behavior that involves having power over others, whereas a woman's attempt at control is often focused on her own body. 56

It would be foolish to suggest that advertising is *the cause* of violence against women—or of alcoholism or eating disorders or any other major problem. These problems are complex and have many contributing factors. There is no doubt that flagrant sexism and sex role stereotyping abound in all forms of the media. There is abundant information about this. It is far more difficult to document the effects of these stereotypes and images on the individuals and institutions exposed to them because, as I've said, it is difficult to separate media effects from other aspects of the socialization process and almost impossible to find a comparison group (just about everyone in America has been exposed to massive doses of advertising). 57

But, at the very least, advertising helps to create a climate in which certain attitudes and values flourish, such as the attitude that women are valuable only as objects of men's desire, that real men are always sexually aggressive, that violence is erotic, and that women who are the victims of sexual assault "asked for it." These attitudes have especially terrible consequences for women abused as children, most of whom grow up feeling like objects and believing they are responsible for their own abuse. These are the very women who are likely to mutilate and starve themselves, to smoke, to become addicted to alcohol and other drugs. As Judith Herman wrote in her classic book *Father-Daughter Incest*: 58

> These women alone suffered the consequences of their psychological impairment. Almost always, their anger and disappointment were expressed in self-destructive action: in unwanted pregnancies, in submission to rape and beatings, in addiction to alcohol and drugs, in attempted suicide.
>
> . . . Consumed with rage, they nevertheless rarely caused trouble to anyone but themselves. In their own flesh, they bore repeated punishment for the crimes committed against them in their childhood.[33]

[33] Herman and Hirschman, 1981, 107–8.

Addictions are not incidental in the lives of women. Most often they are 59
caused by (or at least related to) disturbances in relationships in childhood,
often violent disturbances. They are fueled by a culture that sexualizes children, objectifies, trivializes, and silences women, disparages our interest in
and skill at relating, and constantly threatens us with violence. Feeling isolated
and disconnected, a girl or a woman reaches out to a substance to numb her
pain, to be sure, but also to end her isolation, to relate, to connect. She reaches
for alcohol or other drugs, she reaches for cigarettes, she reaches for men who
don't love her, or she reaches for food. The advertisers are ready for her.

BIBLIOGRAPHY

Abbey, A., Ross, L., and McDuffie, D. (1991). Alcohol's role in sexual assault. In Watson,
    R., ed. *Addictive behaviors in women.* Totowa, NJ: Humana Press.
Associated Press (1999, February 18). Calvin Klein retreats on ad. *Boston Globe,* A7.
Bateson, G. (1972). The cybernetics of self. In *Steps to an ecology of mind.* New York:
    Chandler Publishing.
Bepko, C. (1989). Disorders of power: Women and addiction in the family. In McGold-
    rick, M., Anderson, C. M., and Walsh, F., eds. (1989). *Women in families: A frame-
    work for family therapy.* New York: W. W. Norton, 406–26.
Blumenthal, S. J. (1995, July). *Violence against women.* Washington, DC: Department of
    Health and Human Services.
Brewers can help fight sexism (1991, October 28). *Advertising Age,* 28.
Daley, B., and Vigue, D. I. (1999, February 4). Sex harassment increasing amid students,
    officials say. *Boston Globe,* A1, A12.
Hart, J. (1998, June 8). Northampton confronts a crime, cruelty. *Boston Globe,* A1, A12.
Herbert, B. (1999, May 2). America's littlest shooters. *New York Times,* WK17.
Herman, J. L., and Hirschman, L. (1981). *Father-daughter incest.* Cambridge, MA: Har-
    vard University Press.
Johnson, J. A. (1997, November 10). JonBenet keeps hold on magazines. *Advertising
    Age,* 42.
Kilbourne, J. (1994, May 15). 'Gender bender' ads: Same old sexism. *New York Times,* F13.
Larkin, J., Rice, C., and Russell, V. (1996, Spring). Slipping through the cracks: Sexual
    harassment. *Eating Disorders: The Journal of Treatment and Prevention,* vol. 4, no. 1,
    5–26.
Leo, J. (1994, June 13). Selling the woman-child. *U.S. News and World Report,* 27.
Mackler, C. (1998). Memoirs of a (sorta) ex-shaver. In Edut, O., ed. (1998). *Adios, Barbie.*
    Seattle, WA: Seal Press, 55–61.
Martin, S. (1992). The epidemiology of alcohol-related interpersonal violence. *Alcohol,
    Health and Research World,* vol. 16, no. 3, 230–37.
Novello, A. (1991, October 18). Quoted by Associated Press, AMA to fight wife-beating.
    St. Louis Post Dispatch, 1, 15.
Quindlen, A. (1992, June 28). All of these you are. *New York Times,* E17.
Sandmaier, M. (1980). *The invisible alcoholics: Women and alcohol abuse in America.*
    New York: McGraw-Hill.
Schoolgirls as sex toys. (1997, April 16) *New York Times,* 2E.
Shin, A. (1999, April/May). Testing Title IX. *Ms.,* 32.
Sloan, P. (1996, July 8). Underwear ads caught in bind over sex appeal. *Advertising Age,* 27.
Snell, T. L. (1991). *Women in prison.* Washington, DC: U.S. Department of Justice.
Stein, N. (1993). No laughing matter: Sexual harassment in K–12 schools. In Buchwald,
    E., Fletcher, P. R., and Roth, M. (1993). *Transforming a rape culture.* Minneapolis,
    MN: Milkweed Editions, 311–31.
Tjaden, R., and Thoennes, N. (1998, November). *Prevalence, incidence, and consequences
    of violence against women: Findings from the National Violence Against Women Sur-
    vey.* Washington, DC: U.S. Department of Justice.
Two men and a baby (1990, July/August). *Ms.,* 10.

Vigue, D. I., and Abraham, Y. (1999, February 7). Harassment a daily course for students. *Boston Globe*, B1, B6.

Weil, L. (1999, March). Leaps of faith. *Women's Review of Books*, 21.

Wilsnack, S. C., Plaud, J. J., Wilsnack, R. W., and Klassen, A. D. (1997). Sexuality, gender, and alcohol use. In Wilsnack, R. W., and Wilsnack, S. C., eds. *Gender and alcohol: Individual and social perspectives*. New Brunswick, NJ: Rutgers Center of Alcohol Studies, 262.

Wire and *Times* Staff Reports (1997, May 20). Orange County skate firm's 'destroy all girls' tags won't wash. *Los Angeles Times*, D1.

Wright, R. (1995, September 10). Brutality defines the lives of women around the world. *Boston Globe*, A2.

■ ■ ■

Reading as a Writer: Analyzing Rhetorical Choices

1. Kilbourne spends much of the essay explaining why she finds certain advertisements harmful to women, but she also hints at the damage they do to men. Locate those passages, and, in class, discuss how you could develop her argument that men also are harmed by advertising. How would the essay be different if she had included more material on men?

2. Like many writers who analyze the effects of the media, Kilbourne seeks to show how media images influence us, but she does not establish a simplistic "cause and effect" relationship between the images we see and the ways we act. How *does* she explain the relationship between images and ideas/actions? Locate several places in her essay where she explains this relationship, and discuss what you think of the claims she makes.

Writing as a Reader: Entering the Conversation of Ideas

1. Kilbourne and bell hooks use similar strategies of inviting readers to consider familiar images (in advertising or on the screen) through new lenses, considering the ways viewers are positioned to value (or devalue) people on the screen. Choose as a "test case" a film or series of related advertisements to analyze through the lenses of Kilbourne's and hooks's ideas, in order to see what your test case teaches viewers about gender and class "norms." Consider what these authors say about why it is important to take these images seriously as you draw your own conclusions about your findings.

2. While they take different approaches, Kibourne and Allan G. Johnson (Chapter 14) both analyze the ways representations of male and female bodies foster assumptions about extreme differences between the sexes that are both artificial and damaging. Write an essay in which you place these authors in conversation, noting ways their different insights about women's and men's bodies help you understand the larger significance of what we believe about women and men in our culture.

14

Sociology

How do race, class, and gender influence us?

© Getty Images/Henrik Sorensen

Sociology is the study of human social behaviors, with a particular interest in the origins of these behavior patterns and their significance in the present. As you will see in this chapter's readings, sociologists find meaning in even the smallest rituals, from body hair-removal to the use of the schoolyard taunt, "Dude, you're a fag." Sociologists, like other scholars, often ask us to rethink what we *think* we know about the world.

Agustín Fuentes, one of the authors in this chapter, calls this kind of questioning "myth-busting" and applies this practice to ideas about racial differences that most of us have been taught by our society—even though there is no biological evidence for these ideas. Many of our authors take similar approaches to asking questions about our current cultural assumptions using examples that you might find quite surprising and even foundation-shaking.

Among the topics for myth-busting that you will read and be invited to write about in this chapter, many involve aspects of our identity that seem to be fixed in our biology, such as our gender or our race. However, as Fuentes points out on the topic of racial assumptions, there is no biological proof for many of the ideas we have about race, and he offers us a wide range of evidence to show this is the case. Despite the lack of proof for our racial assumptions, though, Fuentes goes on to argue that there are very real effects on the daily lives of those who are perceived to be in one racial category or another, an idea that is also developed by Peggy McIntosh in her essay about "white privilege." These pieces model ways of talking about race that we do not often hear in a popular culture, and we urge you to pay attention to the ways these authors consider perspectives and evidence as they make their cases.

Other authors in this chapter use "myth-busting" strategies on assumptions about gender, as when Allan G. Johnson asks in the title of his piece the seemingly strange question, "Why Do We Make So Much of Gender?" We have been socialized from birth ("It's a girl!" "It's a boy!") to think that our sex inevitably leads to gender patterns that seem natural, but Johnson invites us to think differently: "From a strictly biological perspective, it's hard to see what all the fuss is about since what actually makes us male or female depends on a tiny bit of genetic information out of all the other factors, genetic and otherwise, that shape who we are" (para. 5). Ultimately, Johnson reveals what he believes to be the fundamental reason that societies have constructed this idea that men and women are very different—and his conclusions might surprise you. Some of our authors focus on the effects on men of these assumptions about gender, such as Matthew Immergut's analysis of male body hair-removal rituals, C. J. Pascoe's consideration of the phrase, "Dude, you're a fag," and Michael Kimmel's exploration of the ways boys and men are often socialized into violent behaviors. Elline Lipkin conducts a similar analysis of the ways girls are raised, examining the long history and implications of socializing girls to see their own bodies as problems in need of solving.

Barbara Ehrenreich's short journalistic essay in this chapter about the ways we often characterize those who are poor as very different from the rest of "us" models a sociological approach at the core of this discipline—examining how some groups come to be seen as "normal" and even "ideal," while some come to be seen as "others." The effects on the daily lives of those who have social power—and those who do not—are enormous. Sociology's premise is that society is *our* creation, and just as we have created these behavior patterns, which so often reinforce existing inequalities (because it is always easier to take the familiar path, the path of least resistance), we can also make the effort to create different patterns. What could the world look like, if we make the effort to become scholarly "myth-busters" ourselves? These readings offer some insights about what is possible.

 Visit **macmillanhighered.com/frominquiry3e** to view a clip from the film *Cracking the Codes: The System of Racial Inequality* that features several speakers reflecting on the personal and social dynamics of "structural racism."

AGUSTÍN FUENTES

From The Myth of Race

Agustín Fuentes is a professor of anthropology at the University of Notre Dame, where his research and teaching specialties include the evolution of social organization, primatology, and biological anthropology. Fuentes frequently writes about anthropological and sociological issues for a more general audience, too, such as in the book from which we draw this excerpt, *Race, Monogamy, and Other Lies They Told You: Busting Myths about Human Nature* (2012). In the chapter titled "The Myth of Race," Fuentes takes on what he calls the "pernicious myth of race," a popular misconception that "if we can see differences, if we can tell people apart, then there must be real (meaning natural) differences between groups of people" (para. 1). Fuentes cautions us to question what we think we know about the concept of "race" in ways that might shake some of your assumptions to the core. The quick guide to "Testing Core Assumptions about Race" that follows paragraph 5 is a preview of Fuentes's argumentative style. You might discuss these "myth-busting" ideas even before you read the full piece.

Fuentes uses a range of examples to demonstrate his claim that while "humans vary biologically, we can demonstrate that this variation does not cluster into racial groups. What we refer to as human races are not biological units" (para. 7). Explaining the significance of this claim in terms of how we understand the world is his main task, and he goes about it by offering many different kinds of evidence. As you read, keep track of the kinds of evidence he offers, and consider which you find most persuasive, and why. His analysis of blood types (which begins in para. 12), for example, uses biological language and charts to demonstrate similar data; which is most helpful to you for understanding his point? Similarly, Figure 5 offers an image that demonstrates claims in paragraph 17. To what extent is visual evidence important to you?

After arguing for half this piece that race is a "myth," Fuentes then makes a different kind of point, starting with the section titled "Myth Busting: Race Is Not Biology, but It Still Matters in Our Society." Fuentes considers the language around the election of President Barack Obama, the categories used by the Census Bureau, and a long bulleted list of statistics from the U.S. Department of Labor and the Pew Research Center (starting with para. 27) to build his argument. Again, what evidence do you find most persuasive, and why?

How optimistic is Fuentes that we can change these deeply rooted myths? Given the seriousness of his subject, it might be surprising that Fuentes ends this selection by quoting the band They Might Be Giants. Consider finding and listening to their song "Your Racist Friend," as you read the lyrics and Fuentes's final thoughts. What call to action does Fuentes make? What, specifically, might you do to become a "myth buster"?

■ ■ ■

> The idea of "race" represents one of the most dangerous myths of our time and one of the most tragic. Myths are most effective and dangerous when they remain unrecognized for what they are.
>
> —ASHLEY MONTAGU (ANTHROPOLOGIST)[1]

Ashley Montagu, one of the most prominent anthropologists of the twentieth century, warned about the pernicious myth of race in 1942, and his warning is still relevant today. In his 2010 book, Guy Harrison challenges the biological reality of race:

> Few things are more real than races in the minds of most people. We are different. Anyone can see that. Look at a "black" person and look at an "Asian" person. If a black Kenyan stands next to a white guy from Finland we all can see that they are not the same kinds of people. Obviously they belong to different groups and these groups are called races, right? (Guy Harrison, journalist)[2]

Guy Harrison is calling into question the most common popular perception of human variation—that if we can see differences, if we can tell people apart, then there must be real (meaning natural) differences between groups of people.[3] The question of whether humans are divided into biological races is answered with a resounding academic "no" by the American Association of Physical Anthropology's (AAPA) statement on the biological aspects of race:

> Humanity cannot be classified into discrete geographic categories with absolute boundaries. Partly as a result of gene flow, the hereditary characteristics of human populations are in a state of perpetual flux. Distinctive local populations are continually coming into and passing out of existence. Such populations do not correspond to breeds of domestic animals, which have been produced by artificial selection over many generations for specific human purposes. There is no necessary concordance between biological characteristics and culturally defined groups. On every continent, there are diverse populations that differ in language, economy, and culture. There is no national, religious, linguistic or cultural group or economic class that constitutes a race . . . there is no causal linkage between these physical and behavioral

traits, and therefore it is not justifiable to attribute cultural characteristics to genetic inheritance.[4]

However, there are others who answer this question with a resounding "yes":

> The three-way pattern of race differences is true for growth rates, life span, personality, family functioning, criminality, and success in social organization. Black babies mature faster than White babies; Oriental babies mature slower than Whites. The same pattern is true for sexual maturity, out of wedlock births, and even child abuse. Around the world, Blacks have the highest crime rate, Orientals the least, Whites fall in between. The same pattern is true for personality. Blacks are the most outgoing and even have the highest self-esteem. Orientals are the most willing to delay gratification. Whites fall in between. Blacks die earliest, Whites next, Orientals last, even when all have good medical care. The three-way racial pattern holds up from cradle to grave. (J. Phillipe Rushton, psychologist)[5]

How can there be two such different answers to Harrison's question? One answer states, in dry academic terms, that the popular concept of biological races is not supported by evidence; the other, in straightforward common language, says that there is a three-way pattern of racial differences. One answer is wrong.

Humans Are Divided into Biological Races, or Are They?

The myth of human biological races is alive and well in our society. Some- 2 one like Phillipe Rushton can make claims about racial patterns, even though they are incorrect, and have some popular success because the categories "black" and "white" make sense to us.[6] He uses simple, common language, that resonates with some of the cultural patterns we hear about via the media, in our daily lives, and in some versions of history. Rushton's claims are a mix of popular assumptions presented as if they were biological facts. Nowhere in his book *Race, Evolution and Behavior* does Rushton provide any real data to support his assertion that "Blacks," "Whites," and "Orientals" are true biological groups, but he does selectively draw from social statistics on crime, income, and mortality to make spurious analogies and then leaps to connect these to the different evolutionary histories of human races. On the other hand the AAPA statement on race (as well as a multitude of similar statements, peer-reviewed articles, books, and Web sites) states unequivocally that these types of associates are not supported and that the concept of clear or determinate biological races in humans today is not justifiable given what we know about human evolution and biology.

While most people would not fully agree with Rushton about the impli- 3 cations of racial differences, more than would care to admit it probably do see things in his proposal that seem to fit with common perceptions of human variation in the United States: Blacks as more athletic and overly sexual, Asians as more bookish and reserved, and whites seem to fall in between, more or less the average everyman. This is because many people today see the division of humanity into races as part of human nature. It's time to bust this myth.

This myth involves the assumption that we can define a specific set of 4 traits that consistently differentiates each race from the other with limited overlap between members. This position also assumes that differences in innate behavior, intelligence, sports abilities, aggression, lawlessness, health and physiology, sexuality, and leadership ability exist between these presumed real clusters of humans and that the clusters can be described as the Asian, black, and white races.[7] Nearly everyone holding these beliefs would accept that these clusters do overlap in many ways and that inter-breeding between them is always possible and not necessarily negative. However, as the journalist Guy Harrison put it so succinctly (and sarcasti-cally), the majority of people regardless of what they might say in public believe to some degree in the natural reality of human races. This "reality" is an assertion that we can test scientifically.

Buying into at least some of this myth about races also suggests a suite 5 of correlates. One is that since these differences are "natural," we should probably be wary of spending much social and economic capital trying to correct them. Some may also feel that the civil rights movement of the last century and the 2008 election of a black American president indicates that U.S. society has already done as much as is possible to ameliorate racial inequality. From this perspective, focusing on race is not really that important anymore. Finally, many might argue that if race is not a bio-logical entity, then how can the actual, and well-documented, differences in health, sports participation, test scores, and economic achievement between the "races" in the United States be explained? In the same vein, what about ancestry tests? How can a company test our DNA and tell us that we are 40 percent Kenyan or 60 percent Irish? Isn't that about race?

Testing Core Assumptions about Race

To bust the myth of race we have to test the core assumptions and refute 6 them.

ASSUMPTION: *Human races are biological units.*

TEST: Is there a set of biological characteristics that naturally divide up humans beings into races? If yes, then the assumption is supported; if no, then it is refuted.

ASSUMPTION: *We live in a (mostly) postracial society.*

TEST: Does our society still use race in assessment, definitions, and daily life? If no, then the assumption is supported; if yes, then it is refuted.

ASSUMPTION: *If race is not a biological category, then racism is not that powerful or important in shaping human lives.*

TEST: Can we demonstrate that racism, without the existence of biological races, is a significant factor affecting human health, well-being, and access to societal goods? If yes, then the assumption is refuted; if no, then it is supported.

ASSUMPTION: *If we can see consistent differences in sports, disease patterns, and other areas tied to physical features between races, these must reflect innate differences between these groups of people.*

TEST: Are these differences consistent over time? Are they due to biological or unique racial characteristics or are they better attributed to other causes? If yes, and they can be linked to biological patterns of human groups, then the assumption is supported; if no, then it is refuted.

If we can refute all four assumptions, the myth is busted.

Myth Busting: Race ≠ Biological Groups

Although humans vary biologically, we can demonstrate that this variation does not cluster into racial groups. "What we refer to as human races are not biological units. Many articles, books, and official statements make this point. However, there are very few brief and succinct overviews of human biological diversity as it relates to racial typologies. Reviewing information about blood groups, genetics, and morphological and physiological variation in the context of evolutionary processes demonstrates unequivocally that there is no way to divide humanity into biological units that correspond to the categories black, white, or Asian, or any other categories.

For close to three hundred years people have been trying to name and classify racial grouping of humans. Carolus Linnaeus, the father of modern taxonomy, made the most important attempt to do so and his classifications still seem very much like current ones.[8] Linnaeus saw the distinction among groups of humans as being rooted in their continental origins (Africa, Asia, Europe, Americas). He saw all humans as belonging to one species, *Homo sapiens*, with a number of subspecies representing the different races.[9] In the tenth edition of his major taxonomy of everything, *Systema Naturae*, published in 1758, Linnaeus proposed four subspecies (races) of *Homo sapiens:* americanus, asiaticus, africanus, and europeanus (he added a fifth category, monstrosous, as a catch-all for wild men and mythical beasts). Unlike his other classifications, which were based on drawings and anatomical analyses of specimens, Linnaeus based his division of humans on what he heard and read about the peoples of the different continents.

> *Homo sapiens americanus* was "red, ill-tempered, subjugated. Hair black, straight, thick; Nostrils wide; Face harsh, Beard scanty. Obstinate, contented, free. Paints himself with red lines. Ruled by custom." *Homo sapiens europeaus* was "white, serious, strong. Hair blond, flowing. Eyes blue. Active, very smart, inventive. Covered by tight clothing. Ruled by laws." *Homo sapiens asiaticus* was "yellow, melancholy, greedy. Hair black. Eyes dark. Severe, haughty, desirous. Covered by loose garments. Ruled by opinion." And last (and

obviously least) *Homo sapiens africanus*: "black, impassive, lazy. Hair kinked. Skin silky. Nose flat. Lips thick. Women with genital flap; breasts large. Crafty, slow, foolish. Anoints himself with grease. Ruled by caprice."[10]

These descriptions initiated the still common mistake of mixing presumed cultural differences with biological realities. The anthropologist Jon Marks has repeatedly pointed out that if you read them carefully, Linnaeus's race descriptions sound a lot like those of Rushton's and other modern racialists.

About half a century after Linnaeus the German naturalist Johann 9 Friedrich Blumenbach developed another set of nonscientific human racial classifications, based on geographical definitions and some facets of skull morphology. His classifications included Caucasian, Mongolian, Malayan, American, and Negroid races, which were also referred to as white, yellow, brown, red, and black (based on serious ignorance about skin colors around the planet). Finally, during the mid-twentieth century the physical anthropologist Carleton Coon developed a derivation of Blumenbach's races with a more refined set of skull measurements that is still used by some racial topologists today: the Capoid race (southern and eastern Africa), Caucasian race (western and northern Europeans), Mongoloid race (Asian and Americans), Negroid (or Congoid) race (all of Africa aside from parts to the south and east), and the Australoid race (Australians). Most importantly Coon proposed that each of these races had a separate evolutionary history and thus a suite of behavioral and other traits that evolved separately.[11]

Despite attempts by researchers over the centuries to divide humans 10 into races based on skull shape, geographic location, and presumed cultural differences, there is absolutely no support for any of these classifications (neither those mentioned above nor the countless others proposed) as actually reflecting the ways in which the human skull, genetic characteristics, or other phenotypes cluster in our species.[12] So what does human biological variation actually look like?

As pointed out in our previous discussion of evolution and genetics 11 in chapter 3, we look at variation in populations. Populations are collections of people that reside in more or less the same place, or in different places but are constantly connected, and mate more with one another than with members of other populations. There are thousands of populations of the species *Homo sapiens* spread across the globe. And in some areas (large international cities like New York, London, or Singapore) individuals from many of those populations congregate. To define a race, then, we need to be able to identify a population or set of populations that has a suite of unique markers that differentiate it from all other such populations and mark it as being affected by slightly different evolutionary forces so as to have altered genetic patterns relative to the rest of the species. Let's look at how we vary biologically between and within populations in our blood, immune system, genetics, body shape and size, skin color, and skull shape.

Blood

For centuries people have looked at blood to tell us about humanity. We *12*
know that blood is important (lose enough and you die) and during the
last century researchers began to discover that blood itself is made up of
a number of different elements, all of which vary a bit! Basically, blood is
made up primarily of red blood cells (for oxygen transport), white blood
cells (defense against infection), platelets (for clotting), and plasma (the
liquid part of blood). There are also a number of other things associated
with these main components and even others that use the circulatory system to get to different parts of the body.[13]

Many sets of proteins serve a variety of functions associated with red *13*
blood cells. We call these protein sets blood types.[14] The best-known blood
type classification is the ABO system, which is often coupled with another
system, the Rhesus blood type, noted as positive (Rh+) or negative (Rh–).
Today we can track more than fifteen blood type systems whose alleles
(forms of genes) are found in variable frequencies across different human
populations.

In the ABO gene there are four alleles: A_1, A_2, B, and O. A_1 and A_2 *14*
are very similar, and mostly respond identically. The three main alleles, A,
B, and O, have a set of relationships with one another, in which A and B
are considered dominant to O and codominant to one another.[15] In other
words, the eventual phenotype of the genotypes AA and AO is A; that of
BB and BO is B; that of OO is O; and that of AB is AB. Across the human
species these alleles are found at the following frequencies: 62.5 percent
O, 21.5 percent A, and 16 percent B. But if we look at the level of different human populations we see different distributions of these alleles. For
example, the frequency of allele B is at, or nearly at, zero in many indigenous populations in South America, southern Africa, northern Siberia,
and Australia, and higher than 16 percent in indigenous populations in
central Asia (Figure 14.1), central West Africa, northern Russia, and main-
land Southeast Asia.[16] Alternatively, the A allele is found at its highest frequencies (more than 40 percent) in the Saami (an indigenous population)
of northernmost Europe and in some groups of Australian Aborigines.[17]
Are populations that share these similar frequencies of A or B more closely
related to one another than to the populations next to them that have different frequencies? No.

Understanding natural selection and gene flow helps us understand *15*
the distributions of blood types. Probably the most common allele is
O because it is the original allele, while A and B are more recent muta-
tions identical to O but with the addition of an extra sugar group. Also,
the different ABO phenotypes confer different slightly different support
against diseases. Specific blood types may increase or decrease chances
of surviving things like malaria or other blood-based parasites. However,
the majority of variation in blood groups comes from the movements of
human populations over the past 50,000 years or so. Gene flow is the major

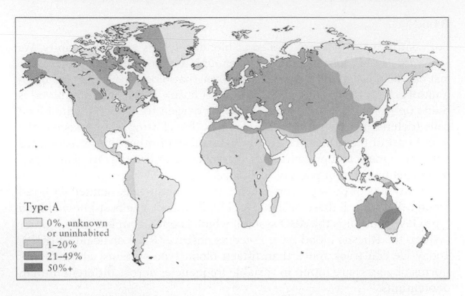

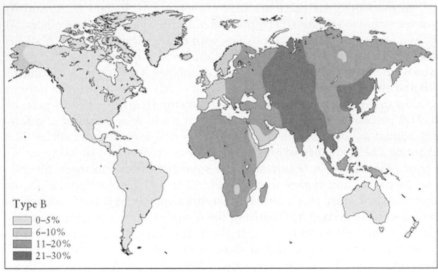

FIGURE 14.1 Geographical distribution and frequencies of the blood types A and B. Note that they do not follow the big three racial divisions of European, African, and Asian. From *Biological Anthropology: Concepts and Connections*, 2E, by A. Fuentes. © McGraw Hill Education 2012.

evolutionary force acting on distribution of the ABO alleles across human populations. None of these alleles are unique to specific populations, nor are their frequencies. And most importantly, none of the patterns, of ABO (or other blood groups) match up with the black-white-Asian model of dividing humans into racial categories. In fact, the full range of blood variation is found in nearly every single human population. The biology of blood does not support biological race.

. . .

There is no support for biological races

We can look to human biology to understand how people vary, how 16 populations differ from one another, and how patterns of adaptation and gene flow shape the way humans look across the planet. Data and results from research into body shapes and size, genetics, skin color, skull shapes, and every other aspect of human biological variation demonstrate unequivocally that we cannot divide humans into discrete biological clusters of white, black and Asian. This does not mean that humans do not vary—populations do differ from one another and this variation can be important. It just means that the racial divisions white, black and Asian do not reflect biology: they are cultural constructs.

Why don't most people know this? In large part it is because of our 17 limited exposure to what humans actually look like. Most people do not have the opportunity to travel across the world and see a large subset of the nearly seven billion members of our species. Nor do they have much opportunity to read concise and accessible summaries of thousands of research efforts documenting human biological variation. As previously established in chapter 2, we are who we meet. Our schemata are shaped and our perceptions of reality structured by what we are exposed to. For example, look at the picture in figure 5 before reading the next few sentences. You should immediately be able to tell that the three children and the young man are from different populations of humans. Given our shared schemata and experiences you can probably as easily place them into two presumed races: The kids are dark with large noses and frizzy hair, so probably of African origin, and therefore "black" and the young man is lighter with sharp facial features and dark hair, probably southern European origin and therefore "white." If you agree with this assessment then you are half right (the guy in the picture with wristwatch is me, a long time ago). I am of European origin (my father is from Spain and my mother's parents from Eastern Europe) and so would be classified in the United States as white (or Hispanic/ Latino, but that is another issue). However, the three kids are not of African descent. We'd call them black here in the United States based on our cultural interpretation of their skin, hair, and faces, assuming these features reflected African descent, but they do not. These kids are members of the Dani people from West Papua (the

Indonesian side of the island of Papua, New Guinea). They are about as far away as you can get from African descent. (I share many more allele frequencies in common with some African populations than they do.) Our limited personal knowledge of human variation cripples our ability to really understand how erroneous racial assumptions are.

Despite everything we've just discussed, many Americans assume that *18* because we seem able to determine a person's race by looking at them or because we can test our DNA and get a percentage of Yoruba or Irish ancestry using AIMs, then the concept of race must have some biological validity. This is wrong; very few people have the background knowledge to make accurate statements regarding the extent and patterns of human biological variation.

Consider an analogy. Nearly all human beings currently accept the *19* notion that the earth is round. We accept it despite the fact that the earth appears to us in our daily experience to be flat. Only a few humans (for example, astronauts or people who sail around the world and arrive back at the same place) have personally seen or experienced the earth as round. The rest of us accept the evidence as scientifically valid even though our personal experience contradicts it. A similar situation holds with the concept of race. Most people do not have the opportunity to see the patterned distribution of humanity across the globe. Although most of us in the United States can generally classify the people we see every day into three to five groups (though not always as easily or reliably as one might think), these groupings might not be valid in other locations. Further, these groupings reflect only a small percentage of the global biological variation in humanity. Thus, as with the shape of the earth, the broader situation is not necessarily obvious from our limited perspectives. If we have the context (broad exposure and the scientific data and understandings reviewed here), we can realize that, although our personal experience and cultural context might seem to show us one thing, the overall pattern of human biological diversity demonstrates something else: that *Homo sapiens* is one species, undivided into races or subspecies. The myth that human races are biological units is busted.

Myth Busting: Race Is Not Biology, but It Still Matters in Our Society

Okay, so if races are not biological units and civil rights has made signifi- *20* cant changes in our society over the last fifty years, then race does not matter, right? Wrong.

> In 2004, fifty years after *Brown v. Board of Education*, the controversies around "race" and racism are raging as brightly as ever. Whether we are talking about the future of affirmative action in elite universities, or what the next U.S. Census form will look like, or what the achievement rates of white

males are versus underrepresented students of color, this conversation is by no means finished. (Yolanda Moses, anthropologist)[18]

The point made by Yolanda Moses is that race matters as a social factor in the United States. The concept of race and how it plays out in our society are core factors in structuring our individual schemata and the maintenance of cultural constructs of, and societal expectations for, human behavior. However, in the first and second decades of the twentieth-first century a chorus of voices has emerged arguing that we are moving toward a post-racial society, or at least a society where race is no longer as powerful or important as it was for much of the twentieth century.[19] This view contradicts what Moses and the entire American Anthropological Association posit: that race matters as an important cultural component of our society.[20] Although the reality of race and racism as part of our society is not being debated, the relative importance of race is a strong current issue, as noted in a recent poll by ABC News and the *Washington Post*.[21] More than twice as many American blacks identified racism as a "big problem" than did American whites.

Since the 2008 election of Barack Obama as U.S. president, there has 21 been a steady series of debates about the relative role of race and racism in our society—not just about blacks or whites but also about Hispanic/ Latinos and Asians. The improvements in civil rights and the election of a black president do not demonstrate that we are in a (mostly) postracial society. Being black, white, Asian, Latino, or other means something in the United States, and although these categories are not biological units, they are social constructs that are central to many aspects of our society: Race is not biology, but it does matter.

Consider the following question: Why is Barack Obama considered 22 black? He is an individual with one parent born in the United States (who would be considered white) and one parent born in Kenya (who would be considered black). Why, when classifying President Obama, do we call him black or African American and not white or European-American or even better yet Afro-Euro-American? Well, interestingly, this last label is not an option in our classification system; moreover, because of his skin color, hair type, and the fact that one of his parents is black, Obama cannot be white. In the United States we have governmentally crafted definitions of race as well as broadly accepted social definitions. We also practice a form of hypodescent, the notion that racial identity is denoted by physical inheritance and by "blood" from a racial group. But this works in a particular way: The lower ranking group is what defines the descent. So throughout U.S. history (and up to today) "looking" black makes you black, as does any black parentage (even great-grandparents). According to popular opinion, having even one drop of "black blood" in your genealogy makes you black, but having many drops of white blood does not make you white.

Why is this? It is tied to the concept that races are biological units   23
and that some races are better than others; thus biological influence (or
contamination) from one race dictates what race you are. This is rooted in
misguided notions about genetics and biology, but nonetheless remains,
subconsciously, a de facto reality for our society. This is one reason why
Barack Obama is considered black and not white.

Another reason has to do with our own government's classification   24
system. The Census Bureau creates and maintains a set of definitions that
we use to officially classify people in our society. The official guidelines
state that

> The Census Bureau collects race data in accordance with guidelines pro-
> vided by the U.S. Office of Management and Budget (OMB), and these data
> are based on self-identification. The race response categories shown on
> the questionnaire are collapsed into the five minimum race groups identi-
> fied by the OMB, and the Census Bureau's "Some other race" category. The
> racial categories included in the following text generally reflect a social
> definition of race recognized in this country, and not an attempt to define race
> biologically, anthropologically or genetically. In addition, it is recognized that
> the categories of the race items include racial and national origin or socio-
> cultural groups. People may choose to report more than one race to indicate
> their racial mixture, such as "American Indian" and "White."[22]

Note that there is a specific statement that these are purely social categories and not intending to define race as biological. However, as you will see
with the following definitions, this is not totally true. Before the census
asks about one's race, it first asks if one is "of Hispanic, Latino, or Spanish
origin." These categories are not officially considered racial categories
(more on this below). Here are the official definitions of race for the U.S.
government:

> Mark the "White" box if this person has origins in any of the original peoples
> of Europe, the Middle East, or North Africa. This includes people who indi-
> cate their race as "White" or report entries such as Irish, German, Italian,
> Lebanese, Near Easterner, Arab, or Polish.

> Mark the "Black, African Am., or Negro" box if this person has origins in any
> of the Black racial groups of Africa. This includes people who indicate their
> race as "Black, African American, or Negro," or provide written entries such
> as African American, Afro-American, Kenyan, Nigerian, or Haitian.

> Mark the "American Indian or Alaska Native" box if this person has origins
> in any of the original peoples of North and South America (including Cen-
> tral America) and who maintain tribal affiliation or community attachment.
> This category includes people who indicate their race as "American Indian
> or Alaska Native," and/or provide written entries such as Navajo, Black-
> feet, Inupiat, Yupik, Canadian Indian, French American Indian, or Spanish
> American Indian.

> Mark any of the Asian boxes if this person has origins of any of the origi-
> nal peoples of the Far East, Southeast Asia, or the Indian subcontinent

including, for example, Cambodia, China, India, Japan, Korea, Malaysia, Pakistan, the Philippine Islands, Thailand, and Vietnam. This includes "Asian Indian," "Chinese," "Filipino," "Korean," "Japanese," "Vietnamese," and "Other Asian."

Mark the "Asian Indian" box if this person indicates their race as "Asian Indian" or identifies themselves as Bengalese, Bharat, Dravidian, East Indian, or Goanese.

Mark the "Chinese" box if this person indicates their race as "Chinese" or identifies themselves as Cantonese, or Chinese American. In some census tabulations, written entries of Taiwanese are included with Chinese while in others they are shown separately.

Mark the "Filipino" box if this person indicates their race as "Filipino" or who reports entries such as Philipino, Philipine, or Filipino American.

Mark the "Japanese" box if this person indicates their race as "Japanese" or who reports entries such as Nipponese or Japanese American.

Mark the "Korean" box if this person indicates their race as "Korean" or who provides a response of Korean American.

Mark the "Vietnamese" box if this person indicates their race as "Vietnamese" or who provides a response of Vietnamese American.

Mark the "Other Asian" box if this person provides a write-in response of an Asian group, such as Bangladeshi, Bhutanese, Burmese, Cambodian, Hmong, Laotian, Indochinese, Indonesian, Iwo Jiman, Madagascar, Malaysian, Maldivian, Nepalese, Okinawan, Pakistani, Singaporean, Sri Lankan, Thai, or Other Asian, not specified.

Mark the "Native Hawaiian" box if this person indicates their race as "Native Hawaiian" or identifies themselves as "Part Hawaiian" or "Hawaiian."

Mark the "Guamanian or Chamorro" box if this person indicates their race as such, including written entries of Chamorro or Guam.

Mark the "Samoan" box if this person indicates their race as "Samoan" or who identifies themselves as American Samoan or Western Samoan.

Mark the "Other Pacific Islander" box if this person provides a write-in response of a Pacific Islander group, such as Carolinian, Chuukese (Trukese), Fijian, Kosraean, Melanesian, Micronesian, Northern Mariana Islander, Palauan, Papua New Guinean, Pohnpeian, Polynesian, Solomon Islander, Tahitian, Tokelauan, Tongan, Yapese, or Other Pacific Islander, not specified.

Mark the "Some other race" box if this person is not included in the "White," "Black or African American," "American Indian or Alaska Native," "Asian," and "Native Hawaiian or Other Pacific Islander" race categories described above. Respondents providing entries such as multiracial, mixed, interracial, or a Hispanic, Latino, or Spanish group (for example, Mexican, Puerto Rican, Cuban, or Spanish) in the "Some other race" write-in space are included in this category.

People who are of two or more races may choose to provide two or more races either by checking two or more race response check boxes, by providing multiple responses, or by some combination of check boxes and other responses.[23]

There are a number of relevant factors to be found in these definitions, but one aspect stands out: "black" is treated differently from all the others. If you look closely at the definitions, you will see that "Black, African Am., or Negro" is the only category where the term "racial groups" is used ("if this person has origins in any of the Black racial groups of Africa"). In all of the other main categories the term "original peoples" is used. This marks the black category as a race, a biologized entity, relative to the other categories. Also, note that it is not just any racial groups, but the "Black racial" groups of Africa. Is there any mention of other types of racial groups in Africa (or anywhere else)? No. There is a clear demarcation of "black" as distinct type of category from the other "original peoples" categories. To be sure, the government does explicitly state that "the racial categories included in the following text generally reflect a social definition of race recognized in this country, and not an attempt to define race biologically, anthropologically or genetically." Yet that is exactly what it is doing, indicating with these categories that in the United States race matters and also that there is a hierarchy of races (one that mimics Phillipe Rushton's analyses). There are no reasons given by the Office of Management and Budget for its use of the terms "racial groups" versus "original peoples," but we can look at the history of naming races from Linnaeus to the modern day to see what is going on here. "Black" is associated with a lower ranking in the hierarchy of races. Race matters. It is worth noting that the U.S. government bureau validates this assertion by stating that it is using the "social definition of race recognized in this country."

Examining the other categories, we also see that these ways of classifying people are clearly nonbiological and in fact emerge largely from events and patterns in U.S. history. The classification of Middle Easterners and Arabs as "white" is certainly left over from a time when the relationship between the United States and the Middle East, especially Muslim countries, was quite different. How many in our society today would define Osama bin Laden, Saddam Hussein, Muammar el-Qaddafi, or anyone from Algeria, Morocco, Iran, or Egypt as "white"? The mandate that to be Native American or American Indian you must hail from the "original peoples of North and South America (including Central America)" and "maintain tribal affiliation or community attachment" stems from the history of treaty signings and manipulation of Indian lands and cultures by the U.S. government. Interestingly, this results in a number of Native Americans without tribal affiliation not being legally classifiable as American Indians. The fact that "Asian" applies to anyone with ancestry in the "Far East, Southeast Asia, or the Indian subcontinent," which is about

70 percent of all humans on the planet and a substantial portion of the overall inhabited landmass, emerges from the limited exposure that the United States has had to the wide range of peoples and populations of Asia. Finally, the "some other race" category is a bit of a catchall (except that you can reinsert Hispanic or Latino as a race at this point) for accounting purposes just in case someone comes up with something else. As part of its normative functioning, the government keeps tabs on the socially defined races (in a very general way) in order to manage the country, which invalidates the assertion that race no longer matters. Race is a core part of the United States.

Let's close this section with a few statistics from the U.S. Department of Labor and the Pew Research Center:[24]

- In tests of housing markets conducted by the U.S. Department of Housing and Urban Development (HUD), black and Hispanic potential renters and buyers are discriminated against (relative to whites) nearly 25 percent of the time.

- Light-skinned immigrants in the United States make more money on average than those with darker complexions, and the chief reason appears to be discrimination.

- Blacks and Hispanics have considerably lower earnings than Asians or whites. In 2009, the median usual weekly earnings of full-time wage and salary workers were $601 for blacks and $541 for Hispanics, compared with $880 for Asians and $757 for whites. The earnings of black men ($621) and Hispanic men ($561) were 65 and 60 percent, respectively, of the earnings of Asian men ($952). The earnings of black women ($582) were 75 percent of the earnings of Asian women ($654), a higher ratio than among black and Asian men. The median earnings for white men and women were 89 and 86 percent of their Asian counterparts in 2009. Median earnings for Hispanic women were $509.

- In 2009, about 90 percent of blacks and Asians (twenty-five years of age and older) in the labor force had received at least a high school diploma, the same proportion as whites. In contrast, about 67 percent of Hispanics had completed high school. Asians were most likely to have graduated from college; 59 percent had a bachelor's degree or higher, compared with 35 percent of whites, 24 percent of blacks, and 16 percent of Hispanics. Although blacks and Hispanics were less likely than whites and Asians to have obtained a college degree, the proportion of college graduates for all groups has increased over time. For all groups, higher levels of education are associated with a greater likelihood of being employed and a lower likelihood of being unemployed. Nonetheless, at nearly every level of education, blacks and Hispanics were more likely to be unemployed in 2009 than Asians or whites.

- The 2008 infant mortality rate per 1,000 births is 5.7 for whites, 13.6 for blacks, 5.6 for Hispanics, and 6.9 for the United States as a whole.

- The 2009 percent of each group living below the poverty level is 11.5 for whites, 32.2 for blacks, 28.4 for Hispanics, 19.4 for other (primarily Asian), and 17.2 for the United States as a whole.

- Percentage of groups without health insurance: 12.2 for whites, 20.9 for blacks, 33.5 for Hispanics, 17.7 for other (primarily Asian), and 17.2 for the United States as a whole.

- The 2009 net worth of U.S. households: white: $113,149, black: $5,677, and Hispanic: $6,325; there is a twentyfold difference between whites and all the others!

I could continue to list statistics, but these are enough to demonstrate *28* the point that, while race is not a biological unit, race as a social reality matters in the United States. The myth that we live mostly in a postracial society and that race does not matter is busted.

. . .

What Race Is and What It Is Not

The anthropologist Clarence Gravlee has suggested that we stop saying *29* that race is a myth, and instead accept that parts of it are myths while other aspects are not. He is correct: The myth part about race is that in modern humans there are biological races. The nonmyth part is that in our society the social categories of race are a reality that affects our lives. Thus, white, black, and Asian are not real biological, evolutionary, or natural categories nor do they reflect true divisions in human nature. However, white, black and Asian are real categories in the United States, for historical, political, and social reasons. People get placed in these categories both by themselves and by others. These social race divisions have real effects on the bodies and minds of the people in the United States. Race is not biology, but race affects biology, experience, and social context. Here are some closing thoughts on what race is and what it is not.

Race is not a valid way to talk about human biological variation

Biological anthropologists widely agree about how to describe and inter- *30* pret variation in the human species. This agreement can be summarized in the following five points that represent our core understanding of biological variation in humanity:[25]

1. There is substantial variation among individuals within populations.

2. Some biological variation is divided up between individuals in different populations and also among larger population groupings.

3. Patterns of within-group and between-group variation have been substantially shaped by culture, language, ecology, and geography.

4. Race is not an accurate or productive way to describe human biological variation.

5. Human variation research has important social, biomedical, and forensic implications.

Race is a social reality that can have lasting biological effects

The work of Clarence Gravlee, Bill Dressler, and others discussed in the   *31*
preceding sections demonstrate this point: race is not biology but it can
affect biology. In a February 2000 editorial, the prestigious, peer-reviewed
journal *Nature Genetics* issued the following guideline:

> The laudable objective to find means to improve the health conditions for
> all or for specific populations must not be compromised by the use of race
> or ethnicity as pseudo-biological variables. From now on, *Nature Genetics*
> will therefore require that authors explain why they make use of particular
> ethnic groups or populations, and how classification was achieved. We will
> ask reviewers to consider these parameters when judging the merits of a
> manuscript—we hope that this will raise awareness and inspire more rigor-
> ous design of genetic and epidemiological studies.

That is, we may use classifications by race and/or ethnicity when talking
about human variation, but we must be clear why and how we are using
these categories and about issues of directionality and reality of biological groupings. Race as a concept and racial inequality (racism) as a social
reality can affect biology.

Race ≠ Ethnicity

Ethnicity is a way of classifying people based on common histories, cultural   *32*
patterns, social ties, language use, symbolic shared identities, and the like.
It lays no claim to biology and is used both by those attempting to classify others and by those within the different ethnic groups as a symbol of
social unity. Ethnicity is not a natural set of divisions in humanity; it is fluid,
changing over time and space. The terms "ethnicity" and "race" are often
used interchangeably, even in commercial ancestry testing; this is wrong.
This mistaken usage is a holdover from the patterns established by eugeni-
cists trying to identify as biological groups the various national and ethnic
groups who were living in, or entering, the United States in the early twentieth century. From that time on the notion of "ethnic" has been used as a
technique for establishing "white" as normal and nonethnic, in contrast to
the "other." Check out the shampoos and hair care products at your neighborhood drugstore: Most places will have an aisle or section marked "hair
care" and another marked "ethnic products" or "ethnic hair care." This is
shorthand for "black," or frizzy, hair care products. Think about the common phrase "ethnic food." Does this refer to what is considered to be typical
U.S. (or white) food like hamburgers, hotdogs, or meatloaf? No, it means all
the other types of foods associated with nonwhite groups or with subdivisions of southern or eastern European origin, those not considered white in
the early parts of the twentieth century, like Jewish, Italian, and Slavic.

The same holds true for commercial ancestry testing. If you submit   *33*
your DNA sample to one of the many companies that offer such services and
your results come back 50 percent Irish, 35 percent German, and 15 percent

Yoruba, you might think you were basically "white" but also 15 percent "black." This is a nonsensical statement. The results suggest only that given the limited genetic samples we have to compare your sample with, certain very small parts of your genetic variation seems to fit with the micro-patterns found most commonly in Irish and German samples but there are some small similarities with the patterns found in our Yoruba sample. At best this means that you have mostly western European ancestors, with possible some West African ancestry mixed in. Or the results might be erroneous given the limited sampling of human populations in the reference samples. Irish/German is not equal to "white" and Yoruba is not equal to "black"; they are simply ethnic labels used to refer to the population samples used in the genetic comparisons. This has nothing to do with "race."

Ethnicity is a valid way to describe social histories and social and symbolic identification, but it is not biology and most definitely is not race.   34

Moving Beyond the Myth

If, as a society, we can move beyond the myth of race as describing natural   35
and biological units, then we can better address the inequalities that the race myth—and its concomitant, the social practices of racism—have created. The myth is strong, even in the face of resounding evidence against it. However, education and information (and access to them) are the main tools of myth busting. We will not move past this myth in this generation, or maybe not even in the next, but it is a possibility for the future of our society. As more and more of the myth-busting information discussed here becomes part of our social context, as children develop their schemata in the context of an accurate,, information-rich social network, the effect on our cultural constructs and societal perceptions can be substantial. Some of these changes are already under way, but the forces maintaining the myth of race are many and massive, especially the current pattern of inertia, or maintenance of the status quo, in adults. We may find it very difficult to change our own views, or once changed, we may find it uncomfortable to speak up against this myth in many situations. Or, maybe we can try out the lyrics of the popular song "Your Racist Friend" by the group They Might Be Giants:[26]

> It was the loveliest party that I've ever attended
> If anything was broken I'm sure it could be mended
> My head can't tolerate this bobbing and pretending
> Listen to some bullet-head and the madness that he's saying
>
> This is where the party ends
> I'll just sit here wondering how you
> Can stand by your racist friend
> I know politics bore you
> But I feel like a hypocrite talking to you
> You and your racist friend

In order to move forward we all have to be active in the discussion 36 about the reality of racism in the United States. We need to confront our racist friends, family, and society. This chapter contains the basic information and references leading you to more in-depth analyses of the myth of race and all the details that refute it. Many of our social norms and cultural constructs stand in our way; they support the inertia and patterns that maintain the myth or at least make it very difficult to challenge it publicly. However, once we have read this kind of information, we cannot be hypocrites, we must be myth busters.

NOTES

1. Ashley Montagu (1942), *Man's Most Dangerous Myth: The Fallacy of Race*.
2. Guy Harrison (2010), *Race and Reality: What Everyone Should Know About Our Biological Diversity*, p. 20.
3. Remember the saying in chapter 2, "I would not have seen it if I hadn't believed it."
4. http://physanth.org/association/position-statements/biological-aspects-of-race/?search term=race. This statement is the official stance of the association of scientists (physical or biological anthropologists) who have spent the last 150 years examining human biological variation.
5. This quote is from J. Phillipe Rushton (2000), *Race, Evolution, Behavior: A Life History Perspective*, 2nd ed., p.17. Rushton is a psychologist focused on "proving" the biological basis for race categories. His work has been reviewed, refuted, and rejected by anthropology and biology journals due to its lack of scientific support and his selective use of fringe datasets. He remains active in self-publishing and also still publishes in a few psychology journals. However, his pronouncements about race differences are worth reading as they receive wide attention and are used by many in the lay public (and racist groups) to shore up assertions about a biological basis for race.
6. There have been numerous refutations of Rushton's work. The American Association of Physical Anthropologists refused his membership request on the grounds of his consistent manipulation of information and his continued pushing of racist ideology in spite of countless refutations of his published works. See the rest of this chapter and the Web sites http://www.understandingrace.org/home.html and http://raceandgenomics.ssrc.org for a whole series of examples and articles that deal with the assertions put forward by Ruston and others supporting the reality of biological races in modern humans.
7. Of course, there are five race systems that add Native American and Hispanic, and other systems that add even more. We address this later in the chapter. For this basic introduction we focus on the standard "big three" division.
8. Taxonomy is the science of naming or classifying organisms based on their phenotypes. Linnaeus developed the system of binomial nomenclature (two names) that we use today. His basic system lumps organisms based on similarity to one another. See http://www.ucmp.berkeley.edu/history/linnaeus. html for a brief overview.
9. A subspecies; also referred to as a biological race, is a unit within a species that is taking an evolutionary path different from the overall trajectory of other populations within the species and thus is becoming increasingly differentiated from them at the genetic level. See A. Templeton (1999), Human races: A genetic and evolutionary perspective, *American Anthropologist* 100: 632 50 and R.A. Kittles and K.M. Weiss (2003), Race, genes and ancestry: Implications for defining disease risk, *Annual Reviews in Human Genetics* 4: 33–67 for overviews.

10. This selection (and translation) is from Jon Marks's 1995 excellent overview of Linnaeus and racial taxonomies (p. 50). I leave out *H. s. monstrosous* as this one was not based any actual peoples at all. See J. Marks (1995), *Human Biodiversity: Genes, Race, and History* for a fuller discussion of this topic.

11. Again see J. Marks (1995), *Human Biodiversity: Genes, Race, and History* for a fuller, and extremely engaging, discussion of this.

12. See for example K.M. Weiss (1998), Coming to terms with human variation, *Annual Reviews in Anthropology,* 27: 273–300; S. Molnar (2002), *Human Variation: Races, Types and Ethnic Groups;* J.H. Relethford (2002), Apportionment of global human genetic diversity based on craniometries and skin color, *American Journal of Physical Anthropology,* 118: 393–98; N.G. Jablonski (2004), The evolution of human skin and skin color, *Annual Reviews in Anthropology,* 33: 585–623; C. Ruff (2002), Variation in human body size and shape, *Annual Reviews in Anthropology,* 31: 211–32; and A. Smedley and B. Smedley (2005), Race as biology is fiction, racism as a social problem is real: Anthropological and historical perspectives on the social construction of race, *American Psychologist* 60(1): 16–26. This is just a small sample of the published, peer-reviewed research and reviews that debunk the race classifications.

13. The circulatory system includes the blood, the blood vessels (arteries, capillaries, and veins), and the heart. This system is the core means of transport for the elements required by the body's tissues for survival.

14. These proteins and their relative compatibility are what set up the problems trying to transfer blood between individuals. In order to be able to transfer blood between humans their blood systems must be very compatible (at least the major ones—ABO and Rh).

15. When talking about alleles, when we say "dominant" we mean that when a dominant allele is paired with a recessive allele in the body only the protein product of the dominant allele is expressed. The recessive allele's protein is not produced, or is produced at very low levels so that the phenotype expressed is that influenced by the dominant alleles. Remember from the last chapter that these alleles are for the same gene and that gene comes in two copies per person.

16. When looking at blood group allele frequencies, it is good to look at indigenous populations or populations that have been in the same location for a long time to see the patterns of allele distribution; if we were to take a random sample from a place like New York City, it would reflect the species-wide averages because of all the gene flow.

17. See S. Molnar (2002), *Human Variation: Races, Types and Ethnic Groups* for a good overview of blood group variation in humans.

18. Yolanda Moses (2004), The continuing power of the concept of "race," *Anthropology and Education Quarterly* 35(1):-146–48.

19. This ranges from commentators on major media outlets (for example see http://www.salon.com/mwt/feature/2010/08/13/dr_laura_the_n_word) to Web sites greeting the postracial society, but at the same time polling indicates that nearly 50 percent of U.S. citizens see racism as a major problem. However, blacks see this as a much greater issue than whites. See the overview of polls related to race in 1999–2009 at http://www.pollingreport.com/race.htm.

20. http://www.aaanet.org/issues/policy-advocacy/AAA-Statement-on-Race.cfm.

21. ABC News/Washington Post poll, January 13–16, 2009.

22. These are directly drawn from the definitions and guidelines for the 2010 census (http://2010.census.gov/partners/pdf/langfiles/qrb_English.pdf). As explained in http://www.understandingracc.org/about/response.html, "the Statistical Policy Division, Office of Information and Regulatory Affairs, of the Office of Management and Budget (OMB) determines federal standards for the. reporting of 'racial' and 'ethnic' statistics. In this capacity, OMB promulgated Directive 15: Race and Ethnic

Standards for Federal Statistics and Administrative Reporting in May, 1977, to standardize the collection of racial and ethnic information among federal agencies and to include data on persons of Hispanic origins, as required by Congress. Directive 15 is used in the collection of information on 'racial' and 'ethnic' populations not only by federal agencies, but also, to be consistent with national information, by researchers, business, and industry as well."

23. http://2010.census.gov/partners/pdf/langfiles/qrb_English.pdf.
24. See the following reports and Web sites for data about racial disparities: Labor Force Characteristics by Race and Ethnicity (2009), U.S. Department of Labor U.S. Bureau of Labor Statistics November 2010 Report 1020; http://www.bls.gov/cps/cpsrace2009.pdf; http://www.msnbc.msn.com/id/l6831909; http://www.kaiseredu.org/topics_reflib.asp?id=329&rID=3&parentid=67; and Pew Research Center Report on Social and Demographic trends (2011), http://pewsocialtrends.org/2011/07/26/wealth-gaps-rise-to-record-highs-between-whites-blacks-hispanics.
25. Heather J.H. Edgar and Keith L. Hunley (2009), Race reconciled? How biological anthropologists view human variation, *American Journal of Physical Anthropology* 139: 1–4.
26. They Might Be Giants (1990) from their song "Your Racist Friend" on the album *Flood*.

■ ■ ■

Reading as a Writer: Analyzing Rhetorical Choices

1. Where and how does Fuentes include writers whose ideas differ from his own? Mark those sections, and discuss the effectiveness of including those voices as a strategy of advancing his own argument. Where and how does he address readers who might disagree with him? How effectively does he address their concerns?

2. In his section titled "Blood," Fuentes includes data that relies on biological discourse about blood types, and accompanies the data with two charts (Figure 14.1). Discuss the effect of offering this kind of data to a generalist audience. How effectively does this approach help him build a case for his own expertise (his ethos)?

Writing as a Reader: Entering the Conversation of Ideas

1. Place Fuentes's text in conversation with Peggy McIntosh's essay and the e-reading for this chapter, a short video clip from the documentary *Cracking the Codes,* in order to write an essay about the methods by which racial stereotypes are reinforced, and how they can be "busted." Based on the evidence in these texts, and perhaps your personal experience, what can you conclude about changing—or unchanging—concepts of race in the United States?

2. While there may be no biological basis for racial difference, Fuentes still argues that race ". . . Still Matters in Our Society." Compose an essay in which you draw on Fuentes's ideas to help explain the social dynamics described in texts by Jonathan Kozol (Chapter 12), Beverly Tatum (Chapter 12), or bell hooks (Chapter 13).

— PEGGY MCINTOSH ——————————————————————

White Privilege: The Invisible Knapsack

Peggy McIntosh is associate director of the Wellesley College Center for Research on Women and has written many well-known articles on multicultural and gender-equitable curricula and is a sought-after lecturer on these topics. The ideas in this very influential essay are drawn from conference presentations in 1986 and 1987 and were published as a working paper in 1988 and reprinted in the Winter 1990 issue of *Independent School*.

When McIntosh first spoke out about white privilege, she was among the first scholars developing an analysis of "whiteness" as a racial category, which involves in part examining the ways European-Americans have become an "invisible norm" against which other racial categories are often measured. In this article, McIntosh traces her own shift from simply seeing nonwhites as "disadvantaged" to seeing her own whiteness as an unearned "privilege." As she explains early in her essay,

> I have come to see white privilege as an invisible package of unearned assets that I can count on cashing in each day, but about which I was "meant" to remain oblivious. White privilege is like an invisible weightless knapsack of special provisions, assurances, tools, maps, guides, codebooks, passports, visas, clothes, compass, emergency gear, and blank checks. (para. 3)

Perhaps the most striking feature of this essay, rare in scholarly writing, is the long personal list in the middle of the piece in which she details the unearned advantages she experiences in her daily life. This strategy of connecting concrete, daily experiences to larger systems of power enables readers to freshly "see" advantages that might come from social class, nationality, educational status, gender, sexuality, nationality, or able-bodied status. In other words, McIntosh's approach is one we might all use to analyze many different aspects of our daily lives.

In her final paragraph, she leaves readers with the provocative question, "What will we do with such knowledge?" In this piece, McIntosh takes risks and reveals her previous ignorance and her slow learning process; in so doing, she invites readers to take similar risks and to begin this important work, as well.

■ ■ ■

Through work to bring materials from women's studies into the rest of the curriculum, I have often noticed men's unwillingness to grant that they are overprivileged, even though they may grant that women are disadvantaged. They may say they will work to raise women's status, in the society, the university, or the curriculum, but they can't or won't support the idea of lessening men's status. Denials that amount to taboos surround the subject of advantages that men gain from women's disadvantages.

These denials protect male privilege from being fully acknowledged, lessened, or ended.

Thinking through unacknowledged male privilege as a phenomenon, *2* I realized that, since hierarchies in our society are interlocking, there was most likely a phenomenon of white privilege that was similarly denied and protected. As a white person, I realized I had been taught about racism as something that puts others at a disadvantage, but had been taught not to see one of its corollary aspects, white privilege, which puts me at an advantage.

I think whites are carefully taught not to recognize white privilege, as *3* males are taught not to recognize male privilege. So I have begun in an untutored way to ask what it is like to have white privilege. I have come to see white privilege as an invisible package of unearned assets that I can count on cashing in each day, but about which I was "meant" to remain oblivious. White privilege is like an invisible weightless knapsack of special provisions, maps, passports, codebooks, visas, clothes, tools, and blank checks.

Describing white privilege makes one newly accountable. As we in *4* women's studies work to reveal male privilege and ask men to give up some of their power, so one who writes about having white privilege must ask, "Having described it, what will I do to lessen or end it?"

After I realized the extent to which men work from a base of un- *5* acknowledged privilege, I understood that much of their oppressiveness was unconscious. Then I remembered the frequent charges from women of color that white women whom they encounter are oppressive. I began to understand why we are just seen as oppressive, even when we don't see ourselves that way. I began to count the ways in which I enjoy unearned skin privilege and have been conditioned into oblivion about its existence.

My schooling gave me no training in seeing myself as an oppressor, as *6* an unfairly advantaged person, or as a participant in a damaged culture. I was taught to see myself as an individual whose moral state depended on her individual moral will. My schooling followed the pattern my colleague Elizabeth Minnich has pointed out: Whites are taught to think of their lives as morally neutral, normative, and average, and also ideal, so that when we work to benefit others, this is seen as work that will allow "them" to be more like "us."

Daily Effects of White Privilege

I decided to try to work on myself at least by identifying some of the daily *7* effects of white privilege in my life. I have chosen those conditions that I think in my case attach somewhat more to skin-color privilege than to class, religion, ethnic status, or geographic location, though of course all these other factors are intricately intertwined. As far as I can tell, my African American coworkers, friends, and acquaintances with whom I come into daily or frequent contact in this particular time, place, and line of work cannot count on most of these conditions.

1. I can, if I wish, arrange to be in the company of people of my race most of the time.

2. I can avoid spending time with people whom I was trained to mistrust and who have learned to mistrust my kind or me.

3. If I should need to move, I can be pretty sure of renting or purchasing housing in an area which I can afford and in which I would want to live.

4. I can be pretty sure that my neighbors in such a location will be neutral or pleasant to me.

5. I can go shopping alone most of the time, pretty well assured that I will not be followed or harassed.

6. I can turn on the television or open to the front page of the paper and see people of my race widely represented.

7. When I am told about our national heritage or about "civilization," I am shown that people of my color made it what it is.

8. I can be sure that my children will be given curricular materials that testify to the existence of their race.

9. If I want to, I can be pretty sure of finding a publisher for this piece on white privilege.

10. I can be pretty sure of having my voice heard in a group in which I am the only member of my race.

11. I can be casual about whether or not to listen to another person's voice in a group in which s/he is the only member of his/her race.

12. I can go into a music shop and count on finding the music of my race represented, into a supermarket and find the staple foods which fit with my cultural traditions, into a hairdresser's shop and find someone who can cut my hair.

13. Whether I use checks, credit cards, or cash, I can count on my skin color not to work against the appearance of financial reliability.

14. I can arrange to protect my children most of the time from people who might not like them.

15. I do not have to educate my children to be aware of systemic racism for their own daily physical protection.

16. I can be pretty sure that my children's teachers and employers will tolerate them if they fit school and workplace norms; my chief worries about them do not concern others' attitudes toward their race.

17. I can talk with my mouth full and not have people put this down to my color.

18. I can swear, or dress in secondhand clothes, or not answer letters, without having people attribute these choices to the bad morals, the poverty, or the illiteracy of my race.

19. I can speak in public to a powerful male group without putting my race on trial.

20. I can do well in a challenging situation without being called a credit to my race.

21. I am never asked to speak for all the people of my racial group.

22. I can remain oblivious of the language and customs of persons of color who constitute the world's majority without feeling in my culture any penalty for such oblivion.

23. I can criticize our government and talk about how much I fear its policies and behavior without being seen as a cultural outsider.

24. I can be pretty sure that if I ask to talk to the "person in charge," I will be facing a person of my race.

25. If a traffic cop pulls me over or if the IRS audits my tax return, I can be sure I haven't been singled out because of my race.

26. I can easily buy posters, postcards, picture books, greeting cards, dolls, toys, and children's magazines featuring people of my race.

27. I can go home from most meetings of organizations I belong to feeling somewhat tied in, rather than isolated, out-of-place, outnumbered, unheard, held at a distance, or feared.

28. I can be pretty sure that an argument with a colleague of another race is more likely to jeopardize her/his chances for advancement than to jeopardize mine.

29. I can be pretty sure that if I argue for the promotion of a person of another race, or a program centering on race, this is not likely to cost me heavily within my present setting, even if my colleagues disagree with me.

30. If I declare there is a racial issue at hand, or there isn't a racial issue at hand, my race will lend me more credibility for either position than a person of color will have.

31. I can choose to ignore developments in minority writing and minority activist programs, or disparage them, or learn from them, but in any case, I can find ways to be more or less protected from negative consequences of any of these choices.

32. My culture gives me little fear about ignoring the perspectives and powers of people of other races.

33. I am not made acutely aware that my shape, bearing, or body odor will be taken as a reflection on my race.

34. I can worry about racism without being seen as self-interested or self-seeking.

35. I can take a job with an affirmative action employer without having my co-workers on the job suspect that I got it because of my race.

36. If my day, week, or year is going badly, I need not ask of each negative episode or situation whether it had racial overtones.

37. I can be pretty sure of finding people who would be willing to talk with me and advise me about my next steps, professionally.

38. I can think over many options, social, political, imaginative, or professional, without asking whether a person of my race would be accepted or allowed to do what I want to do.

39. I can be late to a meeting without having the lateness reflect on my race.

40. I can choose public accommodation without fearing that people of my race cannot get in or will be mistreated in the places I have chosen.

41. I can be sure that if I need legal or medical help, my race will not work against me.

42. I can arrange my activities so that I will never have to experience feelings of rejection owing to my race.

43. If I have low credibility as a leader, I can be sure that my race is not the problem.

44. I can easily find academic courses and institutions which give attention only to people of my race.

45. I can expect figurative language and imagery in all of the arts to testify to experiences of my race.

46. I can choose blemish cover or bandages in "flesh" color and have them more or less match my skin.

47. I can travel alone or with my spouse without expecting embarrassment or hostility in those who deal with us.

48. I have no difficulty finding neighborhoods where people approve of our household.

49. My children are given texts and classes which implicitly support our kind of family unit and do not turn them against my choice of domestic partnership.

50. I will feel welcomed and "normal" in the usual walks of public life, institutional and social.

Elusive and Fugitive

I repeatedly forgot each of the realizations on this list until I wrote it down. [8] For me white privilege has turned out to be an elusive and fugitive subject.

The pressure to avoid it is great, for in facing it I must give up the myth of meritocracy. If these things are true, this is not such a free country; one's life is not what one makes it; many doors open for certain people through no virtues of their own.

In unpacking this invisible knapsack of white privilege, I have listed *9* conditions of daily experience that I once took for granted. Nor did I think of any of these perquisites as bad for the holder. I now think that we need a more finely differentiated taxonomy of privilege, for some of these varieties are only what one would want for everyone in a just society, and others give license to be ignorant, oblivious, arrogant, and destructive.

I see a pattern running through the matrix of white privilege, a pattern *10* of assumptions that were passed on to me as a white person. There was one main piece of cultural turf; it was my own turf, and I was among those who could control the turf. My skin color was an asset for any move I was educated to want to make. I could think of myself as belonging in major ways and of making social systems work for me. I could freely disparage, fear, neglect, or be oblivious to anything outside of the dominant cultural forms. Being of the main culture, I could also criticize it fairly freely.

In proportion as my racial group was being made confident, comfort- *11* able, and oblivious, other groups were likely being made unconfident, uncomfortable, and alienated. Whiteness protected me from many kinds of hostility, distress, and violence, which I was being subtly trained to visit, in turn, upon people of color.

For this reason, the word "privilege" now seems to me misleading. We *12* usually think of privilege as being a favored state, whether earned or conferred by birth or luck. Yet some of the conditions I have described here work systematically to over-empower certain groups. Such privilege simply confers dominance because of one's race or sex.

Earned Strength, Unearned Power

I want, then, to distinguish between earned strength and unearned power. *13* Conferred privilege can look like strength when it is in fact permission to escape or to dominate. But not all of the privileges on my list are inevitably damaging. Some, like the expectation that neighbors will be decent to you, or that your race will not count against you in court, should be the norm in a just society. Others, like the privilege to ignore less powerful people, distort the humanity of the holders as well as the ignored groups.

We might at least start by distinguishing between positive advantages, *14* which we can work to spread, and negative types of advantage, which unless rejected will always reinforce our present hierarchies. For example, the feeling that one belongs within the human circle, as Native Americans say, should not be seen as privilege for a few. Ideally it is an unearned entitlement. At present, since only a few have it, it is an unearned advantage for them. This paper results from a process of coming to see that some of the power that I originally saw as attendant on being a human being in the United States consisted in unearned advantage and conferred dominance.

I have met very few men who are truly distressed about systemic, *15* unearned male advantage and conferred dominance. And so one question for me and others like me is whether we will be like them, or whether we will get truly distressed, even outraged, about unearned race advantage and conferred dominance, and, if so, what we will do to lessen them. In any case, we need to do more work in identifying how they actually affect our daily lives. Many, perhaps most, of our white students in the United States think that racism doesn't affect them because they are not people of color; they do not see "whiteness" as a racial identity. In addition, since race and sex are not the only advantaging systems at work, we need similarly to examine the daily experience of having age advantage, or ethnic advantage, or physical ability, or advantage related to nationality, religion, or sexual orientation.

Difficulties and dangers surrounding the task of finding parallels are *16* many. Since racism, sexism, and heterosexism are not the same, the advantages associated with them should not be seen as the same. In addition, it is hard to disentangle aspects of unearned advantage that rest more on social class, economic class, race, religion, sex, and ethnic identity than on other factors. Still, all of the oppressions are interlocking, as the members of the Combahee River Collective pointed out in their "Black Feminist Statement" of 1977.

One factor seems clear about all of the interlocking oppressions. They *17* take both active forms, which we can see, and embedded forms, which as a member of the dominant groups one is taught not to see. In my class and place, I did not see myself as a racist because I was taught to recognize racism only in individual acts of meanness by members of my group, never in invisible systems conferring unsought racial dominance on my group from birth.

Disapproving of the systems won't be enough to change them. I was *18* taught to think that racism could end if white individuals changed their attitude. But a "white" skin in the United States opens many doors for whites whether or not we approve of the way dominance has been conferred on us. Individual acts can palliate, but cannot end, these problems.

To redesign social systems, we need first to acknowledge their colossal *19* unseen dimensions. The silences and denials surrounding privilege are the key political tool here. They keep the thinking about equality or equity incomplete, protecting unearned advantage and conferred dominance by making these subjects taboo. Most talk by whites about equal opportunity seems to me now to be about equal opportunity to try to get into a position of dominance while denying that systems of dominance exist.

It seems to me that obliviousness about white advantage, like obliviousness about male advantage, is kept strongly inculturated in the United States so as to maintain the myth of meritocracy, the myth that democratic *20*

choice is equally available to all. Keeping most people unaware that freedom of confident action is there for just a small number of people props up
those in power and serves to keep power in the hands of the same groups
that have most of it already.

Although systemic change takes many decades, there are pressing *21*
questions for me and, I imagine, for some others like me if we raise our
daily consciousness on the perquisites of being light-skinned. What will
we do with such knowledge? As we know from watching men, it is an open
question whether we will choose to use unearned advantage, and whether
we will use any of our arbitrarily awarded power to try to reconstruct
power systems on a broader base.

■ ■ ■

Reading as a Writer: Analyzing Rhetorical Choices

1. McIntosh divides her essay into subsections. Read back through each of
   the subsections and describe the purpose of each subsection (including
   that remarkable, long list in the middle). How do the ideas and examples
   in each subsection contribute to the larger goal of her essay? What other
   ways of organizing these ideas might you propose, and with what possible
   effect on readers?

2. Explain in your own words the distinction McIntosh makes in paragraphs
   13 and 14 between "earned strength" and "unearned power." What specific
   examples of these does she urge readers to work against, and how? What
   other suggestions and strategies for change can you add, based on your
   experiences and hopes?

Writing as a Reader: Entering the Conversation of Ideas

1. How do our educational systems work to preserve or undo the kinds of
   race and class divisions McIntosh examines in her text? Draw on the ideas
   in McIntosh's text and connect them to concepts in essays by Beverly
   Tatum and/or Jonathan Kozol (Chapter 12). Write an essay in which you
   use specific examples and ideas in the texts you choose to build an argument about what American education currently accomplishes in relation
   to class and race differences. What do you think it should accomplish?

2. While both McIntosh and Beverly Tatum (Chapter 12) focus primarily on
   the small daily interactions that constitute and perpetuate assumptions
   about racial identity, these authors also bring gender into their analysis of
   these situations. Write an essay in which you consider how each author's
   insights about gender contribute to the observations and analysis they
   make about racial identity and power. You may include your own experiential insights in your essay as you build an argument about what we can
   learn from the ways gender dynamics often intersect with race dynamics.
   How hopeful are these authors, and are you, about changing these dynamics, based on their concluding statements and your own experiences?

ALLAN G. JOHNSON

Why Do We Make So Much of Gender?

This piece is an excerpt from Allan G. Johnson's 1997 book, *The Gender Knot: Unraveling Our Patriarchal Legacy*, frequently used as a college text. Johnson has a PhD in sociology and taught at Wesleyan University and Hartford College for Women before becoming a public speaker on topics related to his research on race and gender. As you can see in this section of his book, Johnson has a knack for helping readers reconsider cultural patterns that may seem to be "just the way things are" with the fresh perspective of sociological inquiry. Here, Johnson challenges us to question why reproductive organs have come to be seen as essential determining aspects of our adult identity.

In his early paragraphs, Johnson explains the difference between biological sex and social interpretations of those organs and notes that cultural ideas about what it means to be male or female change over time and differ by culture. While reproduction is important for societies to continue, Johnson points out, "From a strictly biological perspective, it's hard to see what all the fuss is about since what actually makes us male or female depends on a tiny bit of genetic information out of all the other factors, genetic and otherwise, that shape who we are" (para. 5). As you read these middle paragraphs of his piece, pay attention to the way Johnson acknowledges biological realities and yet questions the cultural assumptions that build from biology. What aspects of his argument surprise you? Which examples most effectively help you grasp his point?

Johnson's central argument arises in paragraph 9, where he states, "None of this means that reproduction doesn't matter. It does suggest, however, that the obsession with sex and gender isn't based on some vital interest in human reproduction. What this obsession *does* serve is the interests of the patriarchy, which uses it to anchor the whole idea of a male-dominated, male-identified, and male-centered society." In paragraph 10, he unpacks what he calls the "peculiar thinking" involved in teaching us all to believe that men and women are fundamentally different from one another, and that this difference creates a rational for men to dominate women. The "cultural slight of hand" (para. 11) that turns traits of adulthood into traits that belong only to men is exactly what Johnson wants us to question.

These ideas may run counter to your—or your family's or friends'—long-held beliefs about the relationship between our sex organs and our identity. Johnson argues in his final paragraphs that while men may seem to have more to gain from these assumptions than do women, the lives of men are seriously shortchanged as well by sorting human traits into two categories and teaching us to believe that we are all only entitled to half of those human traits. Johnson uses strong language for this way of thinking—a "web of lies" (para. 14). What is at stake for men, and for women, if we tell a different kind of truth about our biology and our identities?

Until the 1970s or so, the word "sex" was used to refer to anything related to being female or male—as in "sex roles" or "sex differences" or "sex change operation." "Gender" was about grammatical constructions, which often had nothing to do with sex—such as classifying French and Spanish nouns as masculine or feminine. In French, for example, the gender of the noun "table" is feminine and the gender of the noun "virus" is masculine. In practical terms, all this means is that adjectives used to modify the two kinds of nouns have different endings and the nouns take different articles—*le* and *la* (the masculine and feminine forms of "the")—none of which has much of anything to do with being male or female.

This worked well enough until feminists pointed out the difference between biological and social factors that shape women's and men's lives. From this they argued that patriarchy and women's oppression are rooted in society, not biology, and therefore aren't inevitable or immutable. Having a clitoris, for example, is a matter of biology. The nineteenth-century expectation that women weren't supposed to enjoy sex, however, and the continuing practice in some areas of the world of removing women's clitorises in order to control their sexuality have nothing to do with biology and everything to do with women's position in patriarchal society.[1] To make such distinctions clear, feminists appropriated "gender" from the realm of grammar and gave it a new meaning focused on social aspects of being female or male. In the new version of things, having a clitoris is about sex; ideas and practices about the clitoris are matters of gender.

Although the distinction between biological and social forces is important, it also creates problems by making it seem as though sex isn't in any way social, but rather exists as a concrete biological reality that we're simply naming in an objective way. It is of course true that the human body isn't a cultural creation, but as Michel Foucault has argued, how we think about the body certainly is.[2] When girls reach puberty, for example, the biology of being female dictates that they will rapidly acquire most of what eventually will be their adult body weight. This includes a naturally higher percentage of fat than is usually found in males. In some patriarchal societies, however, women's flesh is so highly devalued that pubescent girls view their own natural growth with a sense of alarm that stays with them for their entire lives.[3] This contrasts sharply with other cultures, such as most of Europe, whose classical art is rich with full-bodied women (and where women today tend to gain far more weight during pregnancy than do women in the United States); Western Samoa, where large women are admired for their erotic dancing during some public events; or even the United States, where not too long ago "sex goddesses" such as Marilyn Monroe were idolized for bodies that would be considered overweight by current standards. The obsession with female thinness—the denial of a natural body fullness rooted in biology—is nothing less than a cultural transformation of what it *means* to be female. In this sense, what a female actually *is* as a living being takes a back seat to the ideas a culture makes available for *thinking* about what she is.

Why cultures would include two categories, male and female, isn't hard 4 to see, since no society can continue without reproducing its human population and it takes males and females to do it. In other words, sex makes a distinction that is certainly relevant to human existence. But it's one thing to make a clear distinction and quite another to give it cosmic importance, as if who people are as female or male were at the core of their lives, the linchpin of personal identity, and the rock foundation of society and social life. As Sam Keen tells it, for example, we are men and women before we arc people, for "God did not make persons . . . only men and women;"[4] and Robert Bly goes even further, deep into every cell where men's and women's bodies supposedly "vibrate" at different frequencies, "sing" different songs, and "dance" a different dance.[5] Jungians (who are especially popular with the mythopoeic men's movement) see human existence as organized around a universal core of male and female archetypes—animus and anima—that presumably exist regardless of time or place.[6]

From a strictly biological perspective, it's hard to see what all the fuss 5 is about since what actually makes us male or female depends on a tiny bit of genetic information out of all the other factors, genetic and otherwise, that shape who we are. Some would argue, however, that however "simple" sex differences may be, they are crucial and central to human life because of their role in human reproduction. This has a lot of intuitive appeal, especially since sexual reproduction brought each of us into the world. It can't, however, carry the weight of explaining why humans have organized so much of social life around an obsession with gender. It can't carry that weight because if we look closely we find that humans and human societies don't assign as much importance to reproduction as we might think.

For thousands of years, societies worshipped fertility and used images 6 of pregnant women as religious symbols. Studies of these traditions suggest, however, that the object of reverence and awe wasn't simply human regeneration or women's part in it, but the seemingly miraculous process through which *all* forms of life are renewed and sustained. It's not at all clear that ancient peoples were obsessed with human reproduction per se rather than with the regeneration of life in general on which human survival depends. Goddess figures were associated with human mothers, for example, but, more important, they were also associated with the Earth itself and all the manifestations of its fertile abundance, much of which is plant based and essentially asexual. In short, before humans worry about reproducing themselves, they have to worry about the ability of all the species that provide food to reproduce *themselves* so that people who are already born can eat.

Of course, there has to be a certain amount of human reproduc- 7 tion in order for social life to continue. This doesn't mean, however, that reproduction and gender are any more important than other necessary ingredients of human existence. This is especially so given that in its fullest sense, reproduction is a long and complicated process that doesn't end with birth. Human societies don't need babies in order to survive. They need fully functioning adults, and compared with what it takes to produce an adult, sexual reproduction is a walk in the park. Some might argue that the socialization of children into adults lacks the grand mystery—and hence the fascination and importance—of sexual reproduction and, by extension, sex and gender. But why limit our capacity for wonder to that? I was awed when I saw my children being born, but my sense of mystery and wonder didn't end there. I will never be able to account for the miracle of children learning to speak and think and struggling with the mysteries of love, death, and loss. I will never be able to explain my feeling that my children are connected to my body and my soul even though I never carried them inside myself, neither birthed nor nursed them—indeed, like every father, had no body experience that unequivocally said they were "mine." Is any of this less miraculous, less mysterious, or less vital to the human condition and experience than the male–female coupling in sexual reproduction? And yet we attribute no cosmic importance to the amazing and difficult process through which people come into being or to the caring work that makes it possible—work that both men and women are capable of doing.[7]

Even reproduction in its fullest sense, however, is not much more important than numerous other human necessities. In fact, it may be less so if we judge from how children are actually treated. Throughout history, for example, the death of babies and infants has been a common and relatively uneventful occurrence, as have abortion and infanticide; and where infant mortality is high, babies are often left unnamed until they show they're likely to survive beyond infancy. For children who do survive, the historical record of child care is unremarkable in much of the world. Children have a long history of being forced to work under appalling conditions or being killed, sold, bartered, and otherwise neglected and abused. This is especially true for females (who, one would think, would be cherished for their reproductive potential) in societies most obsessed with gender distinctions.

None of this means that reproduction doesn't matter. It does suggest, however, that the obsession with sex and gender isn't based on some vital interest in human reproduction. What this obsession *does* serve is the interests of patriarchy, which uses it to anchor the whole idea of a male-dominated, male-identified, and male-centered society. After all, if we were human beings first and women or men second, the patriarchal order wouldn't make much sense. Patriarchy, not some inherent human condition, requires that gender assume mythic proportions and take its place as the most defining and confining human characteristic, one that dwarfs all others by comparison. This is true of most oppressive systems. Race distinctions, for example, would barely matter, without their link to systems of social inequality and privilege.

Using gender to define the core of what makes us human creates huge   *10*
contradictions: It requiring us to define men and women as fundamentally different from each other and yet also as full human beings. On the
one hand, this can't be done, because as soon as human traits are made
gender-specific, each gender is encouraged to alienate itself from a substantial portion of what makes us human. On the other hand, patriarchy
depends on such divisions, because there's no basis for men to dominate
women if we see the genders as fundamentally the same. And this is what
sets up a contradiction that can be sustained only through some peculiar
thinking. This includes, for example, the strange notion that men's place
in society is defined more by their manhood than their adulthood. What it
takes to be an adult is fairly constant across societies—the ability and willingness to take responsibility, for example, to care for others; to be productive and contribute to family, community, and society; to be courageous; to
live creatively and with awareness. Under patriarchy, however, manhood
has to amount to more than this: It has to differ from adult *womanhood*
enough to justify organizing social life in a male-identified, male-centered
way. This calls for a vision of male adulthood based on a social, psychological, spiritual, and physical territory that men can identify with and defend
as exclusively male.

The only way to accomplish this cultural sleight of hand is to gender-   *11*
ize what are essentially human qualities by pretending they define manhood rather than adulthood. The idea of heroism, for example, has been
appropriated almost entirely by patriarchal manhood. From movies and
television to literature to the nightly news, our ideas of who and what is
heroic focus almost entirely on men and what they do. Where the cultural
magic comes in is in the pretense that women are not heroic, which we
can see when we look at what heroism actually consists of. Sam Keen, for
example, describes the "heroic male identity" as a capacity to feel outrage
in the face of cruelty, to protect the powerless, and to heal those who are
broken.[8] This kind of real man knows how

> to take care of the place to which he has been entrusted . . . to practice the art
> of stewardship, to oversee, to make judicious use of things, and to conserve
> for the future . . . to make a decision to be in a place, to make commitments,
> to forge bonds, to put down roots, to translate the feeling of empathy and
> compassion into an action of caring.[9]

These are all wonderful human qualities, but why should we associ-   *12*
ate them primarily with manhood, and not adulthood? The answer is
that genderizing such qualities distinguishes and elevates men in relation to women. The falseness of this practice is even more striking when
we consider that in many ways what Keen described as heroic is more
common among women than men. If anyone puts down roots, commits to relationships, and organizes a life around empathy, compassion,
caring, healing, and even protecting the powerless, it's women. This is
especially true in relation to children, whom many fathers seem all too

willing to abandon and all too unwilling to provide for when the going gets rough. In contrast, women rarely feel they have a choice about whether to stay with and care for their children, and will do what's necessary to hold families together. Why, then, is heroism genderized as an essential element of manhood even though men are no more heroic than women? The answer is that under patriarchy it perpetuates the ruse that women and men are fundamentally different and in the process elevates men by appropriating for them a valuable chunk of symbolic territory.

Robert Bly provides another example of such contradictions when he 13 argues that for "soft" men to get in touch with the true spirit of the "Iron John" wild man, they must overcome their fear of "wildness, irrationality, hairiness, intuition, emotion, the body, and nature."[10] Ironically, almost all of these traits are culturally associated with women, not men. In other words, Bly is telling men to become more like women as a key to being true wild men. He gets into the same kind of trouble when he complains about the suppression of the wild man, because even more striking is the suppression of wildness in women. It is women, not men, who shave the hair from their bodies; who feel compelled to deny their inherent juiciness lest they be accused of being bitches or sluts; who learn to look upon their own flesh as an enemy; who are taught that anger and rage are unbecoming in them. Women's potential wildness so threatens patriarchy that it's been suppressed and twisted to the point of being unrecognizable and shows itself on rare and predictably controversial occasions (such as in the film *Thelma and Louise*). Instead of female wildness, patriarchy churns out images of evil witches, castrating bitches, vengeful feminists, mass media caricatures such as Madonna, and the proverbial "slut," whose wildness, for all the myths about nymphomania, serves men's imaginations more than women's lives.

When we genderize what are inherently human qualities, we lock 14 ourselves in a web of lies whose main consequence is to keep patriarchy going, for if society is to remain male-dominated, male-identified, and male-centered, women and men must be seen as fundamentally different so that men can control women as "other." But the lie cannot abide the underlying truth that all people share a common biological, spiritual, and psychological core, and that qualities such as heroism, caring, and wildness are no more about maleness than they are about femaleness. Rather than confront the contradiction, we obsess about gender and define it as the core of social order and ourselves. And in struggling to hold the lie together, we keep ourselves from knowing what's really going on and what it's got to do with us.

NOTES

1. A form of female genital mutilation that is still common in many regions of Africa and the Middle East. See Fran P. Hosken, *The Hosken Report: Genital and Sexual Mutilation of Females*, 4th rev. ed. (Lexington, Mass.: Women's International Network News, 1994).

2. See Michel Foucault, *The History of Sexuality: An Introduction* (Harmondsworth, England: Penguin, 1981).

3. See S. Bordo, *Unbearable Weight: Feminism, Western Culture, and the Body* (Berkeley: University of California Press, 1993); Kim Chernin, *The Obsession: Reflections on the Tyranny of Slenderness* (New York: Harper and Row, 1981); and Naomi Wolf, *The Beauty Myth: How Images of Beauty Are Used Against Women* (New York: William Morrow, 1991).

4. Sam Keen, *Fire in the Belly: On Being a Man* (New York: Bantam, 1991), 218. Biblical scholar Phyllis Trible has shown Keen to be quite wrong on this. Her translation of the book of Genesis reveals that God created a person named ha'adam, the Hebrew word for person with no specification as to sex. Only when God saw the need for human affiliation did he create women and men. See Trible, *God and the Rhetoric of Sexuality* (Philadelphia: Fortress Press, 1978).

5. Robert Bly, *Iron John: A Book About Men* (Reading, Mass.: Addison-Wesley, 1990), 93–94.

6. See, for example, Eugene Monick, *Phallos: Sacred Image of the Masculine* (Toronto: Inner City Books, 1987); and Robert Moore and Douglas Gillette, *King, Warrior, Magician, Lover: Rediscovering the Archetypes of the Mature Masculine* (San Francisco: HarperCollins, 1990). I'll have much to say about the new men's movement in later chapters.

7. Sara Ruddick describes this as "maternal work" in her powerful and insightful book, *Maternal Thinking: Towards a Politics of Peace* (New York: Ballantine Books, 1989). She emphasizes that it can be performed by both women and men, although it is, of course, almost always women's responsibility.

8. Keen, *Fire in the Belly*, 166.

9. Keen, *Fire in the Belly*, 180.

10. Bly, *Iron John*, 14.

■ ■ ■

Reading as a Writer: Analyzing Rhetorical Choices

1. Some of the key terms Johnson uses that are crucial to his argument are "gender" and "patriarchy." Mark where you find these words, and explain their definitions, given what Johnson says about them. Look up other definitions of these words, and compare those with what you learn from this essay. How do Johnson's examples help you develop your understandings of the definitions?

2. Johnson concludes this section with an extended critique of Robert Bly, a U.S. poet who has become known for his contributions to the "men's movement," which draws on traditional mythology to "reinvigorate" contemporary manhood. Look up information on Bly and this movement on the Internet, and discuss the effectiveness of Johnson's use of Bly to make Johnson's larger point about changing the way we think about biology and gender.

Writing as a Reader: Entering the Conversation of Ideas

1. While Johnson examines the category of gender and Agustín Fuentes analyzes the category of race, both authors are interested in "myth-busting" assumptions about and research on these cultural categories. Compose an essay that uses both authors' insights and examples in order to ana-

lyze the power behind those "myths." How does each author account for the persistence of myths that do not have a biological or scientific basis? What significance do you see in these persistent myths and the challenge of "busting" them?

2. Johnson and Georgia Warnke (Ch. 15) are both interested in the ways research and studies can sometimes be used to reinforce gender stereotypes. Write an essay in which you bring Johnson and Warnke's ideas and examples together to make an argument about the effect of these kinds of studies. Who stands to gain or lose from these studies, how, and why?

MATTHEW IMMERGUT

Manscaping: The Tangle of Nature, Culture, and Male Body Hair

Matthew Immergut is a professor of sociology at the State University of New York–Purchase College, where his sociological research spans from studies of spirituality and meditation, to ethical research dilemmas, to analyses of "personal" practices such as body hair-removal and their social significance. Like many sociologists, Immergut seeks to reframe our commonsense ideas of the way the world works by inviting us to see that even our most "mundane bodily practices can also provide a window into larger cultural currents that define what it means to be human in relationship to the nonhuman world" (para. 4). While scholars have long examined women's hair-removal practices, men's practices have been less commonly analyzed, though the rise of the term "manscaping" gives weight to Immergut's claim that this trend is worth taking seriously now. As he notes, "The body is a bio-physical entity but is also, significantly, a social creation" (para. 16).

Immergut writes his piece generally in the IMRAD style (Introduction, Methods, Research, and Discussion), though he does not divide his essay into clearly labeled sections. As you read, mark in the margins where he shifts from one focus to the next. For example, in paragraph 5, he notes, "A few words about methods are in order" to indicate that he will focus on explaining his use of informal interviews and "discourse and document analysis." What other signposts do you see in other places in his essay that draw the reader's attention to his structure? How does he adapt the IMRAD style to meet his own interests as a writer in providing a range of sources, theories, and examples to build his argument?

In his second paragraph, Immergut explains that he uses the work of Russian social theorist Mikhail Bakhtin to frame his analysis of male body hair. He fleshes out his interest in Bakhtin's ideas in the section titled "Grotesque and Classical Bodies," starting with paragraph 23. How do these historical understandings of the "grotesque natural body" help Immergut make his point about contemporary attitudes toward male body hair? What other examples can you name from popular culture or your own experiences that demonstrate our current attitudes—often contradictory—about "taming" men's bodies?

In his "Conclusion" section, Immergut contextualizes his analysis of body-hair rituals in debates about climate change—perhaps an unexpected place for his argument to end. As you read (and reread) this piece, pay close attention to all the argumentative moves Immergut makes in these dense final paragraphs, including his final two sentences. How did he move from a focus on body hair to considering our fears of "an ecological meltdown"? Immergut models how a "modest examination of all types of body projects and practices" can help us understand big ideas about our relationship to the world. What other bodily practices might be interesting to consider in this light?

■ ■ ■

The first time I took a razor to my body was in college. Not to my wrists or face, but to my stomach. I had this creeping feeling of disdain for the hair growing there. So I locked the bathroom door, grabbed a blade, and scythed the personal scourge. When I finished, I stroked my smooth abdomen and felt proud—like a suburbanite gazing with satisfaction across his freshly mowed lawn. Yet, I was also ashamed of my newly manicured body because it seemed to raise questions about my masculinity—after all, what kind of "guy" shaves . . . his gut? Shouldn't I be celebrating my hairy virility? What I didn't fully realize hiding behind my bathroom door in the 1990s was that I was mired in the middle of a shift in cultural attitude toward male body hair. The days when chest hair and chains were sexy were disappearing, replaced by a new hyper smooth hetero-man. 1

In this chapter, I am interested in exploring this newly deviant hairy "heterosexual" male body and the meanings given to those threadlike segments of keratin sprouting from his skin. What I am particularly interested in exploring is how the contemporary stigma of male body hair has become symbolically linked with all forms of unwanted or grotesque nature. What's my evidence? "Manscaping." Popularized by the television show *Queer Eye for the Straight Guy*, manscaping involves waxing, shaving, lasering, or simply shaping any hairy region of the male body below the head. This connection between manscaping and landscaping is not linguistically arbitrary, a simple humorous flourish, but rather, as I untangle below, reflects a culturally pervasive story about "man" against an untamed "nature." More specifically, appropriating the work of social theorist Mikhail Bakhtin, I argue that the practice of manscaping represents an effort to control the grotesque, messy, and boundary-breaching hairs of the male body in order to cultivate an alluring but nonetheless "natural" and distinct human self. 2

No doubt, women as well as nonwhites have long been associated with a chaotic natural realm in Western intellectual history, and nature has often been construed as an unwieldy feminine force (Adams 1993; Gard 1993; King 1990; Merchant 1980; Plumwood 1993). As such, these 3 "others," their bodies, and their hair have been subjugated to a variety of "civilizing" regimes—including the longstanding normative demand for hairless women (Toerien and Wilkinson 2003; Toerien, Wilkinson, and Choi 2005). Yet increasingly body hair seems to be attaining egalitarian status as a manifestation of nasty and wild nature regardless of the body it sprouts from—and this includes white males. But, you might ask, Do we really want to talk about the body tribulations of white men? And isn't it about time they had a taste of their own medicine? No, I'm not interested in bemoaning the pains of modern men nor celebrating what might be a justified comeuppance. Rather, I'm interested in exploring what this body practice reveals about contemporary understandings of, attitudes toward, and relationship with nature.

The sociological premise that underlies such an investigation is that seemingly mundane bodily practices such as plucking eyebrows or styling hair reflect larger sociocultural arrangements (Conboy, Medina, and Stanbury 1997; Hope 1982; Weitz 2004). I've just stretched this idea to argue that mundane bodily practices can also provide a window into larger cultural currents that define what it means to be human in relationship to the nonhuman world. More than a decade ago eco-feminist Ynestra King said, "there is a terrible confusion about our place in nature" (King 1990). Manscaping, as far as I can tell, discloses the continuation and possible intensification of this confusion.

A few words about methods are in order. There is very little extant research specifically on men's body hair. When male body hair is addressed—usually in passing—scholars tend to hold a view of male body hair as a marker of ideal masculinity (Luciano 2001; Toerien and Wilkinson 2003; Pope, Phillips, and Olvardia 2000; Synott 1987). My first task, therefore, is to present evidence that such a perspective is outdated and that the new hetero-norm is hairlessness. The data I use, as you will see below, are quite heterogeneous, gleaned from a variety of sources such as Internet sites, newspapers, circulating images of men in popular culture, the latest men's depilatory technologies, and so forth. I also performed informal interviews with aestheticians at waxing salons and laser hair removal centers and engaged in limited participation in their services—ouch. Once gathered, this textual- and image-based material was analyzed for nature-based themes in a research method known as discourse and document analysis (Rapley 2007). Two important caveats need to be made here. First, on the basis of deduction from the data, I claim that the men I'm talking about are "heterosexual."[1] I did not, however, conduct interviews or distribute a survey in order to assess sexual preference or other identity variables (which, by the way, I think would make an excellent student research project). Second, I am constructing a fairly big argument on limited data—more empirical research needs to be done. Nevertheless, I consider this a theoretical and exploratory essay, aimed at playfully opening up a space to consider these changing body practices and aesthetics and what they might tell us about the relationship between human embodiment and nature in late modernity. Before getting into this thicket of male body hair, I need to present some concrete evidence that hairy men are truly endangered.

Making the Case for Endangered Hairy Male Bodies

In 1987 sociologist Anthony Synott wrote an excellent article on the sociol- 6 ogy of hair in which he proposes a "theory of opposites." Simply stated, in North America and Britain opposite sexes have opposite head- and body-hair norms. "Hair is not just hair, it is a sex symbol" writes Synott, address-ing this difference relative to body hair,

> and voluminous chest hair is therefore the equivalent of long, glossy, wavy head hair on a woman. Hence the availability of paste-on chest hair. Women seem to feel the same as men about male body hair. . . . Conversely, both men and women are extremely upset by chest hair on women; again, the glory of one gender is the shame of the opposite sex. (393)

Certainly this theory of opposites reflects body hair norms during the time he was writing. Yet the adage, "the glory of one sex is the shame of the other," does not seem viable when one looks at male bodies today. Rather, when it comes to body hair, the shame of one gender now seems to be the shame of the other as well.

To begin making this case, let's look at some numbers. According 7 to the American Society of Plastic Surgeons (ASPS), in 2000 laser hair removal—a very expensive yet effective hair removal technique—was the second most popular noninvasive procedure undertaken by men: 133,142 men, to be more precise (Cooper 2006). Still in second place in 2006, the number of men getting their hair zapped via laser increased to 173,000 (ibid.). Of course, we don't have identity variables for these num-bers, and therefore we might assume, as one salon owner told me in a thick Russian accent, "it's a gay thing . . . gays, they have beautiful bodies but they want no hair on the body." However, a manager of a fairly upscale laser center had a different take: "we're seeing more straight guys all the time. It's not just a gay thing anymore." Even though she admitted to not having records of the sexual preferences of her client base, she did assure me she had excellent "gay-dar."

Stepping away from the numbers, consider the now-iconic image 8 of Burt Reynolds in a 1972 *Cosmopolitan* centerfold. This image of Burt reclining across a bear skin rug, cigar in mouth, hand poised over geni-tals, represented a significant cultural moment—here was a man posing almost completely naked in a traditionally female centerfold. Burt's body became a marker of the feminist movement's progress at equalizing the sexes as well as a signifier of the incorporation of men into an expand-ing consumer market (Bordo 1999). What's interesting to me, however, is Burt's body hair. No paste-on chest pieces here, just his raw hairiness and animal virility on display. Now reflect on the male icons of contemporary popular culture. Compare a hairy Burt Reynolds to completely hairless Brad Pitt. Or for that matter, simply try to find any body hair on any male model in any contemporary magazine—chances are you won't. Actually, what you are likely to find, if you observe closely, is once-hairy male sex symbols becoming increasingly hairless such as David Hasselhoff and John Bon Jovi.

Although there have been no opinion surveys about men's body hair recently, public forums also provide substantiation of this shifting bodily aesthetic. Begin with this Dear Abby column from 1979:

> Hairless in Hilo: Dear Abby: I've never seen a problem like mine in your column. I'm a 33-year-old normal man except that I have absolutely no hair on my chest, arms or legs. And that is where I want hair the most. I have plenty of hair on my head and a thick growth in my pubic hair, so I know I can grow hair, but I'm so ashamed of my hairless body I avoid going to the beach. Is there some kind of treatment I can take to promote the growth of hair where I want it? I am miserable in my hairless state. I want to be like other guys (quoted in Synott 1987, p.392).

Now put Hilo and his hairless dilemma next to this recent Internet posting by SM:

> SM: I wish I was stuck in the '70s where hair was cool and hot. It drives me mad when I hear most women talk about a man they once dated and were horrified to see that he was covered with hair. That's when I usually shy away. I dread the famous "let's all go in the spa!" shouted at parties. Sometimes I brave it anyways but I'd be lying if I said I wasn't nervous as hell.[2]

Although SM presents himself as "excessively" hairy, he is not alone. Internet chat rooms are full of supposed heterosexual men ruminating about the sexual appeal of everything from shaved chests to seal-slick pubic areas.

Newspapers and magazines also provide ample support for the disappearance of hairy men. As an example, consider this op-ed piece by Megan Daum in the *San Francisco Chronicle*:

> my adolescent sources and the grooming industry say men aren't just "the new women"; they're the new seals . . . . it's no secret that larger numbers of men are getting their body hair waxed and lasered off (Daum 2006).

Even though Daum is in San Francisco and therefore might not appear representative, major news outlets from the *New York Times* (see Newman 2007) to Internet magazines (Mondschein 2008) have documented the hairless-man trend. Even Canadians have taken note, as journalist Georgia Binks writes,

> somewhere along the line, after Samson, a few after Rapunzel, and about 30 years after the musical *Hair* lit the Broadway stage in the 1960s, hair became ugly. Not all hair, of course—but body hair. Everything from back and leg hair to pubic hair. And it's not just a female obsession anymore (Binks 2005).

The list of articles, images, and evidence reaches way beyond what I've presented here. However, the more interesting question is, What's going on? Where have all the Burts gone? Why have some facets of American mainstream culture seemingly embraced the ideal of baby-butt-smooth men?

It's challenging to pinpoint the exact cultural factors that contribute *11* to this desire for a hairless body, but I can suggest a few. The rapid spread of muscle culture has played a part (Moore 1997; Klein 1993). Body hair covers up the hours of labor men have spent working out and working up their muscles—or getting "buff," which literally means "to polish or shine." Writing about the growing trend of body hair removal for heterosexual Greek men, Helena Smith says, "What's the point of working up a sweat to acquire macho muscles if they are hidden behind a mat of body hair?" (Smith 2000). A cultural obsession with *youth and youthfulness* also probably has contributed to this hairless movement. If hair sprouting from the body is one of maturity's first biological markers, then to grow hair is to grow older and, thus, in a culture that reveres the *appearance* of youth, body hair must go—for men and women over, say, age twenty-two. More philosophically, the youthful-fit-hairless body also suggests a pervasive denial of mortality—perhaps with every hair plucked, zapped, or shaved one has had a little triumph in a greater war against death (Becker 1973; Shilling 2003). On a more mundane but nevertheless very powerful level, hetero men are simply the newest consumers to be drawn into an increasingly intensifying beauty market. Ever since Burt's appearance in the 1970s, men and their bodies, as Susan Bordo (1999) argues, have been increasingly drawn into an "ever-widening vortex of late-twentieth-century consumerism" (18). Besmirching male body hair and then providing a product to resolve this "problem" seems like a "natural" progression of the market.

Then there is the increasing influence of gay culture on straight men *12* (Gill, Henwood, and McLean 2005; Shilling 2003). Of course there is no singular "gay culture" nor any standardized perfect gay body (Hennen 2005; Connell 2005; Monaghan 2005). Nevertheless, the gay ideal with the most sway on the hetero male, as Monaghan (2005) points out, is the "young, blond, smooth-skinned, gym-buffed model type." The extremely popular show *Queer Eye for the Straight Guy*, in which five gay men give total makeovers to straight men, represents a cultural crystallization of this influence.

Very often makeovers included what Kyan Douglas, the grooming *13* guru, calls "manscaping"—trimming, shaving, waxing, or shaping male body hair. As *Queer Eye*'s popularity demonstrates, manscaping—the practice and the term—appears to have gone mainstream.

More than muscles, youth, mortality, and expanding markets, I'm *14* interested in this landscaping connection. I suspect that this linking between lawn care and male body hair is more than a simple metaphor, but a manifestation of subterranean roots beneath the cultural landscape.

Like a well-manicured lawn, the male body and its hairs have become the site of cultivation—pulling out and clipping back the unwanted to create the desired aesthetic. Like landscaping, manscaping entails human alteration of the external environment, only that environment is not a lawn or land but skin. So too, an expanding market offers various mechanical and chemical technologies for converting a weedy body into the dermal garden of one's dreams. The proverbial weed-whacker has its bodily counterpart in the Mangroomer: The Essential Do-It-Yourself Back Shaver, while chemical herbicides to rid one's lawn of noxious weeds, such as Roundup, have their parallels with products such as Nair for Men.

Whether engaging in landscaping or manscaping, what both practices 15 express is a deep desire for control over land and body. To state the matter differently, the act of manscaping, like landscaping, embodies an enduring effort to control nature. But what is the nature of this nature?

Constructing Nature and Hairy Bodies

The body is a bio-physical entity but is also, significantly, a social creation. 16 The same can be said about "nature." There is a bio-physical reality being referenced when we talk about nature, but the way in which we know and talk about that reality is deeply shaped by our historical and sociocultural position. For example, a photographer, hunter, and real estate developer will understand the same open field bustling with deer quite differently—the photographer sees a natural wonder ("take a picture"), the hunter a five-point buck ("pull the trigger"), and a real estate developer future profits ("bring in the bulldozers"). These differences aren't based on what's "out there" but on social values, meanings, interests, and identities (Greider and Garkovich 1994; Fine 1998). In other words, nature is socially constructed—which also means there's no singular Nature, only multiple natures (see Nash 1982; Oelschlaeger 1991; Murphy 1997; Taylor 2003; Williams 1980; Smith 2001; Cronon 1995; Demeritt 2002; Fine 1998).

Rather than simply an interesting academic insight, this idea that 17 nature is more human product than natural entity has serious environmental and political implications—for the way a group defines a specific nature will influence its feelings and direct its behavior. Consider the simple linguistic shift between calling the same geographic location a "swamp" versus a "wetland." These two names given to the same spot carry very different valuations and direct differing courses of action: namely, draining versus protecting.

Ideas of nature have also been used as ideological weapons to support 18 the intersects of the socially powerful. From the justification of European conquest by labeling indigenous peoples "wild savages" to the scientific racism that secured European superiority on the basis of "natural" skull size differences, the annals of Western history are rife with such examples of the naturalization of social injustice (Sale 2006; Bell 2004). Much of this ideological use of nature stems from a culture/nature dualism at the center of the Western worldview (Peterson 2001; Oelschlaeger 1991; Plumwood 1993; Davidson and Smith 2006; Devall and Sessions 1985; Ruether 1989; Gard 1993; Spretnak 1994). Rather than simply descriptive of the way the world is, this dichotomous worldview is normative—a socially constructed organization of life into mutually exclusive categories in which everything of value resides on the culture side and includes male, mind, reason, spirit, and human, while the devalued side of nature is associated with female, bodies, flesh and fluids, emotions, matter, and animals.

Much of Western history attests to the naturalization of this socially *19* constructed schema as women, indigenous people, and nonwhites were consistently marked as more natural than cultural, more emotional than rational, more animal than human, more savage than civilized, thereby legitimizing their subjugation.[3]

Although certainly not as politically nefarious, hairy male bodies, *20* from this dualistic perspective, are slipping or have slipped into the natural side of the equation. Manscaping, therefore, represents one more modern practice for reestablishing a bulwark against nature, an effort to mark oneself and one's body clearly on the cultural and human side of the equation. In other words, contemporary hairy and hairless males are simply being subsumed within a familiar culture-nature schema—hairless bodies on the culture side and hairy bodies on the nature side.

Sure, this makes sense. Yet, one problem with this dichotomous equa- *21* tion is the pervasive love of nature in the larger culture. We can observe the ever-expanding markets for nature's goods, a growing outdoor recreation and ecological tourism industry, a large section of the entertainment world devoted to the wonders of the wild, and a diverse and increasingly powerful environmental movement. Each of these uniquely testifies to a pervasive desire to protect and connect with rather than escape from or dominate the natural world.

We can account for this, in part, by loosening a strict culture-nature *22* dichotomy and positing that in contemporary society natures are proliferating—in any context multiple natures will be produced and circulated for different purposes. In the case of body hair there are (at least) two prominent natures at work: alluring and grotesque. Alluring nature gains its status from being under some form of physical or symbolic control—nature that stays put, so to speak Grotesque nature is any form of nature that blurs or breaks the symbolic or physical boundaries established by humans—nature that doesn't stay put. Body hair on men is now being symbolically linked with a grotesque nature and thus hairy bodies have become grotesque bodies.

Grotesque and Classical Bodies

I'm drawing this distinction from the work of Russian social theorist 23
Mikhail Bakhtin's (1984) typology of the grotesque and classical body.
From his historical studies of sixteenth-century European literature,
Bakhtin locates the grotesque body within the context of pre-Lenten medieval carnivals. The carnival was a time for the breaching of established
social codes in which "normal" social interactions were subverted — a time
of communal feasting and debauchery in which traditional status and class
hierarchies were broken down as nobleman and peasant joined in mutual
celebration. This type of communal revelry also included public release
of the body and its shared functions, displays of excess and indulgence,
and comic expression that reinforced, rather than excluded, a human and
fleshy (*carn*) commonality. Rich or poor, high or low, the carnival was a
ritualized moment of social equalization in which there was a collective
recognition that every human and nonhuman animal eats, shits, bleeds,
and dies.

From this research, he draws a portrait of the grotesque body as one 24
that penetrates outwards into the world as well as allowing the external
world inside (27). Examining grotesque imagery Bakhtin writes,

> Special attention is given to the shoots and branches, to all that prolongs
> the body and links it to other bodies or to the world outside . . . The grotesque
> body . . . is a body in the act of becoming. Thus the artistic logic of the
> grotesque image ignores the closed, smooth, and impenetrable surface of the
> body and retains only its excrescences (sprouts, buds) and orifices, only that
> which leads beyond the body's limited space or into the body's depth. (316–18)

The grotesque body is a body in constant interchange with its surroundings: a body that is in continual intercourse with other human bodies, the
bodies of nature, and the cycles of death and renewal — in other terms, a
type of "ecological body" (Gardiner 1993; Bell 1994).

With the disintegration of the medieval world and the birth of the 25
modern social order emerged a new "bodily canon" of the "classical body."
Counter to the grotesque's interpenetrating openness, the classical body is
a sealed, closed, individual sphere (321). The classical body is, according
to Bakhtin,

> an entirely finished, completed, strictly limited body, which is shown from the
> outside as something individual, That which protrudes, bulges, sprouts, or
> branches off . . . is eliminated, hidden, or moderated. The basis of the image
> is the individual, strictly limited mass, the impenetrable facade. The opaque
> surface and the body's "valleys" acquire an essential meaning as the border
> of a closed individuality that does not merge with other bodies and with the
> world. (320)

This is the modern "bourgeois ego," according to Bakhtin, a sense of identity based on maintaining an embodied distinction from everything else.

The revelry in the grotesque—in gorging and drinking, in the excesses 26 of the "lower stratum" of bodily life—is deemed dirty, crude, and repulsive to classical sensibilities. "The classic body does not spit. It does not sweat. It does not cry," writes Michael Bell (1994). "It is dirty even to speak of excrement, urine, vomit, ejaculate, and menstrual blood except in polite, disdainful, or scientific language which sanitizes and distances material truth, like plastic wrapping around a supermarket chicken" (73). To follow Bell's imagery of the plastic-wrapped chicken, the archetypal modern expression of the classical body can be found in Barbie and Ken: no openings to stick things in, no protruding genitals that leak fluids out, no nipples, and absolutely no body hair, just sleek, nonbiodegradable, and seamless plastic.

Grotesque Bodies and Grotesque Nature

The hairy male body has become a type of grotesque natural body. It's a 27 body emblematic of a boundary breaching and wild nature and therefore anathema to contemporary-classical aesthetics. No doubt, the physical characteristics of body hair have contributed to this label as grotesque. Body hair breaks borders. Like the shoots of a plant, it pushes beyond the surface of the skin and, at times, reaches beyond the confines of the skin completely as it lands in the shower drain, furrows into a bar of soap, or lodges in food. Body hair also disperses the sweat and odors of the body outward. It is, however, not only its capacity to cast outward but its ability to bring in the outside world by catching smells and other particles that makes body hair particularly susceptible to classical repulsion and efforts of management. Body hair, in other words, can be interpreted as an organ of grotesque interchange between the body and its surroundings. Although head hair has many similar characteristics, only body hair has gained a kind of grotesque status and therefore is seen as in need of contemporary-classical regimes of control—i.e., manscaping.

Popular texts and images clearly attest to male body hair as grotesque. 28 For instance, classical bodies are premised on a sealed purity, a hygienic standard that depends upon the exclusion of all things deemed filthy. Body hair, in that it breaches the boundaries of this enclosed sterility, evokes repulsion from contemporary men and women aiming to adhere to classical standards. "In contemporary Western culture," write Toerien and Wilkinson (2003) on the normative demands of hairlessness for women, "only women's body hair is routinely treated as a cause for disgust, much like other body products (such as blood, faeces, sweat or odours) that are thought to be unclean" (338). For current research, these scholars surprisingly overlook the growing egalitarian status of body hair as filth for both genders. "When it comes to armpits, it is absolutely necessary to maintain the hair growth," advises a "Hair on Men's Body" Internet column, "plus women are totally averse to men with bad body odor. Bushy arm-pits generate heavier perspiration. . . . Taking care of your body hair is the first step towards better personal hygiene" (Jurgita 2003). Or consider the promise of "better hygiene" as a selling point for Nair for Men.[4] According to an Internet article on the importance of shaved male parts, "pubic hair collects sweat and other body fluids that give off strong odors. The warm moist pubic hair provides ideal conditions for bacteria and fungus to grow."[5] Increasingly, body hair is achieving an egalitarian status as unhygienic—a place for mushrooms, bacteria, and other contaminating natural elements to nest and grow. Hairy body parts are thus polluted body parts, and hairless body parts are pure body parts for both men and women striving for classical bodies.

The contaminating potential of body hair runs deeper than issues of hygiene, however. The grotesque quality of body hair threatens to disrupt a much deeper and more cherished human-animal boundary. In the classical-contemporary imagination, body hair appears as a reminder of our connection to other "dirty" creatures, a repulsive memento of our common animal nature. "I have never been a fan of the hairy back," writes Lisa Daily (2006) in her e-article, "Manscaping: The Battle against Hair." "Or hairy shoulders. Most women I know aren't. Frankly, we would like our guy to have more than one degree of separation between him and the banana-eaters down at the zoo." "The hairy bear-y Male," opens a Hair on Men's Body advice column, "a majority of women loathe the sight of an excessively hairy man. They may usually pass him off as some bristly creature" (Jurgita 2003). "If you look like a sasquatch, then you will need to either shave or wax your body hair," counsels the Midlife Bachelor,

> A sasquatch is a large hairy beast (also known as "Big Foot") that supposedly lives in the wilderness of North America. A sasquatch has thick hair every-where—like a bear . . . women do not like the sasquatch look! My point—if you are a sasquatch, it is time to get yourself waxed. Shave that back and chest, at the very least.[6]

Sasquatch, apes, bears, bristly creatures—this type of discourse reveals body hair's potential to disrupt a culturally enduring division between humans and nonhumans. Sure, Darwin made a pretty strong case about our shared evolutionary history, and scientific studies keep discrediting each of the boundaries we've set up to distinguish ourselves from other creatures (see Falk 2007; Peterson 2001). Yet, manscaping seems to reflect a historically and culturally pervasive desire to maintain our humanness through denial—as if by removing body hair women and men are echoing the tortured assertion of the *Elephant Man* (1980), "I am not an animal! I'm a human being!" To not remove these grotesque strands, to let body hair go undomesticated, therefore, is to risk being absorbed back into a primal animalistic and inhuman state.[7]

Inherent in this fear of being stigmatized as a grotesque animal is the   30
creeping fear of the wilderness: after all, where do these inhuman creatures dwell but beyond the edges of society? I am not talking about the
wilderness popularized by the environmental movement—an ecologically
delicate landscape and refuge for poetic and even mystical encounters (see
Cronon 1995). Rather, body hair is symbolically tied to a pre-Romantic,
older, and more chaotic nature, one that has the potential to powerfully
disrupt an orderly civilization (Merchant 1980). This is the wilderness of
the early Puritan settlers of North America, who, guided by their cultivated
sensibilities and a religious script that included dominion and visions of a
sacred garden, set out to cut down and take control of a "cursed" and "chaotic" landscape whose wilds threatened to pollute and possess their bodies
and souls (Finch 2001; Nash 1982).

Yes, most Puritans and the wilderness they knew may have disap-   31
peared, but a Puritanical attitude toward male body hair echoes in the
acts of modern manscapers. Consider Kyan Douglas's definition of manscaping: "manscaping is trimming/shaving/waxing hair to maintain it so it
doesn't look like fur, a sweater or worst of all, a forest."[8] Or how about this
Internet advice: "if your chest/naughty bits are lost in the wilderness rather
than shave, try relaxing the hair a little bit" (Renzi 2007). Reflect on the
implicit association with body hair, wilderness, and the desire for dominion in a review of Norelco's new Bodygroom razor for men: "Norelco is
blazing a path through the largely *unexplored* world of men's body-hair
removal with the release of Bodygroom, a new electric razor designed to
clear-cut dense thickets of chest, back and even pubic hair—without the
nasty irritation" (Creamer 2006; italics added). Associated with either a
threatening forest or a creature dwelling in the wilderness, hairy male
bodies demand civilizing. Just as landscaping cuts back the disorderly and
chaotic—even tall grasses can have dangers such as snakes and ticks lurking about—manscaping tames body hair that has become the symbolic
repository of all forms of unwanted wilderness. This wilderness demands
control because, like all things grotesque, it constantly threatens to creep
across or violently dislocate humanly constructed boundaries. Manscaping
therefore seems to reflect a recent chapter in an old story about an ongoing struggle to civilize the wild; the only difference is that the attitudes and
efforts once primarily reserved for controlling an external savage nature
have become focused on the hairs of male bodies.

Of course, in most cases removal of body hair is not for moral purity   32
but for sexuality—manscapers are not repressed Puritans nor classically
aristocratic bourgeoisie but sexually liberated moderns, right? Maybe.
As critical theorist Herbert Marcuse (1966) argued, human sexuality
does have socially revolutionary potential. Yet, the culture industry of
capitalism transfigures and tames this sexual potential by transforming sex
into one more commodity for consumption—witness the multi-million-
dollar pornography *industry*. Commercialized and therefore controlled,

the apparent sexual freedom that bombards modern men and women is deeply enmeshed with expanding forms of social domination. From this perspective, manscaping with the motive for sexual appeal seems part of this ever-escalating effort of advanced capitalism to domesticate all dimensions of sexuality (and nature). Like a well-manicured lawn, manscaping seems to reflect a commercialized and market-regulated obsession with classically styled, purified, individuated bodies—bodies that are about looking good rather than about indulging in wild pleasure.

To pull this tangle together, male body hair has become a symbolic 33 crystallization of a boundary breaching, animalistic, and wild nature—in a singular term, grotesque nature. As such, the stigma of body hair runs deeper than the skin. Similar to the classical bourgeois-ego fretting about contamination of his pure body or the Puritan worrying about the potential moral stain caused by the wilderness, body hair reflects a type of character flaw—like the neighbor who becomes suspect because he allowed his lawn to grow dense with overgrowth. Manscaping efforts are therefore aimed at control over these grotesque hairs—an effort to transform an uncomely personal wilderness into a well-presented garden. Manscaping, stated differently, can be interpreted as a recent chapter in the ongoing struggle for power over a grotesque nature; a well-manscaped body is a demonstration of control and possession of a distinctly human self.

Classical bodies are not bodies free from nature, but they are bodies 34 ideally composed of an alluring nature. The weedy and wild grotesque elements of the body must be tamed, but the result must appear natural. "Natural Hair Removal" products, for example, promise the use of natural ingredients (read "alluring nature") to remove unwanted hair (read "grotesque nature") as well as promising that the results will look "natural." Hairless classical bodies also desire to commune with and protect an alluring nature—to frolic in emerald rainforests rather than tangled hellish jungles, to protect wetland treasures rather than putrid swamps. Alluring nature, whether on the body or outside the body, is thus premised on a physical and symbolic domination—at root, desired and alluring nature is premised on dominion. Grotesque nature, whether bodily or external, is despised because it disrupts and breaks the symbolic and physical boundaries we've put in place.

Manscaping is, therefore, not simply an effort to distance oneself 35 from nature—after all, the term "manscaping" implies a cultivated nature, not freedom from nature. Rather, shaving and plucking is a reaffirmation and a bulwark to establish the boundary between an alluring controlled-civilized natural body and a grotesque uncontrolled-uncivilized natural body. For those with enough money to afford laser hair removal, mastery over body hair has almost been accomplished. As long as body hair resiliently resurfaces, however, so too does an older chaotic and disobedient nature—a disconcerting reminder that complete control has not yet been achieved.[9]

Conclusion

For women, this battle against the wilds of body hair has been going on 36
for quite some time—for so long that hairless women seem "natural."
This may have something to do with a long-standing Western legacy of
associating women with the frenzied passions of nature's forces and conceptualizing women's bodies as highly grotesque and messy, and therefore
threatening to rational male order (Kristeva 1982; Shildrick 1997). Due
to this association, women and their bodies were, from the perspective of
men, seemingly in need of greater emotional and physical management.
Hairlessness therefore became a type of external sign that expressed an
inner self-containment and, more importantly, a mark of being under the
control of a man's "civilized" dominion. Considering manscaping, however, we are faced with a strange transfiguration in which men seem to
be doing to themselves what they demanded of women as well as women
making those demands on men. Clean up those grotesque, disorganized,
spongy, leaky, and animal bodies!

At one level, this transformation could simply be seen as an expan- 37
sion and incorporation of men's bodies into the beauty market. Linking a
grotesque nature to male body hair is simply a convenient symbolic tool
to stigmatize this male body part and provide new commodities to rid one
of this natural nastiness. After all, human conceptions of nature have long
been a convenient tool for condemnation as well as idealization. However,
I have a theory that the use of this nature is less about symbolic convenience and more about a larger cultural disquiet.

In the face of ecological anxiety induced by issues as overwhelming 38
and potentially disruptive as climate destabilization, one response is an
intensified desire to control the body. A number of highly respected sociological theorists make a similar claim, such as Anthony Giddens (1991),
who argues that the rapid and destabilizing social forces of late modernity
have facilitated an intense focus on personal identity and the body. In her
work *The Body Project* (1998), Joan Brumberg outlines how larger social
anxieties coalesce around adolescent girls' bodies—the body becomes central to her identity, its alteration the only site of control. No doubt, social
anxiety consolidates around those who are most vulnerable, but ecological
anxiety—the anxiety produced from the increasing awareness of an environmental crisis—seems more egalitarian and democratic. Why? Well, simply
put, environmental problems don't respect borders. The hazards of climate
change or radioactive clouds all transgress their point of origin, crossing
over national, class, race, status, and gender boundaries. Certainly pollution
follows the poor and socially marginalized (Bullard 2005, 2000, 1993; Bernier 2007). But because we are all living in what Ulrich Beck (1992, 1999)
calls a "World Risk Society," everyone remains susceptible, even future generations. These environmental hazards penetrate their way into the everyday world, opening up an entire spectrum of questions about the safety of
basic necessities such as food, water, air, and shelter (Edelstein 2000).

So, as the biosphere spins out of control and the old chaotic metaphors 39 for nature return, the body becomes a locus of increasing control. The logic goes something like this: "I might not be able to be in command of an erratic atmosphere but at least I can have some control over my physical being." The body has become the great new hope for dominion at a time when the external natural world seems to be returning with a primordial vengeance. The average man might not be able to exert much influence over these uncontrollable elements of outside nature—and the men that do have the power to change it don't seem very interested in doing so—but if this chaos can be symbolically shifted to the body, then some feeling of control is within grasp. The contemporary manscaping trend is one example of this intensified desire for power over an increasingly chaotic nature. As body hair has become the symbolic repository of a grotesque nature, modern manscapers set upon their body hair with religious zeal and razors to conquer this vestige of natural chaos, to beat back the disquiet caused by a hostile wild, to cultivate a pure body on an increasingly polluted earth.

Now, I am not promoting an antimanscaping campaign or a hairy rev- 40 olution for environmental sustainability as if by "returning" to some idea of the "good old hairy days" when Burt Reynolds was lying on a bearskin rug could somehow reestablish ecological harmony. Such a move seems silly and has been attempted unsuccessfully by the men's movement in the 1990s—in particular by Robert Bly, who implored "the sanitized, hairless, shallow man of the Judeo-Christian corporate world" to get in touch with his "Wild" and "Hairy Man" (Bly in Ross 1992). Bly's return to hairy nature was an effort to resolve a particular male crisis, not an environmental crisis. So, too, while possibly well-intentioned, much of this manly return was laden with sexist, anti-feminist, and ethnocentric sentiments (see Ross 1992). The increasingly stigmatized status of body hair does make it more likely to become a form of dissent to classical body regimes, but stopping manscaping will not accomplish a great deal of ecological good.

What I am proposing is a more modest examination of all types 41 of body projects and practices—from plastic surgery to exercise regimes—in the context of ecological crisis. Drawing out such interconnections and implications may prove not only intellectually interesting for those engaged in body studies but also, for those ecologically engaged scholars and activists, such studies may illuminate what Max Oelschlaeger (1994) has termed the "paradox of environmentalism" (p. 21): After more than three decades of progressive environmental changes why do we appear closer than ever to an ecological meltdown? Manscaping, as far as I can tell, reveals that even with more than three decades of ever-increasing environmental consciousness, there is still a persistent and possibly mounting bewilderment about our embodied relationship to other creatures and our place in the biosphere. This confusion may continue, in part, to thwart even the best-intentioned economic, technological, and legal changes for a sustainable future.

NOTES

1. The quotation marks around "heterosexual" should forewarn you that this term is highly contested and that human sexuality cannot fit into a neat homo-hetero binary.
2. Accessed May 2007, http://www.skinema.com. Also, a simple Internet search brings up a plethora of heterosexual male body hair discussions. For two examples visit http://www.jur-gita.com/articles-id142.html or http://www.carefair.com/Men/Does_She_Mind_1934.html.
3. Although at certain points in modern European history there appears a romantic celebration (often patronizing) of a feminized nature (Merchant 1980) and the "noble savage" (Sale 2006), with the progress and spread of civilization, the idea that triumphed was that nature was to serve culture, animals to serve humans, women to serve men, savages to serve the civilized, and nonwhites to serve whites. Human exceptionalism and distinction, in other words, is a master ideological variable in the domination of nature as well as in different forms of social domination, oppression, and injustice (Spretnak 1999; Adams 1993; Conboy, Medina, and Stanbury 1997).
4. Accessed May 2008, advertisement available at http://www.lovehoney.co.uk/product. cfm?p=l337.
5. Accessed May 2008, http://www.bodyhairremovalnews.com/Men-Shaving-Pubic-Hair-Quiz-Show.htm.
6. Accessed May 5, 2008, http://www.midlifebachelor.com/makeover/makeover-appear-hygiene7.html.
7. Recall your grade-school days and those pictorial representations of the "evolution of man." The posters—probably duplicated in Time-Life books on evolution—show that not only does primal man move from quadra- to bipedal, from a crude club to a refined spear, but he also evolves from hairy to hairless. Although this representation of man's evolution may strive to *describe* the "facts" (i.e., humans were hairier back then and have become progressively less hairy), in the popular imagination this description has become prescription, and the line between facts of body hair and its value becomes fuzzy. The following excerpt from an Internet discussion about body hair illustrates this point:

   > I think that our antipathy against body hair is an evolution thing. Maybe in the past people who didn't have a lot of body hair were considered to be more evolved—So maybe it is an instinctive way of us humans to remove body hair because we don't want to look like our ancestors (whether they were apes or just heavily haired humans).

   Rather than neutral or descriptive, this statement, like so many other public discussions about evolution, is implicitly linked with a value-laden notion of progress—as a species we're not simply evolving but moving toward the "good." Body hair is therefore a primitive marker, a sign that progress has not been made and that hairy men are evolutionary left-behinds in need a civilized shaving or waxing to enter the ranks of homo sapiens.
8. Douglas, Kyan, 2003, "Interesting Questions, Facts, and Information," *FunTrivia* (online 2006). Available at: http://www.funtrivia.com/en/Television/Queer-Eye-for-the-Straight-Guy-10553-html.
9. Although stigmatized, grotesque male body hair does have its place in the public eye—quite often as comic relief. To take one example, in *The Forty-Year-Old Virgin*, actor Steve Carell plays the role of Andy, an earnest yet socially awkward guy who lacks experience with women. In what has become a somewhat classic yet painful scene, Andy, with the guidance of his coworkers who are dedicated to getting him laid, has his chest and stomach hair waxed. Finding humor in grotesque expressions, as Bakhtin argued, helped level social distinctions as well as differences between earthiness and society. Unlike this "laughing with," the new genre of male

body hair humor seems more like a "laughing at"—a form of corrective humor aimed at patrolling the border of the acceptable. In this case, body-hair humor reinforces the increasingly normative demands for a hairless male body.

When not the source of humor, media representations of hairy men often appear as morally suspect and primitive characters. Witness the majority of men on the television show *The Sopranos*, which revolves around the daily-life of New Jersey mobsters. Tony Soprano, played by James Gandolfini, is a contemporary incarnation of grotesque excess—prone to violent emotions, excessive eating and sexuality, and a good deal of body hair. He is the embodiment of all the rejected elements of a classical body and a civilized life. Nevertheless, judging from the ratings, rather than repellent he appears to be a point of popular fascination and possibly idolization. This might be, in some measure, because each of his grotesque characteristics contains what Stallybrass and White (1986) call "the imprint of desire." These grotesque elements, seemingly cast out as the Other to civilization, "return as the object of nostalgia, longing and fascination. Placed at the outer limits of civil life, they become symbolic contents of bourgeois desire" (191). Tony Soprano is an object of fascination because he blurs the distinction that has been constructed between a classical humanity and an uncivilized animal nature.

REFERENCES

Adams, Carol J., ed. 1993. *Ecofeminism and the Sacred*. New York: Continuum.
Bakhtin, Mikhail. 1984. *Rabelais and His World*. Bloomington, IN: Indiana University Press.
Beck, Ulrich. 1992. Risk society: Towards a new modernity. In *Theory, Culture, and Society*. Translated by M. A. Ritter. Edited by M. Featherstone. London: Sage.
——1999. *World Risk Society*. Maiden, MA: Polity Press.
Becker, Ernest. 1973. *The Denial of Death*. New York: Free Press.
Bell, Michael. 2004. An invitation to environmental sociology. In *Sociology for a New Century*. Edited by C. Ragin, W. Griswold, and L. Griffin. Second ed. Thousand Oaks, CA: Pine Forge Press.
Bell, Michael M. 1994. Deep fecology: Mikhail Bakhtin and the call of nature. *Capitalism, nature, socialism* 5 (4):65–84.
Bernier, C. J. Correa. 2007. *Toxic Wastes and Race at Twenty: 1987–2007*. Cleveland, OH: United Church of Christ Justice and Witness Ministries.
Binks, Georgia. 2005. It's a Smooth World. *CBC News*, March 25.
Bordo, Susan. 1999. *The Male Body: A New Look at Men in Public and in Private*. New York: Farrar, Straus, Giroux.
Brumberg, Joan. 1998. *The Body Project: An Intimate History of American Girls*. New York: Random House.
Bullard, Robert. 1993. *Confronting Environmental Racism: Voices from the Grassroots*. Cambridge, MA: South End Press.
——2000. *Dumping in Dixie: Race, Class, and Environmental Quality*. Jackson, TN: West-view Press.
——ed. 2005. *The Quest for Environmental Justice: Human Rights and the Politics of Pollution*. San Francisco: Sierra Club Books.
Conboy, Katie, Nadia Medina, and Sarah Stanbury, eds. 1997. *Writing on the Body: Female Embodiment and Feminist Theory*. New York: Colombia University Press.
Connell, R. W. 2005. *Masculinities*. 2nd ed. Berkeley: University of California Press.
Cooper, Lasandra. 2006. *Cosmetic Surgery for Men Tops 1 Million, Says American Society of Plastic Surgeons*. American Society of Plastic Surgeons 2001 [cited July 2006]. Available from http://www.plasticsurgery.org.
Creamer, Matthew. 2006. Norelco puts the man in manscaping: Testosterone-fueled site for Bodygroom plays up the "optical inch" in attempt to steer clear of metrosexuality. *Advertising Age*, May 15, 45.

Cronon, William. 1995. The trouble with wilderness; or, Getting back to the wrong nature. In *Uncommon Ground: Toward Reinventing Nature*. Edited by W. Cronon. New York: Norton.

——ed. 1995. *Uncommon Ground: Toward Reinventing Nature*. New York: Norton.

Daily, Lisa. 2006. "Manscaping: The Batde against Hair." Available online at http://click.laval-ife.com/datmg/feature/article/manscaping-the-battle-against-hair/rHSA/27764/p1.

Daum, Meghan. 2006. Surveying the cultural manscape. *San Francisco Chronicle*, Sunday, April 16, 8.

Davidson, Joyce, and Mike Smith. 2006. "It makes my skin crawl . . . ": The embodiment of disgust in phobias of "nature." *Body & Society*. 12 (1) 3–67.

Demeritt, David 2002. What is the "social construction of nature"? A typology and sympathetic critique. *Progress in Human Geography*. 26 (2): 767–90.

Devall, Bill, and George Sessions. 1985. *Deep Ecology: Living as if Nature Mattered*. Salt Lake City, UT: Gibbs Smith.

Edelstein, Michael R. 2000. "Outsiders just don't understand": Personalization of risk and the boundary between modernity and postmodernity. *In Risk in the Modern Age: Social Theory, Science, and Environmental Decision-Making*. Edited by M. J. Cohen. New York: St. Martin's.

Falk, William. 2007. Chimps like us. *The Week*, December 28, 35.

Finch, Martha L. 2001. "Civilized" bodies and the "savage" environment of early New Plymouth. In *A Centre of Wonders: The Body in Early America*. Edited by J. M. Lindman and M. L. Tarter. Ithaca, NY: Cornell University Press.

Fine, Gary Alan. 1998. *Morel Tales: The Culture of Mushrooming*. Cambridge, MA: Harvard University Press.

Gard, Greta, ed. 1993. *Ecofeminism: Women, Animals, Nature*. Philadelphia: Temple University Press.

Gardiner, Michael 1993. Ecology and carnival: Traces of a "green" social theory in the writings of M. M. Bakhtin. *Theory and Society* 22 (6):765–812.

Giddens, Anthony. 1991. *Modernity and Self-Identity*. Stanford: Stanford University Press.

Gill, Rosalind, Karen Henwood, and Carl McLean. 2005. Body projects and the regulation of normative masculinity. *Body & Society* 11 (1):37–62.

Greider, Thomas, and Lorraine Garkovich. 1994. Landscapes: The social construction of nature and the environment. *Rural Sociology* 59 (1):1–24.

Hennen, Peter. 2005. Bear bodies, bear masculinity: Recuperation, resistance, or retreat? *Gender & Society* 19 (1):25–43.

Hope, Christine. 1982. Caucasian female body hair and American culture. *The Journal of America Culture*. 5:93–99.

Jurgita. 2003. *Hair on men's body* [Online], 10-26-2006 [cited March 2007]. Available from http://www.jurgita.com/articles-id142.html.

King, Ynestra. 1990. Healing the wounds: Feminism, ecology, and the nature/culture split. In *Reweaving the World: The Emergence of Ecofeminism*. Edited by I. Diamond and G. Oren. stein. San Francisco: Sierra Club Books.

Klein, Alan M. 1993. *Little Big Men: Bodybuilding, Subculture and Gender Construction*. Albany: State University of New York Press.

Kristeva, Julia. 1982. Powers of Horror: *An Essay on Abjection*. Translated by L. Roudiez. New York: Columbia University Press.

Luciano, Lynne. 2001. *Looking Good: Male Body Image in Modern America*. New York: Hill and Wang.

Marcuse, Herbert. 1966. *Eros and Civilization*. Boston: Beacon.

Merchant, Carolyn. 1980. *The Death of Nature: Women, Ecology, and the Scientific Revolution*. New York: HarperSanFrancisco.

Monaghan, Lee F. 2005. Big handsome men, bears, and others: Virtual constructions of "fat male embodiment." *Body & Society*. 11 (2):81–111.

Mondschein, Ken. 2008. *History of Single Life: Public Hair*. Nerve 2007 [cited June 2008]. Available from http://www.nei-ve.com/regulars/singlelife/oo6/.

Moore, Pamela L., ed. 1997. *Building Bodies*. New Brunswick, NJ: Rutgers University Press.

Murphy, Raymond. 1997. *Sociology and Nature: Social Action in Context*. Boulder, CO: West-view Press.

Nash, Roderick. 1982. *Wilderness and the American Mind*. New Haven, CT: Yale University Press.

Newman, Andrew. 2007. Depilatory market moves far beyond the short-shorts. *The New York Times*, September 14, C3.

Oelschlaeger, Max. 1991. *The Idea of Wilderness: From Prehistory to the Age of Ecology*. New Haven, CT: Yale University Press.

—— 1994. *Caring for Creation: An Ecumenical Approach to the Environmental Crisis*. New Haven, CT: Yale University Press.

Peterson, Anna L. 2001. *Being Human: Ethics, Environment, and Our Place in the World*. Berkeley: University of California Press.

Plumwood, Val. 1993. *Feminism and the Mastery of Nature*. London: Routledge.

Pope, Harrison G., Katharine A. Phillips, and Roberto Olvardia. 2000. *The Adonis Complex: The Secret Crisis of Male Body Obsession*. New York: Free Press.

Rapley, Time. 2007. *Doing Conversation, Discourse, and Document Analysis*. Thousand Oaks, CA: Sage Publications.

Renzi, Dan. 2007. *How was your day, Dan?* 2005 [cited March 2007]. Available from http:// danrenzi.typepad.com/stuff/2005/04/after_lett ing_m.html.

Ross, Andrew. 1992. Wet, dark, and low, Eco-Man evolves from Eco-Women. *Boundary 2* 19 (2):205–32.

Ruether, Rosmary Radford. 1989. *Gaia and God: An Ecofeminist Theology of Earth Healing*. New York: HarperSanFrancisco.

Sale, Kirkpatrick. 2006. *Christopher Columbus and the Conquest of Paradise*. Second ed. NewYork Tauris Parke Paperbucks.

Shildrick, M 1997. *Leaky Bodies and Boundaries: Feminism, Postmodernism, and (Bio) Ethics*. New York: Routledge.

Shilling, Chris. 2003. The body and social theory. In *Theory, Culture & Society*, second ed. Edited by M. Featherstone. London: Sage.

Slater, Candace. 1995. Amazonia as Edenic narrative. In *Uncommon Ground: Toward Reinventing Nature*. Edited by W. Cronon, New York: Norton.

Smith, Helena. 2000. Why Zorba can't keep his hair on: Today's Greek gods go late-night loitering in beauty parlours. *New Statesman*, July 10,12.

Smith, Mark. 2001. The face of nature: Environmental ethics and the boundaries of contemporary social theory. *Current Sociology*. 49 (1):49–65.

Spretnak, Charlene. 1994. Critical and constructive contributions of ecofeminism. In *World-views and Ecology: Religion, Philosophy, and the Environment*. Edited by M. E. Tucker and J. A. Grim. Maryknoll, NY: Orbis Books.

—— 1999. *The Resurgence of the Real: Body, Nature, and Place in a Hypermodern World*. New York: Routledge.

Stallybrass, Peter, and Allon White. 1986. *The Politics and Poetics of Transgression*. Ithaca, NY: Cornell University Press.

Synott, Anthony. 1987. Shame and glory: A sociology of hair. *The British Journal of Sociology*. 38 (3):381–413.

Taylor, Sarah McFarland. 2003. Nature. In *Religion and American Cultures: An Encyclopedia of Traditions, Diversity, and Popular Expressions*. Edited by G. Laderman and L. Leon. Santa Barbara, CA: ABC-CLIO.

Toerien, Merran, and Sue Wilkinson. 2003. Gender and body hair: Constructing the feminine woman. *Women's Studies International Forum*. 26 (4):333–44.

Toerien, Merran, Sue Wilkinson, and Precilla Y. L. Choi. 2005. Body hair removal: The "mundane" production of normative femininity. *Sex Roles*. 52:399–406.

Weitz, Rose. 2004, *Rapunzel's Daughters: What Women's Hair Tells Us about Women's Lives*. First ed. New York Farrar, Straus, Giroux.
Williams, Raymond. 1980. *Ideas of Nature*. London: Verso.

■ ■ ■

Reading as a Writer: Analyzing Rhetorical Choices

1. Reread Immergut's description in paragraph 5 of the methods he uses to gather data for this analysis. Take notes on the different sources, which he refers to as "heterogeneous"; why? (You may need to look up this word.) What strengths and limitations does he see in his own research methods, and how does he explain why he uses this approach? What additional strengths and limitations do you see?

2. Like many academic writers, Immergut uses a the ideas of a key theorist—in this case, the ideas of Mikhail Bakhtin—as a lens through which to examine the evidence for his argument. Based on the description of Bakhtin's ideas about the "grotesque body" in the "Grotesque and Classical Bodies" section of this piece, paraphrase Bakhtin's main point about "grotesque" bodies and nature. How does this idea help Immergut make his point about contemporary attitudes about the male body?

Writing as a Reader: Entering the Conversation of Ideas

1. Immergut's ideas about the ways expectations of masculinity are shaped by particular historical and cultural moments are useful to think about in relation to Michael Kimmel's analysis of masculinity and terrorism. Place these authors' ideas and examples in conversation as you write an essay that examines contemporary contradictions in our attitudes toward masculinity. What significance do you see in these contradictions?

2. Both Immergut and Elline Lipkin draw on insights from the cultural historian Joan Jacobs Brumberg, who uses the phrase "body projects" to describe behaviors related to gender performance. Compose an essay that considers the ways Immergut and Lipkin each use Brumberg's idea of "body projects" as you make an argument about the significance you see in these shifting cultural practices.

C. J. PASCOE

"Dude, You're a Fag": Adolescent Masculinity and the Fag Discourse

C. J. Pascoe is a professor of sociology at the University of Oregon who writes and teaches about youth culture, media, and sexuality. This essay comes from the research for her 2007 book, *Dude, You're a Fag: Masculinity and Sexuality in High School*. In this piece, she takes a familiar taunt—"You're a fag"—and examines it through the eyes of a scholar, considering its contexts and meanings. Pascoe argues that rather than being a simple homophobic slur, often used in jest, and so common among school kids that it may seem almost meaningless, if we analyze the contexts in which the phrase is used, we can understand better how adolescent boys often say it to determine what it means to be masculine. Further, Pascoe points out that this "fag discourse is racialized" (para. 6), and is used differently in different communities.

Pascoe calls herself a "feminist" scholar, meaning that she is interested in the effects of gender assumptions on the lived experiences of both women and men. While it might seem unlikely for a feminist scholar to be interested in the lives of men, the study of masculinity is a growing field, as scholars examine the ways our cultural assumptions about what it means to be "masculine" often limit boys' and men's lives.

The essay is organized loosely in what is often called the IMRAD style (Introduction, Methods, Research, and Discussion), common to scientific essays, and also to some social scientists, such as Pascoe. How does the structure of the essay help you follow Pascoe's argument? While you may find the language in the opening pages a bit challenging, as Pascoe lays out the research others have done in the study of masculinity, try to mark key terms and ideas, and look for the definitions she offers of terms like "the sociology of masculinity" (para. 7), "queer theory" (para. 8), and understandings of gender as something made by culture (para. 11). How do these ideas help her make her larger point?

The "Method" and "Research" sections are more descriptive, as Pasco explains how she gathered data firsthand at a high school. What are the effects of describing the high school and the town this way and including direct quotations by students? Consider your own high school experiences as you think about the challenges of obtaining information through personal interviews and observation.

You may be surprised by Pascoe's conclusion that calling someone a "fag" has little do to with homosexuality. She notes, "Looking at 'fag' as a discourse rather than a static identity reveals that the term can be invested with different meanings in different social spaces" (para. 40). By shifting our focus away from simple assumptions about teen homophobia and toward an analysis of specific social situations in which the term "fag" is used, Pascoe argues that we can see how much is at stake, and for whom, when adolescent boys evaluate other boys' masculinity. In Pascoe's final paragraph, she suggests implications for future research and notes that the consequences of this kind of teasing can be deadly.

■ ■ ■

"There's a faggot over there! There's a faggot over there! Come look!" yelled Brian, a senior at River High School, to a group of 10-year-old boys. Following Brian, the 10-year-olds dashed down a hallway. At the end of the hallway Brian's friend, Dan, pursed his lips and began sashaying towards the 10-year-olds. He minced towards them, swinging his hips exaggeratedly and wildly waving his arms. To the boys Brian yelled, "Look at the faggot!

Watch out! He'll get you!" In response the 10-year-olds raced back down the
hallway screaming in terror.

(FROM AUTHOR'S FIELDNOTES)

The relationship between adolescent masculinity and sexuality is   *1*
embedded in the specter of the faggot. Faggots represent a penetrated
masculinity in which "to be penetrated is to abdicate power" (Bersani,
1987: 212). Penetrated men symbolize a masculinity devoid of power,
which, in its contradiction, threatens both psychic and social chaos. It is
precisely this specter of penetrated masculinity that functions as a regulatory mechanism of gender for contemporary American adolescent boys.

Feminist scholars of masculinity have documented the centrality of   *2*
homophobic insults to masculinity (Lehne, 1998; Kimmel, 2001) especially in school settings (Wood, 1984; Smith, 1998; Burn, 2000; Plummer,
2001; Kimmel, 2003). They argue that homophobic teasing often characterizes masculinity in adolescence and early adulthood, and that anti-gay
slurs tend to primarily be directed at other gay boys.

This article both expands on and challenges these accounts of rela-   *3*
tionships between homophobia and masculinity. Homophobia is indeed
a central mechanism in the making of contemporary American adolescent masculinity. This article both critiques and builds on this finding
by (1) pointing to the limits of an argument that focuses centrally on
homophobia, (2) demonstrating that the fag is not only an identity linked
to homosexual boys[1] but an identity that can temporarily adhere to heterosexual boys as well and (3) highlighting the racialized nature of the fag as
a disciplinary mechanism.

"Homophobia" is too facile a term with which to describe the deployment   *4*
of "fag" as an epithet. By calling the use of the word "fag" homophobia—and
letting the argument stop with that point—previous research obscures the
gendered nature of sexualized insults (Plummer, 2001). Invoking homophobia to describe the ways in which boys aggressively tease each other over-
looks the powerful relationship between masculinity and this sort of insult.
Instead, it seems incidental in this conventional line of argument that girls
do not harass each other and are not harassed in this same manner.[2] This
framing naturalizes the relationship between masculinity and homophobia,
thus obscuring the centrality of such harassment in the formation of a gendered identity for boys in a way that it is not for girls.

"Fag" is not necessarily a static identity attached to a particular (homo-   *5*
sexual) boy. Fag talk and fag imitations serve as a discourse with which
boys discipline themselves and each other through joking relationships.[3]
Any boy can temporarily become a fag in a given social space or interaction. This does not mean that those boys who identify as or are perceived
to be homosexual are not subject to intense harassment. But becoming a
fag has as much to do with failing at the masculine tasks of competence,
heterosexual prowess, and strength or in anyway revealing weakness or
femininity, as it does with a sexual identity. This fluidity of the fag identity

is what makes the specter of the fag such a powerful disciplinary mechanism. It is fluid enough that boys police most of their behaviors out of fear of having the fag identity permanently adhere and definitive enough so that boys recognize a fag behavior and strive to avoid it.

The fag discourse is racialized. It is invoked differently by and in relation to white boys' bodies than it is by and in relation to African American boys' bodies. While certain behaviors put all boys at risk for becoming temporarily a fag, some behaviors can be enacted by African American boys without putting them at risk of receiving the label. The racialized meanings of the fag discourse suggest that something more than simple homophobia is involved in these sorts of interactions. An analysis of boys' deployments of the specter of the fag should also extend to the ways in which gendered power works through racialized selves. It is not that this gendered homophobia does not exist in African American communities. Indeed, making fun of "Negro faggotry seems to be a rite of passage among contemporary black male rappers and filmmakers" (Riggs, 1991: 253). However, the fact that "white women and men, gay and straight, have more or less colonized cultural debates about sexual representation" (Julien and Mercer, 1991: 167) obscures varied systems of sexualized meanings among different racialized ethnic groups (Almaguer, 1991; King, 2004).

Theoretical Framing

The sociology of masculinity entails a "critical study of men, their behaviors, practices, values and perspectives" (Whitehead and Barrett, 2001: 14). Recent studies of men emphasize the multiplicity of masculinity (Connell, 1995) detailing the ways in which different configurations of gender practice are promoted, challenged or reinforced in given social situations. This research on how men do masculinities has explored gendered practices in a wide range of social institutions, such as families (Coltrane, 2001), schools (Skelton, 1996; Parker, 1996; Mac and Ghaill, 1996; Francis and Skelton, 2001), workplaces (Cooper, 2000), media (Craig, 1992), and sports (Messner, 1989; Edly and Wetherel, 1997; Curry, 2004). Many of these studies have developed specific typologies of masculinities: gay, Black, Chicano, working class, middle class, Asian, gay Black, gay Chicano, white working class, militarized, transnational business, New Man, negotiated, versatile, healthy, toxic, counter, and cool masculinities, to name a few (Messner, 2004). In this sort of model the fag could be (and often has been) framed as a type of subordinated masculinity attached to homosexual adolescent boys' bodies.

Heeding Timothy Carrigan's admonition that an "analysis of masculinity needs to be related as well to other currents in feminism" (Carrigan et al., 1987: 64), in this article I integrate queer theory's insights about the relationships between gender, sexuality, identities, and power with the attention to men found in the literature on masculinities. Like the sociology of gender, queer theory destabilizes the assumed naturalness of the social order (Lemert, 1996). Queer theory is a "conceptualization which sees sexual power as embedded in different levels of social life" and interrogates areas of the social world not usually seen as sexuality (Stein and Plummer, 1994). In this sense queer theory calls for sexuality to be looked at not only as a discrete arena of sexual practices and identities, but also as a constitutive element of social life (Warner, 1993; Epstein, 1996).

While the masculinities literature rightly highlights very real inequali- *9* ties between gay and straight men (see for instance Connell, 1995), this emphasis on sexuality as inhered in static identities attached to male bodies, rather than major organizing principles of social life (Sedgwick, 1990), limits scholars' ability to analyze the myriad ways in which sexuality, in part, constitutes gender. This article does not seek to establish that there are homosexual boys and heterosexual boys and the homosexual ones are marginalized. Rather this article explores what happens to theories of gender if we look at a *discourse* of sexualized identities in addition to focusing on seemingly static identity categories inhabited by men. This is not to say that gender is reduced only to sexuality, indeed feminist scholars have demonstrated that gender is embedded in and constitutive of a multitude of social structures—the economy, places of work, families and schools. In the tradition of post-structural feminist theorists of race and gender who look at "border cases" that explode taken-for-granted binaries of race and gender (Smith, 1994), queer theory is another tool which enables an integrated analysis of sexuality, gender and race.

As scholars of gender have demonstrated, gender is accomplished *10* through day-to-day interactions (Fine, 1987; Hochschild, 1989; West and Zimmerman, 1991; Thorne, 1993). In this sense gender is the "activity of managing situated conduct in light of normative conceptions of attitudes and activities appropriate for one's sex category" (West and Zimmerman, 1991:127). Similarly, queer theorist Judith Butler argues that gender is accomplished interactionally through "a set of repeated acts within a highly rigid regulatory frame that congeal over time to produce the appearance of substance, of a natural sort of being" (Butler, 1999: 43). Specifically she argues that gendered beings are created through processes of citation and repudiation of a "constitutive outside" (Butler, 1993: 3) in which is contained all that is cast out of a socially recognizable gender category. The "constitutive outside" is inhabited by abject identities, unrecognizably and unacceptably gendered selves. The interactional accomplishment of gender in a Butlerian model consists, in part, of the continual iteration and repudiation of this abject identity. Gender, in this sense, is "constituted through the force of exclusion and abjection, on which produces a constitutive outside to the subject, an abjected outside, which is, after all, 'inside' the subject as its own founding repudiation" (Butler, 1993: 3). This repudiation creates and reaffirms a "threatening specter" (Butler, 1993: 3) of failed, unrecognizable gender, the existence of which must be continually repudiated through interactional processes.

I argue that the "fag" position is an "abject" position and, as such, is *11*
a "threatening specter" constituting contemporary American adolescent
masculinity. The fag discourse is the interactional process through which
boys name and repudiate this abjected identity. Rather than analyzing the
fag as an identity for homosexual boys, I examine uses of the discourse that
imply that any boy can become a fag, regardless of his actual desire or self-
perceived sexual orientation. The threat of the abject position infuses the
faggot with regulatory power. This article provides empirical data to illustrate Butler's approach to gender and indicates that it might be a useful
addition to the sociological literature on masculinities through highlighting one of the ways in which a masculine gender identity is accomplished
through interaction.

Method

Research Site

I conducted fieldwork at a suburban high school in north-central *12*
California which I call River High.[4] River High is a working class, suburban fifty-year-old high school located in a town called Riverton. With
the exception of the median household income and racial diversity (both
of which are elevated due to Riverton's location in California), the town
mirrors national averages in the percentages of white-collar workers, rates
of college attendance, and marriages, and age composition (according
to the 2000 census). It is a politically moderate to conservative, religious
community. Most of the students' parents commute to surrounding cities
for work.

On average Riverton is a middle-class community. However, students *13*
at River are likely to refer to the town as two communities: "Old Riverton" and "New Riverton." A busy highway and railroad tracks bisect the
town into these two sections. River High is literally on the "wrong side
of the tracks," in Old Riverton. Exiting the freeway, heading north to Old
Riverton, one sees a mix of 1950s-era ranch-style homes, some with neatly
trimmed lawns and tidy gardens, others with yards strewn with various
car parts, lawn chairs and appliances. Old Riverton is visually bounded
by smoke-puffing factories. On the other side of the freeway New Riverton
is characterized by wide sidewalk-lined streets and new walled-in home
developments. Instead of smokestacks, a forested mountain, home to
a state park, rises majestically in the background. The teens from these
homes attend Hillside High, River's rival.

River High is attended by 2,000 students. River High's racial/ethnic *14*
breakdown roughly represents California at large: 50 percent white,
9 percent African American, 28 percent Latino and 6 percent Asian (as
compared to California's 46, 6, 32, and 11 percent respectively, according
to census data and school records). The students at River High are primarily working class.

Research

I gathered data using the qualitative method of ethnographic research. 15
I spent a year and a half conducting observations, formally interviewing
forty-nine students at River High (thirty-six boys and thirteen girls), one
male student from Hillside High, and conducting countless informal interviews with students, faculty and administrators. I concentrated on one
school because I explore the richness rather than the breadth of data (for
other examples of this method see Willis, 1981; MacLeod, 1987; Eder et al.,
1995; Ferguson, 2000).

I recruited students for interviews by conducting presentations in a 16
range of classes and hanging around at lunch, before school, after school
and at various events talking to different groups of students about my
research, which I presented as "writing a book about guys." The interviews usually took place at school, unless the student had a car, in which
case he or she met me at one of the local fast food restaurants where I
treated them to a meal. Interviews lasted anywhere from half an hour to
two hours.

The initial interviews I conducted helped me to map a gendered and 17
sexualized geography of the school, from which I chose my observation
sites. I observed a "neutral" site—a senior government classroom, where
sexualized meanings were subdued. I observed three sites that students
marked as "fag" sites—two drama classes and the Gay/Straight Alliance. I also observed two normatively "masculine" sites—auto-shop and
weightlifting.[5] I took daily fieldnotes focusing on how students, faculty
and administrators negotiated, regulated and resisted particular meanings
of gender and sexuality. I attended major school rituals such as Winter
Ball, school rallies, plays, dances, and lunches. I would also occasionally
"ride along" with Mr. Johnson (Mr. J.), the school's security guard, on his
battery-powered golf cart to watch which, how and when students were
disciplined. Observational data provided me with more insight to the
interactional processes of masculinity than simple interviews yielded. If
I had relied only on interview data I would have missed the interactional
processes of masculinity which are central to the fag discourse.

Given the importance of appearance in high school, I gave some 18
thought as to how I would present myself, deciding to both blend in and
set myself apart from the students. In order to blend in I wore my standard
graduate student gear—comfortable, baggy cargo pants, a black t-shirt or
sweater, and tennis shoes. To set myself apart I carried a messenger bag
instead of a back-pack, didn't wear makeup, and spoke slightly differently
than the students by using some slang, but refraining from uttering the
ubiquitous "hecka" and "hella."

The boys were fascinated by the fact that a 30-something white "girl" 19
(their words) was interested in studying them. While at first many would
make sexualized comments asking me about my dating life or saying that
they were going to "hit on" me, it seemed eventually they began to forget
about me as a potential sexual/romantic partner. Part of this, I think, was

related to my knowledge about "guy" things. For instance, I lift weights on a regular basis and as a result the weightlifting coach introduced me as a "weight-lifter from U.C. Berkeley" telling the students they should ask me for weight-lifting advice. Additionally, my taste in movies and television shows often coincided with theirs. I am an avid fan of the movies "Jackass" and "Fight Club," both of which contain high levels of violence and "bathroom" humor. Finally, I garnered a lot of points among boys because I live off a dangerous street in a nearby city famous for drug deals, gang fights, and frequent gun shots.

What Is a Fag?

"Since you were little boys you've been told, 'hey, don't be a little faggot'," 20 explained Darnell, an African American football player, as we sat on a bench next to the athletic field. Indeed, both the boys and girls I interviewed told me that "fag" was the worst epithet one guy could direct at another. Jeff, a slight white sophomore, explained to me that boys call each other fag because "gay people aren't really liked over here and stuff." Jeremy, a Latino junior, told me that this insult literally reduced a boy to nothing, "To call someone gay or fag is like the lowest thing you can call someone. Because that's like saying that you're nothing."

Most guys explained their or others' dislike of fags by claiming that 21 homophobia is just part of what it means to be a guy. For instance Keith, a white soccer-playing senior, explained, "I think guys are just homophobic." However, it is not just homophobia, it is a *gendered* homophobia. Several students told me that these homophobic insults only applied to boys and not girls. For example, while Jake, a handsome white senior, told me that he didn't like gay people, he quickly added, "Lesbians, okay that's *good*." Similarly Cathy, a popular white cheerleader, told me "Being a lesbian is accepted because guys think 'oh that's cool'." Darnell, after telling me that boys were told not to be faggots, said of lesbians, "They're [guys are] fine with girls. I think it's the guy part that they're like ewwww!" In this sense it is not strictly homophobia, but a gendered homophobia that constitutes adolescent masculinity in the culture of this school. However, it is clear, according to these comments, that lesbians are "good" because of their place in heterosexual male fantasy not necessarily because of some enlightened approach to same-sex relationships. It does however, indicate that using only the term "homophobia" to describe boys' repeated use of the word "fag" might be a bit simplistic and misleading.

Additionally, girls at River High rarely deployed the word "fag" and 22 were never called "fags." I recorded girls uttering "fag" only three times during my research. In one instance, Angela, a Latina cheerleader, teased Jeremy, a well-liked white senior involved in student government, for not ditching school with her, "You wouldn't 'cause you're a faggot." However, girls did not use this word as part of their regular lexicon. The sort of gendered homophobia that constitutes adolescent masculinity does not constitute adolescent femininity. Girls were not called dykes or lesbians in any sort of regular or systematic way. Students did tell me that "slut" was the worst thing a girl could be called. However, my fieldnotes indicate that the word "slut" (or its synonym "ho") appears one time for every eight times the word "fag" appears. Even when it does occur, "slut" is rarely deployed as a direct insult against another girl.

Highlighting the difference between the deployment of "gay" and "fag" 23 as insults brings the gendered nature of this homophobia into focus. For boys and girls at River High "gay" is a fairly common synonym for "stupid." While this word shares the sexual origins of "fag," it does not *consistently* have the skew of gender-loaded meaning. Girls and boys often used "gay" as an adjective referring to inanimate objects and male or female people, whereas they used "fag" as a noun that denotes only un-masculine males. Students used "gay" to describe anything from someone's clothes to a new school rule that the students did not like, as in the following encounter:

> In auto-shop Arnie pulled out a large older version black laptop computer and placed it on his desk. Behind him Nick said "That's a gay laptop! It's five inches thick!"

A laptop can be gay, a movie can be gay or a group of people can be gay. Boys used "gay" and "fag" interchangeably when they refer to other boys, but "fag" does not have the non-gendered attributes that "gay" sometimes invokes.

While its meanings are not the same as "gay," "fag" does have multiple 24 meanings which do not necessarily replace its connotations as a homophobic slur, but rather exist alongside. Some boys took pains to say that "fag" is not about sexuality. Darnell told me "It doesn't even have anything to do with being gay." J. L., a white sophomore at Hillside High (River High's cross-town rival), asserted "Fag, seriously, it has nothing to do with sexual preference at all. You could just be calling somebody an idiot you know?" I asked Ben, a quiet, white sophomore who wore heavy metal t-shirts to auto-shop each day, "What kind of things do guys get called a fag for?" Ben answered "Anything . . . literally, anything. Like you were trying to turn a wrench the wrong way, 'dude, you're a fag.' Even if a piece of meat drops out of your sandwich, 'you fag!'" Each time Ben said "you fag" his voice deepened as if he were imitating a more masculine boy. While Ben might rightly *feel* like a guy could be called a fag for "anything . . . literally, anything," there are actually specific behaviors which, when enacted by most boys, can render him more vulnerable to a fag epithet. In this instance Ben's comment highlights the use of "fag" as a generic insult for incompetence, which in the world of River High, is central to a masculine identity. A boy could get called a fag for exhibiting any sort of behavior defined as non-masculine (although not necessarily behaviors aligned with femininity) in the world of River High: being stupid, incompetent, dancing, caring too much about clothing, being too emotional, or expressing interest (sexual or platonic) in other guys. However, given the extent of its deployment and the laundry list of behaviors that could get a boy in trouble it is no wonder that Ben felt like a boy could be called "fag" for "anything."

One-third (13) of the boys I interviewed told me that, while they may liberally insult each other with the term, they would not actually direct it at a homosexual peer. Jabes, a Filipino senior, told me. 25

> I actually say it [fag] quite a lot, except for when I'm in the company of an actual homosexual person. Then I try not to say it at all. But when I'm just hanging out with my friends I'll be like, "shut up, I don't want to hear you any more, you stupid fag."

Similarly J. L. compared homosexuality to a disability, saying there is "no way" he'd call an actually gay guy a fag because

> There's people who are the retarded people who nobody wants to associate with. I'll be so nice to those guys and I hate it when people make fun of them. It's like, "bro do you realize that they can't help that?" And then there's gay people. They were born that way.

According to this group of boys, gay is a legitimate, if marginalized, social identity. If a man is gay, there maybe a chance he could be considered masculine by other men (Connell, 1995). David, a handsome white senior dressed smartly in khaki pants and a white button-down shirt, said, "Being gay is just a lifestyle. It's someone you choose to sleep with. You can still throw around a football and be gay." In other words there is a possibility, however slight, that a boy can be gay and masculine. To be a fag is, by definition, the opposite of masculine, whether or not the word is deployed with sexualized or non-sexualized meanings. In explaining this to me, Jamaal, an African American junior, cited the explanation of popular, rap artist, Eminem. 26

> Although I don't like Eminem, he had a good definition of it. It's like taking away your title. In an interview they were like, "you're always capping on gays, but then you sing with Elton John." He was like "I don't mean gay as in gay."

This is what Riki Wilchins calls the "Eminem Exception. Eminem explains that he doesn't call people 'faggot' because of their sexual orientation but because they're weak and unmanly" (Wilchins, 2003). This is precisely the way in which this group of boys at River High uses the term "faggot." While it is not necessarily acceptable to be gay, at least a man who is gay can do other things that render him acceptably masculine. A fag, by the very definition of the word, indicated by students' usages at River High, cannot be masculine. This distinction between "fag" as an unmasculine and problematic identity and "gay" as a possibly masculine, although marginalized, sexual identity is not limited to a teenage lexicon, but is reflected in both psychological discourses (Sedgwick, 1995) and gay and lesbian activism. 27

Becoming a Fag

"The ubiquity of the word faggot speaks to the reach of its discrediting   28
capacity" (Corbett, 2001: 4). It is almost as if boys cannot help but shout
it out on a regular basis—in the hallway, in class, across campus as a
greeting, or as a joke. In my fieldwork I was amazed by the way in which
the word seemed to pop uncontrollably out of boys' mouths in all kinds of
situations. To quote just one of many instances from my fieldnotes:

> Two boys walked out of the P.E. locker room and one yelled "fucking faggot!"
> at no one in particular.

This spontaneous yelling out of a variation of fag seemingly apropos of
nothing happened repeatedly among boys throughout the school.

The fag discourse is central to boys' joking relationships. Joking   29
cements relationships between boys (Kehily and Nayak, 1997; Lyman,
1998) and helps to manage anxiety and discomfort (Freud, 1905). Boys
invoked the specter of the fag in two ways: through humorous imitation
and through lobbing the epithet at one another. Boys at River High imi-
tated the fag by acting out an exaggerated "femininity," and/or by pretending to sexually desire other boys. As indicated by the introductory vignette
in which a predatory "fag" threatens the little boys, boys at River High link
these performative scenarios with a fag identity. They lobbed the fag epithet at each other in a verbal game of hot potato, each careful to deflect the
insult quickly by hurling it toward someone else. These games and imitations make up a fag discourse which highlights the fag not as a static but
rather as a fluid identity which boys constantly struggle to avoid.

In imitative performances the fag discourse functions as a constant   30
reiteration of the fag's existence, affirming that the fag is out there; at any
moment a boy can become a fag. At the same time these performances
demonstrate that the boy who is invoking the fag is *not* a fag. By invoking
it so often, boys remind themselves and each other that at any point they
can become fags if they are not sufficiently masculine.

> Mr. McNally, disturbed by the noise outside of the classroom, turned to the
> open door saying "We'll shut this unless anyone really wants to watch sweaty
> boys playing basketball." Emir, a tall skinny boy, lisped "I wanna watch the
> boys play!" The rest of the class cracked up at his imitation.

Through imitating a fag, boys assure others that they are not a fag by
immediately becoming masculine again after the performance. They mock
their own performed femininity and/or same-sex desire, assuring themselves and others that such an identity is one deserving of derisive laughter. The fag identity in this instance is fluid, detached from Emir's body. He
can move in and out of this "abject domain" while simultaneously affirming his position as a subject.

Boys also consistently tried to put another in the fag position by lob-   31
bing the fag epithet at one another.

> Going through the junk-filled car in the auto-shop parking lot, Jay poked his head out and asked "Where are Craig and Brian?" Neil responded with "I think they're over there," pointing, then thrusting his hips and pulling his arms back and forth to indicate that Craig and Brian might be having sex. The boys in auto-shop laughed.

This sort of joke temporarily labels both Craig and Brian as faggots. Because the fag discourse is so familiar, the other boys immediately understand that Neil is indicating that Craig and Brian are having sex. However these are not necessarily identities that stick. Nobody actually thinks Craig and Brian are homosexuals. Rather the fag identity is a fluid one, certainly an identity that no boy wants, but one that a boy can escape, usually by engaging in some sort of discursive contest to turn another boy into a fag. However, fag becomes a hot potato that no boy wants to be left holding. In the following example, which occurred soon after the "sex" joke, Brian lobs the fag epithet at someone else, deflecting it from himself:

> Brian initiated a round of a favorite game in auto-shop, the "cock game." Brian quietly, looking at Josh, said, "Josh loves the cock" then slightly louder, "Josh loves the cock." He continued saying this until he was yelling "JOSH LOVES THE COCK!" The rest of the boys laughed hysterically as Josh slinked away saying "I have a bigger dick than all you mother fuckers!"

These two instances show how the fag can be mapped, momentarily, on to one boy's body and how he, in turn, can attach it to another boy, thus deflecting it from himself. In the first instance Neil makes fun of Craig and Brian for simply hanging out together. In the second instance Brian goes from being a fag to making Josh into a fag, through the "cock game." The "fag" is transferable. Boys move in and out of it by discursively creating another as a fag through joking interactions. They, somewhat ironically, can move in and out of the fag position by transforming themselves, temporarily, into a fag, but this has the effect of reaffirming their masculinity when they return to a heterosexual position after imitating the fag.

These examples demonstrate boys invoking the trope of the fag in a 32 discursive struggle in which the boys indicate that they know what a fag is- and that they are not fags. This joking cements bonds between boys as they assure themselves and each other of their masculinity through repeated repudiations of a non-masculine position of the abject.

Racing the Fag

The fag trope is not deployed consistently or identically across social 33 groups at River High. Differences between white boys' and African American boys' meaning making around clothes and dancing reveal ways in which the fag as the abject position is racialized.

Clean, oversized, carefully put together clothing is central to a *34*
hip-hop identity for African American boys who identify with hip-hop
culture.[6] Richard Majors calls this presentation of self a "cool pose"
consisting of "unique, expressive and conspicuous styles of demeanor,
speech, gesture, clothing, hairstyle, walk, stance and handshake," developed by African American men as a symbolic response to institutionalized racism (Majors, 2001: 211). Pants are usually several sizes too big,
hanging low on a boy's waist, usually revealing a pair of boxers beneath.
Shirts and sweaters are similarly oversized, often hanging down to a
boy's knees. Tags are frequently left on baseball hats worn slightly askew
and sit perched high on the head. Meticulously clean, unlaced athletic
shoes with rolled up socks under the tongue complete a typical hip-hop
outfit.

This amount of attention and care given to clothing for white boys not *35*
identified with hip-hop culture (that is, most of the white boys at River
High) would certainly cast them into an abject, fag position. White boys
are not supposed to appear to care about their clothes or appearance,
because only fags care about how they look. Ben illustrates this:

> Ben walked in to the auto-shop classroom from the parking lot where he had
> been working on a particularly oily engine. Grease stains covered his jeans.
> He looked down at them, made a face and walked toward me with limp wrists,
> laughing and lisping in a high pitch, sing-song voice "I got my good pants all
> dirty!"

Ben draws on indicators of a fag identity, such as limp wrists, as do the boys
in the introductory vignette to illustrate that a masculine person certainly
would not care about having dirty clothes. In this sense, masculinity, for
white boys, becomes the carefully crafted appearance of not caring about
appearance, especially in terms of cleanliness.

However, African American boys involved in hip-hop culture talk fre- *36*
quently about whether or not their clothes, specifically their shoes, are
dirty:

> In drama class both Darnell and Marc compared their white Adidas basketball
> shoes. Darnell mocked Marc because black scuff marks covered his shoes,
> asking incredulously "Yours are a week old and they're dirty—I've had mine
> for a month and they're not dirty!" Both laughed.

Monte, River High's star football player, echoed this concern about dirty
shoes when looking at the fancy red shoes he had lent to his cousin the
week before, told me he was frustrated because after his cousin used them,
the "shoes are hella scuffed up." Clothing, for these boys, does not indicate
a fag position, but rather defines membership in a certain cultural and
racial group (Perry, 2002).

Dancing is another arena that carries distinctly fag associated mean- *37*
ings for white boys and masculine meanings for African American boys
who participate in hip-hop culture. White boys often associate dancing with

"fag." J. L. told me that guys think "'NSync's gay" because they can dance. 'NSync is an all white male singing group known for their dance moves. At dances white boys frequently held their female dates tightly, locking their hips together. The boys never danced with one another, unless engaged in a round of "hot potato." White boys often jokingly danced together in order to embarrass each other by making someone else into a fag:

> Lindy danced behind her date, Chris. Chris's friend, Matt, walked up and nudged Lindy aside, imitating her dance moves behind Chris. As Matt rubbed his hands up and down Chris's back, Chris turned around and jumped back startled to see Matt there instead of Lindy. Matt cracked up as Chris turned red.

However dancing does not carry this sort of sexualized gender mean- 38
ing for all boys at River High. For African American boys dancing demonstrates membership in a cultural community (Best, 2000). African
American boys frequently danced together in single sex groups, teaching each other the latest dance moves, showing off a particularly difficult
move or making each other laugh with humorous dance moves. Students recognized K. J. as the most talented dancer at the school. K. J. is
a sophomore of African American and Filipino descent who participated
in the hip-hop culture of River High. He continually wore the latest hip-
hop fashions. K. J. was extremely popular. Girls hollered his name as they
walked down the hall and thrust urgently written love notes folded in complicated designs into his hands as he sauntered to class. For the past two
years K. J. won first place in the talent show for dancing. When he danced
at assemblies the room reverberated with screamed chants of "Go K.J.! Go
K.J.! Go K.J.!" Because dancing for African American boys places them
within a tradition of masculinity, they are not at risk of becoming a fag
for this particular gendered practice. Nobody called K. J. a fag. In fact in
several of my interviews boys of multiple racial/ethnic backgrounds spoke
admiringly of K. J.'s dancing abilities.

Implications

These findings confirm previous studies of masculinity and sexuality that 39
position homophobia as central to contemporary definitions of adolescent
masculinity. These data extend previous research by unpacking multilayered
meanings that boys deploy through their uses of homophobic language and
joking rituals. By attending to these meanings I reframe the discussion as
one of a fag discourse, rather than simply labeling this sort of behavior as
homophobia. The fag is an "abject" position, a position outside of masculinity
that actually constitutes masculinity. Thus, masculinity, in part becomes the
daily interactional work of repudiating the "threatening specter" of the fag.

The fag extends beyond a static sexual identity attached to a gay boy. 40
Few boys are permanently identified as fags; most move in and out of
fag positions. Looking at "fag" as a discourse rather than a static identity

reveals that the term can be invested with different meanings in different social spaces. "Fag" may be used as a weapon with which to temporarily assert one's masculinity by denying it to others. Thus "fag" becomes a symbol around which contests of masculinity take place.

The fag epithet, when hurled at other boys, may or may not have   *41* explicit sexual meanings, but it always has gendered meanings. When a boy calls another boy a fag, it means he is not a man, not necessarily that he is a homosexual. The boys in this study know that they are not supposed to call homosexual boys "fags" because that is mean. This then, has been the limited success of the mainstream gay rights movement. The message absorbed by some of these teenage boys is that "gay men can be masculine, just like you." Instead of challenging gender inequality, this particular discourse of gay rights has reinscribed it. Thus we need to begin to think about how gay men may be in a unique position to challenge gendered as well as sexual norms.

This study indicates that researchers who look at the intersection of   *42* sexuality and masculinity need to attend to the ways in which racialized identities may affect how "fag" is deployed and what it means in various social situations. While researchers have addressed the ways in which masculine identities are racialized (Connell, 1995; Ross, 1998; Bucholtz, 1999; Davis, 1999; Price, 1999; Ferguson, 2000; Majors, 2001) they have not paid equal attention to the ways in which "fag" might be a racialized epithet. It is important to look at when, where and with what meaning "the fag" is deployed in order to get at how masculinity is defined, contested, and invested in among adolescent boys.

Research shows that sexualized teasing often leads to deadly results,   *43* as evidenced by the spate of school shootings in the 1990s (Kimmel, 2003). Clearly the fag discourse affects not just homosexual teens, but all boys, gay and straight. Further research could investigate these processes in a variety of contexts: varied geographic locations, sexualized groups, classed groups, religious groups, and age groups.

Acknowledgments

The author would like to thank Natalie Boero, Leslie Bell, Meg Jay, and Barrie   *44* Thorne for their comments on this article. This work was supported by the Center for the Study of Sexual Culture at University of California, Berkeley.

NOTES

1. While the term "homosexual" is laden with medicalized and normalizing meanings, I use it instead of "gay" because "gay" in the world of River High has multiple meanings apart from sexual practices or identities.
2. Girls do insult one another based on sexualized meanings. But in my own research I found that girls and boys did not harass girls in this manner with the same frequency that boys harassed each other through engaging in joking about the fag.

3. I use discourse in the Foucauldian sense, to describe truth producing practices, not just text or speech (Foucault, 1978).
4. The names of places and respondents have been changed.
5. Auto-shop was a class in which students learned how to build and repair cars. Many of the students in this course were looking into careers as mechanics.
6. While there are several white and Latino boys at River High who identify with hip-hop culture, hip-hop is identified by the majority of students as an African American cultural style.

REFERENCES

Almaguer, Tomas (1991) "ChicanoMen: A Cartography of Homosexual Identity and Behavior," *Differences*. 3:75–100.
Bersani, Leo (1987) "Is the Rectum a Grave?" *October* 43:197–222.
Best, Amy (2000) *Prom Night: Youth, Schools and Popular Culture*. New York: Routledge.
Bucholtz, Mary (1999) "You Da Man: Narrating the Racial Other in the Production of White Masculinity," *Journal of Sociolinguistics*. 3/4: 443–60.
Burn, Shawn M. (2000) "'Heterosexuals' Use of 'Fag' and 'Queer' to Deride One Another: A Contributor to Heterosexism and Stigma," *Journal of Homosexuality*. 40:1–11.
Butler, Judith (1993) *Bodies that Matter*. Routledge: New York.
——. (1999) *Gender Trouble*. New York: Routledge.
Carrigan, Tim, Connell, Bob and Lee, John (1987) "Toward a New Sociology of Masculinity," in Harry Brod (ed.) *The Making of Masculinities: The New Men's Studies*, pp. 188–202. Boston, MA: Allen & Unwin.
Coltrane, Scott (2001) "Selling the Indispensable Father," paper presented at *Pushing the Boundaries Conference: New Conceptualizations of Childhood and Motherhood*, Philadelphia.
Connell, R. W. (1995) *Masculinities*. Berkeley: University of California Press.
Cooper, Marianne (2000) "Being the 'Go-To Guy': Fatherhood, Masculinity and the Organization of Work in Silicon Valley," *Qualitative Sociology*. 23: 379–405.
Corbett, Ken (2001) "Faggot = Loser," *Studies in Gender and Sexuality* 2:3–28.
Craig, Steve (1992) *Men, Masculinity and the Media*. Newbury Park: Sage.
Curry, Timothy J. (2004) "Fraternal Bonding in the Locker Room: A Profeminist Analysis of Talk About Competition and Women" in Michael Messner and Michael Kimmel (eds.) *Men's Lives*. Boston, MA: Pearson.
Davis, James E. (1999) "Forbidden Fruit, Black Males' Constructions of Transgressive Sexualities in Middle School," in William J. Letts IV and James T. Sears (eds.) *Queering Elementary Education: Advancing the Dialogue About Sexualities and Schooling*, pp. 49 ff. Lanham, MD: Rowan & Litdefield.
Eder, Donna, Evans, Catherine and Parker, Stephen (1995) *School Talk: Gender and Adolescent Culture*. New Brunswick, NJ: Rutgers University Press.
Edly, Nigel and Wetherell, Margaret (1997) "Jockeying for Position: The Construction of Masculine Identities," *Discourse and Society* 8: 203–17.
Epstein, Steven (1996) "A Queer Encounter," in Steven Seidman (ed.) *Queer Theory/Sociology*, pp. 188–202. Cambridge, MA: Blackwell.
Ferguson, Ann (2000) *Bad Boys: Public Schools in the Making of Black Masculinity*. Ann Arbor: University of Michigan Press.
Fine, Gary (1987) *With the Boys: Little League Baseball and Preadolescent Culture*. Chicago, IL: University of Chicago Press.
Foucault, Michel (1978). *The History of Sexuality, Volume I*. New York: Vintage Books.
Francis, Becky and Skelton, Christine (2001) "Men Teachers and the Construction of Heterosexual Masculinity in the Classroom," *Sex Education* 1: 9–21.
Freud, Sigmund (1905). *The Basic Writings of Sigmund Freud* (translated and edited by A. A. Brill). New York: The Modern Library.
Hochschild, Arlie (1989). *The Second Shift*. New York: Avon.

Julien, Isaac and Mercer, Kobena (1991) "True Confessions: A Discourse on Images of Black Male Sexuality," in Essex Hemphill (ed.) *Brother to Brother: New Writings by Black Gay Men*, pp. 167–73. Boston, MA: Alyson Publications.

Kehily, Mary Jane and Nayak, Anoop (1997) "Lads and Laughter: Humour and the Production of Heterosexual Masculinities," *Gender and Education*. 9: 69–87.

Kimmel, Michael (2001) "Masculinity as Homophobia: Fear, Shame, and Silence in the Construction of Gender Identity," in Stephen Whitehead and Frank Barrett (eds.) *The Masculinities Reader*, pp. 266–87. Cambridge: Polity.

——. (2003) "Adolescent Masculinity, Homophobia, and Violence: Random School Shootings, 1982–2001," *American Behavioral Scientist* 46: 1439–58.

King, D. L. (2004) *Double Lives on the Down Low*. New York: Broadway Books.

Lehne, Gregory (1998) "Homophobia Among Men: Supporting and Defining the Male Role," in Michael Kimmel and Michael Messner (eds.) *Men's Lives*, pp. 237–149. Boston, MA: Allyn and Bacon.

Lemert, Charles (1996) "Series Editor's Preface," in Steven Seidman (ed.) *Queer Theory/ Sociology*. Cambridge, MA: Blackwell.

Lyman, Peter (1998) "The Fraternal Bond as a Joking Relationship: A Case Study of the Role of Sexist Jokes in Male Group Bonding," in Michael Kimmel and Michael Messner (eds.) *Men's Lives*, pp. 171–93. Boston, MA: Allyn and Bacon.

Mac and Ghaill, Martain (1996) "What about the Boys—School, Class and Crisis Masculinity," *Sociological Review* 44:381–97.

MacLeod, Jay (1987) *Ain't No Makin It: Aspirations and Attainment in a Low Income Neighborhood*. Boulder, CO: Westview Press.

Majors, Richard (2001) "Cool Pose: Black Masculinity and Sports," in Stephen Whitehead and Frank Barrett (eds.). *The Masculinities Reader*, pp. 208–17. Cambridge: Polity.

Messner, Michael (1989) "Sports and the Politics of Inequality," in Michael Kimmel and Michael Messner (eds.) *Men's Lives*. Boston, MA: Allyn and Bacon.

——.(2004) "On Patriarchs and Losers: Rethinking Men's Interests," paper presented at Berkeley *Journal of Sociology* Conference, Berkeley.

Parker, Andrew (1996) "The, Construction of Masculinity Within Boys' Physical Education," *Gender and Education*. 8:141–57.

Perry, Pamela (2002) *Shades of White: White Kids and Racial Identities in High School*. Durham, NC: Duke University Press.

Plummer, David C. (2001) "The Quest for Modern Manhood: Masculine Stereotypes, Peer Culture and the Social Significance of Homophobia," *Journal of Adolescence*. 24:15–23.

Price, Jeremy (1999) "Schooling and Racialized Masculinities: The Diploma, Teachers and Peers in the Lives of Young, African American Men," *Youth and Society*. 31:224–63.

Riggs, Marlon (1991) "Black Macho Revisited: Reflections of a SNAP! Queen," in Essex Hemphill (ed.) *Brother to Brother: New Writings by Black Gay Men*, pp. 153–260. Boston, MA: Alyson Publications.

Ross, Marlon B. (1998) "In Search of Black Men's Masculinities," *Feminist Studies* 24: 599–626.

Sedgwick, Eve K. (1990) *Epistemology of the Closet*. Berkeley: University of California Press.

——. (1995) "Gosh, Boy George, You Must Be Awfully Secure in Your Masculinity!" in Maurice Berger, Brian Wallis and Simon Watson (eds.) *Constructing Masculinity*, pp. 11–20. New York: Routledge.

Skelton, Christine (1996) "Learning to Be Tough: The Fostering of Maleness in One Primary School," *Gender and Education*. 8:185–97.

Smith, George W. (1998) "The Ideology of 'Fag': The School Experience of Gay Students," *The Sociological Quarterly* 39:309–35.

Smith, Valerie (1994) "Split Affinities: The Case of Interracial Rape," in Anne Herrmann and Abigail Stewart (eds.) *Theorizing Feminism*, pp. 155–70. Boulder, CO: Westview Press.

Stein, Arlene and Plummer, Ken (1994) " 'I Can't Even Think Straight': 'Queer' Theory and the Missing Sexual Revolution in Sociology," *Sociological Theory* 12:178 ff.

Thorne, Barrie (1993) *Gender Play: Boys and Girls in School*. New Brunswick, NJ: Rutgers University Press.

Warner, Michael (1993) "Introduction," in Michael Warner (ed.) *Fear of a Queer Planet: Queer Politics and Social Theory*, pp. vii–xxxi. Minneapolis: University of Minnesota Press.

West, Candace and Zimmerman, Don (1991) "Doing Gender," in Judith Lorber (ed.) *The Social Construction of Gender*, pp. 102–21. Newbury Park: Sage.

Whitehead, Stephen and Barrett, Frank (2001) "The Sociology of Masculinity," in Stephen Whitehead and Frank Barrett (eds.) *The Masculinities Reader*, pp. 472–6. Cambridge: Polity.

Wilchins, Riki (2003) "Do You Believe in Fairies?" *The Advocate*, 4 February.

Willis, Paul (1981) *Learning to Labor: How Working Class Kids Get Working Class Jobs*. New York: Columbia University Press.

Wood, Julian (1984) "Groping Toward Sexism: Boy's Sex Talk," in Angela McRobbie and Mica Nava (eds.) *Gender and Generation*. London: Macmillan Publishers.

■ ■ ■

Reading as a Writer: Analyzing Rhetorical Choices

1. After setting up her argument and analyzing a good portion of her data, Pascoe adds another layer to her analysis in the section titled "Racing the Fag." How does the additional analysis of race contribute to Pascoe's central argument? Discuss or write about a few of the examples in this section. What others might you add?

2. Reread the "Method" section of the essay, and consider how Pascoe uses description. How do the details contribute to her larger argument? How does she explain her strategy in this "qualitative method of ethnographic research"? (para. 15). In pairs or as a class, discuss the strengths and possible weaknesses of her methods, given your own experience of high school dynamics.

Writing as a Reader: Entering the Conversation of Ideas

1. Both Pascoe and Allan G. Johnson examine the methods people use to try to make people stay within gender categories. What is at stake, and for whom in this behavior, according to these authors? Write an essay in which you examine the dynamics of this behavior and each author's analysis of problems and possible solutions. If you like, draw on your own insights of learning (and perhaps resisting) gender norms.

2. Pascoe's analysis of adolescent boys is interesting to consider next to Ellen Lipkin's overview of shifting socialization tactics for adolescent girls. Compose an essay that draws out key insights about the ways we socialize boys and girls into gendered behaviors. How is the process similar and different, and what conclusions can you draw? How are forms of resistance to normative masculinity and femininity similar and different, based on your experiences and observations?

MICHAEL S. KIMMEL

Gender, Class, and Terrorism

Michael Kimmel is a professor of sociology at the State University of New York at Stony Brook, and is known internationally for his research and writing on men and masculinity. He is part of a growing group of academics who have followed feminist theorists in thinking about gender as a cultural construct, distinct from biological gender. Kimmel is a spokesperson of NOMAS (The National Organization for Men Against Sexism) and describes himself as a "profeminist man," arguing that it is men's best interest, as well as women's, to work for gender equality.

Kimmel has written many articles and books on the topic of men's socialization that are considered landmark texts in masculinity studies, among them *Manhood in America: A Cultural History* (1996) and *Guyland: The Perilous World Where Boys Become Men* (2008). As a sociologist, Kimmel is interested in the many aspects of everyday life that teach boys to become men who follow specific social scripts that privilege toughness, violence, and displays of power and confidence. This is a key theme in this essay, "Gender, Class, and Terrorism," which appeared in the sixth edition of *Men's Lives* (2004), which Kimmel coedited with Michael A. Messner. For example, look at paragraph 24, where Kimmel describes Mohammed Atta, one of the pilots who crashed a plane into the World Trade Center on 9/11, pointing out that Atta's father urged him as a boy to "toughen up." While Kimmel does not formally cite his sources, he builds his argument on existing research on masculinity and violence, referring to insights from Barbara Ehrenreich, Peter Marsden, and Lothar Machtan, among others.

Before you read, you might think (and talk with your classmates) about your expectations about an essay on gender and terrorism. What kinds of examples do you expect? Consider the images of terrorists you usually see in the media and the explanations you have heard or read about what motivates terrorists. Keep them in mind as you read. Think about Kimmel's strategy in organizing the essay as he does. What surprises do you find, and what do you make of your responses?

Like many scholars of contemporary culture, Kimmel hopes to teach us something beyond what we might read in *Newsweek or Time*. Although the debate he enters here—why people use terrorist tactics that are as deadly to themselves as to others—is certainly a debate we hear in the media, Kimmel uses his sociological insights about masculinity to frame the issue in new ways, to help us make connections we otherwise may not see or *want* to see.

■ ■ ■

The events of September 11 [2001] have sent scholars and pundits alike *1* scrambling to make sense of those seemingly senseless acts. While most analyses have focused on the political economy of globalization or the perversion of Islamic teachings by Al Qaeda, several commentators have raised gender issues.

Some have reminded us that in our haste to lionize the heroes of the *2*
World Trade Center collapse, we ignored the many women firefighters,
police officers, and rescue workers who also risked their lives. We've been
asked to remember the Taliban's vicious policies toward women; indeed,
even Laura Bush seems to be championing women's emancipation.

A few have asked us to consider the other side of the gender coin: *3*
men. Some have rehearsed the rather tired old formulae about masculine
bloodlust or the drive for domination and conquest, with no reference to
the magnificent humanity displayed by so many on September 11. In an
article in *Slate*, the Rutgers anthropologist Lionel Tiger trotted out his old
male-bonding thesis but offered no understanding of why Al Qaeda might
appeal to some men and not others. Only the journalist Barbara Ehrenreich suggests that there may be a link between the misogyny of the Taliban and the masculinity of the terrorists.

As for myself, I've been thinking lately about a letter to the editor of *4*
a small, upstate-New York newspaper, written in 1992 by an American
GI after his return from service in the Gulf War. He complained that the
legacy of the American middle class had been stolen by an indifferent government. The American dream, he wrote, has all but disappeared; instead,
most people are struggling just to buy next week's groceries.

That letter writer was Timothy McVeigh from Lockport, N. Y. Two years *5*
later, he blew up the Murrah federal building in Oklahoma City in what is
now the second-worst act of terrorism ever committed on American soil.

What's startling to me are the ways that McVeigh's complaints were *6*
echoed in some of the fragmentary evidence that we have seen about the
terrorists of September 11, and especially in the portrait of Mohammed
Atta, the suspected mastermind of the operation and the pilot of the first
plane to hit the World Trade Center.

Looking at these two men through the lens of gender may shed some *7*
light on both the method and the madness of the tragedies they wrought.

McVeigh was representative of the small legion of white supremacists— *8*
from older organizations like the John Birch Society, the Ku Klux Klan,
and the American Nazi Party, to newer neo-Nazi, racist-skinhead, white-
power groups like Posse Comitatus and the White Aryan Resistance, to
radical militias.

These white supremacists are mostly younger (in their early 20s), *9*
lower-middle-class men, educated at least through high school and often
beyond. They are the sons of skilled workers in industries like textiles
and tobacco, the sons of the owners of small farms, shops, and grocery
stores. Buffeted by global political and economic forces, the sons have
inherited little of their fathers' legacies. The family farms have been lost to
foreclosure, the small shops squeezed out by Wal-Marts and malls. These
young men face a spiral of downward mobility and economic uncertainty.
They complain that they are squeezed between the omnivorous jaws of
global capital concentration and a federal bureaucracy that is at best indifferent to their plight and at worst complicit in their demise.

As one issue of *The Truth at Last*, a white-supremacist magazine, put it: 10

> Immigrants are flooding into our nation willing to work for the minimum wage (or less). Super-rich corporate executives arc flying all over the world in search of cheaper and cheaper labor so that they can lay off their American employees . . . . Many young White families have no future! They are not going to receive any appreciable wage increases due to job competition from immigrants.

What they want, says one member, is to "take back what is rightfully 11 ours."

Their anger often fixes on "others"—women, members of minor- 12 ity groups, immigrants, gay men, and lesbians—in part because those are the people with whom they compete for entry-level, minimum-wage jobs. Above them all, enjoying the view, hovers the international Jewish conspiracy.

What holds together these "paranoid politics"—antigovernment, 13 anti-global capital but pro-small capitalist, racist, sexist, anti-Semitic, homophobic—is a rhetoric of masculinity. These men feel emasculated by big money and big government—they call the government "the Nanny State"—and they claim that "others" have been handed the birthright of native-born white men.

In the eyes of such downwardly mobile white men, most white 14 American males collude in their own emasculation. They've grown soft, feminized, weak. White supremacists' Web sites abound with complaints about the "whimpering collapse of the blond male"; the "legions of sissies and weaklings, of flabby, limp-wristed, non-aggressive, non-physical, indecisive, slack-jawed, fearful males who, while still heterosexual in theory and practice, have not even a vestige of the old macho spirit."

American white supremacists thus offer American men the restora- 15 tion of their masculinity—a manhood in which individual white men control the fruits of their own labor and are not subject to emasculation by Jewish-owned finance capital or a black- and feminist-controlled welfare state. Theirs is the militarized manhood of the heroic John Rambo, a manhood that celebrates their God-sanctioned right to band together in armed militias if anyone, or any government agency, tries to take it away from them. If the state and the economy emasculate them, and if the masculinity of the "others" is problematic, then only "real" white men can rescue America from a feminized, multicultural, androgynous melting pot.

Sound familiar? For the most part, the terrorists of September 11 come 16 from the same class, and recite the same complaints, as American white supremacists.

Virtually all were under twenty-five, educated, lower middle class or 17 middle class, downwardly mobile. The journalist Nasra Hassan interviewed families of Middle Eastern suicide bombers (as well as some failed

bombers themselves) and found that none of them had the standard motivations ascribed to people who commit suicide, such as depression.

Although several of the leaders of Al Qaeda are wealthy—Osama bin   *18*
Laden is a multimillionaire, and Ayman al-Zawahiri, the fifty-year-old
doctor thought to be bin Laden's closest adviser, is from a fashionable
suburb of Cairo—many of the hijackers were engineering students for
whom job opportunities had been dwindling dramatically. (Judging from
the minimal information I have found, about one-fourth of the hijackers
had studied engineering.) Zacarias Moussaoui, who did not hijack one
of the planes but is the first man to be formally charged in the United
States for crimes related to September 11, earned a degree at London's
South Bank University. Marwan al-Shehhi, the chubby, bespectacled
twenty-three-year-old from the United Arab Emirates who flew the second
plane into the World Trade Center, was an engineering student, while Ziad
Jarrah, the twenty-six-year-old Lebanese who flew the plane that crashed
in Pennsylvania, had studied aircraft design.

Politically, these terrorists opposed globalization and the spread of   *19*
Western values; they opposed what they perceived as corrupt regimes in
several Arab states (notably Saudi Arabia and Egypt), which they claimed
were merely puppets of American domination. "The resulting anger is
naturally directed first against their rulers," writes the historian Bernard
Lewis, "and then against those whom they see as keeping those rulers in
power for selfish reasons."

Central to their political ideology is the recovery of manhood from the   *20*
emasculating politics of globalization. The Taliban saw the Soviet invasion
and westernization of Afghanistan as humiliations. Bin Laden's October 7
videotape describes the "humiliation and disgrace" that Islam has suffered
"for more than eighty years." And over and over, Nasra Hassan writes, she
heard the refrain: "The Israelis humiliate us. They occupy our land, and
deny our history."

Terrorism is fueled by a fatal brew of antiglobalization politics, con-   *21*
voluted Islamic theology, and virulent misogyny. According to Ehrenreich,
while these formerly employed or self-employed males "have lost their traditional status as farmers and breadwinners, women have been entering
the market economy and gaining the marginal independence conferred by
even a paltry wage." As a result, "the man who can no longer make a living,
who has to depend on his wife's earnings, can watch Hollywood sexpots on
pirated videos and begin to think the world has been turned upside down."

The Taliban's policies thus had two purposes: to remasculinize men   *22*
and to refeminize women. Another journalist, Peter Marsden, has observed
that those policies "could be seen as a desperate attempt to keep out that
other world, and to protect Afghan women from influences that could
weaken the society from within." The Taliban prohibited women from
appearing in public unescorted by men, from revealing any part of their
body, and from going to school or holding a job. Men were required to
grow their beards, in accordance with religious images of Muhammad, yes;

but also, perhaps, because wearing beards has always been associated with men's response to women's increased equality in the public sphere, since beards symbolically reaffirm biological differences between men and women, while gender equality tends to blur those differences.

The Taliban's policies removed women as competitors and also shored 23 up masculinity, since they enabled men to triumph over the humiliations of globalization and their own savage, predatory, and violently sexual urges that might be unleashed in the presence of uncovered women.

All of these issues converged in the life of Mohammed Atta, the terror- 24 ist about whom the most has been written and conjectured. Currently, for example, there is much speculation about Atta's sexuality. Was he gay? Was he a repressed homosexual, too ashamed of his sexuality to come out? Such innuendoes are based on no more than a few circumstantial tidbits about his life. He was slim, sweet-faced, neat, meticulous, a snazzy dresser. The youngest child of an ambitious lawyer father and a pampering mother, Atta grew up shy and polite, a mama's boy. "He was so gentle," his father said. "I used to tell him, 'Toughen up, boy!' "

When such revelations are offered, storytellers seem to expect a reac- 25 tion like "Aha! So that explains it!" (Indeed, in a new biography of Adolf Hitler, *The Hidden Hitler*, Lothar Machtan offers exactly that sort of explanation. He argues that many of Hitler's policies—such as the killing of long-time colleague and avowed homosexual Ernst Rohm, or even the systematic persecution and execution of gay men in concentration camps—were, in fact, prompted by a desire to conceal his own homosexuality.)

But what do such accusations actually explain? Do revelations about 26 Hitler's or Atta's possible gay propensities raise troubling connections between homosexuality and mass murder? If so, then one would also have to conclude that the discovery of Shakespeare's "gay" sonnet explains the Bard's genius at explicating Hamlet's existential anguish, or that Michelangelo's sexuality is the decisive factor in his painting of God's touch in the Sistine Chapel.

Such revelations tell us little about the Holocaust or September 11. 27 They do, however, address the consequences of homophobia—both official and informal—on young men who are exploring their sexual identities. What's relevant is not the possible fact of Hitler's or Atta's gayness, but the shame and fear that surround homosexuality in societies that refuse to acknowledge sexual diversity.

Even more troubling is what such speculation leaves out. What unites 28 Atta, McVeigh, and Hitler is not their repressed sexual orientation but gender—their masculinity, their sense of masculine entitlement, and their thwarted ambitions. They accepted cultural definitions of masculinity, and needed someone to blame when they felt that they failed to measure up. (After all, being called a mama's boy, a sissy, and told to toughen up are demands for gender conformity, not matters of sexual desire.) Gender is the issue, not sexuality.

All three failed at their chosen professions. Hitler was a failed *29* artist—indeed, he failed at just about every job he ever tried except dictator. McVeigh, a business-college dropout, found his calling in the military during the Gulf War, where his exemplary service earned him commendations; but he washed out of Green Beret training—his dream job—after only two days. And Atta was the odd man out in his family. His two sisters both became doctors—one a physician and one a university professor. His father constantly reminded him that he wanted "to hear the word 'doctor' in front of his name. We told him, your sisters are doctors and their husbands are doctors and you are the man of the family."

Atta decided to become an engineer, but his degree meant little in a *30* country where thousands of college graduates were unable to find good jobs. After he failed to find employment in Egypt, he went to Hamburg, Germany, to study architecture. He was "meticulous, disciplined, and highly intelligent, an ordinary student, a quiet, friendly guy who was totally focused on his studies," according to another student in Hamburg.

But his ambitions were constantly undone. His only hope for a good *31* job in Egypt was to be hired by an international firm. He applied and was continually rejected. He found work as a draftsman—highly humiliating for someone with engineering and architectural credentials and an imperious and demanding father—for a German firm involved with razing low-income Cairo neighborhoods to provide more scenic vistas for luxury tourist hotels.

Defeated, humiliated, emasculated, a disappointment to his father *32* and a failed rival to his sisters, Atta retreated into increasingly militant Islamic theology By the time he assumed the controls of American Airlines Flight 11, he evinced a hysteria about women. In the message he left in his abandoned rental car, he made clear what mattered to him in the end. "I don't want pregnant women or a person who is not clean to come and say good-bye to me," he wrote. "I don't want women to go to my funeral or later to my grave." Of course, Atta's body was instantly incinerated, and no burial would be likely.

The terrors of emasculation experienced by lower-middle-class men *33* all over the world will no doubt continue, as they struggle to make a place for themselves in shrinking economies and inevitably shifting cultures. They may continue to feel a seething resentment against women, whom they perceive as stealing their rightful place at the head of the table, and against the governments that displace them. Globalization feels to them like a game of musical chairs, in which, when the music stops, all the seats are handed to others by nursemaid governments.

The events of September 11, as well as of April 19, 1995 (the Oklahoma *34* City bombing), resulted from an increasingly common combination of factors—the massive male displacement that accompanies globalization, the spread of American consumerism, and the perceived corruption of local political elites—fused with a masculine sense of entitlement.

Someone else—some "other"—had to be held responsible for the terrorists' downward mobility and failures, and the failure of their fathers to deliver their promised inheritance. The terrorists didn't just get mad. They got even.

Such themes were not lost on the disparate bands of young white 35 supremacists. American Aryans admired the terrorists' courage and chastised their own compatriots. "It's a disgrace that in a population of at least 150 million White/Aryan Americans, we provide so few that are willing to do the same [as the terrorists]," bemoaned Rocky Suhayda, the chairman of the American Nazi Party. "A bunch of towel head/sand niggers put our great White Movement to shame."

It is from such gendered shame that mass murderers are made. 36

■ ■ ■

Reading as a Writer: Analyzing Rhetorical Choices

1. What effect do you think Kimmel hopes to achieve with his comparisons of Timothy McVeigh, Mohammed Atta, and Adolf Hitler? What similarities does he mention? How are these comparisons important to Kimmel's argument?

2. Circle any words that are unfamiliar to you—perhaps *misogyny* or *emasculation*. Look them up so that you feel comfortable defining them in your own words. Based on his vocabulary and examples, who is Kimmel's audience?

Writing as a Reader: Entering the Conversation of Ideas

1. How do Kimmel's insights about us-versus-them dynamics shed light on C. J. Pascoe's analysis of adolescent male culture? How does Pascoe's analysis help use see the dynamic that Kimmel describes in a new way? Compose an essay in which you draw on both authors' ideas and examples in order to make an argument about how and why cultural groups tend to see themselves in terms of "us" versus "them." What is the effect of this pattern of thinking?

2. Kimmel's ideas are interesting to use as a tool for analyzing contemporary film representations of terrorism. Select a film that features terrorism as its theme, and use Kimmel's insights to make sense of the film's connections between violence, masculinity, identity, and motivation. To what extent does the film offer rationale for the behavior of the characters who engage in terrorism? How do concepts of "us" versus "them" play out in the film? Be sure to anchor your claims to specific details in the film as you build your argument.

ELLINE LIPKIN

From Girls' Bodies, Girls' Selves: Body Image, Identity, and Sexuality

Elline Lipkin is a scholar who also writes poetry and nonfiction. Since 2008, she has held the position of Research Scholar at the Center for the Study of Women at the University of California, Los Angeles (UCLA). This excerpt is from her book, *Girls' Studies* (2009), which examines the history and theories of studying girls' lives. "Girls' Studies" is a growing field within research on gender, as scholars focus on the way our earliest experiences shape lifelong expectations of ourselves and our place in society. As Lipkin says, "A girl's body, almost from birth (when her first weight is taken), often reflects cultural expectations and conventions—in how she dresses, how she is allowed to use her body, how she presents it to the world, and how comfortable she feels within it" (para. 5). As you read, you might consider how her examples and arguments might apply to boys' bodies and cultural expectations, too.

In this piece, Lipkin draws extensively from the research of cultural historian Joan Jacobs Brumberg, whose book *The Body Project: An Intimate History of American Girls* (1997) was one of the first to examine the body—particularly the female body—as a "project" in which every part of the body might come to be seen as a "problem" that needs to be solved (often with products). Lipkin notes of "body projects" ranging from hair-removal and weight-loss to makeup and cosmetic procedures, "the effect on the owners of the bodies means often feeling a disquieting angst that they are never good enough as they are, that they are forever being measured and found lacking" (para. 13). Lipkin offers an overview of Brumberg's argument that this problematizing of girls' bodies is hardly a new phenomenon; for hundreds of years, consumer culture has inspired anxiety about and "cures" for the female body.

While Lipkin notes that many beauty standards are set by "Endless images of alluring, flirtatious, slender, usually white, and presumptively heterosexual young women" (para. 2), be sure to read carefully for ways girls of different races and ethnicities are affected by—or resist—these standards. What other examples can you think of that affect girls of all kinds? (The long section on eating disorders offers some useful statistics.) What other examples can you think of that demonstrate how girls of all kinds *resist* them—often in quite creative ways, using social media or other technology?

While a focus on beauty culture may seem frivolous, Lipkin draws on Brumberg's research to argue that our fundamental sense of ourselves as healthy and sexual beings is affected by cultural "norms" that often are harmful physically and psychologically. As you consider the long history of this trend, consider what it would take to change it. How might research, reading, and writing be part of that change?

The signs are everywhere—literally. Look up at a billboard in any major   *1*
American city and what's being sold isn't just the newest soft drink or
face wash. It's usually also an attractive woman, most often below the age
of twenty-five, smiling or posing suggestively. Movies, television shows,
music videos, magazines, video games, and ads for products varying from
clothing to toothpaste to cell phones feature young women, and in American culture, a certain look for these girls and women—slender body; flawless (and more often than not white) skin; delicate, even facial features,
enhanced by makeup; carefully coifed hair—is ubiquitous. This often isn't
even cause for comment—but the images are absorbed and "normalized"
by viewers at almost every turn.

"Children are born anthropologists," girls' historian Joan Jacobs   *2*
Brumberg writes in her foreword to photojournalist Lauren Greenfield's
2002 exposé *Girl Culture*, "able to expertly deconstruct and mimic what
culture offers them, especially in terms of gender roles. Before they even
abandon their teddy bears, contemporary girls embrace the erotic. They
also understand that their power as women will come from their beauty,
and that beauty in American culture is defined, increasingly, by a certain
body type displayed in particular ways." For the most part, advertising,
media, and other cultural vehicles reflect certain physical "standards"
for girls and women—that thinness is attractive, that clear skin and certain kinds of Caucasian features are beautiful, that heterosexuality is
the norm. Endless images of alluring, flirtatious, slender, usually white,
and presumptively heterosexual young women imprint as "normal" and
desirable "standards" of feminine appearance into girls' (and others')
minds, without those viewers necessarily realizing how these values have
infiltrated.

Greenfield's images in *Girl Culture* paint an alarming portrait of how   *3*
different girls respond to this cultural focus on the female body: One
eighteen-year-old is shown being "blind weighed" with her back to the
scale at a treatment center for eating disorders (implying that she can't
face the disheartening result); a five-year-old girl picks out clothing in an
upscale Beverly Hills boutique; and college girls in bikinis strut by hoot-
ing men at spring break competitions, some seeming self-confident, others
seeming uncertain.

The girls in Greenfield's photos often see themselves as too thin, too   *4*
fat, not stylish enough, too trendy, attractive or ugly or desirable or hideous. Comfort with one's body appears all but nonexistent. "I don't know
a girl who's happy with her body," states eighteen-year-old Ashlee in text
accompanying pictures of the debutante Cotton Ball in Chattanooga, Tennessee. Ashlee, a vegan who says she dislikes wearing makeup and dressing up, attended the ball and participated in its rituals, including shaving
her armpits, to appease her family. "I just don't understand shaving every
day," she says. "I like my armpit hair. My boyfriend likes my armpit hair,
too. People just buy into the unattractiveness of unshaven armpits. My
whole family cheered when I shaved."

A girl's body, almost from birth (when her first weight is taken), often 5
reflects cultural expectations and conventions—in how she dresses, how
she is allowed to use her body, how she presents it to the world, and how
comfortable she feels within it. When she is younger, her body is measured
against standards of health and growth, as it would be for any child. But
near adolescence, a girl's growing breasts, widening hips, and changing
skin become the site for many other standards. Her breasts are not just
a physical aspect of her body, but a way in which others will perceive her
as a teenager rather than as a child—custom will dictate that it's time
to wear a bra, parents might deem her old enough to handle more privileges and responsibilities, and she might receive more sexual attention
from acquaintances and strangers. Adolescent girls find themselves on the
receiving end of increasingly sexualized expectations—from peers who
cast a critical eye on girls' appearance and behavior, from parents who
might either assume girls will date or fear that girls will date too soon, and
from a culture that is often uncomfortable with women who don't embody
certain sexualized stereotypes. A changing body means other changes in
a girl's life—some that she might be emotionally able to meet, and some
that she resists. But there is no doubt that as she moves from childhood
to adolescence, an overlay of expectations—sexiness, attractiveness,
availability—can blanket a girl's individual pacing of her desire to venture
into womanhood.

While boys and men are increasingly presented with images that also 6
stray far from the reality of the average male body, the use of male models
to sell mundane products isn't as pervasive, and the presence of a conventionally attractive or sexualized male body isn't considered as strictly
standard to sell a product or tell a story. When women are consistently
objectified—that is, used as vehicles to sway public view through their
sexuality or projected attractiveness—it sends girls a clear message. The
onslaught of images of impossibly perfect-looking, sexually contextualized
female bodies reinforces the idea that physical "perfection" and sexual
attractiveness are both normal and expected of women, and by endlessly
recreating scenarios that reinforce traditional gender roles, advertisers
simultaneously teach girls and women a set of lessons about what it is to
be female in America.

The Body as Battleground

In the 1997 book *The Body Project: An Intimate History of American Girls*, 7
author Joan Jacobs Brumberg traces the history of how teenage girls
within America have made different body parts into "projects." Examining
historical views of aspects of girls' bodies—such as menstruation, body
hair, skin conditions, weight—Brumberg delineates the ways that girls
(and parents, doctors, and advertisers) have conceptualized those aspects
as "problematic" and devised ways of addressing each one. Recollecting

a discussion in which her female college-age students discuss the "necessity" of bikini-line waxes, Brumberg realizes that yet another body part has become a "project" for girls to attend to, mold to a standard, and then maintain. Asking herself why these students were adding another area to manage to the long litany of bodily concerns they already had, she recognizes that girls are now sexualized at a far younger age, and that concern with their bodies is yet more pervasive and rampant, with advertisers eager to instruct on depilation, control, and constant maintenance.

Examining the diaries of girls before World War I, Brumberg explains 8 that the girls whose diaries she finds and reads (most hailing from middle-class families) were often praised for lack of attention to their bodies: Feminine virtue was found in a kind of unself-consciousness in which vanity about one's body was considered immoral or wrong. From decades later, the girlhood diaries that Brumberg collects and reads cite numerous instances of self-consciousness; by the 1950s, girls felt the need to improve their hair, skin, teeth, and weight, among other "body projects" that required honing and then maintenance in order to hew to acceptable standards.

Throughout her book, Brumberg considers how girls' bodies (and 9 specific physical issues such as having clear skin, maintaining virginity, or hiding menstruation) have been commodified and valued as ways in which physical perfection (or the attempt at its attainment) becomes a class-based goal. As print media began to circulate more widely after the turn of the twentieth century, through magazines, newspapers, and books, advertisers also had an opportunity to sell girls (and their parents) products intended to improve overall beauty and health, contributing to anxiety about not meeting a standard of "normalcy," which, as Brumberg shows, historically has altered but has never left American cultural consciousness.

In her chapter "Sanitizing Puberty: The American Way to Menstru- 10 ate," Brumberg writes, "In the effort to sell products, menstruation finally burst out of the closet in the 1920s when popular magazines, such as the *Ladies' Home Journal* and *Good Housekeeping*, began to run ads for Kotex. These advertisements constituted the first real public acknowledgement of menstruation." She writes that later, in the 1930s and 1940s, "Newly established educational divisions within the personal products industry (i.e., Kimberly-Clark . . . Tampax, Inc. . . .) began to supply mothers, teachers, parent-teacher associations and also the Girl Scouts with free, ready-made programs of instruction on 'menstrual health.'" Postwar, "marketing strategists understood that sales to the baby-boom generation—soon to be the largest cohort of adolescents in American history—could turn menstrual blood into gold." With menstruation, as with other functions and features of the female body, Brumberg shows how marketing strategists and cultural scripts intertwine until the messages girls receive are impossible to separate out and are just accepted as part of an overarching gender code.

In her chapter "Perfect Skin," Brumberg looks at the history of teenage 11 acne, noting that as far back as 1885 a physician at New York Hospital realized that girls were three times more likely than boys to seek help for their skin. "Although boys surely suffer from the stigma of acne," Brumberg writes, "girls' pimples get more cultural attention. Because of cultural mandates that link femininity to flawless skin, the burden of maintaining a clear complexion has devolved disproportionately upon women and girls. . . . Skin care was really the first of many body projects endorsed and supported by middle-class parents for their adolescent children." In Brumberg's accounting, a girl's face was a key to her future: a good marriage (i.e., a marriage that put her into the same or an even higher social and economic position than she was in). As twentieth-century advances in dermatology also made acne treatment more available, families could "invest" in a daughter with skin issues so that her visage wasn't marred. Brumberg mentions a Victorian-era skin-care product called Kosmeo that was advertised in the Sears, Roebuck catalog with this copy: "When a man marries, nine times out of ten he chooses a girl with a pretty complexion." Brumberg's research concludes, "In order to avoid an unhappy future as a spinster, thousands of American girls ordered Kosmeo, and then rubbed earnestly with camel's hair brushes and Turkish towels in order to increase friction and improve blood circulation to the face."

Another historical shift Brumberg notes involves girls' response to *12* makeup. She writes, "In the effort to look like the attractive women they saw in movies and magazines, American women in the 1920s put aside long-established objections to face makeup and began to purchase and use a wide range of cosmetics." Brumberg details products marketed specifically to African American girls and women to lighten their skin, and she recounts the "hierarchy of hue in the African American community"; describing 1950s magazines' range of ads for lightening products, she elaborates, "Until recent times—probably the 1960s—the color of a girl's skin was central to her sense of self, as well as her place in the community of people of color. Although skin bleachers are still sold today, they generally are not used by the current generation to bleach the entire face, the way older generations did, before the Black Pride movement of the 1960s and 1970s." Reflecting, again, on how commerce intersects with "standards" that girls are told they must adhere to in order to be pleasing, or attractive, she writes, "The fact that skin bleachers and fade creams sold so well is a painful and compelling reminder of how much class and racial anxiety has been invested in skin in American society, particularly among groups who suffer from exclusion and bigotry."

What makes the female body such a battleground? The claims that *13* parents, advertisers, and culture make on girls' bodies are dizzying—body odor must be banned, underarm hair removed, breasts lifted to a certain perk, skin made clear enough to touch, hair made glossy and enticing. The effect on the owners of the bodies means often feeling a disquieting angst that they are *never good enough* as they are, that they are forever being measured and found lacking. Contemporary "body projects" that girls today might undertake include the ones that Brumberg shows have lasted for decades in girls' awareness: weight, skin, haircut and color, among others. But consider how many other "body projects" are also undertaken in the twenty-first century: eyebrow grooming, development of fuller eyelashes, chemical peels and dermabrasion, tattooing, nail art, "bikini line" maintenance, colored contacts or Lasik surgery, tooth whitening, use of push-up bras or minimizers, contemporary "smoothers" to cover up panty lines, cellulite erasure, and skin buffing. And the list could go on.

Body weight and body shape come up consistently in Brumberg's   14
history as factors to be controlled. In the chapter titled "Body Projects," under the subtitle "The Century of Svelte," Brumberg gives a brief history of the cult of thinness in America, and she also shows how trends in and expectations about girls' body shapes have changed, demonstrating again how subject the female figure has been to cultural trends and demands. She cites 1920 as the first time that "teenage girls made systematic efforts to lower their weight by food restriction and exercise" as adolescent girls "were motivated by a new ideal of female beauty that began to evolve around the turn of the century." New fashion trends that emphasized a trim silhouette replaced more voluptuous Victorian hourglass figures, with small waists and large hips. Instead, the American woman migrated toward the look of the "flapper"—flat chested, long limbed, and decidedly slender. Brumberg writes that girls around this period (starting around 1908 and progressing through the 1920s and 1930s) "bade farewell to corsets, stays, and petticoats, and they began to diet, or internalize control of the body."

The changing fashions of girls' breasts (whether their owners are try-   15
ing to appear flat or large chested) is another point Brumberg explores by looking at the evolution of the training bra and undergarments sold to girls and women, especially around teenage anxiety about "developing" too quickly or too slowly. Different decades dictated that breasts either be disguised or enhanced, but the focus on controlling one's weight remained a constant, as it still seems to be. Another historical trend Brumberg traces is the focus on female legs: "Americans have talked about glamorous 'gams' ever since the Rockettes made good legs a requirement back in the 1930s," she writes. "But American taste in legs has changed considerably in the past half-century." She notes that whereas the Rockettes had "shorter, chunkier limbs than today's long-stemmed, lean favorites," changes in fashion have accounted for an emphasis on "tight, narrow thighs." After miniskirts became popular in the 1960s, girls and women felt more emphasis put on their legs—particularly their thighs, which were meant to be as trim and cellulite free as possible. The phrase "thunder thighs," notes Brumberg, entered the American lexicon "in the early 1980s both as shorthand for female anxiety about the body and as a misogynistic slur." Discussing the cellulite avoidance industry, through use of thigh creams and liposuction, she concludes, "Our national concern about 'thunder thighs' says a lot about what Americans value. . . . Not surprisingly, there is more self-hatred [of the body] among women than men, and women tend to be

especially dissatisfied about the lower body—the waist, hips, thighs, and buttocks. . . . This sad reality needs to be factored into our understanding of girls and the way in which they develop their sense of self."

Without question, being thin is widely held up in American culture   *16* today as an ideal to be achieved. Cultural differences play a large role in these perceptions; what's considered a "normal" body shape in a rural Midwestern community might look very different from what is considered "standard" in Manhattan. A Latina girl might have a fuller, larger frame presented to her as positive, as might an African American girl. But no matter a girl's cultural background, what is seen within American society at large is a narrow standard that's often in direct opposition to the bodies of most real women. And from the scores of models who advertise the "waif look" alongside whatever product they are hawking to the scores of slender television and film stars, the image of the thin woman is everywhere. And recent teen pop-culture icons varying from the Olsen twins to Destiny's Child, Lindsay Lohan, and Miley Cyrus tend to embody the same extremely slender stereotype.

Why value thinness? The concept that women's presentation matches   *17* the status they hold within a patriarchal culture—meant to be diminutive, shrinking, not taking up excessive space, and standing in contrast to a larger male form—is one possible explanation. There are many other viable responses as to why women are told through cultural code that being thinner and smaller is better, including the fact that most women do have smaller body sizes than men do. But the pervasive glorification of taking up less space with one's body, and the idealized feminine body shape being slight rather than large, is a widely accepted tenet of American culture, sometimes with drastic consequences.

The media literacy organization Mind on the Media reports, "Eighty   *18* percent of ten-year-old American girls diet. The number one magic wish for young girls age eleven to seventeen is to be thinner." The media are most often cited as the instigators of pressure to be thin. In many sources the height of the average American women is listed as five feet four inches, and her weight is listed as approximately 140 pounds. In a more recent study by the National Center for Health Statistics, the average American woman's weight is now listed as 163 pounds and her height is listed as just under five feet four inches. The height of the average fashion model, on the other hand, is approximately five feet nine inches to above six feet tall, and her average weight is approximately 117 pounds. This means that fashion models are on average significantly thinner and taller than the majority of the female American population, and yet they present an image to which most women and girls feel they ought to aspire. Seen in this light, the bloatedness of the diet industry—in which book authors, pharmaceutical companies, dieting organizations, makers of special exercise equipment, magazine publishers, and support groups feed anxiety to women about weight while filling their own bank accounts—becomes quietly disturbing.

According to the National Alliance on Mental Illness (NAMI), anorexia *19*
nervosa is "a serious, often chronic, and life-threatening eating disorder
defined by a refusal to maintain minimal body weight within 15 percent of
an individual's normal weight." Asserting that anorexia most often occurs
in pre- and postadolescent girls, NAMI's website explains that "one reason
younger women are particularly vulnerable to eating disorders is their tendency to go on strict diets to achieve an 'ideal' figure. This obsessive dieting behavior reflects today's societal pressure to be thin, which is seen in
advertising and the media."

Bulimia (or bulimia nervosa), another well-known eating disorder, *20*
occurs when girls eat excessively (or "binge") and then purge their food,
whether through vomiting, use of laxatives, or diuretics. With both bulimia and anorexia, overexercising can be common, along with a sense of
"body dysmorphic syndrome"—the sense that one's own body is distorted,
bloated, and unacceptable, despite what a mirror or scale might reveal.
Left untreated, both disorders can be fatal, and even with treatment both
can cause lifelong damage to the body through inadequate nutrition and
through the development of a vexed relationship with food.

Estimating that between one-half to 1 percent of all females in the *21*
United States will develop anorexia, NAMI also states that "because more
than 90 percent of all those who are affected are adolescent and young
women, the disorder has been characterized as primarily a woman's illness." The complex motivations underlying different cases of anorexia are
many—girls might experience starving themselves as a way to exercise
control over their changing bodies, or they may see it as a way to comply
with a cultural standard of extreme thinness, promoted to them daily and
tacitly praised by parents who admire models' or actresses' bodies.

In response to these concerns, activists and girls' advocates have *22*
pushed in recent years for magazines aimed at adolescent girls (and
magazines geared toward women) to employ diverse models with "real"
figures that exemplify different body types. Agitating for change with
how girls and women are perceived by the public—and hence, perceive
their own bodies—is nothing new, although advocating for change has
taken different forms. Feminist activists of the 1960s and 1970s prom-
inently crusaded against the sexist and racist standards of beauty pag-
eants: The group New York Radical Women organized a protest in 1968
in which two hundred activists in Atlantic City, New Jersey, gathered to
express outrage over the Miss America Pageant's objectification of girls
and women, likening them to animals being judged for their physical
attributes. According to Rory Dicker in her work *A History of U.S. Feminisms*, the protesters carried signs with messages such as CAN MAKEUP
COVER THE WOUNDS OF OUR OPPRESSION? and THE REAL MISS AMERICA LIVES
IN HARLEM. Dicker explains that the last sign made reference to the
pageant's embedded racism: "Until 1940, contestants had to be white,
and as of 1968, no black woman had competed in, much less won,
the contest."

These campaigns of the past, and those of the present, have often 23
been met with mixed success. In 2004 the skin- and hair-product company
Dove launched a Campaign for Real Beauty, during which scouts recruited
a variety of "ordinary-looking" women and asked them to pose in basic
white underwear while looking naturally proud of their nonmodel-size
bodies. Dove also set up the Dove Self-Esteem Fund, which sponsored a
series of videos and online resources meant to promote body acceptance
among women and girls, no matter their shape or size.

Dove's campaign sought to use "real women" to defy use of expected 24
body shapes and types, as well as ages, of models, and it pinpointed bolstering self-esteem in girls as a crucial starting point to having grown
women appreciate their bodies as they are. In a "Girls Only" part of its web
site, the campaign offered interactive tools for girls to use to think about
issues of body image and self-esteem, with activities designed to help girls
figure out who best supports them in their lives, identify where their inner
strengths lie, and determine what they need to feel good about themselves. In the site's "Girls Only Interactive Self-Esteem Zone," users could
learn how to decode media messages aimed at girls and women and view
"before" and "after" images of models whose bodies had been cosmetically
retouched and digitally manipulated.

And yet it is critical to look more closely at what this media campaign 25
is selling—just as Dove advises media-literate girls to do. Detractors are
quick to point out that, fundamentally, Dove is still hawking products to
girls and women that they probably don't fundamentally need—but with
different, "affirming," packaging. And a further catch? One of the original
ads for the Dove Real Beauty campaign was for a cellulite-firming cream,
pointing to the disconnect between promoting women's self-acceptance
and selling a product that diminishes the size of women's thighs.

Reporter Rebecca Traister critiqued the campaign—and other media 26
campaigns that use a "feel good about yourself" tactic to fundamentally
tell girls and women that they need to do (or buy) more—in a 2005 Salon.
com article, citing the tagline used in the Dove marketing: "For too long/
beauty has been defined by narrow, stifling sterotypes [sic]./You've told
us it's time to change all that./We agree./Because we believe real beauty
comes/In many shapes, sizes and ages./It is why we started the Campaign
for Real Beauty." Traister, pointing out the cellulite-firming cream conundrum, writes, "As long as you're patting yourself on the back for hiring
real-life models with imperfect bodies, thereby 'challenging today's stereotypical view of beauty and inspiring women to take great care of themselves,' why ask those models to flog a cream that has zero health value
and is just an expensive and temporary Band-Aid for a problem' that the
media has told us we have with our bodies?" Traister also describes a similarly conflicted girl-focused ad campaign, colaunched by Bath and Body
Works and American Girl dolls, that purportedly focuses on "Real Beauty
Inside and Out" by selling young girls "personal care products 'designed
to help girls ages 8 to 12 feel—and be—their best.'" The products—"body

lotions, splashes, soaps and lip balms, all dressed up in girl-friendly 'hues of berry'"—arrived "with an inspirational message like 'Real beauty means no one's smile shines exactly like yours,' 'Real beauty is helping a friend,' or 'Real beauty is trusting in yourself.'"

In 2007, the Campaign for a Commercial-Free Childhood (CCFC) 27 launched a letter-writing campaign to Unilever, Dove's owner, citing the hypocrisy in Dove's hyping its marketing campaign for girls "while simultaneously advertising Axe Body Spray by degrading them." The organization's press release cites CCFC director and cofounder Dr. Susan Linn: "Even as Unilever basks in praise for its Dove Real Beauty campaign, they are profiting from Axe marketing that blatantly objectifies and degrades young women." Unilever's Axe product line, marketed to boys, featured ads trading on the humor of over-the-top sexist, stereotypical gender roles: In one promotional online music video for Axe, the Bom Chicka Wah Wahs, a young female singing trio wearing only panties, bras, garters, and high-heeled boots, gyrate seductively atop a bus, fondle their own breasts, cuddle up to a variety of phallic objects, and sing pantingly about how the scent of Axe "attacks" and overwhelms a woman's "common sense." The singers writhe around stripper poles and along the floor while the camera repeatedly cuts to the women's crotches and bottoms. A "nerdy girl" with glasses who is first seen ironing and mentions she needs to get to work is then transformed into a sex kitten like the other singers; claiming she wants "true love like Romeo and Juliet," she is then "converted" to the other singers' hypersexual look with their implication of sexual licentiousness. "[The group's] suggestive theme song and video is all about how the Axe aroma causes women to lose control sexually," CCFC writes. "Sample lyric: 'If you have that aroma on, you can have our whole band.'" Bob McCannon, copresident of the Action Coalition for Media Education, calls the Dove campaign "marketing masquerading as media literacy." Whether it's viewed positively or negatively, it's certain that the Dove campaign for girls and women has caused a stir—and maybe one that will edge change forward by other marketers. However, if change simply means new types of marketing for products that fundamentally tell women their bodies need improvement, does it really mean true progress?

Freedom and Choices

In the final chapter of *The Body Project*, Brumberg writes, "At the end of 28 the twentieth century, living in a girl's body is more complicated than it was a century ago." She lays out a late-twentieth-century dilemma that still resonates in the twenty-first, in what some still consider a "postfeminist" era: Girls, she explains, are told "on the one hand . . . that being female was no bar to accomplishment. Yet girls of [this] generation learned from a very early age that the power of their gender was tied to what they looked like—and how 'sexy' they were—rather than to character or achievement." Absent the Victorian-era "protective umbrella" that once shielded girls (and restricted them) from sexuality, girls have more freedom than ever, but, according to Brumberg, "their freedom is laced with peril."

Yet openness about sexuality in a post-sexual revolution era also gives *29* girls options they would never before experience: the choice to explore their sexuality before marriage or committed partnership, to understand their own desires and needs, to discover whether or not they are heterosexual, bisexual, lesbian, or want to move between definitions.

"Knowledge is power" is a popular saying, and it is remarkable how *30* much more informed girls can now be—through Internet resources if there isn't open discussion within their own families or good information given through school or other community resources. Knowing more about their bodies and about sex leads girls toward making their own choices, although careful media education is still needed to decode options that are "normalized," such as being sexualized at early ages or at a moment when a girl feels she "should" be, but might not be, ready.

Artist Barbara Kruger's famous statement "Your body is a battle- *31* ground" is often heard within circles where women examine issues pertaining to bodies, gender, and cultural expectations. Girls' more recently won freedoms—to participate in sports, to envision and plan for careers previously limited to (often privileged) men, to access accurate information about sexuality and sexual health—intersect with a consumer culture that sees girls and women as both bait and targets, and a society that has not come as far in abolishing limiting and harmful stereotypes of gender and sexuality as it likes to think. The site of a complex locus of cultural issues surrounding power, identity, and sexuality—often converging at uncomfortable angles—a girl's body is hardly peaceful to inhabit.

■ ■ ■

Reading as a Writer: Analyzing Rhetorical Choices

1. Much of the work of this piece is Lipkin offering an overview of Brumberg's research. Where do you see Lipkin making her own points? Mark out these sections, and be ready to discuss how Lipkin adds to the "conversation" about the body as a "project" that Brumberg starts with her 1997 research.

2. Lipkin devotes paragraphs 23 to 27 to an analysis of the Dove "Campaign for Real Beauty." What varying perspectives on this campaign does she describe? How do the ideas in these paragraphs demonstrate her larger argument? Consider looking up the images and short videos affiliated with this campaign and discuss what you find, in light of Lipkin's points.

Writing as a Reader: Entering the Conversation of Ideas

1. Given the long history of gendered practices that Lipkin describes, it is helpful to consider her text in relation to Allan G. Johnson's text, with its telling title: "Why Do We Make So Much of Gender?" Compose an essay that uses Johnson's ideas about the motivation behind arguments about gender in order to analyze the "body projects" that Lipkin describes. Given the history and present that both authors depict, what conclusions can you draw about what is at stake and for whom in these behaviors and beliefs?

2. How do Lipkin's ideas help you understand the advertising campaigns such as those depicted in essays by Jean Kilbourne (Chapter 13) or Noël Sturgeon (Chapter 16)? Drawing on images and insights from these authors, analyze two or three related visual advertisements for products marketed to women. Reread and implement the strategies in Chapter 8 on analyzing visual rhetoric for this assignment.

BARBARA EHRENREICH
How I Discovered the Truth About Poverty

Barbara Ehrenreich is one of the best-known journalists publishing social commentary in the United States today. She earned a PhD in cell biology but has a voracious appetite for learning and writing about topics far beyond science. She has published and lectured on the state of health care, the history of women as healers, the anxieties of the middle class, and the history of dancing, to name just a few of the topics she's addressed. In addition to the many books she has written, cowritten, and edited, she writes prolifically for newspapers and magazines, including the *New York Times Magazine*, *The Washington Post Magazine*, *The Atlantic*, *The Nation*, and *The New Republic*.

This piece was published in *The Nation* magazine and then republished on Alternet, an online news source for original and republished journalism. This short, pithy essay is written in a journalistic style, with short paragraphs and without footnotes. Ehrenreich does, however, draw on sources; this is not simply an opinion piece, as her extended critique of Michael Harrington's book, *The Other America* (1962), which is part of this essay, demonstrates. Why does Ehrenreich consider the phrase from Harrington's book (which he draws from anthropologist Oscar Lewis), "the culture of poverty," to be so problematic? As you read, pay attention to the way Ehrenreich traces the history and uses of that phrase through time. You might even try to paraphrase her ideas about each different political use of the phrase.

Because Ehrenreich moves so quickly through different political figures and examples, it may be a challenge to keep track of her larger point. Try underlining sentences where she helps us see the big picture she's examining, such as in paragraph 11, where she notes, "Even today, more than a decade later [than Clinton's bill], and four years into a severe economic downturn, as people continue to slide into poverty from the middle classes, the theory maintains its grip. If you're needy, you must be in need of correction, the assumption goes. . . ." Where else do you see her moving from examples to her larger point about the way the poor are characterized as "other"?

In her final paragraph, Ehrenreich returns to her opening point about Harrington having "discovered" poverty, by noting that it's time for a "new discovery" of poverty that reveals a new truth: "if we look closely enough, we'll have to conclude that poverty is not, after all, a cultural aberration or a character flaw. Poverty is a shortage of money" (para. 15). Given your own experiences and knowledge about attitudes toward the poor and rich, how would you chime into this conversation?

■ ■ ■

It's been exactly fifty years since Americans, or at least the non-poor *1* among them, "discovered" poverty, thanks to Michael Harrington's engaging book *The Other America*. If this discovery now seems a little overstated, like Columbus's "discovery" of America, it was because the poor, according to Harrington, were so "hidden" and "invisible" that it took a crusading left-wing journalist to ferret them out.

Harrington's book jolted a nation that then prided itself on its class- *2* lessness and even fretted about the spirit-sapping effects of "too much affluence." He estimated that one quarter of the population lived in poverty—inner-city blacks, Appalachian whites, farm workers, and elderly Americans among them. We could no longer boast, as President Nixon had done in his "kitchen debate" with Soviet Premier Nikita Khrushchev in Moscow just three years earlier, about the splendors of American capitalism.

At the same time that it delivered its gut punch, *The Other America* *3* also offered a view of poverty that seemed designed to comfort the already comfortable. The poor were different from the rest of us, it argued, radically different, and not just in the sense that they were deprived, disadvantaged, poorly housed, or poorly fed. They *felt* different, too, thought differently, and pursued lifestyles characterized by shortsightedness and intemperance. As Harrington wrote, "There is . . . a language of the poor, a psychology of the poor, a worldview of the poor. To be impoverished is to be an internal alien, to grow up in a culture that is radically different from the one that dominates the society."

Harrington did such a good job of making the poor seem "other" *4* that when I read his book in 1963, I did not recognize my own forbears and extended family in it. All right, some of them did lead disorderly lives by middle-class standards, involving drinking, brawling, and out-of-wedlock babies. But they were also hardworking and in some cases fiercely ambitious—qualities that Harrington seemed to reserve for the economically privileged.

According to him, what distinguished the poor was their unique 5 "culture of poverty," a concept he borrowed from anthropologist Oscar Lewis, who had derived it from his study of Mexican slum-dwellers. The culture of poverty gave *The Other America* a trendy academic twist, but it also gave the book a conflicted double message: "We"—the always presumptively affluent readers—needed to find some way to help the poor, but we also needed to understand that there was *something wrong with them*, something that could not be cured by a straightforward redistribution of wealth. Think of the earnest liberal who encounters a panhandler, is moved to pity by the man's obvious destitution, but refrains from offering a quarter—since the hobo might, after all, spend the money on booze.

In his defense, Harrington did not mean that poverty was *caused* by 6 what he called the "twisted" proclivities of the poor. But he certainly opened the floodgates to that interpretation. In 1965, Daniel Patrick Moynihan—a sometime-liberal and one of Harrington's drinking companions at the famed White Horse Tavern in Greenwich Village—blamed inner-city poverty on what he saw as the shaky structure of the "Negro family," clearing the way for decades of victim-blaming. A few years after The Moynihan Report, Harvard urbanologist Edward C. Banfield, who was to go on to serve as an advisor to Ronald Reagan, felt free to claim that:

> The lower-class individual lives from moment to moment. . . . Impulse governs his behavior. . . . He is therefore radically improvident: whatever he cannot consume immediately he considers valueless. . . . [He] has a feeble, attenuated sense of self.

In the "hardest cases," Banfield opined, the poor might need to be cared 7 for in "semi-institutions . . . and to accept a certain amount of surveillance and supervision from a semi-social-worker-semi-policeman."

By the Reagan era, the "culture of poverty" had become a cornerstone 8 of conservative ideology: Poverty was caused, not by low wages or a lack of jobs, but by bad attitudes and faulty lifestyles. The poor were dissolute, promiscuous, prone to addiction and crime, unable to "defer gratification," or possibly even set an alarm clock. The last thing they could be trusted with was money. In fact, Charles Murray argued in his 1984 book *Losing Ground*, any attempt to help the poor with their material circumstances would only have the unexpected consequence of deepening their depravity.

So it was in a spirit of righteousness and even compassion that Demo- 9 crats and Republicans joined together to reconfigure social programs to cure, not poverty, but the "culture of poverty." In 1996, the Clinton administration enacted the "One Strike" rule banning anyone who committed a felony from public housing. A few months later, welfare was replaced by Temporary Assistance to Needy Families (TANF), which in its current form makes cash assistance available only to those who have jobs or are able to participate in government-imposed "workfare."

In a further nod to "culture of poverty" theory, the original welfare 10 reform bill appropriated $250 million over five years for "chastity training" for poor single mothers. (This bill, it should be pointed out, was signed by Bill Clinton.)

Even today, more than a decade later and four years into a severe economic downturn, as people continue to slide into poverty from the middle classes, the theory maintains its grip. If you're needy, you must be in need of correction, the assumption goes, so TANF recipients are routinely instructed in how to improve their attitudes and applicants for a growing number of safety-net programs are subjected to drug testing. Lawmakers in twenty-three states are considering testing people who apply for such programs as job training, food stamps, public housing, welfare, and home heating assistance. And on the theory that the poor are likely to harbor criminal tendencies, applicants for safety net programs are increasingly subjected to fingerprinting and computerized searches for outstanding warrants. 11

Unemployment, with its ample opportunities for slacking off, is another obviously suspect condition, and last year twelve states considered requiring pee tests as a condition for receiving unemployment benefits. Both Mitt Romney and Newt Gingrich have suggested drug testing as a condition for *all* government benefits, presumably including Social Security. If granny insists on handling her arthritis with marijuana, she may have to starve. 12

What would Michael Harrington make of the current uses of the "culture of poverty" theory he did so much to popularize? I worked with him in the 1980s, when we were co-chairs of Democratic Socialists of America, and I suspect he'd have the decency to be chagrined, if not mortified. In all the discussions and debates I had with him, he never said a disparaging word about the down-and-out or, for that matter, uttered the phrase "the culture of poverty." Maurice Isserman, Harrington's biographer, told me that he'd probably latched onto it in the first place only because "he didn't want to come off in the book sounding like a stereotypical Marxist agitator stuck-in-the-thirties." 13

The ruse—if you could call it that—worked. Michael Harrington wasn't red-baited into obscurity. In fact, his book became a bestseller and an inspiration for President Lyndon Johnson's War on Poverty. But he had fatally botched the "discovery" of poverty. What affluent Americans found in his book, and in all the crude conservative diatribes that followed it, was not the poor, but a flattering new way to think about themselves—disciplined, law-abiding, sober, and focused. In other words, not poor. 14

Fifty years later, a new discovery of poverty is long overdue. This time, we'll have to take account not only of stereotypical Skid Row residents and Appalachians, but of foreclosed-upon suburbanites, laid-off tech workers, and America's ever-growing army of the "working poor." And if we look closely enough, we'll have to conclude that poverty is not, after all, a cultural aberration or a character flaw. Poverty is a shortage of money. 15

■ ■ ■

Reading as a Writer: Analyzing Rhetorical Choices

1. Reread Ehrenreich's essay, noting all the different places she describes and analyzes Michael Harrington's writing and ideas. Take notes on the different points she makes about him. Why is he such a crucial touchstone for her argument? How do his ideas help her make her larger point?

2. Ehrenreich mentions several turning-point political moments in attitudes toward poverty, some of which might be new to you. Perhaps working in different groups, look up President Lyndon Johnson's "War on Poverty," *The Moynihan Report*, reviews of Charles Murray's 1984 book *Losing Ground*, and President Bill Clinton's "One Strike" rule, and report your findings to the larger group. How do your findings contribute to your understanding of Ehrenreich's piece?

Writing as a Reader: Entering the Conversation of Ideas

1. Just as Ehrenreich critiques writer Michael Harrington for turning poor people into "others," Allan G. Johnson and Agustín Fuentes write about specific populations who are cast as different from a "norm." How does each author write about the effects of this creation of the category of otherness? How does each talk about the origins of these ideas, and their current iterations? Whose interests are served, and how, by "othering" parts of the population?

2. Both Ehrenreich and bell hooks (Chapter 13) analyze the ways popular understandings of poverty often blame the poor. Place these authors' ideas in conversation in an essay in which you make an argument about the ways policymaking and popular culture often go hand in hand to produce ideas about inequality. What solutions does each author offer, and what do you make of those solutions?

15

Biology and Psychology
How do our physical and cultural selves intersect?

© Getty Images/Alfred Pasieka

The readings in this chapter invite us to think about the fascinating places where our bodies meet culture. These wide-ranging authors reveal the myriad intersections where biology is shaped by psychological and social expectations of what it means to be feminine, masculine, disabled, smart, attractive, a member of an identity group . . . or good at math.

While most of us suspect that the way we see—and feel about—ourselves and others is in part a product of our society, these authors offer fresh perspectives on how this dynamic works, with many eye-opening examples. What we imagine to be "facts" are often not supported by evidence, and the effects of these misunderstandings on people's lives can be dramatic.

Mahzarin R. Banaji and Anthony G. Greenwald challenge us to reconsider our psychological "blindspots" that lead to stereotyping . . . and then somewhat paradoxically claim that stereotyping can be beneficial. Jesse J. Prinz and Georgia Warnke help us unpack common misconceptions about gendered behaviors, placing scientific studies under the microscope for closer analysis.

Some of the authors focus on the ways we alter our bodies, and why. For example, Margaret Talbot looks at the significance of "brain-boosting" drugs, which are gaining popularity on college campuses, and raising the bar for academic performance (particularly when students are also cramming in socializing activities). Coauthors Anahí Viladrich Ming-Chin Yeh, Nancy Bruning, and Rachael Weiss examine the pressures on Latinas to conform to often-conflicting body standards. William J. Peace extends the conversation about body "norms" into the realm of disability studies and challenges us to reframe our ideas of the disabled body by examining adaptive sports.

These readings will take you from theories and research to your very own body, from your daily practices to the largest questions of what it means to be human. We bet you will have strong responses to these ideas, and we invite you to dive into this raucous conversation.

 Visit **macmillanhighered.com/frominquiry3e** to check out a short article and accompanying video that tell the story of Marinalva de Almeida, a Brazilian athlete and 2016 Paralympic hopeful.

 How does biology explain the low numbers of women in computer science? At **macmillanhighered.com/frominquiry3e,** a witty slide show by computer scientist Terri Oda proposes an answer.

MAHZARIN R. BANAJI AND ANTHONY G. GREENWALD

On Stereotypes

Mahzarin R. Banaji and Anthony G. Greenwald are both professors of psychology who met at the Ohio State University when Greenwald supervised Banaji's graduate research. Banaji now teaches at Harvard University and Greenwald teaches at the University of Washington. They have collaborated for more than thirty years on the intersection of psychology and social contexts, particularly the unconscious decisions we make about others, especially those based on social groupings such as gender, age, race, disability, and other identity markers. This piece, "On Stereotypes," is from their 2013 book, *Blindspot: Hidden Biases of Good People*. In it, they explain challenging concepts about the way biases work (even when we think we are being fair-minded) by using the term *blindspot*—likely familiar to you as a term for something hidden from sight (e.g., a car in your blindspot while you are driving). These authors use this idea as a metaphor for the part of the mind that hides assumptions—stereotypes—we do not realize we hold.

Before you read, skim through this piece to see how the authors organize it in subsections. What can you discern about their argument from the titles of these sections, and the organization? You will notice that Banaji and Greenwald use bullet points and charts and lists to make their point; how does this affect the way (and speed at which) you read?

The authors also use interactive strategies to draw the reader into questioning and testing preconceptions. Consider the effect, in paragraphs 13 to 14, of asking us to visualize a person of a certain type . . . and then predicting our responses. They also challenge us to test our assumptions in the lists of "traits" and "groups" of people in paragraphs 30–31. What do you make of your own responses, and their interpretations in the next paragraph?

In their final two sections, Banaji and Greenwald set out their theory that "stereotyping achieves the desirable effect of allowing us to rapidly perceive total strangers as distinctive individuals" (para. 37). What do you think of this paradoxical claim? Ultimately, the authors argue, perhaps surprisingly, that stereotypes can be useful—even beneficial—but they can also have very real and negative consequences. As a reader, you will need to decide how their complex exploration of the idea of stereotyping extends your own understanding of how we all think in categories, and how this affects others, and yourself.

■   ■   ■

Categories

The recognized starting point for modern scientific understanding *1* of stereotypes is Gordon Allport's 1954 book *The Nature of Prejudice*. Allport wrote: "The human mind must think with the aid of categories. . . . Once formed, categories are the basis for normal prejudgment. We cannot possibly avoid this process. Orderly living depends on it."[3]

The term *Homo categoricus* acknowledges the scientific impact of All- *2* port's view of the importance of mental categories. A category is a collection of things having enough in common so that it is convenient to treat them as kin. The similarity among category members does not need to be great. The category of *car* includes things as different as toy cars, cable cars, and railroad cars. But the use of categories has a powerful effect on our behavior—as a quick look at a situation involving some subordinate categories within the *car* category will make clear: If you are driving on a highway and closing rapidly on a fast-moving car in front of you, your own speed in the next few seconds will be drastically different if you categorize that speeding vehicle as *police car* rather than as *sports car*. Another example: You will act very differently toward small white crystals that you categorize as *sugar* than toward ones you categorize as *salt*, even though you can't visibly tell one from the other in a spoon.

The categories that we use for people also affect our behavior in very   3 clear ways. For example:

- In a department store to make a purchase, you readily surrender your credit card to a total stranger whom you categorize as a *salesclerk*. You trust this stranger to be a typical member of the salesclerk category—that is, someone who will not surreptitiously record your account information and then sell it to an identity thief.

- Entering a medical clinic, you assume the obedient role of *patient* (another category). Even though you may never have seen any of the medical staff before, you unquestioningly follow the instructions of people who are dressed in ways that lead you to categorize them as *doctor* or *nurse*. Having so categorized them, you then proceed to trust them with your life—not to mention your willingness to strip naked in their presence.

- Driving on highways, you stay in your proper lane, you obey the traffic lights, and (a remarkably high percentage of the time) you stop at the stop signs. Without giving it a moment's thought, you behave as a member of the category *driver* and trust that others whom you categorize as drivers will be good members of that category and will act likewise.

Consider the alternatives. You might request a criminal-record check for   4 all salesclerks. You might ask for the diplomas and current certifications of all the medical personnel you encounter. And you might refuse to venture out driving, for fear of being crushed under the wheels of other vehicles. If you did actually behave in so cautious a fashion, however, you yourself might be classified as paranoid or agoraphobic (two more categories), as a consequence of which you would experience inconveniences far greater than those you risk just by trusting others to be good members of their categories. Yes, there are tales of salesclerks who engage in identity theft, stories of medical impostors, and news reports of accidents caused by inebriated, incompetent, and sleepy drivers. It is remarkable that, for almost all of us, knowing that these possibilities exist does not stop us from shopping, getting medical help, or driving. Categories are not only extremely convenient—they are essential in permitting us to get about the business of our lives.

A Mind Built to Use Categories

To show how, as Allport put it, "orderly living" depends on the use of   5 categories, we shall describe four of the many feats that our minds perform with the aid of categories. Each of these is carried out so effortlessly that, even while doing them, we remain entirely unaware of the mental virtuosity that they draw upon.

Feat 1: Multidimensional Categories—A Snap!

Can you make sense of this string of sixteen words?   6

> *1991 Subaru Legacy 4-door sedan with 4-cylinder engine, front-wheel drive, and automatic transmission.*

Possibly you understood it in no more than the few seconds it took   7
to read it. Next question: Would you have known that the string identified something quite different if it included "station wagon with standard transmission" in place of "sedan with automatic transmission"? If you can answer yes to both questions, you can regard yourself as the proud owner of a seven-dimensional category structure for automobiles. The seven dimensions are the seven columns of Table 15.1.

The sixteen-word Subaru description is one of thousands of distinct   8
automobile categories that can be formed by stringing together identifiers from the seven columns of the table. The ability to conjure up pictures of a great many distinct automobile categories is one of two important characteristics of Feat 1. The second is the ease and automaticity with which your mind regularly makes use of this seven-dimensional structure.

Because some people are not so familiar with automobiles, not every-   9
one can rapidly decode the sixteen words that describe the 1991 Subaru. If the Subaru example did not work for you, hold on for a moment—the much larger number of groups categorized in Feat 2 should establish the point.

TABLE 15.1   Seven-Dimensional Automobile Category Generator

Model	Year	Body Type	Engine Size	Power Source	Transmission	Drive
Ford Taurus	1990	Hatchback	4-cylinder	Diesel	Manual 4-speed	Front wheel
Cadillac Seville	1991	Station wagon	6-cylinder	Electric	Manual 5-speed	Rear wheel
VW Jetta	1992	Convertible	8-cylinder	Hybrid	Automatic	4-wheel
. . .	. . .	SUV		Gasoline		
Subaru Legacy	2007	Pickup				
Audi Turbo	2008	2-door sedan				
Toyota Camry	2009	4-door sedan				
Mercedes 550SL	2010	Van				

Feat 2: Millions of Person Categories Creatable on the Fly

Table 15.2 shows a small part of a six-dimensional structure that generates   *10*
distinct categories of people by stringing together terms from its six columns. Some of the categories identified by these six-label strings encompass a relatively large number of people. For example, there are many
middle-aged, White, male, Christian, Detroit factory workers. At the same
time, if you don't live in Detroit, there is a good chance, that you may never
have met even one such person. Nevertheless, few Americans will have difficulty in forming an immediate mental conception of that factory worker
on reading or hearing the six-label description. You may think that you
can form an immediate impression of the Detroit factory worker because
you've seen or heard or read about people like him in news media (talking about the closing of factories or being on strike, perhaps), in fiction,
through friends, and so on.

But in fact, your facility with the six dimensions of Table 15.2 can-   *11*
not be explained that simply. Your category-forming capacity is actually
great enough to allow you to instantly conceive even a person described
by an entirely unfamiliar combination of the six dimensions. For example, try thinking about a Black, Muslim, sixtyish, French, lesbian professor. Most readers of this book are unlikely to know even one person who
could be identified by any four of those six identifiers. (Try it!) But that
doesn't make it difficult to imagine one. It's almost a certainty that you
will easily be able to form a picture in your mind of a person quite unlike
anyone you have ever met: A Black, Muslim, sixtyish, French, lesbian
professor.

For people who recognize the four sexuality/gender categories in   *12*
the table, along with five race groups (add Native American to the four
shown), plus approximately fifty nationalities or regions, about ten religions, eight age groups, and perhaps fifty occupations, Table 15.2 will
produce a staggeringly large number of person categories—four million.
The rapidity with which we can use the six identifiers to arrive at a picture of a category of person, however large (the Detroit factory worker) or
small (the French professor) the category, confirms the brain's agility as a
maker and user of categories.

TABLE 15.2   Six-Dimensional Person Category Generator

RACE	RELIGION	AGE	NATIONALITY/ REGION	SEX/ GENDER	OCCUPATION
White	Christian	Young	French	Male	Professor
Asian	Muslim	Middle-aged	Detroit	Female	Homemaker
Black	Jewish	Sixtyish	Australian	Gay	Flight attendant
Hispanic	Zoroastrian	Elderly	American	Lesbian	Factory worker

Feat 3: Leaping beyond the Available Information[4]

How does your brain deal with learning that a person is "American"—for *13*
example, "My English professor is American" or "An American passenger
was held for questioning" or "The American lottery winner remained anonymous"? Before reading the next paragraph, please humor us by forming a
mental image of one of these—say, the anonymous American lottery winner. Try to visualize that person in the process of making a phone call to
claim the winnings.

What characteristics does your imagined person have in addition to *14*
being American? We suspect that your imagined person is very likely also
White, male, and adult. And if your imagined American did have those
three added characteristics, very likely they entered your mind without your having to consciously place them there. You can't form a mental image of a person without attributing a male or female gender to
that person, and usually a race and an age too. That said, you could—in
theory—have imagined a female Hispanic American teenager making the
call to collect the lottery winnings. But there's a much higher likelihood
that your mind generated the image of a White male adult. The characteristics that you added can be thought of as your default values for the
race, gender, and age of a typical American. Why might White, male, and
adult be the default characteristics for an otherwise undescribed "American"? Likely it's because those are the characteristics of Americans whom
you see, hear, and read about in newspapers, radio, television, and conversation most frequently, no matter whether they are the characteristics of
those you meet and talk with most often as you go about your day.

If you are at all skeptical about the idea that in forming these men- *15*
tal pictures we use default characteristics to flesh out and go far beyond
the basic information we've been given, then think about it this way: The
default attributes that we add are so taken for granted and so automatic
that, without thinking about why we do this, we are usually careful to
specify a *different* set of attributes when the default ones don't apply. Thus
you simply say "American" when you are referring to a White American.
But if you're talking about another kind of American, you may instead say
"Asian American" or "African American." Similarly, when you refer to a
"taxi driver" you are almost certainly referring to a male taxi driver. If not,
you may say "lady cab driver."

You can now understand something that might have been puz- *16*
zling when we described the 1933 Princeton stereotype study. . . . The
students were asked to describe typical characteristics of nationality or
race categories that were identified by single words, such as *Americans*,
Germans, *Chinese*, and *Italians*. The Princeton students almost certainly
assumed, without giving it any thought, that when they were asked to
choose characteristics typical of Americans, they were expected to provide
traits characteristic of White, male, adult Americans. The two traits that

they most often selected for Americans, *materialistic* and *ambitious*, are very unlikely to be characteristics that the students would have chosen if they had been asked to describe American women or children.[5]

Feat 4: Cooperative Categorization

People often actively send signals about the categories to which they them-   *17*
selves belong. Thus, on first meeting, we can often read these signals to help us identify a person's occupation. At the service station, we know that the person wearing coveralls is a mechanic, not a customer. In the hospital, the person in the white coat is a nurse or doctor, not a patient. The use of clothing to identify different occupations is just one of many ways in which people routinely help others to easily place them into appropriate categories.

Probably the most common, and arguably the most important, of   *18*
these cooperative categorization strategies are those that help others to categorize us as male or female. If you are puzzled by this statement, wondering, "Who needs help in classifying people as male or female?" your puzzlement indicates only how unthinkingly—and routinely—almost everyone provides this help.

Although it is not difficult to distinguish male from female using natu-   *19*
ral body shape and facial features, we nevertheless use a wide variety of additional aids to help the process along. Women typically wear their hair longer than men. Most men and women wear sex-typical clothes that serve to accentuate body shape differences between male and female. Many people wear styles of collars, sleeves, belts, and shoes that are distinctively masculine or feminine. Cosmetics, manicures, jewelry, and gestures add still more markings that advertise—perhaps *flaunt* is the better word—maleness or femaleness. It could be an interesting exercise in economics to calculate the fraction of American wealth spent on clothing, cosmetics, and other accessories that ease the work of categorizing one another as male or female.

Race is another feature that can usually be identified fairly rapidly   *20*
without help, but it too is a category that people often choose to make, more identifiable by their choice of hairstyle, clothing, speech, gesture, and other signifiers.

Of course, such signifiers can be co-opted by other groups—witness   *21*
the phenomenon of White suburban teenagers dressing "ghetto" to make a particular impression. This brings us to recognize that the cooperative categorization phenomenon also has its uncooperative variant form, in which we send visual signals for the explicit purpose of *mis*representing a category to which we belong.

The most common form of uncooperative categorization is the effort   *22*
that many put into projecting the appearance of an age group younger than their own. A great deal of money is made supplying elders with cosmetics,

hair dyes, surgery, and drugs designed to erase wrinkles, shore up sagging body parts, disguise hair that is turning gray or white, and replace hair that has disappeared. Given the traits stereotypically associated with old age—being slow, forgetful, hard of hearing, feeble, and so on—it is easy enough to see why elderly people might want to make it appear that they belong to a younger age group!

Less often disguised than age are religion and ethnicity, but they too *23* are the object of uncooperative categorization under certain circumstances. A well-known strategy is to replace an ethnically identifiable name, such as Winona Horowitz, Issur Demsky, Anna Maria Louisa Italiano, or Jacob Cohen, with something less ethnically identifiable—like the names Winona Ryder, Kirk Douglas, Anne Bancroft, and Rodney Dangerfield (as these people are better known). A more recent cultural invention of the uncooperative categorization variety is the "whitening" of résumés submitted by African Americans in applying for jobs. This involves removing mentions of memberships and positions in obviously African American organizations and altering or omitting names of traditionally Black colleges or universities.

Notwithstanding the relative ease of engaging in uncooperative cat- *24* egorization, many members of often-stigmatized ethnic, racial, or sexual orientation categories not only avoid misrepresenting their categories but choose to do quite the opposite, making it easy for others to place them in their often-stigmatized categories. This suggests that the advantages of signaling those identities, may often outweigh the disadvantages.

Think, for example, of gays and lesbians. Although they remain *25* stigmatized and disadvantaged in many settings in modern America, many have decided to make their sexual orientation known—at least to other members of their category, and sometimes to the world at large. Such assists to "gaydar" (the ability to assess another's sexual orientation from a distance) make it much easier for gays to identify one another, and—if the signals are not of the secret-handshake type—often for non-gays to do so as well, helping avoid potential embarrassment on both sides.

Of the four feats, cooperative categorization stands apart from the *26* others, being the only one that directly shows the everyday working of stereotypes. When cooperative categorization comes into play, a stereotype operates, interestingly, exactly opposite to the fashion usually expected. Instead of knowing a person's category (for example, female) and expecting a stereotypic trait (for example, long hair), we observe the long hair and infer that the person is female. Another paradox of cooperative categorization is that deliberately displaying a stereotyped characteristic (for example, the male professor's pipe and elbow-patched jacket) can have the possibly unwanted effect of strengthening observers' conception of the stereotype's validity.

The remainder of this chapter will make use of the mental virtuosity of *27* Feats 1, 2, and 3 to describe further how stereotypes function in our daily lives. We reach a conclusion that should be a surprise to those familiar with existing scientific understanding of stereotypes.

How We Use Stereotypes

Most of us think that the statement *Ducks lay eggs* is quite reasonable. But "Ducks lay eggs" is actually false for a substantial majority of the world's ducks, and not for one but two reasons. First, because fewer female than male ducklings survive the hatching process, more than half the world's ducks are non-egg-laying males.[6] Second, among female ducks, many are too young to be egg layers. Without doubt, egg-laying ducks are a distinct minority. We anticipate your reaction: "In agreeing that 'Ducks lay eggs' was reasonable, I meant only that I knew that *some* ducks lay eggs, not that *all* ducks lay eggs."   28

Fair enough. But suppose that the statement had been *Dogs wear clothes*. This is certainly true of *some* dogs. Would you have classified that statement as reasonable? Not likely. In our understanding, "Ducks lay eggs" seems more reasonable than "Dogs wear clothes" because most people have a strong *duck = egg layer* association. And unless you have been greatly influenced by William Wegman's photos of Man Ray, Fay Ray, and their successors, you probably do not have a *dog = clothes wearer* association.   29

The "Ducks lay eggs" example gives a clue to how stereotypes influence our thinking. Just as we may incorrectly assume that a duck seen swimming in a nearby pond can lay eggs, we may—equally unthinkingly—assume that an elderly person we have just met has poor memory. The *old = forgetful* stereotype is valid only to the extent that a greater proportion of elderly than young people have poor memory. Nevertheless, that stereotype may influence your reactions to *all* elderly people, including ones whose memories may be far better than your own.[7]   30

Here is another illustration of the tendency to think in stereotypes. For each of the five traits listed on the left below, do you see that trait as a better description of the first of the two groups named to the right, or the second?   31

TRAIT	GROUPS
Leadership	Men more than women?
Musical talent	African Americans more than Native Americans?
Legal expertise	Jews more than Christians?
Math ability	Asians more than Whites?
Criminality	Italians more than Dutch?

Any yes answer suggests that you possess a stereotype that, undoubtedly, many others also have. It's true that possessing these stereotypes doesn't make it inevitable that you will use them when you are making judgments about   32 individual people, or that you will make important decisions based on them. For example, a corporate manager may believe that the *leader* = *male* stereotype is generally valid but may still be able to recognize that a specific woman who has shown outstanding leadership potential would be a good candidate for an executive position. At the same time, the bar she would have to clear might be higher than for men competing for the same position. Similarly, a teacher with a *math* = *male* stereotype may encourage an obviously gifted girl to pursue her studies in math. But this same teacher may also underestimate the math abilities of many other girls, all the while being more ready to recognize the potential of boys and to single them out for extra help and attention.

Does Stereotyping Have a Useful Purpose?

While we may concede Gordon Allport's point that "the human mind must   33
think with the aid of categories," and that, as he said, orderly living is not possible without using categories, we also have to wonder about the ultimate consequences of our category-making and category-using activities. For, as Allport also told us, "Once formed, categories are the basis for normal prejudgment." Another way of saying this is that the categories that our brains form so easily give rise to stereotypes. Thus we associate certain categories with certain prejudged attributes—Africans with having rhythm, Asians with being good at math, women with being inattentive drivers, and so forth.

Indeed, stereotyping by social category is so widely practiced as to   34
deserve recognition as a universal human trait—as implied by the term *Homo categoricus*, which we used as the title for this chapter. Scientists understand universal traits in terms of the idea of adaptiveness or usefulness. Universal traits are generally assumed either to be presently adaptive or to be unfortunate by-products of other presently adaptive characteristics, or perhaps to be troublesome vestiges of previously (but no longer) adaptive characteristics.

The currently dominant explanation for the pervasiveness of stereo-   35
typing is of the "unfortunate by-product" type—stereotyping is an unfortunate by-product of the otherwise immensely useful human ability to conceive the world in terms of categories. Many social psychologists see this explanation as plausible, and we are among them.

There is also a theory of the "presently adaptive" type. This theory sup-   36
poses that many people derive a useful self-esteem boost because stereotypes allow them to see their own group as superior to other groups. Having unfavorable stereotypes of many other groups makes this fairly easy to do. But this theory is less than compelling, in part because humans have so many other ways to boost self-esteem, and in part because it leads to an expectation that is most likely untrue—that those occupying the higher-status roles in their society or possessing the society's default characteristics should engage in more stereotyping than those lower in the hierarchy.

We offer here a new (and admittedly speculative) theory of the benefits 37
of stereotyping that is also of the "presently adaptive" variety: Stereotyping
achieves the desirable effect of allowing us to rapidly perceive total strangers as distinctive individuals.

We hope you read that last sentence at least twice, trying to find words 38
that you thought you must have missed on first reading. The assertion
"Stereotyping allows us to perceive strangers as distinctive individuals"
may seem incomprehensible, even ludicrous, to anyone who thinks of stereotypes as the one-size-fits-all mental boxes into which we force all members of a group, no matter how different from one another they may be.
Recall the inspiration for Walter Lippmann's coinage in 1922—the print-
er's metal plate that produced many identical copies. If stereotypes cause
us to view all _____ (you name the group: Cheerleaders, Italians,
Muslims, rocket scientists, whatever) as being alike, then it would seem to
follow that stereotypes must undermine, rather than facilitate, our ability
to perceive strangers as distinct individuals.

We come to our seemingly absurd theory courtesy of the second 39
mental feat of which *Homo categoricus* is capable: The ability to simultaneously use six (possibly more) person identifiers to produce mental
images of many distinct categories of people. Applying the stereotypes
associated with these six or so identifiers simultaneously produces a result
very different from Lippmann's "identical copies."

This will be a good time to recall the Black, Muslim, sixtyish, French, les- 40
bian professor we used to illustrate Feat 2. Each of her six identifiers carries
its own set of stereotypic traits. Using one identifier at a time would mean
seeing her only with the Black stereotype, or only the Muslim stereotype, or
only the stereotype for one of her other four category labels. But processing
her six identifiers together, all at once, lets us conceive of a person who is distinctly different from anyone else we know. Maybe they didn't quite break the
mold when they made her, but she'll be seen as a distinct individual, someone
whom we will not readily confuse with anyone else we know.

To make our paradoxical explanation convincing, it may help if we 41
make clear how easy it is to grasp half a dozen or so person identifiers
within a fraction of a second. We do this all the time. Imagine a person
who walks past you while you wait to board an airplane. Five identifiers
will almost always be immediately available—sex, age, race, height, and
weight. Clothing may permit us to add multiple other identifiers, perhaps
including income, social class, religion, ethnicity, and occupation. Each of
these identifiers has stereotypical traits associated with it. When our minds
automatically activate all these stereotypes at once, we get a rich, complex
perception of the person, even though the passerby we are contemplating
is a total stranger. After no more than a brief glance we should be able to
distinguish this passerby from just about everyone else in sight, and quite
possibly from everyone else in the airport. This is why we conclude that
the mental virtuosity described in Feat 2 allows us to use stereotypes to
perceive strangers as distinctive individuals.

Who Uses Stereotypes? Who Gets Stereotyped?

It is not possible to be human and to avoid making use of stereotypes.   *42*
Stereotypes make up a submerged but significant portion of the meaning that we read into words such as *old, female, Asian*, and *Muslim*. These submerged, automatically activated meanings go well beyond dictionary definitions. For example, nowhere in any dictionary of the English language will you find *old* defined as "slow," "forgetful," "hard of hearing," or "feeble," but these are all parts of the stereotype that the category *old* is packaged with. Not having stereotypes to provide meaning to our person categories would be like knowing the words of a language without knowing what they mean. In other words, *everyone uses stereotypes*.

The answer to "Who gets stereotyped?" is less simple. Stereotypes are   *43*
not distributed equally. If you can be described by the default attributes of your society—the attributes that don't need to be mentioned because they are assumed unless explicitly stated otherwise (see Feat 3)—you will be subject to less stereotyping than others. You won't be stereotyped by the members of your in-group—those who share the default characteristics that you have—and you may be stereotyped little by others. In Japan, young Japanese men are unlikely to be stereotyped. However, in the United States, they are likely to be stereotyped. This is perhaps why those who belong to their society's "default" categories may see stereotyping as less of a problem than others do—they are much less likely to be its victims.

On the other hand, those who lack their society's default char-   *44*
acteristics are likely to be stereotyped, and not just by others but by themselves—which can be to their disadvantage. This conclusion has only recently been established in research, and it may be the unkindest cut of all. The stereotypes applied to a group are sometimes self-applied by members of the group to themselves, and in that case the stereotypes may act as self-undermining and self-fulfilling prophecies.

Self-fulfilling prophecies can be beneficial. An own-group stereo-   *45*
type might guide African Americans toward becoming better track athletes, basketball players, or jazz musicians. Asian stereotypes may prompt Asian Americans to work hard in school, win scholarships, and launch themselves into high-paying careers in science, medicine, and engineering.

But when stereotypes are unfavorable, as many are, the forces that   *46*
cause people to act in ways that conform to the stereotype applied to their own group can have damaging effects. Elders who internalize stereotypes of the elderly are at greater risk of declining health; women who internalize gender stereotypes are at risk of underperforming in math and science; African Americans who internalize stereotypes of their own group are at risk of not living up to their academic potential. It doesn't take the (stereotypical) rocket scientist to understand the potential for harm in stereotypes.[8]

REFERENCES

Allport, G. W. (1954). *The nature of prejudice*. Cambridge, MA: Perseus.

Brown, D. E. (1982). Sex ratios, sexual selection and sexual dimorphism in waterfowl. *American Birds, 36*, 259–260.

Bruner, J. S. (1957). Going beyond the information given. In H. Gruber et al. (eds.), *Contemporary approaches to cognition* (pp. 41–69). Cambridge, MA: Harvard University Press.

Dovidio, J. F., Glick, P., & Rudman, L. A. (eds.) (2005). *On the nature of prejudice: Fifty years after Allport*. Malden, MA: Blackwell.

Eagly, A. H., & Kite, M. E. (1987). Are stereotypes of nationalities applied to both women and men? *Journal of Personality and Social Psychology, 53*, 451–462.

Katz, D., & Braly, K. (1933). Racial stereotypes of one hundred college students. *Journal of Abnormal and Social Psychology, 28*, 280–290.

Khemlani, S., Glucksberg, S., & Rubio Fernandez, P. (2007). Do ducks lay eggs? How people interpret generic assertions. In D. S. McNamara & J. G. Trafton (eds.), *Proceedings of the 29th Annual Cognitive Science Society*, 64–70. Austin, TX: Cognitive Science Society.

Levy, B. (2009). Stereotype embodiment: A psycho-social approach to aging. *Current Directions in Psychological Science, 18*, 332–336.

Lippmann, W. (1922). *Public opinion*. New York: Harcourt, Brace.

Madon, S., et al. (2001). Ethnic and national stereotypes: The Princeton trilogy revisited and revised. *Personality and Social Psychology Bulletin, 27*, 996–1010.

Rice, S. A, (1926). "Stereotypes": A source of error in judging human character. *Journal of Personnel Research, 5*, 267–276.

Schneider, D. J. (2004). *The psychology of stereotypes*. New York: Guilford.

Steele, C. M., Spencer, S. J., & Aronson, J. (2002). Contending with group image: The psychology of stereotype and social identity threat. In M. P. Zanna (ed.), *Advances in experimental social psychology*, vol. 34 (pp. 379–440). San Diego, CA: Academic Press.

■ ■ ■

Reading as a Writer: Analyzing Rhetorical Choices

1. After you've made note of the different sections of this piece and their titles, do a reverse outline to sketch out the major points the authors make in each section. What do you conclude about their organization? What is the effect of moving readers back to earlier examples as they make their final point about stereotypes?

2. Working in pairs, try to paraphrase the different perspectives that the authors offer on the usefulness and problems of thinking in categories (or, to put it another way, in stereotypes). Passing the conversation back and forth between you, and without looking back through the text (if you can), explain to your partner which examples stand out to you, and why. How would you each summarize the main point of this text?

Writing as a Reader: Entering the Conversation of Ideas

1. Banaji and Greenwald's insights about gender stereotypes are interesting to consider in light of Jesse J. Prinz's concept of "learned limitations." Take notes on the ways these authors explain the methods and effects of

gender socialization. Write an essay in which you connect examples and ideas from each essay in order to make a point about the significance of these learned behaviors for our understanding of ourselves and others. What is at stake in keeping these practices as they are or in changing them?

2. Banaji and Greenwald believe there can be some usefulness in stereotyping. Consider their support for this claim in light of ideas by bell hooks (who writes about representations of poverty in Chapter 13) or Agustín Fuentes (who writes about race in Chapter 14). Compose an essay in which you build on your chosen authors' ideas and examples, and perhaps specific examples from your own experience, as you make an argument about the effects of stereotyping.

JESSE J. PRINZ

Gender and Geometry

Jesse J. Prinz holds the positions of Distinguished Professor of Philosophy and Director of the Committee for Interdisciplinary Science Studies at the City University of New York's Graduate Center. Prinz's interdisciplinary research involves studying and publishing widely on the complex intersections of emotions and biology, which you can infer from the title of his book from which this excerpt was taken: *Beyond Human Nature: How Culture and Experience Shape the Human Mind* (2012). This section on "Gender and Geometry" focuses on cultural assumptions about the intellectual strength of men and women, using performance in math as an extended example. Before you read, you might think about all you have heard about what boys (and men) and girls (and women) are "naturally" good at. What do you make of these claims? How do those assumptions affect the way others see us? What might the implications be for our sense of ourselves, and for our careers?

Prinz's general strategy is to offer data, and then to analyze the significance of it in relation to his overall argument. It is easy to see the sexism in the historical examples warning of the dangers of educating women (in paras. 4 and 5); you might even find funny some of the ridiculous claims from the past about women's intellectual weaknesses. However, Prinz points out that these assumptions about women's inferiority to men are still common, as he reveals in the comments and practices by Lawrence Summers, then-president of Harvard University. As you read this piece, consider way Prinz presents each bit of data and then offers his analysis. He often proposes more than one possible interpretation of the data; how does this strategy affect the way you consider the data and Prinz's overall argument?

Prinz focuses on brain science in his "Biological Factors" section. Even these biological "facts" about men's and women's brains, though, are "intriguing, but difficult to interpret," as he points out in paragraph 22. He unfolds the complex interactions between environment and cognitive differences a bit more in the "Learned Limitations" section. The examples in paragraph 33 about gender bias in college classrooms will probably make you consider your own experiences (and perhaps your own behavior) through fresh eyes.

Prinz's conclusion moves readers in the direction of *doing* something about the inequalities that are often perpetuated by misuses and misunderstandings of "scientific" studies. Ultimately, he argues that we can—and should—change our assumptions, and change the way we teach children and treat adults, so that we all might fulfill our potential. What do you think? What will you do?

■ ■ ■

When we think about cultural differences, we tend to think about groups who live in different places, speak different languages, and worship different gods. But cultural differences can be very local, as when urban subcultures live side by side in the same town. The most local cultural divide of all, however, is the gender divide. Men and women work the same fields, worship in the same churches, and sleep in the same beds, but they reside in different cultures. Men and women are treated differently, they often do different things with their leisure time, and they are subject to very different cultural expectations. Of course, men and women are also biologically different. And this raises a puzzle for science. If men and women perform differently on tests of intellectual ability, should the difference be pinned on nature or nurture or both?

Difference and Discrimination

The Summers Debacle

On 14 January 2005, Lawrence Summers, the president of Harvard University, sparked a media frenzy by suggesting that innate cognitive differences are a leading cause of the fact that women are underrepresented in the science and engineering faculties of elite universities. He voiced this opinion while speaking at a private conference at the National Bureau of Economic Research, but soon his assessment was being reported by newspapers across the globe. Critics argue that Summers's remarks were uninformed and irresponsible. In his speech, Summers claimed that discrimination and socialization play little role in gender inequity within the academy. There is a considerable body of research to the contrary. Summers also implied that women are biologically inferior to men, in that they are genetically less likely to attain the levels of aptitude demanded by prestigious programmes in science, maths, and engineering. This, we will see, is also at odds with the evidence. Biology may make some contribution to cognitive differences between men and women, but differences in academic achievement may owe more to socialization.

The same people who presume that the cognitive differences between *3* men and women are primarily biological also tend to conclude that these differences are inalterable. If this conclusion is combined with the view that women are cognitively inferior to men, then the inevitable upshot is that they are incapable of achieving the same standards. This is exactly what Summers implied, and that is why his speech was offensive to so many. The offense was compounded by the fact that Harvard has had a depressingly bad record when it comes to hiring women. During Summers's reign as president, only 12 percent of the new tenured faculty appointments went to women. Summers was not in charge of selecting new faculty—departments do that—but he participated in tenure decisions, and he could have encouraged departments to recruit women more actively. Instead, female appointments declined appreciably during his time at the helm. When Summers raised the spectre of biological differences, his detractors inferred that he might be guilty of gender bias, falsely believing that men are more likely than women to be naturally brilliant.

Before presenting the evidence against this conjecture, we should note *4* that it is nothing new. In 1873, a respected Harvard medical professor named Edward Clarke published a book called *Sex in Education, or a Fair Chance for the Girls,* in which he warns that women who attend college risk becoming infertile and hysterical. He conjectured that when women tried to use their underdeveloped cognitive capacities to learn, blood would be diverted to the brain from the uterus, which would then atrophy. In 1889, C.C. Coleman, an American physician, issued a similar warning:

> Women beware. You are on the brink of destruction: You have hitherto been engaged in crushing your waists; now you are attempting to cultivate your mind . . . you are exerting your understanding to learn Greek, and solve propositions in Euclid. Beware!! Science pronounces that the woman who studies is lost.

The French psychologist Gustave Le Bon went even further:

> [T]here are a large number of women whose brains are closer in size to gorillas' than to the most developed male brains. This inferiority is so obvious that no one can contest it for a moment . . . [Women] represent the most inferior forms of human evolution and . . . they are closer to children and savages than to an adult, civilized man . . . A desire to give them the same education, and, as a consequence, to propose the same goals for them, is a dangerous chimera.

Such attitudes were not esoteric or anachronistic. Clarke's book went through seventeen printings, and the scientific community widely believed Le Bon's contention that women are no smarter than children. The fact that women have more youthful proportions than men was taken as incontrovertible physiological evidence for the conclusion that their intellectual development did not advance beyond childhood. The prevailing view throughout the nineteenth century was that women are intellectually inferior to men.

This prejudice had a measurable impact. Most obviously, women were not allowed to vote. Women's suffrage came to Great Britain and Germany in 1918, to the United States in 1920 and to France in 1944. Women were also excluded from many professions. At one time, women were deemed incapable of working as stenographers or secretaries, two fields they came to dominate. The presumption of inequality seriously delimited women's access to education. Women were generally excluded from college education until the nineteenth century. In 1837, Oberlin College in Ohio became the first college to admit female students, but they were assigned a special curriculum, which included cooking and cleaning rather than Latin and Greek. Even the feminist reformers of this period were happy to admit that women could never equal men. In 1823, Harriet Martineau argued that women should be given access to higher education in England, so that they could become "companions to men, instead of playthings or servants."[1] This may sound like a plea for equality, but Martineau was also quick to concede that "the acquirements of women can seldom equal those of men, and it is not desirable that they should." Accordingly, women were often educated in separate schools, and they were discouraged or prevented from pursuing graduate degrees, especially in maths and science. Sofia Kovalevskaya was the first woman to earn a mathematics doctorate in Europe, in 1874. In 1895, Caroline Baldwin Morrison became the first woman in the United States to receive a doctorate in science. The first European woman to receive a doctorate in science was Marie Curie, in 1902; she went on to win two Nobel Prizes. For the majority of women, graduate education was not an option, and, though almost half of all college students were women in the early twentieth century, many went to women's schools that were not always equal to their male counterparts. Widespread coeducation is a recent development. Princeton and Yale opened their doors to women in 1969. Harvard beat them to the punch by conferring degrees to women in 1964, but those women had to be enrolled in Radcliffe Women's College, which did not officially merge with Harvard until 1999.

Summers struck a nerve against this background. His remarks were especially wounding to women in academia who have extensive first-hand knowledge of inequitable treatment. Women are routinely ignored, talked down to, and hit on by male college professors. They are often not encouraged in their academic pursuits and not believed in. Women in academia also know that the struggle for equal treatment is a slow one. Most had many more professional opportunities than their mothers, and it seems implausible that bias would simply evaporate in the space of a single generation.

The Science of Difference

By the 1970s, few people would openly suggest that women are less *7*
intelligent than men, but the same period saw an increase in scientific testing of gender difference. Flagrant claims of male superiority were replaced
by the rhetoric of separate but equal. Scientists began broadcasting
evidence that women think differently, and, more often than not, they
assumed these differences were biologically based.

There is now a considerable body of evidence showing that men per- *8*
form better on some tasks, while women perform better on others. The
male advantage shows up most frequently in two areas: spatial reasoning and maths. In spatial reasoning, men are on average better at imaging
geometrical objects at different orientations ("mental rotation"), finding
an object that has been embedded in a complex picture, and orienting a
rod so that it is perpendicular with the floor of a room. When it comes to
spatial navigation, men are more likely than women to use their sense of
compass directions and geometrical information. In maths, male scores
on standardized tests tend to be higher. In 2004, male high school students
scored 7 percent higher on the maths portion of the Scholastic Assessment Test (SAT), and, in earlier years, those numbers have been as high as
15 percent. Moreover, 78 percent of the students who got perfect scores on
the maths SAT were male.

Women's strengths tend to lie elsewhere. They outperform men on cer- *9*
tain verbal tasks and on tasks that involve recognition of fine details and
contextual information. In terms of language, women do better than men
at coming up with words that begin with a particular letter, and they are
better at recalling words from lists; they also use considerably more words
than men in the course of a day. In visual memory tasks, women also have
some advantages over men. They are better at recalling where an object
was located in an array. Unlike men, women tend to navigate using landmarks rather than compass directions. Where a man might recall that the
bank is three blocks north, a woman might recall that the bank is just past
the post office.

Women tend to be less efficient than men when it comes to spatial *10*
tasks that involve understanding three-dimensional configurations of
objects or object parts. Some of the largest gender differences have been
reported in studies of mental rotation. In mental rotation tasks, subjects
are presented with a picture of two objects at different orientations, and
they are asked whether the two objects are the same. To answer, subjects
must mentally rotate one object to see if it aligns with the other. Women
make more errors than men, and there is some evidence that they tend to
use a different strategy. One way to see how a person solves a problem is
by giving them two tasks at the same time and seeing if one interferes with
the other. Men do badly at mental rotation tasks if they are doing another
spatial task at the same time, such as keeping an arrangement of dots in
their minds. Women are not impaired at mental rotation while they are

memorizing arrangements of dots, but they are impaired if they are trying to hold a list of words in their minds. This suggests that women may be relying on their language skills when they mentally rotate objects. Perhaps they are labelling each part of the object and reasoning about how it would change when rotated.

Some naturists have advanced evolutionary explanations of gender *11* differences. Differences in maths and language are difficult to explain in evolutionary terms, because sophisticated maths and language skills appear recently in human evolution, and it's far from obvious why either sex would have greater use for capacities than the other. Are women with greater vocabulary and men who excel in algebra really more likely to procreate? Most evolutionary speculation has centered around spatial skills. According to one popular view, men are better at spatial cognition because male ancestors were hunters, and hunting requires a high degree of spatial precision. This hypothesis is not really plausible, however. First of all, it's not clear what specific skills such as mental rotation have to do with hunting. Second, some spatial skills, such as finding embedded objects in a complex scene, are equally useful for both hunting and gathering, which is believed to have been dominated by women. Third, the male advantage in spatial cognition has been reported in species that don't hunt, such as rats, who are scavengers by nature. If gender differences in cognition are at all based in biology, we have no good explanation of why they evolved. It is possible that such differences are just a freak by product of how male and female brains happen to be wired.

The differences between men and women are often small, and some *12* people perform in ways that are atypical for their sex. But, however small, the differences do show up reliably on a variety of tests, and they often ring true anecdotally. For example, it's something of a cliché that men have a better sense of direction, and women have a better eye for details. Men refuse to ask for directions because they feel confident about where they are going. Women may be more likely to remember where the car keys are, and they may be more likely to notice an interesting building or odd looking person as they drive along the road.

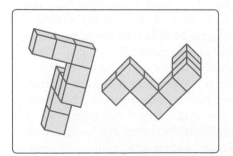 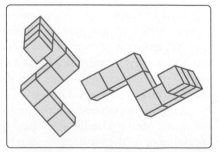

FIGURE 15.1   Mental rotation task. Which pairs are the same?

Gendered Jobs?

In his speech, Summers suggested that gender differences in thinking *13*
might be used to explain why women are underrepresented in certain university departments. In particular, it might explain why there are comparatively few women in maths, engineering, and scientific fields that are
highly quantitative, such as physics. Summers also implied that the cognitive differences are biologically determined. Both of these conjectures
are misguided. Biology contributes to cognitive differences between men
and women, but there are important cultural factors as well, and cultural
factors may be the primary cause of academic hiring inequity.

The underrepresentation of women in university departments may *14*
owe something to cognitive differences, but it owes much more to discrimination. The disproportion of men to women in the academy is far greater
than the extent of the alleged cognitive differences. Based on data from
2001, the National Science Foundation reports that, in American maths
and physics departments, male full professors outnumber female full professors by a ratio of 10 to 1. In engineering departments, the ratio is about
36 to 1. If faculty employment ratios were driven entirely by statistical differences in thinking styles, we might expect women to outnumber men in
fields that rely heavily on language skill, such as English and philosophy.
This is not the case. In Harvard's English department, twenty of fifty-three
faculty members are women, and in the philosophy department, five of
eighteen are women. For all the rhetoric about women being better than
men in some cognitive domains, there is little evidence that their superior
aptitude ever affords greater opportunities for women than for men. Up
until very recently, men have dominated in all areas of the academy. We
mustn't forget that, one hundred years ago, there were virtually no women
teaching in universities. It would have been absurd to think this was due
to differences in cognitive style. Women just weren't given the opportunity.
The current numbers suggest that there has been exponential progress
in women's educational equity, but they also suggest that discrimination
remains a serious problem.

In fact, there is direct evidence for discrimination against women in *15*
hiring. Rhea Steinpreis and her colleagues at the University of Wisconsin
in Milwaukee sent out a CV to a large number of psychology professors
and asked them to assess whether the person named on the CV was worthy of hiring.[3] Each professor received a CV with exactly the same content, but in half the cases, the name on the CV was Brian Miller, and in
the other half it was Karen Miller. Despite the fact that the imaginary
job applicants were equally qualified, those who received the male applicant's CV were about 50 percent more likely to say that he should be
hired than those who received the female applicant's CV. The majority of
professors evaluating the female applicant said she should not be hired,
and the overwhelming majority of professors evaluating the male applicant said that he should be hired. It must be noted that all the professors

who participated in this study probably believe that it is wrong to show preferential treatment to a man, yet that is exactly what they did unwittingly. Female professors were as likely as male professors to show this form of bias. This is direct and powerful evidence for the existence of discrimination in academic hiring. Similar studies have shown that the very same paper is rated as superior if it has a male author's name on it rather than a female name. There is also evidence showing that female professors receive less mentoring than their male counterparts when they are starting out, they are given lower salaries, and they are regarded more negatively when they are assertive. Each of these factors can negatively impact prospects for women in academia.

Given the evidence for discrimination, it is possible that employment   16
inequity has very little to do with cognitive differences. If graduate admissions committees, hiring committees, and tenure committees are unconsciously biased against women, then we have a perfectly good explanation of why men outnumber women in the academy. The fact that inequity is greater in some fields than in others may be the result of residual stereotypes about women's capabilities. There used to be very few women in law and medicine, and now women are catching up with men rapidly. Our conception of what women can do is continually shifting. Given this history, and evidence for continued biases in hiring, there is no reason to think that cognitive differences are a major factor in the current distribution of university jobs.

Explaining Gender Differences

In blaming academic employment inequity on discrimination, I don't   17
mean to deny that there are cognitive differences between men and women. There may be. As we have seen, men and women tend to perform differently on certain tests. Men do better with maths, mental rotation, and embedded pictures, and women do better with verbal memory and fluency and with recalling where objects were located. These differences need to be explained. There are three possibilities. One possibility is that men and women are equally good at the skills in question, but they just perform differently on tests. Another possibility is that there are biological differences that have an impact on cognition. A third possibility is that cultural variables lead men and women to think somewhat differently. It turns out that each of these variables is partially right.

Testing Troubles

Let's begin with the possibility that gender differences in thinking are, in   18
part, an illusion generated by misleading performance, on tests. There is some strong evidence for the suggestion that differences between male and female math scores can be partially explained this way. The primary evidence for male superiority in maths comes from the fact that men do

better on the maths portion of standardized tests, such as the SAT and the Graduate Record Exam (GRE). But these results actually conflict with records of classroom performance. In American high schools, girls take about the same number of mathematics classes as boys, and they get better grades. Women also comprise almost half of the maths majors in American colleges, and they do just as well as men. These indicators suggest that women and men have comparable aptitude for mathematics. "Why, then, do men do better on standardized tests? One possibility is that women underperform because they believe that they are less capable than men. In a simple experiment Claude Steele and his colleagues gave a maths test to a group of male and female college students, after telling them in advance that men tend to do better than women.[4] Lo and behold, the women did worse. Then the experimenters gave the same test to another group of male and female college students without saying anything in advance, and their scores came out the same. This phenomenon, which has been replicated many times, is called stereotype threat; if you make a negative stereotype salient to people, they will inadvertently conform to it. These effects are widespread. If you tell people of color that they do not generally perform as well on a test as whites, their scores will drop, and if you tell white men that their scores are usually lower than Asians', there will also be a significant decline in performance.

A negative stereotype can become salient without even mentioning it. To demonstrate this, Michael Inzlicht and Talia Ben-Zeev gave female college students maths portions from the GRE.[5] The women took the test in a room with other women, with men, or with a combination of men and women. When women were placed in a room with men, their performance declined, and the extent of the decline was proportionate to the number of men in the room. Male performance was not affected by the presence of women. Apparently, when women take standardized tests in the presence of men, they unconsciously recall the stereotype that men are better at maths, and their performance drops off. If the presence of men adversely affects female performance in maths, one might wonder why women do as well as men in their maths courses. One possible explanation is that a male presence has an adverse affect only when women are taking standardized tests. Unlike the ordinary tests that students take for their maths courses, standardized tests are overtly comparative. Everyone knows that the SAT and GRE are used to make college and university admissions decisions, and scores are given as a percentile in comparison to other students. With ordinary classroom tests, students are less likely to see themselves as competing with other students, so stereotypes pertaining to comparative performance (women are worse than men) are less likely to come to mind.

This research suggests that the cognitive differences between men and women may be exaggerated. Some of the variation in test performance may result from the unconscious fulfilment of negative stereotypes. But this probably isn't the whole story. First, it's not clear that there are negative gender stereotypes associated with every cognitive test that shows gender differences. Why, for example, are women better at verbal memory and recalling how objects are arranged? Why are women worse than men at embedded picture tasks? Second, there is a nagging question of where the stereotypes come from. Many stereotypes have no basis in reality; they are merely used to denigrate. We can instill fear by saying that Jews are greedy, and we can justify economic disparity by saying that blacks are lazy. The claim that women are worse than men at mental rotation is potentially insulting, in that it implies that men are more intelligent, but it's hard to see how this particular claim would have been deliberately devised to hold women back. Third, there is evidence that biology has a role in the cognitive differences between men and women.

Biological Factors

The evidence for a link between biology and cognitive differences comes *21* from several sources. First, there is evidence from neuroscience. Compared with women, men seem to have more grey matter, the pinkish grey tissue comprised of cell bodies covering the surface of the brain. But women have more white matter, the connective tissue just below the surface that allows cells to communicate. Male brains are larger overall, but women have faster brains, and some studies suggest that women's brains have more cells and larger areas dedicated to language. There are also differences in how male and female brains function. For men, IQ scores correlate best with activity in the frontal cortex and parietal cortex. In women, IQ scores are correlated with different areas of the frontal cortex, including language areas, and there is little correlation with the parietal cortex.[6] Differences in brain function could explain male and female performance on spatial tasks. For both men and women, mentally rotating an object involves many of the same brain areas, but in women there is greater activity in areas associated with object recognition, and in men there is greater activity in areas associated with motor control. One possibility is that women try to mentally rotate an object by visually analyzing its parts, whereas men are more likely to imagine physically moving the object around.

These findings are intriguing, but difficult to interpret. We often don't *22* know the significant brain differences; for example, we have a very limited understanding of the link between brain size and brain function. Moreover, different labs report different results, and some alleged contrasts between male and female brains have been called into question. For example, it was widely reported that female brains are more symmetrical than male brains, with certain language functions actively involving both hemispheres rather than being predominantly located in the left. But a recent analysis of multiple brain scanning studies suggests that this isn't the case; both male and female brains seem to be equally asymmetrical. Studies of the brain also raise a difficult chicken and egg problem. If male and female brains function differently, those differences could result from differences in socialization. Differences in how the sexes are educated could affect brain function. We know, for example, that trained musicians, mathematicians, and taxi drivers have brains that function somewhat differently from those of the rest of us.

Even if we take current findings from brain science as tentative, there is some reliable evidence for the conjecture that biology contributes to gender differences in cognition. For one thing, gender differences show up in other creatures. Male rhesus monkeys outperform females on a spatial memory task, in which they have to find a food reward that changes locations on each round. The male spatial advantage can even be found in rodents. In rats, mice, and meadow voles, males often outperform females when learning the location of food in mazes. In rats, the pattern changes when the food can be located by memorizing landmarks; females do better than males at using such information. These findings are intriguing, because they confirm the pattern we see in humans: Males in many mammalian species are more adept than females at spatial tasks. 23

Research on animals suggests that some of the cognitive differences between men and women may be deeply rooted in biology, but there are reasons to exercise caution when drawing this conclusion. First, gender differences have not been found in all animals. Male meadow voles are maze masters, but male prairie voles are not. Second, when gender differences are found, they are often ephemeral. In some species, the gender differences disappear with age, training, or at different stages in the reproductive cycle. Third, in some species, the gender differences we find in animals may actually contrast with the human case on closer analysis. As I mentioned, male rhesus monkeys outperform females in remembering the location of objects, but in human beings spatial memory is often better in women. Finally, there is also some risk in drawing inferences from one species to another, because each has its own evolutionary history. Consider an analogous case. Members of polygynous societies might find comfort in knowing that male gorillas keep a harem of females, but it would be a mistake to infer from this comparison that polygyny is the natural arrangement for human beings; a wide range of sexual arrangements can be observed in the animal kingdom. 24

The best evidence for an interaction between biology, gender, and thought comes from hormone studies. Consider testosterone, the principal male hormone. It turns out that fluctuations in testosterone correlate with fluctuations in cognitive performance. As men age, testosterone levels drop, and, when those levels drop, there are correlative drops in performance in maths and spatial skills. Hormone replacement therapy can improve performance. Similar effects have also been observed in women. Women naturally produce some testosterone, but only about a seventh of the amount that men produce. Studies have shown women with comparatively high testosterone levels outperform women with low testosterone 25 levels on spatial tasks and maths tasks. Giving women a single dose of testosterone improves their performance on mental rotation tasks. That doesn't mean we should all take megadoses of testosterone. Optimal performance is associated with moderate levels of the hormone. Women with high testosterone levels and men with low levels perform better than people with too much or too little.

Cognitive effects have also been associated with the principal female 26 hormone, estrogen. In particular, estrogen is positively correlated with verbal memory and verbal fluency, two skills that tend to be better in women than in men. Two to three weeks after menstruation, when estrogen levels are high, women score better on verbal tests. When estrogen levels decline in menopause, there are correlated drops in verbal skills. When men with prostate cancer take estrogen, their verbal memory improves.

These findings suggest that cognitive differences between men and 27 women are influenced by hormonal differences. Testosterone and estrogen can change the way we think. But we should not get too carried away. For one thing, the correlations between hormone levels and cognitive abilities are ceiling high. A maths wiz can have low testosterone, and a verbal savant can have low estrogen. In fact, there is little reason to think that individuals who make great achievements in these domains have impressive levels of the corresponding hormones. For example, it was recently discovered that people working in the hard sciences tend to have low testosterone levels, or at least levels that were low during crucial periods of early development. This underscores the point that women are not being excluded from science because of inadequate biology.

A second reason to doubt the importance of hormones comes from the 28 fact that gender gaps are closing. A few decades ago, the performance gap between men and women was twice as large, but the hormonal differences were, we can presume, just as great as they are today. If hormones were the primary source of cognitive differences between the sexes, we should see greater stability over time.

A third reason for caution is that hormone differences may have 29 social causes. Suppose that hormone levels were perfectly correlated with cognitive skills. It still would not follow that hormones are the *ultimate* cause of gender differences, because variation in hormone levels can be affected by environmental factors including socialization. For example, depression causes testosterone levels to drop. It also happens to be the case that women are twice as likely to be depressed as men. Why? Perhaps it is because women are socialized into feeling inadequate, subordinate, or limited in their opportunities. Thus, socialization can cause depression, depression lowers testosterone, and low testosterone levels in women diminish performance on maths and spatial tasks. Perhaps women do worse than men statistically because societal factors make women more depressed. Hormone levels might be the proximate cause of sex differences, and not the ultimate causes.

Finally, hormones cannot explain all the data on cognitive differences, *30* because there are demonstrable interactions between hormone levels and environmental factors. Here's a case in point. As we have seen, women are more likely to do badly on maths tests when they are reminded of the stereotype that women are less numerically competent than men. It turns out that the effects of stereotype threat are magnified for women who have high levels of testosterone. Remember, these are the women who are ordinarily likely to do best on maths tests. When women who are talented in maths are reminded of negative stereotypes, their performance plummets. Women with low testosterone do not show the same effect. Consequently, when stereotypes are primed, naturally talented women actually perform worse than women who have not had a helping hand from biology.

Learned Limitations

The impact of stereotypes on cognitive performance suggests that social *31* environment plays a role in the cognitive differences between men and women. If drawing attention to a negative stereotype can affect a woman's performance while she is taking a test, imagine what a lifetime of exposure to negative stereotypes can do. There is overwhelming evidence that women are treated differently from men, and these differences begin from the earliest days of life. In the face of such obvious and overt differences in socialization, it is remarkable that researchers ever looked to biology as the primary source of differences in cognition. In the nineteenth century, scientists thought that women's childlike appearance, such as their lack of facial hair, explained the fact that women were more ignorant than men. The more obvious explanation was that women were prevented from having equal education, employment opportunity, government involvement, and personal autonomy. If women were less informed than the men who controlled their lives in the nineteenth century, it was a consequence of the fact that women were treated like children. With 20/20 hindsight we know that biological differences are too small and too ephemeral to explain the gross inequality that existed at that time.

History teaches a sobering lesson. Our contemporary attempt to *32* explain gender differences by appeal to biology alone may look preposterous fifty years from now, when women have had more time to prove themselves in every branch of the academy. Biological differences exist, but they can be swamped, exaggerated, and shaped by culture. In response, a well-intentioned naturist might argue that men and women now enjoy equal education and equal opportunity. In the nineteenth century, women were denied equal access to higher education, but now they are not. So, the naturist will say, any residual cognitive differences must be due to biology. This line of argument is sheer folly. Women and men may attend the same schools, but they are not treated the same way. Attending the same classes does not entail having the same education.

Studies have shown a pervasive and systematic pattern of unequal treat- 33
ment in contemporary classrooms. Dedicated and well-intentioned teachers fall prey to societal gender bias and treat female students inequitably.
Here are some unsettling facts. Male students are given more praise and
criticism than female students; teachers call on male students more often;
male students are given more time to answer questions when called on;
male students are asked harder questions; female students are more frequently asked to report matters of fact, rather than matters of opinion or
analysis; teachers generally give male students more feedback; in that feedback, teachers are more likely to give male students advice that helps them
arrive at correct answers the next time around rather than just telling them
the correct response. This pattern of preferential treatment starts early and
has an impact. By the time women are in college, their style of academic
engagement differs markedly from their male classmates. Where men make
assertions in the classroom, thereby advertising their intelligence, women
are much more likely to ask questions, advertising their ignorance. In fact,
women who make assertions in classrooms tend to make them with the
same intonation as a question, inadvertently playing dumb when they know
the answer.[7] Men speak four times as often and shout out answers eight
times as often.[8] Teachers are more receptive to these male interruptions,
they direct more questions at men, are more likely to develop remarks made
by men, and they offer men more encouragement.

A die-hard naturist or an unrepentant sexist might argue that all these 34
classroom differences are the result of biological differences and not the
other way around. Perhaps teachers treat males as more intelligent because
they are more intelligent. The problem with that explanation is that female
performance on aptitude tests suggests that they are as capable as men in
most areas, and better than men in some areas. Women's aptitude for science is comparable to men's during teenage years, but social factors are
working against them. A recent study shows that teenage boys and girls
have comparable interest in, and aptitude for, science, but parents systematically report that their daughters have less interest and talent.[9] In the same
study, fathers were shown to be significantly more demanding when helping their sons with science projects. The biases at home reinforce the pattern at school. Ultimately, girls lose confidence in their ability to become
good scientists. There is some evidence that these deleterious effects can be
mitigated by sending girls to single-sex schools. Girls who graduate from
single-sex schools have higher educational aspirations than their coed counterparts, they are more likely to attend top universities, and they are more
likely to pursue graduate degrees. These girls are also more confident, and
they are considerably less likely to fall into the stereotypically female pattern
of turning assertions into questions when they contribute to classroom discussion. Girls in single-sex schools are also more likely to profess an interest
in maths.[10] These girls are not biologically different from those who attend
coed schools; they have just been socialized differently. With boys around,
girls become second-class citizens.

Socialization is not restricted to educational settings. Children are 35 exposed to an endless barrage of images showing men and women playing gender-specific sex roles. In movies, television shows, magazines, and pop music, kids learn gender-specific attitudes and behaviors. These differences even show up in sources of entertainment designed for young people. In children's books, male characters are five times more likely than female characters to be portrayed as aggressive, and more than three times as likely to be portrayed as competitive. Girls are more than twice as likely to be portrayed as emotionally expressive, and almost four times as likely to be portrayed as passive.[11]

Gender socialization begins at birth. Girls and boys are named differ- 36 ently, dressed differently, and put in differently decorated rooms. These overt differences cue caregivers into different patterns of socialization. This has been nicely demonstrated by a series of studies in which adults are presented with a baby wearing either pink clothes and bearing a female name or wearing blue clothes and bearing a male name.[12] In these studies, the same baby is used, but some adults think it's a boy and others think it's a girl, and that makes all the difference. For example, when a six-month-old baby is labelled "Beth," adults described "her" as soft, nice and delicate. When the same baby is introduced as "Adam," adults describe "him" as strong, active, and intelligent. If adults see a video clip of a baby reacting to a jack-in-the-box, they will describe that baby as frightened if they think it's a girl and as angry if they think it's a boy. Adults will also play different games with male and female babies. If several toys are present, adults will hand "Beth" a doll. If they think the same baby is named "Adam," they will hand over a toy hammer or truck. Adults also give positive feedback to babies when they pick up toys that fit the gender stereotype. This is not just fun and games. Studies suggest that, regardless of sex, children who play more with stereotypically three-dimensional toys, such as construction sets, do better on maths tests than children who play with dolls. Socialization encourages girls to be less active than boys, more timid and more preoccupied with beauty than brains or brawn. Such socialization could easily affect thinking styles. A typical boy may spend hours making models and building go-carts, and a typical girl may spend hours imagining dialogues between Barbie dolls. The boy gets extensive training in spatial reasoning, and the girl becomes a master of language. Later, when they are given tests as teenagers, the boy will do better at mental rotation, and the girl will show greater verbal fluency. . . .

If there are biological differences between men and women, those 37 differences probably get magnified through socialization. But it need not work that way. If we stop assuming that one sex is inherently better at certain cognitive tasks than the other, we can encourage both sexes to master the same range of important skills. Training would allow men to improve verbal skills and increase their sensitivity to contextual information, such as landmarks, and training would allow women to rival men in maths and spatial skills. If we design curricula to maximize the capacities of both boys and girls, sex differences in cognitive abilities may shrink away. Rather than blaming biology for inequality, we should blame ourselves for not taking steps to even the playing field.

NOTES

1. Martineau, H. (1823). On female education. *Monthly Repository*, 18, 77–81.
2. Based on Shepard, R. N., and Metzler, J. (1971). Mental rotation of three-dimensional objects. *Science*, 171, 701–3.
3. Steinpreis, R., Anders, K. A., and Ritzke, D. (1999). The impact of gender on the review of the curricula vitae of job applicants and tenure candidates: A national empirical study. *Sex Roles*, 41, 509–28.
4. Spencer, S. J., Steele, C. M., and Quinn, D. M. (1999). Stereotype threat and women's math performance. *Journal of Experimental Social Psychology*, 35 4–28.
5. Inzlicht, M., and Ben-Zeev, T. (2000). A threatening intellectual environment: Why females are susceptible to experiencing problem-solving deficits in the presence of males. *Psychological Science*, 11, 365–71.
6. Haier, R. J., Jung, R. E., Yeo, R. A., Head, K., and Alkire, M. T. (2005). The neuroanatomy of general intelligence: Sex matters. *NeuroImage*, 25, 320–27.
7. Tannen, D. (1994). *Talking from 9 to 5*. New York: William Morrow.
8. Swarm, J. (1988). Talk control: An illustration from die classroom of problems in analyzing male dominance of conversation. In J. Coates and D. Cameron (eds.), *Women in their speech communities*. London: Longman.
9. Tenenbaum, H. R., and Leaper, C. (2003). Parent-child conversations about science: The socialization of gender inequities? *Developmental Psychology*, 39, 34–47. See also: Simpkins, S. D., Davis-Kean, P. E., and Eccles, J. S. (2006). Math and science motivation: A longitudinal examination of the links between choices and belief. *Developmental Psychology*, 42, 70–83; Jacobs, J. E., Davis-Kean, P., Bleeker, M., Eccles, J. S. and Malanchuk, 0. (2005). I can, but I don't want to: The impact of parents, interests, and activities on gender differences in math. In A. Gallagher and J. Kaufman (eds.), *Gender differences in mathematics*. Cambridge: Cambridge University Press.
10. Lee, V. E., and Bryk, A. S. (1986). Effects of single sex secondary schools on student achievement and attitudes. *Journal of Educational Psychology*, 78, 381–95.
11. Evans, L., and Davies, K. (2000). No sissy boys here: A content analysis of the representation of masculinity in elementary school reading textbooks. *Sex Roles*, 42, 255–70.
12. Will, J. A., Self, P. A., and Dantan, N. (1976). Maternal behavior and perceived sex of infant. *American Journal of Orthopsychiatry*, 46,135–9; Vogel, D. A., Lake, M. A., Evans, S., and Karraker, K. H. (1991). Children's and adults' sexstereotyped perception of infants. *Sex Roles*, 24, 605–16.

■ ■ ■

Reading as a Writer: Analyzing Rhetorical Choices

1. In pairs or groups, locate what you think are the strongest examples of Prinz's data presentation and analysis. Explain why these examples stand out to you, and how, exactly, these examples help him build his overall point. What can you conclude about offering an effective example to support an argument?

2. Reread paragraph 15, in which Prinz describes the experiment in which both men and women judge the same CVs (this is an academic term for

a résumé and stands for "curriculum vitae") differently, depending on whether they believe it belongs to a man or a woman. What do the results suggest to you? How does Prinz's argument help you understand how these assumptions happen? What can be done to change such discrimination?

Writing as a Reader: Entering the Conversation of Ideas

1. Georgia Warnke, like Prinz, is deeply interested in the ways biological claims are often used to reinforce cultural inequalities, particularly around gender. Where do these authors' analyses overlap, contradict, and extend one another? Write an essay in which you teach your reader what is at stake in these conversations — and for whom — according to these authors, and to you. Where do you stand in this still-evolving debate?

2. How do Prinz's ideas shed light on the classroom behaviors described by Deborah Tannen (Chapter 12) and vice versa? In an essay that draws on insights and examples from both authors, make an argument for the ways we can most effectively understand classroom dynamics and behaviors. Given these authors' ideas, what conclusions can you draw about effective interventions when classrooms become a site of inequality for students?

GEORGIA WARNKE

Sex and Gender: Behavioral Ecology and Hormone Studies

Given this article's extended exploration of hormone studies, it may come as a surprise that the author, Georgia Warnke, is a professor of political science. However, her expertise in political theory includes a focus on issues of identity and issues of sex and gender, which bring her into conversation with the other authors in this chapter who examine the complex relationships between biology and culture.

Warnke opens her piece with a quotation from Robert Wright, a "behavioral ecologist" who asserts that evolution has produced men and women who are "deeply different" from one another. After taking several paragraphs to unfold his argument, she challenges his claims in detail in her second section, "Questioning Behavioral Ecology." Keep track of all the common misconceptions that she lists about supposed biological or evolutionary roots of gender differences. Which do you hear most often? Which do you find most surprising, and why?

In particular, Warnke disputes the conclusions that have been drawn from hormone studies, asking rigorous questions of this research in paragraphs 14 to 17. What do you make of the kinds of questions she asks, and why do you think other researchers might have failed to ask them? What is at stake, and for whom, in maintaining the idea that there is a simple gender binary (masculinity and femininity)?

Warnke's brief final paragraph contains the seeds of a very big idea—that there might be more than two genders: "Numerous questions remain about the relation between sex and gender. Before considering them, however, perhaps we should ask how many of each there are" (para. 20). Spend a few minutes looking up research on this idea (Anne Fausto-Sterling, mentioned in paragraph 19, is a leading thinker on this topic), and share what you learn with your classmates. What possibilities would this open up for thinking about human traits? Warnke's essay invites us to question what we think we know and to consider the possibilities of new understandings of sex and gender.

■ ■ ■

Behavioral Ecology

In his 1994 book *The Moral Animal*, Robert Wright states that some femi- 1
nists "now accept that men and women are deeply different." He continues:

> What exactly "deeply" means is something they're often vague about, and
> many would rather not utter the word *genes* in this context. Until they do, they
> will likely remain in a state of disorientation, aware that the early feminist
> doctrine of innate sexual symmetry was incorrect (and that it may have in
> some ways harmed women) yet afraid to honestly explore the alternative.[1]

Wright's alternative is that sex and gender go hand-in-hand, and that 2
they do so for evolutionary reasons. We can begin, Wright says, with the observation that those of us who are alive today are here because we possess a genetic heritage that worked. Our oldest ancestors survived and reproduced ancestors who also survived and reproduced and, as the family tree continued, eventually produced us. Suppose, then, we ask what traits would have been useful for this survival and reproduction, and suppose that instead of thinking backward from hindsight, we think proactively: What do we have to do to maximize our chances of producing healthy children who can survive at least long enough to have children of their own, thereby allowing our genes to endure through successive generations? Wright claims that in species that reproduce sexually, males and females will have to answer this question in different ways depending on their reproductive roles. Because males and females have different biological roles in reproduction—that is, different sexes—they must devise different strategies to maximize the chances for the birth and survival of their offspring into maturity, and these strategies lead to different masculine and feminine traits—or in other words, to different genders.

Behavioral ecologists like Wright define females as those who pro- 3
duce large gametes or eggs for fertilization.[2] Human females do so, however, only relatively infrequently, and typically, they generate only one or perhaps two fertilized eggs. Moreover, the time between fertilization and birth is a long one, and to make matters worse, a female human being,

once pregnant, cannot become more pregnant. Instead, she has to wait to give birth before she can start the process again. It follows, then, that female human beings have only limited opportunities to produce children. Moreover, in order to maximize their chances for children, they must make the most of the opportunities they have. Hence, they must be careful in their mating decisions, taking up only the most promising opportunities, where "promising" means those opportunities that bode well along two dimensions: First, those with whom females deign to mate must have the potential to produce healthy offspring and, second, these mates must also be both willing and able to provide sufficient resources to help nurture those offspring to maturity.

Males, for behavioral ecologists, are those who, in contrast to females, *4* produce small gametes or sperm. In comparison to the rate at which human females can produce eggs and the effort it takes to do so, human males produce large amounts of sperm both easily and repeatedly. Nor does the circumstance that they may have already impregnated one female limit their ability to impregnate another—indeed, countless others. If males are to try to guarantee that they will produce healthy children who survive into adulthood, their strategy must therefore be quite different from that of females. Indeed, like the proverbial voters in Chicago whom the Daley machine urged to vote early and often, males should also mate early and often, trying to produce as many offspring as possible with the hope that one or more will live to adulthood and carry on their line. Thus, Wright says, we see the evolutionary function of two readily observable gender traits that follow directly from biology. Men, because of their biology, will be promiscuous and possess an interest in maximizing the quantity of mating opportunities irrespective of their quality. Women, because of their different biology, will be choosy and possess an interest in pursuing only the best mating opportunities, not the most. The same holds for mammals in general, Wright insists. To be sure, Wright concedes, female chimpanzees and especially female bonobos "seem particularly amenable to a wild sex life."[3] Yet, he insists, they do not do what males of the species do—namely, "search high and low, risking life and limb, to find sex, and to find as much of it, with as many different partners, as possible."[4] As Wright concludes, "Male license and (relative) female reserve are to some extent innate."[5]

Behavioral ecologists are adept at showing additional gender conse- *5* quences of these strategies. For example, in keeping with an evolutionary history in which the males of the species follow bonobos in searching "high and low, risking life and limb, to find sex," one would expect men to be better than women with numbers, maps, and spatial analysis. And, indeed, some research seems to confirm this expectation. Men have been observed to perform better on mental rotation tests, in which subjects are asked to rotate figures drawn on paper through three dimensions;[6] on spatial tests, in which they are asked to throw and intercept balls;[7] and in virtual maze tests, in which they are asked to learn a novel route through a three-dimensional map.[8] In all cases, males performed the tasks more quickly and more accurately than females, even when controlling for such factors as more experience and, in the last case, more time spent playing computer games. In fact, a thirty-year study published in the late 1990s found that in tests of math and science ability, boys outnumbered girls in the top 10 percent by three to one and, furthermore, that "in the top 1 percent, there were seven boys for every one girl."[9]

Behavioral ecologists often attribute these results to differences in the   6 way the brain structures of men and women have evolved. The human male cerebrum is 9 percent bigger than the female cerebrum, while the ratio of corpus callosum to total cerebrum volume is smaller in males.[10] The male amygdala also grows for an extended period during childhood and is larger than that in the female. Finally, the male cerebral cortex has more neurons than the female cerebral cortex, and they tend to be more tightly packed. This fact suggests that more connections between neurons occur within one hemisphere in men with "decreased interhemispheric connectivity," while women are more "bilateral."[11] Behavioral ecologists trace the explanation for both sets of differences to the brain organizations that would have won out in the evolutionary environment. Women, not racing around the evolutionary environment trying to impregnate people, need not have processed spatial relations as efficiently as men. As a result, they use both sides of the brain to control spatial skills. Hence, each side of their brains must deal with interferences from the activities that the other side may be trying to control. Male brains, in contrast, control spatial abilities more locally, leaving less chance for other activities to interfere.[12]

Questioning Behavioral Ecology

Just as no good deed goes unpunished, no scientific study goes unques-   7 tioned. Take studies of differences in male and female brains and cognition. The late 1990s study showed persistent differences in the mathematical and spatial abilities of boys and girls, but a study published in 2001 reconsidered these results.[13] Using two longitudinal surveys of American children, researchers examined the children's mathematical paths from first through twelfth grade. Few differences were found between boys and girls up to about 11 years of age, but at age 11, girls posted higher average scores. When researchers examined only the scores of the children scoring most highly on the mathematical tests, they found that between the ages of 4 and 7, girls in this group scored higher than boys in this group; between the ages of 8 to 11, the boys scored higher than the girls; and between the ages of 11 and 13, there were no statistically significant differences in the scores of the children the group. With regard to the reasoning skills in this oldest high-scoring group, girls had a slight advantage. In older, college-age individuals, the study found a small and statistically insignificant difference, with male students scoring higher in both math and reasoning. Only with regard to spatial skills in the area of geometry did the study find statistically significant differences, but even these decreased once the girls were taught spatial strategies.

Suppose, however, the studies showed that men did have better math *8* and spatial abilities than women. Would that discovery provide a definitive answer to the question of sex versus gender? In one test for spatial abilities, subjects sit on chairs in darkened rooms with rods balanced within large frames in front of them. Each subject's task is to keep the rod perpendicular to the floor as a reseacher tilts either the frame or the chair. In seven of twelve studies that reseachers examined, men performed better on this task than women.[14] We could point out that in five studies, they did not, but we should also recall that traditionally, boys, but not girls, receive models to build and blocks to play with when they are growing up. Might not another explanation be that for social and cultural reasons, women are distracted and ill at ease in dark rooms, perhaps especially when male investigators surround them?[15]

While conventional wisdom says that boys are better in math and with *9* maps, it also says that girls are better with verbal tasks. The same thirty-year study that found boys to be better in math found girls to be better in reading comprehension and writing, with twice as many girls as boys found among the top scorers and twice as many boys as girls among the bottom.[16] But, if women's comparative weakness in math and spatial abilities all but disappears in recent research, and if we attribute the remaining disparities to cultural factors, what explains boys' comparative weaknesses in reading and writing? Both are required across the elementary and high school curricula, and for this reason alone, a cultural explanation for the gender disparity would seem to be less than plausible. Michael Kimmel thinks it is the correct explanation anyway. Boys' comparative weakness in reading and writing tests, he says, is part of the "ideology of traditional masculinity."[17] Unless they are poets or novelists, men, as a gender, are not meant to be good with words. "What makes a man a man," Kimmel writes, "is that he is reliable in a crisis and what makes a man reliable in a crisis is that he resembles an inanimate object."[18]

Hormone Studies

In the popular imagination, the part of biological sex that is often thought *10* to exert the most influence on gender is hormonal. Indeed, when they were first discovered in the 1920s, the so-called sex hormones were supposed to be all-purpose explanations: Men were men because their bodies possessed testosterone; women were women because their bodies possessed estrogen. It even looked like homosexuality could be explained as an atypical invasion of estrogen into a man's body, whereas agitation for female suffrage could be explained as an atypical invasion of testosterone into a woman's.[19] The hormones themselves were named after the respective sex to which they attached: Androgens from the Greek word for men (*andros*) and estrogens from the English word, estrus, referring to the period immediately preceding ovulation. (Forget for the moment that the hormones associated with the male sex get to derive their name from man while estrus comes from the Latin, *oestrus*, meaning frenzy or gadfly, and from the Greek, *oistros*, meaning gadfly, sting, or mad impulse.[20]) Research today largely rejects the role of hormones on sexuality or female suffrage, but some studies, and certainly the popular imagination, continue to appeal to hormones as a cause for differences in gender. In particular, testosterone is said to lead to what are meant to be the masculine traits of dominance, persistence, energy, libido, and focused attention. One analysis even attributes Celestine's failed papacy in 1294, a papacy that lasted less than five months, to his low baseline level of testosterone.[21]

Behavioral ecologists offer us a different explanation for testosterone's importance: Men would have benefited from sudden bursts of it in pursuing their "live fast and die young" lifestyle, clambering over other males and beating them down to impregnate the available females. Andrew Sullivan is especially rhapsodic about testosterone, linking it to "confidence, competitiveness, tenacity, strength and sexual drive."[22] Noting that he must give himself regular injections of a synthetic version or it for medical reasons ("a biweekly encounter with a syringe full of manhood," as he puts it[23]), Sullivan credits testosterone with an increase in appetite, far less need for sleep, and a complete absence of the depression he says used to plague him. He also feels "better able to recover from life's curve balls more persistent, more alive." In Sullivan's view, what he calls the "Big T" explains the "deeply male" substitution of risk and intense experience for security and longevity, and it "affects every aspect of our society from high divorce rates and adolescent violence to the exploding cults of bodybuilding and professional wrestling."[24]

Anne Moir and David Jessel suggest the opposite effects of estrogen:

> Colin is a quiet boy. He is studious, shy, and tries to avoid games. . . . He has no interest in contact sports. If there's a free-for-all in the playground, Colin simply walks away from it. His mother, who tells him he "should stand up for himself," says that in sixteen years he has only once been involved in a fight. Colin's mother, it transpires, took doses of synthetic female hormone during pregnancy.[25]

Not to be outdone, researchers also examine effects on girls whose mothers took a course of synthetic progestins with androgenlike characteristics during pregnancy. Here, Erika serves as an example:

> She likes rough-and-tumble games, chase games, and activities involving climbing—and trespassing. She dresses in boys' clothes, and prefers their company. She has only once taken her doll out of the cupboard, and that was to put it into the bath "to see if it would float." Her schoolteachers complain of her rowdiness. She frequently starts fights, and is known to have a frequent, and violent temper. She is more self-confident, self-reliant, domineering and ambitious.[26]

11

12

13

The link between testosterone, aggression, and "manhood" is also [14] supposed to show up in comparisons strictly between men, between those with more machismo and those with less. Thus, a 1998 study of male lawyers found what the *New York Times* calls "juris cojones."[27] It turns out that male trial lawyers have higher testosterone levels than other lawyers, even male ones. In fact, according to James Dabbs, the lead author of the study, trial lawyers are so aggressive, they sometimes have to "tone down" their personalities or risk alienating the jury. "There's a certain animal quality to their behavior," he continues, "They're less concerned with pleasing other people."[28] Another study in 1992 measured serum levels of testosterone in former enlisted men who were representative of the United States population as whole in terms of race, education, income, and occupation.[29] What it found was that those with the higher testosterone levels were either unemployed or blue-collar workers, while those with lower testosterone levels were white-collar workers. Moreover, it linked high testosterone to "low verbal intelligence, antisocial behavior and insufficient education, all leading to low occupation status."[30] Of course, the link could go in either of two directions: Either high testosterone levels might cause "low-status" jobs or low-status jobs might increase levels of testosterone. Or perhaps blue-collar workers have more physical confrontations with managers and coworkers, and perhaps these confrontations raise testosterone levels. Still, the study concluded that even if physical confrontations do raise testosterone levels in male blue-collar workers, the effect is not significant enough to explain the extent of the hormone differences between them and male white-collar workers. Testosterone, it seems, is "deeply male"—indeed, sometimes too deeply male. For Sullivan, in fact, testosterone "helps explain, perhaps better than any other single fact, why inequalities between men and women remain so frustratingly resilient in public and private life."[31]

What do critics of the "sex leads to gender" camp have to say, or what [15] could they say, about hormone studies? Erika is meant to be masculine in wanting to see if her doll will float, in possessing a bad temper, and in being self-confident, self-reliant, domineering, and ambitious.[32] Yet, surely we need not think such characteristics are only, or even primarily, masculine. Indeed, rather than demonstrating Erika's masculinity, does the connection of all these characteristics to one another already presuppose it? Otherwise, why suppose the characteristics have anything to do with one another? Certainly, nothing about the trait of self-confidence would link it inherently to an experimental attitude about floating or to a bad temper. Nor is it clear why female hormones should explain Colin's penchant for nonviolence. Should we question Mahatma Gandhi's masculinity or the levels of testosterone in male members of the Society of Friends? Indeed, we might ask whether testosterone is really all it is cracked it up to be. Take, for example, its effects in monkeys. Better yet, compare the neurobiologist Robert Sapolsky's description of a monkey hierarchy to Sullivan's paean to "the Big T."[33] Sapolsky's description is worth quoting at length:

> Round up some male monkeys. Put them in a group together. . . . Give them enough time to form a dominance hierarchy, the sort of linear ranking in which number 3, for example, can pass his day throwing around his weight with numbers 4 and 5, ripping off their monkey chow, forcing them to relinquish the best spots to sit in, but numbers 1 and 2 still expect and receive from him the most obsequious brown-nosing. . . . Take that third-ranking monkey and give him some testosterone . . . inject a ton of it . . . give him enough testosterone to grow antlers and a beard on every neuron in his brain. And, no surprise, when you check the behavioral data, he will probably be participating in more aggressive interactions than before.
>
> So . . . testosterone causes aggression, right? Wrong. Check out number 3 more closely. Is he raining terror on everyone in the group, frothing with indiscriminate violence? Not at all. He's still judiciously kowtowing to numbers 1 and 2 but has become a total bastard to numbers 4 and 5. Testosterone isn't causing aggression, it's exaggerating the aggression that is already there.[34]

We should stress two points in particular here. First, the levels of *16* testosterone that the individual monkeys possess at the beginning of the experiment do not predict which monkey will be dominant or submissive in the hierarchy they establish. Second, flooding them with artificial testosterone does not change the focus of their aggressive behavior or make them assertive against those to whom they were previously submissive. Rather, individual monkeys simply treat in a worse way those they already treated badly.

Other studies show that testosterone rises and falls with emotions. *17* If two tennis players have equal levels of testosterone before they play a match against one another, testosterone levels rise in the one who eventually wins and fall in the one who eventually loses.[35] When the American hostages were released from captivity in Iran in 1981 after 444 days of captivity, immediate physiological and psychological testing found measures of cortisol, catecholamine, and testosterone levels in the men to be extremely elevated. These reflected not aggression, however, but "three strong affects: Distress, anxiety and elation."[36] We might also point out that the authors or the study associating higher levels of testosterone with men in lower-status jobs was stumped when it came to farmers. As it turns out, farmers have the lowest levels of testosterone of all, even lower than white-collar men. This "finding," the researchers admit, "presents a puzzle,"[37] since farming would seem to require toughness and white-collar jobs would seem to have a higher social status. But by way of an answer, the researchers only, and completely enigmatically, quote Willa Cather on the weather: "Men's affairs went on underneath it, as the streams creep under the ice."[38]

Despite its status in popular culture, testosterone is therefore a bit of *18* a disappointment in the attempt to explain gendered behaviors by way of biological sex. It is only fair, however, to point out that estrogen is equally disappointing. In 1934, Bernard Zondek discovered estrogen in the testicles of a virile stallion and, much to his own dismay, thereby destabilized the received understanding of hormones as responsible for masculine dominance and feminine submission. Zondek himself remained confused. "To this day," he said in an interview, "I do not understand how it is that the high concentration of estrogen in stallion testes and blood does not exert an emasculating effect." (The interviewer had a quick response: "It is fortunate for the stallion that he has no chance of knowing your trouble."[39])

Conclusion

Given persistent questions about and differences between scientific studies, what should we conclude about the relation between sex and gender? In recent decades, the unidirectional debate over whether or not sex characteristics cause gender traits has given way to a more reciprocal conception of the causal process. Carol Worthman notes that synthetic organic chemicals affect gonadal steroids and that diet affects hormones.[40] Anne Fausto Sterling makes a similar point using bones: According to a recent study, maintaining at least an average weight is the best predictor of good bone mass density.[41] Yet, in another study of adolescents in the United States, 27 percent of girls who think they weigh the correct amount are nonetheless trying to lose weight, while only 10 percent of the boys who think they weigh the correct amount are trying.[42] We can assume that cultural conceptions of beauty are at work here. Yet, insofar as they affect our bones, they affect our relative weakness and strength, perhaps as much as hormones do. Indeed, it seems uncontroversial that cultural practices affect bodies. Just consider how much vitamin D women can absorb if they are outdoors on a sunny day but clothed in full burkas. On the other hand, Fausto-Sterling also argues that girls and boys may differ in basal metabolism rates that affect food intake. It looks, then, as if many factors, some cultural and some biological, contribute to bone density and to physical bodies in general. As Fausto-Sterling puts the point, "We are always 100 percent nature and 100 percent nurture."[43]

Numerous questions remain about the relation between sex and gender. Before considering them, however, perhaps we should ask how many of each there are.

19

20

NOTES

1. Robert Wright, *The Moral Animal: Why We Are the Way We Are* (New York: Random House Vintage Books, 1995) p. 31
2. See Bobbi S. Low, *Why Sex Matters: A Darwinian Look at Human Behavior* (Princeton, NJ: Princeton University Press, 2000), p. 43.
3. *The Moral Animal*, p. 51.
4. Ibid.

5. Ibid., p. 46.
6. Mary Soares Masters and Barbara Sanders, "Is the gender difference in mental rotation disappearing?" in *Journal of Behavior Genetics*, Vol. 23, No. 4 (1993), pp. 337–41.
7. Neil V. Watson and Doreen Kimura, "Nontrivial sex differences in throwing and intercepting: Relation to psychometrically-defined spatial func-tions" in *Personality and Individual Differences*, Vol. 12, No. 5 (1991), pp. 375–85.
8. Scott Moffat, Elizabeth Hampson, and Maria Hatzipantelis, "Navigation in a 'Virtual' Maze: Sex Differences and Correlation with Psychometric Measures of Spatial Ability in Humans" in *Evolution and Human Behavior*, Vol. 19, No. 2 (1998), pp. 73–87.
9. Deborah Blum, *Sex on the Brain: The Biological Differences between Men and Women* (New York: Penguin Books, 1997), p. 58.
10. Simon Baron-Cohen, Rebecca C. Knickmeyer, and Matthew K. Belmonte, "Sex Differences in the Brain: Implications for Explaining Autism" in *Science*, Vol. 310, No. 5749 (2005), pp. 819–23.
11. Ibid.
12. Anne Moir and David Jessel, *Brain Sex: The Real Difference Between Men and Women* (New York: Dell Publishing, 1991), p. 45.
13. Erin Leahey and Guang Guo, "Gender Differences in Mathematical Trajectories" in *Social Forces*, Vol. 80, No. 2 (2001), pp. 713–32.
14. *Myths of Gender*, p. 31.
15. ibid., p. 35.
16. *Sex on the Brain*, p. 58.
17. Michael S. Kimmel, "'What About the Boys?' What the Current Debates Tell Us—and Don't Tell Us—About Boys in School" in *The Gendered Society Reader*, eds. Michael S. Kimmel with Amy Aronson (Oxford; Oxford University Press, 2004), p. 253.
18. Ibid., p. 251.
19. Anne Fausto-Sterling, *Sexing the Body: Gender Politics and the Construction of Sexuality* (New York: Basic Books, 2000), p. 154.
20. Online Etymology Dictionary, http://www.etymonline.com/index.php? term=estrus
21. Robert A. Josephs, Jennifer Guinn Seller, and Matthew L. Newman, "The Mismatch Effect: When Testosterone and Status Are at Odds" in *Journal of Personality and Social Psychology*, Vol. 9, No. 6 (2006), p. 999.
22. Andrew Sullivan, "The He Hormone" in *New York Times Magazine* (April 2, 2000), http://www.nytimes.com/2000/04/02/magazine/the-he-hormone. html?pagewanted=l,
23. Ibid.
24. Ibid.
25. *Brain Sex*, p. 78.
26. *Brain Sex*, pp. 77–8.
27. "Law; Juris Cojones" in *New York Times Magazine* (November 1, 1998), http://www.nytimes.com/1998/11/01/magazine/sunday-november-l-1998-1aw-juris-cojones.html?pagewanted=1.
28. Ibid.
29. James M. Dabbs, Jr., "Testosterone and Occupational Achievement" in *Social Forces*, Vol. 70, No. 3 (1992), pp. 813–24.
30. Ibid., p. 819.
31. "The He Hormone."
32. *Brain Sex*, pp. 77–8.
33. Ibid., p. 5.
34. Robert Sapolsky, "Testosterone Rules" in *The Gendered Society Reader*, p. 30.
35. Alan Booth et al., "Testosterone and Winning and Losing in Human Competition" in *Hormones and Behavior*, Vol. 23, Issue 4, (December, 1989), pp. 556–71.

36. Richard H. Rahe et al., "Psychological and Physiological Assessments on American Hostages Freed from Captivity in Iran" in *Psychosomatic Medicine* Vol. 52, Issue 1, (1990), p. 1.

37. Cited in "Testosterone and Occupational Achievement," p. 821.

38. ibid..

39. See Adele E. Clark, *Disciplining Reproduction: Modernity, American Life Science and the Problems of Sex* (Berkeley: University of California Press, 1998), p. 126.

40. Carol M. Worthman "Hormones, Sex and Gender" in *Annual Review of Anthropology*, Vol. 24 (1995), p.608.

41. Cited by Anne Fausto-Sterling, "The Bare Bones of Sex: Part 1 — Sex and Gender" in *Signs: Journal of Women in Culture and Society*, Vol. 30, No. 2 (2005), p. 1494.

42. Ibid., p. 1515.

43. Ibid., p. 1510.

■ ■ ■

Reading as a Writer: Analyzing Rhetorical Choices

1. What is the difference between "sex" and "gender," two terms that Warnke raises at the beginning of her essay? Look up the definitions to these terms, and perhaps others that may be new to you (such as "behavioral ecology" or "female suffrage") and explain the difference to a partner. Feel free to divide the work and share the findings.

2. What do you make of Warnke's decision to use her opening paragraphs to paraphrase someone she disagrees with, the behavioral ecologist Robert Wright? This is a strategy that Warnke uses again in the second half of her essay about hormone studies; she sets out the conclusions of those with whom she disagrees, and then challenges the findings. How effective do you find this strategy of argument, and why?

Writing as a Reader: Entering the Conversation of Ideas

1. Both Warnke and Margaret Talbot are fascinated by the intersection of social expectations of bodies (which change over time and depend on cultural contexts) and our biology. Compose an essay in which you place these authors in conversation around these issues, in order to draw out what you think is a significant point about the ways we use (and misuse) appeals to biology as our expectations of people change over time.

2. Like Warnke, Agustín Fuentes (Chapter 14) is interested in the assumptions we make about biological differences and the sociological effects of those ideas. Compose an essay in which you forge connections between each author's examples and analysis in order to draw your own conclusions about the reasons for and effects of these assumptions. You might choose a specific example from the contemporary news or media to examine in light of these author's insights as you make your argument.

MARGARET TALBOT

From Brain Gain: The Underground World of "Neuroenhancing" Drugs

Margaret Talbot is a staff writer at *The New Yorker*, where this article first appeared in 2009. Talbot has also written for *The New Republic* and *The Atlantic Monthly* on a wide range of topics, including changing attitudes toward women's work and family life, the intersection of politics and moral debates, and children's culture. This article on "neuroenhancing" drugs is part of an unfolding conversation among scholars and public intellectuals about the increasingly large role that prescription medication plays in many people's lives. You may be aware of the debates about whether or not we are "overmedicating" patients for depression or attention deficit disorder. In this article, Talbot takes up a more recent side effect of our medically fascinated culture—the nonmedical use of prescription drugs such as Adderall and Ritalin to enhance academic performance, particularly at the college level. In this piece, Talbot describes the stressful dynamics of college life that may be familiar to you—balancing academic demands with other pressures on your time, whether from work or socializing. As you read, compare Talbot's examples to your own experiences and the ways you and your peers struggle to stay on top of the competing demands of contemporary life and college coursework.

Talbot uses an extended example of an anonymous student, "Alex," in order to make a broader point about the ways many college campuses "have become laboratories for experimentation with neuroenhancement" (para. 2). Pay attention to the strategies Talbot uses to move from her close-up example of Alex to her big-picture analysis of the implications of increasing use among college students of prescription "brain-boosting" drugs. How is one person's decision to use drugs in this way more than a "private act," as Talbot claims in paragraph 12? Talbot brings in experts who weigh in on both the negatives and positives of this issue. She also contextualizes this kind of recreational drug use in a long history of people using (or abusing) caffeine and nicotine in order to stay awake and focused at school and at work. What do you make of these comparisons?

If, as Talbot claims, "Every era . . . has its defining drug" (para. 26), she invites us to consider the significance of the current use (or abuse) of "brain-boosting" drugs. What do they tell us about what we—and our professors and our employers—expect? What does it take to be competitive right now, and do we agree with the direction we are heading? Talbot offers multiple perspectives on an issue that is likely to be affecting your life right now, and will surely affect your future.

■ ■ ■

A young man I'll call Alex recently graduated from Harvard. As a his- *1* tory major, Alex wrote about a dozen papers a semester. He also ran a student organization, for which he often worked more than forty hours a week; when he wasn't on the job, he had classes. Weeknights were devoted to all the schoolwork that he couldn't finish during the day, and weekend nights were spent drinking with friends and going to dance parties. "Trite as it sounds," he told me, it seemed important to "maybe appreciate my own youth." Since, in essence, this life was impossible, Alex began taking Adderall to make it possible.

Adderall, a stimulant composed of mixed amphetamine salts, is com- 2 monly prescribed for children and adults who have been given a diagnosis of attention-deficit hyperactivity disorder. But in recent years Adderall and Ritalin, another stimulant, have been adopted as cognitive enhancers: Drugs that high-functioning, overcommitted people take to become higher-functioning and more overcommitted. (Such use is "off label," meaning that it does not have the approval of either the drug's manufacturer or the Food and Drug Administration.) College campuses have become laboratories for experimentation with neuroenhancement, and Alex was an ingenious experimenter. His brother had received a diagnosis of ADHD, and in his freshman year Alex obtained an Adderall prescription for himself by describing to a doctor symptoms that he knew were typical of the disorder. During his college years, Alex took fifteen milligrams of Adderall most evenings, usually after dinner, guaranteeing that he would maintain intense focus while losing "any ability to sleep for approximately eight to ten hours." In his sophomore year, he persuaded the doctor to add a thirty milligram "extended release" capsule to his daily regimen.

Alex recalled one week during his junior year when he had four 3 term papers due. Minutes after waking on Monday morning, around seven-thirty, he swallowed some "immediate release" Adderall. The drug, along with a steady stream of caffeine, helped him to concentrate during classes and meetings, but he noticed some odd effects; at a morning tutorial, he explained to me in an e-mail, "I alternated between speaking too quickly and thoroughly on some subjects and feeling awkwardly quiet during other points of the discussion." Lunch was a blur: "It's always hard to eat much when on Adderall." That afternoon, he went to the library, where he spent "too much time researching a paper rather than actually writing it—a problem, I can assure you, that is common to all intellectually curious students on stimulants." At eight, he attended a two-hour meeting "with a group focussed on student mental-health issues." Alex then "took an extended-release Adderall" and worked productively on the paper all night. At eight the next morning, he attended a meeting of his organization; he felt like "a zombie," but "was there to insure that the semester's work didn't go to waste." After that, Alex explained, "I went back to my room to take advantage of my tired body." He fell asleep until noon, waking "in time to polish my first paper and hand it in."

I met Alex one evening last summer, at an appealingly scruffy bar in 4 the New England city where he lives. Skinny and bearded, and wearing faded hipster jeans, he looked like the lead singer in an indie band. He was ingratiating and articulate and smoked cigarettes with an ironic air of defiance. Alex was happy enough to talk about his frequent use of Adderall at Harvard, but he didn't want to see his name in print; he's involved with an Internet start-up and worried that potential investors might disapprove of his habit.

After we had ordered beers, he said, "One of the most impressive fea- 5 tures of being a student is how aware you are of a twenty-four-hour work cycle. When you conceive of what you have to do for school, it's not in terms of nine to five but in terms of what you can physically do in a week while still achieving a variety of goals in a variety of realms—social, romantic, sexual, extracurricular, résumé-building, academic commitments." Alex was eager to dispel the notion that students who took Adderall were "academic automatons who are using it in order to be first in their class, or in order to be an obvious admit to law school or the first accepted at a consulting firm." In fact, he said, "it's often people"—mainly guys—"who are looking in some way to compensate for activities that are detrimental to their performance." He explained, "At Harvard, at least, most people are to some degree realistic about it. . . . I don't think people who take Adderall are aiming to be the top person in the class. I think they're aiming to be among the best. Or maybe not even among the best. At the most basic level, they aim to do better than they would have otherwise." He went on, "Everyone is aware of the fact that if you were up at 3 a.m. writing this paper it isn't going to be as good as it could have been. The fact that you were partying all weekend, or spent the last week being high, watching *Lost*—that's going to take a toll."

Alex's sense of who uses stimulants for so-called nonmedical purposes 6 is borne out by two dozen or so scientific studies. In 2005, a team led by Sean Esteban McCabe, a professor at the University of Michigan's Substance Abuse Research Center, reported that in the previous year 4.1 percent of American undergraduates had taken prescription stimulants for off-label use; at one school, the figure was 25 percent. Other researchers have found even higher rates: A 2002 study at a small college found that more than 35 percent of the students had used prescription stimulants nonmedically in the previous year.

Drugs such as Adderall can cause nervousness, headaches, sleepless- 7 ness, and decreased appetite, among other side effects. An FDA warning on Adderall's label notes that "amphetamines have a high potential for abuse" and can lead to dependence. (The label also mentions that adults using Adderall have reported serious cardiac problems, though the role of the drug in those cases is unknown.) Yet college students tend to consider Adderall and Ritalin benign, in part because they are likely to know peers who have taken the drugs since childhood for ADHD. Indeed, McCabe reports, most students who use stimulants for cognitive enhancement obtain them from an acquaintance with a prescription. Usually, the pills are given away, but some students sell them.

According to McCabe's research team, white male undergraduates at 8 highly competitive schools—especially in the Northeast—are the most frequent collegiate users of neuroenhancers. Users are also more likely to belong to a fraternity or a sorority and to have a GPA of 3.0 or lower. They are ten times as likely to report that they have smoked marijuana in the past year, and twenty times as likely to say that they have used cocaine. In other words, they are decent students at schools where, to be a great student, you have to give up a lot more partying than they're willing to give up.

The BoredAt Web sites—which allow college students to chat idly 9 while they're ostensibly studying—are filled with messages about Adderall. Posts like these, from the BoredAtPenn site, are typical: "I have some Adderall—I'm sitting by room 101.10 in a grey shirt and headphones"; "I have Adderall for sale 20mg for $15"; "I took Adderall at 8 p.m., it's 6:30 a.m. and I've barely blinked." On the Columbia site, a poster with an e-mail address from CUNY complains that her friends take Adderall "like candy," adding, "I don't want to be at a disadvantage to everyone else. Is it really that dangerous? Will it fuck me up? My grades weren't that great this year and I could do with a bump." A Columbia student responds, "It's probably not a good idea if you're not prescribed," but offers practical advice anyway: "Keep the dose normal and don't grind them up or snort them." Occasional dissents ("I think there should be random drug testing at every exam") are drowned out by testimonials like this one, from the BoredAtHarvard site: "I don't want to be a pusher or start people on something bad, but Adderall is AMAZING."

Alex remains enthusiastic about Adderall, but he also has a slightly 10 jaundiced critique of it. "It only works as a cognitive enhancer insofar as you are dedicated to accomplishing the task at hand," he said. "The number of times I've taken Adderall late at night and decided that, rather than starting my paper, hey, I'll organize my entire music library! I've seen people obsessively cleaning their rooms on it." Alex thought that generally the drug helped him to bear down on his work, but it also tended to produce writing with a characteristic flaw. "Often, I've looked back at papers I've written on Adderall, and they're verbose. They're belaboring a point, trying to create this airtight argument, when if you just got to your point in a more direct manner it would be stronger. But with Adderall I'd produce two pages on something that could be said in a couple of sentences." Nevertheless, his Adderall-assisted papers usually earned him at least a B. They got the job done. As Alex put it, "Productivity is a good thing."

Last April, the scientific journal *Nature* published the results of an infor- 11 mal online poll asking whether readers attempted to sharpen "their focus, concentration, or memory" by taking drugs such as Ritalin and Provigil— a newer kind of stimulant, known generically as modafinil, which was developed to treat narcolepsy. One out of five respondents said that they did. A majority of the 1,400 readers who responded said that healthy adults should be permitted to take brain boosters for nonmedical reasons, and 69 percent said that mild side effects were an acceptable risk. Though a majority said that such drugs should not be made available to children who had no diagnosed medical condition, a third admitted that they would feel pressure to give "smart drugs" to their kids if they learned that other parents were doing so. . . .

If Alex, the Harvard student, . . . [considers his] use of neuroenhancers *12* a private act, Nicholas Seltzer sees his habit as a pursuit that aligns him with a larger movement for improving humanity. Seltzer has a BA from UC Davis and a master's degree in security policy from George Washington University. But the job that he obtained with these credentials—as a researcher at a defense-oriented think tank, in northern Virginia—has not left him feeling as intellectually alive as he would like. To compensate, he writes papers in his spare time on subjects like "human biological evolution and warfare." He also primes his brain with artificial challenges; even when he goes to the rest room at the office, he takes the opportunity to play memory or logic games on his cell phone. Seltzer, who is thirty, told me that he worried that he "didn't have the mental energy, the endurance, the—I don't know what to properly call this—the *sponginess* that I seem to recall having when I was younger."

Suffice it to say that this is not something you notice when you talk *13* to Seltzer. And though our memory is probably at its peak in our early twenties, few thirty-year-olds are aware of a deficit. But Seltzer is the Washington-wonk equivalent of those models and actors in LA who discern tiny wrinkles long before their agent does. His girlfriend, a technology consultant whom he met in a museum, is nine years younger, and he was already thinking about how his mental fitness would stand up next to hers. He told me, "She's twenty-one, and I want to stay young and vigorous and don't want to be a burden on her later in life." He didn't worry about visible signs of aging, but he wanted to keep his mind "nimble and healthy for as long as possible."

Seltzer considers himself a "transhumanist," in the mold of the Oxford *14* philosopher Nick Bostrom and the futurist writer and inventor Ray Kurzweil. Transhumanists are interested in robots, cryogenics, and living a really, really long time; they consider biological limitations that the rest of us might accept, or even appreciate, as creaky obstacles to be aggressively surmounted. On the Imminst forums—"Imminst" stands for "Immortality Institute"—Seltzer and other members discuss life-extension strategies and the potential benefits of cognitive enhancers. Some of the forum members limit themselves to vitamin and mineral supplements. Others use Adderall or modafinil or, like Seltzer, a drug called piracetam, which was first marketed by a Belgian pharmaceutical company in 1972 and, in recent years, has become available in the United States from retailers that sell supplements. Although not approved for any use by the FDA, piracetam has been used experimentally on stroke patients—to little effect—and on patients with a rare neurological condition called progressive myoclonus epilepsy, for whom it proved helpful in alleviating muscle spasms. Data on piracetam's benefits for healthy people are virtually nonexistent, but many users believe that the drug increases blood flow to the brain.

From the time I first talked to Seltzer, it was clear that although he 15 felt cognitive enhancers were of practical use, they also appealed to him on an aesthetic level. Using neuroenhancers, he said, "is like customizing yourself—customizing your brain." For some people, he went on, it was important to enhance their mood, so they took antidepressants; but for people like him it was more important "to increase mental horsepower." He added, "It's fundamentally a choice you're making about how you want to experience consciousness." Whereas the '90s had been about "the personalization of technology," this decade was about the personalization of the brain—what some enthusiasts have begun to call "mind hacking."

Of course, the idea behind mind-hacking isn't exactly new. Fortifying 16 one's mental stamina with drugs of various kinds has a long history. Sir Francis Bacon consumed everything from tobacco to saffron in the hope of goosing his brain. Balzac reputedly fuelled sixteen-hour bouts of writing with copious servings of coffee, which, he wrote, "chases away sleep, and gives us the capacity to engage a little longer in the exercise of our intellects." Sartre dosed himself with speed in order to finish *Critique of Dialectical Reason*. My college friends and I wrote term papers with the sweaty-palmed assistance of NoDoz tablets. And, before smoking bans, entire office cultures chugged along on a collective nicotine buzz—at least, if *Mad Men* is to be believed. Seltzer and his interlocutors on the Imminst forum are just the latest members of a seasoned cohort, even if they have more complex pharmaceuticals at their disposal.

I eventually met Seltzer in an underground food court not far from 17 the Pentagon. We sat down at a Formica table in the dim light. Seltzer was slim, had a shaved head, and wore metal-frame glasses; matching his fastidious look, he spoke precisely, rarely stumbling over his words. I asked him if he had any ethical worries about smart drugs. After a pause, he said that he might have a concern if somebody popped a neuroenhancer before taking a licensing exam that certified him as, say, a brain surgeon, and then stopped using the drug. Other than that, he couldn't see a problem. He said that he was a firm believer in the idea that "we should have a fair degree of liberty to do with our bodies and our minds as we see fit, so long as it doesn't impinge on the basic rights, liberty, and safety of others." He argued, "Why would you want an upward limit on the intellectual capabilities of a human being? And, if you have a very nationalist viewpoint, why wouldn't you want our country to have the advantage over other countries, particularly in what some people call a knowledge-based economy?" He went on, "Think about the complexity of the intellectual tasks that people need to accomplish today. Just trying to understand what Congress is doing is not a simple thing! The complexity of understanding the gamut of scientific and technical and social issues is difficult. If we had a tool that enabled more people to understand the world at a greater level of sophistication, how can we prejudice ourselves against the notion, simply because we don't like athletes to do it? To me, it doesn't seem like the same question. And it deserves its own debate."

Seltzer had never had a diagnosis of any kind of learning disorder. [18] But he added, "Though I wouldn't say I'm dyslexic, sometimes when I type prose, after I look back and read it, I've frequently left out words or interposed words, and sometimes I have difficulty concentrating." In graduate school, he obtained a prescription for Adderall from a doctor who didn't ask a lot of questions. The drug helped him, especially when his ambitions were relatively low. He recalled, "I had this one paper, on nuclear strategy. The professor didn't look favorably on any kind of creative thinking." On Adderall, he pumped out the paper in an evening. "I just bit my tongue, regurgitated, and got a good-enough grade."

On the other hand, Seltzer recalled that he had taken piracetam to [19] write an essay on "the idea of harmony as a trope in Chinese political discourse"—it was one of the papers he was proudest of. He said, "It was really an intellectual challenge to do. I felt that the piracetam helped me to work within the realm of the abstract, and make the kind of associations that I needed—following this idea of harmony from an ancient religious belief as it was translated throughout the centuries into a very important topic in political discourse."

After a hiatus of several years, Seltzer had recently resumed taking [20] neuroenhancers. In addition to piracetam, he took a stack of supplements that he thought helped his brain functioning: Fish oils, five antioxidants, a product called ChocoMind, and a number of others, all available at the health-food store. He was thinking about adding modafinil, but hadn't yet. For breakfast every morning, he concocted a slurry of oatmeal, berries, soy milk, pomegranate juice, flaxseed, almond meal, raw eggs, and protein powder. The goal behind the recipe was efficiency: To rely on "one goop you could eat or drink that would have everything you need nutritionally for your brain and body." He explained, "Taste was the last thing on my mind; I wanted to be able to keep it down—that was it." (He told me this in the kitchen of his apartment; he lives with a roommate, who walked in while we were talking, listened perplexedly for a moment, then put a frozen pizza in the oven.)

Seltzer's decision to take piracetam was based on his own online [21] reading, which included medical-journal abstracts. He hadn't consulted a doctor. Since settling on a daily regimen of supplements, he had sensed an improvement in his intellectual work and his ability to engage in stimulating conversation. He continued, "I feel I'm better able to articulate my thoughts. I'm sure you've been in the zone—you're having a really exciting debate with somebody, your brain feels alive. I feel that more. But I don't want to say that it's this profound change."

I asked him if piracetam made him feel smarter, or just more alert and [22] confident—a little better equipped to marshal the resources he naturally had. "Maybe," he said. "I'm not sure what being smarter means, entirely. It's a difficult quality to measure. It's the gestalt factor, all these qualities coming together—not only your ability to crunch some numbers, or remember some figures or a sequence of numbers, but also your ability to maintain a certain emotional state that is conducive to productive intellectual work. I do feel I'm more intelligent with the drugs, but I can't give you a number of IQ points."

The effects of piracetam on healthy volunteers have been studied even 23 less than those of Adderall or modafinil. Most peer-reviewed studies focus on its effects on dementia, or on people who have suffered a seizure or a concussion. Many of the studies that look at other neurological effects were performed on rats and mice. Piracetam's mechanisms of action are not understood, though it may increase levels of the neurotransmitter acetylcholine. In 2008, a committee of the British Academy of Medical Sciences noted that many of the clinical trials of piracetam for dementia were methodologically flawed. Another published review of the available studies of the drug concluded that the evidence "does not support the use of piracetam in the treatment of people with dementia or cognitive impairment," but suggested that further investigation might be warranted. I asked Seltzer if he thought he should wait for scientific ratification of piracetam. He laughed. "I don't want to," he said. "Because it's working."

It makes no sense to ban the use of neuroenhancers. Too many people 24 are already taking them, and the users tend to be educated and privileged people who proceed with just enough caution to avoid getting into trouble. Besides, [University of Pennsylvania neurologist] Anjan Chatterjee is right that there is an apt analogy with plastic surgery. In a consumer society like ours, if people are properly informed about the risks and benefits of neuroenhancers, they can make their own choices about how to alter their minds, just as they can make their own decisions about shaping their bodies.

Still, even if you acknowledge that cosmetic neurology is here to stay, 25 there is something dispiriting about the way the drugs are used—the kind of aspirations they open up, or don't. Jonathan Eisen, an evolutionary biologist at UC Davis, is skeptical of what he mockingly calls "brain doping." During a recent conversation, he spoke about colleagues who take neuroenhancers in order to grind out grant proposals. "It's weird to me that people are taking these drugs to write grants," he said. "I mean, if you came up with some really interesting paper that was *spurred* by taking some really interesting drug—magic mushrooms or something—that would make more sense to me. In the end, you're only as good as the ideas you've come up with."

But it's not the mind-expanding 60s anymore. Every era, it seems, has 26 its own defining drug. Neuroenhancers are perfectly suited for the anxiety of while-collar competition in a floundering economy. And they have a synergistic relationship with our multiplying digital technologies: The more gadgets we own, the more distracted we become, and the more we need help in order to focus. The experience that neuroenhancement offers is not, for the most part, about opening the doors of perception, or about breaking the bonds of the self, or about experiencing a surge of genius. It's about squeezing out an extra few hours to finish those sales figures when you'd really rather collapse into bed; getting a B instead of a B-minus on the final exam in a lecture class where you spent half your time texting; cramming for the GREs at night, because the information-industry job you got after college turned out to be deadening. Neuroenhancers don't offer freedom. Rather, they facilitate a pinched, unromantic, grindingly efficient form of productivity.

This winter, I spoke again with Alex, the Harvard graduate, and 27 found that, after a break of several months, he had gone back to taking Adderall—a small dose every day. He felt that he was learning to use the drug in a more "disciplined" manner. Now, he said, it was less about staying up late to finish work he should have done earlier, and more "about staying focussed on work, which makes me want to work longer hours." What employer would object to that?

■ ■ ■

Reading as a Writer: Analyzing Rhetorical Choices

1. Talbot offers an extended example of the Harvard student, "Alex," in order to illuminate some of the reasons some college students use neuroenhancing drugs. What strengths and weaknesses can you see in using an extended example to illustrate a larger trend? How effectively do you think Talbot ties this example into her larger argument throughout her essay?

2. After reading this piece carefully, list the different perspectives on "brain-boosting" drugs that Talbot lays out in her essay. Does she seem to take sides on this issue? Provide evidence from the text for your responses.

Writing as a Reader: Entering the Conversation of Ideas

1. Talbot's examples of neuroenhancing drug use focus on the way men use these mind-altering substances, just as Matthew Immergut's study of body hair (Chapter 14) focuses on male bodies and attitudes toward body hair. What can these two essays tell us about our expectations of men in current culture? Compose an essay that brings together examples and insights from both readings in order to make a larger point about our current expectations for men, in mind and body. What is at stake for these men, and for our culture, given the ideas you present to your reader?

2. Like Talbot, Mark Edmudson (Chapter 12) is interested in the expectations that college life makes on students. Are those expectations too high? Not high enough? These authors have different perspectives, and you likely have a strong point of view of your own. Drawing on insights and examples from these authors and your own experiences, compose an essay about the ways you believe college life should challenge students effectively. What recommendations do these authors make for changes in the current system, and where do your ideas fit in?

ANAHI VILADRICH, MING-CHIN YEH,
NANCY BRUNING, RACHAEL WEISS

"Do Real Women Have Curves?" Paradoxical Body Images among Latinas in New York City

The authors of this researched essay share an interest in immigrant health and a connection through the Urban Public Health Program at Hunter College of the City University of New York. Anahí Vladrich is a professor of sociology and medical anthropology, whose research centers on immigration and health. Ming-Chin Yeh is a professor of public health, who focuses on multi-ethnic communities, diet, and health issues. Nancy Bruning teaches community and public health courses and publishes on health and fitness for both scholarly audiences and the general public. Rachael Weiss was a research associate at both Brookdale Center for Healthy Aging & Longevity and the Immigration and Health Initiative/Hunter College and an environmental policy analyst at Environmental Packaging International. These authors' collaborative work with Latinas in New York City fills a gap in the existing research, as they note in paragraph 5: "Until recently, most work on body image had been conducted among Whites, with Blacks and Hispanics usually being comparison groups." As you read, consider how their analysis and conclusions help you expand your own understanding of body image, popular culture, and health.

The authors write their article in the IMRAD style (Introduction, Methods, Research, and Discussion), typical of social science and science writing. They open with a plot summary of the film they mention in their title, *Real Women Have Curves,* pointing out that the storyline is more optimistic than experiences of real Latinas who navigate challenging contemporary expectations of female bodies. In paragraph 7, the authors sketch out their claims about the "contradictory body ideals" faced by their research group. You might return to this paragraph as you read (and reread) this rich essay, to see how the authors' specific claims and analysis lead up to their overall argument.

Take sufficient time to read the "Study Design and Methods" section, so that you understand their rationale for the "mixed methods" the authors use to gather their data. What challenges can you see in working with human subjects? Pay attention to your responses to the statistical/quantitative data and the qualitative data from interviews. Do you find one kind of data more compelling? Why? The subjects of this study have a range of attitudes toward the contradictory expectations of women to be thin or to be curvy—depending on the context or community. What strikes you about their responses?

These authors are interested in both the psychology of these conflicting cultural expectations of women's bodies and the biological health consequences of disordered body image. The "real life" consequences of media ideals can be serious. This study, like many studies, concludes with more questions for further research. See what you think of their proposals for future research, and why it matters. What other questions does this study raise for you? What "multiple cultural commands" might shape your own expectations of "what is desirable and possible" (para. 29)? Considering your own position at the nexus of competing cultural expectations may add an even richer understanding of this study, and why such analysis matters.

■ ■ ■

Introduction: Underscoring Latinas' Curves

In the 2002 film *Real Women Have Curves*, Ana (portrayed by actress *1*
America Ferrera) is an 18-year-old Latina youngster, who is eager to keep
her conspicuously curvy body as an act of rebellion against the thin ideals of womanhood, which her surrounding milieu impinges upon her [1].
The film portrays the protagonist's counter-image as a self-defiant young
woman who boldly confronts conventional ideals of beauty and femininity. The media attention that this movie attracted when it was first released
was not fortuitous. Certainly, the film awoke social anxieties regarding
Latinas' gender roles and body images along with counter-cultural commands that defy mainstream norms.

Contrary to what the actress America Ferrera would do later on in the *2*
sitcom *Ugly Betty*, in which her character undergoes a progressive meta-
morphosis from a supposed overweighed "ugly duckling" into a swan, Ana
will not comply with the norm to shed her extra pounds. And although
she refuses to obey the "thin" and "slim" mandate, she does choose a path
to mainstream success. From where she stands, Ana firmly claims her
Latinidad (Latinness) not necessarily as a counter-normative act but as a
symbolic acceptance of American ideals of personal achievement. At the
end of the movie, she moves to New York City to start college at Columbia
University thanks to a well-deserved fellowship. Ana's farewell also leaves
us to wonder about her future with the cute *White* guy in the story who,
as it would become clear throughout the movie, not only did fall for Ana's
spikey personality and determination but also for her *curves*. The underlying moral is of a Latino heroine conflicted by cultural norms (i.e., getting
married as an ultimate heterosexual female ideal), unattainable models of
femininity as promoted by conventional media, a drive to succeed intellectually, and the difficulties she encounters to navigate among all of them.

If, in the film, the stand taken by Ana to keep (and defend) her body *3*
shape and weight goes along with an ethnic *aggiornated* feminist assertion,
in the real world her extra pounds are metonymies of a less optimistic reality. By the time the film was released, Latinos or Hispanics (these terms
are used interchangeably here) had already become the largest minority in
the United States. In recent years, Latinas/os have experienced the greatest
increase in obesity prevalence of any population subgroups, with Latinas
having higher obesity prevalence than their non-Hispanic white female
counterparts [2–4]. New health problems have made them major protagonists in rising chronic disease rates including type 2 diabetes, cardiovas-
cular disease, hypertension, cancer, cerebrovascular disease (stroke), and
premature death [5, 6].

In this article, we examine Latinas' assessment of their actual and *4*
desired body shapes and weight vis-à-vis their beliefs regarding mainstream
and alternative body images. Body image is usually defined as the way people perceive weight, body size, and appearance [7]. As noted in the literature
[8, 9] body image is a complex and multifaceted construct, and therefore

most research has narrowed its dimensions to body dissatisfaction and body image distortions. Research shows an association between body dissatisfaction and distorted body images as predictors of obesity and eating disorders, including binge eating, excessive laxative use, cessation of all eating, and purging patterns across ethnic groups [10–16]. In addition, the effects of body image and body dissatisfaction on eating habits and disorders may go in opposite directions. In fact, distorted body images may make women believe that they are thinner than they really are, a faulty perception that can lead to underestimating weight-gain, and which has been associated with higher rates of obesity among Black women [17]. Distortions in body image may also do the reverse by leading women to obsess over being fat, even when they are not, a pattern more typically found among White women suffering from eating disorders, particularly anorexia nervosa and bulimia.

Until recently, most work on body image had been conducted among 5 Whites, with Blacks and Hispanics usually being comparison groups (see Lovejoy for a critique [18]). Studies on weight concerns and body image have traditionally underreported the prevalence of eating disorders among minorities in general, and women of color in particular, with findings on White women often generalized to all women [19–21]. As noted in the literature, the myth of White, upper- and middle-class women as the only group suffering from body image dissatisfaction and eating disturbances is still prevalent in our society, in spite of evidence to the contrary [22–25]. In addition, studies that do include Latinas generally sample young women with Latinas over age 35 being neglected [7].

The rising trend in overweight among minority women has prompted 6 innovative studies on body image and body mass index (BMI) across ethnic groups [26]. This promising body of research has looked at the weight and eating habits of diverse ethnic minorities in the United States to counteract the limitations of previous studies that only studied White-Black comparisons [9, 27]. This literature has addressed the impact of acculturative stress in predicting body dissatisfaction and bulimic symptoms [28], as well as the relationship between body image and health outcomes, such as depression and eating disorders among Latinas [29]. Yet, researchers still struggle to understand the specific factors that impinge on minority women's distorted body images and weight concerns [11, 30], including the pressures Latinas experience from a competitive and individualistic job market versus traditional family norms [9, 31].

In this article, we utilize a mixed research methodology, which com- 7 bines individual instruments and group guidelines, to examine some of the complex belief systems underlying Latinas' ideas and attitudes regarding body image, weight, and shape. We particularly explore conflicting body paradigms in tune with discordant female types shaped by the media and by Latinas' dissimilar cultural frameworks (e.g., the United States versus their culture of origin). In the end, we coin the term *Latinas' Paradoxical Body Images* (LAPABI) to refer to the tensions that permeate Latinas' contradictory body ideals, a fact that calls attention to growing obesity trends and the rise of eating disorders, mostly bulimia and anorexia, in this population. We now turn to the findings drawn from the analysis of the literature on Latinas and body image.

Uncovering Body Paradoxes

The literature reports conflicting findings regarding Latinas' body image 8 and body satisfaction. One stream of research suggests that Latinas are more accepting of heavier female figures, and thus suffer from less body dissatisfaction than do White women [13, 32]. In fact, body dissatisfaction and low body esteem have been found to be higher among White women than among Latinas and other ethnic minority women [13, 33]. Proponents of this trend argue that cultural differences in self-perception of obesity/overweight help explain variations in obesity prevalence across populations. Non-Euro-American cultures of origin are assumed to not be fixated with ultra-thin ideals, and therefore able to provide individuals with more realistic options of physical types [11]. Consequently, minorities in the United States would supposedly be less concerned with body image and feel more attracted to larger silhouettes than whites [34]. These findings are supported by the underlying notion of ethnic protective factors, including specific cultural traits, which would keep Latinas from becoming vulnerable to mainstream values [34]. Protective cultural factors specifically include appreciation of a physiologically healthy body-size, stable family and social structures, and emphasis more on personality than on physical appearance [11, 24, 35, 36]. For example, a study on the impact of young Cuban women's eating disorders found that close ties with the Cuban community and culture, including primary use of Spanish language at home and frequent consumption of Cuban meals, were associated with lower and less problematic scores on the Eating Attitudes Test [37].

A very different line of research argues that Latinas face similar, if not 9 greater, concerns regarding body image, low self-esteem, body shame, and fear of weight gain than their White counterparts [38, 39], with studies reporting comparable levels of weight concern and body dissatisfaction in both populations [29, 34]. Goodman [40] found that Latinas present greater body satisfaction than do White women, but equal levels of eating disorders. Cachelin and colleagues [2] noted that after controlling for age, BMI, and education, Latinas, and White women suffered similar levels of body discrepancy. In a study on body image attitudes among Guatemala-American women and their White female counterparts, Franco and Herrera [41] found that although the former group stated more positive attitudes toward obesity, they reported greater body dissatisfaction than did the latter group. Age and degree of acculturation stress also appear to be related to Latinas' distorted body images with second-generation Latina women, who are also less susceptible to cultural protective factors, being more stressed about weight than their first-generation peers [42].

Researchers also argue that higher prevalence of obesity/overweight in *10* Latinas has led to the faulty perception that Hispanic culture is more tolerant of heavy figures, although Latinas actually experience similar body image problems to their White peers [2, 38]. Similarly, Root [24] notes that the impact of pervasive, racism may preclude early diagnosis of eating disorders among women of color. In sum, despite the fact that Latinas face a disproportionate burden from obesity, the interaction of obesity/overweight prevalence and body image is less apparent. While some studies conclude that Latinas are closer to White women in terms of ascribing to ultra-thin Caucasian norms, research has underscored the cultural protective effect that pinpoints Latinas' acceptance of more sizeable curvy ideals. In the following pages, we uncover some of the possible roots of these intriguing, albeit conflicting, research findings.

Study Design and Methods

Six focus groups of Latinas were conducted in New York City, between late *11* Summer 2006 and early Spring 2007. Study participants were recruited through flyers posted at local churches, grocery stores, health clubs, and e-mail bulletin boards, as well as through word-of-mouth. All sessions were held in private classrooms located in public educational facilities in the neighborhood of Washington Heights, in upper Manhattan, to which all women had easy access. Individual questionnaires were filled out at the beginning of the session to collect women's self-reported weight and height; basic sociodemographic characteristics, such as age, education, income, and marital status; and body shape-related questions. The body shape rating scale consisted of nine female silhouettes ranging from very thin (1.0) to very heavy (9.0), and was used to assess the following four items: (1) the participant's current size and shape, (2) the size and shape the participant would most like to be, (3) the size and shape that the participant feels is most attractive, and (4) the size and shape the participant feels that men find the most attractive (see Figure 15.2). These measures estimated whether body satisfaction in Latina women varied as a factor of their BMI and level of physical activity.

The focus group interviews were divided in two sections. The first *12* addressed participants' cultural and personal factors related to their perceptions of body weight and shape, including their body satisfaction vis-à-vis their weight control efforts. Specific themes included women's concerns about gaining weight, their strategies to keep an optimal weight, their perceived gender and ethnic differences in terms of body shape and optimal weight, women's past and present experiences with weight control, and their perceived obstacles to maintaining an optimal weight. The second part of the group interview addressed participants' beliefs and practices regarding physical activity, including their motivations to be physical active and the barriers they experienced to engaging in regular physical activity (e.g., structural, cultural, and personal).

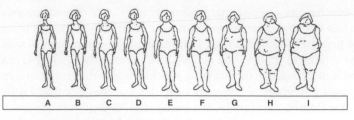

Which of the above figure drawing best represents:

_____ 1. Your current size and shape?

_____ 2. The size and shape you would most like to be?

_____ 3. The size and shape you feel is most attractive?

_____ 4. The size and shape you feel men in general find most attractive?

FIGURE 15.2 Body shape scale

This project received Institutional Review Board (IRB) approval from   *13*
Hunter College and participants signed a consent form and were compen-
sated for their time. All sessions were conducted in English and were led
by team members with experience in facilitating focus group interviews.
Each session lasted approximately 1.5–2 h and was tape-recorded for later
transcription and content analysis. Individual questionnaire data were
entered into Excel before being exported to SPSS for analysis. ANOVA and
t-tests were performed to test group significance at $P < 0.05$ level. Focus
group data were transcribed, entered as text, and then coded using QSR
NVivo software. Focus group transcripts were carefully analyzed by two
researchers on the team who identified recurrent themes, both within and
across groups. Detailed codes were organized along four general categories that included women's concerns about gaining weight, external pressures to keep an optimal weight (media and family), body and weight
satisfaction, and main paradigms influencing body size and shape.

Study Findings: Quantitative Results

A total number of forty-four women participated in the focus groups.   *14*
Seventy percent of the study participants were foreign born, with a
majority from the Dominican Republic (47.7 percent, see Table 15.3). The
average age was 38.7 years old and almost 90 percent had completed some
college or above. In addition, the mean BMI was 27.5 kg/m², with approximately 55 percent being overweight or obese. Analysis revealed signifi-
candy heavier mean scores for participants' current body size (4.4 ± 1.3) as
compared to their desired shape (3.1 ± 0.8), the shape they believed to be
most attractive (2.9 ± 0.7), and the shape thought to be most attractive to
men (2.8 ± 0.9). Table 15.4 shows the results of body shape scores by BMI
patterns.

TABLE 15.3   Participant Demographic Results

CATEGORY	SAMPLE (n)	PERCENT (%)
Foreign born	31	70.5
Dominican Republic	21	47.7
Mexico	2	4.5
Other	8	18.2
Born in United States	13	29.5
Age (Mean 38.7 ± 10.7)		
Age 18–30	13	31.7
Age 31–45	15	36.6
Age 46 Plus	13	31.7
Education level		
Completed high school	4	9.3
Completed collge	30	69.8
College plus	9	20.9
Marital status		
Married	9	20.5
Single	21	47.7
Other	14	31.8
Income level		
Less than $25,000	11	25.6
$25,000–50,000	20	46.5
More than $50,000	12	27.9
BMI (Mean 27.5 ± 7.0)		
Normal	19	45.2
Overweight	12	28.6
Obese	11	26.2

TABLE 15.4   Participants' Mean Body Shape Scores by Body Mass Index

BMI	BS 1	BS 2	BS 3	BS 4
Normal weight	3.5 (±0.8)	2.7 (±0.6)	2.7 (±0.7)	2.9 (±0.9)
Overweight	4.8 (±1.0)	3.1 (±0.6)	2.8 (±0.7)	2.7 (±0.8)
Obese	5.7 (±1.0)	3.9 (±0.7)	3.4 (±0.7)	2.8 (±1.1)

Results indicate a self-identification with higher current body size 15 among obese women compared with overweight and normal weight participants. Findings also revealed a statistical variation in body shape rankings between normal weight (BMI < 25) and obese (BMI ≥ 30)

participants, and between overweight (BMI 25–29) and obese participants. Normal and overweight women wanted to be slimmer and felt that a slimmer figure is more attractive than did the obese women. Also, normal and overweight women preferred smaller shapes and felt that a slimmer figure is more attractive than did obese women. Interestingly, women of all three weight categories shared a similar view point of the body shape most appealing to men; they all thought that a slim body size (with a score of about 3 on the body shape scale) is most attractive to them. Those who participated in monthly or yearly (infrequent) vigorous exercise reported statistically thinner current and desired body shapes, than did those who did not know or did not answer.

Qualitative Assessments of the Impact of Media Images

In agreement with the quantitative results that suggest participants' overall desire to be thinner, women's remarks about body image and their weight-control efforts spontaneously emerged during the group interviews, even before specific questions were addressed. When asked about the reasons for women wanting to control their weight, participants from all groups stressed the role of the media in influencing their attempts to look good, along with the concomitant pressure to fit to mainstream standards. Although generally participants acknowledged the unrealistic expectations set by media images of ultra-thin women, most conveyed that these representations exerted an omnipresent pressure to judge their own weight and shape, along with their on-and-off efforts to lose weight. The ultimate social stereotype was summarized in being thin, tall, and White. In participants' own words: *16*

> Participant 1, group 2: I think the media has an immense part to do with it. I mean, on TV and in the magazines and what you see is these thin women, you know, it's the same thing over and over. On TV and shows it's the same thing, it's the same look, it's the same size . . .
> Moderator: Regardless of race and ethnicity?
> Participant 1: Oh now, I mean, it's usually White, it's usually thin, it's usually bigger chested, bigger breasts . . . Like that's constantly what you see on TV shows. So if you see that, I mean Barbie, HELLO! Like Barbie alone, you know, that's what little girls always want [these] Barbies. And they always want the White Barbie with the blue eyes and blonde hair, and none of them like the darker Barbie! So it's something that girls see from the very beginning and it's almost near impossible to control because, what are you gonna do? I mean, you have little kids watching TV all the time . . .
> Moderator, group 1: So you agree that those models you get from magazines . . .
> Participant 1: Oh yeah! They put a lot of pressure.
> Participant 2: On *Desperate Housewives*, they are so skinny I mean . . ."

Participant 1: They are desperate because they are hungry!
Participant 2: Yeah I know.

A second aspect that emerged from the focus group data relates to the *17* ubiquitous nature of the "American" type, usually defined as the White models that sell in magazines and TV shows.

Moderator, group 2: What is the American type? Participant: Skinny, big breasts. You know your thighs are supposed to be smaller than your top, and very, very skinny as opposed to a lot of the Latina women you know. Your thighs are kind of shaped bigger than the top of your body and that kind of thing

Although participants acknowledged the impact of the thin ideal on *18* how women judged themselves compared to others, most appeared to be conspicuously aware of the distortion between media and reality. We now turn to the analysis of curvier body ideals that also emerged from the focus group data.

From Coca-Cola Shaped Gals to Shrinking Violets: The Rise of *Latinidad*

In spite of mainstream images that privilege thin women as the ideal to *19* be sought, most participants acknowledged that slowly, but increasingly, alternative body types have been capturing the public imagination. Not surprisingly, the rising visibility of Latinas in public media has corresponded to the increasing typecasting of rounded beauties, Jennifer Lopez (J-Lo) being a case in point. Only a few years ago, her prodigious backside catapulted her rise to stardom, and what she called a "guitar body" became the counter-stereotype of her less endowed American peers [43]. Some participants specifically referred to J-Lo as the counter-stereotype that has recently opened new spaces for alternative body types in public media:

Participant 1, group 4:
That's really changed though [referring to the slim norm]. I guess it's kind of like it started with J-Lo because she's in the mainstream and look at her: She obviously has hips! So now you're seeing, like . . . It's weird: You start to see Caucasian and Asian girls that now are going to the gym to work it out [their butts]. They even have butt implants. They're willing to go buy what they didn't want before. That used to be discriminated against!

A remarkable discrepancy emerged from the way in which women *20* saw themselves versus how they thought men wanted them to be. As noted earlier, results from the body shape rating scale indicated that most participants (regardless of body weight) believed that men preferred a very thin body type. However, focus group data revealed an overall belief that Latino men like curvier types. In fact, most participants noted that Latino men like women "who have shape" and "curves" rather than thin ones.

One participant even explained that men's disparate preferences would lead her to change her body weight and shape accordingly:

> Participant, group 5: We control ourselves to look better for them [men]. I think. I'll just say quickly that I'm small and I get more attention from White men and if I'm thicker I get more attention from Latino darker men. So it's like . . . Well, do I want to be with a White man now or do I want to be with a Latino? When I stopped growing, and I stopped growing at 5′4″, I reached 181 pounds and I was much, much thicker and it was like: Oh! The guys used to love it! I mean the Latino darker males. I have dated Asian males, but I find that the White males like me to be small and I seem to attract more [of them] if I'm really skinny. I do find a difference in the way I'm treated and it's like with whoever I end up with, I have to kind of think: "Okay, how do they need me and what they're attracted to, and how can I perpetuate that?" So, if I met you in a much heavier state and you seemed to like that, then I try to be that for you. . . .

Alternative body ideals also emerged when participants reflected 21 upon mainstream media images vis-à-vis different body types being more acceptable in their cultures of origin. Participants marked a clear distinction between Caucasian/White body types and the Latina body shape, graphically symbolized by the "apple" White figure versus the "pear-shaped" Latina type:

> Participant 1, group 6: Another thing that's different from Caucasians. I think Latinas, yes, they eat a lot of things but they're more flexible with their curves. You can be thin but there needs to be curves there. But I think Caucasians like Kate Moss, which is like a thin rail, and it's straight . . . And my friends . . . they don't want to look like that. They don't want to look like a supermodel with no curves.
>
> Moderator, group 6: As Hispanic women the norm is what?
>
> Participant 3: Curves. A pear-shaped woman. Yeah, it's funny because I was with a friend of mine and she was getting her wedding dress put on, and me and another one were looking at this woman, Caucasian. She looked so good in her dress because she had curves, and me and my friend were commenting on it. She couldn't hear us but the first thing she complained about was: "Oh my God: look at these hips!" And me and my friend told her: "Are you kidding me? We were just talking about how good you look in that dress because you have hips." I think for us, it's to our advantage. It's like curves are a good thing. Like it's not necessarily a horror.

Indeed, and despite of the acceptance of the "thin norm," participants 22 acknowledged the increasing recognition of alternative body types, including the pear-shaped type:

> Participant 4, group 2: You know I have friends who are Latina, I have friends who are White . . . but when it comes to my Latina friends, you know: Yeah! They have curves! And she's like: Yes, I'm shapely . . . When it comes to my friends that are White, they are always trying to hide certain things when they go to clubs, and they don't dance. At least that's what comes to the way they use their body, this is what I've seen. . . .

Participant 1, group 3: And you must have all heard about the Dove program, how the Dove commercials [show] about true beauty. And it says basically like: What's beautiful for you is not beautiful for me. You know, and it's all about kind of like self-image and stuff. I actually have the privilege to meet with them and to talk to them about it, because I was planning this thing for them to come to the school to talk to girls and to talk to guys.

Discussion: Narrowing the Gap between Contradictory Findings

Among study participants, contradictory body images seem to be alive as well. While most reflected on the general pressure they feel to stay thin, they also contested this norm by pointing out Latinas' preferences for curvier types. And although participants acknowledged the pervasive influence of mainstream ideas that privilege slim and thin types, they also challenged those paradigms by subscribing to curvier body types and by opposing the idea that one-size-fits-all. These results draw attention to the "double-edge" that many Latina women must deal with, as they endure a conventional culture that privileges excessive thinness vis-à-vis alternative messages that promote full-rounded bodies. These results concord with the conflicting findings reported by the literature reviewed earlier. Indeed, although participants showed discordance with their actual body shape compared to what they would like to be, they supported counter paradigms more permissive of fuller body types [20, 44]. 23

Against simplified bicultural notions that place Latinas amidst two opposed cultural domains (mainstream American norms versus the culture of origin), our research has underscored a more comprehensive picture. On the one hand, mainstream Latina images comply with an Anglo type of beauty; while on the other, subaltern cultural streams are channeled via voluptuous icons more in tune with *real* women in *real life*. We argue that these contradictions are a reflection of overlapping social and cultural constructs that pervade Latina ideals in society. These results are also consistent with growing research that shows that alternative media messages portray a broader span of Latinas' images including fuller bodies and larger sizes [7, 40]. Our findings also accord with a large body of literature that points out the power of western values, and particularly the media, in setting unrealistic slender standards leading to body dissatisfaction [8, 45]. Among Latinas/os, cultural frameworks that associate being healthy with having a curvy shape appear to be dissonant with a media culture obsessed with images of abnormal thin models [24, 46]. 24

Nevertheless, our findings do not explain to what extent the conflicting body paradigms presented above influence women to either lose or gain weight. As noted earlier, the mainstream command to stay thin could actually be counter-effective in helping women to keep a normal weight by setting impossible standards. At the same time, the cultural 25 acceptance of curvicr body types could help encourage (and justify) women's overweight and obesity trends. Cultural factors that may protect some groups may become a risk factor for others, as it has been found among African Americans whose positive body image correlate with high obesity prevalence [18]. In other words, being curvy is not necessarily synonymous with being healthy. In one of our participant's words: "I think what we Latinas don't realize is that you can be curvy and thick and full versus just being curvy because you are overweight or gaining weight" (participant 1, group 6).

In sum, being curvy but not fat may be a path for some, but the fine   26
line between the two is not easily drawn either by those who carefully study this tension or by the women who experience it. And, although there is no conclusive evidence on the mechanisms through which media images influence women's body satisfaction and eating behaviors, studies consistently report a strong correlation between the two [8, 47]. Finally, and despite the fact that mainstream media have steadily become more inclusive of Latinas and Latinos, these remain the most underrepresented segment in non-Spanish language mass media and the most underrepresented population among major minority groups in the U.S. magazine advertisement [7, 48].

Conclusions and Future Steps: Beyond Body Paradoxes

The findings presented here provide firsthand glimpses into Latinas' beliefs   27
regarding body image, including differences between what is considered expected and possible. As revealed by the quantitative data, all participants reported a preference for thinner body types than what they actually considered themselves to be. Although overweight and obese women were more lenient toward bigger body types, all women were conspicuously aware of the mainstream American norm that privilege thinner body types as the predicament to which women should subscribe. Nevertheless, our qualitative analysis also shows that participants acknowledged the acceptance of heavier and curvier body types, in accordance with Latino/a paradigms that are more in tune with fuller shapes. These results also suggest how different (and even contradictory) body ideals can coexist among Latinas. In the end, our coining of the term LAPABI has turned into a working hypothesis that will be the focus of future research and testing.

Still, what we know about the relationship between body image and   28
body satisfaction among Latinas is far from conclusive. Further quantitative and in-depth qualitative work should focus on the multiplicity of Latinas' experiences in the United States, while including multidimensional frameworks to encompass the role of race/ethnicity, class and social status, national origin, migratory histories (first and second generation), and

sexual orientation. Conspicuously, although the social sciences and health literature have consistently reported a relationship between social class (SES) and body type [49], most studies overlook SES as a determinant of intra- and interracial and ethnic differences. Unless differences in SES are taken into account, research cannot conclude that disparities in body-size preferences are solely based on ethnic differences [2, 9]. More work is also needed on the cultural protective factors against distorted body images and eating disorders, including media messages tailored to diverse racial/ethnic groups [11].

Health messages should challenge a uniform model of womanhood, 29 which may have a negative impact on Latinas' efforts to control weight. The promotion of more realistic body types that are in tune with women's differences may be more effective in targeting Latinas in the United States. To be a woman, and to become one, has different connotations among women in the United States. The film that opened this article, *Real Women Have Curves*, reminds us that between fiction and reality, and between what is desirable and possible, there are many different Latinas for whom subjective notions of personal beauty are drawn from multiple cultural commands, leading them to challenge their own boundaries and dare to go where no other women have gone before.

REFERENCES

1. Lewis, JA. Film. Magazine Americana, www.americanpopular. culture.com/archive/film/young_latinas.htm; 2005.
2. Cachelin FM, Rebeck RM, Chung GH, Pelayo E. Does ethnicity influence body-size preference? A comparison of body image and body size. Obes Res. 2002;10(3): 158–66. doi:10.1038/oby. 2002.25.
3. Ogden CL, Carroll MD, Curtin LR, McDowell MA, Tabak CJ, Flegal KM. Prevalence of Overweight and Obesity in the United States, 1999–2004. J Amer Med Assoc. 2006;295(13):1549–55. doi:10.1001/jama.295.13.1549.
4. Wang Y, Beydoun MA. The obesity epidemic in the United States—gender, age, socioeconomic, racial/ethnic, and geographic characteristics: a systematic review and meta-regression analysis. Epidemiol Rev. 2007;29:6–28. doi:10.1093/epirev/mxm007.
5. Shai I, Jiang R, Manson JE, Stampfer MJ, Willett WC, Colditz GA. Ethnicity, obesity, and risk of type 2 diabetes in women: a 20-year follow-up study. Diab Care. 2006;29(7):1585–90. doi: 10.2337/dc06-0057.
6. Stein CJ, Colditz GA. The epidemic of obesity. J Clin Endocrinol Metab. 2004;89(6):2522–5. doi:10.1210/jc.2004-0288.
7. Pompper D, Koenig J. Cross-cultural-generational perceptions of ideal body image: Hispanic women and magazine standards. J Mass Commun Quart. 2004;1:89–107.
8. Grogan S. Body image and health. J Health Psychol. 2006;11(4):523–30. doi: 10.1177/1359105306065013.
9. de Casanova EM. No ugly women. Gend Soc. 2004;18(3):287–308. doi:10.1177/0891243204263351.
10. Sussman NM, Truong N, Lim J. Who experiences "America the beautiful": ethnicity moderating the effect of acculturation on body image and risks for eating disorders among immigrant women. Intl J Intercult Relat. 2007;31(1):29–49. doi:10.1016/j.ijintrel.2006.03.003.

11. Warren CS, Gleaves D, Cepeda-Benito A, Fernandez M, Rodriguez-Ruiz S. Ethnicity as a protective factor against internalization of a thin ideal and body dissatisfaction. Intl J Eat Disord. 2005;35(3):241–9. doi:10.1002/eat.20102.

12. Anderson LA, Eyler AA, Galuska DA, Brown DR, Brownson RC. Relationship of satisfaction with body size and trying to lose weight in a national survey of overweight and obese women aged 40 and older, United States. Prev Med. 2002;35(4):390–6. doi: 10.1006/pmed.2002.1079.

13. Paeratakul S, White MA, Williamson DA, Ryan DH, Bray GA. Sex, race/ethnicity, socioeconomic status, and BMI in relation to self-perception of overweight Obes Res. 2002;10:345–50. doi: 10.1038/oby.2002.48.

14. Mintz LB, O'Halloran MS. The eating attitudes test: validation with DSM-IV eating disorder criteria. J Pers Assess. 2000;74:489–504. doi: 10.1207/S15327752JPA7403_11.

15. Henriques GR, Calhoun LG. Gender and ethnic differences in the relationship between body esteem and self-esteem. J Psychol. 1999;133(4):357.

16. Stice E. Review of the evidence for a sociocultural model of bulimia nervosa and an exploration of the mechanisms of action. Clin Psychol Rev. 1994;14:633–61. doi: 10.1016/0272-7358(94) 90002-7.

17. Sánchez-Johnsen LAP, Fitzgibbon ML, Martinovich Z, Stolley MR, Dyer AR, Van Horn L. Ethnic differences in correlates of obesity between Latin-American and Black women. Obesity Res. 2004;12:652–60. doi: 10.1038/oby.2004.75.

18. Lovejoy M. Disturbances in the social body. Differences in body image and eating problems among African American and White women. Gcnd Soc. 2001;15(2):239–61. doi: 10.1177/08912430 1015002005.

19. Gilbert SC. Eating disorders in women of color. Clin Psychol Sci Pract. 2003; 10(4):444–55. doi:10.1093/clipsy/bpg045.

20. Poran MA. Denying diversity: perceptions of beauty and social comparison processes among Latina, Black, and White women. Sex Role. 2004;47(1–2):65–81.

21. Baca Zinn M. Family, feminism, and race in America. Gend Soc. 1990;4(l):68–82. doi:10.1177/089124390004001006.

22. Hrabosky JI, Grilo CM. Body image and eating disordered behavior in a community sample of Black and Hispanic women. Eat Behav. 2006;8:106–14. doi:10.I016/j.eatbeh.2006.02.005.

23. Yanovski SZ. Eating disorders, race, and mythology. Arch Fam Med. 2000;9(1):88. doi:10.1001/archfami.9.1.88.

24. Root MP. Disordered eating in women of color. Sex Role. l990;22(7–8):525–36. doi:10.1007/BF00288168.

25. Smith JE, Krejci J. Minorities join the majority: eating disturbances among Hispanic and Native American Youth. Intl J Eat Disord. 1991;10(2):179–86. doi: 10.1002/1098-108X(199103)10:2<179:: AID-EAT2260100206>3.0.CO;2-S.

26. Schooler D, Ward LM, Merriwether A, Caruthers A. Who's that girl: television' role in the body image development of young White and Black women. Psychol Women Quart. 2004;28(1):38–47. doi:10.1111/j.l471-6402.2004.00121.x.

27. Molinary R. Beauty, body image and growing up Latina. Emeryville, CA: Seal Press; 2007.

28. Perez M, Voelz ZR, Pettit JW, Joiner TE Jr. The role of acculturative stress and body dissatisfaction in predicting bulimic symptomatology across ethnic groups. Intl J Eat Disord, 2002;4:442–54. doi:10.1002/eat.l0006.

29. Bay-Cheng LY, Zucker AN, Stewart AJ, Pomerleau CS. Linking femininity, weight concern, and mental health among Latina, Black and While women. Psychol Women Quart. 2002;26(1):36–45. doi:10.1111/1471-6402.00041.

30. de Casanova EM. Women's magazines in Ecuador: re-reading "la chica cosmo". Stud Latin Am Pop Cult. 2002;22:89–102.

31. Hyams M. Adolescent Latina bodyspaces: making homegirls, homebodies and homeplaces. Antipode. 2003;35(3):536–58. doi: 10.1111/1467-8330.00338.

32. Fitzgibbon ML, Blackman LR, Avellone ME. The relationship between body image discrepancy and body mass index across ethnic groups. Obes Res. 2000;8(8):582–9. doi: 10.1038/oby.2000.75.

33. Roberts A, Cash TF, Feingold A, Johnson BT. Are black-white differences in females' body dissatisfaction decreasing? A meta-analytic review. J Consult Clin Psychol. 2006;74(6):1121–31. doi: 10.1037/0022-006X.74.6.1121.

34. Altabe M. Ethnicity and body Image: quantitative and qualitative Analysis. The International Journal of Eating Disorders. 1998; (23):153–159. doi:10.1002/(SICI)1098-108X(199803)23:2<153:: AID-EAT5>3.0.CO;2-J.

35. Schooler D. Real women have curves. J Adolesc Res. 2008;23(2):132–53. doi: 10.1177/0743558407310712.

36. Austin JL, Smith JL. Thin ideal internalization in Mexican girls: A test of the sociocultural model of eating disorders. Intl J Eat Disord. 2008;5:448–57. doi:10.1002/eat.20529.

37. Jane DM, Hunter GC, Lozzi BM. Do Cuban American women suffer from eating disorders? Effects of media exposure and acculturation. Hispanic J Behav Sci. 1999;21(2):212–18. doi: 10.1177/0739986399212007.

38. Seo D, Torabi MR. Racial/ethnic differences in body mass index, morbidity and attitudes toward obesity among U.S. adults. J Natl Med Assoc. 2006;08(98):1300–8.

39. Hebl MR, King EB, Lin J. The swimsuit becomes us all: ethnicity, gender, and vulnerability to self-objectification. Personal Soc Psychol Bull. 2004;30(10):1322–31. doi: 10.1177/0146167 204264052.

40. Goodman JR. Flabless is fabulous: How Latina and Anglo women read and incorporate the excessively thin body ideal into everyday experience. J Mass Commun Quart. 2002;79(3):712–27.

41. Franco DL, Herrera I. Body image differences in Guatemalan-American and While college women. Eat Disord. 1993;5(2):119–27. doi: 10.1080/10640269708249215.

42. Chamorro R, Florez-Ortiz Y. Acculturation and disordered eating patterns among Mexican American women. Intl J Eat Disord. 2000;28:125–9. doi:10.1002/(SICI)1098-108X(200007)28:l<125:: AJD-EAT16>3.0.CO;2-9.

43. Beltrán Ma. The Hollywood Latina body as site of social Struggle: media constructions of stardom and Jennifer Lopez's "cross-over butt". Quart Rev Film Video. 2002;19(l):71–86. doi: 10.1080/10509200214823.

44. Diaz VA, Mainous AG, Pope C. Cultural conflicts in the weight loss experience of overweight Latinos. Intl J Obes. 2007;31:328–33. doi:10.1038/sj.ijo.0803387.

45. Spurgas AK. Body image and cultural background. Sociol Inquiry. 2005;75(3):297–316. doi: 10.111 1/j.1475-682X.2005.00124.X.

46. Andrist LC. Media images, body dissatisfaction, and disordered eating in adolescent women. *MCN.* Am J Mater Child Nurs. 2003;28(2): 119–23. doi: 10.1097/00005721-200303000-00014.

47. Thompson JK, Heinberg LJ, Altabe M, Tantleff-Dunn S. Exacting beauty: theory, assessment, and treatment of body image disturbance. Washington, DC: American Psychological Association; 1999.

48. Taylor CR, Bang H. Portrayals of Latinos in magazine advertising. J Mass Commun Quart. 1997;74(2):285–303.

49. Bourdieu P. Distinction: a social critique of the judgement of taste. Cambridge: Harvard University Press; 1984.

■ ■ ■

Reading as a Writer: Analyzing Rhetorical Choices

1. What effects do the authors achieve by opening and closing with references to the movie *Real Women Have Curves*? What other films or media
   examples can you think of that would illustrate some of the claims in this
   essay?

2. Working in pairs or groups, explain aloud exactly what the authors mean
   by "mixed method data collection." Review the sections of the essay where
   the authors present and analyze their data, and discuss the examples you
   find most effective for understanding the authors' argument. As a reader,
   do you respond more to numbers, language—or both? Why?

Writing as a Reader: Entering the Conversation of Ideas

1. This reading considers the often-contradictory effects of stereotypes on
   people. How might Mahzarin R. Banaji and Anthony G. Greenwald's ideas
   about how and why we use stereotypes shed light on the experiences of
   the Latinas in this study? Compose an essay in which you consider theories in each reading in relation to the experiences depicted and draw some
   conclusions about effective ways to understand and counter the negative
   effects of stereotyping.

2. These authors' examination of "contradictory body ideals" (para. 7) faced
   by the Latinas is interesting to consider in light of Jean Kilbourne's ideas
   (Chapter 13) about the mass media's images of women. How do these
   readings complement and extend one another? Write an essay that draws
   on these readings (and their specific examples) in order to make an argument about the significance of the ways women's bodies are depicted in the
   U.S. mass media. How do these authors explain what is at stake in these
   images, and for whom? What solutions do they—and you—recommend?

WILLIAM J. PEACE

Slippery Slopes: Media, Disability, and Adaptive Sports

William J. Peace is a multidisciplinary teacher and scholar who writes
from an anthropological and sociological perspective about attitudes
toward bodies, body modification, and disabilities. Besides his scholarly publications, he writes the provocatively titled blog *Bad Cripple*
(badcripple.blogspot.com), and is working on the memoir *Bad Cripple: A
Protest from an Invisible Man*. This essay examines the effects of the very
narrow media depictions of disability as something to be miraculously
and inspirationally "overcome," with very real consequences: "The negative portrayal of disabled people is not only oppressive but also affirms
that nondisabled people set the terms of the debate about the meaning of
disability" (para. 1). There are a growing number of scholars working in
the field of disability studies, and Peace's often-critical voice is well-known
in this conversation.

Peace claims, "Disabled people have embraced a social model of disability that is based on the belief that disability is a social malady" (para. 3). What do you think this means? As you read, think about your own understanding of "disabilities," and test those ideas against Peace's argument that disability is "a social construct." At the end of paragraph 4, he explains his research methods and overall argument; this is a paragraph to return to after you read the essay. How does he support and explain the claims he sets out here?

In his first subsection, "A Primer on Disability Activism and Disabled Bodies," Peace offers readers a quick background on the history of disability studies. As you learn about the history of this movement, which parallels many other civil rights movements, consider his claims about the challenges of defining the "disabled." Why does such a definition matter, when it comes to the law? How does his call for a more "nuanced" view of disability (paras. 12–15) advance the overall argument in this essay?

Peace's extended example of adaptive sports—particularly his own experiences with adaptive skiing—helps illustrate the challenges and possibilities of thinking about disability in new ways. He concludes with a call to action that critiques many scholars in disability studies: "These efforts are critical but contain one flaw I cannot overlook: Disability studies scholars have not done enough to empower the people they study" (para. 27). What actions is he calling for, and why? His challenge to engage in "action-oriented scholarship and activism" is a challenge for all of us as we consider what we will *do* with what we learn. How will you—and your classmates—respond?

The history and scholarship of mass media have conspicuously ignored the images commonly associated with disability in American society. This is unfortunate because the media is complicit in distorting the cultural perception of disability (Riley 2005). For decades disabled Americans have grown increasingly appalled, offended, and angry about the way they have been exploited by the media. Dominant images associated with disability are largely negative. Stereotypical portrayals of disability abound, as do feel-good stories. Here I refer to archetypical ninety-second television news segments or 500-word stories in national newspapers that focus on the "remarkable," "heart warming" tale of a disabled person. Disabled athletes in this regard provide the media with endless fodder and great visuals: The paralyzed person, blind person, or amputee who finishes a marathon or performs some other "miraculous" feat. What is celebrated is not the athletic or personal achievement but rather the ability of a disabled person to "overcome" a physical deficit; the more profound and visible the disability, the better the story. The negative portrayal of disabled people is not only oppressive but also affirms that nondisabled people set the terms of the debate about the meaning of disability.

The antiquated images of disability have resonated with the gen- 2
eral public and reinforced economic, political, and social oppression
experienced by disabled people. Thus the media has contributed to
and expanded the gulf between disabled and non-disabled people. This
divide and the inequities associated with disability are rarely discussed.
Thanks to the Internet, technological advances, laws such as the Americans with Disability Act (ADA), and rapidly aging Baby Boomers, disabled and non-disabled people are interacting more than at any other
time in American history. The interaction between those with and those
without a disability has led to conflict and misunderstanding. Disabled
people have rights, civil rights guaranteed by the ADA, and are not hesi-
tant to assert them.

Disabled people have embraced a social model of disability that is based 3
on the belief that disability is a social malady. The social model of disability
is at odds with what the average American has been taught about disability: That the primary problem disabled people have is a physical or cognitive impairment. In contrast, disability scholars assert that a bodily deficit
is used to justify the prejudice, discrimination, and oppression associated
with disability. Scholars in the humanities and social sciences such as Simi
Linton (1998, 2006), Paul Longmore (2003), Rosemarie Garland Thomson
(1997), and others have firmly established that disability is a social construct. Disability cannot be studied in isolation or on a case-by-case basis
because it is part of the social structure of American society. This theoretical
shift has had a seismic impact on the disability community and was spearheaded by innovative disability studies scholars. For those with disabilities,
the scholarship produced by the aforementioned scholars provided them
with a way of understanding disability that was empowering. For the first
time in American history, people with disabilities understood that the discrimination they encountered was not of their own making and began to
think of themselves as a single, united, and oppressed minority group.

The media and general public have yet to acknowledge the social 4
model of disability. Thus when disabled people such as myself embrace
the slogan "Disabled and Proud" and assert our civil rights, the average citizen does not know how to respond. The result is a culture clash,
disabled versus nondisabled, one that is being worked out in the media,
online, and in adaptive sport programs across the country. The sporting
arena is of particular interest because the presence of disabled people
is unexpected there. It is assumed that a physical or mental deficit precludes not just an interest in sports but the ability to participate. Concep-
tually, the disabled body from an athletic standpoint is devalued, as are
the lives of disabled people. It is assumed that disabled people should not
be skiing, kayaking, or playing a sport. Instead, they should be focused
on an all-out effort to "fix" their bodies and return to normal (Christopher Reeve's quest for a cure to spinal cord injury is a perfect example).
The fundamental dichotomy between disabled and nondisabled people

forms the core of this chapter. I will detail why adaptive athletic programs are important and how adaptive athletes undermine disability-based prejudice. My research is based on interviews I conducted with adaptive athletes, bloggers, and adaptive sport program co-coordinators in the northeastern United States between 2006 and 2008. I will also draw on my experience as a novice adaptive skier and kayaker.

A Primer on Disability Activism and Disabled Bodies

Disability studies is among the newest fields in American academia. In 5 my estimation, disability scholarship as it is known today began with the publication of the *Body Silent* by Robert Murphy in 1987. I consider this book the Magna Carta for all disabled people. While other scholars such as Irving Zola and Irving Goffman had studied disability for many years, Murphy was the first prestigious scholar based at an Ivy League institution to critically examine disability from a cultural perspective. Murphy did something in the *Body Silent* that no other person had done before: He bared his soul and body and evocatively convinced others that the main problem people with disabilities encounter is not their disability but the social consequences it generates. Given this new perspective, people with disabilities began to "demedicalize" their bodies and push for civil rights legislation while disability studies scholars published ground-breaking books like Nancy Mair's *Waist-High in the World* and Rosemarie Garland Thomson's *Extraordinary Bodies*. The central idea that would emerge from the incipient disability studies field was the belief in a social model of disability. This is the fundamental principle that created and has sustained the disability rights movement. The social model of disability is not complicated: In essence it holds that society disables people with physical and cognitive disabilities. Disability is something imposed on top of a physical impairment that is used to unnecessarily isolate and exclude disabled people from full participation in society.

The origins of disability studies can be found in the 1960s civil rights 6 movement, and the epicenter for disability rights was the San Francisco Bay Area. The efforts of one man, Edward Roberts, known as the "father of the independent movement," stand out. Roberts is remembered for his political prowess and razor-sharp wit. For example, after learning that his doctor had characterized him as a hopeless vegetable, he remarked that if he had to be a vegetable he wanted to be an artichoke—prickly on the outside but with a big heart inside, one that could call on all the other vegetables of the world to unite. Roberts helped lay the foundation for disability pride from which disability studies would emerge. The notion of disability pride is something that is hard for an able-bodied person to grasp. I know this, as do many other disabled people who have been told overtly and covertly that they are inherently defective and incompetent.

Family, friends, and strangers deliver this message as efficiently as a Federal Express package. Roberts was among the first generation of people with a disability to escape institutionalized life and embrace an identity tied to disability. In a letter Roberts sent to Gina Laurie he stated that he was "tired of well-meaning non cripples with their stereotypes of what I can and cannot do directing my life and future. I want cripples to direct their own programs and be able to train others cripples to direct new programs. This is the start of something big—cripple power" (Roberts circa 1970).

For people with disabilities, Roberts became a powerful symbol for all 7 that was wrong with America's perception of disability. He was the Jackie Robinson of the disability rights movement, the single individual around whom others could rally. Like Jackie Robinson, Roberts did not single-handedly end baseless discrimination. He was part of a much larger social movement that produced cataclysmic changes in terms of civil rights. Each civil rights movement was associated with tragic events or charismatic figures: Jerry Rubin was the face of the Students for Democratic Society and encouraged male college students to burn their draft cards. The women's movement burned bras, and Gloria Steinem founded *Ms. Magazine*. The Vietnam War is tied to Lyndon Johnson, the fall of Saigon, and the My Lai Massacre. Martin Luther King Jr. is remembered for his powerful speech "I Have a Dream" and tragic assassination.

What is absent from Americans' general understanding of civil rights 8 is a disability component. Disability rights as civil rights is not a connection people make. Disabled people are an invisible minority and are not considered to be a "distinct and insular minority group." In spite of the fact that I have not walked in over thirty years, I can readily understand why people do not connect disability rights and civil rights. Eighteen years ago the ADA was passed, and since that time the Supreme Court has muddied the meaning of disability in an effort to limit the scope of the law. The definition of disability contained in the ADA was broad by design and was the end product of a generation of lawmaking. The intent of the ADA was to protect the civil rights of all people who were perceived to be disabled. The legislative process to protect the rights of people with disabilities began in 1968 with the Architectural Barriers Act and concluded with the ADA. During this era, 1968 to 1990, fifty acts of Congress were passed designed to protect or enhance the rights of people with a disability (Longmore and Umansky 2001). In spite of all this legislation, the legal definition of disability has not changed since 1973 when it was included as Title V, part of the Rehabilitation Act that barred discrimination against disabled people in programs that receive funding from the federal government. As outlined in the Americans with Disability Act, an "individual with a disability is defined as someone who: (i) has a physical or mental impairment which substantially limits one or more of such person's major life activities, (ii) has a record of such an impairment, or (iii) is regarded as having such an impairment."[1]

Since the ADA was passed, the Supreme Court has used the definition   9
of disability as it relates to the phrases "substantial limitation," "major life
activity," and "regarded as" to narrow the number of people who are considered to be legally disabled. At a theoretical level I understand what the
Supreme Court is trying to do: Identify exactly who is disabled and entitled to protection under the law. However, creating a precise definition of
disability is exceptionally difficult and highlights that disability is a complex construct. There are a multitude of factors involved—social, political, economic, and legal—that make it difficult to identify what all people
with a disability have in common. There is a seemingly endless array of
disabling conditions and no agreement as to what disability means to this
wide cross-section of people. Until we can identify what it means to be disabled, people with disabilities will continue to struggle to defend their civil
rights. Thus the Supreme Court will continue to rule as it has and limit the
scope of the ADA because it perceives disability to be a medical or physical
deficit alone.

In utilizing a medical model of disability, the Supreme Court has   10
ignored the broader ramifications of disability. Here I refer to the fact that
disabled people are as a group uniformly poor, unemployed, and lacking a
basic education. This troika puts disabled people at a distinct disadvantage
before they exit their homes and bars too many from pursuing a rewarding
life. The result is that the Supreme Court has not only narrowed the scope
of the law but also splintered and butchered our understanding of what it
means to be disabled. This has led me to tease my friends that what medical science failed to do—cure my paralyzed body—the Supreme Court
did. In the court's view my disability is "mitigated" by the fact that I use a
wheelchair and all people whose impairments can be alleviated by medication, glasses, or other devices are generally not disabled and so do not
come under the protection of the ADA. In short, the Court determined that
disabled people are not a distinct and insular minority group. Thus people
who are paralyzed, deaf, blind, diabetic, or missing a limb have nothing in
common! This is hard for me to fathom.

Since the Supreme Court narrowed the definition of disability, I do   11
not consider the ADA a mandate that protects the civil rights of disabled
people. The ADA was about far more than ramps for wheelchair users,
braille for the blind, and closed captioning for the deaf. The ADA was
intended to protect anyone who experienced discrimination because he
or she had what was perceived to be a disability. According to Silvia Yee
of the Disability Rights Education and Defense Fund, the ADA was "built
on the conviction that disability prejudice is a fundamental force behind
the exclusion of people with disabilities from a myriad [sic] of social and
economic opportunities." In Yee's estimation there was no question that
disability prejudice existed and that the phenomenon was "not widely
understood or truly accepted among the political and social institutions
that are counted upon to put anti-discrimination laws into practice"
(Yee 2007).[2]

Adaptive Sports: Undermining Stigma Associated with the Disabled Body

Too many people fail to realize that the dichotomy between disabled and   *12*
able-bodied is a fallacy. Life is simply not that definitive. Under the law,
I am not disabled. I am a teacher, writer, father, and provider for my son
and have been since he was born. Provided I can enter a building or my
employer is willing to make a "reasonable accommodation," there is no
reason why I cannot work. My ability to work and care for myself is not
compromised by my physical deficit: Partial paralysis. Yet when I sit in
my wheelchair, a device that supposedly mitigates my disability, I remain
the symbolic representation of disability. I am regularly asked, "What happened to you?"—a question that assumes a significant flaw exists. The person asking this question is making a statement about my disability. He
or she is telling me that there is something inherently "wrong" with my
body. Such a person is also curious or, in some cases, fearful. The tacit
understanding is that I am not a fully functioning adult capable of living
independently. Even if capable, the only reason I can function "normally"
is that I am a remarkable person, one who puts all those other disabled
people to shame. All this is called into question when disabled people participate in adaptive sports. It is the only environment in which people with
a wide range of disabilities interact not only with one another but with
able-bodied people as well.

A nuanced view of disability too often requires personal experience   *13*
with disability. In part, this is why historian Paul K. Longmore (1995) has
argued that the first phase of disability activism centered on civil rights
while the second phase has been a quest for a collective identity. In this
regard, disability rights scholars have been particularly successful. A cur-
sory glance at the literature published in the last ten years reveals a bevy of
exceptionally well-written memoirs and theoretical analyses. For example,
Linton's *Claiming Disability* was the first comprehensive account in disability studies that provided the groundwork for terms and concepts in the
field and linked them with identity politics. Disability as a cultural identity
is well understood by disability studies scholars but has not as yet been
incorporated into the multicultural curriculum. Leonard Davis, an influential disability studies scholar, has noted that faculty members who mandate the inclusion of African American, Latino, and Asian American texts
and novels do not support the inclusion of works about disability (Davis
2002). In contrast, people outside of academia have embraced this literature and disability culture. Disability culture is created by people with disabilities and is based upon the disability experience. Carol Gill, a disability
rights activist, has written that disability culture involves "the pleasure we
take in our own community," maintaining that "the assertion of disability
pride and the celebration of our culture are a massive assault on ablecen-
tric thinking. It also really rocks people when we so clearly reject the superiority of nondisability" (Gill 1995:98).

I contend that the divide between disabled and nondisabled people is   *14*
innately tied to the body and individual difference. According to Bérubé,
disability "is a category whose constituency is contingency itself" (Bérubé
1998:x). For disabled people it is obvious why nondisabled people resist
thinking about disability: The fear of disability itself. It is equally obvious
why this fear must be overcome: Nondisabled people perceive disability
as inherently negative. Corporal variation is perceived to be deviant; there
is a divide between normal and abnormal, disabled and nondisabled. Disabled people know a different reality, one in which "there's no line dividing
us. There are shades of ability, varying talents that surface in surprising
places. This is true for physical and cognitive disabilities. Most of us, in the
course of our lives, discover we have abilities or affinities for some things
and lack talent elsewhere, so this idea that a certain class of people lack
value or ability to contribute inevitably underestimates and wastes human
potential" (Olson 2007).

Like many disabled people, I embrace an identity that is tied to my   *15*
body. I have been made to feel different, inferior, since I began using a
wheelchair thirty years ago and by claiming that I am disabled and proud,
I am empowered. A skeptic at heart, I have always craved tangible proof
that disability rights have advanced. In part this is why I am critical of disability studies. How can disability rights scholars determine whether progress has been made? The proof I sought became evident two years ago on a
ski trip to Vermont. My son had never skied and I had not seen an adaptive
sit ski since I was in college. In the late 1970s one adaptive sport, wheelchair basketball, was dominant (I was on my college team) Modern sit
skis do not resemble the model I saw in college, and I will never forget the
first time I skied in 2006. I had no conception that a veritable technological revolution had taken place. As I looked around I saw an overcrowded
room filled with people. Near me I saw people with a host of physical disabilities: amputees, people with cerebral palsy, the blind, and paralyzed
people. I also saw many people with cognitive disabilities such as autism,
Down Syndrome, and a host of behavioral disorders. Adaptive skiing had
come of age, and it was clear that any person who desired could ski.

Adaptive skiing involves the use of specialized equipment that is as   *16*
diverse as disability itself. Broadly, adaptive skiing can be broken down
into basic groups. Two-trackers are adaptive skiers who use archetypical
equipment, stiff plastic boots, and two skis along with ski poles. An adaptive skier who can ski in this manner usually has a cognitive impairment
such as autism or Down Syndrome. Other two-trackers include visually
impaired skiers. Sometimes these skiers wear a bright orange bib that
identifies them as "Blind Skier" and they ski with a person whose identical
bib identifies him or her as "Blind Guide." The blind skiers I have observed
wore this type of bib and skied with a sighted skier who guided them as
they skied. Three-tracker adaptive skiers usually have one leg. These skiers ski on one leg and instead of traditional ski poles use poles that have
an outrigger or small ski attached to the bottom. The outriggers are used

to control speed and direction. They are also used to brake. Four-tracker adaptive skiers ski on two skis and carry two outriggers. A person who has cerebral palsy or walks with a cane or uses crutches is often a four-tracker.

Mono-skiers are the elite of adaptive skiers, and the rigs they use are 17 akin to Ferraris. Prominent mono-skiers such as Kevin Bramble are on the cutting edge of technology in the ski industry and not only participate in the Paralympic Games but also appear in Warren Miller ski films and the popular X-Games broadcast on ESPN. A typical mono-skier is para-lyzed in his or her lower extremities, has good torso control, and possesses excellent upper body strength. If the reader has ever seen a seated adap-tive skier whiz by, the skier is probably using a mono-ski. A similar device, a bi-ski, exists for those adaptive skiers who cannot master a mono-ski. However, the prestige factor among adaptive athletes is greatly reduced when one uses a bi-ski. The bi-ski is like a mono-ski but has a lower center of gravity and two specially made skis making it easier to master because the two skis actuate independently and the skier is much closer to the ground.

The above clinical description does not convey the effort and knowl- 18 edge needed to ski. It also does not convey the fear I felt when I skied the first time. Skilled volunteers determined the correct rig for a novice such as myself to use. Selecting the appropriate rig is the most important deci-sion an adaptive skier makes. My first season skiing I used a mono-ski. To mono-ski one sits in a small plastic bucket seat that is connected to a single ski with a basic suspension system. To balance and turn one uses two outriggers. What I did not anticipate was exactly how tightly I had to be strapped into the bucket. My body was strapped into the bucket tighter than one's feet in ski boots. The volunteers kept telling me a tight fit was required and the key to success. They also joked that there is no such thing as too tight. I simply tried to focus on being able to breathe. The entire process of getting into the bucket, selecting outriggers, and getting ready takes about an hour for a novice. As I headed outside with two volunteers in tow I was extremely nervous. Having two experienced people at my side helped, but those first few trips up the ski lift and down the slopes were nerve-wracking experiences. By the end of the first season of skiing, I was not only able to enjoy myself but also became aware of what was going on around me. I also learned that I enjoy skiing for many reasons. First, the view from the top of the ski lift was a sight to behold, especially early in the morning. Second, skiing was a physical challenge I could share with my son. It also helped that we each like to go very fast. Third, I liked to socialize with skiers, who struck me as open-minded free spirits. My pres-ence was readily accepted and I felt as though I was an ordinary, nondis-abled person. Finally, the bar was packed and the people who helped me ski drank high-quality micro-brewed ale.

Between 2006 and 2008 I skied at least once a month and talked 19 to adaptive skiers and all those affiliated with the adaptive ski pro-grams I participated in. I learned that adaptive sports in general and adaptive skiers in particular were important because they shed light on the dichotomy between the way people who can and cannot walk perceive disability. Among paralyzed people such as myself, a wheelchair and mono-ski are alternate forms of locomotion. Depending upon the environmental setting, they can be a superior or inferior means of movement. At heart a wheelchair and mono-ski are culturally constructed technological devices that empower the human body. As such they affirm how remarkably adaptable the body is. A wheelchair or mono-ski is a type of human adaptation, a process that was recognized by Charles Darwin and tied to disability by Kenny Fries in his memoir *The History of My Shoes* (Fries 2007). Fries wrote about two interconnected stories, one that concerned Darwin and the other about his struggle to understand the meaning of disability. While this may seem to be a tenuous connection, bodily fitness and disability are directly related. The human body is continuously evolving via variation and adaptation, but it is society that determines how a given variation is perceived. In the case of the disabled body, all adaptive athletes know there are advantages to their physical deficit. For instance, Fries found that his shoes, leg braces, and abnormal gate made him a better mountain climber than an able-bodied person. Likewise, when skiing I use the muscle spasms in my torso caused by bumpy terrain to my advantage in terms of balancing on the edges of my skis.

A great deal of stigma is associated with a wheelchair, which can be characterized as a portable social isolation unit (Murphy 1980). In my experience, when I get out of my wheelchair and am active athletically, this diminishes the stigma and isolation associated with disability. The adaptive sport a person with a disability participates in is not as important as the physical activity itself. This is why many disabled people such as myself are drawn to adaptive sports. Physically departing their wheelchair negates negative stereotypes associated with disability. For example, one man told me, 20

> The minute people see a wheelchair they think of all the things that cannot be done. They consider my life a quasi tragedy. The younger and more physically fit the person using a wheelchair is the worse that person's life is thought to be. If you are a guy, they think you can't have sex or push a chair on anything other than a sidewalk. People assume I live in a nursing home. If you are a disabled woman then you cannot give birth or raise a child. This skewed viewpoint is really hard to overcome—people are conditioned and raised to think this way. There is a fundamental philosophical difference between those that walk and those that do not. I see my wheelchair as a powerful means of freedom while those that can walk see it as horrible, a fate worse than death. In some ways this is why I like to get out of my wheelchair as much as possible. I bike, kayak, sail, and ski. When you are doing a sport regardless of what it is, people see you as capable, you do not need to be a Paralympian. When active I am transformed from being thought of as a pathetic human in a wheelchair whose life sucks into an average person. (interview with a disabled male, age thirty-two)

For disabled men and women who have come of age in the post-ADA   *21*
world, there is growing frustration and anger about the law, specifically
the gap between what the ADA is supposed to do and the reality they experience. Many ski lodges I have been to are grossly inaccessible. They have
met the letter of the law; specifically, they have made "reasonable accommodations." However, these accommodations do not mean that ski resorts
seek to be truly inclusive. Discrimination, though increasingly uncommon, exists in part because the bodily image associated with skiing does
not include the presence of disabled people. All ski resorts have a clientele
and an image they project to draw customers. Thus even at resorts where
adaptive skiers abound, corporations do not place great value on adaptive
ski programs. The severely limited number of employees hired to coordinate adaptive programs evidences this. The ski resorts I have been to in
New England are reliant upon well-trained, poorly paid, and overwhelmed
employees. They are also dependent upon a large staff of volunteers. The
adaptive programs I have skied at usually have a staff of less than three
or four full-time employees. The archetypical person who coordinates an
adaptive ski program is a recent college graduate. Stress, long hours, and
substandard pay insure that most adaptive program coordinators do not
work for more than a few ski seasons.

The adaptive skiers I have met are a dedicated group who love the   *22*
physical and social dimension of the sport. It is one of the few activities
that disabled people participate in that permits social networking. Thus it
should be no surprise that adaptive sports and athletic competitions have
played a major role in the disability rights community. Some of the largest
disability-related organizations in this country and abroad can trace their
origins to adaptive sport. In adaptive sports, the Paralympic movement is
easily the largest international competition for people with physical disabilities. Other well-known programs include the Wounded Warrior Project, Disabled Sports USA, Adaptive Sports Association, Special Olympics,
and the American Association of Adaptive Sport Programs, to mention but
a few prominent groups.

Among accomplished adaptive skiers, adult men and women between   *23*
twenty and twenty-five years old, ski resorts are a safe haven, a place to
let loose and not only be among their peers but also develop personal and
professional relationships. One young man told me,

> Skiing is the one place where I am not looked at with pity or scorn by other peo-
> ple, especially by older people who just don't get how or even why a paralyzed
> person would want to ski. What, I wonder, do they expect me to do? Sit at home
> with a lap blanket? When I am out skiing with friends I am just another guy out
> on the slopes. I just happen to be using a mono-ski. I have even been asked by
> nondisabled people if they can rent sit skis. No idiots ask, "What happened to
> you?" which is rude and pisses me off. No one asks a person who can walk this
> sort of question. Imagine if I asked someone why they were fat or if I went up
> to a woman and asked her why she had small breasts or a big ass. The best part
> of skiing is that a lot of people, snowboarders for example, know mono-skiers

can really rip it up. I don't like the attitude of snowboarders and hate it when they stop and sit down in the middle of a slope, but to these guys I am cool. The X Games helped a lot in this regard as does the fact a lot of skiers dislike snow-boarders. The thing is that when I ski I feel equal to others. I can't tell you how many times I have people yell at me "go for it dude" and I am dumb enough to try and show off. We are all just having fun and I am just another dude sharing the same space. (interview, male, twenty-one)

When I skied I noted that many married couples participated in   24 adaptive programs. The couples I spoke with all felt at ease, that is, their relationship was accepted. For those married or involved in an intimate relationship with a disabled person, such a union is subject to intense pub-lic examination. In my experience, it is common for nondisabled people to question why an able-bodied person would consider having a relationship with someone who has an obvious physical deficit. Friends and strang-ers alike will ask couples intrusive questions that are rude. For example, every nondisabled woman I have been intimately involved with has told me that the first question female friends ask about the relationship is, "Can he have sex?" Apparently the fact that I have a son is not adequate proof of my reproductive ability. Such inappropriate questions place a nondisabled and disabled couple at a distinct disadvantage in that mixed couples are public property, their physical and personal relationship open to scrutiny. Those couples that do not have a disability are exempt from comparable inquiries. One woman who was married to a paralyzed spouse told me,

I love to see my husband play sports. I feel as though we have a mixed mar-riage—he is paralyzed and I am not. By mixed marriage I think what we expe-rience is like what a married black man and white woman went through in the 1950s—that sort of thing was just not socially acceptable. I hate it when people give me that look of pity or want to put a halo over my head for being married to a man in wheelchair. My husband uses a wheelchair, he is not in wheelchair. To me, there is a big difference. I lose no matter what—if I get flowers it is not an ordinary event but as though I deserve them 'cause I am married to a disabled guy. The funny thing to me is that I am not into sports at all. He is a much better skier than I am. He has been skiing for ten years and I finally relented and am learning how to snow board. At the end of the day I am so sore I can barely walk while he is zooming by at a million miles an hour. When people see this, that they know he is a far more skilled athlete, can go on a double diamond while I am still on a bunny hill and holding onto a rope tow as though my life depended upon it makes others think. (interview with female, midtwenties)

The mission statement for most adaptive ski programs focuses on   25 quality-of-life issues and empowerment. For example, New England Disabled Sports at Loon Mountain in Lincoln, New Hampshire, aims to enhance the quality of life of individuals with disabilities through outdoor education. It is believed that participation in outdoor activities in a support-ive, boundary-free environment will endow participants with the opportu-nity to conquer physical challenges that enable them to build self-esteem and confidence. I appreciate the sentiments expressed but know that adaptive skiing is well beyond the economic means of many disabled people. The cost of a mono-ski is prohibitive for many. There are a small number of companies that manufacture adaptive ski equipment. For example, a basic entry-level mono-ski made by Freedom Factory costs $2,600, and two outriggers cost $375. A mono-ski used by a skilled adaptive skier who races can double or triple this amount and often exceeds $5,000. For those who cannot afford to own their own adaptive equipment, all programs rent specialized equipment. Every adaptive program I have participated in has a sliding pay scale and does its best to be inclusive. The cost of adaptive equipment also limits many programs that have tight budgets. The ski season in New England is short, unpredictable, and with the price of gas and lodging, an expensive proposition. Adaptive programs in New England charge disabled skiers between $75 and $110 a day to ski. On average I estimate a weekend of skiing for a disabled person would cost about $500 (this includes gas, an inexpensive motel, food, and ski equipment rental). Adaptive skiing in western states such as Colorado, Utah, and Wyoming is twice as expensive as in New England and restricted to elite skiers.

In spite of the cost, the number of disabled people participating in   26 adaptive sports has increased significantly in the last decade. Although no federal laws such as Title IX, which has helped female athletes, exist, disabled people who cannot afford to ski can find other easily adaptable sports such as kayaking. Disabled kayakers such as myself can afford not only to purchase a reasonably good kayak but also to inexpensively modify it with dry cell foam and duct tape that costs no more than $50. For instance, my kayak cost $500, and required ancillary equipment such as a life vest, paddle, and roof rack brought the total up to about $1,000. This amount is the equivalent of two weekends of skiing or a deposit on a mono-ski. The cost of renting a kayak for one day is half the price of a mono-ski. A disabled person with a limited budget is more likely to be able to afford to purchase or rent a kayak. Kayaking offers disabled people the same feeling of empowerment that skiing does. One kayaker told me economics were a major factor in his decision to paddle instead of ski.

> It took me two minutes to figure out skiing was too expensive. Kayaking is my sport. I am pretty new to kayaking but can get places where I could never dream of being when using my wheelchair. For example, I recently camped on an island in Long Island Sound. Being on the water is relaxing and after using a wheelchair for most of my life it is a different movement. But the best part of kayaking is the feeling of equality. When on the water I am just another kayaker—no one knows I use a wheelchair. I am not Mr. Cripple, a living symbol of how life can go wrong. Shit, why are people so stupid when it comes to disability? No other place in American society offers me the sense of equality as when I am out on the water. I truly feel liberated when I am in my boat. Sometimes when I paddle I really wish I did not have to return to the dock and get back in my wheelchair and the hassles associated with it. (interview with male, forty-five years old)

Conclusion

In this chapter I have constantly referred to the disability rights movement   27
and a number of influential disability studies scholars. While I have tried
not to be biased, it must be apparent that I am drawn to the disability rights
movement. There are two reasons for this: First, in spite of the important contributions disability studies scholars have made, in my estimation the field
has lost its soul. I do not question the dedication, effort, and contributions
made by disability studies scholars. There is no doubt their work is important and intellectually rigorous. I am also aware that the place of disability
studies in academia is by no means secure. Opposition to disability studies
within academia is an ongoing problem because some scholars, perceive disability as degrading or as watering down the integrity of identities. Given this,
disability scholars have focused on the important job of securing a place in
higher education where disability is perceived to be a form of human diversity
as well as an intellectual endeavor. These efforts are critical but contain one
flaw I cannot overlook: Disability studies scholars have not done enough to
empower the people they study. People with disabilities are the most overlooked, disenfranchised, and stigmatized minority group in American society.
Given this reality, I think every disability studies scholar must make a practical contribution to the lives of the disabled people they study. Jim Charlton in
Nothing about Us without Us (2002) has chronicled the history and legacy of
exclusion familiar to disabled people past and present, and this is exactly the
sort of oppression disability scholars must work to end.

Second, thanks to the Internet, people with disabilities are communi-   28
cating daily if not hourly and are not as isolated as they once were. People
with disabilities have embraced the Internet with gusto and have formed a
vibrant cyber community. Disability studies scholars have also embraced
the Internet, but their communication and scholarship is restricted and
exclusionary. This is a significant problem. For example, the journal of
the Society for Disability Studies, *Disability Studies Quarterly*, can only be
read by members. Membership costs $95 a year. This is far too costly when
one considers that dozens of disability-related blogs and web sites exist
that are free to all who can access the Internet. The exclusive nature of disability studies scholarship is particularly unfortunate. I worry about those
who could benefit the most from disability studies but are unable to read
the work intended to empower them. In my estimation this highlights how
far disability studies has distanced itself from the disability rights movement. Disability studies is more than an intellectual endeavor. I know this,
as do many disability scholars who are not only engaged scholars but activists as well. It is imperative for all academics, activists, universities, independent living centers, bloggers, and cultural institutions to work together
and demonstrate the relevance of post-secondary education. This type of
action-oriented scholarship and activism can only enhance the quality of
life for all people—those with and those without disabilities.

NOTES

1. This definition is from Title I of the 1990 Americans with Disabilities Act. Retrieved August 2008 from the U.S. Department of Justice Americans with Disabilities Act, ADA homepage. Available at http://www.eeoc.gov/types/ada.html.
2. Both quotations in this paragraph are from the Disability Rights Education and Defense Fund web site, which is available at http://www.dredf.org/publications/civil_rights_to_ human_rights.pdf.

REFERENCES

Bérubé, Michael. 1998. "Foreword: Pressing the Claim." In *Claiming Disability*, edited by Simi Linton. New York: NYU Press. Pp. vii-xii.

Davis, Leonard. 2002. *Bending over Backwards: Disability, Dismodernism, and Other Difficult Positions*. New York: NYU Press.

Fries, Kenny. 2007. *The History of My Shoes*. New York: Carroll Graf.

Gill, Carol. 1995. "The Pleasure We Take in Our Community." *Disability Rag*, September/October.

Linton, Simi. 1998. *Claiming Disability: Knowledge and Identity*. New York: NYU Press.

——————. 2006. *My Body Politic: A Memoir*. Ann Arbor: University of Michigan Press.

Longmore, Paul K. 1995. "The Second Phase: From Disability Rights to Disability Culture." *Disability Rag*, September/October.

—————— 2003. *Why I Burned My Book and Other Essays on Disability*. Philadelphia: Temple University Press.

Longmore, Paul K., and Lauri Umansky. 2001. *The New Disability History*. New York: NYU Press.

Mairs, Nancy. 1997. *Waist-High in the World: A Life among the Nondisabled*. Boston: Beacon Press.

Murphy, Robert. 1980. *Body Silent*. New York: Norton.

Olson, Kay. 2007. "Updated: CNN, Developmental Disability, and Institutionalization." The Gimp Parade, August 1 (http/www.thegimpparade.com).

Thomson, Rosemarie Garland, 1997. *Extraordinary Bodies: Figuring Physical Disability in American Culture and Literature*. New York: Columbia University Press.

Riley, Charles A. 2005. *Disability and the Media: Prescriptions for Change*. Hanover, NH: University Press of New England.

Roberts, Edward. Ca. 1970. Letter to Gina Laurie, University of California, Bancroft Library Special Collections.

Yee, Sylvia. 2007. "From Civil Rights to Human Rights." Disability Rights Education and Defense Fund, available at http://dredf.org/publications/Civil_rights_to_human_rights.pdf.

Reading as a Writer: Analyzing Rhetorical Choices

1. While Peace draws information from interviews and contextualizes this data in research from the field of disability studies, he also includes himself, and his experiences as a disabled person, as a source of information here. What effect does this have on his piece, particularly when you think about strategies of persuasion through ethos, pathos, and logos?

2. How might you summarize the attitude toward disability that Peace argues against, and that which he argues for? What examples stand out to you, without looking back at your text?

Writing as a Reader: Entering the Conversation of Ideas

1. Peace is interested in the stories that the media tell about disability, just as bell hooks (Chapter 13) is concerned with the media images we most often see of the poor. Drawing on both authors' insights about media representations and their effects, compose an essay in which you draw larger conclusions about the ways the media can be used to uphold or undo stereotypes. Include a specific, brief media example or two, if you like, to help you make your point.

2. Like Peace, Matthew Immergut (Chapter 14) makes an argument about the ways expectations of bodies change, based on historical and cultural context. Compose an essay in which you consider the significance of changing expectations for male bodies in particular, given the ideas and examples in these two readings.

16

Environmental Studies

How do our decisions affect our environment?

© Corbis/Catherine Raillard

In this chapter, you plunge into high-stakes arguments and very personal conversations about our individual relationships to the planet. In the face of climate change and dwindling resources, you have certainly heard the cacophony of voices on television, in the movies, and in newspapers and magazines, addressing these frightening global problems with "green" or "sustainable" solutions. What do these terms mean? More importantly, what do they mean for *you* as you go about your daily activities of getting from one place to the next, eating meals, buying things, learning, and occasionally cleaning your living space?

While "environmental studies" may sound mostly scientific, as you will see, thinkers in many different disciplines are challenging us to reconsider our relationship to the environment in eye-opening and innovative ways. For example, authors Derrick Jensen and Stephanie McMillan use the graphic novel form to invite us to question many of the "easy" ways we have heard to "save the earth." Noël Sturgeon uses visual rhetoric in a different way, teaching us to analyze the arguments in advertising that make often damaging claims about "nature." Carolyn Merchant picks up on the conversation about our desire to "buy nature," often at great cost to producers and ourselves.

Steven D. Levitt and Stephen J. Dubner see environmental issues through the eyes of economists, to try to understand better the human responses to environmental issues. As a scientist and mother, Sandra Steingraber frames the problem differently, but you will see many connections between all these authors' approaches to bringing the personal into conversation with policy making and social patterns.

Other writers focus on the politics of food, in a growing chorus of thinkers whose ideas are captured in Anna Lappé's title, "The Climate Crisis at the End of Our Fork." What is the connection between your supper plate and our planet? Lappé offers surprising statistics about the food industry's enormous contributions to global warming, as well as solutions you might consider. Many of us may not be willing to make the changes we *should* make, both for the health of the planet and for the sake of ethics, according to philosopher Gary Steiner in his impassioned plea for veganism. Why not? Well-known food-writer Michael Pollan reminds us, as do many of the authors in this chapter, that the answers to our environmental problems must go beyond scientific and technological solutions. What can we gain not only by changing what we eat, but by altering what Pollan calls our "cheap-energy minds"?

These writers share the rhetorical challenge of inviting readers to think creatively and more knowledgeably about an issue that is weighted with bad news. What approaches, examples, facts, and personal anecdotes will inspire you to think, make connections, and act? How might you try these strategies in your own conversation and writing?

At **macmillanhighered.com/frominquiry3e** a short trailer for the 2014 documentary *Food Patriots* makes a definitional argument for a new kind of citizen. Are you one?

Visit **macmillanhighered.com/frominquiry3e** to play "The Sins of Greenwashing," an interactive game designed to educate consumers about misleading environmental practices of companies or environmental benefits of products or services.

DERRICK JENSEN AND STEPHANIE McMILLAN

As the World Burns: 50 Simple Things You Can Do to Stay in Denial

Derrick Jensen and Stephanie McMillan are writers and graphic artists who have published individually and who teamed up to write the book-length comic satire *As the World Burns: 50 Simple Things You Can Do to Stay in Denial* (2007). This reading is a section of this satiric graphic novel, which makes a challenging—and somewhat uncomfortable—argument: All the little things we do to help the environment may be making us feel better about ourselves but may not be helping the planet as much as we like to think.

Jensen and McMillan use sarcasm to get across their somewhat counterintuitive argument, as is apparent in the opening exchange between a pig-tailed do-gooder who recycles a can (seemingly a good thing to do, yes?), and the one-eyed rabbit who reveals that her approach does not address the much larger corporate structures that harm the health of the planet and individuals.

What follows is a series of scenarios of "easy" ways to "save the Earth" that will be familiar to most of us—and are likely to be actions we have taken and felt pretty good about. In the witty interplay between two characters, you will hear strategies and statistics that sound persuasive in the mouth of the optimistic environmentalist . . . until the dark-clad character reveals how little these "easy" solutions accomplish, given the enormity of environmental problems. Pay attention to the way each character uses facts to make a point, and also pay attention to your own reactions to this rhetorical approach. How do the images underscore the emotions of this argument?

Jensen and McMillan do not let readers off the hook very easily here, but does this piece suggest that we should simply give up on trying to "save the Earth"? Jensen and McMillan argue that if we really want to work toward better environmental policies, we should know the full facts, the full picture. We would do better, they argue through their graphics, to focus less on changing light bulbs and more on changing corporations' policies and legislation. This is not an "easy" solution to our environmental problems, but it is also not giving up. How does that make you feel?

■ ■ ■

Excerpt from *As the World Burns: 50 Simple Things You Can Do to Stay in Denial.* Copyright © 2007. Reprinted with the permission of The Permissions Company, Inc., on behalf of Seven Stories Press, www.sevenstories.com.

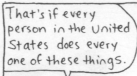

Reading as a Writer: Analyzing Rhetorical Choices

1. How do the drawings underscore the meaning in this text? For example, what do you make of the one-eyed rabbit in the opening sequence? What difference would it make if the characters were older? How does the body language illustrate each character's perspective?

2. There are a lot of statistics in this text. How are they used to make the argument? Given all the numbers that the characters throw at one another, what is the overall point the authors seem to make about the way data are often used in claims about the environment?

Writing as a Reader: Entering the Conversation of Ideas

1. Jensen and McMillan take a different approach to the climate crisis than Michael Pollan, who argues that people should go "personally green" by planting gardens and making different daily choices. Write an essay in which you play these authors' ideas off one another, considering similarities and differences in the ways they understand environmental problems and propose solutions. Evaluate the strengths and weaknesses of their claims, given the evidence they provide. Where do they overlap, if at all, in their vision of how we should — or can — act to "save the earth"?

2. Like Jensen and McMillan, Noël Sturgeon is interested in visual rhetoric in the environmental debate. Write an essay in which you consider the effects of visual argument in these two readings. While their approaches are quite different (drawings versus advertising), what similarities do you see in the effect of making an argument with visual strategies? What can visual rhetoric accomplish that written text cannot? What conclusions can you draw about effective use of visual rhetoric in environmental debates?

NOËL STURGEON

The Politics of the Natural in U.S. History and Popular Culture

Noël Sturgeon is a professor of environmental studies at York University in Ontario, Canada. Her research interests include social movements, theories of globalization and transnationalism, and feminist issues in environmental studies. Her recent publications have focused on sustainability and reproductive health, popular culture, and globalization. This reading comes from her book, *Environmentalism in Popular Culture: Gender, Sexuality, Race, and the Politics of the Natural* (2009), and features her interest in popular advertising.

Sturgeon opens with the claim that "nature plays an important role both materially and ideologically in our culture" (para. 1), and then moves to a series of big questions at the end of paragraph 2 about the effects of misusing the term *natural*. Return to these rich opening paragraphs after you have read the whole text once to test your understanding of her argument. (This is an effective strategy for reading any text.) How do her many examples help her explain and answer these opening questions?

In her section titled "Using Arguments from Nature as a Tool of Power," Sturgeon unfolds the history behind her argument that there are power dynamics involved in claims about what is "natural." You will likely find some of her examples familiar; "natural" order has been used to justify slavery, sexism, and many other inequalities. Can you think of other examples? As Sturgeon points out, though, claims about "nature" also have been used successfully by antislavery activists, to fight for gay rights, and in other social justice campaigns. Thus, claims about what is or isn't "natural" are complicated, and can cut more than one way, for those in power and those without it. Sturgeon calls for "relentlessly critical examinations of claims to the natural" (para. 17).

We see that critical examination at work in the "Patterns of Nature in U.S. Popular Culture" section, in which she discusses her students' analysis of "nature." Consider how your own personal background and experiences have contributed to your understanding of what is—and isn't—natural. Sturgeon notes that advertising culture often plays a key role in developing our understanding of "nature," as well. In the final portions of her essay, she applies her earlier ideas about the power dynamics in claims about "nature" to the visual rhetoric of some sample advertising gathered by her students and herself. See what you think of her interpretations of the images and language in these ads, and their relation to her overall argument.

Sturgeon argues, like other writers in this section, that our attitudes toward "nature" reflect our conflicting and shifting understandings of ourselves and "others." What strategies does Sturgeon offer as you figure out where you stand in this contested territory?

■ ■ ■

Nature plays an important role both materially and ideologically in our culture. Environmental problems, particularly the contemporary concern over global climate change, are crucially important challenges, and we urgently need to be able to think clearly about them. But because "nature" and "natural" have such powerful and complex cultural resonances, the use of these concepts as tropes, metaphors, and dominant cultural narratives has the capacity to confuse and obscure our thinking about environmental policy. In particular, metaphors and narrative frameworks about nature in regard to "human nature"—for example, understandings of human evolution, inherent human capacities for violence and sex, and differences among humans—have often been used to naturalize and therefore justify social inequalities.

There is often quite a gap between how scientists or policymakers approach questions of nature and environment, and dominant ways of thinking and talking about nature and environment found in popular culture. Nevertheless, the latter provides a framework within which the former is often accomplished. Habits of popular and commonsense thinking can be shaken up by a few simple questions: What are the effects (political, rhetorical, ideological) of calling something "natural"? Does the descriptive term *natural* assume or justify social behaviors and relationships that are actually built on inequity and exploitation? What are the consequences for the environment (the land, animals, water, ecosystems, the biosphere) of these inequitable social arrangements, and how does an uncritical understanding of "nature" and the "natural" prevent us from seeing these connections?

One of the commonplace assumptions I want to challenge is that 3 nature and culture, or the natural and the artificial (or "manmade"), are identifiably and completely separate, and should be so. This is one of the major problems with popular and mainstream environmentalist discourses. Challenging this separation goes against the grain for many of us because it troubles the obviousness or transparency of what we think of as "natural." But we only have to look at the daily news to see how often ideas of what is natural and what counts as nature are called into question or called into service to support various claims or positions. Moreover, the lines of separation between artificial and natural, whether or not they were ever clear, are now becoming more and more blurred. New genetic, agricultural, and reproductive technologies (such as cloning, stem cell research, in-vitro fertilization, and genetically modified foods) are serious material challenges to the idea that nature and culture are or should be separate. And assuming that these two realms are separate obscures human environmental responsibilities.

Why, when advanced scientific technologies make pinning down 4 exactly what is meant by the term *natural* harder and harder, does the designation remain so powerful a tool in important contemporary social debates? Arguments from nature have long been used to try to justify social phenomena such as racial and cultural differences in educational outcomes, different gendered athletic, academic, or work abilities, or the rightness or wrongness of gay relationships. None of these arguments have proven to be conclusive, yet attempts to find biological explanations for social differences persist. This is not to say that there are no biological differences between various groups of people, but the effort to find such differences has been historically a suspect project.

All of these examples are about people or about "human nature." Things 5 get even more slippery when we think about the ways in which changing ideas of nature have affected our conceptions of the environment. Are wilderness areas necessary for preserving "wild nature"? Or are they managed and commodified leisure resources in which "wild nature" has to be controlled? (For instance, think about the policy of removing "problem" bears in Yellowstone who have gotten too used to humans and their garbage.) Should every species be saved, from extinction, or should some be allowed to expire because of "natural selection"? But how would we define "natural selection" in today's world, when new bacteria are formed in reaction to antibiotics used for medical purposes and industrial chemicals permeate the biosphere, possibly affecting our own ability to reproduce? If the bioengineering of a better tomato means introducing salmon genes into the tomato, does that violate the integrity of both tomato and fish? Are wild salmon superior to farmed salmon if they are basically the same genetic organism, and on what basis are they superior? Are wild salmon preferred because they are valued by a culinary market, because they may taste better? Or are they better for environmental reasons, because the farming of salmon causes a significant amount of pollution? Should wild salmon be valued just because they are authentic, the "original" fish? Or should salmon be preserved because they are sacred beings to several Northwest tribal peoples, who have developed reciprocal relationships to the fish over thousands of years? Obviously, what is "natural" is highly contested and therefore deeply political.

Using Arguments from Nature as a Tool of Power

The arguments and controversies examined in this book, then, are not about the old debate between nature and nurture. I want to move beyond that way of thinking to critically examine the power of the idea of "the natural" and "nature." The persistence of the debate between nature and nurture begs the question about why those divisions (nature/nurture, nature/culture, biology/society, natural/artificial) have such power in certain cultures, especially U.S. culture. The answer is that these distinctions are tools of power. Historically, calling something "natural" places it in an arena of truth, inevitability, and immutability, beyond the reach of social criticism or democratic dialogue. Understanding the history of these ideological uses of the concept of nature and examining the multiple ways in which the politics of the natural affect our social and environmental policies permits us to critically assess various solutions to environmental problems and social inequalities. Under the world-spanning threat of global climate change, such a critical perspective may make the difference in having a world of elite green fortresses in a sea of poverty and war of having an open, equal, and sustainable society.

Those of us who are engaged in and subjected to Western (that is, Anglo-European), especially U.S., dominant cultural and political discourses (encompassing a major part of the world now) are familiar with the idea of nature being invoked to settle arguments or determine policy directions. This is in part because nature has a special place in the founding of Western and particularly U.S. culture. Since the Enlightenment, nature has played the role of foundation, truth, ground—replacing the older European feudal framework of religious order, divine right, and ordained social hierarchy. The overthrow of traditional European monarchies and the establishment of new republican democracies were based on the idea that "natural law" rather than divine law should be the determining source of the rule of law. This radical shift in political arrangements was based on the idea that (some) men were naturally equal and had natural rights inherent in their status as (male) humans and as such were able to rule themselves rather than be ruled by kings and queens.

However, these revolutionary men did not intend to eliminate racial, 8 gender, and class hierarchies that supported their own privilege and power. (This is why I call their understanding of human rights "huMAN" rights.) Some way of justifying the continuance of certain social hierarchies had to logically fit with arguments for natural law. Thus, the idea that some social inequalities were naturally determined developed hand in hand with the idea that freedom and equality were natural rights. In the same period as a series of revolutions brought modern Western democratic politics into being through a celebration of the natural rights of "man," the new modern sciences of botany, biology, anthropology, and primatology were "discovering" a host of "natural" differences that proved the superiority of white European men over European women and certainly over all Africans, Indians, and other subjugated peoples. Thus, while upper-class white European men were freeing themselves of feudal and monarchical structures, they could conveniently argue that others were naturally unfit for the same rights. Those Others included darker-skinned peoples, European women, and in some cases lower-class European men of particular ethnicities such as Irish, Mediterranean, and Slavic peoples (Merchant 1980; Schiebinger 1993). Such logic even allowed slaveholders to see themselves as champions of freedom, given that freedom was understood to be "natural" to white men while slavery was "natural" to Africans (Africans being understood as less "civilized") (Morgan 1975).

The effect of the legitimating function and long historical dominance 9 of this set of contradictory ideas about nature is that Westerners often use the idea of the natural to justify either the way things are or the way we think things should be. To say that some phenomenon is "natural"—for instance, women doing most of the domestic work and child care around the world or men being more likely to use violence—seems to settle the question for many people. Not surprisingly, arguments from the natural often settle the question for those who benefit from the social arrangement in question, tragically, these arguments can sometimes also convince those who suffer from inequality and exploitation to accept their situation.

Arguing that something is natural tends to prevent an examination of 10 whether the situation is just or right or desirable. For example, instead of questioning the conventions of the contemporary gender division of labor some might argue that women doing most of the domestic work may be unfortunate, but it is part of "nature's plan" (connected to women's biological ability to give birth) and therefore the best arrangement. This argument conveniently obscures the ways in which men can do much domestic and child-care work beyond the actual birthing and breast-feeding that are biologically determined. Women's unequal domestic responsibilities are far from natural, even if they may have been, in specific circumstances, tied to women's biological ability to give birth. Aside from actually giving birth and breast-feeding, other caregiving activities and domestic work have no biological basis for being gendered. Gathering fruits, weeding a field, holding a baby, using a microwave, sewing a shirt, washing a sick elderly person, or driving a kid to day care are not acts determined by nature.

The pattern of seeking a biological or natural basis to justify inequali- *11* ties of sex, ability, race, and class is not merely located in an origin story of Euro-American democracies—in other words, something that happened a long time ago in the 1600s and 1700s—but is repeated throughout the nineteenth and twentieth centuries, in discursive and institutionalized practices such as eugenics, social Darwinism, Nazism, IQ testing, exclusionary immigration laws, sterilization policies, and certain problematic racialized and gendered projects within employment law, educational policies, and scientific research. Because of this history, those less privileged by "naturalized" social arrangements are rightly suspicious of arguments from nature. Are these "natural" justifications for social inequalities continuing into the twenty-first century? Contemporary debates and trends in popular culture suggest that they are.

But the politics of the natural are complicated. Because of the impor- *12* tance of nature as a legitimating idea, there has been a liberatory possibility in strategically arguing from nature against social norms. Several groups of people originally left out of the Enlightenment social contract have used this liberatory aspect of arguments from nature effectively in many historical cases. For instance, antislavery activists (and later, civil rights activists) argued that if one believed that black people were human, then they must deserve full human rights, since the Declaration of Independence stated that "all men are created equal." Those rights, as the U.S. founding documents state, were meant to be conceived as "natural" rights, inherent in the status of being human (or at least male, according to the founders). A more contemporary example of a liberatory argument from the natural is the strategic power of the insistence by many gay and lesbian activists that sexual orientation is biologically innate and thus unchangeable, "natural" and therefore deserving of social acceptance. This point of view argues against hundreds of years of seeing same-sex practices as "unnatural" and seeks to remove the taint of perversity from same-sex relationships by seeing them as just as "natural" as heterosexual relationships.

Finally, arguments from nature have been used to sustain and inspire *13* numerous environmental struggles. Seeing nature as valuable to human society, or as valuable in itself, has been an important basis for struggling to preserve, protect, and respect animals, plants, ecosystems, and the planet. Environmentalists have had their own complicated debates about what is natural and what is artificial, whether humans should manage nature or leave nature alone, whether environmental decisions should be made based on scientific, cultural, or spiritual grounds. But the shared sense that nature should not be damaged and that entities in their "natural" state are valuable and deserving of our protection—for their own sake, as a touchstone for human understanding, and as the basis for human life—is a core concern of environmentalists and has been a strategically effective and liberatory use of arguments from nature.

Looking over these different uses of arguments from nature, we can   *14*
see that the contested and illimitable social meaning of the natural means
that the same kind of arguments can be and have been used strategically
many times for both conservative and progressive ends. One should not
always assume that if an argument is being made that some phenomenon is natural, especially a social phenomenon, then it is necessarily an
argument meant to prop up social inequality. But one can (and should) be
skeptical of such arguments, given their historical uses as justifications for
human and environmental exploitation.

In particular, as environmental activists struggle to preserve and sup-   *15*
port environmental health, integrity, and sustainability, their ways of
thinking about and arguing for nature need to be carefully, examined for
the worrisome possibility that problematic assumptions about nature and
the natural that have been used to oppress groups of marginalized peoples
are being unintentionally promoted. For example, in 2004, the Sierra Club
was thrown into turmoil by some members' attempts to protect against the
"natural" increase in population thought to be caused by Latina/o immigrants who "naturally" had more families and thus, in their view, endangered
the environment. These members tried to have the Sierra Club promote
anti immigration policies as a way to protect U.S. natural resources, despite
the ways these same anti-immigration policies were being used to support
racism and the exploitation of immigrant workers (Chea 2004).

Furthermore, some environmentalist discourses about nature may not   *16*
be the best way to achieve environmental goals, because they may contain
unexamined assumptions or justify problematic arrangements that support
environmental degradation as well as human exploitation. The Sierra Club
example above fits this case as well, since policies that are exploitative of
and harmful to immigrant workers and depend on racist attitudes toward
those workers, such as the lax restrictions on pesticide use in U.S. agriculture, are environmentally polluting of food, water, and soil.

Asking people to become critical of any claim to the natural, from any   *17*
position, sometimes creates anxiety that an insistence on the sociality of
nature means that one is arguing that nature does not exist for itself; that
seeing nature as socially constructed means that we can do whatever we
choose with the nonhuman environment, that nonhuman entities and
places will therefore have no integrity that must be respected by humans.
This conclusion seems extremely problematic to me, and I reject it pas-
sionately. A seriously critical position on claims to the natural need not
leave us in a state in which "nature" is infinitely flexible, always already
socially constructed, immaterial, and endlessly exploitable. To persistently
question the status of the natural does not mean that we should reject the
materiality, the corporeality, the autonomy, or the agency of the nonhuman
(or the human, for that matter) (Haraway 1991, 1992). Nor should we
deny out of hand all indications of biological differences, as long as we can
ensure that social bias does not affect our understanding of them (which,
given the long history of the misuse of arguments from the natural, can

be a very difficult thing to determine). Humans are inside, coexisting, and interdependent with nature rather than outside and independent of it. Human biology is responsive to and changed by our environments, just as part of human nature is to change environments, whether those changes are for the better or worse needs to be carefully judged. Thus, the human and nonhuman environment is co-constructed, and there are material (and should be ethical) limits on our interaction with "nature"—whether land, animal, body, water, air, or the planet (Bird 1987; Cuomo 1998; Sandi-lands 1999). Unless we are willing to recognize the deeply political and ideologically variable status of "nature" in our culture, however, we cannot adequately discuss and decide these important questions about our interaction and use of the environment. So I argue that a relentlessly critical examination of claims to the natural is the best way to learn to respect natural beings and processes (including our own natural status as animal-hurnans or humanimals).

Patterns of Nature in U.S. Popular Culture

What are the dominant uses of symbols of nature and arguments from *18* the natural in U.S. popular culture? In teaching this material as a class for many years, I have learned a lot about these patterns from my students (to whom I owe a giant debt for their questions and contributions).[1] One of the things I always did with my U.S. students, early in the class, was a wonderful exercise suggested by Carolyn Merchant in her useful book *Radical Ecology* (1992). I recommend that readers try this exercise for themselves. In this exercise, students are asked to reflect, in writing, on their personal histories and the relationship between those histories and their understanding of the environment. They are specifically asked what environmental values, or understanding of nature, arose from their social class, their racial/ethnic identity, their gender, and (an element I added to Merchant's framework) their sexuality.

After the essays were written and students had had a chance to con- *19* sider the unusual notion that their social locations might influence their conception of nature, I would usually take some of a class period to ask the students to brainstorm about what "nature" meant to them. I would write these words and phrases so that all could see them, and then we would discuss the patterns that developed. Though a wide variety of things could be associated with the idea of "nature," there were, inevitably, consistent patterns that showed up in the U.S. context. This exercise demonstrates that the concept of nature is immensely flexible and variable, yet there are still repeated patterns of meaning that can be discerned, and these patterns are historically as well as culturally specific.

For my U.S. students, one of these patterns was a sharp split between *20* human and nature ("anything 'not us,'" one student offered), another was the idea of nature as a source of purity and regeneration, another was nature as inevitability (a law of nature, an instinct, a dictate of behavior, whether individual, social, or environmental), another (especially for my students from the small farming communities of eastern Washington) was nature as source of food, as site of labor and economic productivity, another was nature as wildness, unpredictability, another was nature as the source of scientific knowledge, and another was nature as the location for play, leisure, and physical action. It was rare to encounter notions of nature as urban, as community, as constructed in interaction with humans, as autonomous agent, or as self.

These patterns could be predicted, given my usual pool of students *21* (primarily but not only white, middle class, from the state of Washington) and the history of Western ideas about nature. In Raymond Williams's wonderful book of cultural and historical definitions, *Keywords* ([1976] 1983), he says, "Nature is perhaps the most complex word in the [English] language" (219) and goes on to declare, "Any full history of the uses of nature would be a history of a large part of human thought" (221). Williams ([1976] 1983, 219) identifies three main senses of "nature":

(i) the essential quality and character *of* something;

(ii) the inherent force which directs either the world or human beings or both;

(iii) the material world itself, taken as including or not including human beings

In these definitions, one can see the likelihood of confusion between the "is" and the "ought" of nature—how Westerners commonly understand nature both as the ways in which things are materially and as the ways in which they are meant to be, instinctually and essentially.

Another scholar of the meaning of the word *nature*, William Cronon, has *22* come up with a list of meanings of nature quite similar to my students' list but also containing some notions rarely found in our brainstorms in class. In his introductory essay to the important collection *Uncommon Ground* (1996, 34–50), Cronon identifies the following versions of nature that arose out of the conversations among the academics who contributed to the volume:

Nature as naïve reality

Nature as moral imperative

Nature as Eden

Nature as artifice, as self-conscious construction (such as parks)

Nature as virtual reality

Nature as commodity

Nature as demonic other, as avenging angel, as the return of the repressed

My students tended to be comfortable with the first three ideas (nature *23* as real, as right, and as good) and the last (the "fury of Mother Nature" cliché, so often used on the Weather Channel). But the idea of nature as artifice, as virtual reality, and as commodity tended to be rejected vehemently. My students wanted their nature to be "real" in some way or another, revealing a strong and common assumption that the natural and the artificial are essentially different (though, as it turns out, any attempt to define the boundaries between the two always generates a lively, unresolvable debate). They also wanted their nature to be untouched by the dictates of the capitalist market economy. Thinking of nature as co-constructing reality with humans meant to them that the force of nature as a location of immutable rules and dictates, a concept in which they were deeply invested, was uncomfortably diluted. My students were often resistant to the idea that nature had a history, both in the sense of being thought of differently at different times and by different cultures and in the sense of being composed of a changing, dynamic set of interrelated entities (including humans) existing in chronological dimensions. Donna Haraway's important concept of "naturecultures" (2004) is meant to encompass these two meanings of nature as a historical entity and, though resisted, ultimately proved a very useful neologism for my students (and, obviously, for me as well).

Although nature is a concept that is essentially contested (that is, 24 it cannot be resolved into one broadly accepted and fixed meaning), as Cronon and many others have pointed out, it is at the same time a powerful force and flexible source of legitimation. Given the diversity and the inconsistency of both Cronon's and my students' lists of meanings for "nature," it is not surprising to see arguments from the natural made from almost any social or political viewpoint to justify widely divergent and even opposing positions. But identifying common patterns, repeated narratives of nature, allows us to analyze serious social and environmental consequences of the deployment of these repeated ideas.

Advertising Natures

As John Fiske (1989) has pointed out, popular culture is a dynamic loca- 25 tion where important struggles between those more powerful and privileged and those less powerful and privileged are often carried out. Because it is an arena of intense commodification and because postindustrial global capitalism is always seeking out new niche markets, subcultural oppositional meanings expressed in fashion, food, music, art, and other social practices arc constantly being incorporated into dominant expressions of nonoppositional support for buying particular products. At the same time, new oppositional meanings are continually created, sometimes through the very process of consumption itself.

In a chapter called "The Jeaning of America," Fiske describes the 26 process of "excorporation" (subcultural oppositional cultural practice) and "incorporation" (dominant recasting of oppositional meaning into new commodities) as an ongoing dance within the semiotics (or meaning-making practices) of the global economy. Uses of the idea of the "natural" are frequently tokens in this process. His primary example of this process of excorporation and incorporation is jeans, the way in which a garment that at one time referred to the working class in the 1930s and 1940s, was taken up by folk musicians and rockers in the 1950s and 1960s, and was worn torn and faded by young radicals in the 1970s has now become a ubiquitous item of clothing, signaling meanings of youth, status, and high fashion devoid of oppositional content. But even as these meanings changed, Fiske argues, jeans remained symbolic of "naturalness," representing many ideas associated with nature (freedom, comfort, informality, purity, and so forth), thus showing how connections with naturalness can mean many things at the same time that they obscure the sociality and variety of the messages being relayed (Fiske 1989).

Examples from U.S. advertising demonstrate some of the uses of what *27* I have been calling "naturalization." Over the years, my students and I have assembled an archive of hundreds of such ads, only a few of which I can refer to here. These ads exhibit various ways of using images of nature in connection with images of social stereotypes, showing the ubiquitous character of these patterns in U.S. culture. This is not because there is an advertising conspiracy to justify social inequalities with images of nature. Rather, when analyzing ads, you are examining something like a social unconsciousness, since ads are designed to reflect and appeal to our common desires, beliefs, and values. Marita Sturken and Lisa Cartwright (2001, 89) explain,

> Advertising often presents an image of things to be desired, people to be envied, and life as it "should be." As such, it necessarily presents social values and ideologies about what the "good life" is. It is also a central strategy of advertising to invite viewers/consumers to imagine themselves within the world of the advertisement. This is a world that works by abstraction, a potential place or state of being situated not in the present but in an imagined future with the promise to the consumer of things "you" will have, a lifestyle you can take part in.

Because the creators of ads hope to make some powerful symbolic *28* connections with images that will spur people to consume their product, they often draw upon what they assume are widespread commonsense beliefs. Sometimes ads do so in the seemingly opposite approach, by flouting or contradicting widely held assumptions to associate their product with rebellious individualism and freedom from convention. But this move, while often masquerading as resisting conformist attitudes, can still serve to reinforce stereotypes and dominant logics. This might be called "the exception proves the rule" effect; we only notice that something goes against the grain when we accept that there is a grain. Sturken and Cartwright (2001, 206) put it this way: "Advertising uses particular codes and conventions to convey messages quickly and succinctly to viewers. While some ads intend to shock us or capture our attention through their difference, most advertising provides information through the shorthand language of visual and textual conventions. Hence, most ads speak a mixture of familiarity and newness." Ads thus create ideological connections, but often they do so because they reflect preexisting ideological narratives. Because they are designed to appeal to many people, ads are revealing items through which dominant patterns of social meaning in a given cultural context can be ascertained.

A 1994 Discovery Channel ad that tells the viewer to "Explore Your 29 World" (Figure 16.1) is an image that summarizes many of the patterns addressed in this book. The ad shows six "faces": a Mayan or Aztec sun mask, an Aboriginal man, a Native American man, a jet pilot in a helmet and breathing apparatus, a woman in an obscuring headdress, and a leopard or jaguar. Because the ad exhorts the viewer to "find yourself here," I often begin an analysis of this image by asking my students to see whether they can find themselves in any of the images. Are they a wild cat? An Aborigine? The very few of my students who are Native Americans or Middle Eastern women are clearly not assumed to be the likely audience for this ad. Sometimes I ask my students to find the white man in the picture, and they frequently respond by pointing to the mask of the fighter pilot. In stating that these are "the faces of the world," the Discovery Channel ad presents only one face as the face of technology, of "civilization," and my students are used to associating white men with technology and civilization. The other faces—the vaguely Aztec mask, the Aborigine, the American Indian, the leopard, and the Middle Eastern woman (signified as Muslim by her headdress)—are all placed on the same plane, the natural, "primitive" backdrop to the process of exploration and achievement. The

FIGURE 16.1 "The faces of the world" (Discovery Channel 1994)

jungle cat is equivalent to the other "natural" faces, all of whom (except the fighter jet pilot) belong to those who have been colonized in the name of "progress" arid "discovery." In this way, the colonization and exploitation of nature is made equivalent to the colonization and exploitation of darker-skinned peoples. The statement of the ad, "The faces of Discovery are the faces of the world," tells us that all the "nonmodern" faces are the ones to be discovered; the pilot's mask puts "him" in the position of discovery, given the close connections in U.S. cultural mythology among discovery, space exploration, and militarism. This set of assumptions—that "primitive" peoples are closer to nature, that there is a natural evolution from "primitive" to "civilized," and that history inevitably involves "progress" defined as a movement toward modernization and industrialization—makes the cost of such "progress," for nature and for particular people, invisible. The fact that the logo of the Discovery Channel is firmly over the mouth of the Muslim woman in effect symbolically silences the one woman present as well.

Another set of dominant patterns visible in late-twentieth- and early-twenty-first-century ads is various associations of gender and sexuality with nature. The representation of women as natural and nature as female is very common. This often places women in an inferior position in relation to men; they are depicted as closer to nature, the "primitive," the animal, the body, and farther from culture, the "civilized," the human, and the mind. Ads frequently portray women as landscapes, as surrounded or subsumed by nature, while men are often shown physically dominating nature, as in many ads depicting men skiing, driving cars, or rock climbing. Men's nature

FIGURE 16.2   Flower women (Dolce and Gabbana 2006)

is to *control* nature, while women's nature is to *be* nature. (John Berger [1972, 47] made a similar statement on the representation of women in art: "Men act. Women appear.") For instance, you can often see ads that show women (especially white women) as flowers or defined by intense floral or plant-related images. Figure 16.2 depicts women whose flowery dresses embed them so thoroughly in their leafy background that they can barely be distinguished from nature; it takes us a minute to notice that there are two pairs of identical women in this Dolce and Gabbana ad, their individuality matters so little. By contrast, one rarely, if ever, sees men as flowers.

But what *kind* of woman or man is depicted influences how they are visu- *31* ally associated with nature. There are patterns within patterns here, varying meanings of feminized or masculinized nature articulated by differences of race, class, and sexuality. In a rare image of a man surrounded by and subsumed within nature, from an article entitled "Natural Man" (Figure 16.3), the man appears to be Latino, with brown skin and carefully coiffed, dark curly hair, offering a coquettish smile while surrounded by fruit. The accompanying article is about Philip Berkovitz, the founder of a line of skin- and hair-care products called PhilipB, and the text assumes a close connection between the idea of "natural" products and health. The coiffed hair, the smile, and the association of the word *fruit* as a derogatory word for a gay man assists in this image to convey the idea that if a man (especially a brown man) is portrayed as surrounded by or enmeshed in nature, then he is a feminized man (that is, stereotypically gay). When a man is shown actively engaged in and in control of nature, he is usually depicted as white, straight, and very stereotypically masculine. For example, a Stetson cologne ad (Figure 16.4)

FIGURE 16.3 "Natural Man" (Mirabella Magazine 1999)

FIGURE 16.4 Nature is freedom (Stetson Cologne 1999)

© UL LLC. Reproduced with permission.

FIGURE 16.5   Worshipping purity
(White Rain 2001)

shows a white man in the midst of exuberant exploration, escaping from the dark, claustrophobic city to the "freedom" of the country. In splashing his way up a river, he epitomizes strength, control, and manly success.

Another key pattern within 32 a pattern is the association of white women with nature used to represent purity and health, as in an ad for White Rain shampoo in which a naked blonde woman ecstatically raises her arms in supplication to a powerful water-fall (Figure 16.5). Another version of this association of white women with nature as purity is the Evian mermaid who, as part fish, is a sensuous, fabled creature reveling in the purity of water (Figure 16.6). When a man is used in the complementary Evian ad, he represents "l'original" by symbolizing the "primitive"—he is a brown-skinned man dressed as an Inuit, or Eskimo (to use the colonizer's term for these indigenous people, one that is referenced in Figure 16.7 by the "igloo" the man is making). In this Evian ad, in a common visual association,

FIGURE 16.6   Mermaid (Evian n.d.)

FIGURE 16.7   "Eskimo" (Evian n.d.)

indigenous people are closer to nature, depicted as more authentic but less "developed" and lower on the chain of evolution than white people—therefore, they are "l'original" people, whose lost purity consumers can capture by using Evian's product.

Unlike the Evian mermaid, most of the images one encounters that associate women with animality are of a more sexualized and aggressive nature. Leopard patterns or leather clothes are often used to convey the "animal" sexuality of women. Figure 16.8, for example, celebrates a white woman's passionate sexual attraction to the ocean, proposing the medically dubious idea that "natural" tanning products might be healthier for one's skin. The leopard-skin bikini the model is wearing is an advertising cliché, signaling the association of animals and female sexuality.   33

When women of color are represented as animals, these associations of aggressive sexuality tend to take an even more negative cast. An ad for B-Boots shows a brown woman, dressed in leather, displaying a ferociously clawed and aggressive demeanor (Figure 16.9). A handbag ad for Bottega Vega compares the leather of the purse with the textured skin of a black woman. And a Moschino ad shows a very dark African American woman displayed on a wall like a trophy animal, dressed in leopard skin.   34

Some advertising images present lesbians as inherently exhibiting this animal sexuality, as in two women cuddling in leather for Guess jeans. A Hennessy ad combines many of these patterns of naturalization in one image (Figure 16.10). Here, two women who are to be "mixed accordingly,"   35

FIGURE 16.8   Sex, nature, and tanning (Supre 2004)

FIGURE 16.9   "Dressed to kill" (B-Boots 2002)

FIGURE 16.10   "Mix accordingly" (Hennessy n.d.)

vaguely hinting at some nefarious same-sex and cross-racial activity to come, have small labels placed above their heads. The white woman, blonde, slim, and dressed in white—all signs of purity—is a "vegetarian," thus refusing to even eat animals let alone be associated with them. In contrast, the Asian woman, dark, dressed in black, applying very dark lipstick to an open mouth, is designated a "man-eater," not merely a voracious animal herself but a man-hater as lesbians (and feminists) are stereotypically assumed to be. This image repeats a long-standing sexist dualism that women are either pure or corrupted, good girls or bad girls, including the racist overlay of the association of good with white and bad with dark skin. But the messages embedded in this image work also to convey other ideas: the association of female sexuality with animality, of women of color as dangerous and abnormal, of same-sex sexuality as "mixing" those that are naturally meant to be kept apart. At the same time, promises the Hennessy ad, all of this danger and perversion is incorporated as pleasurable and erotic, especially for a male viewer who is in proper control of the situation (which seems to mean buying the right Cognac).

Another common set of patterns in ads shows nature as heteronormative, that is, supporting the idea that heterosexuality is the only natural, 36 normal, and acceptable sexuality. Some examples are images such as a Geo Tracker ad that exhorts the male and female pair to "be two with nature" (Figure 16.11) and a clothing ad that shows a man and woman together and states, "We're all love junkies. Nature made us that way." A Winston ad foregrounding a mule's head clearly wants us to reject any sexual liaison that is

FIGURE 16.11   "Be two with nature" (Geotracker n.d.)

nonreproductive as "unnatural," as it says, "The mule. The offspring of a donkey and a horse. They cannot reproduce. A perfect example of not leaving well enough alone." Thus the idea of purity in tobacco is associated with naturalness, normative sexuality, and health in one move.

Another, very different but pervasive, pattern of naturalization presents 37 nature as something to conquer, to claim, and to control, this pattern is often associated with ideas of nationalism or militarism. The images that use this pattern usually are related to ideas of straight, white masculinity as dominant, hard, powerful, muscular, and competitive. Car ads revel in this imagery, especially those vehicles (such as trucks, SUVs, Jeeps, and Humvees) that are associated with this kind of dominant masculinity. As these tough vehicles bound over a rough, natural landscape, the ads convey a sense of achievement in conquering nature, a thrill of power in being able to penetrate into hidden, desirable, and wild places. These images are often also associated with nationalism as well as masculinism, as in an ad for a ski area that asks, "Should you plant your poles? Or the flag?"

Images of conquest such as these are also frequently associated with 38 the mythology of the frontier and with associations of Native Americans as nature, as objects of colonization and expropriation. One of the richest images that represent this pattern is not actually an ad but part of a story published in the fashion magazine *W* about the private life of Ralph Lauren, the clothing designer, entitled "Ralph's Teepee" (Reginald n.d.). Apparently, when Ralph wants to get away and relax, he can do so in his very own buffalo-hide teepee on his 14,000-acre ranch in Telluride, Colorado, a teepee he designed himself and filled with trendy furniture and furs. His ability to create a teepee, to expropriate Native American culture and land in the West, is celebrated as a mark of his strength, his success, his independence, his individuality, and his competitive drive. "I don't look at anyone else's teepee. I make my own rules about how I want to live," says Lauren in this story, completely obscuring the costs to others of his "lifestyle choices" and the way in which only his wealth allows him to make his own rules.

All of these patterns of naturalization use ideas of nature, sexuality, 39 animals, the earth, and the natural not only to produce the desire to consume a product (which is the function of advertising) but also to reproduce views that underlie many social inequalities: that nature is female, white women are pure, female sexuality is dangerous, women of color are closer to animals, heterosexuality is more natural than homosexuality, "real" men are competitive and violent conquerors of nature, and indigenous peoples are primitive by being closer to nature or are inherently ecological. Though ad designers seldom consciously intend to support these ideas, they do want to use images that are powerful and bring associations of pleasure, desire, and achievement—dominant associations that may depend on ideas that support unequal social hierarchies. They reveal the degree to which the American psyche remains deeply riddled with prejudices that the ads rely on and reinforce.

NOTE

1. For many years, I have taught an upper-level undergraduate class called "Gender, Race and Nature in American Culture" at Washington State University. I have also taught this material in Santa Cruz, California, as well as in Perth, Australia, Berlin, Germany, Taipei, Taiwan, and Kunming, China.

WORKS CITED

Berger, John. 1972. *Ways of seeing*. New York: Penguin.

Bird, Elizabeth. 1987. "The social construction of nature: Theoretical approaches to the history of environmental problems." *Environmental Review* 11, no. 4: 255–64.

Chea, Terence. 2004. "Immigration debate fuels battle over Sierra Club's fate." *Boston Globe*, Feb. 18. http://www.boston.com/news/nation/articles/2004/02/18/immigration_debate_fuels_battle_over_sierra_clubs_fate/.

Cronon, William, ed. 1996. *Uncommon ground: Toward reinventing nature*. New York: W. W. Norton.

Cuomo, Christine. 1998. *Feminism and ecological communities: An ethic of flourishing* New York: Routledge.

Fiske, John. 1989. *Understanding popular culture*. New York: Routledge.

_____ 1992. "The promises of monsters: A regenerated politics for inappropriated others." In *Cultural Studies*, ed. Lawrence Grossberg, Cary Nelson, and Paula Triechler, 295–337. New York: Routledge.

_____ 2004. "Cyborgs to companion species: Reconfiguring kinship in technoscience." In *The Haraway Reader*, 298–320. New York: Routledge.

Haraway, Donna. 1991. *Simians, cyborgs, and women: The reinvention of nature*. New York: Routledge.

Merchant, Carolyn. 1980. *The death of nature: Women, ecology and the scientific revolution*. New York: HarperOne.

Morgan, Edmund S. 19765. *American slavery, Ameican freedom: The ordeal of colonial Virginia*. New York. W. W. Norton.

Reginald, James. n.d. "Ralph's teepee." *W Magazine*, with photographs by Michael Mundy.

Sandilands, Catriona. 1999. *The good-natured feminist: Ecofeminism and the guest for democracy*. Minneapolis: University of Minnesota Press.

Schiebinger, Londa. 1993. *Nature's body: Gender in the making of modern science*. Boston: Beacon Press.

Sturken, Marita, and Lisa Cartwright. 2011. *Practices of looking: An introduction to visual culture*. Oxford: Oxford University Press.

Williams, Raymond. [1976] 1983. *Keywords*. New York: Oxford University Press.

■ ■ ■

Reading as a Writer: Analyzing Rhetorical Choices

1. At the end of paragraph 5, Sturgeon writes, "Obviously what is 'natural' is highly contested and therefore deeply political." Discuss the examples she offers in the previous paragraphs to illustrate this claim. What other examples can you produce and analyze, as she does? What do you conclude about current uses of the term *natural*?

2. Locate some other visual ads that in some way play on ideas about "nature," and apply Sturgeon's analytic strategy to them. To what extent do they illustrate—or extend or contest or complicate—her claims? Share your analysis with your peers.

Writing as a Reader: Entering the Conversation of Ideas

1. Sturgeon and Carolyn Merchant are fascinated by the complex intersec-
    tion of nature and culture. Compose an essay in which you draw on both
    writers' insights and examples to see how these terms overlap, shape one
    another, and contrast with one another. Given these examples, how do you
    define the line between nature and culture? What significance do you see
    in the your definitions of these terms, given the ways the term *natural* is
    misused, according to these authors?

2. Both Sturgeon and Jean Kilbourne (Chapter 13) are interested in the
    visual arguments of advertising. Gather a small set of visual advertise-
    ments that in some way evoke nature or appeals to the natural. Write an
    essay in which you apply Sturgeon's and Kilbourne's analytical perspec-
    tives to the advertising, along with your own insights. What can you con-
    clude about the intersections of gender, culture, and concepts of nature?
    Be sure to tie your claims to specific visual and textual examples in the
    advertisements.

CAROLYN MERCHANT

Eden Commodified

Carolyn Merchant is a professor of environmental history, philosophy,
and ethics in the Department of Conservation and Resource Studies at the
University of California, Berkeley. She has published widely and won many
awards for her work on the interrelationships between these areas of study
in her pursuit to explain better the long-term effects of human behaviors
on the environment. This reading comes from her book, *Reinventing Eden:
The Fate of Nature in Western Culture* (2003, republished in 2013).

Merchant opens with a detailed description of a contemporary mall
as a kind of Garden of Eden, with "pleasures and temptations" that will be
familiar to anyone who has wandered through a shopping mall with indoor
gardens, fountains, and enticingly arrayed treats to purchase and consume. By paragraph 4, though, her argument begins to emerge more fully:
"Malls are designed to be morally uplifting places. Sanitized surroundings,
central surveillance systems, noise restrictions, and strict behavioral rules
regulate the undesirable, homeless, and criminal elements of society, while
socializing both young and old into the acceptable consumer culture of
the new twenty-first century." You might pause to discuss what she might
mean by this list, even before you read the whole essay. What examples
from your own experience might illustrate—or challenge—this depiction
of a typical mall?

Merchant moves from her rich descriptions of the "malling" of the
United States (and the world) to her analysis of biotechnology. How, exactly,
does she make this somewhat unexpected connection? Consider what you
already know about GMOs (genetically modified organisms), and weigh the
examples that Merchant offers here. Which do you find surprising?

Throughout this piece, Merchant weaves together our fascination with the idea of an Edenic nature with our consumerist desires for convenience and "perfection." As she moves back and forth between these two aspects of her argument, consider additionally what this changing technology might mean for workers in these industries, and for you as a consumer (both as a purchaser of products and as someone who literally eats the fruits of biotechnology). Merchant's end notes (especially note 17) help us think about costs of our desires that are not always apparent when we head out, optimistically, to shop.

■ ■ ■

Cora had been in the mall since early morning. Donning her pink jogging suit, she joined twelve other seniors who set out each day to circle the inner mall. As she passed each shop she gazed longingly at the orlon dresses, silk Parisian scarves, blue-steel tennis rackets, DVDs, television sets, cafe lattés, and orange smoothies. Her limited retirement budget prevented her from purchasing more than one little "luxury" a month, but she reveled in her daydreams. After her aerobic fitness exercises ended, she finished her bagel and coffee in the garden café and wandered through the big department stores checking for new fall styles and jotting down ideas for Christmas. How lucky I am, she thought. This beautiful world, right across the street from my house, is an Eden on Earth.

—Carolyn Merchant, 1998

The modern version of the Garden of Eden is the enclosed shopping *1* mall. Surrounded by a desert of parking lots, malls comprise gardens of shops covered by glass domes, accessed by spiral staircases and escalators reaching upward toward heaven. Today's malls feature life-sized trees, trellises decorated with flowers, stone grottoes, birds, animals, and even indoor beaches that simulate nature as a cultivated, benign garden. The "river that went out of the Eden to water the garden" is reclaimed in meandering tree-lined streams and ponds filled with bright orange goldfish. The commodified Eden is the Recovery Narrative's epitome in the modern world.

This garden in the city re-creates the pleasures and temptations *2* of the original Eden, where people can peacefully harvest the fruits of earth with gold grown by the market. Within manicured spaces of trees, flowers, and fountains, we can shop for nature at the Nature Company, purchase "natural" clothing at Esprit, sample organic foods and "rainforest crunch" in kitchen gardens, buy twenty-first-century products at The Sharper Image, and play virtual reality games in which SimEve is reinvented in cyberspace. The spaces and commodities of the shopping mall epitomize consumer capitalism's vision of Recovery from the Fall of Adam and Eve.[1]

Consumer's Nature

Canada's West Edmonton Mall, the first of a generation of megamalls, is   3
eight city blocks long by four blocks wide and covers 5.2 million square
feet. It sports an indoor surfing beach with adjustable wave heights, an
amusement park, an ice-skating rink, a twenty-screen movie theater,
and eight hundred stores. Cul de sacs within the mall replicate New
Orleans's Bourbon Street and Paris's boulevards. It has a 360-room hotel,
with theme rooms inspired by places such as Polynesia, Hollywood, and
Victorian England, along with rooms based on transportation forms such
as sports cars, pickup trucks, and horse-drawn carriages. People from
around the world celebrate honeymoons, anniversaries, and birthdays in
the hotel, while those with recreational vehicles may spend an entire summer camped in the parking lot to maximize shopping access.[2]

Malls are places of light, hope, and promise—transitions to new   4
worlds. People are reinvented and redeemed by the mall. Said one ecstatic
visitor, "I *am* the mall. . . . This place is heaven." In the film *Dawn of the
Dead*, the apocalypse has come and the survivors have gathered in a
shopping mall as the best place to make their last stand. Malls are designed
to be morally uplifting places. Sanitized surroundings, central surveillance
systems, noise restrictions, and strict behavioral rules regulate the undesirable, homeless, and criminal elements of society, while socializing both
young and old into the acceptable consumer culture of the new twenty-first
century. Like the enclosed gardens of the Middle Ages, they are redemptive
places of ecstasy. Like the eighteenth-century gardens of the nobility, they
are displays of power, surprise, and desire. Like the public parks of the
nineteenth century, they uplift, temper, and socialize the masses.[3]

Malls have replaced orange groves, cornfields, and pine forests. Arti-   5
ficial nature has redeemed natural nature. Nature is captured in the West
Edmonton Mall in a palm-lined beach, an artificial lagoon, an underwa-
ter seascape, performing dolphins, caged birds, and tame Siberian tigers.
Sunlit gardens, tree-lined paths, meandering streams, and tropical flowers adorn courtyard restaurants. Nature in the mall is a dense text to be
read by the visitors. It exemplifies not only human control over nonhuman nature, but the reinvention of nature itself as Edenic space. It portrays original innocence and delight in nature, calming the consumer as
she contemplates elements for purchase and duplication in the home.
Just as the mall keeps out the socially undesirable, it rejects the naturally
undesirable—weeds, pests, and garbage.[4]

Outside of Minneapolis is the Mall of America, which aspires to the   6
iconic and totemic status of the Grand Canyon, and in which four hundred trees are planted in interior gardens. At the mall's center is Knott's
Camp Snoopy, a seven-acre theme park that "brings the outdoors in-
doors." "Inspired by Minnesota's natural habitat—forests, meadows, river
banks, and marshes," it feels, smells, and sounds like a perpetual summer of 70-degree temperatures in the Minnesota woods. But those alien

year-around temperatures forced Camp Snoopy to substitute 256 tons of non-Minnesota figs, azaleas, oleanders, jasmine, hibiscus, and olive trees from the tropics. Although marketers for Camp Snoopy assert that the park's mealy bugs, aphids, and spider mites are controlled through the use of integrated pest management methods (such as lady beetles), the staff actually spend nights spraying with pesticides to minimize insect damage.[5]

The Mall of America declares itself "the most environmentally con- 7 scious shopping center in the industry," and claims to recycle up to 80 percent of its refuse, as a "dedication to Mother Earth." Yet Rich Doering of Browning-Ferris Industries, the contractor responsible for dealing with the 700 tons of garbage produced at the mall each month, says that only about one-third of the stores' waste is actually recycled and very little of the shoppers' trash: "The venture is unprofitable to Browning-Ferris, which would find it far cheaper to recycle the mall's refuse somewhere other than in its basement."[6]

Mall culture has diversified to take advantage of changing economic 8 times and consumer habits. The malling of America has become the malling of the world, reconstituting the Shakespearean dictum as, "All the world's a mall and all the men and women merely shoppers." Streets are blocked off to become pedestrian malls. Lifestyle malls target achievers, emulators, and belongers, while class-conscious malls focus on lower income and ethnic consumers. Specialty malls cater to New Age, new chic, and cool commodity shoppers. Boutiques, antiques, museum shops, art galleries, cultural centers, history theme parks, Renaissance fairs, piazzas, and discount malls are featured in a profusion of difference within unity Even "hip teens" for whom malls are "totally uncool" reinvent the East Village streets of New York City, Goodwill, and Salvation Army stores, and warehouse "labs" as "anti-mall Meccas." Malls, they claim, are all look-alikes, are not teen savvy, are designed for parents and kids, and have too many suffocating antinoise, antismoking, and antiskateboarding rules.[7]

As a way of life, consumer culture reclaims pleasure, innocence, tran- 9 quility, youth, and even nature itself as a garden. It replicates "the most enchanting dream which has ever consoled mankind, the myth of a Golden Age in which man lived on the fruits of the earth, peacefully, piously, and with primitive simplicity." As Joseph Addison put it in the eighteenth century, "I look upon the pleasure which we take in a Garden, as one of the most innocent Delights in Human . . . Life. A Garden was the Habitation of our first Parents before the Fall. . . . [The] satisfaction which a Man takes in these Works of Nature, [is] a laudable, if not a virtuous Habit of Mind."

Biotechnology

Just as the mall re-creates the Garden of Eden, biotechnology re-creates 10 the tree of life at the center of the garden. While mechanistic science deciphered the book of nature, biotechnology decodes the book of life. It "improves" on nature's heritage, correcting "her" mistakes by removing genetic flaws, cloning genetically perfect organisms, and banking designer genes for future human brains and bodies. From genetically engineered apples to "Flavr-Savr" tomatoes, the fruits of the original, evolved garden are being redesigned so that the salinated, irrigated desert can continue to blossom as the rose. In the recovered Garden of Eden, fruits will ripen faster, have fewer seeds, need less water, require fewer pesticides, contain less saturated fat, and have longer shelf lives. The human temptation to engineer nature is reaching too close to the powers of God warn the Jeremiahs. Still, the progressive engineers who design the technologies that allow the Recovery of Eden to accelerate see only hope in the new fabrications.[8]

Biotechnology, the Recovery Narrative's newest chapter, illustrates   *11* the reading of nature's bible in sentences, books, and libraries comprising genetic sequences. Information encoded in the DNA of each species can be manipulated to create new books in the library of nature.[9] It assumes:

- DNA is composed of the four bases adenine, thymine, cytosine, and guanine that are the molecular "letters" that form the words needed to create the many hundred-word sentences that comprise the gene—the "universal building block of life."

- Genes are discrete bits of information assembled into "books" of chromosomal messages, "libraries" of bacterial clones, and databanks to be edited, revised, and reorganized.

- Because the gene is the fundamental building block of life, a gene will maintain its identity through change when inserted into the matter of another species and yet continue to function as it did in the original.

- Individual genes can be studied and analyzed in models before being assembled into new combinations.

- Genetically engineered organisms can be introduced into new environmental contexts with little or no risk since the laboratory and the fields are one and continuous.

In the "garden of unearthly delights," genetically engineered food is created by taking genes from one life form and implanting them in another. The process ensures "summertime tastes" year around with "vine-ripened" flavors. Companies such as Calgene, Monsanto, Upjohn, Pioneer, and DeKalb are pioneering efforts to improve the genes of cantaloupes and squash to resist viruses, corn that requires fewer herbicides, potatoes with higher starch content, bell peppers that stay fresh longer, and rice with higher protein value. Calgene's tomatoes have a gene that reverses the action of the enzyme that causes decay, eliminating the need to pick green tomatoes for shipment followed by rapid ripening—degreening—with ethylene gas.[10]

Calgene's "MacGregor" tomato (so named for its warm Farmer   *12* MacGregor and Peter Rabbit feeling) was engineered by inserting a copy of the "rotting" gene backwards, allowing the tomato to stay in the field a few days longer and be picked pink, or vine-ripe, rather than green. The process of implanting this "antisense" gene was patented, so that in the future the company could collect royalties, not only on bioengineered tomatoes, but on any other crop altered by the same technique. The vertically integrated company controlled the entire process, from planting to processing and distributing the tomatoes. The bioengineered tomato, approved by the U.S. Food and Drug Administration (FDA) in early 1994, was the first step toward realizing huge profits on the new DNA technology. Unfortunately for investors, the Farmer MacGregor lacked the taste of a garden ripened tomato and Calgene lost value in the marketplace.[11]

Farmers prepare fields for engineered tomatoes by covering them with *13* black plastic to prevent weed growth and soil erosion. Computer-regulated, plastic drip-irrigation pipes ensure that correct amounts of water at proper times are released to the seedlings. The tomatoes are grown using techniques of sustainable agriculture. Correct amounts of nitrogen are applied to the fields and deep drainage ditches collect the runoff to prevent it from damaging the surrounding environment. Cover crops and fallowing improve soil quality and integrated pest management (IPM) techniques control pests through the use of beneficial insects and minimal pesticides. In the packing house the tomatoes are labeled with a brand-name sticker and boxed stem-side up so the customer will see the fruit in its prime, reminding her or him of its Edenic summer freshness and taste.[12]

Corn is another crop that biotechnology companies such as Monsanto *14* are engineering as new marketplace commodities. Genetically modified varieties can be made resistant to pests, salinization, and drought. A problem arises, however, over the question of genetic pollution—a potential clash between genes versus ecosystems and genetics versus ecology. In some cases, engineered genes (transgenes) may cross over into other corn plants, via pollen from the modified plant that mixes with unmodified plants, thus "contaminating" them with engineered genes. In this way the evolutionary diversity of corn in its center of origin (Mexico) might become polluted with new genetically engineered varieties not heretofore found in nature. Such a situation apparently has occurred in Mexico and could be of concern for other crop cradles (such as rice, barley, wheat, potatoes, and so on) which have been sources of diversity for plant breeders responding to catastrophic diseases (such as the Irish potato blight). In the case of "polluted plants," the transgenes do not decline over time, but instead replicate their genetic information repeatedly.[13]

In the reinvented Eden, animals too would be modified for greater *15* productivity, increasing their share in the commodities markets. Dairy cows produce more milk with less fat when cows are injected with a bovine growth hormone, such as Posilac, marketed by Monsanto Chemicals after FDA approval in November 1993. More milk per cow means more profit for the dairy farmer and for Monsanto. Monsanto's promotional video tells farmers that "Posilac is the single most tested product in history . . . You'll want to inject Posilac in every eligible cow, as every cow not treated is a lost income opportunity." Observes critic Robin Mather, "There are dozens of cows in every [video] segment, but no one ever touches them—except to inject them. Cows are shown eating in long rows stretching to the camera's horizon; cows are shown in milking parlors. . . . There are cows in barns, but not cows in pastures. That's not how cows are 'managed' these days."[14]

Chickens are harder to engineer than cattle or fruit crops because the embryo is encased in the hard eggshell. Nevertheless bioengineers work toward genetically engineered chickens that will resist influenza and salmonella, while also attempting to breed docile chickens that will show less aggressiveness in the close quarters of today's vast poultry houses. Scientists aim to manipulate chicken DNA so that the birds produce more lean white meat, less dark meat, and less fat. If a poultry company could patent its new chicken, it could own it as well as the eggs it produces.[15]   16

While bioengineered domesticated animals may be controlled to some degree, transgenic wild animals are not so easily managed. Transgenic salmon are created by introducing genes from ocean pout fish that promote growth in the salmon. Such "Frankenfish" seem to biotechnologists to be the answer to feeding growing populations with healthy food, without depleting ocean supplies. Environmentalists, on the other hand, fear that transgenic fish might escape their ocean breeding pens, mate with wild fish and contaminate the wild salmon gene pool. In fact, one study showed that not only did wild salmon prefer to mate with transgenic fish, but that the offspring died young, raising fears that the wild fish would die out.[16]   17

Biotechnology contributes the science and technology needed for consumer capitalism's vision of Recovery from the Fall. Not only does bioengineering reinvent the products of fallen nature to make them more perfect, it redeems human labor by introducing new labor-saving technologies. Tomato planting is done by automatic drill and picking by the tomato harvester; dairy cows are milked by automatic carousel milkers; chickens are stunned by electric shock, killed by a spinning blade, plucked by "rubber fingers," and mechanically eviscerated. Now computer-driven robots are being designed to pick apples from the trees, saving Eve the task of reaching for the fruit, but not of tasting it.[17]   18

NOTES

1. Richard Keller Simon, "The Formal Garden in the Age of Consumer Culture: A Reading of the Twentieth-Century Shopping Mall," in *Mapping American Culture*, ed. Wayne Franklin and Michael Steiner (Iowa City. University of Iowa Press, 1992), 124–25, 231–50.
2. Margaret Crawford, "The World in a Shopping Mall," in *Variations on a Theme Park*, ed. Michael Sorkin (New York: Hill and Wang, 1992), 3–30.
3. David Guterson, "Enclosed, Encyclopedic, Endured: One Week at the Mall of America," in *A Forest of Voices: Reading and Writing the Environment*, ed. Chris Anderson and Lex Runciman (Mountain View, Calif.: Mayfield, 1995), 124–36; see esp. 126, 128, quotation on 126; Crawford, "The World in a Shopping Mall," 27; Simon, "The Formal Garden in the Age of Consumer Culture," 244.

4. Crawford, "The World in a Shopping Mall," 7; Simon, "The Formal Garden in the Age of Consumer Culture," 238; Guterson, "Enclosed, Encyclopedic, Endured," 132–34.

5. Guterson, "Enclosed, Encyclopedic, Endured," 133–34.

6. Ibid., 132.

7. Crawford, "The World in a Shopping Mall," 9, 28–30; Bruce Horovitz, "Malls are Like, Totally Uncool, Say Hip Teens," *USA Today*, May 1, 1996, 1–2.

8. Philip Elmer-Dewitt, "Fried Gene Tomatoes," *Time*, May 30, 1994, 54–55.

9. Francesca Lyman, "Are We Redesigning Nature in Our Own Image? An Interview with Jeremy Rifkin," *Environmental Action*, April 1983, 20–25; P. J. Regal, "Models of Genetically Engineered Organisms and their Ecological Impact," in *Ecology of Biological Invasions in North America and Hawaii*, ed. Harold Mooney (New York: Springer-Verlag, 1986); Marc Lappé, *Broken Code: The Exploitation of DNA* (San Francisco, Calif.: Sierra Club Books, 1984); Marc Lappé and Britt Bailey, *Against the Grain: Biotechnology and the Corporate Takeover of Your Food* (Monroe, Maine: Common Courage Press, 1998); Jon Beckwith, *Making Genes, Making Waves* (Cambridge, Mass.: Harvard University Press), 2002.

10. Robin Mather, *A Garden of Unearthly Delights: Bioengineering and the Future of Food* (New York: E. P. Dutton, 1995), 25–49; Elmer-Demitt, "Fried Gene Tomatoes," 54, 55.

11. Mather, *Garden of Unearthly Delights*, 27–30, 42; Herb Greenberg, "Calgene's Biotech Bounty Disappears From Grocers' Shelves," *San Francisco Chronicle*, Jan. 17, 1995, B1, B3.

12. Mather, *Garden of Unearthly Delights*, 31–33, 44–46.

13. Michael Pollan, "Genetic Pollution of Corn in Mexico," *New York Times*, Dec. 9, 2001.

14. Mather, *Garden of Unearthly Delights*, 84–94, quotations on 90, 91–92.

15. Ibid., 121–22.

16. Jane Kay, "Frankenfish Spawning Controversy," *San Francisco Chronicle*, April 29, 2002, A4.

17. Mather, *Garden of Unearthly Delights*, 35, 80, 131–33; Claude Gele, "L'Agriculture manque de robots," *Sciences and Techniques* 26 (1986): 22–29 and cover illustration. Such technology, which delivers perfect fruit, pure milk, and lean meat to the supermarket, masks the labor of the field and processing plant. Much of that labor now comes from Mexico, legally or illegally, via the tomato, chicken, and pork trails. Men and women work on their feet all day grading, packing, and inspecting tomatoes. Men who inject cows, mix feed, and clean milking equipment often labor under bitterly cold or hot, humid conditions. Women who catch and correct chickens missed by the eviscerating machinery work under cold, moist conditions that may cause illnesses leading to job loss. Yet for industry, the problems are offset by the advantages. (Mather, *Garden of Unearthly Delights*, 43–45, 80–82, 132–33.)

■ ■ ■

Reading as a Writer: Analyzing Rhetorical Choices

1. Merchant uses description to do more than depict the places we shop; she uses description to build her point of view. Return to the early paragraphs of her essay in which she describes malls, and mark the passages where you can hear her argument emerging in her choice of details and in her language. What do you conclude about the effectiveness of using description in the service of argument?

2. Merchant includes plenty of science in her discussion and analysis of biotechnology. What effect does this information have on her overall argu-

ment? Consider looking up some recent information about GMOs. What varying perspectives do you find, and from which sources? Share your insights with a partner, small group, or the class.

Writing as a Reader: Entering the Conversation of Ideas

1. Noël Sturgeon shares Merchant's concerns about the way concepts about "nature" are packaged and sold like any other commodity. How do these writers extend, complement, and perhaps complicate one another's ideas? Write an essay in which you bring together the ideas of these authors and your own conclusions about the significance of the trend of "selling nature," given our current environmental problems.

2. Merchant and the co-writers of *Nature's Fortune*, Mark R. Terek and Jonathan S. Adams (Chapter 17), are interested in the complicated and problematic relationship between businesses and nature. While these writers may seem to be on different sides of an argument about the relationship between money-making and the natural world, a close analysis might reveal that they share some of the same values and perspectives. Compose an essay in which you draw on these authors' ideas and examples in order to develop your own perspective on this current and heated debate.

STEVEN D. LEVITT AND STEPHEN J. DUBNER

What Do Al Gore and Mount Pinatubo Have in Common?

Steven D. Levitt is a professor of economics at the University of Chicago who has won many scholarly awards, in addition to being named in 2004 the most influential economist under the age of forty, and one of *Time* magazine's "100 People Who Shape Our World." Stephen J. Dubner is an author of books for adults and children and a journalist on a wide range of topics, from sports to economics. Levitt and Dubner collaborated on the best-selling *Freakonomics: A Rogue Economist Explains the Hidden Side of Everything* (2005), followed by *SuperFreakonomics: Global Cooling, Patriotic Prostitutes, and Why Suicide Bombers Should Buy Life Insurance* (2009), the latter of which is the source of this reading. Their proclivity for lively titles extends to the chapter from which this excerpt comes, "What Do Al Gore and Mount Pinatubo Have in Common?"

You might be surprised to find that economists are interested in far more than the economy, narrowly defined. In this chapter, Levitt and Dubner explore behavioral patterns and their consequences—in this case, focusing on shifting approaches to environmental concerns. They open this chapter with a reminder that not all that long ago (in the 1970s), there had been concern about global *cooling*. Now, as we know, the concern is about warming, and in punchy journalistic prose they suggest how complicated it is to measure humans' effect on the environment: "There is essentially a consensus among climate scientists that the earth's temperature has been rising and, increasingly, agreement that human activity has played an important role. But the ways humans affect the climate aren't always as obvious as they seem" (para. 11). In the paragraphs that follow, they offer many surprising examples as they explain this complexity.

These writers enjoy using unexpected examples; keep track of the information you find most surprising, and why. For example, why do they suggest that eating kangaroos is better for the environment than eating cows? Why do they claim that climate scientists "are more like economists than physicists or biologists"? They do use economic language when they consider "cost-benefit analysis" of climate concerns (para. 22), and why there is no simple way to evaluate this. How do they explain their understanding of the way humans balance their concerns of a catastrophic future and their more immediate desires? Why do they venture into the language of religiosity in their final paragraphs?

Levitt and Dubner, like other writers in this collection, seek to reframe our understanding of contemporary issues. While they do not "solve" the problem of how to understand our concerns about climate change, they invite us to see the problem in a fresh—and perhaps even more complex—way. What will you take from this piece as you read the next report about global warming? How might you apply their insights about human behavior to other issues?

The headlines have been harrowing, to say the least. *1*

"Some experts believe that mankind is on the threshold of a new pattern of adverse global climate for which it is ill-prepared," one *New York Times* article declared. It quoted climate researchers who argued that "this climatic change poses a threat to the people of the world." *2*

A *Newsweek* article, citing a National Academy of Sciences report, warned that climate change "would force economic and social adjustments on a worldwide scale." Worse yet, "climatologists are pessimistic that political leaders will take any positive action to compensate for the climatic change or even to allay its effects." *3*

Who in his or her right mind wouldn't be scared of global warming? *4*

But that's not what these scientists were talking about. These articles, published in the mid-1970s, were predicting the effects of global *cooling*. *5*

Alarm bells had rung because the average ground temperature in the Northern Hemisphere had fallen by .5 degrees Fahrenheit (.28 degrees Celsius) from 1945 to 1968. Furthermore, there had been a large increase in snow cover and, between 1964 and 1972, a decrease of 1.3 percent in the amount of sunshine hitting the United States. *Newsweek* reported that the temperature decline, while relatively small in absolute terms, "has taken the planet about a sixth of the way toward the Ice Age average." *6*

The big fear was a collapse of the agricultural system. In Britain, cool- 7
ing had already shortened the growing season by two weeks. "[T]he resulting famines could be catastrophic," warned the *Newsweek* article. Some
scientists proposed radical warming solutions such as "melting the arctic
ice cap by covering it with black soot."[1]

These days, of course, the threat is the opposite. The earth is no longer 8
thought to be too cool but rather too warm. And black soot, rather than
saving us, is seen as a chief villain. We have cast endless streams of carbon
emissions skyward, the residue of all the fossil fuels we burn to heat and
cool and feed and transport and entertain ourselves.

By so doing, we have apparently turned our tender planet into a green- 9
house, fashioning in the sky a chemical scrim that traps too much of the
sun's warmth and prevents it from escaping back into space. The "global
cooling" phase notwithstanding, the average global ground temperature
over the past hundred years has risen 1.3 degrees Fahrenheit (.7 degrees
Celsius), and this warming has accelerated of late.

"[W]e are now so abusing the Earth," writes James Lovelock, the 10
renowned environmental scientist, "that it may rise and move back to the
hot state it was in fifty-five million years ago, and if it does most of us, and
our descendants, will die."

There is essentially a consensus among climate scientists that the 11
earth's temperature has been rising and, increasingly, agreement that
human activity has played an important role. But the ways humans affect
the climate aren't always as obvious as they seem.

It is generally believed that cars and trucks and airplanes contribute 12
an ungodly share of greenhouse gases. This has recently led many right-
minded people to buy a Prius or other hybrid car. But every time a Prius
owner drives to the grocery store, she may be canceling out its emission-
reducing benefit, at least if she shops in the meat section.

How so? Because cows—as well as sheep and other cud-chewing 13
animals called ruminants—are wicked polluters. Their exhalation and
flatulence and belching and manure emit methane, which by one common
measure is about *twenty-five times more potent* as a greenhouse gas than
the carbon dioxide released by cars (and, by the way, humans). The world's
ruminants are responsible for about 50 percent more greenhouse gas than
the entire transportation sector.

Even the "locavore" movement, which encourages people to eat locally 14
grown food, doesn't help in this regard. A recent study by two Carnegie
Mellon researchers, Christopher Weber and H. Scott Matthews, found
that buying locally produced food actually *increases* greenhouse-gas
emissions. Why?

More than 80 percent of the emissions associated with food are in 15
the production phase, and big farms are far more efficient than small
farms. Transportation represents only 11 percent of food emissions, with
delivery from producer to retailer representing only 4 percent. The best

way to help, Weber and Matthews suggest, is to subtly change your diet. "Shifting less than one day per week's worth of calories from red meat and dairy products to chicken, fish, eggs, or a vegetable-based diet achieves more greenhouse-gas reduction than buying all locally sourced food," they write.

You could also switch from eating beef to eating kangaroo—because 16 kangaroo farts, as fate would have it, don't contain methane. But just imagine the marketing campaign that would be needed to get Americans to take up 'roo-burgers. And think how hard the cattle ranchers would lobby Washington to ban kangaroo meat. Fortunately, a team of Australian scientists is attacking this problem from the opposite direction, trying to replicate the digestive bacteria in kangaroos' stomachs so it can be transplanted to cows.

For a variety of reasons, global warming is a uniquely thorny problem. 17

First, climate scientists can't run experiments. In this regard, they are 18 more like economists than physicists or biologists, their goal being to tease out relationships from existing data without the ability to, say, invoke a ten-year ban on cars (or cows).

Second, the science is extraordinarily complex. The impact of any 19 single human activity—let's pretend we tripled the number of airplane flights, for instance—depends on many different factors: the gases emitted, yes, but also how the planes affect things like convection and cloud formation.

To predict global surface temperatures, one must take into account 20 these and many other factors, including evaporation, rainfall, and, yes, animal emissions. But even the most sophisticated climate models don't do a very good job of representing such variables, and that obviously makes predicting the climatic future very difficult. By comparison, the risk models used by modern financial institutions seem quite reliable—but, as recent banking meltdowns have shown, that isn't always the case.

The imprecision inherent in climate science means we don't know 21 with any certainty whether our current path will lead temperatures to rise two degrees or ten degrees. Nor do we really know if even a steep rise means an inconvenience or the end of civilization as we know it.

It is this specter of catastrophe, no matter how remote, that has pro- 22 pelled global warming to the forefront of public policy. If we were certain that warming would impose large and defined costs, the economics of the problem would come down to a simple cost-benefit analysis. Do the future benefits from cutting emissions outweigh the costs of doing so? Or are we better off waiting to cut emissions later—or even, perhaps, polluting at will and just learning to live in a hotter world?

The economist Martin Weitzman analyzed the best available climate 23 models and concluded the future holds a 5 percent chance of a terrible-case scenario—a rise of more than 10 degrees Celsius.

There is of course great uncertainty even in this estimate of uncer- 24
tainty. So how should we place a value on this relatively small chance of
worldwide catastrophe?

The economist Nicholas Stern, who prepared an encyclopedic report 25
on global warming for the British government, suggested we spend
1.5 percent of global gross domestic product each year—that would be a
$1.2 trillion bill as of today—to attack the problem.

But as most economists know, people are generally unwilling to spend 26
a lot of money to avert a future problem, especially when its likelihood is
so uncertain. One good reason for waiting is that we might have options in
the future to avert the problem that cost far less than today's options.

Although economists are trained to be cold-blooded enough to sit 27
around and calmly discuss the trade-offs involved in global catastrophe,
the rest of us are a bit more excitable. And most people respond to uncertainty with more emotion—fear, blame, paralysis—than might be advis-
able. Uncertainty also has a nasty way of making us conjure up the very
worst possibilities. (Think about the last time you heard a bump in the
night outside your bedroom door.) With global warming, the worst possibilities are downright biblical: rising seas, hellish temperatures, plague
upon plague, a planet in chaos.

It is understandable, therefore, that the movement to stop global 28
warming has taken on the feel of a religion. The core belief is that humankind inherited a pristine Eden, has sinned greatly by polluting it, and must
now suffer lest we all perish in a fiery apocalypse. James Lovelock, who
might be considered a high priest of this religion, writes in a confessional
language that would feel at home in any liturgy: "[W]e misused energy and
overpopulated the Earth . . . [I]t is much too late for sustainable development; what we need is a sustainable retreat."

A "sustainable retreat" sounds a bit like wearing a sackcloth. To citi- 29
zens of the developed world, in particular, this would mean consuming
less, using less, driving less—and, though it's uncouth to say it aloud,
learning to live with a gradual depopulation of the earth.

If the modern conservation movement has a patron saint, it is 30
surely Al Gore, the former vice president and recent Nobel laureate. His
documentary film *An Inconvenient Truth* hammered home for millions
the dangers of overconsumption. He has since founded the Alliance for
Climate Protection, which describes itself as "an unprecedented mass
persuasion exercise." Its centerpiece is a $300 million public-service
campaign called "We," which urges Americans to change their profli-
gate ways.

Any religion, meanwhile, has its heretics, and global warming is no 31
exception. Boris Johnson, a classically educated journalist who managed
to become mayor of London, has read Lovelock—he calls him a "sacer-
dotal figure"—and concluded the following: "Like all the best religions,
fear of climate change satisfies our need for guilt, and self-disgust, and

that eternal human sense that technological progress must be punished by the gods. And the fear of climate change is like a religion in this vital sense, that it is veiled in mystery, and you can never tell whether your acts of propitiation or atonement have been in any way successful."

So while the true believers bemoan the desecration of our earthly ₃₂ Eden, the heretics point out that this Eden, long before humans arrived, once became so naturally thick with methane smog that it was rendered nearly lifeless. When Al Gore urges the citizenry to sacrifice their plastic shopping bags, their air-conditioning, their extraneous travel, the agnostics grumble that human activity accounts for just 2 percent of global carbon-dioxide emissions, with the remainder generated by natural processes like plant decay.

WORKS CITED

738 LET'S MELT THE ICE CAP: For the section on global cooling, see: Harold M. Schmeck Jr., "Climate Changes Endanger World's Food Output," *New York Times*, August 8, 1974; Peter Gwynne, "The Cooling World," *Newsweek*, April 28,1975; Walter Sullivan, "Scientists Ask Why World Climate Is Changing; Major Cooling May Be Ahead," *New York Times*, May 21, 1975. Ground temperatures over the past one hundred years can be found in "Climate Change 2007: Synthesis Report," U.N. Intergovernmental Panel on Climate Change (IPCC).

738 JAMES LOVELOCK: All Lovelock quotes in this chapter can be found in *The Revenge of Gaia: Earth's Climate Crisis and the Fate of Humanity* (Basic Books, 2006). Lovelock is a scientist perhaps best known as the originator of the Gaia hypothesis, which argues that the earth is essentially a living organism much like (but in many ways superior to) a human being. He has written several books on the subject, including the foundational *Gaia: The Practical Science of Planetary Medicine* (Gaia Books, 1991).

738 COWS ARE WICKED POLLUTERS: The potency of methane as a green-house gas as compared with carbon dioxide was calculated by the climate scientist Ken Caldeira, of the Carnegie Institution for Science, based on the IPCC's Third Assessment Report. **Ruminants produce more greenhouse gas than transportation sector:** see "Livestock's Long Shadow: Environmental Issues and Options," Food and Agriculture Organization of the United Nations, Rome, 2006; and Shigeki Kobayashi, "Transport and Its Infrastructure," chapter 5 from IPCC Third Assessment Report, September 25, 2007.

738 WELL-MEANING LOCAVORES: See Christopher L. Weber and H. Scott Matthews, "Food-Miles and the Relative Climate Impacts of Food Choices in the United States," *Environmental Science and Technology* 42, no. 10 (April 2008); see also James McWilliams, "On Locavorism," Freakonomics blog, *New York Times*, August 26, 2008; and McWilliams's forthcoming book, *Just Food* (Little, Brown, 2009).

739 EAT MORE KANGAROO: See "Eco-friendly Kangaroo Farts Could Help Global Warming: Scientists," Agence France-Press, December 5, 2007.

739 GLOBAL WARMING AS A "UNIQUELY THORNY PROBLEM": For the **"terrible-case scenario,"** see Martin L. Weitzman, "On Modeling and Interpreting the Economics of Catastrophic Climate Change," *The Review of Economics and Statistics* 91, no. 1 (February 2009). / 000 **A Stern warning:** see Nicholas Herbert Stern, *The Economics of Climate Change: The Stern Review* (Cambridge University Press, 2007). / 000 There is much to be read about the **Influence of uncertainty**, especially as it compares with its cousin risk. The Israeli psycholo-

gists Amos Tversky and Daniel Kahneman, whose work is generally credited with giving ultimate birth to behavioral economics, conducted pioneering research oh how people make decisions under pressure and found that uncertainty leads to "severe and systematic errors" in judgment. (See "Judgment Under Uncertainty: Heuristics and Biases," from *Judgment Under Uncertainty: Heuristics and Biases*, ed. Daniel Kahneman, Paul Slovic, and Amos Tversky [Cambridge University Press, 1982].) We wrote about the difference between risk and uncertainty in a *New York Times Magazine* column ("The Jane Fonda Effect," September 16, 2007) about the fear over nuclear power: "[The economist Frank Knight] made a distinction between two key factors in decision making: risk and uncertainty. The cardinal difference, Knight declared, is that risk—however great—can be measured, whereas uncertainty cannot. How do people weigh risk versus uncertainty? Consider a famous experiment that illustrates what is known as the Ellsberg Paradox. There are two urns. The first urn, you are told, contains fifty red balls and fifty black balls. The second one also contains one hundred red and black balls, but the number of each color is unknown. If your task is to pick a red ball out of either urn, which urn do you choose? Most people pick the first urn, which suggests that they prefer a measurable risk to an immeasurable uncertainty. (This condition is known to economists as *ambiguity aversion*.) Could it be that nuclear energy, risks and all, is now seen as preferable to the uncertainties of global warming?" / 000 **Al Gore's "We" campaign:** see www.climateprotect.org and Andrew C. Revkin, "Gore Group Plans Ad Blitz on Global Warming," *New York Times*, April 1, 2008. / 000 **The heretic Boris Johnson:** see Boris Johnson, "We've Lost Our Fear of Hellfire, but Put Climate Change in Its Place," *The Telegraph*, February 2, 2006. / 000 **"Rendered nearly lifeless":** see Peter Ward, *The Medea Hypothesis: Is Life on Earth Ultimately Self-Destructive?* (Princeton University Press, 2009); and Drake Bennett, "Dark Green: A Scientist Argues That the Natural World Isn't Benevolent and Sustaining: It's Bent on Self-Destruction," *The Boston Globe*, January 11, 2009.

■ ■ ■

Reading as a Writer: Analyzing Rhetorical Choices

1. How would you characterize the voice in this piece? How does this tone contribute to the approach these authors take to the serious issue of climate change? Locate some sentences that demonstrate your answers, and discuss your conclusions about the effectiveness of this approach for this topic.

2. In their final paragraphs of this selection, the authors claim that "the movement to stop global warming has taken on the feel of a religion" (para. 28). How so? What evidence do they offer, and what do you make of the language they point to? Test your own responses to this language of "guilt" and "self-disgust" (para. 31), and consider how it might and might not be effective to change our behaviors.

Writing as a Reader: Entering the Conversation of Ideas

1. Levitt and Dubner, like Derrick Jensen and Stephanie McMillan, use a lot of statistics to explain the scope of environmental problems. Write an essay in which you analyze these writers' strategies of using quantitative evidence to explain environmental issues, offering examples from each

text. What conclusions can you draw about effective use of quantitative data in this highly charged debate about how we should respond to environmental problems?

2. While Levitt and Dubner do not focus solely on the role of food production in the environmental crisis, they do include an analysis of agriculture in their essay. How do their insights as economists add to the conversation about food and the environment in readings by Anna Lappé and Michael Pollan? Compose an essay in which you consider the differing perspectives in these texts on the problems and solutions of food production and the environment. Given what you have learned, where do you stand in this debate?

SANDRA STEINGRABER

Despair Not

Sandra Steingraber is an ecologist who began her work in the science lab and then expanded her work to write for general audiences about the relationship between environmental and human health. A cancer survivor, she writes frequently of environmental links to cancer, as in her landmark 1997 book, *Living Downstream: An Ecologist's Personal Investigation of Cancer and the Environment*. Steingraber is also a poet and blogger and writes frequent columns such as this one in the online journal, *In These Times*, for their series about whether or not we should "despair" about the issue of climate change. Steingraber's title makes her perspective clear: "Despair Not."

Given readers' expectations that she is writing about climate change, her opening paragraphs might come as a surprise. What is the effect of beginning this conversation with a description of the murder of an abolitionist in 1837? How does she connect the effect of this murder—the increase in antislavery activity—with the contemporary environmental crisis?

Steingraber claims there are "two branches" to the environmental crisis, "although they share a common cause." As you read, follow the ways she distinguishes between these two "branches" and the ways she connects them, in part through her ethos as a scientist and as a mother. What is the effect of her decision to highlight her relationship to her son (and the experience of sewing his "polar bear" Halloween costume) before leading into the data-rich list under "New Morbidities of Childhood"?

Despite her title, Steingraber is not exactly a cheerful optimist when it comes to the issue of climate change. What will you do with the information she offers here? Given this data, why do you think she might still say we should "despair not"? This is a conversation we need to have for ourselves, and, if you are persuaded at all by her claims, for the next generations, too.

■ ■ ■

What will we say when our grandchildren ask us the names of the *1* departed? Or, by then, will the loss of favorite animals be the least of our worries?

In Alton, Ill., downstream from Peoria, the Illinois River town where *2* I grew up, the abolitionist Elijah Lovejoy was pumped full of bullets on a dark November night by a mob intent on silencing the man once and for all. On this evening, they succeeded.

By dawn, Elijah was dead, and his printing press—the means by *3* which he distributed his radical ideas—lay at the bottom of the Mississippi River. The year was 1837. The Rev. Lovejoy, a Presbyterian minister who attended Princeton Theological Seminary, was buried on this thirty-fifth birthday.

But the story doesn't end there.   *4*

Almost immediately, membership in antislavery societies across the *5* nation swelled. Vowing to carry on the work of his fallen friend, Edward Beecher, president of Illinois College in Jacksonville, threw himself into abolitionist efforts and, in so doing, inspired his sister, Harriet Beecher Stowe, who went on to write the most famous abolitionist treatise of all: *Uncle Tom's Cabin*. Meanwhile, Elijah's brother, Owen Lovejoy, turned his own house into a station along the Underground Railroad. Owen went on to win a seat in Congress and, along the way, befriended a young Illinois politician by the name of Abraham Lincoln.

These facts impressed me as a child.   *6*

When I read Reverend Lovejoy's biography as a grown-up and mother, *7* I found other things impressive. Such as the fact that, at the time of his assassination, Elijah had a young family. And yet, in the weeks before his death—when it became clear that the mob pursuing him was growing bolder by the hour—he did not desist from speaking out against slavery. So Elijah declared in one of his final speeches:

> While all around me is violence and tumult, all is peace within. . . . I sleep
> sweetly and undisturbed, except when awakened by the brickbats of the mob.

Truly? With a pregnant wife in the bed next to him and a one-year-old *8* son in the next room? He wasn't worried?

A letter to his mother in Maine tells a more nuanced story: *9*

> Still I cannot but feel that it is harder to "fight valiantly for the truth" when
> I risk not only my own comfort, ease, and reputation, and even life, but also
> that of another beloved one.

And then there's this poignant aside: *10*

> I have a family who are dependent on me. . . . And this is it that adds the
> bitterest ingredient to the cup of sorrow I am called to drink.

Here's something else that I've noticed while reading his words. To the *11* slave owners and murderous thugs, Elijah spoke calmly. He reserved his fierce language for the members of the community who gladly lived in the free state of Illinois but wished to remain above the fray: the ones who added their signatures to a resolution asking him to cease publication of his newspaper and leave town, but would not sign a resolution that urged protection of law against mob rule; the ones who agreed that slavery was a homicidal abomination but who feared that emancipation without recompense to slave owners for loss of property would be socially destabilizing; the ones who believed themselves upstandingly moral but who chose to remain silent about the great moral crisis of the day.

Two Crises, One Cause

In the spirit of Elijah Lovejoy —the man who is the namesake of my nine-year-old son— the time has come for outspoken, full-throated heroism in the face of the great moral issue of our own day: the environmental crisis—an unfolding calamity whose main victims are our own children and grandchildren. *12*

In fact, the environmental crisis is actually two crises, although they share a common cause. You could view it as a tree with two main branches: One branch represents what is happening to our planet through the atmospheric accumulation of heat-trapping gases (most notably, carbon dioxide and methane). The second branch represents what is happening to us through the accumulation of inherently toxic chemical pollutants in our bodies. *13*

Follow the first branch and you find droughts, floods, acidifying oceans, dissolving coral reefs, and faltering plankton stocks (the oceans' plankton provides half of our atmospheric oxygen supply). Follow the second branch and you find pesticides in children's urine, lungs stunted by air pollutants, abbreviated pregnancies, altered hormone levels, and lower scores on cognitive tests. *14*

The trunk of this tree is an economic dependency on fossil fuels, primarily coal (plant fossils) and petroleum and natural gas (animal fossils). When we light them on fire, we threaten the global ecosystem. When we use them as feedstocks for making stuff, we create substances—pesticides, solvents, plastics—that can tinker with our subcellular machinery and various signaling pathways that make it run. *15*

Biologist Rachel Carson first called our attention to these manifold dangers in her 1962 book, *Silent Spring*. She wrote, "Future generations are unlikely to condone our lack of prudent concern for the integrity of the natural world that supports all life." Since then, the scientific evidence for the disintegration of our world has become irrefutable, and members of the future generations to whom she was referring are now occupying our homes. *16*

They are our kids. *17*

I mean this in the most basic ways. When my son Elijah, at age 4, asked to be a polar bear for Halloween, I sewed a polar bear costume—and I did so with the full knowledge that his costume might outlast the species. No other *18* generation of mothers before mine has ever borne such knowledge—nor wondered if we should share this terrible news with our children. Or not. It's a novel situation. Indeed, according to the most recent assessment, one in every four mammal species (and one in every three marine animals) is now threatened with extinction, including that icon of Halloween itself: the little brown bat. Thus, animal costumes whose real-life correspondents have been wiped from Earth may well become commonplace.

This leads me to wonder: What will we say when our grandchildren   19 ask us the names of the departed? When bats, bees, butterflies, whales, polar bears and elephants disappear, will children still read books about them? Will they want to dress up as vanished species? Or, by then, will the loss of favorite animals be the least of their worries?

"New Morbidities of Childhood"

Chronic childhood diseases linked to toxic chemical exposures are rising   20 in prevalence. Here are a few of the current trends:

- One in eight U.S. children is born prematurely. Preterm birth is the leading cause of death in the first months of life and the leading cause of disability. Its price tag is $26 billion per year in medical costs, special services, and lost productivity. Preterm birth has demonstrable links to air pollution, especially maternal exposure to fine particles and combustion byproducts of the type released from coal-burning power plants.

- One in eleven U.S. children has asthma, the most common chronic childhood disease and a leading cause of school absenteeism. Asthma symptoms have been linked to certain ingredients in plastic (phthalates) as well as outdoor air pollution, including traffic exhaust. The annual cost of childhood asthma is estimated at $18 billion. Its incidence has doubled since 1980.

- One in ten U.S. children has a learning disability, and nearly one in ten has attention deficit/hyperactivity disorder. All together, special education services now consume 22 percent of U.S. school spending—about $77.3 billion per year at last count. Neurodevelopmental disorders have significant associations with exposures to air pollution, organophosphate pesticides like diazinon, and the heavy metals lead, mercury, and arsenic, among others.

- One in 110 children has autism or is on the autism spectrum. Annual costs are $35 billion. Causes are unknown, but exposure to chemical agents in early pregnancy is one of several suspected contributors.

- One in ten U.S. white girls and one in five U.S. black girls begin breast development before the age of eight. On average, breast development begins nearly two years earlier (age 9) than it did in the early 1960s (age 11). A risk factor for breast cancer in adulthood, early puberty in girls is associated with increasing body fat as well as exposure to some hormonally active chemical agents known as "estrogen mimickers." We have no cost estimates for the shortened childhoods of girls.

All together, asthma, behavioral problems, intellectual impairments and preterm birth are among the "new morbidities of childhood." So concludes a 2006 federally funded investigation of pediatric environmental health. Ironically, by becoming so familiar a presence among children, these disorders now appear almost normal or inevitable. And yet, with an entirely different chemical regulatory system, farm bill, and energy policy, their prevalence might be much reduced. *21*

The fact that we do not identify and abolish hormone-disrupting, brain-damaging chemicals to which children are routinely exposed raises profound ethical questions. The authors of the pediatric health investigation, published in *Environmental Health Perspectives*, put it this way: *22*

> In the absence of toxicity testing, we are inadvertently employing pregnant women and children as uninformed subjects to warn us of new environmental toxicants. . . . Paradoxically, because industry is not obligated to supply the data on developmental neurotoxicity, the costs of human disease, research, and prevention are socialized whereas the profits are privatized.

In the absence of federal policies that protect child development and the ecology of the planet on which our children's lives depend, we parents have to serve as our own regulatory agencies and departments of interior. *23*

Already manically busy, we are encouraged by popular media reports to read labels, consult Web sites, vet the contents of birthday party goody bags, shrink our carbon footprints, mix our own nontoxic cleaning products, challenge our school districts to embrace pesticide-free soccer fields, and limit the number of ounces of mercury-laced tuna fish consumed by each child per week. *24*

"Well-Informed Futility"

Thoughtful but overwhelmed parents correctly perceive a disconnect between the enormity of the problem and the ability of individual acts of vigilance and self-sacrifice to fix it. Awareness without corresponding political change leads to paralyzing despair. And so, eventually, we begin to discount or ignore the latest evidence of harm. We feel helpless in the face of our knowledge, and we're not sure we want to know anything more. The apt term for this is "well-informed futility syndrome." *25*

"Well-informed futility" refers to a particular kind of learned helplessness. It's a term that was coined in 1973 by psychologist Gerhart Wiebe, who was writing in an age when television had brought war into the living rooms of Americans for the first time. Wiebe noticed that a steady onslaught of information about a problem over which people feel little sense of personal agency gives rise to a sense of futility. Ironically, the more we know about such a problem, the more we are filled with a paralyzing *26* sense of futility. That sense, in turn, forestalls action. And yet, action is the cure for paralysis.

Just down the street from well-informed futility resides denial. Accord- *27* ing to contemporary risk communication expert Peter Sandman, we all instinctively avoid information that triggers intolerable emotions—such as intolerable fear or intolerable guilt. In the face of knowledge too upsetting to bear, there is nothing to do but look away.

Well-informed futility and its inattentive neighbor, denial, especially *28* flourish, says Sandman, when there are discontinuities in the messages we receive, as when we are told that a problem (mass extinctions, melting icecaps) is dire but the proposed solutions (buy new light bulbs) seem trivial. If the problem were really so dire, wouldn't we all be asked to respond with actions of equivalent magnitude? So . . . maybe the problem isn't so dire.

It is such discontinuity that provides the exit doors. And soon enough, *29* we retreat into silent paralysis rather than stand up for *abolition now*.

The Antidote to Despair

Action is the antidote to despair, and by action I do not mean shopping dif- *30* ferently. Indeed, the notion that toxicity should be a consumer choice must be soundly rejected. Instead, we must seek the higher ground of human rights, and from that vantage explore systemic solutions to the ongoing chemical contamination of our children and our biosphere.

The domestic routines of family life with young children—however *31* isolated and detached from public life they seem—are inextricably bound to the most urgent public health issues of our time:

- Risks for asthma are related to transportation and energy policies.
- Bedtime snacks are linked to global systems of agricultural subsidies.
- The highly explosive raw materials used for manufacturing my kitchen floor pose demonstrable threats to national security.
- Sunburn at the beach is linked to the stability of the ozone layer, which, in turn, is threatened by particular pesticides used in the production of tomatoes and strawberries.
- The capture of a rabid bat in the kids' bedroom demonstrates the precautionary principle in action as enlightened public health policy. The proposal to extract natural gas from the Marcellus Shale that lies below my rural county in upstate New York demonstrates the abandonment of that same principle.

From understanding the inter-relatedness of situations like these, two *32* epiphanies emerge.

> **ONE:** Ultimately the environmental crisis is a parenting crisis. It undermines my ability to carry out my two fundamental duties: to protect my children from harm and to plan for their future.

Current environmental policies must be realigned to safeguard the healthy development of children and sustain the planetary life-support systems on which their lives depend.

> **TWO:** Such a realignment necessitates emancipation from our terrible addiction to fossil fuels in all their toxic forms.

Happily, the best science shows us that we can do so. Mark Jacobson and Mark Delucchi, in their 2009 *Scientific American* article, "A Path to Sustainable Energy by 2030," explain how in the course of the next twenty years, we could entirely meet our energy requirements with renewable, non-carbon-based sources, if we cut our energy consumption by half. With the willingness to make deep cuts in consumption, the whole fossil-fuel freedom project becomes doable. And this is a place where a thousand molehills really do a mountain make.

According to Paul Stern, the director of the Committee on the Human 33 Dimensions of Global Climate Change at the National Research Council, in the United States, individuals' homes and vehicles are responsible for 38 percent of carbon dioxide emissions. Therefore, we don't have to wait around for political change before making immediate and radical transformations in our own lives and spheres of influence.

We should not despair. We can break the spell. We can prepare the 34 way. In other words, as Elijah Lovejoy exhorted his fellow citizens when encouraging them to imagine a U.S. economy no longer dependent on the unpaid labor of people held as property: It's time to "come up to the rescue, and let it be known whether the spirit of freedom yet presides."

■ ■ ■

Reading as a Writer: Analyzing Rhetorical Choices

1. Steingraber argues by analogy in this piece, claiming that just as slavery was the moral crisis of the nineteenth century, so the environment is the moral crisis of our day. What evidence does she provide for this claim? How does she link the personal and family lives of people to the larger issue in each case? What do you conclude about the effectiveness of this argumentative strategy?

2. What do you know about Rachel Carson? If this name is new to you, do a quick search on her biography and her writing. You might even read the brief, poetic first chapter of her book, *Silent Spring*, available online. What do you think? Share your findings with your classmates.

Writing as a Reader: Entering the Conversation of Ideas

1. Steingraber and Noël Sturgeon both use appeals to history in their essays. What does this historical background add to their arguments about the environment? Compose an essay in which you consider the effectiveness of these specific uses of history and draw larger conclusions about the role history can (or should?) play in our analysis of contemporary environmental problems.

2. Like many of the writers in this chapter, Steingraber struggles with bal-
    ancing pessimism and optimism while writing about the environment.
    After all, there is reason for pessimism, given the grim news about a range
    of environmental crises. However, without at least a little optimism, it is
    hard to find reasons to act. Other writers who foreground this balancing
    act are Derrick Jensen and Stephanie McMillan and Michael Pollan. Com-
    pose an essay in which you analyze the ways these three texts use opti-
    mism and pessimism to make their points, taking care to cite examples
    and analyze them. What larger conclusions can you draw about effective
    methods of motivating readers to act on difficult issues like environmen-
    tal crises?

ANNA LAPPÉ

The Climate Crisis at the End of Our Fork

Anna Lappé is a best-selling author, public speaker, and founder, along
with her mother, the food activist Frances Moore Lappé, of the Small
Planet Institute, an international network of scholars, activists, and educators who are interested in the intersections of hunger and poverty. Lappé
is a frequent guest writer for the *New York Times, Gourmet, O: The Oprah
Magazine, and Body + Soul*, to name a few of the many publications that
have featured her writing on food politics. She has also edited and written
or cowritten several books, including *Hope's Edge: The Next Diet for a Small
Planet* (2002, with Frances Moore Lappé) and *Grub: Ideas for an Urban
Organic Kitchen* (2006, with chef Bryant Terry). Her most recent book project is *Restoration Agriculture: Real-World Permaculture for Farmers* (2014,
with Mark Shepard). This piece with the same name was published in the
anthology *Food Inc.: A Participant Guide: How Industrial Food Is Making
Us Sicker, Fatter, and Poorer—and What You Can Do about It* (2009), edited
by Karl Weber. The book is a companion to the documentary film *Food,
Inc.*, about the ecological and health effects of the industrialization of the
food chain.

   In this piece, Lappé opens by describing the gasping response of the
audience at a talk at which a climate change scholar discussed the enormous impact of the food system on global warming. She throws at readers the same surprising information she learned at this talk, that "the
global system for producing and distributing food accounts for roughly
one-third of the human-caused global warming effect . . . [and] the livestock sector alone is responsible for 18 percent of the world's total global
warming effect—more than the emissions produced by every plane, train,
and steamer ship on the planet" (para. 5, author's emphasis). This statis-
tic launches her argument that if the food sector is a critical part of the
global-warming problem, it is also critical to the solution. Lappé wants
readers to see that changing the food system is as crucial—or even more
crucial—than any other ecological solutions we commonly think of, such
as changing light bulbs or driving more efficient cars.

As you read, pay close attention to the evidence Lappé offers, in her text and in her copious footnotes. What do you think are the most persuasive examples and statistics she offers to make her point about the problem and how much is at stake? How does she use evidence to propose solutions in her final section?

Lappé is part of a rapidly expanding group of scholars, writers, and activists who are interested in all aspects of food politics. Unlike some forms of consumption, which we can avoid—like smoking, for example—we all need to eat to survive. What will we spear on the end of our fork when we take our next bite of food? Lappé argues that our answer will affect not only our bodies, but the fate of the planet.

＊ ＊ ＊

We could hear audible gasps from the two dozen New York state farmers gathered at the Glynwood Center on a cold December day in 2007 when NASA scientist Cynthia Rosenzweig, one of the world's leading experts on climate change and agriculture, explained the slide glowing on the screen in front of us. 1

The Glynwood Center, an education nonprofit and farm set on 225 acres in the Hudson Valley, had brought Rosenzweig to speak to area farmers about the possible impact of climate change on the region. Pointing to an arrow swooping south from New York, Rosenzweig said: "If we don't drastically reduce greenhouse gas emissions by 2080, farming in New York could feel like farming in Georgia." 2

"It was all projections before. It's not projections now—it's observational science," said Rosenzweig. We are already seeing major impacts of climate change on agriculture: droughts leading to crop loss and salinization of soils, flooding causing waterlogged soils, longer growing seasons leading to new and more pest pressures, and erratic weather shifting harvesting seasons, explained Rosenzweig. 3

When people think about climate change and food, many first think of the aspect of the equation that Rosenzweig focused on that day—the impact of climate change on farming. But when it comes to how the food system impacts global warming, most draw a blank. 4

Challenged to name the human factors that promote climate change, we typically picture industrial smokestacks or oil-thirsty planes and automobiles, not Pop-Tarts or pork chops. Yet the global system for producing and distributing food accounts for roughly *one-third* of the human-caused global warming effect. According to the United Nation's seminal report, *Livestock's Long Shadow*, the livestock sector alone is responsible for 18 percent of the world's total global warming effect—more than the emissions produced by every plane, train, and steamer ship on the planet.[1] 5

Asked what we can do as individuals to help solve the climate change crisis, most of us could recite these eco-mantras from memory: Change our light bulbs! Drive less! Choose energy-efficient appliances! Asked 6 what we can do as a nation, most of us would probably mention promoting renewable energy and ending our addiction to fossil fuels. Few among us would mention changing the way we produce our food or the dietary choices we make.

Unfortunately, the dominant story line about climate change—its biggest drivers and the key solutions—diverts us from understanding how other sectors, particularly the food sector, are critical parts of the *problem*, but even more importantly can be vital strategies for *solutions*. 7

If the role of our food system in global warming comes as news to you, it's understandable. Many of us have gotten the bulk of our information about global warming from Al Gore's wake-up call *An Inconvenient Truth*, the 2006 Oscar-winning documentary that became the fourth-highest grossing nonfiction film in American history.[2] In addition to the record-breaking doc, Gore's train-the-trainer program, which coaches educators on sharing his slideshow, has further spread his central message about the threat posed by human-made climate change. But Gore's program offers little information about the connection between climate change and the food on your plate. 8

Mainstream newspapers in the United States haven't done a much better job of covering the topic. Researchers at Johns Hopkins University analyzed climate change coverage in sixteen leading U.S. newspapers from September 2005 through January 2008. Of the 4,582 articles published on climate change during that period, only 2.4 percent addressed the role of the food production system, and most of those only peripherally. In fact, just half of 1 percent of all climate change articles had "a substantial focus" on food and agriculture.[3] Internationally, the focus hasn't been much different. Until recently, much of the attention from the international climate change community and national coordinating bodies was also mostly focused on polluting industries and the burning of fossil fuels, not on the food sector. 9

This is finally starting to change. In the second half of 2008, writers from *O: The Oprah Magazine* to the *Los Angeles Times* started to cover the topic, increasing the public's awareness of the food and climate change connection. In September 2008, Dr. Rajendra Pachauri, the Indian economist serving his second term as chair of the United Nations Intergovernmental Panel on Climate Change, made a bold statement about the connection between our diet and global warming. Choosing to eat less meat, or eliminating meat entirely, is one of the most important personal choices we can make to address climate change, said Pachauri.[4] "In terms of immediacy of action and the feasibility of bringing about reductions in a short period of time, it clearly is the most attractive opportunity," said Pachauri. "Give up meat for one day [a week] initially, and decrease it from there."[5] 10

Why does our food system play such a significant role in the global warming effect? There are many reasons, including the emissions created by industrial farming processes, such as fertilizer production, and the 11 carbon emissions produced by trucks, ships, and planes as they transport foods across nations and around the world. Among the main sources of the food system's impact on climate are land use changes, especially the expansion of palm oil production, and effects caused by contemporary agricultural practices, including the emissions produced by livestock.

The Land Use Connection

Let's look at land use first. A full 18 percent of the world's global warming effect is associated with "land use changes," mostly from the food system.[6] The biggest factors are the destruction of vital rainforests through burning and clearing and the elimination of wetlands and peat bogs to expand pasture for cattle, feed crops for livestock, and oil palm plantations, especially in a handful of countries, Brazil and Indonesia chief among them.[7]   12

What do Quaker Granola Bars and Girl Scout Cookies have to do with the climate crisis?[8] These processed foods—along with other popular products, including cosmetics, soaps, shampoo, even fabric softeners—share a common ingredient, one with enormous climate implications: palm oil.[9] As the taste for processed foods skyrockets, so does the demand for palm oil, production of which has more that doubled in the last decade.[10] Today, palm oil is the most widely traded vegetable oil in the world, with major growth in the world's top two importing countries, India and China.[11]   13

As oil palm plantations expand on rainforests and peat lands in Southeast Asia, the natural swamp forests that formerly filled those lands are cut down and drained, and the peat-filled soils release carbon dioxide and methane into the atmosphere. (Methane is a key greenhouse gas with twenty-three times the global warming impact of carbon dioxide.) In a recent study, researchers estimate that producing one ton of palm oil can create fifteen to seventy tons of carbon dioxide over a twenty-five year period.[12]   14

Three of the world's biggest agribusiness companies are major players in the palm oil market, which is concentrated in two countries—Malaysia and Indonesia—where in 2007, 43 percent and 44 percent of the world's total palm oil was produced, respectively.[13] Wilmar, an affiliate of the multinational giant Archer Daniels Midland, is the largest palm oil producer in the world;[14] soy behemoth Bunge is a major importer of palm oil into the United States (although at the moment it doesn't own or operate any of its own facilities);[15] and grain-trading Cargill owns palm plantations throughout Indonesia and Malaysia.[16] These three companies and others producing palm oil claim that guidelines from the Roundtable on Sustainable Palm Oil (RSPO), established in 2004 by industry and international nonprofits, ensure sustainable production that minimizes the destruction of forest and peat bogs as well as deleterious effect on the global climate.[17]   15

However, some environmental and human rights groups argue that loopholes in the Roundtable's regulations still leave too much wiggle room.   16

Says Greenpeace, "The existing standards developed by the RSPO will not prevent forest and peat land destruction, and a number of RSPO members are taking no steps to avoid the worst practices of the palm oil industry."[18]

We also know from new data that palm plantation expansion on peat *17* land is not slowing. According to Dr. Susan Page from the University of Leicester, deforestation rates on peat lands have been increasing for twenty years, with one-quarter of all deforestation in Southeast Asia occurring on peat lands in 2005 alone.[19]

The other side of the land use story is deforestation driven by the *18* increased production of livestock, expanding pasture lands and cropland for feed. In Latin America, for instance, nearly three-quarters of formerly forested land is now occupied by pastures; feed crops for livestock cover much of the remainder.[20] Globally, one-third of the world's arable land is dedicated to feed crop production.[21] Poorly managed pastures lead to overgrazing, compaction, and erosion, which release stored carbon into the atmosphere. With livestock now occupying 26 percent of the planet's ice-free land, the impact of this poor land management is significant.[22]

Raising livestock in confinement and feeding them diets of grains and *19* other feedstock—including animal waste by-products—is a relatively recent phenomenon. In the postwar period, intensification of animal production was seen as the path to productivity. As livestock were confined in high stocking densities often far from where their feed was grown, a highly inefficient and environmentally costly system was born.

As a British Government Panel on Sustainable Development said in *20* 1997, "Farming methods in the last half century have changed rapidly as a result of policies which have favored food production at the expense of the conservation of biodiversity and the protection of the landscape."[23] Despite these environmental costs, confined animal feeding operations (CAFOs) spread in the 1960s and 1970s into Europe and Japan and what was then the Soviet Union. Today, CAFOs are becoming increasingly common in East Asia, Latin America, and West Asia.

As the largest U.S.-based multinational meat companies, including *21* Tyson, Cargill, and Smithfield, set their sights overseas, the production of industrial meat globally is growing.[24] In addition, the increasing supply of meat in developing countries flooded with advertising for Western-style eating habits is leading to a potential doubling in demand for industrial livestock production, and therefore feed crops, from 1997–1999 to 2030.[25]

Although the shift from traditional ways of raising livestock to *22* industrial-scale confinement operations is often defended in the name of "efficiency," it's a spurious claim. As a way of producing edible proteins, feedlot livestock production is inherently inefficient. While ruminants such as cattle naturally convert inedible-to-humans grasses into high-grade proteins, under industrial production, grain-fed cattle pass along to humans only a fraction of the protein they consume.[26] Debates about this conversion rate abound. The U.S. Department of Agriculture estimates that it takes seven pounds of grain to produce one pound of beef.[27] However, journalist

Paul Roberts, author of *The End of Food*, argues that the true conversion rate is much higher. While feedlot cattle need at least ten pounds of feed to gain one pound of live weight, Roberts states, nearly two-thirds of this weight gain is for inedible parts, such as bones, other organs, and hide. The true conversion ratio, Roberts estimates, is twenty pounds of grain to produce a single pound of beef, 7.3 pounds for pigs, and 3.5 pounds for poultry.[28]

The inefficiency of turning to grain-fed livestock as a major component of the human diet is devastating in itself, especially in a world where nearly one billion people still go hungry. But now we know there is a climate cost as well. The more consolidation in the livestock industry—where small-scale farmers are pushed out and replaced by large-scale confinement operations—the more land will be turned over to feed production. This production is dependent on fossil fuel—intensive farming, from synthesizing the human-made nitrogen fertilizer to using fossil fuel-based chemicals on feed crops. Each of these production steps cost in emissions contributing to the escalating greenhouse effect undermining our planet's ecological balance. *23*

The Agriculture Connection

One reason we may have been slow to recognize the impact of the food system on climate change may be a certain "carbon bias." While carbon dioxide is the most abundant human-made greenhouse gas in the atmosphere, making up 77 percent of the total human-caused global warming effect, methane and nitrous oxide contribute nearly all the rest.[29] (Other greenhouse gases are also relevant to the global warming effect, but are currently present in much smaller quantities and have a less significant impact.)[30] Agriculture is responsible for most of the human-made methane and nitrous oxide in the atmosphere, which contribute 13.5 percent of total greenhouse gas emissions, primarily from animal waste mismanagement, fertilizer overuse, the natural effects of ruminant digestion, and to a small degree rice production[31] (1.5 percent of total emissions come from methane produced during rice cultivation).[32] *24*

Though livestock only contribute 9 percent or carbon dioxide emissions, the sector is responsible for 37 percent of methane and 65 percent of nitrous oxide.[33] Here again, recent changes in agricultural practices are a significant factor. For centuries, livestock have been a vital part of sustainable food systems, providing muscle for farm work and meat as a vital protein source. Historically, properly grazed livestock produced numerous benefits to the land: Hooves aerate soil, allowing more oxygen in the ground, which helps plant growth; their hoof action also presses grass seed into the earth, fostering plant growth, too; and, of course, their manure provides natural fertilizer. Indeed, new self-described "carbon farmers" are developing best management practices to manage cattle grazing to reduce compaction and overgrazing and, mimicking traditional grazing patterns, increasing carbon sequestration in the soil.[34] *25*

But modern livestock production has steered away from these 26
traditional practices toward the industrial-style production described
above and to highly destructive overgrazing. In sustainable systems tap-
ping nature's wisdom, there is no such thing as waste: Manure is part of
a holistic cycle and serves to fertilize the same lands where the animals
that produce it live. In CAFOs, there is simply too much waste to cycle
back through the system. Instead, waste is stored in manure "lagoons,"
as they're euphemistically called. Without sufficient oxygenation, this
waste emits methane and nitrous oxide gas. As a consequence of industrial
livestock production, the United States scores at the top of the world for
methane emissions from manure. Swine production is king in terms of
methane emissions, responsible for half of the globe's total.[35]

The sheer numbers of livestock exacerbate the problem. In 1965, eight 27
billion livestock animals were alive on the planet at any given moment;
ten billion were slaughtered every year. Today, thanks in part to CAFOs
that spur faster growth and shorter lifespan, twenty billion livestock animals are alive at any moment, while nearly fifty-five billion are slaughtered
annually.[36]

Ruminants, such as cattle, buffalo, sheep, and goats, are among the 28
main agricultural sources of methane. They can't help it; it's in their nature.
Ruminants digest through microbial, or enteric, fermentation, which
produces methane that is then released by the animals, mainly through
belching. While this process enables ruminants to digest fibrous grasses
that we humans can't convert into digestible form, it also contributes to
livestock's climate change impact. (Enteric fermentation accounts for
25 percent of the total emissions from the livestock sector; land use changes
account for another 35.4 percent; manure accounts for 30.5 percent.)[37]

In addition to the ruminants' digestive process, emissions from live- 29
stock can be traced back to the production of the crops they consume.
Globally, 33 percent of the world's cereal harvest and 90 percent of the
world's soy harvest are now being raised for animal feed.[38] Feed crop
farmers are heavily dependent on fossil fuels, used to power the on-farm
machinery as well as used in the production of the petroleum-based chemicals to protect against pests, stave off weeds, and foster soil fertility on
large-scale monoculture fields. In addition, these crops use up immense
quantities of fertilizer. In the United States and Canada, half of all synthetic fertilizer is used for feed crops.[39] In the United Kingdom, the total
is nearly 70 percent.[40] To produce this fertilizer requires tons of natural
gas; on average 1.5 tons of oil equivalents are used up to make one ton of
fertilizer.[41] Yet in the United States, only about half of the nitrogen fertilizer applied to corn is even used by the crop.[42] This needless waste is all
the more alarming because nitrogen fertilizer contributes roughly three-
quarters of the country's nitrous oxide emissions.

Erosion and deterioration of soils on industrial farms is another factor 30
in the food sector's global warming toll. As industrial farms diminish natural soil fertility and disturb soil through tillage, soil carbon is released into

the atmosphere.[43] Because industrialized agriculture also relies on huge amounts of water for irrigation, these farms will be more vulnerable as climate change increases drought frequency and intensity and decreases water availability. Globally, 70 percent of the world's available freshwater is being diverted to irrigation-intensive agriculture.[44]

The Waste and Transportation Connection

The sources of food system emissions on which we've focused so far—   *31* including land use changes and agricultural production—are responsible for nearly one-third of the total human-made global warming effect. That's already quite a lot, but other sectors include emissions from the food chain, including transportation, waste, and manufacturing.

For example, 3.6 percent of global greenhouse gas emissions come   *32* from waste, including landfills, wastewater, and other waste.[45] The food production system contributes its share to this total. After all, where does most of our uneaten food and food ready for harvest that never even makes it to our plates end up? Landfills. Solid waste, including food scraps, produces greenhouse gas emissions from anaerobic decomposition, which produces methane, and from carbon dioxide as a by-product of incineration and waste transportation.[46]

An additional 13.1 percent of the emissions that contribute to the   *33* global warming effect come from transportation, toting everything from people to pork chops.[47] The factory farming industry, in particular, demands energy-intensive shipping. CAFOs, for example, transport feed and live animals to feedlots and then to slaughter. Then the meat must be shipped to retail distribution centers and to the stores where it is sold to us consumers.

Americans, in particular, import and export a lot of meat. In 2007, the   *34* United States exported 1.4 billion pounds of beef and veal (5.4 percent of our total production of beef)[48] and imported 3.1 billion pounds of the same.[49] One could argue that a lot of that transport is unnecessary from a consumer point of view and damaging from an environmental point of view.

Globally, international trade in meat is rapidly accelerating. As   *35* recently as 1995, Brazil was exporting less than half-a-million dollars' worth of beef. A little more than a decade later, the Brazilian Beef Industry and Exporters Association estimates the value of beef exports could reach $5.2 billion and expects revenues of $15 billion from beef exports by 2013.[50]

All of these billions of pounds of meat being shipped around the world   *36* add significantly to the carbon emissions from transportation. So do the Chilean grapes shipped to California, the Australian dairy destined for Japan, or the Twinkies toted across the country—all the meat and dairy, drinks, and processed foods shipped worldwide in today's globalized food market.

The Organic Solution

The globalized and industrialized food system has not only negative health   37
consequences—think of all those Twinkies, that factory-farmed meat, and
that chemically raised produce—but a climate change toll as well. But the
news is not all bad. Once we gaze directly at the connection between food,
farming, and global warming, we see plenty of cause for hope.

First, unlike many other climate change conundrums, we already   38
know many of the steps we can take now to reduce carbon emissions from
the food sector. For instance, we know that compared with industrial
farms, small-scale organic and sustained farms can significantly reduce
the sector's emissions. Small-scale sustainable agriculture relies on people power, not heavy machinery, and depends on working with biological
methods, not human-made chemicals, to increase soil fertility and handle
pests. As a result, small-scale sustained farms use much fewer fossil fuels
and have been found to emit between one-half and two-thirds less carbon
dioxide for every acre of production.[51]

We also are just beginning to see results from long-term studies show-   39
ing how organic farms create healthy soil, which has greater capacity to
store carbon, creating those all-important "carbon sinks."[52] By one estimate, converting 10,000 medium-sized farms to organic would store as
much carbon in the soil as we would save in emissions if we took one million cars off the road.[53]

We're closer than ever to global consensus about the direction in which   40
we need to head. In April 2008, a report on agriculture initiated by the
World Bank, in partnership with the United Nations and representatives
from the private sector, NGOs, and scientific institutions from around the
world, declared that diverse, small-holder sustainable agriculture can play
a vital role in reducing the environment impacts of the agriculture sector.

The result of four years of work by hundreds of scientists and review-   41
ers,[54] the International Assessment of Agriculture Science and Technology
for Development (IAASTD) calls for supporting agroecological systems;
enhancing agricultural biodiversity; promoting small-scale farms; and
encouraging the sustainable management of livestock, forest, and fisher-
ies, as well as supporting "biological substitutes for agrochemicals" and
"reducing the dependency of the agricultural sector on fossil fuels."[55] A civil
society statement timed with the report's release declared that the IAASTD
represents the beginning of a "new era of agriculture" and offers "a sobering account of the failure of industrial farming."[56] Said Greenpeace, the
IAASTD report recommends a "significant departure from the destructive
chemical-dependent, one-size-fits-all model of industrial agriculture."[57]

(Not everyone involved in the process was happy with the final report,   42
which was signed by fifty-seven governments.[58] Chemical giant and agricultural biotechnology leaders Syngenta and Monsanto, for instance,
refused to sign on to the final document. No public statements were given
at the time.[59] But in an interview, Syngenta's Martin Clough told me,

"When it became pretty evident that the breadth of technologies were not getting equal airtime, then I think the view was that there was no point in participating. It's important to represent the technological options and it's equally important to say that they get fair play. That wasn't happening."[60])

Despite the chemical industry holdouts, there is also consensus that [43] sustainable farming practices create more resilient farms, better able to withstand the weather extremes of drought and flooding already afflicting many regions as a result of climate change. In other words, mitigation *is* adaptation. Because organic farms, by their design, build healthy soil, organic soils are better able to absorb water, making them more stable during floods, droughts, and extreme weather changes. In one specific example, conventional rice farmers in a region in Japan were nearly wiped out by an unusually cold summer, while organic farmers in the same region still yielded 60 to 80 percent of their typical production levels.[61]

In ongoing studies by the Pennsylvania-based Rodale Institute, [44] organic crops outperformed nonorganic crops in times of drought, yielding 35 to 100 percent more in drought years than conventional crops.[62] Visiting a Wisconsin organic farmer just after the major Midwest flooding of the summer of 2008, I could see the deep ravines in the surroundings corn fields caused by the recent flooding, while I spent the afternoon walking through a visibly unscathed biodiverse organic farm.

Encouraging sustainable agriculture will not only help us reduce [45] emissions and adapt to the future climate chaos, it will have other beneficial ripples: addressing hunger and poverty, improving public health, and preserving biodiversity. In one study comparing organic and conventional agriculture in Europe, Canada, New Zealand, and the United States, researchers found that organic farming increased biodiversity at "every level of the food chain," from birds and mammals, to flora, all the way down to the bacteria in the soil.[63]

Finally, we know that shifting toward sustainable production need not [46] mean sacrificing production. In one of the largest studies of sustainable agriculture, covering 286 projects in fifty-seven countries and including 12.6 million farmers, researchers from the University of Essex found a yield increase of 79 percent when farmers shifted to sustainable farming across a wide variety of systems and crop types.[64] Harvests of some crops such as maize, potatoes, and beans increased 100 percent.[65]

Here's the other great plus: we all have to eat, so we can each do our [47] part to encourage the shift to organic, sustainable farming every time we make a choice about our food, from our local market, to our local restaurants, to our local food policies.

I was recently talking with Helene York, director of the Bon Appétit Man- [48] agement Company Foundation, an arm of the Bon Appétit catering company, which serves eighty million meals a year at 400 venues across the country. York has been at the forefront of educating consumers and chefs about the impacts of our culinary choices on climate change, including leading the charge of the foundation's "Low Carbon Diet," which has dramatically reduced greenhouse gas emissions associated with their food. She summed up the challenge of awakening people to the food and climate change connection this way: "When you're sitting in front of a steaming plate of macaroni and cheese, you're not imagining plumes of greenhouse gases. You're thinking, dinner."

But the truth is those plumes of gases are there nonetheless, in the background of how our dinners are produced, processed, and shipped to our plates. Thankfully, more and more of us eaters and policymakers are considering the climate crisis at the end of our fork and what we can do to support the organic, local, sustainable food production that's better for the planet, more pleasing to the palate, and healthier for people too.

49

NOTES

1. Henning, Steinfeld et al., *Livestock's Long Shadow: Environmental Issues and Options* (Rome: Food and Agriculture Organization of the United Nations, 2006). While livestock is responsible for 18 percent of total emissions, transportation is responsible for a total of 13 percent of the global warming effect.
2. Film stats from Box Office Mojo. Available online at http://www.boxofficemojo.com/movies/?page=main&id=inconvenienttruth.htm.
3. R. A. Neff, I. L. Chan, and K. A. Smith, "Yesterday's Dinner, Tomorrow's Weather, Today's News?: US Newspaper Coverage of Food System Contributions to Climate Change," *Public Health Nutrition* (2008).
4. Rajendra Pachauri, "Global Warning—The Impact of Meat Production and Consumption on Climate Change," paper presented at the Compassion in World Farming, London, September 8, 2008.
5. Ibid.
6. N. H. Stern, *The Economics of Climate Change: The Stern Review* (Cambridge: Cambridge University Press, 2007), 539.
7. Ibid.
8. Ingredients for Quaker Granola Bar available online: https://www.wegmans.com/webapp/wcs/stores/servlet/ProductDisplay?langId=&storeId=10052&productId=359351&catalogId=10002&krypto=QJrbAudPd0vzXUGByeatog%3D%3D&ddkey=http:Product Display.
9. Marc Gunther, "Eco-Police Find New Target: Oreos," *Money*, August 21, 2008. Available online at http://money.cnn.com/2008/08/21/news/companies/palm_oil.fortune/index.htm?postversion=2008082112.
10. Ibid.
11. USDA FAS, "Indonesia: Palm Oil Production Prospects Continue to Grow," December 31, 2007. Total area for Indonesia palm oil in 2006 is estimated at 6.07 million hectares according to information from the Indonesia Palm Oil Board (IPOB). Available online at http://www.pecad.fas.usda.gov/highlights/2007/12/Indonesia_palmoil/.
12. "New Data Analysis Conclusive About Release of CO_2 When Natural Swamp Forest Is Converted to Oil Palm Plantation," CARBOPEAT Press Release, December 3, 2007. Dr. Sue Page or Dr. Chris Banks (CARBOPEAT Project Office), Department of Geography, University of Leicester, UK.
13. USDA FAS.
14. "Palm Oil Firm Wilmar Harming Indonesia Forests-Group," Reuters, July 3, 2007. Available at http://www.alertnet.org/thenews/newsdesk/SIN344348.htm.
15. Bunge Corporate Web site. Online at http://www.bunge.com/about-bunge/promoting_sustainability.html.

16. See information at Cargill-Malaysia's website, http://www.cargill.com.my/, and Cargill-Indonesia, http://www.cargill.com/news/issues/palm_current.htm.
17. See, for instance, Cargill's position statement: http://www.cargill.com/news/issues /palm_roundtable.htm#TopOfPage. Bunge: http://www.bunge.com/about-bunge /promoting_sustainability.html.
18. Greenpeace. See, for instance, http://www.greenpeace.org.uk/forests/faq-palm-oil-forests-and-climate-change.
19. "New Data Analysis . . ." For more information, see "Carbon-Climate-Human Interactions in Tropical Peatlands: Vulnerabilities, Risks & Mitigation Measures."
20. Steinfield et al., xxi.
21. Ibid., xxi.
22. Ibid.
23. British Government Panel on Sustainable Development, *Third Report*, 1997. Department of the Environment.
24. From company annual reports, Tyson and Smithfield, 2007.
25. Steinfield et al., 45.
26. For further discussion, see Paul Roberts, *The End of Food* (Boston: Houghton Mifflin, 2008), 293. See also Frances Moore Lappé, *Diet for a Small Planet*, 20th anniversary ed. (New York: Ballantine Books, 1991).
27. Conversion ratios from USDA, from Allen Baker, Feed Situation and Outlook staff, ERS, USDA, Washington, D.C.
28. Roberts, quoting "Legume Versus Fertilizer Sources of Nitrogen: Ecological Trade-offs and Human Need," *Agriculture, Ecosystems, and Environment* 102 (2004): 293.
29. World GHG Emissions Flow Chart, World Resources Institute, Washington, D.C. Based on data from 2000. All calculations are based on CO_2 equivalents, using hundred-year global warming potentials from the IPCC (1996). Land use change includes both emissions and absorptions. Available online at http://cait.wri.org /figures.php?page=WorldFlowChart.
30. According to the IPCC, greenhouse gases relevant to radiative forcing include the following (parts per million [ppm] and parts per trillion [ppt] are based on 1998 levels): carbon dioxide (CO_2), 365 ppm; methane (CH_4), 1,745 ppb; nitrous oxide (N_2O), 314 ppb; tetrafluoromethane (CF_2), 80 ppt; hexafluoromethane (C_2F_6), 3 ppt; sulfur hexafluoride (SF_6), 4.2 ppt; trifluoromenthane (CHF_3), 14 ppt; 1,1,1,2-tetra-fluoroethane ($C_2H_2F_4$), 7.5 ppt; 1,1-Difluoroethane ($C_2H_4F_2$), 0.5 ppt.
31. IPCC, *Climate Change 2007: Fourth Assessment Report of the Intergovernmental Panel on Climate Change* (New York: Cambridge University Press, 2007). Graphic 13.5.
32. World GHG Emissions Flow Chart, World Resources Institute.
33. Steinfeld et al., 79. See also, for instance, http://www.fao.org/ag/magazine/0612spl.htm.
34. See, for example, Carbon Farmers of Australia. http://www.carbonfarmersofaustralia. com.au.
35. Steinfeld et al.
36. United Nations FAO, quoting Anthony Weis, *The Global Food Economy: The Battle for the Future of Farming* (London: Zed Books, 2007), 19.
37. J. McMichael et al., "Food, Livestock Production, Energy, Climate Change, and Health," *The Lancet* 370 (2007):1253–63.
38. Pachauri.
39. Steinfeld et al.
40. Ibid.
41. CNN, "All About: Food and Fossil Fuels," March 17, 2008, cnn.com. Available online at http://edition.cnn.com/2008/WORLD/asiapcf/03/16/eco.food.miles/; author communication with Professor Jonathan Lynch, University of Pennsylvania.
42. Author communication with Lynch.
43. Stern.
44. See, for instance, Niles Eldredge, *Life on Earth: An Encyclopedia of Biodiversity, Ecology, and Evolution* (Santa Barbara, Calif.: ABC-CLIO, 2002). Online at http: //www.landinstitute.org/vnews/display.v/ART/2002/08/23/439bd36c9acf1.

45. World GHG Emissions Flow Chart, World Resources Institute.

46. For more detail, see Environmental Protection Agency, "General Information on the Link Between Solid Waste and Greenhouse Gas Emissions." Available online at http://www.epa.gov/climatechange/wycd/waste/generalinfo.html#ql.

47. IPCC. See Figure 1, Chapter 2.

48. Most recent data available from USDA/ERS, U.S. Cattle and Beef Industry, 2002–2007. Available online at http://www.ers.usda.gov/news/BSECoverage.htm.

49. Pounds noted here are measured by commercial carcass weight. U.S. Red Meat and Poultry Forecasts. Source: World Agricultural Supply and Demand Estimates and Supporting Materials. From USDA/ERS. See also http://www.ers.usda.gov/Browse /TradeInternationalMarkets/.

50. Data from Brazilian Beef Industry and Exporters Association. Cited in "Brazilian Beef Break Records in September," October 3, 2008, The Beef Site. Available online at http://www.thebeefsite.com/news/24565/brazilian-beef-break-records-in-september.

51. IPCC.

52. http://www.rodaleinstitute.org.

53. See, for instance, studies from the Rodale Institute, found here: http://www .newfarm.org/depts/NFfield_trials/1003/carbonsequest.shtml.

54. Editorial, "Deserting the Hungry?" *Nature* 451 (17 January 2008):223–24; dio:l0.1038/451223b; published online January 16, 2008. Available at http://www .nature.com/nature/journal/v451 /n7176/full/451223b.html.

55. Executive Summary, 9. IAASTD, "Summary Report," paper presented at the International Assessment of Agricultural Science and Technology for Development, Johannesburg, South Africa, April 2008.

56. "Civil Society Statement from Johannesburg, South Africa: A New Era of Agriculture Begins Today," April 12, 2008. Available online at http://www.agassessment.org /docs/Civil_Society_Statement_on_I AASTD-28Apr08.pdf.

57. Greenpeace Press Release, "Urgent Changes Needed in Global Farming Practices to Avoid Environmental Destruction," April 15, 2008.

58. Fifty-seven governments approved the Executive Summary of the Synthesis Report. An additional three governments—Australia, Canada, and the United States of America—did not fully approve the Executive Summary of the Synthesis Report, and their reservations are entered in the Annex. From the Executive Summary of IAASTD, "Summary Report."

59. *Nature*, 223–24.

60. Author interview with Martin Clough, head of biotech R & D and president of Syngenta Biotechnology, Inc., based in North Carolina; and Anne Birch, director with Corporate Affairs, Syngenta, September 9, 2008.

61. Nadia El-Hage Scialabba and Caroline Hattam, "General Concepts and Issues in Organic Agriculture," in *Organic Agriculture, Environment and Food Security*, ed. Environment and Natural Resources Service Sustainable Development Department (Rome: Food and Agriculture Organization of the United Nations, 2002), chapter 1. Available online at http://www.fao.org/docrep/005/y4137e/y4137e01 .htm#P0_3.

62. "Organic Crops Perform up to 100 Percent Better in Drought and Flood Years," November 7, 2003, Rodale Institute. Online at www.newfarm.org.

63. D. G. Hole et al., "Does Organic Farming Benefit Biodiversity?," *Biological Conservation* 122 (2005):113–30, quoting James Randerson, "Organic Farming Boosts Biodiversity," *New Scientist*, October 11, 2004. Note: *New Scientist* emphasizes that neither of the two groups of researchers—from the government agency, English Nature, and from the Royal Society for the Protection of Birds—" has a vested interest in organic farming."

64. Jules Pretty, *Agroecological Approaches to Agricultural Development* (Essex: University of Essex, 2006).

65. Ibid.

■ ■ ■

Reading as a Writer: Analyzing Rhetorical Choices

1. Lappé offers many different forms of evidence in this piece. Mark at least three different places in the text and three different endnotes where you think the evidence is especially compelling. Explain the strengths you see in these examples. What conclusions can you draw about providing evidence in your own persuasive writing?

2. Like Al Gore, Lappé tells us some fairly "inconvenient truths" about our daily food habits. How does she coax readers into seeing that there is a problem? What solutions does she offer? Locate some specific places where you see her addressing the how challenging it can be to acknowledge the connection between our eating habits and the health of the planet. How and where does she try to bring skeptics to her side? How effective do you think she is, and why?

Writing as a Reader: Entering the Conversation of Ideas

1. Both Lappé and Gary Steiner make claims that we should change the way we eat, and not simply based on what tastes good to us. To what extent do these writers' ideas about consuming food differently overlap? Write an essay in which you place these writers in conversation, considering the ways their arguments about how we ought to consume food are related, even if they may not seem to be at first. How might each author's ideas enhance the other's? What larger point might you make about the connection between what we eat and the larger world?

2. Lappé, like Michael Pollan, urges us to see the connections between our supper plates and the planet. Compose an essay that draws on the ideas and examples in both texts to build your own argument about the problems in the ways most Americans eat, and possible solutions. Develop your evidence with some additional research about food consumption in the United States, if you like.

MICHAEL POLLAN

Why Bother?

When it comes to the politics of food, Michael Pollan is one of the best-known American public intellectuals on the topic. He is also a professor of journalism at the University of California, Berkeley. Pollan's lively critiques of modern agribusiness and the harms our industrial food chain causes our environment and ourselves have appeared in dozens of top-ranked news and literary magazines, including the *New York Times Magazine* and *Harper's Magazine*. His research and writing and dynamic public lectures are interdisciplinary, bringing together history, the sciences, cultural studies, anthropology, sociology, and environmental justice (to name a few) in his focus on food—the ways we think about it, and the ways we do not think about it. His most recent books, *In Defense of Food: An Eater's Manifesto* (2009), *Food Rules: An Eater's Manual* (2009), and *Cooked: A Natural History of Transformation* (2014), are all designed to make readers far more mindful about what we put into our mouths. Pollan reveals to us the ways every bite of food is connected to politics and practices that we might find unsavory if we knew about them.

This is an excerpt of a longer essay that ran in the *New York Times Magazine* (2008). Pollan opens with a question that many of us have asked when faced with the overwhelming problem of climate change. Can small differences in our daily lives really make a difference to our planet's health? In this essay, Pollan works through the doubts many of us have that our personal attempts to "go green" will matter very much when, for example, we see neighbors driving gas-guzzlers or power mowers. For Pollan, the "why bother" question is answered partially by the writing of Wendell Berry, a farmer and writer who for over thirty years has been arguing that the crisis in our relationship to the land is a "disease of the modern character" in which we have become accustomed to specialists solving our problems and therefore no longer see our role in the big picture of personal and planet health (para. 9).

Drawing on Berry's insights and his own interest in industrial food production as a key contributor to global-warming, Pollan offers a very concrete solution: Plant a garden. (If you don't have a yard, Pollan very practically suggests trying to grow some of your food in a planter or buying into a community garden.) Pollan acknowledges that this can seem like too small of a gesture in the face of climate change, but he argues that growing even a little of your own food is "one of the most powerful things an individual can do—to reduce your carbon footprint, to be sure, but more important, to reduce your sense of dependence and dividedness: to change the cheap-energy mind" (para. 18).

Pollan reframes climate change as a call for *personal* change, noting that if we cultivate the ground in a garden, we will be cultivating different "habits of mind" (para. 21). He is part of a growing chorus of scholars who connect our cheap and unhealthy food supply to our increasingly unhealthy planet. Pollan's point is that the solution—changing the way we eat—will be delicious and make us feel better. In the face of so much "feel bad" news about global warming, you might be hungry for his perspective.

■   ■   ■

Why bother? That really is the big question facing us as individuals hop- *1* ing to do something about climate change, and it's not an easy one to answer. I don't know about you, but for me the most upsetting moment in *An Inconvenient Truth* came long after Al Gore scared the hell out of me, constructing an utterly convincing case that the very survival of life on earth as we know it is threatened by climate change. No, the really dark moment came during the closing credits, when we are asked to . . . change our light bulbs. That's when it got really depressing. The immense disproportion between the magnitude of the problem Gore had described and the puniness of what he was asking us to do about it was enough to sink your heart.

But the drop-in-the-bucket issue is not the only problem lurking *2* behind the "why bother" question. Let's say I do bother, big time. I turn my life upside-down, start biking to work, plant a big garden, turn down the thermostat so low I need the Jimmy Carter signature cardigan, forsake the clothes dryer for a laundry line across the yard, trade in the station wagon for a hybrid, get off the beef, go completely local. I could theoretically do all that, but what would be the point when I know full well that halfway around the world there lives my evil twin, some carbon-footprint doppel-ganger in Shanghai or Chongqing who has just bought his first car (Chinese car ownership is where ours was back in 1918), is eager to swallow every bite of meat I forswear, and who's positively itching to replace every last pound of CO_2 I'm struggling no longer to emit. So what exactly would I have to show for all my trouble?

There are so many stories we can tell ourselves to justify doing nothing, but perhaps the most insidious is that, whatever we do manage to do, it will be too little too late. Climate change is upon us, and it has arrived well ahead of schedule. Scientists' projections that seemed dire a decade ago turn out to have been unduly optimistic: The warming and the melting is occurring much faster than the models predicted. Now truly terrifying feedback loops threaten to boost the rate of change exponentially, as the shift from white ice to blue water in the Arctic absorbs more sunlight and warming soils everywhere become more biologically active, causing them to release their vast stores of carbon into the air. Have you looked into the eyes of a climate scientist recently? They look really scared. 3

So do you still want to talk about planting gardens? 4

I do. 5

Whatever we can do as individuals to change the way we live at this 6 suddenly very late date does seem utterly inadequate to the challenge. It's hard to argue with Michael Specter, in a recent *New Yorker* piece on carbon footprints, when he says: "Personal choices, no matter how virtuous, cannot do enough. It will also take laws and money." So it will. Yet it is no less accurate or hardheaded to say that laws and money cannot do enough, either; that it will also take profound changes in the way we live. Why? Because the climate-change crisis is at its very bottom a crisis of lifestyle—of character, even. The Big Problem is nothing more or less than the sum total of countless little everyday choices, most of them made by us (consumer spending represents 70 percent of our economy), and most of the rest of them made in the name of our needs and desires and preferences.

For us to wait for legislation or technology to solve the problem of how 7 we're living our lives suggests we're not really serious about changing— something our politicians cannot fail to notice. They will not move until we do. Indeed, to look to leaders and experts, to laws and money and grand schemes, to save us from our predicament represents precisely the sort of thinking—passive, delegated, dependent for solutions on specialists—that helped get us into this mess in the first place. It's hard to believe that the same sort of thinking could now get us out of it.

Thirty years ago, Wendell Berry, the Kentucky farmer and writer, put 8 forward a blunt analysis of precisely this mentality. He argued that the environmental crisis of the 1970s—an era innocent of climate change; what we would give to have back that environmental crisis!—was at its heart a crisis of character and would have to be addressed first at that level: at home, as it were. He was impatient with people who wrote checks to environmental organizations while thoughtlessly squandering fossil fuel in their everyday lives—the 1970s equivalent of people buying carbon offsets to atone for their Tahoes and Durangos. Nothing was likely to change until we healed the "split between what we think and what we do." For Berry, the "why bother" question came down to a moral imperative: "Once our personal connection to what is wrong becomes clear, then we have to choose: we can go on as before, recognizing our dishonesty and living with it the best we can, or we can begin the effort to change the way we think and live."

For Berry, the deep problem standing behind all the other problems of 9 industrial civilization is "specialization," which he regards as the "disease of the modern character." Our society assigns us a tiny number of roles: We're producers (of one thing) at work, consumers of a great many other things the rest of the time, and then once a year or so we vote as citizens. Virtually all of our needs and desires we delegate to specialists of one kind or another—our meals to agribusiness, health to the doctor, education to the teacher, entertainment to the media, care for the environment to the environmentalist, political action to the politician.

As Adam Smith and many others have pointed out, this division of 10 labor has given us many of the blessings of civilization. Specialization is what allows me to sit at a computer thinking about climate change. Yet this same division of labor obscures the lines of connection—and responsibility—linking our everyday acts to their real-world consequences, making it easy for me to overlook the coal-fired power plant that is lighting my screen, or the mountaintop in Kentucky that had to be destroyed to provide the coal to that plant, or the streams running crimson with heavy metals as a result.

Of course, what made this sort of specialization possible in the first 11 place was cheap energy. Cheap energy, which gives us climate change, fosters precisely the mentality that makes dealing with climate change in our own lives seem impossibly difficult. Specialists ourselves, we can no longer imagine anyone but an expert, or anything but a new technology or law, solving our problems.

The "cheap-energy mind," as Wendell Berry called it, is the mind 12 that asks, "Why bother?" because it is helpless to imagine—much less attempt—a different sort of life, one less divided, less reliant. Since the cheap-energy mind translates everything into money, its proxy, it prefers to put its faith in market-based solutions—carbon taxes and pollution-trading schemes. If we could just get the incentives right, it believes, the economy will properly value everything that matters and nudge our self-interest down the proper channels. The best we can hope for is a greener version of the old invisible hand. Visible hands it has no use for.

But while some such grand scheme may well be necessary, it's doubt- *13* ful that it will be sufficient or that it will be politically sustainable before we've demonstrated to ourselves that change is possible. Merely to give, to spend, even to vote, is not to do, and there is so much that needs to be done—without further delay. In the judgment of James Hansen, the NASA climate scientist who began sounding the alarm on global warming twenty years ago, we have only ten years left to start cutting—not just slowing—the amount of carbon we're emitting or face a "different planet." Hansen said this more than two years ago, however; two years have gone by, and nothing of consequence has been done. So: eight years left to go and a great deal left to do.

Which brings us back to the "why bother" question and how we might *14* better answer it. The reasons not to bother are many and compelling, at least to the cheap-energy mind. But let me offer a few admittedly tentative reasons that we might put on the other side of the scale.

If you do bother, you will set an example for other people. If enough *15* other people bother, each one influencing yet another in a chain reaction of behavioral change, markets for all manner of green products and alternative technologies will prosper and expand. (Just look at the market for hybrid cars.) Consciousness will be raised, perhaps even changed: New moral imperatives and new taboos might take root in the culture.

Going personally green is a bet, nothing more or less, though it's one *16* we probably all should make, even if the odds of it paying off aren't great. Sometimes you have to act as if acting will make a difference, even when you can't prove that it will.

So what would be a comparable bet that the individual might make *17* in the case of the environmental crisis? The idea is to find one thing to do in your life that doesn't involve spending or voting, that may or may not virally rock the world but is real and particular (as well as symbolic) and that, come what may, will offer its own rewards. Maybe you decide to give up meat, an act that would reduce your carbon footprint by as much as a quarter. Or you could try this: Determine to observe the Sabbath. For one day a week, abstain completely from economic activity: no shopping, no driving, no electronics.

But the act I want to talk about is growing some—even just a little—of *18* your own food. Rip out your lawn, if you have one, and if you don't—if you live in a high-rise, or have a yard shrouded in shade—look into getting a plot in a community garden. Measured against the Problem We Face, planting a garden sounds pretty benign, I know, but in fact it's one of the most powerful things an individual can do—to reduce your carbon footprint, sure, but more important, to reduce your sense of dependence and dividedness: to change the cheap-energy mind.

A great many things happen when you plant a vegetable garden, some *19* of them directly related to climate change, others indirect but related nevertheless. Growing food, we forget, comprises the original solar technology: calories produced by means of photosynthesis. Years ago the cheap-energy mind discovered that more food could be produced with less effort by replacing sunlight with fossil-fuel fertilizers and pesticides, with a result that the typical calorie of food energy in your diet now requires about ten calories of fossil-fuel energy to produce. It's estimated that the way we feed ourselves (or rather, allow ourselves to be fed) accounts for about a fifth of the greenhouse gas for which each of us is responsible.

Yet the sun still shines down on your yard, and photosynthesis still   20 works so abundantly that in a thoughtfully organized vegetable garden (one planted from seed, nourished by compost from the kitchen, and involving not too many drives to the garden center), you can grow the proverbial free lunch—CO_2-free and dollar-free. This is the most-local food you can possibly eat (not to mention the freshest, tastiest, and most nutritious). And while we're counting carbon, consider too your compost pile, which shrinks the heap of garbage your household needs trucked away even as it feeds your vegetables and sequesters carbon in your soil. What else? Well, you will probably notice that you're getting a pretty good workout there in your garden, burning calories without having to get into the car to drive to the gym. Also, by engaging both body and mind, time spent in the garden is time (and energy) subtracted from electronic forms of entertainment.

Still more valuable are the habits of mind that growing a little of your   21 own food can yield. You quickly learn that you need not be dependent on specialists to provide for yourself—that your body is still good for something and may actually be enlisted in its own support. If the experts are right, if both oil and time are running out, these are skills and habits of mind we're all very soon going to need. We may also need the food. Could gardens provide it? Well, during World War II, victory gardens supplied as much as 40 percent of the produce Americans ate.

But there are sweeter reasons to plant that garden, to bother. At least   22 in this one corner of your yard and life, you will have begun to heal the split between what you think and what you do, to commingle your identities as consumer and producer and citizen. Chances are, your garden will re-engage you with your neighbors, for you will have produce to give away and the need to borrow their tools. You will have reduced the power of the cheap-energy mind by personally overcoming its most debilitating weakness: its helplessness and the fact that it can't do much of anything that doesn't involve division or subtraction. The garden's season-long transit from seed to ripe fruit—will you get a load of that zucchini?!—suggests that the operations of addition and multiplication still obtain, that the abundance of nature is not exhausted. The single greatest lesson the garden teaches is that our relationship to the planet need not be zero-sum, and that as long as the sun still shines and people still can plan and plant, think and do, we can, if we bother to try, find ways to provide for ourselves without diminishing the world.

■ ■ ■

Reading as a Writer: Analyzing Rhetorical Choices

1. Pollan's title is an indicator that he understands it can be hard to believe our personal actions can have an effect on the environment. Throughout the essay, he addresses this skepticism in various ways. Mark the places where you see him addressing skeptical readers and evaluate how effective you find his strategies for inviting readers to see this issue from his perspective.

2. Pollan draws on the ideas of Wendell Berry, a farmer and well-known environmentalist writer, to develop his argument here. Mark the places where he explicitly mentions Berry. How, exactly, do Berry's concepts help Pollan make his own point in this essay?

Writing as a Reader: Entering the Conversation of Ideas

1. Pollan and co-authors Derrick Jensen and Stephanie McMillan argue that in order to make an impact on climate change, citizens have to do more than tweak their daily behaviors; they have to change their values and understand their relationship to the world differently. Compose an essay in which you draw on the insights and examples in both texts in order to make your own argument about the ways we could and should live more healthful lives, for ourselves and the planet. Be sure to anticipate and address counterarguments to your proposals. (If change were easy, more of us would do it, after all.)

2. Other writers in this chapter argue that changing our daily habits can improve our health and the health of the planet. Compose an essay in which you connect Pollan's ideas about changing our habits to those of the following writers: Gary Steiner or Anna Lappé. Use key ideas and examples from your chosen texts to build an argument about which changes are most pressing, given the evidence you have learned. What challenges do you see, and what benefits?

GARY STEINER

Animal, Vegetable, Miserable

Gary Steiner is a philosophy professor at Bucknell University who has focused his most recent work on the significance of the ways we understand our relationship with animals. This is the topic of his 2005 book, *Anthropocentrism and Its Discontents: The Moral Status of Animals in the History of Western Philosophy* and also his book, *Animals and the Moral Community: Mental Life, Moral Status, and Kinship* (2008). Steiner's key argument is that we should reevaluate the ideas we have inherited from Western philosophy that human animals are morally superior to nonhuman animals. Using both moral reasoning and statistics about the levels of violence that nonhuman animals suffer at the hands of humans, he attempts to open readers' minds about what we assume is "normal" behavior, such as eating meat or enjoying circuses or zoos.

In this short and pointedly argued guest column in the *New York Times*, Steiner raises questions about the ethics of eating even "humanely" raised meat, and he does so in late November (2009), right when millions of Americans are preparing to tuck into roasted turkey. As you read, pay attention to his word choice and examples as he tries to get us to see what he calls our "meat-crazed" culture through his eyes, the eyes of an "ethical vegan" who avoids *all* animal products—not just in food, but in clothing, shoes, and even Band-Aids (para. 13). Steiner knows he is in the minority; how does his affect his argument, and how does he address what he knows to be the enormous opposition to his perspective?

Where do you stand in this heated conversation about ethics and non-human animals? How you respond will affect the very next meal you eat.

■　■　■

Lately more people have begun to express an interest in where the 1
meat they eat comes from and how it was raised. Were the animals humanely treated? Did they have a good quality of life before the death that turned them into someone's dinner?

Some of these questions, which reach a fever pitch in the days lead- 2
ing up to Thanksgiving, pertain to the ways in which animals are treated. (Did your turkey get to live outdoors?) Others focus on the question of how eating the animals in question will affect the consumer's health and well-being. (Was it given hormones and antibiotics?)

None of these questions, however, make any consideration of whether 3
it is wrong to kill animals for human consumption. And even when people ask this question, they almost always find a variety of resourceful answers that purport to justify the killing and consumption of animals in the name of human welfare. Strict ethical vegans, of which I am one, are customarily excoriated for equating our society's treatment of animals with mass murder. Can anyone seriously consider animal suffering even remotely comparable to human suffering? Those who answer with a resounding no typically argue in one of two ways.

Some suggest that human beings but not animals are made in God's 4
image and hence stand in much closer proximity to the divine than any nonhuman animal; according to this line of thought, animals were made expressly for the sake of humans and may be used without scruple to satisfy their needs and desires. There is ample support in the Bible and in the writings of Christian thinkers like Augustine and Thomas Aquinas for this pointedly anthropocentric way of devaluing animals.

Others argue that the human capacity for abstract thought makes us 5
capable of suffering that both qualitatively and quantitatively exceeds the suffering of any nonhuman animal. Philosophers like Jeremy Bentham, who is famous for having based moral status not on linguistic or rational capacities but rather on the capacity to suffer, argue that because animals are incapable of abstract thought, they are imprisoned in an eternal

present, have no sense of the extended future, and hence cannot be said to have an interest in continued existence.

The most penetrating and iconoclastic response to this sort of reason- 6 ing came from the writer Isaac Bashevis Singer in his story "The Letter Writer," in which he called the slaughter of animals the "eternal Treblinka."

The story depicts an encounter between a man and a mouse. The man, 7 Herman Gombiner, contemplates his place in the cosmic scheme of things and concludes that there is an essential connection between his own existence as "a child of God" and the "holy creature" scuffling about on the floor in front of him.

Surely, he reflects, the mouse has some capacity for thought; Gombiner 8 even thinks that the mouse has the capacity to share love and gratitude with him. Not merely a means for the satisfaction of human desires, nor a mere nuisance to be exterminated, this tiny creature possesses the same dignity that any conscious being possesses. In the face of that inherent dignity, Gombiner concludes, the human practice of delivering animals to the table in the form of food is abhorrent and inexcusable.

Many of the people who denounce the ways in which we treat animals 9 in the course of raising them for human consumption never stop to think about this profound contradiction. Instead, they make impassioned calls for more "humanely" raised meat. Many people soothe their consciences by purchasing only free-range fowl and eggs, blissfully ignorant that "free range" has very little if any practical significance. Chickens may be labeled free-range even if they've never been outside or seen a speck of daylight in their entire lives. And that Thanksgiving turkey? Even if it is raised "free range," it still lives a life of pain and confinement that ends with the butcher's knife.

How can intelligent people who purport to be deeply concerned with 10 animal welfare and respectful of life turn a blind eye to such practices? And how can people continue to eat meat when they become aware that nearly 53 billion land animals are slaughtered every year for human consumption? The simple answer is that most people just don't care about the lives or fortunes of animals. If they did care, they would learn as much as possible about the ways in which our society systematically abuses animals, and they would make what is at once a very simple and a very difficult choice: to forswear the consumption of animal products of all kinds.

The easy part of this consists in seeing clearly what ethics requires 11 and then just plain doing it. The difficult part: You just haven't lived until you've tried to function as a strict vegan in a meat-crazed society.

What were once the most straightforward activities become a constant 12 ordeal. You might think that it's as simple as just removing meat, eggs, and dairy products from your diet, but it goes a lot deeper than that.

To be a really strict vegan is to strive to avoid all animal products, 13 and this includes materials like leather, silk, and wool, as well as a panoply of cosmetics and medications. The more you dig, the more you learn about products you would never stop to think might contain or involve animal products in their production—like wine and beer (isinglass, a kind of gelatin derived from fish bladders, is often used to "fine," or purify, these beverages), refined sugar (bone char is sometimes used to bleach it), or Band-Aids (animal products in the adhesive). Just last week I was told that those little comfort strips on most razor blades contain animal fat.

14   To go down this road is to stare headlong into an abyss that, to paraphrase Nietzsche, will ultimately stare back at you.

15   The challenges faced by a vegan don't end with the nuts and bolts of material existence. You face quite a few social difficulties as well, perhaps the chief one being how one should feel about spending time with people who are not vegans.

16   Is it OK to eat dinner with people who are eating meat? What do you say when a dining companion says, "I'm really a vegetarian—I don't eat red meat at home." (I've heard it lots of times, always without any prompting from me.) What do you do when someone starts to grill you (so to speak) about your vegan ethics during dinner? (Wise vegans always defer until food isn't around.) Or when someone starts to lodge accusations to the effect that you consider yourself morally superior to others, or that it is ridiculous to worry so much about animals when there is so much human suffering in the world? (Smile politely and ask them to pass the seitan.)

17   Let me be candid: By and large, meat-eaters are a self-righteous bunch. The number of vegans I know personally is . . . five. And I have been a vegan for almost fifteen years, having been a vegetarian for almost fifteen before that.

18   Five. I have lost more friends than this over arguments about animal ethics. One lapidary conclusion to be drawn here is that people take deadly seriously the prerogative to use animals as sources of satisfaction. Not only for food, but as beasts of burden, as raw materials, and as sources of captive entertainment—which is the way animals are used in zoos, circuses, and the like.

19   These uses of animals are so institutionalized, so normalized, in our society that it is difficult to find the critical distance needed to see them as the horrors that they are: so many forms of subjection, servitude, and—in the case of killing animals for human consumption and other purposes—outright murder.

20   People who are ethical vegans believe that differences in intelligence between human and nonhuman animals have no moral significance whatsoever. The fact that my cat can't appreciate Schubert's late symphonies and can't perform syllogistic logic does not mean that I am entitled to use him as an organic toy, as if I were somehow not only morally superior to him but virtually entitled to treat him as a commodity with minuscule market value.

We have been trained by a history of thinking of which we are *21*
scarcely aware to view nonhuman animals as resources we are entitled
to employ in whatever ways we see fit in order to satisfy our needs and
desires. Yes, there are animal welfare laws. But these laws have been formulated by, and are enforced by, people who proceed from the proposition that animals are fundamentally inferior to human beings. At best,
these laws make living conditions for animals marginally better than they
would be otherwise—right up to the point when we send them to the
slaughterhouse.

Think about that when you're picking out your free-range turkey, *22*
which has absolutely nothing to be thankful for on Thanksgiving. All it
ever had was a short and miserable life, thanks to us intelligent, compas-
sionate humans.

■ ■ ■

Reading as a Writer: Analyzing Rhetorical Choices

1. How and where exactly does Steiner make use of ethos, pathos, and logos
   as he builds his argument in this piece? Discuss the relationship you see
   between these different strategies. Which is most effective? How do they
   complement one another?

2. How does Steiner characterize those who are not vegans? Locate some
   specific passages and discuss the ways you think this serves his argument
   well, or not. How does he characterize himself, and other vegans? Again,
   discuss how you think this serves his argument well, or not.

Writing as a Reader: Entering the Conversation of Ideas

1. Steiner and Anna Lappé both make very strong appeals for changing the
   way we eat as a key strategy (perhaps *the* key strategy) to living more
   humane lives that are healthier for us and healthier for the globe. Compose an essay in which you place these authors in conversation, considering how each describes the problem and solutions. What do you think
   are the most compelling reasons for changing our patterns, and why? You
   might also analyze the rhetorical strategies each author uses as you consider how best to inspire others to change their daily habits.

2. While they may seem unlikely companions, both Steiner and Jean Kilbourne write about levels of violence we have become accustomed to in
   our daily lives, whether on our plates or in the images we consume. Write
   an essay in which you connect the ways each author writes about violence
   and its effects. What connections do you see in the objectification of and
   violence to bodies in each text? What solutions does each author offer, and
   what connections do you see there? Where do you stand?

17

Business and Marketing

What is the present and future of marketing?
Are we what we buy?

© Getty Images/Barisonal

Most of us recognize both the pleasure and problems of the contemporary belief that "to be is to buy"—that who we are is connected in some way to what we wear, eat, drive, and own. Most of us are able to resist the lure of commercial sloganeering a bit (that is, we know we are not literally our Abercrombie and Fitch shirts), and yet we give in, as well (or companies like Abercrombie and Fitch would not be so successful).

The readings in this chapter examine—often quite critically—the methods that corporations use to get us to buy their products, all while somehow making us feel great about handing them our money. Naomi Klein focuses on the shift from mere advertising to "branding," which goes far beyond selling products to selling experiences and lifestyles. John Dicker examines the power of telling an effective story as a marketing technique used by corporations such as Wal-Mart, even if the story does not match the facts.

Some of the writers in this chapter examine the role of science in advertising. For example, psychologists Sally Satel and Scott O. Lilienfeld raise questions about the strategy of neuromarketing, or hiring "buyologists" who make claims that the latest brain science can help target advertising with scientific accuracy. Taking a different approach, Mark R. Tercek and Jonathan S. Adams argue that the scientific challenges in the environmental movement would be better addressed if more companies used marketing insights to sell the idea of conservation. Investing in nature, Tercek and Adams argue, can and should be profitable.

Other writers analyze the role of business in the shifting and complex understandings of diversity within the United States and beyond. Fareed Zakaria contextualizes the place of the United States in a globalized economy that increasingly favors "the rise of the rest." What will the United States do to adapt to this changing market? The anthropologist Shalini Shankar examines the shifting demographics of racial groups within the United States and makes an argument that new advertising strategies aimed at Asian Americans retool old racial stereotypes to fit a contemporary consumerist identity that has problems of its own.

Finally, Ann duCille uses an extended analysis of the marketing of multicultural Barbies to demonstrate how problematic and limited "our" understanding of diversity is—and why it is so unsettling that we continue to sell these ideas to our children.

The diverse perspectives these authors bring to the practices and effects of the current market should inspire you to think carefully about free you are—or are not—to act according to your values when you invest in yourself, your community, and the world.

 At **macmillanhighered.com/frominquiry3e,** flip through an interactive critique of fashion advertising by Paul Mulhauser and Kelly Bradbury that focuses on the rhetoric of gendered assumptions, using examples from the J. Crew catalogue.

NAOMI KLEIN

From No Logo

Naomi Klein is a Canadian journalist who writes on a range of social issues, including feminism, militarism, and environmental injustices, but she is best known for her work on corporate abuses and the effects of glo-balization. She publishes frequently in newspapers and has written several books, including the best-seller, *The Shock Doctrine: The Rise of Disaster Capitalism* (2008). This excerpt is taken from an earlier book, *No Logo* (2000, reissued in 2012), in which she lays out her critique of corporate greed. How have we, as well-meaning consumers, become complicit in that greed by allowing ourselves to become "branded," and with what effects?

Klein opens historically, observing in the mid-1980s a corporate shift from producing products to producing brands. Pay close attention to the way she analyzes this shift from manufacturing to marketing and how she distinguishes between advertising and branding, explained more fully in the section "The Beginning of the Brand." How and why did "brand essence" become more important to consumers than the products themselves? You might test your own responses to products like Kraft or Campbell's Soup or Quaker Oats—or other brands you name as a class—to consider the emo-tions those brands evoke that may have very little do to with the product itself. How do you—and Klein—account for these responses?

In an age when big box stores and generic brands are popular, Klein asserts that branding has a power that goes far beyond consumer common sense. As you read about the rise of brand names from Apple to Starbucks in "The Brands Bounce Back," think about the slogans and the look of the ads and commercials—what Klein calls "brand as experience, as life-style" (para. 31). This idea is probably not totally new to you, but how does Klein's analysis of the historical reasons for this marketing approach help you understand the ways almost all of us have fallen prey—often willingly—to branding?

What's wrong with feeling good about buying a product for an image, or for the social cachet of owning a particular brand name? Klein sug-gests we think less about good and bad, and more about the significance that we have been successfully socialized as consumers to purchase ideas, rather than products. Who gains most from this consumer behavior? Klein argues: It will never be you.

■ ■ ■

As a private person, I have a passion for landscape, and I have never seen one improved by a billboard. Where every prospect pleases, man is at his vilest when he erects a billboard. When I retire from Madison Avenue, I am going to start a secret society of masked vigilantes who will travel around the world on silent motor bicycles, chopping down posters at the dark of the moon. How many juries will convict us when we are caught in these acts of beneficent citizenship?
—DAVID OGILVY, FOUNDER OF THE OGILVY&MATHER
ADVERTISING AGENCY, IN *CONFESSIONS*
OF AN ADVERTISING MAN, 1963

The astronomical growth in the wealth and cultural influence of *1* multinational corporations over the last fifteen years can arguably be traced back to a single, seemingly innocuous idea developed by management theorists in the mid-1980s: that successful corporations must primarily produce brands, as opposed to products.

Until that time, although it was understood in the corporate world that *2* bolstering one's brand name was important, the primary concern of every solid manufacturer was the production of goods. This idea was the very gospel of the machine age. An editorial that appeared in *Fortune* magazine in 1938, for instance, argued that the reason the American economy had yet to recover from the Depression was that America had lost sight of the importance of making *things*.

> This is the proposition that the basic and irreversible function of an industrial economy is *the making of things*: that the more things it makes the bigger will be the income, whether dollar or real; and hence that the key to those lost recuperative powers lies . . . in the factory where the lathes and the drills and the fires and the hammers are. It is in the factory and on the land and under the land that purchasing power *originates*. [italics theirs]

And for the longest time, the making of things remained, at least in *3* principle, the heart of all industrialized economies. But by the eighties, pushed along by that decade's recession, some of the most powerful manufacturers in the world had begun to falter. A consensus emerged that corporations were bloated, oversized; they owned too much, employed too many people, and were weighed down with *too many things*. The very process of producing—running one's own factories, being responsible for tens of thousands of full-time permanent employees—began to look less like the route to success and more a clunky liability.

At around this same time a new kind of corporation began to rival *4* the traditional all-American manufacturers for market share; these were Nikes and Microsofts, and later, the Tommy Hilfigers and Intels. These pioneers made the claim that producing goods was only an incidental part of their operations, and that thanks to recent victories in trade liberalization and labor-law reform, they were able to have their products made for them by contractors, many of them overseas. What these companies produced primarily were not things they said, but *images* of their brands. Their real work lay not in manufacturing but in marketing. This formula, needless to say, has proved enormously profitable, and its success has companies competing in a race toward weightlessness: Whoever owns the least, has the fewest employees on the payroll and produces the most powerful images, as opposed to products, wins the race.

And so the wave of mergers in the corporate world over the last few *5* years is a deceptive phenomenon: It only *looks* as if the giants, by joining forces, are getting bigger and bigger. The true key to understanding these shifts is to realize that in several crucial ways—not their profits, of course—these merged companies are actually shrinking. Their apparent bigness is simply the most effective route toward their real goal: divestment of the world of things.

Since many of today's best-known manufacturers no longer produce 6 products and advertise them, but rather buy products and "brand" them, these companies are forever on the prowl for creative new ways to build and strengthen their brand images. Manufacturing products may require drills, furnaces, hammers, and the like, but creating a brand calls for a completely different set of tools and materials: It requires an endless parade of brand extensions, continuously renewed imagery for marketing, and, most of all, fresh new spaces to disseminate the brand's idea of itself. In this section, I'll look at how, in ways both insidious and overt, this corporate obsession with brand identity is waging a war on public and individual space: on public institutions such as schools, on youthful identities, on the concept of nationality, and on the possibilities for unmarketed space.

The Beginning of the Brand

It's helpful to go back briefly and look at where the idea of branding first 7 began. Though the words are often used interchangeably, branding and advertising are not the same process. Advertising any given product is only one part of branding's grand plan, as are sponsorship and logo licensing. Think of the brand as the core meaning of the modern corporation, and of the advertisement as one vehicle used to convey that meaning to the world.

The first mass-marketing campaigns, starting in the second half of the 8 nineteenth century, had more to do with advertising than with branding as we understand it today. Faced with a range of recently invented products—the radio, phonograph, car, light bulb and so on—advertisers had more pressing tasks than creating a brand identity for any given corporation; first, they had to change the way people lived their lives. Ads had to inform consumers about the existence of some new invention, then convince them that their lives would be better if they used, for example, cars instead of wagons, telephones instead of mail, and electric light instead of oil lamps. Many of these new products bore brand names—some of which are still around today—but these were almost incidental. These products were themselves news; that was almost advertisement enough.

The first brand-based products appeared at around the same time as 9 the invention-based ads, largely because of another relatively recent innovation: the factory. When goods began to be produced in factories, not only were entirely new products being introduced but old products—even basic staples—were appearing in strikingly new forms. What made early branding efforts different from more straightforward salesmanship was that the market was now being flooded with uniform mass-produced products that were virtually indistinguishable from one another. Competitive branding became a necessity of the machine age—within a context of manufactured sameness, image based difference had to be manufactured along with the product.

So the role of advertising changed from delivering product news bul- *10* letins to building an image around a particular brand-name version of a product. The first task of branding was to bestow proper names on generic goods such as sugar, flour, soap, and cereal, which had previously been scooped out of barrels by local shopkeepers. In the 1880s, corporate logos were introduced to mass-produced products like Campbell's Soup, H.J. Heinz pickles and Quaker Oats cereal. As design historians and theorists Ellen Lupton and J. Abbott Miller note, logos were tailored to evoke familiarity and folksiness, in an effort to counteract the new and unsettling anonymity of packaged goods. "Familiar personalities such as Dr. Brown, Uncle Ben, Aunt Jemima, and Old Grand-Dad came to replace the shopkeeper, who was traditionally responsible for measuring bulk foods for customers and acting as an advocate for products . . . a nationwide vocabulary of brand names replaced the small local shopkeeper as the interface between consumer and product." After the product names and characters had been established, advertising gave them a venue to speak directly to would-be consumers. The corporate "personality," uniquely named, packaged and advertised, had arrived.

For the most part, the ad campaigns at the end of the nineteenth cen- *11* tury and the start of the twentieth used a set of rigid, pseudoscientific formulas: Rivals were never mentioned, ad copy used declarative statements only, and headlines had to be large, with lots of white space—according to one turn-of-the-century adman, "an advertisement should be big enough to make an impression but not any bigger than the thing advertised."

But there were those in the industry who understood that advertis- *12* ing wasn't just scientific; it was also spiritual: Brands could conjure a feeling—think of Aunt Jemima's comforting presence—but not only that, entire corporations could themselves embody a meaning of their own. In the early twenties, legendary adman Bruce Barton turned General Motors into a metaphor for the American family, "something personal, warm, and human," while GE was not so much the name of the faceless General Electric Company as, in Barton's words, "the initials of a friend." In 1923 Barton said that the role of advertising was to help corporations find their soul. The son of a preacher, he drew on his religious upbringing for uplifting messages: "I like to think of advertising as something big, something splendid, something which goes deep down into an institution and gets hold of the soul of it. . . . Institutions have souls just as men and nations have souls," he told GM president Pierre du Pont. General Motors ads began to tell about the people who drove its cars—the preacher, the pharmacist, or the country doctor who, thanks to his trusty GM, arrived "at the bedside of a dying child" just in time "to bring it back to life."

By the end of the 1940s, there was a burgeoning awareness that a *13* brand wasn't just a mascot or a catchphrase or a picture printed on the label of a company's product; the company as a whole could have a brand identity or a "corporate consciousness," as this ephemeral quality was termed at the time. As this idea evolved, the adman ceased to see himself as a pitchman and instead saw himself as "the philosopher-king of commercial culture," in the words of ad critic Randall Rothberg. The search for the true meaning of brands—or the "brand essence," as it is often called—gradually took the agencies away from individual products and their attributes and toward a psychological/anthropological examination of what brands mean to the culture and to people's lives. This was seen to be of crucial importance, since corporations may manufacture products, but what consumers buy are brands.

It took several decades for the manufacturing world to adjust to this *14* shift. It clung to the idea that its core business was still production and that branding was an important add-on. Then came the brand equity mania of the eighties, the defining moment of which arrived in 1988 when Philip Morris purchased Kraft for $12.6 billion—six times what the company was worth on paper. The price difference, apparently, was the cost of the word "Kraft." Of course Wall Street was aware that decades of marketing and brand bolstering added value to a company over and above its assets and total annual sales. But with the Kraft purchase, a huge dollar value had been assigned to something that had previously been abstract and unquantifiable—a brand name. This was spectacular news for the ad world, which was now able to make the claim that advertising spending was more than just a sales strategy: It was an investment in cold hard equity. The more you spend, the more your company is worth. Not surprisingly, this led to a considerable increase in spending on advertising. More important, it sparked a renewed interest in puffing up brand identities, a project that involved far more than a few billboards and TV spots. It was about pushing the envelope in sponsorship deals, dreaming up new areas in which to "extend" the brand, as well as perpetually probing the Zeitgeist to ensure that the "essence" selected for one's brand would resonate karmically with its target market. For reasons that will be explored in the rest of this chapter, this radical shift in corporate philosophy has sent manufacturers on a cultural feeding frenzy as they seize upon every corner of unmarketed landscape in search of the oxygen needed to inflate their brands. In the process, virtually nothing has been left unbranded. That's quite an impressive feat, considering that as recently as 1993 Wall Street had pronounced the brand dead, or as good as dead.

The Brand's Death (Rumors of Which Had Been Greatly Exaggerated)

. . . On April 2,1993, advertising itself was called into question by the *15* very brands the industry had been building, in some cases, for over two centuries. That day is known in marketing circles as "Marlboro Friday," and it refers to a sudden announcement from Philip Morris that it would slash the price of Marlboro cigarettes by 20 percent in an attempt to compete with bargain brands that were eating into its market. The pundits went nuts, announcing in frenzied unison that not only was Marlboro dead, all brand names were dead. The reasoning was that if a "prestige" brand like Marlboro, whose image had been carefully groomed, preened, and enhanced with more than a billion advertising dollars, was desperate enough to compete with no-names, then clearly the whole concept of branding had lost its currency. The public had seen the advertising, and the public didn't care. The Marlboro Man, after all, was not any old campaign; launched in 1954, it was the longest-running ad campaign in history. It was a legend. If the Marlboro Man had crashed, well, then, brand equity had crashed as well. The implication that Americans were suddenly thinking for themselves en masse reverberated through Wall Street. The same day Philip Morris announced its price cut, stock prices nose-dived for all the household brands: Heinz, Quaker Oats, Coca-Cola, PepsiCo, Procter and Gamble, and RJR Nabisco. Philip Morris's own stock took the worst beating.

Bob Stanojev, national director of consumer products marketing for 16 Ernst and Young, explained the logic behind Wall Street's panic: "If one or two powerhouse consumer products companies start to cut prices for good, there's going to be an avalanche. Welcome to the value generation."

Yes, it was one of those moments of overstated instant consensus, but 17 it was not entirely without cause. Marlboro had always sold itself on the strength of its iconic image marketing, not on anything so prosaic as its price. As we now know, the Marlboro Man survived the price wars without sustaining too much damage. At the time, however, Wall Street saw Philip Morris's decision as symbolic of a sea change. The price cut was an admission that Marlboro's name was no longer sufficient to sustain the flagship position, which in a context where image is equity meant that Marlboro had blinked. And when Marlboro—one of the quintessential global brands—blinks, it raises questions about branding that reach beyond Wall Street, and way beyond Philip Morris.

The panic of Marlboro Friday was not a reaction to a single incident. 18 Rather, it was the culmination of years of escalating anxiety in the face of some rather dramatic shifts in consumer habits that were seen to be eroding the market share of household-name brands, from Tide to Kraft. Bargain-conscious shoppers, hit hard by the recession, were starting to pay more attention to price than to the prestige bestowed on their products by the yuppie ad campaigns of the 1980s. The public was suffering from a bad case of what is known in the industry as "brand blindness."

Study after study showed that baby boomers, blind to the alluring 19 images of advertising and deaf to the empty promises of celebrity spokespersons, were breaking their lifelong brand loyalties and choosing to feed their families with private-label brands from the supermarket—claiming, heretically, that they couldn't tell the difference. From the beginning of the recession to 1993, Loblaw's President's Choice line, Wal-Mart's Great

Value, and Marks and Spencer's St. Michael prepared foods had nearly doubled their market share in North America and Europe. The computer market, meanwhile, was flooded by inexpensive clones, causing IBM to slash its prices and otherwise impale itself. It appeared to be a return to the proverbial shopkeeper dishing out generic goods from the barrel in a pre-branded era. . . .

The Brands Bounce Back

There were some brands that were watching from the sidelines as Wall *20* Street declared the death of the brand. Funny, they must have thought, we don't feel dead.

Just as the admen had predicted at the beginning of the recession, the *21* companies that exited the downturn running were the ones who opted for marketing over value every time: Nike, Apple, the Body Shop, Calvin Klein, Disney, Levi's, and Starbucks. Not only were these brands doing just fine, thank you very much, but the act of branding was becoming a larger and larger focus of their businesses. For these companies, the ostensible product was mere filler for the real production: the brand. They integrated the idea of branding into the very fabric of their companies. Their corporate cultures were so tight and cloistered that to outsiders they appeared to be a cross between fraternity house, religious cult, and sanitarium. Everything was an ad for the brand: bizarre lexicons for describing employees (partners, baristas, team players, crew members), company chants, superstar CEOs, fanatical attention to design consistency, a propensity for monument-building, and New Age mission statements. Unlike classic household brand names, such as Tide and Marlboro, these logos weren't losing their currency; they were in the midst of breaking every barrier in the marketing world—becoming cultural accessories and lifestyle philosophers. These companies didn't wear this image like a cheap shirt—their image was so integrated with their business that other people wore it as *their* shirt. And when the brands crashed, these companies didn't even notice—they were branded to the bone.

So the real legacy of Marlboro Friday is that it simultaneously brought *22* the two most significant developments in nineties marketing and consumerism into sharp focus: the deeply unhip big-box bargain stores that provide the essentials of life and monopolize a disproportionate share of the market (Wal-Mart *et al.*) and the extra-premium "attitude" brands that provide the essentials of lifestyle and monopolize ever-expanding stretches of cultural space (Nike *et al.*). The way these two tiers of consumerism developed would have a profound impact on the economy in the years to come. When overall ad expenditures took a nosedive in 1991, Nike and Reebok were busy playing advertising chicken, with each company increasing its budget to outspend the other. In 1991 alone, Reebok upped its ad spending by 71.9 percent, while Nike pumped an extra 24.6 percent into its already soaring ad budget, bringing the company's total spending on marketing to a staggering $250 million annually. Far from worrying about competing on price, the sneaker pimps were designing ever more intricate and pseudoscientific air pockets, and driving up prices by signing star athletes to colossal sponsorship deals. The fetish strategy seemed to be working fine: In the six years prior to 1993, Nike had gone from a $750 million company to a $4 billion one and Phil Knight's Beaverton, Oregon, company emerged from the recession with profits 900 percent higher than when it began.

Benetton and Calvin Klein, meanwhile, were also upping their spend- 23 ing on lifestyle marketing, using ads to associate their lines with risqué art and progressive politics. Clothes barely appeared in these high-concept advertisements, let alone prices. Even more abstract was Absolut Vodka, which for some years now had been developing a marketing strategy in which its product disappeared and its brand was nothing but a blank bottle-shaped space that could be filled with whatever content a particular audience most wanted from its brands: intellectual in *Harper's*, futuristic in *Wired*, alternative in *Spin*, loud and proud in *Out*, and "Absolut Centerfold" in *Playboy*. The brand reinvented itself as a cultural sponge, soaking up and morphing to its surroundings.

Saturn, too, came out of nowhere in October 1990 when GM launched 24 a car built not out of steel and rubber but out of New Age spirituality and seventies feminism. After the car had been on the market a few years, the company held a "homecoming" weekend for Saturn owners, during which they could visit the auto plant and have a cookout with the people who made their cars. As the Saturn ads boasted at the time, "44,000 people spent their vacations with us, at a car plant." It was as if Aunt Jemima had come to life and invited you over to her house for dinner.

In 1993, the year the Marlboro Man was temporarily hobbled by 25 "brand-blind" consumers, Microsoft made its striking debut on *Advertising Age*'s list of the top 200 ad spenders — the very same year that Apple computer increased its marketing budget by 30 percent after already making branding history with its Orwellian takeoff ad launch during the 1984 Super Bowl. Like Saturn, both companies were selling a hip new relationship to the machine that left Big Blue IBM looking as clunky and menacing as the now-dead Cold War.

And then there were the companies that had always understood that 26 they were selling brands before product. Coke, Pepsi, McDonald's, Burger King, and Disney weren't fazed by the brand crisis, opting instead to escalate the brand war, especially since they had their eyes firmly fixed on global expansion. They were joined in this project by a wave of sophisticated producer/retailers who hit full stride in the late eighties and early nineties. The Gap, Ikea, and the Body Shop were spreading like wildfire during this period, masterfully transforming the generic into the brand-specific, largely through bold, carefully branded packaging and the promotion of an "experiential" shopping environment. The Body Shop had been a presence in Britain since the seventies, but it wasn't until 1988 that it began sprouting like a green weed on every street corner in the United States. Even during the darkest years of the recession, the company opened between forty and fifty American stores a year. Most baffling of all to Wall Street, it pulled off the expansion without spending a dime on advertising. Who needed billboards and magazine ads when retail outlets were three-dimensional advertisements for an ethical and ecological approach to cosmetics? The Body Shop was all brand.

The Starbucks coffee chain, meanwhile, was also expanding during 27 this period without laying out much in advertising; instead, it was spinning off its name into a wide range of branded projects: Starbucks airline coffee, office coffee, coffee ice cream, coffee beer. Starbucks seemed to understand brand names at a level even deeper than Madison Avenue, incorporating marketing into every fiber of its corporate concept—from the chain's strategic association with books, blues, and jazz to its Euro-latte lingo. What the success of both the Body Shop and Starbucks showed was how far the branding project had come in moving beyond splashing one's logo on a billboard. Here were two companies that had fostered powerful identities by making their brand concept into a virus and sending it out into the culture via a variety of channels: cultural sponsorship, political controversy, the consumer experience, and brand extensions. Direct advertising, in this context, was viewed as a rather clumsy intrusion into a much more organic approach to image building.

Scott Bedbury, Starbucks' vice president of marketing, openly recog- 28 nized that "consumers don't truly believe there's a huge difference between products," which is why brands must "establish emotional ties" with their customers through "the Starbucks Experience." The people who line up for Starbucks, writes CEO Howard Shultz, aren't just there for the coffee. "It's the romance of the coffee experience, the feeling of warmth and community people get in Starbucks stores."

Interestingly, before moving to Starbucks, Bedbury was head of mar- 29 keting at Nike, where he oversaw the launch of the "Just Do It!" slogan, among other watershed branding moments. In the following passage, he explains the common techniques used to infuse the two very different brands with meaning:

> Nike, for example, is leveraging the deep emotional connection that people have with sports and fitness. With Starbucks, we see how coffee has woven itself into the fabric of people's lives, and that's our opportunity for emotional leverage . . . A great brand raises the bar—it adds a greater sense of purpose to the experience, whether it's the challenge to do your best in sports and fitness or the affirmation that the cup of coffee you're drinking really matters.

This was the secret, it seemed, of all the success stories of the late 30 eighties and early nineties. The lesson of Marlboro Friday was that there never really was a brand crisis—only brands that had crises of confidence. The brands would be okay, Wall Street concluded, so long as they believed fervently in the principles of branding and never, ever blinked. Overnight,

"Brands, not products!" became the rallying cry for a marketing renaissance led by a new breed of companies that saw themselves as "meaning brokers" instead of product producers. What was changing was the idea of what—in both advertising and branding—was being sold. The old paradigm had it that all marketing was selling a product. In the new model, however, the product always takes a back seat to the real product, the brand, and the selling of the brand acquired an extra component that can only be described as spiritual. Advertising is about hawking product. Branding, in its truest and most advanced incarnations, is about corporate transcendence.

It may sound flaky, but that's precisely the point. On Marlboro Friday, *31* a line was drawn in the sand between the lowly price slashers and the high-concept brand builders. The brand builders conquered, and a new consensus was born: The products that will flourish in the future will be the ones presented not as "commodities" but as concepts: the brand as experience, as lifestyle.

Ever since, a select group of corporations has been attempting to *32* free itself from the corporeal world of commodities, manufacturing, and products to exist on another plane. Anyone can manufacture a product, they reason (and as the success of private-label brands during the recession proved, anyone did). Such menial tasks, therefore, can and should be farmed out to contractors and subcontractors whose only concern is filling the order on time and under budget (ideally in the Third World, where labor is dirt cheap, laws are lax, and tax breaks come by the bushel). Headquarters, meanwhile, is free to focus on the real business at hand—creating a corporate mythology powerful enough to infuse meaning into these raw objects just by signing its name.

The corporate world has always had a deep New Age streak, fed—it *33* has become clear—by a profound need that could not be met simply by trading widgets for cash. But when branding captured the corporate imagination, New Age vision quests took center stage. As Nike CEO Phil Knight explains, "For years we thought of ourselves as a production-oriented company, meaning we put all our emphasis on designing and manufacturing the product. But now we understand that the most important thing we do is market the product. We've come around to saying that Nike is a marketing-oriented company, and the product is our most important marketing tool." This project has since been taken to an even more advanced level with the emergence of online corporate giants such as Amazon.com. It is online that the purest brands are being built: Liberated from the real-world burdens of stores and product manufacturing, these brands are free to soar, less as the disseminators of goods or services than as collective hallucinations.

Tom Peters, who has long coddled the inner flake in many a hard-nosed *34* CEO, latched on to the branding craze as the secret to financial success, separating the transcendental logos and the earthbound products into two distinct categories of companies. "The top half—Coca-Cola, Microsoft,

Disney, and so on—are pure 'players' in brainware. The bottom half [Ford and GM] are still lumpy-object purveyors, though automobiles are much 'smarter' than they used to be," Peters writes in *The Circle of Innovation* (1997), an ode to the power of marketing over production.

When Levi's began to lose market share in the late nineties, the 35 trend was widely attributed to the company's failure—despite lavish ad spending—to transcend its products and become a free-standing meaning. "Maybe one of Levi's problems is that it has no Cola," speculated Jennifer Steinhauer in *The New York Times*. "It has no denim-toned house paint. Levi makes what is essentially a commodity: blue jeans. Its ads may evoke rugged outdoorsmanship, but Levi hasn't promoted any particular life style to sell other products."

In this high-stakes new context, the cutting-edge ad agencies no lon- 36 ger sold companies on individual campaigns but on their ability to act as "brand stewards": identifying, articulating, and protecting the corporate soul. Not surprisingly, this spelled good news for the U.S. advertising industry, which in 1994 saw a spending increase of 8.6 percent over the previous year. In one year, the ad industry went from a near crisis to another "best year yet." And that was only the beginning of triumphs to come. By 1997, corporate advertising, defined as "ads that position a corporation, its values, its personality and character," were up 18 percent from the year before.

With this wave of brand mania has come a new breed of businessman, 37 one who will proudly inform you that Brand X is not a product but a way of life, an attitude, a set of values, a look, an idea. And it sounds really great—way better than that Brand X is a screwdriver, or a hamburger chain, or a pair of jeans, or even a very successful line of running shoes. Nike, Phil Knight announced in the late eighties, is "a sports company"; its mission is not to sell shoes but to "enhance people's lives through sports and fitness" and to keep "the magic of sports alive." Company president-cum-sneaker-shaman Tom Clark explains that "the inspiration of sports allows us to rebirth ourselves constantly."

Reports of such "brand vision" epiphanies began surfacing from all 38 corners. "Polaroid's problem," diagnosed the chairman of its advertising agency, John Hegarty, "was that they kept thinking of themselves as a camera. But the '[brand] vision' process taught us something: Polaroid is not a camera—it's a social lubricant." IBM isn't selling computers; it's selling business "solutions." Swatch is not about watches; it is about the idea of time. At Diesel Jeans, owner Renzo Rosso told *Paper* magazine, "We don't sell a product, we sell a style of life. I think we have created a movement. . . . The Diesel concept is everything. It's the way to live, it's the way to wear, it's the way to do something." And as Body Shop founder Anita Roddick explained to me, her stores aren't about what they sell; they are the conveyers of a grand idea—a political philosophy about women, the environment and ethical business. "I just use the company that I surprisingly created as a success—it shouldn't have been like this, it wasn't meant to be like this—to stand on the products to shout out on these issues," Roddick says.

The famous late graphic designer Tibor Kalman summed up the *39* shifting role of the brand this way: "The original notion of the brand was quality, but now brand is a stylistic badge of courage."

The idea of selling the courageous message of a brand, as opposed *40* to a product, intoxicated these CEOs, providing as it did an opportunity for seemingly limitless expansion. After all, if a brand was not a product, it could be anything! And nobody embraced branding theory with more evangelical zeal than Richard Branson, whose Virgin Group has branded joint ventures in everything from music to bridal gowns to airlines to cola to financial services. Branson refers derisively to the "stilted Anglo-Saxon view of consumers," which holds that a name should be associated with a product like sneakers or soft drinks, and opts instead for "the Asian 'trick'" of the *keiretsus* (a Japanese term meaning a network of linked corporations). The idea, he explains, is to "build brands not around products but around reputation. The great Asian names imply quality, price and innovation rather than a specific item. I call these 'attribute' brands: They do not relate directly to one product—such as a Mars bar or a Coca-Cola—but instead to a set of values."

Tommy Hilfiger, meanwhile, is less in the business of manufacturing *41* clothes than he is in the business of signing his name. The company is run entirely through licensing agreements, with Hilfiger commissioning all its products from a group of other companies: Jockey International makes Hilfiger underwear, Pepe Jeans London makes Hilfiger jeans, Oxford Industries make Tommy shirts, the Stride Rite Corporation makes its footwear. What does Tommy Hilfiger manufacture? Nothing at all.

So passé had products become in the age of lifestyle branding that *42* by the late nineties newer companies like Lush cosmetics and Old Navy clothing began playing with the idea of old-style commodities as a source of retro marketing imagery. The Lush chain serves up its face masks and moisturizers out of refrigerated stainless-steel bowls, spooned into plastic containers with grocery-store labels. Old Navy showcases its shrink-wrapped T-shirts and sweatshirts in deli-style chrome refrigerators, as if they were meat or cheese. When you are a pure, concept-driven brand, the aesthetics of raw product can prove as "authentic" as loft living.

And lest the branding business be dismissed as the playground *43* of trendy consumer items such as sneakers, jeans, and New Age beverages, think again. Caterpillar, best known for building tractors and busting unions, has barreled into the branding business, launching the Cat accessories line: boots, back-packs, hats, and anything else calling out for a postindustrial *je ne sais quoi*. Intel Corp., which makes computer parts no one sees and few understand, transformed its processors into a fetish brand with TV ads featuring line workers in funky metallic space suits dancing to "Shake Your Groove Thing." The Intel mascots proved so popular that the company has sold hundreds of thousands of bean-filled dolls modeled on the shimmery dancing technicians. Little wonder, then, that when asked about the company's decision to diversify its products, the senior vice president for sales and marketing, Paul S. Otellini, replied that Intel is "like Coke. One brand, many different products."

And if Caterpillar and Intel can brand, surely anyone can. *44*

There is, in fact, a new strain in marketing theory that holds that even *45* the lowliest natural resources, barely processed, can develop brand identities, thus giving way to hefty premium-price markups. In an essay appropriately titled "How to Brand Sand," advertising executives Sam Hill, Jack McGrath and Sandeep Dayal team up to tell the corporate world that with the right marketing plan, nobody has to stay stuck in the stuff business. "Based on extensive research, we would argue that you can indeed brand not only sand, but also wheat, beef, brick, metals, concrete, chemicals, corn grits, and an endless variety of commodities traditionally considered immune to the process."

Over the past six years, spooked by the near-death experience of Marl- *46* boro Friday, global corporations have leaped on the brand-wagon with what can only be described as a religious fervor. Never again would the corporate world stoop to praying at the altar of the commodity market. From now on they would worship only graven media images. Or to quote Tom Peters, the brand man himself: "Brand! Brand!! Brand!!! That's the message . . . for the late '90s and beyond."

■ ■ ■

Reading as a Writer: Analyzing Rhetorical Choices:

1. Try to summarize Klein's argument about how and why brands became more important than products starting in the mid-1980s. What is the difference between advertising and branding, according to Klein?

2. Divide into pairs/teams and look up the advertising costs and production information of a few popular brands, including some of your favorites. Also consult the costs of generic versions of these products. What conclusions can you draw, using Klein's insights?

Writing as a Reader: Entering the Conversation of Ideas

1. How might Klein's ideas enhance the claims that Shalini Shankar makes about marketing to specific ethnic groups? How do Shankar's ideas extend Klein's insights? Write an essay in which you teach your reader what you have learned about marketing, branding, and ethnicity using the ideas and examples in these readings. Explain the significance of your findings.

2. Klein's ideas about branding are interesting to consider in light of the ideas about marketing and "nature" found in essays by co-authors Mark R. Tercek and Jonathan S. Adams, and by Noël Sturgeon (Chapter 16). In an essay that draws together insights and examples from Klein and one or both of the additional readings, construct an argument about an effective approach to branding or marketing environmental products or issues. What are the possible hazards? What might be good about this kind of marketing? If you like, include an example of an environmental issue that could be marketed, keeping the cautionary ideas of these authors in mind.

JOHN DICKER

From The United States of Wal-Mart

John Dicker is a freelance writer whose work has appeared in *The Nation* and *Salon*, among other publications. The book from which this excerpt comes, *The United States of Wal-Mart* (2005), is written for the general public and takes a polemical stance on Wal-Mart as troubling corporation.

Dicker's focus is on "the story" of Wal-Mart, and why this company, among so many other gigantic corporations, has garnered so much media attention. As you read, keep track of the evidence Dicker provides for what sets Wal-Mart apart from other "big box" stores. In paragraph 10, Dicker offers a bulleted list of conflicts that come up frequently in stories about Wal-Mart and then suggests that the "binaries" might be more complicated. Take a moment to consider and discuss the oppositions in that list, given what you know about Wal-Mart as a business.

Dicker's perspective in this piece is pretty clear. How and where does he include oppositional points of view? How does he use these oppositional claims to further his own argument? Given Dicker's punchy tone and rhetorical approach, how effective do you think he might be at persuading someone who does not already agree with him, and why?

In his final section, Dicker returns to the idea of "storytelling," and argues that Wal-Mart is having a difficult time telling a flattering story because the facts are not flattering. Must companies "tell a story" about themselves in order to be appealing to consumers? If you research the facts about many companies you support, you might find that Wal-Mart hardly stands alone in hiding less appealing facts about its business. Ultimately, who should get to tell the end of the story—the corporations, or the consumers?

■ ■ ■

The Story That Won't Die

In an age of global terrorism and preemptive war it may seem strange that *1* a chain of discount stores should keep finding its way into the news. In 2003 the *Los Angeles Times* bagged a Pulitzer Prize for a three-part series on the chain's global influence. *The New York Times* has told of workers being locked inside stores overnight, of its use of illegal immigrants, and its effects on book and magazine publishing. *The Wall Street Journal* has provided some of the most rigorous Wal-Mart coverage, on everything from the company's healthcare plan to the growing power of its Washington lobby. And state and regional papers have all chimed in with their own versions of "Dude, where's my neighborhood grocer?"

Business Week wonders, "Is Wal-Mart Too Powerful?" *Fortune* asks, "Should *2* We Admire Wal-Mart?" *The Economist* claims that it's "Learning to Love Wal-Mart"; *Fast Company* tells us about "The Wal-Mart You Don't Know." According to *Forbes*, "Sam Walton Made Us a Promise." And outlets far too numerous to name have been unable to resist some version of "Up Against the Wal."

Each week brings fresh outrages. In the month of September 2004, 3 Wal-Mart opened a store on the site of an ancient tribal burial ground on the Hawaiian island of Maui. The same year, Wal-Mart announced plans to plop a Supercenter at San Juan Teotihuacán, northeast of Mexico City—a Supercenter that would be visible from the top of nearby ancient pyramids. (The announcement triggered multiple hunger strikes.)

Given all this coverage, it's easy to forget that to most people, 4 Wal-Mart is *just* a store. A place to buy batteries, dog food, and paper towels to a soundtrack of barcode blips and infant apoplexy. As former *Atlantic Monthly* columnist and author Thomas Hine notes, "Never before has so much been available to so many. And never before has it seemed so dull."[1]

Harp too long on Wal-Mart and people may want to know if it's 5 really that bad. What about all the Targets, Kohl's, Home Depots, Costcos, Kmarts, Petsmarts, Office Maxes, Whole Foods, Best Buys, Circuit Citys, and BJ's Wholesale Clubs? Why isn't anyone talking about them? They have to be doing something wrong, right? That so many news outlets should be so consumed with one company's doings suggests either an outbreak of monomania or, as some have claimed, a political agenda.

One reason Wal-Mart is a story as fixed in the news cycle as the war 6 on terrorism is apparent in the second paragraph of every article written about it: Wal-Mart is big. It's so big it takes several paragraphs just to catalogue its bigness. As predictable as these second paragraphs have become, it is difficult to understate the company's scope. Consider:

- Wal-Mart alone represents a staggering 2 percent of the GDP of the United States of America.
- Wal-Mart employs one out of every 115 American workers.
- Wal-Mart is more than four times the size of its largest retail rival, Home Depot.

Other stores may look and feel and behave in similar ways, but com- 7 paring why they're treated differently in the media is like asking why Britney is always in *Us Weekly* instead of the third runner-up on *American Idol*. As much as Wal-Mart might smell like the media's flavor of the month, the avalanche of stories does not reflect an ephemeral interest.

But what gives the Wal-Mart story legs is more than impressive statis- 8 tics. As *The New Yorker*'s Ken Auletta writes, the mainstream media are not so much biased toward a political camp as they are toward conflict itself. And Wal-Mart has provided enough scandals, lawsuits, and irresistible storylines to keep journalists busy for years beyond the rapture.

When Wal-Mart first blipped on the public's radar, the narrative, however 9 nascent, was framed as a feel-good story, in which the main character was a good ol' boy from Arkansas, the quixotic figure of Sam Walton. Despite being the country's richest man, he drove a beater pickup, flew coach class, and got five-dollar haircuts. The concept of the "backwoods billionaire" was new, intriguing, and, perhaps most important, it appealed to a nation that, although growing increasingly cynical, still celebrated the self-made man.

As Walton's company became a national powerhouse, spreading *10* beyond the Ozarks and the Sunbelt, skirmishes erupted between the company and the communities it served, between the company and the states in which it operated, between the company and a vociferous and growing antiglobalization movement, and even between the company and its employees. All of this attracted media attention, and the story was too good to drop. The more the media investigated, the more conflict it uncovered. It's nearly impossible to cite all the ongoing battles in this escalating war between Wal-Mart and the media. A few of the most notorious:

- the "mom-and-pop" shops versus the corporate behemoth that puts them out of business
- the popularity of low prices versus the unpopularity of their social costs
- First World consumers versus Third World producers
- union solidarity versus the "the Wal-Mart family"
- blue-state quaint versus red-state pragmatic
- retail spaces that are big, cheap, and no-frills versus those that are small, distinct, and where, at least in theory, everybody *could* know your name

Not all of these oppositions are as binary as presented, but they offer *11* convenient frameworks on which stories can be built and then published—again and again and again. But is this bad? Is it antibusiness to ask questions about a company's business practices? And if it's not, then what, exactly, is the point to these stories? To change policy? To change consumers' minds? Maybe Wal-Mart is just a convenient target, a very visible corporate villain whose success is the very thing that people hate about it. Or maybe the company represents an unstoppable force in American capitalism, one that is destined to erase regional identity by giving every state in the union the Wal-Mart Makeover.

It's hard to know what the real story is, because the real story is *12* complicated.

A Macro-Sized Microcosm

Wal-Mart serves as a macro-sized microcosm of many of America's biggest *13* socioeconomic problems. Take the ongoing loss of American manufacturing jobs to China, Bangladesh, India, and beyond. A result of new technology and the global marketplace, and spurned by that "retro" conflict between labor and capital, outsourcing has decimated the U.S. manufacturing base, which has been hemorrhaging jobs for seven straight years. Wal-Mart didn't start this trend; and because it relies mostly on suppliers and subcontractors rather than foreign firms directly, the company's hands usually stay clean. As Lee Scott told the *Wall Street Journal* in 2004, "I am not familiar with the idea that Wal-Mart brings anyone in and says you need to take this item offshore. I can't say it never happened, but I can say that is not our policy."[2]

As the CEO suggests, no Bentonville buyer is ever going to whisper   *14* the equivalent to "Michigan bad, Guangdong Province good!" in a supplier's ear. That's because they don't have to. It's no secret the company plays hardball with its suppliers (from whom Bentonville's buyers are forbidden from accepting so much as a soft drink). Not only do the buyers demand the lowest price, as any business would, they also require seven to eight "points of improvement" a year. These can range from adding cost efficiencies to their supply line to more consistent sizing on garments. They're burdensome, and sometimes next to impossible to achieve: Wal-Mart's demands make it difficult for its suppliers to offer their employees livable wages and good working conditions—not when you've got the world's largest retailer holding your leash. . . .

Then there's the ubiquity of Wal-Mart itself, the way it is altering the   *15* American landscape. Conservatives have argued that the building of Wal-Marts and Supercenters in economically depressed areas is *the solution* for urban blight. In a column on the alternative news web site "The Raw Story," columnist Brian Holley wonders if the Wal-Marts that are popping up in urban areas, where lower-income families seek out low-price goods, are like the pox-infested blankets freshly landed Europeans gave to Native Americans. Great in the short term; devastating over time. The very concept of "sprawl" evokes visions of Wal-Mart, as the typical Supercenter requires a twenty-plus-acre lot—space for 1,000 parking spots—and generates an estimated 7,000 to 10,000 car trips per day.

And a widely publicized report from Good Jobs First, a nonprofit think   *16* tank, revealed that the federal and state governments have subsidized Wal-Mart to the tune of nearly $4 billion. These subsidies come in a rainbow of colors: free or reduced-price land, tax breaks, sales tax rebates, state corporate income tax credits, and so on. The other subsidy that Wal-Mart receives from the government is endorsement for its near-poverty wages: The amount of money Wal-Mart employees and their dependents cost the states in which they operate in welfare benefits, which many workers rely on to make ends meet, numbers in the hundreds of millions of dollars—per year. The Good Jobs First report estimated that a full 90 percent of all Wal-Marts and Supercenters built on U.S. soil receive some kind of government subsidy. . . .

We Provide Jobs!

For the depressed communities that Wal-Mart approaches, invariably the   *17* carrot is the promise of jobs and more jobs. And yet one of the most widely and publicly leveled charges against Wal-Mart is that its jobs [stink]. In 2004 the company claimed that a full-time worker averaged $9.64 per hour, up from only $8.27 two years earlier. Since full time is thirty-two hours a week, the average annual take-home pay totals around $18,000 a year (assuming hours aren't cut, as they often are). For a family of four, the figure is nearly $1,000 *below* the poverty line.[3] Add to this that Wal-Mart's health insurance is priced so far beyond the reach of most of its associates that states from Washington to Georgia have found the company's workers to be among the largest groups seeking public assistance, and Wal-Mart's carrot begins to look like a very meager meal.

Hardly a season goes by without a new Wal-Mart scandal: 2,000 ille- *18* gal immigrants working for subminimum wages as janitors; workers on overnight shifts are locked inside stores; lawsuits in twenty-eight states alleging unpaid overtime on behalf of thousands of current and former workers. And the real doozy: a class-action lawsuit alleging systematic gender discrimination against 1.6 million female workers. When certified in the spring of 2004 it became the largest civil rights lawsuit in American history. In fact, it is estimated that Wal-Mart faces roughly 5,000 lawsuits each year,[4] an average of about thirteen new suits *each day*.

Workers who so much as dabble in union organizing are subjected *19* to surveillance by management and onslaughts of antiunion meetings, videos, and reprisals. When workers have managed to persevere and elect union representation, Wal-Mart has responded by eliminating entire job classifications, and threatening to close stores.[5]

When confronted with this information, the company response is: *20* "Wal-Mart provides good jobs." It's like some sort of corporate mantra designed to soothe troubled souls and put worried minds at ease. Wait: I can't make ends meet on this wage. *Wal-Mart provides good jobs.* But the deductible is 42 percent of my yearly salary; I can't afford that. *Wal-Mart provides good jobs.*

The hypnotist act works well on desperate communities with high *21* unemployment numbers. They don't need too much convincing. The message is clear: You need us more than we need you.

"We opened a store last year in Valley Stream [a Long Island suburb *22* just across the border from New York City] where we had over 15,000 applicants for 300 jobs," Michael Duke, CEO of the Wal-Mart Stores division said in spring of 2004. "They all wanted to wear that Wal-Mart badge. When I visit with our associates, I can see their pride. They know they were the very best from more than 15,000 applicants. They feel like the chosen ones."[6]

The hordes of applicants don't merely want a job; they want a Wal- *23* Mart job. As a pleased-as-pork Lee Scott told an industry panel about a store opening in Phoenix, "We had 500 job openings, we had 5,000 applications. Maybe it is different where you live, but where we live, people don't line up to get a new job that pays less and has less benefits. The world does not work that way."

Except when it does. Wal-Mart's moral calculus is a strange hybrid of *24*
know-nothing and spin: The stock market fallout of 2000, the slow recession that veered dangerously close to a minor depression after September 11, and a recovery unprecedented in the amount of jobs it *didn't* create
played no role in the formation of Wal-Mart's rationale for continuing
business as usual despite the bad press. And though few call the company
out on such twisted logic, Wal-Mart's claim that the number of applicants
for its jobs reflects the quality of its jobs is like saying soup-kitchen lines
are a referendum on soup.

From executives like Duke and Scott, the overriding message is: Trust *25*
us. Even if our associates make a fraction of our annual bonuses, hey, we
know them and they *love* it.

"People who write about the quality of jobs at Wal-Mart don't under- *26*
stand or know anything about our associates," Duke explains. "When you
get to know our people, their dedication and loyalty, and you see firsthand
their level of commitment, you realize these are quality jobs."[7]

But don't take it from Duke. Lee Scott, whose 2003 salary and bonus *27*
(including stock grants of $17.4 million) was 966 times the salary of a full-
time associate explains it this way: "It is not forced labor. The truth is, I go
to the stores and shake hands with the associates, and they like working at
Wal-Mart."[8]

More than 500,000 associates leave Wal-Mart each year. In fact, the *28*
company's 2003 turnover rate of 44 percent was actually the *lowest* it
had seen in recent years. Just two years earlier, it was churning through
over 56 percent of its employees annually. Within the first ninety days of
employment, when the majority of turnover occurs, the figure was a staggering 70 percent. Even at its current "low" of 44 percent, with a roster of
1.2 million associates, Wal-Mart must hire 660,000 fresh bodies a year just
to maintain homeostasis.

Storytelling

The consensus in Bentonville is that times have changed. Wal-Mart, they *29*
say, *must* do a better job of using the media to tell its story. However, for
much of its history, Wal-Mart didn't need the media. Unlike an Internet
start-up (remember those?) or a Tina Brown publication (remember that?),
no "buzz" is required to get people into its stores. While it'll often christen
a new store with a pep rally, complete with marching bands, cheerleaders,
and other wholesome incarnations of American rah rah rah, these fetes
are not intended to draw media attention or trigger sales. With the exception of certain hotel heiresses, everybody has heard of Wal-Mart.

But times have changed for Wal-Mart. Its anonymity is gone, as is its *30*
underdog status. Unflattering and unfortunate episodes that might have
fallen by the wayside in Sam Walton's day will now make fast headlines.
But implicit in the oft-stated presumption that effective storytelling is all

that's required is the idea that if more people could just understand *the real Wal-Mart*, and not the one portrayed in the newspapers and TV, perhaps have a Massengill moment with a smiling associate or two, then its unaffordable health insurance, low wages, and cutthroat business practices would dissolve into the ether.

In January of 2005, Lee Scott went on the offensive against the company's critics. Taking out more than one hundred full-page newspaper ads trumpeting the company's wages and benefits, Scott told the Associated Press that he felt Wal-Mart was being "nibbled to death by guppies."

"We're taking this time to say, 'Hold on a minute, we have good jobs,'" he said.[9] Scott intended to spread this good news through a series of planned meetings with various organizations in which he vowed to explain Wal-Mart's labor practices, its environmental policies, and the way it conducts business with its suppliers. He refused to name the organizations.

"If you're a company with a budget the size of Wal-Mart and you're claiming to be misunderstood, it's pretty pathetic frankly," says PR consultant and industry analyst Paul Holmes, who sees Wal-Mart's PR efforts as being quick and cosmetic in nature. "It's a lot easier to get a face-lift than to change your whole personality, or change your character."

It might be hard to believe, but critical press is not always the result of bad or inadequate PR, or an ideological agenda. Sometimes unflattering stories can actually come from unflattering facts. As a *New York Times* editorial put it, "If Wal-Mart wants to do a better job in telling its story, it needs to work on having a better story to tell."[10]

But for now, at least, the story isn't pretty.

NOTES

1. Thomas Hine, I *Want That!* (New York: HarperCollins, 2002).
2. Ann Zimmerman, "Defending Wal-Mart," *Wall Street Journal*, October 6, 2004.
3. *Federal Register*, vol. 69, no. 30 (February 13, 2004), pp. 7336–38.
4. Elizabeth MacDonald, "Giant Slayer," *Forbes*, September 6, 2004.
5. Steven Greenhouse, "Labor Department Wins $1.9 Million in Back Pay for Janitors," *New York Times*, August 26, 2004. Sadly, such practices aren't limited to the house of Wal-Mart. In 2003, the Minneapolis-based Target organization eliminated health insurance for part-time associates. It also put the kibosh on "shift differential," or a wage premium, for those working the graveyard shift. A few months after Wal-Mart felt the heat on janitorial subcontractors using illegal immigrants, Target paid nearly $2 million in unpaid overtime to more than 700 immigrant janitors exploited in an arrangement nearly identical to Wal-Mart's. Insomuch as it offers a model for competitors, Wal-Mart also serves its industry as an effective buffer against bad PR.
6. Don Longo, "Fighting a Bad Rap," *Retail Merchandiser*, May 1, 2004.
7. Ibid.
8. Abigail Goldman and Nancy Cleeland, "An Empire Built on Bargains Remakes the Working World," *Los Angeles Times*, November 23, 2002.
9. "Wal-Mart's CEO on Offensive Against Critics," Associated Press, January 13, 2005.
10. "Wal-Mart's New Spin," *New York Times*, September 14, 2004.

■ ■ ■

Reading as a Writer: Analyzing Rhetorical Choices

1. What does Dicker mean in paragraph 13 when he claims that "Wal-Mart serves as a macro-sized microcosm" of many socioeconomic problems in the United States? Try to paraphrase his claim (aloud in class, or in writing) and then point to the evidence he offers. How would you evaluate the strength of his claim, and why?

2. Look up some current statistics and news stories about Wal-Mart. What has—and hasn't—changed in the Wal-Mart "story"? What numbers and facts strike you as most interesting as you consider Wal-Mart's effect on workers, communities, and consumers?

Writing as a Reader: Entering the Conversation of Ideas

1. Naomi Klein suggests that branding has more power than the produces themselves, and includes a section on big box stores, including Wal-Mart, in her essay. John Dicker takes a different approach to the Wal-Mart story. Compose an essay in which you draw on both writers' insights to examine what you consider to be the weaknesses and strengths of Wal-Mart's corporate story. What is at stake, and for whom, when you consider the perspective of the storyteller? What conclusions can you draw about the way we tell stories of business success?

2. Dicker's analysis of Wal-Mart's strategy is similar to that of Carolyn Merchant (Chapter 16) in her analysis of the "malling" of the United States. Write an essay in which you place these authors in conversation about the significance of current strategies used to sell commodities to customers. What might each author say about the other's examples? What larger point can you draw from these texts about what seems to work—and why—in current marketing tactics? What conclusions can you draw about U.S. consumers, based on these examples?

SALLY SATEL AND SCOTT O. LILIENFELD

From The Buyologist Is In: The Rise of Neuromarketing

Sally Satel, a psychiatrist and a lecturer at Yale University School of Medicine, has ties to the American Enterprise Institute, a conservative think tank. She writes occasionally for the *New York Times* and has written several books about the intersection of policy and medical treatment. Scott O. Lilienfeld is a professor of psychology at Emory University. These authors share an interest in challenging the current popular infatuation with neuroscience, which you can observe in the title of the 2013 book this reading comes from *Brainwashed: The Seductive Appeal of Mindless Neuroscience*. In this excerpt, from the chapter "The Buyologist Is In: The Rise of Neuromarketing," they question the ability of neuroscience to predict effective marketing tactics.

Satel and Lilienfeld coin the term *buyologist* to "denote marketers who routinely exaggerate what neuroscience can do" to sell almost anything (para. 3). They open their argument by laying out broad claims in the popular media that studying the brain will allow us to understand "scientifically" how and why we desire some products over others. These claims are naïve and simplistic, according to Satel and Lilenfeld, and yet large corporations such as Google, Facebook, and Disney—among many others—have hired neuromarketers to help them develop advertising campaigns. These authors seek to explain this current trend and to raise questions for consumers.

Like other authors in this section, Satel and Lilenfeld provide an historical backdrop for their argument, contextualizing our current infatuation with neuroscience in a long history of psychological approaches to marketing products. Pay attention to the ways they build their argument into this history; where do you hear their perspective most clearly? The examples they provide of corporations that use neuromarketers on their campaigns—Coca-Cola, Warner Brothers, and Pantene—also are aimed to persuade the reader (paras. 18–21). How effectively do their examples support their claims about the limits of neuromarketing?

Ultimately, Satel and Lilienfeld's critique is less about neuroscience and more about analyzing the popular desire to believe that brain scans are the new answer to understanding human motivation. In their concluding paragraphs, they urge readers to avoid simple conclusions "for" or "against" the value of neuromarketing. They recontextualize the phrase "buyer beware" in a way that is consistent with effective scholarly research: Ask questions! The answers, they argue, are rarely simple.

▨ ▨ ▨

"The ultimate no-bullshit zone." This is how globetrotting Danish 1 branding expert Martin Lindstrom refers to the human brain. "Our truest selves react to stimuli at a level far deeper than conscious thought," he writes, estimating that a whopping 90 percent of our buying decisions take place at this level. As a result, "we can't actually explain our preferences, or likely buying decisions, with any accuracy." The author of the 2008 business bestseller *Buyology: Truth and Lies about Why We Buy* and one of *Time* magazine's top 100 "Scientists and Thinkers," Lindstrom advises marketers to cut out the middlemen—the buyers themselves—and ask their brains directly: Will you buy our product? Forget focus groups and questionnaires. The brain is the route to the heart's desire.[1]

Lindstrom is a high-profile member of an upstart generation of Mad 2 Men known as neuromarketers. They apply the tools of neuroscience, such as fMRI and brain-wave technologies, to learn how consumers' brains instantly react to ads and products. It's all in the service of answering elusive questions as old as advertising itself: What do customers want? What motivates them to buy? And how can I get them to buy *my* product? "Half the money I spend on advertising is wasted. The trouble is I don't know which half," Gilded Age department-store magnate John Wanamaker famously said. His lament still echoes today. American businesses spend billions on advertising each year—$114 billion in 2011. Yet, according to marketing experts, 80 percent of all new products either fail within six months of launch or fall significantly short of their profit forecasts.[2]

Corporations such as Google, Facebook, Motorola, Unilever, and Dis-   3 ney have hired neuromarketers to help them improve those odds. Has this hiring paid off? It's hard to know. Neuromarketing is a controversial practice without an established track record. Many of its purveyors lean heavily on hype. One buyologist—we use the term "buyologist" to denote marketers who routinely exaggerate what neuroscience can do to sell widgets—is A. K. Pradeep, head of the U.S. firm NeuroFocus, which, Pradeep says, can offer its corporate clients "secrets for selling to the subconscious mind." FKF Applied Research (which sponsored the notorious swing-voter study) touts its "scientifically sound, empirically precise brain scan approach." To the nonexpert, neuromarketing seems able to drill down to the physiological essence of desire. Consumer choice "is an inescapably biological process," claims Neuroco, a neuromarketing firm located in the United Kingdom.[3]

The media routinely abet the mystique. "They mine your brain so they   4 can blow your mind with products you deeply desire," gushed a 2011 article in the business magazine *Fast Company*. When reporters first began to cover neuromarketing around 2004, the consumer's "buy button in the brain" was a favorite metaphor. Other versions of a discrete buying "center" now animate the small army of neuromarketing boosters—coaches, consultants, and workshop leaders—that has formed. A company called SalesBrain, for example, touts its ability to show marketers how to "maximize your ability to influence the part of the brain that decides: the Reptilian Brain. . . . You will walk away [from the seminar] with a clear and simple methodology that brings proven science to the act of selling and persuasion."[4]

Claims such as these led the prestigious journal *Nature Neuroscience*   5 to editorialize in a 2004 column titled "Brain Scam?" that "neuromarketing [might be] little more than a new fad, exploited by scientists and marketing consultants to blind corporate clients with science." Even friendly critics say that it is hard to judge the rigor and value of neuromarketing in the absence of clear and detailed documentation of the complex methods and research protocols that neuromarketers use. Still, the fact that an impressive cohort of esteemed scientists have joined the advisory boards of various neuromarketing companies—one even boasts a Nobel Prize winner in medicine—suggests at least some kernel of promise in the neuromarketing enterprise.[5]

By conventional metrics, neuromarketing has not yet penetrated   6 all that deeply into the advertising world. A 2011 survey of almost 700 marketing professionals revealed that only 6 percent used imaging and brain-wave analysis in client work. Yet *Advertising Age*, the leading industry publication, has speculated that the use of neuromarketing by some of the biggest names in consumer goods "suggests that the early adopters are seeing results." Perhaps companies are indeed seeing results, but the evidence is largely under wraps. Firms do not publish their research, both to keep contractual agreements with their clients and to protect their own proprietary methodologies and mathematical algorithms. As a result, few detailed case studies of neuroscience influencing real marketing decisions by named companies are publicly available for review. "Until there are publications in peer-reviewed journals, there will always be a whiff of pseudo-science surrounding neuromarketing," admits Roger Dooley, host of a well-regarded blog on the subject.[6]

That whiff of pseudoscience is a common problem that plagues 7 many efforts to apply brain imaging and other brain-based technologies outside the lab and the clinic. In this respect, neuromarketing is a microcosm of the far broader tendency within popular neuroscience to engage in neurohype. At its worst, neuromarketing succumbs to the kinds of errors in interpretation, such as reverse inference, neurocentrism, and neuroredundancy—using brain science to demonstrate what we could find out more simply by asking people directly—that can give brain imaging an undeservedly bad name. And when profits are involved, the threshold for playing fast and loose with brain science may be lowered even more.

Lindstrom, for example, has made headlines by proclaiming that the 8 brains of Apple product users show neural patterns identical to those displayed by the brains of devoted Christians viewing a religious figure or icon. (Is it a coincidence that Lindstrom routinely advises his corporate clients to "treat your brand as a religion"?) Later, Lindstrom claimed that iPhone users are "in love" with their phones because, like love, the gadget activates the insula; never mind that the structure mediates other emotions as well. Furthermore, neuromarketing lapses too readily into neurocentrist cheerleading. Although there is little debate among cognitive psychologists that immediate emotional responses operating outside awareness influence many of our decisions, neuromarketers often take this conclusion too far. They relentlessly drive home the debatable point that immediate neural responses are inherently more authentic and predictive of consumer behavior than is conscious reflection.[7]

Since the turn of the twentieth century, businessmen have sought the advice 9 of psychological experts to unlock the secrets of the consumer mind. In the 1920s, the influential American psychologist John B. Watson promoted a basic learning theory of advertising: Consumers buy a product when they have an incentive to do so. One surefire way to cultivate this desire, Watson advised companies, was to appeal to people's self-image—and the emotions and cultural associations that went with it.[8]

As a behaviorist, Watson famously treated the mind as a "black box." *10* He was not interested in its inner workings, only its behavioral outputs. But the idea that the consumer has a strong irrational streak that marketers need to harness was persistent. Melvin Cope-land's 1924 textbook *Principles of Merchandising* attributed buying behavior to both rational and irrational drives. "Motives have their origins in human instincts, and emotions represent the impulsive or unreasoning promptings to action," he wrote.

The idea that most of our actions, desires, and fantasies contain hid- *11* den meaning created a niche for Freudian theory in marketing. By the 1930s, a psychodynamic model of the consumer mind came to the fore, embodied in the writings of Ernest Dichter, an ambitious émigré from Vienna who arrived in America in 1938.[9] "You would be amazed to find how often we mislead ourselves, regardless of how smart we think we are, when we attempt to explain why we are behaving the way we do," Dichter observed. He developed a system called "motivational research." Trained interviewers administered Rorschach inkblot tests and "depth" interviews in which participants free-associated to products, and investigators then examined their narratives for themes of Freudian conflict, sex, and aggression. Dichter is perhaps best known for advising General Mills to design a cake mix that required an egg for its Betty Crocker cake mix, partly to assuage the housewife's unconscious guilt for taking a baking shortcut by using a mix, and partly because the egg symbolized a fertility offering to her husband.[10]

With the darkness of the Depression era lifting after World War II, *12* household austerity gave way to a marketer's bounty. Although Madison Avenue was no less interested in manipulating the consumer, it was becoming increasingly disillusioned with the ability of Freudian theory to predict buyer behavior. By the mid-1960s, most agencies had abandoned the analytic approach because they found it too unscientific and its sensational claims unfulfilled.[11]

Madison Avenue was already turning to a more straightforward *13* approach: market research. Rather than attempting to uncover customers' secret motivations, it simply asked them what they thought of a product and whether they would buy it. Focused group interviews (not known as "focus groups" until the late 1970s) combined the interview approach with polling. The groups typically consisted of a dozen or so individuals, mainly homemakers, who were led by a professional moderator in a free-form but comprehensive discussion of their reasons for liking a product, ad, radio spot, or commercial. On the basis of participants' enthusiasm, or lack thereof, executives decided to kill a product, modify it, or push it further down the production pipeline.[12]

Although focus groups remain a useful method in electoral politics *14* and public opinion research, they have notorious weaknesses. Sometimes, a single forceful participant may sway or intimidate the others in the group. Participants often tell moderators what they think the moderators want to hear, rather than giving truthful answers, or censor their true reactions so they will fit in with the group.

A deeper issue, though, is the premise that group participants are *15*
valid informants. "The groups were basically a waste of time because there is often such a tenuous relationship between a participant's expressed intention to purchase and actual buying behavior," explains Gerald Zaltman, an emeritus professor at the Harvard School of Business who once ran such groups. The typical participant knows what she likes but not *why* she likes it or, more crucially, whether she will buy the featured product. This is because, as Dichter and earlier consumer psychologists recognized, decisions are shaped by a multitude of factors, many of them operating outside awareness, such as past experiences and personal and cultural influences that would take too long to consider individually.[13]

This insight led advertisers to the lab, where they tried to measure *16*
consumers' physiological responses to advertising. In the early 1960s, researchers experimented with pupillometry, or measures of spontaneous pupil dilation, to gauge interest in features of package designs or print advertisements. (Of course, pupillary dilation can reflect anxiety, fear, or stress, as well as interest.) They examined skin conductance response, a measure of the sweatiness of the palms, as an indicator of people's emotional response to advertisements and employed eye tracking to reveal where on a page or TV screen people's eyes traveled. In the 1970s, researchers first used electroencephalography (EEG), which measures the electrical activity of the brain by means of electrodes placed on the scalp, to examine left- and right-brain activations in response to marketing stimuli. A decade later, they added steady-state topography (a cousin of EEG that is highly sensitive to the speed of neural processing) to ascertain whether long-term memory encoding during advertising is linked to changes in consumers' preferences for certain brands. In the end, however, experts did not find these approaches particularly revelatory.[14]

Within the past two decades, refinements in brain-wave technology *17*
(primarily EEG) and the advent of brain-imaging technology have revived a biological approach to the consumer mind. Zaltman, sometimes called "the Father of Neuromarketing," conducted some of the earliest studies using PET scans in the 1980s and fMRI a decade later. From his Mind of the Market lab at Harvard Business School, Zaltman and colleagues showed advertisements and products to subjects to evoke neural patterns related to emotion, preference, or memory. In one study, the team scanned subjects while half of them examined a detailed cartoon sketching for an ad and the other half looked at the finished ad as it might appear in a magazine. Neural activity was comparable under both conditions, which prompting the team to suggest that the client need not take the very expensive step of going from the artists' rendering to a finished ad. In 1999, British neuroscientist Gemma Calvert established Neurosense hi Oxford, England,

the first company to apply brain imaging to consumer psychology. In the United States, the Atlanta-based BrightHouse Neurostrategies Group was established in 2002.[15] Such corporate giants as Coca-Cola, Home Depot, and Delta. Airlines were among BrightHouse's earliest clients.

Neuromarketers differ from consumer neuroscientists. The former are less [18] interested in how the brain operates during choice making than in what its human proprietor "chooses"—and in how to tempt the brain to "choose" their clients' products. Neuromarketers' services don't come cheap; an average EEG or fMRI marketing study costs around $40,000 to $50,000.[16] Still, there seems to be no shortage of willing clients.

For example, a Coca-Cola marketing team used EEG to help edit an [19] ad for Super Bowl XLII in 2008. After screening several possible commercials for volunteers, the marketers noticed that the viewers appeared to be more "engaged" when the music in one version of the commercial was built to a crescendo. The ad team altered its original version of the commercial accordingly. Reportedly, creative teams working with a number of modern big-budget films, including *Avatar,* used EEG measures of viewers' brain responses to different scenes and sequences to help them refine film elements, such as scripts, characters, plots, scenes, effects, and even cast selection. MindSign, a neuromarketing company in San Diego, deployed fMRI to help develop the most engaging movie trailer possible for Warner Brothers' *Harry Potter and the Half-Blood Prince.* The researchers showed film sequences to test audiences to measure their level of attention and emotional reactions, such as pleasure, fear, boredom, or empathy. [17]

When Pantene, a maker of hair products, wanted to explore wom- [20] en's "overall feelings about their hair," in the words of a lead scientists at Procter and Gamble, it enlisted NeuroFocus. The NeuroFocus analysts recorded electrical signals as the surface of women's heads as they watched a Pantene commercial, creating a millisecond-by-millisecond picture of activity in the brain. According to the brain wave data, the women became "distracted" as the point in the commercial when a model appeared frustrated as she tried to deal with her unruly hair. Procter and Gamble revised the ad to focus more on the model's hair and less on her facial expression.[18]

But how meaningful are these conclusions? One is tempted to assume [21] that they have value, given that reputable companies use brain-generated information. Yet the lack of transparency surrounding neuromarketers' interpretation of these data opens them to challenge by critics. Columbia University researchers recently reviewed the websites of sixteen neuromarketing firms and found that few described their methodology with enough detail to verify their claims. Almost half of the companies did not use EEG or fMRI but rather relied on old technologies like skin conductance response or measures of pupil size. Moreover, neuromarketing companies' use of different proprietary formulas for interpreting brain-wave data makes it even more difficult to assess their utility.

So is neuromarketing "hidden persuasion or junk science," as *Advertising* 22 *Age* asked in 2007? It is neither. There are limits to influencing, human behavior, in general, and there is no specific evidence that neuromarket-ers can manipulate information they glean from our brains to turn us into passive, unconscious consumers of things we don't need. As esteemed market researcher Andrew S. C. Ehrenberg wrote in 1982, "Advertising is in an odd position. Its extreme protagonists claim it has extraordinary powers . . . and its severest critics believe them." Three decades later, his observation is just as true. Nor is it fair to allow buyologists' exaggerated claims to taint all neuromarketing and dismiss it out of hand as junk sci-ence. For one thing, its premise is sound: Namely, that people are drawn to certain products and disposed to purchase them for motives to which they are often not privy. It may turn out that neuromarketing is best suited for generating and testing early hypotheses about the optimal way to grab viewers' attention and engage them emotionally. For example, if moments in the initial versions of a commercial or movie clip arouse only very weak responses, the team may want to go back to the drawing board.[19]

At bottom, however, the predictive value of neural information will 23 take on real marketplace significance only if it outperforms what people say they will buy or what they say they like about a product. If this is already happening—and given the paucity of available, replicated evidence, we are skeptical—neuromarketers are not sharing their in-house proprietary data and their methods. What's more, the "neuro" part of marketing needs to be worth it compared with conventional methods. "If I can spend $1,000 to do a traditional market study that gets me 80 percent of what a $24,000 fMRI study does, then the return on my neuromarketing investment is not great," says neuroscientist Craig Bennett, of dead salmon fame.[20]

Nonetheless, the burden falls on neuromarketing to prove itself. In 24 2010, the Advertising Research Foundation began a long-term project to develop neuromarketing guidelines. After a review of methods used by a number of neuromarketing firms, the foundation concluded that "the complexity of the science underlying these methods makes it difficult to assess their validity." The project's reviewers noted what they saw as neuro-marketers' too-frequent exaggeration of what their tests could deliver and asserted that "documentation of methods, research protocols, and clarity about what was done are essential," given the complexities involved.[21]

For now, the basics of advertising remain intact. Effective advertis- 25 ing must be seen, read, believed, remembered, and acted on—much as pioneering market researcher Daniel Starch concluded in the 1920s. Mar-keters still evaluate promotional campaigns and products according to tra-ditional constructs: Are viewers paying attention to an ad, do they like it, can they recognize and recall the product, do they identify with the brand image, and do they intend to purchase? Marketers continue to rely heavily on surveys, market tests of product samples, one-on-one interviews with consumers, and, yes, old-fashioned focus groups. Whether neuromarketing will flourish, burn out, or flicker on the periphery of the advertising world remains to be seen. Right now, the promises are bright and shiny, but behind the scenes, the fallacies and pitfalls of overhyped neuroscience give the "[corporate] buyer beware" truism a new twist.[22]

NOTES

1. Martin Lindstrom, *Buyology: Truth and Lies About Why We Buy* (New York: Broadway Books, 2008), 15. Lindstrom followed up with *Brandwashed: Tricks Companies Use to Manipulate Our Minds and Persuade Us to Buy* (New York: Crown Business, 2011). A sample of recent neuromarketing books (some careful and realistic, and others more superficial and slick) includes Erik du Plessis, *The Branded Mind: What Neuroscience Really Tells Us About the Puzzle of the Brain and the Brand* (London: Kogan Page, 2011); Roger Dooley, *Brainfluence*: 100 *Ways to Persuade and Convince Consumers with Neuromarketing* (Hoboken, NJ: Wiley, 2011); A. K. Pradeep, *The Buying Brain: Secrets for Selling to the Subconscious Mind* (New York: Wiley, 2010); Susan M. Weinschenk, *Neuro Web Design: What Makes Them Click?* (Indianapolis, IN: New Riders Press, 2009); and Patrick Renvoisé and Christophe Morin, *Neuromarketing: Is There a "Buy Button" in the Brain? Selling to the Old Brain for Instant Success* (San Francisco, CA: SalesBrain, 2005). The Lindstrom quotations are from *Buyology*, 11; and Martin Lindstrom, "Our Buyology: The Personal Coach," http://thepersonalcoach.ca/documents/Buyology_chapter_x(4) .pdf. On Lindstrom being named as one of *Time's* top 100, see "*Time* Top 100, 2009," http:/www.martinlindstrom.com/index.php/cmsid_buyology_TIME100. Katie Bayne, chief marketing officer of Coca-Cola North America, praised neuromarketing as "provid[ing] you with more natural and unedited responses than you get when you force people through the cognitive loop of having to annunciate how they feel," in Steve McClellan, "Mind over Matter," *Adweek*, February 18, 2008, http://www.adweek.com/news/television/mind-over-matter-94955. See also Rachel Kaufman, "Neuromarketers Get Inside Buyers' Brains," *CNNMoney.com*, March 18, 2010, http://money.cnn.com/2010/03/17/smallbusiness/neuromarketing/index .htm?section=money_smbusiness; and Joseph Plambeck, "Brain Waves and Newsstands," *New York Times*, September 5, 2010, http://mediadecoder.blogs.nytimes .com/2010/09/05/brain-waves-and-newsstands/.

2. The term "neuromarketing" is widely attributed to Ale Smidts, a marketing professor at Erasmus University in Rotterdam, per Thomas K. Grose, "Marketing: What Makes Us Buy?," *Time*, September 17, 2006. On application of the tools of neuroscience, see Carl Erik Fisher, L. Chin, and Robert Klitzman, "Marketing: Practices and Professional Challenges," *Harvard Review of Psychiatry* 18 (2010): 230–237; Laurie Burkitt, "Neuromarketing: Companies Use Neuroscience for Consumer Insights," *Forbes*, November 16, 2009, http://www.allbusiness.com/marketing-advertising /market-research-analysis/13397400-1.html; and Graham Lawton and Clare Wilson, "MindReading Marketers Have Ways of Making You Buy," *New Scientist* 2772 (2010), http://www.newscientist.com/article/mg20727721.300-mindreading-marketers-have-ways-of-making-you-buy.html?page=1. Wanamaker is quoted in Edward L. Lach Jr., "Wanamaker, John," *American National Biography Online*, February 2000, http: //www.anb.org/articles/10/10-01706.html. On advertising spending for television, internet, radio, and print, see "Kantar Media Reports U.S. Advertising Expenditures Increased 0.8 Percent in 2011," March 12, 2012, http://www.kantarmedia .com/sites/default/files/press/Kantar_Media_2011_Q4_US_Ad__Spend.pdf. On the

failure rate of new products, see Gerald Zaltman, *How Customers Think: Essential Insights into the Mind of the Market* (Boston: Harvard Business Review Press, 2003), 3.

3. Natasha Singer, "Making Ads That Whisper to the Brain," *New York Times*, November 13, 2010, http://www.nytimes.com/2010/11/14/business/14stream.html; Kevin Randall, "Neuromarketing Hope and Hype: 5 Brands Conducting Brain Research," *Fast Company*, September 15, 2009, http://www.fastcompany.com/1357239/neuromarketing-hope-and-hype-5-brands-conducting-brain-research. Carl E. Fisher and colleagues reviewed the Web sites of sixteen neuromarketing firms and reported the following: Thirteen companies "described their methodology, but these descriptions were often insufficient to determine what was being done." The authors concluded that there was "a paucity" of peer-reviewed reports on the company sites. Eleven Web sites referenced none at all, and only one company "provided citations for its specific claims." Nine of the companies, however, listed staff members with advanced science degrees. See Fisher, Chin, and Klitzman, "Defining Neuromarketing." See also Pradeep, *Buying Brain*. Nielsen acquired Neurofocus in May 2011, prompting insiders to ask, "Is-this the start of a stampede for mainstream market research firms & ad agencies to have their own neuromarketing units?" See Roger Dooley, "Nielsen to Acquire Neurofocus," May 20, 2011, http://www.neurosciencemarketing.com/blog/articles/nielsen-to-acquire-neurofocus.htm. FKF presents a vastly oversimplified lesson in the functional anatomy of the brain. "A key part of that data is how the brain reacts in nine well known and well mapped areas, such as the Ventral Striatum (reward), Orbitofrontal Prefrontal Cortex (wanting), Medial Prefrontal Cortex (feeling connected), Anterior Cingulate Cortex (conflict) and the Amygdala (threat/challenge)." See http://www.fkfappliedresearch.com/AboutUs.html. "Neuromarketing is the study of how humans choose, and choice is inescapably a biplogical process," says David Lewis of Neuroco, a neuromarketing firm in the UK, in Thomas Mucha, "This Is Your Brain on Advertising," August 1, 2005, http://money.cnn.com/magazines/business2/business2_archive/2005/08/01/8269671/index.htm.

4. Adam L. Penenberg, "NeuroFocus Uses Neuromarketing to Hack Your Brain," *Fast Company*, August 8, 2011, http://www.fastcompany.com/magazine/158/neuromarketing-intel-paypal. See also Stuart Elliott, "Is the Ad a Success? Brainwaves Tell All," *New York Times*, March 31, 2008; and Nick Carr, "Neuromarketing Could Make Mind Reading the Ad-Man's Ultimate Tool," *Guardian*, April 1, 2008, http://www.guardian.co.uk/technology/2008/apr/03/news.advertising. On the "buy button," see Clint Witchalls, "Pushing the Buy Button," *Newsweek*, March 22, 2004. On Sales-Brain, see "Neuromarketing: Understanding the Buy Buttons in Your Customer's Brain," http://www.salesbrain.com/are-you-delivering-with-impact-on-the-brain/speaking-engagements/. The BrightHouse Institute for Thought Sciences partnered with leading neuroscience professors from Emory University to better understand human thought and apply the knowledge to societal and business concerns. BrightHouse used Emory-owned fMRI scanners to "unlock the consumer mind," as its promotional material put it. BrightHouse Institute for Thought Sciences news release, June 22, 2002, http://www.prweb.com/releases/2002/06/prweb40936.htm. "Imagine being able to observe and quantify a consumer's true response to something without the influence of groupthink and other biases that plague current research approaches," said Brian Hankin, president of Bright-House, quoted in Scott LaFee, "Brain Sales: Through Imaging, Marketers Hope to Peer Inside Consumers' Minds," *San Diego Union Tribune*, July 28, 2004, http://legacy.utsandiego.com/news/.../20040728-9999-lzic28brain.html.

5. Michael Brammer, "Brain Scam?," *Nature Neuroscience* 7, no. 7 (2004): 683, http://www.nature.com/neuro/journal/v7/n7/pdf/nn0704-683.pdf. Brammer notes that "cognitive scientists, many of whom watched from the sidelines as their molecular colleagues got rich, are now jumping on the commercial bandwagon." On the absence of documentation, see "NeuroStandards Project White Paper," *Advertising*

Research Foundation NeuroStandards Collaboration Project 1.0, October 2011, 7, http://neurospire.com/pdfs/arfwhitepaper.pdf. NeuroFocus has Eric Kandel, a 2000 Nobel Prize winner in medicine/physiology, on its advisory board.

6.   Lisa Terry, "Learning What Motivates Shoppers (Quarterly Trend Report)," *Advertising Age*, July 25, 2011, 2–19, citing a spring 2011 survey by Greenbook Industry Trends Report. The director general of the European Society for Opinion and Market Research (a global market research association) said in 2011, "As far as [we are] concerned, it is clear that Neuroscience has a growing commercial following and application, but that there also remain a number of key questions, the three main ones [being]: Why is there very little peer-reviewed literature on the topic? Are these methods truly immune from subjectivity and bias? What is the true dollar value of neuroscientific research?" Remarks by ESOMAR director Finn Raben on June 8, 2011, http://rwconnect.esomar.org/2011/06/08/neuroscience-seminar-2011/. The quotation from Roger Dooley is in a personal communication with authors, September 17, 2010, http://www.neuroscience marketing.com/blog/.

7.   Martin Lindstrom, "10 Points Business Leaders Can Learn from Steve Jobs," *Fast Company*, October 15, 2001, http://www.martinlindstrom.com/fast-company-10-points-business-leaders-can-learn-from-steve-jobs/; Martin Lindstrom, "You Love Your Phone, Literally," *New York Times*, September 30, 2011; Ben R. Newell and David R. Shanks, "Unconscious Influences on Decision Making: A Critical Review," *Behavioral and Brain Sciences* (in press).

8.   P. J. Kreshel, "John B. Watson at J. Walter Thompson: The Legitimation of 'Science' in Advertising," *Journal of Advertising* 19, no. 2 (1990): 49–59.

9.   Melvin Thomas Copeland, *Principles of Merchandising* (Chicago: A. W. Shaw Company, 1924), 162. On Freudian theory in marketing, see Lawrence R. Samuel, *Freud on Madison Avenue: Motivation Research and Subliminal Advertising in America* (Philadelphia: University of Pennsylvania Press, 2010); and Stephen Fox, *The Mirror Makers* (Urbana: University of Illinois Press, 1997). Fans of *Mad Men* may recall the first episode (July 19, 2007), in which Don Draper, a smoker, is advised by his agency's head of research, a German-accented woman, to deploy the concept of the Freudian death wish to sell Lucky Strike cigarettes. "I find your whole approach perverse," he tells her, repelled by the idea of a death wish, and drops her report in the garbage can. On Dichter, see "How Ernest Dichter, an Acolyte of Sigmund Freud, Revolutionised Marketing," *Economist*, December 17, 2011, www.economist.com/node/21541706. "His larger philosophy was that a marketer who tries to sell a self-indulgent product must assuage the guilt that goes with it." Morton Hunt, *The History of Psychology* (New York: Doubleday, 1993), 620.

10.   Ernest Dichter, *The Strategy of Desire* (Garden City, NY: Doubleday and Company, 1960; rcpr., New Brunswick, NJ: Transaction Publishers, 2004), 31. Dichter claimed, for example, that smokers liked to use lighters because they fulfilled the human desire to "summon fire . . . the desire for mastery and power. . . . It is also bound up with the idea of sexual potency'" (*Strategy of Desire*, xi). "He sought to scrub the public of a puritanical tradition which, he said, equated consumption, especially of self-indulgent products, with moral transgression"; Daniel Horowitz, *The Anxieties of Affluence* (Amherst: University of Massachusetts Press, 2004), 61. See generally Ernest Dichter, *Handbook of Consumer Motivation: The Psychology of the World of Objects* (New York: McGraw-Hill, 1964); and "How Ernest Dichter, an Acolyte of Sigmund Freud, Revolutionised Marketing." The big emphasis on the "fresh eggs" can be seen in a Betty Crocker commercial from the 1950s at http://www.youtube.com/watch?v-KxdXWw94NgY. Feminist author Betty Friedan would later take Dichter to task for being "paid approximately a million dollars a year for his professional services in manipulating the emotions of American women to serve the needs of business." Betty Friedan, *The Feminine Mystique*

(New York: W. W. Norton and Company, 1963; New York: W. W. Norton and Company, 2001), 300. Citations are from the 2001 Tenth Anniversary edition.

11. "Unless all advertising is to become simply a variation on the themes of the Oedipus complex, the death instinct, or toilet training we must recognize that the motives with which we deal should be the manipulable ones," Albert J. Wood, a distinguished Philadelphia businessman and market researcher, told the American Marketing Association in the mid-1950s; cited in Vance Packard, *The Hidden Persuaders* (Philadelphia: D. McKay Company, 1957), 246. See generally Anthony Pratkanis and Elliot Aronson, *Age of Propaganda: The Everyday Use and Abuse of Persuasion* (New York: W. H. Freeman and Co., New York, 1992), 22.

12. In the 1950s, Madison Avenue began to break with its tradition of conformist, follow-the-crowd messaging and targeted particular groups (e.g., young single men, older women, and high-income seniors) for specific products, brands, and services. In differentiating between types of consumer mentality, advertisers gave more sophisticated treatment to the better-educated consumer. "Instead of bludgeoning the customer with razzle-dazzle headlines and ranting copy, admen are buttonholing him with quiet humor, soft talk and attractive art"; "The Sophisticated Sell: Advertisers' Swing to Subtlety," *Time*, September 3, 1956, 68–69, http://www.time.com/time/magazine/article/0,9171,824378,00.html. An influential model for setting advertising objectives and measuring the results was established in 1961. Its acronym was DAGMAR, for Defining Advertising Goals for Measured Advertising Results. The idea was that advertising needed to take a consumer through four levels of progressive understanding, from unawareness to awareness, understanding the product and its benefits, and actually buying the product. See Solomon Dutka and Russell Colley, *DAGMAR: Defining Advertising Goals for Measured Advertising Results* (Lincolnwood, IL: NTC Business Books, 1995). On focus groups, see "Lexicon Valley Takes on Mad Men," in *On the Media*, National Public Radio, June 16, 2012, http://www.onthemedia.org/2012/jun/15/lexicon-valley-takes-mad-men/.

13. Gerald Zaltman, personal communication with authors, October 28, 2010. "A great mismatch exists between the way consumers experience and think about their world and the methods marketers use to collect this information," Zaltman wrote in *How Customers Think*, 37. The Mind of the Market Lab was established in 1997 at Harvard Business School and ended when he retired in 2003. Richard Nisbett and Timothy Wilson, "Telling More Than We Can Know: Verbal Reports on Mental Processes," *Psychological Review* 84 (1977): 231–259, is a classic essay on how people are good at introspecting on the content of their thoughts and desires but are often unable to explain why they think this or want that. As the late advertising magnate David Ogilvy once put it, "People don't think how they feel, they don't say what they think, and they don't do what they say." Sharif Sakr, "Market Research and the Primitive Mind of the Consumer," BBC News, March 11, 2006, http://www.bbc.co.Uk/news/mobile/business-12581446.

14. Herbert E. Krugman, "Some Applications of Pupil Measurement," *Journal of Marketing Research* 1, no. 4 (1964): 15, 19. The Leo Burnett agency even wired the fingers of a group of housewives to polygraphs to test their reactions to newly filmed TV commercials. Stuart Ewen, "Leo Burnett, Sultan of Sell," *Time*, December 7,1998. On the use of EEG, see Flemming Hansen, "Hemispheral Lateralization: Implications for Understanding Consumer Behavior," *Journal of Consuer Research* 8, no. 1 (1981): 23–36. Greater electrical asymmetry supposedly reveals affinity or aversion to the product. An increase in left frontal activation suggests a greater affinity for the product and lower scores of right frontal activation indicate not liking a stimulus. Richard J. Davidson, "Affect, Cognition and Hemispheric Specialization," in *Emotions, Cognition and Behavior*, ed. Carroll E. Izard, Jerome Kagan, and Robert B. Zajonc (Cambridge: Cambridge University Press, 1984), 320–365. On steady-state topography, see Max Sutherland, "Neuromarketing:

What's It All About?" (originally a talk delivered in February 2007 at Swinburne University in Melbourne), http://www.sutherland.com/Column_pages/Neuromarketing_whats_it_all_about.htm. Anthony Pratkanis, personal communication with authors, May 15, 2012. "Physiological research is not good at predicting success of advertising, and certainly not better than verbal data, though perhaps no worse." Herbert E. Krugman, "A Personal Retrospective on the Use of Physiological Measures of Advertising Response," undated manuscript, ca. 1986, in Edward P. Krugman, *The Selected Works of Herbert E. Krugman: Consumer Behavior and Advertising Involvement* (London: Routledge, 2008), 217.

15. In 1997, Zaltman started the Mind of the Market Laboratory at the Harvard Business School, conducted neuroimaging research with corporate funding, and then shared the results with its sponsors; personal communication to Sally Satel, October 28, 2010. In 2000, Zaltman and colleague, psychologist Stephen Kosslyn, received patent approval to use neuroimaging as a means for validating whether a stimulus such as an advertisement, a communication, or a product evokes a certain mental response, such as emotion, preference, or memory, or to predict the consequences of the stimulus on later behavior, such as consumption or purchasing; http://www.google.com/patcnts?vid=USPAT6o99319. The patent was granted in 2000 and in 2008 was sold to NeuroFocus, when Kosslyn joined the Neurofocus scientific advisory board; see "Neuromarketing Patent Changes Hands," *Neuromarketing*, September 4, 2008, http://www.neurosciencemarketing.com/blog/articles/neuromarketing-patent-changes-hands.htm. On the study, see Gerald Zaltman, *How Customers Think* (Boston: Harvard Business School Press, 2003), 119–121. Zaltman has since shifted his focus to the so-called Zaltman Metaphor Elicitation Technique, an interview protocol that plumbs the unconscious values underlying consumers' reactions to products and marketing campaigns. See the Olson Zaltman Associates website, http://www.olsonzaltman.com/, for more details. "Brain-based research has little deep to say about the meanings and motives that steer individuals' choices," Zaltman told the authors in a personal communication, October 28, 2010.

16. Neuroco charges an average of $90,000 per study. And its list of services is growing: The firm will evaluate the subliminal power of colors, logos, or product features. It measures the mental might of music or jingles, the heft of celebrity endorsers, and the most brain-wave-soothing designs for store layouts. The company is even testing neurological reactions to smell and tough, and has worked with U.K. auto dealers to gauge responses to the feel of automobile upholstery and the sound of a car as it slams; see Thomas Mucha, "This Is Your Brain on Advertising," *CNN Money*, August 1, 2005, http://money.cnn.com/magazines/business2/business2_archive/2005/08/OI/826967I/index.htm.

17. McClellan, "Mind over Matter"; Kevin Randli, "The Rise of Neurocinema—How Hollywood Studies Harness Brain Waves to Win Oscars," *Fast Company*, February 25, 2011; Jessica Hamzelou, "Brain Scans Can Predict How You'll React to a Movie Scene," *Gizmodo*, September 9, 2010, http://www.gizmodo.com.au/2010/09/brain-scans-can-predict-how-youll-react-to-a-movie-scene/#more-416708; April Gardner, "Neurocinematics: Your Brain on Film," *NewEnglandFilm.com*, June 30, 2009, http://newenglandfilm.com/magazine/2009/07/neuro.

18. Mya Frazier, "Hidden persuasion or Junk Science," Advertising Age, September 10, 2007, http://adage.com/article/news/hidden-persuasion-junk-science/120335/A.S.C. Ehrenberg, "Repetitive Advertising and the Consumer," *Journal of Advertising Research* 1 (1982): 70–79, 70. "It is not yet whether neuroimaging provides better data than other marketing methods, but through the use of MVPA methods it might be possible to reveal the 'holy grail' of hidden information"; Ariely and Berus, "Neuromarketing," 287.

19. Ellen Byron, "Wash Away Bad Hair Days," Wall Street Journal, June 30, 2010.

20. Craig Bennett, "The Seven Sins of Neuromarketing," April 22, 2011, http://prefrontal.org/blog/2011/o4/the-seven-sins-of-neuromarketing/. The typical cost of neuromarketing research ranges from about $30 million to $100 million (with Super

Bowl spots being sold for an average $2.6 to $2.7 million), as cited in Rachel Kauffman, "Neuromarketers Get Inside Buyers' Brains," *CNNMoney.com*, March 18, 2010, http://money.cnn.com/2010/03/17/smallbusiness/neuromarketing/index .htm?section=money_smbusiness. According to Burkitt, "A marketer can hook 30 consumers up to an EEG device for $50,000. An MRI trial with 20 people would cost more like $40,000," in Burkitt, "Neuromarketing."

21. "NeuroStandards Project White Paper," 7, 30.

22. On Starch, see Sean Brierley, *The Advertising Handbook* (London: Routledge, 1995), 182. Indeed, most marketers still recommend focus groups as useful for obtaining feedback on how consumers view a product. "Far too often a single cutting-edge technology is deployed into projects for technology's sake, without recognizing the importance of cross-method support/validation." MattTullman, CEO of Merchant Mechanics, Inc., comment on Roger Dooley, "Your Brain on Soup," *Neuromarketing: Where Brain Science and Marketing Meet* (blog), February 20, 2010, http://www.neurosciencemarketing.com/blog/articles/your-brain-on-soup .htm.

■ ■ ■

Reading as a Writer: Analyzing Rhetorical Choices

1. Satel and Lilienfeld have a definite perspective on the misuses of neuro-science. Mark and discuss passages where their argument is particularly clear. How would you characterize their tone? To what extent do they include oppositional perspectives? What do you conclude about effective argumentative strategies, based on their approach?

2. Given their assumption (probably accurate) that their readers are not neu-roscientists, where and how in this piece do the authors offer explanations of the neuroscientific research? How effective do you find their strategy of including this information, and why?

Writing as a Reader: Entering the Conversation of Ideas

1. Satel and Lilienfeld, like the co-authors Mark R. Tercek and Jonathan S. Adams, are interested in uses and misuses of science for business. How do their ideas intersect or complement one another? Compose an essay in which you build on the examples and ideas in these readings in order to make an argument for an effective relationship between science and marketing. What are the risks and benefits of incorporating science into business and marketing? Offer a specific example or two beyond these readings if you like.

2. Readings by Satel and Lilienfeld and Agustín Fuentes (Chapter 14) use "myth busting" to shatter what we think we know about topics by apply-ing research to commonplace ideas. While these essays have different topics, their rhetorical approach is similar. Write an essay in which you evaluate the effectiveness of this strategy of presenting common ideas and then skewering them with research. To what extent might this be a successful—or unsuccessful—approach for different kinds of readers? What other issues might benefit from this approach? Offer specific exam-ples to illustrate your claims.

MARK R. TERCEK AND JONATHAN S. ADAMS

From Nature's Fortune: How Business and Society Thrive by Investing in Nature

Mark R. Tercek is president of the Nature Conservancy, a conservation organization with a presence in every U.S. state and in thirty-five countries. A quick look at their Web site (www.nature.org) will give you a preview of the argument that Tercek builds in this excerpt from his 2013 book, *Nature's Fortune: How Business and Society Thrive by Investing in Nature*. The book is coauthored by science writer Jonathan S. Adams, a conservationist and program director of the Nature Conservancy. The book seeks to dispel the argument that what is good for business must be bad for the environment, and vice versa. Instead, Tercek builds on his experience as a managing director at the investment banking firm Goldman Sachs to claim that investing in the environment can be profitable in many different ways.

The "I" in this text is Tercek's. Consider how he uses his personal background to help build his argument. What details from his private and professional life contribute more effectively to the overall point of this piece? How would this piece be different without biographical information to build his ethos?

The authors frequently draw on the language of business, using terms that may not be familiar to you. (Look up any terms you could not explain clearly to a friend.) You might mark these phrases with a different color so that you can see how this language is threaded through the argument. How do the authors speak to multiple audiences by bringing together the language of conservation and the language of business? (Their extended metaphor of the "three-legged stool" is one place where they work out these connections.) Who is their ideal audience, and how can you tell? What can be gained from reading this, if you do not consider yourself the targeted audience of this piece?

Like many of the authors in our Environmental Studies chapter, Tercek and Adams seek to reframe how we understand "nature." By weaving together personal, psychological, scientific, and business relationships into our ideas about "nature," the authors invite you to reconsider your assumptions about what is "profitable." Tercek claims he is an "optimist." After reading this, are you?

■ ■ ■

How I Got Here

Unlike many conservationists, especially leaders of environmental non-   *1*
profits, I didn't spend my childhood in the late 1960s and early 1970s
roaming the great outdoors. I wasn't a backpacker, hiker, kayaker, tree
climber, or bug collector. I didn't bale hay or herd sheep. I was a city boy.
Born and raised in a working-class area of Cleveland, I spent plenty of

time outside—shooting baskets, delivering the *Cleveland Plain Dealer*, shoveling snow, mowing lawns—but not in contemplating "nature" in the grand sense of the word.

In college, I majored in English and busied myself with acting or try- 2 ing to write poetry, not spending time outdoors or immersed in environmental causes. After I graduated in 1979 I moved to Japan, where I taught English and studied martial arts, then worked for Bank of America. From there, it was on to Harvard Business School and then to a twenty-four-year career at the rapidly growing investment firm Goldman Sachs.

My evolution into a conservationist began as I worked as an invest- 3 ment banker for Goldman Sachs—and, more tellingly, when I became a parent. Like many, I struggled to pry my kids away from their computers and televisions. Hiking and camping were my tools. I found that I enjoyed nature in ways I never had when I was young.

I read *The New Economy of Nature: The Quest to Make Conservation* 4 *Profitable*, the 2002 book by Stanford University's Gretchen Daily, a professor of environmental science. The book explained the workings of ecosystems and how they delivered goods and services to people. This scientific examination of nature delivering value began to build my appreciation for nature and prompted me to reflect on opportunities and price tags.

After reading Gretchen's book, I called her. Our first conversation, 5 with Gretchen talking biology and me talking finance, was a bit awkward, but it had a lasting impact on me. I started asking the same questions about ecology as my MBA training had taught me to apply to corporate finance: What is nature's value? Who invests in it, when and why? What rates of return can an investment in nature produce? When is protecting nature a good investment? Isn't conservation really about building natural capital? . . .

The Idea of Natural Capital

I left Goldman Sachs in 2008 to become president and CEO of TNC. When 6 my cell phone rang with the news that I might get the job, I was so excited that I backed my car right into a tree. My back window was shattered. The tree was fine.

TNC seemed to be a perfect fit for me. A sixty-year-old organization 7 with some 4000 staff members pursuing conservation in all fifty states and thirty-five countries around the world, TNC has a reputation for getting things done in a pragmatic, science-based, and no-nonsense style. TNC reminded me of an investment bank—but one whose client was nature itself. I thought TNC was the ideal organization to champion the idea of natural capital, putting a value on nature as an asset.

Putting a value on nature is a tricky and even controversial task. Envi- 8 ronmentalists tend to love nature for its own sake, love being outdoors, and believe their children and generations beyond should inherit a world as vibrant and as diverse as the one they experienced. These are all enormously important reasons to protect nature. A business perspective, however, reveals other, perhaps less lofty but no less important reasons to do so—for example, securing the clean water nature provides, and the timber people need to manufacture houses and furniture. Valuing nature does not mean replacing one set of compelling arguments for conservation with another, but it provides an additional and important rationale for supporting the environment.

I began to think systematically about business, business principles, and *9* what nature really means. *Nature* is a complicated word—more complicated than I knew. People often speak about human nature, or Mother Nature. But in thinking about this word, I realized that people generally also consider nature as something separate from themselves—something distant, out there in national parks and in the wilderness.

I want to get away from that simple dichotomy. Nature is not just *10* something to preserve in a few special places and degrade in others. Nature is everywhere. Yet nature is also not just a source of practical, tangible benefits to people. It has a deeper meaning to people around the world. By my definition, nature means all species of animals and plants, their habitats and the ecological processes that support them. This broad definition includes human beings but does not include all the things that humans have built, often in a misguided attempt to control nature. Trying to dominate nature will likely fail, but bringing nature back into how people organize society, run businesses, design cities, and even how we live our daily lives can give us reason to hope.

Business as an Environmental Partner

Thinking about the value of nature leads to other ways of thinking famil- *11* iar to business analysts. For example, concepts such as *maximize returns, invest in your assets, manage your risks, diversify,* and *promote innovation* are the common parlance of business and banking. These are rarely applied to nature, but they should be.

Viewing nature through these basic business principles focuses more *12* attention on the benefits of conservation. You may not become a conservationist, but you will realize that conservation—protection of nature—is a central and important driver of economic activity, every bit as important as manufacturing, finance, agriculture, and so on.

My experience as an environmentalist at Goldman Sachs revealed *13* new possibilities, but I recognize that relationships with businesses can be complicated and risky for environmental organizations. Hardcore environmentalists can be quick to criticize organizations such as TNC when they build alliances with companies. They sometimes see such collaborations as consorting with the enemy. Nevertheless, in my view, seizing the opportunity to work with companies as they pursue environmental strategies to strengthen their business provides the chance to create significant conservation gains.

Companies can be good partners for environmentalists in other ways 14 as well. Large businesses control huge amounts of natural resources, often more than governments. Contrary to popular opinion, companies can be better at making long-term plans for those resources than governments, which often get hamstrung by political divides and the short-term thinking driven by the next election cycle. Companies that have short time horizons and neglect long-term planning and investing generally lose out in the marketplace. Most companies also do a good job of dealing with reality. For example, they tend to accept rather than deny the conclusions of science; otherwise, again, they get punished in the marketplace. There are exceptions—some bad actors in the business community seek to exploit loopholes, break regulations, or mislead the public—usually in misguided pursuit of short-term gain. But in an era of increasing transparency, more companies understand that it is ultimately going to be in their own best interest to follow the rules and to try to do the right thing. They also increasingly understand that investments in nature can produce big financial returns.

Still, nothing is free from risk. Critics sometimes challenge me—"Are 15 you sure working with business will produce environmental benefits?" Of course I'm not sure. But I believe we should try. If other organizations have alternative strategies, I say that's great, too. Let's see what works best. We need more environmental strategies, and we need to pursue them with vigor and confidence, as well as a receptivity to critiques and ideas about how to improve them.

A Three-Legged Stool

All of these considerations lead to an important question. How should 16 environmentalists work with business? I believe the best way forward is to think of business as one of the legs of a three-legged stool. The other two are governments and individuals. Saving the world from environmental degradation requires all three.

Governments and individuals should encourage and welcome volun- 17 tary environmental initiatives by business. But to scale such initiatives up in a meaningful way, governments will need to enact strong and effective policies. The role of government goes even further than this regulatory responsibility. Think of the billions of dollars governments invest in infrastructure every year. More of these investments should be made in natural capital.

In turn, to get governments and businesses to do the right thing, indi- *18* viduals need to motivate them as voters and consumers, respectively. These three actors—businesses, governments, and individuals—now have the opportunity to come together to create new practices in pursuit of conservation as a means to invest in and benefit from natural capital. Conservation organizations should do all they can to make this happen.

Environmentalists generally believe in nature's inherent value. That *19* idea is the bedrock of the environmental movement. However, environmentalists cannot persuade everyone to think along the same lines. Focusing only on the innate wonders of nature risks alienating potential supporters and limits the environmental community's ability to reach a broader audience and to mine sources of new ideas. The "Isn't nature wonderful?" argument can leave the impression that nature offers solely aesthetic benefits, or worse, that nature is a luxury only rich people or rich countries can afford. We need to *get* business, government, and individuals to understand that nature is not only wonderful, it is also economically valuable. Indeed, nature is the fundamental underpinning to human well-being.

One way is to connect nature to what concerns people most—how *20* to make lives better, protect health, create jobs, and strengthen the economy. Whether they grew up in the city or the country, in the United States, Brazil, or Indonesia, and no matter what they've studied or read, every person shares these concerns. In many places around the world people believe they have more pressing concerns than conserving nature, and those concerns will take precedence unless they better understand what nature provides.

The Way Forward

I'm an optimist. I see nature as remarkably resilient and ready to rally *21* if we make smart investments. Optimism notwithstanding, finding workable, science-driven solutions means looking unflinchingly at the facts. And the facts are troubling. Despite the best efforts of the world's passionate and hardworking conservationists, we are simply not getting the job done. We need to move fast to set things on the right path.

To be sure, conservation has won some crucial victories. Over the past *22* half century in the United States alone, the government banned DDT, created the Environmental Protection Agency, and passed the Endangered Species, Clean Water, and Clean Air Acts. Deforestation in the Amazon has slowed and new marine-protected areas have been created across the Pacific. Scientists and activists have worked with government agencies to bring species back from the brink of extinction and to protect some of the world's greatest places.

Still, nearly every precious bit of nature—teeming coral reefs, sweep- *23* ing grasslands, lush forests, the rich diversity of life itself—is in decline. Everything humanity should reduce—suburban sprawl, deforestation, overfishing, carbon emissions—has increased. The thirteen warmest years for the entire planet have all occurred since 1998, and 2012 was the warmest year on record for the United States. Although daily weather fluctuations cannot be definitively linked to climate change, the collection of droughts, floods, heat waves, enormous storms, and record rainfalls unmistakably signals the need for action.

Communities and nations have made conservation break-throughs *24* before, and they can do so again. This time, instead of the towering figures of conservation history such as Theodore Roosevelt and Rachel Carson, the catalyst may be newly emerging and highly innovative environmentalists—innovators like Kenya's Wangari Maathai, who passed away too soon, in 2011. Wangari successfully and courageously brought together conservation, economic development, human rights, and democracy goals as a way to make substantial environmental progress, first in Kenya and later around the world. Looking ahead, we need more people to challenge convention, take risks, and tackle the world's big environmental challenges. Unlikely alliances should emerge—businesses, investors, and governments joining farmers, ranchers, students, and urbanites—to pursue strategies based on a shared understanding that we all depend on nature.

These new alliances will enable us to conserve nature at a scale never *25* before achieved. The point is not just to help businesses and governments do less harm, but to make them become part of something far bigger. Saving nature means saving wild species and wild places, but it also means saving ourselves. This opportunity is real, it may not come again, and it should be humankind's priority to achieve it fully and achieve it now.

■ ■ ■

Reading as a Writer: Analyzing Rhetorical Choices

1. Some of the business terms in this piece may be unfamiliar to you. Underline and be sure to look up phrases that might need some clarification, such as "rates of return," "building capital," "investing in assets," and others that you may not know. You might divide up the work of researching these definitions and then share the results with your peers.

2. Visit the Web site of the Nature Conservancy, and do a close analysis of the visual and linguistic information. In what ways does the Web site bring together the language of science, business, and environmental appeals? What aspects of the Web site do you find most interesting and persuasive, and why?

Writing as a Reader: Entering the Conversation of Ideas

1. Tercek and Adams are interested in telling a story about business, as is John Dicker in his examination of the story of Wal-Mart. To what extent is the story of companies important to consumers? Should it be? Compose an essay in which you consider these authors' perspectives on the significance of corporations' stories, drawing on their insights and examples. Consider examining the Web sites of both corporations and doing some additional research to test their claims. What conclusions can you draw about whether it is important for consumers to know the backstory of a business?

2. Tercek and Adams strive to demonstrate that business need not be seen as bad for nature. Carolyn Merchant and Noël Sturgeon (Chapter 16) have different perspectives on the relationship between business and "the natural." Imagine a conversation these writers might have on this topic. Write an essay in which you play these authors' ideas off one another in order to explore what you see as the significant challenges and opportunities of balancing the safety of the environment and the success of businesses. Where do you stand in this debate? Offer evidence from another company if it will help you strengthen your claims.

FAREED ZAKARIA

The Rise of the Rest

Fareed Zakaria has a PhD in political science from Harvard and has been the editor of *Newsweek International* since 2000. He is well known for the political columns he writes for *Newsweek* and the *Washington Post,* and he is a frequent guest on political analysis television shows. His many awards for columns and leading essays include his October 2001 *Newsweek* cover story, "Why They Hate Us." In addition to his columns, he has written several best-selling books, including *The Future of Freedom* (2003) and *The Post-American World* (2008), from which this reading was excerpted. Included here is his first chapter, "The Rise of the Rest," and two sections of his second chapter, "The Rise of Nationalism" and "The Last Superpower."

   You can hear in Zakaria's opening line that he is interested in helping us see the world in a new way: "This is a book not about the decline of America but rather about the rise of everyone else" (para. 1). In the paragraphs that follow, Zakaria lists at length various kinds of evidence that we are on the cusp of the third great "tectonic power shift" of the last 500 years. As he describes these three power shifts, test your own knowledge of history against his claims, and see what comes into focus for you in this description.

   Zakaria's general approach is to look back in *history* to see how we have arrived at this globalizing moment, to examine the *present* through myriad examples and data, and to begin to consider the globalized *future* with the "rise of the rest." As you read, pay particular attention to how and where he makes these moves backward and forward in time, to see how Zakaria uses this historical contextualization to make his argument. Which examples are most compelling to you, and why?

Like many of the authors in this book, Zakaria hopes to reveal aspects of contemporary life that we might miss if we fail to understand certain contexts or make particular connections. He does not have a crystal ball to reveal the future, but he argues that if we look carefully at the evidence around us, we will see that the United States will have to make some changes in order to have a place in the new world order. Will the United States be willing to "globalize itself"? Zakaria provides evidence that should help us ponder possible answers to a very big question that certainly will affect all our lives.

■ ■ ■

This is a book not about the decline of America but rather about the *1* rise of everyone else. It is about the great transformation taking place around the world, a transformation that, though often discussed, remains poorly understood. This is natural. Changes, even sea changes, take place gradually. Though we talk about a new era, the world seems to be one with which we are familiar. But in fact, it is very different.

There have been three tectonic power shifts over the last 500 years, *2* fundamental changes in the distribution of power that have reshaped international life—its politics, economics, and culture. The first was the rise of the Western world, a process that began in the fifteenth century and accelerated dramatically in the late eighteenth century. It produced modernity as we know it: science and technology, commerce and capitalism, the agricultural and industrial revolutions. It also produced the prolonged political dominance of the nations of the West.

The second shift, which took place in the closing years of the nine- *3* teenth century, was the rise of the United States. Soon after it industrialized, the United States became the most powerful nation since imperial Rome, and the only one that was stronger than any likely combination of other nations. For most of the last century, the United States has dominated global economics, politics, science, and culture. For the last twenty years, that dominance has been unrivaled, a phenomenon unprecedented in modern history.

We are now living through the third great power shift of the modern *4* era. It could be called "the rise of the rest." Over the past few decades, countries all over the world have been experiencing rates of economic growth that were once unthinkable. While they have had booms and busts, the overall trend has been unambiguously upward. This growth has been most visible in Asia but is no longer confined to it. That is why to call this shift "the rise of Asia" does not describe it accurately. In 2006 and 2007, 124 countries grew at a rate of 4 percent or more. That includes more than thirty countries in Africa, two-thirds of the continent. Antoine van Agtmael, the fund manager who coined the term "emerging markets," has identified the twenty-five companies most likely to be the world's next great multinationals. His list includes four companies each from Brazil, Mexico, South Korea, and Taiwan; three from India; two from China; and one each from Argentina, Chile, Malaysia, and South Africa.

Look around. The tallest building in the world is now in Taipei, and 5 it will soon be overtaken by one being built in Dubai. The world's richest man is Mexican, and its largest publicly traded corporation is Chinese. The world's biggest plane is built in Russia and Ukraine, its leading refinery is under construction in India, and its largest factories are all in China. By many measures, London is becoming the leading financial center, and the United Arab Emirates is home to the most richly endowed investment fund. Once quintessentially American icons have been appropriated by foreigners. The world's largest Ferris wheel is in Singapore. Its number one casino is not in Las Vegas but in Macao, which has also overtaken Vegas in annual gambling revenues. The biggest movie industry, in terms of both movies made and tickets sold, is Bollywood, not Hollywood. Even shopping, America's greatest sporting activity, has gone global. Of the top ten malls in the world, only one is in the United States; the world's biggest is in Beijing. Such lists are arbitrary, but it is striking that only ten years ago, America was at the top in many, if not most, of these categories.

It might seem strange to focus on growing prosperity when there are 6 still hundreds of millions of people living in desperate poverty. But in fact, the share of people living on a dollar a day or less plummeted from 40 per cent in 1981 to 18 percent in 2004, and is estimated to fall to 12 percent by 2015. China's growth alone has lifted more than 400 million people out of poverty. Poverty is falling in countries housing 80 percent of the world's population. The fifty countries where the earth's poorest people live are basket cases that need urgent attention. In the other 142—which include China, India, Brazil, Russia, Indonesia, Turkey, Kenya, and South Africa— the poor are slowly being absorbed into productive and growing economies. For the first time ever, we are witnessing genuinely global growth. This is creating an international system in which countries in all parts of the world are no longer objects or observers but players in their own right. It is the birth of a truly global order.

A related aspect of this new era is the diffusion of power from states 7 to other actors. The "rest" that is rising includes many nonstate actors. Groups and individuals have been empowered, and hierarchy, centralization, and control are being undermined. Functions that were once controlled by governments are now shared with international bodies like the World Trade Organization and the European Union. Nongovernmental groups are mushrooming every day on every issue country. Corporations and capital are moving from place to place, finding the best location in which to do business, rewarding some governments while punishing others. Terrorists like Al Qaeda, drug cartels, insurgents, and militias of all kinds arc finding space to operate within the nooks and crannies of the international system. Power is shifting away from nation-states, up, down, and sideways. In such an atmosphere, the traditional applications of national power, both economic and military, have become less effective.

The emerging international system is likely to be quite different from *8* those that have preceded it. One hundred years ago, there was a multipolar order run by a collection of European governments, with constantly shifting alliances, rivalries, miscalculations, and wars. Then came the bipolar duopoly of the Cold War, more stable in many ways, but with the super powers reacting and overreacting to each other's every move. Since 1991, we have lived under an American imperium, a unique, unipolar world in which the open global economy has expanded and accelerated dramatically. This expansion is now driving the next change in the nature of the international order.

At the politico-military level, we remain in a single-superpower world. *9* But in every other dimension—industrial, financial, educational, social, cultural—the distribution of power is shifting, moving away from American dominance. That does not mean we are entering an anti-American world. But we are moving into a *post-American world*, one defined and directed from many places and by many people.

What kinds of opportunities and challenges do these changes present? *10* What do they portend for the United States and its dominant position? What will this new era look like in terms of war and peace, economics and business, ideas and culture?

In short, what will it mean to live in a post-American world? . . . *11*

The Rise of Nationalism

In a globalized world, almost all problems spill over borders. Whether *12* it's terrorism, nuclear proliferation, disease, environmental degradation, economic crisis, or water scarcity, no issue can be addressed without significant coordination and cooperation among many countries. But while economics, information, and even culture might have become globalized, formal political power remains firmly tethered to the nation-state, even as the nation-state has become less able to solve most of these problems unilaterally. And increasingly, nation-states are becoming less willing to come together to solve common problems. As the number of players—governmental and nongovernmental—increases and each one's power and confidence grows, the prospects for agreement and common action diminish. This is the central challenge of the rise of the rest—to stop the forces of global growth from turning into the forces of global disorder and disintegration.

The rise of pride and confidence among other nations, particularly the *13* largest and most successful ones, is readily apparent. For me, it was vividly illustrated a few years ago in an Internet café in Shanghai, where I was chatting with a young Chinese executive. He was describing the extraordinary growth that was taking place in his country and a future in which China would be modern and prosperous. He was thoroughly Westernized in dress and demeanor, spoke excellent English, and could comfortably discuss the latest business trends or gossip about American pop culture. He seemed the consummate product of globalization, the person who bridges cultures and makes the world a smaller, more cosmopolitan place. But when we began talking about Taiwan, Japan, and the United States, his responses were filled with bile. He explained in furious tones that were Taiwan to dare to declare independence, China should instantly invade it. He said that Japan was an aggressor nation that could never be trusted. He was sure that the United States deliberately bombed the Chinese embassy during the Kosovo war in 1999, to terrify the Chinese people with its military might. And so on. I felt as if I were in Berlin in 1910, speaking to a young German professional, who in those days would have also been both thoroughly modern and thoroughly nationalist.

As economic fortunes rise, so does nationalism. This is understand- *14* able. Imagine that you lived in a country that had been poor and unstable for centuries. And then, finally, things turn and your nation is on the rise. You would be proud and anxious to be seen. This desire for recognition and respect is surging throughout the world. It may seem paradoxical that globalization and economic modernization are breeding political nationalism, but that is so only if we view nationalism as a backward ideology, certain to be erased by the onward march of progress.

Nationalism has always perplexed Americans. When the United States *15* involves itself abroad, it always believes that it is genuinely trying to help other countries better themselves. From the Philippines and Haiti to Vietnam and Iraq, the natives' reaction to U.S. efforts has taken Americans by surprise. Americans take justified pride in their own country—we call it patriotism—and yet are genuinely startled when other people are proud and possessive of theirs.

In the waning days of Britain's rule in India, its last viceroy, Lord Louis *16* Mountbatten, turned to the great Indian leader Mahatma Gandhi and said in exasperation, "If we just leave, there will be chaos." Gandhi replied, "Yes, but it will be *our* chaos." That sense of being governed by one's "own," without interference, is a powerful feeling in emerging countries, especially those that were once colonies or quasi-colonies of the West.

Zbigniew Brzezinski recently called attention to what he terms a *17* "global political awakening." He pointed to rising mass passions, fueled by various forces—economic success, national pride, higher levels of education, greater information and transparency, and memories of the past. Brzezinski noted the disruptive aspects of this new force. "The population of much of the developing world is politically stirring and in many places seething with unrest," he wrote. "It is acutely conscious of social injustice to an unprecedented degree . . . [and this] is creating a community of shared perceptions and envy that can be galvanized and channeled by demagogic political or religious passions. These energies transcend sovereign borders and pose a challenge both to existing states as well as to the existing global hierarchy, on top of which America still perches."[1]

In many countries outside the Western world, there is pent-up frus- *18* tration with having had to accept an entirely Western or American narrative of world history—one in which they either are miscast or remain bit players. Russians have long chafed at the standard narrative about World War II, in which Britain and the United States heroically defeat the forces of fascist Germany and Japan. Given mainstream U.S. historical accounts, from Stephen Ambrose to Ken Burns, Americans could be forgiven for believing that Russia played a minor part in the decisive battles against Hitler and Tojo. In fact, the eastern front was the central arena of World War II. It involved more land combat than all other theaters of the war put together and resulted in thirty million deaths. It was where three-quarters of all German forces fought and where Germany incurred 70 percent of its casualties. The European front was in many ways a sideshow, but in the West it is treated as the main event. As the writer Benjamin Schwarz has pointed out, Stephen Ambrose "lavishes [attention] on the U.S.-British invasion of Sicily, which drove 60,000 Germans from the island, but completely ignores Kursk—the largest battle in history, in which at least 1.5 million Soviets and Germans fought, and which occurred at exactly the same time. . . . [M]uch as it may make us squirm, we must admit that the struggle against Nazi Germany . . . was primarily, as the great military historian John Erickson called it, 'Stalin's war.'"[2]

Or consider the perspective on the same war from another spot on the   *19* map. An Indian friend explained to me, "For Britain and America, World War II is a heroic struggle in which freedom triumphs over evil. For us, it was a battle to which Britain committed India and its armed forces without bothering to consult us. London told us to the for an idea of freedom that it was at that very moment brutally denying to us."

Such divergent national perspectives have always existed, but today,   *20* thanks to greater education, information, and confidence, they are widely disseminated on new news networks, cable channels, and Internet sites of the emerging world. Many of the "rest" are dissecting the narratives, arguments, and assumptions of the West and countering them with a different view of the world. "When you tell us that we support a dictatorship in Sudan to have access to its oil," a young Chinese official told me in 2006, "what I want to say is, 'And how is that different from your support for a medieval monarchy in Saudi Arabia?' We see the hypocrisy, we just don't say anything, yet."

After the Cold War ended, there was a general hope and expectation   *21* that China and Russia would move inexorably into the post-World War II Western political and economic system. When George H. W. Bush spoke of "a new world order," he meant simply that the old Western one would be extended worldwide. Perhaps this view stemmed from the postwar experience with Japan and Germany, both of which rose to the heights of economic power and yet were accommodating, cooperative, and largely silent members of the existing order. But perhaps those were special circumstances. The two countries had unique histories, having waged aggressive wars and become pariahs as a consequence, and they faced a new threat from Soviet communism and relied on American military power for their protection. The next round of rising powers might not be so eager to "fit in."

We still think of a world in which a rising power must choose between   *22* two stark options: integrate into the Western order, or reject it, becoming a rogue nation and facing the penalties of excommunication. In fact, rising powers appear to be following a third way: entering the Western order but doing so on their own terms—thus reshaping the system itself. As the political scientists Naazneen Barma, Ely Ratner, and Steven Weber point out, in a world where everyone feels empowered, countries can choose to bypass this Western "center" entirely and forge their own ties with one another.[3] In a post-American world, there may be no center to integrate into. U.S. Secretary of State James Baker suggested in 1991 that the world was moving toward a hub-and-spoke system, with every country going through the United States to get to its destination. The twenty-first-century world might be better described as one of point-to-point routes, with new flight patterns being mapped every day. (This is true even in a physical sense: In just ten years, the number of Russian visitors to China increased more than fourfold, from 489,000 in 1995 to 2.2 million in 2005.) The focus has shifted. Countries are increasingly interested in themselves—the story of their rise—and pay less attention to the West and the United States. As a result, the urgent discussions on the presidential campaign trail throughout 2007 about the need to lessen anti-Americanism are somewhat off-point. The world is moving from anger to indifference, from anti-Americanism to post-Americanism.

The fact that new powers are more strongly asserting their interests is   23 the reality of the post-American world. It also raises the political conundrum of how to achieve international objectives in a world of many actors, state and nonstate. According to the old model of getting things done, the United States and a few Western allies directed the show while the Third World either played along or stayed outside the box and remained irrelevant as a result. Nongovernmental players were too few and too weak to worry about. Now, look at something like trade negotiations, and you see the developing world acting with greater and greater force. Where they might once have taken any deal offered by the West or ignored the process altogether, countries like Brazil and India play hardball until they get the deal of their choice. They have heard Western CEOs explain [in an analysis of the economies of Brazil, Russia, India, and China] where the future lies. They have read the Goldman Sachs BRIC report. They know that the balance of power has shifted.

The Kyoto accord (now treated as sacred because of President Bush's   24 cavalier rejection of them) is in fact a treaty marked by its adherence to the old worldview. Kyoto assumed that if the West came together and settled on a plan, the Third World would adopt the new framework and the problem would be solved. That may be the way things have been done in international affairs for decades, but it makes little sense today. China, India, Brazil, and other emerging powers will not follow along with a Western-led process in which they have not participated. What's more, governments on their own can do only so much to tackle a problem like climate change. A real solution requires creating a much broader coalition that includes the private sector, nongovernmental groups, cities and localities, and the media. In a globalized, democratized, and decentralized world, we need to get to individuals to alter their behavior. Taxes, tariffs, and wars are the old ways to do this, but states now have less room to maneuver on these fronts. They need more subtle and sophisticated ways to effect change.

The traditional mechanisms of international cooperation are relics of 25
another era. The United Nations system represents an outdated configuration of power. The permanent members of the UN Security Council are the
victors of a war that ended sixty years ago. The body does not include Japan
or Germany, the world's second- and third-largest economies (at market
exchange rates), or India, the world's largest democracy, or any Latin American or African country. The Security Council exemplifies the antique structure of global governance more broadly. The G-8 does not include China,
already the world's fourth-largest economy, or India and South Korea, the
twelfth and thirteenth. By tradition, the IMF is always headed by a European and the World Bank by an American. This "tradition," like the customs of an old segregated country club, may be charming and amusing to
insiders, but to outsiders it is bigoted and outrageous.

A further complication: When I write of the rise of nationalism, I am 26
describing a broader phenomenon—the assertion of identity. The nation-
state is a relatively new invention, often no more than a hundred years old.
Much older are the religious, ethnic, and linguistic groups that live within
nation-states. And these bonds have stayed strong, in fact grown, as economic interdependence has deepened. In Europe, the Flemish and French
in Belgium remain as distinct as ever. In Britain, the Scots have elected
a ruling party that proposes ending the three-hundred-year-old Acts of
Union that created the United Kingdom of England, Scotland, and Wales.
In India, national parties are losing ground to regional ones. In Kenya,
tribal distinctions are becoming more important. In much of the world,
these core identities—deeper than the nation-state—remain the defining
features of life. It is why people vote, and what they die for. In an open
world economy, these groups know that they need the central government less and less. And in a democratic age, they gain greater and greater
power if they stay together as a group. This twin ascendancy of identity
means that, when relating to the United States or the United Nations or
the world at large, Chinese and Indian nationalism grows. But within their
own countries, sub-nationalism is also growing. What is happening on the
global stage—the rise of identity in the midst of economic growth—is
also happening on the local stage. The bottom line: It makes purposeful
national action far more difficult.

As power becomes diversified and diffuse, legitimacy becomes even 27
more important—because it is the only way to appeal to all the disparate
actors on the world stage. Today, no solution, no matter how sensible, is
sustainable if it is seen as illegitimate. Imposing it will not work if it is
seen as the product of one country's power and preferences, no matter
how powerful that country. The massacres in Darfur, for example, are hor-
rific, and yet military intervention there—the most effective way of stopping it—would succeed only if sanctioned by the major powers as well as
Sudan's African neighbors. If the United States acted alone or with a small
coalition—invading its third Muslim country in five years—the attempt
would almost certainly backfire, providing the Sudanese government with
a fiery rallying cry against "U.S. imperialism." The Bush administration's
foreign policy record offers a perfect illustration of the practical necessity

of legitimacy. And yet, beyond Bush's failures, the dilemma remains: If many countries need to cooperate to get things done, how to make this happen in a world with more players, many of them more powerful?

The Last Superpower

Many observers and commentators have looked at the vitality of this   28
emerging world and concluded that the United States has had its day. Andy Grove, the founder of Intel, puts it bluntly. "America is in danger of following Europe down the tubes," he says, "and the worst part is that nobody knows it. They're all in denial, patting themselves on the back as the *Titanic* heads straight for the iceberg full speed ahead." Thomas Friedman describes watching waves of young Indian professionals get to work for the night shift at Infosys in Bangalore. "Oh, my God, there are so many of them, and they just keep coming, wave after wave. How in the world can it possibly be good for my daughters and millions of other Americans that these Indians can do the same jobs as they can for a fraction of the wages?"[4] "Globalization is striking back," writes Gabor Steingart, an editor at Germany's leading news magazine, *Der Spiegel*, in a bestselling book. As its rivals have prospered, he argues, the United States has lost key industries, its people have stopped saving money, and its government has become increasingly indebted to Asian central banks.[5]

What's puzzling, however, is that these trends have been around for   29
a while—and they have actually helped America's bottom line. Over the past twenty years, as globalization and outsourcing have accelerated dramatically, America's growth rate has averaged just over 3 percent, a full percentage point higher than that of Germany and France. (Japan averaged 2.3 percent over the same period.) Productivity growth, the elixir of modern economics, has been over 2.5 percent for a decade now, again a full percentage point higher than the European average. Even American exports held up, despite a decade-long spike in the value of the dollar that ended recently. In 1980, U.S. exports represented 10 percent of the world total; in 2007, that figure was still almost 9 percent. According to the World Economic Forum, the United States remains the most competitive economy in the world and ranks first in innovation, ninth in technological readiness, second in company spending for research and technology, and second in the quality of its research institutions. China does not come within thirty countries of the United States in any of these, and India breaks the top ten on only one count: market size. In virtually every sector that advanced industrial countries participate in, U.S. firms lead the world in productivity and profits.

The United States' share of the global economy has been remark-   30
ably steady through wars, depressions, and a slew of other powers rising. With 5 percent of the world's population, the United States has generated between 20 and 30 percent of world output for 125 years. There will surely be some slippage of America's position over the next few decades. This is not a political statement but a mathematical one. As other countries grow faster, America's relative economic weight will fall. But the decline need

not be large-scale, rapid, or consequential, as long as the United States can adapt to new challenges as well as it adapted to those it confronted over the last century. In the next few decades, the rise of the emerging nations is likely to come mostly at the expense of Western Europe and Japan, which are locked in a slow, demographically determined decline.

America will face the most intense economic competition it has ever *31* faced. The American economic and social system knows how to respond and adjust to such pressures. The reforms needed are obvious but because they mean some pain now for long-term gain, the political system cannot make them. The more difficult challenge that the United States faces is international. It will confront a global order quite different from the one it is used to operating in. For now, the United States remains the most powerful player. But every year the balance shifts.

For the roughly two decades since 1989, the power of the United States *32* has defined the international order. All roads have led to Washington, and American ideas about politics, economics, and foreign policy have been the starting points for global action. Washington has been the most powerful outside actor on every continent in the world, dominating the Western Hemisphere, remaining the crucial outside balancer in Europe and East Asia, expanding its role in the Middle East and Central and South Asia, and everywhere remaining the only country that can provide the muscle for any serious global military operation. For every country—from Russia and China to South Africa and India—its most important relationship in the world has been the relationship with the United States.

That influence reached its apogee with Iraq. Despite the reluctance, *33* opposition, or active hostility of much of the world, the United States was able to launch an unprovoked attack on a sovereign country and to enlist dozens of countries and international agencies to assist it during and after the invasion. It is not just the complications of Iraq that have unwound this order. Even had Iraq been a glorious success, the method of its execution would have made utterly clear the unchallenged power of the United States— and it is this exercise of unipolarity that has provoked a reaction around the world. The unipolar order of the last two decades is waning not because of Iraq but because of the broader diffusion of power across the world.

On some matters, unipolarity seems already to have ended. The *34* European Union now represents the largest trade bloc on the globe, creating bipolarity, and as China and then other emerging giants gain size, the bipolar realm of trade might become tripolar and then multipolar. In every realm except military, similar shifts are underway. In general, however, the notion of a multipolar world, with four or five players of roughly equal weight, does not describe reality today or in the near future. Europe can not act militarily or even politically as one. Japan and Germany are hamstrung by their past. China and India are still developing. Instead, the international system is more accurately described by Samuel Huntington's term "uni-multipolarity," or what Chinese geopoliticians call "many powers and one superpower." The messy language reflects the messy reality. The United States remains by far the most powerful country but in a world with several other important great powers and with greater assertiveness and activity from all actors. This hybrid international system—more democratic, more dynamic, more open, more connected—is one we are likely to live with for several decades. It is easier to define what it is not than what it is, easier to describe the era it is moving away from than the era it is moving toward—hence *the post-American world*.

The United States occupies the top spot in the emerging system, 35 but it is also the country that is most challenged by the new order. Most other great powers will see their role in the world expand. That process is already underway. China and India are becoming bigger players in their neighbor hoods and beyond. Russia has ended its post-Soviet accommodation and is becoming more forceful, even aggressive. Japan, though not a rising power, is now more willing to voice its views and positions to its neighbors. Europe acts on matters of trade and economics with immense strength and purpose. Brazil and Mexico are becoming more vocal on Latin American issues. South Africa has positioned itself as a leader of the African continent. All these countries are taking up more space in the international arena than they did before.

For the United States, the arrow is pointing in the opposite direction. 36 Economics is not a zero-sum game—the rise of other players expands the pie, which is good for all—but geopolitics is a struggle for influence and control. As other countries become more active, America's enormous space for action will inevitably diminish. Can the United States accommodate itself to the rise of other powers, of various political stripes, on several continents? This does not mean becoming resigned to chaos or aggression; far from it. But the only way for the United States to deter rogue actions will be to create a broad, durable coalition against them. And that will be possible only if Washington can show that it is willing to allow other countries to become stakeholders in the new order. In today's international order, progress means compromise. No country will get its way entirely. These are easy words to write or say but difficult to implement. They mean accepting the growth in power and influence of other countries, the prominence of interests and concerns. This balance—between accommodation and deterrence—is the chief challenge for American foreign policy in the next few decades.

I began . . . by arguing that the new order did not herald American 37 decline, because I believe that America has enormous strengths and that the new world will not throw up a new superpower but rather a diversity of forces that Washington can navigate and even help direct. But still, as the rest of the world rises, in purely economic terms, America will experience relative decline. As others grow faster, its share of the pie will be smaller (though the shift will likely be small for many years). In addition, the new nongovernmental forces that are increasingly active will constrain Washington substantially.

This is a challenge for Washington but also for everyone else. For 38 almost three centuries, the world has been undergirded by the presence of a large liberal hegemon—first Britain, then the United States. These two superpowers helped create and maintain an open world economy, protecting trade routes and sea lanes, acting as lenders of last resort, holding the reserve currency, investing abroad, and keeping their own markets open.

They also tipped the military balance against the great aggressors of their ages, from Napoleon's France, to Germany, to the Soviet Union. For all its abuses of power, the United States has been the creator and sustainer of the current order of open trade and democratic government—an order that has been benign and beneficial for the vast majority of humankind. As things change, and as America's role changes, that order could begin to fracture. The collapse of the dollar—to the point where there was no global reserve currency—would be a problem for the world just as much as for America. And solving common problems in an era of diffusion and decentralization could turn out to be far more difficult without a superpower.

Some Americans have become acutely conscious of the changing 39 world. American business is increasingly aware of the shifts taking place around the world and is responding to them rapidly and unsentimentally. Large U.S.-based multinationals almost uniformly report that their growth now relies on penetrating new foreign markets. With annual revenue growth of 2–3 percent a year in the United States and 10–15 percent a year abroad, they know they have to adapt to a post-American world—or else lose out in it. A similar awareness is visible in America's universities, where more and more students study and travel abroad and interact with foreign students. Younger Americans live comfortably with the knowledge that the latest trends—in finance, architecture, art, technology—might originate in London, Shanghai, Seoul, Tallinn, or Mumbai.

But this outward orientation is not yet common in American soci- 40 ety more broadly. The American economy remains internally focused, though this is changing, with trade making up 28 percent of GDP (compared with 38 percent for Germany). Insularity has been one of nature's blessings to America, bordered as it is by two vast oceans and two benign neighbors. America has not been sullied by the machinations and weariness of the Old World and has always been able to imagine a new and different order—whether in Germany, Japan, or even Iraq. But at the same time, this isolation has left Americans quite unaware of the world beyond their borders. Americans speak few languages, know little about foreign cultures, and remain unconvinced that they need to rectify this. Americans rarely benchmark to global standards because they are sure that their way must be the best and most advanced. The result is that they are increasingly suspicious of this emerging global era. There is a growing gap between America's worldly business elite and cosmopolitan class, on the one hand, and the majority of the American people, on the other. Without real efforts to bridge it, this divide could destroy America's competitive edge and its political future.

Popular suspicions are fed and encouraged by an irresponsible 41 national political culture. In Washington, new thinking about a new world is sorely lacking. It is easy enough to criticize the Bush administration for its arrogance and unilateralism, which have handicapped America abroad. But the problem is not confined to Bush, Cheney, Rumsfeld, or the Republicans, even though they have become the party of chest-thumping machismo, proud to be despised abroad. Listen to some Democrats in Washington, and you hear a weaker unilateralism—on trade, labor standards, and various pet human rights issues. On terrorism, both parties continue to speak in language entirely designed for a domestic audience with no concern for the poisonous effect it has everywhere else. American politicians constantly and promiscuously demand, label, sanction, and condemn whole countries for myriad failings. Over the last fifteen years, the United States has placed sanctions on half the world's population. We are the only country in the world to issue annual report cards on every other country's behavior. Washington, D.C., has become a bubble, smug and out of touch with the world outside.

The 2007 Pew Global Attitudes Survey showed a remarkable increase   42 worldwide in positive views about free trade, markets, and democracy. Large majorities in countries from China and Germany to Bangladesh and Nigeria said that growing trade ties between countries were good. Of the forty-seven countries polled, however, the one that came in dead last in terms of support for free trade was the United States. In the five years the survey has been done, no country has seen as great a drop-off as the United States.

Or take a look at the attitudes toward foreign companies. When   43 asked whether they had a positive impact, a surprisingly large number of people in countries like Brazil, Nigeria, India, and Bangladesh said yes. Those countries have typically been suspicious of Western multinationals. (South Asia's unease has some basis; after all, it was initially colonized by a multinational corporation, the British East India Company.) And yet, 73 present in India, 75 percent in Bangladesh, 70 percent in Brazil, and 82 percent in Nigeria now have positive views of these companies. The figure for America, in contrast, is 45 percent, which places us in the bottom five. We want the world to accept American companies with open arms, but when they come here — that's a different matter. Attitudes on immigration represent an even larger reversal. On an issue where the United States has been the model for the world, the country has regressed toward an angry defensive crouch. Where we once wanted to pioneer every new technology, we now look at innovation fearfully, wondering how it will change things.

The irony is that the rise of the rest is a consequence of American ideas   44 and actions. For sixty years, American politicians and diplomats have traveled around the world pushing countries to open their markets, free up their politics, and embrace trade technology. We have urged peoples in distant lands to take up the challenge of competing in the global economy, freeing up their currencies, and developing new industries. We counseled them to be unafraid of change and learn the secrets of our success. And it worked: The natives have gotten good at capitalism. But now we are becoming suspicious of the very things we have long celebrated—free markets, trade, immigration, and technological change. And all this is happening when the tide is going our way. Just as the world is opening up, America is closing down.

Generations from now, when historian write about these times, they   45 might note that, in the early decades of the twenty-first century, the United

States succeeded in its great and historic mission—it globalized the world. But along the way, they might write, it forgot to globalize itself.

NOTES

1. Zbigniew Brzezinski, "The Dilemma of the Last Sovereign," *American Interest* I, no. 1 (Autumn 2005).
2. Benjamin Schwarz, review of Stephen E. Ambrose, *The Good Fight*, in *Atlantic Monthly*, June 2001, p. 103.
3. Naazneen Barma et al., "The World Without the West," *National Interest*, no. 90 (July/Aug. 2007): 23–30.
4. Thomas L. Friedman, *The World Is Flat: A Brief History of the Twenty-first Century* (New York: Farrar, Straus and Giroux, 2006), 226. Andy Grove's statement is quoted in Clyde Prestowitz, *Three Billion New Capitalists: The Great Shift of Wealth and Power to the East* (New York: Basic Books, 2005), 8.
5. Gabor Steingart, *The War for Wealth: Why Globalization Is Bleeding the West of Its Prosperity* (New York: McGraw-Hill, 2008).

■ ■ ■

Reading as a Writer: Analyzing Rhetorical Choices

1. Zakaria is careful to point out that the evidence he presents "does not mean we are entering an anti-American world. But we are moving into a *post-American world*, one defined and directed from many places and by many people" (para. 9). What is the significance of phrasing his argument this way? How do his examples illustrate his definition?

2. Part of Zakaria's argumentative strategy is to situate the present in relation to the past. Which historical details that Zakaria includes are most surprising and interesting to you? How does this history relate to his larger point about where "we" are now and what might come next?

Writing as a Reader: Entering the Conversation of Ideas

1. Zakaria is interested in analyzing the economic shifts that are coming with globalization, and not only from a U.S. perspective. Write an essay in which you link Zakaria's insights about the United States' role in a "post-American" world to ideas about business and racial and ethnic differences raised by Shalini Shankar and/or Ann duCille. What do the writers you choose have to say about what might be next for the United States, based on the evidence they provide? What path do you think the United States should take to engage effectively with a globalized market, and why, given this evidence?

2. Both Zakaria and John Dicker are fascinated by the effects of stories "we" tell about our place in the world and on the economic market. Locate specific examples in each author's text where the author raises the problem of biased history (Zakaria calls this an "entirely Western or American narrative of world history" in para. 18). Compose an essay in which you examine the effect of these stories, and the corrective measures each author proposes. What conclusions do you draw about the uses and dangers of crafting stories about ourselves?

SHALINI SHANKAR

Creating Model Consumers: Producing Ethnicity, Race, and Class in Asian American Advertising

Shalini Shankar is a professor of sociocultural and linguistic anthropology at Northwestern University, where she specializes in media, youth culture, and race and ethnicity, particularly Asian American identity. This article from the journal *American Ethnologist* is part of the research for her forthcoming book, *Advertising Diversity, Producing Language and Ethnicity in American Advertising*. As the title of this 2012 article suggests, Shankar is interested in the idea of Asian Americans as a "model minority" with purchasing power.

Shankar's language is pitched to an academic audience, but her ideas are of popular interest, as she investigates the complicated and often problematic ways that advertisers market their products to a particular group. As she notes in paragraph 3, she bases her analysis on two recent case studies of advertising campaigns in order to build her larger point about the effects of mass-mediated representations of ethnicity and race (para. 2) through advertising. Shankar argues, as do other theorists, that the "message" of advertising can shape and recontextualize ideas and values — in this case about ethnic and racial identity — in order to sell products. Her term for this is *metaproduction*, an idea she develops throughout this article. Be sure to note where and how she uses this term to make her argument.

As Shankar notes, there are many groups that constitute the umbrella term "Asian American," and so her case studies trace the process of designing advertising for a specific ethnicity (in one case, Chinese American, and in another, South Asian American), drawing on language and cultural ideas that speak very particularly to that audience. Shankar's detailed description of the lively advertising-development meetings she observed for her research offer a peek into the ways marketers work with clients to design an effective campaign. What details from these meetings surprise you (or don't), and why? What patterns do you notice in the conversations for the Allied Country Insurance and Financial Services ad campaign, and the campaign for the "Deluxis Winter Sales Event"?

The core of Shankar's argument is in her sections titled "Creating Model Consumers" and "Linking Metaproduction and Racialization," so take some time to read (and reread) these sections carefully. How, according to Shankar, are old racial stereotypes being retooled to fit a contemporary consumerist identity? Given the shifting U.S. demographic information that Shankar provides in her final paragraphs, what are the implications for our senses of ourselves that go far beyond advertising? If our differences are becoming less pronounced, the dynamic that draws us together — buying products — might give us pause.

Fortune, wealth; luck, you know, those are all common themes. You know, I could go to a marketer [and] he may not know the Asian American market well. I could say to him, "You know, Chinese love the color red and the number eight and the number nine and gold, and so here's our ad." And the client would think, "Oh wow! I'm really touching this Asian American market now, because I've got all the cues that resonate with them, right? You know, I got the red, I got the dragon, I got the eight, I got the nine." And then when I see it, it's just this cliché thing, you know? It doesn't say anything to me.
—STEVE, ACCOUNT EXECUTIVE, ASIAN COLLABORATION
ADVERTISING AND MARKETING AGENCY, NEW YORK[1]

S itting in his modern, minimalist, loft-style office on Madison Avenue, *1* Steve conveyed a central tension in the creation and development of advertising aimed at Asian American audiences. He and his client bring conflicting notions to bear on the creative process, in that each believes a different set of signs will be most appealing to Asian audiences in the United States. According to Steve's performance of his client, the latter is drawn to signifiers that are neither American nor Asian American per se; they are perhaps best understood as icons that signify Asia in the broad U.S. imagination. Although icons such as dragons and numerology certainly could conjure images of Asia for Asian Americans more particularly, Steve indicates that he, like his audiences, would find them simplistic and ineffective. Executives like Steve pride themselves on avoiding icons that might diminish the complex subjectivity of Asians in the United States. They approach their creative work on a "meta" level that reveals their knowledge of broader historical and cultural narratives about Asian Americans, their familiarity with language varieties and uses of speech, and their ability to create indexes for different Asian ethnic groups. All the while, they aim to please clients who expect to maintain brand identity and to see evidence of Asian American language and culture that will reach this emerging market.

In this article, I examine the ideological underpinnings of racial and *2* ethnic formation while also foregrounding the processes and practices of media production. To connect numerous levels of development and production and draw attention to the impact of finished ads on mass-mediated racial and ethnic formation, I introduce the concept of "metaproduction." As an analytic, metaproduction offers a way to understand how Asian American–niche advertising executives transform census and marketing data into representations suitable for commercial consumption by populating them with indexes of ethnicity and class. Executives' goal in this media production is to compel corporate clients wishing to reach this niche market to look beyond iconic signs that conjure Asia in mainstream U.S. culture and to opt instead for those signs that index ways of being Asian American. Through metaproduction, executives like Steve are remaking the racial category of "Asian American" and the ethnic groups it encompasses in the neoliberal United States. Neoliberal notions of success and diversity invite a theoretical framework that can connect broader pub-lic-sphere ideologies with the microlevel cultural and linguistic work of advertising development and production. One outcome I trace here is a shift in the perception of Asian Americans from model minority producers in the U.S. economy to sophisticated, upwardly mobile model minority consumers.

In what follows, I flesh out the theoretical underpinnings of metapro-   3 duction, present two case studies drawn from my ethnographic research in ad agencies, and offer an analysis of racial and ethnic formation in media production. I analyze discussions among "creatives" who are responsible for generating concepts, original artwork, and writing copy for ads; agency executives' interactions with clients, those corporate entities who commission advertising; and the activities of other industry personnel, including account executives who oversee the entire process, producers responsible for casting, directing, and postproduction of print, TV, radio, and Internet ads, and media buyers who place ads in various media.

Metaproduction and Message

Metaproduction is a process of material and linguistic signification that   4 uses values already deemed "meta" in some sense, specifically, those that are metacultural and metalinguistic. Metaculture, or reflections about culture, and metalanguage, talk about language and its use, tend to be routine parts of advertising production, but the creation of racially and ethnically specific communications requires a heightened degree of reflexivity. Just as the metalevel has been useful in theorizing the consumption of media, it is also quite relevant to understanding how signs are generated, vetted, and put into circulation in the production of commercial communications (see also Davila 2001; Foster 2007; Kemper 2001; Mazzerella 2003; Moeran 1996a).[2] As an analytic, metaproduction connects microlevel cultural and linguistic signification with broader categories of brand identity and racial meaning. The notion of "meta" is well suited to capture the time-space compression of late capitalism characterized by the acceleration of communication and the circulation of cultural forms in the neoliberal era (Harvey 1989; Jameson 1991). Greg Urban observes that the metacultural "focuses attention on the cultural thing, helps to make it an object of interest, and hence, facilitates its circulation . . . metaculture is a supplement to culture" (2001:4). Also remarking on the metacultural dimensions of advertising development and production, Daniel Miller (1997) contends that, in the Trinidadian case, "meta-symbols" such as Coca-Cola should be considered not simply material culture but also the debate about it. The metalevel is especially revealing because it involves the coordination of different moments of signification (Lee 1997:201). Nowhere is this more evident than in language, in which the metalinguistic is a level at which speakers express socially informed assessments of their own utterances and those of others. Building on Roman Jakobson's conception of the "metalingual," the ways in which speakers reflect on language, Michael Silverstein's (1993) discussion of "metapragmatics" links the relevance of talk about language use to broader social formations. Metaproduction uses such assessments of language and culture as a starting point for the creation of racial and ethnic representations.

Metaproduction here attends not only to the deployment of linguistic and material signs in advertisements but also to the political economy that underpins Asian American advertising production. In industry parlance, the term category "niche market" includes agencies that create and produce advertising and marketing for specific segments of the U.S. population. Asian American advertising is considered niche market because it is expected to contain cultural and linguistic signs that appeal to Americans of Chinese, Korean, South Asian,[3] Filipino, and Vietnamese descent—a complicated assumption that I investigate here. Contrasting yet overlapping with niche markets, the category of "general market" (GM) ostensibly encompasses all groups in the United States. The "in-language" and "in-culture" ads that Asian American executives produce differ from general market advertising in terms of language, culture, media placement, and, sometimes, overall creative approach. As talent for hire, executives are asked to generate complex indexes within narrow constraints of time and budget. Managing and furthering brand identity certainly play a role in this process, as I discuss to some degree here, but what metaproduction reveals most clearly is the formation of mass-mediated representations of ethnicity and race through the manipulation of signs.[4]

In the medium of advertising, metaproduction is not only focused on content but also on form. Jane H. Hill (2000) develops Roman Jacobson's concept of "poetics" to consider "message" in ways that draw attention to nonverbal communication along with the "word." She elaborates on the concept of "message" as it pertains to the performance of politicians: "Message includes talk and text, but it is dominated by the poetic function, with thematic material encapsulated in sound bites and slogans. The construction of message lies in the realm of art, with colors, lighting, music, costume, posture, and a variety of other signaling media at least as important as text itself" (Hill 2000:264). Also interested in message, Silverstein discusses "creativity in the poetics of advertising" (2005:12) by emphasizing the affective dimensions of the propositional claims of ads, what Richard Parmentier (1994) has described as "puffery." Aspects of message, poetics, and beyond are integral to metaproduction. In my case, metacultural and metalinguistic levels work in tandem because Asian American advertising is marked both culturally and linguistically. Language, already a rich site of inquiry in advertising (Lefkowitz 2003; Silverstein 2006), is dynamically intertwined with visual elements to signify additional levels of meaning.

Creatives do not simply reflect existing values about race and ethnicity 7
but approach the process of signification as one in which they generate
new indexical values or recontextualize existing ones for particular purposes. The meanings speakers associate with the indexical values of utterances create tiered levels of meanings, or "indexical orders" (Silverstein
2003). In indexical orders, metapragmatic assessments and other types
of metalanguage shape indexical values about language use, such that
each subsequent order builds on a previous one (Silverstein 2003:196).
Utilizing the concept of "indexical orders" allows one to consider cultural
indexes alongside linguistic ones and how they interact to create message. Accordingly, message and metaproduction consider both material
and linguistic elements in the creation of semiotic meaning (see Cavanaugh 2005; Keane 2003; Moore 2003; Shankar 2006, 2008). Metaproduction thus offers a lens through which to understand the complex interplay
of linguistic and material signs as well as their success and efficacy in
advertising.

Creating the Genre of Asian American Advertising

Executives aspire to reach Asian American consumers through special- 8
ized communications that transform general market brand identities into
ethnically and racially specific communications for Asians in the United
States. Ethnographic studies of advertising have illustrated the localized
ways in which this industry does not simply reflect existing values but
actively formulates and creates them (Mazzerella 2003; Miller 1997). Likewise, executives make the category of "Asian American" and the five most
profitable ethnic groups it encompasses—Chinese, Korean, Vietnamese,
Filipino, and South Asian—meaningful and recognizable among themselves, their clients, and their audiences. Understanding regional ideologies, values, and norms specific to a target audience is paramount to
effectively constructing consumers and markets (Davila 2001; Foster 2007;
Kemper 2001; Malefyt and Moeran 2003; Moeran 1996a). Asian American
executives make ads that are "in-language," meaning they include an
Asian language or Asian variety of English, and "in-culture," meaning they
include nonlinguistic signs that represent one or more Asian American
ethnic groups.

Advertising agencies that cater exclusively to the Asian American 9
market emerged in the mid-1980s and are concentrated in New York,
Los Angeles, and San Francisco. These ten or so major agencies offer a
range of services that include producing advertisements for print (ethnic
newspapers and magazines), television (local access cable and satellite
channels), the Web, and social media platforms (Twitter and smartphone
applications). Additionally, they do direct marketing and e-mail blasts
(commonly known as junk mail and spam, respectively) as well as

community-level event sponsorship and public relations. Goods and services categories such as automotive, telecommunications, liquor, insurance, banking, casinos, and fast food have been especially invested in marketing directly to Asian American consumers. The majority of executives working at these agencies are themselves first- or second-generation Asian Americans, and many are fluent in one of the languages used for writing advertising copy (Hindi, Korean, Mandarin, Tagalog, or Vietnamese). This ethnolinguistic heritage forms a major part of the expertise these advertising executives project, a point I develop in greater detail elsewhere (Shankar n.d.).

The two case studies below are based on observations and audio *10* recordings I collected during four months of research conducted in 2009 at "Asian Ads." Asian Ads is a seventy-five-person pan-Asian advertising agency that was cofounded in 1986 by three first-generation Chinese Americans and is currently owned by one of them. On a daily basis, I observed and audio-recorded creative brainstorms, account status meetings, production activities, client calls, and industry events. This work was part of a multiyear, multisited research project I began in 2008 that includes fieldwork in Asian American ad agencies and their industry events and more limited fieldwork in general market agencies. As a university professor, I found my way into Asian American advertising agencies with relative ease. I used the Asian American Advertising Association's Web site to contact major agencies in New York, Los Angeles, and San Francisco. Eight of the leading Asian American agencies were exceedingly gracious in inviting "the professor" to visit them and conduct interviews. At some, my visit was brief, involving an extended interview with a single representative and viewing an "agency reel" of the firm's best work. At others, I spent several days observing meetings, production sessions, and interviewing numerous executives. New York City–based Asian Ads allowed me to conduct longer-term fieldwork and to audio-record meetings, and I have included transcripts from that research here. I was required to sign nondisclosure agreements at every agency in which I spent an extended period of time, and I have adhered to their terms by using pseudonyms and omitting information deemed proprietary. I believe people allowed me access to their rarified corporate world because very little work has been done on this relatively new niche in U.S. advertising and because my research is funded by the National Science Foundation, is for educational purposes, and has no commercial affiliation. As a South Asian American conversant and literate in Hindi, I best understood communications made for this audience but closely followed all accounts I was permitted to observe. This was feasible because in this multilingual workplace, meetings were conducted in English and English back translations (verbatim translations of phrases originally in English but now in-language) were provided for clients and coworkers.

"Allied Country Dividend" Print Ad

BRIEF 1   Allied Country Dividend Brief.

CREATIVE AGENCY BRIEF	
Client	Allied Country
Agency	Asian Ads, New York, NY
Brand managers	Mike and Janet
Project	Dividend Ad: In-language, in-culture print ad for Chinese, Korean, and South Asian American segments.
Overview	This is a campaign for financial services that emphasizes monetary dividends.
Objective	We want to increase brand presence among target segments so that they use Allied Country for their financial service needs.
Target audience	Primary target will be men, 35–64-year-olds, with household incomes of $80k+.
Reasons to believe and buy	Allied Country is a trusted company that can help build and plan your financial future.

NOTE: The briefs that appear in this article are simulations of the originals, per the terms of my nondisclosure agreement with the agency.

In a print ad campaign for Allied Country Insurance and Financial *11*
Services (hereafter, AC), the client asked Asian Ads to produce versions of a general market ad for the Chinese, Korean, and South Asian American market "segments," as they are called in this industry. Asian Ads had an excellent relationship with AC, which regularly commissioned ads and even sent representatives to the annual Asian American Advertising Federation conference to demonstrate its investment in Asian American marketing. In some AC campaigns, those on the account team had been given free rein to generate original concepts for the layout, message, and style of the ad, provided they maintain brand identity—an evaluation reserved for the client. For this campaign, however, AC had requested Asian Ads to make versions of a general market print ad for each segment. Once the account supervisor received the agency brief from the client (see Brief 1), head of creative An Rong delegated the job to three members of his department. On this job, Jun Yi, a first-generation Taiwanese American man, Esther, a 1.5-generation Chinese American woman, and Andrew, a first-generation Filipino American man, worked together on a creative brainstorm. Presenting the "concept" of the ad, or what would be communicated, was an important step in the Asian Ads creative process. After creatives Esther and Jun Yi worked independently to generate ideas, they met with copywriter Andrew to discuss them. The team convened in a casual meeting area in the front of the office, their ideas and sentences punctuated by the chimes of approaching elevators, which opened directly into the loft-style office.

In their meeting, the team searched for the most relevant ways to rep-   *12*
resent Chinese American ethnicity while also preserving the message of
the general market print ad. They began by distilling the key messages of
the GM ad and considering how they might tailor them for Chinese Americans. The broader aim was to generate creative concepts that could later
be adapted for Korean and South Asian American segments, but the work
at hand was to create a winning Chinese American version of what the
client called the "dividend ad." The very notion of "dividends" signals a
level of financial security and well-being that might be a distant memory
for many Americans in the current economic climate, but the task was to
present this idea as a natural and unquestioned part of everyday Chinese
American life. Both Jun Yi and Esther had studied the GM print ad, which
featured a cheerful white father and son dressed in matching white oxford
shirts and rolled-up khakis, walking on a log of driftwood at the beach with
their arms outstretched for balance. They brought several hand-sketched
concepts that conveyed the main themes they associated with the notion
of "dividend," including security, prosperity, and empowerment. Each concept also featured a round visual element that would allow for the incorporation of AC's circular logo—an innovative flourish that the clients loved
in Asian Ads' previous work.

At this stage of the metaproduction process, Esther and Jun Yi pre-   *13*
sented concepts that reflected the themes of the GM ad in ways that would
resonate with Chinese Americans. For instance, "risk and reward" was
represented in one image by a rock climber ascending a cliff, a large circular knot holding him steady, and in another by whitewater rafters in
circular rafts holding their paddles triumphantly up in the air, signaling
their safety. Another theme, "skill and accomplishment," was conveyed by
two ice skaters "making a figure eight on the ice and signifying infinite
peace of mind," Esther explained. Jun Yi added to this category by offering sketches of a father teaching his son how to hit a golf ball out of a
sand trap, a hand holding Chinese exercise balls against pressure points to
build strength, and a gymnast balancing on a beam and exhibiting agility.
A third set of images that directly addressed the theme "benefit" included
a child eating an ice cream cone, a woman in a difficult yoga pose, and a
father and son peering into a bird's nest filled with three small eggs. The
team agreed that all of these had strong potential and that it was time to
call in creative director An Rong to narrow down the list.

As in other metacultural and metalinguistic assessments, evalua-   *14*
tion and judgment constitute an integral part of metaproduction. In this
case, a critical discussion ensued about which ads would have the greatest resonance with a Chinese American audience. Andrew, the copywriter,
reminded the team that they needed to find a concept that "works across
different Asian segments and conveys security without signaling insecurity." As they waited for An Rong, Esther cycled through the short list
of concepts by embodying a Chinese American consumer and voicing
engagements with each creative idea. She mused, "The rock presents risk,

but the knot is security, so I choose [AC]." Narrating each concept, she tested the efficacy of her metaproduction work by assessing whether the correct reading of signs led to the "choice" of AC. Throughout, the team offered critical feedback to one another about select concepts, such as the ice cream and yoga, which showed end results but not how one could achieve them. Esther asserted that the idea of yoga could work for all three segments, but Jun Yi countered that it was irrelevant to financial services and did not address the notion of "dividend." When creative director An Rong finally arrived, he preempted Esther and Jun Yi's presentation with his own reading of the general market ad, which he called "the sea." Remarking that the sea is dangerous and unstable, but one can still enjoy it, he strategized, "we need to show some unpredictable environment but the family still enjoying it." The quizzical expressions on Esther's and Jun Yi's faces suggested that their reading of the GM ad had been somewhat different than that of their creative director, but they nonetheless proceeded with the presentation. After taking in the concepts, An Rong was sharp and focused in his critique. Arguing that rock climbing offered little cultural insight, he challenged, "Is this in-culture? Why not just use the general market ad?" Jun Yi conceded that it did not have any apparent significance for Chinese American audiences and, unlike the GM ad, it did not meld notions of family and security. They all agreed, however, that golf would provide an ideal concept because of its popularity among Chinese and Korean Americans.

With Asian Ads's initial stage of the metaproduction process com- 15 pleted, the team faced the task of obtaining client approval for two print ad concepts on their short list. On a conference call with AC, account executive Sunil began by priming his client: "They are gonna sell their concept to you today, if you will buy it!" Asian Ads cycled through the concepts the team had sent to AC in advance, beginning with the golf idea. The client swiftly and politely declined, explaining that it had already been done too many times in AC's GM ads. A wave of disappointment was palpable in the Asian Ads conference room, especially as the team had found this message to be particularly apt for Chinese American and Korean American audiences. The bird nest concept, however, seemed to hold the client's imagination longer, and Jun Yi seized the opportunity to narrate the concept's indexical value: "All their hard work for the family, for their loved ones, the bird nest is protection. First-generation immigrants want to make a good future for their children. The father and son look at the bird nest, and [AC] gives you the benefit and strength to protect your family." Approval of a second concept followed the client's acceptance of the bird nest concept: The team agreed to the client's recommendation to use a graphic design program to modify the general market "sea" ad by splicing Asian American faces onto it. In conjunction with the Chinese copy, the client thought the visual would suffice, and the ad could be produced on schedule and within budget.

In this campaign, executives chose signs to represent Chinese *16*
Americans in sophisticated, cosmopolitan ways that also convey the
essence of the AC brand. Like the general market ad that features a middle-
class man who is able to reap the benefit of financial dividends by spending
leisure time with his son at the beach, the nest signifies a lifestyle in which
Asian Americans already flush with capital would be well advised to manage this wealth effectively. Similar to the now-Chinese American father
walking with his son on the beach in oxford shirts and rolled-up khaki
pants, the Chinese American father who takes time to explore the wonders of nature with his son is pleased with the boy's reaction to the perfect
robin's eggs they find. Also notable in this case of metaproduction is the
partial success of the agency's creative strategies. For instance, the client
rejected the golf concept on the grounds that it had already been used in
the GM ads. The need for differentiation in the Asian American ads, then,
is reflected both in the inclusion of individuals who index particular Asian
American ethnic groups—in this case, Chinese Americans—and in scenarios that will resonate with the ads' audiences. Although the rejection
of the golf ad was something of a setback, the polysemy of the bird's nest
allowed for multiple indexical readings.

The Genre of Asian American Advertising

The AC case illustrates several processes, including the emergence of Asian *17*
American advertising as a genre. If one considers general market advertising in the United States and Chinese advertising in China as genres with
conventional characteristics and features that both resonate, to an extent,
with Chinese Americans, then Asian American advertising targeting that
group fills an intertextual gap; that is, it emerges between these two well-
defined genres and draws from them to produce a third. Intertextuality,
a process by which elements from one text are referenced in another in
ways that index the former and may be resignified as a result, contributes
to the creation of genre in this way: "By choosing to make certain features explicit (and particularly by foregrounding some elements through
repetition and metapragmatic framing), producers of discourse actively
(re)construct and reconfigure genres" (Bauman and Briggs 1992:584). Producers of Asian American advertising, likewise, select and showcase features from advertising genres in Asian countries, the United States, and
other relevant sources.

Conventions and content from general market advertising cannot be *18*
altogether overlooked, as brand identity must be preserved across genres.
Chinese representations of family, security, and financial planning are signified in ways that dovetail with AC's general market brand identity. Recall
the rejection, for instance, of the golf idea that Asian Ads thought would
work well for Chinese Americans but that AC thought had already become
overdone in its general market campaigns. Creating representations that
are in-culture, as An Rong pointed out, in this case led to the use of certain

ethnically marked signs, such as Chinese American actors and Mandarin text. It also meant recreating genre features from the general market campaign, such as fathers and sons exploring nature. In other executions for AC, Asian Ads created far more marked indexes of ethnicity, such as a traditional Indian wedding scene and a jade pendant handed down between generations of women. In those ads, as in the AC ad, the genre of Asian American advertising is most effective when executives are able to find the right indexical references to convey general market brand identity.

The use of ethnically marked signs, as in advertising elsewhere (see   *19* Bhatia 1992; Piller 2001), is indeed an important way in which the genre of Asian American advertising is distinguishable from general market advertising. Arlene Davila (2001) skillfully demonstrates how Latino executives downplay key ethnonational and linguistic differences in favor of a more uniform cultural and linguistic identity, and she makes a compelling case for the remaking of the Latino for marketing and consumption. In her research and mine, clients value the inclusion of recognizable emblems of ethnicity in ads because it enables them to justify spending advertising dollars to reach niche audiences, but executives note the shortcomings in this approach. Steve put it to me like this: "How can you touch them in this 'Asian' way, but be relevant, not cliché, and not overdone?" The AC ad offers an example of how this process worked smoothly for the most part and demonstrates how the client, like the customer, is always right. Even though executives would prefer to stay with their creative strategies, they change course as a matter of survival.

Reflexivity is thus a central part of the metaproduction process, among   *20* creatives, between creatives and their director, and between agency and client. Assessments about culture, language, and what constitutes ethnicity are articulated, and choices are made about the efficacy of representations. The political economy of the advertising process contributes to the conditions by which creatives sometimes rely on indexical shortcuts, and metaproduction allows for this type of shorthand for particular values. In this sense, the messages produced fall somewhere on a continuum between essentialist and antiessentialist representations. In the AC case, creativity and originality that are prized in general market advertising are openly curtailed by constraints imposed by clients with limited advertising budgets and established brand identities. The ads should exhibit the right sensibilities—material and linguistic—of Asian American culture and language but also the correct brand message, one that correlates with the general market brand identity. To produce the genre of Asian American advertising, then, executives deentextualize and reentextualize elements from genres of general market and Asian advertising.

Executives additionally define the genre of Asian American advertis-   *21* ing through their promotion of it as a vital and effective way to reach Asian American consumers. For instance, many were quick to explain to clients, and to me, that ads created for audiences in Asia do not resonate with Asian audiences in the United States, even though they may feature faces, voices, and ways of speaking and interacting that index a degree of familiarity. They also pointed out that general market ads lack the cultural and linguistic markers that are signature elements of Asian American niche advertising and are, accordingly, less effective forms of communication. On the one hand, this disposition is typical of agency executives who want to convince their corporate clients that only specialized communication will effectively reach consumers (see Mazzerella 2003; Miller 1997 for similar arguments). On the other hand, the link between racialized representation and consumerism is so fundamental to niche marketing that there is something substantive to be learned from the process of creating a marketable semiotic link between ideas, texts, and the Asian American consumer's wallet. The Chinese American case I discuss here, as well as the South Asian American case I discuss next, further contribute to the emergence and definition of the Asian American genre in advertising.

Creating Model Consumers

Ad executives do not simply use racialized identities but actively create [22] them through the process of making advertising. If, in fact, "we do not yet know all that is involved in the essentialization process whereby such a metadiscursive category—a category of contingently achieved role inhabitance—is projected onto the world" (Silverstein and Urban 1996:8), then metaproduction can contribute to understanding how this essentialization is accomplished. What is at stake, then, is the "continual back and forth interplay between the metadiscursive category and the actual instances of discourse that are used to categorize and interpret it" (Silverstein and Urban 1996:8). As a fairly new category that has been featured in media since the mid-1960s, Asian American advertising is playing the double role of inhabiting the category as well as projecting it into society. Executives use earlier discourses of racialized capitalism along with current ideologies of neoliberalism to shape representations of the Asian American consumer. Numerous insights have been offered about the rise of neoliberalism and its attendant cultural shifts (see di Leonardo 2008; Goldberg 2009; Harvey 2005); here I am most concerned with the remaking of public discourse that results from the production of racial representation. In neoliberal discourse, meanings of race and ethnicity that are rooted in political economy are recoded simply as "differences" that can be considered equal (Comaroff and Comaroff 2001). Neoliberalism especially idealizes the notion that individuals can thrive in capitalism without state assistance and that market deregulation creates opportunities for unlimited financial growth and accumulation (Harvey 2005).

Neoliberalism is a contemporary logic in a racialized capitalism [23] that has long positioned Asian Americans as ideal, especially compared to other racial minorities. Introduced in 1966 by the *New York Times* and *U.S. News and World Report*, the model minority stereotype portrayed

Asian Americans as self-sufficient, good citizens at a time when the state was looking to cut social services overall. Asian Americans were lauded as productive members of U.S. society, whereas other minority populations, especially African Americans, were unfavorably depicted for their reliance on state welfare (Kim 1999; Prashad 2000). Attributes such as strong familial ties, educational attainment, good citizenship, and economic mobility meld easily with market research and with executives' use of 2000 and 2010 census data to show that Asian Americans have the highest per capita income, are a rapidly growing population with spending power in the billions, and have been less affected by the economic downturn than the average American. In other words, they are ideal consumers to target through specialized advertising. Account supervisor Suzie, a first-generation Chinese American woman at a New York City agency, underscores the importance of contemporary Asian American representations that reflect these ideologies:

> Our clients always want us to have cultural nuances in the ads, but we don't want to do it too much. You want to think about your audience as modern customers that are really in sync with today's appeal and today's look. You don't really want to put too much of these so-called cultural nuances in there, but rather, something that speaks to the family, because Asians are very family-centric and they really focus on their kids' education. It could still be very modern and not outdated. We don't want to seem outdated.

Suzie's comments, like Steve's, suggest the existence of competing representations based on different signs that ad executives and clients each promote for different purposes. To best reach their Asian American audiences, executives avoid obvious icons of Asia, what Suzie calls "so-called cultural nuances," such as numerology or Chinese characters, that might index outdated notions of what it means to be Chinese in China as well as in the United States. By contrast, the model minority stereotype offers the potential to provide a modern narrative from which to create indexical signs that valorize family and education. In the AC ad, the model minority stereotype allows for the depiction of second-order indexical meanings (Silverstein 2003). For instance, the nest egg featured in the ad fits perfectly with the neoliberal ideology of self-sufficiency and financial wherewithal. Likewise, the sea ad also indexes class mobility and leisure through its tasteful depiction of beach activity. These representations reinforce the model minority stereotype while they also affirm the current success of Asian Americans. As refined, cultured individuals who are connected to nature and the corporate world, these Asian Americans are able to enjoy upper-middle-class life in ways that still prioritize family. These are not huddled masses of immigrants simply yearning for a better life; rather, they are middle-class professionals who are being shown the value of financial planning. Ad executives expect their clients to appreciate the complex subjectivities indexed through these signs, but clients can counter with their own signs of what they believe will work better.

The Deluxis "Winter Sates Event" Print Ad

Creating a South Asian American print ad for the "Deluxis Winter Sales 24 Event" should have been a fairly smooth process, considering the Asian Ads team had done a number of well-received Deluxis ads for Chinese American and South Asian American audiences. Asian Ads had been working with Deluxis for about a year and a half and was very familiar with the luxury automaker's brand identity and style of advertising. Asian Ads worked in tandem with Latino and African American agencies to promote Deluxis cars to a broad multicultural market. For the winter sales event, each multicultural agency was asked to create in-culture and in-language copy for a print ad sent by Deluxis's general market agency—a glamour shot of two silver cars on an icy surface in front of a bright blue sky, large snowflakes, and trees with ice-coated fronds (see Brief 2). The GM ad read, "This holiday season, celebrate two decades of inspired performance," and the multicultural agencies were asked to keep this message as consistent as possible in their in-language versions. Of the three versions Asian Ads was commissioned to make—Chinese Mandarin, Chinese Cantonese, and South Asian—I focus on the third, both because I understand Hindi and because it was the most contentious. The executives on the account included creative Stanley, a first-generation Chinese American man; account executive Joyce, a first-generation Chinese American woman; and freelance copywriter Jayshree, a South Asian American woman who had previously worked on Deluxis ads. The account team also asked Priya, a South Asian American account executive, to assist because Asian Ads did not then have a creative from this ethnic group.

BRIEF 2   Deluxis Winter Sales Event Brief

CREATIVE AGENCY BRIEF	
Client	Deluxis Automobiles
Agency	Asian Ads, New York, NY
Brand managers	Mike and Josie
Project	Winter Sales Event: In-language, in-culture print ad for South Asian American segment.
Overview	This is a campaign for the December holiday sales event.
Objective	We want our South Asian American consumers to buy a Deluxis car during a season they may not associate with holidays or car buying.
Target audience	Primary target will be 35–59-year-old men, with total household incomes of $100k+. The audience is familiar with the luxury car market and may already own one.
Reasons to believe and buy	Deluxis is a high-performing luxury automobile. We want them to know about our new financing options and cash back incentives.

Because the visuals were predetermined, the team focused on writ- *25*
ing copy with metalinguistic connotations that would work well with the
featured imagery. Jayshree admitted to me that it was a formidable challenge to find suitable terms for certain concepts and words in the GM
ad, including snowflakes and a winter "holiday season." Of course, many
South Asian Americans had experienced winter in the United States, but
snowflakes are not a preferred indexical sign for this audience. Moreover, the December holiday season is not one that most Hindu or Muslim
South Asian Americans associate with celebration in South Asia. Nonetheless, some culturally relevant sign was required to compel this group to
embrace the consumerism of the Judeo-Christian holidays. On Monday of
the week the ad copy was to be submitted to the client, Jayshree remarked
to account executive Sunil and me that the Deluxis copy had "vexed her
all weekend." She explained that car companies rely on their winter sales
events and that a seasonal promotion was a perfectly natural idea for
Deluxis but that she was having trouble generating a catchy phrase that
closely resembled the GM copy and that also had the right cultural resonance. Her copy, *"Dhoom machao, jashn manao! Yeh hai* two decades of
inspired performance," which she translated as "Have a blast, celebrate!
This is (here's to) two decades of inspired performance," was sent to the
client for review.

In a conference call with the client, the indexical meanings of this *26*
utterance came under intense scrutiny and debate. About twenty-eight
minutes into the call, when the client had already approved the Latino
concept as well as the two Chinese concepts, he voiced hesitation and
concern about the English back translation of the South Asian American
copy. In the following excerpt, Stanley, the creative, has just finished reading the transliterated Hindi copy for Mike, the client, and after a sizable
pause, Mike responds. Priya, the only Hindi speaker on the call, attempts
to address Mike's concerns.[5]

Excerpt: "Have a blast!"

1. Mike: Okay, so the: have a blast, celebration, is that,
2. what is the context in which that term would typically
3. be used?
4. (Team looks to Priya, who takes it as a cue to speak)
5. Priya: Um, typically for Indians, celebration and
6. festivity is larger than life, it means a punch line.
7. So "Dhoom machao! Jashn manao!" it's not as if you're
8. **going partying** and you're saying "Have a blast!"
9. It's more the background for have a blast, it's more
10. celebration, festivity. It's an expression, it's an

11. emotion, it's larger than life, happy. Being Indian
12. myself, I relate. When I read the line, I relate to it very
13. well. I think it is happy. It's happy thoughts, and
14. you read the line, and you immediately connect it
15. to what the message is, even in the body copy.
16. Mike: So it's basically saying "celebrate this, this event"
17. cele[brate, come celebrate with us]
18. Priya: [yes, right. Yes, celebrate the winter sales event.]
19. Be a part of it, have a blast.
20. Mike: And this is kind of arguing with that, but I guess
21. I shouldn't.
22. Many: ((Laughter))
23. Mike: My question is more content as I don't really
24. understand, the content feels a little over the top.
25. (Team looks to Priya again)
26. Priya: It's actually not too over the top. The actual
27. general market headline is "This holiday season,
28. celebrate two decades of inspired performance."
29. The Indian line is actually very similar to that, in fact
30. it's almost the same, it's just a little happier. Indians
31. are a little, it's a very common expression,
32. many Bollywood movies have this expression, it's
33. actually very common. I mean I—even in India
34. you see this line very commonly used, so I don't
35. think it's very over the top.

In this excerpt, Mike and the Asian Ads team introduce different indexical values for "Dhoom machao, jashn manao!" Even though Mike politely prefaces his disapproval with "and this is kind of arguing with that, but I guess I shouldn't" (lines 20–21), he nonetheless cannot reconcile the back translation of "Have a blast!" with the Deluxis brand identity and calls it "a little over the top" (line 24). In response, Priya defends the phrase's relevance and offers a justification for the choice. As a smart young executive with a newly minted marketing degree from a prestigious U.S. university, Priya seems to understand that what Mike is getting at is context: Is the phrase in question too irreverent or déclassé for this luxury brand? She attempts to clarify the connotations of the phrase in lines 5–15 though in doing so betrays her recent college graduate status: "It's not as if you're going partying and you're saying 'Have a blast' . . . it's more celebration, festivity." Additionally, she makes linkages with Bollywood and downplays the idea that the phrase is "over the top," but Mike remains skeptical. The call ended with Mike indicating that he will again consult his Indian American colleagues at Deluxis (who work in information technology, not marketing) to see how they respond to the copy. Asian Ads was soon notified that the client's colleagues did not respond favorably and that revised copy was required as soon as possible.

In this instance of metaproduction, Asian Ads' message was deemed potentially incongruous with the Deluxis brand and the identity of the intended consumer. Asif Agha's (1998, 2007) extensive investigations of the ways in which people make sense of speakers' identities offer another way to consider this outcome. He asserts, "Since our ideas about the identities of others are ideas about pragmatic phenomena, they are in principle metapragmatic constructs. In particular, such ideas are metapragmatic stereotypes about pragmatic phenomena" (Agha 1998:151). As values that are openly reportable, contestable, and consciously grasped, metapragmatic stereotypes of Asian American speakers are used to imagine audiences. What the average consumer sounds like and how he or she would respond to the talk of others are at stake here. Even though the Asian Ads team did not perceive a disconnect between their message and the brand identity, the client did. So did Sunil, the other Hindi speaker in the office. After learning that the client had rejected the team's idea, he joked quietly with Priya and me that for the summer sales event, "Jashn manao!" should be reworded "Garmi banao!"—"Make heat!"—which, of course, would be even more inappropriate for Deluxis because of its lewd connotations.

The case was particularly vexing for Jayshree because the client loved the copy she had written for earlier ads. For instance, in an ad for the G-series sedan fall sales event, the client had approved the playful phrase "G is for *josh*," A Hindi-Urdu speaker reading this ad may appreciate the clever play on the phoneme /j/ and its bivalent meaning in both English and Hindi. In the ad, the English G refers to the featured sedan model, and the same phoneme begins the word *josh*, which means "excitement." In this successful use of a metalinguistic sign, the second-order indexical value connotes sophistication and literacy. The intended consumer is not only wealdiy enough to purchase a luxury sedan but is also educated enough to be lured in by the wordplay in the ad. The message is refined, and the consumer is expected to be the same. To get to this place in the winter sales event, Jayshree offered a new version in which she removed "dhoom machao" and retooled the rest of the copy to read "Jashn manao! This is two decades of inspired performance," and translated it as "Celebrate! This is two decades of inspired performance." She also offered a second option, both of which were sent to the client for review.

During the next conference call, the Asian Ads team and client were finally able to agree on a metalinguistic sign that offered pleasing indexical meanings to both parties. Stanley described revisions made to the first option, "jashn manao," and then moved on to the second: "Additionally we also came up with another option, which if we pair with the visual, this would be an elegant visual, and that line reads 'Is haseen mausam, celebrate two decades of inspired performance.' The back translation is 'This beautiful, festive season, celebrate two decades of inspired performance.' And also with this I think we feel like we captured the [Deluxis] brand."

Stanley underscored those qualities indexed by the new copy and linked them to the visuals and the Deluxis brand identity. His use of the adjectives *elegant* and *beautiful* stands in stark contrast to "have a blast." To a Hindi-Urdu speaker, the poetic value of "Is haseen mausam" is indisputable. *Haseen* is an Urdu word conveying stunning beauty, and *mausam* is a word for weather with positive connotations of harvest, fertility, and traditional celebration. Both work well with the notion of a well-educated, wealthy, and discerning South Asian American consumer. The client ultimately approved this copy, and the Asian Ads team was pleased with and relieved by the outcome.

In this example of metaproduction, executives and clients clashed over the metapragmatic meaning of signs. Asian Ads considered the phrase "Dhoom machao, jashn manao!" to be an apt signifier of the wealth and refinement connoted by a luxury car. Hindi-Urdu speakers might positively associate it with weddings, lively festivals such as holi, in which colored powder is thrown on passersby, or even the short-lived Disney Channel India children's show whose title bears part of the phrase *(Dhoom Machao!)*. But in this instance, the client countered with its own second-order indexical meaning based on the English back translation and internal opinions to which the Asian Ads team was not privy.

Noteworthy here is the process by which the genre of Asian American advertising is created through the continuity it forms with ongoing representations of Asian Americans as model minorities. Richard Bauman and Charles L. Briggs note the "leakiness" and contingency of genre and argue, "Some elements of contextualization creep in, fashioning indexical connections to the ongoing discourse, social interaction, broader social relations, and the particular historical juncture(s) at which the discourse is produced and received" (1992:585). Drawing on Silverstein (1993), they add that metapragmatics must be considered when seeking to understand the production and reception of genre and that such a process may suppress some forms of intertextual variation and expand others (Bauman and Briggs 1992:586–587). In keeping with the elegant, refined identity of Deluxis, the Hindi phrase ultimately chosen offers second-order indexical values of education and sophistication. As Stanley's comments suggest, these are attributes of the modern identities the team wished to portray. Moreover, the ad offers new indexical meanings about seasons and holidays that are distinctly South Asian American.

The genre of Asian American advertising thus comprises the numerous campaigns and ads aimed at specific ethnic groups within the larger category. Here, the Deluxis ad offers a media-based representation of the ethnic group South Asian American as wealthy luxury-automobile drivers.

The final copy the client chose is arguably the more refined of the two options presented and indexes a more prestigious consumer. Likewise, the AC ad presents Chinese Americans as cultured, wealthy consumers. Taken together, these ads, along with scores of other campaigns, reflect the emergence of the genre of Asian American advertising as well as the racialization of Asian Americans. Metacultural and metalinguistic signs together index a new generation of powerful consumers and bring broader questions of racialization, metaproduction, and message to the fore.

Linking Metaproduction and Racialization

The above examples of metaproduction and message illustrate how executives create indexes for Asian American ethnic groups and, in turn, create the broader advertising genre. The work of Asian American ad executives raises questions of where Asian Americans fit in the sliding scale of U.S. racialization and what to make of the broader political-economic framework that governs ethnic advertising production. By observing their open discussions of negative stereotypes in agencies, at their annual conference, and in casual conversation, I came to believe that many who work in niche advertising are acutely aware of mass-mediated stereotypes of Asian Americans and the role advertising has played in perpetuating them. They are not only proud of the work they do but also see it as a counterpoint to past and current racist imagery of Asian Americans. For instance, during the early twentieth century, xenophobic sentiment crystallized in an ideology referred to as the "yellow peril" that at once characterized Asian Americans as dangerous invaders who required containment and as licentious, amoral, and infantile individuals in need of patriarchal control (Okihiro 1994). "Orientals," as they were called, were depicted on business or "trade" cards and their representations thus circulated through this mass-produced form of advertising (Matsukawa 2002; Metrick-Chen 2007). These earlier racializations underlay Asian exclusion acts and anti-Asian sentiment, ranging from anticitizenship and antimiscegenation laws to the World War II internment of Japanese Americans, and they continued to contribute to subsequent waves of hostility due to U.S. military conflict in Korea, Vietnam, and, most recently, the Middle East and Pakistan in a post–9/11 era.

The representations executives produce through metaproduction enable them to circulate a more modern and complex Asian American subjectivity than that tied to the anti-immigrant sentiment prevalent in previous generations of ads as well as in some contemporary general market advertising. Their work certainly differs from mainstream advertisements that have been critiqued for racist imagery that furthers xenophobic and anti-immigrant sentiment (Chávez 2001; Steele 2000), especially general market advertising that still features racist representations of Asian Americans (see Kim and Chung 2005; Knobloch-Westerwick and Coates

2006; Ono and Pham 2009). Just as in other studies that have demonstrated advertising to be an effective arena for cultural production that challenges dominant social meanings (Moeran 1996b), here metaproduction plays an important role in remaking the racial category of Asian American by countering simplistic racializations.

Through the genre of Asian American advertising, executives remake 36 core elements of the model minority stereotype into contemporary narratives of the economic solvency championed by neoliberalism to depict Asian Americans as refined professionals with sophisticated identities and tastes. The hardworking Asian American model minority producer, a staple of capitalist rhetoric and public policy since its 1960s introduction, emerges in a new form as the sophisticated model minority consumer. Executives use census and market research data to illustrate Asian Americans' high per capita income and willingness to spend money—even in the current recession. Their overall purchasing power outstrips their numbers—they make up a mere 5 percent of the total U.S. population. The newly minted version of the model Asian American enables ad executives to enter the marketplace of multicultural advertising and work alongside agencies that target the Latino and black markets in the United States. In this sense, neoliberal logics make this version of the Asian American appear new for marketing purposes, but it can also be considered another version of the same model minority stereotype that emerged from racialized capitalism. In this sense, this genre may be "no more than the reentextualization of what a different metadiscourse recognizes as an old text" (Silverstein and Urban 1996:13; cf. Bauman and Briggs 1992).

In attempting to counter negative general market representations of 37 Asian Americans while also reaching target audiences, Asian American advertising is delimiting this category to include a far more elite subsection of the population than the original model minority stereotype. In her astute analysis of the myriad gaps and erasures in the creation of the Latino category for advertising and marketing, Davila (2001) demonstrates how ethnonational history, varieties of Spanish, postcolonial histories, and numerous other inequalities are subsumed to make "Latinos Inc." Inasmuch as executives might like to make an analogous Asian Americans Inc., this unified category does not allow them to emphasize the very cultural and linguistic specificities that they must stress to reach individual Asian American ethnic groups. Apart from the occasional public-service ads for health issues or the U.S. Census, for instance, it is rarely beneficial for them to combine Chinese, Korean, South Asian, Filipino, and Vietnamese American populations under a single cultural and linguistic rubric. Language differences are a concern even within ethnic groups, as South Asian Americans may speak one of fifteen major languages and Chinese Americans may have strong ties to either Mandarin or Cantonese. Because the range of nations encompassed in the category "Asian" is so wide, and because different languages are needed for each, executives and their clients know that Asian American marketing almost always involves making several versions of an ad, each in-culture or in-language for a particular ethnic group. Despite admitting the impossibility of subsuming all of these specificities into a larger group, executives know that to win accounts alongside Latino and African American niche agencies, they have to convince clients that the category of Asian American, despite its myriad differences, is viable.

Through metaproducdon, executives shape individual ethnic groups   38 as they make campaigns, but they also conceive of and present the broader racial category of Asian American as a unified entity to survive in an industry that struggles with ethnic differentiation. In their everyday work, executives embrace this category by performing it for clients and to one another (see Shankar n.d.). As Asian Americans, they participate in complex social and economic networks, such as outsourcing aspects of media production to colleagues in Hong Kong, Taipei, Mumbai, Manila, and Shanghai; using contacts with agencies in Asia to find jobs in the United States, and collaborating with other Asian American ad agencies on various projects and objectives. Although they rarely used the term *diaspora*, the types of connections they maintained, the networks they leveraged, and the global nature of their work all confirmed the role of Asian diasporas in the creative and economic aspects of their industry. Especially at a time when clients are looking to commission fewer ads that reach more people, managing the somewhat unruly ethnolinguistic diversity of Asian Americans is critical for capitalist success.

The second-order indexical values used in metaproduction offer   39 insight into another dimension of racial refashioning: making model minority consumers that are so idealized that they obscure the diversity that this group includes. Executives capitalize on depicting immigrants of Asian descent as good citizens and good consumers by focusing on family, consumption, and other favorable attributes, but these emergent racial and ethnic definitions are detached from the politics of globalization that engender their conception. The complexity of the ever-shifting geopolitical relationship the United States has with different Asian nations is exactly what this type of advertising (and, to be fair, advertising anywhere) wants to sidestep altogether, and neoliberal discourses of individual economic success enable them to do this with considerable ease. Indeed, everyday realities of outsourcing jobs and production to Asia, the rising dominance of China and India in the global economy, and other indicators that draw attention to the powerful production capabilities of Asia, and, by extension, many members of its diasporas, are here dramatically downplayed.

In niche advertising, only the five most profitable Asian American   40 ethnic groups are included; others are excluded either because they are too small, such as Pacific Islanders, or because they are considered too assimilated, as in the case of Japanese Americans. Even within the five major groups, populations that are currently targets of political and social tension, including Muslims in a post–9/11 United States, tend to be avoided (see also Rana 2011). Working-class Asian Americans who may not be succeeding economically or socially or are otherwise not performing up to model minority expectations also fall through the cracks of this racial refashioning process. Of course, this "spin" is what disengages these representations from the political economy that underpins them, as Davila (2008) argues in the case of the "whitewashing" that occurs with Latinos. A significant point of contrast to note here between Latinos and Asian Americans is that the model minority stereotype seems to have addressed the issue of "whitewashing" already. Indeed, the notion of Asian Americans as "part of a solution," as Vijay Prashad (2000) puts it, has prevailed in popular media (see also Jun 2011; Lee 1997; Tuan 1998). In these ways, niche advertising is creating a racialized identity for Asian Americans that is distinct from that of white Americans but nonetheless positions them as good racial minorities and, of course, as good consumers.

From Media Margins to the U.S. Mainstream

I have offered metaproduction as a way to understand how messages cre- 41 ated by niche advertising and marketing play a central role in creating and circulating neoliberal meanings of race and ethnicity. A move from productive workers to neoliberal consumers can only be fully understood through a metaproduction framework, which illustrates how these values are created, negotiated, and put into circulation. Metaproduction relies on both metaculture and metalanguage, and message is hewn of linguistic and material elements. In this way, metaproduction can be seen as an example of "language materiality," a framework that draws attention to the ways in which the intertwining of the linguistic and material enable particular types of commodification and circulation in capitalism (Shankar and Cavanaugh 2012). As an analytic, metaproduction may also be useful to anthropological studies of cultural production more broadly, especially of art, festivals, and other types of media.

As the United States continues to diversify and move toward the 42 "majority minority" paradigm predicted by demographers, several points arise that constitute an agenda for further inquiry in this nascent niche industry. Longitudinal issues to consider include the question of language use and the second generation as immigration patterns shift. If the large-scale post-1965 professional immigration from Asia and subsequent waves are not to be repeated, and immigration is now curtailed in a United States gripped by the Patriot Act and the outsourcing of service and production work that previously drew new immigrants, what will become of the ethnic-language periodicals and satellite television stations? Will these media continue to be relevant to second- and third-generation Asian Americans, and will the need for niche advertising continue to grow? Equally pressing is the general market's treatment of ethnic and racial difference. As general market advertising struggles to keep pace with demographic shifts, such as the more than 100 million minority individuals counted in the 2010 census, who make up a third of the nation's population, will it turn to Asian American, Latino, and other niche executives for their expertise? There is already some evidence of this, as ads created for the Asian American niche market cross over into the mainstream.

Indeed, even though Asian American executives are making ads for 43 ethnic television stations, print periodicals, and Internet sites, these ads are beginning to shape broader racial and ethnic formation as they cross over to and circulate in mainstream media. Several of the campaigns I observed have at least one spot that executives identify as having "crossover potential," meaning it could effectively communicate brand identity to Asian American as well as mainstream audiences. Robert, a creative director at a prominent Los Angeles–based Asian American ad agency, confirmed this aspiration: "We really want to have creative strong enough to be used in the general market." He referred to a spot his agency had filmed just the day before our conversation, one that features a flirtatious dance battle between a male hip-hop dancer dressed in yellow and a female modern dancer dressed in red. Each does a dance in his or her own style to a steady bass backbeat and the occasional twangs of a Chinese stringed instrument, but ultimately the red and yellow come together, as they do in the featured product, "blended strawberry lemonade." Robert remarked that the client loved the spot and was considering running it in the general market, and that is precisely what happened. During spring 2011, this ad for McDonald's aired during prime time on NBC and other major West Coast television stations.

In this skillful execution of metaproduction, executives cast attractive 44 Asian American dancers, used music that blends hip-hop and a classical Chinese instrument, and set the spot in an airy, loft-style dance studio in downtown Los Angeles. The absence of dialogue in the ad makes it ready for general market consumption, and the result is an ad that easily appeals to youth, urban audiences, and, of course, Asian Americans. Comments posted on the YouTube page for the spot (see victorvictorkim 2011) reveal viewer excitement about seeing this ad on NBC, MTV, and several local and digital Asian channels and offer praise for the execution of the ad. Examples like these demonstrate that, as niche advertising crosses over into mainstream media, it reshapes edmicity and remakes race according to commercial agendas. These refashioned racializations, which may well be decontextualized from the political economy of the ethnic groups they feature, become embedded in that same neoliberal political economy as they circulate.

Acknowledgments

Research featured in this article was funded by the National Science Foundation Cultural Anthropology Program (grant 0924472) and Northwestern University. I am deeply indebted to the Asian American advertising agencies and advertising executives that supported my field research. I am grateful to Jillian Cavanaugh for ongoing conversations about this article and project as well as to Micaela di Leonardo, Jessica Winegar, and four anonymous reviewers for their thoughtful comments on drafts. My thanks to audiences at the University of Chicago, Emory University, and the University of Illinois at Urbana-Champaign for critical feedback on portions of this article, and to Angelique Haugerud for her editorial support. All errors are my own.

NOTES

1. I have replaced the names of individuals, agencies, corporate clients, and brands with pseudonyms. Names of places have not been changed.
2. Deborah Spitulnik's (1996) ethnographic analysis of how Zambian radio discourse is reentextualized in everyday talk has paved the way for understanding many such mediatized encounters. One of the key points of departure between metaproduction and mediatization is that the former addresses how individuals (in this case, ad executives) use metacultural and metalinguistic values in the process of production, whereas the latter investigates the generative capacity of mediated forms to shape local ideologies and identities through consumption. See *Journal of Linguistic Anthropology* 2010 and Agha 2011 for a variety of case studies about language and media consumption.
3. For consistency with other academic literature, I have chosen to use *South Asian American* rather than *Asian Indian*, the census term commonly used by executives. The latter designates a U.S. Census category that has since been refined to differentiate between Indians, Pakistanis, Bangladeshis, Sri Lankans, and others in the South Asian diaspora.
4. Elsewhere I examine the creation and development of brand in greater detail (Shankar n.d.). See also numerous recent works that offer critical insights on the production and management of brands (Arvidsson 2006; Lury 2006; Manning 2010; Moore 2003; Schroder and Salzer-Morling 2006)
5. Transcription key. "[ ]" overlap; "**bold**" speaker emphasis; "?" rising intonation.

REFERENCES CITED

Agha, Asif
    1998 Stereotypes and Registers of Honorific Language. Language in Society 27; 151–193.
    2007 Language and Social Relations. New York: Cambridge University Press.
Agha, Asif, ed.
    2011 Mediatized Communication in Complex Societies. Special issue, Language and Communication 31(3).
Arvidsson, Adam
    2006 Brands: Meaning and Value in Media Culture. London: Roudedge.
Bauman, Richard, and Charles L. Briggs
    1992 Genre, Intertextuality, and Social Power. In Language, Culture, and Society. Ben G. Blount, ed. Pp. 567–591. New York: Waveland.
Bhatia, T. K.
    1992 Discourse Functions and the Pragmatics of Mixing: Advertising across Cultures. World Englishes 11(1):195–215.
Cavanaugh, Jillian
    2005 Accent Matters: Material Consequences of Sounding Local in Northern Italy. Language and Communication 25:127–148.
Chávez, Leo
    2001 Covering Immigration: Popular Images and the Politics of the Nation. Berkeley: University of California Press.

Comaroff, John L., and Jean Comaroff
    2001 First Thoughts on a Second Coming. *In* Millennial Capitalism and the Culture
        of Neoliberalism. Jean Comaroff and John Comaroff, eds. Pp. 1–58. Durham,
        NC: Duke University Press.
Davila, Arlene
    2001. Latinos Inc.: The Marketing and Making of a People. Berkeley: University of
        California Press.
    2008 Latino Spin: Public Image and the Whitewashing of Race. New York: New
        York University Press, di Leonardo, Micaela
    2008 Introduction: New Global and American Landscapes of Inequality. *In* land-
        scapes of Inequality: Neoliberalism and the Erosion of Democracy in America.
        Jane Collins, Micaela di Leonardo, and Brett Williams, eds. Pp. 3–20. Santa Fe,
        NM: School for Advanced Research Press.
Foster, Robert
    2007 The Work of the New Economy: Consumers, Brands, and Value Creation.
        Cultural Anthropology 22(4):707–731.
Goldberg, David
    2009 The Threat of Race: Reflections on Racial Neoliberalism. Maiden, MA: Blackwell.
Harvey, David
    1989 The Condition of Postmodernity: An Enquiry into the Origins of Cultural
        Change. Malden, MA: Blackwell.
    2005 A Brief History of Neoliberalism. New York: Oxford University Press.
Hill, Jane H.
    2000 Ideological Complexity and the Overdetermination of Promising in Ameri-
        can Presidential Politics. *In* Regimes of Language. Paul V. Kroskrity, ed.
        Pp. 259–291. Santa Fe, NM: School of American Research Press.
Jameson, Frederic
    1991 Postmodernism or, the Cultural Logic of Late Capitalism. Durham, NC: Duke
        University Press.
Journal of Linguistic Anthropology
    2010 Media Ideologies. Special issue, Journal of Linguistic Anthropology 20(2).
Jun, Helen
    2011. Race for Citizenship: Black Orientalism and Asian Uplift from Pre-
        Emancipation to Neoliberal America. New York: New York University Press.
Keanc, Webb
    2003 Semiotics and the Social Analysis of Material Things. Language and Commu-
        nication 23 (3–4):409–425.
Kemper, Steven
    2001 Buying and Believing: Sri Lankan Advertising and Consumers in a Trans-
        national World. Chicago: University of Chicago Press.
Kim, Claire
    1999 The Racial Triangulation of Model Minorities. Politics and Society 27(1):
        105–138.
Kim, Minjeong, and Angie Chung
    2005 Consuming Orientalism: Images of Asian/American Women in Multicultural
        Advertising. Qualitative Sociology 28(1):67–91.
Knobloch-Westerwick, Silvia, and Brendon Coates
    2006 Minority Models in Advertisements in Magazines Popular with Minorities.
        Journalism and Mass Communication Quarterly B3(3):596–614.
Lee, Benjamin
    1997 Talking Heads: Language, Metalanguage, and the Semiotics of Subjectivity.
        Durham, NC: Duke University Press.
Lefkowitz, Daniel
    2003 Investing in Emotion: Love and Anger in Financial Advertising. Journal of
        Linguistic Andiropology 13(l):7l–97.
Lury, Celia
    2006 Brands: The Logos of the Global Economy. London: Routledge.

Malefyt, Timothy, and Brian Moeran, cds.
    2003 Advertising Cultures. Oxford: Berg.
Manning, Paul
    2010 The Semiotics of Brand. Annual Review of Anthropology 39:33–49.
Matsukawa, Yuko
    2002 Representing the Oriental in Nineteenth-Century Trade Cards. *In* Re-Collecting
        Early Asian America: Essays in Cultural History. Josephine Lee, Imogene Lim,
        and Yuko Matsukawa,eds. Pp. 200–217. Philadelphia: Temple University Press.
Mazzerella, William
    2003 Shoveling Smoke: Advertising and Globalization in Contemporary India.
        Durham, NC: Duke University Press.
Metrick-Chen, Lenore
    2007 The Chinese in the American Imagination: 19th Century Trade Card Images.
        Visual Anthropology Review 23(2):115–136.
Miller, Daniel
    1997 Capitalism: An Ethnographic Approach. London: Berg.
Moeran, Brian
    1996a A Japanese Advertising Agency: An Anthropology of Media and Markets.
        Honolulu: University of Hawai'i Press.
    1996b The Orient Strikes Back: Advertising and Imaging in Japan. Theory, Culture,
        and Society 13(3):77–112.
Moore, Robert
    2003 Prom Genericide to Viral Marketing: On Brand. Language and Communica-
        tion 23(3–4):331–358.
Okihiro, Gary
    1994 Margins and Mainstreams: Asians in American History and Culture. Seattle:
        University of Washington Press.
Ono, Kent A., and Vincent N. Pham
    2009 Asian Americans and the Media. Cambridge: Polity.
Parmentier, Richard J.
    1994 Signs in Society Studies in Semiotic Anthropology. Bloomington: Indiana
        University Press.
Piller, Ingrid
    2001 Identity Constructions in Multilingual Advertising. Language in Society 30:153–186.
Prashad, Vijay
    2000 The Karma of Brown Polk. Minneapolis: University of Minnesota Press.
Rana, Junaid
    2011 Terrifying Muslims: Race and Labor in the South Asian Diaspora. Durham,
        NC: Duke University Press.
Schroder, Jonadian E., and Miriam Salzer-Morling, eds.
    2006 Brand Culture. New York: Routledge.
Shankar, Shalini
    2006 Metaconsumption and the Circulation of Objectifications. Journal of Material
        Culture 11(3):293–317.
    2008 Desi J. and: Teen Culture, Class, and Success in Silicon Valley. Durham, NC:
        Duke University Press.
    N.d. Creating Model Consumers: Producing Race, Ethnicity, Gender, and Class in
        Asian American Advertising. Duke University Press (in preparation).
Shankar, Shalini, and Jillian Cavanaugh
    2012 Language and Materiality in Global Capitalism. Annual Review of Anthropol-
        ogy 41:355–369.
Silverstein, Michael
    1993 Metapragmatic Discourse and Metapragmatic Function. In Reflexive Lan-
        guage: Reported Speech and Metapragmatics. John A. Lucy, ed. Pp. 33–58.
        Cambridge: Cambridge University Press.
    2003 Indexical Order and the Dialectics of Sociolinguistic Life, Language and Com-
        munication 23(3–4): 193–229.

2005 Axes of Evals: Token Versus Type Interdiscursivity. Journal of Linguistic Anthropology 15(1):6–22.

2006 Old Wine, New Ethnographic Lexicography. Annual Review of Anthropology 35:481–496.

Silverstein, Michael, and Greg Urban
1996 The Natural History of Discourse. In The Natural Histories of Discourse. Michael Silverstein and Greg Urban, eds. Pp. 1–17. Chicago: University of Chicago Press.

Spitulnik, Deborah
1996 The Social Circulation of Media Discourse and the Mediation of Communities. Journal of Linguistic Anthropology 6(2):161–187.

Steele, Jeffrey
2000 Reduced to Images: American Indians in Nineteenth Century Advertising. In The Gender and Consumer Culture Reader. Jennifer R. Scanlon, ed. Pp. 109–128. New York: New York University Press.

Tuan, Mia
1998 Forever Foreigners or Honorary Whites? The Asian Ethnic Experience Today. New Brunswick, NJ: Rutgers University Press.

Urban, Greg
2001 Metaculture: How Cultures Move through the World. Minneapolis: University of Minnesota Press.

Victorvictorkim
2011 My McDonald's Commercial :). http://www.youtube.com/watch?v=qqlFuB7/2BA, accessed April 20, 2012.

■ ■ ■

Reading as a Writer: Analyzing Rhetorical Choices

1. There are likely some specialized words in Shankar's article that are new to you; mark them and look them up. In particular, you might look up the term *neoliberalism*, which she raises early in her piece and then explains in the context of her argument in her section titled "Creating Model Consumers."

2. How does Shankar's decision to include the advertising "briefs" and exact quotations from the marketing meetings contribute to your understanding of her argument?

Writing as a Reader: Entering the Conversation of Ideas

1. Both Shankar and Ann duCille are interested in the marketing of ethnicity. These writers explore the ways that concepts of difference and unique aspects of race and ethnicity are shaped by a market that must appeal effectively to many consumers. Place these writers in conversation with one another as you write an essay that explores the complexities and challenges of marketing the concept of "difference." Draw on some additional specific advertising examples beyond those in these readings if they will help you support your claims.

2. Like Shankar, Noël Sturgeon (Chapter 16), is interested in the process of training consumers to find certain products appealing. Compose an essay in which you consider the different ways each writer analyzes this process, and draw some conclusions about the significance you see in this strategy of marketing. What is at stake, and for whom, in this kind of marketing? What conclusions can you draw about the ethical dimension of this aspect of consumerism?

ANN DUCILLE

From Multicultural Barbie and the Merchandising of Difference

Ann duCille has served as the chair and director of the Center for African American Studies at Wesleyan University. She has published widely on black women writers and on race and popular culture, particularly in her book *Skin Trade* (1996), which won the Myers Center Award for the Study of Human rights in 1997. The essay here originally appeared in the Spring 1994 issue of *differences: A Journal of Feminist Cultural Studies.* In this piece about Barbie, you'll hear one of duCille's key interests in popular culture—the ways we all help establish cultural norms through producing and consuming goods and ideas.

A quick look through duCille's MLA-style Works Cited list at the end of the essay shows that she draws on a range of academic conversations to frame her analysis of Barbie. She responds not only to scholars who write about Barbie but also to those who write about adolescent self-image, raising African American children, and various aspects of multiculturalism and diversity. As you read duCille's essay, keep track of when and how she draws on those she calls "Barbiologists" and those whose ideas give context to her broader analysis of culture. You will have to make similar moves in your own writing as you use various sources to help you build your own point.

While she draws on many other scholars' ideas to help her build her point, duCille also invites readers to identify with her personal experiences, particularly in the opening and closing sections of the essay. How effectively do these personal anecdotes—her own and others'—draw you into the piece? How might they shed new light on toys you played with as a child, toys you may have forgotten all about? Considering the way culture teaches us to pay attention to both race and physical appearance as we think about who "we" are, duCille ends her essay by asking, "Is Barbie bad?" Her answer: "Barbie is just a piece of plastic, but what she says about the economic base of our society—what she suggests about gender and race in our world—ain't good." duCille should invite you to reconsider your own experiences with the "ideological work of child's play" (para. 5). If you ask the kinds of questions duCille asks of Barbie, you should discover similarly eye-opening answers

■ ■ ■

The white missionaries who came to Saint Aug's from New England were darling to us. They gave Bessie and me these beautiful china dolls that probably were very expensive. Those dolls were white, of course. You couldn't get a colored doll like that in those days. Well, I loved mine, just the way it was, but do you know what Bessie did? She took an artist's palette they had also given us and sat down and mixed the paints until she came up with a shade of brown that matched her skin. Then she painted that white doll's face! None of the white missionaries ever said a word about it. Mama and Papa just smiled. (Sarah Delany)

> This is my doll story (because every black journalist who writes about race gets around to it sometime). Back when I started playing with Barbie, there were no Christies (Barbie's black friend, born in 1968) or black Barbies (born in 1980, brown plastic poured into blond Barbie's mold). I had two blonds, which I bought with Christmas money from girls at school.
>
> I cut off their hair and dressed them in African-print fabric. They lived together (polygamy, I guess) with a black G.I. Joe bartered from the Shepp boys, my downstairs neighbors. After an "incident" at school (where all of the girls looked like Barbie and none of them looked like me), I galloped down our stairs with one Barbie, her blond head hitting each spoke of the banister, thud, thud, thud. And galloped up the stairs, thud, thud, thud, until her head popped off, lost to the graveyard behind the stairwell. Then I tore off each limb, and sat on the stairs for a long time twirling the torso like a baton. (Lisa Jones)

G rowing up in the 1950s, in the shadow of the second world war, it *1* was natural for children—including little black children like my two brothers and me—to want to play war, to mimic what we heard on the radio, what we watched in black and white on our brand new floor model Motorola. In these war games, everyone wanted to be the Allied troops—the fearless, conquering white male heroes who had made the world safe for democracy, yet again, and saved us all from yellow peril. No one, of course, wanted to play the enemy—who most often was not the Germans or the Italians but the Japanese. So the enemy became or, more rightly, remained invisible, lurking in bushes we shot at with sticks we pretended were rifles and slabbed at with make-believe bayonets. "Take that," we shouted, liberally peppering our verbal assaults with racial epithets. "And that! And that!" It was all in fun—our venom and vigor. All's fair in wars of words. We understood little of what we said and nothing of how much our child's play reflected the sentiments of a nation that even in its finer, pre-war moments had not embraced as citizens its Asian immigrants or claimed as countrymen and women their American-born offspring.

However naively imitative, our diatribe was interrupted forever one *2* summer afternoon by the angry voice of our mother, chastising us through the open window. "Stop that," she said. "Stop that this minute. It's not nice. You're talking about the Japanese. *Japanese*, do you understand? And don't let me ever hear you call them anything else." In the lecture that accompanied dinner that evening, we were made to understand not the history of Japanese-Americans, the injustice of internment, or the horror of Hiroshima, but simply that there were real people behind the names we called; that name-calling always hurts somebody, always undermines someone's humanity. Our young minds were led on the short journey from "Jap" to "nigger"; and if we were too young then to understand the origins and line points of all such pejoratives, we were old enough to know firsthand the pain of one of them.

I cannot claim that this early experience left me free of prejudice, but *3* it did assist me in growing up at once aware of my own status as "different" and conscious of the exclusion of others so labeled. It is important to note, however, that my sense of my own difference was affirmed and confirmed not simply by parental intervention but also by the unrelenting sameness of the tiny, almost exclusively white town in which I was raised. There in the country confines of East Bridgewater, Massachusetts, the adults who surrounded me (except for my parents) were all white, as were the teachers who taught me, the authors who thrilled me (and instilled in me a love of literature), and the neighborhood children who called me nigger one moment and friend the next. And when my brothers and I went our separate ways into properly gendered spheres, the dolls I played with—like almost everything else about my environment—were also white: Betsy Wetsy, Tiny Tears, and Patty Play Pal.

It seems remarkable to me now, as I remember these childish things 4 long since put away, that, for all the daily reminders of my blackness, I did not take note of its absence among the rubber-skin pinkness of Betsy Wetsy, the bald-headed whiteness of Tiny Tears, and the blue-eyed blondness of Patty Play Pal. I was never tempted like Sarah Delany to paint the dolls I played with brown like me or to dress them in African-print fabric like Lisa Jones. (Indeed, I had no notion of such fabrics and little knowledge of the "dark continent" from which they came.) Caught up in fantasy, completely given over to the realm of make-believe, for most of my childhood I neither noticed nor cared that the dolls I played with did not look like me. The make-believe world to which I willingly surrendered more than just my disbelief was thoroughly and profoundly white. That is to say, the "me" I invented, the "I" I imagined, the Self I day-dreamed in technicolor fantasies was no more black like me than the dolls I played with. In the fifties and well into the sixties of my childhood, the black Other who was my Self, much like the enemy Other who was the foreign body of our war games, could only be imagined as faceless, far away, and utterly unfamiliar.

As suggested by my title, I am going to use the figure of multicultural 5 Barbie to talk about the commodification of race and gender difference. I wanted to back into the present topic, however, into what I have to say about Barbie as a gendered, racialized icon of contemporary commodity culture, by reaching into the past—into the admittedly contested terrain of the personal—to evoke the ideological work of child's play. More than simple instruments of pleasure and amusement, toys and games play crucial roles in helping children determine what is valuable in and around them. Dolls in particular invite children to replicate them, to imagine themselves in their dolls' images. What does it mean, then, when little girls are given dolls to play with that in no way resemble them? What did it mean for me that I was nowhere in the toys I played with?

If the Japan and the Africa of my youth were beyond the grasp (if not the 6 reach) of my imagination, children today are granted instant global gratification in their play—immediate, hands-on access to both Self and Other. Or so we are told by many of the leading fantasy manufacturers— Disney,

Hasbro, and Mattel, in particular—whose contributions to multicultural education include such play things as Aladdin (movie, video, and dolls), G.I. Joe (male "action figures" in black and white), and Barbie (now available in a variety of colors and ethnicities). Disneyland's river ride through different nations, like Mattel's Dolls of the World Collection, instructs us that "It's a Small World After All." Those once distant lands of Africa, Asia, Australia, and even the Arctic regions of the North Pole (yes, Virginia, there is an Eskimo Barbie) are now as close to home as the local Toys R Us and F.A.O. Schwarz. And lo and behold, the inhabitants of these foreign lands—from Disney's Princess Jasmine to Mattel's Jamaican Barbie—are just like us, dye-dipped versions of archetypal white American beauty. It is not only a small world after all, but, as the Grammy award-winning theme from *Aladdin* informs us, "it's a whole new world."

Many of the major toy manufacturers have taken on a global perspec-   7
tive, a kind of nearsightedness that constructs this whole new world as small and cultural difference as consumable. Perhaps nowhere is this universalizing myopia more conspicuous than in the production, marketing, and consumption of Barbie dolls. By Mattel's reckoning, Barbie enjoys 100 percent brand name recognition among girls ages three to ten, 96 percent of whom own at least one doll, with most owning an average of eight. Five years ago, as Barbie turned thirty, *Newsweek* noted that nearly 500 million Barbies had been sold, along with 200 million G.I. Joes—"enough for every man, woman, and child in the United States and Europe" (Kantrowitz 59–60). Those figures have increased dramatically in the past five years, bringing the current world-wide Barbie population to 800 million. In 1992 alone, $1 billion worth of Barbies and accessories were sold. Last year, Barbie dolls sold at an average of one million per week, with overall sales exceeding the $1 billion all-time high set the year before. As the *Boston Globe* reported on the occasion of Barbies thirty-fifth birthday on March 9, 1994, nearly two Barbie dolls are sold every second somewhere in the world; about 50 percent of the dolls sold are purchased here in the United States (Dembner 16).

The current Barbie boom may be in part the result of new, multicul-   8
turally oriented developments both in the dolls and in their marketing. In the fall of 1990, Mattel, Inc. announced a new marketing strategy to boost its sales: the corporation would "go ethnic" in its advertising by launching an ad campaign for the black and Hispanic versions of the already popular doll. Despite the existence of black, Asian, and Latina Barbies, prior to the fall of 1990 Mattel's print and TV ads featured only white dolls. In what *Newsweek* described as an attempt to capitalize on ethnic spending power, Mattel began placing ads for multicultural Barbies in such Afrocentric publications as *Essence* magazine and on such Latin-oriented shows as *Pepe Plata* after market research revealed that most black and Hispanic consumers were unaware of the company's ethnic dolls. This targeted advertising was a smart move, according to the industry analysts cited by *Newsweek*, because "Hispanics buy about $170 billion worth of

goods each year, [and] blacks spend even more." Indeed, sales of black Barbie dolls reportedly doubled in the year following this new ethnically-oriented ad campaign.[1] But determined to present itself as politically correct as well as financially savvy, Mattel was quick to point out that ethnic audiences, who are now able to purchase dolls who look like them, also have profited from the corporation's new marketing priorities. Barbie is a role model for all of her owners, according to product manager Deborah Mitchell, herself an African American. "Barbie allows little girls to dream," she asserted—to which the *Newsweek* reporter added (seemingly without irony): "now, ethnic Barbie lovers will be able to dream in their own image" (Berkwitz 48).

Dream in their own image? The *Newsweek* columnist inadvertently *9* put his finger on precisely what is so troubling to many parents, feminist scholars, and cultural critics about Barbie and dolls like her. Such toys invite, inspire, and even demand a potentially damaging process not simply of imagining but of interpellation. When little girls fantasize themselves into the conspicuous consumption, glamour, perfection, and, some have argued, anorexia of Barbie's world, it is rarely, if ever, "in their own image that they dream."[2] Regardless of what color dyes the dolls are dipped in or what costumes they are adorned with, the image they present is of the same mythically thin, long-legged, luxuriously-haired, buxom beauty. And while Mattel and other toy manufacturers may claim to have the best interests of ethnic audiences in mind in peddling their integrated wares, one does not have to be a cynic to suggest that profit remains the motivating factor behind this merchandising of difference.[3]

Far from simply playing with the sixty or so dolls I have acquired in *10* the past year, then, I take them very seriously. In fact, I regard Barbie and similar dolls as Louis Althusser might have regarded them: as objects

[1] Mattel introduced the Shani doll—a black, Barbie-like doll—in 1991, which also may have contributed to the rise in sales, particularly since the company engaged the services of a PR firm that specializes in targeting ethnic audiences.

[2] Of course, the notion of "dreaming in one's own image" is always problematic since dreams, by definition, engage something other than the "real."

[3] Olmec Toys, a black-owned company headed by an African American woman named Yla Eason, markets a line of black and Latina Barbie-like dolls called the Imani Collection. Billed on their boxes as "African American Princess" and "Latin American Fantasy," these dolls are also presented as having been designed with the self images of black children in mind. "We've got one thing in mind with all our products," the blurbs on the Imani boxes read: "let's build self-esteem. Our children gain a sense of self importance through toys. So we make them look like them." Given their obvious resemblance to Barbie dolls—their long, straight hair and pencil-thin plastic bodies—Imani dolls look no more "like them," like "real" black children, than their prototype. Eason, who we are told was devastated by her son's announcement that he couldn't be a superhero because he wasn't white, may indeed want to give black children toys to play with that "look like them." Yet, in order to compete in a market long dominated by Mattel and Hasbro, her company, it seems, has little choice but to conform to the Barbie mold.

that do the dirty work of patriarchy and capitalism in the most insidious way—in the guise of child's play. But, as feminists have protested almost from the moment she hit the market, Barbie is not simply a child's toy or just a teenage fashion doll; she is an icon—perhaps *the* icon—of true white womanhood and femininity, a symbol of the far from innocent ideological stuff of which the (Miss) American dream and other mystiques of race and gender are made.

Invented by Ruth Handler, one of the founders of Mattel, and named *11* after her daughter, Barbie dolls have been a very real force in the toy market since Mattel first introduced them at the American Toy Fair in 1959. In fact, despite the skepticism of toy store buyers—who at the time were primarily men—the first shipment of a half million dolls and a million costumes sold out immediately (Larcen A7). The first Barbies, which were modeled after a sexy German doll and comic strip character named Lilli, were all white, but in 1967 Mattel premiered a black version of the doll called "Colored Francie." "Colored Francie," like white "Francie Fairchild" introduced the year before, was supposed to be Barbie's "MODern" younger cousin. As a white doll modeled and marketed in the image of Hollywood's Gidget, white Francie had been an international sensation, but Colored Francie was not destined to duplicate her prototype's success. Although the "black is beautiful" theme of both the civil rights and black power movements may have suggested a ready market for a beautiful black doll, Colored Francie in fact did not sell well.

Evelyn Burkhalter, owner, operator, and curator of the Barbie Hall of *12* Fame in Palo Alto, California—home to 16,000 Barbie dolls—attributes Colored Francie's commercial failure to the racial climate of the times. Doll purchasing patterns, it seems, reflected the same resistance to integration that was felt elsewhere in the nation. In her implied family ties to white Barbie, Colored Francie suggested more than simple integration. She implied miscegenation: a make-believe mixing of races that may have jeopardized the doll's real market value. Cynthia Roberts, author of Barbie: *Thirty Years of America's Doll* (1989), maintains that Colored Francie flopped because of her straight hair and Caucasian features (44), which seemingly were less acceptable then than now. No doubt Mattel's decision to call its first black Barbie "Colored Francie" also contributed to the doll's demise. The use of the outmoded, even racist term "colored" in the midst of civil rights and black power activism suggested that while Francie might be "MODern," Mattel was still in the dark(y) ages. In any case, neither black nor white audiences bought the idea of Barbie's colored relations, and Mattel promptly took the doll off the market, replacing her with a black doll called Christie in 1968.

While a number of other black dolls appeared throughout the late *13* sixties and seventies—including the Julia doll, modeled after the TV character played by black singer and actress Diahann Carroll—it was not until 1980 that Mattel introduced black dolls that were called Barbie like their white counterparts. Today, Barbie dolls come in a virtual rainbow coalition of colors, races, ethnicities, and nationalities—most of which look remarkably like the prototypical white Barbie, modified only by a dash of color and a change of costume. It is these would-be multicultural "dolls of the world"—Jamaican Barbie, Nigerian and Kenyan Barbie, Malaysian Barbie, Chinese Barbie, Mexican, Spanish, and Brazilian Barbie, et cetera, etcetera, etcetera—that interest me. For me these dolls are at once a symbol and a symptom of what multiculturalism has become at the hands of contemporary commodity culture: an easy and immensely profitable way off the hook of Eurocentrism that gives us the face of cultural diversity without the particulars of racial difference.

If I could line up across the page the ninety "different" colors, cultures, and other incarnations in which Barbie currently exists, the fact of her unrelenting sameness (or at least similarity) would become immediately apparent. Even two dolls might do the trick: "My First Barbie" in white and "My First Barbie" in black, for example, or white "Western Fun Barbie" and black "Western Fun Barbie." Except for their dye jobs, the dolls are identical: the same body, size, shape, and apparel. Or perhaps I should say *nearly* identical because in some instances—with black and Asian dolls in particular—coloring and other subtle changes (stereotypically slanted eyes in the Asian dolls, thicker lips in the black dolls) suggest differently coded facial features. _14_

In other instances, when Barbie moves across cultural as opposed to racial lines, it is costume rather than color that distinguishes one ethnic group or nation from another. Nigeria and Jamaica, for instance, are represented by the same basic brown body, dolled-up in different native garbs—or Mattel's interpretation thereof.[4] With other costume changes, this generic black body becomes Western Fun Barbie or Marine Barbie or Desert Storm Barbie, and even Presidential Candidate Barbie, who, by the way, comes with a Nancy Reagan-red taking-care-of-business suit as well as a red, white, and blue inaugural ball gown. Much the same is true of the generic Asian doll—sometimes called Kira—who reappears in a variety of different dress-defined ethnicities. In other words, where Barbie is concerned, clothes not only make the woman, they mark the racial and/or cultural difference. _15_

[4]After many calls to the Jamaican Embassy in Washington, D.C., and to various cultural organizations in Jamaica, I have determined that Jamaican Barbie's costume—a floor-length granny-style dress with apron and headrag—bears some resemblance to what is considered the island's traditional folk costume. I am still left wondering about the decision-making process, however: why the doll representing Jamaica is figured as a maid, while the doll representing Great Britain, for example, is presented as a lady—a blonde, blue-eyed Barbie doll dressed in a fancy riding habit with boots and hat.

Such difference is marked as well by the cultural history and language   *16*
lessons that accompany each doll in Mattel's international collection. The
back of Jamaican Barbie's box tells us, for example, *"How-you-du* (Hello)
from the land of Jamaica, a tropical paradise known for its exotic fruit,
sugar cane, breathtaking beaches, and reggae beat!" The box goes on to
explain that most Jamaicans have ancestors from Africa. Therefore, "even
though our official language is English, we speak patois, a kind of *'Jamaica
Talk,'* filled with English and African words." The lesson ends with a brief
glossary (eight words) and a few more examples of this "Jamaica Talk,"
complete with translations: *"A hope yu wi come-a Jamaica!* (I hope you will
come to Jamaica!)" and *"Teck care a yusself, mi fren!* (Take care of yourself,
my friend!)."* A nice idea, I suppose, but for me these quick-and-dirty eth-
nographies only enhance the extent to which these would-be multicultural
dolls treat race and ethnic difference like collectibles, contributing more
to commodity culture than to the intercultural awareness they claim to
inspire.

Is the current fascination with the black or colored body—especially   *17*
the female body—a contemporary version of the primitivism of the 1920s?
Is multiculturalism to postmodernism what primitivism was to modernism? It was while on my way to a round table discussion on precisely this
question lhal I bought my first black Barbie dolls in March of 1993. As
carbon copies of an already problematic original, these colorized Mattel
toys seemed to me the perfect tools with which to illustrate the point I
wanted to make about the collapse of multiculturalism into an easy pluralism that simply adds what it constructs as the Other without upsetting the
fundamental precepts and paradigms of Western culture or, in the case of
Mattel, without changing the mold.

Not entirely immune to such critiques, Mattel sought expert advice   *18*
from black parents and early childhood specialists in the development
and marketing of its newest line of black Barbie dolls. Chief among the
expert witnesses was clinical psychologist Darlene Powell Hopson, who
coauthored with her husband Derek S. Hopson a study of racism and child
development entitled *Different and Wonderful: Raising Black Children in a
Race-Conscious Society* (1990). As part of their research for the book, the
Hopsons repeated a ground-breaking study conducted by black psychologists Kenneth and Mamie Clark in the 1940s.

The Clarks used black and white dolls to demonstrate the negative   *19*
effects of racism and segregation on black children. When given a choice
between a white doll and a black doll, nearly 70 percent of the black children in the study chose the white doll. The Clarks' findings became an
important factor in *Brown v. the Board of Education* in 1954. More recently,
some scholars have called into question not necessarily the Clarks' findings
but their interpretation: the assumption that, in the realm of make-believe,
a black child's choosing a white doll necessarily reflects a negative self

concept.[5] For the Hopsons, however, the Clarks' research remains compelling. In 1985 they repeated the Clarks' doll test and found that an alarming 65 percent of the black children in their sample chose a white doll over a black one. Moreover, 76 percent of the children interviewed said that the black dolls "looked bad" to them (Hopson xix).

In addition to the clinical uses they make of dolls in their experiments, *20* the Hopsons also give considerable attention to what they call "doll play" in their book, specifically mentioning Barbie. "If your daughter likes 'Barbie' dolls, by all means get her Barbie," they advise black parents. "But also choose Black characters from the Barbie world. *You do not want your child to grow up thinking that only White dolls, and by extension White people, are attractive and nice*" (Hopsons 127, emphasis original). (Note that "Barbie," unmodified in the preceding passage, seems to mean white Barbie dolls.) The Hopsons suggest that parents should not only provide their children with black and other ethnic dolls but that they should get involved in their children's doll play. "Help them dress and groom the dolls while you compliment them both," they advise, offering the following suggested routine: "'This is a beautiful doll. It looks just like you. Look at her hair. It's just like yours. Did you know your nose is as pretty as your doll's?'" (119). They also suggest that parents use "complimentary words such as *lovely, pretty, or nice* so that [the] child will learn to associate them with his or her own image" (124).

Certainly it is important to help children feel good about themselves. *21* One might argue, however, that the "just like you" simile and the beautiful doll imagery so central to these suggestions for what the Hopsons call positive play run the risk of transmitting to the child a colorized version of the same old beauty myth. Like Barbie dolls themselves, they make beauty—and by implication worth—a matter of physical characteristics.

In spite of their own good intentions, the Hopsons, in linking play *22* with "beautiful" dolls to positive self-imagining, echoed Mattel's own marketing campaign. It is not surprising, then, that the Hopsons' findings and the interventional strategies they designed for using dolls to instill ethnic pride caught the attention of Mattel. In 1990 Darlene Hopson was asked to consult with the corporation's product manager Deborah Mitchell and designer Kitty Black-Perkins—both African Americans—in the development of a new line of "realistically sculpted" black fashion dolls. Hopson agreed and about a year later Shani and her friends Asha and Nichelle became the newest members of Barbie's ever-expanding family.

---

[5] See among others Morris Rosenberg's books Conceiving the Self (1979) and Society and the Adolescent Self-image (1989) and William E. Cross's Shades of Black: Diversity in African American Identity (1991), all of which challenge the Clarks' findings. Cross argues, for example, that the Clarks confounded or conflated two different issues: attitude toward race in general and attitude toward the self in particular. How one feels about race is not necessarily an index of one's self-esteem

Shani means "marvelous" in Swahili, according to the dolls' press kit. *23*
But as *Village Voice* columnist Lisa Jones has noted, the name has other
meanings as well: "startling, a wonder, a novelty" (36). My own research
indicates that while Shani is a Swahili female name meaning marvelous, the Kiswahili word "shani" translates as "an adventure, something
unusual" (Stewart 120). So it seems that Mattel's new play thing is not just
marvelous, too marvelous for words, but, as her name also suggests, she is
difference incarnate—a novelty, a new enterprise, or, perhaps, as the black
female Other so often is, an exotic. Mattel, it seems to me, both plays up
and plays on what it presents as the doll's exotic black-is-beautiful difference. As the back of her package reads:

> Shani means marvelous in the Swahili language . . . and marvelous she is!
> With her friends Asha and Nichelle, Shani brings to life the special style and
> beauty of the African American woman.
>
> Each one is beautiful in her own way, with her own lovely skin shade and
> unique facial features. Each has a different hair color and texture, perfect
> for braiding, twisting, and creating fabulous hair styles! Their clothes, too,
> reflect the vivid colors and ethnic accents that showcase their *exotic looks*
> and fashion flair!
>
> Shani, Asha, and Nichelle invite you into their glamorous world to share
> the fun and excitement of being a top model. Imagine appearing on maga-
> zine covers, starring in fashion shows, and going to Hollywood parties as
> you, Shani, Asha, and Nichelle live your dreams of beauty and success,
> loving every marvelous minute! (emphasis added)

While these words attempt to convey a message of black pride—after the
fashion of the Hopsons' recommendations for positive play—that message is clearly tied to bountiful hair, lavish and exotic clothes, and other
outward and visible signs not of brains but of beauty, wealth, and success.
Shani may be a top fashion model, but don't look for her (or, if Mattel's
own oft-articulated theory of Barbie as role model holds, yourself or your
child) at M.I.T.

Like any other proud, well-to-do parents of a debutante, Mattel gave *24*
Shani her own coming out party at the International Toy Fair in February of 1991. This gala event included a tribute to black designers and an
appearance by En Vogue singing the Negro National Anthem, "Lift Every
Voice and Sing!"—evidently the song of choice of the doll Mattel describes
as "tomorrow's African American woman." Also making their debuts were
Shani's friends Asha and Nichelle, notable for the different hues in which
their black plastic skin comes—an innovation due in part to Darlene Hopson's influence. Shani, the signature doll of the line, is what we call in the
culture "brown-skinned"; Asha is honey-colored (some would say "high-
yella"); and Nichelle is deep mahogany. Their male friend Jamal, added in
1992, completes the collection.

For the un(make-)believing, the three-to-one ratio of the Shani *25*
quartet—three black females to one black male—may be the most realistic thing about these dolls. In the eyes and the advertising of Mattel,

however, Shani and her friends are the most authentic black female thing the mainstream toy market has yet produced. "Tomorrow's African American woman" (an appellation which, as Lisa Jones has noted, both riffs and one-ups *Essence's* "Today's Black Woman") has broader hips, fuller lips, and a broader nose, according to product manager Deborah Mitchell. Principal designer Kitty Black-Perkins, who has dressed black Barbies since their birth in 1980, adds that the Shani dolls are also distinguished by their unique, culturally-specific clothes in "spice tones, [and] ethnic fabrics," rather than "fantasy colors like pink or lavender" (qtd. in Jones 36)—evidently the colors of the faint of skin.

The notion that fuller lips, broader noses, wider hips, and higher der-   26
riéres somehow make the Shani dolls more realistically African American raises many difficult questions about authenticity, truth, and the ever-problematic categories of the real and the symbolic, the typical and the stereotypical. Just what are we saying when we claim that a doll does or does not "look black"? How does black look? What would it take to make a doll look authentically African American? What preconceived, prescriptive ideals of legitimate blackness are inscribed in such claims of authenticity? How can doll manufacturers or any other image makers—the film industry, for example—attend to cultural, racial, and phenotypical differences without merely engaging the same simplistic big-lips/broad-hips stereotypes that make so many of us—blacks in particular—grit our (pearly white) teeth? What would it take to produce a line of dolls that more fully reflects the wide variety of sizes, shapes, colors, hair styles, occupations, abilities, and disabilities that African Americans—like all people—come in? In other words: what price difference? . . .

The Body Politic(s) of Barbie

> Barbie's body is a consumer object itself, a vehicle for the display of clothing and the spectacular trappings of a wealthy teenage fantasy life. Her extraordinary body exists not simply as an example of the fetishized female form typical of those offered up to the male gaze, but as a commodity vehicle itself whose form seduces the beholder and sells accessories, the real source of corporate profit. Like Lay's chips, no one can buy just one outfit for the doll. Barbie is the late capitalist girl incarnate. (McCombie)

In focusing thus far on the merchandising of racial, perhaps more   27
so than gender, difference, I do not mean to imply that racial and gender identities are divisible, even in dolls. Nor, in observing that most if not all of Mattel's "dolls of the world" look remarkably like what the company calls the "traditional, blond, blue-eyed Barbie," do I mean to suggest that the seemingly endless recapitulation of the white prototype is the only way in which these dolls are problematic. In fact, the most alarming thing about Barbie may well be the extent to which she functions as what M. G. Lord calls a teaching tool for femininity, whatever her race or ethnicity.

Lord, the author of *Forever Barbie: The Unauthorized Biography of a Real Doll*, due out later this year, describes Barbie as a "space-age fertility icon. She looks like a modern woman, but she's a very primitive totem of female power" (qtd. in Dembner 1).

Barbie has long had the eye and ire of feminists, who, for the most 28
part, have reviled her as another manifestation of the damaging myths of female beauty and the feminine body that patriarchy perpetuates through such vehicles as popular and commodity culture. A counter narrative also exists, however, one in which Barbie is not an empty-headed, material girl bimbo, for whom math class is tough, but a feminist heroine, who has been first in war (a soldier who served in the Gulf, she has worn the colors oi her country as well as the United Colors of Benetton), first in peace (she held her own summit in 1990 and she's a long-time friend of UNICEF, who "loves all the children of the world"), and always first in the hearts of her country (Americans buy her at the rate of one doll every second). While time does not allow me to reiterate or to assess here all the known critiques and defenses of Barbie, I do want to discuss briefly some of the gender ideals that I think are encoded in and transmitted by this larger than-life little woman and what Barbie's escalating popularity says about contemporary American culture.

In *Touching Liberty: Abolition, Feminism, and the Politics of the Body* 29
(1993), Karen Sanchez-Eppler argues that all dolls are intended to teach little girls about domesticity (133). If such tutelage is Barbie's not so secret mission, her methodology is far more complex and contradictory than that of the Betsy Welsy and Tiny Tears baby dolls I played with thirty-five years ago. Those dolls invoked and evoked the maternal, as they and the baby bottles and diapers with which they were packaged invited us to nestle, nurse, and nurture. Barbie's curvaceous, big-busted, almost fully female body, on the other hand, summons not the maternal but the sexual, not the nurturant mother but the sensuous woman. As Mel McCombie has argued, rather than rehearsing parenting, as a baby doll does, Barbie's adult body encourages children to dress and redress a fashion doll that yields lessons about sexuality, consumption, and teenage life (3). Put another way, we might say that Barbie is literally and figuratively a titillating toy.

Bodacious as they may be, however, Barbie's firm plastic breasts have 30
no nipples—nothing that might offend, nothing that might suggest her own pleasure. And if her protruding plastic mounds signify a simmering sensuality, what are we to make of her missing genitalia? McCombie suggests that Barbie's genital ambiguity can be read as an "homage to 'good taste'" and as a "reflection of the regnant mores for teenage girls—to be both sexy and adult yet remain virginal" (4). I agree that her body invites such readings, but it also seems to me that there is nothing ambiguous about Barbie's crotch. It's missing in inaction. While male dolls like Ken and Jamal have bumps "down there" and in some instances simulated underwear etched into the plastic, most Barbies come neither with drawers nor with even a hint of anything that needs covering, even as "it" is

already covered or erased. As an icon of idealized femininity, then, Barbie is locked into a never-never land in which she must be always already sexual without the possibility of sex. Conspicuously sensual on top but definitively nonsexual below, her plastic body indeed has inscribed within it the very contradictory, whore/madonna messages with which patriarchy taunts and even traumatizes young women in particular.

This kind of speculation about Barbie's breasts has led the doll's creator, Ruth Handler, to chide adults for their nasty minds. "In my opinion people make too much of breasts," Handler has complained. "They are just part of the body" (qtd. in BillyBoy 20). Mrs. Handler has a point (or maybe two). I feel more than just a little ridiculous myself as I sit here contemplating the body parts and sex life of a piece of plastic. What is fascinating, however, what I think is worth studying, what both invites and resists theorizing, is not the lump of molded plastic that is Barbie, but the imaginary life that is not—that is our invention. Barbie as a cultural artifact may be able to tell us more about ourselves and our society—more about society's attitudes toward its women—than anything we might say about the doll her or, rather, *itself*.

In the nineteenth century, Alexis de Tocqueville and others argued that you could judge the character, quality, and degree of advancement of a civilization by the status and treatment of its women. What is the status of women in soon to be twenty-first-century America, and can Barbie serve as a barometer for measuring that status? Barbie, it seems to me, is a key player in the process of socialization—of engendering and racialization—that begins in infancy and is furthered by almost everything about our society, including the books children read, the toys they play with, and the cartoons they watch on television.

While changing channels one Saturday morning, I happened upon a cartoon, just a glimpse of which impelled me to watch on. At the point that I tuned in, a big, gray, menacingly male bulldog was barking furiously at a pretty, petite, light-colored cat, who simply batted her long lashes, meowed coquettishly, and rubbed her tiny feline body against his huge canine leg in response. The more the dog barked and growled, the softer the cat meowed, using her slinky feline body and her feminine wiles to win the dog over. Her strategy worked; before my eyes—and, I imagine, the eyes of millions of children—the ferocious beast was transformed into a lovesick puppy dog, who followed the cat everywhere, repeatedly saving her from all manner of evil and danger. Time and time again, the bulldog rescued the helpless, accident-prone pussy from falling girders, oncoming traffic, and other hazards to which she, in her innocent frailty, was entirely oblivious. By the end, the once ferocious bulldog was completely domesticated, as his no longer menacing body became a kind of bed for the cat to nestle in.

There are, of course, a number of ways to read the gender and racial politics of this cartoon. I suppose that the same thought process that theorizes Barbie as a feminist heroine for whom men are mere accessories might claim the kitty cat, too, as a kind of feminist feline, who uses her feminine wiles to get her way. What resonates for me in the cartoon, however, are its beauty and the beast, light/dark, good/evil, female/male, race and gender codes: light, bright, cat-like femininity tames menacing black male bestiality. Make no mistake, however; it is not wit that wins out over barbarism but a mindless, can't-take-care-of-herself femininity.

Interestingly enough, these are the kinds of messages of which fairy 35 tales and children's stories are often made. White knights rescue fair damsels in distress from dark, forbidding evils of one kind or another. As Darlene and Derek Hopson argue: "Some of the most blatant and simplistic representations of white as good and black as evil are found in children's literature," where evil black witches and good white fairies—heroes in white and villains in black—abound (121).

What Barbie dolls, cartoons like the one outlined above, and even the 36 seemingly innocent fairy tales we read to our children seem to me to have in common are the mythologies of race and gender that are encoded in them. Jacqueline Urla and Alan Swedlund maintain that Barbie's body type constructs the bodies of other women as deviant and perpetuates an impossible standard of beauty. Attempting to live up to the Barbie ideal, others argue, fosters eating and shopping disorders in teenage girls—nightmares instead of dreams. BillyBoy, one of Barbie's most ardent supporters, defends his heroine against such charges by insisting that there is nothing abnormal about the proportions of Barbie's body. Rather, he asserts, "she has the ideal that Western culture has insisted upon since the 1920s: long legs, long arms, small waist, high round bosom, and long neck" (22). The irony is that BillyBoy may be right. "Unrealistic" or not, Barbie's weight and measurements (which if proportionate to those of a woman 5'6" tall would be something like 110 pounds and a top-heavy 39–18–33) are not much different from those of the beauty queens to whom Bert Parks used to sing "Here she is, Miss America. Here she is, our ideal."[6] If Barbie is a monster, she is our monster, our ideal.

"But is Barbie bad?" Someone asked me the other day if a black doll 37 that looks like a white doll isn't better than no black doll at all. I must admit that I have no ready answer for this and a number of other questions posed by my own critique. Although, as I acknowledged in the beginning, the dolls I played with as a child were white, I still remember the first time I saw a black doll. To me, she was the most beautiful thing I had ever seen; I wanted her desperately, and I was never again satisfied with white Betsy Wetsy and blonde, blue-eyed Patty Play Pal. She was something else,

---

[6]In response to criticism from feminists in particular, the Miss America Pageant has attempted to transform itself from a beauty contest to a talent competition, whose real aim is to give college scholarships to smart, talented women (who just happen to look good in bathing suits and evening gowns). As part of its effort to appear more concerned with a woman's IQ than with her bra size, the pageant did away with its long-standing practice of broadcasting the chest, waist, and hip measurements, as well as the height and weight, of each contestant.

something *Other*, like me, and that, I imagine, was the source of her charm and my desire.

If I did not consciously note my own absence in the toys I played with, that absence, I suspect, had a profound effect on me nevertheless. We have only to read Toni Morrison's chilling tale *The Bluest Eye* to see the effect of the white beauty myth on the black child. And while they were by no means as dire for me as for Morrison's character Pecola Breedlove, I was not exempt from the consequences of growing up black in a white world that barely acknowledged my existence. I grew up believing I was ugly: my kinky hair, my big hips, the gap between my teeth. I have spent half my life smiling with my hand over my mouth to hide that gap, a habit I only began to get over in graduate school when a couple of Nigerian men told me that in their culture, where my body type is prized much more than Barbie's, such gaps are a sign of great beauty. I wonder what it would have meant for me as a child to see a black doll—or any doll—with big hips and a gap between her two front teeth.

Today, for $24.99, Mattel reaches halfway around the world and gives little girls—black like me—Nigerian Barbies to play with. Through the wonders of plastic, dyes, and mass production, the company brings into the homes of African American children a Nigeria that I as a young child did not even know existed. The problem is that Mattel's Nigeria does not exist either. The would be ethnic dolls of the world Mattel sells, like their "traditional, blond, blue-eyed" all-American girl prototype, have no gaps, no big ears, no chubby thighs or other "imperfections." For a modest price, I can dream myself into Barbie's perfect world, so long as I dream myself in her image. It may be a small world, a whole new world, but there is still no place for me as *me* in it.

This, then, is my final doll story. Groucho Marx said that he wouldn't want to belong to a club that would have him as a member. In that same vein, I am not so sure that most of us would want to buy a doll that "looked like us." Indeed, efforts to produce and market such truer-to-life dolls have not met with much commercial success. Cultural critics like me can throw theoretical stones at her all we want, but part of Barbies infinite appeal is her very perfection, the extent to which she is both product and purveyor of the dominant white Western ideal of beauty.

And what of black beauty? If Colored Francie failed thirty years ago in part because of her Caucasian features, what are we to make of the current popularity and commercial success of Black Barbie and Shani, straight hair and all? Have we progressed to a point where "difference" makes no difference? Or have we regressed to such a degree that "difference" is only conceivable as similarity—as a mediated text that no matter what its dye job ultimately must be readable as white. Listen to our language: we *"tolerate difference"*; we practice "racial tolerance." Through the compound fractures of interpellation and universalization, the Other is reproduced not in her own image but in ours. If we have gotten away from "Us" and "Them," it may be only because Them R Us.

Is Barbie bad? Barbie is just a piece of plastic, but what she says about   42
the economic base of our society—what she suggests about gender and
race in our world—ain't good.

WORKS CITED

Berkwitz, David N. "Finally, Barbie Doll Ads Go Ethnic." *Newsweek* 13 Aug. 1990: 48.

BillyBoy. Barbie: *Her Life and Times*. New York: Crown, 1987.

Cross, William E., Jr. *Shades of Black: Diversity in African American Identity*. Philadelphia: Temple UP, 1991.

Delany, Sarah, and Delany, A. Elizabeth. *Having Our Say: The Delany Sisters' First 100
Years*. New York: Kodansha, 1993.

Dembner, Alice. "Thirty-five and Still a Da\\." *Boston Globe* 9 Mar. 1994: 1+.

Jones, Lisa. "A Doll Is Born." Village Voice 26 Mar. 1991: 36.

Kantrowitz, Barbara. "Hot Date: Barbie and G.I. Joe." *Newsweek* 20 Feb. 1989: 59–60.

Hopson, Darlene Powell and Derek S. *Different and Wonderful: Raising Black Children in
a Race-Conscious Society*. New York: Simon, 1990.

Larcen, Donna. "Barbie Bond Doesn't Diminish with Age." *Hartford Courant* 17 Aug.
1993: A6–7.

Lord, M. G. *Forever Barbie: The Unauthorized Biography of a Real Doll*. New York:
Morrow, 1994.

McCombie, Mel. "Barbie: Toys Are Us." Unpublished essay.

Morrison, Toni. *The Bluest Eye*. New York: Washington Square, 1970.

Roberts, Cynthia. *Barbie: Thirty Years of America's Doll*. Chicago: Contemporary, 1989.

Rosenberg, Morris. Conceiving the Self. New York: Basic, 1979.

——.*Society and the Adolescent Self-image*. Middletown: Wesleyan UP, 1989.

Sanchez-Eppler, Karen. *Touching Liberty: Abolition, Feminism, and the Politics of the
Body*. Berkeley: U of California P, 1993.

Stewart, Julia. African Names. New York: Carol, 1993.

Urla, Jacqueline, and Alan Swcdlund. "The Anthropometry of Barbie: Unsettling Ideals
of the Feminine in Popular Culture." *Deviant Bodies*. Ed. Jennifer Terry and Jacqueline Urla. Bloomington: Indiana UP, [1995].

■ ■ ■

Reading as a Writer: Analyzing Rhetorical Choices

1. List the key phrases duCille uses to build her argument in her early paragraphs (you might look in particular at paragraphs 5, 9 and 10), and be
   ready to explain them in your own words. Be sure you look up words that
   are new to you. For example, what do you think duCille means by "the
   commodification of race and gender difference" in paragraph 5? Work in
   pairs or groups to help make sense of some of these challenging phrases
   that are important to duCille's argument about Barbie.

2. Find two passages where duCille uses a specific doll as an example to illustrate her larger argument. What words and phrases does she use to move
   between her detailed descriptions of the dolls and their packaging, and her
   analysis of those details? How persuasive do you find her claims, based on
   the evidence in these passages? Explain your answer.

Writing as a Reader: Entering the Conversation of Ideas

1. While they examine marketing to different age brackets, duCille and Shalini Shankar both examine the ways attitudes toward racial differences are constructed through marketing. Compose an essay in which you draw on these authors' ideas and limited examples to consider the relationship between marketing to children and marketing to adults. Given the small sample size of the examples, what conclusions can you draw about marketing and its relationship to attitudes toward racial differences? Consider using these authors' ideas to analyze an additional advertisement or two that helps you make your point.

2. duCille's emphasis on women's bodies and the marketplace intersects with the concerns of Jean Kilbourne (Chapter 13) and Elline Lipkin (Chapter 14). Write an essay in which you use insights from duCille and either Kilbourne or Lipkin (or both) in order to analyze a specific product related to gendered bodies and its marketing. What do you conclude about the significance and effects of gendered marketing, based on your example and analysis?

Assignment Sequences

The assignment sequences invite different kinds of inquiry from the writing exercises in the questions following each reading. Those questions ask you to consider what you have just read, paying attention to specific aspects of the text and seeking new understanding by placing each reading next to others for examination and written response. In contrast, the assignments here are sequences, which define a subject for extended inquiry and offer a series of steps through readings and writing assignments that build on one another. For example, you may write an essay in which you analyze a film about American education through the lens of two authors in this collection. Your next essay may consider the same film in light of different readings and research that gives context to your ideas by describing the ongoing conversation on the issue you are exploring. And yet another assignment in the sequence may invite you to analyze test cases or texts from your own college's promotional materials, to see how the issues raised in the film are played out in those publications.

In other words, instead of writing one essay in response to an assignment and then moving on to a new topic, these assignment sequences allow you to pursue an issue in depth by writing an essay that prepares you to develop an idea in your next essay, considering one central issue from different perspectives and a range of sources. You will be asked to consider texts from different chapters of the reader, to play a wider range of ideas off one another. As you draw on various combinations of resources over a series of assignments and contribute your own research—from the library or from data you have gathered yourself—your ideas about the issues you write about will become richer and more complex. Through reading, researching, and writing, you become an academic writer in conversation with other academic writers. In addition, these assignments can help you see the world around you—from your daily life at college to a Saturday night at the movies to your next meal—in unexpected and insightful ways.

As an academic writer, you will need to document your sources carefully, using the guidelines for quoting and citing sources explained in Chapter 7. We have not included page length requirements on these assignments; your instructor will determine this, in accordance with your program's guidelines.

■ SEQUENCE ONE: What Do Media Representations Tell Us about American Education? [hooks, Gillam and Wooden, Tannen, Tatum, Edmundson, Talbot, original research]

These assignments address the stories we tell ourselves through the media about American education. The readings in this sequence act as lenses you can use to examine representations of American education, not to label them true or false, good or bad, but to consider what they tell us about the positive possibilities, the anxieties, and maybe the dangers we see played out in classrooms. What does it really mean to be educated in America? These assignments begin an inquiry into this always relevant issue.

ASSIGNMENT 1: *Educated by the Movies* [hooks, Gillam and Wooden]

This assignment asks you to interpret the way a particular film of your choosing represents American education and to make an argument about the film's attitudes toward this subject by paying attention to the role of stereotypes in the film. What key issue is raised in the film, and what resolutions are offered? Who is the intended audience, and how does it shape the film's issues and point?

The film you choose might be one that celebrates teachers' relationships with students (*Stand and Deliver, Dangerous Minds, Dead Poets Society, Freedom Writers, The School of Rock*, or the *Harry Potter* films, for example) or depicts them in vicious or even mortal conflict (*Teaching Mrs. Tingle, The Faculty, Cheaters*, or the *Harry Potter* films) or somewhere in between. Or, you might choose a film that illuminates high school social dynamics, like *Napoleon Dynamite, Juno,* or *Charlie Bartlett*. Choose a visual text that really interests you so you can convey that interest through an argument richly supported with details from the film. You will need to choose scenes and images to describe and analyze in detail as you build an argument about the significance of the way education is represented in this visual text.

To help you sharpen your focus and analyze your visual text, use strategies drawn from bell hooks's and Gillam and Wooden's analyses of stereotypes and gender roles in films. These authors show how to look for the unquestioned assumptions about people and to consider how representations of main characters and sidekick characters serve to advance the plot. Use their methods for a close analysis of particular scenes and images, and then draw your own conclusions about a central issue of interest to you in the film. What is this film teaching us about American education? What do you learn about the function of stereotyping in the process?

ASSIGNMENT 2: *What Does Gender or Race Have to Do with It?*
[Tannen, Tatum]

Return to the media example you use for Assignment 1, but analyze the film through the lens of gender or race dynamics. (Choose a focus you did not take in your first essay.) Draw on Deborah Tannen's or Beverly Daniel Tatum's claims that behaviors we often consider to be intrinsic to a person (gender and race) are actually learned behaviors and that school is often a place that reinforces these limiting patterns. Using the author whose ideas are most pertinent for your focus, reconsider the scenes you wrote about for Assignment 1 to analyze the way the film confirms or re-imagines (or both) stereotypes relating to gender and race in educational settings. What new issues and details come into focus when you apply Tannen's or Tatum's specific insights to the scenes? (You may also draw on scenes you did not discuss in your previous paper.) Write a paper that uses these fresh insights to make a point about the way your film teaches viewers to see education in relation to gender or race stereotypes.

ASSIGNMENT 3: *Broadening the Conversation* [Adding original research to Assignment 1 or 2]

Develop the essay you wrote for Assignment 1 or 2 further with research in your college library. What conversations are unfolding among academic writers on the issue you focused on in that essay? Speak with a librarian about which research tools will be most effective for finding two or three recent scholarly articles on this issue. Consider drawing not only on resources from education but also on materials from sociology, psychology, or other fields that may give you a broader understanding of the dynamics you analyzed in your essay. (Your instructor and librarian can show you library databases that focus on specific disciplines.)

The object of this assignment is not simply to add more secondary sources to your paper, but to use those sources to help you reconsider your position, and, perhaps, see significant new details in your film—maybe in the very scenes you have already analyzed. You may find you need to revise your thesis as you develop a broader understanding of the issue from your research. You also may find you no longer want to use one or more of the readings from this collection in your final draft if other framing concepts and examples from your new research are more useful for supporting the argument you make in your essay.

ASSIGNMENT 4: *Focusing on Your Campus* [Edmundson, Talbot, original research]

Analyze representations of your college on its Web site, on promotional videos, and in brochures and student catalogues through the lenses of Mark Edmundson's and Margaret Talbot's texts. For example, how does Edmundson's argument that students expect college to be "lite entertainment," with an emphasis on recreation and enjoyable learning experiences, apply to the images and text in these materials? How does Talbot's analysis of the extreme study habits and intense academic pressure apply to these materials?

This assignment asks you to read college materials closely, in the same way you analyzed the film, looking for visual and textual details to help you determine the arguments these promotional materials make about education at your institution. You will need to select specific examples to analyze—perhaps a section of the college's Web site and a brochure, or one promotional film and one brochure. How do these materials make an argument about both the pleasures and rigors of education at your institution? What do you want to teach your readers about these materials, and what they tell us about what "we" value about American education?

■ SEQUENCE TWO: Reading Bodies [Kilbourne, Immergut, Lipkin, Pascoe, Fuentes, McIntosh, original research]

This sequence asks you to analyze bodies as cultural texts, to consider what we can learn about cultural beliefs from the ways we learn to appear, move, and act. These readings and assignments ask you to consider, from different perspectives, how our bodies display cultural values. An awareness of the arguments bodies make may allow you to explore popular culture in a new way, as well as reflect on the ways your own body is capable of confirming or challenging cultural expectations.

ASSIGNMENT 1: Selling "Normality": How Does Popular Culture Shape Our Sense of What Is Normal? [Kilbourne, Immergut]

Read Jean Kilbourne's analysis of the particular kinds of bodies—especially female bodies—that are "sold" to us as normal and desirable in advertising. How do her ideas about the effects of these images intersect with Matthew Immergut's analysis of contemporary representations of masculinity?

In your own essay, use Kilbourne's and Immergut's ideas to help you think about the significance of these images. What traits do these images teach us to value, and what are the effects? What are these authors pessimistic or optimistic about, and where do you place yourself in this conversation? Use specific insights and examples from each text, and, if you like, analyze a few additional images that you find on your own to enhance your argument. Teach your readers what you find most significant about what you have learned about the bodies we are most often shown in popular culture, and, perhaps, how we can push back.

ASSIGNMENT 2: Gender Projects: How Do We Learn (or Resist) Lessons in Gender? [Lipkin and Pascoe]

Reconsider the ideas you wrote about for Assignment 1 in the context of "body projects," the concept that Elline Lipkin describes as rituals and interactions that shape our sense of our bodies and ourselves. Both Lipkin and C. J. Pascoe examine the effects of these highly gendered practices on children and teenagers.

Using concepts and examples from Lipkin and Pascoe, write an essay in which you consider the significance of these body projects on young people. Don't leave behind the ideas you explored in your first essay; instead, think about how Kilbourne's and Immergut's insights might add context to the implications of your findings. How do these body projects of our youth feed into the images of gendered bodies that are sold to us in advertising when we are older? What kinds of resistance are possible? Consider using some specific examples of teen body projects that you describe and are familiar with as you build your argument.

ASSIGNMENT 3: What Role Does Race Play? [McIntosh, Fuentes, original research]

Return to the essays you wrote for Assignments 1 and 2, and choose one to develop in light of the role race plays in the way we "read" bodies. Peggy McIntosh or Agustín Fuentes should help you think about the ways we "see" or "don't see" race in the examples, images, and body projects you examine. Whichever essay of yours you choose to develop with a focus on race, reread your sources with fresh eyes to find passages that will help you develop your thinking about the role race plays in our interpretations and expectations of bodies.

In addition, investigate the broader scholarly conversation about the significance of the ways we interpret racial differences. Use your library's search tools, indexes such as EBSCOhost or JSTOR, or another source recommended by a librarian or your instructor to find an article that helps you analyze the role of race in the context of your essay. Work with a librarian to develop search terms that will yield the best results—an article that offers you the analytical tools you need for a fresh focus.

ASSIGNMENT 4: Hearing from Your Peers [Using a focus group to develop your ideas]

Use a focus group to find out what your peers think about an issue you have written about in this sequence. (Refer to the discussion in Chapter 11 about designing and conducting an effective focus group.) Given the topics and issues you have explored in these essays, decide on a specific focus for this final paper that can be enriched with the kind of data you can collect in a focus group. Think carefully about the kinds of information you need as you choose participants for the focus group and write your questions for them. (See Chapter 11 for a discussion of the kinds of claims you can make based on focus-group data.) As you consider how best to analyze and contextualize the material you gather in your focus group, return to your previous essays and library research and the readings themselves to choose the most useful tools to make sense of your findings. Be sure to shape your essay so that you teach your readers something specific about a body issue and its significance.

■ SEQUENCE THREE: Visualizing Meaning: How Do Images Make Arguments? [Kilbourne, Sturgeon, Jensen and McMillan, images from Chapter 8, "From Ethos to Logos: Appealing to Your Readers," original research]

This sequence gives you the opportunity to practice analyzing images in order to consider how visual arguments work. As we discuss in Chapter 8, we are surrounded by images in our culture, so it is crucial to learn to make sense of what these images tell us about cultural values and aspirations. The readings in this sequence offer concrete strategies for analyzing visual arguments in advertisements and graphic novels. You will have the opportunity to pursue areas of interest to you, both through your research and the test cases you analyze. Reading, researching, collecting, and writing about visual arguments will help you see the world around you with new—and perhaps startling—clarity.

ASSIGNMENT 1: *Analyzing Advertising* [Kilbourne, Sturgeon]

Consider the strategies Jean Kilbourne and Noël Sturgeon use to analyze advertisements, and apply their insights to three advertisements of your choice. Kilbourne and Sturgeon argue that images are not neutral, but that like any text, they project perspectives and arguments. Reread the authors' essays to determine their most effective strategies for analyzing the images and language in advertisements. How are their strategies similar? How are they different?

Choose three visual advertisements that share a focus or theme that interests you (you could use the images in Chapter 8 as a starting place), and, using tools drawn from Kilbourne, Sturgeon, and Chapter 8's "Analyzing Visual Rhetoric" section, write an essay about what these images argue and how they do so. Consider the assumptions the ads make about their audience and the ideas and associations they play on in order to sell the product. How does the language of each ad work in relation to the image? As you teach your reader how Kilbourne and Sturgeon help you analyze these visual arguments, be sure to describe and analyze specific details in the advertisement to illustrate your claims. Be clear about what you want your readers to see in these advertisements, and why these insights matter.

ASSIGNMENT 2: *Considering the Visual Arguments of Graphic Novels* [Jensen and McMillan, Kilbourne, or Sturgeon]

Derrik Jensen and Stephanie McMillan's graphic novel can be analyzed with at least some of the same tools you used in your first essay. Select a series of frames in Jensen and McMillan's text that work interestingly with some of the advertisements you analyzed in your first essay (or find a few new advertisements, if you like), and write another essay that explains the way visual rhetoric works to build an argument in both the advertisements and the graphic novel. You might consider the way the images are framed, for example, and the relationship between the images and words.

In your essay, teach your reader about the parallels you see between analyzing these two different kinds of visual rhetorics, and the differences, as well. What do these similarities and differences tell us about the importance of visual literacy? What kinds of skills do we need for visual analysis? What might be lost in the case of the advertisements and the graphic novel if a reader did not bring these tools of visual analysis to bear on these images? What conclusions can you draw?

ASSIGNMENT 3: *Broadening the Conversation about Visual Arguments* [Adding original research to Assignment 1 or 2]

Develop one of the papers you wrote in response to Assignment 1 or 2 through scholarly research. Which ideas and issues in that paper spark your ideas and interest the most? Building on those ideas, use your library's databases to find out what other scholars have said on this particular topic or issue. For example, you might begin with a general database like EBSCOhost and a search on "advertising and gender" or "graphic novels and politics"—to name just two of the possibilities. Your instructor or librarian can help you narrow your search and find the most useful database for your needs. Read broadly enough in your search results to gain a clear sense of the scholarly conversation on your issue, and select at least two articles that will help you further develop the ideas you have written about for this sequence.

Depending on the direction your essay takes, you may wish to return to the examples you used in the previous assignments or you may decide to use fresh passages and examples to support the focus and argument in this essay. Drawing on the broader conversation you have researched and now joined, what new ideas can you teach your readers about the significance of visual rhetoric?

ASSIGNMENT 4: *Working with a Larger Archive* [Developing your ideas with test cases]

This assignment requires you to gather a broader "archive," or collection, of materials to analyze, using the readings in this sequence and the tools in Chapter 8. Depending on your interests, collect a larger "archive" of images (advertisements, graphic novel excerpts, book covers, posters, etc.) to use as your data for this essay. Think carefully about what you would like to learn from this process to be sure the materials you collect will address your interest. Your instructor and classmates can also help you reflect on how best to develop a collection and how large your collection should be to answer your research question responsibly. (For example, if you wish to analyze a pattern of a particular kind of image on magazine covers, you would need to decide if you will only analyze one magazine or several, and how many issues, as well as over how many years.)

Draw on the theories and ideas you have read and learned in the assignments in this sequence, and apply them to the samples in your archive in order to address your focus in this essay. What can you teach your readers about the significance of the patterns you see in these images, using the tools of visual analysis? This essay is your opportunity to contribute to the scholarly conversation on how visual arguments work, because you will be the expert on the collection of materials you are using for your essay. Be clear about what you want your readers to learn, and why your ideas about these images matter.

■ SEQUENCE FOUR: The "I" in the "We": Exploring Tensions between Individual and Group Identities [Banaji and Greenwald, hooks, Ehrenreich, McGonigal, Turkle, original research]

This sequence gives you an opportunity to reflect on the many ways in which individuals understand their relationship to their communities (real or virtual), and the evidence we use to understand this relationship between others and ourselves. It also asks you to evaluate the rhetorical tactic of drawing on personal experiences and researched data when making a larger argument: What are the advantages and possible problems of each strategy?

ASSIGNMENT 1: Seeing a Social Group through the Writer's Eye/"I"
[Banaji and Greenwald, hooks, Ehrenreich]

Use Mahzarin R. Banaji and Anthony G. Greenwald's analysis of the ways humans tend to think in categories to examine the assumptions about the poor in texts by bell hooks and Barbara Ehrenreich in Chapter 14. How do Banaji and Greenwald's ideas about "blindspots" and stereotyping help you make sense of the strategies that hooks and Ehrenreich use to examine poverty through both personal experiences and scholarly insights? How do these writers position themselves in relation to the poor?

Write an essay in which you respond to these questions in order to draw out a larger point about effective ways that writers can help readers think beyond categories when it comes to addressing social problems such as poverty. How do hooks's and Ehrenreich's rhetorical strategies help support their arguments? What can you conclude about the uses (personal, political, social) of seeing oneself as part of a community or different from a social group when it comes to analyzing a social issue?

ASSIGNMENT 2: Virtual Communities and Their Effects [Banaji and Greenwald, McGonigal, Turkle]

Reconsider Assignment 1's analysis of categorical thinking and stereotyping "blindspots" in light of the ideas about virtual communities raised by Jane McGonigal and Sherry Turkle. McGonigal and Turkle in Chapter 13 offer readers contrasting ways to understand the relationship between the individual and social groups, as structured and enabled by the Internet. How does shifting from the "real" world problem of poverty to the tensions in virtual worlds extend or test the limits of Banaji and Greenwald's claims about the ways we tend to think in categories?

As you address these questions in your own essay, be sure to draw on examples from McGonigal and Turkle, and perhaps from additional specific examples from your own virtual experiences. What happens to stereotypes in virtual worlds? What happens to the sense of self? What is gained and/or lost when we join communities that exist "only" virtually?

ASSIGNMENT 3: Researching the Relationship between Individuals and Their Communities [Adding original research to Assignment 1 or 2]

Now that you have written two essays, choose one to develop further with insights drawn from scholarly research on your subject. Using your library's research databases, find at least two articles that enrich your understanding of the relationship between individuals and their communities, focused on the issues and examples of the essay you have chosen to develop. Your librarian (and perhaps your instructors and peers) can help you brainstorm keywords to search and databases that might be particularly helpful.

The purpose of your research is to find at least two articles that will help you develop, extend, and perhaps change your ideas in the essay you are revising. You will need to be willing to rethink and rewrite your essay substantially as you return to your ideas with a fresh perspective and the new meanings you've discovered in the material. Establish a clear thesis to draw through the whole essay as you teach your readers about the ways your research has extended your thinking in your original essay with new framing theories, insights, and examples. What significance do you see in these additional ideas?

ASSIGNMENT 4: Adding Other Voices through Original Research
[Using interviews or a focus group to develop your ideas]

In this assignment, you have the opportunity to use interviews or a focus group (see Chapter 11) to discover how others have negotiated the relationship between their individual and community identities, particularly thinking about the hazards of stereotyping others. Look back through your previous three essays and draw out the most compelling issues and ideas from the readings and research you have done. Based on this work, decide on the form your original research should take. That is, are you more likely to obtain useful material for developing your ideas through interviews with individuals who have experience with these issues, or through a focus group?

Be sure to make good use of the framing theories and concepts you have explored in the readings and in your research as you plan questions for your interviews or focus group. For example, you might choose to concentrate on lived social justice issues (such as poverty or the effects of stereotyping groups) or virtual communities.

Whatever the focus of your original research, have a clear goal in mind about the material you want to gather so that you will have rich data to analyze as you develop a thesis for your final essay of this sequence. You may find that you will need to do more library research to make sense of your new findings. You may also decide to use passages in the textbook readings that you have not used before, or you may return to familiar passages but use them in new ways to teach your readers something you find significant about the relationship between individual and community identities.

APPENDIX:
Citing and Documenting Sources

You must provide a brief citation in the text of your paper for every quotation or an idea taken from another writer, and you must list complete information at the end of your paper for the sources you use. This information is essential for readers who want to read the source to understand a quotation or an idea in its original context. How you cite sources in the body of your paper and document them at the end of your paper varies from discipline to discipline, so it is important to ask your instructor what documentation style he or she prefers.

Even within academic disciplines, documentation styles can vary. Specific academic journals within disciplines will sometimes have their own set of style guidelines. The important thing is to adhere faithfully to your chosen (or assigned) style throughout your paper, observing all the niceties of form prescribed by the style. You may have noticed small differences in the citation styles in the examples throughout Chapter 7. That's because the examples are taken from the work of a variety of writers, both professionals and students, who had to conform to the documentation requirements of their publication venues or of their teachers.

Here we briefly introduce two common documentation styles that may be useful in your college career: the Modern Language Association (MLA) style for listing bibliographic information in the humanities, and the American Psychological Association (APA) style, in the social sciences. The information is basic, for use when you begin drafting your paper. In the final stages of writing, you should consult either the *MLA Handbook for Writers of Research Papers* (7th ed.) or the *Publication Manual of the American Psychological Association* (6th ed.).

Although you'll need the manuals for complete style information, both the MLA (http://www.mla.org/style_faq/) and the APA (http://www.apastyle .org/learn/faqs/) maintain Web sites for frequently asked questions. Again, before you start your research, check with your instructor to find out whether you should use either of these styles or if there's another style he or she prefers.

MLA and APA styles have many similarities—for example, both require short citations in the body of an essay linked to a list of sources at the end of the essay. But it is their differences, though subtle, that are crucial. To a great extent, these differences reflect the assumptions writers in the humanities and in the social sciences bring to working with sources. In particular, you should understand each style's treatment of the source's author, publication date, and page numbers in in-text citations, and verb use in referring to sources.

Author.   MLA style requires that you give the author's full name on first mention in your paper; APA style uses last names throughout. The humanities emphasize "the human element"—the individual as creative force— so MLA style uses the complete name at first mention to imply the author's importance. Because the social sciences emphasize the primacy of data in studies of human activity, in APA style last names are deemed sufficient.

Publication Date.   In-text citations using MLA style leave out the date of publication. The assumption is that the insights of the past may be as useful as those of the present. By contrast, APA style gives the date of the study after the author's name, reflecting a belief in the progress of research, that recent findings may supersede earlier ones.

Page Numbers.   MLA style requires that page numbers be included with paraphrases and summaries as well as quotations (the written text is so important that a reader may want to check the exact language of the original). By contrast, APA style requires attribution but not page numbers for paraphrases and summaries (it is the findings, not how they are described, that are most important).

Verb Use.   MLA style uses the present tense of verbs ("Writer X claims") to introduce cited material, assuming the cited text's timelessness, whether written last week or centuries ago. By contrast, the verbs introducing citations in APA style acknowledge the "pastness" of research ("Writer X claimed" or "Writer Y has claimed") on the assumption that new data may emerge to challenge older research.

Although it is useful to understand that different citation styles reflect different attitudes toward inquiry and research in different disciplines, for the purposes of your writing it is mainly important to know the style you have to follow in your paper, and to stick to it scrupulously. Whenever you

TABLE A.1   Basic Information Needed for Citing Sources

Books	Chapters in Books	Journal Articles	Online Sources
Author(s) or editor(s)	Author(s)	Author(s)	Author(s)
Title and subtitle	Chapter title and subtitle	Article title and subtitle	Document title and subtitle
Edition information	Book editor(s)	Journal title	Print publication information, if any
Place of publication	Book title	Volume and issue number	Site sponsor
Publisher	Edition information	Date of publication	Site title
Year of publication	Place of publication	Page numbers	Year of publication
Medium of publication	Publisher	Medium of publication	Medium of publication
	Year of publication		Date accessed
	Page numbers		
	Medium of publication		

consult a source—even if you don't end up using it in your paper—write down complete citation information so that you can cite it fully and accurately if you need to. Table A.1 shows the basic information needed to cite books, chapters in books, journal articles, and online sources. You also should note any other information that could be relevant—a translator's name, for example, or a series title and editor. Ideally, you want to be able to cite a source fully without having to go back to it to get more information.

THE BASICS OF MLA STYLE

In-Text Citations.   In MLA style, you must provide a brief citation in the body of your essay (1) when you quote directly from a source, (2) when you paraphrase or summarize what someone else has written, and (3) even when you use an idea or a concept that originated with someone else.

In the excerpt below, the citation tells readers that the student writer's argument about the evolution of Ebonics is rooted in a well-established source of information. Because the writer does not mention the author in the paraphrase of her source in the text, she gives the author's name in the citation:

> The evolution of U.S. Ebonics can be traced from the year 1557 to the present day. In times of great oppression, such as the beginning of the slave codes in 1661, the language of the black community was at its most "ebonified" levels, whereas in times of racial progress, for example during the abolitionist movement, the language as a source of community identity was forsaken for greater assimilation (Smitherman 119).

The parenthetical citation refers to page 119 of Geneva Smitherman's book *Talkin and Testifyin: The Language of Black America* (1977). Smitherman is a recognized authority on Ebonics. Had the student mentioned Smitherman's name in her introduction to the paraphrase, she would not have had to repeat it in the citation. Notice that there is no punctuation within the parentheses and no *p.* before the page number. Also notice that the citation is considered part of the sentence in which it appears, so the period ending the sentence follows the closing parenthesis.

By contrast, in the example that follows, the student quotes directly from Richard Rodriguez's book *Hunger of Memory: The Education of Richard Rodriguez* (1982):

> Many minority cultures in today's society feel that it is more important to maintain cultural bonds than to extend themselves into the larger community. People who do not speak English may feel a similar sense of community and consequently lose some of the individuality and cultural ties that come with speaking their native or home language. This shared language within a home or community also adds to the unity of the community. Richard Rodriguez attests to this fact in his essay "Aria." He then goes on to say that "it is not healthy to distinguish public words from private sounds so easily" (183).

Because the student mentions Rodriguez in her text right before the quotation ("Richard Rodriguez attests"), she does not need to include his name in the citation; the page number is sufficient.

Works Cited.   At the end of your researched essay, and starting on a new page, you must provide a list of works cited, a list of all the sources you have used (leaving out sources you consulted but did not cite). Entries should be listed alphabetically by author's last name or by title if no author is identified. Figure A.1 is a sample works cited page in MLA style that illustrates a few (very few) of the basic types of documentation.

Steps to Compiling an MLA List of Works Cited

1 Begin your list of works cited on a new page at the end of your paper.

2 Put your last name and page number in the upper-right corner.

3 Double-space throughout.

4 Center the heading ("Works Cited") on the page.

5 Arrange the list of sources alphabetically by author's last name or by title if no author is identified.

6 Begin the first line of each source flush left; second and subsequent lines should be indented ½ inch.

7 Invert the author's name, last name first. In the case of multiple authors, only the first author's name is inverted.

8 Italicize the titles of books, journals, magazines, and newspapers. Put the titles of book chapters and articles in quotation marks. Capitalize each word in all titles except for articles, short prepositions, and coordinating conjunctions.

9 For books, list the place of publication, the name of the publisher, and the year of publication. For chapters, list the editors of the book, the book title, and the publication information. For articles, list the journal title, volume and issue numbers, and the date of publication.

10 List the relevant page numbers for articles and selections from longer works.

11 Give the medium of publication, such as Print, Web, CD, DVD, Film, Lecture, Performance, Radio, Television, PDF file, MP3 file, or E-mail.

The steps outlined here for compiling a list of works cited apply to printed sources. MLA formats for citing online sources vary, but this is an example of the basic format:

> Author. "Document Title." *Name of Site.* Site Sponsor, date posted/revised. Medium. Date you accessed the site.

Things to remember:

- Invert the author's name or the first author's name.
- Italicize the name of the site.
- If the site sponsor—usually an institution or organization—isn't clear, check the copyright notice at the bottom of the Web page.
- MLA style uses the day-month-year format for dates in the works-cited list.
- Notice that there's a comma between the sponsor and the publication date.
- In general, the medium of publication for online sources is "Web."
- Notice that you do not need to include a URL after the date of access.

In addition to online sources, you will likely use other nonprint sources in researching your papers. Our students, for example, regularly analyze films, recordings, television and radio programs, paintings, and photographs. For details on how to format these sources, consult the *MLA Handbook* or go to Purdue University's Online Writing Lab (OWL) site (http://owl.english.purdue.edu/owl/section/2/11).

Works Cited

Gutiérrez, Kris D., Patricia Baquedano-López, and Jolynn Asato. "English for the Children: The New Literacy of the Old World Order." *Bilingual Review Journal* 24.1&2 (2000): 87-112. Print.

Online scholarly journal/article, no author

"History of Bilingual Education." *Rethinking Schools* 12.3 (1998): n. pag. Web. 15 Feb. 2008.

Article in a scholarly journal

Lanehart, Sonja L. "African American Vernacular English and Education." *Journal of English Linguistics* 26.2 (1998): 122-36. Print.

Article in a magazine

Pompa, Delia. "Bilingual Success: Why Two-Language Education Is Critical for Latinos." *Hispanic* Oct. 1996: 96. Print.

Rawls, John. *Political Liberalism*. New York: Columbia UP, 1993. Print.

Essay in an edited collection; second source by same writer

---. "Social Unity and Primary Goods." *Utilitarianism and Beyond*. Ed. Amartya Sen and Bernard Williams. Cambridge, Eng.: Cambridge UP, 1982. 159-85. Print.

Rodriguez, Richard. "Aria." *Hunger of Memory: The Education of Richard Rodriguez*. New York: Bantam, 1982. 11-40. Print.

Schrag, Peter. "Language Barrier." *New Republic* 9 Mar. 1998: 14-15. Print.

A book

Smitherman, Geneva. *Talkin and Testifyin: The Language of Black America*. Detroit: Wayne State UP, 1977. Print.

Willis, Arlette. "Reading the World of School Literacy: Contextualizing the Experience of a Young American Male." *Harvard Educational Review* 65.1 (1995): 30-49. Print.

FIGURE A.1   Sample List of Works Cited, MLA Format

THE BASICS OF APA STYLE

In-Text Citations.   In APA style, in-text citations identify the author or authors of a source and the publication date. If the author or authors are mentioned in the text, only the publication date is needed:

> Feingold (1992) documented the fact that males perform much better than females in math and science and other "masculine" areas.

Notice that the in-text citation does not include a page number. Because Feingold is only cited, not quoted, no page reference is necessary. If the source is quoted directly, a page number is added in parentheses following the quote:

> Feingold (1992) argued that "men scored significantly higher than women in situations designed to test aptitude in mathematics and hard sciences" (p. 92).

APA style uses the abbreviation *p.* or *pp.* before page numbers, which MLA style does not. If the author is not identified with a signal phrase, the name, year, and page number would be noted parenthetically after the quotation:

> One study found that "men scored significantly higher than women in situations designed to test aptitude in mathematics and hard sciences" (Feingold, 1992, p. 92).

Many studies in the social sciences have multiple authors. In a work with two authors, cite both authors every time:

> Dlugos and Friedlander (2000) wrote that "sustaining passionate commitment to work as a psychotherapist reflects passionate commitment in other areas of life" (p. 298).

Here, too, if you do not identify the authors in a signal phrase, include their names, the year the source was published, and the relevant page number parenthetically after the quotation—but use an ampersand (&) instead of the word *and* between the authors' names:

> Some believe that "sustaining passionate commitment to work as a psychotherapist reflects passionate commitment in other areas of life" (Dlugos & Friedlander, 2000, p. 298).

Use the same principles the first time you cite a work with three to five authors:

> Booth-Butterfield, Anderson, and Williams (2000) tested . . .
> (Booth-Butterfield, Anderson, & Williams, 2000, p. 5)

Thereafter, you can use the name of the first author followed by the abbreviation *et al.* (Latin for "and others") in roman type:

Booth-Butterfield et al. (2000) tested . . .

(Booth-Butterfield et al., 2000, p. 5)

For a work with six or more authors, use *et al.* from the first mention.

These are only some of the most basic examples of APA in-text citation. Consult the APA manual for other guidelines.

References. APA style, like MLA style, requires a separate list of sources at the end of a research paper. This list is called "References," not "Works Cited." The list of references starts on a new page at the end of your paper and lists sources alphabetically by author (or title if no author is identified). Figure A.2 shows a sample list of references with sources cited in APA style.

Steps to Compiling an APA List of References

1 Begin your list of references on a new page at the end of your paper.

2 Put a shortened version of the paper's title (not your last name) in all caps in the upper-left corner; put the page number in the upper-right corner.

3 Double-space throughout.

4 Center the heading ("References") on the page.

5 Arrange the list of sources alphabetically by author's last name or by title if no author is identified.

6 Begin the first line of each source flush left; second and subsequent lines should be indented ½ inch.

7 Invert all authors' names. If a source has more than one author, use an ampersand (not *and*) before the last name.

8 Insert the date in parentheses after the last author's name.

9 Italicize the titles of books, capitalizing only the first letter of the title and subtitle and proper nouns.

10 Follow the same capitalization for the titles of book chapters and articles. Do not use quotation marks around chapter and article titles.

11 Italicize the titles of journals, magazines, and newspapers, capitalizing the initial letters of all key words.

12 For books, list the place of publication and the name of the publisher. For chapters, list the book editor(s), the book title, the relevant page numbers, and the place of publication and the name of the publisher. For articles, list the journal title, the volume number, the issue number if each issue of the volume begins on page 1, the relevant pages, and the DOI (digital object identifier) number if available. If you retrieve a journal article online and there is no DOI, include the URL of the journal's home page.

GENDER AND TEACHING   15

References

Journal article with no DOI

Campbell, R. J. (1969). Co-education: Attitudes and self-concepts of girls at three schools. *British Journal of Educational Psychology, 39*, 87.

Report, seven authors

Coleman, J., Campbell, E., Hobson, C., McPartland, J., Mood, A., Weinfeld, F., & York, R. (1966). *Equality of educational opportunity (The Coleman report)*. Washington, DC: U.S. Government Printing Office.

Journal article with a DOI

Feingold, A. (1992). Sex differences in variability in intellectual abilities: A new look at an old controversy. *Review of Educational Research, 62*, 61-84. doi:10.3102/00346543062001061

Online source

Haag, P. (2003). *K-12 single-sex education: What does the research say?* Retrieved from http://www.ericdigests.org/2001-2/sex.html

Journal article retrieved online with no DOI

Hallinan, M. T. (1994). Tracking: From theory to practice. *Sociology of Education, 67*, 79-84. Retrieved from http://www.asanet.org/journals/soe/

Hanson, S. L. (1994). Lost talent: Unrealized educational aspirations and expectations among U.S. youth. *Sociology of Education, 67*, 159-183. Retrieved from http://www.asanet.org/journals/soe/

Jovanovic, J., & King, S. S. (1998). Boys and girls in the performance-based science classroom: Who's doing the performing? *American Educational Research Journal, 35*, 477-496. doi:10.3102/00028312035003477

FIGURE A.2   Sample List of References, APA Format

Lee, V. E., & Marks, H. M. (1990). Sustained effects of the single-sex secondary school experience on attitudes, behaviors, and values in college. *Journal of Educational Psychology, 82,* 578-592.

Mickelson, R. A. (1989). Why does Jane read and write so well? The anomaly of women's achievement. *Sociology of Education, 62,* 47-63. Retrieved from http://www.asanet.org /journals/soe/

Scholarly book   Rosenberg, M. (1965). *Society and the adolescent self-image.* Princeton, NJ: Princeton University Press.

Schneider, F. W., & Coutts, L. M. (1982). The high school environment: A comparison of coeducational and single-sex schools. *Journal of Educational Psychology, 74,* 898-906.

Essay in edited collection   Spade, J. Z. (2001). Gender education in the United States. In J. H. Ballantine & J. Z. Spade (Eds.), *Schools and society: A sociological approach to education* (pp. 270-278). Belmont, CA: Wadsworth/Thomson Learning.

Streitmatter, J. L. (1999). *For girls ONLY: Making a case for single-sex schooling.* Albany, NY: State University of New York Press.

Dissertation from a database   Winslow, M. A. (1995). *Where the boys are: The educational aspirations and future expectations of working-class girls in an all-female high school* (Doctoral dissertation). University of Arizona. Retrieved from ProQuest Dissertations and Theses database. (AAT 9622975)

The *APA Manual* is your best resource for formatting online sources, but here is an example of a basic reference to an online source:

Author. (Date posted/revised). *Document title.* Retrieved from URL

- If no author is identified, alphabetize the entry under the title.
- Capitalize an online document title like an article title, and italicize it; don't enclose it in quotes.
- Include a retrieval date after the word "Retrieved" only if the content is likely to change.
- Notice that there is no end punctuation after the DOI or URL.

- APA style asks you to break lengthy DOIs or URLs after a slash or before a period, being sure that your program doesn't insert a hyphen at the line break.

The *APA Manual* is also your best resource for formatting references to other nonprint sources. You should know that certain nonprint sources you are likely to rely on in your research in the social sciences—interviews and focus groups, for example—do not have to be included in your list of references. Instead, you would cite the person you interviewed or the focus group you conducted in the text of your paper. For example:

(J. Long, personal interview, April 7, 2007)

ACKNOWLEDGMENTS

Joni Adamson. "Indigenous Literatures, Multinaturalism, and *Avatar:* The Emergence of Indigenous Cosmopolitics." Adapted from *American Literary History*, Spring 2012. Reprinted by permission.

Mahzarin R. Banaji and Anthony G. Greenwald. "On Stereotypes." From *Blindspot: The Hidden Biases of Good People.* Copyright © 2013 Mahzarin R. Banaji and Anthony G. Greenwald. Used by permission of Bantam Books, an imprint of Random House, a division of Random House LLC. All rights reserved.

Susan Blum. "The United States of (Non)Reading: The End of Civilization or a New Era?" From *HuffPost College*, October, 8, 2013. Copyright © 2013 by Susan Blum. Reprinted with permission.

William Deresiewicz. "The End of Solitude." From *The Chronicle of Higher Education*, January 2009. Used with permission of The Chronicle of Higher Education. Copyright © 2014. All rights reserved.

John Dicker. Excerpt from *The United States of Wal-Mart.* Copyright © 2005 John Dicker. Used by permission of Jeremy P. Tarcher, an imprint of Penguin Group (USA) LLC.

John Dickerson. "Don't Fear Twitter." From *Nieman Reports*, Summer 2008. Nieman Foundation for Journalism at Harvard. Reprinted by permission.

Anne duCille. Excerpt from "Multicultural Barbie and the Merchandising of Difference." From *differences: A Journal of Feminist Cultural Studies*, Spring 1994, Volume 6, no. 1, pp. 46–68. Copyright © 1994, Brown University and differences: a Journal of Feminist Cultural Studies. All rights reserved. Republished by permission of the copyright holder, and the present publisher, Duke University Press. www.dukeupress.edu.

Mark Edmundson. "On the Uses of a Liberal Education." From *Harper's Magazine*, September 1997. Copyright © 1997 by Harper's Magazine and Mark Edmundson. All rights reserved. Reproduced from the September issue by special permission.

Barbara Ehrenreich. "Cultural Baggage." From *The New York Times Magazine*, April 5, 1992. Copyright © 1992 by Barbara Ehrenreich. Reprinted with permission.

Barbara Ehrenreich. "How I Discovered the Truth about Poverty." From *The Nation*, March 15, 2012. Reprinted with permission of The Nation. For subscription information, call 1-800-333-8536. Portions of each week's Nation magazine can be accessed at http://www.thenation.com.

Agustín Fuentes. "The Myth of Race." From *Race, Monogamy, and Other Lies They Told You: Busting Myths about Human Nature.* © 2012 Regents of the University of California. Published by the University of California Press. Reprinted with permission.

Ken Gillam and Shannon R. Wooden. "Post-Princess Models of Gender: The New Man in Disney/Pixar." From *Journal of Popular Film and Television*, 2008, Volume 36(1). Copyright © 2008 Taylor & Francis Ltd. Reprinted by permission of the publisher. www.tandf.co.uk/journals.

Gerald Graff. "Hidden Meaning, or, Disliking Books at an Early Age." From *Beyond the Culture Wars: How Teaching the Conflicts Can Revitalize American Education.* Copyright © 1992 Gerald Graff. Used by permission of W.W. Norton & Company, Inc.

Steve Grove. "You Tube: The Flattening of Politics." From *Nieman Reports*. Nieman Foundation for Journalism at Harvard University. Summer 2008. Reprinted by permission.

Kris Gutiérrez. Excerpt from "Teaching Toward Possibility: Building Cultural Supports for Robust Learning." From *PowerPlay,* 2011, Volume 3(1): 22–3. Reprinted by permission.

Cynthia Haven. "The New Literacy: Stanford Study Finds Richness and Complexity in Student Writing." From *Stanford University News*, Stanford Report, October 12, 2009. Reprinted by permission.

Gary Steiner. "Animal Vegetable Miserable." From *The New York Times*, November 22, 2009. © 2009 The New York Times. All rights reserved. Used by permission and protected by the copyright laws of the United States. The printing, copying, redistribution, or retransmission of this Content without express written permission is prohibited.

Sandra Steingraber. "Despair Not." From *In These Times*, May 25, 2011, adapted from an excerpt of *Raising Elijah: Protecting Our Children in an Age of Environmental Crisis*. Copyright © April 23, 2013 Sandra Steingraber. Reprinted by permission of Da Capo Press, a member of the Perseus Books Group.

Constance Steinkuehler and Sean Duncan. "Scientific Habits of Mind in Virtual Worlds." From *Journal of Science Education and Technology*, December 2008, Volume 17(6). Republished with permission of Springer Science+Business Media. Permission conveyed through Copyright Clearance Center, Inc.

Noël Sturgeon. "The Politics of the Natural in U.S. History and Popular Culture." From *Environmentalism in Popular Culture: Gender, Sexuality, Race, and the Politics of the Natural*. © 2009 Noël Sturgeon. Reprinted by permission of the University of Arizona Press.

Margaret Talbot. "Brain Gain: The Underground World of 'Neuroenhancing' Drugs." From *The New Yorker*, April 27, 2009. Copyright © 2009 Margaret Talbot, used by permission of The Wylie Agency LLC.

Deborah Tannen. "How Male and Female Students Use Language Differently." From *The Chronicle of Higher Education*, March 31, 2000. Used with permission of The Chronicle of Higher Education. Copyright © 2000. All rights reserved.

Beverly Daniel Tatum. Excerpt from *Why Are All the Black Kids Sitting Together in the Cafeteria?* Copyright © 2002. Reprinted by permission of Basic Books, a member of The Perseus Books Group.

Mark R. Tercek and Jonathan S. Adams. From *Nature's Fortune: How Business and Society Thrive by Investing in Nature*. Copyright © 2013. Reprinted by permission of Basic Books, a member of The Perseus Books Group.

Clive Thompson. "The New Literacy." From *Wired Magazine*, August 24, 2009. Copyright © WIRED Magazine/Clive Thompson. Reprinted with permission.

Sherry Turkle. "The Flight from Conversation." From *The New York Times Magazine*, April 22, 2012. © 2012 The New York Times. All rights reserved. Used by permission and protected by the Copyright Laws of the United States. The printing, copying, redistribution, or retransmission of this Content without express written permission is prohibited.

Sherry Turkle. "Growing up Tethered." From *Alone Together: Why We Expect More from Technology and Less from Each Other*. Copyright © 2011. Reprinted by permission of Basic Books, a member of The Perseus Books Group.

David Tyack. "Whither History Textbooks?" From *Seeking Common Ground: Public Schools in a Diverse Society*, pp. 59–63, Cambridge, Mass.: Harvard University Press. Copyright © 2003 President and Fellows of Harvard College. Reprinted by permission of the publisher.

Anahí Viladrich, Ming-Chin Yeh, Nancy Bruning, and Rachael Weiss. "'Do Real Women Have Curves?' Paradoxical Body Images among Latinas in New York City." From *Journal of Immigrant and Minority Health*, Febraury 2009, Volume 11(1). Republished with permission of Springer Science+Business Media. Permission conveyed through Copyright Clearance Center, Inc.

Georgia Warnke. "Sex and Gender: Behavioral Ecology and Hormone Studies." From *Debating Sex and Gender*, (2011): 20–28, 124–126. Copyright © Oxford University Press. By permission of Oxford University Press, USA.

Fareed Zakaria. "The Rise of the Rest." From *The Post-American World*. © 2008 Fareed Zakaria. Used by permission of W.W. Norton & Company, Inc.

Index of Authors, Titles, and Key Terms